AN ECONOMIC HISTORY OF THE IBERIAN PENINSULA, 700-2000

This is a comprehensive long-run history of economic and political change in the Iberian Peninsula. Beginning with the development of the old medieval kingdoms, it goes on to explore two countries, Portugal and Spain, which during the early modern period possessed vast empires and played an essential role in the global economic and political developments. It traces how and why both countries began to fall behind during the first stages of industrialization and modern economic growth only to achieve remarkable economic development during the second half of the twentieth century. Written by a team of leading historians, the book sheds new light on all aspects of economic history from population, agriculture, manufacturing and international trade to government, finance and welfare. The book includes extensive new data and will be an essential work of reference for scholars of Portugal and Spain and also of comparative European economic development.

PEDRO LAINS was Senior Research Professor at the University of Lisbon. He was the author of *An Economic History of Portugal* (2016), *A History of Public Banking in Portugal in the 19th and 20th Centuries* (2021) and editor of *An Agrarian History of Portugal* (2017). He was president of the Portuguese Economic and Social History Association from 2003 to 2007.

LEONOR FREIRE COSTA is Professor in Economic History at the ISEG, University of Lisbon. She has published articles on Portugal's economic and financial history in the early modern period. Together with Pedro Lains and Susana Miranda she authored *An Economic History of Portugal* (2016).

REGINA GRAFE is Professor of Early Modern History at the European University Institute in Florence. She is a global economic and social historian who has published widely on the political economy of Spain and the Spanish Empire including *Distant Tyranny: Markets, Power and Backwardness in Spain, 1650-1800* (2012).

ALFONSO HERRANZ-LONCÁN is Professor of Economic History at the University of Barcelona. He has published articles on the history of transport, infrastructure, public policies, market integration and economic growth in Spain and Latin America during the nineteenth and twentieth centuries.

DAVID IGUAL-LUIS is Professor in Medieval History at the University of Castilla-La Mancha. He is a specialist on social and economic history. His previous publications include his collaborations in the collective volumes *The Routledge Handbook of Maritime Trade around Europe, 1300–1600* (2017), *Social Mobility in Medieval Italy, 1100–1500* (2018) and *Faire son marché au Moyen Âge: Méditerranée occidentale, XIIIe-XVIe siècle* (2018).

VICENTE PINILLA is Professor in Economic History at the University of Zaragoza and researcher at the Instituto Agroalimentario de Aragón. His previous publications include *Wine Globalization* (2018), *Agricultural Development in the World Periphery: A Global Economic History Approach* (2018) and *Natural Resources and Economic Growth: Learning from History* (2015).

HERMÍNIA VASCONCELOS VILAR is Professor of Medieval History at the University of Évora. She is author of articles and book chapters on political and economic structures, social mobility and political legitimation in the Iberian kingdoms of the late Middle Ages.

AN ECONOMIC HISTORY OF THE IBERIAN PENINSULA, 700–2000

EDITED BY

PEDRO LAINS
University of Lisbon

LEONOR FREIRE COSTA
University of Lisbon

REGINA GRAFE
European University Institute

ALFONSO HERRANZ-LONCÁN
University of Barcelona

DAVID IGUAL-LUIS
University of Castilla-La Mancha

VICENTE PINILLA
University of Zaragoza

HERMÍNIA VASCONCELOS VILAR
University of Évora

Shaftesbury Road, Cambridge CB2 8EA, United Kingdom

One Liberty Plaza, 20th Floor, New York, NY 10006, USA

477 Williamstown Road, Port Melbourne, VIC 3207, Australia

314–321, 3rd Floor, Plot 3, Splendor Forum, Jasola District Centre, New Delhi – 110025, India

103 Penang Road, #05–06/07, Visioncrest Commercial, Singapore 238467

Cambridge University Press is part of Cambridge University Press & Assessment, a department of the University of Cambridge.

We share the University's mission to contribute to society through the pursuit of education, learning and research at the highest international levels of excellence.

www.cambridge.org
Information on this title: www.cambridge.org/9781108488327
DOI: 10.1017/9781108770217

© Cambridge University Press & Assessment 2024

This publication is in copyright. Subject to statutory exception and to the provisions of relevant collective licensing agreements, no reproduction of any part may take place without the written permission of Cambridge University Press & Assessment.

First published 2024

A catalogue record for this publication is available from the British Library

A Cataloging-in-Publication data record for this book is available from the Library of Congress

ISBN 978-1-108-48832-7 Hardback

Cambridge University Press & Assessment has no responsibility for the persistence or accuracy of URLs for external or third-party internet websites referred to in this publication and does not guarantee that any content on such websites is, or will remain, accurate or appropriate.

CONTENTS

List of Figures   *page* viii
List of Tables   xi
List of Contributors   xiii
Preface: By Way of Presentation   xv
PEDRO LAINS

Introduction   1
LEONOR FREIRE COSTA, REGINA GRAFE, ALFONSO HERRANZ-LONCÁN, DAVID IGUAL-LUIS, VICENTE PINILLA AND HERMÍNIA VASCONCELOS VILAR

PART I   **The Making of Iberia, 700–1500**   23
Edited by David Igual-Luis and Hermínia Vasconcelos Vilar

SECTION I   **The Early Middle Ages, 700–1200**   25

1   Muslim and Christian Polities, 700–1200   25
HERMENEGILDO FERNANDES AND FLOCEL SABATÉ

SECTION II   **The Medieval Economy, 1000–1500**   47

2   Production, 1000–1500   47
MARÍA ASENJO-GONZÁLEZ AND ANTONI FURIÓ

3   Population, 1000–1500   76
LUÍS MIGUEL DUARTE, IGNACIO ÁLVAREZ BORGE AND MARIO LAFUENTE GÓMEZ

4   The Polity, 1000–1500   102
MARIA HELENA COELHO, FRANCISCO FRANCO-SÁNCHEZ, JESÚS ÁNGEL SOLÓRZANO TELECHEA AND HERMÍNIA VASCONCELOS VILAR

5   Money, Credit and Banking, 1000–1500   130
    DAVID CARVAJAL, ANTÓNIO HENRIQUES AND PERE VERDÉS

6   Technology, 1000–1500   158
    ARNALDO SOUSA MELO, GERMÁN NAVARRO ESPINACH AND
    RICARDO CÓRDOBA DE LA LLAVE

7   Living Standards, 1000–1500   175
    HIPÓLITO RAFAEL OLIVA HERRER, PERE BENITO I MONCLÚS AND
    ISABEL DOS GUIMARÃES SÁ

8   International Trade and Commerce, 1000–1500   199
    HILARIO CASADO ALONSO, DAVID IGUAL-LUIS, FLÁVIO MIRANDA
    AND JOANA SEQUEIRA

9   The Iberian Economy in Global Perspective, 700–1500   221
    JEFF FYNN-PAUL

PART II **Globalization and Enlightenment, 1500–1800**   249
Edited by Leonor Freire Costa and Regina Grafe

10 Patterns of Iberian Economic Growth in the Early Modern Period   251
    NUNO PALMA AND CARLOS SANTIAGO-CABALLERO

11 Population of the Iberian Peninsula in the Early Modern Period: A Comparative and Regional Perspective   278
    ANDREIA DURÃES AND VICENTE PÉREZ MOREDA

12 Institutions and Policy, 1500–1800   310
    MAFALDA SOARES DA CUNHA, FRANCISCO GIL MARTÍNEZ AND ANA SOFIA RIBEIRO

13 Early Modern Financial Development in the Iberian Peninsula   335
    LEONOR FREIRE COSTA, SUSANA MÜNCH MIRANDA AND PILAR NOGUES-MARCO

14 Science, Knowledge and Technology, 1500–1800   358
    CARLOS ÁLVAREZ-NOGAL, ALEJANDRO GARCÍA-MONTÓN AND PEDRO LAINS

15 Living Standards, Inequality and Consumption, 1500–1800   385
    ESTEBAN NICOLINI, FERNANDA OLIVAL AND FERNANDO RAMOS-PALENCIA

16 Trade and the Colonial Economies, 1500–1828   409
CÁTIA ANTUNES, REGINA GRAFE AND XABIER LAMIKIZ

17 The Economic History of Iberia in a Wider Context, 1500–1800   443
BARTOLOMÉ YUN-CASALILLA

PART III **Industrialization and Catching Up, 1800–2000**   471
Edited by Alfonso Herranz-Loncán and Vicente Pinilla

18 Economic Growth and the Spatial Distribution of Income, 1800–2000   473
ALFONSO HERRANZ-LONCÁN, M. TERESA SANCHIS-LLOPIS AND DANIEL A. TIRADO-FABREGAT

19 Population Growth, Composition and Educational Levels   496
AMÉLIA BRANCO AND FERNANDO COLLANTES

20 Economic Policies and Institutions   519
JOSÉ LUÍS CARDOSO AND FRANCISCO COMÍN

21 Iberian Financial System, 1800–2000   546
PABLO MARTÍN-ACEÑA AND RITA MARTINS DE SOUSA

22 Economic Growth and Structural Change in the Iberian Economies, 1800–2000   567
LUCIANO AMARAL, CONCHA BETRÁN AND VICENTE PINILLA

23 Living Standards in Iberia, 1800–2010   592
ALFONSO DÍEZ-MINGUELA, JORDI GUILERA AND JULIO MARTINEZ-GALARRAGA

24 Iberian Globalization and Catching Up in the Poor South European Periphery, 1830–2010   617
ANTONIO TENA-JUNGUITO, GIOVANNI FEDERICO AND ESTER G. SILVA

25 The Iberian Economy in Comparative Perspective, 1800–2000   648
STEPHEN BROADBERRY AND RUI PEDRO ESTEVES

References   679
Index   768

FIGURES

1.1 The Iberian Peninsula in the eighth–twelfth centuries. *page* 39
3.1 Evolution of the population in the Iberian states in the late Middle Ages. 79
3.2 Evolution of the population in the Crown of Aragon: number of inhabitants in 1300 and 1500. 81
8.1 The Iberian Peninsula in the mid-fifteenth century. 214
10.1 GDP per capita in constant, Geary–Khamis (GK) 'international' 1990 dollars for Spain, Portugal and England, 1500–1800. 252
10.2 Map of Spain. 254
10.3 Agricultural output in Spain, 1500–1800 (11 years moving average). 258
10.4 Agricultural output per head in Spain, 1500–1800. 259
10.5 Urbanization rates in Spain, 1530–1857. 262
10.6 Map of Portugal. 265
10.7 CPI for four regions of Portugal, 1527–1850. 266
10.8 Skilled real wages for four regions of Portugal, 1527–1850. 266
10.9 Portugal's GDP per capita, in constant prices (GK 'international' 1990 dollars). 267
10.10 Land rents index for 1565–1850, in constant prices. 272
10.11 Index of agricultural GDP per capita for 1527–1850, in constant prices. 272
11.1 (a) Portuguese administrative divisions, 1758. (b) Historical regions of Spain. 282
11.2 Estimates of the Portuguese population, 1527–1864. 286
11.3 Portugal: population estimates per region, 1500–1860. 286
11.4 Estimates of Spanish population, 1600–1800. 295
11.5 Median age at first marriage for women in Iberia (Spain, 1787–1797; Portugal, eighteenth century). 299
11.6 Growth of towns over 5,000 inhabitants in Spain (1591 and 1787) and Portugal (1527–1532 and 1801). 304
13.1 (a) Long-term debt, Castile, 1504–1800. (b) Interest payments to tax revenues (%), Castile. 342
13.2 Interest rates on the nominal value of long-term bonds (*juros*) (%), Castile. 345

LIST OF FIGURES

13.3 Interest rates on the nominal value of long-term bonds (*juros*) (%) (weighted average), Portugal.   347
13.4 Commercial annual interest rates (%), Cádiz, 1729–1789.   351
13.5 Annual market interest rates (%) – short-term obligations, Lisbon, 1719–1800.   353
13.6 Interest rates at issuance (%): private perpetuities in Portugal.   355
15.1 Prices and wages in Iberia, 1500–1800.   387
15.2 Real wages in Spain and Portugal, 1500–1800.   388
16.1 Number of enslaved Africans disembarked in Iberoamerica, 1500–1800.   415
16.2 New World gold output, 1492–1810 (by decade, in millions of pesos of 272 *maravedís*).   430
16.3 Cotton exports from Maranhao and Pernambuco, 1758–1815 (in *arrobas*).   431
16.4 Total tonnage of merchant ships sailing from the western Andalusian ports (Seville, Sanlúcar and Cádiz) and the Canary Islands to Spanish America, 1550–1778 (tons of 1.376 m^3).   432
16.5 Sugar exports from Cuba, 1750–1815 (in *arrobas*).   434
16.6 Spanish private imports from the Indies, 1747–1820 (by quinquennium in millions of pesos of 272 *maravedís*).   435
16.7 Total shipping movements between western Andalusian ports (Seville, Sanlúcar and Cádiz) and Spanish America, 1506–1796.   436
16.8 New World silver and gold output, 1492–1810 (by decade in millions of pesos of 272 *maravedís*).   439
17.1 European urban networks, 1800.   464
17.2 European urban growth.   465
18.1 Spanish and Portuguese GDP per capita, 1800–2018 (Geary–Khamis 'international' 1990 dollars).   475
18.2 Portuguese and Spanish GDP per capita as a percentage of the average of Western European economies.   477
18.3 Regional inequality in Iberia, 1900–2000 (Williamson index).   481
18.4 GDP per capita in the Iberian regions, 1900 (quartiles).   481
18.5 GDP per capita in the Iberian regions, 1960 (quartiles).   482
18.6 GDP per capita in the Iberian regions, 2000 (quartiles).   482
19.1 Iberian population change and its sources.   498
19.2 The demographic transition.   500
20.1 Government revenue/GDP (%).   527
20.2 Government expenditures/GDP (%).   527
20.3 Budget balance/GDP (%).   531
20.4 Outstanding public debt/GDP (%).   532
23.1 Real per capita income in Iberia (Spain and Portugal), 1850–2010 (Geary–Khamis 'international' 1990 dollars).   594
23.2 Share of consumption expenditure in Spain and Iberia by category.   595

LIST OF FIGURES

23.3 Life expectancy at birth (years) in Spain/Iberia and Western Europe, 1850–2011.   602
23.4 The Human Development Index: the narrowing of the gap between Spain/Iberia and Western Europe.   604
23.5 Gini indices for Portugal and Spain.   608
23.6 Extraction ratio in Spain and Portugal.   612
23.7 Top income shares (10% left axis; 0.01% right axis) in Spain and Portugal.   614
24.1 Exports/GDP (Geary–Khamis 'international' 1990 dollars).   619
24.2 Per capita exports relative to Rich Europe (1913$; Rich Europe = 1).   622
24.3 Exports/GDP ratio of tradables in current dollars, 1850–2007.   624
24.4 Revealed comparative advantage indices (Portugal, 1842–2014).   629
24.5 Tariff average in Spain and Portugal, 1842–1980 (import duties as a percentage of import value).   632
24.6 Portugal main export destinations, 1842–2010.   634
24.7 Spain main export destinations, 1826–2010.   635
24.8 Net capital flows (absolute value of the current account as a percentage of GDP, Spain, Portugal, Italy, Europe and world, 1870–2017).   637
24.9 Net migration rate per 1,000 population (absolute figures).   638
24.10 Portugal's balance of payments and financial capacity/financial need (% of GDP; 1948–2018).   641
24.11 Spain's balance of payments and financial capacity/financial need (% of GDP; 1850–2018): (a) 1850–1913; (b) 1931–2018.   643
25.1 GDP per capita in Spain and Portugal, 1800–2016.   649
25.2 Spanish and Portuguese GDP per capita as a percentage of the UK and US economies: (a) comparison with the UK; (b) comparison with the US.   650
25.3 Spanish and Portuguese GDP per capita compared with the maximum and minimum in the rest of Western Europe.   651
25.4 Spanish and Portuguese GDP per capita compared with India and China.   652
25.5 Globalization forces, 1830–2000: (a) Spain; (b) Portugal.   664
25.6 GDP per capita in Iberian regions, relative to the average: (a) 1900; (b) 2000.   671
25.7 Growth of the credit system, 1870–2016: (a) Spain; (b) Portugal.   676

TABLES

2.1 Evolution of cereal production in the archbishopric of Seville in the fifteenth century.   *page* 55
10.1 Total output per head (Spain in 1857 = 100).   256
10.2 Portugal's population shares by total by occupation.   269
10.3 Output per capita in Western Europe (GK 'international' 1990 dollars), using the Maddison method.   274
10.4 Output per capita in Europe (GK 'international' 1990 dollars), using the Prados method.   276
11.1 European population, 1500–1820 (thousands of inhabitants).   280
11.2 Spanish and Portuguese populations according to the *vecindarios*, official censuses and estimates (millions).   280
11.3 Population of continental Spain by region, c. 1530–1800.   285
11.4 Estimates of the population in Portugal by region, c. 1530–1800.   285
11.5 Average annual growth rate (%), 1591–1787.   295
11.6 Standardized marital fertility (I_G), expectation of life at birth (E_0) and singular mean age at first marriage for females ($SMAM_F$).   298
11.7 Average age of women's first marriage by region (Portugal, eighteenth century).   300
11.8 Urbanization rates in Europe between 1500 and 1800, considering towns with 5,000 inhabitants (%) or more.   301
11.9 Sectoral distribution of the active population in Spain, 1797.   306
11.10 Portuguese population by sectors.   307
12.1 Fiscal revenues of the Hispanic monarchy, 1560–1805 (without imperial revenues).   321
12.2 Fiscal revenues of Portugal, 1527–1804 (without imperial revenues).   321
13.1 Decennial remittances to Spain and Portugal, 1487–1660.   337
13.2 Decennial remittances to Spain and Portugal, 1700–1800.   341
13.3 Consolidated debt in Portugal, 1607–1812.   348
15.1 Inequality in Portugal, 1565–1770.   392
15.2 Income inequality in Spanish cities, towns and villages, c. 1750.   393
16.1 Sugar production in the Portuguese colonial empire, 1515–1617 (*arrobas*).   412

LIST OF TABLES

18.1 Iberian growth accounting: annual average growth rates.   487
18.2 Contribution of factors and TFP to GDP growth (%).   491
19.1 Basic population figures for Portugal, Spain and 'Iberia' (Portugal + Spain).   497
19.2 Sources of population change (average annual per thousand rates).   499
19.3 Occupation and activity.   505
19.4 Percentage share of population living in nuclei of 5,000 inhabitants or more.   508
19.5 Education.   512
19.6 Iberian demographic and economic change in a comparative perspective.   516
22.1 Economic growth, structural change and labour productivity (%), Spain.   569
22.2 Structural change and labour productivity (%), Portugal.   569
22.3 Share of each sector in GDP (%).   571
22.4 Share of each sector in employment (%).   571
22.5 Structure of agricultural output (%).   574
22.6 Agricultural annual growth rates of outputs, inputs and TFP between 1950 and 2005.   578
22.7 Share of manufacturing valued added (%).   581
22.8 Share of service sector value added (%).   587
23.1 Average male adult height by birth decade in Western Europe and Iberia, 1860–1980.   598
23.2 Life expectancy at birth by sex.   603
24.1 Composition of exports: main WTO categories (Portugal and Spain, 1877–2014).   626
24.2 Composition of imports: main WTO categories (Portugal and Spain, 1877–2014).   627
24.3 Revealed comparative advantage indices (Spain, 1877–2014).   630
25.1 Accounting for the growth of output: average annual growth rates.   654
25.2 Accounting for the growth of labour productivity: average annual growth rates (%).   655
25.3 Sectoral shares of employment (headcount), 1870–2007 (%).   657
25.4 Structural change and labour productivity growth (% per annum).   658
25.5 Political and economic institutions, 1800–2019.   667
25.6 Macroeconomic policy and imbalances.   674

CONTRIBUTORS

Ignacio Álvarez Borge	University of La Rioja, Spain
Carlos Álvarez-Nogal	University Carlos III of Madrid, Spain
Luciano Amaral	Nova University of Lisbon, Portugal
Cátia Antunes	Leiden University, The Netherlands
María Asenjo-González	Complutense University of Madrid, Spain
Pere Benito i Monclús	University of Lleida, Spain
Concha Betrán	University of Valencia, Spain
Amélia Branco	University of Lisbon, Portugal
Stephen Broadberry,	University of Oxford, United Kingdom
David Carvajal	University of Valladolid, Spain
José Luís Cardoso	University of Lisbon, Portugal
Hilario Casado Alonso	University of Valladolid, Spain
Maria Helena Coelho	University of Coimbra, Portugal
Fernando Collantes	University of Oviedo, Spain
Francisco Comín	University of Alcala, Spain
Ricardo Córdoba de la Llave	University of Córdoba, Spain
Leonor Freire Costa	University of Lisbon, Portugal
Mafalda Soares da Cunha	University of Évora, Portugal
Alfonso Díez-Minguela	University of Valencia, Spain
Luís Miguel Duarte	University of Porto, Portugal
Andreia Durães	University of Minho, Portugal
Rui Pedro Esteves	Graduate Institute, Geneva, Switzerland
Hermenegildo Fernandes	University of Lisbon, Portugal
Francisco Franco-Sánchez	University of Alicante, Spain
Giovanni Federico	NYU Abu Dhabi, UAE
Antoni Furió	University of Valencia, Spain
Jeff Fynn-Paul	Leiden University, The Netherlands
Alejandro García-Montón	University of Granada, Spain
Francisco Gil Martínez	University of Almería, Spain
Regina Grafe	European University Institute
Jordi Guilera	Independent Researcher
António Henriques	University of Porto, Portugal
Alfonso Herranz-Loncán	University of Barcelona, Spain

David Igual-Luis	University of Castilla-La Mancha, Spain
Mario Lafuente Gómez	University of Zaragoza, Spain
Pedro Lains	University of Lisbon, Portugal
Xabier Lamikiz	University of the Basque Country, Spain
Pablo Martín-Aceña	University of Alcalá, Spain
Julio Martinez-Galarraga	University of Barcelona, Spain
Arnaldo Sousa Melo	University of Minho, Portugal
Flávio Miranda	University of Porto, Portugal
Susana Münch Miranda	Nova University of Lisbon, Portugal
Germán Navarro Espinach	University of Zaragoza, Spain
Esteban Nicolini	Universidad del Norte Santo Tomás de Aquino, Argentine; University Carlos III of Madrid, Spain
Pilar Nogues-Marco	University of Geneva, Switzerland
Hipólito Rafael Oliva Herrer	University of Seville, Spain
Fernanda Olival	University of Évora, Portugal
Nuno Palma	University of Manchester, United Kingdom; University of Lisbon, Portugal
Vicente Pérez Moreda	Complutense University of Madrid, Spain
Vicente Pinilla	University of Zaragoza, Spain
Fernando Ramos-Palencia	Pablo de Olavide University, Spain
Ana Sofia Ribeiro	University of Évora, Portugal
Isabel dos Guimarães Sá	University of Minho, Portugal
Flocel Sabaté	University of Lleida, Spain
M. Teresa Sanchis-Llopis	University of Valencia, Spain
Carlos Santiago-Caballero	University Carlos III of Madrid, Spain
Joana Sequeira	University of Minho, Portugal
Ester G. Silva	University of Porto, Portugal
Jesús Ángel Solórzano Telechea	University of Cantabria, Spain
Rita Martins de Sousa	University of Lisbon, Portugal
Antonio Tena-Junguito	University Carlos III of Madrid, Spain
Daniel A. Tirado-Fabregat	University of Valencia, Spain
Pere Verdés	Spanish National Research Council (CSIC), Barcelona
Hermínia Vasconcelos Vilar	University of Évora, Portugal
Bartolomé Yun-Casalilla	Pablo de Olavide University, Spain

PREFACE: BY WAY OF PRESENTATION

PEDRO LAINS[1]

The Iberian Peninsula stands out as a well-defined regional unit cut from the rest of Europe by the Pyrenees and encircled by the Mediterranean Sea and the Atlantic Ocean. It was ruled by successive empires or polities, including Romans, Celts, Visigoths, Muslims and Christians, with varying degree of political integration within its borders, and in regard to the rest of Europe and the world. For most of its history, Iberia was at the periphery of larger political units, particularly, the Romans and the Muslim empires and served as a bridge between different parts of the world. Since late medieval times, it was the centre of overseas empires that stretched from Africa to Asia and the Americas. Within its territory, borders between different political and cultural entities moved across time and space, following geographical discontinuities, such as rivers and mountains, particularly during Antiquity and up to the Muslim period, and for a long period of time the political borders were mostly between the north and the south. Since the Medieval period, borders have been mostly politically defined and the north–south division has become less important. Yet the old divide could still be noticed possibly up to present times, in a complex net of political and natural divisions. The level of political integration increased, as Spain was formed as a dynastic union in the fifteenth century, and from 1580 to 1640 Spain and Portugal were ruled under the crown of the Habsburgs. Clearly, the Iberian Peninsula, with all its internal differences, should be taken as a unit of historical study.

Economically, the Iberian Peninsula is as diverse as probably any other part of the European continent of a similar size, due to differences in geography, climate and resource endowments, and the level of economic integration certainly has varied across the centuries. However, the economic divide has not necessarily followed the political divide. Recent research on long swings of economic development for Portugal and Spain has pointed to the possibility that the performance across the political border was rather disparate until well into the industrialization period. As economic development proceeded, the

---

[1] Text written in September 2018.

level of economic integration within the peninsula increased, although certainly not at a regular rate. Iberia diverged from the core European economies for a long period of time, and converged only from the mid-twentieth century on.

Why do some nations prosper and others lag behind? This is probably the most researched question in Economic History and one of the most important in the field of Economics. Answers to the question will always be incomplete and provisional, and have changed considerably across time, as we learn more about the past, in terms of time and space. The study of the economic history of the Iberian Peninsula should be set in the context of understanding different paths of growth within Europe.

The divide in levels of economic development between northern and southern Europe is quite clear and well documented in the period since the Industrial Revolution. It is of utmost relevance to understand why that happened and the literature on the contemporary period provide several answers that range from the role of the state and private institutions, the limitations imposed by the structure of resource endowments, or cultural factors. Those factors, however, need to be revisited in order to assess whether they can survive the light of new evidence regarding the varieties of experiences within the European continent that have been revealed by the new research on patterns of growth and retardation. The understanding of economic performance during the industrialization period and its aftermath is much dependent on our perception regarding the starting point. Due to the increased interest in research in long-term economic growth and development, we are now closer than ever in identifying the long swings of the economic performance of Spain and Portugal since the Middle Ages, as well as the relative levels of income, as compared to the rest of Europe.

The aim of the present book is to provide a global interpretation of the evolution of the Iberian economies in the second Millennium. The project gathers a number of specialists in the field, with joint contributions, and is divided into three epochs: *The Making of Iberia, 700–1500*; *Globalization and the Enlightenment, 1500–1800*; and *Industrialization and Catching Up, 1800–2000*. Each epoch comprises eight or nine chapters covering an equal number of topics, including the institutional framework, population, money and banking, domestic product and factor markets, international trade, economic output, economic well-being and international comparisons. The book is the outcome of two preliminary workshops, held in Lisbon and Zaragoza, where the structure and contents of the project were widely discussed, and most chapters are written in co-authorship by specialists on different parts of the Iberian Peninsula.

Introduction

LEONOR FREIRE COSTA, REGINA GRAFE, ALFONSO
HERRANZ-LONCÁN, DAVID IGUAL-LUIS, VICENTE PINILLA
AND HERMÍNIA VASCONCELOS VILAR

An Economic History of Iberia: The Dream and Project of Pedro Lains

We can consider, quite rightly, that this book, while being the collective work of more than 70 authors, is overall the posthumous work of Pedro Lains, who sadly passed away on 16 May 2021. Pedro always expressed concern about southern Europe not being sufficiently represented in the analyses of the continent's economic past. Therefore, he believed that the countries of the Iberian Peninsula shared sufficient common features so as to deserve a monograph, published in English, to address their trajectory and facilitate their integration in European economic history.

His efforts with this book were titanic. He designed the structure of a text that had to span from the Early Middle Ages to the present day. The perspective that he sought was not to analyse the Iberian territories separately but to integrate them in a common vision. This implied integrating the economic past of the Christian and Muslim territories from the early Middle Ages, of Aragon, Castile and Portugal in early modern times and finally of Spain and Portugal in the contemporary age. Furthermore, he selected authors to write the different chapters and editors to assist him in this immense task. He organized two conferences in Lisbon (2016) and Zaragoza (2019), where the authors were able to discuss the project and the drafts of the different chapters.

Pedro's academic trajectory allows us to understand his project. After having published extensively on the economic history of Portugal, he considered that its parallelisms with that of Spain justified this effort. It has to be said that he had a profound knowledge of Spanish economic history. Not only did he carry out a post-doctoral stay in the Universidad Carlos III of Madrid, with which he always maintained close contact as a member of the Instituto Laureano Figuerola, but he also participated in many research projects developed in the universities of Barcelona and Zaragoza, collaborating with their economic historians over many years and forging close friendships with them.

Sadly, a cruel illness prevented Pedro from completing a task in which he had invested many years and a lot of effort and enthusiasm. The editors and authors of this volume wish to offer this book as a warm tribute to an admirable person and an excellent economic historian.

From a very young age, Pedro dreamed of becoming a university professor.[2] This vocation was reinforced by his idea that this profession would give him great freedom of movement and also commitment. After finishing his baccalaureate studies, he chose to study Economics at the Universidade Nova of Lisbon, as he considered that some of the subjects in which he had obtained the best results, such as Mathematics, Geography or English, had prepared him well for it. In the Faculty, from which he graduated in 1983, early on he developed a concern for the lower level of economic development of Portugal compared with other European countries. After finishing his degree, he considered that, with its theoretical models or mathematical instruments, his field did not allow him to respond to his big question and what he had studied was merely an instrument to bring him closer to real economics. This is when he found economic history, a discipline which he felt would help him to resolve his questions about Portugal's backwardness.

Although he joined the Instituto de Ciências Sociais (ICS) of the Universidade de Lisboa in 1984, shortly afterwards he went abroad to complete his training. First, he went to the University of Oxford and immediately afterwards to the European University Institute (EUI) in Florence to undertake his doctorate, which he finished in 1992. He returned to the ICS after conducting a post-doctoral stay in the Universidad Carlos III in Madrid. He spent the rest of his academic life in this centre, except for a year in the United States in Brown University.

His thesis addressed the effect of Portugal's international integration during the first globalization on the country's backwardness, concluding that the unfavourable starting point made it impossible to correct this backwardness with a few decades of internationalization. This constituted one of his main fields of study over many years; the analysis of the relation between Portugal's economic growth and international integration, from a comparative and long-term perspective. At that time, as he recognized later, Pedro did not contemplate publishing his thesis in English in book form or as articles in international journals. He translated it into Portuguese and published it as a book (Lains, 1995), which was translated a few years later into French (Lains, 1999). As we previously mentioned, his analysis of Portugal's economic past was a constant theme throughout his career, with monographs such as Lains (2002a) (Spanish translation, Lains, 2006a) or the formidable work co-authored with Leonor Freire Costa and Susana M. Miranda (Costa et al., 2014), analysing the economic

---

[2] Responding to the request of the Portuguese Association of Economic and Social History, Pedro Lains wrote a text published online in May 2020 in which he summarizes his life and academic career: www.aphes.pt/images/Docs.pdf/thomas/APHES_Lains_2020_05_18_Revisao_final.pdf

history of Portugal over a period of 900 years, which had enormous success, with several editions and an English translation published a few years later (Costa et al., 2016).

Many other topics of the Portuguese economy also captured Pedro's attention. We can highlight his studies on the Portuguese financial system, particularly the books on the Caixa Geral de Depósitos (Lains, 2002b and 2008), the loss of the Brazilian empire, or the integration into the European Union and Portugal's economic growth.

But in recent years, although Pedro published many of his studies as articles in prominent journals, mainly specialized in economic history, he began focusing on leading ambitious projects to publish books that would enable him to answer complex questions, something which, in his opinion, was not possible through articles. The ambition of the studies in which he was involved, normally as a co-editor, is remarkable. He addressed broad subject areas such as the relationship between agriculture and economic growth in Europe in the nineteenth and twentieth centuries (Lains and Pinilla, 2009), public finance and the construction of liberal states in this same continent in the nineteenth century (Cardoso and Lains, 2010a) or the agricultural history of Portugal in the second millennium (Freire and Lains, 2017). This was an activity that aroused passion and excitement in him, as he expressed to many of his friends in recent years. It is within this context that the book that we are presenting in this introduction can be framed.

But Pedro was not only a great researcher. He also taught classes in universities such as La Católica in Lisbon or Évora, and tried to make his knowledge as an economic historian useful to society, furthering the understanding of current problems with a historical perspective. He wrote for the most important Portuguese newspapers, participated in television programmes, wrote a blog commenting on Portugal's problems during the crisis beginning in 2008 and published two books that included his journalistic interventions (Lains, 2007a and 2014). Finally, he also devoted substantial effort to the Economic History profession, being secretary of the European Historical Economics Society, president of the Portuguese Association of Economic and Social History and the director of the journal *Analise Social*.

This is the trajectory of a prominent and exemplary academic and an excellent person, without whom this book would never have been published. All co-editors and authors of this volume have worked over the last two years, without his direction, in order to conclude it as he would have liked. He was able to read all chapters and made many suggestions to improve them. There is no doubt that his direction has profoundly marked this project. Pedro launched and developed a magnificent idea which authors and editors have all also made our own. We believe that having completed it satisfactorily is the best way to pay tribute to him. Pedro will always be remembered among European economic historians and this is our tribute to his memory.

As Pedro Lains' preface reminds us, the peninsula is as much a European gateway to different parts of the world as a peripheral point at the western end of a continental mass. Both attributes would merit consideration in economic history and, indeed, their far-reaching implications cut across the book's 25 chapters. However, this collective effort very dear to Pedro Lains is not based on the aprioristic identification of an area on a map. It fills a gap in current knowledge by addressing a European area from an overarching perspective. A growing scholarly interest in Spain and Portugal economic performance in different timespans has brought about new data supporting this entirely new view on the peninsula as a whole. That output contributes to a comparative history of regional dynamics in the face of economic integration.

From almost complete insertion into Muslim polities to full membership in the European Union, the Iberian Peninsula has experienced over the last thousand years shifting political boundaries and changing patterns of economic integration, but has also comprised cultural and linguistic resilience. If economic growth has been widely studied in the framework of the sovereign state, it is also true that Iberian diversity is not simply the result of the formation of nation-states and domestic integrated markets over the last two centuries. Diversity involves climatic and resource specificities at the regional level, and, for the subject under consideration in the design of the book, it reflects income inequality that has accompanied a long-term process of economic change. This book tackles the factors for some areas to prosper, and others to decline. Apart from Madrid district bolstering the very continental core of the peninsula, the most dynamic regions have been located on the Mediterranean and Atlantic coastlines, thus contemporary economic geography questions the economic role of the north–south divide between the Iberian countries since the medieval period. This book's approach is free from pre-defined political borders, but it does not ignore them either.

We start in the year 711 with the Islamic conquest of large parts of the peninsula. But we take the symbolic date of the year 1000 to begin a detailed analysis of the economic development of all Iberian regions over the past millennium. The book unfolds in three separate parts. The Iberian transformations and their intersection with major transformations taking course in the rest of the world construct each part. Part I – The Making of Iberia – observes the peninsula under Muslim influence and the subsequent creation of kingdoms in the orbit of the expansion of the Christianity in Europe; Part II – Globalization and Enlightenment – considers Iberia's participation in the globalization of the world economy and the relative alienation of this area from the major reforms of the Enlightenment; Part III – Industrialization and Catching Up – addresses the virtually synchronic performance of the two Iberian national economies, both undergoing economic divergence in the nineteenth century and catching up after 1950. Despite particularities inherent to the chronological periods covered, the three parts bear a similar structure.

Each of the chapters of one part focuses on a theme or a set of themes that finds a corresponding chapter in the other two. This arrangement allows the reader to use the book to explore a single theme in diachrony, or several themes in a single period.

Part I: The Making of Iberia

The Historical Context

From the eighth century onwards, the medieval history of the Iberian Peninsula was marked by the consequences of the Muslim expansion and occupation of much of the territory, the establishment of a Christian zone in the north and a number of kingdoms and territories that gradually developed in both Christian- and Muslim-controlled regions. The characteristics of these circumstances can be found in the nine chapters that make up this part of the book, and are dealt with in greater or lesser detail.

By way of introduction, it is worth noting that the Muslim space (al-Andalus) evolved from a unified political structure to the fragmentation which characterized the so-called *taifa* kingdoms between the eleventh and thirteenth centuries, and also, thereafter, by the influence of the Almoravids and Almohads, dynasties originating in North Africa. Granada was the only Muslim kingdom that persisted up until the fifteenth century. Meanwhile, in the Christian sphere, a number of polities were gradually established which ended up, especially from the twelfth and thirteenth centuries, as the kingdoms of Portugal, Castile, Navarre and Aragon. The overall picture is one of changes in the military and territorial balance of power between Christians and Muslims throughout the period, with Muslims predominant until the twelfth century, when there was a shift in favour of Christians.

This pattern of political and territorial diversity was also a reality in the economic sphere, and the specific characteristics and patterns of evolution of the economies of the different Iberian spaces were manifestly diverse. The most marked differences were those between Christians and Muslims: the two worlds displayed differences in terms of economic organization and patterns of development over time. Three major stages can be identified in the development of the Christian economies: first, establishment and gradual expansion from the eighth century; second, a period of growth from the eleventh century; and third, the difficulties and transformations experienced from the fourteenth century. In the Islamic side there are indications of the hegemony and strength of the Muslim economy from its origins, and its vitality was evident up until the thirteenth century, despite the inevitable setbacks and fluctuations that characterized the history of al-Andalus.

In terms of the Iberian Peninsula, this helps to put into perspective the significance that historians of medieval Europe have assigned to the year 1000 as the starting point for the expansion of Western Christian countries and their overall domination of the societies based in the east (Islam and Byzantium). Although the year has been taken as delimiting periods examined in these chapters, it should be noted that if it can be held true for Christian territories, it is not for Muslim territories.

Questions of Research and Historiography

The available studies on the period clearly reflect the aspects of plurality and differentiation indicated above, with a clear divide between authors who focus on periods either before or after the eleventh or the fourteenth century and those who cover al-Andalus or the Christian areas. In turn, each of these two groups is divided between studies focusing on the various states and/or regions that were established.

It should also be noted that comparatively fewer written sources are available for the Early Middle Ages than for the late Middle Ages, and for Muslim territories than for Christian spaces and, among Christians, for the kingdoms of Portugal and Castile than for the kingdoms of Navarre and Aragon. In this regard, the contribution of archaeological research is crucial, especially in relation to the Muslim world and periods prior to the year 1000, although this does not always compensate for the lack of archival documentation.

The content and intrinsic characteristics of the majority of available manuscript sources, as well as the theoretical and methodological approaches of the majority of experts in medieval Iberian economics, explain the existence of research in which qualitative approaches predominate over quantitative ones. Whatever the case, the difficulty of the synthesis has been classically and strongly felt, which is a result of the diverse characteristics of medieval Iberia and the academic and historiographical traditions of Spain and Portugal.

In fact, two elements posed a challenge, at both the academic and personal level, for the 25 authors who contribute to this first part: the need to break down barriers between different historiographical approaches and the need to include in the analysis ideas (and perspectives) as diverse as those required not only by the historical reality of medieval Iberia but also by the distribution of chapters and themes for this part of the book.

In fact, we are unaware of any other work with similar aims to those of the studies included in this part of the book: a reasonable attempt to produce a synthesis of the array of Iberian economic scenarios during the Middle Ages, covering the different stages of the development of the economy in the different territories from the eighth century while adopting a perspective that, besides allowing for the separate treatment of kingdoms and societies, attempts to focus on the great issues of economic history: production, population, politics and institutions, currency and credit, technology, living standards and trade.

Structure and Content of the Chapters

What has been said above provides the rationale for the structure of Part I, which is divided into two sections: the first, composed of a single chapter, covers the period from 700 to 1200; the second, comprising seven chapters, deals with the period from 1000 to 1500. The aim of the ninth and final chapter is to draw overall conclusions and contextualize the medieval Iberian economy from a global perspective over the long term. The chronological overlap of Sections I and II is explained by the interest in demonstrating in practice how the economies of Christian and Muslim Iberia developed at a different pace, a fact that has already been commented on. And, at the same time, taking into account the influences these spaces had on each other, as well as factors of continuity in terms of spaces, powers and economies; thus, this overlap is more apparent than real.

Section I deals with the initial prolonged prominence of al-Andalus at a number of different levels during the period examined (from 700 to 1200), as well as with all aspects regarding Christian territories from 700 to 1000 and the links between these and al-Andalus from 1000 to 1200, the period during which we witness the transition of the peninsula from Muslim to Christian control. The chapter in this section deals with these aspects and, to this end, is divided into two parts. The first copes with al-Andalus and its characteristics as a monetary economy, in which the role of state institutions and their policies are examined, covering aspects such as urban development and the integration of the al-Andalus economy in the Mediterranean context. The role of power centres as regards the minting of coinage, market regulation and the creation of a tax system is highlighted, the last of these emerging as particularly burdensome during the period when the *taifa* kingdoms were required to pay *parias* to Christian kingdoms. The second part of this chapter focuses on the Christian kingdoms and counties of the north of the peninsula, their initial economic features and gradual expansion, closely linked to the perception of the frontier with Muslim territories as a zone for occupation, the accumulation of wealth, and social and economic prosperity. Particular attention is paid to the geographical diversity of spaces, the different political solutions that took shape in the northernmost regions of the peninsula, and to the models for the appropriation of the territories that were gradually integrated into areas under Christian control.

Section II focuses on the development of Iberian Christian societies from 1000 to 1500, involving processes that began with the growth of such societies from the eleventh century, and culminated in their expansion beyond the peninsula from the fifteenth century. Of course, this focus on the Christian world does not mean that the Muslim sphere is ignored. On the contrary the Muslim sphere is dealt in the different chapters taking in account: (1) a focus on the kingdom of Granada from 1200 to 1500, although there are also notes on the *taifa* kingdoms and the Almoravids and Almohads from 1000 to 1200, especially when they serve the purposes of contrast and comparison with the Christian world or as essential elements for gaining an understanding of the latter; and (2) the legacy of al-Andalus and its later influence on the Iberian Christian kingdoms following the conquest of the former by the latter.

Deriving from an analysis of peninsular productive patterns, the first chapter in this section, Chapter 2, sets out the main chronological and territorial milestones in the development of the Christian economy: (a) the period of growth and expansion of the eleventh to thirteenth centuries, and that of the crisis and recovery of the fourteenth to fifteenth centuries; and (b) the spaces in which economic activities were carried out, taking into account landscape features and different forms of resource use by agricultural, manufacturing and commercial activities. In both cases, and despite the difficulty involved, the discussion in this chapter is accompanied by the available quantitative estimates on, for example, agricultural production and productivity.

Chapter 3 deals with population: demographic trends and human mobility, as well as patterns of rural and urban settlement and the distribution of occupations. Serious limits are placed on research deriving from the lack of documentary sources and difficulties regarding the production of reliable population figures. Even the use of coefficients for the conversion of households into inhabitants does not ensure the reliability of the figures analysed, since these always depend on the value of the coefficient adopted. This chapter also highlights the specificities of population growth and population distribution over the different regions and discusses the consequences of the effects of the so-called 'crisis of the fourteenth century' on the evolution of population figures.

Chapter 4 deals with politics and institutions, mainly focusing on their relationship with the economy. Similar to Chapter 1, the political and institutional narrative is unfolded separately for the Muslim and the Christian worlds, highlighting in the latter case the distinction between the periods before and after 1300. In particular, the process of the territorial and political construction of the Iberian monarchies is analysed, as well as the way in which they played a role as economic protagonists in an economically and politically fragmented world. Also highlighted is the role of taxation as a source of revenue for central governments and how the imposition of a tax structure involved the creation of a collection system and led to the growing complexity of the administrative structure.

Chapter 5 focuses on currency, credit and banking, by means of an analysis that underlines the complexity of these aspects, and especially the monetary system, in the peninsula and also, for example, the gradual expansion of private and public credit mechanisms in the Christian kingdoms. Emphasis is thus given to the way in which the political fragmentation of the Christian space led to the emergence of different monetary systems, as an alternative to the Islamic model, while they were nevertheless influenced by the latter, but also by the Carolingian and Visigoth heritage. Despite the scarcity of precious metals, which marked the monetary and minting policy of the different kingdoms, the chapter highlights the tendency to an increasing integration of the monetary systems of the peninsular kingdoms in international circuits.

Chapter 6 examines technology. It begins with some conceptual considerations and then moves on to an explanation of technology in agriculture, manufacturing, energy sources and transport. It also highlights the importance of the Islamic influence on the dissemination of certain techniques in the Iberian case, in particular associated with agriculture.

Chapter 7 examines standards of living and deals with the problems involved in researching the subject for the medieval period. This does not preclude an approach to the issue through the analysis of prices and wages, the distribution of income in the peninsula and existing models of the consumption of food, housing and clothing. In the context of this analysis the negative image prevalent in part of the historiography on peninsular standards of living is called into question by means of a comparison with regions outside the peninsula, while improvements in food, housing and clothing during the course of the late Middle Ages are highlighted.

Chapter 8 is concerned with trade and, above all, with its international dimension. The focus is on trade routes, the products that circulated within Iberia and those which were traded with other countries, local and foreign agents for trade, the institutions that formed the framework within which these agents operated, and the variables that underpinned the development of Iberian trade in the late Middle Ages in the case of Aragon and, especially, Portugal and Castile. This chapter also highlights the process of transition from the eleventh-century trade marked by the dominant influence of al-Andalus to the development of trade by Christian kingdoms from the twelfth century.

As has already been said, the last chapter in this part, Chapter 9, serves to contextualize the medieval Iberian economy in a global and long-term perspective. Global because it compares the Iberian economy with other European and Mediterranean regions. Long-term because it deals not only with the specific period from 700 to 1500 but also aspects of the prehistoric and ancient eras, including references to the post-Roman or Visigoth period. The chapter proceeds to an analysis of Iberian regional economies at the end of the Middle Ages, which completes and complements what is set out on the subject in previous chapters.

Compared with Parts II and III of the book, what stands out is the specificity of the peninsular economy of the Middle Ages and the differences (and difficulties) involved in researching the topic as compared with early and late modern times. Also, throughout the nine chapters, several notable aspects are evident, which while well known are presented here in a combined approach: the multiple effects of the contrast and contact between Christian and Muslim communities; the social and economic bases of the peninsular states that were established from the eighth to the tenth century; the consequences of the great Christian military and territorial expansion that occurred from the eleventh to the thirteenth century; the dual perception of the fourteenth to fifteenth centuries as a period of crisis and recovery on the one hand and difficulty and transformation on the other hand (although with differences among territories and economic sectors). And at last the idea, which may be applied to the entire period from 700 to 1500, that factors working for diversity and fragmentation in the peninsula developed in parallel with other factors involving interaction and even integration between spaces, countries, cultures and individuals.

As emphasized in the chapters in this part of the book, there were no closed and isolated Iberian medieval economies: on the contrary, they were at all times willing to connect with other areas – the rest of Europe and the Mediterranean. In addition, the peninsular economies shared many similarities with these 'other worlds', and in some cases can even be regarded as pioneering or relatively advanced. These elements, along with many others that are described in detail in the chapters, help to confirm not only the fact that the peninsula never played a subordinate or 'peripheral' role at the European level in the Middle Ages, but also that, as we approach the end of the Middle Ages, the characteristics of its economy provided the essential foundations for the overseas expansion of Iberian societies, which started in the fifteenth century and culminated in the period following 1500.

Part II: Globalization and Enlightenment

A Historical Context

Throughout the centuries covered by Part II, Iberia became the first European region to push the economic frontiers beyond the 'Old Continent'. The first move forward began in the fifteenth century with the conquest of Islamic territories in North Africa, still before the full Christian conquest of the Iberian Peninsula. The integration of Granada (1492) in the south-east of the peninsula consolidated the political borders of the united Castilian–Aragonese polity. Portugal's conquest of Ceuta (1415) and Tanger (1437) in Morocco pushed the border between Islamic and Christian polities beyond the peninsula. The pursuit of a Christian 'holy war' in North Africa would lead to the death of Portugal's young king Sebastião at the battle of Ksar el Kebir (1578) without issue. The ensuing succession crisis resulted in the Habsburg Philip II to claim the Portuguese crown in addition to those of Castile and Aragon. Thus, between 1581 and 1640 all Iberian territories were for the first and the last time ruled by the same monarchy.

The shifting political boundaries within the peninsula coincided with early expansion beyond the sea. By the sixteenth century, two biological effects of Iberian geographical and nautical innovations were felt from Asia to the Americas. One consisted of demographic shocks and labour flows on an unprecedented scale; the other entailed the intercontinental exchange of plant and animal DNA that positively impacted productivity in the regions involved. The demographic disaster among the indigenous population that the conquistadores caused in the Americas was aggravated by the socio-cultural dislocation and the imposition of various forms of forced labour services, especially in agriculture and to a lesser extent in mining (the *mita* in today's Bolivia though not in Mexico). Almost from the start Iberians also used the forced migration of enslaved Africans to America to substitute for the indigenous labour force. Slavery would become the dominant labour system in many sectors of the economy in Brazil. In the Spanish colonies slavery was very widespread and until the mid-seventeenth century even more numerous than in Brazil. However, it was much less concentrated in specific sectors until the introduction of plantation systems in the late eighteenth century.

The second biological consequence of the Iberian offshoots in America was the arrival of large draft animals (oxen, horses) and several crops in America, and that of important staple crops, maize and especially potatoes, and dyestuffs in Europe. They offered a range of opportunities for investment that diversified the consumer baskets across all social sectors in Iberia. More and cheaper foodstuffs combined with additional attractive consumption goods, such as sugar, cocoa and tobacco, to transform patterns of consumption and production in a process known as an 'Industrious Revolution' in Europe.

Iberian rule over territories on distinct continents rested on a political system that scholars defined as a composite monarchy, which implied a polycentric decision-making system. The Dynastic Union of the Portuguese and Castilian crowns (1580–1640), which respected the principle of jurisdictional autonomy, did not prevent the intensification of transcultural commercial networks that blurred the formal borders between both kingdoms' colonial offshoots. Direct navigation across the Atlantic, Pacific, Indian Ocean, Arabian Sea and the Mediterranean eased the integration of markets for certain crucial commodities. The global flows of silver became integrated with the shipment of enslaved Africans and the trade in Asian goods, either directly through Manila to China or indirectly through the Cape route via Europe and Africa. Arguably, Iberian investment in American mining and the means through which silver and gold were spread through the world ensured that the growth of the world economy would not be constrained by monetary restrictions.

The impressive scale of the Habsburg empire became a factor in its breakdown. Imperialist strategies on a world scale put enormous pressure on resources to protect this geographically diverse political unit, with consequences for taxpayer discontent and ultimately the political independence of the United Provinces and Portugal. The occupation of North-eastern Brazil by the Westindische Compagnie (WIC) extended the Eighty Years' War to the waters of the South Atlantic (1630-1654), while attacks by the Vereenigde Oostindische Compagnie (VOC) on Asian possessions, also under military threat from the British East India Company (EIC), also stretched the defensive forces required. Although not implying a clear recession on all fronts of Portuguese or Castilian colonial trade, the north-western European powers eventually undermined Portugal's returns from colonial investments, which made the kingdom vulnerable to any conflict affecting the Habsburg geostrategic goals in Europe. The seventeenth-century crisis of the Castilian economy was thus the context of the War of Restoration of Portugal (1640-1668). The war definitively separated the two major political formations within the peninsula and sustained a lasting division into two diplomatic blocs.

Arguably the crisis and the intra-Iberian war of the mid-seventeenth century were a watershed of internal disintegrations and external integration of Iberia. Portugal's Atlantic orientation contributed to its alignment with England and the United Provinces, which the war of the Spanish succession (1701-1714) reinforced through a defensive Treaty (1703). The alliance conditioned Portugal's geostrategy throughout the eighteenth century and culminated in 1808 in the flight of the Royal Court to Brazil in English vessels following Napoleon's invasion of the peninsula. In contrast, on the Spanish side, the War of Spanish Succession sealed the transition from Habsburg to Bourbon rule and with it an alignment with France in the major conflicts of the eighteenth century. The War also reduced the network of Spain's European possessions significantly, but maintained the American Empire intact.

A new balance between the two Iberian monarchies, with Spain and Portugal undergoing significant reform processes, marks the eighteenth century. The direction of reforms was, however, quite distinct in the two countries. In Spain reforms began mostly directed at overcoming the legacy of jurisdictional fragmentation within the polycentric structure of the peninsular and colonial economy. They addressed the Aragonese territories, which had overwhelmingly supported the losing side in the conflict of the Spanish succession (the Austrian Archduke Karl with the support of England and the Netherlands). The first Bourbon, Philip V, used victory as a pretext to align the legal and fiscal organization of the formerly Aragonese territories of Aragon, Valencia and Catalonia more closely with Castilian institutions under the *decretos de Nueva Planta*. Though the de iure change in the institutions took a long time to alter the juridical and political structures in the Aragonese territories de facto, over the course of the eighteenth century a realignment was driven by increasing fiscal pressure.

As the century progressed, a focus on improving colonial governance, strengthening the struggling silver mining sectors in Mexico and Peru, and fostering manufacturing through active policies meant to attract specialists was added. Most historians now distinguish an early eighteenth-century phase of Spanish reforms that failed to impact more deeply but set the stage for a more intense reforming impetus in the second half of the century and especially during the reign of Carlos III. In Portugal, the legacy of jurisdictional fragmentation did not have the same significance and reforms mostly begun under the ministry of the Marquis de Pombal were more clearly focused on the basic features of a colonial exclusive. Fiscal reforms were accompanied by active policies to concentrate the processing of colonial products in the metropolis, while at the same time supporting a limited strategy of what could be somewhat anachronistically called import substitution. In spite of the different character of each kingdom reforms, the impetus had in common a widespread contemporary perception that the Iberian economies were notably falling behind developments in France, England or the Netherlands, but also intellectual changes brought about by the enlightenment.

The State of the Art

Long before any quantification by macroeconomic aggregate indicators was available, Iberian economic history discussed the problem of economic backwardness as being rooted in the early modern period. Debates about the ultimate causes of the divergence vis-a-vis north-western Europe and between Iberian regions have centred around political and economic institutions, including the development of state and fiscal capacity, property rights regimes, and the empires, as well as potential limitations to agricultural improvements and market integration. Part of the challenge in the debate has been that economic historians long dismissed as dead ends all processes of economic growth that did not lead to industrialization, thus probably underestimating the impact a specialization based on the entrepôt trade (the re-export of unprocessed imperial goods) or on the export of local agricultural goods – such as wine, olive oil or wool – could have. Though the mechanisms identified in the Portuguese and Spanish historiographies over the past half century diverge one can usefully identify four major themes:

First, overall growth over the period from 1500 to 1800 was slower in Iberia than in north-western Europe. The proximate cause was on the whole not permanently slower rates of economic growth but the fact that Iberian economies still went occasionally into reverse gear. Nevertheless, the economic transformations that took place in the early modern period did lay the foundations for industrialization in the nineteenth century. That in turn set Iberia's growth path apart from that of most of the rest of the world, including its former colonies in America and Africa, where industrialization only began at different points in the twentieth century.

Second, growth trends were not uniform across regions or between Spain and Portugal. Negative growth was more often a regional than a 'national' phenomenon. In Spain the centre of economic activity moved from the Castilian interior to the coastal regions starting in the late sixteenth century. In many ways this mirrored the rise of regions with access to maritime trade elsewhere in Europe. But questions remain for example over the impact of the disintegration between regions in the context of Portugal's Restoration War (1640–1668) or the potential for more integration between the Castilian and Aragonese territories after the War of the Spanish Succession.

Third, the impact of imperial expansion also differed regionally and between Spain and Portugal in the aggregate. A number of potential hypotheses have been put forward to explain these outcomes. The regulatory framework and territorial structures of empire differed from the start between the Spanish/Castilian expansion and that of Portugal. Both countries embarked on significant reforms to regulatory frameworks that underpinned colonial trade in the eighteenth century, but the direction of reforms diverged. In addition, the cycles related to particular commodities traded in the Atlantic were far more pronounced in the Portuguese case than in the Spanish.

Fourth, differences in the relative size of the metropolitan and imperial economies meant that colonial revenues and their indirect impact on the fiscal capacity of each economy differed by a degree of magnitude in the two countries with consequences regarding the social implications of taxation. In Portugal economic historians have suggested that the crown's large fiscal windfall from imperial trade removed the need for innovative fiscal solutions and allowed the privileged social groups to keep their income dependent on quasi-fiscal rights whose roots were in the occupation of the territory in the Middle Ages. In sharp contrast, in Spain the argument has been advanced that the much smaller fiscal return from empire led to the creation of very innovative fiscal instruments in the later sixteenth century which, however, allowed the monarchy to (over-) leverage the limited funds from the Americas in order to finance its European wars. Here the consequence was a mortgaging of the fiscal system for at least a century and a half, which would overburden urban taxpayers for generations.

As agriculture continued to be the most important occupation in Iberia throughout this period, agrarian historiography offers another set of explanatory factors. It has been concerned with the role of manorial and ecclesiastical institutions in the distribution of land and produce, assuming that institutions such as perpetual contracts, *mayorazgo* property and emphyteusis, if they did not have direct effects on productivity, had indirect effects through their impact on the liquidity of the land market. Although the recent literature stresses significant processes of specialization in agricultural production over the period under consideration as well as the impact of new crops, questions still exist as to the causes of the relative slowness of change. On the one hand, techniques directed towards the improvement of productivity in land were of limited use. On the other hand, specific forms of landholding may have held back innovation in agriculture.

Structure and Content of the Chapters

The present part mirrors Part I in structure and revises these debates with new quantitative data and a different way of observing Iberian regional economies in comparative terms. Chapter 10 offers overall trends by presenting the evolution of real incomes per capita of the Iberian economies, the changes experienced in the main sectors of the economy, as well as the distribution of economic activity across the peninsula. Importantly, the chapter provides evidence that the seventeenth-century crisis in Castile has no counterpart in Portugal, and the pace of growth of the eighteenth century is also distinct. There is no common growth pattern of the two Iberian national economies in the early modern period.

The notion of significant regional differences is also a theme in Chapter 11, which deals with demographic patterns. The common phases of growth and contraction at the Iberian level were accompanied by diverse regional dynamics. The overview of the Iberian Peninsula shows not only a movement towards more dynamic coastal regions; but also finds a northeast-southwest divide. The late age of marriage in the north and especially north-east in the eighteenth century compares well with the so-called European marriage pattern, denoting cultural particularities conditioning these differences.

The regional approach in Chapter 12 takes into account the political structures and explores the concept of composite monarchy to highlight the significance of jurisdictional particularism. The eighteenth-century reformism questioned this model by introducing what were thought to be the best practices observed in other parts of Europe, promoting a set of measures of political, fiscal and administrative centralization. Beyond jurisdictional differences, and without the reform impulse affecting it, these kingdoms show a common pattern of taxation, with indirect taxes prevailing from an early stage.

Chapter 13 connects public finance with the circumstances of Spain and Portugal becoming first-order receivers of precious metals. The institutional characterization and quantitative assessment of inflows allows the liquidity effect of remittances in the credit markets to be questioned. The financial development in Iberia displays divergent paths regarding private and public credit, on the one hand, and the workings of markets for long- and short-term maturities, on the other hand, suggesting that capital markets remained segmented. Notwithstanding diverse trends in interest rates, and considering in particular long-term maturities, the cost of capital was not critically higher than elsewhere in Europe in the late eighteenth century, which cast doubts on the lack of capital as a cause of the Iberian slower growth path.

In analysing Iberian economic performance through the supply side, Chapter 14 reassesses the role of technological change and innovation. However, the authors argue that major changes appear to have been demand-driven. The process of specialization in agriculture appears as the result of population growth rather than major technological improvements. Still, the chapter stresses that Iberia exported knowledge and technology in the sixteenth century – especially in sectors more directly related to maritime expansion. In the eighteenth century, to keep pace with major changes in the European industrial sector, technology had to be imported. It remains open to discussion, therefore, why population growth and increased demand, together with technology imports, did not improve productivity and prevent Iberia from falling behind European peers.

Chapter 15 analyses income levels and consumption. The combination of low and declining real wages with high levels of inequality in Spain and Portugal define the framework of the Iberian divergence in the early modern period. Notwithstanding significant regional variations, low wages stimulated a rise in the workload but at the same time continued to limit the expansion of demand. Any positive effect on growth derived from an industrious revolution was not enough to compensate the other, more pessimistic, effect of the low living standards of the largest mid–low and low social ranks.

Chapter 16 reassesses the role of trade and in particular the colonial expansion in the long-term growth performance of the Iberian economy. Starting off with the institutional foundations of the regulatory systems that governed colonial trade, the trends and cycles of external commerce in Asia and America are discussed. The chapter looks at the importance of particular commodity cycles as well as the extension of the slave trade. Finally the authors offer a short summary of the backward and forward linkages that trade may have had in the Iberian economies.

As a conclusion to this part, Chapter 17 provides an overview of the Iberian world in the early modern period. It places the development of the Iberian economies not just in their wider European context but within a consideration of the Empires of the early modern period spanning Eurasia and America. The secular trends that saw the relative disintegration of interior Spain also left evidence of economic dynamism shifting to the coastal regions. Finally, it offers a concise summary of the complex developments from the French Revolution to the dissolution of the Old Regime in Spain and Portugal and the loss of most of their colonies.

Part III: Industrialization and Catching Up

Historical Context

The third part of the book analyses the economic evolution of Iberia from the early nineteenth century to the present. Unlike in earlier times, no border changes have taken place during this period, and Portugal and Spain have consolidated their previous path as independent and unified nation-states. Despite some substantial differences between both Iberian economies, these two centuries have been characterized by parallel national economic histories and a similar periodization. The Napoleonic Wars represented a dramatic break in the history of both countries. With the Portuguese royal family taking refuge in Brazil and the Spanish one kept imprisoned in France, the war involved an irreversible institutional discontinuity in the evolution of both monarchies. Ferdinand VII and John VI would eventually return to their home countries in 1814 and 1821, respectively, but the political context had completely changed by then. On the one hand, Brazil and most of Spanish America were breaking their colonial bonds. Both Portugal and Spain would keep some colonies thereafter, some of which, like Cuba or Angola and Mozambique, would perform a significant role in the Iberian economy in some periods. However, the loss of most of the American empires in the early nineteenth century reduced both countries to secondary players in the international arena for the time being.

On the other hand, in the absence of the monarchs, the war set off a revolutionary process that put into question the early modern institutional framework. The struggle between liberals and absolutists would dominate the history of both countries during several decades, reaching its peak in the Portuguese Miguelista war (1828–1834) and the Spanish Carlista war (1833–1840). In both cases, the liberal victory gave place to a long-lasting process of institutional development and state building. The initial political strife of the new liberal regimes would be replaced in the 1870s by agreements between the main parties to alternate in power (the Portuguese *rotativismo* and the Spanish *turno pacífico*), which would increase stability at the expense of electoral fraud. The end of the liberal wars also allowed for a gradual process of economic growth and early industrialization, which was too slow, though, to bring convergence with the core European economies.

At the end of the nineteenth century, colonial troubles would again be the starting point of profound crises with long-lasting consequences for both liberal regimes. In 1890, the British Ultimatum thwarted Portuguese ambitions of imperial expansion in Africa; eight years later, Spain lost the last remnants of her old transatlantic empire (Cuba, Puerto Rico and the Philippines). The subsequent decrease in legitimacy of the two Iberian monarchies was made worse by an increasingly active labour movement and growing democratization demands and, as a consequence, both liberal regimes eventually collapsed.

In Portugal, Manuel II was deposed in 1910 and his reign was replaced by the I Portuguese Republic, while in Spain Alfonso XIII tried to extend his rule by replacing the Parliament by an authoritarian regime led by General Primo de Rivera. The end of the dictatorship, however, was also the end of the monarchy, with the II Spanish Republic being established in 1931.

Those democratic experiences, though, would be short lived and were followed by long-lasting dictatorships both in Portugal (1926–1974) and in Spain (1939–1976). In the Spanish case, the end of democracy was the final outcome of a disastrous Civil War with huge human and economic costs. In addition, the new dictatorships applied a set of inward-looking policies that isolated Iberia from the rest of Western Europe and brought its income levels to a minimum in comparative terms. Starting from this low point, however, the mid-twentieth century represented a new turning point in Iberian economic history. Economic modernization and structural change accelerated in the 1950s and 1960s, and the region started to catch up with the most developed countries of Europe. Convergence was consolidated from the 1970s onwards, when Portugal and Spain launched their respective processes of democratic transition and integration in the European Union. Catching up would only reach a halt in the early twenty-first century. By then, the region had recovered from the setback of the nineteenth and early twentieth centuries and the levels of Iberian gross domestic product (GDP) per capita, relative to the European core countries, were similar to those in the 1800s.

Throughout those two centuries, both Iberian economies have experienced radical transformations in their institutions, infrastructure, sectoral composition, technology and productivity, and their standards of living have undertaken revolutionary changes. By the early twenty-first century, although still plagued with different social and economic problems, Spain and Portugal have joined the club of the world's most developed countries, and their population enjoy welfare levels that are below but not that far from those prevailing in the richest European countries. Despite the hardship of the process and the low international relevance of both countries (compared with early modern times), this final outcome would allow the long-term economic evolution of Iberia since the early nineteenth century to be characterized as a rather troubled but relatively successful story. The chapters of this volume provide an overview of the different dimensions of that story.

The State of the Art

With some important precedents in the 1970s, the analysis of the economic history of Iberia in the nineteenth and twentieth century experienced a boom in the 1980s and has thereafter benefitted from a vast accumulation of new knowledge. Moreover, in contrast with previous periods, for which quantitative data are relatively scarce, the Portuguese and Spanish economic historiography has provided in recent years an enormous amount of quantitative evidence on all dimensions of those economies, which are reflected, for instance, in the collections of historical statistics published for both countries. The substantial quantification efforts carried out by scholars in both nations has resulted in a large number of long-term series focusing on different economic aspects such as economic growth, demography, foreign trade, public finance, and monetary variables. These efforts, though, have generally been constrained to the national borders and, to our knowledge, this is the first time that the different dimensions of the economic history of the whole Iberian space have been paid joint and detailed attention.

Although it is not easy to summarize the historiographical debates that have taken place in the last few decades on the late modern Iberian economies, some topics stand out as specially important. The first one is economic growth and convergence, with a large amount of works trying to quantify the growth record of both countries, compare it with the most developed world economies and identify the reasons for the different periods of catching up and divergence. Second, as in early modern times, the reasons for regional inequality have also been object of careful attention in both countries, trying to ascertain why industrialization took off in some areas in the late eighteenth and early nineteenth centuries, then spread to other territories and eventually relocated. Third, the impact of international relations (including the economic role of the remaining colonies) and the fluctuations of trade policies have been discussed as some of the key elements explaining the cycles of convergence and divergence. The alternation of openness and closure policies has received a lot of attention by scholars, who have held intense debates on the benefits and costs of liberal and protectionist policies.

Structure and Content of the Chapters

In the context of all the aforementioned debates, the third part of the book provides a joint perspective that includes both Iberian countries together. The chapters of this part are the result of the collective work of twenty scholars. They focus on the different dimensions of Iberian economic history in late modern times and have benefitted from the huge accumulation of historical evidence that was mentioned above. The main challenge in each of these chapters has been the need to overcome the barriers of the national historiographies and to provide a joint view of the Iberian Peninsula, stressing the common features of the Portuguese and Spanish historical experiences, but also their differences. The main outcome of this volume is precisely the first joint view of modern economic growth in Iberia as a European region with its own defining features, which make it clearly different from its north-western neighbours but also from other peripheral areas of the continent. The picture that emerges from these nine chapters indicates that the differences between the experiences of Spain and Portugal, although significant, become relatively minor when analysed side-by-side with the common defining features of Iberian history. Thus, for instance, the crisis of the early nineteenth century, directly associated to the loss of massive empires, or the long-lasting conservative dictatorship of the twentieth century, single out the Iberian experience in the European context and turn the Iberian space into a clearly meaningful unit of analysis for the historians of late modern times.

The analysis of the Iberian economy since the early nineteenth century starts in Chapter 18 with the description of the long-term growth pattern of both countries, which shows the alternation of long-lasting periods of divergence (until 1950) and convergence (from 1950 on). The chapter also provides a growth accounting exercise, which shows the differences across time and space in the main proximate factors of growth. This analysis indicates that, generally speaking, both Iberian economies have been unable to take full advantage of technological change and have tended to grow largely based on the accumulation of production factors, with the exception of Spain in the second half of the twentieth century, when total factor productivity (TFP) increases became the main explanatory factor of economic growth. Finally, the chapter approaches the evolution of regional differences in income per capita. It shows how, after a long period in which rich and poor regions were scattered throughout both Iberian states, the acceleration of economic growth since the 1950s has been accompanied by the emergence of clearly defined clusters of rich regions (in the north-east of the Peninsula and around the two capital cities) and poor territories, particularly concentrated around the border between Portugal and Spain.

The next chapters focus on different explanatory factors for the long-term economic growth record: population and human capital, institutions and the financial system. Chapter 19 analyses demographic change and the accumulation of human capital, distinguishing between several stages of the population history of Iberia. During most of the nineteenth century, population grew slowly in the context of a traditional (high mortality and high fertility) demographic regime, which was to a large extent the continuation of the situation in early modern times. Demographic transition unfolded in the second period, from the 1890s to 1980. Old demographic structures disappeared, being replaced by a process of decreasing mortality and (with some delay) fertility, massive internal and external migrations, urbanization and industrialization. This was also the time in which human capital accumulation accelerated. From 1980 onwards, mortality, fertility and natural population growth have remained low, and regional concentration and urbanization have reached their limits.

In Chapter 20, the different stages of institutional change in the Iberian countries are studied in detail. The chapter describes the conflict between liberalism and absolutism in the early nineteenth century, the construction of the liberal state and the authoritarian regimes of the twentieth century, and highlights the common features and differences of the institutional evolution of both countries. The authors stress how both countries' histories have reached their maximum level of coincidence since the 1970s, when they both entered democracy at the same time and started the path that would bring them to the European Union on the same day in 1986.

Chapter 21 includes a comparative history of the banking system in Spain in Portugal. This took off almost at the same time (the central decades of the nineteenth century) in both countries and its development level was clearly backward by European standards until recently. The small size of credit institutions, the absence of foreign banks or a low level of banking penetration in the economy was characteristic of the Iberian financial system until the early twentieth century, when a process of slow growth and convergence with the neighbouring Western European countries started. The chapter also stresses some differences between both countries, such as the absence of a public banking system in Portugal or the earlier origin of central banking in Spain.

Chapter 22 goes back to the characterization of the process of economic growth, focusing in this case on structural change and the gradual transformation of each production sector. Structural change started comparatively late in the Iberian economies and the progress of industrialization was modest until the early twentieth century. The main push to the process came in the interwar period and, especially, in the second half of the century, when new technology and the evolution of international markets were specially favourable to the Iberian factor endowments. In this context, Portugal and Spain followed different paths, with the Portuguese economy experiencing a slower structural transformation. The Portuguese industry was also less focused on heavy and skilled-labour intensive sectors, and de-industrialization started much later than in Spain. Finally, in both economies, the modernization of the economic structure has been hindered for a long time by insufficient investment in human capital and research and development.

One of the main consequences of economic growth was the sustained improvement in the living standards of the Iberian populations. The remarkable achievements that have taken place in this area are studied in Chapter 23, together with the remaining disadvantages between Iberia and its European neighbours. In terms of the Human Development Index (HDI) or life expectancy, Spain and Portugal are now among the most advanced countries in the world, although the growth of well-being indicators was deferred by the belated establishment of the Welfare State and the long dictatorships that affected both countries until the 1970s. Together with the delay in reaching political freedom levels comparable to other Western European countries, Iberia has also suffered from persistent high inequality, which explains why today the Portuguese and Spanish Gini indices are among the highest in Europe.

Chapter 24 analyses the degree of internationalization of the Iberian economies, which is also to a large extent a reflection of their process of economic growth. The period of economic divergence during the nineteenth century was also a time of globalization backlash in Spain and Portugal, which participated only partially in the process of reduction of trade barriers that was taking place in Europe at the time. In the case of Portugal this was partly compensated by a significant outflow of migrants, while in Spain international movements of capital and labour remained moderate. Such low degree of internationalization was consolidated in the first half of the twentieth century by the establishment of isolationist dictatorships. The 1950s, though, were not only a turning point in terms of international convergence but also in terms of openness, which reached unprecedented levels at the end of the century and was especially encouraged by integration in the European Union.

As a conclusion to this part, Chapter 25 carries out a systematic comparative approach to the economic performance of the Iberian economies, including GDP per capita, the causes and consequences of growth, and macroeconomic policies and fluctuations. While the authors of this chapter recognize that both countries had to face multiple growth obstacles during the nineteenth and twentieth century, they specifically stress the political history of the Peninsula, where differences with the rest of Western Europe clearly stand out. The long-lasting dictatorships of the twentieth century hindered the growth potential of both economies and it was their gradual reopening, first economic and then political, which allowed the partial recovery of the losses associated with the inward-looking policies of the authoritarian regimes.

PART I

The Making of Iberia, 700–1500

Edited by David Igual-Luis and Hermínia Vasconcelos Vilar

SECTION I THE EARLY MIDDLE AGES, 700–1200

1

Muslim and Christian Polities, 700–1200

HERMENEGILDO FERNANDES AND FLOCEL SABATÉ

1.1 Introduction

At the beginning of the eighth century, the old Visigoth kingdom was in social and political crisis. Consequently, it collapsed easily under the expansion of the Muslims after they crossed the Straits of Gibraltar in 711. The collapse of the monarchy left power in the hands of the local elites and ecclesiastic hierarchy of the cities. The scant interest of the Muslims in the rugged northern lands and the Carolingian intervention in the north-east of the Peninsula facilitated the rise of Christian kingdoms and counties, separated by the frontier. This was a territorial strip, which immediately served as a stimulus to precipitate the internal processes of both societies, and which thus had a strong impact on economic evolution and articulation.

South of this frontier the lands were in the cultural and economic framework of the Muslim Mediterranean with shared links as far as the Middle East. This relation was maintained despite the political split, because in 756 al-Andalus became an Umayyad emirate separate from the Abbasid caliphate, and in 929 it was turned into a caliphate. Ibn Hawqal (1964) testified to the strong artisanal and commercial prosperity reached then, just when the Andalusian capital, Córdoba, occupied a position only surpassed by Baghdad and Byzantium. This, however, did not give enough cohesion to the multi-ethnic Islamic society of al-Andalus, which entered into crisis on the turn of the tenth to the eleventh centuries, to the extent that it was about to collapse and split into small kingdoms centred on their respective urban capitals ruled by ethnically cohesive lineages, the so-called *taifas* or petty kingdoms.

This scenario was one of weakness compared to the Christian kingdoms established on the northern side, where the aristocracy and the ecclesiastic hierarchy had consolidated their domains over territories seized on the frontier where, especially from the eleventh century on, feudalism linked lords, peasantry and land, while prominent urban centres, well communicated commercially, were gaining ground. The northern economy came to be identified with an expansive dynamic, precisely justified by the ideological discourse that supplied the political will to religious arguments to delegitimize the Muslim presence. The frontier stopped being a strip of land to become a line that the northern kingdoms gradually pushed southwards with the aim of gaining new domains. Al-Andalus could do little more than trust in its renewal from the African empires, first the Almoravid, before the end of the eleventh century, and, from the mid-twelfth century, the Almohad, which was definitively defeated in 1212, however. Thus, by the end of the twelfth century, the Christian kingdoms in the north had taken the lead, not only to occupy most of the territory of the Peninsula but had also stabilized rural and urban, feudal and bourgeois societies, well prepared to face the imminent late Middle Ages.

1.2 Hispania Under Muslim Rule

Several challenges opened up for the economy after the Islamic occupation of the Iberian Peninsula. First, the settlement of a new population, in general repeating its tribal and traditional structure and, in many cases, combining with respect for the native population ('Muwallads'), implied changes in the tenure and exploitation of agricultural systems. Second, the consolidation of cities and towns, so typical of Muslim culture, would facilitate the action of the urban elites over the surrounding rural environment, interfering in such aspects as property and production. Third, urban production would lead to important trade routes, which connected al-Andalus, maintaining strong relations with Muslim lands on the other side of the Mediterranean, as well as stimulating specific relations with northern lands. This way, the bulk of the rich Roman (Visigoth) urban and commercial network continued under the new rulers and in the new Mediterranean scenario. The southern half of Iberia was closer to the contemporary patterns of development in the Middle East and Byzantium than to its northern neighbours in the Frankish dominated areas. Most of its commercial activities were related preferably to Mediterranean-based networks that spread from Misr (Egypt) and al-Sham (Syria), but also from Iraq and eastern Islam, at least from the point of view of technological and intellectual transfers. At the same time, the close relation between state structure and economic development led to an economic scenario marked by monetary consolidation, economic policies and urban development.

1.2.1 State and Consolidation of a Monetary Economy

From the mid-eighth century, the emirs of al-Andalus minted silver coins (*dirhams*), although without their names on them. The supply fluctuated: they became scarce in moments of turmoil, like the mid-eighth century coinciding with the great Berber uprising, or in the late eighth and early ninth centuries (the early years of Emir al-Hakam I); while, in contrast, they were much more common at times of economic growth, as in the second quarter of the ninth century (the reign of Abd-al Rahman II). During the periods of absence of a mint, coins would enter al-Andalus from the east and Maghreb through exports of agricultural goods and minerals. Praise is not spared for the consequences, both political and economic, of the creation of the mint generating widespread prosperity and encouraging the trade in luxury goods.

The coherence between the state and the authority of the emir was strongly compromised by internal upheaval and the victory of regional dynasties (*duwal*). Some of these clearly clashed with Umayyad rule; others negotiated a sort of symbolic acknowledgment of their authority. In every case, tax flows stopped, which may account for the data concerning coinage in this period. Very little survives from 272–285 AH (885–898 CE), corresponding to the reign of al-Mundhir and the early stages of 'Abdallah. Almost nothing remains (two examples from 293 AH/906 CE) from 285 to 316 AH (898–928 CE). Some of this information should be updated taking into consideration Alberto Canto's data (Canto, 2012). A drop in the activity of the mint may thus be seen as a result of a political crisis, lack of power and centrality from the emir with consequences for the state of economy. The result of this state of affairs in urban life can be observed during Ordoño II's attack on the medium-sized city of Évora (912 CE), seized by surprise thanks to the poor state and lack of repair of its walls.

In 316 AH/928–929 CE, Abderraman III defeated the rebel Banu Hafsun in Bobastro, assumed the minting of gold coinage (*dinar*) and proclaimed the caliphate. Minting gold coins was a caliphal prerogative, in concordance with the Roman assimilation of minting gold with imperial *munus*. The adoption of the title of caliph formed part of the competition between the Umayyads in al-Andalus and Fatimids in northern Africa's Kayrawan. Such competition was political but also for markets and control of the gold trade, Andalusian links to the Maghreb already being notable in the ninth century during the emirate of 'Abd al-Rahman II. Minting was then linked to the economic recovery, overcoming the serious problems that had persisted since the emirate of Al-Mundhir, from the late ninth century, until 928. The issuance of gold coinage brought numerous gains. According to Ibn Hawqal's testimony, while the caliphate of Kayrawan collected between 700,000 and 800,000 *dinars* annually through different taxes, in al-Andalus, only the rent from the mint would supply an annual income of 200,000 *dinars* (gold) or 3,400,000 *dirhams* (silver), using a conversion rate of 1/17 that was probably too high (Ibn Hawqal, 1964: I, 94–95, 107).

The minting of gold coinage continued in Córdoba during the following 20 years before the transfer of the capital (and the mint) to the one newly built at Madina al-Zahra according to the eastern Abbasid models. In these years, the great increase in the amount of silver delivered to the mint is noticeable (from 316 to 336 AH/928–948 CE a variable number of surviving coins is registered, but this rises to 106 coins in 331 AH/943 CE). The huge investment implied by the construction and establishment in al-Zahra of a costly court society required large-scale minting of both gold and silver, the first represented by up to 24 surviving examples from 336 to 364 AH, and the latter also by high levels of coinage in the same period. Stability seems to describe the altogether brief al-Zahra period until the end of the reign of al-Hakam II. A change in the regime followed, with the minister (*hadjib*) al-Mansur taking power. In spite of this, nothing substantial seems to have changed from an economic point of view. The minting of silver coins characterizes the period of the economic recovery from 366 AH (976–977 CE) and that affected the last years of al-Hakam and then the caliphate of Hisham, particularly after 378 AH/988 CE. Al-Mansur Ibn Abi Amir's ability to benefit from war with northern Christian kingdoms and the revenues brought to the state from booty and putting captives on the market, may account for the last moments of economic splendour before another major political crisis.

The great turmoil (*Fitna*) that led to the disintegration of the Umayyad caliphate (1009–1031) was accompanied by a severe fall in coinage, clearly perceived after 403 AH/1012 CE. The *taifa* regime based on the urban economy and local power followed the path of the caliphal state, in this respect as in many others. The mint, promoted by the new *taifa* kingdoms, acted as a show of power and a form of appropriation of Umayyad ideology. At the same time, it was a sign of the economic prosperity of al-Andalus in the eleventh century while it financed both investments in luxury goods and court society. Finally, it was the vehicle for a policy of buying truce *vis-a-vis* the rising northern Christian kingdoms, now much more aggressive, through the payment of tributes (*parias*), which became very high.

The major transformation in the eleventh century was a result of a political and religious event external to al-Andalus but with huge impact on Andalusian society. The rise of the *maliki* Berber Almoravid empire allowed integration into an economic network that controlled the continuous flux of gold from Timbuktu. That allowed a stimulation of the economy of al-Andalus, which had been exhausted under the pressure of the Christians kingdoms to the north, including strict fiscal policy required to be able to meet the payment of the *parias*. At the same time, the conquest of al-Andalus by an empire based in the Maghreb allowed monetary integration at a level never experienced before, in spite of the existing interdependence of both economies. The impact of North-African gold on the economy of Iberia (and not only al-Andalus), probably pre-dates the Almoravid conquest (in 1091, the conquest of Seville) as may be observed through documents from the frontier region of Coimbra, although it is not clear that all the early references to 'morabitinos' in the Christian area refer to Almoravid coinage (Menéndez Pidal et al., 2003). The fact that not until the eleventh century did the Christian kings begin to issue their own currency helped to establish Andalusian money, either minted in al-Andalus or later on in the Maghreb, as the key element in the Iberian economy. Even more so because the Almohad conquest in the mid-twelfth was accompanied by the takeover of the Almoravid *dinar*, which the Almohads adopted, changing very little in this respect (*dobra*, *masmudi*), and which were in circulation in Iberia together with the currency issued by the Christian kings in line with Islamic models. The fact that all these coins tended to circulate somewhat indistinctly make it hard to picture the actual provenance of such treasures as that amassed by the second Portuguese king Sancho I (d. 1211), mainly through a war economy, which amounted to 720,200 '*morabitinos*' (Almoravid *dinars*?, *dobras*?), 195 gold marks and 4.5 ounces of gold and 1400 silver marks.

The Berber empire's control of the gold supply enabled them to create an economic area in the western Mediterranean ruled with the double monetary pattern of gold/silver (*dinar/dirham*), in which gold coinage played a decisive role, fuelling both the dynamic Andalusian urban-based economy and the growth of Christian northern Iberia, even if a significant part of the transactions in that region were still not monetized. Its decline in the thirteenth century was a direct result of the crisis of the Almohad empire and stressed the close connection between state building and the monetary economy, always usual in al-Andalus.

1.2.2 Economic Policies

The role of the state and its impact on the medieval Andalusian economy may be asserted not only by taking minting activity as a measure of the evolution of the economy but also by observing the impact of public expenditure, taxation and market regulation.

An important motor for economic growth in tributary Islamic society was the policy of propaganda through a pattern of luxury consumption and a building programme. This can be appreciated when the court of 'Abd al-Rahman II hosted the singer and trendsetter Ziryab freshly arrived from Baghdad in or just after 822. The amounts given to him in *dinars* (directly and in rents) and in kind (palace, properties, goods, enslaved people and servants), as well as the focus on his impact on collective mores, material culture and patterns of consumption, show al-Andalus as a rich society closely connected by taste and refinement with the Abbasid east, then at its peak.

The construction of the new complex of Madinat al-Zahra, west of Córdoba between 937 and 961, brought the splendours of Byzantine and Abbasid palaces to the Iberian Peninsula. Before the end of that century, the palaces of the court aristocracy were added, along with the enlargement of the Aljama mosque, all under al-Hakam II, and the construction of a second courtly city, al-Madina al-Zahira, under the Amirids. Al-Makkari, quoting Ibn Ḥayyān, mentions a cost of 300,000 *dinars* per year, for a total sum of 7.5 million *dinars* (Makkari,1840–1843: II, 187ff). The caliph reserved a third of its annual revenue from the treasure for the construction site, a sum that can easily match the investment by the emperor Justinian in the Hagia Sophia, four centuries earlier. This was made possible by a huge increase of the state's revenues during the tenth century. This denotes the good state of the economy, as well as a model of society that promoted specialized work as it supported a court of luxury and consumer goods.

The ideological and economic impact of Madina al-Zahara became the model followed by the *taifa* kings in the eleventh century. The latter reproduced on their own scale the magnificence of the palaces and the ostentation of the royal courts as a base for their power. This can be seen both in the large capitals, like Seville, Zaragoza, Málaga or Granada, and in the lesser ones. Even the kings of Lleida had a second palace built in the nearby town of Balaguer that condensed the best the artists of the time knew how to do. All together it reflects an urban setting conducive for developing a rich material culture, with the production and dealing in silk fabrics, rugs, glazed pottery and ivory items, among others. Later, during the twelfth century, the Berber empires, especially the Almohads, also financed relevant construction programs in al-Andalus. In the late twelfth century, in their capital of Seville, the latter completely restructured the palace and the city around it, which required a heavy tax burden.

Flaunting power through building requires fiscal power. The Muslim territory was always a tributary state. The first *wali* (governor), 'Abd al-Aziz, negotiated advantageous conditions for the surrender of the Visigoth lord Theodomirus in 713. These terms ensured religious freedom for the Christians and political independence for his territory but reserving for themselves the tax (a *dinar* per capita, plus part of the produce from the land). The system of distribution after the conquest awarded a fifth of the land to the state, which is why it later had in these fiscal lands its main source of revenue. In any case the model of a strong fiscal state seems to be inherent to al-Andalus, this being directly connected to the strengthening of central power. Therefore, when this model did not predominate, we can understand it as a deviation from the normal and a testimony that the central state went through moments of weakness, as evidenced by having to cede tax revenue to local or regional authorities.

Precisely the reinforcing of central power under 'Abd al-Rahman II, in the second quarter of the ninth century, led to a reform of the treasury (Hizanah) and the institution of registers of tax collection (Ibn Ḥayyān, 2001; II-2, 181–182). That facilitated the increase in tax income, which, according to al-Shabinasi's calculations, approached one million *dinars* of *dirhams* (silver), thanks to a great extent to the tax on real estate (haraj), which played an important part in the overall state income. This figure of tax income diminished with the later political crisis, which included agreements (or the lack of them) with the insurgents, giving them autonomy from central taxation. This was the case of the Banu Marwan in the west and the Banu Hafsun in the south of Córdoba.

The reinforcement of the state and the recuperation of the mint under 'Abd al-Rahman III facilitated that, as Ibn Hawqal states (Ibn Hawqal, 1964: I, 111), the tax revenues until 340 AH/951 CE amounted to about 20 million *dinars*, not counting those on trade in merchandise and luxury goods, a number which is in line with the estimate that the 7.5 million spent on Madina al-Zahra corresponded to a third of the general revenue. In 961, on the death of 'Abd al-Rahman III, his son al-Hakam II confiscated the courtesan's fortunes, which enabled him to raise 20 million *dinars*.

The signs of a growing economy continued during the Amirid period between the last decades of the tenth century and the first decade of the eleventh. Military expenses undoubtedly rose to a new level but, as a consequence, booty also became part of the income. The collapse of the caliphate led to fragmentation into the *taifa* kingdoms, centred around urban capitals, each ruled by an ethnic elite (Andalusian, Berber or Slavic). They attempted to reproduce the caliphal administrative model, including its taxation. Precisely, the economic growth evident in the eleventh century was not enough to keep pace with the ostentatious courts of the rulers and, especially, pay the *parias* that the Christian kingdoms to the north demanded in return for peace. This led to high fiscal pressure, which generated popular unrest and disqualification by influential Islamic scholars, who considered this taxation illegal as it was not supported by Islamic law. Thus, at the end of the eleventh century, intellectuals and the general population supported the Berber Almoravid invaders. The crisis of the latter in the mid-twelfth century was followed by a brief second *taifa* period and the arrival, also from Africa, of the Almohads. At the centre of the policies of both Berber empires was a religious reform expressed also through a different fiscal policy which was less damaging to a rich but already fragile and socially unequal Andalusian society. Based in the Maghreb and with control of the Saharan gold, both the Almoravids and the Almohads could afford this.

A tributary society like al-Andalus may be dependent on taxes but is not necessarily focused on market regulation. A leading study on trade in late Andalusian society (Constable, 1994: 110) seems to point in the opposite direction, showing how the Christian conquest reinforced control of the markets in which the previous Muslim princes had shown little interest. The lengthy classic study on the market by Chalmeta (1973), recently enlarged, analyses the institutional framework considering the evolution of trades (Ibn Ḥayyān, 2001: 393–494) and bearing in mind the data collected, one could ask if there is no contradiction between the idea of losing control and establishing an institutional framework for the markets. Also, the frequency of treatises concerning the urban police (*Hisba*), like those of al-Saqati or Ibn 'Abdun in which control of the market and regulation played a major part, seems to contradict that notion. Perhaps the idea, prevalent in the tenth century, that taxation was light referred preferably to market activities but does not mean an absence of regulation. It is true that no general laws were issued, unlike in the thirteenth-century Christian Iberian kingdoms. *Hisba* treatises are in their stead and would probably be in use for determining market good practices. Also, the ulama played a very important part in regulating the market and economic activities in general as documented in the collection of *fatawa* by al-Wansharisi. Nevertheless, direct princely intervention cannot be excluded, as demonstrated by the Almohad caliph's commitment to building markets, as in the case study of Seville, the Suq being part of the aljama mosque complex (Ibn Ṣāḥib aṣ-Ṣalā, 1969). A concession made to some major ex-Andalusian towns after the conquest by the Portuguese king may shed some light on this issue: by transferring his rights to regulate the market (Almotaçaria) to local authorities he acknowledged that those rights were public and inherited from the Andalusian princely authorities.

1.2.3 Urban Development and Economic Growth

The overall importance of trade in al-Andalus, shown even more through archaeology than the texts, must be put in the context of indisputable urban growth. The rise in trade was closely linked to the state polities, while urban growth was connected to the state-building processes even if in a different way from mint activities. The position of Córdoba as the capital seems to have played a key role in the process, not only because it served as a role model for other cities but also because nowhere else in the west was there a similar concentration of political and economic power that converged with such a large population. The capital of al-Andalus enjoyed an economic influence going beyond the Mediterranean to the south and the Pyrenees to the north, acting as a huge hub of consumption and production that recalls the role played in the Near and Middle East, at different moments, by Constantinople, Baghdad, Samarra or Cairo (al-Qahira).

In the second quarter of the ninth century, under 'Abd al-Rahman II, Córdoba was not only the seat of power but also the site of considerable industries, among them the Tiraz, the state manufacturer of luxury fabrics. However, the key issue here would be to measure how the network of cities inherited from the late Antiquity benefited from the growth of the capital. Everything seems to indicate the survival of the late Roman cities in Iberia, many of which (Mérida, Toledo, Zaragoza and Seville) retained their position as regional capitals, although other cities were newly created as a result of political choices, like Badajoz and Almería. Precisely, the transfer of the regional capital from Pechina to Almería, which would become a major port city, was a sign of the growing connection of al-Andalus with Mediterranean trade as well as the rise of Murcia, another Levantine city. All this shows the importance of the arrival of irrigated agriculture and intensive production systems associated with small plots of land, but which also allowed very impressive urban growth, particularly in eastern Iberia (Sharq).

The eleventh-century fragmentation of the *taifa* was based precisely on urban dynamism. These cities had grown notably in the second half of the tenth century, often using material from the earlier Roman city to reinforce the new central points: the main mosque, the souk and the palace complex, Zaragoza being a good example. The physical embodiment of royal power was the *zuda* or palace, like those in Zaragoza, Lleida (with Balaguer) and Tortosa, or the kasbahs, which had risen to protect the governors from the ninth century onwards. This was the early case of Mérida, and then Seville or the Gharb in Lisbon, creating an urban landscape common to every Andalusian city, much like Aleppo or Damascus in contemporary Syria, where walls began to segregate a military elite from the rest of the population. Zudas and kasbahs housed micro-court societies that emulated the caliphal court cities, with a corresponding economic stimulus.

The walled suburbs that encircled many of the main cities from this period onwards also show that Andalusian cities were not only getting richer but bigger and more populous. This is surely the case of Lisbon, an interesting example if we consider the peripheral position and function of this Atlantic city during the emiral and caliphal periods. Not being a capital of a *taifa*, nor a key city for the Almoravids, its growth in the century before the Christian conquest of 1147, attested to by the two new neighbourhoods, particularly the western, was not due to any political relevance but to trade, navigation and a rich hinterland. For this reason, Lisbon can be used as a case study for the overall growth of the Andalusian urban system during the eleventh and twelfth centuries, a growth resulting both from decentralizing political processes, which stimulated markets at a regional and local level, and the impact of technology on agricultural production, even if considerable differences can be seen in the use of irrigation techniques, particularly between the dry eastern part of al-Andalus and its more humid western regions. In the Sharq, in fact, urban growth during this period seems to have been sustained by intensive agriculture, which accounts for the prevalence of such regional capitals as Valencia and Murcia, and in another sense, is mostly connected to silk production in Granada, a new city that had replaced Elvira in the eleventh century. At the same time, in northern areas near the frontier, like the north of the Ebro Valley, agriculture was based on rural nuclei well protected thanks to public investments, whether central, regional or local.

In the twelfth century, under the Berber empires, the multi-polarized structure of the state, at the central and regional levels, again linked urban development with a central political position. In the first half of the century, Seville and

Valencia took on the role of capitals under the Almoravids. Not only these cities but also regional capitals, like Badajoz, Granada or Jaén, grew to a relevance that would be acknowledged after the Christian conquest with the status of kingdoms they were granted. The state capitals, including Marrakesh and the failed attempt in Rabat in Africa, as well as Seville, all underwent extensive programmes of urban renewal involving huge financial and human resources. Some minor centres, like Beja, are also examples of efforts to revive urban structures wherever and whenever widespread warfare had damaged them.

One final issue concerns the impact of this monetized, market-based economy, strongly connected to statal ability to invest, on the Christian northern neighbours. The presence of Andalusian coins can be attested very early and will be enhanced by the payment of *parias* during the eleventh and again in the mid-twelfth centuries, this time particularly in the extreme west and the east. It is beyond any doubt that this was the model for Christian kings' coinage activities and also that the contribution made by the input of gold coinage from the south had a major role on the northern principalities' economic development to an extent difficult to measure. Some other issues, equally important, remain less visible: commercial networks linking northern and southern Iberia, transfers of technology and artisanship, transfer of market institutions and, above all, the development of patterns of consumption in northern societies that some objects we refer to in this chapter seem to attest.

1.3 The Northern Kingdoms and Counties

The northern territories combined continuity with earlier periods and a development that led them to occupy the frontier strip. This expansion led to the consolidation of a feudal society that benefited from urban development and trade links.

1.3.1 The Early Medieval Society

The disinterest of Muslim society in unattractive northern areas of the Iberian Peninsula combined with Frankish pressure, especially in the Eastern sector, disconnected the northern lands from the rest of al-Andalus. In all of them, a strong Roman tradition was maintained, as reflected in the territorial references (*villa, strata*) or the regional structure. The ease with which the Visigoth kingdom had collapsed does not imply that its interior lived in a state of poverty. The archaeological remains of Visigoth rural centres destroyed in the conquest (Bovalar in Catalonia, Pla de Nadal in Valencia) show active, populated communities, and with currency circulating. Nor is poverty perceived in the journey Eulogius of Córdoba made in the mid-ninth century to the numerous monasteries in the Pyrenees of Navarre. However, it is true that there was a growing regionalization, which meant a progressive ruralization, links between cities and the central state, and the social consolidation of magnates. Accordingly, the latter, mixed with the regional aristocracy, played a role as representatives before the new lords after the central Visigoth state collapsed.

Continuity is perceived in the cities that maintained a leading role, with the local magnates continuing to exercise a guiding hand, as in Pamplona. Also, the most exposed rural areas like the landscape of hilltop sites in Castile highlights the evolution from earlier centuries, which is why the pottery found reflects local structures and poor external connections. Even the Frankish penetration into the north-east of the peninsula accentuated the existing relation with the northern side of the Pyrenees through the former Septimania.

This scenario shows agrarian communities with communal assets and free peasant owners, as seen in Galicia. They were busy buying and selling land on a non-monetary market as well as establishing networks of friendship and patronage, which facilitated the rise of a local elite around the tenth century. Consequently, inequality between farmers grew. In the Pyrenees of Navarre and Aragon, the difficult geography, coupled with an ever-present Muslim danger that increased in the tenth century, invigorated the weight of the aristocracy and led to an early rise in peasant servitude. In the east, the documentation from the Catalan counties shows some allodiums belonging to lords but worked by enslaved people or fiscal servants; some lands were ceded to free peasants under various agreements and others under contract (*precaria*) established according to agreements. However, in both the east and the west, the magnates stood out (many of whom were initially neither nobles or clergy) and accumulated a large number of properties. On this base, they founded monasteries and churches and became close to the Asturian and Navarrese monarchies, which from the mid-eighth century tried to assert their pre-eminence.

Hunting for small game was important in peasant production at that time. Agriculture based on growing cereals was spreading. Wheat was very unusual, even on aristocratic tables. Instead, the barley was the staple, followed by rye, which was better adapted to poor soils. Other cereals were also grown, including millet, spelt or other variants of millet such as *pámula* and *panizo*. Vineyards were also expanding, in smaller plots and with a low output. Other plants, such as flax and hemp, were always needed for textile production. Irrigation was valued, which is why it was specified in contracts – *subtus rego* – and the *insulae* in the rivers were negotiated. The canals for mills were used for irrigation and specific small channels were used in tenth century in the Barcelona region and Roussillon, for instance. The use of manure as a fertilizer is documented in the same century, but the effects of a shortage of tools and draft animals and variability in the weather contributed to irregular crops, with some really bad years, as explicitly documented in the eastern counties in 990.

Nevertheless, the general tendency was for growth. Everywhere there was an important and continued increase in agricultural land in the eighth and ninth centuries, through the *presura* or *aprisio*. This principle, according to Visigoth legislation, granted a right to ownership after 30 years working land that had no known owner. The increase in farmed areas had previously happened in northern regions, such as Septimania, and reflected growing population density and the necessary growth in agricultural production. From this, some historiography has emphasized the increase in full ownership by family units, giving an image of a society full of free peasants who were small landowners. In any case, the documentation leaves no doubt that the dynamics of economic expansion benefited, above all, the magnates, including the groups close to power (as is the case of viscount and vicar lineages in the Catalan counties) and the ecclesiastic hierarchy formed by monasteries and bishops. Between the eighth and tenth centuries, all of these accumulated great landed estates as the basis of their power.

Livestock was also becoming increasingly significant. The contents of wills reflect the importance given to the ownership of small numbers of animals. In any case, magnates and monasteries were soon accumulating larger herds, as documented in negotiations for pastures by monasteries such as those in Arles in 878, Sant Joan de les Abadesses in 977 and Sant Pere de Besalú in 978. In the tenth century, livestock farming was regulated by properly organizing the areas of grass and pastures, although conflicts could not be avoided, like the one in the delta of the River Llobregat. Mountain territories such as Aragon received an economic boost from livestock. At that time, transhumance routes worked more on a basis of altitude than distance. This livestock was mainly sheep and goats, in addition to pigs, but with smaller numbers of oxen and horses given their high price.

The increase in production encouraged the work of blacksmiths and the spread of metal instruments. By 860, there was already a documented demand in Andorra for 'decimis Andorrensis pagi ferri et piscis quae aeclesie sue debentur' (Abadal, 1952: 287). In the ninth and tenth centuries, the demand for arms and tools given the expansion of agriculture stimulated metal production in the Pyrenees (using water power often under the control of monasteries), but also in the new lands, where smithies were set up, especially working on repairing implements. The increase in mills had a greater economic and social impact. *Molinarem anticuum* was stated in Lillet, in the Pyrenean zone, in 833. The construction of a mill was complex, requiring a dam, a canal and a reservoir, in addition to the mill itself. However, in the ninth and tenth centuries, these spread along the rivers following the expansion of agriculture. This reflected the growing demand for flour, which was part of a change in eating habits. Secondary cereals are more digestible cooked than baked, which explains that in the Early Middle Ages the most important food was a stew based on cereal served as semolina or porridge combined with portions of meat and other products, often according to what was foraged in the forests. Focusing agriculture on cereals and dedicating the majority to flour processing implied the spread of bread and, with it, the progressive implementation of a new dietary model, based on the three items that would dominate the late medieval table: bread, wine and meat.

Consistent with this dynamic, at that time, the tax burdens fell mainly on agricultural production, in contrast with what was seen at the beginning of the eighth century in the eastern counties with their taxes on livestock and, above all, on trade. In fact, commercial activity had remained at a high level in the north-east of the Peninsula. This is perceived in the continuity of the markets in the cities and, notably, by the desires to possess the teloneum, a toll on the movement of merchandise to the market. In the ninth century, the ecclesiastic authorities asked the Carolingian sovereigns for control of this tax, a request that was granted partially. In 834, Lothair of Aquitaine gave the bishop of Elne 'mediam parte mercati', and in the same year, Louis the Pious conceded 'tertia parte de pascuario et teloneo' to the bishop of Girona in the 'pagus' of Girona and Besalú. Similarly, in 889, Eudes granted the bishop of Osona 'theloneis mercatorum terre'. The internal movement and the relationship with long-distance trade were combined. In 860, the bishop of Urgell obtained the right to part of the teloneum on goods crossing his large dioceses in the Pyrenees and the bishops of Girona in 844 and Barcelona in 878 obtained a similar concession on merchandise arriving by land or sea.

However, there were other mountainous areas that seem to have had low levels of trade, such as Aragon. Similarly, the inward-looking nature and scarce outward orientation that characterized the Cantabrian area was a continuity of the disconnection in the fifth century following the fall of the Roman Empire as the region was closely linked to the economic and political needs of the Imperial power structures. The former Roman structures were also maintained in the western areas (Asturias and Galicia). They had little connection with the outside world and, instead, there was a continuity of regional markets and a network of urban capitals in rural regions.

The increase in space and agricultural production was consistent with a significant growth in trade, which combined the distribution of regional produce and other transported from afar, especially in the second half of the tenth century. The spread of hostels for pilgrims and travellers at the same time makes sense. At the end of the century, markets are documented in large cities and middle-sized towns, especially those with good communications. This is clear in many places in the eastern counties (Elna, Girona, Barcelona, Vic, Cardona, Urgell, Anglès, Gerri, Bages, Llor and Llavorsí). Also in the west, markets in Sahagún and León were complimented with those in Zamora or Cea. Some markets, like the one in Villafuentes (Burgos), clearly redistributed local produce. In other cases, they enabled a connection with products brought from afar. Luxury goods were usually from al-Andalus. These included silk, cotton, brocades, skins and leather goods, as well as perfumes and precious objects. Exports to the south were very specific, such as weapons made of Pyrenean metal or coral from Empúries, already documented in the ninth century. In fact, testimonies from the eighth and ninth centuries, such as the request from the bishop Elipandus of Toledo to Felix of Urgell who sent him a letter *cum mercaturios*, or the French clergy who journeyed seeking relics, show a network of communications travelled by merchants. The central role in this connection with Europe was played by Barcelona ('via Mercaderia' was the name given in the tenth century to the route continued to the Pyrenees via Girona) and secondarily through Pamplona, both cities connected to Muslim Zaragoza, where the routes linked to the heart of al-Andalus via Toledo.

Nevertheless, commercial investment was scarce, because credit responded more to consumption than investment, if we look at its short terms – the return dates coinciding with the harvest of cereal or wine and high interest rates, which in some cases reached 50%, despite the formal legal limitation included in the Visigoth legislation. The currency was, primarily, the benchmark for calculating sales, contracts and credits 'ad rem valentem'. Reiterated references like the 'solido' of Galicia in the tenth century were not to a real currency but rather to units of account. Only in the north-east of the Peninsula, under Carolingian domain, were coins minted in the ninth century in Barcelona, Girona, Empúries and Roda de Ter (identification disputed with Roses). The bishops intended to monopolize the inherent profits. In 862, the emperor yielded a third of the profits from the currency of Barcelona to the bishop. This was also applied in Osona county in favour of the bishop of Vic with a disputed interpretation of Wilfred II's will when he died in 911, and then in 934, when Count Sunyer granted it to the Bishop of Girona. The lack of precious metals and even the legitimist ideology of the Asturian monarchy impeded the issuance of coinage in the west. However, during the second half of the tenth century, Muslim currency circulated all through the north, although geographically unequally distributed.

1.3.2 *The Frontier and Its Occupation*

The frontier was stabilized in the mid-eighth century as a wide strip of territory between the Christian North and the Islamic South (see Figure 1.1). It covered the entire Douro Valley, a small strip north of the Ebro Valley and the lands east of the Muslim cities of Lleida and Tortosa. The historiography had imagined an empty territory that was occupied by the legitimate population who would recover their lands after retreating to the mountains; or a space open to spontaneous settlers who would find land and freedom until the nobles seized it through the feudal revolution in the following century. In reality, it

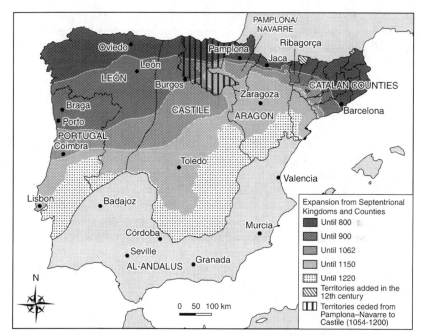

Figure 1.1 The Iberian Peninsula in the eighth–twelfth centuries.
Source: Flocel Sabaté and Servei Científicotècnic de Cartografia i Sistemes d'Informació Geogràfica de la Universitat de Lleida.

was not barren, unoccupied territory but a disorganized one, that is to say atomized into various local communities and scattered settlements.

Since the late Roman crisis, the population in the Douro Valley had been concentrated in 'castra', usually on local roads dominating a space with other minor occupations – 'penellas', 'populaturas' – and always in scattered, inward-looking, settlements. This included the continuity of populations like Castelhos Velhos or 'civitas' like Zamora. These peasant communities produced small local elites who acted as intermediaries with the outside, although contacts were scarce. Coherently, pottery remains are common local products and some imitations of *sigillata*, combining domestic pottery done on a slow wheel with other larger pieces done by hand. The scenario encouraged the lords of the north to lead incursions against notable populations that survived independently, as was the case of the 'civitates' in the Douro Valley attacked by the Asturians.

On the north-eastern side of the Peninsula, the frontier strip was narrower. This accentuated its function linking two peoples through raids between them (Muslims against Christian settlements and vice-versa in nightly expeditions), as Ibn Ḥayyān explained as happening in 975 (Bramon, 2000: 326) and all kind of human relations. Many documents describe the no-man's land of this frontier as a place full of ruins – 'villa herema', 'ancient parietes', 'altos parietos' – but with sufficient continuity to maintain the place names and inhabited by farmers and gatherers who lived between the two sides of the frontier. They appeared as an amalgam made up of remnants of the original population, early Islamic settlers, some fugitives and spontaneous settlers, all in a suspicious position, who coexisted with each other. From the Christian side, they were seen as 'gentem paganam, perversos cristianos [...] male insidiantes' (Junyent, 1992: 132).

The cohesion of these frontier territories could only come from outside. The growing economic power of the northern territories in the ninth century had boosted their elites, who projected their vigour onto the frontier strip. Therefore, the sovereign of the Asturian kingdom intended to repopulate attractive places on the frontier, such as Zamora in 893, and led armed interventions, such as the repopulation of various cities after the battle of Simancas in 940. From the last decade of the ninth century, Alfonso III of Asturias led a successful conquest to the south and east, thanks to attracting the local elites and their respective (often independent) efforts to conquer domains and occupy regions, who, in exchange, increased their status sheltering under royal protection. In fact, by serving the king they obtained donations in land, or his approval of pressures already applied. This was started by the counts of Castile in the tenth century. They ended up controlling the eastern side of the kingdom through their own conquests. In this way, numerous nobles expanded the frontier of the Asturian kingdom from Viseu, Santiago or Astorga in the west to Amaia or Osma in the east.

In the tenth century, the frontier everywhere benefited the aristocracy and the ecclesiastical hierarchy, formed by bishops and monasteries. Throughout this century, viscount and vicar lineages and ecclesiastical hierarchies from the former Carolingian counties led a systematic occupation of the eastern strip. They seized coherent areas within the frontier, marked them and built castles to rule this space. This transformed the border into a dense network of castle districts. In Aragon and Pamplona, north of the Ebro, the occupation of the border fringe was similar, under more direct control from the sovereign, who granted the territory as 'honores' for his barons. Similarly, in the centre of the peninsula, the '*alfoz*' defined the new districts.

The real aim of occupying the frontier fringe was to establish perennial systems of territorial organization, trying to link the population permanently to their lords and the agricultural production to seigniorial and jurisdictional levies. The landscape was therefore covered with aristocrats' castles controlling well-defined districts. The profits from this occupation could only be obtained from due agricultural development of the land. Therefore, the lords systematically called for new population – 'agricultores ibi obducas ad habitandum et ad excolendum opus rusticum in eo' – the scope being defined as 'ipsa terra erema perducas ad cultura' (Font Rius, 1969: 24, 25–26). The tax burden was initially weak to encourage occupation, while the population already residing on the frontier was initially respected in its allodial right despite becoming subject to the new jurisdiction. This direct relationship between the owner and the person with the right to work it soon became complicated by the progressive accumulation of rights over the property, with intermediate owners, often monasteries, appearing which lengthened the chain of those who held rights over the property.

Thus, the occupation of the frontier in the tenth century continued the social and agrarian densification seen in the interior in the previous century. Agriculture based on cereal and vineyards was consolidated, contracts for the development of vineyards were disseminated, like the *complantatio* in the eastern counties and the rivers was used for the construction of mills. Some spaces taken from the border were suitable for livestock, such as the mountains of Salamanca and Ávila. The changes in ownership and landscape were justified by the Christian doctrine that supported the expulsion of the invading Muslim who had occupied these lands and also the Christian duty to transform the 'eremum' into 'cultum'. The development of these territories strengthened towns and cities as central places for services and exchange, which consolidated the power of their elites and at the same time blurred the disquisition between the urban and rural spaces. The old frontier as a fringe of separation disappeared, absorbed and converted into a well-articulated space, one which was fully integrated into the northern domains. From this moment on, the frontier would become a line, which led to warlike relations in the eleventh-century feudal context.

The expansion of the eleventh century penetrated into Islamic territories in the east, where the infrastructure was used either to displace the population, change crops and impose a new feudal structure under the formula of castles districts, if necessary divided into minor sub-districts called *quadres*. In the centre of the Peninsula, south of the Douro, especially in the second half of the century, the new territories combined military defence, repopulation and rural and agrarian colonization under royal jurisdiction. They were organized into extensive '*alfoces*', a kind of territorial and administrative unit that brought together numerous villages dependent on the respective town council. At the end of the eleventh century and throughout the twelfth important towns and cities grew up presiding over extensive *alfoces*. These included Sepúlveda, Segovia, Ávila, Plasencia or Toledo in Castile and Calatayud, Daroca, Teruel and Albarracín in Aragon.

The circulation of people and goods and the complexity of the occupation of the territory transformed the social and economic reality both in the new lands and in the interior. The prosperity of the interior lands cannot be understood without the wealth coming from the border. It was not only about the loot or commercial relationship with al-Andalus but, notably, the establishment of a permanent system to extract income, one which greatly benefited the aristocracy and ecclesiastical hierarchy. All the urban capitals and indoor market centres benefited from this system. The emergence of Barcelona, as a clear example, was related to its opening to the Mediterranean as well as its hinterland, which included prosperous cities (three episcopal seats: Barcelona, Vic and Girona), but directly because of the profits that enriched aristocrats and clergy from the nearby border settled in the surroundings of Barcelona. On its part, the institutionalization of royal powers in León, Castile and Navarre was mainly based on the frontier, which produced immediate profits, a place where durable social and economic links were established and the framework to take the various holders of power into the royal orbit.

1.3.3 Societies in Expansion

The Asturian monarchy was gaining ground thanks to ensuring its links with aristocrats and magnates, and in 910, it moved its seat southwards, from Oviedo to León. This city was consolidated as the *urbs regia*, as Fernando I reinforced it, initially settled on the eastern frontier of the kingdom, as count of Castile, and who in 1037 assumed, now as king, the thrones of León and Castile. He based his rise on the promotion of different *clienteles* in his curia and in administrative roles outside the court, together with successful conquests and new ways of promoting the settlement of the newly added areas. Royal wealth enabled him to undertake notable projects, like the collegiate church in León in 1063. In 1085, when Alfonso VI of Castile conquered Toledo, one of the Muslim capitals and ideological reference for the Visigoth monarchy, the territorial expansion offered him the way to solidify his power through presiding over a structure of magnates converted into his vassals.

The movement on the frontier and the wealth of all the northern kingdoms and counties was shaped in the eleventh century by the supply of financial contributions the *taifa* kingdoms in the Muslim south were obliged to hand over, the tributes called *parias*. Previously, trade, booties and ransoms made the Andalusian currency familiar, like the profit Alfonso III of Asturias earned in 878 for returning to Muhammad I one of his leading 'consiliarius'. Muslim gold coins were circulating more regularly in the northern lands at the end of the tenth century. The eleventh-century *parias* benefited all the northern kingdoms and counties, as well as leading warlords like El Cid or Arnau Mir de Tost. Incomes from these were very high between 1048 and 1073 but diminished from then on. They injected a great deal of cash, especially gold, into the northern territories, favouring an increase in wealth that had immediate political, social and economic effects. It is thus no surprise that, in the 1080s, the county of Barcelona focused its efforts on applying pressure to the *taifa* kingdoms in the east of the Peninsula to ensure this important source of income. The *parias* disappeared with the arrival of the Almoravids and did not reappear until this empire entered into crisis between 1130 and 1170. It was precisely then, from this context, that Ibn Mardanīš, the Wolf King, aimed to build an Andalusian kingdom around Murcia in the south-east of the Peninsula, but found himself obliged to pay important *parias,* agreed in a pact between Alfonso the Chaste of Aragon and Alfonso VIII of Castile.

The issuance of currency had only been maintained in Barcelona but during the tenth century and the beginning of the eleventh, the counties of Besalú, Cerdanya-Berga, Empúries, Roussillon, Urgell joined it, as probably did Ribagorça, as well as Girona, which belonged to the same count of Barcelona. The bishops of Girona, Urgell and, especially, Vic also issued money, as did the Viscount of Cardona, who occasionally put it into circulation at the end of the eleventh century in Calaf. While population growth and economic development stimulated the circulation of cash, the link between the issuance of currency and royal power explains why Alfonso VI issued money for the first time in Castile shortly after the conquest of Toledo (1085) and that Sancho of Aragon did the same soon after taking Pamplona (1076), a move that turned him into the sovereign of both kingdoms. Soon after, around 1085 Aragonese currency was minted in Jaca. At the same time, the circulation of Andalusian currency was made compatible with the arrival of European money. From the end of the eleventh century and even more in the twelfth, a lot circulated from the Camino de Santiago, especially Angevin, Tours and Melgueil shillings (*solidos*), while the latter also spread across the north and Catalonia. In the twelfth century, various cities in León and Castile issued currency. These included León, Toledo, Santiago, Salamanca, Ávila, Palencia, and probably Oviedo, Osma, Nájera and Burgos, the profits from these issues coinciding with certain cathedrals and monasteries. At the end of the twelfth century, in the east, the main reference currencies were defined, such as the Jaca and Barcelona shillings (*solidos*) and other local coinage was strengthened like that of Agramunt in Urgell, while the importance of the Melgueil shilling in the Catalan north-east reflected the cultural and economic proximity between Catalonia and Provence, and in Navarre at the end of the twelfth century there were the *sanchetes* in reference to Sancho VII.

Around 1018 gold coinage began to be issued in Barcelona, and this would continue regularly throughout the century. These were the *mancusos* that imitated Andalusian currency. The initiative for these issued was private, linked to the financial strategies in a context of a great deal of wealth circulating. The count of Barcelona worked to control the currency issues, and did so between 1069 and 1076. Precisely, in 1069 gold *mancusos* were coined with his name ('RAIMUNDUS COMES'). Gold coins may occasionally have been minted in Besalú between 988 and 1020, coinciding with a moment of splendour for this county, similarly to what happened in the final years of the century with the city of Jaca in Aragon. In another context, Almoravid gold coins were occasionally imitated by Alfonso VII of Castile around 1150, these being issued in Baeza in the brief period he held the city. However, it was from 1176 under Alfonso VIII when imitation Andalusian *morabatinos* were issued. These were prestigious coins that circulated throughout the Peninsula, including both Navarre and the Catalan counties. The emission of gold *morabatinos* or *maravedíes* also happened in León, under Ferdinand II from 1177. Precisely the Leonese king ceded the rights to the currency to the Church; in 1186 to Salamanca Cathedral and in 1193-1194 to the Cathedral in Santiago de Compostela. In Portugal gold coins were minted under Sancho I, in 1185-1189.

Trade allowed the surpluses from one area to be redistributed and, at the same time, luxury articles to be exchanged. These included luxurious fabrics and objects made of precious metals or ivory from al-Andalus, not infrequently from the Orient, that were used by the aristocracy and in the Christian liturgy. On occasions these objects were very unusual, like the three chess sets made of 96 pieces of rock crystal, produced between the end of the tenth and beginning of the eleventh century, which reached Arnau Mir de Tost, lord of Àger. In other cases, they produced a multiplier effect and were replicated, which is why in the eleventh century in Valdesaz, near León, artisan *tiraceros* imitated silk cloth.

Initially, the Jews tended to stand out in long-distance trade. It was Jews who, shortly before the mid-eleventh century, transported products for leading magnates in the west of the Peninsula, especially Menendo González, but were assaulted by rival aristocrats, losing 1,700 pounds of silk, 30 tunics and 30 linen canvases. A large part of credit was also entrusted to the Jews, like near Coimbra in 1018 when an enslaved man sought them to obtain the money with which to buy his freedom. However, the increase in wealth in the mid-tenth century generalized the participation in long-distance trade, as denoted by the traders in Barcelona from various places or the permission granted by Borrell II to subjects from Sant Cugat to fish and carry *mercaderias* by boat, a privilege confirmed by the count's son, Ramon Borrell of Barcelona, in 1011. Very significantly, the Peace and Truce conceded by Bishop Oliba of Vic in 1030 protected all participants in the markets: 'quicumque mercatores ad mercata venientes aut in mercata manentes aut inde redeuntes' (Gonzalvo, 1994: 7).

The increase in trade meant the development of artisanal activities, which appeared in the urban fabric, like the 'tendas' documented in the tenth century in both Barcelona and León. The high immigration of 'francos' from Europe, from the end of the eleventh century was mainly of those dedicated to urban trades centred around commerce, artisanal activity or construction. Unquestionably, between the end of the eleventh century and early decades of the twelfth, all the towns and cities on the line marked by the Camino de Santiago, across the kingdoms of Pamplona and Aragon and Castile and León, received a large number of immigrants. This led to the growth of specific neighbourhoods for these 'francos', with a customized legal status, especially in Navarre. This way, the *inventio* of Santiago de Compostela not only generated a nucleus of great consequences at the ecclesiastic, political and social levels, but that the way that led Christendom to this centre worked as a route for pilgrimage and trade, generating great wealth, with a multiplier effect that benefited all sectors of society, which explains the royal backing, with explicit actions like the establishment of hospitals under Alfonso VI. It coincided with a political opening to France, which facilitated the entry of the Gregorian reform, the influence of Cluny and elites of French origin around Alfonso VI. Meanwhile, the Pyrenean territories, Pamplona, Aragon and the Catalan counties with Barcelona to the fore, were interrelated with Occitania and Provence, establishing a political, economic and cultural link highlighted in the twelfth century.

The urban development consolidated a specific bourgeois social group, denomination that appeared in the *fuero* of Jaca in 1077, differentiating between *burguensis*, *miles* and *rusticos*. The urban setting was clearly stratified with elites like those found in the twelfth century in Pamplona, Burgos, León, Sahagún, Santiago de Compostela, Barcelona or Lleida. The documentation conserved referring to the latter two shows an urban elite dedicated foremost to investment in properties, and all kinds of rights, rents and activities, thus reinforcing a leading position from which they assumed the representation of the city before the respective lord. The numerous weekly markets established all over the territories from the eleventh century reinforced the vitality of the urban nuclei as regional centres. The central role of these towns and cities and the attraction of long-distance trade was strengthened with the annual fairs, beginning with the one in Belorado in 1116, to which others, like Valladolid, Sahagún and Jaca, were added during the same century. In this context, at the end of the twelfth century, the axis established by the Camino de Santiago lost its uniqueness due to the drastic reduction in immigrants in the last third of the century and, especially, because the urban fabric showed the entrenchment of the cities that grew on the old frontier, as well as the emergence of those on the Cantabrian Coast. For its part, from the end of the eleventh century and notably throughout the twelfth, Barcelona had risen as a trading port open to the Mediterranean, which explains its permanently fluctuating relations with Genoa.

1.4 Conclusion

The long evolution that had been transforming the Iberian economy since the fifth century found its excipient in the Islamic invasion at the beginning of the eighth century. The establishment of the frontier and then its transformation were its main consequences. The social and economic transformations that occurred between the eighth and tenth centuries were at the base of the social model that would be developed in the Christian world during the rest of the

Middle Ages, including the forms of seigneuralization and extraction of rents and income. The overwhelming transformation of the landscape guaranteed the agrarian base of the economy, with the predominance of cereal and vineyards, at the same time that a network of urban capitals with their markets was reinforced to articulate internal distribution and external relations. From this moment on, the border would be, first and foremost, a line that separated two cultures, which remained related by cultural and economic exchanges. This path did not lead to inward looking but rather to an opening to the exterior, well illustrated by the economic momentum around the Camino de Santiago, the establishment of an inextricable political, social and economic connection between both sides of the Pyrenees and, at the same time, the opening of trade to the Mediterranean.

SECTION II THE MEDIEVAL ECONOMY, 1000–1500

2

Production, 1000–1500

MARÍA ASENJO-GONZÁLEZ AND ANTONI FURIÓ

2.1 Introduction

Traditionally, historians have divided the central and late centuries of the Middle Ages into two periods: a first phase of growth and expansion, which would have begun around 1000, and would have lasted up to the end of the thirteenth century or the first decades of the fourteenth; and a second phase of crisis and recovery, which would characterize the last two medieval centuries, separated by the calamities of the fourteenth century (epidemics, war, famines). This chronological division has recently been questioned and the very concept of 'crisis' has not resisted the scrutiny of the new empirical evidence and new interpretations, which have led to the conclusion of economic readjustment and reconversion, rather than crisis and depression.

This applies to the whole of Western Europe, but particularly to the Iberian Peninsula, where, from the eleventh to the thirteenth centuries, the Christian kingdoms expanded to the south, at the expense of al-Andalus, a movement that was accompanied by extensive economic expansion in agriculture, commerce and manufacturing. The subsequent repopulation effort required a strong demographic contribution by the Christian kingdoms of the north, so demographic and economic growth hardly could have peaked or shown the first signs of exhaustion at the end of the century. Iberia had just 'entered' in Europe, and begun to homologate its economic and social structures with those of the rest of the continent and insert itself in a privileged position, as a bridge, between the Mediterranean and Atlantic worlds. It had motives and, above all, the possibilities to continue growing.

Without denying the strong impact of the calamities of the fourteenth century, and particularly their economic and social consequences, which will be discussed in this chapter, recent studies show, however, that the last and a half century of the Middle Ages was not one of a strong economic depression.

The states of the Iberian Peninsula continued growing, with the gradual sedentarization of the population (linked to the land and to the organization of agricultural areas), the introduction of new crops, the application of new technologies, especially irrigation that increased yields, and more productive investments. All this resulted in a significant improvement in productivity, mainly agricultural, and quality, especially in industry, which would make Iberian production more competitive and strengthen its position within the great international trade. Far from staying in the margins or the periphery of Western Europe, Iberia occupied an important place, thanks to its demographic strength, its high levels of urbanization, increasing commercialization, the development of its institutions, and the state-building process of the polities who shared the peninsula and competed to impose their hegemony.

2.2 Phases of Output Expansion and Retraction

By the year 1000, most of the Iberian Peninsula was dominated by Muslims, and only in the northern part had some small Christian states developed, formed autonomously or by the advance of the Carolingian Empire. By the end of the Middle Ages, almost all of Iberia was already Christian, with the sole exception of Granada, which would eventually be annexed by Castile in 1492. The phenomenon that marked the history of the peninsula in these five centuries, and in particular the first three, from the eleventh to the thirteenth, was the so-called *Reconquista*, that is, the territorial expansion of the Christian kingdoms at the expense of al-Andalus. In just two and a half centuries, from 1000 to 1250, Portugal went from some 12,000 km^2 to about 92,000 km^2, while the Crown of Aragon, which did not even exist in 1000, went from some 28,000 km^2 (20,000 km^2 in Catalonia and 8,000 km^2 in Aragon) to about 103,000 km^2, and Castile from some 70,000 km^2 (when it was still the Asturias kingdom in the tenth century) to about 350,000 km^2. In the same period the total population of the peninsula, also including the territory under Muslim domination, went from about four million inhabitants to five and a half million.

The magnitude of these figures allows us to understand the importance of the *Reconquista* in the medieval history of Iberia and its influence both in shaping the productive structures and the phases and rhythms of its economy. In general, Iberia followed a pattern very similar to that of the rest of Western Europe, with a first phase of growth from the eleventh to the thirteenth century or even well into the fourteenth century, interrupted by a brief but intense interval of crisis and depression in the central decades of this century, followed in turn by a new period of recovery in the fifteenth century, which in Castile was already noticeable from the end of the fourteenth. However, each of these phases was conditioned in the case of the peninsula by territorial expansion and by the demographic, economic and social changes associated with the

Reconquista. Indeed, the Christian conquest was not limited to a mere military occupation that left the defeated population in the territory. Instead, it involved the replacement of the native Muslim population by Christian settlers, the transformation of productive structures, and the change of the legal and institutional framework; in short, the substitution of one society for another and the implementation of a new economic and social order.

2.2.1 Growth and Expansion

The eleventh to thirteenth centuries were of great economic growth in both the Muslim and Christian parts of the Iberian Peninsula. The collapse of the caliphate weakened al-Andalus politically and militarily, but it boosted and favoured local and regional growth dynamics, especially by allocating the product of taxation that was previously directed towards Córdoba to investments in the territory itself. In particular, the *taifas* gave great impetus to the development of irrigation, with the construction of new ditches leading to an expansion of the watered area and the introduction of new crops, which would lead to a true agricultural or 'green' revolution. The Arabic texts of the time also allude to the great importance of livestock, both in the mountains of Lorca and Tudela and in the marshes of the lower Guadalquivir, as well as the breeding of numerous cattle and lamb herds in the central mountain massif. Certainly, Andalusian agriculture differed from Christian agriculture because of the importance of irrigation and the cultivation of vegetables and other plants and fruits, but in both the cultivation of cereals food base and livestock were fundamental. The growing importance of the urban population, both in the capitals of the *taifas* and in other medium-sized nuclei, reinforced the commercial orientation of agricultural production, a large part of which was destined to meet the supply needs of the towns.

In the Christian north of the peninsula, the economic growth of this first phase, from the eleventh to the thirteenth century, was concretized and is attested by the strong demographic increase already noted, the agrarian expansion, the urban renaissance and the development of industrial and commercial activity. Despite the lack of reliable figures, demographic growth must have been remarkable and sustained, since, otherwise, the reconquering progress of the early Christian nuclei in more than 400,000 km^2 and the corresponding repopulation process of the conquered territory would be difficult to explain (Vaca, 2014). The advances of the *Reconquista* allowed to give way to the surplus population of the Christian kingdoms, but their rhythm and strength were very different according to the periods and the major or minor importance of the previous Muslim population. Settlement and land occupation were more intense in the northern areas, which were conquered throughout the eleventh and twelfth centuries. In Portugal, for example, and despite Almoravid and Almohad counterattacks, the forest and heathland south of

Coimbra continued to be claimed, whereas a little later, after the double conquest of Santarém and Lisbon in 1147, the region was intensely populated and organized – in contrast with the Muslim neglect of it in the previous centuries. This was witnessed first by the string of towns built around the existing castles and then by the multiplication of new villages surrounding the towns and established near the best soils. On the contrary, colonization was much slower in the next hundred years, until the capture in 1249 of the last Muslim strongholds in the Algarve, due both to the speed of the military advance and the vast extent of the occupied territory, as well as to the permanence of pockets of Moorish population (Silva, 1996; Gomes, 2009; Henriques, 2017).

The same happened in the rest of the peninsula, where both the Castilian-Leonese conquest in the centre and south and the Catalan-Aragonese in the east entailed the incorporation of thousands and thousands of square kilometres, with many fertile lands from which their previous Muslim owners were dispossessed, but also many unfarmed terrains to be claimed and put into cultivation. In contrast to the peasant initiative that had characterized the preceding centuries, settlement and cultivation was now a directed and controlled process. According to the different areas, the protagonists of this control were the monarch and the monasteries, within the framework of the process of seigniorialization that followed the feudal revolution of the eleventh century, and then, in the second half of the twelfth century, by military orders (the Templars, the Knights Hospitallar and others of a strictly Iberian nature), which played a decisive role in the spatial articulation of border areas. Other protagonists were also the so-called *concejos* (urban councils), key elements in the consolidation of the frontiers and in the first economic take-off. Their large number and their organizational potential explain the urban substratum of some areas, especially in Castile, in which neither commercial nor artisan stimuli played an important role. The new spaces were organized around large towns, surrounded by a large subsidiary rural territory (*alfoz*) and dependent villages and hamlets. However, and contrary to the northernmost territories, the Muslim kingdoms of Toledo and Zaragoza, located in the centre of the peninsula and in the Ebro valley, respectively, had at the time of their conquest (in 1085 and 1118, respectively) a denser and more consistent settlement. The repopulation, therefore, was limited to favouring the presence of Christian immigrants that balanced the Muslims who continued to live under Christian rule (Miranda & Guerrero, 2008).

South of this new territorial advance, the border stabilized for more than a century, with continual attacks and counterattacks by Christians and Muslims. These territories were largely entrusted to military orders, which privileged sheep farming, both for their own economic interests and because the instability of a frontier zone hindered both settlement and a stable crop system. On the other hand, as Christian settlers descended south, they encountered the irrigation systems developed by Muslims. Irrigation was not only an Andalusian legacy, but was extended and improved by the new Christian-feudal society. The agriculture of the Christian kingdoms was not limited to the fertile irrigated lands taken from the Muslims. Everywhere, from Galicia to the newly conquered southern territories, the *ager* advanced at the expense of the *saltus*, the wasteland, new lands were reclaimed, the forest was pushed back, the marshes were dried and agriculture began to climb the mountains. Even as late as 1340, shortly before the Black Death made its appearance, forest clearances and drainage of swamps continued on the outskirts of Leiria or Santarém (Gonçalves, 1989; Viana, 2007; Gomes, 2009), while the heathlands around Coina (south of Lisbon) was gradually converted into vineyards and grain fields (Pontes, 2006; Henriques, 2017).

By the mid-thirteenth century, virtually the entire peninsula had passed into Christian rule, with the sole exception of the stronghold of Granada. The kingdom that expanded the most was Castile, occupying the entire central axis of the peninsula, from the Cantabrian coast to Cádiz. A huge territory was gained in a short time and that, given the limited demographic resources available, established a very favourable land to labour ratio. The thirteenth and first half of the fourteenth century, then, were times of a fundamentally extensive growth – colonization of the vast occupied territory, enlargement of the cultivated space, advance of cereal farming and livestock, extension and improvement of the irrigation system – which was far from touching the ceiling when the calamities of the fourteenth century ensued. Long before the Black Death made its appearance in Iberia in the summer of 1348, the peninsula had been suffering from severe food shortages, hungers and famines. The one in 1333 was particularly critical. In Catalonia it was known as 'the bad first year' (*lo mal any primer*), but the effects of the famine were also felt severely in other cities of the Crown of Aragon and in the kingdoms of Navarre (where a third of the population died), Castile (particularly in the northern *Meseta*) and Portugal. In the latter, the situation became truly critical and a chronicle of the time qualifies this year as 'a bad year throughout Portugal' (*mao anno por todo Portugal*), not only because of food shortages and price escalation, but also because of the great deaths caused by famine, of proportions unknown until then.

That of 1333 was not, however, the first of the great shortages that the Iberian kingdoms suffered in the fourteenth century. There were others in 1302, 1311, 1315, 1322, 1324 and, later, in 1347 and 1374, and even more, if believing the urban councils, who continually complained to the monarchs of the difficulties they had in ensuring the supply of their cities and the immoderate rise in the price of cereals, asking the monarchs to ban grain exports outside the kingdom and guarantee their redistribution inside. Famine and hunger had become a regular, structural phenomenon, and it is not surprising that municipal documentation records shortages almost every year, while, on the contrary, contemporary chronicles, forced to be more selective, and the studies of historians coincide in highlighting the intensity and uniqueness of three of them: those of 1333, 1347 and 1374, which were truly catastrophic years, when hunger ruled over the peninsula.

2.2.2 Crisis and Recovery

Famines, epidemics and wars (particularly the war between Castile and the Crown of Aragon in the third quarter of the fourteenth century, which in Castile was also a civil war) interrupted the growth that Iberia had been experiencing since the eleventh century. The effects of this conjunction of adversities, particularly of the Black Death, were very different in the different kingdoms. However, the demographic decline and the disorganization of productive structures were neither general nor continued. They did not affect the entire peninsula, being more pronounced in some regions than in others, and, beyond the immediate and drastic effects of the plague, with very high losses in some areas, the result was not so much a regression, a reversal of the previous trend, as a momentary interruption of the growth, a stagnation phase, of balances even negative but punctual, which alternated with equally transient recovery intervals.

The population decline resulted in the abandonment of many farms and, in particular, in the reduction of the cultivated area. Less farmland in absolute terms, but more, proportionally, for the surviving peasants, who increased average productivity, since agricultural production remained fairly stable and even increased at some times. However, the decline in cultivated space is a topic of debate, for example in Castile. On the one hand, it is possible to underline both the scarcity of the empirical basis for considering this idea, and the fact that depopulated places could also be the result of the mobility of settlements (Castán, 2020). On the other hand, the available evidence has shown that the decline may not only have been the result of the decrease in the number of peasants, but also of the abandonment by the lords of the direct cultivation of their large farms, which were no longer economically profitable. According to this interpretation, the setback seems to have been selective and have affected the cereal lands more than, for example, the vineyards, which had demanded a greater investment for their exploitation and on which the attention of the lords was concentrated (Vaca, 2014).

Both factors, the reduction of the cultivated area and the decrease in the number of people to work it, would in turn affect the fall of the seigniorial income, in a percentage that ranged between a third (for the bishopric of Oviedo) and half (for the monastery of Sahagún). Consequently, many lords left their lands uncultivated or transformed them into pastures. In this sense, and as Ángel Vaca recalls, it has been possible to say that the Mesta, the powerful organization of livestock farmers in Castile, was 'daughter' of the

Black Death, although it had been born much earlier, as we will explain better later on: the sheep farming allowed people to take advantage of the empty spaces that the Christian conquest and colonization had created in the centre and south of the peninsula and that had been increased by the demographic regression of the fourteenth century. Many herd owners found in the increase in the number of their sheep and in the rise of international wool trade, compensation for the loss of the number of their vassals and the degradation of their seignorial rents.

In reality, and despite its immediate devastating effects, the crisis led to a profound transformation and readjustment of productive structures. In Castile, according to Miguel Ángel Ladero (1992), the crisis hit bottom towards 1390, then began a timid recovery until 1420 and reached a stage of maximum Castilian economic growth between 1420 and 1460. In the Crown of Aragon, the recovery was later, but it is also true that the impact of the crisis was very different according to the territories: stronger in Catalonia and lower in Aragon and Valencia. In general, it can be said that the recovery came with or resulted in an intensification of agricultural and livestock production, its increasing adaptation to the market, a growing specialization of crops and a redistribution and concentration of land ownership. This last process benefited in particular the most affluent farmers, the *labradores* in Castile or the *pagesos grassos* in Catalonia, who incorporated into their farms those abandoned by their less fortunate neighbours and were also the main drivers of technical (in particular, the extension of irrigation) and productive innovations (the diffusion of much more lucrative new crops such as rice, sugar, mulberry, flax, hemp and saffron). Rural elites, which included this upper stratum of the peasantry but also notaries, artisans and merchants, gathered in their hands economic power and political power in rural communities and small towns, and their sphere of activities and interests included both the cultivation of land and livestock farming, the commercialization of agricultural production, the leasing of mills, ovens and other monopolies, of royal and municipal taxes, of seignorial rents or ecclesiastical tithe and the credit to individuals and institutions. From these rural elites also came, in part, the recovery of demand, which was no longer, as it had been until then, fundamentally aristocratic and urban.

The wide agrarian reconversion also translated into productive specialization and greater commercialization of agricultural and livestock production. The increase in sheep farming (livestock would become the main wealth and economic activity not only of much of Castile, but also of Aragon, the Valencian north and even Mallorca), as well as the cultivation of flax, hemp or mulberry, were closely related to the development of the textile and silk industry, both in the peninsula and in other countries where raw materials and, to a lesser extent, finished products were exported. On the other hand, both in Castile and in the Crown of Aragon and Portugal, the vineyard became a regular crop on the outskirts of cities and towns, just to supply the urban demand. Foreign demand was also important: wines from Alicante and the Algarve were exported to Flanders and England.

Other specialized crops that experienced a great expansion during the fifteenth century, due to their high commercial demand, were olives (mainly produced in Andalusia), rice (cultivated in the Valencian marshes), sugar (also produced in Valencia and Granada), mulberry (in Valencia and Murcia, whose cultivation was related to both the export of raw silk and the development of the silk industry), vegetables (especially in irrigated *huertas*), as well as the so-called industrial (flax and hemp) and dye plants (madder, weld, woad, saffron and sumac). Everywhere, however, agricultural recovery and growth were linked to wheat expansion, although that did not mean that it was a totally traditional and stagnant economy. After all, wheat was still the most commercial of all crops, since in addition to its own consumption, much of the production was destined for the market and even for export.

We do not yet have data on the total production of Iberia and its evolution, although regional data is increasingly abundant, especially for this third phase of recovery, which would begin in the late fourteenth and early fifteenth centuries. According to the calculations of a chronicler from the second half of the fifteenth century, the city of Valencia needed 600 hl of wheat every day, that is, more than 220,000 hl per year. This figure fits well with the 60,000 inhabitants that the city had at that time, considering that historians estimate annual consumption at 4 hl of wheat per person. Extrapolating these figures to the kingdom as a whole, this would mean a million hectolitres by 1400, when the population was around 250,000 inhabitants, and 1,200,000 hl by 1500, when the population had risen to 300,000. The wheat production in the kingdom of Valencia, with all its strong oscillations from one year to the next, and with the exported grain compensating for imported grain, had to be around one million hectolitres in general annually, that is, about 75,000 tons. In the last two decades of the fifteenth century the kingdom of Seville produced approximately double that: about 150,000 tons per year. But this kingdom, which included the archbishopric of Seville and the bishoprics of Cádiz, Córdoba and Jaén, was one of the main producing regions of Castile. According to Ladero and González Jiménez, based on data from the ecclesiastical tithe, wheat production alone in the archbishopric of Seville went from about 30,000–33,000 tons in the first third of the fifteenth century to double in the central years (1451–1467), 77,000 tons in 1484 and 92,000 tons in 1503. As Table 2.1 shows, data from the tithe (measured in Castilian *fanegas*: 1 *fanega* is equal to about 43 kg) indicates that, at least since 1420, agricultural production experienced strong growth, which the authors attribute to both the expansion of cultivated space and the increase in demand, motivated in turn by the population boom and the best functioning of the markets (Ladero & González Jiménez, 1978).

Table 2.1 *Evolution of cereal production in the archbishopric of Seville in the fifteenth century*

Years	Wheat
1408	602,772
1420	713,992
1431	1,011,824
1432	1,210,693
1451	1,331,806
1461	1,410,273
1470	1,579,659
1480	1,696,735
1491	1,656,743
1503	2,120,319

Source: Ladero & González Jiménez (1978)

In the Crown of Aragon, the regional rhythms of the recovery were very diverse. In the northern and central regions of the kingdom of Valencia, where the crisis was most pronounced in the fifteenth century, recovery did not begin until the early sixteenth. In the southern regions it was not only earlier, but agricultural production increased by 70% in just over a hundred years, between 1420 and 1530. In any case, the last decades of the fifteenth and the first of the sixteenth were of vigorous agricultural growth, attested by multiple indications: by the lease of the tithe in the first place, but also by other more secondary ones such as the increase in the number of mills. In the territory of Ontinyent, of six mills that existed up to 1463 and seven between this date and 1502, the number rose to eight in 1504, eleven in 1508, fifteen in 1526 and seventeen in 1528; in the same period, the number of fulling mills went from five to eighteen, and the set of milling facilities, including oil mills, from eleven to forty-one. Production increased, but so did productivity. In the Albaida valley and the Alcoi region, always in the kingdom of Valencia, the population increased by 45% between 1421 and 1530, while production increased by almost 70%.

We do not have similar data for the same period for Portugal. However, António Henriques, also from the ecclesiastical tithe, has offered an estimate of the agricultural output of this country for the second decade of the fourteenth century (1311–1320) and 1530, expressed not in units of capacity (hl) or of weight (tons) but in currency: about 15 million Portuguese pounds, equivalent to 180.7 tons of pure silver for the period before the Black Death, when Portugal counted between 0.9 and 1.2 million inhabitants, and 240.5 tons of silver at the beginning of the sixteenth century, for a population of around 1.27 million. These figures document a decline of the real agrarian output per head from the 1320 benchmark to the sixteenth century (Henriques, 2015).

2.3 The Landscape

Iberia is very diverse in its landscapes, both for climatic and historical reasons. The western half of the peninsula is influenced by the Atlantic climate while the eastern half is influenced by the Mediterranean climate. There are therefore two Iberias: one that is wet and green and the other dry and arid, with no more vegetation than the thicket and bushes. Here water is a scarce and vital resource, indispensable. Not only agriculture is not possible without water, but also life itself. Historically, both population and agriculture have been conditioned by the existence of water resources for both consumption and irrigation. And if in the western and northern half of the peninsula the extension of agriculture has been done against the trees, clearing and receding the forest, in the central and southern part it has been done against the water, both against its scarcity and against its excess. Mediterranean climate is irregular and characterized by long and persistent droughts, especially during the summer months, but also by torrential rains, especially in autumn, which devastate everything – crops, agricultural infrastructure and even houses. Farmers have learned since prehistoric times to domesticate water, to channel it through dams and *azudes* and to use it for consumption and irrigation. The first major hydraulic works are from the Roman era, but many of them stopped being used and deteriorated during the early Middle Ages. It was the Arabs who *reinvented* irrigation in Iberia, both on a small (*micro*) scale, to irrigate a few hectares with water from springs, fountains and wells, and on a large (*macro*) scale, with the design and construction of large watered perimeters – the large Mediterranean *huertas*, especially in Valencia, Murcia and Granada – irrigated with river water, diverted through dams and channelled to the fields through a complex network of ditches and trenches. In addition to the technical aspects, this also required a complex social and institutional organization for the distribution of available water, the management and maintenance of the system and the settlement of conflicts.

Both in dryland and irrigated areas, Iberia's landscape was heavily anthropized by the end of the Middle Ages. Natural landscape can hardly be spoken of, because both the one cultivated and the one dedicated to meadows and pastures formed a humanized landscape, deeply transformed by human intervention. All this was carried out precisely during the medieval centuries, with the deforestation of woodlands and mountains and the desiccation and reclamation of marshes and wetlands. Agriculture advanced through the occupation and cultivation of these wastelands. However, the economy of the peasant communities and even of the inhabitants of towns and cities was not only limited to the exploitation of the *ager*, but also included the use of *saltus*, forested and mountainous areas, lagoons and swamps, which constituted the base of the communal lands and where an intense silvopastoral activity of hunting, fishing and collection of wild plants and fruits was developed.

To the structural, Atlantic or Mediterranean climate regime, climate change must also be added. Between the years 900 and 1300 there seems to have been a warming in the northern hemisphere known by historians as the 'Medieval Warm Period', which would have had important consequences for the environment, landscape, settlement and economic activity, primarily agriculture. According to Henriques (2017), increases in temperature allowed for extending the grown area and diversifying cultures, in particular more valuable and nutritional species like vines and olive trees. Better ecological conditions for men, animals and plants allowed large villages to be settled at altitudes that were not met again in any historical period, in the same way that, for example, vines reached altitudes that would not be seen again (Durand, 1982; Henriques, 2003; Fontes & Roriz, 2007; Gouveia, 2012). The effects of warming, however, were contradictory. In the mountainous or humid areas of the Atlantic Iberia (Portugal, Galicia, Asturias, Cantabria and even in the Pyrenean regions), it made the cultivation of hitherto unusable land possible and fostered both the intensification and the extensification of agrarian production, increasing the cultivated area and diversifying the crops. In contrast, it made the dry, low-lying southern plains more arid. Perhaps the development of Mediterranean irrigated spaces, from small systems designed and created by rural communities, and expanded and turned into large and complex *huertas* in the tenth and eleventh centuries, is related, together with the urban expansion, to this warming. Conversely, the cooling period that followed later, known as the 'Little Ice Age' and starting around 1300, badly affected the late medieval economy, with a succession of heavy rains and droughts resulting in bad harvests, poor livestock survival and famines. It is also possible that this climatic cooling contributed, along with the other calamities of the fourteenth century (plague, war and famine), to interrupt the age-old economic growth. However, its effects do not seem to have been very prolonged, since the recovery of the fifteenth century would occur in this same framework of cooling that would last until the nineteenth century.

In any case, medieval Iberian societies were no longer totally dependent on natural conditions, both climate and environment, and, on the other hand, they were increasingly concerned with their conservation. In addition to the forest clearance to expand cultivated space, some crops and industries were very harmful to the environment, and public authorities tried to ban them or at least control them. Rice cultivation in stagnant waters and the treatment of woad and other dye products were forbidden in the vicinity of towns because of its infectious nature in the first case and polluting in the second. On the other hand, sugar mills consumed a huge amount of firewood, which led, together with the use of wood in the naval industry and, above all, the great summer fires, to the deforestation of entire regions, especially in the more arid Mediterranean part of the peninsula. Hence the repetition of municipal ordinances punishing with harsh penalties the illegal logging of trees or burning stubble that could cause serious fires. These environmental conservation measures were added to those that protected the cultivated space from the destruction caused by the passage of animals. It was not about protecting only the *ager*, the arable land, but also the *saltus*, the forests and the lagoons, which were generally communal property, and from where peasants extracted an important part of their diet and other daily utilities.

2.4 Agriculture, Manufacturing and Commerce

2.4.1 *Agriculture*

Agriculture was the main productive sector in Iberia in the Middle Ages and the one that occupied most of the active population. The growth of agricultural output allowed more and more people to engage in non-agrarian activities and contributed greatly to the development of cities and towns. However, within the urban centres, even in the larger ones, a good part of the population remained as farmers dedicated to the cultivation of land in the immediate countryside. In some towns this productive dedication was so predominant that historians have coined the term 'agrotowns' to define them. Conversely, not all the inhabitants of the rural areas were peasants or engaged in agricultural activities. In recent years, historians have highlighted the importance of rural industry and the presence of artisans and merchants in medium-sized towns and villages (Furió, 2010a, 2017; Igual-Luis, 2017a; Navarro & Villanueva, 2017). The borders between the urban and rural worlds were not as airtight as had been supposed until now, but were much more fluid and, rather than separate, they brought into contact two closely related and complementary worlds. The cities, it is true, were born from the first rural boom between the eleventh and thirteenth centuries. But the agrarian development of the late Middle Ages is explained only by the progress of commercialization and, in particular, by the increase in urban demand, which conditioned the productive dedication of the nearby regions, absorbing most of their production. Take for example the case of Valencia. The city developed strongly from the eleventh century thanks in particular to the neighbouring *huerta* (the irrigated plain), which covered its food needs. Later, in the fourteenth century, when the city had already reached 30,000 inhabitants and neither the *huerta* nor the production of the entire kingdom could already guarantee its supply, it had to resort to the importation of grains from abroad, financed by the city council (Furió, 2015a). In many parts of the peninsula, especially in its eastern part, when one left the city walls behind, one did not enter a purely rural, backward and autarkic world, enclosed in itself, but one that was heavily commercialized and urbanized, that is, subject to the influence of the city and urban capital. We see it in Barcelona, Mallorca and Zaragoza, but also in Segovia, Seville and many other Castilian cities (Borrero Fernández, 1983; Asenjo, 1986; Cuadrada, 1990–1991; Jover, 1997; Falcón, 2011).

The predominance of the primary sector, both agriculture and livestock farming, also does not imply a lack of investment and technical and productive innovation. Probably the area in which this innovation was most important, in terms of technical and social complexity as well as funding, was irrigation. In this field the cultural transfer from the Islamic to the Christian world was very important, bringing to Iberia techniques and irrigation systems from the Middle East and even further away, transmitted by the Arab civilization. Closely linked to the development of irrigation was also the diffusion of the hydraulic mill, usually of horizontal wheel, widespread in both the Christian-feudal and Muslim parts of the peninsula. This type of mill has been documented, both in al-Andalus and in the Christian north, since long before the eleventh century. The following century sees the first mentions of tidal water mills, a very innovative technology, widespread in Portugal and the north-west of the peninsula, from Galicia to Cantabria, and to windmills, attested in Lisbon in 1182 and in Tarragona also in the twelfth century.

The Christian conquest profoundly modified the previous Andalusian productive spaces. This is particularly evident in the parcel system. Faced with the irregular layout of the fields in Muslim agriculture, since their limits were adapted to the terrain conditions and contour lines, the Christian settlers imposed a more regular, orthogonal grid, often a result of the distribution of land after the conquest and reminiscent of the Roman centuriation. They came from a cereal ecosystem, based on fallow and plough, and what they valued most were the large areas of flat land and open spaces, although they did not renounce irrigated lands and vegetables, but kept and improved them. In northern Catalonia settlement was dispersed and plots grouped in compact farms (*masos*) of generally about 10 ha. In Valencia these compact granges were called *alqueries* and their size was smaller, between 1.5 and 6 ha, well below the 10–15 ha that the affluent farmers could own. However, the general trend was the opposite, that of a concentrated settlement and an atomized and dispersed plot. This was partly a consequence of the inheritance system, which fragmented the peasant holdings in each generation, as well as of the land market, which built these holdings with plots scattered throughout the territory. In Alzira and Manises, the immense majority of the plots did not reach half a hectare, while in Castelló the average plot was half a hectare in the irrigated area and just over one hectare in the dry land. The size of the parcels was larger in Extremadura, where cereal plots were normally between two and eight *fanegas*, i.e., between 1.28 and 5.12 ha (in Pozuelo, for example, the average size was 4 *fanegas*, i.e., 2.5 ha), although the smallest ones could be less than one and a half *fanegas*, and the largest, especially in the case of *rozas* (clearings), were more than 10 *fanegas* (6.4 ha). Here, the peasant holdings were made up of several plots located in different parts of the territory and together they were on average between 5 and 7.7 ha; however, holdings of more than 9.6 ha (59.77% of the farmed area) and even more than 19.2 ha (28.12% of the farmed area), which only accounted for a quarter of the total, covered almost 90% of the cultivated area. In any case, according to Clemente, the hierarchy of peasant farms around 1300 was much greater – with a higher number of large farms – in the south than in the north of Castile (Clemente, 1989; 2003; 2004; 2005). As for Portugal, calculations based on the case of Póvoa d'El Rey at the end of the fourteenth century give an average of 2.9 ha per holding, although the majority, nearly two thirds, were less than 4 ha, with less than 15% of the total acreage, holdings between 4 and 6 ha (28% of the farms) accounting for 44.3% of the farmed area and those larger than 6 ha (only three: two of 6 ha and one of 13 ha, or 9.4% of the number of farms) owning almost 28% of the farmed area (Hoffman & Johnson, 1971).

Cereals and essentially wheat were the hegemonic crop, generally occupying more than a half to 80% or more of the cultivated space. There was a wide variety of cereals, which can be grouped into two large types: those planted in the winter and harvested in early summer, such as wheat, barley and rye, and those planted in spring and harvested in the autumn, like barley, oats, millet or sorghum. Wheat was the most prized grain and the most suitable for making white bread, but it fatigued the soil excessively and only in irrigated lands were the fields not to be abandoned to fallow. On the contrary, the other cereals were more robust, depleted the soil less and were more productive, in addition to the fact that their production costs were lower than those of wheat (Garcia-Oliver, 2004). In Castile and León, the quintessential crop system was that of *año y vez*, which meant one year of planting and one year of fallow; the three-year rotation is documented as early as the fourteenth century, in Ávila and Burgos (Martín Cea, 1996; Casado, 1987), although it does not seem to have generalized until early-modern times, although some studies advance its chronology to the thirteenth century (Alfonso, 1982; Riesco, 2015). For its part, in addition to adapting better to all types of soils, barley had the advantage of serving both human and animal consumption, and in some regions its production was double that of wheat. It was also the most used cereal to associate with wheat in the sowing of meslin. Millet and other similar varieties (*panizo*) were used to feed poultry, while spelt and especially barley were intended for horses.

Traditionally, historians have calculated very low yields per unit of wheat or barley sown – from 1:4 for wheat and 1:3.2 for barley around 1300 (García de Cortázar, 1988; Reglero, 1994). The most recent research raises this to at least 1:4.5 (1:4.46 for Póvoa d'El Rey, in Portugal) or even 1:5 for wheat and 1:5 and 1:6 for barley, with the highest quality lands, such as those of the Andalusian countryside, giving average yields of between 1:10 and 1:12, according to Antonio Collantes, Mercedes Borrero and Miguel Ángel Ladero. These figures correspond to rainfed or dry land crops. In the irrigated lands, they were much higher, and this was the reason why cereals (and also vines and olive groves), in addition to vegetables, were watered. Normally they were around 1:10 or 1:12, but in early-modern times they had doubled up to 1:20 or 1:30 (Furió, 2015b). Yields were also higher in the suburban *huertas* and fields, where the investments of the landowners residing in cities and towns were more substantial. Some of them even tried to apply to their farms the technical and productive improvements they read in agronomy books, translated first from Arabic and then directly from Latin into Romance languages. The widespread dissemination of these agronomy treaties in the late Middle Ages, some of them commented and adapted by their translators, as well as their presence in private libraries, shows that they were not just scholarly works, but had a practical application (Furió, 2021). As regards yields per hectare, estimates for Portugal range from the 8.9 hl proposed by Hoffman and Johnson for Póvoa d'El Rey to 10 hl/ha for Mondego (Coelho, 1989) and to the 20 hl/ha suggested by Henriques for wheat and second-rate cereal in optimal land. In Tenerife, at the beginning of the sixteenth century, the yield on fertile dry land was 10.5 hl/ha (calculations based on Aznar, 1983 and Macías, 2011). These figures are much higher than those obtained in the Valencian Country and the Balearic Islands for rainfed wheat (around 5 hl/ha) and barley (around 10 hl/ha), although in irrigated areas they could reach 12–24 hl/ha (Ardit, 1997). However, the rates should not have been very high, since average yields of 6.5 hl/ha for wheat and 8.3 hl/ha for barley have been estimated for early modern Castile (Bringas, 2012). For vines, yields have been estimated at between 4.5 and 5 hl/ha for Valladolid (Rucquoi, 1997), an average that in the mid-eighteenth century was between 5.5 and 7 hl for the whole of Castile and León (Blanco & Bragado, 2003), while in Portugal in the fifteenth century the average was as high as 30–38 hl/ha (Viana, 1998) or even 50 hl/ha (Coelho, 1989).

The vineyard was present everywhere, both in the dry and irrigated lands. In addition to liturgical reasons, its cultivation was driven by the lords in the settlement charters that followed the great conquests of the thirteenth century, as it was a product that could be stored well and transported and commercialized easily. Later, urban demand determined its production by urban landowners on the outskirts of cities. For climatic and ecological reasons, the olive groves were reduced mainly but not exclusively to the southern and eastern half of the peninsula. In addition to consumption, the oil was also used for lighting, for making soap and for multiple applications in medicine and pharmacopoeia. Other regionally important tree crops were figs, almonds, hazelnuts, carob, as well as fruit (apples, pears, plums, cherries, pomegranates). The variety of crops was completed with legumes, vegetables and industrial (flax, hemp) and dye plants (madder, weld, woad, henna, safflower, saffron). Broadly speaking, the cultivated space was organized in rings around the population centres. The first ring and closest to the city was occupied by orchards and gardens, often fenced, where vegetables and fruit trees were grown, followed by *huertas* and vineyards, sometimes also watered. Beyond, the arable land extended, dedicated mainly to cereals, in a landscape of open fields, and further still, pastures and meadows. Finally, in the limits of the territory came the forests, the marshes and the lagoons, often shared by several towns and villages, in communal property or exploitation regime.

Livestock has always played an important role in Iberia, both a standing and transhumant one. Although it was undoubtedly benefited by the *Reconquista*, the transhumance is prior to it, especially to the great territorial expansion of the twelfth and thirteenth centuries, and the cattle went up and down the *cañadas* (ravines) that crossed the peninsula from north to south regardless of political and military borders. Transhumance, of greater or lesser distance, was important in Portugal and the Crown of Aragon, but it was especially in Castile that it reached a greater development. This was caused, in addition to traditional ancestral practices, by the extreme breadth of the border strip between Islam and Christianity in the centre of the peninsula, which did not allow the cultivation of the land due to the continual military and looting incursions into one another, and the strong commercial demand for wool, which increased markedly after the appearance of the merino sheep. Sheep farmers gathered in assemblies or councils, called *mestas*, which are at the origin of the *Honrado Concejo de la Mesta*, created in 1273 by Alfonso X to bring together all the breeders of Castile and León, mainly the large owners of flocks, both lay and ecclesiastical. The Mesta, object of numerous privileges on the part of the monarchs, mainly in terms of rights of passage and grazing, was also born to defend the interests of the ranchers against the farmers (Bishko, 1996). The transhumance was organized through three vertical routes in the central part of the peninsula: from León to Extremadura, from Logroño to Andalusia and from Cuenca to Murcia and Andalusia. The commercialization of wool stimulated the growth of the sheep population, which doubled from one and a half million heads in 1400 to three million in 1500 (Ladero, 2017). This increase in wool production had an impact on the development of the textile industry, especially in the regions most linked to sheep farming, such as Cuenca (Iradiel, 1974).

In Portugal, the transhumance routes descended from the Douro Valley and the Central System to the Alentejo, sometimes passing to the Castilian

Extremadura. In turn, the Castilian cattle entered Portugal from the North (Minho and Trás-os-Montes). Faced with the interest of the Portuguese monarchs to favour the entry of Castilian merino sheep, local shepherds complained that they consumed all the available grass. The *Cortes* of 1481- 1482 numbered between 50,000 and 60,000 the number of Castilian sheep that entered Riba d'Ondiana every year, depleting pastures and harming Portuguese breeders who had no way to feed their flocks (Sequeira, 2014). On the contrary, the passage and sale of Portuguese cattle in Castile was prohibited in order to prevent the departure of such an important resource. This protectionist measure did not prevent, however, the smuggling of sheep and other animals and, in short, the exchange of raw materials for manufactured products, such as the Castilian cloths that the smugglers brought back (Duarte, 1998; 2001).

In the Crown of Aragon, the main transhumance routes were those that had united since the thirteenth century the north-eastern mountain ranges of the Iberian System with the Valencian coast and Andalusia. In Aragon, the areas of origin of the livestock were located in the mountains of Albarracín and Teruel, while the fresh winter pastures were located in the central Valencian plain, delimited by the Millars, Turia and Xúquer rivers, the middle and lower irrigated plain of the Segura River, in Orihuela, and the high valley of the Guadalquivir, in Andalusia. As in Castile, the growth of livestock was favoured by the commercial demand for wool, mostly by Tuscan merchants, who imported it from southern Aragon and northern Valencia. Although we do not have global figures, we know that in the fourteenth century the breeders of the community of Teruel had reached agreements to graze 10,000 annual heads in the territory of Llíria and 25,000 in that of Castelló, and that the total number of Aragonese sheep entering each year in the kingdom of Valencia can be estimated at 150,000 heads (Castán, 1994). Unlike in Castile, in the Crown of Aragon an institution like the Mesta did not exist and the transhumance was organized by local or regional sheep farmers associations or by the urban communities themselves (Teruel, Albarracín . . .). These institutions were known as *ligallo* (sometimes also as *mesta*), and in addition to Aragon they were also found in Southern Catalonia and in the kingdom of Valencia (since the thirteenth century), where they generally took care of collecting and guarding lost or unowned animals.

Along with the long-distance transhumance, a shorter, regional one was developed, from the valleys to the nearby mountain pastures, which also had its own *mestas* and brotherhoods. Less known, however, is the standing livestock, which could account for half or more of the total and has been estimated, only for sheep, as 'two million cattle' in 1500 (Ladero, 2017). It was more or less specialized regionally. Cows were important in the north, from Galicia to the Basque Country, while pigs were in Extremadura and sheep and goats in Andalusia. But in general, animal husbandry was found throughout the peninsula. Also important was the farming of horses, donkeys and mules, both as draft animals and for transport. In many territories, especially in the western part of the peninsula, there were limited and reserved pastures for the exclusive use of certain breeders, known as *dehesas*. In the eastern part, in addition to these preserves, there were also delimited areas of grass called *bovalars* so that the draft animals and those of the butchers could graze. It was a way to protect the cultivated *huerta*, but also to ensure the meat supply.

2.4.2 Manufacturing and Industrial Production

The first mentions of people engaged in non-agricultural activities in both León and Catalonia, at either end of the northern Iberian Peninsula, date from the end of the tenth century, initially associated with self-supply and very soon with a view to the nearest local market (Sánchez-Albornoz, 1980; Feliu Monfort, 1998). In these early times, iron tools, farm implements and harnesses for horses are mainly documented. However, very soon, between the eleventh and twelfth centuries, the presence of artisans in the reconquered and repopulated cities both in Castile and in the Crown of Aragon increased, especially in trades related to construction, the clothing industry, leather, and tools made of iron and other metals. This was mainly due to three factors: the relative transfer of artisanship from the countryside to the city, the Muslim heritage, and the immigration of artisans of ultra-Pyrenean origin (Feliu Monfort, 1998). As far as Portugal is concerned, references to manufacturing activities are somewhat later, dating back to the thirteenth century, and although its development seemed for a long time to be linked to the Muslim and Jewish communities, more recent studies have relativized, if not its prominence, at least its exclusivity. For example, despite the importance of the Muslim community in silk production in Lisbon from the thirteenth century onwards, the expansion of this industry would have been stronger in the Trás-os-Montes region, an area with little or no Islamic influence (Sequeira, 2014, 2017).

Throughout the peninsula, as in Europe in general, the textile industry was the most important of all, especially from the thirteenth century onwards. In Catalonia, for example, and fundamentally in Barcelona, although at the beginning leather and fur work predominated, from the end of the twelfth century and especially the thirteenth century, the woollen cloth industry began to stand out, with the transition from a phase of domestic production, for self-consumption or by order of local consumers, to a manufacturing stage linked to trade, in which part of the fabrics became merchandise and crossed regional borders (Riera, 2005). Similarly, in Castile, artisanship was developed mainly to meet domestic demand, but also for export. Such is the case of the forges of Biscay and Guipúzcoa, the ceramics of Talavera, the leather and cordobanes of Córdoba and Andalusia and the arms and silks of Toledo. By the end of the

Middle Ages, Castile already had the three elements necessary to activate any craft production system: labour, capital and natural resources. This favoured the increase in urban craft output, which was assisted by significant rural immigration to the cities and innovation in work systems. The situation of growth and wealth provided sufficient capital to ensure investments and to increase the demand of large sectors of the population for medium quality and luxury products.

The mercantile activity benefited from this favourable situation. Merchants focused on attracting trades and artisan work for their businesses, with the aim of modelling the production process according to demand. The aim was to merge the craft and commercial enterprise, which ensured higher profits and diversified risks. The number of trades was adjusted to an extraordinary division of artisan labour. Thus, a document from 1481 mentions all the trades practised in the city of Segovia and lists 83 different activities practised by men and women, involved in productive tasks, services and agricultural activities (Asenjo, 1986). The many trades that developed in the cities gave the appearance of a self-sufficient microcosm, but soon the artisans were organized and guided by precise rules, whether written or unwritten, which conformed to professional criteria of quality, in terms of product manufacture, and sought to avoid internal competition (Contreras y López de Ayala, 1921).

Textile production was the leading industrial sector throughout Iberia, although its trends and pace varied greatly in the different kingdoms. In the major urban centres of the Crown of Aragon (Barcelona, Perpignan, Girona, Lleida, Zaragoza, Palma and Valencia), a true degree of industrial concentration was reached, with high numbers of artisans and trades. A few figures give a glimpse of the number of people involved in the drapery. In Barcelona, a municipal source estimates that in the fifteenth century a third of the city's inhabitants worked in the textile industry, while at the same time, in Palma, calculations show that between 30 and 50% of the registered artisans worked in this sector. For its part, in Zaragoza, a count of 1495 included 109 textile artisans from 16 different professions, among which *pelaires* (carders) and weavers were the most significant. The combination of these larger cities with medium-sized centres of lesser importance (Puigcerdà, Granollers, Sant Mateu, Xàtiva, Oriola, Huesca, Calatayud and Daroca), especially after 1400, facilitated the design of authentic productive constellations, which even incorporated the dynamics of dispersed rural industry and helped the economic integration of each region or territory (Igual-Luis, forthcoming). However, from 1450 onwards, particularly in Barcelona and Mallorca, signs of weakness and recovery could be seen in the cloth industry, in a context – also in Valencia – of a struggle between the protectionist stances of local industry and those more permissive towards imports.

Craft work had a markedly family character, with the help of apprentices and enslaved people and the temporary assistance of day labourers and wage labourers. Nevertheless, some fairly solvent weavers, *pelaires* and dyers were able to achieve the role of artisan-entrepreneurs, either on their own or by forming mixed companies, by placing all the stages of cloth manufacture under their management or by taking on the tasks of purchasing raw materials, paying for the work carried out and selling the resulting fabrics. But the channels of entrepreneurial control of the industry also emerged from outside it, from the commercial sphere, in which case the image of the masters is less optimistic. Indeed, the limited financial power of many artisans, or their inability to cope with the demands of the market with guarantees, favoured the action of merchant-entrepreneurs in the textile industry in the late Middle Ages, who ended up becoming true 'lords' of production, and the subjugation of workers to commercial capital became generalized (Igual-Luis, forthcoming).

As for Castile, urban drapery showed signs of stagnation until the mid-fifteenth century. In fact, until the mid-fourteenth century, luxurious and expensive Flemish cloths flooded the Castilian markets, but were then replaced by cloths from the Lys region and, in the first half of the fifteenth century, by English cloths. Some 8,000 pieces a year were imported at that time, and this number increased until the middle of the sixteenth century (Childs, 1978). These last two types of cloths were of medium quality, more affordable in price and highly prized by large urban and peasant sectors. It was the changes in domestic demand that stimulated the indigenous crafts, which by the end of the fifteenth century had become involved in a better adaptation to these demands, in particular the drapery of the south of the Tagus and Andalusia (Toledo, Cuenca, Murcia, Córdoba-Los Pedroches and Seville) as opposed to the more traditional drapery represented by Segovia, Ávila, Palencia and Zamora, at a time, moreover, when other textile centres (Úbeda, Baeza, Ciudad Real, Huete and Ágreda) had not yet surpassed the level of domestic and local production (Asenjo, 1991).

From the fifteenth century onwards, a new rural industry emerged in Castile, which was an obvious response to the new trends in demand and form of organization, and capable of offering quality goods at a good price. This 'rural industry', however, was not the primitive family or local crafts for self-consumption of earlier times, but now the countryside represented only an appendix to the urban crafts which threatened to become competitive. A case in point is Seville, whose census shows 2,000 people of both sexes engaged in the textile trades in its *Tierra* (countryside), while only 66 appear in the city (Collantes, 1977). The reaction of urban producers to the arrival of cloth from the *tierra* and from other localities was unequal. Thus, in Murcia, the entry of cloths manufactured in Cartagena, Lorca, Mula, Librilla, Alhama, Caravaca and its bailiwick was prohibited, while those from Molinaseca, Villena, Yeste and Cieza were sold at the same prices as those from Murcia. In other cities, such as Córdoba, which benefited from the manufacturing activity in Los

Pedroches and other places in the *Sierra*, it was decided to promote this rural industry, complementing urban production, while the existence of a putting-out system made the Úbeda–Baeza–Baena triangle one of the most dynamic areas of textile production (Edwards, 1987; Fortea, 1981).

In general, the take-off of cloth production in Castile is confirmed by fiscal sources (*alcabalas* rates) and the reasons for this growth coincide with those of other craft sectors, which benefited from the monetary stability of the reign of the Catholic Monarchs, the improvement in the purchasing power of the peasantry and the better organization of work (Asenjo, 1986). The techniques and organization of the Castilian cloth industry were in the target of the 'bullionist' policy of the Catholic Monarchs, who reacted and tried to curb the unequal imports that led to the outflow of gold from the kingdom, stimulating internal production and adapting it to this demand through the promulgation of general cloths ordinances in 1500 that were compulsory for artisans (Asenjo, 1991). On the other hand, everything seems to indicate that, as the case of Segovia shows, the improvement in the conditions of demand was the cause that boosted drapery in the fifteenth century and the development of artisanship to competitive levels. In this stimulus, the architects may have been the merchants who were able to take advantage of the weak corporate response of the artisans to enter the production process and stimulate the manufacture of cloth with investment. The intervention of the merchants gave greater versatility to the manufacture of cloths, as they did not hesitate to carry out certain manufacturing processes, relying on peasant labour that was cheaper and more docile than urban artisans. The new pre-capitalist forms of production were thus introduced in Castile, with little resistance from the guilds in the cloth-making cities of the kingdom. It was an industrial activity coordinated by the merchant-entrepreneur, who directed production from the city to sell it on an external market. And although artisans continued to sell the finished product to merchants and, in rural areas, crafts could benefit from the small size of the urban workshops and production, numerous factors indicate the gradual loss of independence of the artisan, which would become greater as money loans were added.

For its part, Portugal was for most of the late Middle Ages a clear importer of Flemish, English and Castilian woollen cloths. However, this did not prevent the production of cloths in the kingdom, especially in the area of cattle traffic in the interior region, in Beira Baixa and in the Alentejo, where several centres of textile industry emerged. Indeed, an important pole was located in the Beira Interior, where herds circulated in transhumance, while the inland strip of the Alto and Baixo Alentejo emerged as an important producer of medium/low-quality woollen fabrics, capable of creating its own brands such as the *manta* (blanket) *do Alentejo* or the *manta de Évora*, revealing the existence of an industry in the true sense of the term, by placing on the market products that were mass-produced, manufactured in series and of constant quality. A third producer region was located in Santarém, where the *bureles* (coarser and browner) and the fine cloths of Alcobaça and those of Leiria, commercialized nationally, both in the north and south of the kingdom, stood out. Despite the importance of these three regions, the cloth industry was somewhat dispersed throughout the kingdom, although confined to the sphere of domestic production destined for self-consumption. These were the 'cloths of the land' (*manta da terra*), products of low quality, unable to compete with Flemish, English or even Castilian cloths.

As regards linen cloths, the most important production centre was Guimarães, from where it was transported to Porto and, from there, redistributed to other markets. In 1512 alone, the production of Guimarães was 100,000 *varas* (1.1 metres each) of linen and tow clothes. From the sixteenth century onwards, and in relation to America, the cotton industry also developed. Finally, unlike wool, linen and cotton, silk production was not part of the self-consumption economy. This was therefore concentrated in the main cities of the kingdom – particularly in Lisbon, where the importance of the Muslim community contributed to its development from the thirteenth century onwards – and in the Trás-os-Montes region, where the main centres were Bragança and Lamego. It is also worth noting that, at the end of the fifteenth century, the geographical distribution of the silk industry was related to the presence of ethnic or foreign minorities in the cities, although, as mentioned above, it experienced a stronger expansion in a region – Trás-os-Montes – with little or no Muslim influence (Sequeira, 2014, 2017).

Also in the Crown of Aragon, the progress of the silk industry, especially in Valencia, mobilized new resources and introduced productive, labour and technological reorientations (Navarro, 1999). In Castile, meanwhile, leather artisanship was prominent, associated with easy access to sheep and goat skins (Mendo Carmona, 1990). The leather trades were grouped into tanners, shoemakers, boot makers, glove makers, saddlers and needle makers, among others, each with different processes and techniques. The councils exercised strong control over these activities, both in the manufacturing process and in quality control and the location of the tasks outside the town, given their polluting effects and bad smells. Finally, another prominent industrial sector, especially in the north, in the Basque provinces, as well as in Catalonia, were the forges. Iron working required ore, water and also wood as fuel. Iron pyrite is abundant in nature, but large quantities were made in the north from ore from Biscay and Guipúzcoa. Under the cover of iron, minor crafts such as nail making, naval equipment, weapons, and agricultural implements also arose. At the end of the fifteenth century there were some 115 forges in Guipúzcoa, each producing between 1,500 and 1,800 quintals (1 quintal = 73.8 kg), totalling 100,000 quintals/year (Díez de Salazar, 1985). Some 2,750 families (12,375 inhabitants) depended on the iron and steel industry, plus those who made a living from iron manufacturing, which would bring the number to some

60,000 inhabitants, 20.5% of the population of the whole province. The forges were owned by the large families in the area, although in some cases they were acquired by purchase by some of the towns. Alongside these industries, in all the Iberian kingdoms there were many other trades linked to construction, shipbuilding, ceramics, glass, wood, wax, sugar processing and foodstuffs (mills, ovens and butchers), which increased the number of people engaged in non-agricultural activities.

2.4.3 Trade

If in general terms from the year 1000 to the thirteenth century the primary sector had been the driving force of the economy, in the fourteenth and fifteenth centuries the tertiary sector achieved greater prominence. Trade and commercial capital were obviously related to the productive elements, as we have seen in the previous points of this chapter. Their characteristics are also important in defining the economic geography of medieval Iberia, in terms of both internal and external trade.

Internal trade was a basic activity, closely linked to agriculture and manufacturing. The exchange networks generated in this economic sector, supported by certain institutional variables, were an essential substratum for the development of large-scale international trade around the Iberian kingdoms. However, this trade developed in the midst of certain structural constraints. The difficulties of a mountainous orography combined with the non-existence of navigable rivers, except at the end of their course, placed the transport of goods in the hands of muleteers capable of adapting to mountain passes and other geographical features. This problem may have led to an increase in the cost of trade and, probably, to a market that adapted to different parameters in order to remain competitive.

For the Iberian kingdoms as a whole we can distinguish between, on the one hand, the trade organized around the cities, both to supply them and as a vehicle for industrial production, and, on the other hand, the networks of markets and fairs spread throughout the peninsula. The cities were the result of a social organization rooted in the agricultural exploitation of the territory, sometimes from before the Christian repopulation, and in the urban capacity to project itself spatially and create a hinterland. At least from the thirteenth century onwards, there are several striking examples. In the case of Lisbon, its economic influence was not limited to its administrative region or to the Low River Tagus area, where it exercised greater control in terms of direct interference in market regulation, jurisdiction and taxation, but extended to the whole kingdom, with a constant movement of peoples and commodities from all northern (Ponte de Lima, Viana, Fão, Vila do Conde, Porto and Aveiro) and southern port towns (Lagos, Faro, Tavira and Mértola) (Andrade & Miranda, 2017). The same was true in Valencia, capital of a kingdom that bore its name and which had to resort regularly to cereal imports to ensure its supply (Furió, 2015a), and to a lesser extent also in Seville, which, like most Castilian cities, had strong jurisdictional and fiscal prerogatives and an institutional apparatus that guaranteed the city's dominion over the countryside, control over unified weights and measures and the surveillance of coordinated tariffs, all of which were necessary factors to achieve lower market costs (Collantes, 1991). This coercion reduced supply costs and lowered the risks of investment in manufacturing by giving artisans an outlet for their products in the territory, while providing peasants with stable markets. Urban markets meant a great deal for economic growth as they contributed to the homogenization of space, in economic, social, legal, cultural and mental terms, while establishing points of exchange that encouraged the production and redistribution of goods.

Such situations have also made it possible to connect urban markets with the regional level. Always in the last centuries of the Middle Ages, this regional and even interregional trade was marked in Portugal by the contrast between the Atlantic coastline, dominated by maritime towns where salt and dried fish production, shipbuilding and pottery were prominent, and the interior, where the weight of the cereal and livestock economy gave rise to large fairs, such as that of Trancoso, and to rural and urban markets with domestic economies that interacted with the Castilian food and textile markets (Gomes, 2017). For its part, the Crown of Aragon achieved a certain economic complementarity between cereal agriculture and wool from Aragon, the commercial and export agriculture of Valencia, Catalan drapery and Mallorcan trade, to which must be added the importance of foreign demand for the development of local economies, in particular wool from Teruel and from Morella and Sant Mateu in northern Valencia, the relevance of Tortosa as the beginning and end of the Ebro route and the role of the Valencian ports of Dénia, Xàbia and Alicante in the interconnection between the Mediterranean and the Atlantic (Riera, 2017).

Commercial activity in the interior also developed from the markets and fairs held in the cities and towns, which had a regional scope that allowed the direct commercialization of some peasant products, while at the same time bringing urban manufactured goods and imported products to remote areas. Their number multiplied from the thirteenth century onwards. In Portugal alone, 31 fairs were created between 1320 and 1475 (Marques, 1987). In Castile, 67 fairs were granted between 1150 and 1310 and another 88 between 1350 and 1499, located in four large areas: Galicia and the Cantabrian lands, Castile and León, Extremadura and New Castile, and Andalusia and Murcia (Ladero, 1994). The fairs not only favoured the integration of those territories that, although peripheral and marginal, had an abundant population and varied agricultural wealth, but also allowed for the connection of local, regional and continental market activity and the creation of complex business networks of great scope that trafficked different products on an international scale

(Igual-Luis, 2001). Some fairs, such as those of Medina del Campo, founded at the beginning of the fifteenth century, achieved great national and international renown – from 1444 they were considered 'general fairs' of the kingdom and took place in two annual periods of 50 days each. In contrast, the large cities – such as Seville and Burgos in Castile or Barcelona and Valencia in the Crown of Aragon – did not need fairs to boost their trade, as their commercial activity alone exceeded that of the fairs.

With regard to foreign trade, the precocity of its development in Catalonia, and particularly in Barcelona, stands out, in comparison with the rest of the Christian peninsula. As early as the eleventh century, the distribution of Asian spices and cloth from France was known there, and the flows of trade that crossed the Pyrenees or that contacted al-Andalus are noteworthy. During the twelfth century, Barcelona consolidated its international maritime presence, which by the thirteenth century was already reflected in an activity that extended along the whole of the Christian and Muslim coasts of the Mediterranean, to which were added some intense ramifications towards the interior of the Iberian Peninsula and Western Europe and, to a lesser extent, towards the Atlantic routes (Riera, 2017). Mainly in the following centuries up to 1500, Barcelona, a financial hub of the first order and a centre of redistribution and intermediation between the Mediterranean East and West and, later, the Atlantic, was in the Crown of Aragon also the cardinal pole of a triangle formed together with Palma and Valencia, to which Zaragoza should also be added as the fourth vertex of a system of relations in which ties of competition, concurrence and complementarity were combined. The Catalan capital continued to be a very important mercantile and maritime power, although it could lose its leadership in some routes and sectors, and its prominence showed signs of contraction towards the end of the fifteenth century at the edges of some of its main routes of action (the East and Flanders) (Igual-Luis, 2014).

As for Castile, relying on the strength of the domestic substratum of trade, external exchanges were directly or indirectly stimulated from the thirteenth century onwards thanks to the liberalizing measures adopted by the kings. Of particular note in this respect was Alfonso X's decision to alleviate the strong protectionism that had marked the previous period, both to increase fiscal resources and under pressure from the nobility, who wished to export certain goods. Alfonso decided to open up all products for export except precious metals, whether in metal or coin, horses and cereals. However, the most widespread intervention was the manipulation of the currency, in order to improve the royal income and due to the lack of precious metals, which is why devaluations were frequently carried out. But these controversial operations, although they accentuated inflation, also favoured exports (Ladero, 1990–1991). Nevertheless, the great development of Castilian foreign trade took place from 1300 onwards, largely linked to the export of wool and to the traditional aspiration to maintain a double exit route to the Atlantic, of course, but also to the Mediterranean via the Murcian and Valencian coasts. The long-distance routes were those that took products such as wool and cloth from Toledo to Burgos, passing through Segovia, and from there to the ports of the Cantabrian Sea. Other routes towards the south and east, passing through Madrid and Toledo, took products to Córdoba and Seville, and from Cuenca and Moya to Valencia. On these routes, the products of foreign trade coincided with the goods from the interior of the kingdom. From the beginning of the fourteenth century, merchants from Narbonne used Valencia as a point of penetration for their cloth to spread the Languedoc cloth to Castile and to bring agricultural products and manufactured goods. From 1415, people came from all over to the fairs of Medina, while in the south the points of reference were Seville and Cádiz, where the routes from Toledo and the Sierra Morena converged (Córdoba de la Llave, 1995). Dyed products also travelled along the routes of the great inter-regional trade to the inland dyeing centres. The people of Burgos who controlled this trade also had access to woad from Toulouse, via Bearn and Navarre, to distribute it among the cities of Segovia, Cuenca and Toledo, while Italian woad reached these lands through Genoese merchants, via Valencia (Casado, 1990; Bonachía, 1994). Silk was another product much sought after by the Italians, in an attempt to replace imports from the road to Cathay. Silk was obtained in Granada, which was accessed from Málaga, and from there its production spread to the region of Murcia (Garzón, 1972).

Data on foreign trade are later for Portugal, where wine and oil were mainstays among exports in the Middle Ages. Wine was shipped in very large quantities to almost every market in Atlantic Europe, mainly to England, but as Bristol customs records show for the second half of the fifteenth century, it was not the only Portuguese merchandise imported by the English. If 18% of the wine and 33% of the olive oil landed in Bristol came from Portugal, wax and sugar exceeded the threshold of 70%, to which should be added other products such as oranges, dates, marmalade, soap and vinegar, among others. Availability and surely the price must have been factors influencing the choice of Portuguese commodities (Childs, 2013; Miranda & Casado, 2018). Sugar, first from Lisbon and then from Madeira, was a really important product of Portuguese exports. In 1498, Madeira produced more than two thousand tons of sugar, of which 588 tons were sold to Flanders, 191 tons to Venice, Genoa and Constantinople each, and about 90 tons to England (Rau & De Macedo, 1962). For its part, the records of the Italian company Salviati, based in Pisa, show that 22% of the hides imported by the firm came from Portugal, and 13% from Ireland – meaning in the opinion of the authors who have studied it that 35% of this trade was managed through Lisbon (Carlomagno, 2010; Sequeira & Miranda 2019).

2.5 Conclusion

The economic model of Iberia in the Middle Ages coincided with some of the European patterns, although it presented original aspects and particular challenges linked, for example, to the Christian war against al-Andalus, to the demands of military supplies and to the role of the spoils of war in the construction of individual and collective fortunes. On the whole, however, the results of economic development were remarkable and do not support the undoubtedly hasty images of Iberia as a peripheral region, located in the extreme south-west of the European continent, whose economy, which was not very developed, was based on the production and export of foodstuffs and raw materials and on the import of processed products, mainly cloths. In the late Middle Ages, Portugal exported – to England, but also to northern Italy and other countries – wine, oil, sugar, wax and hides. Castile exported mainly its highly prized merino wool, but also wheat; the kingdom of Granada, still Muslim, exported silk; and the Crown of Aragon exported wool, saffron, sugar and silk. All of them in turn imported Flemish, French, English and Italian cloth. However, Iberia also exported manufactured goods, both leatherwork from Granada and cloths from Catalonia, which were distributed throughout the western Mediterranean and, in particular, in the area of influence of the Crown of Aragon. In any case, production was not only limited to goods destined for export. Despite the political, administrative and fiscal borders between the various kingdoms, Iberia itself constituted a large internal market, the demand for which was decisive for the development of both agriculture and its own industry.

The supply of the large cities, with tens of thousands of inhabitants, conditioned the economic production of the surrounding regions and sometimes even of more distant territories, as was the case with Lisbon, Granada, Valencia, Barcelona, Burgos, Valladolid, Toledo and Seville. It is not surprising, therefore, that agriculture was the main productive sector and the one that occupied most of the active population. The interior of the peninsula – Aragon, the north and south of Castile, especially Andalusia, and the Portuguese inland – were the main wheat-producing areas, mostly on dry land. However, in some areas of southern Portugal and especially on the Mediterranean coast of the peninsula, from Valencia to Murcia and Andalusia, a much more productive irrigated agriculture developed, allowing yields to multiply not only for cereals and vines but also for mulberry, vegetables and fruit trees. These water lands were also the ideal place for the cultivation of rice and, above all, sugar, whose techniques were tested in Gandia, Oliva, Motril and the coast of Granada, the Canary Islands and Madeira before being transferred to the Caribbean. In the introduction and expansion of new plants and crops, as well as in the spread of new agricultural techniques, especially irrigation, the cultural transfer of the Muslim/Andalusian legacy was very important, which around the year 1000 had known a true 'green revolution', whose main achievements were recorded in the numerous books on agronomy, later translated from Arabic into Latin and Romance languages.

Alongside agriculture, Iberia was also the scene of a prodigious development of livestock farming, especially transhumance, not only in Castile, where it was regulated by the Mesta, but also in Portugal and Aragon. In the latter, as well as in the north of Valencia, wool was exported, mainly to northern Italy. In Castile, although the Mesta was founded earlier (1273), the expansion of livestock farming took place mainly from the second half of the fourteenth century and, even more, from the fifteenth century. In turn, the increase in wool production had an impact on the development of the textile industry, especially, but not only, in the regions most closely linked to sheep farming.

Notwithstanding having the best quality raw material, merino wool, Castile was flooded, until well into the fifteenth century, by Flemish, French and English cloths. Towards the end of the century, however, a type of cloth-making developed, especially south of the Tagus and in Andalusia, which was better adapted to the needs and tastes of domestic demand, and capable of offering quality goods at a good price. In Portugal, too, a textile industry developed around the same time, scattered throughout the kingdom, producing woollen fabrics of medium/low quality. The most industrialized region, however, was Catalonia, where the drapery soon shifted from domestic production for home consumption to production for export. In Barcelona, a third of its inhabitants worked in the textile industry in the fifteenth century and, alongside it, many other medium-sized centres also produced cloths for the market, although from 1450 onwards the cloth industry began to show signs of weakness and stagnation. It was precisely at this time that, as had already happened in northern Italy, the silk industry developed as a substitute for or in competition with wool, for example in Toledo and especially in Valencia, a region that also produced raw silk and mulberry leaves for silkworms.

In all sectors, from agriculture to industry, the decisive step was the shift from domestic production for self-consumption to production for the market and the increasing integration of the latter. Iberia was not only a peninsula divided politically into various kingdoms, but within each of these there was also great regional diversity, which generated complementarity, but at the same time had to deal with a great productive competition. Integration was first local, at the level of the cities and their respective hinterlands. Urban domination of the countryside contributed to this, as did the proliferation of markets and fairs regulated and organized at this level, including the homogenization of weights and measures, currency and the legal framework. In turn, these local spheres were articulated and integrated into larger spaces around the great regional capitals, which made their influence felt beyond their immediate territory. Such regional integration was not only incomplete, but also did not give rise to true inter-regional integration within the same kingdom, much less in the peninsula as a whole. This was prevented by the diversity of laws, jurisdictions, usages, customs, currencies and measures. However, some of the most important fairs, such as those of Medina del Campo, acquired the character of 'general fairs' and were attended by merchants not only from all the kingdoms of the peninsula but also from other countries. For its part, the presence of foreign trading and banking companies, also contributed to overcoming internal barriers and promoting economic links between the different territories. At the same time the Iberian merchants – Catalans in the Mediterranean and Castilians and Portuguese in the Atlantic – were expanding their commercial and business networks further and further afield. If foreign demand and the participation of Iberian merchants in the great international trade would contribute to economic recovery after the difficulties of the fourteenth century, the discovery of America in 1492 and the transfer of the geostrategic centre from the Mediterranean to the Atlantic would open a new stage in the economic history of the peninsula, with very different results for the various kingdoms and territories.

3

Population, 1000–1500

LUÍS MIGUEL DUARTE, IGNACIO ÁLVAREZ BORGE
AND MARIO LAFUENTE GÓMEZ

3.1 Introduction

In recent years, Iberian medieval historiography has not prioritized population and demography, hence much of what we know on these problems comes from papers of the 1980s and 1990s. Nevertheless, studies on taxation have developed significantly and it is these that provide us with a good part of the data for analyzing the population of the late medieval period. On the other hand, among the available studies, those of a local or district nature abound, regional ones are less frequent and those that propose a vision of the global evolution are very scarce, especially in the case of the Crown of Castile and the kingdom of Portugal, although for the Crown of Aragon and Navarre we do have joint works in this field. Thus, it is very difficult to offer a general approach that, in addition, must necessarily be hypothetical and provisional.

The primary sources that allow us a more accurate approach to the study of the population consist of tax information and these are more abundant from approximately 1350. Up to that time, the assessment of the demographic evolution has been derived from the analysis of other indirect sources that make quantitative conclusions difficult, but instead permit qualitative approaches: the indicators that allow us to bear witness to agricultural growth; the evidence of the increase in the number of populated sites and settlement densification; and also the cities, of which we will speak later, in both the greater number of urban centres and the quantity of their inhabitants. Furthermore, in recent years our knowledge has also become more precise through the archaeological investigations of rural and urban settlements. We also have some inventories, inquiries or partial surveys for specific sites or areas.

From the fourteenth century, documented recording is notably enriched, although irregularly, on the peninsular scale. Beginning with the Crown of Castile, the 'tax roll' (i.e. the assignment to each place of a certain number of taxpayers or of a certain quantity of money that must be collected) led to the realization of censuses and 'equalizations' that established the number of taxpayers who were subject to taxation in each site. A very singular text of enormous importance is the *Becerro de las Behetrías*, produced in 1352 for the district known as the 'Merindad Mayor de Castilla' (Castilla la Vieja to the north of the Douro River) prepared for tax purposes and in order to know the feudal status of all the places of the area (Estepa, 2003).

For the Crown of Aragon, the sources of a fiscal nature most used in historical demographic papers are basically two: the *'monedajes'* and the *'fogajes'*. The *monedajes* were nominal lists or counting of hearths drawn up at the request of the royal power, with the purpose of locating all those persons subject to the payment of a tax belonging to the monarchy, called *maravedí* or simply *monedaje*, which was collected every seven years and which was established in the first quarter of the thirteenth century. Despite the fact that groups of privileged population, that is, the nobility, the urban elites ('caballeros villanos') and the clergy, were exempted from paying this tax, the lists drawn up for this purpose usually identify them along with the population subject to the exaction, indicating, to be sure, their condition of being exempt. However, the persons considered poor and, logically, the floating population, remained outside the count (Feliu, 2010: 32–35).

The *fogajes*, for their part, had a different purpose. In general terms, a *fogaje* was a register of houses or hearths belonging to a certain place, where the names of the persons considered heads of family were noted, along with any significant feature in order to facilitate their identification, normally their profession. The principal difference with the *monedaje* is that, in this case, the preparation of the count was not for the purpose of the payment of an ordinary tax to the monarchy, but rather the collection of a general service, negotiated and approved in the *Cortes*. For this reason, the *fogajes* were drawn up with the intention of including the totality of the territory of each State, regardless of their jurisdictional affiliation, and to the overall population based in each place, apart from their statutory condition. The use of the *fogajes* as an instrument to identify the taxpayers began at the end of the decade of the 1350s, that is, at the time in which State taxation was established in the Crown of Aragon, whose management depended exclusively on the political elite represented in the *Cortes* and institutionally organized in the territorial Provinces of Aragon, Catalonia-Mallorca and Valencia (Ortí, 1999; Sesma, 2004a).

In the kingdom of Navarre, there also exists a considerable volume of tax sources susceptible of being interpreted as demographical information. Due to their nature, these records are quite similar to those existing in the Crown of Aragon, and they shared, in fact, the same name and nature. The preserved *monedajes* of Navarre started in the first third of the fourteenth century and referred, principally, to the city of Estella and its land, to the district of the Navarrería area of Pamplona and to the city of Tudela. Furthermore, several hearth records (*libros de fuegos*) were preserved in relation to the council districts (*merindades*) of Tudela, Sangüesa, Pamplona-Mountains and Estella (Carrasco, 1973: 69–86). On the other hand, for conducting demographic studies, the researchers have also used the records of the *Comptos* section of the Royal and General Archive of Navarre, which collects the accounts rendered by the treasurer of the kingdom and that refer to the entire territory, although their preservation is not fully homogeneous (Monteano, 2000: 34–46).

With respect to Portugal, which created a general taxation system with the *sisas* (a local tax appropriated by the Crown in the 1370s), the repertoire of available sources is considerably less, since we barely have a handful of hearth records which were prepared, as in the previous cases, for fiscal purposes. Among the most important of the other sources appear, in chronological order, the hardly reliable list of *tabeliães* from the end of the thirteenth century (which does not include the Algarve); a count of churches with royal patronage, dated 1320–1321; the list of archers that had to ensure the safety of each village, town or city for the royal armies, from 1421 (a total of 5,000 soldiers); and especially the *Numeramento de 1527–1532*, the first national quantitative source, of which we will speak later. The analysis of the indications has led some researchers to estimate the population of the country as a whole, at the end of the Middle Ages, to be between 1.2 and 1.5 million inhabitants (Marques, 1987), but the calculations are very debatable,[3] based on problematic readings of the sources. In parallel, there exists another type of documents that partially allows the visualization of the demographic volume on a local scale and especially the regional distribution.

3.2 Patterns of Population Change and Migration

3.2.1 Evolution of the Population in the Peninsular Kingdoms

From these sources, some estimates have been made that provide an approximate idea, although they have always been taken with caution (see Figure 3.1). Thus, there is a considerable agreement in proposing a figure of around three million inhabitants for the Crown of Castile up to 1300, at the end of the expansion process and growth in the high Middle Ages and at the threshold of the crisis of the late Middle Ages. In accordance with its greater territorial extension, it is a figure that is higher than that of the rest of the peninsular kingdoms all together. And it should be warned that it is not an universally accepted figure (but it is, generally) and that some authors propose increasing it significantly. In the case of the Crown of Aragon, the estimates made for the moments immediately prior to the Black Death plague fluctuate around 1,200,000 inhabitants, distributed unequally among the three Peninsular States and the kingdom of Mallorca. Specifically, the most populated territory in this context was Catalonia, which would bring together around 50% of the total population of the Crown, while the kingdoms of Aragon and Valencia

---

[3] As an example of the possible debates, see Chapter 11.

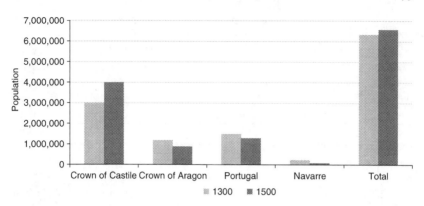

Figure 3.1 Evolution of the population in the Iberian states in the late Middle Ages. Sources: see references in the text.

had 25% and 20%, respectively, with Mallorca having an approximate share of 5% (Feliu, 2010: 45–47; Laliena, 2010a: 64). In Navarre, the most recent research supports that, after uninterrupted growth between the eleventh and thirteenth centuries, in 1300 the population of Navarre was around 60,000 hearths (an intentionally rounded figure), distributed between approximately a thousand villages (Monteano, 2000: 93, 95). In the kingdom of Portugal, in turn, the estimates made offer a much higher margin of error than the rest of the Hispanic territories, due, mainly, to the bias and insufficiency of the preserved sources. Nonetheless, it is considered that the Portuguese population was nearly 1.5 million inhabitants around 1300, descending to approximately one million a century later (Coelho, 1996a); the recovery, irregular and differentiated according to the local situations and social means, was confirmed when the first large national survey was conducted, between 1527 and 1532. This 'Numeramento', with a very complex methodological analysis, indicates to us that Portugal had 282,708 hearths, which gives a total of between about 1,215,687 and 1,357,046 inhabitants (depending on whether we apply coefficients of 4.3 or 4.8 suggested by a scholar of this document). We repeat: it is a rather classic estimate, but with evident weaknesses; we do not have any initial figure, not even partial; reliable indicators show that in 1300, although taken as a symbolic date, the growth of the population had already stalled; lastly, we do not have a way to quantify the losses caused by several factors of that debated 'crisis of the fourteenth century', certainly due to the 'Black Death'. For this reason, the 'Numeramento de 1527–1532' is so valuable.

The evolution of the population throughout the peninsular territories is framed in the general context of the rest of western Europe, but it also presents some nuances that deserve to be taken into account (see Figure 3.1). The high

Middle Ages, between 1000 and 1300, is a period of growth and expansion in all aspects, followed by the crisis of the fourteenth century (Álvarez Borge, 2003). The crisis has many facets, but in reference to the demographic evolution, the Black Death of 1348–1350 (and subsequent recurrences) and the famines and shortages caused by poor harvests and wars have to be mentioned. Afterwards, the fifteenth century (perhaps from approximately 1420, but not always coinciding at the local level) was a period of recovery. At the end of the fifteenth century, Castile had somewhat more than four million inhabitants, exceeding by a third the population of about 200 years earlier. In Portugal, qualitative indications suggest a similar evolution, although we are not able to propose absolute figures, which in that period varied between 1.3 and 1.5 million: while until 1500 the Crown of Aragon had still not exceeded the figures of around 1300, being situated at about a million inhabitants, perhaps somewhat less in the latest of the indicated dates (Feliu, 2010: 46). For its part, the kingdom of Navarre had reduced its population in that period, going from around 240,000 inhabitants in 1300 (an amount estimated by applying a coefficient of 4 to the figure of 60,000 hearths proposed by Peio Monteano (2000: 93, 95)) to 85,000 in 1514 (if we apply the same coefficient to the figure of 21,274 hearths provided by the fiscal count of 1514) (Monteano, 2001: 40). Such a different evolution between Castile, on the one hand, and Portugal, Aragon and Navarre on the other, indicates to us a very uneven demographic impact of the crisis, especially in reference to the Black Death, and also the different paces and intensities of the recovery (of the Black Death and subsequent recovery, we continue to know very little, especially for Portugal).

As for al-Andalus, its population was being reduced as the Andalusian territory was reduced with the advance of the reconquest and feudal colonization. We do not have conclusive figures, but we do have estimates that allow us to make some comparisons. At the end of the Caliphate, that is, at the beginning of the period that we are studying here, it has been calculated that there could have been between six and ten million inhabitants (the first figure is probably closer); while the population of the Nasrid kingdom (Nazarí, in Spanish) of Granada before the reconquest was around 300,000, after having suffered in the fourteenth century the consequences of the Black Death, which had probably reduced its population by a third. But, as we will see, in addition to comparing figures, the fact has to be considered that the distribution of the population in al-Andalus was quite different due to the importance of the cities and urban life.

3.2.2 *Regional Distribution of the Population in Christian Kingdoms*

In the Crown of Castile, the population was distributed very unevenly – an irregular distribution that will have economic reasons, but that found its main explanation in the pace and characteristics of the process of political and territorial expansion. Around 1500, of the approximately four million inhabitants that Castile could count, somewhat less than half, around 40%, were concentrated in the northern plateau (León and Castile); a quarter in the southern plateau and Extremadura, more or less 24%; in Andalusia and Murcia, around 22%; and in the coastal area of the north (Galicia, Asturias, Cantabria and the Basque Country) approximately another 14%. These differences in the large areas must be fine-tuned further because, for example, in the southern plateau, in La Mancha, the largest population concentration occurred in the basin of the Tagus River (Monsalvo, 2014: 313).

With respect to the Crown of Aragon (see Figure 3.2), according to the general *fogajes* drawn up around 1500, it can be affirmed that, at the end of the Middle Ages, Catalonia represented a little more than a third of the population (59,929 hearths), far from the 51% estimated on the eve of the Black Death. Valencia, in turn, had at that time somewhat less than a third (55,631), slightly exceeding Aragon (51,540) and far from Mallorca, which continued representing around 5% of the total (9,207). In all, at the end of the Middle Ages the Crown of Aragon had 176,307 hearths – always from the fiscal counts with a general scope – an amount that could be translated into 881,535 inhabitants (Feliu, 2010: 46).

Along this same line, Navarre did not recover the demographic volume prior to the Black Death before 1500, in fact it did not do so until the nineteenth century. In general, in the last two centuries of the Middle Ages, a significant decrease was noted in Navarre in the number of inhabited sites, going from 997 to 790, and a decrease in the number of hearths exceeding 40% in some areas of the kingdom (Monteano, 2000: 65–67; 2001: 108–111). It must not be forgotten, along with the effects of the epidemic crises, that other impoverishing factors particularly affected the weakest sectors of the rural

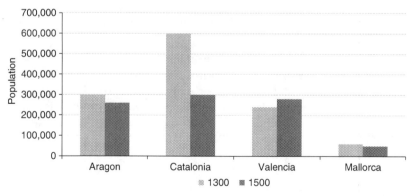

Figure 3.2 Evolution of the population in the Crown of Aragon: number of inhabitants in 1300 and 1500.
Source: Feliu (2010: 45–47); Laliena (2010a: 64).

population, such as the subsistence crises and wars, phenomena that motivated the disappearance of some families and the migration of many others. The effects of all these factors could be reflected circumstantially on the settlements, by means of the redistribution of the population from the southern part of the kingdom towards the capital and the districts of Central Navarre and the Mountains, but the demographic weight of the different areas did not change substantially throughout the entire period. The largest part of the population settled in the core area of Navarre, that is, the valleys of the Pre-Pyrenees and Central Navarre (Monteano, 1996: 327-332).

Historical demographic studies in Portugal have yielded conclusions very similar to those obtained for the rest of the Iberian Peninsula. For example, in the region of the Baixo Mondego, it was confirmed that the demographic deceleration began in the fourth decade of the thirteenth century (Coelho, 1989, I: 89-90); and, along this same line, the region Entre-Douro-e-Minho, by far the most populated, had lost in 1284 a relevant portion of its settlers (Marques, 1999). The occurrence of the Black Death was, as in all areas, very uneven, but everything indicated that it had a greater impact on the urban cores than on the rural environment. Having overcome this situation, regional studies point towards a slow recovery of the previous levels. This was observed, for example, in the case of the archdiocese of Braga, which during the fifteenth century experienced a trend comparable to the neighbouring kingdoms, that is, a gradual tendency of the number of hearths to grow and the consolidation of the urban milieu (Marques, 1988).

The population change in the Christian kingdoms was also determined by other factors. The movements of population in relation to the repopulating of the areas that were conquered and the migrations from the countryside to the city had special importance. We will refer to both later on.

3.2.3 The Muslim Population after the Christian Reconquest: The Mudejar Issue

The population figures that we have mentioned and specifically in the case of Andalusia reveal the issue of the Muslim population in the areas that were being annexed. Many of the most important reconquests were done by means of capitulation and the agreements frequently included maintaining the majority of the Muslim population. But, either because it did not take long for the capitulation agreements to be breached or for other reasons, a good part of the Muslim population emigrated towards other areas.

This occurred in Toledo after the reconquest in 1085. It was one of the most important cities of al-Andalus and the urban centre of reference in the basin of the Tagus River. The rest of the kingdom of Toledo surely never had a high population density and the instability of the border situation in the decades following the reconquest contributed to the depopulation of the area. This was done in such a way that the Christian occupation took place on a scarcely populated territory and led to the formation of the large domains of the military orders. But Andalusia and Murcia did have an important population when they were reconquered in the thirteenth century. The conditions of the capitulation agreements determined the fate of the Muslim population at first. In general, the Muslim settlers had to abandon the main cities, but they could continue to live in the rural areas. This meant the initial continuance of an important Muslim population (Mudejars) that, in principle, ensured the work in the fields and the continuance of the substance of the productive system. But between 1264 and 1266 an important revolt of the Muslim population took place and, after being beaten, the Mudejars of Andalusia and Murcia had to abandon Castile. The expulsion of the Castilian Mudejars entailed a very notable difference with the Crown of Aragon, where a significant volume of Muslim population, the Moorish, remained. In Castile, some groups of Mudejars also survived, but they were small communities especially in urban centres, where the Moorish quarters, along with those of the Jews, had a certain economic identity. A figure of 20,000 Mudejars in the Crown of Castile at the end of the Middle Ages has been given, which supposes around 0.5% of the population (Ladero, 2010). For the Crown of Aragon, at the end of the fifteenth century, it is calculated that the Muslim population was around 30% in the kingdom of Valencia, 11.1% in Aragon and 1.5% in Catalonia (Ferrer Mallol, 2002: 36, 43, 64). The Mudejar population in Navarre, according to the count drawn up in the second half of the fourteenth century, reached a modest 1.1%, accompanied in this kingdom by a Jewish population of 3.3% (Carrasco, 1973: 153). Portugal, for its part, experienced an important Islamic settlement between the Tagus River and the Algarve. In the north of the country, however, the presence of this community was hardly felt, whose vestiges were limited to a handful of place names. The largest Moorish areas were located in Évora, Lisbon, Santarém and Elvas (Coelho, 1996a; Barros, 2007), being important in agriculture and crafts, but without political expression and always in decreasing numbers.

3.2.4 Some Debates and Pending Questions

However, if these are the large lines of evolution that can be commonly accepted, there are also important discussions and lively debates on some aspects. We will point them out in a much-summarized form in this section.

The first aspect that arouses controversy among researchers is about methodology and involves the interpretation of the fiscal sources, especially those of a general nature, and their translation into demographic terms. To solve this problem, historians have opted, generally, to use coefficients of 4 or 5 when converting the number of taxpayers into individuals. However, in those territories in which it is possible to compare this type of source with other records, the detected population volume increases considerably. Thus, in the territories of the Crown of Aragon, the scrutiny of sources coming from the municipal authorities in villages, cities and communities of towns, along with the notary records, offers sufficient indications so as to think that the criteria with which the counting of a general character has been interpreted, that is, the *monedajes* (controlled by the royal power) and the *fogajes* (generated by the territorial governments) should be revised upwards. It is not possible, for the moment, to establish conclusions globally, but the conducted local studies argue that, at least in some circumscriptions, the number of solvent houses registered by the officers of the king or of the territorial governments was only part of those that actually existed, and that many times their number was fixed through negotiation between the local authorities and the officers in charge of carrying out the count. When it was necessary to have a nominal list of residents, it was sufficient to put in writing as many names of taxpayers as had been previously agreed (Medrano, 2006: 211–213). Furthermore, studies of social history show, in an increasingly more evident manner, that the number of persons who lived in each dwelling greatly exceeded the coefficients of 4 and even 5, especially in the mountain areas and in the rural environment (Tomás Faci, 2016: 340–345).

In addition, in the historiography related to Castile, there has been an interesting debate on the scope of the repopulation of Andalusia and its economic consequences. Some authors suggest that the needs of the Christian population to ensure the reconquests and the transfer of the population from the north towards the south was, if not the cause, indeed one of the causes, of the economic crisis, a crisis that would appear clearly in the last decades of the thirteenth century (Ruiz, 1994). Other authors deny that the arrival of the settlers from the north was so significant; on the contrary, they sustain that there was a 'failure of the repopulation of Andalusia', a failure that would be expressed in a crisis especially in agricultural operations and particularly after the expulsion of the Mudejars (González Jiménez, 1995). In this way, what is suggested, both in one case and in the other, is an inadequacy in the ratio between population and resources, because there was a lack of people. The late Middle Ages in Castile would not be, in general terms, a Malthusian crisis originated by an excess of population (although it could be true in very specific areas, but not on a general level). There was no shortage of land, there was a shortage of people.

In Portugal, there were no 'Distributions' (*sesmarias*) and today we do not accept the classic theses of the 'depopulating' and of the repopulating of the south by people from the north. There was a spontaneous formation of towns, almost unknown, but the great majority of charters, granted by the Crown, by military orders or by the clergy, basically intended the reorganization of the already existing towns. Furthermore, although many times there were complaints that people were leaving and that the generalized depopulation was a danger for the defence of the kingdom and a threat to its economy, the structural problem of this country was rather always the contrary: the flagrant lack of labour opportunities for its small population. Hence the resulting emigration towards the Atlantic islands (from the fifteenth century), Africa, Brazil and India, in great uninterrupted waves up to our days.

Moreover, there is a quite distance to go to determine with more precision the impact of the Black Death (Amasuno, 1996; Castán, 2020). In general, there is a broad consensus in admitting that the Crown of Castile was less affected than the territories of the Crown of Aragon and in Navarre, but even so the impact of the disease offered a quite variable situation in the different areas and even in its local impact. The depopulated areas have been used as an indicator of the impact of the Black Death, but, given that the sources used are fiscal ones, their data have to be analysed considering that their objective is not to reflect population centres, but rather tax collection units. On the other hand, the depopulated areas sometimes do not reflect the total population loss, but rather their regrouping in certain centres.

The role of the wars, agricultural crises and poor harvests that generated shortages and famines are not perfectly clear (Oliva & Benito, 2007). The references in the first half of the fourteenth century are frequent, but each text, each news item must be situated in its context. In addition, the political instability, in any case, had already begun in the last decades of the thirteenth century. A shortage or famine could be the consequence of a simple disturbance in the cereal distribution, frequently affecting, for example, Lisbon, but not the rest of Portugal – and without it necessarily having demographic consequences.

3.3 Rural and Urban Settlements

As in the rest of the medieval western Europe, in the Iberian territories the majority of the population lived in rural settings and their fundamental economic dedication was agriculture and livestock. It will surely not be inaccurate to propose that around 80% or 85% of the population were farmers and of them a very significant percentage were vassals of seigniories, although with important differences in the diverse areas. Also, the period that we study in the Christian kingdoms was one of, first, the emergence (or re-emergence) of cities and, afterwards, their growth and the extension of the urban phenomenon – the 'urban renaissance', common to all the peninsular kingdoms and to other areas of western Europe, although also with its own characteristics. This phenomenon caused notable growth in the percentage of the urban population in the late Middle Ages, but a clear majority of the rural population was always maintained. In any case, it is advisable to point out that there is no urban world, on the one hand, and rural world, on the other; there is a gradation of cases and situations more or less rural or more or less urban. Thus, we can assess much better the role of the numerous 'small cities' that are key to the political and economic articulation of the medieval world.

It must be considered that the vision we can offer on the population and the settling of people in the different areas of the peninsula is conditioned to a considerable degree on the different historiographies that have been developed on the peninsular states in the Middle Ages; historiographies that offer many common elements, but also many peculiarities.

3.3.1 Territories and Society in Castile

The differences in the population of the diverse areas of Castile that we have expressed above also existed with regard to the settlements and the social and political organization, being able to point out large areas from north to south (always with an excess of simplification), defined over time and with the advance of the territorial expansion (García de Cortázar, 1985). The territories between the Cantabrian Sea and the Douro River correspond to the 'ancient territories', they are the most densely populated and through which the domains and seigniories were vigorously extended. Afterwards, the areas between the Douro River and the Central System were incorporated, whose control was consolidated with the reconquest of Toledo in 1085 when the border was situated at the Tagus River. They were royal areas and were organized around extensive municipal territories (sometimes very extensive), governed by the councils of the main head villages, councils that were dominated by oligarchies of village knights. They are areas where livestock acquired great importance. To the south of the Central System in the Transierra to the Tagus River, the system of the large royal councils was replicated in part, but the territories of the Episcopal See of Toledo were also important. The Tagus marked the border for decades and when the feudal colonization advanced towards the south (La Mancha and Extremadura), scarcely populated areas were incorporated through which extended large (on occasion, very large) domains of military orders, also often clearly dedicated to livestock. Afterwards, approximately between 1230 and 1250 the great expansion took place with the reconquests of Baetica Andalusia and Murcia, with only the Nasrid kingdom of Granada remaining in Muslim hands. Their incorporation into the Christian Castilian domains was done by distributing the reconquered lands among new settlers or new Christian owners coming from the north. They were very rich areas with an abundant population under Muslim rule.

There are sources that offer us partial data on the importance of the seigniories in some areas of Castile. The *Becerro de las Behetrías* shows that in Castile to the north of the Douro the significance of lordships was very important in the middle of the fourteenth century. In Andalusia, the 'distributions' (*repartimientos*), such as that of Seville, provide sufficient detail of the structure of land ownership after the reconquest, although the map of the extension of the large ownership in Andalusia did not remain, by any means, fixed at that time (Cabrera, 1999). In the late Middle Ages an increase in seigneuries occurred, not only in Andalusia, but also in general in the entire territory of Castile, although it was greater in some areas than in others. In the first place, there was a geographical extension of the seigniorial regime. If before the lordships were more numerous to the north of the Douro, the seigniorial regime now extended through all of Castile. Thus, in Andalusia at the end of the fifteenth century, the seigniories occupied approximately half of the territory (Collantes, 1979). And, although to a lesser degree, the seigniories of nobility were also extended through the areas of the large town councils and the seigniorial councils (Monsalvo, 1997). But it did not deal solely with a larger geographic extension, but rather the new concessions contained broader and better-defined seigniorial rights from the legal viewpoint. It is what the scholars of the seigniorial regime call 'jurisdictional seigniories'. All this would lead to the formation of the so-called 'seigniorial states'.

In addition, the urban phenomenon, which extended throughout all parts from the second half of the eleventh century, had different origins in Castile. In the first place, it saw the evolution of core sites that in the previous period could be considered urban or, better stated, pre-urban. Some were of Roman origin (León) and others arose later (Santiago, Oviedo, Burgos). It is difficult to see in them authentic cities around the year 1000, but they developed and grew throughout the following centuries. Another urbanizing factor was the formation of new cities; in this sense, the first allusion must refer to the Camino de Santiago and to the very important stimulus brought on by pilgrimages and, especially, the settlement of new inhabitants and Frankish merchants. It was not only the Camino de Santiago, but it was also a royal policy, expressed in jurisdictions, that achieved the formation of numerous 'royal villages' or 'new villages' by means of the so-called 'interior repopulations' (Martínez Sopena, 1995).

3.3.2 Settling and Organization of the Territory in Aragon

For its part, the distribution of the settlements in the Crown of Aragon was characterized by its integration and its internal hierarchy, expressed in demographic terms as well as with respect to the organization and structuring of the territory. At the peak of the system were found the four large political centres, one for each of the peninsular territories along with Mallorca, which constituted actual metropolises on the supra-regional scale. These four cities were placed in the vertices of a rhombus of approximately 320 km per side and they controlled, furthermore, other economic spaces, structures around urban settlements of lesser importance and, especially, a dense rural settling. On its westernmost end, the city of Zaragoza was set up as the most populated centre of the kingdom of Aragon, dominating the commercial traffic on the Ebro

River and acting as an exchange centre with the kingdom of Navarre (Pamplona), the Cantabrian coast (Bilbao), the south-east of France (Toulouse, Pau, Bordeaux, Oloron) and the northern Castilian plateau (Burgos, Valladolid, Medina del Campo). In the centre, and on the Mediterranean coast, Barcelona in the north and Valencia in the south headed the urban tapestry of the principality of Catalonia and the kingdom of Valencia, functioning in turn as export centres of the interior production and of receiving goods coming from the entire Mediterranean arch. And, on the easternmost point, the city of Mallorca acted, from its definitive incorporation into the Crown in 1344, as a fundamental hub for ensuring the functioning of the system, as proof of its enormous economic potential during all the late Middle Ages (Sesma, 2003: 156-160). In demographic terms, Barcelona was the most populated city until, at least, the end of the fourteenth century, where around 7,000 or 8,000 hearths were concentrated. Shortly afterwards, Valencia exceeded the Catalonia capital, reaching 9,000 hearths in the first quarter of the fifteenth century, while Zaragoza and Mallorca were somewhat less populated, with around 4,000 and 6,000 hearths, respectively, at the end of the Middle Ages (Sesma, 2003: 181-186).

On a second level, the integration of the land in the territories of the Crown of Aragon was established in the promotion and development of a series of medium-sized population centres, capable of functioning as mid-distance production and marketing centres, but also as structural hubs of the population for legal and administrative purposes (Sesma, 2003: 186-187). The small and large cities and large villages that made up this section were maintained during the entire Middle Ages in modest dimensions, compared to the four capitals cited earlier, varying between 1,000 and 1,500 hearths in the best of the cases. The consolidation of this second populating level, with an eminently urban aspect, took place during the period of expansion and feudal conquest, in such a way that around 1300 it was already fully constituted around four large areas, connected, in turn, with other economic regions adjacent to the territories of the Crown of Aragon.

From north to south, those four areas are the following: in the first place, the area situated to the north of the axis between Zaragoza and Barcelona, driven from two intermediate centres, the cities of Huesca and Lleida, and enlivened by the profitability of the exchanges with the southern part of the kingdom of France. A second area is that which constitutes the Ebro waterway, very economically and legally controlled by the oligarchy of Zaragoza and, especially, by the corporation of merchants of the city. The geographic conditions and the actions of the royal power as well as of the Zaragoza merchants favoured the development of several centres located on the river basin, situated precisely on the channels of some of its principal rivers. At the end of the route, the city and port of Tortosa absorbed a constant flow of goods from Aragon's production, but also imports coming from Biscay and Navarre, destined for the markets of Catalonia and Valencia, as well as to other places of the Mediterranean arch. The third of the indicated areas involves the land borders between the kingdoms of Aragon and Valencia, where some urban populations also developed, spurred on by the profitability of wool production, specialized agriculture and manufacturing destined for the regional market. Among them, several seigniorial towns situated on the right bank of the River Ebro can be highlighted, such as Montalbán, Alcañiz, Maella, Caspe, Morella and Sant Mateu. Furthermore, it is necessary to also highlight the town of Teruel, located on the communication route between Zaragoza and Valencia (Sesma, 2003: 159–160; 2004b: 58–60; 2006: 205–207). And finally, in fourth place are the urban centres located on the Mediterranean coast, which, on a smaller scale than Barcelona, Valencia and the city of Mallorca, also played a fundamental role in connecting the lands of the interior with the exterior markets. Thus, in addition to the already noted city of Tortosa, the role of the ports of Rosas and Tarragona, in Catalonia, along with those of Peñíscola, Sagunto and Alicante in Valencia can be highlighted (Furió, 2010a: 400–409).

3.3.3 The Urban Network in Navarre: Villages and Cities

The population of the kingdom of Navarre was structured by an urban network that included a dozen cities and villages of diverse origin, since among them were centres of Roman origin or even earlier, along with those founded in the Islam era and newly created boroughs from between the eleventh and thirteenth centuries. The urban stimulus in this case came from the growing importance acquired by the Camino de Santiago, within the Hispanic context, from the year 1000 and this factor is essential for understanding the economic and social development of the urban environment of Navarre during the entire Middle Ages. From north to south, and following the Camino de Santiago, the area that garnered a higher number of centres with urban characteristics corresponded to northern and central Navarre, between the lands of Ultrapuertos (San Juan de Pie de Puerto) and that of Middle Navarre (Puente la Reina and Estella, to the west; Monreal and Sangüesa to the east), a strongly hierarchical territory from the capital of the kingdom, Pamplona. Towards the south-west are found the towns of the Ribera (Olite, Tafalla and Artajona), whose origin is due to the colonizing thrust of the twelfth and thirteenth centuries, and, on the border of Castile, Laguardia and Viana. The fluidity of commercial exchanges between the capital and the interior markets of northern Castile led to the development of a second urban network in this area, integrated by towns such as Larraga, Falces, Lerín and Miranda, whose population varied between 400 and 700 hearths on the eve of the Black Death. Lastly, the southern area of the kingdom, for its part, experienced the development of an urban centre of great importance on the regional scale, the city of Tudela, which carried out a relevant invigorating role in the economy in the northern section of the Ebro waterway (Carrasco, 2006).

Many of these villages and cities acted as control instruments of the rural environment, from the political-administrative viewpoint, by means of the seigniorial dominion of rural districts (e.g. Viana, from 1219) (Carrasco, 2006: 227), and all of them exercised an indirect influence on the population of their setting, by concentrating the functions of transformation and commercialization of all types of goods. In addition, in all of these centres the financial activities developed rapidly, thus becoming authentic loan markets and exchange centres of capital (Carrasco, 2003). The case of Monreal can be highlighted in this sense, where, due to its proximity to the capital of the kingdom, one of the minting houses was located, which was a decisive element in it receiving, at the beginning of the fourteenth century, the condition of '*buena villa*', thereby giving it the capacity to participate in the meetings of the *Cortes* (Carrasco, 2006: 233). In addition, it is important to point out that a good part of the economic stimulus detected in the urban milieu of Navarre up to this time is due to the installation of boroughs of tax-free population, that is, privileged in the economic and fiscal aspect, in a large part having arrived from other peninsular or European territories (like Toulouse), along with the Jewish communities that tended to concentrate, precisely, in the cities. The case of Olite serves as an example: during the thirteenth century it housed more than a thousand Christian families and more than five hundred Jewish families, becoming in this way a commercial centre (with a fair and a market) at the top level on the scale of the kingdom (Carrasco, 2006: 234–235).

3.3.4 Settlement and Territories in Portugal

In Portugal, the Minho, the present district of Porto and the valley of the Douro (the Entre-Douro-e-Minho) were areas of intense and disperse settlement. In the centre, the population was more concentrated, especially in the current districts of Viseu, Guarda, Aveiro and Coimbra. In this area of the country there existed important population centres, surrounded mostly by areas with very low demographic density: in Ribatejo, Extremadura, Beira Baixa, Alentejo (called Entre-Tejo-e-Guadiana) and Algarve. Apparently, the less populated regions of Portugal were the central transmontana strip that crossed the district of Vila Real; the one that in the eastern part runs through the region of Bragança; the north-west part of the district of Viseu; the Atlantic coastal part between Aveiro and Coimbra; the mountains of Estrela and its derivations; a large part of the current districts of Leiria and Castelo Branco; Ribatejo, to the south of the Tagus River; and vast regions of Alentejo and the interior of Algarve (Marques, 1987: 18).

As for the distribution of urban settling, in addition to a powerful and indisputable capital from the middle of the thirteenth century, Lisbon, and three second-level cities (Évora, Santarém and Porto; the last of which from the end of the fifteenth century would assume an outstanding second place), the researchers have made clear the existence of two well-differentiated areas: on the one hand, the interior area, sustained by agriculture and livestock, where towns such as Vila Real, Lamego, Guarda, Estremoz, Serpa, Moura, Évora, Beja and Montemor-o-Novo are found; and on the other, the coast, with very few villages, among which stand out Vila do Conde, Viana, Aveiro, Salir, Torres Vedras, Setúbal, Sines, Portimão, Silves, Lagos, Loulé, Faro and Tavira (some of these more dedicated to fishing and to naval construction than to naval trade). In the long term, between the thirteenth and fifteenth centuries, a certain development of the coast and a slight loss of importance of the interior was noted, with the growth of Lisbon, Porto, Setúbal and Faro (the principal centre of fruit exports of the Algarve) (Reis, A. M., 2007). Special mention should be given to the Jewish communities, which in Portugal had few episodes of violence, although the assault on the Jewish quarter of Lisbon of 1449 should be pointed out. Partially due to this state of relative peace, the number of Jewish communities experienced a marked increase in Portugal during the fifteenth century, stimulated precisely by the problems that arose in other peninsular territories. Maria José Ferro Tavares has counted 32 communities for the fourteenth century and 139 in the fifteenth, with a total population of approximately 30,000 persons around the year 1500 (Tavares, 1982–1984).

The cities grew in number and inhabitants throughout the Middle Ages, mainly attracting people from the countryside, but the figures are always estimated and we hardly have a general impression of the pace (Monsalvo, 2010: 268) and the areas of attraction.

3.3.5 The Cities of al-Andalus

Likewise, one has to consider that as the feudal reconquest advanced, numerous Islamic cities became incorporated into Christian Castile, some of which were very important, whose inhabitants multiplied by far those of any of the larger cities of the kingdoms of León and Castile. The importance of the urban life in al-Andalus was much greater. In this way, the percentage of its inhabitants that lived in cities was also much greater than in the Christian kingdoms, perhaps half of the population or even more. Some of their cities were enormous in comparison to those of the Christian kingdoms. The evolution of each one presents its own characteristics. Some decreased, like Córdoba, but others maintained their importance or increased it in the following centuries, under the Maghreb empires or in the *taifas*. From the classic studies of Torres Balbás (1971) several estimates have been made with different methodologies (size of the cities, size of the mosques or of the cemeteries) that, although not fully coinciding, did permit the importance of the cities of al-Andalus and their population to be highlighted. For example, Toledo, when it was reconquered in 1085, although perhaps no longer with the somewhat more than 35,000 inhabitants that it may once have had, still multiplied by far the more or less 1,500, perhaps 2,000 inhabitants that León had at that time. Afterwards, the reconquest of Baetica Andalusia and Murcia in the first half of the thirteenth century supposed the incorporation of many and very important cities; among them, the most important of all at that time was Seville, the Almohad capital in the peninsula, which probably surpassed 80,000 inhabitants, perhaps even 90,000. Other cities would also exceed 15,000 inhabitants, such as Córdoba, Almería, Granada, Mallorca, Zaragoza, Málaga and Valencia. Added to them was a dense network of smaller cities, which included cities of Roman origin as well as new cities founded by Muslims, especially in the Umayyad Period.

3.4 Labourers, Artisans and Merchants

The social structure in the cities was different and more complete than in the rural areas. A greater social complexity featured, in the first place, the different skilled workers, merchants and artisans that formed the largest group, which in Castile was called 'the common'. These were almost always free men, but were still subject to forms of hegemony – not legal, but indeed the social, economic and political hegemony of oligarchical groups. The oligarchies, with different scales and compositions, dominated and controlled the cities, and their economic power was quite distinct from one area to another: trade and liberal professions or service to the Crown in some cases (citizens or 'honourable citizens'), war and livestock in others (the urban elite). The cities also contained a variable number of 'misfits' and the poor. Finally, the landscape of the urban society is completed with the minorities – Frankish at first and later Moors and Jews above all.

On the other hand, it is also advisable to consider that neither the urban population was detached from the agricultural and livestock activities nor the rural population was detached from the small handicraft production, or much less the participation in the local markets; each day we understand better how abundant the circulation of currency was in the countryside. Thus, one must focus on the economic structure of the feudal society. The urban and the rural were not, at all, distinct worlds far from each other. One of the best examples is the patriciate or urban oligarchy of the councils of the historical Extremaduras of Castile and León (the areas between the Douro and the Central System), the urban elite of cities such as Ávila, Salamanca, and Segovia or in Portugal, Évora or Beja, whose economic position, as mentioned, derived to a great extent from livestock. Or the feminine participation in the textile industry, by means of the *Verlagssystem*.

In fact, the study of women's history has been a very significant development in recent years and, among other things, has contributed to placing a value on their economic and political roles, which had been obscured by traditional historiography, which placed priority only on the social or family value of women, and in the best of the cases also religious, while ignoring their contribution to economic development in all fields, from agriculture to commerce and handicraft production (García Herrero, 2009; del Val Valdivieso & Jiménez Alcázar, 2013). As we said, their importance is very clear in the textile industry, and their presence, and that of children, in public works is sure but not documented.

3.4.1 Qualified People and Minorities in Castile

In the case of the Crown of Castile, we cannot offer figures on the importance of the different economic sectors, or calibrate their evolution throughout the period, beyond some general traces. Only at the end of the Middle Ages some tax records offer information on the composition of the population of some cities. Thus, a census of 1384 allows us to know the composition by professions of the population of Seville (or at least of the 2,613 residents registered): the marine professions stand out with 13.7% of the population, the textile sector occupied 11.9%, public posts and officers made up 11.5%, the liberal professions 8.4%, construction and pottery 7.2%, the professions considered as maintenance 7.2%, leather and hides 6.5%, servants 6%, commerce 5.1%, metalworking 5.5%, transport 3.7%, etc. (Álvarez, Ariza & Mendoza, 2001). Meanwhile, in the small city of Logroño the tax censuses preserved from the middle of the fifteenth century (on 717 residents) indicate to us that the majority of the population was dedicated to the primary sector; within the secondary, the sectors that had a greater number of artisans were textiles, leather and metal work, followed by construction and the artistic professions; and in the tertiary sector were the liberal professions, health, food and commerce (Díaz de Durana & García Fernández, 1991).

After the expulsion of the Mudejars, the great majority of the population in Castile were Christian. Jews and Moors formed minority groups, particularly in urban centres and with a legal and, to a certain degree, economic standing. The number of Jews in Castile grew in the thirteenth century, partially coming from al-Andalus, eventually adding up to perhaps some 100,000 persons around 1300. The thirteenth century, in general, was one of tolerance and coexistence (beyond the doctrinal debates), but antisemitism was growing, resulting at the end of the fourteenth century in persecutions and killings (1391), and which afterwards led to forced conversions and to Crypto-Judaism and the problem of converting – in contrast with the pacific situation in Portugal. Any generalization is excessive, but among the economic dedications that can be highlighted are those related to financial activities, trade, the textile industry or the practice of medicine, although too many stereotypes have been established, especially in relation to usury, and perhaps underestimating their participation in agriculture (Cantera, 1986; Monsalvo, 1985).

As for the Mudejars, unlike Aragon, where important rural communities continued, in Castile the communities of Mudejars were mostly urban. This was also a minority with an economic standing, with a greater orientation towards construction and pottery. But before the Jews and Mudejars formed significant minorities there was also another minority group, although not one based on religious differences, that likewise had an economic projection. This group was the Frankish, who from the second half of the eleventh century and throughout the twelfth and thirteenth were installed in a significant number of locations along the Camino de Santiago (but not only there, also in other cities) and contributed to the development of trade and of the cities (Martínez Sopena, 2004).

3.4.2 Social Groups and Professional Sectors in Aragon

For its part, in the Crown of Aragon, the nominal lists of residents prepared for fiscal purposes allow a quite general estimation of the overall potential of the active population at between 90 and 95% of the total existing population, while the rest, between 5 and 10% of the total, were framed socially and legally in some of the privileged groups, that is, the clergy, the medium and high nobility, and the specific categories typical of the urban oligarchies, such as the honoured citizens or the urban elite (Sesma, 2004a). In this regard, the case of the low nobility, whose members were called *infanzones* or *hidalgos* in Aragon, and *generosos* or *hombres de paraje* in Catalonia, Valencia and Mallorca, is particularly complex, since their legal condition was usually incompatible with the performance of a profession and, very especially, with the exercise of manual work. However, the practical application of this principle was very heterogeneous and materialized in very difficult ways, according to the legal framework and social context. It is necessary to distinguish, for example, the low urban nobility, generally rentiers and, from the last quarter of the thirteenth century, also dedicated to the practice of law and the judiciary, and even partially to trade at medium and long distance (Laliena & Iranzo, 1998: 47–50), from the rural low nobility and, more specifically, from the *infanzona* population established in the towns of the north kingdom of Aragon, who benefitted, from the end of the thirteenth century, from the so-called privileges of universal *infanzonia* and whose professional dedication did not differ much from the rest of the rural population (Tomás Faci, 2015: 343–344).

Furthermore, as occurred in Castile, in the Crown of Aragon the bulk of the active population preferably carried out professional activities that could be recorded in the primary sector, while the rest (i.e. a small part of the total) carried out tasks typical of what today we would call the secondary sector, which suppose the transformation and production of goods elaborated in the framework of a socially recognized profession. According to the available sources, even before the demographic crisis of the fourteenth century, both in the medium-sized urban centres and, especially, in the large cities, there existed a group of residents identified by the professions they carried out and that, with the exercise of their professions, covered some of the basic needs of the population. Thus, in the nominal lists prepared for fiscal purposes during the entire thirteenth century, it is frequent to find professionals related to the production of consumer goods (butchers, bakers, etc.) and of objects derived from the manipulation of leather or textile (furriers and wool workers, etc.). Their specific importance, within the whole, was still minor, since normally it represents a small percentage of the total of the consigned residents, but their importance for the community was fundamental, and, moreover, also relevant for the functioning of the State and the reproduction of the system, since their activities were usually taxed with exactions by the royal or seigniorial power (Sesma, 2006: 212–214). In this respect, it must be considered that many persons could carry out more than one activity during their working life, and even perform two or more activities simultaneously during prolonged periods of time. This crossover has been detected among the urban population and among the inhabitants of the rural environment and, especially, in the case of the women contracted in the area of domestic service (García Herrero, 2009: 575–579), for which reason any general assessment on the sectorial distribution of the labour market must be contrasted with the corresponding analyses of the local or regional area.

But, independently of the greater or lesser degree of crossover as regards the labour activities of the active population, what is certain is that during the Middle Ages a sustained development of professional specialization took place in the Crown of Aragon. The most significant social group or, at least, the most visible in this process was, without doubt, that of the 'master craftsmen', mostly established in cities and villages, whose businesses were based on forms of domestic production. At the beginning of the thirteenth century, these began to be integrated in associations of a corporate character, in charge, among other functions, of ensuring the preservation of the technical knowledge typical of each profession (Riera, 1992). The masters – and, at the same time, businessmen – were also the ones in charge of transmitting the technical qualification necessary for the correct exercise of each profession, to the benefit of the apprentices contracted for the purpose (Navarro, 2004).

If we make a brief review of the more dynamic professional activities, due to their capacity to assume technical innovations and to concentrate a higher share of the active population, within the secondary sector, it is necessary to start with the textile industry, clearly dominant in Barcelona, Valencia, Mallorca and Zaragoza from the thirteenth century, and which congregated an important volume of specialized manpower among the male population as well as among the female (Comas, Muntaner & Vinyoles, 2008: 25–35, 37–41).

A significant sampling of it is found in the evolution of the so-called 'silk art' in Barcelona and Valencia, spurred on by a new group of businessmen of both local and foreign origin, with broad technical knowledge, well connected within the sector and capable of mobilizing large quantities of capital, individually or associated in forms or commercial companies (Iradiel, 2003: 295–296). The particular aspect of the silk industry is that it is exclusively urban, compared to others of older tradition, such as leather, metalworking and construction, professions that had a much more disperse presence, although it is in the large cities where we find the most outstanding professionals in their field. Among them are frequently found persons belonging to the Mudejar and Jewish minorities, as shown in the contracts carried out to raise constructions as relevant as the royal palace of the Aljafería, in Zaragoza, or in order to fabricate quality pieces of metal used to manufacture weapons in that city (Martínez García, 2006; Lafuente Gómez, 2018: 53, 58–59).

3.4.3 Merchants and Artisans in Navarre

The professionals of production (masters and labourers) and trade in the kingdom of Navarre, although they are similar to their contemporaries in Castile and Aragon as regards the sectors of activity and practical implementation of their professions, present some singularities that have to do with their area of specialization, but also with other factors. In the first place, if we focus on the more distinctly urban environment, it is necessary to indicate that the economic activity was driven from the practice of trade and credit, more than from the area of production of goods (Carrasco, 2003: 246). This characteristic is logical if we consider that, as we have pointed out in Section 3.3.3, the main villages of Navarre, along with the capital of the kingdom, underwent their process of urbanization by being integrated into the route of Camino de Santiago which was so densely transited from the eleventh century onwards. The city of Pamplona and the village of Estella provide two significant examples of the productive and, especially, commercial structure of the urban environment in Navarre. The first, organized from the integration of three different boroughs (Navarrería, San Cernin and San Nicolás), had a very special incentive, as was the continued presence of the royal court, whose levels of demand for all types of products were always very high. This fact fostered the arrival of merchants from the south of France (Bayonne, Oloron, Nantes, Avignon and Montpellier), but also from more distant places (Paris, northern Italy) and, especially, from the principal cities of the north-eastern quadrant of the Iberian Peninsula (Burgos, Zaragoza or Barcelona, among others). Although the information on commercial societies is scarce, those that were located inform us of the interest of these economic agents in the credit sector and through the participation in the lease payments of the royal income (Carrasco, 2003: 254–265). The village of Estella, for its part, offered a similar scenario on a lesser scale, logically, than in the previous case. On an urban fabric characterized also by the juxtaposition of three different boroughs (San Martín, San Miguel and San Juan), in Estella an active cloth trade developed during the entire fourteenth century, controlled by individuals of French heritage, such as Lohan de Limoges, who in 1385 ran an establishment in the village and also supplied English cloth (from Bristol and London) to the royal court. The credit market, in this case, presented a clear specialization among the Christian lenders, focused more specifically on consumer loans (Carrasco, 2003: 266–270).

The leading role of the commercial and banking sectors should not be an impediment for recognizing that in the cities of the kingdom of Navarre a flourishing productive sector also developed, aimed mainly at satisfying the local and regional demand. Thus, for example, we know that in 1427 the textile sector comprised 82 persons in Pamplona and 9 in Estella; that leatherworks involved at that time 111 persons in Pamplona and 21 in Estella; and that the metal sector employed 25 persons and that of construction 49 carpenters, just in the capital. In 1328 in Tudela 7 weavers and 14 esparto weavers worked; along with 26 shoemakers, 5 belt-makers and 5 chair-makers; beside 22 blacksmiths and 16 carpenters. And, to cite just one more example, in Olite, at as early a date as 1264, two corporations of professions coexisted, related to the textile sector: that of the weavers and that of the furriers (Mugueta, 2017: 147). As a distinctive feature of all this activity, it is worthwhile to point out that it was the leather industry that acquired, generally, a greater leading role, and that the textile sector remained in second place. This fact kept active the demand for cloth from abroad and, with it, the occupation of many of the merchants to which we referred in the previous paragraph (Mugueta, 2017: 148).

Without yet abandoning the scenario of Navarre, it is important to point out at least three productive sectors of great importance in this area that were developed, mainly, in the rural environment. First, there were the ironworks, organized by means of contracts carried out between the monarchy and individual businessmen, which paid an agreed economic amount, supplied the means of production and contracted the manpower, all in exchange for receiving an operating licence on the subsoil and the mountains. This activity is documented from the end of the thirteenth century and its growth can be verified up to the beginning of the fifteenth, when there were 40 ironworks working simultaneously. However, at the end of that century their number had declined to 33. According to data from 1376, the annual production of these enterprises was somewhere between 2.7 tons of iron (the smallest) and 53 tons (the largest). The second sector was salt mining, which was very important in the council districts of Sangüesa, Pamplona and Estella; along with copper and silver mining operations, which were much more localized and less profitable. Lastly, the production of charcoal was also important in the southern part of the kingdom, driven by the demand for this product in the city of Tudela, where there was an important collective of Mudejar blacksmiths (Mugueta, 2017: 164–170).

3.4.4 Population and Social Groups in Portugal

The structure of the Portuguese population was estimated above all by Oliveira Marques, who proposed, after risky but very valid projections, the existence of between 8,000 and 10,000 clergymen before the Black Death and around 7,000 for the fifteenth century (Marques, 1987: 222–226); a very high figure, which could explain the long runs of the first printed books. For the nobility, the same author has suggested the existence of approximately a thousand families, with between five and six members each (although these figures are problematic), during the fifteenth century. Together, clergy and nobility barely reached 3% of the entire population, so that the remaining 97% were represented by the 'people', characterized, in turn, by accommodating an infinity of social categories, legal statuses and professional profiles. Thus, in the urban milieu, merchants and teachers can be highlighted, accompanied by groups of professional artisans and the persons who worked for others.

Evidently, the social mapping of the coastal centres differed notably from the rural population of the interior. And it was not always easy to distinguish 'statuses': there were many knights and squires who were not nobles, but rather belonged to the higher strata of the 'people'. And with the income crisis, that very interesting figure of the merchant-knight multiplied.

3.4.5 Cities and Society in al-Andalus

With reference to al-Andalus, at the end of the caliphate the process of Islamization had extended notably, and perhaps around 80% of its inhabitants were Muslim, the rest being Mozarabic Christians with a significant Jewish population. Later, in the eleventh and twelfth centuries, the importance of Christians and Jews was reduced by the religious pressure of the Almoravids and the Almohads. Then in the Nasrid period, to a scant but not irrelevant Christian population, integrated mainly by colonies of merchants, was added a Jewish population that increased after the persecutions in the Christian kingdoms at the end of the fourteenth century.

In al-Andalus there was a very close relationship between agricultural development and urban life (Malpica, 2010); especially due to the importance of intensive agriculture in peri-urban areas and frequently aimed at production for the market (textile crops such as cotton, esparto or flax, fruit and vegetables). In addition to that intensive irrigated agriculture, which is the most significant, one must not forget the intensive rain-fed agriculture, where the more important sectors were cereals and olive groves.

The importance of urban life, as has been stated, was based on a good number of important cities. This dense urban network was founded on a compact network of commercial exchanges. The manufactured products also corresponded to the development of agriculture for the market. Metalwork, the textile sector and ceramics stand out, not only in local or regional productions, but also in products of high quality aimed at provisioning the networks of big trade. This is because another of the factors that favoured the development of the urban world was the inclusion of al-Andalus in the broad Islamic world, where the commercial relations were conducted on a global scale.

In the Nasrid era, the most important city by far was the capital, Granada, which in times of the reconquest may have had around 50,000 inhabitants (Ladero, 1969) (other authors have even spoken of 100,000). Quite a distance below that figure, Málaga had around 15,000 and Almería perhaps 5,000, and to them was united other minor urban centres (Arié, 1992). It is worthwhile to highlight the development achieved by some industries of luxury products, such as silk, precious metal works and the exploitation of mining resources. In the fourteenth and fifteenth centuries, part of the trade of these products was carried out by Christian merchants, first Catalans, then Valencians and, above all, Genoese.

3.5 Conclusion

As in the other chapters referring to the Middle Ages, this chapter has had to square the circle: in studying the very diverse area of the Iberian Peninsula throughout 500 years, with its respective political fragmentations, which almost never correspond to the geographic areas; in wrestling with the specific political histories, although with common aspects, such as the struggle of the Christian kingdoms to occupy the territories in the hands of the Muslims, which ended in Portugal in 1249 but in Castile it lasted until 1492; in grappling with the different traditions and historiographic schools, to a great degree inherited from that political fragmentation in nearly constant evolution and that in certain eras and for certain subjects strongly conditioned the selection and interpretation of the sources; lastly, in integrating in the same discourse on demography and history of the population, regions or kingdoms with abundant and rich *sources comptables* (Aragon), with others that hardly have written records, beyond qualitative suggestions of the regional distribution of the population and of its evolution.

The difficulties arose from the start: how to propose an estimated calculation of the number of inhabitants (for convenience we have based ourselves on the 'peninsula of the five kingdoms' – Portugal, Castile, Navarre, Aragon, Granada – although this was not always the political reality). In the best of the cases, we have lists of 'hearths'. Demographers have long preferred to work with hearths and not with the multiplying coefficients. But finally, we resigned ourselves to proposing those multiplications, in an attempt to translate realities of six or seven centuries ago into numbers that correspond to our mental tools. And a round or absolute number that many years ago an authority in the subject awarded to a city or region is very difficult to question; but, between those classic proposals that today offer us justified doubts and the pure and simple void, we usually look for the reassurance of the first, which does not always help to advance the research.

We have tried to highlight the local and regional specificities: the strong economic integration of the territories of the Crown of Aragon; the unique case of the cities of Navarre, especially those in which the court remained longer and therefore became animated centres of consumption of luxury products and, moreover, in credit markets (with the very interesting difference between Christian and Jewish credit); the particular history of the Portuguese settlements, also dependent on geography and the political history of the kingdom, with the ancient nobility opting to remain to the north of the Douro, without accompanying Afonso Henriques and his successors in the war against the Muslims in the south, and in this way losing any role in the reorganization of the population of the majority of the kingdom and, therefore, being limited in its seigniorial, patrimonial, political and military dimensions; or finally, the centripetal force of the Castilian colossus, including such diverse regions as Galicia, the Cantabrian Coast, Extremadura or Andalusia, regions that many times corresponded to levels and forms of settlements and social structures and different policies. The different documental traditions, which generated written records that are very diverse from each other, can be added to the geographic and human differences among all these areas.

We end as we began, with demography, whose knowledge is essential in order to understand the economy, society and politics, after decades of stagnation, which returns to life, reinventing focuses of 'classic' sources and trying to discover and use other new ones. We continue basing our work on the traditional scheme of European evolution, which is very schematic but still sufficiently accepted: growth, sometimes very rapid, between 1000 and 1300; and the increasingly more debated 'crisis of the fourteenth century', with the 'Great Famine' (1315–1322) and a succession of epidemics that preceded the worst of all, the Black Death (1347–1351) and that was prolonged with mortal and uninterrupted sequelae. Therefore, from 1300 to 1500 a cycle of brutal rupture was followed by a stage of recovery. We are increasingly less satisfied with these generic characteristics: we have seen signs of population loss from the middle of the thirteenth century, signs that were very clear in the last quarter of century; we are still searching for minimally reliable figures for the Black Death and its respective economic and social consequences, or we try to explain their apparent absence. Finally, we continue analyzing at the local and regional level, to determine when the population reached its minimum and when and at what pace it began to recover itself, in order to understand when the optimum of the thirteenth century was reached.

It was once said disapprovingly of an English politician that he used numbers as adjectives. We are condemned to do the same, but also to use adjectives as numbers.

4

The Polity, 1000–1500

MARIA HELENA COELHO, FRANCISCO FRANCO-SÁNCHEZ, JESÚS ÁNGEL SOLÓRZANO TELECHEA AND HERMÍNIA VASCONCELOS VILAR

4.1 Introduction

The period from the eleventh to the fifteenth century was one of profound political and economic change in the Iberian Peninsula during which several expansionist processes combined. These changes led to successive reconfigurations of the political map.

Although these processes were interlinked and common trends may be identified, a range of different political solutions and economic structures were present in the peninsula during this period which necessarily conditioned the scope of action of institutions responsible for decision making.

Thus, it is important to be aware not only of the different stages in this process but also of the role of different powers. By the end of the Middle Ages the political configuration of the peninsula was reasonably well established and there was a complex and diverse economy in terms of both production and levels of monetarization and trade, increasingly controlled by an interventionist policy pursued by the Iberian monarchies (Ladero, 1997).

During this period, we witness the long-term process of the political formation of the Iberian kingdoms, the establishment of new political and military powers in the peninsula as a result of the Christian conquest of Muslim lands, the subsequent redrawing of boundaries, and the emergence of new economic protagonists. The fifteenth century was also a period of the new expansion of the kingdoms: from Aragon into the Mediterranean; from Castile to Granada, the Canary Islands and the Americas; and from Portugal to the Atlantic islands, South Atlantic coast and into North African territory. Iberians' horizons extended as contact was made with new cultures and civilizations, while the period also saw the beginnings of the establishment of a large-scale economy spanning several continents.

This work is funded by Portuguese national funds through the Foundation for Science and Technology, under the project UIDP/00057/2020, and by the Spanish National Research Agency and FEDER funds, under the project PID2020-118105GBI00.

The organization of this chapter reflects what is set out above and is divided into two parts: the first deals with al-Andalus, while the second focuses on the Christian kingdoms. In the first part, an attempt is made to provide an account of the evolution of the territory controlled by the Muslims, looking at transversal aspects of economic policy and also to the implications deriving from the development of the territory. In the second part, which focuses on the construction of the Iberian kingdoms, we emphasize the role of monarchies and political institutions in the establishment of the economic framework.

4.2 Al-Andalus

4.2.1 Al-Andalus: Different and Heterogeneous States in the Iberian Peninsula (711–1492)

In economic terms, al-Andalus should be regarded as a society whose resources derived mostly from agriculture and trade. A distinguishing feature of the territory is the fact that from 711 its society and economy became part of the Islamic empire, first as part of the Umayyad Caliphate, and later as an independent state, while close links were maintained with the Abbasid empire. This provided access to a trans-Mediterranean world in which journeys undertaken to make the Muslim pilgrimage (*ḥaǧǧ*), trade and the flow of goods were a constant feature throughout its history.

Similarly, as an Islamic society, cities took on a central religious, social and economic role, becoming centres of artisanal and mercantile activity. Indeed, as Islamologist Míkel de Epalza (1991a) states, Islamic civilization was above all urban-based, with the city as the hub of religious, administrative, legal, social and economic life. At the same time, large numbers of people lived in rural areas under the control of urban administrative centres to a varying degree, in accordance with different eras and states, as Pierre Guichard (2001) has shown, especially during the twelfth and thirteenth centuries. A large proportion of the income earned from agriculture and trade, which was prosperous, ended up in the state coffers as a result of the collection of taxes.

Al-Andalus is the name given to a number of states ranging in area that were established in the Iberian Peninsula following the conquest of the territory by Muslim forces during the period 711–716 up to the conquest of the so-called Nasrid kingdom of Granada by the Castilian forces of the Catholic Monarchs in 1492. During this period, spanning 781 years, the name al-Andalus covered a series of very different types of states organized in very different ways, of a range of sizes and features, that developed over time in the Iberian Peninsula. In different epochs several different independent Muslim states existed at the same time (generally known as the *taifa* kingdoms, or *mulūk al-ṭawā'if*), where a single state previously existed. Whether constituting a single state or several states, the name al-Andalus was always used.

In all these states, the common factor and the agent for cohesion was a shared religion and culture: *Mālikī* Sunni Islam shaped the identity of the different Andalusian states. They were states rather than kingdoms because their rulers were not strictly kings, the exercise of regal power having a religious dimension that, depending on the means of the ruler's accession to the throne, either legitimized the government or not (Franco, 2010).

Organizational and macroeconomic aspects, linked to the idea of continuity and the relative uniformity of the different states during the history of al-Andalus, have been generally associated with an economic vision that is based on Islam and was expressed in daily life in the form of socio-economic regulations; this was common to all states over time, although there was an evident degree of evolution in this regard. Let us begin by discussing it, and then go on to describe the most salient aspects of the economic policy of each state (or period, in accordance with the traditional approach).

4.2.2 Transversal Aspects of Economic Policy Deriving From the Application of Islamic legislation

The institutions of al-Andalus developed in parallel with the established Islamic religion, law and morality current in the Ḥiǧāz, the holy land of Islam.

The economy of the various states of al-Andalus can be described as being based on the development of productive sectors, especially taxes and coinage, while some synthetic studies have been produced on this topic (Chalmeta, 1992; Benaboud, 1994; Kassis, 1997; Molina, 1997; Trillo, 2000; Torres, 2000). Therefore, let us carry out a different type of analysis, differentiating between socio-economic processes that are common to different eras and states, and those that are characteristic of specific times and places.

In *Sunnī* Islam there are some very well-established precepts associated with the economic sphere. Below there is a list of these, outlining their influence on the economic administration of the state.

4.2.2.1 The Payment of Taxes, the Religious Basis of the Muslim Economy

The 'pyramid of sovereignty' in *Mālikī* Sunni Islam helps to show how power was exercised in the medieval Muslim West (Franco, 2010). Governance over Muslims was possible due to the basic legitimacy enjoyed by the caliph, whose status was in turn based on requirements of a kinship and legal nature. The delegation of this sovereignty provided legitimacy for the governance of the rest of the administrative and military structure, both central and provincial, provided that the caliph's representatives had been legitimately appointed, and if officials had been appointed legitimately, the population was obliged to obey them. Muslims were bound to 'recognize the sovereignty' of the caliph at Friday prayers, and also by paying an official tax.

Revenue from this compulsory tax is what sustained the Muslim community, that is, the state; non-payment represented a form of rebellion against the entire community of Islam, and was punished extremely harshly. The Quran is somewhat vague as to its name, but it is generally accepted that it is the *zakāt*, based on income that had been earned in the previous year, and it became a fixed tax whose regulation led to the various treatises known as *Kitāb al-ḥarāğ*. These provide an account of the basic rules regarding the payment of the tax, that is, the economic norms applied in the Umayyad states, and in the later 'abbāsī. In the Muslim West the provisions of *Mālikī* law were put into practice, and from the tenth century several treatises appeared on economic theory, although we know only of the *Kitāb al-amwāl* by al-Dāwūdī and a few others (Franco Sánchez, 1999). These treatises defined the obligations of the sultan regarding the distribution of the spoils of war, the payment of taxes and the administration of the treasury of the palace or the state. Another matter of a different nature is how the economy and the royal finances of the al-Andalus Umayyad state actually worked.

One question concerns what was envisaged for the embryonic Muslim society of a city like Medina in the early days of Islam while another regards economies of scale that involved the administration of states. Economic matters were always the cause of serious disagreement between the *ulama* and *faqīhs* (who demanded a return to the essential principles of Islam, the abolishing of any taxes other than the compulsory *zakāt* and little else) on the one hand and on the other hand governments, which were forced to levy taxes on both goods entering and leaving the souks of the city as well as local produce, in addition to the already generally applied poll tax, the tax on the ownership of land, and so on. These supplementary taxes were known by many names, such as *mukūs*, *ḍarā'ib*, *maġārim*, *ġanīma*, among others, all of which had a pejorative connection from a religious point of view.

The debate regarding the abolition of illegal taxes (i.e. those not prescribed by the Quran and the sunnah) continued throughout the history of al-Andalus, punctuated by periods of intensity with the rise to power of figures or dynasties that sought a return to purist origins. Thus, when Almanzor was appointed *ḥāğib* the first thing he did was abolish the tax on olives, which was despised by the people of Córdoba; and following the annexation of al-Andalus the Almoravids issued an edict abolishing the illegal taxes that the kings of the *taifas* had imposed on local people, while the Almohad state did the same after the conquest of al-Andalus.

4.2.2.2 *Waqf* Property, Aid and the Distribution of Resources to Meet Social Needs

In Islam inheritance is subject to extremely strict rules, and their complex mode of enforcement led to the study of arithmetic by *faqīhs*, experts in matters of inheritance. Soon a system developed which, with the blessing of the Quran, was frequently used as a way to circumvent the rigid rules of inheritance. The ḥab (plural ḥubūs) – in the east, waqf (plural wuqūf) – is a type of contract drawn up with the mosque involving an arrangement by which a bequest is transferred to it, with ownership and responsibility for administering it being transferred to the 'economic office' (bayt al-māl) of the mosque. Administrators thus became the legitimate heirs of the first party to the waqf contract: the mosque became the legal owner of the property while the heirs continued sine die to be able to use what was known as 'waqf property' in accordance with the arrangement. In accordance with the contract, the heirs were bound to make an annual payment to the bayt al māl based on the income earned on the property in question.

The most interesting thing about this arrangement is that, on drawing up the waqf contract, the heirs usually made it explicit what the money in question should be used for; thus, waqf income paid to the bayt al māl might be used for funding social assistance (the payment of a dowry to young married women, help for the sick and needy, sustenance for travellers and the sick and so on), and thus we witness what could be described as the working of a medieval social security system. Other uses for funds included: the various overheads of the Mosque (building repairs, the salaries of the sacristan and the imam, oil for lamps, purchase of copies of the Quran for religious instruction, and pay for teachers of young children); the defence of Muslim territory and the city (repairs to the city walls or fortress; travel expenses, lodging, horses and weapons for those defending frontiers); and urban public works (repairs to roads and bridges).

Thus, a system which might have led to the division of property-holdings and an ever-increasing rise in the number of smallholdings in fact provided for social assistance and a means for financing the defence of borders and the repair of the military and urban infrastructure. A register of waqf contracts was kept at the bayt al-māl of the mosque and extensive documentation was found by the Castilian conquerors at the mosques of the city of Granada. During the era, waqf property administered both by mosques and principally by the ṭariqāt, or mystical brotherhoods, contributed to alleviating the effects of famines and meeting the needs of the people of Granada, deriving from the overpopulation of the city and surrounding plain, and helping towards meeting the needs of disadvantaged strata of society.

4.2.2.3 Control of the Economy of the Souk, the ṣāḥib al-sūq and the ḥisbah Treatises

One instrument used by the state to control the local economy, namely in the al-Andalus Umayyad Caliphate, was the appointment of a judicial officer, designated ṣāḥib al-sūq or 'lord of the souk', who had judicial responsibilities in addition to certain police functions.

Detailing the kind of shady dealings that went on at the souk, a list of transgressions and forms of deception of all kinds began to be drawn up in *ḥisba* (accountability or moral rectitude) treatises, describing all kinds of misdemeanours, from tampering with weights and measures to those relating to enslaved people (the disguise of diseases, especially conditions of the skin and those associated with pregnancy), and food offences, thus providing an overview of the fraudulent acts that took place and information about how frequently they occurred and to what extent the judicial authorities were engaged in curbing them.

Later, in the Almoravid and Almohad states it was the *muḥtasib*, a subordinate judicial officer, who was responsible for preventing and punishing such acts: according to the treatise of Ibn ʿAbdūn (eleventh to twelfth centuries), the mission of these judicial officials was to provide security for commercial transactions at the souk, and monitor conduct and compliance with the public morals of Islam, especially that of the women of the city.

4.2.2.4 Prohibition of Usury: *ribā'*

The Quran forbids usury, regarding it as *ribā'*, the earning of interest on loans or debts. This led to the production of treatises that defined *ribā'* and demonstrated how to avoid practising it while taking advantage of opportunities for doing business, in accordance with the doctrine of *mālikī*, as detailed in the treatise of ʿAbd al-Malik Ibn Ḥabīb (c. 790–853). In order to enable commercial transactions to be conducted, legal experts determined what kind of deals were regarded as being susceptible to usury and what courses of action were available to avoid being accused of *ribā'* (Hernández, 2016).

4.2.2.5 The Positive Religious Stance of Islam with Regard to Commercial Success: Paper Money, Marine Insurance and High Tax Revenues for the State

To end this section, let us examine two aspects of the economy that are not the direct result of the direct policy of states, but which concern important taxes. As they have their origin in Islamic concepts, they applied to all Sunni Mediterranean states.

Commercial success and wealth are regarded in Islam as blessings of Allāh, and are therefore held in high regard socially. The concept of *rizq* appears in the few Quranic verses that mention travel 'by land and sea', trade (*tiğāra*) and money in general (*māl*). In his providence, Allāh bestows success on those who undertake new business initiatives (Epalza, 1989: 189–90; 1991a). The positive social regard for success in business also led to consequences of a different kind: trust in God and the provision for misfortune go hand in hand and underlie the concept of maritime insurance during the last Islamic era, the protection of commercial risk thus reflecting an aspect of trust in God and safeguarding against misfortune as a result of plans made in the sphere of worldly affairs.

Also associated with the Mediterranean maritime trade in al-Andalus from the ninth century, there are reports of the first paper money, in the form of a written guarantee establishing fiduciary obligations in connection with trade operations carried out by the agents of a single shipping company who were based in different ports.

This helps to provide an understanding of the character and development of maritime trade and shows how those who devised tax collection policies saw it as an essential source of fiscal revenue. While states sought to maintain a high level of maritime trade, private businessmen developed sophisticated mechanisms for protecting themselves against the risk of loss of vessels by means of maritime insurance and against the theft of coins and precious metals through the use of paper money.

4.2.3 Transversal Macroeconomic Aspects of al-Andalus in Different Eras and States (1000–1492)

4.2.3.1 The Monetary Policy of the Almoravid State (1090–1147)

The *taifa* kingdoms were doomed to economic collapse due to the demand for the payment of increasingly high *parias* to the kingdom of Castile, in addition to the stagnation of agricultural production owing to the ongoing state of war. Some *faqīhs* sent missives to the Almoravids begging for their aid, and even some *taifa* kings, such as al-Mu'tamid of Seville, personally crossed the Strait of Gibraltar to seek their intervention in al-Andalus. In the Maghreb, the Almoravid state had already been consolidated following the founding of Marrākuš as its new capital in 1062. In response to requests, the emir crossed the strait with his troops, passing to the Iberian Peninsula on four occasions, and on the third of these, in 1090, several *taifa* states were conquered, turning al-Andalus into one more province of a unified state, with its capital in Marrakech, from 1090 to 1147.

Having conquered Siğilmāsa in 1054, the Almoravids gained control of the gateway to the Saharan caravan routes. The gold obtained from the trans-Saharan trade enabled them to mint gold and silver coins of great quality, which were highly sought all over the state and throughout the rest of Western Europe. The demise of the Almoravids, defeated in a series of Almohad victories, did not lead to the disappearance of Almoravid coinage in al-Andalus, however. It was so highly prized that both gold and silver coins continued to be minted by the *taifas* during the post-Almoravid period, with the meaning of the words of a religious and political nature they bore being adapted to the new situation. Even the kingdom of Castile imitated the dinars of the Almoravids during the reign of Alfonso VII, and *morabetinos*, or *maravedís*, were minted by Alfonso VIII and Henry I.

The end of the Almoravid period came following Almohad attacks on Marrakesh and led to the emergence of a second period of *taifa*s in al-Andalus. Among them, the *taifa* of the dynasty of Ibn Mardanīš, with its capital in the kingdom of Murcia, is notable for its strength, territorial extension and durability.

4.2.3.2 The Segmented Economy of the Almohad States and the Third *taifa* Period (1147–1232)

The new Almohad state (1147–1232) emerged as the result of a revolution of a religious nature that led to the demise of the ailing Almoravid state. Several Iberian Peninsula states, including the eastern territories of Ibn Mardanīš, were annexed by this new state.

During the Almohad era, there was a great surge in economic development, reflected in the huge scale of rural development. The settlement of Muslims who had migrated from Christian lands led to the expansion of cultivation into mountainous areas of the southern and eastern peninsula. This migration was controlled to an extent, and local governors exercised direct control over the new settlers in order to be able to levy taxes on them. There was an expansion of cultivation in the south, with new crops such as sugar cane, cotton, flax and silk, mostly grown by large landowners. Their action, along with that of urban-based groups of irrigators, led to the proliferation of waterwheels and irrigation systems in river valleys. Moreover, as a result of the development of the local economy in different states, mining enjoyed a revival at this time, and maritime salt flats expanded to their maximum extension on the Atlantic and Mediterranean coast.

In the field of economic policy, changes were made to the tax system and, over a period of almost a century and a half, a system of centralized tax-collection was re-established. Far from the capital of Marrākuš, the growth of the rural population led to the emergence of small self-sufficient regions based on local castles, mosques and rural markets that were no longer dependent on nearby urban centres (Guichard & Lagardère, 1990; Kassis, 1997; Molina, 1997). This trend intensified at the end of the Almohad period, and we witness the emergence of the third period of *taifas*: kingdoms independent of the control of the ailing Almohad state.

4.2.3.3 The Economy of the Nasrid Kingdom of Granada (1232–1492)

Of these kingdoms, only the *taifa* of Arjona, ruled by its sovereign Muḥammad Ibn Yūsuf Ibn Naṣr, survived, as it was a fortified stronghold and was protected by the Subbaetic mountains. Thus, for almost two and a half centuries (between 1232 and 1492), a rump *taifa* state was heir to al-Andalus.

Despite the long list of sovereigns who ruled from the Alhambra fortress palace in Granada, this period displayed a degree of homogeneity that was more marked than Castilian sources indicate. It was a kingdom of large cities, the result of large-scale migration from all over al-Andalus, not only to the mountains but also to cities and the plain surrounding the capital, Granada.

In socio-economic terms, the Nasrid kingdom of Granada was characterized by its extreme overpopulation, from the twelfth century onwards, caused by people fleeing from all over Al-Andalus, by its powerful army and also by its important intensive agricultural sector and range of crafts, especially silks and textiles. Evidence from the tenth century shows that silk was produced and traded in al-Andalus and the trade of silk held importance for the agricultural, manufacturing and commercial sectors, while it was produced at state factories (*tirāz*). There were mulberry plantations for the breeding of silkworms at Jaén, Elvira (Granada), Málaga, Guadix, Baza, the Alpujarras and Almería, and textiles were produced as a cottage industry in these places and in the main cities. During the Almoravid era, the silk industry reached its peak at the beginning of the twelfth century, in Almería, where, according to al-Idrīsī, there were 800 looms. No clear idea of the Nasrid economy can be gained without a knowledge of the huge scale of the production and processing of various qualities of silk, with centres spread all over the kingdom (Álvarez de Cienfuegos, 1958; Torres Delgado, 2000; Trillo San José, 2000).

The *rábitas* and confraternities of mystics were organizations that provided aid and fostered social cohesion as well as enjoying high social standing, and the large amount of *waqf* property they controlled contributed to their work. As agents for social welfare, they succeeded in reducing levels of inequality and helped feed, though not always contain, the poorest social classes.

4.3 The Institutions of the Christian Kingdoms, 1: 1000–1280

4.3.1 The Construction of the Christian Kingdoms and the Monarchies

4.3.1.1 An Economy of War

The fall of the Caliphate of Córdoba in 1031 led to the fragmentation of al-Andalus into dozens of *taifas*, small warring kingdoms that were forced to accept the protection of Christian kingdoms in exchange for the payment of tributes, known as *parias*, in the form of large amounts of coinage and precious metals. Along with other factors, these taxes were key to the strategy of weakening the *taifa* kingdoms and the success of the advance of Christian forces to the south (Abd Allāh, 1980; García Fitz, 2002). Although the *parias* were initially instituted on a temporary basis, they eventually provided a permanent source of income for the Christian kings; albeit the defeat of the Christians by the Almoravids at Zalaca (1086) led to a temporary interruption in the payment of these tributes. We cannot be sure how much was received by kings since we do not know how regularly tributes were made to the Christian kingdoms and it is even difficult to have a clear idea of the impact of *parias* on the economy of the Christian kingdoms. We know that the *parias* paid by Badajoz *taifa* to the King of León amounted to 5,000 dinars per year between 1058 and 1063. In 1064, the set of *parias* of the Badajoz, Toledo and Zaragoza *taifas* amounted to around 20,000 dinars per year and 36,000 dinars a year in 1087 (Negro, 2020).

In fact, the minting of coins by Alfonso VI of Castile had, apparently, little effect on the economy. There has been some discussion of the negative influence of *parias* on Castilian artisanal production, since it was with these funds that artisans' products were purchased from the *taifa* kingdoms. In Castile, these tributes swelled the royal treasury, leading to the strengthening of royal authority, and kings counted on this source of income for funding military expeditions, the payment of debts, the arrangement of marriages, the forging of alliances and for making donations to the Church. However, much of the money deriving from *parias* was used for the payment to *infanzón* nobles and knights, the enrichment of grandees and their petrification in liturgical objects, and to the construction of churches and cathedrals (Moreta, 1989).

The Catalan counts, especially those of Barcelona, were the first Christian leaders to collect taxes in the *taifa* kingdoms, as was the case with those of Zaragoza and Tortosa, as early as the eleventh century. The tributes collected increased the central political and military character of these counts and reinforced the role they played as a warrior elite in the framework of an ideology of expansion.

In a context in which *parias* are perhaps one of the best indicators of the importance of war for the Christian kingdoms, it should be borne in mind that the process of expansion constituted a profitable economic prospect not only for the Iberian monarchs but also for other political entities. Cities organized annual armed raids on Muslim territory for the sole purpose of obtaining plunder (livestock, enslaved people and precious items). Forces were mobilized as veritable business enterprises, as reflected in the terms of several charters.

For the nobility, taking part in military expeditions provided an opportunity for increasing their wealth and receiving donations from kings in reward for their loyalty and the support they provided.

4.3.1.2 The Imposition of Regional Diversity

The marriage of Petronilla, heiress to the kingdom of Aragon and daughter of Ramiro, and Raymond Berenguer IV, Count of Barcelona, in 1150, laid the foundations for a new political entity, whose durability and specificities would mark the eastern Iberian Peninsula during the following centuries (Bisson, 1991).

The union of Aragon and the county of Barcelona highlights, on the one hand, Aragonese concern to free itself from domination by the kingdom of León and Castile and, on the other hand, the primacy achieved by Barcelonese counts over other Catalan counts. Despite the alliance forged between Aragon and Catalonia by marriage, the union led neither to regional differences being eliminated nor to the abatement of the latent conflict between the two territories, which would be felt during the following centuries.

Catalonia was already a highly feudalized region by the eleventh to twelfth centuries. The Carolingian heritage was reflected in a hierarchical power structure based on the existence of a warrior class of nobles and organized in accordance with bonds of vassalage and dependence based on land and a network of fortified strongholds (Manzano, 2015: 372-376).

In addition to the existence of a highly feudalized society, during the course of the eleventh century Barcelona asserted itself as a city in the process of expansion, despite the limited political representation enjoyed by its urban elites and the impact of the crisis in the twelfth century (Bensch, 1995).

Meanwhile in Aragon, perhaps due to its small size, the county system does not seem to have developed in a similar manner. The feudal regime was based on both lineages, which were already present (Miranda & Guerrero 2008), and tenancies of different types and duration. Also, in border areas, especially the Ebro valley region, conquered territory was controlled by means of 'honours' bestowed by monarchs on lineages that provided for the defence of the territory in the name of the king (Laliena Corbera, 2014: 337-366).

The war of conquest that continued throughout the twelfth century led to the annexation of new territories in the regions of Aragon and Catalonia, for example Zaragoza, Tortosa and Lleida in the mid-century. It assured Raymond Berenguer IV and his descendants a leading role on the political stage in the Christian Iberian Peninsula. In 1179, in accordance with the terms of the treaty of Cazola, Alfonso II of Aragon and Alfonso VIII of Castile agreed the establishment of separate zones of expansion in Muslim territory.

In that year, on the other side of the Peninsula, Afonso Henriques was granted recognition as king of Portugal in the papal bull *Manifestis Probatum Est* issued by Pope Alexander III. Alexander invoked the war against the Muslims led by Afonso Henriques as justification for this recognition, while proclaiming the inalienable character of the conquered territory.

The war waged by the first king of Portugal led to the incorporation into the new kingdom of vast regions conquered between the 1120s and the 1160s whose borders were initially established on the northern bank of the River Tagus, including urban centres such as Lisbon and Santarém, and later on the southern bank, taking in cities such as Évora. The class of nobles that supported and sustained the early stages of this expansion underwent significant changes throughout the twelfth century due to the rise of Afonso Henriques and his consolidation as military chief. The *nobreza de infanções* (from the medieval Latin *infantione*) was consolidated in the eleventh to twelfth centuries, joined by new families from the region of Coimbra and further south who rose to prominence thanks to their active role in war and their loyalty to the king and royal circles (Mattoso, 1985).

War not only served as an instrument for the establishment of the legitimacy of power but also as an important source of income and upward social mobility. The assets detailed in the wills of the first monarchs, especially those of Sancho I, dating from about 1188 and 1210, provide examples of this kind of wealth as a result of pillage and the collection of taxes in the conquered lands (Branco, 2006; Vilar, 2019). This wealth was still visible up until the mid-thirteenth century in the minting of gold coins that were imitations of the *marabotins* or *maravedís* of the Muslims.

Also, in Portugal the constitution of tenancies was aimed at strengthening links between powerful magnates and the king, and their names appear as signatories of royal documents. As in Aragon, the terms of the donations involved are not always clear, much less their duration, but the aims are similar: ensuring the control and exploitation of conquered territory.

Following the restoration of the kingdom of Pamplona in 1134, after separation from the kingdom of Aragon, the key to the success of the Navarrese monarchy recently established by King García Ramírez was tax reform leading to an increase in Crown income. First, Sancho the Wise introduced an annual tax on the use of the plots on which the residents of the new urban centres created from 1157 had built their houses (Fortún Pérez de Ciriza & Jusué Simonena, 1993). Meanwhile, from 1189, the Navarrese monarchs renewed the old system of manorial charges on the peasantry on Crown estates involving unified *pechas*, paid either individually by each household or by the community. Likewise, monarchs renewed their toll rights imposing charges on goods, thus taking advantage of the mercantile boom of the era. The spoils of war of royal campaigns should also be mentioned, which brought in a sizeable amount of income between 1212 and 1223. Thanks to these new sources of revenue, the Navarrese monarchy was able to increase the extent of Crown patrimony through purchases from private lords, fortifying the boundaries of the kingdom by means of the acquisition of towns and fortresses. Nevertheless, the collectors of this royal income were still barons and *ricoshombres* (literally 'rich men' – the highest-ranking nobles), who were assigned responsibility for the administration of honours or districts. The tendency of these administrators was to patrimonialize income, although the development of the royal estate and the deployment of *claveros* (knights of the military orders) and *comarca* (county) deposits reduced the significance of the role of the barons.

4.3.1.3 Changes During the Thirteenth Century: The Case of Castile

The battle of Navas de Tolosa (1212) marks a turning point in the military balance of power in the peninsula, following the victory of an alliance consisting of Alfonso VIII of Castile, Peter II of Aragon, Sancho VII of Navarre and several Portuguese knights over Muslim forces. Besides the ideological struggle involved in the battle, it is worth noting the importance of fact that the thirteenth century marked the high point of the Christian conquest, roughly up until the conquest of the kingdom of Granada. During this period the economy of the Iberian Peninsula evolved from one in which war was a source of income to a situation in which war was a source of expenditure. This resulted in changes in the pattern of the sources of the income of both royalty and seigniorial groups leading, in some cases, to an increase of the degree of seignioral dominance and to the extension of state taxation.

Meanwhile, for all the Christian kingdoms of the peninsula, the first few decades of the thirteenth century were a period of territorial expansion. The military successes that enabled Castile to reach Murcia (1245) and Seville (1248), Portugal conquer the kingdom of the Algarve (1249), and Aragon take the Balearic Islands (1235) and Valencia (1245), preceded new stages of seigniorial dominance and the expansion of Christian societies which were a feature of the thirteenth century (Guinot Rodríguez, 2014). As a result, from the mid-twelfth century to the late thirteenth century the kingdom of Aragon almost tripled in size (Sánchez et al., 2008).

In Portugal, the thirteenth century was also marked by territorial advances on the south bank of the Tagus and the left bank of the Guadiana, owing largely to the action of the military Order of Santiago, whose establishment in the south of the kingdom would prove to be crucial, and more important than that due to royal initiative. In 1249, Alfonso III officially ended the occupation of the Algarve, although discussion with Castile regarding his tenure stretched out over the following decades until the signing of the Badajoz agreement in 1267. A few years later, the Kingdom of Portugal completely defined its eastern borders with Castile by the treaty of Alcañices in 1297.

Thanks to the conquests of the first half of the thirteenth century, Castile became the largest kingdom in terms of territory and the only one bordering Islamic land (Miranda & Guerrero, 2008).

In the context of this phase of expansion, monarchs acquired a new role as the drivers of processes of the settlement of population and constitution of new areas of seignioral governance in the new territories, which was evident in particular in the organization of *repartimientos* (settlements), the multiplication of Crown donations as a basis for the formation of new secular and ecclesiastical landholdings, and the constitution of *realengos*, or royal jurisdictions, but also by the allocation of municipal areas and jurisdictions recognized by charters.

However, the second half of the thirteenth century brought the first indications of economic difficulties in almost all the Iberian kingdoms, especially Castile. The kingdom of Castile experienced a serious economic crisis as a result of inflation and the devaluation of the currency. The initial political action of the monarchs in the economic sphere was aimed at stimulating production: they implemented measures aimed at combating increases in wages, which led to a rise in prices, as well as making several attempts to control and prohibit trade fraternities, in Castile beginning in the reign of Alfonso X and in Aragon from the reign of James I (Miranda & Guerrero, 2008). One of the first measures took by Alfonso X at the beginning of his reign in 1252 was aimed at regaining control of prices following the devaluation of the currency, since the rise in wages and prices spelt ruin for all those who depended on a fixed income. The *Cortes* were the assembly to which representatives of the towns were summoned by the king to join his noble and clerical advisers as royal counsellors on issues of far-reaching importance to the kingdom. The first *Cortes* were set up in León in 1188, and were joined with the *Cortes* of Castile after the union of the Kingdoms of León and Castile in 1230. The *Cortes* provided the monarch with a means of fixing prices and wages in the different regions of the kingdom, thus establishing a monetary policy and consequently an economic policy; they were also able to place limits on extravagant expenditure and devised a series of sumptuary laws aimed at reducing private and public spending (Martín, 1993).

In 1268, the *Cortes* of Jerez approved a series of laws aimed at aiding the Castilian economy. For example, the king promised not to devalue the currency and to standardize weights and measures, and regulations were introduced to restrict the export of goods to certain ports, which were mostly, but not only, located on the Cantabrian coast: San Sebastián, Fuenterrabía, Castro Urdiales, Laredo, Santander, Avilés, Ribadeo, Vivero, Betanzos, La Coruña, among others (Solórzano Telechea, 2018).

For the first time, during the reign of Alfonso X, the Castilian economy was organized bearing in mind economic institutions. The foundations of Castilian industry were laid, by prohibiting the export of important goods and regulating imports, as well as establishing customs posts at ports and ensuring the compulsory payment of duties. Likewise, an attempt was made to ensure that production satisfied demand. In Castile, monarchs protected the Mesta from the date of its establishment in 1273. The measures adopted by Alfonso X and continued by his successors up until the mid-fourteenth century created a tax system that hardly changed during the following centuries (Ladero, 2011).

The kings implemented a series of measures to ensure a balance of trade surplus with the exterior and guarantee the supply of goods to the inhabitants of the territory, a basic feature of the policies of late medieval monarchies, as was the creation of the mercantile courts which were held at the *consulados* of merchants, the reorganization of economic spaces involving the creation of fairs and markets, Castilian expansion in the Atlantic and that of Aragon in the Mediterranean, and laws to protect the wealth of the kingdom (Miranda & Guerrero, 2008).

4.3.2 Manorialism and the Urban World

4.3.2.1 The Military Orders as Protagonists

Based on the role of monarchies in the conquest the Crown was able, in virtually all Iberian kingdoms, to play an important role in the distribution of goods and rights and consequently in establishing links between the king and royal circles on the one hand and privileged groups on the other, although the degree to which this occurred varied in accordance with the territories and circumstances in question.

New and old entities gained prominence in the drive to occupy conquered lands. Along with the nobility the secular and regular clergy were key figures in this process. The imposition of the diocesan map, which accompanied the Conquest process itself, laid the foundations for a process of appropriation of territory and collection of income from parish units, with particular emphasis on the tithe, which gradually spread from the twelfth century onwards. At the same time, religious orders such as the Benedictines and Cistercians promoted, from their monasteries, centres of development and agricultural exploitation and settlement of the conquered territories.

Among the new protagonists, the military orders took an important role, both those of peninsular origin, such as the orders of Calatrava, Avis and Santiago, and the so-called international orders, such as the Knights Hospitaller and the Templars (Ayala Martínez, 2003). Although they emerged within the context of the crusades against Muslim power, the role and importance of these orders went far beyond the bounds of military conflict and during subsequent centuries they played an active role in the control, exploitation and integration of the conquered territories, where they not only collected rents from tenant farmers and tributes resulting from the exercise of jurisdiction, but also imposed taxes of a religious nature.

The system of *comendas* (commanderies) underlying the organization of these orders was initially associated with a network of fortresses whose purpose was to defend border zones and areas of latent conflict (Bonet Donato & Pavón Benito, 2013: 5–54), but they soon became hubs for the management of assets and revenues, and, in some cases, political centres for the orders, as was the case of Amposta in Aragon and Avis and Palmela in Portugal, throughout the late Middle Ages. In Aragon, the Hospitallers were perhaps the order that brought together most goods and vassals under their purview even before the dissolution of the Order of the Templars (Bonet Donato & Pavón Benito, 2013).

In Portugal, especially in the first half of the thirteenth century, both peninsular and international military orders also assumed a prominent role in the occupation and organization of the territory, in particular south of the Tagus, thanks to an important series of royal donations made in the first half of the thirteenth century to the Order of Santiago in the Palmela area and the border region with the Kingdom of the Algarve, to the Order of Hospitallers around Crato, and to the Order of Avis-Calatrava in northern Alentejo.

The first Castilian order was that of Calatrava, founded in 1158 by the warrior monks of the Cistercian monastery of Fitero, who were responsible for the defence of the castle of Calatrava, conquered in 1147 and a strategic bulwark between the Tagus and the Guadiana. A few years later, the other great military orders of Santiago and Alcántara were founded in Castile. These orders played a leading role in much of the campaign of conquest of the southern peninsula. After the victory of the Christian hosts in the battle of Las Navas de Tolosa in 1212, the military orders began to manage economic and human resources on a large scale, in La Mancha and Andalusia, which were granted by the monarchs in recognition of the help they provided in the reconquest of the southern peninsula. For example, the order of Santiago administered 23,000 km^2 in more than 200 places with a total population of around 200,000 people at the end of the fifteenth century (Ayala Martínez, 2003). The patrimony accumulated by the military orders enabled them to draw huge manorial benefits deriving from income from the land, jurisdictional rights and the spoils of war. A high proportion of this came from commercial income. For example, the orders benefited from trade between al-Andalus and Christian territories and also held royal licences for allowing the holding of fairs and markets in places under their jurisdiction. Likewise, they enjoyed the right to receive a fifth of the spoils of the knights under their jurisdiction and the tithe of royal booty, as well as *parias* received by monarchs. Finally, the Hispanic military orders had an important role to play in pastoral farming involving livestock such as sheep, cattle and swine, thanks to the fact that monarchs had granted them exemption from the tax on livestock. Such is the case of the Order of Calatrava, which enjoyed exemption for its 15,000 cattle, 8,000 sheep and 8,000 pigs (Ayala Martínez, 2003).

The small size of the Navarrese kingdom and its remoteness from the border with al-Andalus, as well as its complicated orography in the north of the kingdom, led to the emergence of a singular system of *comiendas*, with a rural base. The income of the orders derived from agricultural estates and tolls on the use of trade routes (Pavón & García de la Borbolla, 2000).

Thus, the political and military importance of the military orders was enormous. In addition, initially the Castilian–Leonese orders were instrumentalized by the Crown, up until the middle of the thirteenth century, since they had been founded by the monarchs, unlike the universal military orders, which were the outcome of pontifical designs. The military orders were responsible for reconquering and colonizing the new territories, thereby enabling monarchs to achieve their political aims, but this also led to the politicization of the orders and growing tension with the Crown, which led to their total submission to the monarchs from the fourteenth century.

In Portugal, the end of the Middle Ages also saw the 'nationalization' of the military orders, growing royal intervention in the appointment of their leaders (Oliveira, 2009), and the gradual incorporation of their assets and benefits within the sphere controlled by royal families and the system of reward dependent on kingly favour.

4.3.2.2 Cities and Urban Elites as Economic Protagonists

In the final decades of the twelfth century and the first half of the thirteenth century, the Christian kingdoms saw an increase in their territorial extension and the emergence of new forms of urban organization. This included cities characterized by the continuity of religious and political power, especially those located in the north of the peninsula, as well as those with an important mercantile function and a role as hubs for the organization of trade, such as Barcelona and Mallorca in Aragon, Seville and Valladolid in Castile, and to a lesser extent Lisbon in Portugal. It also included centres for domestic trade with regional links, such as Zaragoza in Aragon, Santarém in Portugal, and Burgos in Castile, and new cities, whose construction or development took place under the aegis and the protection of new powers.

In Castile from the twelfth century, the system of urban settlement was characterized by the subordination of rural spaces to urban centres. This system, known as *villa y tierra* (town and land), was generally used for the organization of local administration in the territory, from the north to the south of the kingdom, during subsequent centuries, on which the dynamic energy of Castilian-Leonese urban centres was based. The incipient urban elites strove to secure territorial dominance, the means of the negotiation of charter concessions from kings and the purchase of small settlements.

The incorporation of these spaces brought with it the challenge of making a warrior and seigniorial economy work alongside new market structures, with access to new sources of income deriving not only from trade but also from the exploitation of real estates by privileged groups and the king himself, and problems arising from the integration of new groups into the political sphere.

These groups were characterized by different features and a variety of different names: *cavaleiros-vilãos* (villein knights) and *homens-bons* (literally, good men – men with status in the local community) in Portugal, honourable citizens in Aragon, and knights in Castile are just some of the terms used to characterize a diverse and differentiated universe, marked by a distinct internal hierarchy established on the basis not only of wealth and the ability to access sources of income but also access to local government. The thirteenth century was the pivotal moment in the development of these urban elites linked to the exercise of urban power (Laliena Corbera, 2010b: 65–96). The end of the war of conquest brought an inevitable reassessment of the way urban groups thought about themselves and represented themselves to others. The distinction dictated by the war effort whereby local men were organized into groups of knights and foot-soldiers, as mentioned in the charters bestowed on different Portuguese localities in the twelfth and thirteenth centuries, was gradually replaced by an economic and political hierarchy consisting of citizens, good men, merchants and simple artisans.

Migration resulting from the conquest of new territories, both within individual regions and between regions (Igual-Luis, 2018: 101–118), provided a means of social mobility and the reorganization of urban elites (Vilar, 2012: 145–212), as did access to municipal magistracies, among which the positions of judge and *almotacé* were highly prized, as were proximity to royal circles and active roles in them (Coelho & Magalhães, 2008: 23–43). In Lisbon there are many examples of families whose members served at municipal magistracies and at the same time held office in the royal administration, in particular from the second half of the thirteenth century.

As far as the urban sphere is concerned, thirteenth-century Aragon is synonymous with an attempt to consolidate and standardize municipal judiciaries of an elective character, for example those of Barcelona, Mallorca and Valencia. At the same time, the management of mounting fiscal pressure from the Crown throughout the fourteenth century had an evident impact on the development of urban tax systems, whose officials were under pressure from the royal treasury while being responsible for collecting payments and taxes and contributed to the strengthening of urban political elites (Sánchez, Furió & Sesma Muñoz, 2008: 99–130).

From the time of their foundation, the inhabitants of Castilian cities and towns were represented by those who spoke on their behalf and small groups of *vecinos* (local residents), an elite who exercised power in the pre-urban and urban community and maintained a dialogue with the monarchy. These elites were composed of *caballeros y hombres principales* (knights and important men), whose ideals were typical of the aristocracy. These urban oligarchies controlled local political and social life, although they were not totally closed groups, as new members were admitted on account of their wealth or relationship with central power. The usual form of the organization of the members of these oligarchies was on the basis of lineage, that is, a number of kinship groups, and belonging to one of them was a prerequisite for access to council posts in almost all cities and towns in Castile from the thirteenth century. By the fourteenth century, the policy of Alfonso XI encouraged the transformation of lineages into political groupings, which controlled sources of urban power during subsequent centuries. However, there were some places where this did not occur and some lineages were even replaced by representatives of the common people, especially in northern peninsular towns (Solórzano, 2013a).

Councils played an important role in the fiscal policy formulated by the Castilian monarchs. The Crown estate was founded on the levying of direct taxes and *derramas*. Cities had to deal with requests from kings in the *Cortes* and pay their dues in a timely manner, so councils were forced to collect local taxes from *vecinos* in order to cover the amounts required by monarchs. The lack of royal tax collectors prevented the direct collection of royal taxes, and the task was assigned to tax farmers. From this time, the *alcabala* (a key royal sales tax) was farmed out to tax-farmers and sub-contractors.

4.4 The Institutions of the Christian Kingdoms, 2: 1280–1500

4.4.1 King and Kingdom: A Range of Different Political Systems

Legislative production, the complexification of the administrative structure and the control of the territory, the development of royal taxation, and the management of warfare and military practice are all features which signal a process of consolidation of royal power within the framework of the plurality of powers and overlapping of jurisdictions.

In the Iberian kingdoms, the period from the second half of the thirteenth century to the mid-fifteenth century is perhaps the key period in the development of these processes, despite the differences between the political systems of the kingdoms. This apparent extension of royal power should not blind us to the weaknesses inherent in the process. The occasion of a change of monarch or the final years of a reign were, as far as Portugal, Castile and Aragon are concerned, in many cases marked by political crisis, and there is evidence of attempts to reconfigure groups present in political society.

In Portugal, the period from the 1280s to the mid-fifteenth century was marked by civil strife and conflict, in particular during a change of king or a dynasty, such as the end of the reigns of Denis, Alfonso IV and Ferdinand. In the fifteenth century, the troubled regency of Peter came to an end with his death at the battle of Alfarrobeira (1449), and was set against a backdrop of confrontation between noble houses linked to the royal family and centres with a clientele which was both new and wide-ranging.

Viewed from a global standpoint, these successive crises, marked by military clashes involving varying degrees of violence, which always ended up with participants entrenched in opposing camps, demonstrate on the one hand the apparent security of the position of the royal family, whose legitimacy was not openly questioned, even though minor changes were introduced with regard to succession affecting the lineage, and on the other hand the importance of pressure from the nobles, which was felt especially at times when the royal family was particularly vulnerable, such as when an expected succession loomed.

In Castile, the period between the end of the thirteenth century and the end of the fourteenth century is marked by great tension between the king and the nobility, with a great deal of pressure being put on collateral members of the royal family by noble families in many cases. This tension was defused on the death of Peter the Cruel and the imposition of the Trastámara dynasty, following the reign of Alfonso XI marked by a policy aiming at the strengthening of the Crown.

Neither is the process of royal succession in Aragon seen by some historians as one that called into question the role of the dominant lineage, at least until the death of Martin I and the Compromise of Caspe (Sesma Muñoz, 2014: 55–84). This interpretation is based on the understanding that royalty was a key element in maintaining the cohesion of the Crown of Aragon, despite the central role assigned to the *Cortes* and the political and economic autonomy of the territories that made up the kingdom of Aragon. Attempts to explain this apparent contradiction have led to a debate surrounding the specificity of the Aragonese system of government, centred, in the opinion of some, on the pact between the monarch and the privileged social groups present in the *Cortes* and municipalities, while the monarch's scope for action was severely limited by overwhelming financial dependency and the burden of a growing public debt. For others, the apparent succession of a lineage in control of the throne does not call into question the vulnerability of the Crown throughout the Middle Ages and the predominance of collective prominence that the Compromise of Caspe reflects (Sabaté i Curull, 2015: 279–290).

From this discussion emerges a traditional conclusion about the existence of the two opposing systems of governance mentioned above in the Iberian space – that is, on the one hand territories based at an early stage on the king and royal power, of which Portugal and Castile provide good examples, and on the other hand the case of the Crown of Aragon, a system characterized by diversity or a greater degree of weakness of royal power, which nevertheless remained in place until the end of the fifteenth century with no serious attempts at fragmentation or rupture. With regard to the establishment of the central role of the king at an early stage and the ongoing weakness of the king's position, it should be borne in mind that the construction of royal power is an ongoing process in which the king and the power of the Crown are responsible for the organization of the political space and its cohesion, and that it is also necessary to look to the territorial specificities of the territories involved as well as the financial constraints of each individual kingdom.

Moreover, processes of the fostering of domestic cohesion in the kingdoms and the imposition of royal power present evident similarities, both at the administrative level through the increase in the number of representatives for peripheral areas in all Iberian kingdoms (Abulafia & Garí, 1996; Coelho, 1996b; Miranda & Guerrero, 2008) and at the judicial level through the promulgation of a series of laws aimed at strengthening the image and powers of the king as legislator and the recognition of the maintenance of the exercise of supreme justice by monarchs (Laliena Corbera, 2010b: 65–96).

4.4.2   Crown Revenues and Taxation

The gradual establishment of a fiscal system and a network of collectors for the numerous taxes that were levied are key features of the process of the extension of the power of the Crown to territories of the Iberian Peninsula from the thirteenth to fifteenth centuries.

In the kingdom of Aragon, by the mid-thirteenth century revenue from the exploitation of royal domains plus the collection of a wide range of taxes was manifestly insufficient to meet the increase in expenditure resulting from the conquest and the system of governance. To the tributes derived from old feudal practices, such as the *cenas* in Navarre and Aragon and *jantares* in Portugal, are added those that were levied on Moors and Jews, as well as others that were imposed on cities in particular, such as the *pechas* in Aragon, *questias* in Catalonia and *peitas* in Valencia (Sanchéz, Furió & Sesma Muñoz, 2008: 99–130). In addition to these taxes, which were either levied locally or restricted to certain places or to certain social groups, the thirteenth century was also characterized by the appearance of taxes of a wider scope. Imposed either as result of decisions of the *Cortes* or in the wake of more or less arbitrary decisions, they led to the idea of levying a general tax, as a result or not of a process of negotiation. The *monedage* was collected every seven years in order to provide a safeguard against the devaluation of the currency by the king, appearing initially in Aragon in the early thirteenth century and later in Valencia and Mallorca in the second half of the century. Meanwhile, the *bovatge*, which was exclusively levied in Catalonia and linked to the accession to the throne by a new king, gradually disappeared from 1300.

It was undoubtedly the extraordinary taxes, whose introduction was negotiated in the *Cortes*, especially throughout the fourteenth and fifteenth centuries, that were a hallmark of Aragonese governance. Growing royal dependence on these taxes, agreement on which was laboriously thrashed out in the *Cortes* of the different territories of the kingdom of Aragon, increased royal dependence, which was already great due to the gradual alienation of royal patrimony, and strengthened the hand of individual territories in negotiations. Understood as partly forming the basis of 'pactism', this financial dependence undoubtedly limited the ability of the Crown to carry out its role and strengthened the autonomy of individual territories. This was all the more so when the number of interlocutors tended to increase with cities as taxpayers and protagonists of the campaign for additional taxes, which was aimed particularly at funding campaigns in the Mediterranean in the second half of the fourteenth century and throughout the fifteenth century (Sánchez, Furió & Sesma Muñoz, 2008: 99–130), while the nobility and clergy refused to pay them.

Thus, the stage for negotiations was not restricted to the *Cortes*, just as the scope of negotiation was not restricted to maintaining or altering the status quo between the territories of the kingdom of Aragon, but also involved different kinds of disagreement between groups within each territory. While urban groups may have been the main financial beneficiaries of the growing public debt, the increase in the number of borrowers and lenders conferred a new kind of power on cities and their elites, accentuated the importance of the role of the nobility and clergy as the king's interlocutors, and increased the financially dependent role of royal power, while it also turned the king into a by no means negligible source of income and additional speculation for groups of lenders. This is probably important to take into account when considering the longevity of the royalty of the kingdom of Aragon.

The process of establishing and imposing a tax system in Portugal presented differences, which were to be expected, but there were also similarities, showing that there was common ground in the political and economic spheres. Particular concerns about the royal heritage were also felt from the second half of the thirteenth century and the end of the campaign of conquest. Royal commissions, *inquirições*, were launched at an early stage, in 1220, during the reign of Afonso II, and were continued and extended in scope during subsequent reigns – in 1258, 1301, 1303–1304, 1307 and 1315. At the same time, monarchs consolidated their presence in the urban sphere by means of the acquisition of new patrimony, especially in the most important cities of the kingdom.

The Crown continued to exact payment for royal rights associated with its property and means of production and collect taxes on commerce in the form of tolls, customs duties, tithes and services, such as notaries' pensions, chancellery rights and rights over groups of people, such as Jews and Moors, as well as the *monetagio* (a fixed tax paid by the burgher to the Crown) that was introduced during the reign of Alfonso III in the 1250s.

From the reign of Ferdinand I, in 1387, general *sisas* were introduced: taxes levied on the buyers and sellers of any goods, introduced to pay for the defence of the kingdom and the cost of the royal household. The Crown began to collect the *sisa* as a general, permanent tax covering all subjects of the kingdom, and it was therefore of great political and fiscal significance (Sousa, 1990: 521–524). The resulting revenues entering the Crown coffers were so great that a series of laws were introduced to regulate its collection. However, it is not clear whether the imposition of the new tax led to an increase in the burden of taxation, given the decrease in revenue from royal rights (Henriques, 2019).

We thus witness a process of evolution towards a wide-ranging financial system in the kingdom, which revenues from overseas made all the more essential, involving the reorganization of customs duties, the systematic monitoring of public finances, and the introduction of regulations for bookkeeping and tax collection at the local level, while improvements were made in the field of warehouse management and bookkeeping, and estimates of Crown revenue and expenditure were drawn up from 1473.

Local people were also repeatedly urged to support the monarchy. Key elements in the implementation of Crown policy, cities and their elites were also essential sources of revenue deriving from extraordinary *pedidos* (levies) and taxes. Throughout the fifteenth century, especially between the reign of John I and the end of the reign of John II, the *Cortes* met 54 times (Sousa, 1990), the agenda of no less than 41 meetings including a discussion regarding the proposal for an extraordinary *pedidos* and taxes, which is why in a few cases the agenda featured an attempt to reform the financial system.

To a large extent, the effectiveness of the Castilian monarchy in the fourteenth and fifteenth centuries was based on the successful creation of a new taxation system to meet its needs, which meant that it was no longer dependent on traditional feudal resources. In the kingdom of Castile from the early thirteenth century, the privilege of minting coinage led to the creation of new forms of indirect taxation, such as the *moneda forera*, which involved on a pact between the king and the kingdom, represented in *Cortes*, by which the king agreed not to devalue the currency for seven years in exchange for a payment by the people of the kingdom.

The monarchs of Castile gradually introduced their fiscal system from the mid-thirteenth century. Alfonso X imposed new taxes (royal *tercias, décimas, diezmos* [tithes], *portazgos, servicios* and *montazgos*) and modified old ones (the *martiniega*, the *fonsadera*, royalties, and others). However, as a result of a declining population and economic depression, revenue from direct taxes stagnated and they were replaced by indirect taxes, especially on commercial transactions, such as the customs tithe and the *alcabala*. The former, levied by Alfonso X in 1268, proved very profitable for the Crown: customs duties collected on Portuguese goods amounting to 30,000 *maravedíes* in 1294, while maritime customs duties collected in Galicia, not counting La Coruña, brought in 40,000 *maravedíes* in 1285. The ports of the Cantabrian coast were even more lucrative, as half a million *maravedíes* were collected annually and San Vicente de la Barquera alone accounted for as much as the port of Seville. The tithes collected at ports along the coast from Fuenterrabía to San Vicente de la Barquera, known as the tithes of the Sea of Castile, were the most profitable in the kingdom, accounting for total duties of two million *maravedíes* on 812 different types of goods in 1453.

Customs tithes became a regular source of income for the royal treasury, complemented by the *almojarifazgos* and the so-called *cosas vedadas* or 'forbidden things'. The former was a legacy of urban taxation in al-Andalus, and were made up of the revenue of the king in the most important cities from Toledo to Seville, accounting for 10% of the value of imports, or sometimes less – in the case of the cities of Murcia, Alicante and Cartagena – or more – as was the case with the kingdom of Granada. As for income from the 'forbidden things', at the *Cortes* of Guadalajara held in 1390 John I promulgated the first *Cuaderno de sacas*, or list of outgoings, in which from the mid-thirteenth century all the information on the provisions concerning expenditure was to be collected, and which provides a list of goods involved and the competences of the *alcaldes* and *guardas de las sacas*. As foreign trade developed, the monarchy lifted the ban on the export of most items except for cereals, horses, silver, gold, currency and weapons.

As for the *alcabala*, this indirect tax on the consumption of goods became an extraordinary Crown tax in 1342 when the *Cortes*, meeting in Burgos, granted Alfonso XI the right to levy the tax for three years to finance the frontier war, and this arrangement was later made permanent by the *Cortes* of Alcalá de Henares in 1393. The *alcabala* was paid by the purchaser of goods, withheld by the seller and later paid to the taxman. From 1400, it became a regular tax on all purchases of both movable goods and property, and in 1429 it accounted for 80% of regular Crown income. Other regular sources of income were the tithe and the Moorish half tithe, *portazgos*, the *servicio y montazgo* and the *moneda*, among others. Due to the transfer of these taxes into the hands of the noble elites of the kingdom, the use of extraordinary direct taxes such as *servicios* and those sanctioned by papal bulls associated with the crusades became widespread from the time of the Catholic Monarchs. In addition, the Catholic Monarchs faced the problem of public debt, especially for financing extraordinary expenditure due to war, and they resorted to borrowing from the local banks that had emerged or began to appear, based in the main cities of Castile and Aragon.

Another source of revenue for the Castilian monarchy derived from its share of the income of the Church. These were extraordinary resources, but they were resorted to more and more frequently. The two most important of them were the *tercias* (thirds) and *décimas* (tenths): a third of the ecclesiastical tithe was earmarked for the maintenance of churches, but in accordance with a papal concession kings began to collect a proportion of this amount, which they called the royal *tercia*. In Castile in 1247, on the occasion of the conquest of Seville, Ferdinand III was granted the *tercias* of the whole kingdom for three years and after that they were collected regularly. Other revenue deriving from the Church was in the form of tithes, collected in accordance with a papal concession, which provided a ready source of income for the monarchy. The kings of Navarre and Aragon also received tithes from the 1460s.

In Navarre, Theobald I's installation of the house of Champagne on the Navarrese throne in 1234 brought great change to the kingdom, the new Crown administration bringing in a series of administrative innovations from France, where progress had been made in this field. One of these was the new Crown accounting system, and the development of the system of bookkeeping by the *Registros de Cuentas*, which provided a record of the income and expenditure of the kingdom. The revenue of the kingdom derived mainly from agricultural incomes, as its economy was largely rurally based. These revenues were the main source of income of the Navarrese monarchy, since kings used them to defray the expenses of both the royal household and those of the administration of the kingdom (Ramírez Vaquero, 2006).

From 1274, following the death of King Henry I, Navarre fell under the direct control of the French Capetians, and as a result the territory was governed from Paris. Thus, those who received the accounts of *merindades* and *bailías* (administrative areas) would come from France and the bookkeeping records would be sent to Paris every year. These circumstances held until the coming of a new dynasty, the Evreux, in 1328, following a series of Capetian kings who never set foot on Navarrese soil.

Thenceforth, the accounts ceased to be sent to Paris and a new important office, that of receiver general or treasurer, responsible for the accounts of the kingdom, was created. Auditors or inspectors of accounts were also appointed, who were in charge of inspecting the accounts presented by those who received revenues from the *merindades*. A specialist Crown finance accounting body, the Cámara de Comptos, was established for these inspectors in 1365 during the reign of Charles II. In 1400, he created a new post, that of *procurador patrimonial*, responsible for inspecting, investigating and recovering the royal income that had been misappropriated (Lacarra, 1981).

There were few changes with regard to regular sources of income in the late Middle Ages. *Pechas*, accounting for 65% of total revenues, were paid by rural workers who did not enjoy *hidalgo* noble status. Other sources of regular income included tolls, *pechas* levied on Jews, iron mines and sentences. One profitable source of income for the Navarrese monarchy was iron mining, which had been a royal monopoly since 1368 and was either exploited directly by the Crown or farmed out to third parties under certain conditions, such as the king having first option on the purchase of extracted minerals, which could then be sold at a profit.

Regular incomes were insufficient to cover the expenditure deriving from the political intervention of Charles II (1349–1387), especially during a period in which the Navarrese population was stricken with the plague and as a result *pechas* were reduced.

For this reason, the king resorted to making requests for extraordinary annual aid, which had to be approved by the *Cortes*. Philip III of Evreux had already used general *derramas* twice, first for the minting of coinage and later to pay for the dowry of his daughter in 1338. During the reign of his son, Charles II, requests for extraordinary income were made every year. When even this was not enough, monarchs resorted to seeking loans from Jews, councils and ecclesiastics, lodging the crown jewels as surety or promising exemption from tax.

Extraordinary aid was a burden on the entire population of the kingdom – clerics, nobles, burghers, peasants and religious minorities – levied in accordance with individual means. Payments were made in four instalments or *cuarteles* to special officials responsible for tax collection.

Other sources of Crown income were the *monedaje* and the *alcabala*. The *monedaje* was a special source of aid used occasionally, involving the minting of a monarch's own coinage, once only, following their coronation, whose value was fixed for the duration of the reign.

The *alcabala* was introduced by Charles II and was similar to measures that had been implemented in other kingdoms: a tax on commercial transactions at fairs and markets. Requiring the approval of the *Cortes*, it was originally intended as a special tax, to be used once only, but soon turned into an annual levy, which monarchs farmed out to private individuals – usually Jews or councils – whereby the Crown secured an advance on tax to be collected. During the reign of Charles III, the rate of the *alcabala* was fixed (Ramírez Vaquero, 2006).

4.4.3 The Crisis of the Fourteenth Century and the Waves of Expansion of the Fifteenth Century

In 1458, Alfonso V of Aragon died in Naples, and that year another Afonso V, king of Portugal, conquered the town of Alcácer Ceguer in North Africa. These two events occurred at a great distance and were apparently completely unrelated, all they had in common being the fact that they took place outside the kingdoms of the respective monarchs. The Aragonese king's demise brought to an end a long reign which had begun in 1416 and was focused on Mediterranean expansion, while the Portuguese king's success was due to a number of expeditions carried out during the first decades of the fifteenth century, targeting North African settlements, which took place in parallel with expansion along the Atlantic coast.

Both kings apparently limited themselves to recovering traditional spaces for military and economic expansion of their kingdoms, but it reminds us of the new expansionist phenomenon that marked fifteenth-century peninsular history, in which Castile certainly also took part. The Portuguese policy of expansion, which resulted in the colonization of the Atlantic islands and later the exploration of the African coast, opened up new trade routes. The establishment of the trading posts of Arguim and Mina enabled the Portuguese to trade along the African coast, and the proceeds, which included enslaved people, gold, ivory and pepper, were controlled in the African space by the *Casa da Guiné* and later from Portuguese Guinea and Mina.

Much of the profits were used for the remuneration of those most closely connected with royalty, in the form of *pensions* and dowries, involving huge expenditure, while enabling one of the obligations of the Crown during the era to be fulfilled: that of providing reward for services rendered, granting favours and providing protection in the form of money and the granting of special rights. A new stage in the growth of seigniorial power is notable throughout the fifteenth century.

In Aragon, the final centuries of the Middle Ages saw the consolidation of large urban centres, despite the devastating effects of the civil war in Catalonia. The development of textile production and the consolidation of new crops were features of a wider process of economic integration carried out in Aragon during this period, focusing on four major urban centres: Barcelona, Valencia, Zaragoza and Mallorca. The integration of local and regional markets into a wider trade network led to the reorganization of the production system and alleviated the impact of the demographic and social crisis.

In Castile, monarchs introduced a large number of laws aimed at protecting commercial activity, for example setting up official bodies of merchants, such as the *consulados*. The creation of the Consulado de Burgos on 21 July 1494 was aimed at bringing together the professional organizations of seafarers and merchants in order to protect their interests by setting up a special court to resolve disputes. Following the establishment of the Consulado de Burgos, competition between the merchants of Burgos and those of the Cantabrian coast was fierce, since it included under its jurisdiction all the towns from Merindad de Trasmiera to Fuenterrabía, leading to inevitable conflict between the merchants of Burgos and those based on the coast. A dispute between the two communities arose as a result of the refusal of the merchants of Cantabria to subordinate their interests to those of the merchants of Burgos, while the latter attempted to avoid dependence on the shipowners of the coast who controlled the trade in wool to Flanders. In Bilbao, the most important port on the Bay of Biscay at the end of the fifteenth century, the network of interests, made up of the council, the fraternity of merchants and the shipowners of Santiago, set up the *Nación de la Costa de España* in 1489 and began to work together to establish their own *consulado*, the Universidad de Mercaderes de Bilbao, similar to that of Burgos, with the aim of controlling goods passing through the port. In 1495, the Catholic Monarchs exempted the Lordship of Biscay from the jurisdiction of the Consulado de Burgos, and in 1499 areas of influence were delimited, assigning the four coastal towns plus Logroño, Nájera and Medina de Pomar to the Consulado de Burgos, while Biscay Guipúzcoa and Álava were assigned to the Universidad de Mercaderes de Bilbao. A few years later, on 22 June 1511, Queen Joanna granted the establishment of the Consulado de Bilbao, which henceforth enjoyed the same rights as that of Burgos.

During the era of Castilian expansion in northern Europe from the mid-fourteenth century, monarchs turned their eyes towards the African coast and the Atlantic islands, although no expeditions took place until the end of the century. The rivalry between Castile and Portugal over the Canary Islands was not settled until 1454, when the two kingdoms agreed to establish spheres of influence, placing the archipelago in the orbit of the former, though the conquest of the islands of Gran Canaria, Tenerife and Las Palmas was not carried out until the reign of the Catholic Monarchs. The papal bull *Romanus Pontifex* promulgated by Nicholas V on 8 January 1455 left European expansion south of Cape Bojador exclusively in the hands of Portugal while the issue of the Canaries was resolved by the treaty of Alcaçovas of 1479, according to which Castile could explore and conquer territories north of a parallel set at the latitude of the islands while the Portuguese were given free rein south of it, which provided the conditions for the discovery of the passage to India.

4.5 Conclusion

In conclusion, despite the homogenizing role of the monarchies of the Iberian Peninsula and the fact that their economies followed a similar pattern of development, the kingdoms cannot be analysed as a homogeneous economic unit since their individual patterns of economic development differed due to the influence of foreign, regional and local agents, ranging from the colonies and mercantile companies, merchant-bankers and large landowners (the military orders, the Church and the nobility), to the urban elites that controlled the policies of urban local governments. All these players were involved in the formulation and implementation of the economic policies of kings, which formed the basis of the diverse range of Crown economic policies. Thus, the results of the economic policy of each peninsular monarchy were different in scope, despite the fact that the political powers in each territory sought to homogenize and favour economic relations in the Iberian Peninsula through monetary, commercial and fiscal policy. Even within each territory, change was uneven, as is evident in Aragon, where within the Catalan sphere the economy developed and the difficulties of the crisis of the fourteenth century were alleviated to an extent. The Catalan civil war of 1462 brought a setback, the city of Valencia seizing the advantage to become the financial and mercantile centre of the kingdom of Aragon, spurred on by the close relations it enjoyed with the main mercantile centres of Italy and Castile. As for Castile itself, due to its great territorial extension, some regions that had close links with the exterior were more prosperous than other more isolated regions. Castilian economic policy was based on support for the export of agricultural products and livestock, as well as support for the owners of land and livestock, who were generally aristocrats and important Castilian and foreign merchants, which led to the emergence of an economic policy that derived from the increased availability of gold, stimulated international trade and provided kings with a greater degree of autonomy in relation to the nobility. Meanwhile, the Kingdom of Portugal was deeply committed to the exploration and consolidation of new maritime routes and overseas markets, thus laying the foundations of a solid economy.

5

Money, Credit and Banking, 1000–1500

DAVID CARVAJAL, ANTÓNIO HENRIQUES AND PERE VERDÉS

5.1 Introduction

Throughout the Iberian Peninsula, the period from 1000 to 1500 saw profound transformations as monetary systems were renewed and credit markets emerged. These markets were underpinned by specialized financial agents who dealt with increasingly sophisticated contracts, institutions and instruments. The emergence of monetary systems, credit markets and specialized agents were complex and multifaceted processes that cannot be studied without close consideration of cultural and political factors. Also, these developments did not proceed at the same pace in all peninsular realms and did not lead to the same results everywhere.

This analysis benefits from distinguishing two main issues: money and coinage, on the one hand, and credit on the other. To some extent this is both a logical and a chronological sequence: the formation of credible monetary systems can be seen as a precondition for a credit market. The stable and intense interaction between economic agents typically stimulates their specialization.

These two issues naturally cannot be fully understood without reference to the wider European and Mediterranean context. It should also be added that the evolution of coinage, credit and banking in the peninsula during the five centuries from 1000 to 1500 does not lend itself easily to a synthetic, unified perspective. Apart from the difficulties created by such a long time span, constructing such a perspective requires facing four challenges.

A very important challenge is that the timing of the major changes in coinage, on one side, and credit and banking, on the other, did not coincide. Although, as we will show, there was an interaction between these dimensions, they were strongly influenced by mutually independent forces, which in turn vary from state to state. Monetary issues were affected by the availability of metals and by the political and constitutional tussle regarding debasement and minting rights. On the other hand, credit and banking were conditioned by usury laws and by the changing strength of the great players in this market, that is, the institutions and social groups devoted to credit.

The political fragmentation of the peninsula during this period also constitutes a considerable challenge. The different, and competing, polities did not always tread the same paths in terms of coinage and finances. From the outset, there is the great divide between the Islamic and Christian sides of the peninsula. Within each of these two cultures, there were important political and institutional fault-lines. The political and territorial fragmentation had a decisive impact in the financial and monetary histories of these kingdoms, which did not attain uniformity in any given moment.

A third major challenge is the nature and the spread of the available sources. As we will see, sources for the study of Muslim coinage, credit and banking are considerably scarcer than those available for the Christian kingdoms. Archaeological research has been very important for the study of the Andalusian coinage, whereas the studies on credit and banking are buttressed on the surviving collections of Islamic rulings. The history of coinage and credit in the Christian kingdoms before the thirteenth century relies on such sources, but after this period the fiscal and notarial sources provide the foundations for a far more thorough analysis. On account of the exceptional wealth of its archival sources for the thirteenth and fourteenth centuries, the studies dedicated to the Crown of Aragon are particularly detailed. These circumstances dictate that it is possible to provide far less information on the Muslim states than on their Christian counterparts and, among these, on Aragon.

The shortcomings of the sources create yet another major obstacle in the form of limitations for comparative quantitative history. The available literature does not allow us to know, for instance, mint outputs for the different monarchies. It is not even possible to estimate the number of mints that were active at any point during the five centuries presented here. Also, the comparative studies on interest rates face the unevenness of the sources and the complexities of the different institutions. For instance, in the Crown of Aragon, where sources are relatively abundant, it is possible to estimate the interest rates charged to the sovereign in perpetuities and life annuities, but there is little research on the private market.

Despite these limitations, it is nevertheless possible to portray the evolution of the peninsular money, credit and banking issues during the epoch considered as well as pointing out the broad trends and the main differences between al-Andalus and the Christian territories, and within the various kingdoms, across five centuries.

5.2 Coinage and Monetary Systems

After the fall of the Roman Empire, the use of coins and the development of the monetary systems in the peninsula were hampered by the political crisis and economic frailty of a region in conflict, with one exception – al-Andalus.

The eleventh century saw the re-emergence of coinage as a means of payment across the Christian lands while the monetary system survived the dissolution of the Caliphate of Córdoba on the Muslim side. Despite political fragmentation, the existence of means of payment drove a lively economy that went considerably beyond subsistence, with a seemingly important regional and even peninsular trade. Overall, and up until the fifteenth century, this period saw the progressive consolidation of different monetary systems, that is, the articulation of means of payment and the agents who controlled the rules regarding the issue and circulation of money.

Although many peninsular monetary systems were ultimately rooted in the Roman origin and in the coinages struck by the Germanic rulers (Swabians, Visigoths, etc.), by 1000 the two main traditions were the Carolingian and the Muslim. In the former, widely spread in the Christian polities, coinages followed the standard set by Charlemagne and his successors, in which silver *denarii* and bullion coinage dominated circulation. Most of the peninsula, however, inherited the stable and relatively homogeneous bimetallic monetary system boosted by the caliphate of Córdoba which subsisted long after its end.

Against a backdrop of political and legal change and diversity, the period that goes from the late eleventh century until the year 1500 saw the emergence and consolidation of five monetary systems, each with its own specific features and trajectory: the Muslim, the Aragonese, the Navarre, the Castilian-Leonese and the Portuguese. It is hard to claim that all Iberian rulers intentionally sought to create stable monetary systems; it seems more likely that the monetary systems were instead the result of a process of adaptation to political and economic changes (Riera, 2000).

One of the main issues for the Iberian monetary systems was the availability of precious metals. Periodic shortages limited the issue of coinage and led to the modification of the existing types and/or fineness of the coins. These phases also stimulated stopgap remedies like recoinage or procuring precious metals from other territories. On the other hand, the Iberian realms also enjoyed favourable periods, in which precious metals flowed to the peninsula from different sources. Silver, which was widely available in eleventh to thirteenth century Europe, arrived from the north of the peninsula, thus benefitting the monetary systems tied to the Carolingian world. After this period, silver became scarcer relative to its demand and the debasement of bullion became more frequent. Due to its strategic position, Iberia played a role as the linchpin between Europe and the non-European sources of precious metals, especially sub-Saharan Africa. From the eleventh century onwards, African gold flowed to the peninsular *taifa* kingdoms via the Almoravid and Almohad empires and, through tribute, plunder and trade, some of it streamed northwards to Castile and León, and Portugal, where the Muslim gold coins circulated and were even adopted as money of account. Finally, Portuguese Atlantic navigation found the sources of West African gold and integrated them with the European economy. Muslim gold coins also circulated in Aragon but were eventually replaced by the *florin* during its heyday, that is, when African and Hungarian gold irrigated the Mediterranean and late medieval Europe (Spufford, 1988).

5.2.1 The Monetary System of Al-Andalus

The monetary system of al-Andalus inherited the Byzantine traditions. For centuries, the Ummayad caliphs of Córdoba minted stable gold (*dinar*) and especially silver (*dirham*) coinages, following older imperial models. The *dinar* had about 4 grams of gold (with a fineness of 90%) and the *dirham* had 3 grams of silver with a fineness of 80%. As such, cities under Islamic domination enjoyed a higher degree of monetization than the Christian lands. Both coinages were geared towards a functioning fiscal system, in which coin was used for receiving tributes and disbursing wages, mostly military but also administrative. The high value of these coinages and the demand for small change led to the issuing of coins with lower denominations or to the splitting of existing coins into smaller parts, which acted as fractions of the monetary unit. At a lower level, we find fiduciary copper coins (*fals*), which were well-suited for the needs of everyday trade and of the local fairs and markets (Canto, 2012). Despite the overall stability of the Muslim monetary system in comparison with its Christian counterparts, the uses and the physical dimensions of the circulating gold *dinars* were affected by the political upheaval that followed the fragmentation of the Ummayad Caliphate of Córdoba in 1031.

In the early stages of the complex political map born out of the fragmentation of the Caliphate, the caliphal currency continued to circulate and only in few cases, such as the *taifa* of Málaga, struck new coins. Eventually, the new *taifa* rulers claimed minting prerogatives, which they saw as a source of legitimacy for their newly acquired power. The ensuing result was the growing variety of coin types and the popping up of new mints or *cecas* (Doménech-Belda, 2016). From the late eleventh century the new coinages were of inferior quality, especially the *dirham*, which underwent a drastic reduction in its fineness (in some cases down to 30% silver). The *dinar* and its fractions kept their importance and monies of account, although the *parias* collected by the Christian kingdoms drained this coinage leading to its scarcity. The Almoravids resumed the minting of this coin until the arrival of the Almohads in the middle of the twelfth century. This dynasty imposed a new metrology, temporarily lowering the weight of the golden *dinar* from 4.25 down to 2.27 grams of fine gold and further debased the *dirham*.

After this eventful period, the foundation of the Nasrid kingdom of Granada in 1238 meant a lasting return to the old models. The early Nasrid monarchs issued golden *dinars* – and their submultiples – each weighting 4.66 grams with a 972‰ fineness of 23.3 carats, as well as *dirhams* with 1.51 grams and a roughly similar fineness. From then and until their final defeat in 1492, its rulers used their full control over the mint to gradually debase their currency (Canto, 2012).

5.2.2 Control of Monetary Systems and Monetary Policy

The control of the Iberian monetary systems, that is, the minting rights, was in the hands of the highest political authority, whether they were kings, sultans or caliphs. During the eleventh and twelfth centuries, the *taifa* rulers claimed this right, which had not been challenged during the time of the Caliphate. Nonetheless, their doubtful legitimacy caused no small measure of instability, which was reflected in small issuances, with the exception of those by the *taifas* of Málaga and Algeciras. Unlike the Almoravids, the Almohad rulers went on to seize the control of minting. Thusly, *taifas* like the Murcia *taifa* achieved a stability that would become a staple of the *nasri* polities from the thirteenth century up until 1492. On their part, the Christian kings sought to recover the minting prerogative of the Visigoth times, although with varying results. By means of the law, they claimed the power to mint and change the type, the value and the 'titre'. Nevertheless, the monarchs did not always retain an effective control over the monetary systems: jurisdictional diversity, the demand for wider supply of money and the profits of seigniorage led to a tug-of-war between the lords and the monarchy, which was leveraging its increasing strength to recover its original prerogative.

The evolution of the monetary system of the Crown of Aragon reflected its territorial diversity and the constitutional limits that bounded royal authority. After the Carolingian period, the right to mint was distributed among different authorities (king, counts, bishops, seignorial lords) which, together, would form the future crown. Regardless, during the twelfth century, the new monarchy acquired full control over the Aragonese currency (*jaquesa*) and over that of Barcelona. In the territories wrested from the Moors, like Valencia and Mallorca, during the thirteenth century, the control was even more stringent (Crusafont, 2015). The frequent debasements and changes by tale are a clear example of the pre-eminence of the monarchy. Like its peninsular counterparts, the Crown of Aragon exacted taxes known as *monedajes*, which were paid to the king as a compensation for not debasing. Nevertheless, the growing needs of the monarch forced him to cede the control of the mint to the estates of Aragon (1236) and then to the municipality of Barcelona (1256) (Feliu Monfort, 2014; Torró, 2014). Until the end of the fifteenth century, under Fernando II, the repeated intents of the monarchy to recover its prerogatives had limited and uneven results. The only area in which the monarchy kept its pre-eminence was the gold coin (the *florin*). In spite of this, the result of this situation was monetary stability imposed by the *Cortes* of Aragon and, most of all, by the *Consell de Cent* of Barcelona, with positive results but, as we will see in Section 5.2.4, also with some negative consequences (Feliu Monfort, 2016b).

Unlike Aragon, in Castile and León, Navarre and Portugal, the monarchy gradually attained full control of the monetary system. In an initial stage, from the eleventh to the twelfth centuries, the kings of Castile and León granted minting rights to private parties like the Cathedral of Santiago de Compostela and some cities, with the goal of increasing the money in circulation. During these early centuries, the main power players in Castilian politics (monarch, church, nobility and municipalities) attempted to profit from the minting, a circumstance that invalidates any talk of a common monetary policy. Nevertheless, from the reign of Alfonso VII (1126–1157) onwards, the monarchy slowly but surely reclaimed this right. A clear example thereof is the fact that from 1202 onwards Castilian and Leonese kings collected the *moneda forera*, a tax that was originally a compensation for not changing the value of circulating coinages.

The consolidation of royal power under Alfonso X (1252–1284) was supported by the enactment of laws pertaining to Castilian coinage, as occurred in the *Las Partidas* and in the books of the *Cortes*, an institution that allowed the municipalities to defend their monetary interests vis-à-vis the Crown. From then, despite clashes with the nobility and the municipalities, we can speak of a veritable monetary policy under the control of the monarch (MacKay, 1981; Ladero, 1988a; Castán, 2000), which culminated in the time of the Catholic Kings. The goals of Castilian monetary policy, which had often to be negotiated with the *Cortes* and others, balanced between the defence of the royal interest, which meant the accumulation of resources to finance military expenditure, and the demands created by the economic life of the kingdom. Kings like Sancho IV, Enrique II, III and IV were all very interventive and repeatedly resorted to three devices: recoinage, debasement or change of the coins' physical characteristics, and the introduction of new types (Roma, 2000).

In Portugal, as in the remaining peninsular realms, the firm grip on minting by the Crown was a source of instability for the markets. Unlike other European countries, the Portuguese kings did not have to fight with feudal lords for centralizing minting powers. In Portugal, all the households became liable to a tax in exchange for keeping the weight and fineness of coinage each seven years, not unlike the *moneda forera* of Castile and León. The monarchy resorted to its minting powers and issued gold coinage along the features of the *dinar*, as this coin was used both as a means of payment and as a money off account. For the monarchy, debasements were first seen as a handy alternative to creating demanding fiscal systems. Under Afonso III (1248–1279), a century of stability began as the political problems with the manipulation of coinage became evident and the monarchy started to build its own domain state. As wars raged on, from 1369 onwards the development of trade and investment was often disrupted by severe devaluations and other episodes of monetary mischief. Eventually, negotiation between these parts settled in moderate tax demands in exchange for stable coinage.

There were differences between the crowns under study. We argue that during this period it is possible to contrast Castile, on the one hand, and Aragon, on the other. The latter developed a far more complex system in which the *Cortes* retained a greater say in decision making. In the long term, the Aragonese coinage also proved more stable. The Castilians, Portuguese and Navarrese, however, had more centralized systems and, as a consequence, their currency underwent periods of severe debasement from the end of the fourteenth century until the middle decades of the fifteenth century, when the former two countries successfully reformed their monetary systems.

5.2.3 The Monetary Systems of the Christian Kingdoms

For five centuries, the different monetary systems built by the Christian polities were conditioned by their main political, geographical and economic situations. Whereas the Crown of Aragon did not centralize the issue of coins and had a strong foreign influence on account of its Mediterranean position and constitutional structure, in Castile and León and Portugal stronger central powers exerted their minting prerogatives and broke with earlier Muslim influences.

5.2.3.1 The Crown of Aragon

The Aragonese monetary systems were derived from the Carolingian model. As elsewhere in Europe, the accounting system was based on the *libra*, which was worth 20 *sueldos*, which in turn was equal to 12 *dineros*. The different polities that made up the Crown of Aragon followed considerably different trajectories. Nevertheless, it is possible to pinpoint some common features. First, all these systems were monometallic and, from the eleventh century, the Aragonese polities minted bullion *dineros*. As a large quantity of Andalusian gold coins (*mancusos* and *morabatines*) were in circulation in the twelfth century, some rulers imitated the model and used it as a money of account in the payment of land rents and some important transactions. Along with the local currency, Andalusian silver coins and Castilian or Leonese *morabatines alfonsinos* also circulated (Crusafont, 2015).

The thirteenth century saw the reduction of the circulation of gold coinage, which was progressively replaced by massive issues of bullion. Initially, bullion appeared in the form of a *dinero* called *de cuaterno* (with a silver content of about one-third) in both the Barcelona-influenced area and Aragon proper. After some markedly inferior issues of *quaternos*, struck for paying debts, the Crown created a *dinero* called *de terno* (with 25% silver content), which, as happened with the *dinero de cuaterno*, was issued in different types in Aragon (1234), Valencia (1247) and Barcelona (1256).

As in many other territories, in Catalonia by the late thirteenth century the demand for larger value coins for transactions led to the creation of the *croat*, also known as the *dinero barcelonés* (1285). This coin also circulated in the Kingdom of Valencia until 1393 (when this polity started to struck its own silver coinage) and in the continental territories of the Kingdom of Mallorca. In 1300, a peculiar, French-influenced system monetary emerged in this insular territory of realm with bullion, silver and gold coins. On the other hand, Aragon never minted silver *dineros* or gold coins and as such the monetary system remained based upon the *dinero de terno*, until the end of the fifteenth century. As happened with bullion coins, the different silver species were struck with different designs but with the same denomination, which made their exchange easier (Feliu Monfort, 2014; Torró, 2014).

The minting of gold coin took longer than in most European states. In 1346, Pedro 'the Ceremonious' (1336–1387) minted the Aragonese *florin*, inspired by the Florentine coinage. This coin went on to become commonly used throughout all territories of the Crown and also in Castile and Navarre, until the middle of the fifteenth century. The decadence of the Florentine coinage vis-à-vis the Venetian *ducato* and the Portuguese *cruzado* led to the minting of the *pacífico* (modelled upon the Portuguese *cruzado*) by Pedro de Portugal and the *ducado* by his opponent Juan II (an imitation of the Venetian *ducato*) during the Catalan Civil War of 1467.

The system was reformed in 1493 by Fernando II (1479–1516) who debased the *dinero de terno*, reducing its silver content to 60% of its previous state, and issued a new golden coin, the *principado*, which eventually became known as the *ducado*, after its original Venetian model. This debasement was meant as a solution to the shortages of bullion, which had been produced in small quantities from the late fourteenth century. This was due to the low profitability of minting, due to its high silver content. This explains the entry of foreign bullion in the lands of the Crown, which is shown by the wide circulation of foreign species as well as local copper currencies (Feliu Monfort, 2014).

5.2.3.2 Castile and León

Castile and León took the first steps towards a monetary system of its own in the late eleventh century, discarding the earlier Carolingian models. The new system drew from two main inspirations: contemporary France with its reliance on bullion and al-Andalus with its strong gold and silver coinages. The issue of *dineros*, which initially had a high content of silver but were later debased, started in the year 1087 (Roma, 2000). Despite their separation between 1157 and 1230, Castile and León kept parallel monetary systems. During this phase, the exaction of *parias* from the Muslim *taifa* rulers favoured the circulation of Muslim currency in the two realms. As such, the Castilian-Leonese monetary system incorporated some Muslim features and were essentially bimetallic and had their own gold coinage. The crucial innovation took place between 1172 and 1177, when the Castilian *maravedí* was minted, following the Muslim *morabetino*. Although its coinage ceased in the first half of the thirteenth century, the *maravedí* stuck as a money of account.

Alfonso X (1252-1284) sought to unify the different monetary systems within Castile and León and consolidate the minting of new types of coinage, like the golden *dobla*. However, the growing demand for money and the political instability during the second half of the thirteenth century increased the number and variety of coinages in circulation, especially those of lower quality and value. This, in turn, generated a rise in prices and wide discontent among the population and the most powerful sectors, namely the nobility and the clergy (Castán, 2000).

The scarcity of precious metals and the complexity of the monetary system led to further reforms in the reign of Alfonso XI (1312-1350). The latter's successor, Pedro I (1350-1369), attempted to stabilize the system by creating a new silver coin, the *real*, but the political instability of his reign and the Civil War (1366-1369) against his brother Enrique II aggravated this uncertainty (Roma, 2000). In the transition from the late fourteenth to the early fifteenth centuries, Castilian demand for money was growing at a fast pace, due to the needs of a growing economy that was increasingly connected to the European markets. Also, the Castilian monarchs were hard-pressed for means of payment in order to pay their debts and finance new military projects. As usual, the solution was to strike low-quality coins and further debase the currencies, contributing to instability and conflict, like the anti-Jewish violence of 1391 (Ladero, 1988a).

Juan II (1406-1454) tried also to stabilize the Castilian monetary system. In order to achieve this goal, he issued a new, lighter golden coin called the *dobla de la banda*, which represented an approximation to European models like the *florin* or the *ducado*, but kept the silver content of the silver *real*. Nevertheless, under his successor Enrique IV (1454-1474) further debasements took place, as well as numerous changes in the types and value of existing coins (MacKay, 1981), as occurred with the new gold coins: the *enriques* and later the *enriques nuevos* or *castellanos*. Given an apparent impossibility of minting further strong gold and silver coins, the monarchs resorted to excessive coining of bullion. By 1470, the situation was clearly untenable, and the monarchy tried to eliminate bullion and foster the minting of gold and silver. While urgent and widely demanded, broader monetary reform had to wait until 1497, when Isabel I reorganized the entire system (de Francisco, 1999). Her objective was to stabilize the issuing of money, which was attained by restricting the number of mints, rigorously setting the fineness of the coinage and using a stable system of denominations: bullion (*moneda blanca*), silver (*real*) and gold (*excelente*), with the latter following the model of the *ducado*. This reform finally endowed Castile with a three-centuries-old aspiration: monetary stability (Ladero, 1988a).

5.2.3.3 Portugal

The Portuguese monetary system emerged out of two interrelated processes: the *Reconquista* and the consolidation of Portuguese independence. By 1140, before the emergence of the Portuguese monarchy, monetization was far from complete, and the circulation of coins was dominated by Almoravid and Castilian *morabitinos*. By the 1260s, monetization was complete, and the use of Portuguese coinage was enforced, with bullion and gold coinages circulating according to parities set by the state. By then, Portuguese coinage was geared to the European, silver-dominated markets, wherefrom the system took its money of account: the *libra* (Marques, 1996).

Up to the middle of the twelfth century, the north-west of the peninsula underwent a severe shortage of currency. The emergence of a monarchy autonomous to the western shores of the peninsula was a game-changer in monetization, as in many other aspects. The kings of Portugal duly claimed as theirs the prerogative to mint coins. In fact, at least nine issues of bullion pence (*dinheiros*) are attributed to Afonso I (1140–1185). The plunder, the ransoms and the *párias* obtained by the Portuguese kings in the twelfth century contributed to a steady northward inflow of metals and strong coinages (Henriques, 2008). Tellingly, the money used as a money of account throughout the country until the middle of the thirteenth century was the *morabitino*.

In Portugal, like in the neighbouring kingdoms, the intrinsic value of the circulating coinage became depleted. The bimetallic system was unstable until it ended in 1261. Afonso III issued a new type of *dinheiro* with higher metallic content and simultaneously decrying the value of the current *dinheiros*. In 1261, the monarch had to solemnly swear an oath that he would not change coinage ever again and that the new *dinheiro* coins he issued had to circulate by tale (of 1.3 *dinheiros*), leaving the old *dinheiro* coinage denominated as 1 *dinheiro*. Under the terms of the *Juramentum super Facto Monete* sworn by King Afonso III in 1261, not only had the fineness of the coinage to be kept (one *dinheiro novo* had 0.06 grams of silver) but also the quantity the money issued was limited (Henriques, 2020: 109). From that date until 1369, the king of Portugal operated under strict constitutional limits that forbade the monarch from significantly changing the money supply in the economy. Prices did rise after then but at moderate rates.

After the end of a long century in which the *libra* retained its metallic value, the Wars with Castile triggered violent devaluations of the currency. In 1369 Fernando I broke the monetary constitution and minted a whole new system of coins (*barbuda, pilarte, coroado*) (Marques, 1996). The effect of these changes was disruptive, at the exchange counters the new Portuguese money was worth one-third of its previous value (Farelo, 2018). The monarch summoned the

Cortes in 1371 and 1372 and agreed to adjust the tales of the new coins to the old silver content of the Portuguese *libra*. In 1368, one *libra* contained nearly 12 grams of silver, whereas in the following year it was only worth 1.08 grams (Marques, 1996).

In the fifteenth century, rents were often expressed in kind or in foreign strong coinages: *florins* from Florence, *doblas* (Moorish and Castilian), *ducati* and *écus à la couronne* were commonly used as currency or as money of account. It was at this point that the *real* emerged as the new money of account in the first regnal year of João I (1385). The *real* took a long time to attain stability. Scarcity of metals, opportunism on behalf of the king and, perhaps, the influence of merchants dealing with foreign trade contributed to further debasements. João I made at least two reforms aimed at monetary stability in 1398 and 1407, while his son Duarte I (1433–1438) tried in 1435 to create a new, monometallic silver system, anchored in a *leal*. However, stability would come later, namely when the caravels started to bring African gold to the royal mint. This led to the issuance of a stable gold coinage: the *cruzado* in 1457, which copied the Venetian *ducato*. This coin (known in Europe as 'Portuguese') was the pinnacle of a system comprising the *real* and large amounts of copper species (*ceitis* or *reais pretos*). A few decades later, in 1485, João II (1480–1495) ordered a general recoinage with the likely aim of mopping up earlier species that had been issued throughout the century (*chinfrão*, *cotrim*, *espadim*). Some defensive devaluations notwithstanding, in the second half of the fifteenth century the intrinsic value of the Portuguese currency stabilized (Marques, 1996). Essentially, landlords, lenders and others counted on a functional monetary unit that broadly conformed to their expectations (Henriques, 2019).

5.2.3.4 Navarre

Changes in the monetary system of the Kingdom of Navarre were largely determined by what happened in its larger neighbours: Castile, Aragon and France. Under the reign of Sancho Ramírez (1076–1094), the mint of Jaca became active and it struck the golden *mancusos* (with a weight of 3.5 grams), which followed the *morabetino* of the *taifa* Kingdom of Zaragoza, and the *dineros jaqueses*. The influence of the Muslim monetary systems, whose *morabetino* circulated in Navarre, was decisive until the mid-twelfth century. However, increasing contacts with French lands led to an inflow of silver. As such, in the time of Sancho VI, new types of *dineros* (*navarros* and later *sanchetes*) and *óbolos* were struck. The tensions over recoinage and the associated tax between the monarch and the towns led to the latter being granted minting rights. Accordingly, the town started to issue their own *dineros torneses* (following French models), which in turn coexisted with the *sanchetes*, keeping a rate of exchange of 14/12 in the early twelfth century.

Due to the military expenditure of the Capet monarchs and other factors, Navarre underwent a period of money shortage and growing debt between 1330 and 1428. This situation led to the minting of false coins, the emergence of new monetary types and the creation of small change, as demanded by the market. By 1336, the circulation of the Castilian gold coin decayed vis-a-vis the Aragonese *florin* and French *écu*. New *dineros carlines* ('black' or 'white' according to the fineness) minted by 1330 replaced the *sanchetes*. In that period, Navarre issued for the first time a large money of account (the *gros*), which was a poor imitation of the French *gros tournés* and it was valued at 1 *sueldo* or 12 *carlines* (Carrasco, 2009).

In the second half of the fourteenth century, the Navarrese monetary system was centred on a gold coin (whose name is uncertain, but it had similar metrics to those of its neighbours), the silver *gros tornés* and three types of bullion: *dineros torneses chicos* or *cornados*, *dineros carlines negros* and *meajas* or *medios dineros*. Nevertheless, late in the fourteenth century, the shortage of silver, the strong demand for a wider money supply and the king's spending led to further issues of lower-value silver coins. Thus, debasements led to the flooding of Navarre by lowly bullion, and as such after the large great issue of 1393, there would be no other until 1428. From then, and until the end of the century, the situation of the Navarrese monetary system was chaotic. Attempts to stabilize the system by eliminating bullion failed on account of the war with Castile and metal shortages. Finally, the minting of the golden *escudo* (with 22.75 carats) and the silver *gros* (valued at 72 *groses* for each *castellano* and 36 for each Aragonese *florin*) between 1492 and 1496 stabilized the situation, although earlier *reales* of gold and silver and their divisors continued. The fifteenth century was a time of monetary shortage (Carrasco, 2000), which certainly favoured the use of other means of payment.

5.2.4 Problems and Shortcomings: Variety, Shortage, Debasement and Falsification

At some point, the Iberian monetary systems faced one or all of the following four main problems: the confusing variety of currencies resulting from an unstable monetary policy; the progressive debasement as a response to the scarcity of precious metals and the need for increasing the money supply; the falsification of coinage during times of shortage; and, lastly, the outflow of precious metals to other European regions on account of the high metal content of some coinages.

Not only were the Iberian systems monetary very complex, but they each contained many different types of coins. Despite the resistance of lords and urban elites, debasements were a policy tool increasingly used by the kings, who also regarded coinage as a propaganda vehicle. Frequent changes in typology were compounded by changes in design and by a long-term trend of debasement. Nonetheless, each kingdom has some distinctive traits. Thus, from the thirteenth century onward the political ascendancy of the nobility and towns over the kings of Aragon, like in Portugal, instilled stability in the monetary system and protected the kingdom from the debasement that ravaged Castile and France. The steadiness of the money favoured the economic development of the Crown of Aragon, but the rigidity of the authorities in Barcelona and the representative assemblies of the different realms also prevented the Aragonese currency from adapting to the changes in the European market. In a context of widespread devaluation, this fact ended up causing major problems from the late fourteenth century onward, as a consequence of the inconsistency between the value of the bullion *dinero* and the *croat* with its high silver content. In Aragon, bullion coins ceased to be coined in 1381 for their lack of profitability, while the silver *croats* started to disappear from circulation, as they were hoarded or, together with the *florins*, exported. The authorities attempted to attenuate the scarcity of divisional money and the invasion of overvalued foreign currencies (most of all Castilian *blancas* and French *écus*), but the problems persisted, due to the conservatism of the urban oligarchies. The relative stability introduced by this readjustment was short-lived because of the Catalan Civil War (1462–1472), whose effects were felt until the monetary reform of 1493 (Crusafont, 2015; Feliu Monfort, 2016b).

In Castile and León, the political troubles, the pressing need for revenue and the silver famine led the monarchy to nearly constant recoinages. The problems caused by the disorderly minting of low-grade coin were especially acute during the reigns of Alfonso X and Sancho IV (1252–1295), as well as Juan II and Enrique IV (fifteenth century). This devaluation affected mainly the bullion, with the gold coins (*morabetinos, doblas, doblas de la banda, enriques, castellanos* and *excelentes*) keeping their stability, a situation that led to outflows of Castilian coinage. In spite of what the penalties and Castilian laws (namely, in the *Partidas* and in various statutes approved in *Cortes*), currency outflows did not stop and became a serious problem in the transition from the fourteenth to the fifteenth century, when Castilian international trade was flourishing. Finally, the falsification of coins was another worrisome issue. The scarcity of coins and the need for means of payment tempted many to the forgery of coins. Because of the well-known negative effects of introducing inferior coinage on the circulating money, new laws issued by the rulers severely condemned this practice (Sáinz, 1994). Nevertheless, counterfeiting was especially intense during the fifteenth century, at a time when bullion flooded the Castilian economy.

The intensity of these same practices varied in the remaining peninsular kingdoms. The peninsular monetary systems successfully transitioned to centralized models that were well-articulated with their European counterparts. Nonetheless, the incapacity to accommodate late medieval economic growth and the stringent demand for money on behalf of kings, merchants and other agents stimulated the development of new means of payment and, thus, credit.

5.3 Credit and Banking

As in other places of the European West, in the twelfth and thirteenth centuries, economic growth in the peninsular kingdoms compounded by all issues related to the shaping of monetary systems led to a demand for other credit-based means of payment. Thus far credit had been reduced to small operations on a local level (Postan, 1973). With this backdrop, credit became more and more important and, according to available sources, we see it spread out over all Christian polities. While the nature of the available sources does not allow us to define exact timings, volumes or many of its traits, there is also enough documentation for al-Andalus to testify to financial operations.

In spite of it not being a response to a single intellectual tradition, concerns over usury are common to the Christian and Muslim polities. As is common knowledge, usury (*riba*) was banned in the Muslim world, especially in the areas with a *maliki* legal background, like al-Andalus. There are many hints, however, that, under the guise of various tricks, interest-bearing loans were present in Andalusian society. As for the Christian world, the doctrine was stated unambiguously in the Council of Lateran in 1215, building upon the Patristic ideas of good will, which seamlessly converged with Roman law and Biblical norms. Loans should not generate any reward as they had to be *gratis et pro amore*. Twelfth and thirteenth century preachers aimed their criticism at the lenders whom they describe as preying upon the vulnerable poor. As in other areas of the European West, the condemnation of interest had one important consequence in terms of credit agents: it paved the way for the Jewish minorities to act as financiers. Regardless, many of these problems were relegated to the theoretical plane, as loans, consumer credit or the sale of public debt became everyday affairs (Munro, 2013).

As a result of this credit expansion, an innovative financial system emerged and grew in complexity over time. As stated before, in the beginning Jews specialized in operations like loans, but soon other financing agents came to the fore, in both the Christian and Muslim worlds. As we will demonstrate, moneychangers played an increasingly important role and went from mere exchangers of currency to bankers. Merchants, local and foreign, also diversified their portfolios to offer lucrative financing services. Generally, most of the Iberian medieval society, including the various political powers that acted as catalysts for all this financial development, ended up taking part in credit activities.

5.3.1 Credit and Banking in Al-Andalus

Even if only a limited number of sources attest to the daily use of credit, its existence and expansion in al-Andalus from early times can be inferred from the various references in notarial formulas, from the treatises of *hisba* and from the legal doctrine on usury (Guichard & Legardère, 1990). Contemporary documents created by the issuance of credit in other Muslim territories of the Mediterranean allows us to also infer the existence of similar practices in the Iberian Peninsula, especially considering the trade relations existing between those territories (Goitein, 1967). Yet another source that bears witness to regular credit operations in the Muslim areas are the documents generated by Christian traders who, in the late Middle Ages, traded in the Kingdom of Granada. Beyond attesting to its existence, it is hard to establish the financial evolution in al-Andalus during the period we analyse. However, we can safely assume that the Muslim system developed earlier than the Christian one and not all possible interactions between both worlds have been the subject of study.

Under the legal doctrine at the time, we initially find that loans were posing as agricultural or cattle-producing business partnerships, as shown by the discussions between *faqihs* on the division of tasks and benefits among the partners. The generalized development of trade all over the Mediterranean during the eleventh and twelfth centuries increased the need for credit as well as for various transactions to conceal interest-generating credit. Often these transactions themselves hid small personal loans, meant to cover different needs, like the purchase of food, clothing or sundry, unforeseen issues. Some donations, deposits or other seemingly free legal acts served the same function. Lastly, we can surmise that the Andalusian rulers resorted to credit from early times in order to meet the demands of expensive military campaigns, support envoys or face other governmental needs.

Many signs point to the fact that many of the larger loans to rulers were made in a courtly context by Jews, who were then the experts in fiscal and financial matters. Similarly, there is clear evidence of loans of agricultural, commercial or personal nature granted by this *dhimmi* minority even if experts warn against speaking of the stereotype of the Jewish loan shark. Laws make no direct reference to financial transactions with the *harbi*, but in the late Middle Ages we can infer these actions from the context of international trade. Regarding the Muslims, we have already stressed that neither usury (*riba*) nor any ploys to practice usury (*hiyal*) were condoned in the Maliki school in al-Andalus. Nevertheless its very existence in the legal doctrine of the time is clear *a contrario* evidence that it was widespread in all layers of the Andalusian society.

There was no shortage of instruments used to skirt the prohibition of usury. We have already mentioned the relevance of different forms of partnerships for sowing, irrigating, co-harvesting or cattle-raising. Other trade mechanisms were frequently documented to cover up interest-generating loans, such as several types of contracts that disguised two transactions into one, such as the *mujatara*. Similar to what happened in the Christian areas, there is also evidence for several types of contracts to disguise loans: interest-free loans, simple loans, gifts, pawns, redeemable loans, sales with advance payment (e.g. of crops), etc., founded on trade partnerships. Lastly, considering the legal sources available, we must recall the existence of contracts geared towards preserving the assets of a debtor or the use of enslaved people as go-betweens to circumvent the prohibition of usury (Hernández, 2011; 2016).

As for banks, some are already mentioned in the eighth century, and some authors speak of the proliferation of moneychangers (*sayarifa*) and banking merchants (*jahbadh*) during the tenth century in the Muslim lands of the Middle East. These exchangers and merchants would exchange and verify currency, recover debts and provide financial services both to private persons and to rulers (Udovitch, 1979). In al-Andalus, there is no direct evidence of this activity, only signs that it did exist in the shape of legal sources regulating interest. In effect, the *Kitab al-Riba* by Ibn-Habib (d. 238 AH/852 CE) presents moneychangers as one of the groups that practiced usury (*riba*). This idea will remain for all the medieval period in the *fiqh* of the Maliki school to the extent that it claimed that one should not accept anything from moneychangers, not even water, or the shade made by the walls of their homes (Hernández, 2011; 2016).

There are several references of various types of credit-related operations associated with usury practiced by Andalusian moneychangers. One can easily guess that the exchange of cash (*sarf*), making the best use of the fluctuations in value of the currency, was one such operation. Regarding this practice, several legal scholars from al-Andalus and North Africa suggested the exchange be according to weight (*muratala*) rather than to the number of coins (Hernández, 2016). On the other hand, the assignment of credit (*hawala*) to bankers or exchangers who practiced usury was also frowned upon. These assignments were particularly useful for long distance trade, like the *suftaya*. Even if there is no mention of it in the *fiqh* of the Maliki school, the *suftaya* is documented by an *ulema* who travelled to al-Andalus carrying this type of letter of credit and 5,000 *dirhams* in cash. Lastly, moneychangers were also barred from acting as intermediaries, from participating in double sales or from conducting advanced sales, etc.

There is usually no mention of who these moneychangers were, but we can infer that there were both Muslim and Jewish ones from a reference made by Ibn 'Abd al-Ra'uf (fourth century AH/tenth century CE) who recommended the prohibition of *dhimmi* to exert that trade (Hernández, 2016). As for the Muslim moneychangers, some historians believe that between the sixth century AH/twelfth century CE they organized some type of professional guild. This is the interpretation made of a reference by Ibn Abdun in the Treatise of *Hisba*, written in Seville near the end of the *taifa* period. This idea, however, is not shared by all authors (García Sanjuan, 1997). Legal Muslim sources make no reference to *harbi* moneychangers, but the Christian ones do track financial activity of Italian merchants-bankers in Nasrid territory. This is the case with the Spinola or Centurione, two Genoese families who, from the late fourteenth century, provided much financial support to Nasrid rulers in exchange for trade advantages and for the power to manage the Crown's resources (Fábregas, 2007).

5.3.2 The Configuration of Credit in the Christian Kingdoms: Institutions and Instruments

The information available on the expansion of credit in the Christian lands, particularly after the thirteenth century is considerably better. Before this period, mentions of credit are generally very limited and we can only document credit activity in some northern regions and always with a local scope. Such is the case of eleventh-century Catalonia, when loans flourished right when the emergence of the feudal market (Bensch, 1995). The first contracts were short-term loans, funded by the pledging of movable assets or real estate worth more than the principal debt. Initially, during the eleventh century, these pledges would be the 'mortgage' (*prenda muerta*), but in the twelfth century the creditor would reap some benefits from the pledge for the duration of the debt (*prenda viva*) (Feliu Monfort, 1992). This is similarly documented in Navarre, where throughout the twelfth century we see the creation of the first rules governing credit contracts in local charters or *cartas pueblas* (Carrasco, 2001). We must lastly mention also the case of León, where there are also early occurrences of loans guaranteed by pledges (of both aforementioned types, *muertas* or *vivas*), usually provided by the church or great landowners (Ladero, 1990–1991).

However, as stated before, it was in the thirteenth century and within the context of economic growth and urban expansion that credit became mainstream in all Christian kingdoms. Accordingly, and assuming that informal credit was an everyday occurrence in the medieval Iberian Peninsula, we must stress that in mid-thirteenth century due to the recovery of Roman Law and Italian influence, credit became fully integrated in many legal systems, like the case with *Las Partidas* in Castile. Here, there types of credit are mentioned, from loans (*mutuum* and *commodatum*), bonds, exchange or deposits. In the late Middle Ages praxis and other Castilian legal documents, such as the *Ordenamientos de Cortes*, incorporated these operations into credit instruments (Carvajal, 2017). But also in Navarre, during the thirteenth century, we see an increase in legislation on both the local and central levels. In the first case, to the provisions in the *fuero de Estella*, we can add those from the charters of Novenera, Tudela, Viguera-Val de Funes or from Pamplona, in the fourteenth century. In a more general manner, during the thirteenth century there is plenty of legislation concerning loans, pawns and other credit-related issues. Legal provisions on these matters did increase during the *amejoramiento* of 1330 and 1418 (Carrasco, 2001; 2019). The legal systems of the different polities of the Crown of Aragon contained many laws on credit.

During the thirteenth century, the goal of many of these provisions was to regulate lending activities, above all establishing a 20% interest rate cap for Jews when Catalonia set also the interest rate for Christians at 12%. Later, in the fourteenth and fifteenth centuries, laws in the Aragonese Crown aimed at regulating the very active market of perpetual and life annuities: *censales muertos* and *violarios* (Feliu Monfort, 1992; García Marsilla, 2002). In closing we have to mention legal provisions published in Portugal during the thirteenth and fourteenth centuries on usury and other credit-related issues (Costa, 1961).

All this regulation also played a relevant role in the spread of credit, as well as institutions like notaries and the various judicial bodies. In effect, the consolidation of notaries has been documented from the thirteenth century onward in all Christian territories, even if we have not been able to find complete notarial registers with credit contracts from such early dates (likely because they were not kept). Only in Catalonia, a place with a distinct record-keeping culture, can we find notarial registers from the thirteenth century onward describing many credit operations. In other polities, like Castile, only in the 1330s do we find the first notarial credit registers, even if notaries had been regulated there from the thirteenth century. References to credit in the fourteenth century are still scarce and only in the following century did Castilian notaries begin keeping regular records of credit instruments.

Navarre deserves a special mention. Again, there is little information on credit to be gleaned from the notary records, as this type of documents is only available for later dates. There is, however, a very important source for studying credit in Navarre in the late Middle Ages: the records sealed with the royal seal containing the notarial contracts (Carrasco, 2019). The royal seal, for which an *ad valorem* fee was paid, endowed the contract with an additional strength for the credit market which, as stated before, also benefited from the existence of different judicial bodies which judged financial litigation. In the particular case of Castile, courts played a key role and the courts – both local and the superior ones, the *Reales Chancillerías* – were bolstered to ensure the rights of debtors, creditors and guarantors (Carvajal, 2017). In other case, like in the Aragonese Crown, this process was more decentralized, and the manorial courts, together with royal and ecclesiastic bodies, granted legal security to credit operations (Sales, 2014).

As well as all these institutions, the spread of credit across urban and rural areas and among different social strata was made possible by a diversity of financial instruments in all the countries considered. There were similarities, but differences between instruments in different countries.

In Portugal, the credit markets were segmented and there is little evidence of interaction between them. At the lower level, there were the local credit markets which relied on private agreements (known as *obrigações*).

These involved small sums of money, were light on formalities and could be enforced at local courts. They comprised bridging loans to obtain grain and seed between the harvests and for petty trade. A second stratum was the credit market for commercial credit. This market was dominated by the short-time debt instruments called *mutua*, although other forms existed (Durand, 1982; Barbosa, 1991). Although not exclusively, the market for *mutua* was essentially found in cities and townships. Savings flowed from the countryside to the towns and vice-versa. Formally usury-free and recorded by the notary public, the *mutuum* allowed for the parts to agree some under-the-table interest and use courts to enforce them, if necessary (Henriques, 2020). There were alternatives to the *mutua* which allowed for nearly overt interest, like bottomry contracts. Finally, rent charges or perpetual annuities (*censos, juros*) provided less risky instruments and lower interest rates, two useful features for landed church institutions and private investors to meet their immediate needs or for investing. In Portugal, they became very common after the monetary stability brought by Afonso III (not coincidentally, the first known perpetuity was issued in 1261, the year of the *Juramentum Super Facto Monete*) (Costa, 1961; Henriques, 2020).

In Castile, the main credit instruments were the *obligación* and the rent charge or annuity (*censo*). The former was a public instrument that became more and more popular, especially in the fifteenth century. It was usually a short-term instrument that included a payment commitment and was simple and very flexible, which made it popular in trade and finance. The interest rate was around 10%. The latter, and especially the *censo consignativo*, stemming from the *mutuum*, included relinquishing assets or cash in exchange for a regular payment until the creditor received the principal back. The diverse forms assumed by the *censo* (until payback *consignativo* or *al quitar*, for life, on rent or *enfiteutico*) and its long maturity were meant to match the financing needs of certain groups with the financing capabilities of others – nobility, clergy, etc. Nevertheless, the *censo consignativo* only truly expanded towards the end of the fifteenth century. The diversity in credit operations stimulated the use of other instruments like private contracts and operations registered in merchant's books. Later in the fifteenth century we see a proliferation of the bill of exchange in markets and large cities, like Seville, stimulated by the Italian presence or the contact with Aragonese merchants.

In Navarre, the most common credit instrument was the *carta de deuda* (letter of debt), also called *carta de obligança* when the credit was backed by one or more underwriters. Both Jews and Christians alike used this type of letter, but the latter would resort more to *comandas* or deposits, which had to be returned when demanded by the creditor. We must also mention the *cartas judevencas* (Jewish letters), drafted in Hebrew and used for credit between Jews, even when prohibited by their laws. When claimed before the bailiff, who was the royal representative in the Jewry, they became *tornadas* or *quenaces*, which as sources show were used as credit notes. Notarial protocols in the fifteenth century show the existence of credit operations after purchasing with advance payment, especially in the scope of agriculture. Still, considering legal provisions alluding to that and other types of financial subterfuge, these must have already existed in much earlier times (Carrasco, 2019). The same is not true for the *censos consignativos*, which were only regulated in Navarre after the mid-sixteenth century, and the annuities sold by the Tudela municipality in 1499 and 1507 with a moderate interest rate of 5% seem to be an exception (Ramírez, 2006).

Lastly, in Aragon, among the main credit instruments, we find the *obligaciones*. In these contracts, which were recorded by a court official, the debtor acknowledges the debt and commits to repaying it within a set period and presents an underwriter. These *obligaciones* were used for loans of modest size. For larger amounts there was a notarial record and procedures similar to the ones recorded in other parts of the Iberian Peninsula. This comprised the *mutuum*, the *comandas* for cash on deposit or the fake sale with a buyback clause (*carta de gracia*). All these instruments were used for short-term loans. For long-term operations, and typically larger amounts, the lender sold life (*violaris*) or perpetual (*censals*) annuities, with interest rates ranging from 16% to 2.5% and underwritten by a piece of land or by someone's income and goods. Finally, outside of the court and notarial records, we find credit activities in the books of merchants and shopkeepers, who registered the sales made to their clients on credit (García Marsilla, 2002).

5.3.3 The Expansion of Credit: Consumption, Investment, Trade and Public Debt

The later medieval centuries saw the consolidation and spread of credit across all the territories of Christian Iberia. As credit expanded within different institutions and social groups, financial dealings became increasingly more secure. As with other European regions, three main factors explain the spread of credit in the different kingdoms of the peninsula: investment in trade and production (both urban and rural); internal consumption; and public expenditure.

Although quantitative evidence falters, most historians agree that the development of credit was more advanced in the Crown of Aragon, on account of its early and intense contacts with the Mediterranean world, especially with Italy. In effect, from the thirteenth century onwards, credit was a key element in the urban, commercial and territorial development of the Aragonese polities. Coastal cities like Barcelona, Valencia and Mallorca, whose ports were connected with the Mediterranean commercial and financial networks, were the pioneers of the development of mercantile credit. Nevertheless, as recent historiography has demonstrated, from the thirteenth century onwards, the

Aragonese rural hinterlands were not left out of the expansion of the market for credit, as this activity became increasingly prevalent in the country's market economy (de la Torre, 2018). As mentioned, there are many indications about the spread of credit across all layers of medieval society in response to a growing demand for loans. An important feature of the Crown of Aragon was the widespread sale of rents, which started at the end of the thirteenth century. In the following century, this form of credit became a normal expedient for all types of physical and legal persons. From the middle decades of the fourteenth century onwards, public powers (the monarchy and the municipalities) started resorting to the financial market, a move that generated further development of the credit (Furió, 1998).

Like the other polities, the Crown of Aragon relied on loans in order to meet its diverse needs from the late twelfth century onward. The reliance on credit became more frequent during the following century, as the Crown increased its administrative capacity and its ambitious territorial expansion in the peninsula and the Mediterranean. Initially, the kings of Aragon resorted to loans by Jewish financiers, to short-term loans and to the pawning their demesne and other revenues. Nevertheless, during the fourteenth century, these expedients were visibly insufficient to meet the incessant and growing military needs. In this context, the monarchy was forced to require financial support from the cities in the royal domain and, then, from the representatives assembled in the *Cortes*. As stated, starting in the mid-fourteenth century, the urban authorities of the various polities started massively resorting to long-term credit (life and perpetual annuities) in order to meet these ever-growing demands and other needs in their communities. Later, the entities represented in the *Cortes* (nobility, church and towns) also ended up by issuing long-term debt on behalf of their entire political community (i.e. Catalonia, Aragon or Valencia) and created commissions (*diputationes*) to manage the debt service. The success of the sales of revenue was such that no political body ignored the opportunities offered by this expedient. The sources show that the very monarchy, the nobility and even the church sold annuities (*censales*) paid with regular revenues.

The stock of public debt issued by the cities and the Crown quickly ballooned and its consequences were not always positive. There were negative events like the bankruptcy of the commonality (*Universitat*) of the city and realm of Mallorca, whose revenues were eventually managed by the powerful syndicate of creditors of Barcelona in the late fourteenth century. Such episodes, nevertheless, do not offset the notion that the development of public debt was overall beneficial to the country. The capital markets proved very stable and allowed for increasing the Crown of Aragon's state capacity and boosted the political and economic development of the country (Ortí & Verdés, 2016).

The expansion of credit was less spectacular in the other Christian polities (Ladero, 1990–1991). During the first centuries, we know that Castilian kings and lords went into debt to finance their expenses, especially to the Jewish community. But the economic growth of late-fourteenth-century Castile, built on improvements in demographic growth, output increases production and international trade, triggered the development of all types of credit. In the fifteenth century, fast-growing cities like Burgos, Seville, Toledo or Valladolid attracted financiers and, during the following centuries, the main markets and fairs of the northern half of the kingdom (Villalón, Medina de Rioseco and Medina del Campo) also acquired considerable importance as financial centres. Likewise, credit also spread to the Castilian countryside, as farmers sought to acquire more property, working animals and tools. Rural and urban population also turned to credit to finance production and increase their consumption. In Castile, both the monarchy and the cities resorted to credit as a means to meet extraordinary expenses. Castilian institutions – monarchy and city councils – financed a share of their spending with tax-farming and, occasionally, with short-term loans. It was only at the end of the fifteenth century that the monarchy started to sell rights on fiscal revenues. Thus emerged the *juro al quitar* (literally the 'right' of the buyer to receive every year a given sum from the Crown). This yearly payment serviced by the royal revenues essentially amounted to an interest for the principal handed in by the buyer. After their issuance became common from 1489 onwards, the *juros* became the key instrument for financing military projects in the fifteenth and sixteenth centuries.

As previously stated, in Navarre, there are several indications that point to a progressive expansion of credit in the thirteenth century. However, in the following century we observe a decisive increase in the number of credit operations as well as the consolidation of the country's financial centres of Estella, Pamplona and Tudela. As elsewhere in the peninsula, nearly all layers of society, including the Jewish and Muslim minorities, resorted to credit even if the aims were somewhat distinct. The main borrowers in the kingdom appear to have been farmers in the rural areas (normally borrowing from the Jewry) and, in the urban areas, artisans, merchants and the iron and textile industries. The credit advanced to noblemen, officeholders, local communities, lay confraternities (*cofradías*) and the monarchy itself was less important (Elía, 1995; Carrasco, 2019). Long-term public debt did not consolidate in the medieval period. In the surviving sources, the most frequent solution was resorting to short-term credit both by the monarchy and the local municipalities. Regarding the monarchy, examples abound of the credit given by Jews, moneychangers, courtiers and other financiers to the king and his entourage to allow them to meet the various demands of the Crown (Mugueta, 2008). There were also several examples of local communities who resorted to financiers or to their neighbours to pay for the Crown's services or to purchase wheat.

As mentioned, only in Tudela can we find the sale of long-term *censales* with an interest rate of 5%, an event occurring in 1499 and 1507 (Ramírez, 2006).

Finally, in Portugal the demand for capital came from the rise in private consumption and investment in the productive sectors, but not from state expenditure. In the thirteenth century, with a fully monetized economy, a stable coinage and well-defined property rights, capital flowed both from savings in the countryside to the city and vice-versa. This resulted in comparatively low interest rates (Henriques, 2020). Although the main stimuli were similar to Aragon (maritime expansion, state expenditure and also endogenous growth), the development of financial markets occurred at a somewhat later date. Nevertheless, in the period considered, Portugal did not develop a consolidated public debt. Portuguese kings occasionally obtained funds from their moneyed subjects but such loans were raised and paid for in an ad hoc fashion. These loans were treated as debts to the monarch and no state revenues were pledged to their payment. As should, they were not the foundation for a public debt system based on perpetual annuities, as in Aragon and in Castile under the Catholic Kings.

5.3.4 Financial Agents and the Development of Banking

Despite the different paces of financial development, the final outcome was the consolidation of capital markets that thus became able to provide the wider economy with the necessary capital for investment. This capital came from various social groups, but three collectives stood out as financial intermediaries and as the pioneers of banking in the peninsula: Jews, moneychangers and the so-called merchant-bankers, both of Italian and local stock. Some credit institutions deserve a special reference, especially the municipal banks of the Crown of Aragon.

As in the case of al-Andalus and other polities of the Christian West, the financial activity of the Jewry can be documented in each and every one of the Christian kingdoms of the Iberian Peninsula, lending to both kings and private investors. Although we are aware of financial dealing in the twelfth century, it was in the thirteenth century that the Jewish presence was consolidated in the financial markets, as shown by the abundant legislation passed against usury and lending by Jews in that century in the various territories of the peninsula. The literature shows that, during the fourteenth and fifteenth centuries, Jewish lenders gradually focused on rural areas, where they supplied mostly short-term loans, as the role of Christian financiers grew in urban settings. Their contribution to the royal and municipal coffers and on those of other bodies was reduced further. The service by the Jews to the various Iberian monarchies was particularly relevant from the twelfth century. For the late fifteenth century, we should stress the growing relevance of the *converso* financiers.

The role played by the Ruiz, Sánchez, Santángel or Coronel at the sworn moneychanger service of the Catholic Kings is widely known.

We find references to moneychangers from the twelfth century in the northern part of the peninsula (they are first documented in Barcelona, in 1125). Initially, their business was limited to the exchange of local and foreign currency in major cities or along the Camino de Santiago. In Navarre, for instance, there is evidence for a street called the Rua Mayor de los Cambios in Pamplona, where the presence of the king's court and its financial needs also fostered exchange (Carrasco, 2001).

However, during the thirteenth century, there is documental evidence of the first banking deals: the legislation issued in Catalonia (1248) separated simple moneychangers from proper certified moneychangers with an official ledger. Later, sources tell of a quick growth of financial activity in the Crown of Aragon with an increase in the numbers of moneychangers, the emergence of the first banking companies and the increase in legislation meant to strengthen the moneychangers against from the crises that began to unfold towards late thirteenth century (Feliu Monfort, 1992; 2016a). Regardless of their risks, all along the fourteenth century, there is evidence of the increasing role of exchangers who served the Crown, the municipalities and other entities (the church, nobility, *Diputaciones*, etc.) at the time. Banking continued to develop in the Crown of Aragon during the fifteenth century, when Valencia, not far from Barcelona, acquired importance as a major financial hub (Igual-Luis, 2000).

As was the case in other areas of credit, the development of banking in the remaining Christian territories happened later. Take the example of Portugal, where the first moneychangers or *cambhadores* are cited in a 1242 contract in Lisbon. The needs of traders were likely important for this emergence in a commercial city like Lisbon. However, decades later, inland towns like Guarda and Viseu also have *cambhadores* of their own (1305 and 1309, respectively). These are two episcopal cities and they suggest another major influence in the growth of money changing: the integration between the Portuguese Church and the papal finances. The Vatican sources from the fourteenth-century papal collectors provide an interesting viewpoint on the financial life of the country. Those of Bertrand Du Mazel, for instance, show that by 1370 it was possible to exchange different currencies and gold in small towns like Serpa (Farelo, 2018). For the monarchy, the regulation of the moneychangers was a major issue as gold and silver flowed in and out of the realm through their hands. Clearly, as fiscal issues became more pressing and papal authority weaker, the monarchy had higher incentives to regulate the profession. In 1375, Fernando I (1367–1383) issued the first statutes for the moneychangers, naturally including a large set of restrictions. This was even more visible under João I (1385–1433), who created the office of the *cambiador-mor*. The first known *cambiador-mor* was Messer Percival, a naturalized merchant from Piacenza.

As for Castile, the business of exchange emerged in some cities connected with trade flows and other centres related with the Camino de Santiago. But some of these moneychangers specialized in banking operations like deposits and loans when the Jews started to see their position deteriorate after the 1391 pogroms (Crespo, 2002). Despite the presence of moneychangers being recorded in fourteenth-century Seville or Burgos, their activity only became mainstream during the first half of the fifteenth century. At this time the kings of Castile attempted to regulate moneychangers. Juan II used the *Cortes* in 1436 and 1455 to legislate on this matter and set the conditions that should be met in order to establish a public bank and to be able to exchange money and ply their trade in towns and marketplaces (Carvajal, 2015). Public moneychangers and the so-called court moneychangers, bound to the royal coffers, saw their roles increase in relevance all through the fifteenth and early sixteenth century. They established banks in cities like Seville, Valladolid, Toledo and Burgos. In this flurry of activity, other moneychangers set up private banks in these and other cities, especially those that hosted major markets, where the typical banking operations took place in late fifteenth century: deposits, loans, exchanges, money orders and payments and financial mediation services (Carvajal, 2015).

As well as the Jews and moneychangers, there was a third group devoted to financial mediation in the late medieval period: the merchant-bankers. These were merchants that both traded and performed banking operations, often blurring the lines between the two. From the thirteenth century, these financiers plied their trade by making the best of the growing business opportunities offered by credit in all its aspects, as well as of the need to bring several cities in the peninsula into the commercial and financial networks that were forming in the west of Europe. Traditionally, historians have stressed the role of the great Italian (Genoese and Florentine) merchant-bankers. The spread of commercial and finance techniques over the Iberian territories from the early fourteenth century was due to the large Italian family firms and societies, including the Alberti, Datini, Strozzi, Scarampi, Tecchini, Spannochi, Centurione, Lomellini, Bonini, Cassini, etc. We have already highlighted how early and relevant was their presence in the main cities of the Aragonese Crown, but there is also documental evidence of their presence in other places like Lisbon, Seville, Toledo or Valladolid. Just like we observed in Granada, some of these Italian merchants mixed their private businesses with financial services offered to the various peninsular monarchies, in exchange for the farming of royal revenues and other trade-related privileges (Igual-Luis, 2000).

Even if slightly less relevant, the existence of native merchant bankers is also well documented. They were especially active in the Crown of Aragon, where we find them entwined in the trade networks and taking part in the construction of the monarchy's financial system in the fourteenth and fifteenth centuries. This is the case of the Cortielles, Casasàgia, Donsancho, Casaldàliga, Coscó, Marrades, Pujades and others (Igual-Luis, 2000; de La Torre, 2018; Cruselles, 2019). They were also important in Navarre: despite the absence of documented evidence of banking corporations as such, credit activities in the main cities of the kingdom in the fourteenth and fifteenth centuries were controlled by several lineages, who also offered their services to the kings. They were also part of a merchant networks linking Paris, Bayonne, Barcelona and other financial hubs of their time. In Pamplona, for example, the main families involved in this trade were the Cruzat, Jurdán, Marcel, Eza, Caritat or Laceilla (Carrasco, 2001).

We have had the opportunity to state that, as well as the various groups of financial mediators, in the late medieval years, there were also several institutions that devoted their resources to credit. As in Italy, this is what happened with some hospitals in the Crown of Aragon or with Castilian institutions that collected alms to help the poor: *arcas de limosna y misericordia*. However, the most noteworthy fact in the Iberian finances at this time are the municipal banks, or *Taules de Canvi*, created in some cities or the Aragonese Crown (Feliu Monfort, 2016a). These bodies were created during the fifteenth century with the purpose of procuring liquidity to face, mostly, the long-term debt of the cities without further adding to it. The first documentary hints for the creation of these banks stem from the fourteenth century and are concurrent with a financial crisis and the ensuing loss of trust in the private bankers, who, from the late thirteenth century, had been acting on behalf of many municipalities and of the monarchy. There is documented evidence of the creation of *Taules de canvi* – or attempts to create them – in Barcelona and Mallorca (1401), Perpignan (1404), Valencia (1407), Tarragona (1416, 1420) and Girona (1443).

Of all these endeavours, only the *Taula de Canvi* in Barcelona consolidated. In Valencia, the municipal bank only operated between 1407 and 1416, and in Perpignan there are signs of activity in the fifteenth century but no record of its later evolution. Barcelona's *Taula* is considered by many historians as the first public bank in Europe and it is well documented. This institution was entitled to receive all types of judicial deposits or will trusts (*albaceazgos*) in the city as well as the proceedings of the municipal income. They also received voluntary and individual deposits from private citizens. These voluntary deposits collected no interest and no credit was given to the public. The sole services given to the depositors were the safekeeping, administration and transfers to third parties. As stated, the main function of the bank was to provide liquidity to the municipality and to control the city's debt. The *Taula de Canvi* in Barcelona went through some turbulence and had to be reformed several times (1412, 1436, 1468); however, recent historians have considered that this institution had a positive effect on both the municipal finances and the financial system as a whole (Feliu Monfort, 2016a; Ortí & Verdés, 2016).

5.4 Conclusion

Like elsewhere in Europe, there are numerous signs that there was a slow, but steady recovery of economic activity in the Iberian Peninsula in the early eleventh century. This process ran parallel to the formation of new Christian kingdoms headed by monarchs who, making use of the power vacuum created by the end of the Córdoba Caliphate, created administrative structures and expanded southwards. This period saw the emergence of currency as a means of payment and exchange, as well as a symbol of the rising power of the northern kingdoms. Recovering the Carolingian and Visigothic legacies and adapting elements from the Andalusian systems, the Christian monarchs brought in new monetary systems that, albeit archaic, provided an alternative to the Islamic model that had functioned until then and was in force until 1492 in the Nasrid kingdom of Granada.

The peninsular monetary systems were initially constrained by both territorial and jurisdictional complexity as well as by other factors: the unification and separation of the various kingdoms according to dynastic politics; the power struggles between the Crown, the nobility, the church and the cities; and the scarcity of precious metals. Different combinations of these factors led to the contrasting evolutions of the peninsular monetary systems in the early centuries.

As elsewhere in Europe, the thirteenth century saw an increase of output and trade, buttressed by the development of political institutions. The king, the *Cortes*, legal codes and other institutions also fostered the improvement of the economy. This growth was conditioned by the scarcity of coinage and successive bullion debasements, two factors that set apart the peninsula from the more dynamic regions of Europe, like centre-north Italy and the Low Countries, where such events were less common.

Overall, debasements and the increasing size of bullion issues responded to the demand for currency. On account of this demand, credit became a necessary resource to bolster economic activity. The availability of short- and long-term instruments, the advantages it offered for purchasers, the existence of experts (often Jewish) and state borrowing by Aragonese countries and cities made credit into a key factor for the economic, commercial and financial development of all Christian polities. Meanwhile, in the *taifa* kingdoms and in Granada, Jewish-provided credit and financial activity played an essential role in the economic development, despite the condemnation of usury.

From the fourteenth century onwards, the strong opening of trade in all the kingdoms in the peninsula, especially the Crown of Aragon, brought about great changes in currency, as their systems had to adjust to European and/or Mediterranean patterns; and it also contributed to the increasing flows of capital and goods. Thus, Italian merchants and bankers, as well as others, turned the Iberian Peninsula into a business space, where they could find local merchants who assimilated their mercantile and financial techniques, especially in urban markets like Barcelona or Valencia. Both the Christian kingdoms and Muslim territories alike attracted great business dynasties, notably the Genoese, who in turn stimulated the financial dealing of both Andalusian and Christian moneychangers and bankers.

In the fifteenth century, the currency and credit systems of the peninsular kingdoms allowed them to connect with each other and with various areas of Europe. Hence, a city like Barcelona could count from the early fifteenth century on an institution like the *Taula de Canvi*. This happened at a time when Portugal started to send its ships in search of new horizons, markets and conquests in the Atlantic and the East, and when Castile was starting a steady economic growth that ultimately became the foundation for another global empire, one century later. The financial and economic momentum of this century meant that the various peninsular kingdoms, especially Castile and Portugal, were at the forefront of European economic growth.

6

Technology, 1000–1500

ARNALDO SOUSA MELO, GERMÁN NAVARRO ESPINACH
AND RICARDO CÓRDOBA DE LA LLAVE

6.1 Introduction

The combination of production, labour, capital and natural resources in economic systems can vary according to various factors, including technology, market size and production models. As such, widely different combinations can coexist in the same economic system, even if technology is evenly distributed and production systems are homogenous. Technology is, therefore, a factor of production, and cannot be explained simply in the context of a history of economic events, but must be integrated into the history of economic systems and their evolution in relation to the institutional setting (Cipolla, 1974: chap. 6). Recently, Iradiel has put forward a proposal to define and measure medieval economic growth; he argues that the subject must be analysed systemically, combining the potential of microanalysis with a macro perspective that takes into consideration the role of production and demand in the economic development of medieval polities (Iradiel, 2017: 41–68). From a broader perspective, another recent publication has examined the issue with regard to medieval markets and consumers in the Iberian Peninsula and the Mediterranean (Petrowiste & Lafuente, 2018).

Excessive focus on economic growth has led us to a vision of history marked by a great chasm, that which divides the 'industrial revolution', seen as the beginning of modernity (even of the concept of 'technology'), from the periods that preceded it, which are abusively qualified under the umbrella term 'pre-industrial' (while their technology is demoted to the inferior rank of 'technique'). This conceptual antinomy between technology and technique is absolutely fallacious. In fact, the 'industrial revolution' cannot be explained without the millennium of growth that preceded it, which laid the foundations of market relations – the real stimulus behind technological change (Gimpel, 1982). The greater the size of the market, the more specialized and segmented technical operations were, especially in densely populated urban environments. It was the market, and the constant pressure that it posed, that lay behind many technological innovations, the concentration or dispersion of productive processes, and the formation of the earliest urban industrial quarters. Therefore, the history of production techniques and, in particular, the history of how they evolved over time, is crucial for any analysis of economic and social development, as one of the key factors that define the means of production and, it follows, production itself.

Philippe Braunstein argues that 'Europe showed a clear interest for technical endeavours at two critical junctures for economic development. From the second half of the thirteenth century, a first impulse lasting three-quarters of a century, European systems of energy generation developed, systematically applying hydraulic energy to industrial processing and introducing forestry regulations. In a second phase, starting in the first half of the fifteenth century and approximately spanning 50 years, space and time became rationally divided, at a time when the known world was becoming wider and information circulated as never before' (Braunstein, 2007: 12).

Technical innovations can be a new production technique or a new product, an invention that generally follows an incremental path of small steps and simple mechanisms – optimizing a woodworking tool or improving hide-processing by adding new ingredients or combining existing ones differently are examples of the small technical gestures that must have been at the root of multiple innovations (Hilaire-Pérez & Verna, 2006: 539). The humble nature of these gestures suggests that truly ground-breaking innovations were few and far between, and that they generally took place in a limited number of fields, including the application of water power to industrial processes, the textile industry and ceramic production.

On the other hand, examining technical variables and their evolution over time allows us to raise another set of variables that are of capital importance for economic history: yields, productivity and production costs. These are key variables for the analysis of accumulation and profit rates and of the impact of the specific costs of each stage of production in the final costs. Our ultimate aim is to incorporate these variables into the objective and comparative examination of economic growth. Productivity determines the quantity and quality of production (output), given the quantity, quality and combination of the different factors present in any production system (inputs): labour, capital and natural resources. According to Cipolla (1974: chap. 3), productivity was low in the Middle Ages because its economic system was not capitalistic. In feudal economies, labour was very intensive and the capital input small, and in consequence technological innovation was rare, although it is rather arguable whether this notion applies to all economic sectors.

We must avoid explaining invention and the dissemination of technical innovations in diffusionist terms. In cultural anthropology, diffusionism argues that human progress relies on the dissemination of cultural traits from more advanced societies to less advanced ones. However, it is now understood that the main channel for the dissemination of technology is the emigration of human capital. We must not forget that skilled workers' attachment to a given place was directly proportional to their living conditions and that, conversely, the migration of a person or group of people who possess knowledge about an innovation does not guarantee that said innovation will automatically work in the new environment. This depends on the specific context. The social profile of emigrants in their places of origin must be taken into consideration, as well as how they integrate in the host society, which will, to a large extent, depend on the size and form of organization of this society.

Medieval techniques were primarily based on praxis; not only knowing how something was made, but also having the ability to make it. That is, there was not a sharp distinction between theoretical instructions and practical training. Moreover, training is not limited to the passing and processing of information, but also includes various embodied processes of muscular, neuronal and sensorial adaptation. Ultimately, work is a cultural activity, and often this crystallizes in the need for public recognition, in the wish for one's labour to be regarded as an 'art', and not simply work. This distinction between the practical and the cognitive components of know-how is essential to understand the key problems of technological change in Iberia or, indeed, anywhere else (Navarro, 2012).

6.2 Agriculture

Agricultural practice[4] in the West was to a large extent determined by Islamic heritage. Andalusian agronomy treatises (*Kitab al-filaha*) included multiple innovations concerning irrigation agricultural practices, especially the use of fertilizers and the allocation of irrigation slots; particularly well known are the works by Ibn Wafid and Ibn al-Bassal, both writing in the eleventh century, Ibn al Awwan, in the early thirteenth century, and the Almería-born Ibn Luyun, writing in the Nasrid kingdom of Granada in the fourteenth century. These works were synthetized and compiled in Gabriel Alonso de Herrera's *Tratado de Agricultura* (1503), the pinnacle of agronomic studies in late medieval Christian Spain. The introduction of new crops into the Iberian Peninsula from the eighth and ninth centuries is also a well-known phenomenon: citrus fruits, such as lemons and oranges, date palms, sugar cane, silk worms, and industrial crops such as cotton. Most innovations involved the adaptation of irrigation crops from the Near East, which were grown near water courses but also in veritable *green belts* around major cities and villages. These green belts were the origin of many of the areas of *huerta* that were to remain in place after the Christian conquest, for instance in Valencia, Murcia, and the Ebro and Guadalquivir valleys (Nuez, 2002).

From the eleventh century onwards, land became the basis of feudal power in Iberia, and stock-keeping and agriculture the main sources of

---

[4] On the matter of this whole section, see also Chapter 2.

wealth. The land colonization programmes that followed the feudal conquest of al-Andalus resulted in a substantial increase in the amount of agricultural land; wasteland and areas of undergrowth were cleared and broken up, especially for sowing cereal and vines. This agrarian expansion resulted in the contraction of woodland. The agricultural regime was dominated by low-yield cereal crops, which were very vulnerable to adverse climatic conditions; this added to difficulties in food transport and conservation to present a general picture dominated by hunger and epidemics, long before the arrival of the Black Death. Fallow and crop traditional rotation systems were the norm. More productive rotation systems, such as the triennial system, are documented in some areas of Galicia or the hinterland of Córdoba and in some Portuguese western areas, such as Coimbra and Alcobaça. These areas had to strike a fine balance between agricultural and stock-keeping practices. In good-quality soils, for instance in the Andalusian farmlands, yields were above 1:10 on average in the early fourteenth century, so they were probably not as low as has sometimes been suggested, although there are significant disparities in yield-related data from different cereal-growing regions.

Meanwhile, irrigation, inspired by the Islamic tradition, was a minor practice in the general context of Iberian agriculture, which was largely based on dry land agriculture. However, from the thirteenth century onwards irrigation systems tended to increase in size, and this had a multiplier effect on labour, as these practices were labour-intensive. The expansion of cereal crops and vines in irrigated areas changed the agricultural landscape of some regions in the Kingdom of Valencia, which also witnessed the proliferation of grazing areas for sheep, often with an eye on the international markets. In the Crown of Aragon, the most important irrigation areas were located in Zaragoza, Lleida, Huesca, Bajo Cinca, Alcañiz, the Middle Ebro Valley, Tortosa, Plana de Castelló, Valencia, Ribera del Xúquer (from Alzira to Xàtiva) and Gandia. However, hydraulic archaeology has shown that, apart from major areas of *huerta*, multiple small irrigation areas existed alongside river courses, for instance the Guadalaviar, the Cinca and the Aguasvivas, in the Kingdom of Aragon. The most important change witnessed by the late Middle Ages in this regard was the increasing specialization of industrial crops: oil, rice, dyes, sugar cane, mulberry (for silk worms), cotton and saffron, among others. Irrigation agriculture was of paramount importance in the Crown of Aragon, with cereal yields of 1:5 compared to 1:2 for dry land agriculture (Ayala Martínez et al., 2004: 169–170, 296–299).

In some areas of Portugal, the more fertile areas were located in wetlands, where canals and other structures were built to divert and regularize excess water for intensive agriculture, for instance in the Mondego valley, near Coimbra, and the coastal area to the south-southwest of Coimbra, towards Lisbon; in the region around Leiria, cereal crop yields ranged from 1:5 to 1:8 (Marques, 1978: 44–50; 1987: 96–97; Coelho, 1989, I: 139–142; Gonçalves,

1989: 88). In the Portuguese north-west, as well as in Galicia, the prevailing Atlantic climate allowed the formation of naturally irrigated agricultural systems; this, in turn, led to denser settlement patterns from at least the eleventh century onwards, if not earlier (Marques, 1978; 1987; Ribeiro, 1986; Mattoso, 1993; Sousa, 1993).

Industrial crops, such as textile fibres (flax, hemp), dyes and mordents became increasingly common. Woad, although originally imported from Toulouse, was soon being produced in Levante; sumac, quite abundant in the Douro valley in León and Portugal, also expanded significantly in the fifteenth century in some areas of Sierra Morena and the Baetic Systems (Andalusia); cochineal and madder were found mostly in southern Spain (modern regions of Castilla-La Mancha, Murcia and Andalusia); litmus (*roccella tinctoria*) became one of the main economic assets in the Canaries after the Castilian conquest in the late fifteenth century; and woad in Azores was much produced in the early colonizations of Azores, for export to textile industries. The expansion of industrial crops is a reflection of the intensification of textile production in the Iberian Peninsula between the thirteenth and the fifteenth centuries (Córdoba, 2002: 241-242).

This was also reflected in the appearance of large flocks of *merino* sheep for the production of wool, which was highly appreciated in European markets (England, Italy, the Low Countries). Although transhumance had been a common practice throughout the Middle Ages, the conquest of large territories in the south in the thirteenth century created the opportunity to develop long-haul transhumant routes between northern Castile and Sierra Morena, leading to the foundation by Alfonso X of the *Honrado Concejo de la Mesta* in 1273, the aim of which was to represent the interests of major flock-owners. In addition to transhumance, stockbreeding was an important economic sector in some regions, for instance the farmlands of La Mancha and the Guadalquivir Valley. These flocks were owned by feudal lords and the urban oligarchies, who every year sold the wool to the Burgos-based merchant that controlled the export trade. This practice greatly contributed to the development of mercantile and financial practices, as well as transport technologies, during this period (Córdoba, 2002: 247-249).

There was also a substantial expansion of horse-breeding practices. Equids were used in agriculture (e.g. horses were used in cereal agriculture and to power waterwheels), transport (mule trains became a common sight, as we shall see in Section 6.4) war and sports such as jousts, which were as popular among the common people as they were among the aristocracy. Breed selection became a widespread practice; the so-called Arabic or *Morisco* horse – from the influence posed on horse-breeding in al-Andalus by the arrival of eastern horse breeds – is at the roots of the modern Andalusian horse and the *Lusitano* in Portugal.

From the eleventh century, the use of the heavy mouldboard plough with wheels (*carruca*) became widespread in the Iberian Peninsula as in much of Europe, pulled by a yoke of oxen or by a pair of horses. Despite this, simpler light ploughs pulled by a single animal continued to be used to cut furrows for planting. The grain of the cereal was sown on the fly and then a leash was passed through the field to cover the seeds with earth. The cultivation of the vine, however, required the participation of a greater number of workers, as evidenced by the accounting documents on vineyard management studied in the Kingdom of Valencia during the fifteenth century (Sueca, Segorbe).

6.3 Manufactures and Energy

6.3.1 Technology and Innovation

In general, in the Middle Ages the use of easy-to-access raw materials was at a premium, in order to minimize extraction and transport costs, but some areas specialized in the production of certain products. Basque iron, which was both abundant and high quality, reached nearly all cities in the Iberian Peninsula; it was cheaper and easier than exploiting local mines. As a result, the Basque Country underwent substantial industrial growth in the fifteenth and sixteenth centuries, and its commercial networks reached the whole of the Iberian Peninsula and Western Europe (Córdoba, 2017a: 41–44). Alum was originally imported from the eastern Mediterranean (Turkey and Egypt) and the exploitation of western mines began in the second half of the fifteenth century (Tolfa in Italy, Mazarrón in Murcia) (Marques, 1987: 148–171; Melo & Ribeiro, 2012).

New industrial developments that used traditional energy sources more efficiently contributed to considerable industrial growth in the Iberian Peninsula during the late Middle Ages. Derivation dams, which diverted water courses towards hydraulic infrastructures, were greatly improved with the dissemination of *estacadas*, wood and stone dams placed in the river stream which were much more resistant to water pressure than the traditional wooden dams. The development of the camshaft, which was used to transform the rotation of waterwheels into a vertical motion, in the eleventh and twelfth centuries, was a game-changing event: camshafts were used to propel the large hammers used in fulling mills and also to depurate iron. As a result, fulling mills and iron-smelting facilities proliferated all over the Iberian Peninsula, alongside the traditional water-geared flourmills. John Munro points out the importance of camshafts and cranks in the design of multi-purpose mechanisms used in the textile and tanning industries, metallurgy and paper production; in camshafts, the axis attached to the wheel is encircled by a series of spoon-shaped paddles which, as they turn, push the rear end of a series of hammers, elevating them, which then fall using their own weight; in cranks, a U-shaped piece causes an oscillating motion which was particularly useful in water-powered sawmills, splendid examples of which have been attested in the Alps, the Pyrenees and other heavily wooded areas (Munro, 2003). The use of new or existing energy sources applied in new mechanical devices is the greatest episode of technological innovation in the Middle Ages, triggering the concentration of industrial facilities in the vicinity of these sources (water courses, coal-producing areas and wind-swept slopes).

Wind energy started to be used for milling flour in the thirteenth century: windmills were built in cities such as Seville and Zaragoza, and in 1258 Alfonso X authorized their construction in the region of Murcia. Some examples are documented near Lisbon and in Alcobaça (Leiria) at least from 1262, perhaps earlier, but never in great numbers (Marques, 1987: 49). Their use was never very widespread, being limited to milling grain; their location was restricted to high areas with constant winds. The earliest windmills were made of wood and were placed on an axis which allowed them to be oriented towards the wind. The use of tower-like fixed windmills, made of masonry and ending in a conical roof, upon which the sails were mounted, seems to become common from the fifteenth century onwards (Rodas, Mallorca, Santarém), reaching a peak of popularity during the sixteenth and seventeenth centuries (Córdoba, 2017b: 34). From the thirteenth century on, new high-energy fuels (holm oak, heather) allowed higher temperatures to be reached inside iron smelting furnaces. The use of firewood was still widespread in domestic and industrial contexts (fulling mills, bakeries).

Innovations in the use of energy sources were accompanied by the introduction of revolutionary machinery, tools and industrial processes. Concerning the use of hydraulic energy, the camshaft was not the only significant innovation: for example, the connection rod permitted the invention of water-geared sawmills, and from the early sixteenth century on, traditional penstocks were progressively replaced with horizontal wheels in flourmills – they used energy just as efficiently but were much cheaper to maintain. A debate exists as to whether these *regolfo* mills (a name derived from the whirlpool of water that formed in the cylindrical wells in which the driving wheels were located) originated in the Iberian Peninsula, and the fact is that several applications for implementing a new system of water mills are attested during the reign of the Catholic Monarchs. In addition, water-powered hammers completely replaced foot hammers in fulling mills.

Some of the most significant innovations, which greatly contributed to increasing productivity and capacity, took place in the textile industry, which underwent a kind of early industrial revolution in Europe between the eleventh and thirteenth centuries. The dissemination of the spinning wheel reduced spinning time by three-quarters, although traditional spindle whorls were still in use. In the late Middle Ages, the *torno de torcer seda* became widespread; this device used a series of wheels to give the silk thread bobbins and spindle whorls a regular motion. The horizontal loom with pedals, which was introduced in the twelfth century, was a leap forward for the textile industry. New looms permitted the weaving of more complex patterns in much less time while also being amenable to the use of new fabrics, especially silk, which could be variously combined with other types of fabric. According to Paolo Malanima, rather than the spinning wheel and even the horizontal loom, water-powered fulling mills attached to a camshaft was the most important among all the innovations adopted by the textile industry, as it allowed productivity to reach levels that were 35 to 50 times greater than those of manual workers (Malanima, 1988; Cardon, 1999; Sequeira, 2014; Franch & Navarro, 2017).

Pottery benefited from the general substitution of traditional lead-rich glazing for the new tin-rich formula, previously used in al-Andalus from the tenth century onwards. This led to the development of the typical late medieval glazed wares (enamels) and new decorative motifs, such as the lustreware that characterized the production of cities such as Málaga and Paterna, near Valencia (Gerrard et al., 1995).

Another important innovation concerned the production of sugar cane. The cultivation of this crop was restricted to Mediterranean subtropical climates, and as a result cultivation areas and production techniques were intimately linked to the Mediterranean coast, for instance in Cyprus, Syria and Sicily. The production of sugar cane was an important economic sector in the coast of Granada between the period of the caliphate and the Nasrid kingdom in the fourteenth and fifteenth centuries. In fact, sugar cane continued to be one of the main agricultural crops in the area after the Christian conquest. Between the early sixteenth century and the twentieth century, the coast between Nerja and Motril was peppered with *trapiches*, or sugar cane-processing plants. It was also an important crop in the Spanish Levante and in Southern Portugal (Algarve) until its introduction in Madeira in 1452, if not earlier, in the Canaries in the fifteenth century, and in Brazil and the Caribbean in the sixteenth century. The facilities where sugar was refined were known as *trapiches*, after the Latin word *trapetum*, which referred to primitive oil presses, which is illustrative of the technical similarities between sugar refining and oil pressing. The *trapiche* was equipped with one or several millstones to crush the canes, a press to extract the juice, several ovens to heat it and a storage area to deposit the crystallization moulds (Malpica, 1996). In Portugal, including Madeira, however, *trapiche* was used to refer to human-powered machinery, while the hydraulic structures used to make sugar were called *engenho de açucar* or simply *engenho*, a word that also originally applied to other hydraulic devices. Soon, however, the word became synonymous with sugar production and was the usual term in Brazil after the development there of large-scale sugar plantations (Marques, 1987: 51–52; Vieira, n.d.).

Some of these innovations seem to have reached the Iberian Peninsula through al-Andalus. This may be the case with the horizontal loom (used in al-Andalus from the tenth century onwards); the camshaft and its application in bark and paper mills (also attested in al-Andalus from the tenth century); techniques for processing sugar cane; the use of wind power as a source of energy (the windmill is attested in al-Andalus from the twelfth century); and, naturally, pottery glazing. This was not only the result of the secular cultural contacts across the Iberian frontiers, or the progressive occupation of Andalusian territory, which allowed the Christian rulers to control production centres and a specialized workforce, but also of the imitation of Andalusian fashions and products in the Christian kingdoms during the late Middle Ages (Córdoba, 2007: 741). Other innovations were simply the result of the development of techniques inherited from Antiquity (for instance, the application of water power, which was known but remained underdeveloped in the ancient world) or borrowed from the Eastern Mediterranean, that is, Byzantine, influence (Córdoba, 2017b: 24).

Another innovative manufacturing activity was paper production: it was elaborated from old linen and tow rags, previously crushed in a water-powered mill or fulling mill. Following the introduction of the camshaft in the Iberian Peninsula, seemingly through al-Andalus, this technique soon spread to urban centres such as Xàtiva and Toledo, as well as Leiria, north of Lisbon, where it is attested from at least 1441, although the technique may have arrived as early as 1411 (Marques, 1987: 52–53). In turn, the widespread use of paper in the late Middle Ages encouraged writing, as paper was much cheaper than parchment. Constant improvements in quality allowed for ever neater reading material, which was a key factor in the development of printing and, with it, the possibility to produce multiple copies of texts.

The impact of this development in the promotion of scientific progress in Renaissance Europe cannot be overstated. For instance, the use of weights and measures and the arithmetic knowledge that was essential to alloy metal to the required levels of purity. The chemical knowledge involved in assaying gold and silver, reducing, blanching and striking with dies made the issuing of coinage the most paradigmatic example of how technical knowledge developed in the workshop contributed to scientific progress (Córdoba, 2009). For the first time, these innovations were being put down in writing for the benefit of apprentices and workers. Recipe books, which described the technical and industrial processes in detail, including recommendations on the best way to carry out each step, started appearing in the Iberian Peninsula in the fourteenth and fifteenth centuries: for instance, the arithmetic book in the Collegiate of Saint Isidore, León (ms. 46), dating to the fourteenth century, contains an impressive description of silver assaying techniques; the *Book of Trades*, preserved in the Monastery of Guadalupe (Cáceres), contains detailed instructions for hide tanning and dyeing; and Joanot Valero's *Manual for*

Dyers, compiled in Valencia in 1497 and currently in the Library of the University of Valencia (Córdoba, 2017b: 22).

6.3.2 The Organization of Productive, Commercial and Financial Activities

The organization of productive, commercial and financial activities presented a combination of traditional practices with new techniques that were in themselves sources of economic growth, promoting the economic and social development of fourteenth- and fifteenth-century Iberia. Naturally, the impact and nature of these practices varied from region to region and from craft to craft, and not all of them were adopted everywhere at the same time (Navarro & Villanueva, 2017). Concerning production, traditional crafts and industrial activities coexisted side by side. On the one hand, there were the traditional small-scale workshops that operated with a small workforce – barely the master, two or three skilled workers and several unskilled labourers, comprising a mixture of relatives, servants, and wage labourers. These involved little capital investment, and constituted small cells capable of operating almost autonomously. This was the typical model followed by such trades as shoemakers, goldsmiths, and smiths. On the other hand, new manufacturing models and institutional frameworks began to appear from the thirteenth century onwards, but especially in the fourteenth and fifteenth centuries. It is possible that they emerged even earlier, but they are rarely mentioned in the record before the thirteenth and fourteenth centuries.

These new labour and production models had a clearer entrepreneurial profile, that is, they involved putting together the means required to assemble a chain of production to respond to a specific demand. For instance, the leather production (*couros*) in Évora, in the late fourteenth century was in the hands of merchants and other entrepreneurs, including many shoemakers. The whole 'enterprise' was organized as a chain from the start: the entrepreneurs bought the hides, hired both skilled and unskilled workers, bought all the raw materials needed for tanning, and rented the vats, tanks (*pelames*) and all the rest of the equipment. The entrepreneurs covered all labour and production costs, controlled and supervised the process and, in consequence, owned the final product. When the process came to an end – and that could take from a few weeks to several months – the enterprise could easily be dissolved, unless there were more hides to be tanned. The capitalist would then proceed to sell the leather to other craftspeople, send it away to be sold in regional or international markets or use them for their own craft, in the case of shoemakers (Barros & Viana, 2012: 67–71).

Capitalist entrepreneurs that controlled the whole chain of production – including merchants, aristocrats, members of the church and even kings – were common in other sectors as well: the textile industry in Portugal, Castile and Aragon; shipyards everywhere in Iberia, for example in Portugal, Catalonia and Valencia; and major building projects, such as cathedrals and royal palaces (Sequeira, 2014; Melo & Ribeiro, 2015; Igual-Luis & Navarro, 2018). Naturally, this does not mean that simpler forms of organization did not exist, namely smaller-scale independent productions units. But sometimes even those independent small units were part of more complex production networks that they did not control. These different production models coexisted and combined in different ways from city to city, from region to region, and from craft to craft, as well as over time. Sometimes, even within the same craft and the same city, different production models existed, for instance weavers and *teceleos* in the textile industry. As such, craftspeople could sometimes act independently and sometimes become part of a more complex production system that depended on an 'external' capitalist entrepreneur.

Medieval cities pursued an ideal of autarchy, and most raw materials were sourced from the city's own hinterlands, although some, which could not be found nearby or required highly specialized processing, came from distant places, leading to long-range commerce networks that involved merchants as well as urban craftspeople. Catherine Verna highlights that, in addition to the local production, Barcelona imported iron from Roussillon, Liguria and Germany, while the city of Valencia was using Pisan, Savoyan, Genoese and Basque iron. Basque iron was almost the only kind to be found in Andalusian cities in the fifteenth century (Verna, 2011). In Portugal, granitic stone and oak timber were sent from Porto, in the north, to the southern regions of the kingdom, where these resources were scarce. Timber and iron were also imported, namely from Biscay, whereas sea salt from Aveiro, together with fish, leather and wine were shipped from Porto, Lisbon and a number of small coastal towns to northern Europe and the Mediterranean (Marques, 1987: 148–171). Some merchants, mostly based in Porto, Lisbon, Burgos, Biscay, Catalonia and Genoa, made enormous profits from the export of wool and hides.

6.4 Transport

6.4.1 Time, Space, Measures and Land Transport

Before we analyse the matter of transport in Medieval Iberia, we need to remember that mental perceptions of space and time changed towards the end of the period. Measurement systems and arithmetic practices changed in response to the crisis of the feudal system. In many cities in the Crown of Castile, Aragon, Navarre and Portugal traditional ecclesiastical time frameworks were replaced by the merchants' time regime. Mechanical clocks became widespread; they were generally placed in the main square and maintained by urban councils. Progressively, this new time regime took over, and by the late fifteenth century many documents mention 'the time o'clock' as a reference for contracts. Public authorities tried to homogenize weights and measures and tried to make them more easily comparable to other systems. Commercial accounting and notaries were latent phenomena in major cities by the mid-thirteenth century, especially in the Crown of Aragon (Sabaté, 2017).

The road network was at the centre of commerce and communications. Medieval roads tried to follow the shortest and most direct route between two points, using river valleys and plains and avoiding, if possible, steep slopes. Antoni Riera, analysing the Catalonian case, refers to foot routes, around 1 m wide, which were used by pedestrians and riders, and wheel roads, up to 4 m wide, which were smoothed out to allow carts to use them. The only major engineering works to be found in these roads were the bridges built to go over rivers and streams; natural fords were also commonly taken advantage of. Many of the bridges had only one arch, but multi-arched bridges built to go across major rivers were not rare. Bridges were generally paved, and their access was often barred by gates and towers. Travelling was a slow affair that generally took many days, and inns and other services on the roadsides provided travellers with lodging and refreshment. According to José Ángel García de Cortázar (1994), a mule train could travel approximately 30–40 km per day, whereas carts could do approximately 20–30 km, and inns tended to be spaced accordingly (García de Cortázar, 1994). The most common form of land transport was the mule train: carts were only used to transport very heavy goods, like iron, building stone or wood. The importance of properly keeping horses and other pack animals was remarked upon in numerous manuals published in the Iberian Peninsula, such as the *Libro de fecho de los cavallos* or *Libro de los Caballos*, written in Alfonso XI's court, the *Llibre de la menescalia*, written by the Valencian author Manuel Dies in the fifteenth century (Córdoba, 2006), and in Portugal the *Livro da Ensinança de Bem Cavalgar toda a sela*, written by King Duarte.

Increasingly, the work of cosmographers and geographers was linked to commercial travels and the exploration of distant lands. Apart from the famous late medieval treatises – the *Libro de viajes* dictated to the Nasrid scholar Ibn Yuzayyi (1349) by the Tangier-born Ibn Battuta, after 20 years of travels in the East; the *Embajada a Tamerlán* by Ruy Martínez de Clavijo (1406); and the *Andanzas e Viajes*, by Pero Tafur (1476) – Antonio de Nebrija's (1499) *Cosmographia* is a clear precursor of this genre. The first authors to put on paper what was known about America were Pedro Mártir de Anglería, who compiled different accounts of the earliest trips to the Indies, between 1494 and 1526, and Martín Fernández de Enciso in his *Tratado de Náutica* (1519). And the Portuguese *Crónica dos feitos da Guiné* (1452/1460), written by Zurara, or the *Esmeraldo de situ orbis* (1505–1508), by Duarte Pacheco Pereira with information about the Portuguese voyages and geographical information about Brazil, Africa and Asian shores and ports. Another very important development was in cartography. An important tradition developed in the Catalan–Aragonese area namely in Mallorca, which, following Mediterranean tradition, achieved an enormous development, innovation and quality in the late fourteenth century; one of the most important and best-known examples is the famous Mediterranean-centred *Atles Català* (c. 1375). From that tradition the Portuguese developed their own cartography knowledge, with further advanced cartographic innovations from the early fifteenth century onwards, in order to chart the new Atlantic routes and lands that their seafarers were discovering, such as the *Portulano de Pedro Reinel* (1485), with the West African coast well represented; or the *Atlas de Lopo Homem* (1519), which includes the Brazilian coast, the north and southern Atlantic, as well as the Indic Ocean and Molucas, by Pedro Reinel, Jorge Reinel and Lopo Homem. The Mallorcan, Catalan and Portuguese cartographers of the fourteenth and fifteenth centuries gave an enormous contribution to the advancement of cartography techniques.

6.4.2 Navigation into and around Medieval Iberia

Concerning sea travel, the merchants of the Peninsula frequented three main areas. The first was the Cantabrian Sea, which connected the Iberian and the Atlantic European markets through the Galician, Asturian and Basque harbours. The second included the Atlantic shores of the Bay of Cádiz, the Portuguese coast and the Western African coast – Pierre Chaunu's 'Atlantic Mediterranean' – which became especially important in the second half of the fifteenth century, owing to the colonization of the Canaries, trade links with Madeira and Azores, and the discovery of America. Cities such as Lisbon, Porto, Sanlúcar and Seville played an exceptionally active role in this area. The third area was the western Mediterranean, which was the natural sphere of influence of the Crown of Aragon, where Valencian, Catalan, Portuguese and Italian merchants (especially Pisan and Genoese) created an extraordinarily active commercial zone in which the harbours of Valencia, Barcelona and Palma de Mallorca played a prominent role until the end of the Middle Ages.

Technical advances in ship construction led to the design of faster and safer ships. The most commonly used types were *naos* and *cocas*, large ships with a symmetric layout (prow and stern), a rotund shape, a single mast with square sails, and a sternpost rudder. In Portugal, the written documents also suggest the frequent use of *barcas*, *pinaças*, carracks and caravels (*caravelas*). References to caravels are found in Portuguese documents as early as the thirteenth century, although the caravel with the famous Latin sail, characteristic of the fifteenth-century Atlantic expansion may not have been developed until this century (Marques, 1987: 136–137). In the Mediterranean, rowing ships, such as galleys, fustas and galiots, were more common. New shipbuilding and navigation techniques provided the Iberian kingdoms with the right tools for political and commercial expansion overseas in the late Middle Ages and the Early Modern Age. Concerning river sailing, most Iberian rivers were only traversed by small craft (*barcas*) and ferries at busy crossings (trade routes, transhumance roads, foot roads). These barges are abundantly attested on the Minho, Douro, Ebro, Tagus and Guadalquivir rivers, as well as on many other rivers in connexion with land routes (Casado, 2002; Pujol, 2015).

Some rivers, however, were navigable in their lower courses, sometimes very far inland, for instance the Ebro and the Guadalquivir, and in Portugal the Minho, Lima, Douro and Tagus. The Ebro and the Guadalquivir are very similar rivers, and both are neatly divided into two parts: the lower course of the Ebro, between Tortosa and Mequinenza, is similar to the lower course of the Guadalquivir, between Sanlúcar and Seville; both slope gently and their flow is abundant, and were navigable even for large craft; upriver from Mequinenza and Seville, respectively, the Ebro and the Guadalquivir change radically. Between Mequinenza and Tudela and between Seville and Córdoba, the river can be navigated only by much smaller ships and the conditions are much harsher. Similarly, the lower course of the Tagus, around Lisbon, is fully navigable and, to some extent, this is also the case with the Douro, so large Atlantic ships could easily access the city of Porto (Córdoba, 2006). From Lisbon and from Porto, smaller vessels like barcas linked the river mouths with the interior, sometimes as far as 100 km upriver. In northern Portugal, the Minho River, up to Valença, and the Lima River, up to Ponte de Lima, were also navigable for oceanic ships until the fifteenth century. Fluvial routes, through the combined sailing of oceanic and smaller craft, ensured that these coastal enclaves remained linked with the interior of the kingdom. This greatly enhanced the position of Lisbon and Porto, which became commercial hubs at the centre of a dense network of sea, fluvial and land routes (Marques, 1987: 123-131; Melo, 2009, I: 175-203). Timber rafting, especially pine, used as a construction material, was another important activity: from the Albarracín range, the timber was floated down the Tagus, the Ebro and the Júcar towards Catalonia, Valencia, Toledo and Portugal; and from the Cazorla and Segura ranges, down the Guadalquivir and Segura rivers towards Córdoba, Seville and Murcia. Finally, it is interesting to note that the development of trade and industry often led to the settlement of foreign communities in commercial harbours, for example Portuguese in Valencia in the late fifteenth century (Muñoz et al., 2019).

6.5 Conclusion

Concerning technical innovation and scientific progress, the evidence does not justify the belief that the Iberian Peninsula was during this period in any way backward or 'peripheral' to other centres in the Mediterranean and Northern Europe. The innovations affecting production were the same, appeared at similar times, and had the same influence on productivity as anywhere else.

If anything, the Iberian Peninsula benefitted from the presence of al-Andalus, of contacts with the east and its texts, including translations by members of the different cultures that coexisted within it (Christians, Muslims and Jews).

The invention of the printing press in the mid-fifteenth century had an enormous impact in the dissemination of knowledge and scientific works. Although technical and scientific works were never more than 10% of all books produced, their numbers clearly increased in the sixteenth century. Half of the scientific volumes published during this period were medical treatises, and the other half dealt with such topics as cosmography, mathematics, artillery and nautical science. Vernacular tongues became an important vehicle for the dissemination of science; approximately 70% of the books published in this period in the Iberian Peninsula were in the vernacular, and the rest in Latin (López Piñero et al., 1981–1986).

One of the clearest exponents of technical progress in the Iberian kingdoms lies with naval construction and navigation in the fourteenth and fifteenth centuries. Initially, this allowed Catalan merchants to achieve a predominant position in Mediterranean trade between the thirteenth and fifteenth centuries; later, these advances made possible the colonization of the Canaries, Azores and Madeira by Castilian and Portuguese navigators; the opening of the west coast of Africa to trade; the opening of the route around the Cape of Good Hope by Bartolomeu Dias in 1488; the discovery by Vasco da Gama in 1497–1499 of the maritime route that led to India and south-east Asia; the conquest and colonization of America (after Columbus' first voyage in 1492); and, finally, the symbolic joint enterprise that resulted in the first circumnavigation of the globe (Magallanes–Elcano, 1519–1522).

One should remember the political framework of Iberia and its evolution from the thirteenth to the fifteenth centuries, as a general context in which the economic evolution and technological patterns we have been talking about should be considered. Particularly it must be taken into account the political context related with the existence of different political entities in Iberia and its evolution during those medieval centuries. Each one with its different political organization, different jurisdictional and juridical features, as well as dissimilar social, economic and cultural realities. The features and evolution of economic and technological patterns were also affected by that political entourage. Therefore, even though this book is about economic evolution and not the political one, the reader should always keep in mind the political reality of Iberia in these centuries. So, we will rapidly and briefly comment on the relationship between the technological evolutions and the political context, summing up some general perspectives.[5]

It should be pointed out that those realities could differ greatly in certain aspects between those Iberian states or kingdoms, as well as within each one,

---

[5] For more information, see Chapter 4.

while they could also be quite similar in other aspects: the Crown of Aragon (Aragon, Catalonia, Mallorca and the Balearic Islands); Navarre; Castile and León; Portugal; and the Muslim territories: Al-Andalus/Kingdom of Granada. At the end of the historical period studied here, in the late fifteenth century, these five main political structures will become only two kingdoms from 1492 onwards: Portugal and Spain. In all these different political entities, the cultural and technological influences that came from certain origins, combined in different proportions with their diverse internal features, led to certain particularities and diversity in the technological and economic features of each one.

The ancient Iberian traditions (from Roman and Germanic times) and Islamic features were differently felt in the northern regions, with their reduced period of Islamic rule, and in the south with a much stronger and lasting presence. Its influence was present throughout Iberia in a more or less direct or important way. On the other hand, the influence of southern European regions, such as France and Italy, was particularly felt by land and by the Mediterranean in the Crown of Aragon, while Navarre was particularly connected with France. For Castile and León a double or triple influence of those regions came from the southern Mediterranean and Atlantic (Seville) and the border with the Moorish kingdom of Granada. The control of the northern part of the Strait of Gibraltar from the thirteenth century onwards was of major importance for the opening of regular maritime trips from the Mediterranean to northern Europe.

In northern Iberia, the Atlantic Biscaia shores and north-west Galicia had some strong connections with the Basque Country, France and England, as well as Portugal. Finally, Portugal with its western and southern Atlantic coast was strongly connected with the Mediterranean Catalan–Aragonese area and Italy, as well as with the northern European England, Ireland, France and Flanders (Bruges), as well as Galicia. And from the fifteenth century onwards there were increasing contacts with the Atlantic islands of Azores and Madeira and the Canaries, the North African Moroccan shores and southwards along the Atlantic African coast to the Gulf of Guinea.

In this context we believe that technological innovation, whether imported from other regions or whether as the result of local development of traditional innovations, was particular important in the development of certain economic activities and, at the same time, those enhanced economic areas produced or contributed, in turn, to further knowledge and technical innovation. The important developments, both in quality and production levels, connected with the markets in several industrial activities, such as the textile industries (e.g. silk in Catalonia and Portugal; wool all over Iberia) and their diverse specializations; or tanning and leather production, some of it of high quality, as with the famous *cordovão*, produced in different Iberian locations, which both benefited from the Islamic tradition that was incorporated in some late medieval innovations. The same could be said of iron production in the Basque region, which seems to have benefited from a local tradition that was itself strongly influenced by important technological innovations in iron imported from France.

In the same way, we can find examples of the importance of technology for economic development in rural production, such as in wines. These were increasingly produced to accommodate the needs and tastes of north European markets, and at the same time assure the ability to make transportation in time for to those markets with good quality conditions. The same could be said about the widespread use of hydraulic energy, as anywhere else in late medieval Europe.

Furthermore, the use of commercial and accounting and financial tools, new technologies created in Italy that were 'imported' to Catalonia and, to a lesser extent, to Castile and Portugal, were very important in enhancing the maritime and commercial activities that many Iberian peoples strongly developed in the Mediterranean and in the Atlantic from the fourteenth century onwards.

Finally, the importance of maritime techniques and navigation for the expansion of Iberian kingdoms during the fifteenth century must also be stressed. This expansion was related to the development of naval construction, as well as to the development of orientation and navigation techniques for Atlantic and oceanic travels. The continuous evolution of these techniques is seen during the fourteenth and fifteenth centuries in Portugal, Castile, Aragon and Catalonia, as well as in the use of new naval warfare techniques, such as the intensive use of artillery on board, and the definition and regular use of new maritime trade routes to the Americas, Africa and the Cape route to India. It was thanks to the evolution of naval construction and improvements in navigation techniques and tools for the open ocean that such evolution was made possible. At the same time, existing techniques were further improved in order to allow the creation of new and more accurate cartography, such as the *portolanos*, showing not just coastal areas but also the dominant winds and ocean currents, allowing safer but also more rigorous voyages.

7

Living Standards, 1000–1500

HIPÓLITO RAFAEL OLIVA HERRER, PERE BENITO I MONCLÚS AND ISABEL DOS GUIMARÃES SÁ

7.1 Introduction

By the year 1000 the Andalusian caliphate constituted a highly urbanized society, where the largest cities in Europe were located, while the economy of the Christian kingdoms of Iberia was characterized by a low level of urbanization and a poor market development. Five hundred years later, the territory of al-Andalus had disappeared, and its economy had been absorbed and transformed into the Christian kingdoms. Certainly, there were regional differences; however, at the end of the period they were integrated into the international economy, their rate of relative urbanization was high in a European context and living standards had improved.

The territorial expansion led by the Christian kingdoms appears as a factor to consider, as well as a series of internal dynamics that modified the structure of demand, such as the endogenous growth of cities, the impact of trade on the agrarian economy and the increase in rural stratification that, at different levels, made the market important for the satisfaction of needs and peasant consumption. Also, the jurisdictional fragmentation that characterizes the beginning of this period acted as an important stimulus to the start and evolution of these processes.

Series of prices and wages are difficult to elaborate from medieval sources, but the available evidence allows us to analyse the evolution of consumption levels and living standards, in direct relation with social hierarchy. Food, housing, clothing and furniture functioned as markers of these social differences. In the Christian kingdoms, a strong increase in noble spending dedicated to the conspicuous consumption of products partially purchased on the international market is documented throughout the period. Urban elites tried to emulate such patterns. The most relevant factor, however, was the improvement in the living conditions of large sectors of the population. After the Black Death, with the consolidation of a rural elite, important sectors of the population were attracted by the lifestyle of the urban elites. This evolution can also be detectable in the lifestyle of vast sectors of the urban population. Besides the satisfaction of basic needs, homes were improved and there was an investment in furniture and textiles. The diet also underwent substantial improvements, but this did not prevent those who depended mostly on bread from being highly vulnerable to death and famine.

This chapter will analyse these developments and their causes in detail, and incorporates a gender approach, since it is possible to determine different consumption patterns among women and men. Women's work was important for the support of family economies and the dowry constituted an important device for the transfer of assets among most social strata.

The structure of public spending and investment was different in the Andalusian sphere and in the Christian kingdoms. While in al-Andalus a greater weight of the state in the construction of infrastructures is perceptible, in the Christian kingdoms, with the exception of some specific interventions by the monarchs, the cities or ecclesiastical institutions carried out most of the public spending, including the expenses of charitable institutions. Also, the importance of the war cannot be underestimated, because a significant part of the spending at all levels was directed to the construction and repair of walls, fortresses and the acquisition of military equipment.

In general terms, the structure of aristocratic expenditure was more focused on guaranteeing reproduction than on innovation or the development of investments aimed at the expansion and reproduction of capital. In contrast, this type of investment took place on a different scale; for example, the integration of the rural economy into the market created the conditions for a rural elite to accumulate capital and invest in the land market aimed at rationalizing their exploitations and increasing productivity. The urban elites themselves invested in the creation of rural industries that generated specialized productions, in some cases with high added value.

The analysis of income distribution must take into account the differences between the Christian kingdoms and the Andalusian world, where a developed tax system had been implemented. In the former, agrarian production was subjected to both royal levies and seigneurial exactions, and as such the analysis of lordship is relevant. The landscape was remarkably modified in the last centuries of the Middle Ages with the implementation of a fiscal system that financed war and supported the ongoing building of the various political units of the Iberian Peninsula, and which became the main source of income for the aristocracies. The fact that cities implemented their own taxation must also be taken into consideration. In any case, the consolidation of the fiscal system was compatible with the improvement of the population's standard of living, thus constituting good evidence of the extent of the growth experienced.

Our knowledge of the economic history of the Nasrid kingdom of Granada is more limited. While we are well informed about the productive structures and about the richness and diversity of its material culture, a history of consumption and living standards able to compensate for the serious deficits in historical sources is still to be undertaken, forcing us to draw a somewhat blurred and impressionistic picture.

7.2 Living Standards

Unlike the studies carried out for later historical periods, it is difficult to make a complete approximation to the evolution of living standards relying on prices, wages and consumption models for the medieval period. Regardless of the transformations that occurred in the socioeconomic structure of those societies throughout the whole period, the available series of prices and wages are still scarce and cover unevenly the fourteenth and fifteenth centuries. They also raise issues of representativity. For instance, the most complete series have been established using construction wages, which are not necessarily representative of all wage earners. In fact, the various trades had their particularities and they contributed differently to the labour market; besides, not all wages were entirely paid in currency. This does not deny the value of the evolution of wages as an indicator, but the comparison between series that may have been built on different materials, and reflect disparate situations, must be approached with caution.

Hamilton, in his now classic work on prices and wages in Aragon, Valencia and Navarre between 1351 and 1500, pointed out three cycles or phases of evolution of wages that, broadly speaking, coincide with the evolution observed in most regions of Western Europe: a sharp increase in wages between 1340 and 1380, attributed to labour shortages; a continuation of the upward trend between 1380 and 1420 with regional differences; and, lastly, a phase characterized by oscillations that took place during a good part of the fifteenth century and that defined a cycle of real wages significantly higher than the pre-plague period. Wages began to fall in Aragon in 1420 and in Navarre in 1425, although recoveries occurred throughout the fifteenth century. In Valencia, the decline in real wages began around 1470 and would not recover the previous levels (Hamilton, 1936), a decline that reflected the increase in the availability of labour.

Further research has introduced nuances to this general picture by adding regional variants. In the kingdom of Aragon, the index of real wages, deflated according to the price of cereal, shows three great cycles between 1300 and 1430. The first one, during the first half of the fourteenth century, was a cycle of low wages followed by a doubling of wages in the years after the plague, lasting until 1380. Finally, after a brief fall between 1383 and 1386, wages would resume an upward path until 1410, then suffer a brief relapse, to recover their high levels around 1420 (Zulaica, 1994: 203–205). Zulaica also shows the contextual impact of dynamics of an extra-economic nature on the evolution of wages, such as the start of the war with Castile, before the plague, or the attempts to regulate construction wages in 1358.

For Catalonia we have recent series: the nominal wages compiled for Manresa by Fynn-Paul show increases of around 50% after the Black Death and 200% in the 1380s and 1390s in relation to pre-plague levels (Fynn-Paul, 2015). The series compiled by Maltas, which offers deflated real wages from a commodity shopping basket, is even more illustrative. It distinguishes a period between 1290 and 1348 of relatively stable wages, and a second phase, between 1348 and 1400, of a strong rise in real wages. His analysis also introduces nuances that reflect the failure of the wage appraisals of 1348–1350 and the impact of short-term crises: whether these are cycles of famine, in which the price of cereal shoots up and the purchasing power of wages plummets, as in the episodes of 1291–1292, 1324–1325, 1333–1334, 1346–1347 and 1374–1375; or the sensitivity of wages to mortality crises, as in 1334, 1348, 1362, 1371, 1375, 1381 and 1384 (Maltas, 2019). Fifteenth-century information available for Catalonia is more limited, although it seems to confirm a trend of falling wages from 1440 onwards (Argilés, 2010).

Data concerning the Crown of Castile covers mainly the fifteenth century. The analysis of real wages carried out for Burgos and Toledo shows a trend towards stability in the first half of the century and a decrease in real wages beginning in its second half, in line with population growth, with a critical stage between 1460 and 1480, a moment of great political instability and continuous monetary changes (Izquierdo, 1983; Casado, 1991). However, some data available for the fourteenth century, in cities such as Toledo, show that, despite this decline, real salaries in 1384 were equivalent to those received in 1475. This suggests a scenario of high wages for almost a century, from the second half of the fourteenth century, accentuated by the stability or decrease in the prices of products such as meat or textiles (Izquierdo, 1983), or other indirect indicators, such as the increase in the quality of the textile products consumed by the popular classes during the period (Oliva, 2001). A similar trend can be detected in Portugal. From 1261 to 1368, stability prevailed and the amount of money in circulation increased, confirming the beginning of the monetization process of the economy. Wages appear to have increased until 1369, although subsequent currency devaluations until 1415 meant a decrease in real wages. However, until the last years of the fifteenth century, the real wages of artisans enjoyed a high degree of stability and their purchasing power increased significantly, thanks to the contribution of lower prices in manufactured products (Ferreira, 2014).

The determination of living standards based on prices and wages for the medieval period continues to be problematic, either because we do not know basic factors such as the number of working days per year and its variation over time or the combined volume of household income apart from male work, also because it is difficult to transfer the estimates made for urban workers to the rural world, where the majority of the population lived.

Besides the existence of salaried work, which can be verified during a large part of the period, living standards in the rural world are directly related to the ability to access land and its evolution throughout the period. Also, peasant food consumption cannot be understood without taking into account the resources available for an important part of rural strata: small orchards, domestic animals, fruits of the forest or hunting. In any case, there is a general consensus on the increasing role of the market in the rural world. The model of commercialization of the economy, initially developed for England, has been successfully tested and transferred, albeit with some modifications, to the Mediterranean societies and, to a lesser extent, to the Iberian Peninsula. All in all, the densification of the exchange relations seems evident for most of the Iberian territories from the thirteenth century onwards, which has transformed significantly our perception of peasants as economic agents (Oliva, 2007; Furió, 2019) and also as active consumers.

Consumption models have not been developed in order to allow geographic comparison between economies whose behaviour over the period could have been different. In any case, the available evidence suggests a generalized pattern of increase in living standards after the Black Death that is consistent with other indicators. The drop in cereal prices may have had a major effect. This is suggested by the series of prices for Barcelona in silver, which registered a significant decrease after 1380. Of course, this downward trend lasts until 1495, in what seems to reflect a dynamic of stagnation typical of the Catalan territory. In the Crown of Castile, the prices of cereal were comparatively lower in the last quarter of the fifteenth than in the first half of the century (Ladero, 1988b; Casado, 1991), but real wages were already falling at that time, perhaps reflecting a dynamic of demographic and economic growth that is consistent with what is known for other peninsular territories.

In any case, the available sources, the insufficiency of recent research and difficulties in quantification make it necessary in most cases to determine living standards based on the analysis of consumption patterns and their evolution, which begin to be better known in the late Middle Ages. The problems in obtaining quantitative evidence for Muslim Iberia are even greater. There are even difficulties in obtaining sources that allow, if not quantification, a description of the consumption patterns of the different social strata.

In short, the determination of living standards before the Black Death is very problematic. Available data on prices and wages for the first half of the fourteenth century documents a stagnation or a relative deterioration of the living conditions of urban wage earners. The evolution in the rural world is related to the possible changes in the structure of peasant farms and the expansion of the peasant segment with insufficient properties for the maintenance of the family unit, with the consequent need to resort to wage labour, either part-time or as the main source of income. At the height of the thirteenth century, there was no significant expansion of this segment

(Clemente, 2004), and phenomena comparable to the wide fragmentation of farms observed in other European regions seem not to have occurred (Campbell, 2005), thus making improbable the pauperization of a significant part of the peasantry. Lower demographic pressure and the possibility of acquiring land in conquered territories seem to provide an explanation for this phenomenon.

The first half of the fourteenth century was undoubtedly a period of difficulties in the Iberian Peninsula, although historiography no longer conceives it as a period of systemic economic depression (Furió, 2010b; Oliva, 2013). What seems clear is that the demographic impact of the plague of 1348 and other epidemics during the second half of the fourteenth century pushed up wages sharply, giving rise to a phenomenon comparable to what British historiography call the 'golden age of wage earners'. The decline in wages would fall unevenly: early in Catalonia and well into the second half of the fifteenth century in the Crown of Castile and Valencia. This was not an obstacle to the fact that, during the entire medieval period, consumption capacity was recurrently affected during short-term crises, when cereal prices skyrocketed, and whose effects on family economies, partly to be studied, were prolonged in time. The most serious subsistence crises, such as the fourteenth-century famines of 1334 and 1374–1376, or the episodes of 1422, 1438, 1473–1474, and 1477, 1494–1495 and 1502–1504 in the fifteenth century, seem to have affected the whole of the Iberian Peninsula, although only in some of these critical cycles (Oliva & Benito, 2007).

7.3 Distribution of Income

7.3.1 Seigneurial Regime and Tax System

The analysis of the distribution of income in the peninsular Christian kingdoms must begin by taking into account the seigneurial regime, which operated as a mechanism of absorption of income by kings, nobles and ecclesiastical institutions, through the taxation of agricultural production. The nobility did not constitute a defined social category until the twelfth century. Its formation took place through a complex process related to the territorial expansion and consolidation of the political territories of the different peninsular Christian kingdoms, within the context of a dynamic tension with the monarchy, through which aristocrats obtained resources and consolidated positions of power. The internal social differentiation itself in the local communities was another factor that made it possible to integrate the lowest ranks of this social group. The income of the nobles came mainly from the income they obtained from their domains and from the benefits that war provided them in the form of spoils and new land acquisitions. However, accounts that allow a quantification of this income are available only for the fourteenth and fifteenth centuries. Certainly, there were significant differences of wealth and hierarchy among the nobility, designated *ricos hombres* in Castile and León, *ricos-homens* in Portugal, or the twelfth-century Catalonian *comitores* and *varvasores* and the lower nobility, whose properties, manors and income were located on a regional or local scale.

The peasants exploited the land autonomously, but their integration into a lordship implied the payment of some rents to the landlords and to a varied number of beneficiaries. They received income from the transfer of tenures via inheritance or sale, in recognition of their lordship and also rents derived from the exercise of justice on the territory. In some places of the North, peasants carried out labour services for a few days a year in the plots directly exploited by the landlords. There was a huge disparity of conditions, even if, for the Crown of Castile, the seigneurial exactions, not including tithes, took between 10% and 20% of the gross output of an average peasant (Clemente Ramos, 2004: 238) and in the Barcelona county, including tithes, it summed up between 18% and 45% of cereal production (Benito, 2003: 354).

Tithes represented a very important part of seigniorial rents because they taxed, with different rules for each product and territory, a great variety of agricultural products. They can be documented as early as 878 in the *Marca Hispánica*, being claimed and appropriated by the church throughout the twelfth and thirteenth centuries, although its collection was divided into the hands of a multitude of beneficiaries, including members of the small nobility (Mallorquí, 2011: 98–136).

It is generally accepted that manorial incomes were lower in the Iberian Peninsula as a whole than in other European territories. The increased availability of land and the processes of colonization to the south provide an accepted explanation for this phenomenon. But in reality, the seigniorial system never disappeared from the Iberian Peninsula. The conquest of new territories was followed by the establishment of lordships in a diversified but constant way. The alienation of jurisdictions by the kings during the fourteenth and fifteenth centuries constitutes a substantive part of the process, although the characteristics of this structure were substantially transformed from the fourteenth century onwards, the elements that taxed agricultural production becoming less and less relevant.

Until well into the fourteenth century the characteristic of the patrimonies and manorial rights of the great lineages was fragmentation and dispersion. In Castile and Portugal, the egalitarian system of inheritance partitions also implied the need to rebuild the heritage in each generation. Although the most recent studies are re-evaluating the processes traditionally linked to the crisis of the fourteenth century, the perception of the period remains as a time of difficulty for the noble estates. Its overcoming occurred thanks to the appearance of new sources of income, the concession by the kings of tax revenue being one example. The process can be traced in Portugal, Aragon and Navarre and reaches its highest levels in Castile, where it has been calculated that up to 70% of the income of some aristocratic families came from these new sources. In Catalonia, from the thirteenth century onwards, land transfer incomes became more important, thus encumbering the transactions of fiefs, land holdings and the perception of jurisdictional rights.

As a result, at the end of the period, if we discount the benefits brought by the production of wool intended for the export market to some noble families and ecclesiastical institutions, or some productions of high value in the market, such as olive oil, agricultural production as a whole no longer constituted a significant source of income for the various peninsular nobilities.

At the same time, other institutions developed, such as the *mayorazgo* or *morgadio*, transforming aristocratic wealth into inalienable heritages and favouring their integral transmission to the first-born along male lines, or other systems such as the freedom to test in Aragon that could avoid fragmentation (Álvarez, 2016). Otherwise, these restructurings also involved adjustments within the nobility itself, even if we cannot quantify them. The increase in inequality within this social group seems to be one of the consequences of the process. Henceforth, an important segment of the lower nobility had to be remunerated for their services to the great aristocratic lineages in order to obtain its main source of revenue.

The construction of fiscal systems follows different rhythms in the various peninsular kingdoms, although some features are common to all of them. Its formation was precocious in the Crown of Castile, because it developed from 1269 onwards, from the reign of Alfonso X, although there had been previous attempts to establish a taxation that would encompass all the subjects of the kingdom. In the Crown of Aragon, the succession of armed conflicts in the mid-fourteenth century and the growing needs of the monarchy explain the rapid development of a complex fiscal system. In Portugal, the process developed from 1371 in the context of the Wars with Castile (Henriques, 2014).

Although war appears as a determining factor, the various peninsular territories implemented different fiscal systems. Thus, in the different territories of the Crown of Aragon the development of taxation is linked to the *imposiciones* (direct taxes) and the emergence of a market for public debt of local institutions (Verdés, 2015: 243-272), which did not develop to the same extent in other peninsular kingdoms. In any case, the new tax systems contributed to finance military campaigns, royal policies and the increasingly complex administrative machinery of the different kingdoms, regardless of whether a very significant part of these incomes was transferred to the nobilities, as previously mentioned. Also, taxes generated an important business that benefited intermediaries, either at the level of the kingdom or locally, and the debt holders of the different institutions. In some territories, such as Valencia, the Crown managed to withhold only between a quarter and a third of its own taxes (Mira, 1997: 549-550).

The impact of the implementation of the tax system on family economies has not been calculated. Specific studies show that the increase in fiscal pressure is directly related to the harshness of some short-term crises, and to indebtedness and even loss of property of the most vulnerable social segments. Regarding the long-term impact of the tax system, although it has been pointed out that fiscal indebtedness was one of the factors that engulfed economic growth in Catalonia during the fifteenth century, in the rest of the peninsula its implementation was compatible with intense economic growth during the same period.

In close connection with the development of royal taxation, local tax systems were also implemented during the fourteenth and fifteenth centuries. Previously, the existing taxation in the cities was limited to the amounts needed to cover the costs of construction, repair of walls and some basic infrastructure. The new municipal revenues were generally collected through indirect taxes imposed on the consumption of basic products, such as meat or fish, although there were also direct taxes levied from the inhabitants of the city. City walls continued to be important, but local governments increasingly developed a set of policies for urban investment and the provision of infrastructures for trade, construction of water pipes and fountains, repair of bridges, maintenance of roads, prestigious constructions and even (although undoubtedly insufficient) charitable practices (Sánchez Martínez & Menjot, 2006).

7.3.2 Cities

The development of an urban network of cities and towns of different magnitude, together with the movement of pilgrimages (along the Camino de Santiago) and the colonization of the borders, started in the eleventh century, and led to the emergence of new social groups such as the bourgeois owners of suburban estates, merchants and specialized craftsmen. The former lived on the exploitation of orchards and vineyards, the latter profited from regional and interregional trade (maritime in the case of the Mediterranean and Atlantic ports) of luxury products, spices, manufactured products, and cereal, while the masters and officials of the artisan guilds, with more modest incomes, produced to satisfy the needs of a local demand.

Membership to the local elites was defined everywhere in terms of wealth. In numerous inland cities, more or less close to the border, military activities and land and livestock ownership constituted the primary source of income, forming a group defined by land ownership and military dedication. Economic growth and the development of commercial activities promoted a process of upward mobility. Thus, beginning in the thirteenth century, the maritime cities of the Crown of Aragon experienced a great expansion and specialization of the merchant and artisan groups. In Castilian and Portuguese cities, merchants, financiers and moneychangers during the fourteenth and fifteenth centuries also underwent processes of incorporation into the economic elites, which were never completely closed (Igual-Luis, 2018).

All these elites developed a common pattern of emulation of the nobility. During the fourteenth and fifteenth centuries the great bourgeoisie of Barcelona invested in the purchase of land and lordships. A comparable process of land acquisition and constitution of seigniorial domains is observable in Burgos during the fifteenth and sixteenth centuries (Casado, 1987) and the purchase of land in the peri-urban environments by wealthy citizens is documented in practically all the peninsular cities (Collantes, 1984; Bensch, 1995: 170-233). As a result, the income of the elites at the end of the period was very diverse in nature, including rents from rural properties and urban real estates, commercial activities, taxes and credit. The very peculiarities of the economic structure of the different cities are related to the predominance of one or more of such activities.

With the development of artisanal production from the thirteenth century onwards, some workshop owners reached a certain level of wealth. The large cities experienced an exponential increase in the population of young apprentices and wage earners of rural origin who worked in the workshops of the artisans, in suburban agriculture and in domestic service. Non-salaried workers earned between two-thirds and three-quarters of the value of the profit generated by the manufactured object. At the lowest level, unskilled workers were hired on a daily or seasonal basis (Carrère, 1967: 478-481; Bonnassie, 1975: 95-96). In the world of urban crafts, the guilds, which had originated in confraternal associations, regulated access to the trade, but also acted as mutual aid structures that provided financial aid in case of illness or during old age (González, 2009).

The contribution of women was important for the support of family economies, as well as to production and demand in general. The initial constitution of the family unit was carried out with contributions from both men and women. The bride's dowry was anticipated as part of the subsequent inheritance and the woman controlled its assets that reverted to her family in the case of death without descendants. A part of the dowry was delivered in furniture and domestic equipment used to set up the conjugal home. More affluent families could include land or money, although the transfer of land depended on the type of hereditary system. In old Catalonia, tradition imposed the undivided transfer of land to the first-born and the dowries were liquid (Aventín, 1996: 459-538; To Figueras, 1997). In other territories with more egalitarian inheritance systems, land could be part of the dowry, although families, and even legal compilations themselves, tried to minimize the dispersion of assets (Garcia-Oliver, 1991: 101-103).

Work at home had a clear feminine component, but women also worked in various trades outside the family: in the domestic market as vendors or resellers of food and artisanal production. In fact, some specific tasks of textile production, such as flax production or spinning, were mostly gender specific (Sequeira & Melo, 2012). The Castilian guild ordinances also document their work in crafts under the supervision of the father or husband, although widowed women could continue to exercise the trade on their own. Women's work is also documented as assistants in construction, in the fish preservation industry and even unloading goods in ports, although their wages were lower than those of men (López, 2010).

In the countryside, women took over work in the absence of men. However, their regular participation in a whole series of tasks related to agricultural production is also documented (Borrero Fernández, 1988). If sowing and harvesting were men's work, there were specifically female seasonal tasks, such as digging, performed by the most disadvantaged members of rural communities. Women also worked in the vineyards and participated in crops, either in the family farm or as wage labourers with lower remuneration than men (Coelho, 1990).

7.3.3 Peasants

The situation of seigniorial dependence was a unifying element for a good part of the peasants during the Middle Ages. It translated into the obligation to deliver a part of their production and even in some places in the satisfaction of free labour services, which practically disappeared during the fourteenth and fifteenth centuries. During this period, in most of the peninsula, changes in the seigneurial system led to a loss of interest by the nobility in the direct exploitation of the land, to which was added the devaluation of the old agricultural rents. Precarial grants or grants *in emphyteusis* to the peasants became a current form of cession of these lands for their exploitation.

The availability of land and livestock by peasant families is a key factor in the analysis of the distribution of income within the rural world. From the twelfth century onwards, the configuration of a rural elite that owned more land and extended their tenures through purchase or succession mechanisms can be observed, in comparison with a peasant stratum that worked, in part, on others' farms. However, the late medieval centuries saw an increase of differentiation in peasant communities. Without undervaluing the impact of mortality crises and factors such as emigration to the city, this evolution can be explained by the policy of seigniorial intermediaries and especially by the centrality acquired by the market and credit in the rural economy. The consolidation of a segment of wealthy peasants capable of producing for the urban market, of investing in land, and even of improving the productivity of their farms, appears as a general guideline. They also benefited from their role as seigneurial agents or as local creditors.

The effect, observable during the fifteenth century in a significant part of the peninsula, was the increase of inequality, in a context of population growth and of the rise of pressure over the production of cultivated land, although with some exceptions, such as depopulated old Catalonia. The expansion of the segment of peasants with insufficient properties that were forced to supplement their income by working on others' farms, in which Andalusia represented an extreme case, can also be observed in large areas of Castile or Valencia (Oliva, 2002; Viciano, 2012).

However, the long-term survival of rural communities was not threatened by increasing inequality. The income of rural communities was partially linked to the exploitation of a small cattle herd, poultry, and resources obtained from hunting, fishing or forest exploitation. Access to communal goods, although more restricted, continued to be important for the support of less favoured peasants. There were also reciprocal solidarity networks that made possible the sustainability of the rural community. Rural institutions themselves carried out these roles, thus explaining the survival of agrarian collectivism throughout the early modern period.

7.3.4 The Nasrid Kingdom

The distribution of income in the Nasrid kingdom is less well known. The documentation preserved for the period is limited and the reconstruction of numerous issues requires reading the documentation generated after the Castilian conquest. Also, historiography has until recently been especially interested in highlighting the comparison between the Nasrid and the Christian kingdoms concerning the different logics of political and social structuring, rather than in analysing sources of income and processes of social differentiation. Unlike the medieval Christian kingdoms, there were no seigneurial structures in the Nasrid world dedicated to tax production. The model of state political organization was based on a highly developed tax system that was very expensive for producers, although no quantifications can be established. The defensive needs of the emirate from the moment of its creation implied the multiplication of tax burdens well above those established by Islamic law. Apart from the capitation paid by all individuals, agricultural production was taxed with 10% for cereal, legumes and other products, and 2.5% for the vineyard, whereas a series of additional taxes were levied on the ownership of livestock. Other taxes were created regarding commercial transactions, transmission of inheritances and public works. A series of minor taxes of various characteristics completed the system (Galán, 1991).

Agriculture was characterized by the importance of irrigation and a high level of commercialization. Although the basis of agrarian production in the Nasrid kingdom consisted of small properties organized within the framework of rural communities (*alquerías*), the Crown had an important land and property heritage. Aside from the royal patrimony, the emir had his own assets, although it is difficult to differentiate between them. Additionally, a significant part of the cultivated land, that could reach 20%, exploited through leasing, was ascribed to the mosques for charitable or pious deeds (Trillo, 2000–2001).

There were also large estates in the surroundings of the cities that belonged to the aristocracy, which were exploited for lease or through sharecropping. We are little informed about their forms of acquisition, but we know that their numbers increased during the fifteenth century. The lineages close to the emir fattened their heritage at the expense of the public purse, either as concessions in payment of services or through purchases generated by the increasing economic needs of the emirs. At the end of the period, it is also clear that urban elites acquired properties in the suburbs (Rodríguez, 2016). These processes of formation of large properties multiplied after the conquest, accompanied by a parallel process of formation of seigniorial domains.

Inequality among the inhabitants of the *alquerías* is a proven element in the Nasrid world. Calculations for Almuñécar show that 10% of the most affluent peasants owned more than one-third of irrigated land (Trillo, 2000–2001). Paradoxically, the distribution of income in cities is less known, except for generic perceptions about the existence of an elite formed by state officials and wealthy merchants who invested in peri-urban farms. Or from approximations of material culture, which show the consumption of ceramics, fabrics and other highly refined products. It is difficult to define precise contours in what concerns the rest of the urban population, although we are aware of the existence of significant inequalities, both in income and consumption patterns.

7.4 Patterns of Consumption

7.4.1 Food

In the peninsular medieval Christian kingdoms, consumption patterns differed as much as, or more than, legal statutes or income. Food, clothing and housing are some of the fields where these distinctions are most evident and have been best studied. The difficulties lie, not so much in documenting distinctions in social consumption patterns, but in establishing the precise chronology and scope of the changes based upon very few quantitative indicators.

Religion played a fundamental role in the construction of different food systems for Christians, Jews and Muslims. Among lay Christians, the basic triad of the diet consisted of bread, wine and meat, while the hermitic diet consisted of bread, water and vegetables. The diets of the religious orders were codified with precision by specific rules and the usages of each community, which established the prohibitions and days of fasting according to the liturgical calendar. The latter could include more than 140 fasting days, during which fish and shellfish were mandatory, as well as abstinence from meat and animal fats (Coelho, 1995: 97). Among the laity, the patterns of food consumption differentiated the aristocracy and the high clergy from the underprivileged groups, the city dwellers from the rural inhabitants, the merchants from the small artisans and wage earners, and the wealthy peasants from the poor ones. Some have ventured the existence of a food system for each social group – a controversial issue because some basic components of the diet were shared by a large part of the urban and rural population. In any case, food was one of the fields in which the hierarchies and social distinctions of wealth and power were most evident. The abundance of food and the variety of dishes and delicacies were the prerogative of the wealthy, and medieval sumptuary laws attempted to limit the number of dishes served at their meals (Marques, 1965: 145–147).

Eating was a status symbol and food was ostentatiously displayed on court tables, where it assumed political significance and the clear function of exhibiting power. The consumption of meat was one of the distinctive features of the diet of the king and the nobility. In the fourteenth century, in the Aragonese royal court, mutton and goat meat were purchased and consumed almost daily, while pork and veal were eaten on public holidays or at certain times of the year. Poultry was widely accepted: chickens often appeared on the table, but the costlier capons, peacocks and geese were reserved for large banquets. The presence of game was much inferior to that of livestock and poultry, and it had an ostentation and representation character. Wine never lacked, from the fine reds or whites to the sweet and aromatic ones. Mutton was by far the most common meat at the tables of the lay aristocracy. Pork was consumed salted or used as cooking fat, while beef consumption had limited scope (García Marsilla, 1993; Riera, 1993: 195; 1995: 181–205).

The diet of the popular groups was based on the daily consumption of large amounts of cereals in the form of bread and soups, in contrast with the diet of the privileged social groups. However, the real food frontier during the medieval period separated the inhabitants of the countryside from the inhabitants of the city, who were protected by their privileges. Indeed, during the Middle Ages the oligarchies of towns, cities and even rural centres of greater importance, provided themselves with institutions, magistracies, skills and resources in order to fulfil a key purpose: to ensure the supply of cereals, and the access of their inhabitants to them. City councils also organized the supply of meat, fish and wine in the most populated cities, intervened in fruit markets, and implemented laws and devices to guarantee quality control and hygiene in their sale.

Consequently, the changes in the patterns of food consumption in the cities were strongly conditioned by the policies and circumstances of municipal and royal provisioning. The evolution towards the widespread consumption of wheat bread begins to be documented in Barcelona in the twelfth and thirteenth centuries. During the fourteenth and fifteenth centuries, in normal years, the majority of the city's inhabitants consumed wheat bread (about 164 kg of wheat a year per capita), although it is possible to find lower quality breads. In times of famine, the differences between consumption patterns, quality and quantity of bread between rich and poor increased, and cheaper loaves, which incorporated other cereals, multiplied. Vegetables were highly prized in both urban and rural markets, but their demand was lower than that of cereals. The urban authorities did not develop specific public policies to guarantee their supply, thus bearing proof to their secondary position in the markets.

The largest cities also organized the supply of meat through the annual negotiation of agreements with butchers, strongly limiting the profits of their trade. Meat was therefore a product of mass consumption, eaten by all the inhabitants of the city, although the quantities and qualities varied among social groups. The hierarchy of qualities and prices of meat for sale was designed to satisfy the needs of a heterogeneous population with a very different purchasing power. The consumption of meat of the urban elite did not differ much from the small nobility. The most consumed meat was mutton; veal had a seasonal consumption and poultry was reserved for festive days. The most disadvantaged groups aspired to eat mutton, but could not always afford it. They bought cheaper meat, such as sheep and goat, and viscera (Banegas, 2016: 34–39).

Saltwater and freshwater fish originating from the main seaports and from riverine populations was transported to urban markets in the mainland, where it was consumed fresh, dried, soaked or smoked, either during Lent or in other fasting days (Rodrigo, 2009: 547–577). The urban supply of wine was ensured by the production of the suburban vineyards, and by the import of quality wines, whose consumption was reserved for the social groups with greater purchasing power.

In quantitative terms, between 60% and 70% of the food budget was devoted to the purchase of cereal, meat and wine and the remaining 30–40% was distributed among other products. In the case of the salaried population, the purchase of cereal could absorb two-thirds of the annual budget. By the end of the period, the popular eating pattern should not be very far from the recent estimates made for Seville in the early sixteenth century, where the average daily consumption of an employee consisted of 450 grams of bread, 150 grams of meat, 41 grams of fish and 0.4 litres of wine (González, 2015).

Unlike the cities, in the rural world, formed by peasant producers, small artisans and wage earners, the food supply was not institutionally guaranteed, at least in small population centres. An added factor to consider is that part of the peasant diet was based on products obtained from their orchards (although not all peasants had them), their own livestock and poultry, products collected in forest areas and from fishing. Peasants reserved part of their production for home consumption and a variable portion of its surplus to the local market, once rents had been paid to the landlords. The development from the eleventh to twelfth centuries of a dense network of local markets allowed wealthy peasants to implement marketing strategies for production that would have an impact on their food consumption patterns. One of them was to send the wheat to the market, taking full advantage of the price fluctuations, and to reserve the cheaper grains for their own consumption. Thus, compared to the citizens' preference for white bread, in the rural world, barley and *mediado* or *terciado* breads, that is to say, mixtures of wheat, barley, rye, millet or spelt, were consumed, although well-off peasants also ate white bread (Riera, 1998: 37; Maltas Montoro, 2019: 179). After wheat, rye was the most sought-after cereal and probably one of the most consumed in mountain areas (Clemente, 2004: 118-119). The evolution in the late Middle Ages also developed towards the consumption of higher quality breads. At the end of the period, in wide parts of the Crown of Castile, wheat appears to have been the only bread-making cereal. Recourse to other breads survived in the north facade, part of Catalonia and in areas where the conditions of the soil for growing wheat were limited, such as northern Portugal.

Pigs played an important role in the peasant diet, and their meat was eaten fresh in winter and salted or as sausage during the rest of the year. They also produced lard, the most used cooking fat, as well as bacon (Santos, 2006). Sheep and goats, on the other hand, were eaten old, when their capacity to produce wool and milk was exhausted. Milk was transformed into cheese and butter, but its consumption in raw form is documented only among the wealthy.

Overall, it can be said that the period witnessed a clear trend towards a consumption of higher quality breads with a predominance of wheat and a greater consumption of meat. This evolution was propitiated both by a higher consumption capacity of the populations and by the implementation of systems that guaranteed supply. In the countryside, the consumption of pork replaced the meats that were more present and appreciated in the city.

Quantifying food consumption and its evolution in the kingdom of Granada is more difficult, although we are informed about the basic components of food systems from culinary and medical treatises and, in particular, from the *hisba* treatises of market regulation. Food markets were regulated in Muslim cities, although food prices were only set in times of famine. Cereal formed the basis of the diet of a large part of the population. The best quality wheat bread was reserved for the consumption of the upper classes, while the rest consumed second-class flours and mixed breads that incorporated barley, panic grass, or millet. In periods of scarcity, wild plants and leguminous were used to make bread. In addition to bread, most of the population consumed cereals in the form of porridge to which fat, cheap meat or giblets could be added. The introduction of pasta and wheat semolina, used to make couscous, was late in al-Andalus, although it was already widespread in the Nasrid period (García Sánchez, 1996).

Archaeological studies in Andalusian sites have shown that the main meats consumed were sheep and goats, the latter more affordable for most of the population, followed by poultry and, to a lesser extent, beef (Vaquerizo Gil, 2017). The most precious meat was lamb, which functioned as marker of status and was consumed by elites, whereas the rest of the population ate it only on festive occasions. Roast meats were also considered luxury products. Meat was generally eaten in the form of stews prepared with vegetables and social differences were expressed through the quantity and quality of the meat. Meatballs and meat sausages made with fat and spices were another popular way of consuming meat.

Nasrid elites did not greatly appreciate fish, which was used by the popular groups as a substitute for meat. Cooking used primarily olive oil, of which there were different qualities and prices, whereas cooking with butter was restricted to the wealthy. Diet in the kingdom of Granada was also characterized by a high intake of legumes, fruit and vegetables, due to the extensive development of irrigated agriculture in the Nasrid kingdom and to the variety of conservation techniques. The consumption of sweets was abundant, since they were made with low-price products, the most popular being fritters with honey or cheese (García Sánchez, 1986). Regardless of the legal and cultural norms that limited its consumption, drinking wine was a common practice in court and aristocratic circles, and there were even famous wines, such as those from Málaga. The peasant diet is less known, although some differences can be perceived if compared to urban consumption patterns, such as the consumption of lower quality breads, made with cheaper cereals and a higher presence of game.

7.4.2 Housing

In the cities of the Christian kingdoms, despite the existence of important regional differences, it is possible to reconstruct the essential features of the urban hamlet from the records of late medieval ecclesiastical properties. The typical construction model consisted of narrow plots with patios at the rear of the houses, where orchards could be located, and sheds for storage. Some of these houses had multiple storeys that projected outwards over public space or even formed passageways over the streets. Although for a long time the dominant typology was the single-storey house, by the end of the Middle Ages houses with several floors had become common in many cities (Duarte, 2003; Peribáñez, 2014).

In any case, there was a wide variety of houses with three main features making the difference: their location in the city, the quality of the construction and, finally, their size and number of rooms. Certainly, most houses were small. Thus, in Coimbra, the habitable part of 80% of the houses did not exceed 50 m² (Trindade, 2002). In Palencia, a typical craftsman's house had three rooms, one of which could be used as a small workshop; a kitchen where the hearth was located; and some small auxiliary units such as a loft, a stockyard and a stable. The homes of individuals below this social stratum were much smaller and had only a single room and another compartment where the oven was located (Valdeón & Esteban, 1985). A seemingly consolidated trend at the end of the fifteenth century is the subdivision of houses, a probable correlate of the demographic growth of the cities and perhaps worsening the living conditions of a segment of the population from the second half of the fifteenth century onward (Duarte, 2003; Collantes, 2007).

The houses of the urban elite are better known. They were tall and generally consisted of a well-kept facade, a patio, numerous rooms and corridors, and a private garden. In addition, they also contained several storage rooms for agricultural products, by a cellar and a barn, and a shed for animals. The abundance of stone in their construction was another differential element. The same can be said of aristocratic urban residences. Seigneurial castles were gaining in constructive and ornamentation complexity, but by the late Middle Ages aristocrats had clearly taken up residence in cities and palaces that constituted one of the quintessential symbols of social distinction. The latter were formed of a large number of rooms, private gardens, oratorios, and a main hall where public activities took place. The inventories also include their furniture and other housewares. The rooms were adorned with narrative tapestries that reproduced scenes from the Bible or classical mythology, made in Arras or Tournai. In addition to precious jewellery, clothing and textiles, the presence of weapons, altarpieces, images, religious ornaments and books also stands out. In fact, the possession of book collections had become an important element of prestige.

In the cities of al-Andalus, the houses had undergone important transformations during the thirteenth century. While the traditional model organized around a central courtyard persisted, designed to accommodate an extended family, many houses had already been parcelled out and became smaller, as a result of successive hereditary partitions and the formation of nuclear families. In fact, the distribution of those houses following the Christian conquest shows that their size was small by Christian standards (Navarro & Jiménez, 2001). Excavations in the Islamic quarters of Évora demonstrate the persistence of two-roomed houses with an area between 40 and 50 m² and construction materials similar to the Christian ones, with the exception of paved floors (Leite, 2014). The Christian conquest promoted some adaptations in the configuration of the houses, although in cities like Toledo and Seville the organizational model around a central courtyard persisted. The subdivision of the largest houses began only at the end of the fifteenth century as a result of demographic pressure (Collantes, 2007; Passini, 2015). The conquest of the kingdom of Granada was not followed by an immediate transformation of the housing model, as that process continued well into the sixteenth century (Cañavate, 2006). Similar continuities have been documented in the late Middle Ages in rural enclaves where the Muslim population survived after the Christian conquest (Torró, 2009).

Rural housing does not sustain the traditional image of rusticity and simplicity. At the height of the twelfth century, houses were a single story high and divided between residential space and a number of outbuildings, and often organized around a courtyard, of either agricultural or livestock use (Clemente, 2011). Excavations in fourteenth-century sites show that the residential space already had several rooms, in addition to the one that contained the hearth (Reglero, 2001).

Fifteenth-century inventories document the increasing complexity of rural housing. In an increasing number of houses, the central hall constitutes a clear element of distinction between the peasantry. In Catalonia we also find the tower attached to some isolated farmhouses (*masos*). Here, the room (*sala*) functioned as a distributor for the upper floor compartments and was used as a dining room on special occasions, during festivities and family celebrations. It usually housed the best furniture in the house, including the *tinell*, which exhibited ceramic and glass objects, weapons, etc. (Benito, 2008).

Furthermore, the homes of the richest peasants had more than one storey and included a considerable number of rooms, being comparable to many urban homes (Oliva, 2003). An important aspect of late medieval rural housing is that the role of peasants in its construction was increasingly limited and restricted to secondary tasks. The wooden structure was built by carpenters, and professionals were hired to build the walls. Straw roofs became less frequent. Construction elements varied, although the use of stone was limited to the foundations. Of course, not all peasants owned their houses. Studies show that a quarter of the rural population did not own them, and that the acquisition process could be quite arduous (Ruiz, 1990; Oliva, 2003).

By the end of the fifteenth century, notarial protocols allow the study in depth of furniture in some localities, and their analysis also contributes to refute the idea of simplicity. Certainly, the range of types of furniture was limited. However, there was a great variation in quality and a taste for ornamentation, which can be clearly perceived in the houses of wealthy peasants. By the end of the period, their houses were adorned with lavishly decorated draperies, or with carpets or bedding originated from international trade, and presented elements with a clear ostentatious character, such as silver goblets. This desire for decoration can also be perceived in other less affluent peasant strata. In contrast, the inventories show that the furniture of individuals who rented their houses and worked for others was simpler: a bed, with its corresponding clothing, some storage chests, a table, and crockery composed of different elements (Oliva, 2000).

In sum, the analysis of housing and the evolution of housewares shows not only the increasing consumption capacity of some segments of the population, but also their integration into complex circuits of exchange at all levels.

7.4.3 Dress

External appearance was the most visible indicator of the status of individuals within medieval society. During the late Middle Ages, technical improvements, the appearance of new manufacturing centres and the development of trade increased the supply of fabrics, furs, jewellery and ornaments, making them accessible to ever-expanding sectors of the population.

From the thirteenth century onwards, increasingly refined fabrics began to be manufactured and marketed in the Iberian Peninsula: woollen cloths from Castilian cities (Segovia, Palencia and Cuenca) and from the Crown of Aragon, Occitania and Italy; fabrics imported from Flanders and from northern France (Arras, Cambrai, Valenciennes, Yprès, Chalons and Provins); cotton fabrics from Barcelona and Valencia; in addition to the luxurious and exclusive silk fabrics of Almería, Lucca and other Italian cities. The most attractive and socially distinctive element of these fabrics was colour, since dyes represented a significant proportion of the cost of the final product (Iradiel, 1974; Riera, 2005: 821–901; García Marsilla, 2012: 622–624).

The increasing commercialization of imported textiles lowered their prices and made its consumption accessible, not only to the aristocracy and the urban middle classes, but also to broad sectors of the peasantry. Marriage contracts from Vic reveal the precocity of a phenomenon that has also been observed in other parts of Catalonia, Valencia and Castile: the increase in the number of outfits in bridal trousseaus between 1230 and 1315 and the hegemony of imported fabrics from France and Flanders (85% between 1291 and 1300) not only among the inhabitants of the city, but also among the peasants of the region (To Figueras, 2016). The image offered by post-mortem inventories for other territories in the fourteenth and fifteenth centuries completes this picture and allows us to observe differences in consumption among the peasants. If the presence of imported fabrics is very abundant in a rich peasant's trousseau, an average peasant could have fabrics imported from Flanders or London, although most of his trousseau was formed by lower quality cloths produced locally. Probably, marriage was a privileged moment for the acquisition of these fine clothes and credit played an important role. As we go down the social scale, trousseaus became less abundant and were formed by a limited number of garments made from locally woven textiles (Oliva, 2000; Furió, 2019: 183–184), sometimes acquired in the second-hand market. The study of the circuits of distribution shows the existence of complex social networks designed to satisfy the demand of a diversified clientele, which encompassed all the rural world (Oliva, 2001; Casado, 2008) and which operated both the distribution of luxury products and that of the indigenous production of low- and medium-quality wool or linen cloths at affordable prices. Local productions included cloths of different qualities and finishes, although as a whole their quality was higher than those traditionally manufactured for popular consumption. Thus, in Castile, during the fifteenth century, traditional textile cities such as Palencia or Zamora changed their production of rough cloths (*picotes*) to satisfy modifications in the structure of demand (Iradiel, 1974; Oliva, 2001). This type of products also spread in the rural areas, through *verlagssystem*-type organizational formulas, which involved female labour at different stages of its production (Ferreira, 1983; Sequeira & Melo, 2012; Sequeira, 2014: 169).

On the other hand, throughout the thirteenth century, specialized clothing professionals appeared in the cities, executing increasingly complex garments constituted by different pieces, and lined with fur. The increasingly longer pieces of clothing became multiplied and diversified (García Marsilla, 2012: 627–630). Being well dressed meant wearing several layers of high-quality coloured clothing, as well as accessories (chains, belts, buckles) and very varied ornaments, and they ceased to be exclusive to the privileged groups and the most affluent strata of the society.

This dynamic made privileged groups feel that their identity was threatened, and they tried to safeguard it by establishing status barriers in relation to appearance. The first 'sumptuary laws', promulgated by Jaime I of Aragon in 1234 and Alfonso X the Wise of Castile in 1252, reinforced social differences, establishing limits to the spending possibilities of each social group. The ordinances of Alfonso X the Wise in 1252, for example, prohibited anyone below the status of a *rico hombre* to wear silver ornaments, glasses, buttons and linings. These sumptuary laws were subsequently updated by the *Cortes* and by municipal ordinances. However, the number of full costumes stipulated was low even for the elites, and luxury resided in imported textiles and expensive dyes, as is confirmed by the Portuguese sumptuary law of 1340. The number of complete garments allowed to *ricos-homens* (the highest status degree among the nobility) was set at three. The *escarlata*, a very expensive fabric made of wool or silk and dyed in bright red, was exclusive to the king and his family (Marques, 1965: 145–154). Even so, this law omitted liturgical vestments, which were increasingly expensive and luxurious, the painted linen cloths of the previous centuries being replaced by damasks and brocades during the fifteenth century.

Most peasants, artisans and wage labourers owned little else besides the clothes they wore and restrained the purchase of new garments for the great events. They wore pieces of clothing made of wool or linen, generally not dyed, single coloured or in whitish or brownish tones. The peasant dress was composed of a shirt and pants, a skirt and a light overcoat. During winter, the farmer wrapped himself in a cloak with variable characteristics, and a hood. This outfit remained broadly unchanged throughout the thirteenth and fourteenth centuries, changes occurring during the fifteenth century, when peasants started to wear a skirt and a garment with a hood that covered the head. This garment could be a cape, an overcoat or a cloak, made up of two rectangular cloths joined at the shoulders. Among these, the sheepskin coat, made of lambskin, was the most common outerwear. Leggings were replaced by rolled stockings that did not reach the knee (Clemente, 2011: 228–230).

The processes of cultural hybridization diminished the differences in dress between the Nasrid kingdom and the Christian kingdoms. If during the fourteenth century the influence and import of North African textiles was noticeable in Granada, during the fifteenth century the Castilian influence took hold. All in all, the transfers between the different peninsular kingdoms were reciprocal and the Granada textiles spread to the rest of the peninsula. Thus, the use of high-quality Nasrid luxury textiles became popular among the Castilian aristocracy, giving rise to a specific fashion if compared to that of other European aristocracies. In regions bordering the kingdom of Granada, such as Andalusia or Murcia, the use of garments of Nasrid origin or typology is documented at all social levels. Conversely, gothic fashion had an impact on Andalusian attire and the use of the turban in the kingdom of Granada declined due to Castilian influence.

In the wealthier groups, men wore a shirt overlaid by blouses and tunics; the latter were broad, long and straight, equipped with wide sleeves and lavishly decorated. They protected their legs with stockings and their heads were either bare or covered with a woollen cap or a turban. In contrast, popular dress was much simpler and consisted of a tunic tied at the waist and wide leggings, the *zaragüelles*.

Women, regardless of their social status, wore dresses of a similar typology. The difference was marked by the richness of the fabrics and their ornaments and jewellery. They wore a shirt that reached below the navel, wide *zaragüelles* and thick, wrinkled stockings made of fabric or woven. Over the shirt they wore a short dress and a jacket. They covered the head with a handkerchief fastened with a diadem and outdoors they wore a veil that fell down their backs and covered part of the face. While upper-class women wore silk dresses with rich brocade and gold embroidery, those of the rest of the population were generally in cotton. All women adorned themselves profusely with earrings, necklaces, bracelets and foot rings, also of different quality according to social rank (Arié, 1965).

7.5 Conclusion

Before the fourteenth century, Hispanic medieval sources present significant problems in what concerns the quantification of living standards. The series of prices and wages that can be elaborated after this period demonstrate the existence of substantial improvements in the consumption capacity of broad sectors of the population after the Black Death. The indicators of the evolution of real wages show their exponential increase during the second half of the fourteenth century and show a cycle of wages, lasting for much of the fifteenth century, with regional fluctuations and variations considerably higher than those of the pre-plague era. Certainly, comparative studies of prices and wages still require additional work to refine comparisons at the peninsular and European level, but all the types of evidence compiled in recent decades do not support the traditionally negative image furthered by international historiography about the living standards of peninsular societies.

The last centuries of the medieval period saw substantial improvements in the diet of broad sectors of the population: it became more diversified, with a greater consumption of meat and bread of higher quality. The political implementation of urban supply systems provides an essential interpretative key. The improvements are also evident from a construction point of view, in both the city and countryside. However, textile consumption allows us a better perception of these issues. Recent historiography on consumption and living standards has stressed the importance of conspicuous consumption, of phenomena such as fashion, and patterns of social emulation. By the end of the Middle Ages, in the Iberian Peninsula, the nobility and the urban elites fully participated in this culture of ostentation and acquisition of high-quality goods, many of which were imported. However, and at another level, the consumption of textiles imported from Flanders or England, or quality cloths produced by peninsular industries had already spread to rural elites and probably to a broader segment of urban societies. The archetype of the rich peasant with a high level of spending, as portrayed by Cervantes, was consolidated at the end of the Middle Ages. The sumptuary laws that tried to limit this phenomenon to the socially privileged are revealing in this regard.

Textile consumption of the rest the population also saw improvements. The cloths made by local industries were of better quality than those of the previous period. It is precisely the increase in demand and commercialization that explains the growth experienced by these industries throughout the fifteenth century, and also the expansion of textile production in the rural areas under organizational forms of the *verlagssystem* type, which were produced for the lower strata of the population.

The Christian kingdoms underwent an intense process of urbanization (Fortea, 1995: 23; Laliena, 2016: 25; Freire & Lains, 2017: 75), which placed the peninsula among the most densely urbanized areas in Europe. Specific studies on commercial networks have also shown that, in parallel, during the last centuries of the Middle Ages, there was an intensification of the process of market creation, commercial integration and the creation of exchange networks, enabling the distribution of consumer goods to broader social sectors, thus satisfying a widely stratified demand. The commercialization of the economy spread to all levels and the improvement in wages from the second half of the fourteenth century, and with it the increase in aggregate demand, should have been a strong stimulus to growth in large areas of the peninsula. There were undoubtedly exceptions that can be explained by factors of a different nature. Catalonia during the fifteenth century provides the most relevant example.

In sum, all the evidence points to a significant improvement in the living standards of most of the population after 1350, even though this optimistic picture requires some nuances. In reality, we are little informed about the ensemble of incomes amassed by family economic units, as well as about the number of working days and daily work schedules, or the impact of women's economic contribution, which is absolutely indispensable in solving questions about family income. Our ignorance extends to other factors such as the impact on family budgets of the fiscal system that was implemented in the last centuries of the Middle Ages. What we know for certain is that the increases in cereal prices that occurred during periods of famine posed enormous difficulties for all those who relied on their salaries to make a living. Otherwise, the available evidence points to the beginning of worsening wages in the second half of the fifteenth century, perhaps initiating a change of cycle.

8

International Trade and Commerce, 1000–1500

HILARIO CASADO ALONSO, DAVID IGUAL-LUIS, FLÁVIO MIRANDA AND JOANA SEQUEIRA

8.1 Introduction

During the Middle Ages in the westernmost end of Europe, the Iberian Peninsula was a miscellany of Christian and Muslim political structures. Each such structure came with its own geomorphology, climate, languages and agro-industrial traditions. These physical, institutional and cultural differences, however, were not insuperable for the traders who were constantly traversing the several kingdoms, from the Atlantic Ocean to the Mediterranean Sea and from Iberia to the rest of Europe. How were the Iberian trade ties forged? How did the Iberian economies integrate with the Mediterranean and north-European markets? What role did Iberian and foreign traders play in the commercial gamble?

This chapter will provide answers to these questions, as well as others. It will analyse foreign trade and trade routes in the Iberian Peninsula between the eleventh and the fifteenth centuries – from year 1000 to 1500. It will overview the dual circumstances of the Christian kingdoms and of the Muslim al-Andalus over the long term. This effort at synthesis is doubtlessly encumbered by the broad time span, the diverse territorial and historical realities, the different source collection processes over time and space and, lastly, the discrepancies in the historiography that has touched upon this issue. Also, the following pages will focus especially on the period between the thirteenth and the fifteenth centuries, and on events taking place in Castile, Aragon and Portugal. This is due to both the circumstances above and our own research specialization. It is our belief, however, that none of this will stand in the way of a clear understanding of the evolution that allowed Iberia, at the end of this period, to take on a very crucial role in international trade, due to the output and quality of its various activities.

European and Iberian historians working specifically on foreign trade have already highlighted the substance of Iberian commerce. They have also

---

This paper is financed by National Funds through the FCT – Foundation for Science and Technology (Portugal), under the project UIDB/04059/2020.

emphasized the relationship between institutions and economic growth, the interplay between domestic and foreign trade, the dynamic nature of Iberia's economies and the influence of cultural and informal variables on the market and the economic agents. Iberian trade performance in the Middle Ages provides interesting contributions to all these topics. The available documents, however, do not always give away sufficient reliable figures, resulting in a predilection for qualitative, rather than quantitative, research work.

We shall be analysing the Iberian trade from three different angles. First, from the routes and the goods traded among the Iberian kingdoms as well as outside Iberia, during two periods: from the eleventh to the thirteenth centuries and from the fourteenth to the fifteenth centuries. We will then approach the role of agents and institutions. This will involve an analysis of the distinction between local and foreign traders, as well as the influence of institutional frameworks on foreign trade, via the intervention of public authorities in the market and the establishment of institutions devoted specifically to trade. Finally, we will clarify the reasons why Iberia achieved a leading position in European trade during the later Middle Ages, and why it spearheaded foreign trade at the dawn of the sixteenth century and the so-called 'First Global Age'.

8.2 Routes and Commodities

8.2.1 Foreign Trade, 1000–1300

When analysing Iberian trade over a long period of time, transformation processes – of varying degrees of intensity – become visible in the shape of commercial hubs and trade routes. Focusing on the itineraries leading away from Iberia, it becomes clear that central and secondary spaces coexisted within the relationship in the period between the eleventh and the thirteenth centuries. Christian kingdoms with maritime access to the Atlantic (Navarre, Castile and León), for instance, made contact with markets in Flanders, England, Ireland and western France. It was, however, much more difficult for them to engage in the Mediterranean trade. On the other hand, Catalonian traders developed connections with the Frankish, al-Andalusian and Mediterranean spheres. Although incursions in England and Flanders were infrequent, the Champagne fairs brought the Catalonians and Northern Europe closer. As for al-Andalus, besides the relationship with the Christian territories, its position among the remaining Muslim countries was essential.

These first impressions notwithstanding, the global trade balance highlighted two circumstances. To begin with, the precocious nature of Catalonia's rise to trade prominence. Most notably from the twelfth century onwards, Catalonia's inclination for seafaring trade and the rise of its own textile industry stimulated the production of drapery adequate for multiple export destinations. These circumstances secured its merchants a place, however modest, in the distribution chain of products as valuable as Mediterranean and oriental spices (Riera Melis, 2017: 203-233). The second circumstance is the fact that Andalusian large-scale trade was still very dynamic. The obvious difficulties facing al-Andalus from the eleventh century onwards, paralleled by the growth of the Christian societies, were somewhat compensated by the regionalization of economic efforts prompted by the rise of the different *taifas* (independent Muslim principalities), which took on the roles of both production and distribution centres and divided between themselves the old Caliphal fleet (Constable, 1994: 1-51).

As for the Muslim world, Andalusian exports until the thirteenth century proved very stable and quite diverse, featuring luxury items (such as amber), common products (such as olive oil), raw materials (silk, leather, dyes, copper, mercury and pewter), items sometimes crafted by highly skilled labourers (silk cloths, cordovan, copper tableware and pottery) and peninsular products or resources from other regions that were redistributed through al-Andalus, such as furs from Northern and Eastern Europe, gold from Sudan or enslaved people from Europe and the north of Iberia. Imports at the time were similarly diverse, most notably cereal and other foodstuffs, metals and gems, fabric, pottery, enslaved people, and spices and dyes that were brought in from the East (Constable, 1994: 149-208).

Lisbon provides a good example of the myriad trade routes that still focused on al-Andalus. Known as al-Lixbûnâ under Islamic rule during the eleventh century, the city became a pioneer of the 'First Global Age'. In earlier periods, Lisbon's economy had expanded towards the south of Iberia and North Africa. When Afonso Henriques, the first king of Portugal, conquered the city in 1147, an English chronicler described a wide array of commodities coming from the Mediterranean and Africa. The ports of Faro and Tavira, on the south of the Gharb al-Andalus, and of Mértola, on the River Guadiana, were the point of entry for much of this trade (Andrade & Miranda, 2017: 333-336).

On the opposite side, as previously mentioned, many Iberian kingdoms traded with Northern Europe. Again, this was mostly visible from the twelfth century onwards. Some sources describe the traded assets and their origin. In 1200, a Flemish chronicler listed 34 countries shipping products to Bruges (Gilliodts-Van Severen, 1904, I: 19-20). The list includes Navarre (liquor, almonds and leather), Aragon (saffron and rice), Castile (kermes, wool and iron), León (wax, leather and almonds), Andalusia (honey, olive oil, raisins and dried figs), Granada (wax and dried fruits), Galicia (wine, hides and leather) and Portugal (honey, leather and dried fruits). The list also features products from Mallorca, Fez, Tunis, Constantinople, Egypt and Jerusalem. This reflects the wide expanses travelled by these goods before they reached their consumers, and the viability of the Muslim-dominated Strait of Gibraltar for Christian trade navigation.

Regarding this viability, however, it bears mentioning that Christian navigation through the Strait only became more intense after the major conquests of territory from the Muslims in Iberia, during the thirteenth century. Therefore, the conquests of Mallorca, Valencia, Seville, Cádiz and Faro (between 1229 and 1249) and, somewhat later, Tarifa (1292) and Gibraltar (1309), by the kingdoms of Aragon, Castile and Portugal, were extremely important. These incursions provided the regions newly added to Christendom with a combination of elements of both continuity and rupture regarding the previous history of Muslim trade. The conquests undoubtedly benefitted Christian trade and sailing, in that they assimilated regions as productive as Valencia, Murcia, Andalusia and Algarve, which strategically were also located on the maritime routes. The Portuguese occupation of Algarve gave the kingdom's traders access to fertile land for agriculture. Until the end of the Middle Ages, large amounts of wine, olive oil, dried figs and raisins were regularly shipped from Algarve to Northern Europe.

The territorial accomplishments of the thirteenth century stimulated the previously limited trade routes of the Christian kingdoms. Other contributing factors were the consolidation of Aragon as a Mediterranean power (in control of Sicily since 1282 and of Sardinia from 1326) and, simultaneously, the increasing pursuits of Castile and Portugal in the Atlantic (with proven instances of Castilian trading in London, Rouen and La Rochelle during the thirteenth century). Clearly, Castile and Portugal were not as agile as other Iberian and European regions when it came to actively profiting from the effects of shifting trade outwards. The initial delay notwithstanding, both countries would later experience a truly prosperous age. Regardless, all of the aforementioned gave way to changes in the trade routes during the thirteenth century. These changes were felt in every kingdom, regarding the connections that each one had with the remaining regions in the Mediterranean and Western Europe and also in the relationships among Iberian regions.

This evolution bore an obvious impact on the routes that favoured the links within Iberia itself, whether by short or mid-range sailing or by horizontal (east–west) or vertical (north–south) land and river routes. The early development, from the eleventh century onwards, of the Camino de Santiago, from the Pyrenees to Compostela, established a connection between the regions located along it, in Aragon, Navarre, Castile and León. There is ample written evidence to prove the relevance of the River Ebro for trade connections between the Cantabrian Sea, the northern *Meseta* (plateau) and the Mediterranean from the twelfth century onward. Similarly, from the thirteenth century, Andalusia reaped the benefits of the River Guadalquivir as a conduit towards the Atlantic. At a certain point – during the twelfth and the thirteenth centuries, depending on the region – it becomes easier to identify the paths (sometimes of Roman origin) linking together regions such as Catalonia and Valencia to Murcia and

Granada, the southern *Meseta* of Castile to Granada, and in Portugal, Braga and Lisbon to Elvas, Mértola and Tavira.

8.2.2 Markets and Borders Within Iberia

Connection routes inside Iberia were typically strewn with meeting places, adequate for hosting formal commercial exchanges. These took the form of (weekly) markets and (annual) fairs, which eventually became omnipresent throughout Iberia. The same was true of al-Andalus, albeit little information survives about them. Regardless, souks are known to have existed in rural Granada since the thirteenth century, possibly related to holy places and aimed at the local population. *Alcaicerías* (silk markets), *alhóndigas* (establishments or trading stations) and shops, in Granada's countryside as well as towns, supported domestic transactions in multiple directions (Fábregas García, 2017: 81-91). For the Christian countries, on the other hand, there is plentiful data for until the fifteenth century, allowing for some chronological detail. In Castile, for example, markets and fairs between the eleventh and the fourteenth centuries were interconnected, and there was no great distinction between each other, as only seldom did they extend beyond their regional, or even local, sphere. During the fifteenth century, however, a stricter hierarchy was in place among local, regional and general markets and fairs. The top tier was reserved for the cycle of fairs that included Medina del Campo, Villalón and Medina de Rioseco (Ladero Quesada, 1994).

Within Christendom, markets and fairs, as well as other institutionalized trade locations such as ports, helped establish a wide commercial framework. The mercantile environment gradually took root in communities of variable shapes and sizes. These might be rural as well as urban, including some larger towns that were the centre of daily, stable economic activity and where trade became one of the foundations of their growth. This network ultimately presupposed multiple relationship layers. Again, they become visible mostly from the thirteenth century onwards, as connectors between: production and consumption locations; the countryside and the city; the seaboard and the hinterland; local and international commerce; and, finally, intra- and extra-Iberian trade realities. Researchers have discussed the features, magnitude and meaning of these multiple relationships, in unison with concerns common to European historiography, highlighting the conditions (of convergence or divergence) associated with these levels.

Regarding this matter, it is important to consider the influence of borders on the development of trade between the Iberian kingdoms. The segmentation of states and borders in Iberia clearly hindered the circulation of goods. In addition to circumstances related to political and military conflicts between countries and to their fiscal frameworks, rulers would frequently leave certain items out of the list of products approved for cross-border trade: gold, silver, livestock, weapons and other goods. This was commonplace in Castile, Aragon, Navarre and Portugal, most noticeably from the fourteenth century onwards. There were two ways to circumvent bans: transporting the prohibited products under *licencias de sacas* (transportation permits) issued by the king or through payment of a specific tax; alternatively, engaging in smuggling, an activity amply described in contemporary documents. Portuguese livestock, for instance, was often illicitly traded in Castile, despite the bans.

Traders from areas near the borders would frequently cross them, either legally or by clandestine means. As before, land-based trade between Castile and Portugal is a good example: merchants from both sides frequently ventured outside their region and travelled with raw materials and manufactured items for the corresponding industries or end markets and consumers. This exchange became more frequent from the thirteenth century onwards, particularly in regions with limited access to seaports. In the fifteenth century, Portugal had about 16 dry ports (i.e. landlocked trading posts) to allow the import of Castilian fabrics. Food items were also shipped from Castile to Portugal, while the Castilians purchased mostly salt, fish, olive oil, wax, linen and raw materials for textile manufacturing (Medrano Fernández, 2010). During the last centuries of the Middle Ages, salt had undoubtedly become one of the trademarks of Portuguese exports, earning the interest of virtually every foreign agent in the country and often serving as exchange currency (the Basques, for instance, traded their iron for Portuguese salt).

The crossing of political borders by trade circuits also happened in eastern Iberia. From 1300 onwards, the ports of Catalonia, Mallorca and Valencia had strong connections to the Kingdom of Granada's towns of Málaga and Almería, a clear example of intercultural trade. The former shipped drapery, leather and animal and agricultural produce sourced domestically or in other European or Mediterranean regions. The latter, in turn, sold fresh and dried fruits, sugar, linen and silk fabrics, leather, wax and wheat, also domestic or re-exported from the Maghreb (Salicrú i Lluch, 2007). In fact, the Aragon–Granada route lay along a multilateral context of relationships between the Mediterranean and the Atlantic, one that converged in the Strait of Gibraltar. By the end of the Middle Ages, the Strait was a complex frontier setting, witnessing clashes between Granada, Castile, Portugal and the North African kingdoms. Still, Christian traders were able to establish connections between the enclaves located in both the Iberian and African coasts.

It was commonplace to use a given route within wider networks, such as in the links between Iberia's eastern and western coasts. Fifteenth-century trade between Valencia and Portugal profited from the exchange of Portuguese fish and hides for Valencian manufactured goods and agricultural products (Barata, 1998). Yet this traffic was not exclusively bilateral, since the Italians used Valencia in order to obtain access to Portugal, while Valencian trade groups extended their businesses to Flanders through Lisbon. Similarly, the

Italian merchants themselves accessed the Irish hides market through Lisbon, which by then had gained prominence as a redistributing outlet for such goods (Sequeira & Miranda, 2019: 345–346).

8.2.3 The Christian Trade Expansion, 1300–1500

Iberian trade was supported by the circulation of domestic and foreign products, on the one hand, and agricultural and other types of manufactured goods, on the other. While it may appear obvious, historians not always have given the composite nature of the Iberian markets' due relevance. Product binomials (domestic–foreign, agricultural–manufactured) were discernible between the eleventh and the thirteenth centuries. Still, as hinted at in the previous section, they were more clearly outlined from 1300, owing to the commercial development of Iberian societies. These societies benefitted from the global economic scenario and from achievements specific to Iberia. These included an early recovery from the fourteenth-century crisis and the direct benefits reaped from the increasing trade conducted by Christians through Gibraltar.

Coming back to the maritime routes leading outside the Iberian Peninsula, trade remained connected to both its traditional stages in the Mediterranean and the Atlantic. Such was the case with the Kingdom of Granada (Fábregas García, 2013), though the main role was now mostly played by the Christian kingdoms. During the fourteenth and fifteenth centuries, the latter experienced several circumstances and readjustments, yet the period can generally be seen as one of expansion, especially regarding Portugal and Castile. This unquestionably resulted in the increase of trade, both in absolute and relative terms. All of this occurred simultaneously with the expanding amount and variety of products circulating over the seas and across Europe by land.

Expanding towards the North Atlantic, Aragon, Castile and Portugal traded with France, Flanders and England, while redistribution channels further extended these connections into Germany and the Baltic. Iberian exports mostly involved raw materials (iron, wool, hides, kermes and woad) and foodstuff, some of which also came from Granada (dried figs, dates, raisins, rice, salt, sugar and especially wine and olive oil). In the opposite direction, imports from those regions took on the same dual nature, featuring both raw materials (alabaster, tar and metals) and food items (herring, cheese, beer and wheat). In this case, however, the manufacturing sector (luxury fabrics) seized a considerable share of the Iberian market. Accordingly, the connections with Northern Europe proved very relevant to the Iberian Peninsula, as the two markets matched up thereby providing the commercial agents – such as the Castilians and the Portuguese, mostly from the fifteenth century onwards – with business opportunities and a chance for expansion in that region (Casado Alonso, 2003; Miranda & Faria, 2016).

Italian merchants also benefitted from the Iberian Peninsula's role as a gateway into the North Atlantic markets and from its role as an intermediary between them and the Mediterranean. Their activities were already noticeable in Catalonia and al-Andalus before the mid-thirteenth century. Afterwards, their presence grew and consolidated in every Christian territory and in Granada, reaching its apogee from the end of the fourteenth century onwards (d'Arienzo, 2010). Essentially, the Italians used Iberia as a wholesale market for the raw materials necessary for their textile (silk, wool and dyes) and tanning (hides) industries. At the same time, the Iberian kingdoms became increasingly receptive of Italian manufactured products while they were also able to reallocate merchandises originating from the Atlantic and Africa.

Concerning the Mediterranean, Iberian ties to Italy were noteworthy but by no means exclusive. Castile and Portugal both targeted the Mediterranean, and this grew in intensity from the mid-fourteenth century onwards. However, Aragon's partaking in the Mediterranean routes was both older and deeper. This resulted from the kingdom's political and military expansion process, as well as the strategies of its economic agents: Catalonians, from the start, closely followed by the Mallorcans and Valencians. These traders' pursuits reached the entire Mediterranean coasts, but after 1300 they focused on three particular areas: the eastern region, encompassing Byzantium, Syria and Egypt, which was the main hub for the trading of Asian spices and silk for western fabrics; the central region, surrounding Sicily and Sardinia and – in the fifteenth century – Naples, where fabrics from the Iberian regions of Aragon was sold and cereal, along with other, local agricultural goods, was purchased; and the Maghreb, yet another destination for the kingdom's fabrics, where products such as gold, hides, silk, kermes, spices and enslaved people were purchased (Ferrer Mallol, 2012: 162–178).

The Aragon–Maghreb relationship was deeply tied to the route connecting Catalonia, Mallorca and Valencia to Granada. Granada itself, favourably integrated in the Mediterranean routes, traded intensely with North Africa, purchasing leathers, hides, wool, fabrics, dyestuff, gold and metal. Regardless, the nature of the connections between the Iberian Peninsula and Africa changed during the fifteenth century, as a result of Portugal and Castile's endeavours in Morocco, the Atlantic Islands (the Canary Islands, Madeira, Cabo Verde and, further away, the Azores) and the West Africa coast in general. As for Portugal, the military expeditions in Ceuta (1415), Ksar es-Seghir (1458), and Asilah and Tangier (1471) unravelled new possibilities for trade deployment. In addition, owing to exploration journeys in Africa, Portugal received shipments of fabrics, cotton, malaguetta pepper, ivory, gold, exotic animals and enslaved people (Godinho, 2008: 337). The allure of these goods opened specific trade avenues with local communities. These were interested in purchasing fabrics from Portugal, Castile and, especially, England and Flanders, which reinforced the latter's Iberian supply routes.

8.3 Agents and Institutions

8.3.1 The Domestic Traders

The activities abovementioned were carried out by countless agents of various types. In every territory, be it Muslim or Christian, all social groups engaged in trade, in one way or another. By the late fifteenth century, the merchant peasants of Castile and Aragon, the knights-merchants of Portugal, and the Nasrid kings, who were personally implicated in Granada's foreign trade, all bear testimony to the spreading of mercantile exchanges socially and across Iberia. Nevertheless, as with the other regions of medieval Europe, the most prominent trade roles were taken on by those who might be described simply as 'merchants', everyone who engaged in the trading of goods and money, albeit with different degrees of specialization and investment.

Concerning al-Andalus, even Muslim treatises written before the eleventh century distinguished between several merchant profiles: the sedentary agent, the travelling trader and the importer/exporter merchant. Among them, some were involved in international or long-distance business, while others were economically less powerful and operated at a local or regional scale only (Constable, 1994: 52–54). Ultimately, these categories were applicable to all regions of medieval Europe. In practical terms, elite Muslim traders had business during the fourteenth and fifteenth centuries in Granada and in the Moorish quarters of some Christian towns. They were interested in foreign trade and partook in well-established business models, such as the organization of trade companies and the execution of given credit and product exchange mechanisms (Fábregas García, 2017: 80–81).

Jewish merchants also traded in Iberia. Once again, the most important records are from the fourteenth and fifteenth centuries. They show the involvement, within the Christian kingdoms, in credit operations, in the financing of political and social powers, and more generally in the routes connecting Iberia with the Maghreb and the rest of North Africa. However, the analysis of Jewish quarters in certain Christian settings reveals the heterogeneity of those agents, who were involved in local and regional trade networks and took on multiple professions (Tavares, 1982–1984). The conversion of many Jews, especially during the fifteenth century, gave them access to the Christian trade circle. Still, no credit should be given to the old, clichéd notion that either everyone in this circle was of Jewish descent or that most of the Christian trade was controlled by Jews or Jewish converts.

In fact, as far at the Christian mercantile activities went, they were the outcome of an evolution process which between the eleventh and the thirteenth centuries consisted in the slow growth of trade as a profession, and later, between the fourteenth and the fifteenth centuries, in the consolidation and expansion of that profession. The first stage is noticeable in the territories of the Crown of Aragon. In those regions, the circumstances prompting the surfacing of specific merchant groups were related to the result of migration movements both narrow and wide, and to the effects of social-economic processes of accumulation and transformation, promoted by peasants and artisans, by some sectors of the trade and capital circles (drapers, shopkeepers and moneychangers, for instance) and by noblemen. Documental evidence of the second stage surfaced in every Christian region. It is most visible among the dozens and hundreds of merchants who had settled, particularly during the fifteenth century, in cities such as Barcelona, Valencia, Zaragoza, Burgos, Valladolid, Toledo, Seville and Lisbon.

From the varied evidence identified for the thirteenth century and later, the biggest merchants in each territory usually stand out due to material elements (such as the availability of capital, the robustness of their trade companies, the wide areas where they operated or the multiplicity of businesses), cultural elements (the investment in training, their clear professional identity) and social elements (such as prestige, the proximity to political and social powers, the sporadic belonging in the institutions). Regardless, both the major agents – true businesspeople – and medium and smaller traders exhibited economic tactics equal to their European counterparts.

Several types of capital association, and of capital–labour association, emerged from this context. Short-term contracts were widespread mostly in the coastal settlements, due to the specific nature of maritime transportation and business. Investment was scarce and organizational demands modest. This was no obstacle for the creation of permanent, ambitious companies both along Iberia's seaboard and its hinterland. This required somewhat larger, specialized workforces: partners, factors, servants and proxies, for instance. Yet, associations between family and business were constant to such an extent that kinship became one of the foundations for the development and establishment of trade companies. At its logical extreme, this occasioned the birth of actual trade dynasties. In such cases, there was even a (not always successful) revamping of labour contracts and economic cooperation over generations, both between relatives and between them and agents foreign to the main family. Evidence of these practices appears everywhere, though some of the most researched examples are found in Catalonia during the fourteenth century (the Mitjavila), in Zaragoza between the fourteenth and the fifteenth centuries (the Coscó and the Casaldáguila), and in Burgos (the Sanchester, Bonifaz, Castro, Bernuy, Maluenda and Salamanca) and Toledo (the De la Fuente) from the mid-fifteenth century onwards (Casado Alonso, 2003; Igual-Luis, 2014: 19–21; de la Torre Gonzalo, 2018).

Relationships between Christian, Jewish and Muslim merchants, on the one hand, and between Christian merchants from among the Christian Iberian kingdoms, on the other, induced different phenomena: cooperation, complementarity and mutual influence; conversely, competition and conflict. These situations became particularly relevant when paralleled by political/institutional interference or rivalries due to war, religion or foreign status. This also applied to the relationships with fellow Christian merchants from outside Iberia, particularly since their presence was constant and had an impact all over the territory. On this matter, the Italian activities have already been mentioned, though many other non-Iberian agents operated in this trade.

8.3.2 Foreign Traders

In the eleventh and twelfth centuries, the initial opening to Europe of regions in the north and the repercussions of the Camino de Santiago made the settlement of Frankish traders in Catalonia, Aragon, Navarre and Castile easier. From the twelfth and, especially, the thirteenth century, economic circumstances led to an increasing influx of foreigners. As previously stated, Italians were by then present in every region, and they were eventually joined by other foreigners. In the case of Lisbon, the Genoese had settled in the city from 1270, the English from around 1311 and the Florentines from 1338 (Sequeira & Miranda, 2019: 350). Before 1500, the English were already found in Andalusia and Burgos, the Flemish had settled in Valencia, Lisbon and the Atlantic Islands (the Canaries, Azores and Madeira) and there were Germans and French living in the territories of the Crown of Aragon. The most intense foreign presence was doubtlessly that which was recorded in the fifteenth century.

Foreigners' activities helped improve Iberia's international standing. Yet Iberia itself was never relegated to a subordinate, 'colonial' position. Foreigners never monopolized Iberian trade circles, never held an exclusive sway over foreign trade nor did they stifle the enterprising spirit of Iberian traders. Indeed, as far as the links with the local societies went, foreign business operators required domestic agents for several actions, usually in order to gain access to producers and consumers. They were also subject to the rules imposed by Iberian institutions, regardless of how favourable to foreigners these might have been.

Still, their presence in Iberia was differently characterized. This was also true of the Italians. Their communities were the most plentiful and long-lasting of foreign settlers in Iberia, particularly the Genoese and the Tuscans. For example, in the fourteenth and fifteenth centuries it was easy to find traders and companies belonging to the Centurione, Grimaldi, Lomellini, Pinello and Spinola families from Genoa, or the Bardi, Cambini, Capponi, Datini and Salviati families from Tuscany. But their strategies were not identical. Initially, that is after 1300, the Genoese foreign interventions were characterized by their conspicuous numbers, small-scale companies and the ability to permeate the areas where they settled. Conversely, the Tuscans (spearheaded by the Florentines) were not as many, though their companies were larger and more robust, with greater financial vigour and capacity for business accumulation. In territorial terms, the Ligurians created a few complex settlements. In Granada and Lower Andalusia (from Seville to Cádiz), the Genoese took advantage of diplomatic agreements and prerogatives granted by the sovereigns to establish populous communities that, unlike other foreign groups, were not exclusively devoted to trade. Their members integrated their respective societies and cooperated at a political level. In Lower Andalusia, some Genoese were naturalized, took on roles in the municipal and aristocratic administrations and sometimes even joined the ranks of the local oligarchy and nobility (Igual-Luis, 2005: 309–316).

In addition, the Genoese in Granada, Seville and Cádiz shared a very clear collective identity as a trade 'nation' from the thirteenth century onwards. Their identity was stimulated by fiscal exemptions, the use of specific sites (neighbourhoods, temples, *alhóndigas* and other types of infrastructure) and consulates. The documental evidence shows, however, that such circumstances surfaced in several regions of Iberia for both the Ligurians and other foreign agents. While between the thirteenth and the fifteenth centuries there appeared in Lisbon either fraternities or chapels attached to communities from Germany, Flanders and England, as well as a Florentine consulate, fifteenth-century Valencia housed Genoese, Lombard and German fraternities or chapels, as well as Genoese, Florentine, Venetian, Lombard and French consulates. Several reasons justified the creation of these institutions and the granting of certain privileges to foreigners. Some of those reasons probably related to the will (or consent) of local social and political forces and, at times, the foreigners' ability to negotiate with such powers.

8.3.3 *Commercial Development and the Institutions*

The previous argument, as well as others presented in this section of the chapter, might be employed to connect trade, in its international features, with the role of politics and institutions. This is a matter for wide debate, and the discussion finds its expression also at the Iberian scale. The question revolves around the ultimate role of institutions for trade development, though this formulation can be separated into two aspects: first, the measures taken by public authorities, especially monarchs, towards the market and its external protection; and second, the meaning of specific institutions created by trade and transportation, either directly or through sanction and incentives from the aforementioned public authorities. All this relates, in one way or another, to the possible creation of institutional frameworks adequate for trade, such as the deployment of elements that helped bring down transaction costs, spread information and diversify businesses and company management.

Within the context of the Iberian Peninsula in the Middle Ages, the empiric evidence is not ample enough to analyse these questions. Still, at least from the thirteenth century onwards, numerous pieces of indirect evidence shed light on this matter. Considerable amounts of direct data are also available, showing how trade was affected, at first, by the political decisions of kingdoms and by the diplomatic and military ebb and flow of inter-country relationships. Therefore, an initial approach will highlight the obvious: the successive wars and pacts between the Iberian kingdoms, or between these kingdoms and those outside Iberia, either facilitated or hindered foreign trade and even imposed changes on the nature of the traffic. For example, Portuguese participation in the Hundred Years' War between 1369 and 1385 brought changes to its maritime trade and intensified contact with England. Also, the treaties established from the thirteenth century onward between Granada and Genoa, Aragon and Castile, as well as those which bound Castile to England, to the Low Countries and to the Holy Roman Empire during the reign of the Catholic Monarchs, were considered as essential for the international expansion of both territories.

Such circumstances were especially helpful in terms of the context in which they happened, although the interaction between politics and trade in Iberia – to become structural by the end of the Middle Ages – should be stressed. In fact, regarding the Christian kingdoms, the political treatment of commercial matters became part of the wider processes of state consolidation. The continued attention of the Iberian monarchs, including those of Granada, to trade from the thirteenth century has been unanimously acknowledged. Likewise, there is a common perception that monarchical support for trade development was frequent and that the resources generated by trade were employed for the benefit of the state's structures, mostly resorting to fiscal tools. In this context, the conception of an official map of trading locations became essential, inasmuch as such places provided trade with a scheduling and geographical arrangement, helped apply fiscal restrictions or incentives, and gave legal assurances to traders.

In the Christian kingdoms, this map included the markets and fairs which appeared everywhere, as far back as the eleventh century. This has been mentioned previously, when referring to the role of markets and fairs for the material articulation of trade routes and the different scales at which they operated. Their institutional significance, however, was even more important when considering that the concession of a fair was essentially a political act – it emanated from the royal prerogative, though it might also involve the interest, and even incentive, of local lords and communities. Therefore, the documented privileges given to markets and fairs in this context attest the extent to which political powers were involved. The numbers speak for themselves. In Aragon, a little over 150 markets and somewhat less than 200 fairs were held between the eleventh and the fifteenth centuries (Furió Diego, 2010a: 419–420). In Portugal, at least 133 fairs were held between the twelfth and the fifteenth centuries (Cunha, 2019). In the same period, Castile held 155 fairs and around 200 markets (Ladero Quesada, 1994).

8.3.4 Trade Institutions

News of specific trade institutions proliferated from the thirteenth century onwards. The foundation of the *Universitat dels Prohoms de la Ribera de Barcelona* (the Corporation of the Notables of La Ribera in Barcelona) in 1258, and of the *Hermandad de la Marina de Castilla* (the Brotherhood of the Castilian Coastland) on the Cantabrian seaboard in 1296, are an example of the mechanisms that traders and seafarers from the North of Iberia began to employ in order to self-regulate and protect their activities. In Portugal, a *bolsa de mercadores*, a risk-sharing system, was established in 1293, to support expenses related to merchants' business, judicial costs, and other mishaps involving their professional activity in Portugal and abroad. The *bolsa* evolved into the *Companhia das Naus* (the Company of the Carracks), established in 1380 (Marques, 1944: 21–22, 171–173). Still in the thirteenth century, a Muslim tradition was adopted in Aragon and Portugal, and preserved in Nasrid Granada – the *funduq*, *alfòndec* or *alhóndiga*, a space providing housing to traders and the storage of goods, subject to legal rulings. There were *alfòndecs* in Christian-dominated Valencia, while they were also used by Catalan traders throughout the Mediterranean as hubs for their trade and even as the headquarters for Catalan consulates abroad.

The development of consular institutions until 1500 was definitely significant for Aragon in two different ways. On the one hand, the foundation of the *Consolats del Mar* (Consulates of the Sea), which between 1283 and 1443 extended to the main coastal towns (Barcelona, Valencia and Mallorca) as well as other places, eventually serving as mercantile courts of law and corporations for traders and seafarers. On the other hand, the establishment of trade consulates in the Mediterranean as well as in the Atlantic (Seville and Bruges), where Catalonian traders operated. These overseas consulates (of which 33 were established in the fourteenth century and 29 in the fifteenth century) were similar to those from other European countries, taking on the typical responsibilities of providing legal, representative and protective support to fellow citizens (Riera Melis, 2017: 277–278). Castile would also emulate the consular system at a later date, especially from the fifteenth century onwards, while Portugal simultaneously established certain mechanisms essential for the control of routes in Europe and Africa: negotiating with the papacy exploration monopolies on African goods, establishing specialized entities such as the *Casa de Ceuta* (House of Ceuta) or the *Casa da Mina* (House of Elmina), and especially creating *feitorias*, that is, the trading posts used in Africa to represent the king for business purposes, and in Europe (in Flanders, for instance) for that same purpose and also to exert control over royal monopolies.

In addition to this, there are copious examples of brotherhoods and other associations of traders and carriers between the thirteenth and the fifteenth centuries, at least for Castile and Aragon. Notwithstanding the specific nature of each element mentioned, all of those helped provide Iberian trade and its agents with channels for identity, organization, representation, solidarity, security and conflict management. They were, therefore, in line with what was happening elsewhere in Europe, although some of the aforementioned mechanisms (such as the Consulates of the Sea) were comparatively pioneering, original even, in the European setting. Nevertheless, the set of institutional policies (both general and trade-specific) commented upon above outlined the framework of trade operation in various ways. These dynamics might at times culminate in the real 'bureaucratization' of commercial exchange, which some argue to have been the case with Portuguese trade in Africa during the fifteenth century (Costa, J., 2013: 111). Regardless of this concept's validity, its very formulation is further proof of the medieval parallelisms to be found between trade and institutional activity, as well as of its possible impact on Iberia's foreign standing.

8.4 The Rise of Iberia

8.4.1 The Foundations of Iberian Mercantile Success

Iberia's geographical location, between the Mediterranean and the Atlantic and between Europe and Africa, was especially privileged. Yet only by providing adequate political, social, economic and even cultural conditions, could the region have reaped the maximum benefits from its placement. With specific nuances, this applied to both the Muslim and Christian universes during the two large historical phases covered in this paper: between the eleventh and the thirteenth centuries, and between the fourteenth and the fifteenth centuries. From a Christian perspective, however, the passing of the years certainly consolidated the synergies that gradually developed around trade. This process culminated in the fifteenth century (see Figure 8.1), when Iberia, thanks to the active roles of Portugal and Castile, took on a leading position in the continental expansion across Africa, Asia and America. This resulted from an evolution process, involving several factors, among which was the early resolution of the fourteenth-century crisis in Iberia, as previously mentioned. However similar to other Mediterranean regions, the lesser incidence of this phenomenon distinguished the Iberian case from those of several regions in Central and Northern Europe. Yet, understanding later medieval Iberian trade requires including other factors, some of which were visible already in the fourteenth century and especially after 1400 (Casado Alonso, 2014: 89-94).

In this regard, the period changed the European business world, which in turn helped promote Iberian trade. The commercial upswing in the Atlantic

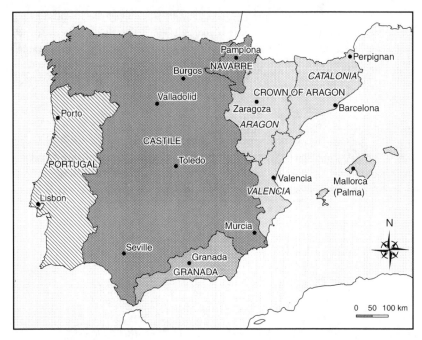

Figure 8.1 The Iberian Peninsula in the mid-fifteenth century.
Source: Flocel Sabaté and Servei Científicotècnic de Cartografia i Sistemes d'Informació Geogràfica de la Universitat de Lleida.

façade, as well as the long-standing dynamic nature of the Mediterranean trade, naturally advanced Iberia's position as an axis between both settings and, thanks to this, its complementary connection with seafaring along the African coasts and, later on, with the routes towards Asia and America. In addition, new products and goods proliferated, thanks to both global changes in trends and demand, and to technological advances in the European industry. Wealthy social groups now increased their expenditure on luxury items, purchasing goods such as tapestries, furniture, glassware, jewellery, and objects made of metal and alabaster. This period also reflected phenomena such as the merino wool boom (caused by the changes brought on the spinning process by the carding technique), the practice of salting food, the consumption of sugar cane, raisins and dried fruits, the increased usage of spices, the expansion of new dyes such as woad (*isatis tinctoria*) or litmus (*roccella tinctoria*), the improvements in wine conservation, and the demand for African gold and ivory. The Iberian kingdoms and their traders had easily adapted to the requirements of the production and distribution of these new articles.

As for the Iberian economic agents, they showed great ability to assimilate and disseminate techniques in trade, finance and accounting, while also creating relationship and information networks. They were definitely advanced as regards the embedded knowledge of trading, reducing long-distance transaction costs by using tools such as double-entry bookkeeping, the Tuscan system of companies, bills of exchange, marine insurance and commercial mathematics. Such techniques originated in Italy and were disseminated, in varying degrees, across the whole of Iberia, starting in Catalonia and ending probably in Portugal (Cardoso & Sequeira, 2020). Indeed, it was Castilian traders who spread some of these techniques throughout France and England, from the second half of the fifteenth century onwards. Such progress was paralleled by vast improvements in the art of sailing. Once more, European developments such as safer ships, larger sails and bigger tonnage were fully implemented in Iberia. In the fifteenth century, Portuguese and Castilian seafaring became the most advanced in the continent thanks to the caravels, the *naos* (carracks) and the pinnaces being built in Basque, Cantabrian, Portuguese and Andalusian shipyards, the nautical knowledge of the Catalonian–Mallorcan cartography, and the improvements to navigational instruments (compass, sextant and astrolabe). In addition, it should be noted that, in support of the external activities of Iberian traders and sailors, the different kingdoms promoted exchange policies via already familiar tools (international diplomacy and supporting the establishment of trade consulates) or by pinning down laws such as those concerning the right of property, which directly affected trade.

One last factor to consider was the robust development of domestic markets, resulting from both the increase in agricultural and industrial production and the boost generated by commercial exchange. Peasants would satisfy their needs in the market more often, even resorting to credit. Consequently, all sorts of traders journeyed throughout the hinterland and the coasts of Iberia. This was encouraged by the existence of groups of carters and mule-drivers, which reduced the costs and simplified transportation overland. This level of trade was visibly strengthened in the inner regions of Castile and Aragon (Sesma Muñoz, 2013). An outstanding example is the Castilian Douro Valley in the fifteenth and sixteenth centuries. It had a dense urban network, comparable to Italy or other European areas, with densely populated towns and villages, close to each other and with strong commercial activities. Trade was articulated here by merchants and carriers who travelled around the local markets and fairs. More generally, these markets and fairs had properly interconnected all over Iberia by the fifteenth century. Castile clearly spearheaded the large fairs: the *ferias generales* (general trade fairs) of Medina del Campo, Villalón and Medina de Rioseco, featuring large-scale international merchants, medium-level traders, peddlers and simple shopkeepers alike. By the end of the century, at which point a system of bills of exchange issued in several points in Europe had become established, these fairs had converted into international business venues for the trade of such bills (Casado Alonso, 2001).

In addition to this element of the Villalón fair and the two Medina fairs, the cycle of Iberian commercial and financial development was completed by the international economic reputation of cities such as Lisbon, Seville, Valencia and Barcelona. It is not, therefore, surprising that the recorded fiscal data reflect the global growth in trade, since there is evidence of a significant increase in trade tax revenue throughout the whole century. Thus, such taxes became one of the key contributions to national treasuries.

Building on these foundations, Iberia's trade success in the fifteenth century proved omnidirectional, with connections to the Mediterranean, the Atlantic, Europe and Africa. However, there was neither competition nor dissonance between the several markets and agents involved. The connections, via land and sea, between locations were more frequent than rivalry. Thanks to the wealth of business opportunities, traders and companies were able to operate everywhere, even as foreigners intervening in Iberian commerce. The heightened presence of those foreigners bears testimony to the attractiveness of Iberian markets. In turn, it helped develop them even further.

8.4.2 The Aragonese Case

Aragon was part of this success, though its foreign trade peak had already taken place. Ignoring a few background elements for the moment, the so-called 'Mediterranean expansion of the Crown of Aragon' began in the thirteenth century and remained in force until the end of the Middle Ages. The previously mentioned conquests of Mallorca, Valencia, Sicily and Sardinia, between the thirteenth and the fourteenth centuries, the military actions in the fourteenth century (including in Greece) and the conquest of Naples in 1442 provided solid political grounding to the expansion process. Yet these elements were indissociable from economic and trade interests. If, on the one hand, kings amassed territories resorting to the traders' financial and material support, the latter, in turn, were given access to ports of call for maritime trading and to markets where they held an advantage over their competitors.

Traders from Barcelona and, by extension, Catalonia, took on leading roles in these processes, though the expansion's effects were also felt by those from Mallorca, Valencia and inland Aragon, with Zaragoza at the helm. These agents channelled a multitude of exports through the entire Mediterranean and even the Atlantic. In turn, they functioned as trade intermediaries between the East and West Mediterranean, and between those regions and other European areas. It bears recalling that they provided different markets with products such as spices, fabrics, agricultural goods and multiple raw materials and manufactured items. Such exchange schemes gave these traders – particularly those from Catalonia – a key role in the late medieval period, analogous to their counterparts from Venice, Genoa and Tuscany. Therefore, especially between the end of the fourteenth century and the beginning of the fifteenth century, Barcelona (around 30,000 inhabitants during the period) became a very important trading and financial market in Europe. Its agents and consulates were present in a number of seaports in the continent and in North Africa (Riera Melis, 2017: 261–277).

Catalonian supremacy receded, however, as the fifteenth century unfolded. This owed to several circumstances: economic troubles in Catalonia; domestic political conflict; changes in the international trade prompted by the rise of the European Atlantic façade; and the qualities of other trade groups, both traditional (the Italians) and ascending (the Castilians). Consequently, Catalonia and Barcelona lost part of the positions they had garnered, though they maintained their status as important focal points – indeed, from the end of the century onwards, taking advantage of the new opportunities generated by the Atlantic trade (Armenteros Martínez, 2012). As for Mallorca, its notable role remained untouched, as it sat in the middle of the numerous routes that supported the Mediterranean. Meanwhile, Valencia evolved into a large commercial hub. Its traders operated as intermediaries for their own goods and those imported from Castile and Aragon. The city also attracted a plethora of foreign merchants, mostly Italian. By the end of the fifteenth century, it had one of the largest populations in Iberia and was one of its main financial centres (Igual-Luis, 2017b). Aragon, the other kingdom in the Crown, never reached such heights, although it managed to solidify its intermediary role in the circuits connecting the Mediterranean to the Atlantic and to Southern France, via the Ebro valley. The kingdom of Navarre, neighbouring Aragon, took on a lesser role, exporting domestic and foreign goods via the Basque ports and the Béarn.

8.4.3 Portugal and Castile

From the end of the fourteenth century, Portugal and Castile both accelerated their economic and trade growth, a process stimulated by their incursions in the Atlantic islands and the African coast, towards the Gulf of Guinea. During the fifteenth century, this expansion helped project the economies of the southern coast of Iberia, from Cádiz to Algarve, under Seville's increasing role as a leading player, with about 50,000 inhabitants by 1530. It also allowed for the creation of an area sometimes called *Mediterráneo atlántico* (the 'Atlantic Mediterranean'), between the islands and Africa – a trading space focusing greatly on the exchange of new products (goods from Africa and, especially, sugar from Madeira), which were much sought after in Europe by a clientele with high purchasing power (Magalhães, 2009). Among other elements, the establishment by the Portuguese of commercial enclaves in Africa (such as the castle and entrepôt of Elmina, in 1481) secured the existence of support interfaces for inter-continental transactions.

In Portugal, two great commercial hubs emerged in Lisbon and Porto, although smaller ports also contributed to the expansion of trade. An increase was recorded in exports such as wine, fish, sugar, salt, spices, dyestuff and other raw materials, targeted especially at Italy, France, the Low Countries and England. This accomplishment encouraged the creation of Portuguese commercial networks in Valencia, Bordeaux, Saint-Malo, Harfleur, Bristol, London, Middelburg, Bruges and Antwerp (Miranda & Faria, 2016: 248–257). An excellent late-fifteenth-century example is Álvaro Dinis, a prominent Portuguese businessman living in Bruges. Of all the Iberian markets, Lisbon (around 60,000 residents near 1530) was one of the most sought after by Italian traders, mostly from Genoa and Florence. These took advantage of the city to export Portuguese products, to exploit the route towards Northern Europe, and to meet the high domestic demand with Italian and Flemish goods. They also benefitted from the arrival to Europe of new products from the African and insular Atlantic. The Tuscan Bartolomeo Marchionni, Lisbon's 'most prominent alien merchant', provides an excellent example of the cosmopolitan nature of some Iberian ports, in the decades after 1470 (Guidi-Bruscoli, 2014).

As for Castile, the growth it experienced led its trade to becoming one of the most dynamic in late medieval Europe. The territories within Castile stimulated international exchange, starting with domestic goods (such as wool, hides, iron, wine, olive oil, dyestuff and fish) and later operating as an intermediary for foreign products. Its influence was mainly felt in the Atlantic – in the north around the English Channel and the Bay of Biscay, and in the south towards Africa. Yet Castilian traders, backed by a powerful local fleet, also expanded their businesses in the Mediterranean, especially along the routes connecting to Italy. This resulted in the creation of a dense trade network, from Hamburg and Antwerp to the Chios island. Castilian natives settled in many ports along that network, managing their communities as corporations. The origins of some of those communities go back as far as the twelfth century, but their growth and especially their legal structure developed more sharply from the 1420s onwards, reaching their peak by the end of the fifteenth century, also due to the support of the crown.

Burgos dominated foreign trade in Castile. The role of Burgos, an inland city that may have had 10,000 inhabitants around 1500, can be understood by the mercantile power of the whole of the Douro valley and by the fact that, from the thirteenth century onwards, it became a centre where commercial information converged thanks to the agents that the city's families and companies had in different parts of Europe. The *Universidad de Mercaderes* (Corporation of Merchants) was founded in mid-fifteenth-century Burgos for the purposes of organizing the different settlements, supervising commercial exchanges and providing aid to Castilians operating abroad. The institution was converted into the Burgos Consulate in 1494, taking on the role of trade high court for the kingdom. It oversaw the Castilian consulates of Bruges, Rouen, Nantes and Florence, as well as the Castilian colonies in Bristol, London, Antwerp, La Rochelle, Bordeaux, Lisbon, Valencia, Barcelona, Genoa, Pisa and Naples. With this thick web of establishments, Castilian traders benefitted from economies of scale, gaining advantage over their competitors. They were able to properly channel information, employ and disseminate trading techniques and resort to collective support structures. This explains the success of companies from certain families – in Burgos, in addition to the Castro, Bernuy, Maluenda or Salamanca, examples include the Arbieto, Astudillo, Gallo, Miranda, Pardo and Soria. It also allowed such merchants to dominate trade in Europe and benefit from advantageous conditions to approach the challenges posed by the geographical discoveries and colonial trade (Casado Alonso, 2003).

8.5 Conclusion

The period between the mid-fourteenth century and 1500 was one of the most glorious ever for Iberian trade. Domestic and foreign commerce increased, public and private institutions were established for the development of exchange, and Iberian traders settled in the main economic centres of Europe, the Mediterranean and West Africa. Iberia then took on a pivotal role within the context of international trade. It was the culmination of a 500-year journey, though interspersed with various distinct circumstances.

In the eleventh century, foreign trade had been much influenced by the powerful Muslim territories of al-Andalus, which kept strong bonds with North Africa and the eastern Mediterranean. However, from the twelfth century and, especially, the thirteenth century onwards, the Christian kingdoms inherited that dynamic trade approach, while broadening their domains through military conquest. These became areas of exchange between the Mediterranean territories and France, England and the Low Countries, also taking advantage of important land routes, such as the Camino de Santiago. Also, from the thirteenth century onwards, the increased circulation of Christian vessels through the Strait of Gibraltar further benefitted these trends, opening the way for the arrival of foreign traders. In parallel, the Crown of Aragon expanded its commercial status. The fourteenth-century crisis did not disrupt this scenario for long. As an example, between the late 1300s and the mid-fifteenth century, the robust nature of Barcelona's trade became evident. However, as the fifteenth century unfolded, the leading role in Iberia would gradually become Portugal and Castile's.

Throughout the course of such an evolution, though mostly from the thirteenth century onwards, Iberia always stood out for the diversity of its trading spheres. These were located along routes heading for multiple directions, and featured various sorts of products, Iberian and non-Iberian traders of various origins, and Christian, Muslim and Jewish agents. All these elements, combined with institutional frameworks, defined the status of Iberian trade, at a point when expansion towards Africa and the Atlantic advanced, overseen by the monarchs, especially in Portugal. These factors granted the Iberian markets some uniqueness when compared to the rest of Europe.

Going back to the fifteenth century, a lack of definite, quantitative documents notwithstanding, the Iberian balance of trade appears to have been positive. In addition, Iberian trade was remarkably dynamic during the period, comparable to regions such as Italy and Flanders. Both elements help corroborate the notion of Iberia as no longer being a peripheral space. Indeed, it was quite the opposite. Its kingdoms and traders were perfectly able to integrate the 'First Global Age'. The interest of Iberian agents in new products and exchanges, their subsequent support for new consumption patterns, and their mastery of navigation and negotiation techniques explain how such agents backed the policy of the Spanish and Portuguese kings, seeking routes to Africa, Asia and the Americas. The establishment of a new type of colonial trade, from the sixteenth century onwards, with the arrival of precious metals, spices, exotic products and enslaved people, prompted the increase in the tendency for commercial growth already visible in the earlier periods.

9

The Iberian Economy in Global Perspective, 700–1500

JEFF FYNN-PAUL

9.1 The Iberian Economy in the Middle Ages: An Overview

Section 9.1 of this chapter contours the main economic developments within Iberia over the medieval millennium, from the Visigothic period through to the Mediterranean and Atlantic expansions. Section 9.2 will place these Iberian developments in a regional and global context, with a look at how Iberia fared at the beginning of the Middle Ages relative to other post-Roman provinces, the peninsula's later incorporation into the Islamic global economy, and finally the participation of Iberian economies in the emerging European macroeconomy at the end of the medieval period. Section 9.3 will then examine the four regional economies of later medieval Iberia in a little more detail: the northern Atlantic trade, the internal economy, the Mediterranean economy and the south-western Atlantic economy. The aim is to emphasize how the medieval 'Iberian economy' should be seen as a set of distinct yet important 'Iberian economies'. Finally, in Section 9.4 we will briefly touch upon a few general conclusions as to the place of the medieval Iberian economy in a global and long-term perspective.

Let us begin at the beginning. Iberia is first and foremost a geographical expression. It is a peninsula that faces both the Mediterranean and the Atlantic in equal measure. It contains a mix of rich land and desert, but it is fairly mountainous. It is not as mountainous as Greece, but it is more mountainous than Italy, and the disposition of its ranges both cut it off from mainland Europe and favour the western part of the peninsula. This bars most of the landmass – except the medieval Crown of Aragon – from effective communication with the Mediterranean. The Guadalquivir valley is among the richest areas of the peninsula, and its mouth was just accessible enough from the Pillars of Hercules that ancient mariners braved the brief foray into the Atlantic in order to take advantage of its mineral and agricultural riches. It was the metals of the greater Guadalquivir region – particularly its copper and tin, which are required to make bronze – that first drew the Iberians into a wider web of exchange.

Iberia has been connected with a wider Mediterranean economy from at least 3,000 BCE, when complex sites based on the exchange of metals and other mineral wealth were constructed. Not only copper and tin, but also silver, gold, iron and amber were mined and sought after by the more advanced states of the eastern Mediterranean. The remarkable fortified mining settlement of Los Millares near Almería, which was continuously inhabited for over two millennia, is a notable example of this late prehistoric phenomenon. With the advent of Greeks, Carthaginians and Romans, Iberian tribes were slowly incorporated into deeper trade networks and, later, into political entities of increasing size and complexity. The Roman economy saw the deliberate creation of hundreds of urban nodes throughout Iberia. These facilitated the introduction of specialized manufacture, the large-scale transportation of cash crops, and an increasing availability of luxury goods to a wealthy, cosmopolitan and relatively large elite. Roman engineers brought tremendous improvements to infrastructure, including a road network that lasted until modern times, and water supplies to cities and fields that formed the basis of successful Islamic irrigation networks. It is safe to say that by bringing material advances such as urbanization, irrigation and an improved road network, along with organizational and human capital advances such as literacy, numeracy and fiscality, the Romans created a permanent improvement to the GDP of the Iberian Peninsula.

The Visigothic period was often unsettled. It saw the diminution of specialized manufacture and cash cropping, and it saw urban shrinkage or abandonment coupled with a decreased spending power and human capital among elites and artisans. The Visigothic monarchy, aided by the episcopate, were somewhat successful in sustaining Roman notions of public authority. They were helped by surviving urban nodes, the Roman road network and a lingering sense of centralized fiscality. However, it is safe to say that by 700, the Iberian economy was much more fragmented and less integrated into global networks than it had been in 500. In particular, large sections of the peninsula had reverted to a near-total localism. Had it not been for the Islamic invasions, we can imagine that Iberian economic growth would have mirrored the relative stagnation of France during this period.

The coming of the Muslim armies after 711 integrated most of Iberia into the new, bourgeoning Islamic economy that stretched across the southern Mediterranean and Western Asia. Until the year 1031, most of the peninsula was united under a single strong central authority, the Emirate (later Caliphate) of Córdoba. The Iberian Emirate/Caliphate was, like other Islamic polities of the time, highly focused on urban life. Cities grew rapidly, with new housing developments that only sometimes respected Roman street plans. Large, important cities fostered artisanal specialization, cash cropping, long-distance trade, literacy and the creation of other forms of human capital. The Emirate/Caliphate maintained roads, public safety, an elaborate central fiscal regime, and it introduced advanced irrigation techniques that substantially improved agricultural yields over Roman ones. Dozens of new crops such as the orange and the fig, the aubergine and carrot, and spices such as cinnamon and cloves were introduced, and manufactured products such as paper and silk were introduced with an eye to export production. Using the rich Guadalquivir valley as its base, with good connections to global trade routes, the Emirate/Caliphate became one of the most successful global economies of the eighth to the tenth centuries outside of China. With the break-up of the Caliphate into dozens of city-state *taifas* in the eleventh century, the individual cities and their rulers remained very wealthy for a time. But cut off as they were from their Muslim brethren across the straits of Gibraltar, individual *taifa* kingdoms proved vulnerable to depredation from the increasingly organized Christian kingdoms to the north. Even so (and partly with the help of Christian capital, as we shall see), the Nasrid kingdom of Granada maintained a level of wealth, organization, material abundance and economic sophistication which easily matched that of the Christian kingdoms, right up to its conquest in 1492.

As late as the year 1200, one could be forgiven for doubting that the economic future of the peninsula was to lie with the small Christian kingdoms of the mountainous north. What accounts for their ultimate success as political entities? There are two main reasons for this: demography, and demography. That is to say, demography within the peninsula, and the demography of the surrounding regions. It is claimed that early Christians hardly knew whether to count Muslims as Christian heretics or another religion altogether. Nevertheless, the Muslim conquest of 711 CE did drive large numbers of Christians into refuge in the north of the peninsula. We know this because of the relatively large, relatively early and relatively wealthy churches that are scattered from Santiago to Navarre and Catalonia across the north. In this way, the religious ideology of the early medieval period gave a significant demographic impulse to the subsequent economic and political history of the peninsula. It is also true that parts of the north receive much more than the average Iberian rainfall, thus supporting a larger population in the absence of irrigation. The Christian kingdoms therefore began with a demographic strength somewhat disproportionate to their small size. The second, and probably more decisive, factor that favoured the eventual re-Christianization of the peninsula is that France is a much agriculturally richer land than Morocco. In a Malthusian pre-industrial world, more food means more population. In the end, many more Christians were available to migrate into Iberia than Muslims. The early success of the Camino de Santiago, attested from the ninth century, brought much needed external contact, some wealth and continuous trickles of migration into the region. Even if in-migration seldom happened in an organized way, the fact is that Western Europe could support a much larger population than North-West Africa. And naturally, the presence of a water barrier made northward migration by ordinary people that much more difficult than southward migration via the Pyrenean passes. Thus, for the same reason that the Romans eventually defeated the Carthaginians

(Italy can support many more people than Tunisia), the weight of regional demography made it likely (though by no means inevitable) that Iberia would tend towards Christianity rather than Islam.

We have argued that it was a combination of geography (mountains to hide in, a water barrier), demography and Islamic political disorganization after the break-up of the Caliphate that turned the tide towards Christian domination of the peninsula. What did that mean in economic terms? For many centuries, the economic record of the Christian kingdoms was not very impressive. About the only thing the Christian communities of the north had going for them around the year 1000 was their Christianity, which notionally connected them to the nebulous but not completely insignificant institutions of Christendom at large. In general this was a de-urbanized, localized and politically fragmented landscape, with little human capital development, small amounts of elite wealth, and, despite the Camino, minimal long-distance trade. Such a localized world developed different dialects of Iberian Romance, and preserved at least one pre-Roman language (Basque, in Navarre). The Carolingian conquest of northern Catalonia brought that region into the Frankish orbit. Catalan and Occitan are much closer to each other than to other dialects of modern Spanish or northern French, and this linguistic affinity helped to keep Catalonia focused on south-central France until the battle of Muret in 1213. In the longer term, the linguistic divide which developed during these centuries between Catalonia, Navarre, Portugal, and the distinct-but-closer dialects of the rest of the Peninsula helped to sustain politically centrifugal forces until the end of the Middle Ages. Of course this linguistically based political factionalism has remained part of Iberian politics and economics to the present day. Until the year 1000, then, the Christian kingdoms of the north were somewhat prosperous, but intensely local, agricultural and economically unremarkable economic entities.

The high medieval period saw the expansion of these kingdoms into the south. The impetus for this expansion was a slowly improving machinery of public administration, which became evident in the twelfth and especially the thirteenth, centuries. Things did not start well for the Christians: the process of feudalization, which took place during the tenth and eleventh centuries, saw a nearly complete collapse of Visigothic and Carolingian-era public authority. But from about 1100 we see a slow mapping of public monarchy back onto the Christian parts of the peninsula. Monarchs subverted the nobility by appointing commoners as royal officials in place of the old counts and viscounts. This was done with the help of the bishops; eventually, the nobility was also brought on board. As price for their aid in reconstructing a more centralized monarchy, these two 'estates' maintained outsized privileges until the very end of the Ancien Régime (Wickham, 2016).

As precarious as this institutional reorganization was, it proved to be enough. By the year 1248 Seville was in Christian hands – permanently, as it turned out. The preponderance of the peninsula was now Christian; it is only after this time that we can talk about the prehistory of the modern state of Spain in any meaningful sense. (We will bracket Portugal for the moment – on which more below.) Compared with other European states, one could make a case that Spain is a young state – akin to Poland or Prussia in this regard. And yet its core institutions, from places like Asturias, León and Catalonia, do date back to the early medieval period. These institutions, as shaky as they were, by the twelfth century enabled Christian Spanish monarchs to take advantage of the disintegration of the Caliphate, which gained them large swathes of populated land. Most important of these was the Guadalquivir valley. Unlike some European polities – Germany and Italy come to mind – much of Iberia was re-centralized under the Crown of Castile about the same time as France, just at the end of the Middle Ages. Castile and Aragon were dynastically united from 1479, and the Crown of Portugal was added to this union in 1581 until 1640. Despite its federal nature, this political consolidation under Castile proved strong by contemporary standards. It enabled Spanish monarchs to project superpower-levels of international influence throughout the sixteenth and seventeenth centuries. But this early modern projection of Iberian power was highly path dependent on economic and political developments of the later medieval period, as we shall see.

Economically, the watershed conquest of Seville in 1248 leads us to several observations. Regarding the causes of the conquest, we observe first that the Christian political reorganization of the previous centuries had a genuine economic significance. It enabled the Christian kings to preside over a primitive yet effective fiscal machinery, which paid enough troops, for long enough, to win sustained wars of conquest. This was never an easy feat, at any time in the medieval period. Much of this was possible because of the reintroduction of money and account-keeping, which were among the principal economic developments of the high medieval period. Second, the conquest of Seville reflects a demographic increase which accelerated around the year 1000, continued until the Black Death, and (especially in the western parts of the peninsula) picked up again throughout the fifteenth century. Already by 1348, many parts of the peninsula had reached something like the limit of what existing agricultural regimes could support. That being said, large sections of the peninsula, especially the drier regions of the centre and south-east, remained relatively empty due in part to centuries of border warfare, and were given over to grazing. This would have an economic impact only after the upsurge in European and Mediterranean trade in the later thirteenth century increased international demand for wool. On the effects side of the balance sheet, the conquest of Seville meant that the Christian kingdoms – including Portugal and Aragon whose conquests advanced roughly along with those of the Castilians – now disposed of a far richer land from which to draw tax revenues. In the Guadalquivir valley, the Castilian kings were the latest to inherit that rich, well-exploited agricultural land with strong urban traditions and a good transportation network.

Still, it was not until the years around 1300 that the 'modern' economic trajectory of the Iberian Peninsula really got underway. The fourteenth century brought an explosion of economic developments that distanced the peninsula from previous centuries of agricultural stagnation: Hilario Casado Alonso has gone so far as to call this a period of '*destrucción creadora*' (Casado Alonso, 2012). Though we do not have space to discuss these advances in detail, a brief list can be attempted. First, there were spillover effects of demographic increase. It was the years around 1300 that saw the creation of a booming land market in the urban hinterlands. Cities had grown, and society had become monetized to the point that speculation and the rapid growth of private portfolios was possible for non-noble urban elites. The establishment of *notariates* was encouraged in most cities and towns (with an early preponderance in the Crown of Aragon) and this further supported the creation of definite property rights among non-nobles. This also fostered the creation of 'modern' forms of accounting, and an enormous proliferation of credit. Early innovations by Italian merchants were taken up by Catalan and other Iberian merchants, and contracts such as the bill of exchange and the *commenda* were used to pool wealth, spread risk and mobilize capital by hundreds of thousands of small investors on an unprecedented scale. The use of such credit instruments was not only common in maritime trade – as is often believed – but throughout the interior. By the later fourteenth century, Aragonese financiers had successfully completed the first national 'financial revolution' in the world, which preceded the more famous 'Habsburg Financial Revolution' of the Burgundian Netherlands by some two hundred years.[6] From the mid-fourteenth century, Aragonese investors were able to purchase government bonds, as well as arrange older forms of credit and investment such as the life annuity. These innovations were only fitfully adopted in Castile and Portugal, however. The home mortgage, which was to become a staple of northern investment portfolios, was not, however, prevalent in southern Europe, including Iberia. It was during the fourteenth century that the Christian states began to reintroduce a bimetallic monetary system, although gold remained a prestige coinage and silver remained the basis of exchange. Most accounting was done in silver-based units of account, with gold units being favoured by government when this worked to their advantage.

By 1300, manufacturing specialization was fully established in most cities and small towns. Certain cities specialized in cloth, leather, metal work, pottery or agricultural cash crops, as befitted the resources prevalent in a given region. In Castile, a greater proportion of manufacturing was also done in the

---

[6] For the financial revolution as a concept see Tracy (1985). For the Aragonese financial revolution of the fourteenth century, see Fynn-Paul (2015a), esp. Chapter 6.

countryside. Lords such as bishops and counts became keen to promote urban growth, even though their somewhat arbitrary fiscal demands meant that royal towns outperformed seigneurial foundations as a rule. As city elites became wealthy, they began to demand representation in national parliaments, as was then the habit throughout Europe. They also attempted to create trade guilds, although Iberian kings were successful in suppressing these groups' public influence, preventing the types of guild-based political upheaval that had caused such tumult in regions such as northern Italy, Germany and the Low Countries. We see a tremendous regional difference in the ability of urban elites to compete with the nobility and the church hierarchy. In Catalonia, urban elites briefly achieved something like parity with the first and second estates, while elsewhere, including in Valencia and Castile, urban elites remained intermixed with chivalric ideas of knighthood. In Castile, this meant that artisans remained as *pecheros*, taxpayers, while a stratum of urban knights gained tax exemption through their (often nominal) role in the military. This single institution of the tax-exempt *caballeros villanos* (urban knights) seems to have permanently weakened the artisan classes of Castile. One does not wish to paint too negative a picture, but compared with Catalan urban elites, Castilian institutions created difficulties for Castilian merchants that were simply not present in all other parts of Western Europe. In this regard, Castilian and French merchants laboured under similar burdens of excess taxation, a rampant honour culture, and arbitrary impositions by clergy and nobility, which made the emergence of an empowered 'burgher' class less likely.[7]

Nevertheless, the vastly increased economic bases of the Iberian cities did help to spur massive development in their agricultural hinterlands by 1300. In much of Castile and Portugal this growth continued, after the hiccup of the Black Death, even more forcefully in the fifteenth century, while in the northeastern peninsula growth slowed somewhat. All over, agricultural surplus fostered the development of elite and middle-class demand, and thus of regional and long-distance trade networks. It seems that the Christian Iberians learned relatively little from Islamic traders, presumably due to linguistic and cultural differences – though this does not seem to have been the case in the eastern Mediterranean (Constable, 1994). Further study might reveal links of which we remain unaware. It seems as though Italian merchants were the principal models and teachers in the late medieval Iberian take off. This began with the arrival of increasing numbers of Italian merchants in Iberian ports after the mid-thirteenth century. In their quest for deals on raw

---

[7] For arguments against this 'weak Castilian merchant class' stereotype, see Chapter 8 by Hilario Casado Alonso and other authors, in this volume. For the argument that smaller states, and/or states with weak monarchies, tended to experience greater financial innovation in the late medieval and early modern periods, see especially Stasavage (2011).

materials and finished goods, these merchants helped to deepen human and material capital networks throughout Iberia. It was in this way that the central Iberian wool network, later known as the Mesta, became integrated into the fairs of Champagne, and also into Italian-dominated Mediterranean trading networks.

It is in long-distance trade of the later medieval period that the three major Iberian kingdoms – Portugal, Castile and Aragon – really showed the economic promise that political decentralization (and competition) could offer. Castilian merchants participated in a number of regional trades, which will be addressed in Section 9.3 below. But the high and late medieval Castilian kings did not as a rule go out of their way, as the Aragonese and then Portuguese monarchs would do, to create favourable conditions for Castilian merchants overseas.[8] This likely has to do with the very size of the kingdom, as well as with the numerous royal minorities that afflicted the Castilian throne in the fourteenth and early fifteenth centuries. Like the kings of France, the Castilian kings were often preoccupied by conflicts with a vast and powerful landed gentry, which tended to relegate merchants to an even more marginal role in their policymaking. Despite this, we shall see how the northern merchants, centred on Burgos and the Basque ports, were able to carry on a respectable trade with Western France, and to connect via Bruges to the Baltic network then emerging in Northern Europe. In the south, Castile's focus on Seville meant that it did not enter into Mediterranean trade networks until later on. Well into the fourteenth century, the kings of Castile were content to rely on Italian merchants, Italian naval mercenaries and Italian bankers, for much of their naval expertise, capital and long-distance trade. For example, during the War of the Two Peters (1356–1375), Pedro of Castile relied heavily on Genoese mercenaries, leadership and financiers in order to organize his war effort, while the Aragonese under Pere III relied primarily on native sailors, shipbuilders and financiers.

The Aragonese, for their part, capitalized on their proximity to the Mediterranean trade routes early on. The thirteenth-century kings were feudally minded, and long insisted on a division of their lands among all of their surviving sons. But the kings from Jaume II (1291–1327) onwards were decidedly centralizing and entrepreneurial. They encouraged the growth of a merchant class at the expense of a feudal nobility, and this merchant class facilitated the adoption of the Italian financial techniques mentioned above. These techniques were so effective that Aragon not only withstood a full-scale

---

[8] Even Castilian kings such as Alfonso X, who are known for their commercial legislation, tended to promote inter-regional trade, rather than overseas trade. Even in the early modern period, when Castilian merchants were more prevalent around the world, the Crown was seldom particularly merchant-friendly compared with some other contemporary rulers. Even in the Middle Ages there were, of course exceptions to this general rule. See for example González Arévalo (2020) and García Díaz (2011).

invasion by Castile in the 1360s, but it was able to wrest Sardinia from the Genoese, effectively ending Genoese extra-territorial imperialism. They had already been able to annex Mallorca and Sicily in the thirteenth century, and they now re-added both of these after brief periods of independence. Particularly spectacular – and this should be seen as a triumph of Aragonese finance – was the conquest in of all of southern Italy by Alfonso V (1416–1458) in the 1440s. Measured in terms of land acquisition, the Crown of Aragon was one of the most successful later medieval states. However, the fifteenth-century Turkish conquests in the eastern Mediterranean cut off the Aragonese from lucrative eastern markets. As increasingly effective state organization began to favour larger states in the sixteenth century, the Aragonese found themselves surrounded, in the midst of a Mediterranean economy that looked increasingly like a backwater.[9] The Aragonese therefore suffered from the same economic downturn as the northern Italian states, while economic momentum swung decisively towards the Atlantic.

By the high medieval period, the Portuguese were forging trading ties all along the Atlantic coast of Europe, including with the southernmost Hanse cities, and Britain. This trade gradually increased throughout the later medieval centuries. Portuguese merchants and traders were also the beneficiaries of a state-sponsored exploration programme; this channelled resources into the foundations of what would later become the Portuguese global empire. As early as the later fourteenth century, it is clear that merchants from all three Iberian kingdoms, as well as some Italians, were probing the west coast of Africa in hopes of reaching the fabled 'land of the blacks' and Prester John. The economic goal was to bypass the Muslim-controlled Saharan trade routes that brought gold and spices to the North African coast. The Portuguese royal house, including its most famous scion Prince Henry the Navigator (d. 1460), gave direction to expeditions that steadily explored the coast of Africa. The Portuguese reached the Cape Verde islands in 1456, the equatorial islands of São Tomé and Príncipe by 1470, and rounded the Cape of Good Hope in 1488. Once this milestone was reached, full-scale Portuguese intervention all along the Indian Ocean littoral was underway scarcely a generation later.

We now understand, however, that the role of the Portuguese Crown in 'directing discovery' has likely been overstated. State sponsorship was often little more than attempt to 'rubber stamp' an already bourgeoning trade network run by merchants and adventurers with financial and personal ties across Europe. The fact is, already by the later fourteenth century, maritime south-west Europe was abuzz with tales of strange islands, peoples and a possible route to the fabulous wealth of the Indies. The general direction of events, coupled with aggressive Portuguese state sponsorship, encouraged Castile to launch its own state-sponsored expeditions into the Atlantic and

[9] For this phenomenon in general, see Ruiz (2014).

African waters. Making use of Italian financial and human capital, the Castilians hit paydirt with the voyages of Columbus and related journeys. The subsequent Treaty of Tordesillas (1494) divided the newly revealed spoils of the 'ocean sea' between Portugal and Castile. The treaty, incidentally, shows how aware authorities already were of the scale and scope of their new discoveries. Rather than being seen as a surprisingly 'premature' division of the spoils (as traditional historiography asserts), Tordesillas should be seen as a culmination of 150 years of determined, entrepreneurial and ongoing exploration.

Even in our age of anti-imperial cynicism, it is impossible to underestimate the economic significance to the global economy of the Portuguese and Castilian discoveries in the fifteenth and early sixteenth centuries. Not for nothing did Wallerstein call this the beginning of modern globalization (Wallerstein, 2011). Already conquerors of Goa in India by 1510, the Portuguese took a dominant place in the Indian Ocean trade networks, supplanting centuries-old Islamic networks at an astonishing pace. As Janet Abu-Lughod has pointed out, this 'Indian Ocean World' of Muslim-dominated trade stretched from the Horn of Africa around India, and to modern-day Malaysia and Indonesia – the famed 'spice islands'. Still, Portugal's heyday as an independent trading empire was relatively short-lived. Like Aragon, Portugal found itself under increasing pressure from rapidly centralizing Spanish might during the sixteenth century, and by 1580 it was forced into a dynastic union and annexation by Spain. It is likely that the economic consequences of Iberian centralization were negative in the main, especially since the state that ended up dominating the Iberian union had a less developed entrepreneurial and financial regime than Aragon or Portugal, and the loss of competitive edge when Portugal was subsumed into the union after 1580 seems palpable.

As to the economic effects of the early trading empire on Iberia before 1500, these seem relatively slight. Portugal probably reaped the greatest benefit, followed by the port of Seville – though the greatest rewards would not accrue to Seville until later in the Golden Age (*Siglo de Oro*). More gold and more capital became available, though much of this was channelled into conspicuous consumption by the church and the nobility. Even the most entrepreneurial nobles often combined trading activity with a disdain for common people, hobbling their chances for long-term success. Spanish and Portuguese merchants, in turn, found it difficult to raise or pool capital without interference by noble patrons or the church. In this regard, the difference between Portuguese and Castilian enterprises with those of the Catalan and Italian merchants is noticeable. The financial regimes of Portugal and Castile, in particular, continued to lag behind Italian and Catalan models, and this remained a significant obstacle. Despite these limitations, trade networks did flourish; new products were introduced into the western peninsula, and cash crops such as sugar and wine were cultivated by a small but influential group of adventurers and speculators. The Portuguese shipping industry and its many affiliated sectors benefitted and expanded greatly.

On the other hand the scourge of slavery, which was economically retrograde because of the social problems that it caused, also increased in southwestern Iberia with the arrival of the first enslaved Africans from the 1440s. In brief, medieval Iberia experienced four phases of slavery. First was the lingering tradition of ancient slavery, which was not completely phased out in favour of serfdom until about the year 1000. Muslim-Christian slavery was always present due to border wars, but after 1300 this was reduced to minor levels, as increasing diplomatic ties between Christian and Muslim states led to the prevalence of ransom over enslavement. The third phase began as labour costs skyrocketed in the wake of the Black Death. Italian merchants had been dealing in enslaved 'pagans', such as Tartars, sold on the shores of the Black Sea, for some centuries. But they had never found a market for these in Western Europe until the Black Death. From that time until the capture of Constantinople in 1453 cut off the main trade routes, enslaved people from the Black Sea were sold and purchased in the port cities of Mediterranean Europe. While some elites enthusiastically embraced this new and economical form of labour, many cities quickly acted to limit the uses to which enslaved people could be put. In Aragon, there is strong evidence that craft guilds were behind this push to limit the legal uses of enslaved labour. This reduced the attractiveness of slavery as an investment. By the time the fourth phase began with the arrival of enslaved Africans in the mid-fifteenth century, there was a declining market for enslaved people in Barcelona or Valencia.[10] The south-west port cities remained the epicentre of this small but noticeable market in enslaved Africans, which continued for some centuries after 1440. Before 1600, numbers arriving from Africa were probably in the neighbourhood of a few hundred per year. Many were trans-shipped to the Canary Islands or the Azores. Such was the scale of the Iberian slave trade until the capitalization of sugar plantations after 1600 incentivized rapid upscaling, and the growth of what we now call the Atlantic System.

9.2 The Medieval Iberian Economy in Wider Context

The previous section focused on the economic developments during the medieval period within Iberia itself, while providing a sketch of the trade routes that nourished parts of the peninsula at various stages. The present

---

[10] The Valencian economy is thought to have taken over from Barcelona during the middle of the fifteenth century, and especially during and after the Catalan Civil War of 1462–1472. For the latest on this, with a possible revision on the relative decline of Barcelona, see Armenteros Martínez (2012).

section will compare the Iberian case with the general economic history of the surrounding European and Mediterranean worlds.

From prehistoric times, Iberia participated in the broad cultural trends that were prevalent in other parts of Europe. Northern Iberians participated in one of the earliest artistic revolutions on the globe, when they created cave paintings beginning about 30,000 BCE. Much later, megalithic stone building and pottery, the metallurgical revolutions of the bronze and iron ages, and the Celtic culture with its distinctive beliefs and practices, were carried into Iberia from the surrounding regions. These were often practised with particular vigour and creativity in various locations in the peninsula. We have already seen how Iberia was a major node in the prehistoric Mediterranean metallurgical trade, drawing seafaring people from all across the Mediterranean to its deposits of tin, copper, iron, lead, gold and silver. These resources helped to make numbers of local chiefdoms relatively prosperous for their time.

Iberia's integration into the wider European and Mediterranean economy was therefore thousands of years old when the Greeks and Carthaginians began to arrive in the 700s BCE. It is from this time that Iberia slowly moves beyond the realm of archaeology and comes into the light of history. The Greeks set up trading posts along the north-east coast, most notably at Empúries (near modern Rosas) and territories south. Meanwhile the Phoenicians set up a number of trading post-forts along the southern coast of the peninsula, from Cartagena in the south-east (where there were lead mines), to the lower Guadalquivir valley in the south-west. There were various outposts along the south-central coast including Málaga, and a group of western strongholds focused on Cádiz. Of the two cultures, the Carthaginian was to prove more impactful. The Greek colonizers' main focus was southern Italy and Sicily, and to a much lesser extent the area around the mouth of the Rhone. The Carthaginians were attracted to the southern peninsula on account of its mining exports, the wealth of the semi-legendary Tartessos, and more practically, to the fertility of the Guadalquivir valley. But before the Carthaginians could settle into a definitive pattern of colonization and influence, the Iberian Peninsula was wrested from their control by the armies of the Roman Republic. The Romans proved to be much more ambitious than the Carthaginians had been. Rather than contenting themselves with coastal strongholds, the Romans undertook the wholesale submission of every Iberian tribe. They were determined to plant permanent cities in the most far-flung portions of the peninsula, and their plan to settle Latin-speaking veteran soldiers in these new colonies must be accorded an unmitigated success. The fact that most Iberians still speak a version of vulgar Latin attests to this. As noted above, the modern urban network in Iberia owes much to these Roman colonizers of the two centuries surrounding the reign of Augustus. Zaragoza, for example, far inland up the Ebro River, is a contraction of the original Latin *Caesarea Augusta*, and one is amazed to learn that cities as far inland as Mérida

(*Augusta Emerita*) and León (*Castra Legionis*) have flourished more or less continually since their foundation.

The previous section has already described how the medieval Iberian economy was path-dependent on the foundations and improvements made by the Romans. The focus of this section, however, is to gauge the relative position of the Spanish economy on a European- and Mediterranean-wide scale during the later Roman and early medieval periods. As we know, the Romans were remarkably consistent in their desire to spread urbanization and other improvements equally throughout their provinces. So *Hispania* benefitted from this GDP-boosting infrastructural improvement in much the way that Gaul, Britain and North Africa did. Angus Maddison has helpfully conjectured some GDP statistics for the various Roman provinces. According to his calculations, Hispania ranked in the second quartile, that is, among the lower end of the wealthy provinces. While Italy, Egypt, Anatolia and Gaul were wealthier, Hispania's GDP was not terribly far behind that of Gaul. However, the eastern Mediterranean urban network was much denser, on account of its ancientness, than that of the western provinces. Thus, when Rome fell, the western provinces suffered a more precipitous decline in urbanization and thus GDP.

On the other hand, while the empire lasted, Hispania produced far more GDP than any of the smaller or more marginal provinces including Mauretania (Morocco), Greece, Africa (Carthage) and Britannia. Some of the cities of Hispania, including Córdoba and Hispalis near Seville, produced such towering Roman personalities as Seneca and Trajan. Metallurgy continued to be a major part of the Spanish economy throughout the Roman period; ice cores from Greenland have enabled us to pinpoint the peak of Roman lead production to the first century CE – perhaps 40% of global lead production at this time occurred in Spain. Furthermore, almost all Roman gold production also occurred in the peninsula. Of course, the fruits of this labour, as with many other Roman crafts, were concentrated in the hands of a few ultra-high net worth individuals (such as Seneca himself). They often employed thousands of enslaved people in their industrial operations. Not that slavery was inherently inimical to entrepreneurialism – the medieval Muslim world shows this clearly – but the Roman mentality towards business never evolved in this direction. Besides mineral wealth, the Tarraconensis (roughly the Ebro valley in the north-east, later the basis of the Crown of Aragon) was famed for its olive oil. This was exported in vast quantities to Rome and throughout the empire; likewise wine was produced as a cash crop. Amphorae were mass produced in various locations around the peninsula to facilitate this trade. Salted fish and the ubiquitous fish sauce (*garum*) had been exported since pre-Carthaginian times, and its production was ramped up during the imperial period.

Recent work by Chris Wickham (2005) has done much to synthesize the bewildering variety of local archaeological studies on various parts of the Roman empire during the late- and post-Roman periods. It is to his work that we must turn in order to gauge how well post-Roman Iberia weathered the storms of the pre-Islamic period. Wickham emphasizes, among other things, that late Roman Iberia consisted of a number of interlocking regional economies, some of which were more linked to neighbouring non-Iberian regions than to the rest of Iberia. This is an important point, because 1,000 years later, a very similar pattern of interlocking regional economies would emerge in the late medieval Iberian economy. Prior to 500 CE, Iberia was connected into a broader western Mediterranean trading network. The main lines ran between Western Italy, Africa, Iberia and southern Gaul. The south-east coast of the peninsula was dependent on North Africa for the majority of manufactured products and commodities. In the interior there was a flourishing regional pottery style, which was mass produced and high quality. The western provinces of Baetica, Lusitania and the western Tarraconensis were dependent on one another in a large-scale, high-demand, highly interlinked economy. The central and eastern Tarraconensis benefited from its location near the Mediterranean trade routes, but it was also more self-sufficient than the south-east; it showed a high degree of aristocratic wealth and villa continuity compared with some other parts of Iberia, even as society began to simplify after 500.

By 700 CE, there is evidence for an almost universal decline in the long-standing Western Mediterranean exchange system. This had struggled on haphazardly, despite the break-up of the Roman Empire. The demise of this exchange system happened by degrees, affecting different sub-Roman provinces in various ways. One clear pattern is that the advancing Muslim conquest was a boon to those provinces which were incorporated into it, and economically disastrous to those provinces that were left out. In south-east Iberia, the system of imports from Africa seems to have collapsed roughly around the time of the Arabic conquest of Carthage in 698. The internal economy of the *Meseta* had already collapsed into pure localism during the sixth and seventh centuries, with lingering concentrations of aristocratic wealth found in Mérida. In the decades before 700, the cities of the Tarraconensis fell to their lowest recorded levels of urban continuity – meaning that the continued occupation of many sites cannot even be proven. Long-distance and high-volume pottery exchanges fell precipitously, and pre-dressed stones ceased to be produced or traded in large volumes. A result of this latter development was that Iberians began to build their buildings almost exclusively in wood, or (very occasionally) in re-used stone. The indication is of a general collapse of demand across not only Iberia, but also southern Gaul and Mauretania/the Western Maghreb. Meanwhile the economy of northern Gaul collapsed much earlier and more precipitously than southern Gaul or Iberia. Only Italy showed higher concentrations of urban continuity and economic exchange, although here too there was a marked slackening of demand, which only picked up in Lombardy in the years after 700.

Thus it was that the Christian Iberian economy had dwindled to a fairly primitive level on the eve of the Muslim conquest of 711. As it turned out, the peninsula still had all of the ingredients for a flourishing economy. It was simply that it did not, under the Visigoths, possess political institutions particularly well suited to directing them. One is tempted to draw a parallel between the Celtiberians who were superseded by the Romans, and the Visigoths who were superseded by the Muslims. In both cases, the succeeding peoples proved capable of a full-scale economic revolution, while the former peoples proved, for various reasons, but modest stewards of the peninsular resources. In any event, a major economic kickstart was provided by the establishment of the Emirate – later the independent Caliphate – centred on Córdoba. Lest we doubt that al-Andalus was one of the most successful global economies in the years between 700 and 1000, we need only look at the population estimates of the capital city. This might have reached 500,000 souls: all the more remarkable because it was a period of extremely low population density around the Mediterranean littoral. Clearly, Córdoba was a place that many people wanted to live. Within a century of the conquest, the Andalusian economy had rocketed ahead of the rest of Europe outside Byzantium. As a city, Córdoba's only global rivals were Constantinople, at the heart of the still-successful Byzantine Empire, the Abbasid capital of Baghdad, and certain of the largest cities in China.

We have stated above that the early period of al-Andalus was marked by a tremendous growth in economic potential. This was not only significant on a regional or intra-Iberian level. By incorporating Iberia into an Arabic-speaking trade network spanning much of the Mediterranean, Africa, even to central Asia and the Indian Ocean, al-Andalus provided many channels for imports and exports, together with a culture geared for trade. Many mercantile fortunes were made, and elite demand soared. Their gold coinage was the envy of the surrounding Christian states. The impressiveness of the Andalusian markets, architecture, cultural life and amenities were envied throughout Europe. Indeed, the Caliphate and its successor states remained so economically successful that they attracted some of the greatest minds in the Arabic-speaking world, even during the *taifa* period of the eleventh and twelfth centuries. The intellectual reputation of al-Andalus was such that European philosophers drew on its knowledge to help fuel the European renaissance of the high Middle Ages. Within the Islamic world, al-Andalus was regarded for a period of some half millennium as one of the richest and most successful provinces in the Dar al-Islam. Most societies of Latin Europe could scarcely hold a candle to the economy of al-Andalus until well into the 1100s.

The Italians were the early exception. By the eleventh century, Italian expansion and the nascent 'commercial revolution' helped turn the economic tide in favour of Christian Europe. In this regard, what happened in the Iberian Peninsula can serve as a microcosm of what was happening in the Mediterranean generally. The establishment of the Crusader states in the Levant, tended by newly emboldened Italian merchants, and the driving of Islamic navies from most of the Mediterranean, helped to flip the Mediterranean shipping routes into a Christian-dominated trade network, beginning soon after the year 1000. Slowly, Christian shipping also became dominant in the waters around Iberia. The conquest of Mallorca in 1229 was a major turning point in the east; in the west, the conquest of Seville in 1248 and the Algarve (southern Portugal) in 1249 helped to secure the west coast from the majority of Islamic pirate raids. Of course, Islamic Granada maintained a naval presence until the end of the Middle Ages, and pirate raids from North Africa remained endemic until the nineteenth century. But from the thirteenth century onwards, Christian domination of peri-Iberian trade routes would not be seriously challenged. From the later 1100s onwards, Italian merchants established trading quarters in the great entrepots of Constantinople and Alexandria, and increasingly 'colonized' these cities' Mediterranean trade. This provided opportunities for east Iberian merchants. Catalans, Valencians, Mallorcans and other Aragonese traders provided some competition to the north Italian trade monopolies of some eastern Mediterranean cities, especially during the thirteenth and fourteenth centuries. This trade deepened capital networks in eastern Iberia and helped cause a surge in the material prosperity of these regions.

From around 1300, an explosion of documentation enables us to focus on many more details of Western European economic developments. The complexity of European economies grew considerably during the later medieval centuries; in this period the foundations for 'modern' developments in fiscality and finance were laid. The years after 1300 also witnessed major strides in political organization and centralization; this is evident throughout Western Europe as a whole. The modern nation state, with its central government, its bureaucratic departments with specific competencies, and parliaments, was a product of these centuries. Rudimentary economic policy, enacted at a national scale, became more common. Government borrowing as a means of war finance was also pioneered at this time. In terms of fiscality, the Crown of Aragon and Italy were world-leading, while Castile and Portugal lagged noticeably behind. That being said, the Islamic states lagged even further behind, due to stronger linguistic and cultural barriers; as a rule Islamic states did not begin to move beyond medieval methods of tax farming until the Ottoman Empire started experimenting with modern finance in the aftermath of the Crimean War. By the fourteenth century, then, the initiative in all manner of fiscality and microeconomic organization lay with parts of

Christian Europe. The sixteenth- and seventeenth-century Northern European systems of public debt and fiscality known as the 'financial revolution' were based on these Southern European experiments of the late medieval period.

Meanwhile, in the realm of microeconomics, advances such as double-entry bookkeeping, the concept of the audit, limited liability partnerships, personal lines of credit, and other forms of detailed accounting and recordkeeping were also widely adopted for private and public business. The Castilian Crown adopted the notion of the audit with particular zeal, once the Catholic Monarchs adopted it as part of their strategy of bureaucratic centralization. It would serve them well as an important tool for administering their far-flung empire.

It is notable that we can speak of pan-European fiscal and financial advancements during the later medieval period. Perhaps even more remarkable is that we can also begin, for the first time since the Roman Empire, to speak meaningfully of a pan-European macroeconomy. This occurred as the trading activity of individual merchants increased across the continent, and as individual merchants and bankers became wealthy enough to gain international reputations. The consolidation of a pan-European credit market began in the late thirteenth century. We know of several bankruptcies of famous Italian banking families (the Bardi and Peruzzi are only two of the best known), which occurred after monarchs forced these families to lend to them on threat of confiscation of their goods, only to turn around and default a few years later. Thus began the early modern trend of rulers courting wealthy bankers. But the lessons of the Bardi and Peruzzi fiasco were never forgotten; monarchs soon found that the price of default was astronomical interest rates the next time around. It is well known that Charles V and Philip II availed themselves of Genoese bankers to finance their wars, many of whom were based at Lyon (and thus conspicuously out of direct reach). It is probably inevitable that banking families thrived in smaller or less centralized states, where (as today), weak or cash-strapped governments were happier to accommodate the lending practices of the ultra-rich.

Evidence also shows that European specie markets were well integrated by the fourteenth century. The prices of gold and silver were remarkably similar in most European regions; opportunities for arbitrage were quickly closed by trading. Likewise, the progress of interest rates across Latin Europe shows a remarkable convergence: for example, the supply shocks of the 1360s and 1370s, which saw wages rise precipitously almost everywhere, led to a decreased demand for cash, which facilitated a permanent fall in the level of interest rates across the continent from some 12–20% down to 5 or 4% for high-grade commercial lending. This permanent decline was not mirrored in the Islamic or South Asian worlds. By sheer accident, this would provide early modern European states and individuals access to the cheapest capital anywhere in the world. Cheap capital is a fundamental but often overlooked factor underpinning the so-called 'Age of Exploration'. This 'Great Interest Rate Shift' of the 1370s was not purely accidental however: it was facilitated by increasing financial efficiency, which cut transaction costs and risk. A third contributing factor was the establishment of government debt systems in several influential polities. This gave governments a strong incentive to keep interest rates low. While government debt initially offered high rates of c. 15% to compete with commercial lending, familiarity led to a realization on the part of investors that these were safe, reliable investments. This led to a decreased price elasticity of demand in states that managed their debt burdens responsibly, enabling well-run governments to cut interest rates and thus their own fiscal burden. After the Great Interest Rate Shift, governments saw to it that future issues of debt paid in the order of 1–5%, rather than the 12–20% that was normative before 1370. Over time, the private sector learned to operate at similar margins, even after prosperity returned in the sixteenth and seventeenth centuries.

Commodity markets were likewise well integrated by the later medieval period. Gone were the days of the Champagne fairs, when opportunities for intra-European arbitrage might stand at 20, 50 or 100%. By the fourteenth century we know that hundreds of merchants, such as the famous Francesco Datini (1335–1410), were keeping track of commodity prices across the continent. This was done via branch operations set up in major economic hubs. It would be some centuries until the Dutch and English pioneered the daily commodities report, but individual merchants had learned to keep track of such information, and broadcast it over long distances to facilitate trading, during the later centuries of the medieval period.

Increasing state power also led to the creation of state protection and organization of merchants, often by specially organized offices located in overseas trading locales. These generally go under the heading of 'Consulates of the Sea'. First pioneered by the Italian trading cities, this idea of state organization of trade fleets was taken up by the Aragonese, Castilian and Portuguese governments from the thirteenth century. The downside of these consulates was that private initiative could be crowded out, as states organized flotillas, regulated trade and taxed it as well. Often, monopolies were granted to individuals who might interfere to the point of hindering or even ruining an existing trade network. At the same time, these consulates did offer much-needed protection to many merchants who got on board with the official regulators, and in any event, a certain amount of private initiative (including outright smuggling) was always carried on. Overall, the Consulates probably did much to increase the volume of trade, lower risks, increase quality and lower transaction costs, all across Western Europe.

Another important development that has been too-little remarked by late medievalists, is what I term the 'material revolution' of the second half of the fourteenth century. This watershed should be seen as the beginning of the 'Industrious Revolution' beloved by early modernists. As attested in my own studies of Catalonia, the home interiors of urban elites and country knights in the early part of the century were furnished in a spartan and primitive manner, apart from a few prestige possessions (Fynn-Paul, 2015a; 2015b; 2017). By the end of the century, however, the homes of urban elites and country knights contained a much more elaborate and articulate set of furnishings and implements, so much so that a visitor from the early nineteenth century might hardly distinguish a difference, except in terms of style. This reflects an increasing appetite for elaborately finished products, home furnishings and new commodities that spread across the European continent in the wake of the Black Death. The *Arnolfini Portrait* of 1434, though it depicts the interior of an Italian merchant's house in Bruges, gives a sense of just how 'modern' middle-class domestic interiors – including those in Iberia – had become in the wake of the Black Death. Why was this? It may have been that surviving households used inherited capital to increase their material environments; but for whatever reason the break is palpable and would characterize 'bourgeoise' patterns of consumption in Europe ever since. This new appetite served to drive increasing demand for a whole range of luxury products such as sugar (see below), and highly wrought, high-value-added artisanal products.

9.3 The Iberian Regional Economies in the Later Middle Ages

In all of these pan-European developments, the various Iberian kingdoms were participants; sometimes, they were pioneers. It is nonetheless crucial to recognize that regionalism remained a very important unit of economic reality in late medieval Europe. During the early modern era, national centralization continued to advance until, by the turn of the nineteenth century, one can speak realistically of national economies. Regionalism still mattered, but not in the way that it had done some three or four centuries earlier. In the late medieval centuries, however, each city or region in Iberia was profoundly affected by the orientation of its trade towards one of several regional trades, which might have little to do with one another.

We can therefore identify at least four regional economies that connected Iberia to surrounding economies in the last medieval centuries and provide a basis of comparison for the rest of this chapter. The first of these four is the northern trading economy, which connected the Bay of Biscay and its hinterland, along with Portugal, to the Baltic markets. The second of these is the economy of the Iberian interior. The third is the south-western economy centred on Portugal and Seville, with its increasing ties to the Atlantic Islands and Western Africa. And the fourth is the Aragonese-dominated economy in the Mediterranean.

9.3.1 The Northern Trade

The north Iberian trade with parts north had been building for centuries. By the later thirteenth century, Castilian merchants had created a merchant colony in Bruges. The two principal nodes for the northern trade route were Burgos in northern Spain and Bruges, in modern day Belgium. Burgos, for its part, became the leading commercial centre of northern Castile by the fourteenth century. It was here that the majority of the wool from the Mesta guild was collected, before being shipped through the Asturian passes and on to the seaports of the Cantabrian coast such as Santander and Bilbao. This trade had become extremely lucrative as the wool-hungry cities of the southern Low Countries became the leading industrial centres for textile production in Northern Europe. Bruges rose to prominence during the high Middle Ages, because it was a political and geographical enclave between the economies of England, the Baltic, the Atlantic coast and the Mediterranean. It benefitted from being semi-independent, due to the fact that the Counts of Flanders, the city's nominal overlords, gave the citizens a measure of fiscal and policymaking autonomy. By the later fourteenth century, the Baltic trade was increasingly organized under the great trading port of Lübeck and its Hanseatic League, as a result the northern markets became increasingly lucrative. As one of the westernmost entrepots of this expanding greater Baltic economy, Bruges became even wealthier. This attracted an increasing number of Iberian merchants. The economic weight of Bruges and the Flemish wool markets, coupled with a Castilian desire to outmanoeuvre the French Crown, led to increasing diplomatic ties with the Burgundian Netherlands. As a result, a marriage alliance was negotiated between the Castilian and Burgundian houses in the later fifteenth century. As ties multiplied, the number of Castilian merchants resident at Bruges grew to several hundred by the sixteenth century (Phillips, 1986). Many of these merchants owned real estate and lived there semi-permanently. Meanwhile, the world-leading artistic advances of Flanders attracted the interest of Castilian and Portuguese patrons, who admired paintings and other *objets d'art* brought back by merchants and diplomats. A strong Flemish imprint on Castilian churches and material culture also dates from this period, and is a result of this elusive but important economy of trade and diplomacy (Kasl, 2012). And of course, the Burgos–Bilbao route was only the most important route among many. There were numbers of regional traders who traded up the Bay of Biscay, and directly to England, at various points (Ruiz, 2015). Portuguese traders, too, engaged in a broad trade with the northern markets. Carla Rahn Phillips gives a sense of the breadth of the northward trade already by the high medieval centuries:

> Portugal exported salt, wine, fresh and dried fruit, oil, honey and dried shellfish to northern Europe as well as cork, hops, and other industrial raw materials. In return northern Europe sent grain and flour, dried and salted fish, dairy products, metals, wood and other forest products for shipbuilding, and textiles and other manufactured goods. (Phillips, 1990: 47)

9.3.2 The Iberian Interior

It used to be believed that the economy of the Iberian interior in the later Middle Ages was characterized by dependence, poverty, lack of integration, noble violence, ecclesiastical intransigence, absence of manufacturing, a dependence on raw material exports and excessive exploitation by the Crown and the Mesta. Viewed in the long term, and from and external perspective, one can still argue that the internal economy of late medieval Castile, like that of France, was not one of the industrial, entrepreneurial or innovative hotspots of Europe. It remains true that travellers in early eighteenth-century Spain found the land to be ill-connected by land or water routes, infested by murderous bandits, and they noted that sheep in many regions wore spiked collars to prevent their being taken by wolves. The interior has always been vast, often dry, often difficult, and it is still underpopulated by comparison with much of the rest of Europe.

At the same time, to view the internal economy in a purely negative light is to miss out on a good deal of economic growth and increasing sophistication which took place, particularly in the two centuries following the Black Death. It is now understood that, particularly during the fifteenth century, the internal economy of Northern and Central Castile experienced a significant demographic increase, which was paralleled by a tremendous increase in agricultural capacity. Viticulture was spread to many regions by entrepreneurial landowners. Increasingly sophisticated financial techniques increased some families' ability to provide credit to merchants, which in turn sparked the growth of short- and medium-distance enterprise all along internal trade routes. Thousands of such enterprises specialized in the movement of commodities between hinterlands and cities, and also between cities which were connected by obvious land or water routes. These ranged in scale from local pedlars to national-level financiers and suppliers. Cartage was a major mode of transport throughout Iberia until the advent of the railroads, but a gradual increase in traffic occurred with the demographic explosion of the fifteenth century. The fifteenth century was marked by an increase in incidents of rural manufacture in leather and also in metallic products, as well as in textiles. The above-mentioned material revolution also occurred in cities throughout the Iberian interior, meaning that demand or well-wrought items of glass, ceramic, metal, leather and cloth all increased. Much of this demand was met by regional producers, whose produce was collected and distributed by regional merchants. Various types of wool and dyestuffs were transported to and from manufacturing points, and fashions for various types of finished cloth and other goods drove regional demand, which ebbed and flowed. This is to say nothing of the Mesta, which famously organized transhumance and the export of wool across much of the interior. The techniques that enabled the exploitation of Merino wool only increased demand for this product in ports as far afield as Bruges and Florence during the late medieval period. Though much of their greatness depended on this trade in raw materials, trading hubs such as Burgos served also as transhipment points for interior locales. Many international goods, including the artistic products mentioned above, were sold and resold at various locations throughout the interior, adding to the capital depth of the interior cities. By the sixteenth century, many of these cities were impressive by any European standards. But it is important to realize that while some of the flashiest artefacts, such as church altarpieces, come from an exploitation of New World silver in the sixteenth and seventeenth centuries, in fact many of the monuments and impressive houses of the cities of the interior were built from capital that had been accumulated via the internal economy of the peninsula during the centuries of later medieval growth.

9.3.3 The South-West

The south-west Iberian economy was exceptionally dynamic during the last medieval centuries, not least because it would soon become a cornerstone for the globalization of maritime trade during the sixteenth century. Economic historians have long recognized that the Portuguese 'voyages of exploration', not to mention the voyages of Columbus, can only be understood in the context of centuries of slow advance, marked by a gradual deepening of material and human capital networks. Historians such as William Phillips and David Abulafia have noted the continuity between Italian colonizing voyages to the Levant and the Black Sea during the high Middle Ages with the later Portuguese and Castilian expansion into the Atlantic Islands and West Africa (Phillips, 1992). In particular, European merchants had learned the techniques not only of navigation, but also of bookkeeping, finance, maritime insurance and long-distance commodities trading, by trial and error, over a period of centuries. Many still find it surprising that such a tiny state as Portugal should have such an outsize impact on the bourgeoning Atlantic economy. This is strange, since we take for granted that tiny states such as Venice, Genoa and later the Netherlands would also carve out large trading empires for themselves. It seems that a small physical area could act as a boon for mercantile communities during the long centuries from the late Middle Ages through to the heyday of the British Empire. The traditional explanation contains elements of truth: small coastal countries had fewer great landed nobles and churchmen to interfere in top-level politics; they naturally looked to the sea for opportunity; and their rulers knew that without heightened amounts of cash, they would quickly succumb to their larger neighbours. Thus it was that, by the fourteenth century if not earlier, the kings of small states such as Aragon, Portugal, Flanders and to some extent England adopted aspects of the Italian model of proto-capitalism as a simple fiscal expedient. By adopting the idea of the maritime consulate to its own ends, the Portuguese

Crown began to actively oversee the mercantile exploration of the West African coast. It naturally combined this with political goals. A slight variant of this peculiarly European alliance between merchants and state would later be adopted by the Dutch and the English with their famed East India Companies.

At any event, we can briefly trace the steps by which the south-western trade became vigorous. By the later thirteenth century, as the fairs of Champagne waned due to political interference, Mediterranean merchants increasingly made the sea voyage to Bruges. This route was characterized by both bulky goods and specialty textiles. As a consequence, small communities of Italian merchants began to congregate in ports along the southern and western Iberian coasts. This contact increased the appetite of Iberian merchants to exploit distant markets in their own right, and their expanding network was fuelled in part by Genoese banking capital. By the later fourteenth century, as noted, the Atlantic islands had been discovered, which quickly set off a race to colonize them and exploit them for sugar. As a luxury product, sugar reflected the rising living standards of Europeans (i.e. the 'material revolution') in the wake of the Black Death. David Abulafia has made the case that sugar was one of the major crops which drove colonization and profiteering efforts of the Portuguese, Castilians and Italians in this growing south-west Iberian economy (Abulafia, 2008). Sugar was originally grown and obtained in the eastern Mediterranean; it was subsequently transferred to Sicily by its Arab rulers, whence it was inherited by the island's Aragonese conquerors. Injections of Italian capital into the Kingdom of Granada, to finance sugar-growing operations there, ironically helped that kingdom to stay afloat for a century longer than it otherwise might have done. Thus sugar was already a cash crop when the Atlantic Islands were discovered – meaning that they could be put to immediate economic use. Familiarity with Ocean navigation encouraged further exploration along the African coast; already by the 1440s this trade was characterized by an importation of gold, enslaved people, pepper and ivory from sub-Saharan Africa. The rest is a story best left to the subsequent parts of this economic history.

9.3.4 The Mediterranean

It is easy for non-medievalists to look down upon the Mediterranean sector of the Iberian economy in the later Middle Ages, since hindsight reveals it as an economic 'dead end'. In most minds, the glorious future of Iberia was to lie elsewhere on the peninsula. But to do this would be a mistake on several fronts. We have already noted how Mediterranean trade significantly and permanently deepened capital networks across eastern Iberia. The natives of Barcelona, Valencia, Mallorca and the other Mediterranean ports were likewise some of the most skilled and daring merchants of their day; they were also some of the best naval officers, and the only Iberian financiers on a par with the Italians. As noted above, the Catalan navy was able to facilitate the conquest and re-conquest of Sicily; it drove the Genoese from Sardinia and facilitated a takeover of all of southern Italy. For a while, the Catalans even counted the Duchy of Athens as part of their Mediterranean Empire. In this time as later, the ability to build and maintain a world-leading navy came down to an abundance of liquid capital and well-oiled capital markets. The Aragonese 'financial revolution' of the later fourteenth century was instrumental in setting the stage for further conquest and integration. Indeed, from the 1450s, the Aragonese monarchs were able to rule eastern Iberia from Naples; under Ferdinand the Catholic and Charles V, the cadet branches of Naples and Sicily were brought into a single monarchy. All of this presupposes the financial and logistical ability to hold such a far-flung naval empire together.

Under the aegis of this increasingly coherent political entity, Catalan merchants were able to fend off Italian, Castilian, Granadan, North African and Ottoman competitors, and establish a regular trade between Sicily, Naples and eastern Iberia, together with voyages to the Levant. These were regulated under increasingly comprehensive maritime law and customs, as adjudicated in the famous Catalan 'Consulates of the Sea'. The Catalan presence in Alexandria and Constantinople was the most significant of any European power after the Venetians and the Genoese, even as the Genoese were driven from the Mediterranean after the mid-fourteenth century. The Black Death played a role in blunting the Catalan initiatives to the Levant, as did the increasing power of the Ottomans. But these factors would naturally have affected the Italians equally as well. Like the Genoese, however, who famously proved incapable of governing their own affairs, the Catalans suffered their own share of self-inflicted misfortune. Particularly the Catalan Civil War of the 1460s had the effect of driving mercantile capital from Barcelona (the epicentre of the war, and seat of opposition to the Crown), and toward Valencia. The result was a flourishing of Valencian trade in the later fifteenth century, which was, however, paralleled by an eclipse of Barcelonese trade lasting some centuries. Barcelonese trade was not the only casualty of the bitter wars of John II (1458-1479) against his Catalan subjects.[11] Evidence suggests that many of the Catalan towns lost a great deal of their wealth and population as a result of destruction and flight. This ruined the commercial prosperity of the Barcelonese hinterland and permanently hobbled the economy of the Catalan capital.

The fifteenth century therefore witnessed both a shift of economic gravity in eastern Iberia from Barcelona to Valencia, and also a gradual downturn, which had begun sometime earlier. Before the decline, however, Catalan merchants from the later 1200s enjoyed at least a century of expansion. There is evidence

---

[11] On this war see in addition to the work of Armenteros Martínez (2012), also Ryder (2007).

that by the mid-fourteenth century, Catalan merchants from even the regional cities were expanding operations far afield. For a few decades, we see small enterprises and partnerships sending employees to regional markets from Valencia to Mallorca, westward to Zaragoza, and along the northern coast through Marseille and Montpellier. Products involved in this trade here were as varied as anywhere else at the time and included fruits, cheeses, leather and leather goods, saffron, dried fish and meat, salt, alum for tanning, paper, sugar, beeswax, silk, textiles and – particularly for the century between about 1350 and 1450 – enslaved people from the Black Sea. However, the continued disruption of labour markets by ongoing bouts of plague, coupled with some 20 years of war with Castile from 1355 to 1375, led to shrinking profit margins. By the 1380s, long-distance voyages had dwindled in number. Many families gained less utility from engaging in trade than from investing in the new government annuities, with a result that many eastern Iberians, along with some of their Italian counterparts, turned away from active trading.[12] Thus, while the Valencian-led phase of the trade was reduced in scope by the later fifteenth century, it certainly remained active as a regional trade among the various Iberian possessions in the western Mediterranean. In the sixteenth century, while the world turned its attention to the wonders coming from India, Indonesia and the New World, the craftspeople and merchants of eastern Iberia continued to generate wealth on a humbler, but by no means insignificant, scale.

9.4 Conclusion

Viewed over the long centuries of the ancient and medieval periods, perhaps the most important corrective we can suggest to our preconceptions of Iberian economic history is that Iberia has, for most of its recorded history, been anything but 'poor', 'underdeveloped' or 'unenlightened' in comparison with neighbouring regions of the globe. We must emphatically lay to rest anything like a 'Black Legend' when considering the ancient or medieval Spanish economy. From a purely geographical perspective, some have lamented the disadvantage afforded by Iberia's location at the extreme west of the Mediterranean. And yet, we have seen that from Neolithic times, this did not prevent the integration of Iberia into Mediterranean-wide trading networks. A second potential 'disadvantage' was that Iberia's most fertile river valley, the Guadalquivir, faces south-west, rather than east. Still, this did not prevent the creation of great wealth there, almost continually from the legendary age of

---

[12] The *locus classicus* of this idea that the Italian merchant families gradually turned away from trading after the 1370s (after what I have subsequently identified as the Great Interest Rate shift) is Kedar (1976). For Catalonia, Jaume Aurell (1996) subsequently reported on a similar occurrence.

Tartessos through the Carthaginian, Roman, Islamic and Castilian periods. A third potential 'disadvantage' was that the Western Mediterranean lay further from the epicentre of civilization in the Nile and Mesopotamian river valleys. This did not stop Iberia from being increasingly integrated into the Greek, Carthaginian and Roman empires by late ancient times. A fourth potential 'disadvantage' is the mountainous nature of the peninsula, which made communication difficult; at the same time, this did not prevent the creation of two or three major Roman provinces in Iberia, or the creation of the Caliphate of Córdoba, or of the unified state of Spain by the end of the medieval period. In comparison with many regions of the Mediterranean, such as the Balkans, Greece, Morocco or Anatolia, Iberia contains vast tracts of rich, fertile and productive land. Finally, a fifth potential disadvantage, which also worked to its advantage by the end of our period, was that Morocco and the North African coast was relatively infertile due to the encroaching Sahara. This was bad for economic growth because it meant that there was always a very small population directly to the south of the peninsula with which to trade. But this geographical 'splendid isolation' often proved an advantage, because when they were well organized, the Iberians had little to fear from incursions from most directions. In this regard the parallels with Egyptian civilization – surrounded as it always has been by deserts – are manifest.

So we have seen that almost all of the 'disadvantages' sometimes raised about the geography of the peninsula were, throughout the ancient and medieval periods, nothing of the sort. The combination of mineral wealth, the fertility of the river valleys, the temperate climate, and the navigability of the Mediterranean meant that Iberia must be put near the top of any global economic ranking by province or region prior to 1500. During the period 700–1000, Muslim Iberia was one of the richest regions of the world. From the eleventh century onwards, the kingdoms of both Castile and Granada were among the wealthiest provinces of their size in the world. By the later medieval period, the Kingdom of Aragon was a major economic powerhouse, and the northern economy centred on Burgos was likewise globally significant. Nor was the internal economy shabby or under-developed by global standards. And no one speaks of geographical disadvantage when it comes to the opening of the Atlantic economy: as soon as we reach the end of the medieval period, economic historians wax eloquent at the perfect location for Portugal and Castile to act as entrepots between European demand and world markets.

But more than simple geography was at play in this story of economic development, and this is even more important for dispelling any lingering economic version of the 'Black Legend'. This chapter has been at pains to emphasize the importance of institutions in creating or hindering the creation of wealth. Throughout its ancient and medieval history, Iberians have shown time and again that they could create world-leading economies, due to their ability to organize polities and exploit the abundant resources of the peninsula.

This was in part due to the accessibility of the peninsula to trade routes, whether Greek, Carthaginian, Roman, Islamic, Mediterranean or Atlantic. It was also due to the receptiveness of Iberians to regional and global developments, which saw them respond in highly successful ways during the majority of centuries under scrutiny. All three major Iberian states were, by the end of the medieval period, highly successful by any global measure. Not only politically, but in economic terms. And living standards in the Iberian regions were likewise very high by global standards.

Throughout the ancient and medieval periods, then, Iberia played host to some of the most interesting and dynamic economies on the globe. Infrastructure, material capital and human capital were often at world-leading levels in comparison with regions of comparable size. Sometimes, the Iberian economies approached a peninsula-wide scale; more often, these economies were regional. But they were nearly always connected with neighbouring regions and larger, semi-global or global trading networks. For all of these reasons, Iberian economic history is an important object of study. If a reader takes away two main lessons from a study of medieval Iberian economic history, they should be the following. First, Iberia did not 'suddenly' emerge as a world-leading economy in the sixteenth century. It had already been playing a pivotal role on the world economic stage for many centuries – indeed for millennia – prior to the Golden Age. Second, readers should take with them an understanding of how the Iberian economy of the Golden Age was in fact a regional one, with multiple interlocking parts, a complex system that had been developing over the course of centuries. These long-enduring structures added both strengths and weaknesses to the overall economy of Spain's Golden Age, and provide layers of insight for those who wish to understand the rise and fall of Spain as a global superpower.

PART II

Globalization and Enlightenment, 1500–1800

Edited by Leonor Freire Costa and Regina Grafe

10

Patterns of Iberian Economic Growth in the Early Modern Period

NUNO PALMA AND CARLOS SANTIAGO-CABALLERO

10.1 Introduction

In the late Middle Ages, Western Europe was the richest region of the world, and Spain and Portugal were, even in the least favourable estimations, at average Western European income levels.[13] Three hundred years later, however, the Iberian economies had lost considerable ground and fallen behind all the main European powers. In this chapter, we describe the comparative aggregate performance of the Spanish and Portuguese economies during the early modern period. First, we present the evolution of incomes per capita, and the changes experienced in the main sectors of these economies. Second, we discuss the regional dynamics to reveal whether the general trends present were common or whether we can find significant internal differences. Finally, we study the Spanish and Portuguese cases in a broader context, comparing their incomes per head with those of the main European powers. This reveals the moment when the Iberian countries diverged from north-western and central Europe.

Before diving into details, we provide some background on the overall performance of Iberia, by comparing it with that of England (Figure 10.1).[14]

We are thankful to Leonor Freire Costa, António Henriques, Leandro Prados de la Escosura, Regina Grafe, Jaime Reis and Joan Rosés for discussions. The usual disclaimer applies. Nuno Palma gratefully acknowledges funding from Fundação para a Ciência e a Tecnologia (CEECIND/04197/2017). Carlos Santiago-Caballero acknowledges grant PID2020-117468GB-I00 funded by CIN/AEI/10.13039/501100011033.

[13] See Broadberry et al. (2018: 989) for evidence that Europe was already ahead by 1500. In Section 10.4 we discuss comparative Western European GDP per capita levels in detail. For a discussion of methodologies and sources used to build premodern GDPs, see Jong & Palma (2018) and Palma (2020b).

[14] These estimates result from recent quantitative research. They are far from set in stone, since their construction implies multiple methodological and data-related challenges (Jong & Palma, 2018; Palma, 2020b). But they are certainly much better than the only alternative, the 'guesstimates' of Maddison (2006: 249), who writes: 'I assumed a growth rate of Spanish GDP per capita of 0.25 per cent a year from 1500 to 1600, no advance in the seventeenth century, and some mild progress from 1700 to 1820. I adopted a similar profile for Portugal'. We now know that this last assumption, for instance, does not work

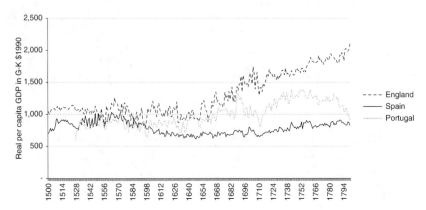

Figure 10.1 GDP per capita in constant, Geary–Khamis (GK) 'international' 1990 dollars for Spain, Portugal and England, 1500–1800.
Sources: for Spain, Prados de la Escosura et al. (2020); for Portugal, Palma & Reis (2019); for England, Broadberry et al. (2015a). In the latter case, levels are extrapolated backwards from the 1870 level for Great Britain, with growth rates corresponding to the borders of England until 1700 and Great Britain afterwards.

The divergence started relatively late – the English economy only took off relative to Spain from the mid-seventeenth century, and relatively to Portugal from the late seventeenth century.[15]

In Spain, the sixteenth century was a period of sustained but slow economic growth, with flourishing production of raw wool that was also exported to international markets, at the same as the country forged its empire (Álvarez Nogal & Prados de la Escosura, 2013).[16] Spain was especially affected by the crisis that started in the late sixteenth century, when increasing fiscal pressure hit urban economies and together with environmental deterioration reduced agrarian production (Álvarez Nogal et al., 2016). It would not be until the

---

well. As Figure 10.1 shows, Spanish and Portuguese early modern macroeconomic history was considerably different.

[15] In Figure 10.1, the levels for England for 1700–1850 in fact correspond more rigorously to Great Britain. If the line is indeed interpreted in this fashion, linking the indexes in 1700 and continuing to go back in time means implicitly assuming that Scotland grew at the same rates as England prior to 1700. Given that the growth data is only available for the borders of England prior to 1700 and Britain thereafter, there is no perfect solution to this problem. However, any adjustment that could be made to the English series would lie within the reasonable margins of error which must be attributed to the series shown in Figure 10.1. Since there is less uncertainty about trends than levels, we prefer to call the line 'England' to emphasize that there was no growth in that territory over the 1500–1650 period.

[16] However, production of woollen textiles (as opposed to raw wool) declined.

eighteenth century that sluggish growth would resume, although by the end of the century income per capita was still below the maximum reached 200 years before.

As for Portugal, there was persistent growth in per capita incomes for long periods of time from the early sixteenth century onwards, but especially during c. 1630–1760, despite this being a period of population growth (Palma et al., 2020). The dynastic union of 1580–1640 was a period of convergence of Portuguese per capita incomes with those of Spain. In 1580, Portugal stood at 725 Geary–Khamis (GK) 'international' 1990 dollars per head, compared with Spain's 920. By contrast, by the restoration of the Portuguese monarchy in 1640, Portugal was richer, at 895 GK 'international' 1990 dollars per capita, compared with Spain's 819. The first half of the eighteenth century was a period of relatively fast imperial and commodity-driven growth, which also interacted positively with agricultural productivity (Costa et al., 2015; Reis, 2016). However, the second half of the eighteenth century was characterized by a period of no growth, in turn followed by fast decline from about 1790. The process of decline would continue persistently well into the nineteenth century (Palma & Reis, 2019).

While knowing the timing of divergence does not give us direct answers with regards to the causes, it is sufficient to exclude some hypotheses. For example, for both Spain and Portugal, the divergence comes too late to have any medieval origins, whether cultural or institutional. At the same time, it comes too early, in both countries, for the Napoleonic invasions to be blamed. However, perhaps Iberia's macroeconomic performance vis-à-vis England is not so surprising in view of the fact that Spanish and Portuguese political institutions became visibly worse than those of England from the middle of the seventeenth century (Henriques & Palma, 2023). Indeed, it is remarkable that there is such a good temporal match between the timing of the political and economic divergence. This chapter will provide a long-term view of Spanish and Portuguese economic performance from an interdisciplinary approach, considering key factors such as climate, natural endowments, economic integration, and the effects of the empires on elements like fiscal policies and the arrival of bullion.

10.2 Spain

Overall, the study of Spanish economic history has been framed by the notion of a poor economy in decline, but recent work has suggested that far from being a backward economy, Spain was an affluent nation (by the standards of the time) prior to early modern imperial expansion (Álvarez Nogal and Prados de la Escosura, 2007a, 2013; Álvarez Nogal et al., 2016; Prados de la Escosura et al., 2020). The new estimations of preindustrial GDP in Spain are based on the use of urbanization rates for the estimation of the secondary and tertiary sector and on indirect and direct estimations of agricultural production. Although they use different sources, these different studies show consistent results which define very similar long-term trends. However, we should note that far from being a homogeneous economy, Spain was the combination of a number of regions that often presented very different economic experiences, following trends that over time became particularly divergent between its interior and periphery. Figure 10.2 shows a map of early modern Spain.

Output per head was relatively high in Spain in the mid-fourteenth century, but the effects of the Black Death were very different to those observed in other countries in Europe. In the Spanish case, instead of improving output per capita, the demographic shock produced a sharp decline. The Malthusian pressures that were present in other parts of Europe did not exist in Spain, which was characterized by a low demographic pressure economy. The Black Death not only diminished the already scarce labour available, but also destroyed the market networks that existed in the country (Alvarez Nogal & Prados de la Escosura, 2013). The sixteenth century was in turn a period of recovery and by the 1590s Spain had almost recovered the output per capita

Figure 10.2 Map of Spain. Early modern regional divisions are as presented in Álvarez Nogal & Prados de la Escosura (2007a).
Source: redrawn based on a map originally published in Álvarez Nogal & Prados de la Escosura (2007a).

reached in the mid-fourteenth century. However, the crisis hit Spain particularly hard in the late sixteenth century, and output per capita fell rapidly once more, in a decline that continued until the early seventeenth century.

The contraction of the Spanish economy was the result of a combination of internal and external factors. Climate change that took place in the late sixteenth century, and that extended its effects during the first half of the seventeenth century, had remarkably negative effects in Spain (Alvarez Nogal et al., 2016). The so-called 'initial oscillation' reduced temperatures and increased floods, with a consequent significant impact on the agrarian economy (Barriendos, 1994; Rodrigo et al., 1999). At the same time, the enormous increase in military expenditure led the king to stop payments to the bankers in Genoa between 1575 and 1577, affecting local bankers and small merchants. The country also suffered monetary instability from the 1590s onwards, namely due to the devaluation of the *vellón*.[17] The urban centres were hit particularly hard and the market economy that had emerged during the sixteenth century was dismantled.[18] During the eighteenth century, Spain was finally able to achieve steady sluggish growth, but it was not until the middle of the nineteenth century that the country was able to recover the output per capita levels of the mid-fourteenth century.

10.2.1 Income per Capita

The territories that currently form Spain were neither a perfectly unified economy nor a single political entity. Part of the explanation behind the different regional growth paths is related to the different institutions that dominated the territories that form current Spain. Land distribution was more equal in the northern coast from Galicia to Navarre and produced more egalitarian societies. The situation was different in the *Meseta* where lords were able to exercise higher coercive power against peasants often through the election of officials in key administrative positions, while the existence of large *latifundia* in the south increased inequality. In Aragon, the power of the lords was almost complete, and the influence of the King limited, offering less room to peasants to organize their own production, a situation similar to Valencia where lords also had a great independence from the King. In Catalonia, on the other hand, institutional changes derived from the late

---

[17] Between 1566 and the early 1580s Spanish coinage had a considerable amount of silver (*vellón rico*). But while from the 1580s to 1596 it had 8 grams of silver per coin, this fell to only 1 gram during 1596–1598, and continued to fall thereafter, especially after 1602.

[18] The increase in fiscal charges in Castile in the wake of the revolt of the Comuneros was also significant. The *alcabalas*, a tax that had to be collected by the cities in Castile, was doubled, new taxes for the consumption of goods like wine, meat and oil were introduced (Álvarez Nogal et al., 2016).

sixteenth century decreased the power of the lords and made the continuation of bad practices more difficult (Yun Casalilla, 2019: 30). Inheritance systems also played a key role in the distribution of economic assets. Indivisible inheritance dominated large areas including the Crown of Aragon and most of the north, while inheritance laws in the rest of the country imposed a more equal distribution of assets (Ferrer Alòs, 2011: 268). The regions of the Crown of Aragon also made extensive use of *enfiteusis* (life-long leases on land), which provided stability for peasants, encouraged investments and gave peasants more control over their production.

Therefore, the large climatic, economic and institutional diversity present at the time meant that the economic history of Spain during the early modern age should be framed within the existence of regional economic histories.

The growth of the sixteenth century was dominated by the regions of the interior where the economic expansion took place thanks to dynamic urban economies and the wool trade, which at the same time increased the demand of a more diversified agrarian economy. The environmental limitations of the interior pushed peasants to look for alternative sources of income in activities like transports that helped and reinforced trade and the system of fairs (Yun Casalilla, 2019: 109). New Castile was also heavily influenced by the presence of Madrid (declared the capital of the country in 1561), which, according to some authors, determined the economic fate of the whole region (see, for instance, Ringrose, 1983: 15). As Table 10.1 shows, GDP per capita grew rapidly between 1530 and 1591, presenting the highest growth rates of all the regions with an average yearly growth rate of 0.69%. Without the economic push of the capital and less room for agrarian expansion, the growth in Old Castile was more moderate. The peripheral regions present a much-differentiated growth pattern in the long term. On the eastern coast, and in contrast to the interior, both

Table 10.1 *Total output per head (Spain in 1857 = 100).*

	Spain	New Castile	Andalusia	Murcia	Old Castile/León	Valencia	Balearic Islands	Catalonia
1530	87	99	114	90	90	97	128	88
1591	93	150	93	96	93	94	134	79
1700	83	110	109	105	70	72	146	89
1750	80	154	101	98	62	79	110	73
1787	81	143	100	93	61	85	97	100
1857	100	145	117	78	82	95	133	128

Source: Álvarez Nogal & Prados de la Escosura (2007a).

Catalonia and Valencia show a moderate decrease of their income per capita levels during the sixteenth century that lasted longer in the case of Valencia. In the south, Andalusia did not benefit as much as the interior from the growth experienced in the sixteenth century, and in fact income per capita levels decreased between 1530 and 1591.

The late sixteenth-century crisis was harder in those regions that had grown more during the previous century. In the interior, New Castile had declined considerably by 1700, and although the crisis was not as hard in Old Castile, it lasted longer and the recovery did not appear until the eighteenth century. In the periphery, the crisis was milder in Catalonia and Valencia, although the recovery in the latter region would take longer than in the former. In Andalusia, the seventeenth century was a period of growth that, although moderate, contrasted with the sharp decline experienced in the interior and also in other peripheral territories.

The different recovery rates that followed the crisis mark the beginning of a little divergence within the Spanish economy with the rise of the periphery and the relative decline of the interior. By 1700 Catalonia had already recovered the income lost during the crisis and although Valencia had to wait longer, it also presented a very intense recovery during the eighteenth century. The expansion was also intense in the case of New Castile in the first half of the eighteenth century but stopped abruptly afterwards, while Old Castile remained immersed in a long period of stagnation with income per capita levels in 1787 well below those achieved in 1591. The lack of a growth pole like Madrid, and especially the disintegration of the urban networks including the collapse of Valladolid, deepened the crisis (Yun Casalilla, 1990: 569). The resilience that Andalusia displayed to the effects of the general crisis weakened in the eighteenth century, which was a period of stagnation with income per capita remaining relatively stable.

10.2.2 National Trends in Agriculture

The lack of official records for premodern times makes necessary the use of alternative sources for the estimation of agrarian production. The payment of the tithe, usually 10% of the output generated by each producer, has been extensively used by economic historians to estimate long-term changes of agrarian production in the past.[19] We should, however, take into account that its payment became less common in the late eighteenth century, and after the Napoleonic invasion the source becomes very unreliable. Nonetheless, the source is a solid option to proxy long swings in the agrarian sector, particularly in the case of Spain where the amount of information available is higher than for other countries. Figure 10.3 shows the estimation

---

[19] See Santiago-Caballero (2014) for a detailed description.

of total production in Spain using tithe series between 1500 and 1800. The estimation includes a wide range of products including the three that dominated Spanish agriculture (grain, olive oil and wine), as well as other sectors like livestock or vegetables.[20]

Total production increased between 1500 and 1800, although there were clear long-term swings within the period. Agrarian production in Spain increased between 1500 and the 1570s, with a growth that was particularly intense during the second half of the century. The primary sector experienced a severe contraction during the following decades that coincides with the general crisis of the seventeenth century, where Spanish agrarian output continued to decline until the first decade of the century. A period of relative stagnation followed, until growth resumed in the mid seventeenth century and continued peaking in the 1750s, to suffer a quick contraction and later recovery. Nonetheless, by 1800 total agricultural production had barely recovered the maximum levels achieved 50 years before.

If we take into account the evolution of population to estimate Spanish agrarian output in per capita levels, the long-term trends and particularly the levels present some important differences. Figure 10.4 shows the estimation of agrarian output per head using tithe records.

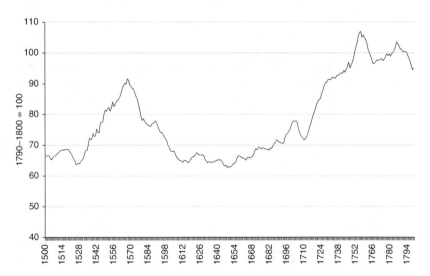

Figure 10.3 Agricultural output in Spain, 1500–1800 (11 years moving average).
Source: Prados de la Escosura et al. (2020)

---

[20] For a detailed description of the series used and the products included, see Prados de la Escosura et al. (2020).

Figure 10.4 Agricultural output per head in Spain, 1500–1800.
Source: Prados de la Escosura et al. (2020).

In per head terms, agrarian production remained relatively stable during most of the sixteenth century, although it experienced a sharp decline during the last decades that lasted until the 1620s. A process of recovery took place until the 1750s followed by a decline. Therefore, we can distinguish three main features in Spanish agriculture between 1500 and 1800: first, the maximum levels of agrarian production per head in Spain were reached in the early sixteenth century; second, the sharp contraction that followed until the early seventeenth century; and third, the slow recovery that was not enough to reach the levels achieved in the late sixteenth century followed by a further decline at the end of the period.

The early affluence achieved by Spanish agrarian producers was also manifested relative to other European economies. In the first decades of the sixteenth century, agrarian output per capita was around 20% higher than in Holland and almost 40% higher than in Britain (Álvarez Nogal et al., 2016: 466). The success of agriculture in Spain during the sixteenth century can be understood linked to the development of urban economies that, driven by domestic and international trade, increased the demand of primary products and fostered the development in the countryside. However, from the late sixteenth century, rampant fiscal pressure, which was especially hard in the cities, monetary instability and the alteration of international trade due to the increasing political conflicts had a devastating effect on the trade networks that were the engine of urban wealth.[21]

---

[21] See Ruiz Martín (1968), Álvarez Nogal (2005) and Álvarez Nogal & Chamley (2014, 2016). Note, however, that the observed fiscal policies were endogenous to the political environment (Charotti et al. 2022).

Between 1500 and 1800, the economically active population moved together with agrarian production per capita. This suggests that, far from being subject to Malthusian forces, Spanish agriculture could be better defined as a frontier economy. Therefore, demographic shocks like the one suffered in the seventeenth century, instead of benefiting output per worker, dismantled a system where the collapse of the urban economies decreased agrarian production not only in absolute but also in per capita terms. The situation was worsened by a deterioration of climatic conditions, which as a consequence of the effects of the Little Ice Age became colder and wetter in key periods of agrarian recession, such as from the late sixteenth to mid-seventeenth century or the second half of the eighteenth century (Rodrigo et al., 2001). The combined forces of an urban economy pushed to its limits, unfavourable climatic conditions and the negative spill-overs from the economic and institutional negative effects of American silver (Palma, 2020a; Arroyo Abad & Palma, 2021; Charotti et al. 2022) produced a deep crisis in Spanish agriculture, which would not recover for centuries.

10.2.3 Regional Trends in Agriculture

Climate has played a vital role in the creation of different regional agrarian systems in Spain and helps us to understand the different patterns followed at regional level. The large region occupying most of the northern coast from Galicia to Navarre enjoys high rainfall levels that allowed the development of animal husbandry and helped peasants in the event of harvest failures. The lower rainfall levels and more extreme climate in the interior developed a system of dry crops and livestock dominated by large flocks of sheep controlled by the *Mesta*, a key institution created to maintain and control the production of wool. The milder ecosystem of the Mediterranean coast made possible the creation of a mixed system with a more diversified agriculture.

Although we can find some general trends, the evolution of agrarian production in Spain at regional level between 1500 and 1800 also presents important differences. The growth that took place during the sixteenth century was dominated by the eastern Mediterranean coast and also New Castile. New crops gained importance in the Mediterranean coast, including rice, sugar, mulberry trees or wine, each of which in areas of Valencia represented up to one-fifth of total production (Furió, 1995: 279). The growth in New Castile was possible thanks to the combination of large portions of uncultivated land and migratory movements from the northern regions that participated in the harvests of wheat and silk (Yun Casalilla, 2019: 127).

Andalusia and the eastern Mediterranean were also the regions where the agrarian crisis appeared first and was more intense during the last decades of the sixteenth century, while the fall in agrarian production began later and was harder in the interior. The crisis was especially hard in Old Castile, where the dismantling of the urban trade networks was more intense (Garcia Sanz, 1982: 376). The north, on the other hand, presented a very different and distinctive pattern during the seventeenth century, characterized by growth that was possible thanks to the introduction of new products like maize that also allowed the expansion of arable lands into areas that were not so suitable for traditional crops (Bilbao Bilbao & Fernández de Pinedo, 2018: 123). The large presence of animal husbandry mitigated part of the crisis, while the increase of fiscal pressure was less damaging thanks to the high levels of self-consumption (Yun Casalilla, 2019: 425).

The eastern Mediterranean recovered quickly during the second half of the seventeenth century and until 1800 presented higher growth rates in total agrarian output than the interior, supported by local demographic growth (Palop Ramos, 1982: 410). Catalonia experienced a rapid increase of viticulture from the late seventeenth century onward encouraged by exports to England and the introduction of more efficient contracts like the *rabassa morta* (Carmona & Simson, 1999). Following the expansion of irrigated land, agriculture also diversified in Valencia with the extension of rice, wine and mulberry trees, which in some areas occupied almost half of all cultivated land (Furió, 1995: 327). The damage caused by the expulsion of the *moriscos* was quickly compensated for by repopulation through internal migrations. The crisis of the seventeenth century was longer in the interior and Andalusia, which also presented lower growth rates than the peripheries during the following century. Therefore, between the mid seventeenth century and 1800 a process of divergence took place between a more dynamic periphery and the interior of the country. As explained earlier, this regional divergence resulted from a combination of several factors, including the limitations imposed in the interior by natural endowments to adopt new crops, the hard effect that increasing fiscal pressure had in the urban markets in large areas of Castile, and the existence of regional markets that, although highly integrated, were not geographically connected with each other.[22]

10.2.4 Secondary and Tertiary Sectors

Urbanization rates, commonly used in the literature to proxy the evolution of the secondary and tertiary sectors, increased in Spain during the sixteenth century thanks to the development of domestic and international trade, particularly of wool, and also to imperial expansion. A decline that was especially sharp in the Crown of Castile took place during the seventeenth century and was connected with the dismantlement of trade networks, partially as a consequence of increasing taxation, which was especially hard in the

---

[22] See Grafe (2012) and Cermeño & Santiago-Caballero (2020) for alternative views on the causes and effects of regional market integration.

Castilian cities. The recovery that followed after 1700 was very intense and, on average, by 1750 Spain had recovered the urbanization levels of 1591. However, the national averages hide the existence of regional dynamics where the economic centre of the country moved from the interior to the periphery (Figure 10.5).

The sixteenth century was dominated by the pre-eminence of the interior and particularly by the role of its urban and trade networks. In New Castile, urbanization rates increased from 6.7% in 1530 to more than 24% in 1591 in a process that followed the expansion of the agrarian sector, which was also important in the case of Extremadura. Textile production linked to wool experienced an intense growth in cities such as Cuenca and Segovia, which became probably the largest textile producers in the Iberian Peninsula thanks to their privileged position within the *Mesta* system (Reher, 1990: 16). The increase in urbanization in Old Castile was more moderate, as it was on the periphery, in cities like Catalonia, Valencia and Aragon, which saw a modest growth during the sixteenth century, albeit starting from already very high levels in the case of the first two. There were important improvements in key sectors like coastal trade, which increased thanks to improvements in security against the actions of northern African pirates and increasing connections with Genoa and its merchants (Furió, 1995: 285). On average, the regions of the north also presented small increases in urbanization, with the exception of Navarre where it more than doubled. In the south, the share of the population living in urban areas of Andalusia also increased, as in the case of Catalonia and Valencia from already very high levels.

The impact of the crisis that started in the late sixteenth century was felt in all regions, with the exception of Andalusia, where the cities from the coast,

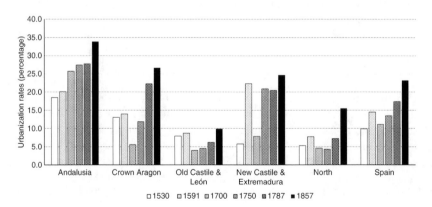

Figure 10.5 Urbanization rates in Spain, 1530–1857.
Source: created from Álvarez Nogal & Prados de la Escosura (2007a).

particularly Seville and later Cádiz, benefited from the expanding empire. The decline was sharp in the interior, especially in Extremadura and Old and New Castile, which suffered the collapse of trade networks and increasing taxation. The manufacturing growth poles that dominated the expansion of the sixteenth century almost disappeared, as in the case of Cuenca where in 1721 there were almost 1,485 houses abandoned and in ruins (Reher, 1990: 16). Although not as much as in the interior, in the periphery the effects of the crisis were severe, too, especially in Valencia. The crisis set in a bit later in Catalonia. Urbanization remained stable in Catalonia until 1700, while in the case of Valencia the percentage of urban population decreased sharply during the crisis. Silk manufacturers in Valencia were particularly hit by the expulsion of the *moriscos* that were key to its production (Gonzalez Enciso et al., 1992: 123). Aragon showed very similar trends to Catalonia and especially Valencia. The northern regions also present a decrease, although one that was not as hard as in the interior.

The recovery that followed the general crisis reinforced the divergence that took place in the agrarian sector between a stagnating interior and a dynamic periphery, with the exception of New Castile, where the growth of Madrid compensated for the decrease of other traditional urban centres. In Old Castile and Extremadura, the recovery of the eighteenth century was so slow that it would not be until 1857 that both regions would reach the urbanization levels achieved in 1591. In large areas of Castile urban centres lost ground, and a ruralization process took place with the primary sector increasing its weight in the cities (Marcos Martín, 2000: 513). In addition to the quantitative loss, textile manufacturers in cities like Segovia or Palencia also had to reduce the quality of their products to adapt them to a different market (Garcia Sanz, 1985: 18). In the periphery, the recovery was very intense in Catalonia, Valencia and Aragon, particularly during the eighteenth century when urbanization rates grew rapidly to historical maximum levels by the end of the century. While fiscal pressure increased particularly in the Crown of Castile, cities in Catalonia or Valencia were not taxed as much as those in the interior, allowing a more efficient allocation of disposable capital (Yun Casalilla, 2019: 428). The experience in the north was diverse with Galicia stagnating, Navarre presenting a moderate growth and the Basque Country experiencing a very intense growth especially during the second half of the eighteenth century. Although the growth of urbanization rates in Andalusia decreased, the region maintained a steady increase.

Summarizing, activity in the secondary and tertiary sectors present significant regional differences that, as in the case of agriculture, moved the economic centre of Spain from the interior to the periphery. The long-lasting effects of the late sixteenth century crisis in the cities of the interior and the sluggish recovery that followed contrasted with the quick and intense recovery that was experienced in the periphery, reinforcing the effects of the little divergence within the Spanish economy. The process implied a shift in the location of key activities like manufacturing, from the traditional textile producers of the interior in the sixteenth century, to the modern textile producers of Catalonia that would take the lead in the nineteenth century, a process that some authors have also linked with the unequal regional distribution of natural endowments and human capital (Rosés, 2003).

10.3 Portugal

While the economic history literature has long considered Portugal to have been backward and in decline, or at least stagnating, during the early modern period (see, for instance, Allen, 2005 or van Zanden, 2009), actual data on GDP or real wages did not exist until recently. Using a large dataset for prices, wages and rents taken from the archives of a variety of institutions, such as hospitals and monasteries, Palma and Reis (2019) have recently put together the first GDP series for Portugal from 1527 and 1850.[23]

Regional trends did not usually differ markedly from the national trend, though there are some caveats. Figure 10.6 shows the location of the four regions used in the construction of the national GDP by Palma and Reis (2019): the hinterlands of the country's main cities, Porto, Coimbra, Lisbon and Évora. In turn, Figure 10.7 shows the consumer price index (CPI) for these four regions, and Figure 10.8 the skilled real wage indexes. These figures show that commodities and labour markets were highly integrated in Portugal.

10.3.1 Income per Capita

Figure 10.9 shows Portugal's GDP per capita in constant prices. Portugal's macroeconomic history is highly nonlinear, far from an oversimplified Malthusian situation. The late Middle Ages corresponded to a favourable situation (Cardoso & Garcia 2009; Henriques & Reis, 2015), but was followed by a period of decline lasting until about 1550. Portugal's economy grew but did not perform particularly well during the sixteenth century, even if this may seem surprising to those who feel that trade associated with the overseas empire must have had central importance. This is explained by the small volumes of that trade in comparison to the overall size of the economy (Costa et al., 2015).

Intensive (per capita) output growth is clearly noticeable from the 1630s, but a third-degree polynomial suggests that it may have started earlier, in the last

---

[23] In contrast to the Palma and Reis (2019) approach, which is based on data from contemporary sources, Maddison (2006: 249) simply assumed his figures for Portugal, as we have noted.

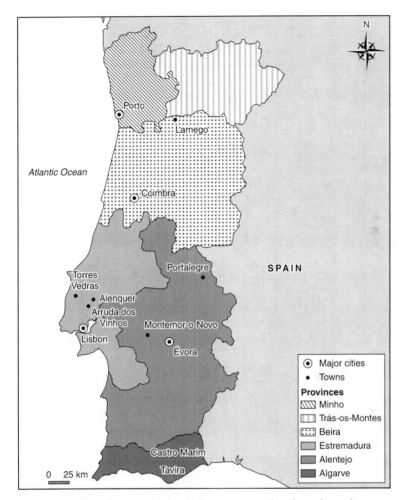

Figure 10.6 Map of Portugal. The borders correspond to the eighteenth-century provinces and the map indicates locations referred to in Palma and Reis (2019). Source: redrawn based on a map originally published in Palma and Reis (2019).

quarter of the sixteenth century.[24] Remarkably, economic growth was accompanied by demographic growth until the mid-eighteenth century, when returns from the imperial economy were at its peak (Costa et al., 2015;

---

[24] As is often the case with historical data and methods, there is some uncertainly about the exact timings.

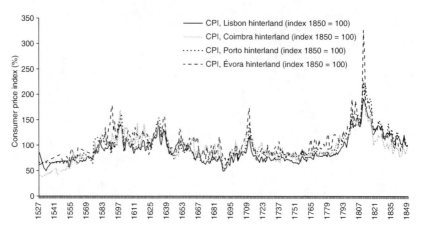

Figure 10.7 CPI for four regions of Portugal, 1527–1850 (in silver units).
Source: Palma and Reis (2019).

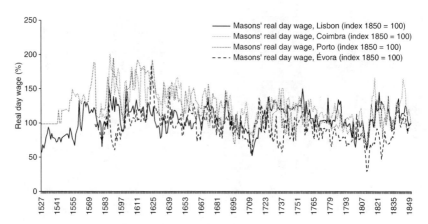

Figure 10.8 Skilled real wages for four regions of Portugal, 1527–1850.
Source: Palma & Reis (2019).

Palma et al., 2019).[25] Around the time of the 1755 earthquake, Portugal stopped growing, though income levels stayed at a comparatively high plateau;

---

[25] Modern tests of the Malthusian model have relied primarily on the Wrigley–Schofield demographic data for England, the most well-known source of annual national data on population stocks for a premodern economy. But Portugal does not fit the model well because it had a period of about 200 years of simultaneous growth of population and income per capita (Palma & Reis 2019; Palma et al., 2020). The combination of intensive and extensive growth is uncommon in premodern economies, as it is a feature of modern economic growth (Kuznets, 1966: 34–85; Broadberry et al., 2015a: 3).

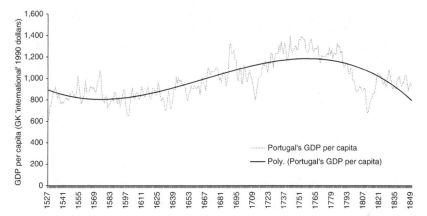

Figure 10.9 Portugal's GDP per capita, in constant prices (GK 'international' 1990 dollars).
Source: Palma and Reis (2019).

then in the 1790s a persistent period of decline began that was to continue well into the nineteenth century. As a consequence, Portugal became Western Europe's poorest country by 1850, with the process of modern economic growth only starting a century later, in the 1950s.

It is difficult to pinpoint the exact reasons for the dismal performance of the Portuguese economy from the mid-eighteenth century onwards.[26] One proximate reason must have been that the engines of much of the growth during the previous decades were exhausted, but no new sources of growth appeared. Progress had been driven by the effects of maize on agriculture, by the boom generated by Brazilian growth and perhaps by the lagged effects of some earlier institutional progress.[27] The imperial economy also had an increasing impact as time went by, but commodity-driven growth could not last forever, and indeed came to a sudden stop with the opening of Brazil's ports to direct international trade in 1808, followed by the loss of Brazil itself in 1822.

---

[26] One popular explanation concerns the differentially negative effects of the Catholic religion compared with, for instance, Protestantism. It is to be noted, however, that Portugal had a numeracy rate close to the most advanced countries in Europe as late as the mid-eighteenth century (Stolz et al. 2013: 562–564). Following Pombal's politically-motivated expulsion of the Jesuits, this situation was to change dramatically.

[27] A series of legal reforms (*Ordenações Manuelinas*), which were progressively issued from 1512 to 1605, encouraged the standardization of weights and measures, and may have prompted specialization gains from additional market integration. It is not clear how much these legal changes were enforced, since the laws were periodically reissued – a sign of previous limited enforcement. Furthermore, a regional diversity of weights and measures persisted well into the nineteenth century.

Additionally, Portugal's productive specialization and other internal conditions did not favour the development of a formalized schooling system, which became increasingly important for more successful European economies as the nineteenth century rolled in. In turn, economic geography favoured more central regions of Europe. Finally, institutional evolution was not favourable from the late seventeenth century onward (Henriques & Palma, 2023), a development due at least partially to a resource curse caused by the discovery of Brazilian gold (Macedo, 1982a; Palma, 2020a; Arroyo Abad & Palma, 2021; Kedrosky & Palma, 2021).[28]

10.3.2 National Trends in Agriculture

The most important factor underlying Portugal's positive growth performance from around 1600 until the mid-eighteenth century was the extent of structural transformation. Table 10.2 shows the remarkable progress that took place over the 1600–1750 period.[29] As column 4 shows, the percentage of the population working in the secondary and tertiary sectors grew from 31% in 1600 to a remarkable 47% in 1750. This progress, however, not sustained. As late as 1800 it was still at 45% but it then declined to only 33% by 1850. This process of 'de-industrialization' (which, to be rigorous, also represented a decline of the service sector) is the most salient feature of Portuguese macroeconomic history, and it largely determined the fall in GDP per capita observed in the late eighteenth century and for much of the first half of the nineteenth. Structural change would fail to take place for a long time. Going beyond the years of Table 10.2, the percentage of the population working outside agriculture remained comparatively low, at 34% in 1862 and 1890, only growing to 37% by 1900. As late as 1911, it was still considerably lower than it had been in 1750, at 39%.[30]

The principal alteration in Portugal's agriculture over the early modern period consisted of the gradual replacement of pastoral by arable production (Reis, 2017: 174), the rise of wine and oil production, and an important shift from wheat, rye and millet to American corn (maize).[31] Initially, in the two or three decades following 1500, there was a tendency for incomes to decline,

---

[28] There were also notable problems of judicial enforcement (Rodrigues, 2019b), though more comparative evidence on this matter, from an international perspective, would be welcome.
[29] Ribeiro da Silva and Carvalhal (2017), using a different methodology and sources as compared with Table 10.2, nevertheless reach similar conclusions both in terms of magnitude and the timing of structural change.
[30] The percentages for 1862, 1890, 1900 and 1911 are from Reis (2005).
[31] See Magalhães (2010). The shift from animal to grain production corresponds to a shift from a land to a labour-intensive mode of production, which suggests increased population pressure on the land (Henriques & Reis, 2019).

Table 10.2 *Portugal's population shares by total by occupation.*

Year	(1) Urban	(2) Rural non-agricultural	(3) Agricultural	(4) = (1) + (2) Total non-agricultural	(5) = (1) / (4) Urban/total non-agricultural
1500	0.155	0.169	0.676	0.324	0.479
1550	0.151	0.161	0.688	0.312	0.485
1600	0.132	0.173	0.695	0.305	0.432
1650	0.124	0.239	0.637	0.363	0.343
1700	0.125	0.286	0.589	0.411	0.304
1750	0.173	0.291	0.535	0.465	0.373
1800	0.162	0.289	0.549	0.451	0.359
1850	0.176	0.155	0.669	0.331	0.531

Note: Urban corresponds to population >5,000.
Source: Palma and Reis (2019).

a trend shared with some other European economies. This corresponded to continued population catch up from the post-bubonic plague population levels. In the absence of sufficient trade, technical or institutional change, incomes fell.[32]

Agriculture, which in the fifteenth and early sixteenth centuries had been predominantly pastoral (Medeiros, 1993), gradually switched to arable, a change that – given individuals' taste for variety in food intake – they were only too willing to incur since it was a way to feed more people without improvements in technology. For around 200 years from the mid-sixteenth century onward, incomes tended to grow both intensively and extensively, caused by a combination of factors of varying degrees of importance. Land clearances were capital-intensive and appeared to have played a role. They led to more intensive usage of the land and hence to higher levels of production (Miranda, 2016). The introduction of maize also took place in this period, and spread considerably, especially in the north of the country (Reis, 2016).

By the early eighteenth century, several irrigation projects were needed to allow for the expansion of maize and viticulture. These often required considerable fixed costs to be implemented. The gold windfall may have helped finance these projects, as it affected people's income both directly through remittances and indirectly through higher land–labour ratios resulting from the emigration of people to Brazil during the gold rush. The cash that was

---

[32] The returns from the empire were growing but were still too small at this point to matter a great deal (Costa et al., 2015).

available for investments was complemented by a vibrant credit market, which lasted until about the time of the 1755 earthquake (Costa et al., 2018a).

Wine cultivation also expanded considerably in the Douro region following the 1703 Methuen treaty with England – a treaty that was closely related to the incoming gold windfall (Fisher, 1971; Macedo, 1982a: 45), and which concerned military and geopolitical matters as much as trade in a strict sense. The increased availability of means of payment increased incomes both directly and also indirectly, by decreasing the transaction costs of participating in the market, allowing for a more monetized and specialized economy. For a few decades, at least, the net effects of the gold windfall were positive. But this was not to last (Palma, 2020a; Kedrosky & Palma, 2021).

The economic expansion boom up to the 1755 earthquake was followed by a period of stagnation that lasted until the 1780s. Afterwards, a period of persistent decline was initiated, continuing well into the nineteenth century, with a noticeable short-lived rebound only during the 1810s. This decline had multiple causes. From the mid-eighteenth century onwards, many of the previous sources of growth became progressively exhausted: gold remittances declined and further expansion of maize was not possible, while the lack of executive constraints had negative consequences for the economy (Henriques & Palma, 2023).

Eventually, following the invasion by Napoleon's troops in 1807, the court escaped to Brazil. As a delayed but direct consequence of the latter, that empire was lost in 1822. The loss of Brazil, albeit sooner or later inevitable, may have at the time mattered a good deal, in light of the fact that, according to one estimate, severing colonial trade around 1800 led to a real wage between one-fifth and one-fourth lower than observed (Costa et al., 2015).

While in several parts of the European periphery the increased usage of iron agricultural improvements was a source of growth from the eighteenth century (Edvinsson, 2013), the evidence that exists for parts of Portugal suggests their usage was still limited well into the nineteenth century (Fonseca and Reis, 2011). Some internal industries became less competitive because the windfall from increased specie availability led to adverse effects in other sections in a Dutch-disease type scenario (Macedo, 1982a: 55–56). But, in addition, the negative effects of institutional change started to be felt, and these political changes were likely to have been at least as important as the strictly economic aspects (and to have had repercussions for the latter). The eighteenth century experienced unfavourable institutional change, with the Cortes not meeting over the entire century, in sharp contrast with what had happened in previous centuries (Henriques & Palma, 2023). But the possible role of political economic factors in arresting the development of the economy after the mid-eighteenth century has been subject to different, and sometimes conflicting, interpretations in the Portuguese literature. For example, Pereira (2009) claims, unconvincingly, that the 1755 earthquake led to benevolent political changes; see Madureira (1997), Salvado (2019) and Henriques and Palma (2023) for contrary evidence. In turn, Macedo (1982a) argues that the windfall of Brazilian gold had negative consequences, though not much detail is given. Palma (2020a) shows that Spain and Portugal, being first-order receivers of the American windfall, did suffer from Dutch disease and institutional resource curse as a consequence. In turn, Pedreira (1994) claims that the economy was recovering in the latter half of the eighteenth century, but this is now rejected by the income series of Palma and Reis (2019).

10.3.3 Secondary and Tertiary Sectors

Portugal underwent considerable structural transformation during 1600–1750: the percentage of people working outside agriculture went from 31% to 46% (Table 10.2, column 3). The transformation was gradual. As previously mentioned, there was economic growth from the last quarter of the sixteenth century until about 1690. This was largely due to structural change: the percentage of workers outside agriculture rose to 41% by 1700 (Table 10.2, column 3). After 1690 Portugal entered a period of decline that lasted less than two decades, before growing considerably until around the time of the 1755 earthquake, when the share of workers outside agriculture stood at a remarkably high 46%. See Figures 10.10 and 10.11 for indexes of land rents and agricultural GDP per capita from the sixteenth century to the mid-nineteenth century.

Incomes per head then declined a little but stayed at a comparatively high plateau, before starting to fall precipitously from the 1780s, a decline that would continue until the 1810s. This was followed by a partial, short-lived recovery, but then incomes per person stayed constant in the following decades. As late as 1800, the percentage of workers outside of agriculture was 45%. Over the first half of the nineteenth century there was a return to agriculture, with this percentage falling to 33% by 1850 (Table 10.2, column 3).

The productive structure of the Portuguese economy did not change dramatically during the early modern period but neither was it static. Industry consisted of wool and linen textiles, leather, construction and all the other provisions for the necessities of daily life. Luxuries and manufactured exports occupied secondary positions. In the tertiary (services) sector, apart from the normal contribution of transport, trade, administration and shipping in such economies, it is worth noting the significant element of colonially oriented activity.[33]

Portugal's industry had at times enjoyed a moderate degree of success, but two factors hampered its future growth. First, it had often enjoyed access to privileged overseas markets, first and foremost Brazil; this access began to be

---

[33] For a measurement of the contribution of the colonial empire to the domestic economy, see Costa et al. (2015).

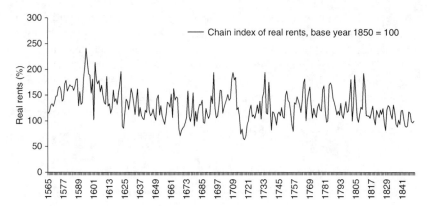

Figure 10.10 Land rents index for 1565–1850, in constant prices.
Source: Palma and Reis (2019), which for nominal rents rely on two series consisting of cash rents from large commercial estates, with leases between 3 and 10 years. These correspond to the Archive of the Hospital of All Saints in Lisbon (10 estates) and a set of 32 estates in Alentejo (Santos, 2003); see Reis (2017) for details. The nominal amounts were spliced and deflated by the CPI of Palma and Reis (2019).

Figure 10.11 Index of agricultural GDP per capita for 1527–1850, in constant prices.
Source: Palma and Reis (2019).

disrupted from the 1790s by the geopolitical situation, and was further hampered by the opening of Brazil's ports to trade with Britain in 1808. Privileged access ended with Brazil's independence in 1822. Second, the part of Portugal's industry that was directed at the internal market had often been located in the provinces, at least in part a side effect of the 1703 Methuen treaty (Macedo

1982a). The arrival of large quantities of gold from Brazil led to an increase in the relative price of non-tradables, to the appreciation of the real exchange rate, and to the loss of competitiveness of Portugal's industry, which persisted for a long period of time (Kedrosky & Palma, 2021).

10.4 Comparisons

10.4.1 Iberian Comparative Performance

The comparative performance of the two Iberian economies, shown in Figure 10.1, suggests that while both economies ended up in a similar position in the very long run, they followed rather different trends as time went by. They started from similar levels around 1550. Spain's economy performed better than that of Portugal in the third quarter of the sixteenth century, but the period of the 1580–1640 dynastic union was one of convergence: Portugal grew and Spain declined. By the time of the restoration of the Portuguese monarchy in 1640, Portugal's per capita income was higher.[34] Then during the second half of the seventeenth century, Spain's economy began a slow recovery, although it lost ground to Portugal in relative terms and even by 1800 it had not reached the level of the late sixteenth century. In Portugal, by contrast, incomes grew much faster in the first half of the eighteenth century, then stagnated, after which decline set in, and this continued into the nineteenth century. While Portugal was able to achieve higher income levels than Spain during most of the century, Spain achieved higher output per capita than Portugal around 1810, and the countries continued to diverge thereafter.

10.4.2 International comparisons

We now shift the discussion from index-based measures to comparison of income levels.[35] There are two options. The most widely used standard is GK 'international' 1990 dollars (Table 10.3). This method ('Maddison's method') starts with a benchmark and moves back using real per capita growth rates. The results in Table 10.3 are shown using the benchmark at which each volume index's series ends. For instance, for England/Britain, the Broadberry et al. (2015a) series ends in 1870, so we are using the 1870 benchmark.[36] Due to

---

[34] When interpreting the results discussed in this subsection, one should keep in mind that while there is considerable uncertainty about income levels, we can place high confidence in general trends.

[35] There is much more uncertainly about levels than trends (Jong & Palma, 2018).

[36] We use the benchmark which Broadberry et al. (2015a) use for Britain in 1870. This differs from Maddison's (2006) lower benchmark for the United Kingdom in 1870. It makes sense to exclude Ireland since the volume indexes do not include it, and it was it was much poorer than the rest of the United Kingdom (Britain).

Table 10.3 *Output per capita in Western Europe (GK 'international' 1990 dollars), using the Maddison method.*

	England/ Great Britain	Holland	Germany	France	Italy	Sweden	Spain	Portugal
1500	1,041	1,454	1,146	935	1,367	1,195	807	1,125
1550	1,014	1,798	—	809	1,278	1,125	945	836
1600	1,037	2,662	806	901	1,216	853	820	790
1650	887	2,691	948	965	1,247	941	689	830
1700	1,513	2,105	939	992	1,317	1,357	772	987
1750	1,694	2,355	1,050	1,010	1,367	1,061	849	1372
1800	2,097	2,609	986	1,045	1,216	930	890	916
1850	2,718	2,355	1,428	1,597	1,321	1,171	1,079	923

Sources: Annual growth rates from the following sources. For England, Broadberry et al. (2015a); for Holland, van Zanden and van Leeuwen (2012); for Germany, Pfister (2011); for France until 1789, Ridolfi (2016); for Italy, Malanima (2011); for Spain, Prados de la Escosura et al. (2020); for Sweden, Schön and Krantz (2012) and Krantz (2017) for 1500–1560. For Portugal, Henriques et al. (2021) for 1500–1527 and Palma and Reis (2019) for 1527–1850. The levels in this table are calculated by applying these volume indexes to benchmarks corresponding to the endpoint year of each index. In the case of England, figures correspond to the volume indexes of England before 1700 and Great Britain afterwards applied to the 1870 level of Great Britain (Broadberry et al., 2015: 375–376). In the case of Holland, borders correspond to Holland until 1800 and the Netherlands for 1850; a benchmark for 1807 was used for the data prior to 1800 (van Zanden and van Leeuwen, 2012: 121), and the 1850 level is from Smits et al. (2000). The other benchmarks are from Maddison (2006) and correspond to 1820 for France (with additional assumptions; see Ridolfi, 2016: 196), 1850 for Germany, Spain and Portugal, and 1913 for Italy and Sweden. The 1800 level shown for France in the table is Ridolfi's 1789 level. For France in 1850, the level is that given in Álvarez Nogal and Prados de la Escosura (2013: 23). Italy corresponds to north and central Italy only; Germany corresponds to the present-day borders of Germany.

index number problems, this can sometimes give rather different results from what one would obtain by linking these 'premodern' series with later series. Take Spain as an example. The Prados de la Escosura et al. (2022) series stops in 1850. Using the 1850 benchmark together with volume indexes, Spain's income per capita level in 1500 becomes 807 GK 'international' 1990 dollars. This is clearly above subsistence, but relatively low by Western European standards. However, using an apparently similar methodology leads to a higher level of 1,112 GK 'international' 1990 dollars.[37] As another example, consider Sweden. While in Table 10.3 we give 853 GK 'international' 1990 dollars for Sweden in 1600, an apparently similar alternative would lead to much lower levels – only 761 GK 'international' 1990 dollars in the same year.[38]

The alternative to the Maddison method is the indirect method of Prados de la Escosura's (2000), which we call the Prados method (see Table 10.4).[39] Using the 1850 relative levels from Prados de la Escosura (2000) as the baseline implies that during the early sixteenth century Spain and Portugal were among the richest economies of Western Europe, only clearly behind the small republics of northern and central Italy. By 1600 Spain was losing ground but it was still able to retain a considerable income per head, higher than the level observed in England. The seventeenth century saw the origin of the little divergence between the Iberian economies and those in the 'core' of Europe, as output per capita fell considerably in the case of Spain and stagnated in Portugal, while it increased in all the major economies of the continent except the Netherlands. The latter was nonetheless able to maintain its considerable advantage over the southern economies. Finally (and despite Portugal's temporary boom during the period 1700–1755), overall the Iberian recovery of the eighteenth century was too short lived and not strong enough to close the gap with the richest countries in Europe by 1800.

While during the first half of the nineteenth century all the main economies of Western Europe increased their output per head, the decrease experienced by Portugal meant that the country fell considerably behind. The case of Spain was different in absolute but not in relative terms. Although GDP per capita levels increased in Spain, the growth was much slower than that achieved by the main European economies. Therefore, the Iberian economies were not able to take advantage of the first industrial revolution in the way that most of north-western Europe did, increasing the gap and therefore the divergence between the south and the north that had already started in the seventeenth century. This differential timing is the important message from the income

---

[37] This alternative consists of taking GDP per capita at current dollars in 1990, converted to GK 'international' 1990 dollars with the Purchasing Power Parities of the International Comparison Program, projected back using Prados de la Escosura's (2017) indexes for 1850–1990, and linking them in 1850 to those of Prados de la Escosura et al. (2020). See also Prados de la Escosura (2016b).

[38] This alternative consists of going back from Sweden's 1990 benchmark using data from The Conference Board, Total Economy Database for 1950–1990, linked with data from Schön and Krantz (2012) for 1560–1950.

[39] While more common, the GK method has a number of disadvantages (Prados de la Escosura, 2000; Deaton and Heston, 2010; Allen, 2013). For example, Álvarez Nogal and Prados de la Escosura (2013: 36) show that using the GK method, in 1850 the price level for Spain would have been 109 (relative to UK =100), which suggests that Spanish real GDP per capita is probably under-estimated for that benchmark.

Table 10.4 *Output per capita in Europe (GK 'international' 1990 dollars), using the Prados method.*

	England/ Great Britain	Holland	Germany	France	Italy	Sweden	Spain	Portugal
1500	1,050	1,138	1,139	1,065	1,546	1,236	1,112	1,295
1550	1,023	1,407		922	1,445	1,164	1,302	962
1600	1,046	2,083	801	1,027	1,375	883	1,130	909
1650	895	2,106	942	1,100	1,410	974	949	955
1700	1,526	1,647	933	1,130	1,489	1,404	1,064	1,136
1750	1,708	1,843	1,043	1,151	1,546	1,098	1,170	1,579
1800	2,115	2,042	980	1,191	1,375	962	1,226	1,054
1850	2,741	1,843	1,419	1,820	1,494	1,212	1,487	1,062

Notes: Purchasing power parities for 1850 are from Prados de la Escosura (2000: 24); the same borders and time series were used to calculate earlier incomes. Holland's 1850 benchmark is assumed to be the same as the Netherlands', which is what is given by Prados de la Escosura. Italy's 1860 level is assumed to be that of 1850. The relative levels were transformed by using the UK to GB ratio of 0.85 (where the UK level for 1850 of $2,330 'international' GK dollars is from Maddison, 2006: 437).

Sources: see Table 10.3.

data, especially as we can be much more certain about growth rates than levels (Jong & Palma, 2018; Palma, 2020b).

10.5 Conclusion

Recent research in the long-term evolution of income per capita in Iberia has challenged the traditional view of Spain and Portugal as perpetually backward and underdeveloped economies.[40] The use of new archival material such as wages, rents or tithes has shown that, in fact, by 1500 Spain and Portugal were among the richest regions in Europe. It is also the case that – unlike the claim of Acemoglu et al. (2005) – by 1500 the Iberian economies did not have 'worse' institutions than England or the Netherlands. Henriques and Palma (2023) show that a political divergence is noticeable from the mid-seventeenth century, hence taking place before the Glorious Revolution of 1688–1689, which

---

[40] A Malthusian view of permanent stagnation is also not appropriate, though it is true that by 1800 these economies were not considerably better off than they had been 300 years earlier.

several scholars identify as the watershed moment that prompted the English economy forward (e.g. North & Weingast, 1989).

In the Spanish case, the levels reached in the sixteenth century corresponded to a recovery from the long and deep crisis that followed the Black Death, an event which had severe consequences, destroying the foundations of a frontier economy that had already reached significant income levels by the mid-fourteenth century. However, the recovery experienced reversed in the seventeenth century, when Spain suffered a considerable contraction of its economy. The recovery started in the last decades of the seventeenth century and continued during the following, a process that speeded up during the first decades of the nineteenth century, when Spain was finally able to recover the income per capita levels reached before the Black Death.

Although Portugal started from a similar income level compared with Spain, it followed a rather different growth pattern over the early modern period. During the first two decades of the sixteenth century, the Portuguese economy suffered an intense crisis. This was followed by a recovery that lasted until the mid-seventeenth century. The second half of the seventeenth century had periods of growth and recession, but then most of the first half of the eighteenth century was a period of sustained growth, and Portugal was able to match and surpass the income levels reached around 1500. However, the recovery did not last long and from the second half of the eighteenth century the Portuguese economy declined, losing most of the advances achieved during the early modern period. Preliminary estimates by Henriques et al. (2021) suggest that it was not until the 1920s that the country would be able to enjoy the same real income per head level of the mid-eighteenth century.

Therefore, we conclude that, in the long run, we cannot observe a common growth pattern in the Iberian economies, in opposition to Maddison (2006: 249), who considered that the economies of Spain and Portugal were similar. The comparison with the main economies of north-western Europe in fact show that, as explained before, Spain and Portugal were initially among the most affluent nations. Their relative position did not change much during the sixteenth century. The divergence between Iberia and the main economies of Europe only became clear in the seventeenth century for Spain, and as late as the second half of the eighteenth century for Portugal. In both cases this was a net effect that was at least partially the result of earlier forces (Palma, 2020a). The divergence widened during the late eighteenth and nineteenth centuries, when the effects of the industrial revolutions were felt in the 'core' of the European economies, but were weakly felt in Iberia. By the middle of the nineteenth century, the relative position of Iberia in Europe had changed radically compared to the situation in 1500: both Spain and Portugal had fallen from the top to the bottom of the income distribution.

11

Population of the Iberian Peninsula in the Early Modern Period: A Comparative and Regional Perspective

ANDREIA DURÃES AND VICENTE PÉREZ MOREDA

11.1 Introduction

Research has shown that during the early modern period economic growth did not take place equally across the whole of Europe. In fact, even though by 1500 Spain and Portugal were among the richest regions in the continent, by 1850, the relative position of Iberia in Europe had changed radically, and both Spain and Portugal had fallen from the top to the bottom of the rankings income. There is evidence that a small divergence between Iberia and the main economies of Europe started in the seventeenth century for Spain, and in the second half of the eighteenth century for Portugal, and accelerated during the late eighteenth and nineteenth centuries (see Chapter 10).

The main goal of this chapter is to analyse the demographic dynamics in Iberia between 1500 and 1800, from a regional and European perspective, comparing the pattern of population growth, demographic distribution, urbanization and socio-professional composition of the population of the Iberian Peninsula with that of the rest of Europe in the same period, and in particular England and the Dutch Republic, in order to understand the 'little divergence' (Pleijt & van Zanden, 2016).

To achieve this goal, Section 11.2 reconstructs the trajectory of the total population for both Iberian countries in order to establish the national trends, and to compare these trends and patterns of growth with other European countries and regions. It also focuses on population distribution across regions and highlights regional differences. Variables and components of population growth in many regions are analysed through the study of nuptiality and fertility, and especially of mortality (its trajectory and components, its cyclical variations, their determinants and economic consequences, and the chronology of major crises and their intensity). Attention is also paid to the prevailing 'demographic system' in both Iberian kingdoms, including a comparison with other European countries, and to the available data on emigration especially towards the colonial areas.

Section 11.3 offers an overview of Iberian urbanization between 1500 and 1800. This is an important point since there is a strong connection between urbanization and the productivity of an economic system. But since the focus is population distribution, the analysis of the urban dynamic takes into account not only the percentage of the total population living in urban areas (the urbanization rate), but also the morphology of the urban structure.

Finally, in Section 11.4, special attention will be paid to the qualitative aspects of the population and its structure, with a portrayal of the socio-professional composition of the population to determine the prevalence of individuals involved in primary, secondary and tertiary occupations, which contributes to the investigation of long-running economic trends. The main goal is to build an overall picture of the socio-professional composition of the population in both countries and, whenever possible, to stress the geographical contrasts.

11.2 Secular Trends of Population and Distribution Across Regions

Despite the variable reliability of the available figures, there is much data and many demographic studies that allow us to trace the main trends of Iberian population during the early modern period. Based on different data and studies, in this section we will reconstruct the trajectory of the total population for the Iberian countries, showing national trends and regional differences, and compare these trends and patterns of growth with other European countries and regions.

11.2.1 Growth in the Sixteenth Century

As Table 11.1 shows, in the sixteenth century, demographic development in Spain followed the European growth trend. This long-term movement, which can be seen as Iberian, would diminish by the end of the century.

To put this growth tendency in context, it should be noted that almost all the territories in the Iberian Peninsula – the exceptions being Catalonia and the kingdom of Navarre – underwent a remarkable demographic boost in the second half of the fifteenth century that started in Castile before 1430–1440, and meant a quickly recovery from the epidemics of the previous century. Notwithstanding, the Spain of the Catholic Kings (1479–1504) had but five million people, and the numbers were not much higher (around 5.3 million) by the time the first 'census' was undertaken, around 1530 (see Table 11.2) (Ladero Quesada, 1978: 29–31; Pérez Moreda, 1995: 227–43; 2002: 13–38).

Between that point and the famous *vecindario* of 1591, the Spanish population grew by almost 42%, at an annual rate of approximately 0.6%. That of

Table 11.1 *European population, 1500–1820 (thousands of inhabitants).*

	1500	1600	1700	1820
France	15,000	18,500	21,471	31,246
Germany	12,000	16,000	15,000	24,905
Italy	10,500	13,100	13,300	20,176
Netherlands	950	1,500	1,900	2,355
United Kingdom	3,942	6,170	8,565	21,226
Portugal	1,088[a]	1,769[b]	2,100[c]	2,893[d]
Spain[e]	5,000	6,800	7,500	11,000[f]
Iberian Peninsula[g]	6,088	8,569	9,600	13,293
Western Europe	57,268	73,780	81,460	132,888

Source: Madison (2006: 241).
Sources: [a] Rodrigues (2008: 176). [b] Serrão (1996: 66). [c] Moreira & Veiga (2005: 36–37). [d] Portuguese population in 1801 (Moreira & Veiga, 2005: 36–37). [e] Pérez Moreda (see Table 11.2). [f] Spanish population in 1800. [g] Authors' own results.

Table 11.2 *Spanish and Portuguese populations according to the* vecindarios,[*] *official censuses and estimates (millions).*

	1500	1600	1712–1717	1768–1769	1787	1797
Spain	5[a]/5.3[b]	6.8[c]	7.5–8[d]	9.3[e]	10.4[f]	10.5[g]/11[h]
Portugal	1[i]/1.1[j]	1.8[k]	2.1[l]	2.5[m]	–	2.9[n]

Note: [*]*Vecindarios* were nosecounts or countings of *vecinos* (household heads) undertaken by the Spanish monarchs between the sixteenth and eighteenth centuries mainly for fiscal purposes.
Sources: [a] Estimate by Pérez Moreda (see text). [b] Estimate from the Castilian *vecindario* of c. 1530. [c] Estimate based on the Castilian *vecindario* of 1591 and contemporary ones from the other regions. [d] Data from the *vecindario* of Campoflorido (1712–1717). [e] Data from the Census of Aranda (1768–1769). [f] Data from the Census of Floridablanca (1787). [g] Data from the Census of Godoy (1797). [h] Estimate by Pérez Moreda (see text). [i] Estimate by Rodrigues (2008: 176). [j] Estimate based on the *Numeramento de 1527–1532* (Dias, 1998: 18). [k] Rodrigues (2008: 176). [l] Estimate based on the *Corografia* by Father Carvalho da Costa (c. 1700) (Rodrigues, 2008: 176). [m] Estimate based on *Memórias Paroquiais* (1758) (Magalhães, 1993). [n] Estimate based on the Census of 1801 (Sousa, 1979: 148–149).

Castile – which represented four-fifths of the country's total population – grew even more, at a rate of 0.64% per year.[41] It is very likely that by 1600, overall, the Spanish kingdoms did not surpass seven million residents (Pérez Moreda, 1995: 236). It was still a small population, but the country would never again know such rapid growth in a similar time span until the modern demographic transition in the twentieth century (see Table 11.3).

In the central decades of the sixteenth century, the population of the outer regions of the Crown of Castile – such as Galicia to the north, and Córdoba, Seville and Murcia to the south and south-east – grew more than that of many inland areas, and the urban population of the centre and south of the country (both Castiles – Castilla la Vieja and Castilla la Nueva – and Andalucía) grew much more than the rest of the crown (see Figure 11.1(b)). Toledo and Talavera de la Reina doubled their residents; Seville's population quadrupled between 1530 and 1588; and Madrid – which had less than 15,000 habitants before being chosen as seat of the court by Felipe II, in 1561 – became the second Spanish city within four decades, second only to Seville, with 100,000 residents by 1600. The spectacular growth of the seat of the monarchy was due to the waves of migration from both Castiles – especially the areas close to the south of Madrid, as was the case of Toledo – and from the Atlantic regions of the north of the country, such as Galicia, which were contributing the most to the fast population growth in its early days as the capital city (Carbajo Isla, 1987).

The death rate in sixteenth-century Spain was high and suffered the impact of frequent and varied epidemic crises. The century began with the plague epidemic of 1506–1507, which was particularly severe in Andalucía, and finished with the even more serious and longer-lasting 'Atlantic plague' of 1596–1602, which hit the centre and north of the Castilian territories especially hard (Bennassar, 1969; Vincent, 1976; Pérez Moreda, 1980: 257ff.). Between these two, there were several other plague epidemics: in the 1520 and 1530s; in Catalonia in 1558; again in many areas of the Peninsula, including the Portuguese coastlines and Andalucía, between 1563 and 1569; and again in 1584–1587 in Castilla la Vieja and Catalonia. Typhus, in turn – the great endemic disease from that moment onwards – was recorded for the first time in 1570, and in 1580 a general epidemic broke out, with an unprecise diagnosis but that may well have been a highly virulent flu.

Likewise, the sixteenth-century demographic growth cannot be explained by an exceptional increase in immigration numbers. It is true that estimates for the second half of the century indicate that to up to a fifth of the Catalonian population was of French origin (Nadal & Giralt, 1960), and that in the kingdom of Aragon (another region with a Pyrenean border) around 20% of the population in 1577 (and up to 25% in 1609) also came from France. The presence of large communities of European migrants can equally be observed

---

[41] According to original data obtained by Ruiz Martín (1967: 189–202).

in many areas in central and southern Castile, especially in the region's main cities. By 1600, there were around 200,000 Frenchmen in total settled in Spain. Nevertheless, emigration to the New World, most of which came from Castile, probably surpassed the number of French immigrants living under the Aragonese Crown in Aragon and Catalonia. Some estimates for 1574 point to 150,000 Spanish residents in America, which might be as many as 200,000 to 250,000 by the end of the century, and could even have trebled (to about

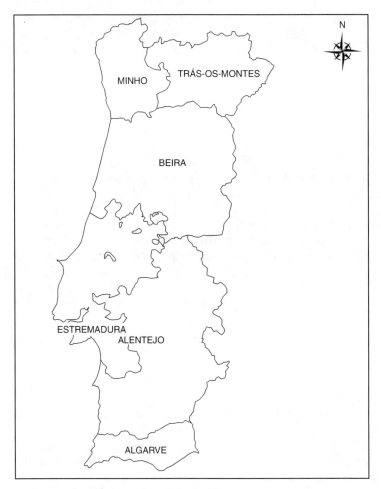

Figure 11.1a Portuguese administrative divisions, 1758.
Source: Memórias Paroquiais, 1758 (http://atlas.fcsh.unl.pt/cartoweb35/atlas.php?lang=pt).

Figure 11.1b Historical regions of Spain.
Source: Javier de Burgos, according to the Royal Decree of 30 November 1833.

450,000) around 1628 (Pérez Moreda, 1988a: 374). Hence, the migratory balance could not have had a significant influence on the demographic growth of the sixteenth century, since it was likely negative, as the outflow of Spanish towards America seems to have been greater than the inflow of people from Europe – and especially France – into Spain in search of jobs, high salaries and the many trading opportunities offered by the Spanish economy of the time.

One is therefore led to conclude that the population growth in this century is explained mostly, or exclusively, by a high birth rate, which in turn resulted from an early age of first marriage (20 years old for Christian women and 18–19 for Muslim women), an intense marriage rate (lifelong celibacy was rare among lay people) and from a very high fertility rate, as suggested by a simple indicator: the ratio between baptisms and marriages, which was higher (4–5) in the sixteenth century than in the seventeenth (3–3.5).

As for Portugal, by 1500 the country appeared to have recovered from the demographic depression into which – like many other European regions – it had sunk as a result of the Black Death and other plagues that struck the population throughout the fourteenth century, and the cereal crises that cyclically blighted populations, engendering lasting famines and sharp increases in mortality rates. Signs of change first appeared in 1480, or even a little earlier. From then on, just as in Spain and the rest of Europe, stagnation gradually gave way to general demographic growth, albeit with regional differences (Dias, 1998: 11; Rodrigues, 2008: 166 and 168). Estimates put the Portuguese population close to one million by 1500 (Rodrigues, 2008: 176). In comparison with its European counterparts, the country presented limited human resources, representing 1.7% of the continent's population and less than 20% of that in Iberia.

The *Numeramento de 1527-1532* provides – for the first time in Portugal – a relatively reliable picture of the Kingdom's residents. According to this source, Portugal had 282,708 households in 1527–1532, corresponding to 1,088,426 individuals (if a coefficient of 3.85 per household is applied). In a European context, Portugal still had a small population; however, if the indicators for population density are taken into account, levels are higher, the country holding a mid-position within Christian Europe, with a mean density of 12 to 18 inhabitants per square kilometre (Dias, 1998: 13; Rodrigues, 2008: 176).

The distribution of the population across the six provinces into which Portugal was then divided – Entre-Douro-e-Minho, Trás-os-Montes, Beira, Estremadura, Alentejo (also known as Entre-Tejo-e-Odiana) and the Algarve – followed a pattern that reached the present day. Around 20% of people lived in Entre-Douro-e-Minho, the smallest of the administrative areas, corresponding to about one-tenth of the country's territory; at the same time another 20% were scattered through the Alentejo and the Algarve, which combined represented almost half the territory (Serrão, 1996: 67–68; Dias, 1998: 14; Rodrigues, 2008: 171–173) (see Figure 11.1(a) and Table 11.4).

To piece together the development of the population in the early modern period, Palma et al. have constructed the first annual series for Portugal's population for the period 1527–1850, using a combination of stocks from population counts and censuses, and flows from the registers of several dozen parishes. Results are shown in Figure 11.2. Another result of this study was six long-running population estimates, for each region of Portugal, from 1527 to 1864 (Figure 11.3). These show that the different regions followed divergent demographic patterns: the south, Alentejo and Algarve exhibited minimal change over time; the north-east interior, Trás-os-Montes, had a mostly stagnant population; and the three regions in the centre and north of the country, with a total growth of around 80–90% per century, were the drivers of Portugal's demographic growth (Palma et al., 2020). The issue will be revisited later in the text.

Regarding national-level growth dynamics, Figure 11.2 shows that between 1527–1532 and 1580 the population expanded steeply (around 0.8% per year). In the following decades, and at least until 1620, the growth trend persisted, although with a slower rhythm (Serrão, 1996: 65; Rodrigues, 2008: 177). Partly

Table 11.3 *Population of continental Spain by region, c. 1530–1800.*

Regions	c. 1530 Inhabitants (thousands)	1591–1600 Inhabitants (thousands)	1787–1800 Inhabitants (thousands)
Andalucía	762	1,067	1,847
Asturias	81	133	348
Castilla la Nueva	614	1,145	1,142
Castilla la Vieja	1,049	1,254	1,232
Extremadura	305	451	417
Galicia	263	504	1,346
León	503	633	628
Murcia	74	115	338
Basque Country – Navarre	268	296	535
Crown of Castile	**3,919**	**5,598**	**7,833**
Aragon	255	310	623
Catalonia	251	364	899
Valencia	273	360	783
Crown of Aragon	**779**	**1,034**	**2,305**
Total Spain	**4,698**	**6,632**	**10,138**

Source: Nadal (1984: 74).

Table 11.4 *Estimates of the population in Portugal by region, c. 1530–1800.*

Provinces	1527–1532* Households (H)	Inhabitants H × 3.85	1700* Households (H)	Inhabitants H × 3.85	1800** Households (H)	Inhabitants
Entre-Douro-e-Minho	55,016	211,812	131,183	505,055	172,172	667,176
Trás-os-Montes	35,629	137,172	59,438	205,736	68,779	265,852
Beira	67,696	260,630	120,586	464,256	239,245	933,384
Estremadura	65,515	252,233	132,928	511,773	173,955	672,180
Entre-Tejo-e-Odiana	48,934	188,396	104,178	401,085	75,717	270,774
Algarve	9,918	38,184	16,148	62,170	28,218	103,307
Total Portugal	**282,708**	**1,088,426**	**558,461**	**2,150,075**	**758,086**	**2,912,673**

Sources: * Rodrigues (2008: 177); ** Sousa (1979: 149).

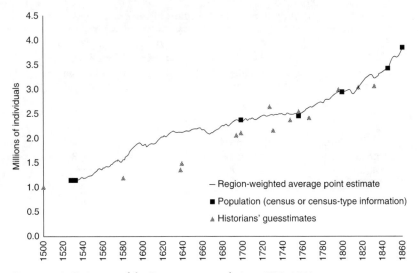

Figure 11.2 Estimates of the Portuguese population, 1527–1864.
Source: Palma et al. (2020).

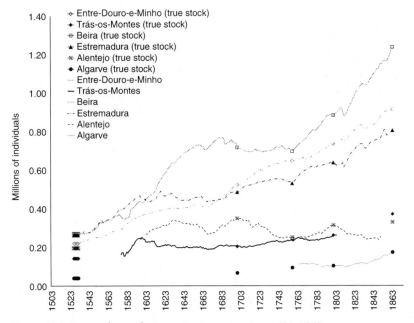

Figure 11.3 Portugal: population estimates per region, 1500–1860.
Source: Palma et al. (2020).

to blame for this slowdown were the mortality crises of 1569, 1579–1580 and 1598–1602, which resulted from the movement pattern of the pathogenic agents of the Black Death within Europe, affecting all the Portuguese territory, as well as from epidemics of pneumonic flu, smallpox and syphilis. The situation was made worse by the gradual decrease of the arrival of enslaved people, mostly from Africa, and European migrants, the increase of emigration overseas, particularly towards Brazil, and in the 1580s and 1590s the latent climate of imminent war (Rodrigues, 2008: 169, 178–182, 229–232).

The crisis intensified at the turn of the century. Although it unfolded in the following century, it had its beginnings in the sixteenth century and should therefore be addressed here. Indeed, the period between 1596 and 1603 was especially difficult due to a number of factors: a plague outbreak which, as noted, affected most of the Iberian Peninsula, as well as some of the main European Atlantic ports; a succession of four bad harvests that led to grain shortages and, consequently, the temporary disarticulation of production and distribution; and the looming prospect of war, with fears of an English attack (Rodrigues, 2008: 181–182; Salgado, 2009). The crises of extraordinary mortality that marked the sixteenth and the beginning of the seventeenth centuries were typically intense but of short duration (Rodrigues, 2008: 229–231). Despite their devastating effects, in the last decades of the sixteenth century life was ahead of death, the rates of baptisms soon overtaking mortality rates, thus allowing numerical recovery. In sum, the impact of these crises explains the slowdown, but it was not strong enough to reverse the century's growth trend (Serrão, 1993: 51).

In broad terms, the sixteenth century also saw remarkable urban development. Although hard to quantify, this growth was fuelled by an internal flux mainly from rural areas, and external migration, especially from Galicia and Castile. Movement was mostly local or regional. Only Lisbon had national and international appeal, and had, from an early time, attracted people from Minho, Alentejo, Beira, the Algarve and around the coast, as well as from overseas, namely from England, Flanders, and German and Italian cities (Rodrigues, 2008: 234–236).

Besides contributing to urban development, the demographic growth in the sixteenth century made the settlement of Madeira, the Azores, Cape Verde, São Tomé and Príncipe and Brazil possible, and the taking of strategic points, like the strongholds in northern Africa, and key economic areas, such as India. Estimates put Madeira at 18,000 inhabitants (of whom 2,000 were enslaved) in 1500, reaching 29,000 in 1598 (Pinto and Rodrigues, 2013). The beginning of the century saw many people leaving the country, especially towards India. During the second half of the century the outflow towards Brazil intensified, the territory becoming the largest and most populous Portuguese colony in the first decades of the seventeenth century (Serrão, 1970: 599–601; Rodrigues, 2008: 239–241). Between 1500 and 1580, 280,000 people left the country, an average of 3,500 per year. During the reigns of kings Felipe I, II and III (1580–1640) the outflow intensified, estimates pointing to between 300,000 and 360,000 people, or 5,000 to 6,000 per year (Godinho, 1977: 57; Rodrigues, 2008: 239).

This outflow – always more male than female – was only partly compensated by immigration. At the beginning of the sixteenth century, the only incoming group of significant volume was that of the Jews expelled from Castile in 1492, 20,000 of whom arrived in Portugal (Tavares, 1982–1984; Sousa, 2007: 122, 128–129). From the middle of the century, the number of enslaved Africans also started to grow, reaching 10% of the population in Lisbon and Évora (Saunders, 1982; Lahon, 2001; Fonseca, 1997; 2010). In comparison, despite the Portuguese population remaining a minuscule fraction of the European population, its development stood out both regarding Europe and the Iberian Peninsula. The sixteenth century was marked by pronounced demographic growth, reaching 30% in Europe and 40% in Spain. In Portugal, however, it was particularly intense, with estimates pointing to 60% growth.

11.2.2 The 'Decadence' of the Seventeenth Century

During the seventeenth century, European population dropped, stagnated or, at best, grew at a slow pace. In Spain, historians – even the most modern – tend to follow the generalized opinion of the economic and political writers of the time, who portrayed the seventeenth as the century of the Spanish crisis or 'decadence'. They described not only a long economic crisis and a political 'decline', but also – and above all else – a process of shrinkage, a 'depopulation' that was one of the first alarm signals of the general downfall the country was undergoing. And they discussed what they believed were its main causes: among others, epidemics throughout the century; problems in agriculture and their repercussions on the population; drops in marriage and birth rates; rural depopulation and, in many areas, also urban depopulation, contrasting – and indeed partly resulting from – the growth of the city of Madrid; and loss of population through forced emigration (the expulsion of the Moors in 1609), administrative reasons or the voluntary decision to leave, as with many of those going to America.

However, the demographic balance of the century does not warrant such pessimistic conclusions. If, by the end of the reign of Felipe II (1527–1598), Spain hardly had seven million people, comparison with Gerónimo de Uztáriz's estimate of 7.5 million at the beginning of the eighteenth century – or the more optimistic range of 7.7 and 8.2 million offered by F. Bustelo – would point to an *increase* of the Spanish population in the seventeenth century, of probably close to one million. It is, however, true that this would be a very modest growth for one century, barely surpassing an annual rate of 0.1%, and which, furthermore, masks a downturn – steeper and longer in some areas than others – stretching especially throughout the first half of the century (Bustelo, 1972; 1973; 1975; Pérez Moreda, 1988a: 375ff.).

This downturn resulted from the famous 'pestilences', as well as from other events with catastrophic mortality hitting both the crowns of Castile and Aragon. It should be noted that only two great plagues were widespread throughout the Spanish territory in this century: the so-called 'Atlantic plague', which spread through the Castilian territories between 1596 and 1602 (Bennassar, 1969; Vincent, 1976; Pérez Moreda, 1980: 280, 300–303), and the epidemic affecting Andalusia and all the Spanish Mediterranean territories, including the Balearic archipelago, Catalonia and part of the kingdom of Aragon, between 1647 and 1654 (Biraben, 1975; Castells, 1987; Pérez Moreda, 1987; Camps i Surroca & Camps i Clement, 1985; Betrán, 1996).[42] It is possible that each of these caused around half a million deaths. Neither the 'Milanese plague' of 1629–1631, which only affected the Catalan territory, nor the last epidemic of this aetiology in Iberian history – which hit only parts of the south-eastern region and specific points of Andalusia between 1676 and 1682 – had any comparable demographic consequences.

Mortality remained very high, not only because of the plague but also owing to the regular presence of equally serious diseases (typhus, diphtheria, etc.), whose consequences often blended with, or were mistaken for, those of bad harvests and famine. That was the case around 1631 in several regions, especially in the north of the Peninsula and in areas of central Castile; and around 1661, and between 1676 and 1685 (with special incidence in 1684), when there was sharp excess mortality in many areas of peninsular Spain, as a result mostly of typhus and malaria, spreading from Andalusia to both Castiles (Pérez Moreda, 1980: 313–314; Kamen, 1981: 92–94). The crisis of 1693–1694 was especially serious, particularly in Galicia and Castile; as well as that of 1699, when the problems derived from shortage provoked riots and political upheaval in the Castilian court (Egido López, 1980).

Besides the excess death rate and the 'regular' death rate, the negative influence of other factors must be taken into account, such as fertility and migration of various kinds towards different destinations. Regarding these, it is worth noting the most credible estimates of net emigration flows towards America: Domínguez Ortiz pointed to an annual average of 4,000–5,000 people, which is a much more modest (and likely) number than those proposed by several contemporary authors; the same author later even reduced that estimate to 3,000 a year (Domínguez Ortiz, 1963: 90; 1973: 272, 429–430). To these must be added, of course, the (minimum) 300,000 Moors (*Moriscos*) expelled between 1609 and 1614; unevenly distributed throughout peninsular Spain, these corresponded to a significant proportion of the population in

---

[42] The plague in the 1650s destroyed 'between 15 and 20% of Catalonia's human potential', according to Nadal (1992a: 66).

some of the territories, especially in the kingdoms of Aragon and Valencia (Domínguez Ortiz & Vincent, 1978). And perhaps a similar number of Spanish subjects lost throughout Europe in the wars the Crown maintained throughout this century.

As to fertility, it has already been noted that the ratio of baptisms to marriages – as an approximate measure of legitimate fertility – had its lowest levels both in rural and urban areas of the Castilian crown in the seventeenth century, especially during its first half. The few family reconstitutions undertaken in different Spanish regions covering at least partially this century, show that the highest levels of legitimate fertility (final descendants) were located on the Mediterranean coast, specifically in Valencia. This doubtless helps explain the high growth rate of this region, hastened in the numerous places that had to be slowly repopulated after the Moors were expelled (Casey, 1983: 26; Pérez Garcia & Ardit Lucas, 1988). Regarding the nuptiality rate – which had a direct impact on fertility levels – the average age of marriage seems to have been slightly delayed since the sixteenth and seventeenth centuries, judging from the much more solid data for the eighteenth century, which will be analysed below (Valero Lobo, 1984; Pérez Moreda, 1988b: 593–594; Dopico & Rowland, 1990: 609–610). Furthermore, all that can be known regarding the intensity of marriage should be seen through definite celibacy. It is possible celibacy increased from the beginning of the seventeenth century, when obstacles to marriage started to proliferate, as decried by so many contemporary writers as cause for the concurrent depopulation.[43]

The demographic 'decadence' of the seventeenth century is surely reflected in the decline in many areas of the country, mostly during the first half of the century. Regional baptism rates show a drop of 30–50% in that period in many parts of Castile's hinterland.[44] In Extremadura too – or at least in Cáceres – there was a drop of over 30% throughout the whole century. The fall seems to be less marked in rural areas of Aragon (around 20%, although the number rises if the sample is widened to include some urban centres). In Andalucía, on the other hand, the births trend throughout the century was rather flat with a small rise at the end, and the information available for Mallorca follows a similar pattern. The curves in Catalonia record a striking fall between approximately 1630 and 1660, reflecting the effects of the war and the plague of the middle of the century; the last third of the century already shows a clear recovery. Similarly, in Valencia, there is a very slight rise until 1660, which increases noticeably henceforth. An important work of reconstitution of the

---

[43] Cellorigo, Leruela, Sancho de Moncada, among others; see Pérez Moreda (1986: 36–37) and Martín Rodríguez (1984).

[44] From a sample of more than 200 communities of the different historical regions, used in previous studies (by J. Nadal, Pérez Moreda-Reher, among others), to which were added the provincial statistics collected by different authors (Pérez Moreda 1999a).

region's population using the inverse projection method confirms this trend in the seventeenth century and shows much more pronounced growth in the eighteenth (Ardit Lucas, 1991). The region of Murcia, in turn, underwent a significant drop until 1650-1660, after which it experienced remarkable growth, from 1670 until at least 1720.

The northern areas of the Castilian crown – forming the Cantabrian coast, and including the Basque Country and Navarre – were those with the highest demographic growth in the seventeenth century. At least since 1630-1640 – when the growing of the new cereal, maize, spread throughout these regions – Galicia and Asturias underwent intense growth, allowing the population to approximately double in this period. A similar situation happened in Cantabria and the Basque Country, at least in Guipúzcoa, where continuous – albeit more moderate – growth could be observed throughout the century. Growth was much stronger in the rural centres in the north of Navarre for which there is available information (Pérez Moreda, 1988a: 384).

As in Spain and most European countries, the seventeenth-century demographic growth rate also slowed down in Portugal. Notwithstanding, by 1700 the Portuguese population had doubled from the values estimated for 1500, while for whole of Europe the population had increased by 40%.

Regarding demographic development in Portugal throughout the seventeenth century, it has already been noted that in the last decades of the previous century and at least until 1620, the growth trend of the sixteenth century remained, even if it had lost pace. Indeed, since 1606 and at least until 1620, there was a medium intensity downturn in the whole kingdom, leading to a generalized increase in the number of deaths and a decrease in the marriage and baptism rate (Rodrigues, 2008: 182-183).

Estimates point to 475,000 households by 1620, and 466,000 twenty years later, which represents estimates of a total population between 1,800,000 and 2,100,000, depending on the applied coefficient, 3.85 or 4.6 (Rodrigues, 2008: 175). Between 1620 and 1660, there was a phase of stagnation or recession, with the most critical point in 1640 (Magalhães, 1987: 23; Serrão, 1996: 65). Political instability will have been a main factor for this situation, namely the War of Portuguese Independence (1640-1668), which led to a peak in mortality and a drop in births. To make things worse, adverse weather conditions and subsequent crop crises led to food shortages, aggravated by outbreaks of diphtheria, typhus and dysentery, typhoid, flu and smallpox, and bubonic plague (1647-1650), leading to abrupt rises in mortality in several regions of the country. In the 1650s and 1660s, typhus, typhoid and flu returned, culminating in a general crisis between 1657-1659 and 1662-1663 (Rodrigues, 2008: 182-184; Costa et al., 2014: 167-168).

Contributing to this scenario of stagnation was the fact that in the seventeenth century the migratory flux towards the colonies, in particular to Brazil, increased. This movement, which initially had a colonizing character, intensified and became purely migratory, leading the state to take measures to restrict the impact of the population's out migration from 1645 onwards. Indeed, in the first half of the seventeenth century, the gross emigration rate increased compared to the previous century, standing at 3.5‰. In the second half of the seventeenth century, the gross emigration rate decreased, but from 1690, due to discovery of gold mines in Brazil, it rose again (to 4‰) (Serrão, 1970: 599–601; Rodrigues, 2008: 142–246).

In 1660, a new, more modest, growth period began, with annual population growth rates of around 0.43% (Serrão, 1996: 65). This expansion was limited by bad harvests, which generated subsistence crises across the country. Food scarcity, hunger and precarious conditions were, in turn, linked to what are believed to be the last episodes of plague in Lisbon, between 1679 and 1682, and in the Alentejo, in 1673, 1676, 1680, 1681 and 1685, and new outbreaks of epidemic typhus in Lisbon (1692, 1694 and 1698), which affected nearby councils and the Algarve (Rodrigues, 2008: 184–185). The low growth that marked the end of the seventeenth century reflected a rise in mortality levels and a decrease in birth rates that generally reduced and, occasionally, reversed the numerical advantage of life over death.

It should be noted that this growth rate stands out in the European context, since between 1650–1660 and 1700 most countries had lower values (Costa et al., 2014: 167–168). The change in the pattern of mortality crises in Portugal was certainly a contributing factor for this scenario. In fact, in the second half of the seventeenth century mortality crises, although more frequent, became less severe and their impact on demographic evolution decreased. Likewise, the causes of these crises themselves changed. While in the sixteenth century plague was the great cause of death, in the seventeenth the impact and frequency of typhus-related crises increased (Rodrigues, 2008: 229–232).

Between the end of the seventeenth century and the beginning of the eighteenth, growth again stagnated, giving rise to a recession that marked the first decades of the eighteenth century (Serrão, 1996: 65). The *Corografia Portugueza* – whose date is uncertain, but certainly corresponds to the end of the seventeenth century or beginning of the eighteenth – points to a total of 593,628 households in continental Portugal, a value corrected by Serrão to 586,461, and by Pinto et al. to 535,000, representing an estimated population of 2,050,000 inhabitants (Pinto et al., 2001: 388–399; Rodrigues, 2008: 175). An analysis of the development of the Portuguese population throughout the sixteenth and seventeenth centuries shows there was indeed growth. However, as seen, this was unequal from region to region, the north and centre of the country growing more pronouncedly than the south (see Figures 11.2 and 11.3).

11.2.3 'Traditional' Growth in the Eighteenth Century

The eighteenth century was a period of growth in Iberia and throughout Europe. The numbers stated by Uztáriz (and the *Vecindario de Campoflorido*, of 1712-1717) for the total population for these dates – after the serious crisis of 1709-1711 – was 7.5 million people. Extrapolating the data contained in the *Vecindario y Censo del Marqués de la Ensenada para la Corona de Castilla* (in 1752) to the Spanish territory as a whole results in a figure close to that given by the *Censo de Aranda* of 1768-1769 (9.3 million inhabitants). The best-known censuses, from the end of the century, register totals of 10.4 million (Floridablanca, 1787) and 10.5 million (Godoy, 1797), which could be rounded up to 11 million people by the end of the century (see above, Table 11.2). Demographic growth throughout this century was therefore a remarkable – even if not dramatic – 0.42% per year, with notable differences by period and region. It must be noted that, although significant, this was a 'traditional' kind of growth, far from a 'demographic transition'. In fact, it was lower than that recorded for a good part of the sixteenth century, and was still subject to the checks and limitations weighing on the populations of the *Ancien Régime*, specifically, and above all, very high mortality rates, averaging close to 40‰.

Throughout the century, catastrophic mortality decreased in Spain without, however, disappearing. There were no longer 'plagues', but other diseases spread such as malaria and, especially, smallpox. Their consequences were aggravated by wars and the agricultural downturns, such as that of the severe crisis of the 1760s, which culminated in the famous mutinies of 1766, and worsened towards the last decades of the century (Anes, 1970: 340-346; 1974; Vilar, 1972; Rodríguez, 1973; Pérez Moreda, 1980: 363-366; 2017: 57).

Infant mortality (0–1 years = q_0) and that of children in general remained very high: on the whole, 250-300‰ in the first year of life, and only slightly lower (200-250‰) in some of the regions, such as Galicia and Catalonia, where it appears to dip below 200‰ at the end of the century. The rate was even higher during the difficult Napoleonic period (1800-1814), with q_0 levels rising above 300‰ in many Spanish inland regions (Pérez Moreda, 1980: 150-155; Sanz Gimeno & Ramiro Fariñas, 2002: 403). For this reason, life expectancy at birth (e_0) was still very low (not above 26-27 years), not much higher than the 23-24 years estimated for some rural and urban areas in the previous century.[45]

The regional contrasts concerning population growth during this century can once again be followed through regional baptism rates, updated with an extensive documentary base thanks to the work of E. Llopis and colleagues

---

[45] For the eighteenth century, see Livi-Bacci (1968: 90-91); Dopico & Rowland (1990: 601). For the seventeenth century, for data concerning Mocejón (Toledo), see Pérez Moreda (1980: 143-144), and the parish of San Pablo – Zaragoza – see Ansón Calvo (1977: 119).

(Llopis Agelán, 2004a: 10-24).[46] The area of the Cantabrian coast, and especially Asturias and Galicia, which had grown significantly in the seventeenth century, recorded a more moderate growth (maybe as low as 25-30% for the whole period in Galicia, the Basque Country, Navarre and Cantabria), lower − except in Asturias (50%) − than that of the whole Spanish territory (40-45%). In Andalusia, the population grew at the same rate as the country as a whole, although the rate was lower in the western part of the region. Baptismal rates on the island of Mallorca increased less than 20%, while in Menorca it rose more than 80%. However, the Catalan population underwent significant growth between 1717 (508,000) and 1787 (900,000), an absolute growth of 77% at an average annual rate of 0.82% (Nadal, 1992b: 108), while the number of baptisms doubled between the beginning and the end of the century. The Valencian Kingdom and Murcia more than doubled, or even trebled their population numbers in this century, with an annual growth rate above 1% in Valencia, and possibly even greater in Murcia. This suggests an intense process of immigration or colonization of these regions, still heavily depopulated at the beginning of the eighteenth century because of the expulsion of the *morisco* population of 1609-1614 (Bustelo, 1975). Some regional samples of inland Castilla la Vieja showed a growth rate of 40-45%, similar to the country as a whole; the Aragonese cases available show growth clearly greater than the national average. In Extremadura, the rate (49%) is similar to that in both Castiles, since a large number of parishes in Castilla la Nueva saw birth numbers increase by around 45%. The city of Madrid − which had developed so much between 1561 and 1630, reaching almost 130,000 inhabitants − only started expanding again when the eighteenth century was well under way, reaching a maximum of 187,000 in 1797, representing a growth of 40% during this century − or, rather, in its second half.

Thus, extensive areas in the Castilian inland − the two Castiles, León and Extremadura − which had undergone a sharp decline in the seventeenth century, grew during the eighteenth century, albeit at a moderate pace. The 1591 population levels had not been surpassed in some of these regions two centuries later, in 1787, as Table 11.5 shows.

The figures thus show a long-term stagnation or a very modest growth in the Spanish inland regions between the end of the sixteenth and the end of the eighteenth century. This trend hides a sharp depression in the seventeenth century, from which the country only recovered − partially in some areas and fully in others − with the growth trend recorded in the last third of that century and in the following one. The northern-Atlantic provinces and those of the Mediterranean coast, including Andalusia, show a much more positive outcome for these same two centuries. This reflects the centuries-old trend of the Spanish population to settle in the periphery of the country, to the detriment of

---

[46] The national sample is based on over 1,050 rural locations from all the Spanish regions.

Table 11.5 *Average annual growth rate (%), 1591–1787.*

Region	%	Region	%
Murcia	0.55	Basque Country – Navarre	0.30
Galicia	0.50	Andalucia	0.28
Asturias	0.49	Castilla la Nueva	0.00
Catalonia	0.46	León	0.00
Valencia	0.40	Castilla la Vieja	−0.01
Aragon	0.36	Extremadura	−0.04
Crown of Aragon	**0.41**	**Crown of Castile**	**0.17**
Spanish mainland	**0.22**		

Source: Nadal (1984: 74).

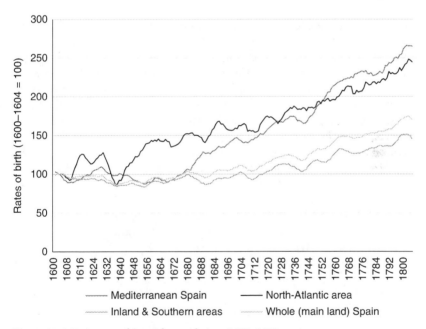

Figure 11.4 Estimates of Spanish population, 1600–1800.
Source: regional birth rates (1600–1604 = 100). See footnotes 4 and 7.

wide inland regions – a tendency that persisted after 1800, and even deepened in the contemporary age up to the present day.

As for Portugal, the conclusion is that, in general in the eighteenth century, demographic development followed the European and Iberian trends, showing a global tendency toward growing. Despite the uncertain quality of the available figures, estimates point to a total population of around 2,100,000 inhabitants in 1700, 2,500,000 in 1750, and almost 3,000,000 in 1801 (Moreira & Veiga, 2005: 36–37; Serrão, 1993: 50–54; Palma et al., 2020). With three million inhabitants, Portugal was still a sparsely populated country at the European scale. Nevertheless, its development in the early modern period allowed it to slightly strengthen its position within Iberia and Europe. At the beginning of the nineteenth century, the population of Portugal was 2% of the European total and 22% of that of the Iberian Peninsula. Unlike in previous centuries, the Portuguese demographic growth rate in the eighteenth century was below the European average. While the latter grew around 60% between 1700 and 1800, Portugal's population increased by only 37% (a rate similar to that of Spain – see Table 11.2).

It should also be noted that even though the period's keynote was growth, the trend was not uniform throughout the century. Indeed, as elsewhere in Europe, the eighteenth century in Portugal was marked by two distinct and opposite tendencies. The first was recession, in the first third of the century, corresponding to a period of slow decline of around 0.2% per year. This is linked to the intense migration outflow, estimated at around 10,000 people leaving the country annually, attracted by the gold and diamonds of Brazil; to mortality crises resulting from the proliferation of epidemics; Portugal's role in the Spanish Succession War; and the dearth of grain, which marked the end of the seventeenth and the first half of the eighteenth century (Moreira & Veiga, 2005: 39, 61, 64).

From the 1730s, the declining trend reversed, and a phase of lasting growth began, even if of uneven rate. From 1732 to 1758 there was a rapid rise, with an annual growth rate of around 0.64%. This was followed by a sharp slowdown between 1758 and 1801, with a rate of 0.31% per year (Moreira, 2008, 256). This slowdown was a result of the various crises of the 1760s and 1770s, marked by the rise of extraordinary mortality, subsistence problems and the so-called 'Fantastic War' (Moreira & Veiga, 2005: 39).

As in Spain, the eighteenth century brought no significant change to the demographic trend. Even at its peak, population growth followed the traditional pattern. Equally, there were no changes in the patterns of geographical distribution of the population, but rather the regional imbalances and asymmetries of previous centuries intensified. Minho maintained its greater demographic dynamism and strengthened its relative weighting, accounting for 25% of the country's population, mostly thanks to the 'corn revolution'. This growth was neither dampened by the migration outflow towards the other provinces of the kingdom nor towards the empire (Moreira & Veiga, 2005: 40, 42, 64; Costa et al., 2014: 214–215). There was also growth in the Algarve (Magalhães, 1993; Moreira & Veiga, 2005: 40, 42). In the Alentejo, on the other hand, the population shrank, and the region's relative weighting diminished

(Serrão, 1993: 54; Moreira & Veiga, 2005: 40, 42). During this century, the contrast between north and south was sharpened. In 1801, the four provinces north of the Tagus river accounted for 83% of the national population, with a population density of 12 households per km², while the provinces to the south had a density of 3.5 households per km². At the same time, the northern and central coastal regions kept a higher growth rate than the country as a whole (Serrão, 1993: 55, 58).

11.2.4 Demographic Patterns and Determinant Factors of Growth

We have already mentioned some of the demographic indices – mortality, marriage rates and fertility – which help explain the growth (sixteenth century), the stagnation or depression (seventeenth century) and then the moderate growth in the eighteenth century. In Spain, the crude mortality rate during these centuries always ranged around 40‰. A more significant indicator is the infant mortality rate (q_0), which in different areas and periods was around 200–250‰, and in some cases – even at the end of the eighteenth century and just after 1800 – came close to 300‰. For this reason, life expectancy at birth for this period (second half of the eighteenth century) was 27 years (26.8, according to Livi-Bacci, 1968), and in the previous century it was probably 25 at best in many areas (Pérez Moreda, 1980: 150–155; Sanz Gimeno & Ramiro Fariñas, 2002: 403 and footnote 6).

Portugal's demographic pattern was equally 'traditional', characterized by high birth and mortality rates (around 30‰ and 40‰). Generally, there was a positive balance, which was often curbed by exogenous causes (Barbosa & Godinho, 2001; Moreira, 2008: 268; Rodrigues, 2008: 221). Regarding the mortality crises in Portugal, there is remarkable continuity into the eighteenth from the preceding centuries. Recurrence, proximate causes, conducive conditions, and impacts remain the same. Their origins are still hunger, epidemics and war. However, during the eighteenth century the main causes behind epidemic death change (typhus, cholera and yellow fever), and so do the mortality crises, whose peaks tend to become more regular, longer, but less serious and concentrated in areas with higher population density (Moreira & Veiga, 2005: 50–54).

Although the scarcity of data does not allow safe conclusions, the available data on infant mortality point to a more favourable scenario for Portugal, where values below 150‰ are common throughout the period under analysis. Apparently, regional differences have an impact on life expectancy at birth – for instance, in the second half of the eighteenth century, this was estimated to be 45 years of age in Minho, while in the Alentejo it was 33 (Amorim, 2004: 160–162).[47]

---

[47] However, in light of those from the mid-twentieth century, these figures seem to be overestimates, or valid only for some periods and regions.

Together with the small but significant improvement of survival rates, eighteenth-century Spain also saw noticeable changes in the marriage and fertility rates. The only explanation for the very low fertility in the seventeenth century is delayed nuptiality and a more limited number of marriages, due to the increasing rate of lifelong celibacy. The combination of high mortality and low fertility explains the weak natural growth seen in the seventeenth century – or no growth at all, in many regions for long periods throughout the century. The progressive delay in the marriage age, probably starting during the worst moments of the seventeenth century, can be seen clearly in the data regarding the middle of the eighteenth century, when the average age of marriage for women in the country reached 23.5 years of age (25 for men); it was around 25 in all the northern area called Green Spain, from Galicia to Navarre (and over 26 in the Basque Country), while the southern half of the kingdom retained an average between 21 and 22 years (Pérez Moreda, 1988b: 594) (see Table 11.6 and Figure 11.5).

Table 11.6 *Standardized marital fertility (I_G), expectation of life at birth (E_0) and singular mean age at first marriage for females ($SMAM_F$)*.

Region	I_G (1787)	E_0 (1787)	$SMAM_F$ (1787–1797)
Andalusia	0.673	29.9	22.3
Aragon	0.716	27.0	23.2
Asturias	0.844	26.3	24.5
Balearic Islands	0.702	27.8	22.4
Castilla la Vieja	0.779	25.2	23.7
Castilla la Nueva	0.653	27.8	23.3
Catalonia	0.819	29.7	23.4
Extremadura	0.702	25.9	21.9
Galicia	0.757	30.8	25.3
León	0.807	25.0	24.2
Murcia	0.656	29.0	22.2
Navarre	0.769	28.1	24.2
Basque Country	0.762	32.0	26.1
Valencia	0.644	32.2	22.7
Spain	**0.723**	**28.1**	**23.5**

Sources: data from 1787 (I_G and E_o) taken from Dopico and Rowland (1990: 607–609). $SMAM_F$ (1787–1797) are from regional estimates undertaken from the information in the censuses of Floridablanca and Godoy (Pérez Moreda, 1988b: 594).

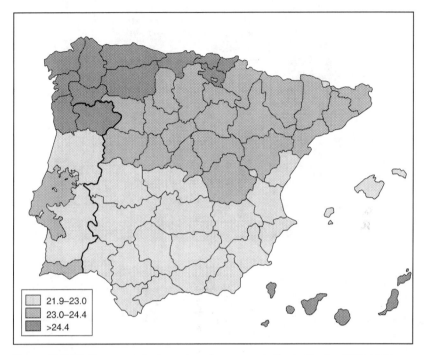

Figure 11.5 Median age at first marriage for women in Iberia (Spain, 1787–1797; Portugal, eighteenth century).

Though the marriage age was delayed, it was not as late as Hajnal's 'model' for Western Europe suggested to which only the country's northern regions come close, particularly the Basque provinces, with figures similar to those seen on the northern side of the Pyrenees. Definitive celibacy (the proportion of single men and women between 40 and 50 years of age) was also on the rise, reaching, in 1787, 11.4% among women and almost 12% among men.[48] The figure rises to 17% when including the ecclesiastic population of both sexes according to the data in the Census of Godoy (1797).

The average real offspring of women in the northern regions was not vastly different from the rest of the country. This was mainly due to the increase in marriage age, which avoided the economic insecurity of excessively young couples and provided some guarantee of minimum living standards for the new families. These were some of the advantages of this demographic behaviour, which in Malthusian terms might be called 'prudential' or 'preventive'. However, fertility

---

[48] In some regions, like Galicia or the Canary Islands, female lifelong celibacy approached or exceeded 20% for this period (Livi-Bacci, 1968: 219).

Table 11.7 *Average age of women's first marriage by region (Portugal, eighteenth century).*

Provinces	Obs.	Age
Minho	5	26.0
Estremadura	6	23.5
Trás-os-Montes	4	27.0
Alentejo	1	21.2
Algarve	1	23.8

Sources: Rowland (1989, 1997); Rodrigues (2008); Amorim et al. (2016).

rates were higher in the northern regions. The higher legitimate fertility offset the potential lower birth rate of later, less universal marriage, as shown in Table 11.6.

Data from local studies on marriage patterns of the Portuguese population emphasize relative stability in regional matrimonial regimes and the contrast between two different regional zones regarding the average age at first marriage for women (Rowland, 1989: 516–529; 1997; Amorim, 2004: 158; Moreira, 2008: 278–279). For reasons of comparability in the Iberian context, we used Portuguese local studies to calculate the average age of women's first marriage by region, to show regional differences in the eighteenth century (Table 11.7 and Figure 11.5).

It is clear that the mean marrying age of women was higher in the north than in the south. The contrast is rather sharp: in the southern regions it tended to be around or below 23, while most of the northern regions had values above 24. With regard to family systems, Portugal was therefore split into two marked types, in the north, large families prevailed, while in the south (Alentejo and Algarve), there was a tendency towards nuclear families. This shows a continuation regarding the tendencies already found in Spain, suggesting that their reading and interpretation must be framed in the context of the whole peninsula (Rowland, 1989: 539–546).

11.3 Urbanization

This section offers an overview of Iberian urbanization between 1500 and 1800. From an economic point of view, in the pre-modern world, cities were stable settlements characterized by a prevalence of individuals involved in secondary and tertiary jobs, agrarian families usually being a minority (Malanima, 2005: 98). Many authors see a strong connection between urbanization, the socio-professional composition of population, agrarian productivity, and the development of economic system in that period (Wrigley, 1987; Persson, 1991; Malanima, 2005). However, an analysis of the urbanization is dependent on the quality of the available sources and deeply compromised by the complexity of the concept of 'urban centre' and by the multitude of criteria used in its definition (Bairoch et al., 1988: 254; de Vries, 1995: 43-60; Silva, 1997: 781-786). For practical reasons, many scholars choose a quantitative criterion, but disagree on the minimum threshold to classify a population as urban. Since this chapter is meant to allow comparison with rates in other European territories, one of the thresholds commonly used in international literature on the modern period was chosen: 5,000 people (Bairoch et al., 1988).

Table 11.8 shows a comparison of the Iberian urbanization rate with other European territories between 1500 and 1800, considering towns with more than 5,000 inhabitants.

Table 11.8 *Urbanization rates in Europe between 1500 and 1800, considering towns with 5,000 inhabitants (%) or more.*

	1500	1600	1700	1800
England and Wales	5.25[v]	8.25[v]	17.0[v]	27.5[v]
'Great Britain' and Ireland	4.6	7.9	11.8	20.8
Belgium (Southern Low Countries)	28.0	29.3	30.6	21.7
Netherlands	29.5	34.7	38.9	34.1
Germany	8.2	8.5	7.7	9.4
France	8.8	10.8	12.3	12.9
Italy	21.0[ii]	18.4[ii]	16.9[ii]	17.5[ii]
Spain		23.3[i]		24.3[i]
Portugal	**10.3**[iii]		**15.2**[iv]	**14.9**[iv]
Europe	**10.3**	**11.7**	**11.4**	**11.9**
Western Europe[a]	8.9	10.7	12.0	14.0
Southern Europe[b]	18.0	19.9	19.4	18.3
Eastern Europe[c]	5.1	5.5	4.7	5.5

Notes: [a] Germany, Belgium, France, Netherlands, 'Great Britain' and Ireland, Scandinavian Countries and Switzerland. [b] The Balkan states and the Mediterranean countries (Spain, Italy and Portugal). [c] Austria, Hungary, Czechoslovakia, Poland, Romania and European Russia.
Sources: Bairoch et al. (1988, 259). Additional data from: [i] Pérez Moreda and Reher (1997: 130); [ii] Malanima (2005: 103); [iii] figures reckoned from the data contained in the *Numeramento de 1527-1532* using the coefficient 3.85 (Dias, 1998); [iv] Serrão (1996: 75); [v] Wrigley (1987: 162).

As the table shows, between 1500 and 1800, the European urbanization rate was relatively stable, rising only from 10.3% to 11.9%. However, this was far from a uniform growth. In the first place, it is clear it was at its highest during the sixteenth century, slowing down in the following two centuries (Bairoch et al., 1988: 253-259). In 1500, Southern Europe – which included Portugal and Spain, but also Italy and the Balkans – was the most urbanized area in the Old Continent, second only to the Northern Netherlands and the Southern Netherlands (mostly Flanders, today's Belgium).

Second, the data highlights that between 1500 and 1800 urbanization rates in Southern and Eastern Europe tended to stabilize, while Western Europe showed continuous growth (from 8.9% to 14%). Globally, the figures show that during this period the centre of gravity moved from Mediterranean Europe to the Atlantic Coast (Bairoch et al., 1988: 259-260). Malanima draws attention to the parallel between urbanization rate and economic dynamism in these regions (Malanima, 2005: 104-105).

Let us now focus on the Iberian situation. In both the sixteenth and the eighteenth centuries, Spain's urbanization rate – especially while using the 5,000 inhabitant minimum to define a town – was very high, respectively at 23.3% and 24.3%. These figures position Spain as one of the most urbanized countries in Europe during this period, second only to the Northern and Southern Netherlands in the sixteenth century, and to the Netherlands and England and Wales in 1800 (Pérez Moreda & Reher, 1997: 130; Wrigley, 1987: 162; 1990: 107). However, regarding the Spanish case, it should be noted that many of the 'towns' in Andalusia and Murcia then had – as until recently – a high percentage of people employed in agriculture. These so-called agro-towns bring down urbanization rates, not only of those regions but, to a point, of the country for the whole period under analysis (Pérez Moreda & Reher, 2003; Llopis & González Mariscal, 2006).

Naturally, this urban development process was not uniform. As mentioned, growth was much stronger in towns than in the countryside in the sixteenth century. For example, Madrid was a unique case, undergoing very rapid population increase from 1561. Furthermore, other towns in the centre of Castile and Andalusia also experienced remarkable growth in that century. However, demographic decline in the following century was especially hard on Castilian towns (except Madrid, which endured a long-lived stagnation from around 1630). It also had a negative effect on the inland towns of Andalusia, including the biggest of them all, Seville, which recorded a considerable loss of people as a consequence of the 1649 plague. At the same time, the southern towns, on the Mediterranean (Málaga) and Atlantic (Cádiz, around which the first Spanish conurbation would be formed, in the eighteenth century) coasts, started gaining increasing importance.

By the end of the sixteenth century, the territories of the former Crown of Aragon (Aragon, Catalonia, Valencia and Balearic Islands) showed a feeble urbanization rate, with only five or six towns or population centres over 10,000 people.[49] Notwithstanding, there was very significant urban growth in all the regions of the Mediterranean coast – including in the Atlantic Andalusian provinces of Cádiz and Huelva – while the demographic depression in the inland towns of Castile, which had started in the seventeenth century or even the end of the sixteenth, continued.

In 1787, while many of the old Castilian towns were now reduced to much smaller population levels than they had at the end of the sixteenth century, the highest urbanization rates were in the Mediterranean periphery and Andalusian coast. There was also remarkable relative development of the urban phenomenon in the northern provinces of the Cantabrian coast, where in previous centuries there were practically no real 'towns'. All this is clearly shown by Figure 11.6.

The figures in the *Numeramento de 1527-1532* are sufficient to allow a determination of the urbanization rate in Portugal, and to retrace the urban network at the beginning of the early modern period. Considering the population centres over 5,000 inhabitants, the country's urbanization rate at the time was around 10.3%, placing it at the European average and above that of Western Europe, but significantly below Spain.[50]

In the sixteenth century, Portugal had an uneven urban network, with the various regions displaying different levels of urbanization: the coast particularly the north-west and the Algarve being ahead of the inland territories, and the south prevailing over the north, reflecting an urban tradition dating to the Muslim period, or even further back to the Roman era. This uneven network was also the result of the proliferation of small population centres, the shortage of medium-sized towns, and the polarization of the phenomenon around the city of Lisbon, beyond which there were only much smaller population centres (Godinho, 1977: 39; Serrão, 1996: 72-73; Rodrigues, 2008: 186-189). Throughout the sixteenth century a slow process of concentration of coastal dwellers began, mostly linked to the development of business and overseas trade (Magalhães, 1993; Serrão, 1994: 346; Rodrigues, 2008: 190-191).

Comparing the number of urban centres of over 5,000 people at the beginning of the sixteenth century with the figures available for the end of the seventeenth (1695) or beginning of the eighteenth (1706) shows a significant increase in urban centres. The same is true for the urbanization rate, which, following the same criterium, rises from 10% to 15.2%. This was a general rise, touching all the regions in the country (Serrão, 1996: 72-75; Rodrigues, 2008: 192-193).

---

[49] The capital cities of the four territories of the Crown: Zaragoza, Barcelona, Valencia and Palma de Mallorca, plus Orihuela and maybe Xátiva, in the Kingdom of Valencia. These territories included only 13 towns with at least 5,000 people, that is, 10% of the 131 towns that Spain had at the time (Reher, 1994: 27-29; Pérez Moreda & Reher, 1997: 130).

[50] Rate based on the data from *Numeramento de 1527-1532*, using a coefficient of 4.6 inhabitants/household.

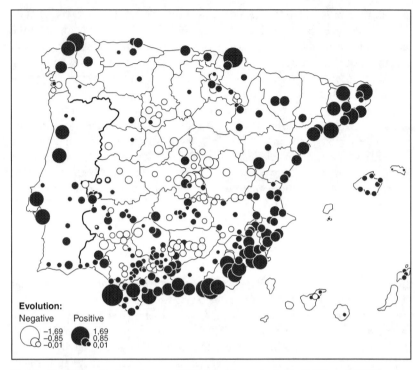

Figure 11.6 Growth of towns over 5,000 inhabitants in Spain (1591 and 1787) and Portugal (1527–1532 and 1801).
Sources: for Spain, Pérez Moreda and Reher (1997: 139). For Portugal, estimated results based on data available in Dias (1998) and Sousa (1979), considering cities with more than 5,000 inhabitants in 1527–1532 and 1801.

Throughout the eighteenth century, urban structuring showed no relevant changes. The proportion of people living in urban centres over 5,000 inhabitants was practically the same (15.2% in 1700 and 14.9% in 1800) and the regional disparities remained. Even so, with this indicator as reference, the Portuguese urbanization rate was still relatively high in European terms. In sum, figures show that the urbanization rate in Portugal tended to stabilize throughout the eighteenth century, in contrast with the fast urban growth between 1527 and 1700 (Serrão, 1993: 62). The authors suggest that, in Portugal – unlike in Northern Europe – population growth was not accompanied by a change in settlement configuration, or by economic transformations able to support urbanization-boosting agricultural productivity (Costa et al., 2014: 219–236).

Once the focus is changed to population distribution, however, the analysis of urban dynamics will take into account not only the percentage of the total population living in urban areas (urbanization rate) but also the morphology of the urban structure or, in other words, the urban system and its infrastructure (Berry, 1961: 573-588; Smith, 1995: 20-42). During this period, the urban structure in Portugal was rather uneven. Imbalances widened between the sixteenth and the eighteenth centuries, and particularly during the latter. These were expressed in the uneven distribution of urbanization rates, urban density and number of urban settlements in the different regions (north-south; coast-inland), as well as their configuration and Lisbon-centric architecture. Lisbon was the greatest city in the kingdom and one of the largest in Europe. According to Bairoch et al., by 1500, the Portuguese capital was the seventh most populous city in the continent, and by 1700 it had risen to fifth, after London, Paris, Naples and Amsterdam, keeping that position until 1750. By then, it was the biggest city in the Iberian Peninsula (Hohenberg & Lees, 1985: 227; Bairoch et al., 1988: 278-280).

In 1527-1532, Lisbon held 5% of the population of the country and more than 40% of the urban population, considering settlements over 5,000 people. The situation was the same in the beginning of the eighteenth century. A century later, 6% of the population was concentrated in Lisbon, which represented 32% of the urban population. Throughout this period, the rate of growth of Lisbon (56%) and Porto (148%) contrasted sharply with the national average (30%) (Serrão, 1993: 62-63). According to Álvaro Ferreira da Silva, 1801 marks the height of Lisbon's primacy relative to the remaining urban centres of the country, but, paradoxically, it also represents the final moments in the evolution of growth and structure Portuguese towns had followed for the three previous centuries (Silva, 1997). From then on, the macrocephaly (Lisbon) became a bicephaly (Lisbon and Porto) (Moreira & Veiga, 2005: 45-46).

The prevailing urban structure during the period under analysis here, together with the lack of a solid network of medium-sized towns, hampered the construction of a nation-wide market around Lisbon and, ultimately, was not favourable to the economic development of the country (Pedreira, 1995: 55). Indeed, the Portuguese urban network at the end of the *Ancien Régime* was marked by the absence of a coherent urban system, which resulted in the fragmentation of the national economic space, compartmentalized into dispersed, poorly integrated markets (Justino, 1989, I: 169-171, 352-356; Pedreira, 1987: 585-586; 1995: 55-56; Costa et al., 2014: 218).

11.4 Socio-Professional Composition

Analysis of the professional activity of the Spanish population can be carried out with a reasonable degree of accuracy, both at regional and national level, based on the 'modern' censuses of Floridablanca (1787) and

Table 11.9 *Sectoral distribution of the active population in Spain, 1797.*

Region	Sector I	%	Sector II	%	Sector III	%	Total
Andalusia	362,487	61.7	92,122	15.7	132,915	22.6	587,524
Castilla la V.	222,764	63.6	55,951	16.0	71,345	20.4	350,060
Castilla la N.	190,390	55.2	58,434	16.9	96,120	27.9	344,944
Galicia	185,262	69.2	28,342	10.6	54,035	20.2	267,639
Valencia	156,103	64.2	46,360	19.1	40,702	16.7	243,165
Catalonia	115,321	52.4	55,138	25.1	49,487	22.5	219,946
Aragon	113,940	63.2	28,191	15.6	38,140	21.2	180,271
León	111,736	66.9	18,061	10.8	37,255	22.3	167,052
Murcia	76,454	59.6	19,877	15.5	31,936	24.9	128,267
Extremadura	85,308	70.4	11,285	9.3	24,529	20.3	121,122
Asturias	60,616	72.0	6,106	7.3	17,512	20.8	84,234
Basque Country	52,974	69.3	8,237	10.8	15,194	19.9	76,405
Navarre	42,091	64.3	10,403	15.9	12,931	19.8	65,425
Balearic Islands	30,605	55.1	8,091	14.6	16,900	30.4	55,596
Canary Islands	27,038	52.5	2,817	5.5	21,611	42.0	51,466
Spain	**1,835,310**	**62.1**	**450,709**	**15.2**	**670,891**	**22.7**	**2,956,910**

Source: Authors' own elaboration of the data from the Godoy Census (1797). With slight differences, this data can also be found in Llopis (2001: 510–511).

especially that of Godoy (1797), that is, at the end point of the period covered by this chapter. However, the results, or those relating to most of the Spanish regions, could be applied without too much risk to at least much of the eighteenth century.

Table 11.9 shows the total values (population employed in each of the three 'classic' or typical sectors of activity), and the percentage with respect to the total active/employed[51] in each historical region, as well as those corresponding to the entire Spanish population. They refer mostly (or almost exclusively) to the adult male population, as female employment and child labour, while very important in some sectors of activity – since it was not limited to the temporary activities of women and children in agricultural tasks – has been obscured in the official sources of the time, and is therefore invisible in the historiography until recently. At this time, it is risky to advance regional and national employment figures that

---

[51] It is practically impossible to differentiate between activity and actual occupation from the official records of this time.

include all ages and overcome gender bias, although there are interesting local and provincial studies in this regard.[52] Nonetheless, the data in the chart allows the already proto-industrial level of the Catalan region to be highlighted, followed to a lesser extent, by that of Valencia, in comparison to the rest of the country, which was predominantly agrarian. This data should undoubtedly serve as a starting point for the analysis of economic activity, which can be followed with increasing precision through population censuses and other official statistics from the mid-nineteenth century onwards.

Portuguese historiography does not have equivalent sources. However, in a recent study, Palma and Reis began by cross-referencing estimates of the general and urban population with data and studies on the population's occupational structure in certain periods and geographical spaces, in order to reconstruct the population that was dedicated to the two basic economic sectors – agriculture and non-agriculture – between 1500 and 1850 (Table 11.10). It should be noted that, as in Spain, sources in this period take the family as a fiscal unit, referring only to the primary, but not necessarily exclusive, activity of the head of the household, not taking into account the work of women and children, introducing some bias in the analysis (Sá, 2005: 96–104). In addition, the data considers the total population, not just the active population. Even so, it

Table 11.10 *Portuguese population by sectors.*

Year	Urban (1)	Rural non-agricultural (2)	Agricultural (3)	Total non-agricultural (4) (1) + (2)	Agricultural (5) %
1500	0.155	0.169	0.676	0.324	68
1550	0.193	0.205	0.877	0.398	69
1600	0.242	0.318	1.277	0.560	70
1650	0.267	0.512	1.369	0.779	64
1700	0.293	0.672	1.384	0.965	59
1750	0.429	0.721	1.325	1.150	54
1800	0.476	0.848	1.612	1.324	55

Notes: millions of inhabitants in columns (1), (2), (3) and (4); % in column (5). Urban (1) corresponds to population >5,000.
Source: Palma and Reis (2019: 483–485).

---

[52] On female labour, see Sarasúa García (1997), Humphries and Sarasúa (2012) and Hernández García (2013a). On child labour, see Sarasúa (2013) and Hernández García (2013b).

is an important advance in the knowledge of the occupational structure of the Portuguese population during the *Ancien Régime*.

First, this analysis shows that between 1500 and 1800 the majority of the male labour force was engaged in agricultural work, which held an overwhelming weight in the country's economy (Sá, 2005: 96-104). The diachronic reading of the data makes it possible to capture some changes in the socioeconomic structure and conclude that, between 1500 and 1700, around 60% to 70% of the population was linked to this activity (a percentage in line with the figure calculated for Spain at the end of the eighteenth century). In 1750 and 1800, this percentage dropped to 55 and 54%, respectively, a value below that of both Spain for the same period, and later periods in Portugal (Palma & Reis, 2019). It is possible to conclude that imperial expansion had a significant impact on the economic weight of agriculture only in the eighteenth century, during the colonial expansion in Brazil and that the higher productivity of secondary and tertiary sectors gained ground from 1500 to 1750, slowing after 1750 (Palma & Reis, 2019: 484-485). This trend is in line with previous conclusions on population growth and the rate of urbanization in Portugal, allowing us to chronologically situate a relative loss of dynamism in the trend of economic and demographic growth when compared with some regions in Europe, in the second half of the eighteenth century.

11.5 Conclusion

In the three centuries of the early modern period that elapse between 1500 and 1800, the Spanish population passed through the three major phases that characterize, with variable intensity, most European populations: growth in the sixteenth century; stagnation or depression in the seventeenth; and new growth in the eighteenth. The growth of the sixteenth century was general and intense; the recession of the seventeenth century – which persisted especially during the first half of the century – was acute in the Spanish interior regions, particularly affecting the cities; and the recovery of the eighteenth century was more modest, with an annual growth rate in the order of 0.4%, lower than that of the sixteenth century. Throughout the entire period (1591-1787), the average annual growth was only 0.22%, and even lower in the Castilian interior (0.17%), when compared to the Aragonese Crown (0.41%) or the northern Cantabrian provinces (>0.50%). From the middle or the end of the seventeenth century, a greater growth can be observed in the Mediterranean provinces and the Andalusian coasts, accompanied by a gradual process of urbanization, in contrast to the sluggishness of the inland urban world.

But the signs of modernization of the demographic regime remain weak and scattered, limited almost exclusively to a slight easing of mortality. There are also partial changes in the professional structure of the population, which at least since the second half of the eighteenth century shows itself as progressively less agrarian and more 'industrial' in regions such as Catalonia or, to a lesser extent, Valencia. The process of ruralization and the 'emptying' of interior Spain seems to have its roots in the 'crisis' of the seventeenth century, and from the end of that century or from the beginning of the eighteenth a clear advantage has been observed in the processes of urbanization and economic modernization of peripheral regions.

In Portugal, the population grew rapidly during the period under consideration. The number of total inhabitants rose from around 1,088 million in 1527, the earliest available national figure, to 2,893 million in 1801. However, this period was marked by different rhythms, intensities and dynamics. As in Spain, the sixteenth century was marked globally by a strong demographic dynamism. In the seventeenth century, as with Spain and Europe in general, the dynamics of growth eased, although Portugal stood out, showing a higher growth intensity than the European average. The eighteenth century, in turn, was marked by growth, although it is possible to detect two different dynamics, first of growth and then of deceleration. It is important to point out that between 1500 and 1800 there was considerable regional variation in terms of total population, density, growth and degree of urbanization. The north of the country and the coast were more populous than the south and the interior, and these differences increased from the sixteenth to the eighteenth century, with the same happening to the density.

The comparative analysis of the demographic dynamics of the two Iberian countries showed that overall, despite some differences in pace, Spain and Portugal showed similar growth dynamics and, in general, in line with European trends. The inequality in growth of the different regions that make up the two countries was also evident, with a common pattern emerging, according to which the accentuated demographic and urban dynamism of coastal areas contrasts with the stagnation of inland regions. The reading of the data in the Iberian table also made it possible to detect other similarities and continuities, such as the demographic dynamism of the northern regions, which, despite significant emigration, continued to show strong growth, and the division between north and south of the peninsula with regard to nuptiality indicators, highlighting the relevance of studying Iberian historical demography in a comparative regional perspective.

12

Institutions and Policy, 1500–1800

MAFALDA SOARES DA CUNHA, FRANCISCO GIL MARTÍNEZ
AND ANA SOFIA RIBEIRO

12.1 Introduction

This chapter analyses the institutional architecture and political reforms of the Iberian monarchies from the sixteenth century to the end of the eighteenth century with the aim of providing a contribution to the discussion on the possible causes of their limited institutional change in the eighteenth century. As a result of the many studies that have been produced there seems to be some agreement as to the existence of signs of divergence between European political units from the mid seventeenth century and throughout the eighteenth century. Some researchers point to the Dutch and British institutional models in order to provide justification for this, but the issue is not straightforward (Acemoglu et al., 2005). The monarchies of Spain and Portugal have been characterized as absolutist regimes since the sixteenth century. They were supported by powerful privileged groups that influenced the Royal Court to obtain economic advantages by controlling monopolistic economic enterprises. The administrative structure of Iberian monarchies was settled in a multitude of political institutions which heavily constrained an effective state power that would allow measures for improving economic growth and state fiscal capacity (North, 1990; Bonney, 1995; Hough & Grier, 2015).

Section 12.2 describes the main characteristics of the constitutional framework of the monarchies of Spain and Portugal up until the end of the seventeenth century. We explain how until the end of the century both countries followed the corporate, or jurisdictional, institutional model, whose rationale was aimed at the harmonious functioning of the system as a whole. It is argued that the use of this model implied the existence of institutional mechanisms aimed at ensuring political participation by the different social bodies, as well as negotiation between the various entities involved, while protecting the rights belonging to and acquired by each. It is

This study received domestic funding from the Foundation for Science and Technology under project UIDB/00057/2020. The authors are grateful to Francisco Andújar Castillo, who reviewed the text and provided comments, and Michael W. Lewis, who translated it from the original Portuguese.

also suggested that the constitutional framework responded in a particularly effective and innovative way in adapting to successive changes in the social and economic context, although the legal guarantee of acquired rights also conferred on it a certain degree of rigidity.

In Section 12.3, this idea is explored through the analysis of the constraints that political culture imposed on the capacity of the Iberian crowns and their main social orders for tax collection. It is noteworthy, however, that in times of heightened financial tension the jurisdictional institutional structure did not preclude the introduction of effective new tax arrangements, while the coexistence of different tax collection systems imposed financial constraints on the monarchy's freedom of political action.

In the final section, Section 12.4, the negative consequences of this financial pressure and its impact on the progressive erosion of the jurisdictional political model are dealt with. We show how this institutional model underwent changes in the eighteenth century partially due to the reduction of the institutional diversity and the active promotion of territorial institutional uniformity of the Iberian political units. Whether these reforms had significant impacts will be questioned.

12.2 Constitutional Framework

The institutional architecture of the Iberian monarchies from the sixteenth to the eighteenth centuries was shaped by the evolution of their territorial configuration as it was dependent not only on their capacity for imperial expansion but also the power strategies that played out in the international arena. The sixteenth and seventeenth centuries marked the period during which the monarchies achieved their maximum territorial reach and dispersion. Spatial discontinuity was a predominant feature of the Portuguese overseas empire, the zones of occupation extending to the Atlantic islands of Madeira, the Azores, Cape Verde, and São Tomé and Príncipe, as well as coastal enclaves on the American, African and Asian continents. This contrasted with the huge continuous extension of the Spanish overseas empire, with large-scale occupation of the Americas from the beginning of the sixteenth century (Bethencourt and Curto, 2007; Elliott, 2007; Cardim & Hespanha, 2018; Yun-Casalilla, 2019). The European territories of the Spanish empire were also characterized by discontinuity, but their incorporation of these territories took place between the mid fifteenth century and the third quarter of the sixteenth century, with the exception of the dominions of the Kingdom of Aragon within the Iberian Peninsula.

Whereas the extent and importance of the Portuguese and Spanish empires boosted the prestige of the Iberian kingdoms on the global political stage, especially in Europe, their institutional architecture also posed enormous challenges for the two kingdoms, while there was also a marked economic impact. Their pre-existing European institutional frameworks did not offer readily adaptable models of governance, especially in view of the multi-territorial configuration of the overseas imperial territories.

The political culture of the era featured a distinction drawn between territories added by means of conquest and those that were integrated through the process of aggregation. In the case of the former, the imposition of models of government by the conquerors on the vanquished was regarded as legitimate. This was the case throughout the Middle Ages, during which the Christians conquered the Muslim territories of the Iberian Peninsula, and this model was later applied to the extra-European territories of the two kingdoms. In the case of the Portuguese overseas empire, its governance structures were established from the mid fifteenth century, and the pace of this process accelerated from the first half of the following century with the establishment of Portuguese settings and factories in Asia, Brazil and Africa. With regard to Spanish America, the structure of the institutional framework was established during the early sixteenth century. Thus, in the conquered territories, mostly located in the overseas empire, the establishment of the legal framework and institutional structures was marked by a process of continuity, with the adoption of medieval Iberian models (as detailed in Chapter 4).

The aggregated territories had a history of political autonomy and had been incorporated into the Iberian kingdoms because of dynastic policies and unforeseen successional circumstances. While all these territories owed allegiance to a single monarch, each retained its own jurisdiction or, in the parlance of the era, their customs, *fueros*, freedoms and particular privileges, which covered languages, borders, currency, legal and tax systems, institutional arrangements, and *Cortes* or parliaments. It should also be noted that aggregation processes were, in general, previously agreed with the parliaments of the different territories. Under the authority of the Castilian monarch, the principle of diversity is evident not only in relation to the Crown of Castile but also to the Crown of Aragon associated with Catalonia, Valencia and Mallorca, Naples, Sicily, and Sardinia, and also Milan, the Low Countries and, from 1580 to 1640, the Crown of Portugal. The model of political governance thus created was described by Felipe II (1556–1598) as *reinos juntos, pero apartados* – kingdoms together but separate – and designated by historians as composite monarchy, multiple kingdoms or aggregation monarchy (Elliott, 1992, Gil Pujol, 2012; Cardim et al., 2019). However, this style of governance, rather than deriving from Iberian particularism of any kind, was a consequence of the political culture of the time and was present in many other European political units, as may be observed in the case of Great Britain, where Scotland was an aggregated kingdom and Ireland a conquered territory, or even the Holy Roman Empire of the German Nation (Elliott, 2018).

In addition to the legal basis for the persistence of particular customs in each territory, the contemporary political culture was also characterized by a natural law and organicist conception of the monarchical political body. The head of state was the king who, in addition to representing all the territories, had as his main role striving for the harmonious functioning of each part of the corporate bodies, 'attributing to each what is due to it, while guaranteeing the status of each (jurisdiction, rights and privileges); in sum, ensuring that justice is done' (Hespanha, 1993: 123). Thus, society was regarded as comprising a group of corporate states, or bodies, each having its own jurisdiction and, therefore, capacity for self-government. In the wake of the historiographic renovation fostered by A. M. Hespanha and B. Clavero, among other authors, the consequences of this corporate conception of society have been clearly set out: 'society ended up comprising a cluster of juxtaposed and coexisting corporate bodies, which communicated with each other through jurisdictional channels' (Cardim, 1998: 19). Moreover, in accordance with this system, the king was bound to ensure the participation of the different corporate groups in governance through the specialized representative bodies of the different jurisdictions that comprised the monarchy (the councils, the Parliaments, the courts, the municipalities, the professional guilds, etc.).

The constitutional framework was, hence, built to govern *ex post* rather than *ex ante*; all political action was oriented to solve conflicts between distinct spheres of interests, observing and maintaining the harmony of the monarchy and the social order. It did not intervene or regulate aprioristically.

The monarchies of Castile and Portugal met the challenge with great efficiency and flexibility by maintaining in existence a plurality of jurisdictional systems both in European territories and in the overseas. It should be stressed, however, that the concrete formula for the application of these principles was also conditioned by the scarcity of material and human resources for ruling the two empires from afar, characterized as they were by their vast extension, extreme dispersal and deep-rooted political and cultural diversity (Santos and Lobato, 2006).

In accordance with such a political conception, Iberian kingdoms were able to provide an institutional response at an early stage. Territorial councils were set up to represent each aggregated political unit, and thematic councils were established with jurisdiction over the entire empire, as it existed, for example, Councils of State, the Treasury and War. In both types of councils two distinct roles coexisted: the administration of a territory or a specific domain and the resolution of conflicts concerning certain aspects, as the Council of Indies, Council of War or the Council of the Inquisition, in Spanish domains. In the Spanish case, apart from the Council of Navarre, which was based in Pamplona, all these bodies were located at the royal court and exercised advisory functions based on a collegial decision-making process. This meant that reports issued by the councillors on the range of matters dealt with by each council were used by the king for decision-making purposes, and the most important were discussed in the Council of State.

The system of conciliar government was also followed in Portugal from the early sixteenth century and, although councils were institutionalized a little later, a similar organizational structure was employed. However, in stark contrast to the situation in Castile, the king of Portugal ruled a territory that in Europe coincided almost entirely with the limits of a single kingdom, while other Portuguese dominions were the result of extra-European conquests. That is why it took such a long time for a council to be set up in Portugal with jurisdiction over all the overseas possessions, the *Conselho Ultramarino* (Overseas Council), although there were much earlier institutional experiences (as the ephemeral Council of India [1604–1614]). However, the consolidation of the Portuguese institutional system only occurred after the separation from Castile with the establishment of the War Council on 11 December 1640, the Overseas Council in 1642 and the *Junta dos Três Estados* – Board of Three States – in 1643. All these bodies sought to address the pressing military, economic and tax-collection issues that the new Braganza dynasty faced, and they survived well beyond the Restoration War also called the War of Independence of Portugal (1640–1668). Thus, it is worth noting that the Spanish-style institutional model persisted in Portugal despite the dynastic change.

Historians have designated this form of government the polysynodial system, reflecting the idea that rather than ruling alone the king should rule with the active participation of a number of different political bodies. A general appraisal shows that the evolution of the range of councils and courts throughout the sixteenth and seventeenth centuries reveals a tendency for the widening of their scope of action, and growing organizational complexity, marked by an increase in the number of officials and a rise in operating costs. This indicates the vibrant expansion of the central government bureaucratic structure (Tomás Valiente, 1982: 1–214; Hespanha, 1994: 259–294). From the point of view of the political goals that the administrative apparatus aimed to achieve, matters of justice remained pre-eminent, despite the increasing pressure of military affairs caused by the European wars in which the Spanish monarchy had been involved from the sixteenth century and, from 1640 onwards, also with Portugal. This led to increased priority for matters regarding the treasury (finance and taxation) and the military apparatus. Equally worthy of note is the remarkable stability of this system of governance in the two kingdoms, which remained fully functional until at least the early eighteenth century. The jurisdictional character of the system and the overlapping competences of bodies, however, generated serious institutional conflict, besides the unwieldiness and slowness of the decision-making process. To overcome these difficulties, the Iberian monarchies frequently resorted to an institutional expedient designed to increase control over the execution of certain matters – juntas or boards – which led to a great deal of opposition among council members. Comprised of people who were close to the king, the juntas ensured the effectiveness of the executive action of the Crown and indicate what some authors characterize as a gradual abandonment of the jurisdictional model in favour of an administrative-type model (Subtil, 2010; Cardim et al., 2019). Whatever the case, it should be emphasized that the modus operandi of the council system contributed towards limiting attempts by individual councils and the interest groups associated with them to assume a dominant role.

But the jurisdictional system of government was still evident in the way the political-administrative system was organized in the territories, and especially at the local level, with the *concelhos* or municipalities in Portugal, the *concejos* of the Castilian system, the *cabildos* in the Spanish Indies and the *consells* of Aragon, which some contemporary authors also term *respublicas* (Herrero Sánchez, 2017). They were a feature of all the Iberian territories and were also present in the extra-European dominions, providing an important means for self-government and self-regulation, which historians today recognize as being incompatible with the argument in favour of the ongoing centralization of monarchical power. In fact, the municipalities had their own privileges and local governmental structures, regulated by agreements between communities and the king or the landlords which, in most cases, had medieval origins (*cartas de foral* or *ordenanzas* – charters). Municipalities were extremely variable in size although they tended to be smaller in northern regions of the peninsula and were characterized by a high degree of institutional uniformity within the Iberian space. In the case of Portugal, the town council (*vereação*) was elected by local people who were members of the elites in each municipality, and the result of the election was later approved by the monarch or by landlords. In the case of Castile, *regidorias* were subject to election or appointment, or sold, and it is noteworthy that the degree of venality of such positions increased from the seventeenth century onwards. In Aragon, *jurados* were subject to a raffle proceeding (*insaculación*) within the members of local oligarchies. Day-to-day administration was carried out by a wide variety of officials whose rights to these positions were gradually transferred to their holders, thus becoming their personal assets, which contributed to accentuating social distinctions in such territories.

Local municipal governments issued local laws (*posturas* and *ordenanzas*), they were invested with judicial powers in the first instance and administrative responsibilities, and also played a significant role in matters of sanitation, taxation and economic governance in the local region, the last of these including the licensing of services, price fixing, supplying essential goods, holding fairs and markets, and the management of community resources. In Portugal, a third of the sum of the revenues collected locally on assets in each municipality was transferred to the Crown for the purpose of carrying out defence works.

At the same time, of key importance were responsibilities assigned to the municipalities for the distribution and collection of certain general taxes in the

Iberian kingdoms, as was the case of *sisas* in Portugal and *alcabalas* in Spain. Of medieval origin, these taxes were levied on individuals at the rate of 10% on all private transactions, though de facto at a wide variety of rates across jurisdictions and goods. In Portugal, from the sixteenth century to the late eighteenth century, members of the clergy were exempt, unlike in Castile, where the nobility was not exempt and members of the clergy only paid if transactions were not mercantile in nature, as in the case of donations, for example, while they tried as hard as they could to circumvent the tax.

As so many authors have pointed out, one of the main aims of local governance was achieving economic self-sufficiency for the community, with the maintenance of fiscal barriers between municipalities, thus contributing to the non-regional and anti-regional character of their political action (Magalhães, 1994). Indeed, despite the high degree of uniformity of the basic legal framework, the defence of particularism at the municipal level was a recurring theme in petitions put forward by residents, complaints made by municipal representatives in the parliaments against repeated abuses by royal and seigneurial officials and also the grievances of residents of neighbouring municipalities regarding the illegal use of common resources (e.g. pasture or water). The political representation of these urban bodies in the *Cortes* in Portugal and Aragon resulted from the election of representatives of the Povo, the Third Estate or cities, while their private communication with the royal court was also able to be conducted in a permanent manner through agents based there. The same occurred in Castile, with the particularity that cities and their appointed agents were the only members of the *Cortes*. Municipalities could, however, appoint and send agents to negotiate directly with the king, a good example being the ambassador that the city of Naples sent to the court of Carlos II (1665–1700) (Álvarez-Ossorio, 2016).

The nobility and the clergy, and the Church as an institution, played an important role in the jurisdictional system. Although these groups were made up of an extremely wide range of members in terms of social status, political power and wealth, the picture of false homogeneity that is attributed to them stems from the medieval trifunctional representative portrayal of society that persisted in the legal order of the Iberian kingdoms as well as in the system of representation in the *Cortes* throughout the early modern period. What differentiated these groups from the rest of society was their privileged legal status, which meant that, in contrast with members of the Third Estate, they benefited from certain fiscal, judicial and military privileges. Yet there was a tendency for the extent of their tax exemption to decrease, especially regarding taxes which were levied on the population in general, such as *sisas* and *alcabalas*, and later *décimas* in Portugal (1641).

The relationship between the Iberian monarchies and the Church contributed to empower the Crowns. First, the papal privileges of Royal Patronage granted first to Portugal (1455) and then to Castile (1486–1523) meant that

Iberian monarchs were the patrons and protectors of the Church in their respective territories, and thus emerged as an answer to the lack of ecclesiastical structures and evangelization activities in the new conquered overseas territories. The monarch had the right to nominate the bishops and other clerics, and manage the ecclesiast administrative territories both within European territories – in this case, from the eighteenth century onwards – and within their respective overseas domains. These prerogatives meant an increase of expenses for Iberian Treasuries, but also legitimized the collection of part of the parish tithes in favour of the Crowns, although in Portugal only in its imperial domains. Still, the Castilian privilege soon became wider and a stronger regalist position of the Crown appeared during the early sixteenth century, reaching its zenith during the eighteenth century, since the *Patronato Regio* became an 'inherent right of Crown' rather than a pontifical concession (Egido, 2011; Xavier and Olival, 2018).

One of the duties of the *Patronato* was to maintain the unity of the catholic faith and the zeal for religious orthodoxy. In such pursuit, the Iberian crowns were responsible for the creation of the Inquisition, first in Castile and Aragon and later in Portugal (1536). Inquisitorial tribunals strove for the homogeneity of faith in their respective Iberian dominions (the home country and the overseas territories), thus signalling the inseparable link between political and religious aims. However, these tribunals were extremely territorialized and decentralized institutions which determined that the targets of their religious persecutions varied across time and space. How great their economic impact was is a matter of debate, but it seems safe to say that the trend towards the exclusion of New Christian minorities traditionally involved in the commercial and financial life of the two monarchies had an impact on the level of reproduction of mercantile groups and that the expulsion of the *Moriscos* (1604–1619) led to fluctuations in the health of the agricultural sector, which had up until then been extremely dynamic in southern and eastern regions of the peninsula. Although rural population decreased in former *Moriscos* areas, recent literature points out a long-term increase in agricultural output and output per capita in those regions due to the persistence of a severe extractive system imposed by landlords upon *Moriscos* farmers. The system had been created previously to 1609 as a means for social distinction and stigmatization (Chaney & Hornbeck, 2016).

The most significant indicator of the prominence of the nobility and clergy is the wide extension of their jurisdictional power in the dominions of Iberian kingdoms, which resulted both in the capacity for political control of these territories and revenues that they derived from them. The area under the jurisdiction of Aragonese nobles in the early sixteenth century is estimated at around 28.5% of the kingdom, which had increased to 40% by the early nineteenth century (Abadía Irache, 2017). In Portugal, meanwhile, the proportion of seigneurial jurisdictions rose from 38% in the early sixteenth century to 44% in 1640, thereafter declining sharply as they were absorbed into the royal domain (Monteiro, 1996: 54). As for ecclesiastical landownership, it is estimated that in the mid eighteenth century it accounted for between 16% and 17% of the total territory of the Spanish monarchy (Barrio Gozalo, 2002: 76-77), in stark contrast with the figures for Portugal in the mid seventeenth century, as presented by A. M. Hespanha (1994: 429-30), who attributed no more than 4% of the area of the kingdom to them.

The clergy and the nobility remained, along with municipalities, the main political interlocutors of the monarchy until the end of the *Ancien Régime*, as kings entrusted them with a wide range of senior government positions among which were the organizational structures of the polysynodial system, the most important military and diplomatic posts and the main overseas government offices.

The coincidence of government elites and privileged orders tended to become more nuanced in the peninsula from the early seventeenth century, although for Portugal this was the case only in the second half of the century. As we shall see, reforms of the eighteenth century led to a progressive exhaustion of decision-making functions of councils and higher courts. State secretariats emerged as the central organ for governance, and those who were most powerful in the Iberian monarchies gradually lost influence to professional political staff recruited from much less select social strata (Subtil, 1993; Monteiro, 2003).

The participation of the various social orders in the political decision-making processes mentioned above is particularly evident in the *Cortes* or *Corts* (parliaments) in the Iberian territories. Continuing with practices that had medieval origins, these assemblies were convened by Iberian monarchs throughout the sixteenth and seventeenth centuries and were always held in the respective territories. Following the *Nueva Planta* decrees, the eighteenth-century *Cortes* of Castile became the *Cortes generales*, or general assembly, with representatives from the other territories of the Spanish monarchy (except for Navarre), even though the matters dealt with mainly concerned succession issues. While in Aragon four estates sat, although with a clear predominance of seigneurial power, in the Portuguese and Castilian *Cortes* the nobility, clergy and commoners were represented. Meanwhile, it should be noted that in the Kingdom of Castile from 1538, the parliament excluded privileged groups, comprising only the Third Estate, with representatives of the 16 main cities, increasing to 18 in the seventeenth century.

In at least one territory, the Kingdom of Aragon, such assemblies had effective legislative functions, while in others (the Kingdoms of Castile and Portugal) they had a merely consultative role. But the operational model characterized by separate orders was common to all of them in keeping with the above-mentioned corporate or jurisdictional conception of society, in accordance with the historical trifunctional system. Although the purpose of some assemblies was solely to swear in the crown prince, especially in Spain during the eighteenth century (Lorenzana, 2014), according to some authors, the issues that took up most time were the introduction of new fiscal measures (Henriques & Palma, 2023) and requests for financial aid addressed to cities in the kingdom. They were also a key space for the presentation of the complaints, grievances and demands of the different social groups represented. These assemblies' negotiations regarding the amount and manner of distribution of tax-collection responsibilities were invariably tense, and concessions would have been made by both parties. The frequency with which assemblies were held varied over time and according to territory. The parliament of Castile met more frequently than those of Aragon and Portugal. However, because of their institutional structure, the Castilian assemblies had less power of revindication in fiscal matters than that of Aragon. Nonetheless, it is worthwhile underlining that between 1588 and 1590 King Philip II negotiated with the Castilian *Cortes* for the amount and form of collection of a tax of 8 million *maravedis* over a six-year period. The *Millones* were levied upon the consumption of wine, olive oil, meat and vinegar, and the cities imposed that the money should be managed by a joint group of representatives of the Crown and the cities of Castile, called the *Cámara de Millones*. Despite the Castilian *Cortes* being rarely assembled since the end of the seventeenth century, the *Cámara de Millones* or *Sala de Millones* persisted until the liberal regime was instituted in Spain. Whatever the case, throughout the Iberian Peninsula the *Cortes* constituted institutional arrangements that provided not only for the political participation of the different social groups but also an important opportunity for the king to consult the different communities. This evidence enables some authors to discuss the role of the parliaments as an embryonic space for public participation, while recognizing that these assemblies effectively limited the exercise of discretionary power by monarchs (Fernández Albaladejo, 1992; Cardim, 1998; Fortea, 2008).

12.3 Fiscal Policy and the Social Distribution of Taxation

The financial resources providing for the governance of the Iberian kingdoms derived from several different sources. Regarding crown resources, the medieval political theory with scholastic origins that persisted until the early eighteenth century held that the king should live on his own revenue deriving from his properties and rights. Since there was no separation between the king's wealth and that of the kingdom, it was assumed that the king should finance crown expenses out of his own personal income. If this was not sufficient, then he should resort to taxation, which had to be lawful and fair; these two conditions decisively affected the scope of the imposition of new taxes, requiring prior consent by those affected and ensuring that ethical and religious norms were considered. At the same time, agreement on the applicability of the domestic *oeconomia* model to the governance of the kingdom, including the duty of liberality, also affected political and financial government. The royal obligation to make donations and provide remuneration was an inherent part of the bargain with vassals for the rendering of services to the Crown. This question is particularly important in providing an explanation for constant royal donations (including seigneurial rights, pensions, *mercedes* and titles of the military orders), which were aimed at preserving social harmony in the two monarchies (Yun-Casalilla, 2004; Hespanha, 2013).

A breakdown of Crown revenues shows the following items: the king's personal assets, taxes, *servicios* (extraordinary financial help for the Crown requested by the monarch), *estancos* or monopolies, and convictions, patronage rights or other extraordinary sources of income. The first of these included mainly revenues from kings' properties (rural and urban), and the royal rights set out in charters, as well as revenues from salt production and mines (exploration rights over the gold or silver mining), among other items. Revenues were almost always paid in kind and gradually diminished in economic importance. Some were donated by the king to private individuals or given in return for services rendered.

In addition to these forms of revenue, in the case of Castile, there were shipments of precious metals, mainly silver sent to the home country from the Americas. Although silver commerce was not a Crown monopoly, taxes levied on the shipment of bullion and seignorage provided an essential means by which the Crown earned income and met its financial commitments. Revenues associated with silver extraction and trade accounted for 22% of Crown revenue in 1566 and remained at around 20% of the total throughout the following century (Tortella and Comín, 2001). Despite a continuous increase in the Indies silver output during the eighteenth century, most of the silver remained in the Americas. Less than 11% of the extraction reached the Spanish central Treasury in the second half of the century, with the exception of the decade of 1790 (TePaske, 2010; Torres Sánchez, 2015).

Tables 12.1 and 12.2 divide the revenues of the Iberian monarchies into direct and indirect taxation and consider different units of account in the case of Castile. Within the typology of direct revenues are included rights of exploration owed by the monarch, patrimonial and ecclesiastical taxes, and every tax levied upon different income sources, or fixed amounts of extraordinary subsidies imposed or negotiated by the Crowns (*servicios*, *subsídios* or *fintas*); indirect taxation covers taxes upon consumption, monopolies and customs rights. In both the Hispanic territories and Portugal, indirect taxation revenues prevailed between the sixteenth and the eighteenth centuries until the beginning of the Napoleonic Wars in the Peninsula, despite a progressive trend of growth in total fiscal revenue, namely from the eighteenth century and in nominal terms.

Table 12.1 *Fiscal revenues of the Hispanic monarchy, 1560–1805 (without imperial revenues). Nominal values.*

Coin unit	Year	Direct taxation revenues Nominal	%	Indirect taxation revenues Nominal	%	Total fiscal revenues
Maravedis	1560	151,500,000	15.8	804,375,000	84.2	955,875,000
	1577	619,494,000	25.2	1,840,135,880	74.8	2,459,629,880
	1599	824,207,133	30.5	1,878,830,490	69.5	2,703,037,623
	1613	823,884,000	21.4	3,027,000,000	78.6	3,850,884,000
	1640	634,078,000	12.1	4,622,029,000	87.9	5,256,107,000
	1666	611,857,000	10.5	5,198,209,000	89.5	5,810,066,000
	1688	556,765,000	16.2	2,882,529,000	83.8	3,439,294,000
Reales de vellon	1713	5,657,138	6.4	82,192,166	93.6	87,849,304
	1750	47,995,176	18.1	216,668,056	81.9	264,663,232
	1779	61,611,822	21.3	227,796,535	78.7	289,408,357
	1790	61,153,684	11	493,378,006	89	554,531,690
	1805	47,623,114	10	427,655,302	90	475,278,416

Sources: Artola (1982); Merino (1987); Andrés and Lanza (2009); Drelichman and Voth (2010); Torres Sánchez (2015).

Table 12.2 *Fiscal revenues of Portugal, 1527–1804 (réis)(without imperial revenues).*

Year	Direct taxation revenues Nominal	%	Indirect taxation revenues Nominal	%	Total fiscal revenues
1527	5,570,000	3.2	169,471,000	96.8	175,041,000
1588	74,044,588	14.3	443,168,919	85.7	517,213,507
1607	86,248,080	9.5	825,146,350	90.5	911,394,430
1619	135,713,646	16.2	701,629,941	83.8	837,343,587
1640–1645	592,000,000	46.8	674,114,651	53.2	1,269,514,651
1660	720,000,000	40.2	1,068,959,000	59.8	1,788,959,000
1680	223,938,248	13.9	1,390,082,865	86.1	1,614,021,113
1730	600,000,000	12.6	4,156,000,000	87.4	4,756,000,000
1766	851,218,830	20.6	3,278,308,927	79.4	4,129,527,757
1804	1,454,000,000	15	8,211,000,000	85	9,665,000,000

Source: Costa et al. (2022).

Within indirect taxes, the most relevant source of revenues for the Iberian crowns was *sisas* in Portugal and *alcabalas* in Spain. In the sixteenth century, *sisas* were one of the main sources of Portuguese Crown revenues covering budgetary expenditure. It is estimated that in the first half of the seventeenth century they still accounted for 40% of Portugal's domestic revenue, although it had declined to about 10% by the end of the century (Hespanha, 1994: 141); by 1717 it had dropped to 5.2%, and in 1804 accounted for a mere 3.4% (Macedo, 1982a). The main reason for the initial fall was changes in the form of collection that, at the request of the *Povos*, or Third Estate, were set out in a contract drawn up by the *Cortes* (parliament) of 1525. It replaced the system of collection of a variable amount at the local level, corresponding to 10% of the value of all transactions, with the collection of a fixed amount charged at the municipal level and sometimes farmed out to private individuals: the *cabeção das sisas*. Now, while this system produced predictable annual revenues for the royal treasury, the rise in the prices of commodities led to a continuous need to update the totals agreed with municipalities, reducing the importance of this tax on internal commercial transactions in the overall assessment of Crown revenues, in the long run. This is why such updates were the subject of several rounds of negotiations with the Povos in the parliaments, but, as already mentioned, they never regained their previous level of budgetary importance. For municipalities, such agreements had more positive effects, since the difference between what was actually charged and that which was contracted to be paid (*sobejos*, or the remainder of the revenues from *sisas*) accounted for a significant proportion of municipal income (Hespanha, 1994; Silva, 2015).

The situation regarding Castilian *alcabalas* was similar: in 1522 they accounted for the main source of revenue for the Real Hacienda – the royal treasury – 53.5% of total revenues collected, while in the late sixteenth century, the figure fell to a mere 20%. In addition, as in the case of Portugal, this tax was increasingly collected by means of *encabezamientos*, which were institutionalized during the reign of Charles V (1516–1556/1558) with the Encabezamiento General de Alcabalas and later fixed definitively in 1636 (Carande, 1987). It is difficult to assess the value of this tax in the eighteenth century. Due to the reorganization of the Spanish treasury, *alcabalas* along with *millones* and other taxes paid at the local level, were associated in the subtreasury of *rentas provinciales*. Several authors have shown that *alcabalas* made up the largest portion of these sources of revenue. Thus, as we know that *rentas provinciales* accounted for 20% of revenues from 1753 to 1765, decreasing in 1807 to 13.7%, *alcabalas* also gradually lost their importance as a source of revenue in Spain (Pieper, 1992).

Periods during which there was an increase in military expenditure by monarchies invariably placed extraordinary demands on a kingdom's finances, especially when they coincided with periods during which there was a decrease or stagnation in taxation on foreign trade. For the Castilian monarchy these demands led to the introduction of *servicios de millones*, approved by successive parliaments as an extraordinary measure. The *servicio de 8 millones* approved in 1590 started out as a temporary measure, but was successively renewed and then increased, becoming one of the main sources of income of the Crown, so that by the mid seventeenth century it accounted for around 30% of overall Crown revenues (Andrés & Lanza, 2009). This *servicio de millones* was not only dependent on the approval of the parliament but its collection was also managed by local oligarchies, who decided what taxes were to be paid in order that the amounts agreed might be reached. The same occurred with other types of *servicios*, and this taxation mechanism persisted up until the eighteenth century. This provides further evidence for the central role played by municipalities in the Castilian tax system, as mentioned above. However, in the eighteenth century they became (although informally) permanent taxes, since the reunion of the *Cortes* to negotiate them was no longer convened.

The taxation revenues growth, first from the beginning of the seventeenth century until mid-century, then during the eighteenth century, is marked by three main strategies followed by the Iberian crowns. Until the reign of Philip IV (1621–1665) the main strategy used to increase treasury revenues was to increase the tax-burden by creating new additional taxation, mainly indirect, although some first attempts at income taxation should be pointed out. It should also be stressed that tax increases sometimes went against the established constitutional principle of the need for prior approval by the *Cortes* – for example, the introduction of the *media-anata*, a tax involving the retention of half the annual income of royal officials assessed at the time at which each royal favour was granted, and a stamp-impressed paper tax levied on bureaucratic operations regardless of the social status of those in whose name they were carried out. Other extraordinary arrangements were also resorted to, such as the creation of numerous donations, both in the Iberian Peninsula as a whole and overseas, with an increasingly broad tax base, and, in the case of Castile and Aragon, the sale of Crown assets such as seigneurial rights, common land, offices and distinctions. This kind of fiscal policy undoubtedly had a more negative impact in the Crown of Castile than the other Habsburg dominions, although it should be noted that the tax burden in Portugal increased by around 55%. Increases in taxation led to vehement protests in several of the Spanish aggregated territories, and has been pointed to as one of the causes of the exacerbation of tensions that arose in the 1640s, when the Catalan, Portuguese and Neapolitan uprisings took place (Elliott, 1963; Oliveira, 1991; 2002; Hugon, 2014).

In Portugal, the tax burden actually doubled after the rupture with the Hispanic monarchy, despite taxes being calculated in a different way, and the system was approved by the *Cortes* of 1641. A rapid form of revenue was needed to support military expenses during the Restoration War, and consequently a new tax called the *décima* was introduced, being levied on 10% of individual income, and applying equally to people at all social levels, with only one exception: members of the clergy were able to pay the tax in the form of a donation. Unsurprisingly, after the conflict, the rate was lowered to 4.5%. While it is true that the level of revenue forecast was never achieved, it is estimated that in many years of war the effective rate of tax collected ranged from 72% to 81% (Costa et al., 2016: 116–119).

As Table 12.2 shows, the mid seventeenth century evidences the higher level of direct taxation in an Iberian territory in the early modern Peninsula. It is difficult to explain this fact by a higher state efficiency or capacity of the Portuguese monarchy, since it continued to be dependent on local structures, such as municipalities, for tax collection. Hypothetically, the success of the *décima* could be related to the lower territorial fragmentation and autonomies of different territories or reigns in Portugal, than in the Spanish monarchy, and with the notion that taxes were authorized by the *Cortes* of 1641. The notion that autonomy was a common cause mobilized the local elites to be directly engaged in the collection design of the tax.

In the face of the increase in spending caused by the Seven Years' War, the military *décima* (1762) was reformed: it was again levied on 10% of income, as well as interest on loans and the land rents. From 1766 to 1772 this tax accounted for 12% of the kingdom's revenues, a figure that fell to 9% in 1781, and later rose to 11% in 1804 (Macedo, 1982a). Such a situation did not, however, prevent it from being the target of scathing criticism by Dom Rodrigo de Sousa Coutinho, a late eighteenth-century Portuguese politician with liberal tendencies, accompanying his 1786 proposals for reforms to increase the effectiveness of taxation and clean up the financial system; he criticized the fact that there were so many taxes and their poor distribution, which placed an especially heavy burden on agriculture, and to resolve this problem suggested abolishing the *décima*, the tithe and the *jugadas* and replacing them with a single tax (Mansuy-Diniz Silva, 1993: 233–239).

While in the Portuguese case there was an option for using a direct form of taxation to face military expenditure, from the reign of Carlos II and during the eighteenth century, in Castile there was a clear option for not increasing the tax burden upon subjects. Up to the 1680s, the first option was to devalue the currency by creating a new monetary unit, the *realles de vellon*. Then, replacing the various indirect taxes that existed until the end of the seventeenth century with a lump sum that each municipality had to collect and transfer to the treasury, as *rentas provinciales*.

A second option was to incentivize freedom of trade, which naturally increased customs revenues, which in the eighteenth century were designated as *rentas generales*. The Spanish Crown began by ending the Cádiz trading monopoly with the Spanish Indies (1765) and in 1778 the Reglamento y Aranceles Reales para el Comercio Libre de España a Indias provided for the implementation of a liberal trade regime with the Indies, opening up a large number of ports in the Iberian Peninsula and the Americas to private enterprise, establishing *ad valorem* duties with a 3% tariff for Spanish commodities and 7% for foreign. Although it was not a great success, data reveals that while in 1740 *rentas generales* represented 6% of Spanish treasury revenues, in 1790 they amounted to 17%. In 1780 and 1795 the revenues coming from Spanish customs surpassed those obtained through Crown monopolies (Torres Sánchez, 2015: 131–132).

Estancos or monopolies consisted of the exclusive right to sell certain goods or exploit certain resources and became extremely crucial for revenue increasing from the seventeenth century for both Iberian crowns. They generated extraordinary revenues for the Crown and were of medieval origin, but unlike taxes their levying did not require the prior consent of the parliament. They are distinguished from the king's personal assets since they were not royal assets but rather the property rights or exploration rights were detained by the Crown (*regalías*). They covered certain products originating in the Iberian Peninsula, such as soap and salt – in Castile from 1564 and in Portugal in 1631; and overseas, such as pepper or cinnamon, brazilwood, the supply of enslaved Africans to Spanish America (1595); also the sale of mercury and of tobacco in the Peninsula – in Castile from 1636 and in Portugal from 1634 (Salvado, 2014).

This exclusive right of commerce or even transformation was subject to the regulation of the prices of the products involved. Logistical difficulties and the operating costs of such commercial circuits led to the concession of monopolies to private individuals, similar to that which occurred with the collection of certain taxes. In addition, as some authors have shown, powerful financial groups profited from these arrangements to a greater degree than royal treasuries, exercising discretionary power over their management and collection (Costa & Salvado, 2018).

Tobacco is the monopoly for which most evidence exists, and seems to have been most profitable for both crowns, accounting, perhaps exaggeratedly, for about 19.5% of total Crown revenues in Portugal in 1681 (Hespanha, 1993), 14% in 1717, 21.5% in 1766 and 19.5% in 1804–1810 (Costa & Salvado, 2018). Recent estimates for Spanish tobacco revenues place them as 6.7% of the total revenue of the royal treasury, 13.7% in 1750, 19.7% between 1775 and 1785, dropping to 8% around 1800–1804 (Escobedo Romero, 2008; Torres Sánchez, 2015). However, unlike Portugal, the Spanish monarchy tried to control directly all the administrative process, ending the farming out of the tobacco monopoly contract, which is argued by historians as the decisive factor for the growth in tobacco revenues (González Enciso, 2003).

Although the impact of Bourbon fiscal reforms on the Spanish empire are not considered in this chapter, and the imperial net revenues reaching the

Peninsula gradually increased along the early modern period, historians agree they were much more important to the Portuguese Crown than its Castilian counterpart. However, they never placed the Iberian monarchies under a financial dependence. Thus, while in the case of Portugal the evidence demonstrates the overwhelming importance of foreign trade (Pedreira, 2007: 71-72), it appears that Castile was much less dependent on it, if silver from the Americas is excluded (Comín & Yun-Casalilla, 2012).

As part of the analysis of taxation in the Iberian crowns, there is also a need to examine the share of Crown financial resources transferred to privileged groups, through an examination of the structure of their revenue. No such study has as yet been made of these groups as a whole for the period from 1500 to 1800, but some partial examinations enable us to arrive at consistent estimates. For example, a study by Monteiro focusing on the elite Portuguese nobility in the second half of the eighteenth century provides evidence of structural elements of the composition of the group's income and the characteristics that differentiated it from its counterpart in Castile (Monteiro, 1998; 2003).

Approximately 55% of the income of the most powerful nobles in Portugal derived from *bens da coroa e ordens*,[53] while the rest consisted of pensions and interest, agricultural revenues, often charged under a system of *emphyteusis*, and, to a lesser extent, income deriving from rural properties of the noble houses (Monteiro, 2003: 148-151). The important percentage associated with assets of the Crown and military orders demonstrates, first of all, the overwhelming dependence of the Portuguese nobility on the Crown for the role that it played in the inheritance of such assets, in accordance with the *Lei Mental*, or Mental Law, of 1434 and the fact that such rights were almost always granted for one, two or three lifetimes, and required periodic royal confirmation.

At the same time, with regard to forms of exploitation of landholdings, indirect exploitation overwhelmingly prevailed, which enables the conclusion to be drawn that the Portuguese nobility cannot be regarded as large landowners and that it adopted an 'ultra-rentier' model of asset management (Monteiro, 1998; 2003). In this particular field, and perhaps with the exception of Galicia and Valencia, the situation differs greatly from that of the Crowns of Castile and Aragon, where the nobility held extensive properties that they exploited directly, the most striking example being western Andalusia.

The situation described above for the elite Portuguese nobility is markedly different from its Spanish counterpart, for whom seigneurial rights and many

---

[53] *Bens da coroa e ordens* (Assets of the Crown and Military Orders) is the designation of the era for the jurisdictions and revenues that belonged to the Crown, while *bens das ordens* refer mostly to ecclesiastical tithes that constitute the greater part of the income of the military orders.

other distinctions donated by the king could also be purchased. Venality was extremely widespread, and such practices were used especially by the kings of Castile to resolve the financial difficulties of the treasury, and enshrined processes of social mobility for urban and mercantile elites who became *señores de vassalos*. In the Crowns of Castile and Aragon, the portion of economic production levied in the form of taxation was much more significant, since in addition to the taxing of seigneurial rights similar to those in Portugal, it also included *alcabalas* and *tercias reales*. At the same time, the Spanish nobility was dependent on the monarchy to a lesser extent than its Portuguese counterpart, not only because royal donations of jurisdictional estates were perpetual and did not include reversion clauses such as those provided for in the Mental Law of 1434, but also because the portion of patrimonial assets under direct exploitation was higher.

Church revenues benefited ecclesiastics, who accounted for just over 1% of the total population of the Hispanic kingdoms in the late sixteenth century, a figure that rose to 2% in the early eighteenth century and had fallen by the late eighteenth century to a level similar to that of the sixteenth century (Barrio Gozalo, 2002: 53). It has been estimated that the income from ecclesiastical tithes in Portugal was equivalent to three times the income deriving from *sisas*, although this is surely an exaggeration (Hespanha, 1994: 144). In the beginning of the eighteenth century, diplomat Dom Luís da Cunha stated as such, suggesting that the estates belonging to the Church totalled one third of the kingdom of Portugal.

Church revenues derived from a variety of sources, but it can be safely said that for the Iberian Peninsula as a whole the most significant was the *dízima* or tithe (levied on about 10% of agricultural production). A second source of revenue was income from numerous properties on which income was paid in kind, resulting mainly from forms of concession in accordance with a variety of institutional arrangements (emphyteutic contracts in perpetuity, for life or short-term leases) and to a lesser extent from the direct exploitation of properties. Although relatively unimportant in the overall picture, the direct exploitation of ecclesiastical land was significant for certain ecclesiastical bodies, such as the wealthy Alcobaça Monastery in Portugal, with estimated rates of property exploited ranging from 15% to 20% of total landownership. Thus, most of the landed properties from which members of the clergy derived their income were worked by individuals who belonged to other social groups. As with landholdings belonging to nobles, the origin of the confusing situation that existed, very often with rights over landholdings and rights of exploitation belonging to multiple entitles, was due to the very nature of the assets in question, which might have been purchased, but were mostly the object of royal or private donations known as *legados pios*, which grew steadily in importance. However, contrary to that which characterized most of the landholdings of the Portuguese nobility, such donations were not associated with precarious land rights. This is one of the reasons why such dead-handed estates were unavailable for transfer, remaining under the administration of the Church until the disentailment process carried out by the liberal Iberian regimes (Monteiro, 2010).

12.4 Political Economy and Reformism

In the early eighteenth century, the political and financial difficulties of the corporate constitutional system for the administration of the Iberian kingdoms were already clear, and new solutions were sought by means of the introduction of a vigorous reform policy, which led to the growth of state intervention in the economy.

While the eighteenth century was the period during which the principles of the polysynodial system and the composite monarchy were most widely abandoned, it should be stressed that an awareness of the limitations of this form of government and the first proposals for discarding this political model date from the late sixteenth century. They consist of 'memorials' written by *arbitristas*, that is, literate figures on the fringes of the institutional power centres. Concern at signs of decline in Spain and Portugal led the *arbitristas* to put forward diagnoses of the failings of the monarchy and proposals for reform. Despite some of these texts being of relatively poor quality or little relevance, others demonstrate a good inside knowledge of the failures of the corporate system and, in the wake of the findings of G. Botero, they advocate the role of the king as being more interventionist in character, and propose increasing income by introducing cuts on expenditure and providing stimuli for the recovery of some sectors of the economy (Cardoso, 2001; Dubet, 2003; Fuentes Quintana, 2005). They also note that the system of *mercês*, or grants, and the lack of interest in the economy shown by social groups who were dependent on the Crown for their living, such as the nobility, had led to the destruction of the productive sectors of the economy in Spain and Portugal. Among the suggestions made by these individuals (Martín González de Cellorigo, Sancho de Moncada and Duarte Ribeiro de Macedo), those that appear most frequently are economic and fiscal measures that approach what were later designated as mercantilist practices: they argued in favour of the intervention of the Crown in the two kingdoms in order to promote manufacturing, restrict the transfer of currency out of the country, and introduce legislation to limit the consumption of luxury goods. Other *arbitristas*, such as Gerónimo Cevallos and Fernando Alvarez de Toledo, made proposals of a more political nature, including a reduction in the granting of royal pensions and grants; a reduction in the number of councils; the recruitment of presidents of councils and courts based on merit; and the creation of a union of the kingdoms that made up the Hispanic monarchy, aimed at reducing internal rivalries (Gutierrez Nieto, 1986).

Some of the *memorials* influenced the great reform plans carried out by the Count-Duke of Olivares, whose reforms were aimed at achieving a greater balance in the distribution of military spending and increased cohesion between the different kingdoms by means of the *Unión de Armas* and the implementation of other measures contained in his well-known *Gran Memorial* (1624). This reform plan, which was never fully carried out, sought to consolidate the range of different forums and privileges in each kingdom that made up the 'composite monarchy', bringing them into line with the model of Castile. It was aimed at reducing the tensions that the greater fiscal impact had caused in this territory while increasing revenue and widening the scope of recruitment, thereby building a monarchy that would go beyond a merely dynastic union, introducing a more organic model of institutional unification (Elliott, 1990).

Debate on the need for institutional changes continued in the eighteenth century, with reformist thinkers who held prominent positions in the central administration putting forward their ideas, such as secretaries of state José Patiño and Cardeal da Mota, and diplomats Dom Luís da Cunha and Sebastião José de Carvalho e Melo (the future Marquis of Pombal). Thus, in the kingdom of Spain from the reign of Felipe V (1700–1746), and in Portugal from the reign of João V (1706–1750), and above all during the reign of Dom José (1750–1777), regimes began to develop a new institutional model in which the king was not only the ruler of the kingdom, but his sphere of action was extended and superimposed on all other bodies in society. The monarch was responsible for ruling according to principles of reason of State, free from corporate constraints, even when he confronted established interests (Subtil, 1993: 160; Dedieu, 2011).

The chronology and scope of the institutional reforms that took place in the Iberian monarchies in the eighteenth century is a subject on which much has been written but there is not always consensus (González Enciso, 2003; Lains & Silva, 2005c; Albareda, 2012; Grafe, 2012). There is similar controversy about the extent to which the concept of the Enlightenment may be applied to the different stages of the reformist movement. Recent works have signalled the importance of the reign of Felipe V, while the degree of rupture they represented with the Habsburg administration is also discussed (Dubet, 2008). It has been suggested that both the Spanish and Portuguese monarchies experienced two waves of reforms: the first, in the first half of the eighteenth century in Spain, was mercantilist in character, while in the case of Portugal it lasted until the end of the Pombaline consulate (1750–1777); the second, occurring in subsequent periods, was more enlightened and perhaps more liberal, particularly in Spain (López-Cordón & Monteiro, 2019). While it can be said unequivocally that a wave of reforms took place, one of the main issues for debate is the degree of impact this had, since there is a reasonable degree of consensus that the reforms did not always produce economic growth in the

Iberian Peninsula territories. This is not the place to examine these questions in great detail, but some general points can be made.

Among Spanish reformist policies, it is worth mentioning, in the first place, the attempts at Bourbon uniformization and centralization that were contained in the *Nueva Planta* decrees (1707-1716), which wrought changes in the constitutional framework of the dominions of the Crown of Aragon. In response to these territories taking up arms against his claim to the throne of Spain, Felipe V henceforth treated them as having been conquered. Most of the *fueros* and privileges peculiar to each territory were abolished, including individual parliaments and particular laws, as well as the language used in administration, and significant changes to tax systems and institutional organization were introduced. It should be noted, therefore, that these legal provisions marked one of the first ruptures with the model of composite monarchy that up until then had provided the structure of the Hispanic monarchy, within which, from now on, only the Basque Country and Navarre retained their autonomy. Second, it is important to highlight the territorial losses that the Spanish Crown experienced as a result of the War of Spanish Succession (1701-1713), which led to a drastic reduction in the extent of its European territory. Therefore, the impact of the contraction of the Spanish monarchy coupled with the profound institutional changes which occurred in the territories that remained under its sovereignty should be noted.

As part of the *Nueva Planta* and the uniformization process of the Spanish monarchy mentioned above, a measure that had great impact was the abolition of *puertos secos*, or terrestrial customs duties, between the Crowns of Aragon and Castile (1708-1714), while promoting the establishment of an internal market by providing stimuli for inter-regional trade. Also the idea of a more equitable system for sharing the fiscal burden among the various kingdoms of the monarchy was taken up again with redoubled vigour. The entire tax system in the kingdom of Aragon was overhauled, with the imposition of new taxes, *equivalentes*, which were designed to be proportionate to the taxes paid in the province of Castile. Following the creation of the *Secretaría de Estado y del Despacho Universal de Hacienda*, efforts were made to centralize the Crown's direct management of Castilian revenues, while transferring taxes which were farmed out and direct responsibility for the collection of *encabezamientos* to the treasury. Ensenada, the enlightened politician who served Fernando VI (1746-1759) and Carlos III (1759-1788), was responsible for an attempt to redistribute the burden on taxpayers by introducing a new direct tax on income, the *única contribución*. However, despite the production of the *Catastro* (the Castile tax census conducted from 1749 to 1759), the new tax foundered as a result of resistance from those who enjoyed tax privileges and the difficulty of assessing the wealth and income of each individual and entity. He also realized the impossibility for the direct collection of taxes by Crown officials (Dedieu, 2000; Torres Sánchez, 2015). Eliminating intermediaries was an impossible task to accomplish, as the Crown did not possess the required human capital, logistic organization and management infrastructure.

Third, another blow to the previous jurisdictional model – that of polysynodial government – was the emergence of secretaries of state, leading to the later creation of ministries. In the case of Portugal, Monteiro suggests that their creation and the progressive decline in the sphere of responsibility of the councils began in the reign of João V (Monteiro, 2001), while other authors maintain that the great political rupture was caused by the Pombaline reforms (Hespanha, 1994; Subtil, 2007). The relevance of this change at the political centre is not, however, to be underestimated, since it restricted the political role of traditionally privileged groups while widening that of secretaries of state. Endowed with a technocratic and professional profile, they formed a nucleus of political coordinators who distanced themselves from corporate interests and were able to speed up the decision-making process. In addition, the secretaries of state (three in Portugal and five in Spain) operated within a hierarchical structure, each with a well-defined jurisdiction, leading to a reduction in the level of inter-institutional conflict that characterized the council system of previous centuries (López-Cordón & Monteiro, 2019).

For Portugal, the creation of the *Erário Régio* (1761) in the reign of Dom José was one of the main changes to the institutional framework. It was aimed at implementing a more rational and more centralized revenue collection system in the kingdom, replacing the many collection and payment centres that characterized the previous system. The new institutional arrangements also led to the introduction of new accounting techniques and the creation of an administrative structure covering the whole territory (Lains & Silva, 2005c; Subtil, 2010).

Another central argument of the reformist discourse of the eighteenth century was the need to provide for the well-being and safety of the king's subjects through the improvement of material conditions for productive activity in order to limit the transfer of money abroad. This was one of the bases for direct intervention in economic life in the two monarchies during the eighteenth century, first, by either stimulating or protecting commercial interests, and second, by promoting industrial and agrarian activities by fostering the use of new technical know-how. This was also why the Iberian crowns managed the economic development of their territories through the promotion of privileged economic groups or those that counted on the direct protection of the Crown. To this end, *Juntas de Comércio* – Boards of Trade – were either created or re-established, aimed at coordinating all operations concerned with industrial and commercial activity in an effort to reduce the weight of foreign intervention in the domestic economy and increase the kingdoms' revenues (Molas i Ribalta, 1978; 1996; Pedreira 1995; Madureira 1997).

In order to achieve a direct intervention in productive sectors of the economy, promoting private entrepreneurship, the improvement of economic activity and fiscal control from the early eighteenth century, the Iberian monarchs created a more technically competent administrative body of staff to implement their new policies. These new agents of the Crown's peripheral administration – inspectors, intendants and superintendents (1749) – represented royal authority and answered to the secretaries of state. They were assigned commissary status, jurisdiction over other magistracies and a field of intervention that was not coincident with the jurisdictional administrative network. Moreover, although there were relatively few of them, they collaborated in efforts to break with the previous model of economic governance. In Spain, this reform strengthened fiscal control of the territory, both with regard to *rentas provinciales* of the Crown and the replacement of the indirect system of tax-collection (through intermediaries as the municipalities and *asientos* contractors) with a direct system, in which royal officials were reassigned responsibility for levying taxes (Torres Sánchez, 2015).

Apart from the greatest reformist projects such as the ones mentioned, the eighteenth century was characterized by a constant improvement in the administration practice. The implementation and development of different *cursus honorum* inside the royal service established positive incentives in order to ensure a good performance from the officials for their own benefit and prevented corruption. In addition, legislation and bureaucratization of many economic aspects and the recovery of several transferred taxes and offices contributed to give the Crown the opportunity to make greater interventions in economic activity. These other reforms were partial and limited, but their number and consistency contributed to a general improvement.

Despite the attempt of gradual replacement of the jurisdictional and privilege model with a political and meritocratic paradigm (Subtil, 1993), many of the main offices in the Iberian kingdoms remained in the hands of the nobility, just as many of the councils continued to function. Likewise, in both Spain and Portugal, privileged groups retained a prominent role in the appropriation of income. Even so, an increasingly well-prepared civil service and specialized ministers and secretaries of state emerged, such as the Marquis of Pombal, Rodrigo de Sousa Coutinho, Campomanes and Ensenada, who sought, through the creation of new institutions and the execution of reformist plans with the introduction of new laws, to increase the revenue of the Iberian crowns and stimulate productivity. The economy became a field for direct intervention by the Crown in these territories, although the monopoly regimes and privileges of the social orders with economic power that the monarchies were interested in retaining were maintained.

These practices generated immediate extraordinary revenues for royal treasuries and succeeded in preserving the relative social order. In this regard, it is worth noting the persistence of the institutional framework, as shown by the frequent occurrence of privative jurisdictions associated with the various traditional players, such as the nobility, the Church and the *Misericórdias*, for the execution of the debts, to the detriment of the equal access to property rights of creditors in all sectors of economic activity. The failure of the territorial reform of 1790 in Portugal is yet another example of the resistance put up by both the municipalities and the corporate power of crown magistrates with their conservative and parochial outlook, which worked against a more rational and uniform understanding of the political organization of the territory, more in line with enlightened ideas (Silva, 1998). Thus, it may be said that the Iberian reforms of the eighteenth century were more successful in the fiscal sphere than in that of justice.

12.5 Conclusion

To conclude, two observations may be made: first, regarding the comparative evolution of the institutional systems of the two Iberian kingdoms, and second, on the causes of the limited institutional changes in Iberian kingdoms in the eighteenth century.

An analysis of the history of the institutions of governance in the two Iberian kingdoms from the sixteenth to eighteenth centuries shows that they were remarkably similar with regard to jurisdictional political culture, the modus operandi of government, early overseas expansion and the reformist practices of the eighteenth century. Such similarities should not, however, serve to hide the many differences between them, especially with regard to territorial composition and its institutional implications. It should be noted that the initial proposal for dealing with the complex problems of articulation between the various dominions which had been either aggregated or conquered was to recognize both the particularities of each and their privileged social groups, by means of the maintenance of jurisdictional pluralism. Thus Iberian monarchs and their ministers were able to establish alliances with local oligarchies, important noble houses, guilds and, of course, the Church. At certain times, these pacts were explicit, as is the case of parliamentary negotiations, in which the bargaining chip for the acceptance of tax liens was the transfer of control over the management of tax-collection; at other times, they were more subtle, as shown by the progressive transformation of the Iberian aristocracy into a nobility of the court which was increasingly dependent on royal favour. Moreover, although there were periods of great social and political tension, such as those that led to revolts in various aggregated dominions, the truth is that royal power was strengthened not in opposition to elites, but rather with their collaboration.

Although the political pressure displayed by the municipal authorities over the monarchs' discretionary power was limited within the framework of the parliaments, particularly in Castile, they were able to negotiate how new fiscal impositions could be implemented. Despite this limited influence, the municipalities enjoyed a significant local and regional autonomy since their role was to regulate the daily local economic activity and, more importantly, they were crucial for tax collection, since Iberian crowns did not have an efficient fiscal administration structure and logistic organization. It was the role of the municipalities to channel the fiscal contribution of the people to the treasuries of the Iberian crowns.

However, it is worth mentioning that the persistence of a political culture based on compromise and negotiation hindered the effective reform of the political system, despite the increasing consolidation of the power of monarchs. Furthermore, this occurred due to the resistance of the different political orders to radical changes in the current institutional, social and economic order rather than a lack of diagnostic capacity or proposals for reform, as is evident from the survey of *arbitrist* literature. The failure of Olivares' constitutional reform programme is an example of this, but the same explanation can, at least in part, be applied to the failure of reformist plans of the eighteenth century.

In the eighteenth century a wealth of reforms was carried out in both Iberian kingdoms, signalling the Crown's growing intervention in the economy. As seen above, measures were almost always introduced in the context of attempts to rationalize the administrative apparatus, including the fiscal and accounting system. While the efficiency of the royal treasuries improved and as they sought to impose more meritocratic criteria on access to a range of administrative positions, they did not succeed in breaking with the privilege inherent to the traditional system of the social orders. This had negative consequences, especially in the field of justice, due to a political culture characterized by a greater interest in preserving a society based in privilege than the economic rationality of markets, which we now take for granted. Perhaps this is why liberal ideas were put into practice so rarely, and they can be detected more readily in plans for economic policy reform in the Iberian kingdoms than in proposals for the radical transformation of the political system, which most members of the enlightened elites sought to preserve.

Thus, perhaps the difficulties encountered in the process of removing the remnants of the jurisdictional system, which had served the kingdoms well in the sixteenth and seventeenth centuries, explain the apparent paradox between the intense reformist movement of the eighteenth century and the limited extent of the institutional change of the two kingdoms achieved in that century. This suggests that an understanding of the institutional causes of the divergence between the Iberian kingdoms and the countries of Northern Europe should be sought in the shortcomings which characterized the second half of the eighteenth century.

13

Early Modern Financial Development in the Iberian Peninsula

LEONOR FREIRE COSTA, SUSANA MÜNCH MIRANDA
AND PILAR NOGUES-MARCO

13.1 Introduction

Monetary systems of early modern Europe were commodity–money systems composed mainly of gold and silver (Esteves & Nogues-Marco, 2021). The Iberian colonial expansion granted Europe access to precious metals, with acceptance as a means of payment, at a worldwide scale. The first major increase in Europe's stock of gold in the early modern period occurred between 1480 and 1560 through trade with the West African coast while, from the mid-sixteenth until the late eighteenth century, mines in South America became suppliers of an unprecedented quantity of gold and silver. In total, Iberian colonies produced nearly 85% of the world's silver, and more than 70% of the world's gold in the early modern period (TePaske, 2010; Costa et al., 2013).

The production of precious metals in their colonies impacted the financial systems of both Castile and Portugal. In this chapter we focus on the relationship between liquidity and financial development – including other relevant variables such as instruments and institutions – to examine the efficiency of the financial systems in Iberia. For this purpose, we first analyse the volume and the institutional structure of the remittances of precious metals. Second, we consider the relationship between remittances and their liquidity effects as well as the structures and instruments of financial markets. We start by looking into public credit to consider debt management and the cost of public debt service. Then we turn to the private credit market and focus on financial instruments and trends in interest rates to estimate the cost of private capital. Finally, we summarize our perspective on the main similarities and differences in the development of the financial systems of Castile and Portugal.

We are especially grateful to Rui Esteves, Nuno Palma and Bartolome Yun-Casalilla for their feedback. We are also very grateful to Paco Comín and Carlos Álvarez-Nogal for sharing data with us. Leonor Freire Costa and Susana Münch Miranda acknowledge the funding provided by the Fundação para a Ciência e Tecnologia for the project *Sovereign debt and private credit in Portugal (1668–1797)* (PTDC/HAR-HIS/28809/2017).

13.2 Remittances

The Iberian colonial empires gave access to entirely new mining resources that pushed the supply of international means of payment and ultimately allowed the growth of long-distance trade (Flynn et al., 2003; Findlay & O'Rourke, 2007; Palma, 2020a). The quest for gold is one of the traditional explanations for Portugal's conquest of Ceuta in 1415 when Europe faced an increasing scarcity of metallic species. This military success, however, did not pave the way to Timbuktu and the gold mines in the more southerly Mali Empire. Only after the conquest of Tangier in 1436 did the Portuguese presence in the region provide intelligence on trans-Saharan trade routes to the sources of gold. From 1440 onwards, Portuguese maritime expeditions along the West African coast were designed to bypass the trans-Saharan ancestral routes in order to tap into Timbuktu's gold resources.

Investments in the exploration of the West African coast began to show profits in the 1480s. In the Portuguese *El Mina* fortress, commodities purchased in the military strongholds of North Africa (woollen textiles) or imported from Europe (copper and iron goods) were exchanged for gold dust. Once arrived in Lisbon, this gold was coined in the Lisbon Mint House, the main institution empowered to strike coins in Portugal since the foundation of the kingdom.[54] In addition to earlier African Coast gold, the Iberian Empires obtained precious metals from the American colonies. Mexico, Bolivia and Peru mainly produced silver, while gold was extracted in Brazil and Colombia and, to a lesser extent, in Mexico, Bolivia, Chile and Peru (TePaske, 2010; Costa et al., 2013).

The America discovery created the mirage of precious metals mining wealth as the measure of economic success in Spain (Bernal, 1999; Stein & Stein, 2000). The Castilian legislation forbade the free trade of gold and silver, so their legal exchange was regulated through the institution that administered colonial trade: The *Casa de Contratación* (House of Trade). Merchants had to register the private remittances as soon as their vessels tied up in Seville (or Cádiz from the early eighteenth century) and pay the import tax for both ingots and coins. Hamilton (1934), who used the official registers of the *Casa de Contratación*, firstly collected information about bullion inflows from the Americas to Spain.

Table 13.1 shows legal remittances of precious metals – both gold and silver – from American colonies to Spain for the period 1503–1660. Unfortunately, official registers have not been preserved after 1660. Similarly, Vogt (1979) collected quantities traded from the African West Coast to Portugal for the period 1487–1561. It is self-explanatory that the

---

[54] The Mint House of Porto closed in 1590. It resumed its functions between 1688 and 1721.

Table 13.1 Decennial remittances to Spain and Portugal, 1487–1660

	Spain						Portugal			
	Silver (tons)	Gold (tons)	Royal remittances (%)	Private remittances (%)	Total (thousand pieces of eight)		Royal remittances (tons)	Private remittances (tons)	Total Gold (tons)	Total Gold (thousand pieces of eight)
1487–1490							0.7	0.1	0.8	320.3
1491–1500							3.43	0.69	4.12	1,622.9
1501–1510		5.0	26.2	73.8	1,964.3		1.60	0.32	1.92	755.6
1511–1520		9.2	26.2	73.8	3,621.1		3.44	0.69	4.13	1,626.5
1521–1530	0.1	4.9	26.2	73.8	1,940.0		2.05	0.41	2.47	971.3
1531–1540	86.2	14.5	31.9	68.1	9,245.1		1.86	0.37	2.23	880.2
1541–1550	177.6	25.0	22.5	77.5	17,309.6		1.20	0.24	1.44	566.9
1551–1560	303.1	42.6	29.1	70.9	29,555.3		1.20	0.24	1.43	565.2
1561–1570	942.9	11.5	22.1	77.9	41,937.3		0.14	0.03	0.17	68.5
1571–1580	1,118.6	9.4	34.1	65.9	48,240.2					
1581–1590	2,103.0	12.1	29.3	70.7	88,026.7					
1591–1600	2,707.6	19.5	30.2	69.8	115,169.2					
1601–1610	2,213.6	11.8	27.0	73.0	92,330.3					

Table 13.1 (cont.)

	Spain					Portugal			
	Silver (tons)	Gold (tons)	Royal remittances (%)	Private remittances (%)	Total (thousand pieces of eight)	Royal remittances (tons)	Private remittances (tons)	Total Gold (tons)	Total Gold (thousand pieces of eight)
1611–1620	2,192.3	8.9	21.2	78.8	90,398.0				
1621–1630	2,145.3	3.9	18.3	81.7	85,971.8				
1631–1640	1,396.8	1.2	28.2	71.8	55,299.5				
1641–1650	1,056.4	1.5	24.7	75.3	42,244.3				
1651–1660	443.3	0.5	26.7	73.3	17,627.6				

Sources: for Spain, Hamilton (1934), Table 1 and Table 3. Hamilton (1934) provided data in *peso de mina* of 450 *maravedies*. We converted the data to pieces of eight of exchange of 272 *maravedies* of old silver and 512 *maravedies* of *vellon* (Kelly, 1835: 318). For Portugal, Vogt (1979: Appendix). To convert Portuguese gold from the physical quantities (tons) to a value comparable with Spanish precious metals, we convert tons to pieces of eight of exchange according to the following equivalences: the par rate of exchange between Portugal and Castile was one crusado of exchange (old crusado of 400 *réis*) equivalent to one ducat of exchange (375 *maravedies*) (Denzel, 1995: 141). Therefore, one piece of eight of exchange is equivalent to 272/375 crusados. The gross weight of the old crusado of 400 *réis* was equivalent to 3.5 grams, according to 'museu casa da moeda' (www.museucasadamoeda.pt). Fineness is 22 carats (Kelly, 1835: 210–211). We assume that the fineness of gold measured in tons is the same as gold coins.

minimal contribution of the African posts in supplying gold shortly after the expedition of Cortés, allowed the *Carrera de Indias* (Spanish trade with American colonies) to dominate in this regard.

Royal rights over trade and taxation respectively, determined the state's share of the amounts that flowed to the Iberian kingdoms. In the case of Portugal, the gold trade on the African Coast was a royal monopoly. The Crown bore the costs of the military and administrative staff in *El Mina* fortress and claimed all the profits. Monopoly rights may have been routinely handed out to private investors, but the overwhelming portion of the remittances from the African Coast was the property of the Portuguese Crown (83.3% of the total). The Crown's prominent role was a unique feature of this earlier stage of colonial expansion and was exclusive to the African gold trade, while bullion exports from the Americas to Spain had been mainly a private business since the inception of the *Carrera de Indias*. The extraction tax for precious metals was 20% (*quinto real* – royal fifth) in the sixteenth and seventeenth centuries, but was reduced to 10% (*diezmo real* – royal tenth) in the eighteenth century (in 1716 for Mexico and in 1735 for Peru) (Haring, 1939: 198). For the period 1503–1660 the percentages were, on average, 26.5% for royal remittances, and 73.5% for private remittances (Table 13.1).

Morineau (1985) questioned the quantities counted by Hamilton (1934) with the divergence in results originating from the different sources consulted. Hamilton used the official registers in the *Casa de Contratación*, whereas Morineau focused his research on Dutch mercantile gazettes, consular reports and merchants' correspondence. Later, Morineau's quantities for the eighteenth century were re-counted by García-Baquero (1996), using the data obtained from the vessels' registers. Counting accurate quantities is complex in the case of Spain, due to the high level of smuggling.

Table 13.2 reports South American remittances in the eighteenth century for Spain and Portugal. In the case of Spain, bullion regulations were intended to prevent bullion outflows. On the one hand, private remittances paid a high import tax (more than 7% for gold and 10% for silver in the eighteenth century) (Nogues-Marco, 2010: 81–82), while on the other hand, the export of precious metals from Spain was forbidden without a licence. Fraud emerged as an inevitable consequence of these bullion regulations because smuggling enabled exporters to ignore the export ban and importers to save the high import tax. In the eighteenth century, smuggling accounted for around 20% of the total precious metals imported from America (Table 13.2). The smuggling of gold and silver, commodities that were mainly the concern of private business, was led by a cartel of foreign merchants with diplomatic immunity and the necessary international connections to illegally extract and distribute the precious metals outside Spain (Nogues-Marco, 2010). Royal remittances were reduced during the eighteenth century from 16% in the 1710s to only 7.5% in the 1770s. They represented, on average, 12% of the total precious metals legally imported to Spain (in comparison to the average share of 26.5% for the period 1503–1660), but the share is smaller if we consider the illegal trade of precious metals (Tables 13.1. and 13.2). Remittances experienced a significant reduction in absolute value during the seventeenth century (Tables 13.1 and 13.2). This was not due to a contraction in mining production in the Americas, but mainly to a dramatic decrease in the amount of precious metals sent to Castile (Yun-Casalilla, 2019: 369).

From the early 1700s up to 1780, Brazil became the main supplier to the world market (Table 13.2). By then, private business controlled an overwhelming share of Brazilian gold remittances, signalling that the Portuguese institutional framework for mining activities was similar to the Spanish one. The royal share of Brazilian gold stemmed from the collection of the one-fifth tax on the gold extracted, whose yield the Crown expected to be shipped to Portugal. In addition, the state levied a 1% *ad valorem* fee on private agents' shipped gold in order to pay for protection costs, which left representative data on the institutional structure of inflows from 1716 to 1808. Costa et al. (2013) calculated the quantities based on the official registers generated to control the import tax (1%). Although this documental source is based on official registers and thereby prone to distortion due to evasion, twenty-five annual observations between 1700 and 1760 point to amounts higher than those reported by the Dutch Gazettes used by Morineau (1985). For this reason, Morineau underestimated the inflows in the 1740s and 1760s, while conversely overestimating them in the 1730s (Table 13.2). In any event, data from Portuguese archives providing a complete series for the whole eighteenth century – which Morineau's series do not – ensure that gold remittances had a higher significance in the mid-eighteenth century than previously estimated. Additionally, this source permits us to conclude that private remittances hovered around 76% of the total (Table 13.2). In eighteenth-century Portugal, as in Spain, precious metals were commodities that were mainly the concern of private business.

Despite the high level of smuggling, Spain and Portugal were first-order receivers of precious metals. Either private or royal property, the overwhelming volume of remittances arrived already minted in coins of different denominations, thus causing silver and gold to be key inputs for producing commodity money in colonial mint houses. In the following sections, we will look further into the relationship between remittances, liquidity cycles, market structure and financial development in the Iberian Peninsula, and will consider both public and private credit markets.

Table 13.2 Decennial remittances to Spain and Portugal, 1700–1800.

	Spain							Portugal		
	Royal remittances (%)	Private remittances to Spain (%)	Total Spain (thousand pieces of eight)	Total Europe (including Spain) (thousand pieces of eight)	Silver Europe (including Spain) (thousand pieces of eight)	Gold Europe (including Spain) (thousand pieces of eight)	Royal remittances (%)	Private remittances (%)	Gold (tons)	Gold (thousand pieces of eight)
1701–1710			78,500	121,800	104,000	17,800				
1711–1720	16.3	83.7	65,200	102,000	86,900	15,100				
1721–1730	19.2	82.0	128,800	162,800	138,900	23,900	23.4	76.9	84.40	33,247
1731–1740	14.9	85.1	90,600	122,100	105,500	16,600	22.6	77.7	91.53	36,054
1741–1750	8.7	91.3	118,600	160,200	136,600	23,600	14.5	85.5	110.30	43,448
1751–1760	12.5	87.5	163,800	170,800	145,300	25,500	24.1	75.9	90.48	35,643
1761–1770	5.5	94.5	154,000	159,400	135,900	23,500	29.6	70.4	80.05	31,532
1771–1780	7.5	92.5	135,300	143,300	122,400	20,900	17.0	83.0	50.91	20,054
1781–1790			260,000	297,800	254,000	43,800	36.9	63.1	18.11	7,134
1791–1800			186,400	206,400	175,700	30,700	23.6	76.3	15.94	6,279

Sources: for Spain: quantities from Morineau (1985), Tables 70, 72 and 73. Morineau (1985) provided data in *piastres*, which is the name of the piece of eight of exchange in the French language, whose value is 272 *maravedies* of old silver and 512 *maravedies* of *vellon* (Kelly, 1835: 318). The proportion of royal remittances versus private remittances comes from García-Baquero (1985, Appendix). Data for Portugal is taken from Costa et al. (2013). For the conversion of Portuguese gold from the physical quantities (tons) to a monetary unit (pieces of eight of exchange), see Table 13.1.

13.3 Public Credit: Debt Management and Creditworthiness

War expenditure was sustained in early modern Europe by the issuing of sovereign debt. In Spain, scholars have stressed the consequences of the Habsburgs' imperial policy on debt increase in the sixteenth and seventeenth centuries due to the intense war activity in Europe and overseas. By contrast, the Spanish Bourbon dynasty almost balanced their fiscal budgets and hardly issued any sovereign debt during the eighteenth century. It was not until the end of the eighteenth century that debt again increased significantly as a consequence of wars against England and France (Comín, 2016; see Figure 13.1).

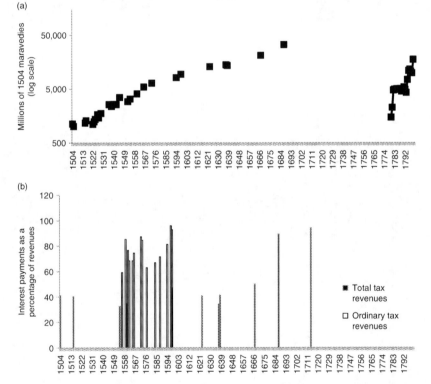

Figure 13.1 (a) Long-term debt, Castile, 1504–1800. (b) Interest payments to tax revenues (%), Castile.
Sources: Dominguez Ortiz (1960), Ruiz Martín (1968; 1990), Artola (1982), Toboso Sánchez (1987), Andrés Ucendo (1999) and Marcos (2006), compiled in Comín (2016, Graphs 7 and 9); and Álvarez-Nogal and Chamley (2014, Figure 2). Long-term debt for years 1714 and 1687 might be overestimated (see Álvarez-Nogal, 2009, Table 1.2, footnote b). Ordinary tax revenues were mainly direct taxes and sales taxes. Total tax revenues include public remittances of precious metals. Blanks mean missing data.

Sovereign debt was funded by two debt instruments: *asientos* and *juros*. *Asientos* were short-term debt contracts between the Crown and private bankers, mainly German, Portuguese and Italian, with the Genoese being the main group that contracted *asientos* in the sixteenth and seventeenth centuries (Ruiz Martín, 1968; Carande, 1987). *Juros* were long-term bonds issued against a specific revenue stream and subscribed mainly by the Spanish (Toboso Sánchez, 1987; Álvarez-Nogal, 2009). Both instruments were related, as contracts with Genoese bankers introduced the practice of collateralizing *asientos* with *juros* in the sixteenth century, which the Genoese then sold in the secondary market (Ruiz Martín, 1968).

Spain defaulted on sovereign debt 13 times in the early modern period under the following: Philip II in 1557, 1560, 1575 and 1596, Philip III in 1607, Philip IV in 1627, 1647, 1652, 1660 and 1662, Charles II in 1688 and Philip V in 1727 and 1739 (see Artola, 1982 for a general overview). This sequence of defaults resulted from different financing problems that eventually led the monarchy to deal with difficulties in accessing long-term credit as the seventeenth century progressed. Starting with suspensions of payments and resettlements of *asientos*, there followed a period in which *juros* serviced by taxes negotiated in the *Cortes*, increasingly secured the loans provided by Genoese bankers, who made a profit from selling them in the secondary market. Thus, the most serious problems in financing the war arose when cuts and deferments affected the service of the *juros*, a situation that tended to worsen from 1620 onwards. The study of these developments has attracted the attention of a broad historiography interested in questioning the institutional framework affecting the credibility of sovereign debt.

In a sovereign debt system without third-party enforcement, Conklin (1998) argues that Philip II's Genoese lenders linked short-term debt (*asientos*) to international specie deliveries from Spain to the Low Countries in order to create a penalty as an enforcement mechanism. According to Drelichman and Voth (2011; 2014), the early defaults of Philip II appear not to have damaged the long-term lending relationship between the bankers and the Crown, because the losses sustained during defaults were more than compensated for by profits garnered in tranquil periods. The reconstruction of the fiscal accounts of Castile during the period 1556–1596 shows that Philip II's debts were sustainable. Silver remittances were used to fund short-term borrowing (*asientos*), but silver revenue was volatile because of the fluctuation in yields of American mines, as well as the challenges of shipping across the Atlantic. Sizable dips in remittances in the years preceding the default coincided with three of the four defaults of Philip's reign (Drelichman & Voth, 2010; 2014).

According to Drelichman and Voth (2010), defaults ultimately helped strengthen the fiscal powers of the State because Philip II used them as a negotiating device to raise relevant ordinary taxes, that is, mainly direct taxes (*servicios*) and sales taxes (*alcabalas*) that had to be authorized by the representative assembly of Castilian municipalities (*Cortes*). The rise in taxes permitted the issuing of new *juros*, which were collateralized by specific taxes. As a consequence, in each default, short-term loans (*asientos*) were converted into long-term debt (*juros*) to repay *asientos* through a *juros* swap.

Álvarez-Nogal and Chamley (2014) argue that, indeed, the suspension of payments on the short-term debt (*asientos*) of Philip II were not caused by short-term liquidity crises, but happened when the interest payments of the long-term bonds (*juros*) had reached the ceiling of ordinary taxes (see Figure 13.1). The suspension of payments on *asientos* initiated the negotiations between the Crown and municipalities represented in the *Cortes* to raise the tax ceiling that then permitted the new issuing of *juros* to refinance *asientos*.

Interest rates on long-term debt decreased in the long run, mainly during the sixteenth century (see Figure 13.2). Indeed, in the sixteenth century and at least until the mid-seventeenth century, Castile's interest rate on the nominal value of public debt was lower than that of the English or Dutch debt, and at the same level as debt issued by the reputable city-republics of Italy (Yun and Ramos, 2012: 20–25; Yun-Casalilla, 2019: 169). According to Álvarez-Nogal (2009), there was a growing demand for long-term bonds until the 1620s, which permitted the government to reduce the interest rate on the nominal value from 10% in the early sixteenth century to 5% in 1625. The most relevant type of *juros* – *juros al quitar* – had an embedded option that gave the Crown the legal right to redeem the *juro* at any time. This feature was used to reduce *de facto* the interest rate on the nominal value by increasing the principal (an operation known as '*crecimiento*') (Álvarez-Nogal, 2009; Álvarez-Nogal & Chamley, 2014; 2018). But *juros* depreciated from the 1560s (although mainly after the 1620s) as a consequence of excessive issuing, default and restructuring, as well as subsequent seizures and delays in the payment of interest. Forced loans to the Crown such as the expropriation of private remittances in exchange for *juros* were used to fund public expenditures (Toboso Sánchez, 1987). The demand for *juros* plunged in the seventeenth century and they were redeemed from 1685 onwards, and more intensely from 1748 (Toboso Sánchez, 1987).

Interest rates on the nominal value, however, are not the proper measure of the cost of capital because debt depreciated, that is, it was traded at a lower value than the nominal value of the bond. Therefore, some evidence on yields is needed. Here two problems arise. On the one hand, the calculation of the yield is complicated because *juros* were financial derivatives that contained embedded options, meaning that the Crown could redeem the bond at any time. Despite the existence of embedded options and other clauses, financial scholars accept the use of the ratio between the interest rate and the market value of the bond as a reasonable approximation of the yields for bonds issued at a very long maturity (Mauro et al., 2006). On the other hand, the sovereign debt of early modern Spain traded in decentralized markets. As a consequence,

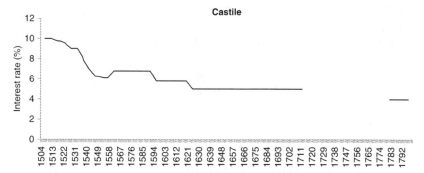

Figure 13.2 Interest rates on the nominal value of long-term bonds (*juros*) (%), Castile. Source: Dominguez Ortiz (1960), Ruiz Martín (1968; 1990), Artola (1982), Toboso Sánchez (1987) and Marcos (2006), compiled in Comín (2016, Graph 10). Blanks indicate missing data.

information about market values is elusive and we have only anecdotal evidence. For instance, Toboso Sánchez (1987: 147–148) has documented that the market value of *juros* depreciated by one-third after the default of 1575; the yield was 10.17% for an interest rate of 6.78% on the nominal value (Figure 13.2). The market value of *juros* depreciated again during the crisis of 1590s and in that instance, the average depreciation was 18.7% (in 1594), so the yield was around 7.6% for an interest rate of 6.2% on the nominal value (Figure 13.2). Similarly, Álvarez Vázquez (1987: 265–267) finds that the yield of *juros* bought by the Cathedral of Zamora at the end of the seventeenth century was between 8% and 9% for the years 1663–1676 and 9% on average for the years 1675–1704, while the interest rate at the time was 5% on the nominal value (Figure 13.2). Yield of *juros* is consistent with the effective interest rates paid for other kind of public investment: the primary sales on credit of venal offices in Castile paid in average an interest rate of 7.875% (average for the period 1543–1710 for the limited sample of primary sales on credit) (Gómez-Blanco, 2021: 172) Unfortunately, empirical evidence on yields is scarce, and more research is needed to extract robust conclusions.

In the case of the Aragon Crown, the limited evidence on effective interest rates shows a higher cost of public capital than in Castile. Short-term fiscal deficits in Catalonia were funded with *asientos* and with credit operations that used bills of exchange. In the case of *asientos*, local private agents charged high interest rates of a minimum of 12% per year (or more in some cases) in 1581 (Hernández, 2003: 201–204). Bill-of-exchange credit operations used change-and-rechange operations between Barcelona and Lyon to fund *de facto* local credit in Barcelona. These operations permitted the circumvention of usury laws and charged high interest rates that fluctuated between 10% per year (in 1582) and 21% per year (in 1585) (Hernández, 1997: 71; 2003: 201–204) (see Nogues-Marco, 2018: 10 on the concept of change-and-rechange).

At the end of the eighteenth century, Spanish debt was traded in the Amsterdam stock market. Tomz (2007: 42–45) reports a yield of 6.1% on Spanish sovereign debt in July 1771 and 5.4% in October 1783, while the interest rate for Castilian holders of domestic *juros* was 4% on the nominal value (Figure 13.2). Additionally, we observe that the yield was higher for Spain than for any other European country in the Amsterdam stock market at the end of the eighteenth century.[55] However, the yield of the Spanish debt traded in Amsterdam decreased from 5.4% to 4% between 1783 and 1793. Through a policy of regular payments of the interest rates and punctual amortization, the Spanish government signalled its creditworthiness in the Amsterdam capital market, which decreased yields (Tomz, 2007: 46).

Like the *juro al quitar* in Spain, the Dutch *losrenten* and the French *rentes*, the Portuguese *padrão de juro* was a redeemable long-term bond, with annual payments earmarked to a specific fiscal income. It was fully transferable and negotiable in secondary markets, as a whole or in fractions. While the first *juros* were issued in the early 1500s, the stock of long-term debt increased consistently from the 1540s onwards and at a faster pace when Portugal was ruled by Spanish Habsburg kings (1580–1640). The latter phase of outstanding debt growth took place, nevertheless, under a slow erosion of the credibility of *juros*. Routine deferments and suspensions first, followed by cuts in the annuity payments, as happened regularly in the 1630s, dried up the market for these securities. As the financial stress increased, the government routinely tapped into the financial resources of the towns. Forced loans from the Lisbon municipality, for example, were backed up by *padrões de juro*, while the municipality sold annuities earmarked to local taxes to meet the required loans (Gomes, 1883, 201–206, 307–311; Hespanha, 1993, 224–225).

Funded public debt slowly regained credibility in the framework of the restoration of the Portuguese monarchy. To restore creditors' trust, the government refrained from issuing new debt and sought to punctually service payments on the old *juros*. Short-term loans tided over regular budget deficits during the Restoration War, while creditors faced the consequences of monetary measures taken by the government. Debasements decreased the real value of the outstanding debt until 1688 (Costa & Miranda, 2023).

By the late seventeenth century, new rules regarding the payment of *juros* strengthened the confidence of royal investors, while some marginal operations, including an attempt to introduce tontines, enabled the state to sell

---

[55] July 1771 and October 1783, respectively: Austria 3.8% and 3.5%; France 4% and 3.9%; Saxony 4% and 4.9%; Danzig 4.9% and 5%; Denmark 4% (both dates); Leipzig 4.2% and 3.5%; Brunswick Luneburg 5.1% and 4.9%; Mecklenburg 5% and 4%; Sweden 5% and 4.1%; and Russia 5.1% and 4.2%.

some new *juros* at 4.5% (Gomes, 1883: 46, 72–73, 79). The vast majority (71%) of *padrões de juro*, however, paid 5% interest, with the rest still paying 6.25%, therefore allowing us to estimate the debt stock at some 3,767 million *réis* in 1680 (Costa & Miranda, 2023). This long-term debt grew further to fund Portugal's participation in the War of the Spanish Succession (1701–1714), when 1,102 million *réis* (35 tons of silver) were raised through the issuance of *juros* at 5% and 6.25%, partly to consolidate short-term loans supplied by English merchants who had ensured military provisioning. From the 1750s and up to the early 1790s, new *padrões* were issued first at 4% and then at 3.5%, in both cases at a rate lower than the legal ceiling – 5% – set on private interest rates in 1757 (Gomes, 1883: 78–79; 321; Costa et al., 2018a).

Hence, throughout three centuries, the issued interest rates on *juros* trended downward from 8% to 3.5%. This trend can partially be attributed to interest payment reductions that became standard practice after 1563 when the first operation was set in motion. These debt management operations qualify as voluntary since bondholders were given the option to reject the reduction and cash the payment of the principal at par. Consequently, these campaigns placed concomitantly new *juros* in the market at a lower rate, as this was key to ensure the liquidity to pay off any holders of old annuities who rejected the reduction (Gomes, 1883, pp. 220–21, 314–316). The last refinancing episode occurred in 1743. Starting with the expressed aim to reduce the last bonds that still yielded 6.25%, the operation further included the consolidation of short-term debt and the redemption and reselling of 5% *juros*. It resulted in the

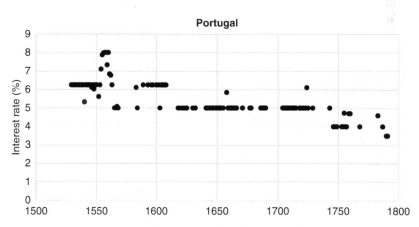

Figure 13.3 Interest rates on the nominal value of long-term bonds (*juros*) (%) (weighted average), Portugal.
Source: Costa, L. Freire, DEBT.PT – Sovereign debt and private credit in Portugal (Dívida Soberana e Crédito Privado em Portugal 1668–1797), https://debt.pt (accessed 11 March 2022).

transference of approximately 5,000 million *réis* of debt to a single ecclesiastical institution, the patriarchal church (*Sé Patriarcal*) (Azevedo, 1973: 374–375).

The relative weight of debt service on state revenues tended to decrease throughout the seventeenth and eighteenth centuries, before weighting more heavily under the Napoleonic Wars (Table 13.3). While indirect taxes, mostly the excise and custom duties, backed the interest rate payment of *juros* during most of the early modern period, by the eighteenth century the government started to earmark new *juros* on specific colonial resources. Taking 1760 as a benchmark, approximately 24% refer to tax streams provided by the colonial empire, including the 1% tax on gold shipment, the monopoly on Brazilian dyewood trade, the transference of tax surpluses from Brazil through the jurisdiction of the Overseas Council, and customs duties on Brazilian tobacco and Asian imports.[56] A similar pattern can be found in the *padrões de juro* belonging to the *Misericórdia*, a lay brotherhood that was the wealthiest welfare institution in Portugal and its empire (Sá, 1997; Abreu, 2016). The branch of the brotherhood in Lisbon, a major lender to the state in the 1700s,

Table 13.3 *Consolidated debt in Portugal, 1607–1812.*

	Crown's revenues (million *réis*)	interest payments (million *réis*)	Debt service on total revenues (%)
1607	1,302	206	15.8
1625	1,173	179	15.3
1641(*)	1,612	180	11.2
1680	1,671	195	11.7
1766	6,138	518	8.4
1802	9,511	1,113	11.7
1812	8,121	2,285	28.1

* Without revenues from the empire.
Sources: Falcão (1859); Dias (1985); Silveira (1987); Thomaz (1988); Hespanha (1994); Biblioteca da Ajuda, cód. 51-VI-19. Interest payments in 1641, 1680 and 1766: dataset from Costa, L. Freire, DEBT.PT – Sovereign debt and private credit in Portugal (Dívida Soberana e Crédito Privado em Portugal 1668–1797), https://debt.pt (accessed 11 March 2022).

[56] DEBT.PT- Sovereign debt and private credit in Portugal (Dívida Soberana e Crédito Privado em Portugal 1668–1797) (www.debt.pt).

held 195.5 million *réis* in *juros*, whose payment was mostly assigned to taxes managed by the Overseas Council (50 million *réis*), and to the tobacco monopoly and Lisbon's custom house, the country's major hub for colonial trade (72.4 million *réis*). Finally, in the late eighteenth century, when new perpetuities were sold at 3.5% interest on the nominal value, the *Misericórdia* bought *padrões de juro*. Allegedly, this investment was less uncertain compared to real estate, which required expenditure for refurbishing and additional costs for monitoring and finding new tenants (Rodrigues, L., 2019a). The empire allowed a gradual trade-off with creditors, whereby higher interest rates were foregone in favour of secure payments at a lower interest rate.

Although prices and yields are difficult to find without a thorough research on notarial deeds, the full property rights assigned to investors promoted the secondary market of *juros*. The *Misericórdia* invested idle money from its coffers by buying *padrões de juro* at par from other creditors. Moreover, *padrões de juro* were used as collateral for private credit obligations (Costa et al., 2018b). We may argue that such a low-risk instrument captured the savings of a range of wealthy people and institutions unaware of options with higher returns. For that reason, when the state endorsed the foundation of joint stock companies, it was stated that the possession of shares was as safe as the ownership of *padrões de juro* (Marcos, 1997: 184, 189). Overall, with the exception of the early and mid-seventeenth century, *padrões de juro* remained credible until 1797, when the Portuguese state issued bearer bonds for the first time.

13.4 Private Credit: The Efficiency of Capital Markets

The credit market in the Iberian Peninsula evolved despite the vagaries of an embryonic banking system. At the outset of the early modern period, banks played a significant role in private markets in Spain, contrary to what happened in Portugal, which had not any form of financial intermediation based on banks.

In the late Middle Ages, the 'primitive bank of deposit' developed in Spain as well as in other European commercial centres such as Genoa, Venice, Florence and Bruges (Usher, 1934; 1943; De Roover, 1948; 1968; Mueller, 1977). Within the Crown of Aragon, these banks originated in Barcelona, Valencia, Girona, Zaragoza and Calatayud between the thirteenth and the fifteenth centuries (Sánchez Sarto, 1934; Ruiz Martín, 1970). In Castile, these institutions, which had already existed in the fifteenth century, expanded during the sixteenth century in the main commercial centres, such as Burgos, Valladolid, Toledo, Segovia, Granada, Madrid and Seville, because of the inflow of American precious metals (Ruiz Martín, 1970; Carande, 1987, book 1; Tinoco Rubiales, 1988). Castilian primitive banks of deposit needed municipal authorization for establishment as well as bankers' personal assets and third-party guarantees as proof of solvency. Despite being known as 'public banks' they nevertheless were private banks whose accounting books were public documents that served as the legal registers of banking activity (Tinoco Rubiales, 1979: 112). The primitive bank of deposit executed the functions of exchange, deposit, *giro* and credit.

Banking activity developed without a proper regulatory framework; as a consequence, bankruptcies were recurrent. On the one hand, bank runs were frequent and permeated the banking system in the absence of modern protective mechanisms such as deposit insurance or the intervention of a lender of last resort. On the other hand, banks invested in high risk and non-diversified activities, such as large-scale investment in sovereign debt as well as commercial and financial activities related to trade with American colonies (Basas, 1964; Ruiz Martín, 1970; Tinoco Rubiales, 1988). From the end of the sixteenth century to the early seventeenth century, the primitive bank of deposit became extinct, as bankruptcies had caused their closure (Lorenzo Sanz, 1979: 155–168). From then on, private merchant-bankers funded credit from their own resources, but no institution centralized *giro* activities until the creation of the *Real Giro* in 1752 and, later, the Banco de San Carlos in 1782 (Tedde de Lorca, 1988).

In sixteenth-century Castile, the primitive bank of deposit paid an interest rate of 7–7.5% for deposits and usury laws established a maximum legal interest rate for credit of 10% (Ruiz Martín, 1970: 24; Martín-Aceña & Nogues-Marco, 2013: 145). This legal ceiling was the same as England had at that time, although the effective interest rate there was *de facto* between 15 and 20% (Flandreau et al., 2009a: 171–172). In the case of Castile, Álvarez-Nogal (2017: 541) has documented an example of a prominent primitive bank of deposit that formally charged an interest rate of 6.67–7.14% on loans, which implies a net interest spread – the difference between borrowing and lending rates – near zero or even negative, inconsistent with the prevalent high-risk of banking activity. As is evident from studies of other European centres such as Italy and France that were also regulated by maximum legal interest rates for credit, it is probable that simple devices camouflaged the effective interest rate, where, for example, a banker might record a debt larger than the sum actually paid to the borrower (Nogues-Marco, 2018). As a result of usury regulations on interest rates, effective interest rates are usually unknown, except for those exceptional cases where private records registered the 'true' loan. Therefore, the interest rates registered in official records are only a biased measure of the cost of capital.

To address the efficiency of private capital markets, we should focus on bills of exchange. They constitute the benchmark to calculate private interest rates because this instrument circumvented usury regulations, as the interest rate was hidden in the exchange rate at maturity (Flandreau et al., 2009a). The bill-of-exchange was an instrument developed to transfer money and provide credit between distant centres in pre-industrial Europe. Braudel (1992, vol. II: 248) described the boundaries of commercial finance as a 'Bell Jar' within early modern capitalism that connected European commercial centres. These connections can be tracked through bill-of-exchange quotations registered in the financial and commercial press as well as merchants' correspondence (Flandreau et al., 2009b). In addition, they facilitate the calculation of the interest rates embedded in exchange rates. For Cádiz in the eighteenth century, Nogues-Marco (2011: 65–92) estimated that the hidden interest rates of bills of exchange averaged 8.79% for the period 1729–1788 (see Figure 13.4). This estimate is consistent with the very scarce direct evidence available in primary sources. For instance, according to the archive of the Banco de San Carlos, the discount rate in Cádiz in 1786 was 8% (Tedde de Lorca, 1988: 131). Cádiz's interest rate was above that of the main financial markets in the eighteenth century (1720–1789): Amsterdam averaged an interest rate of 3.92%, London 3.8% and Paris 4.59% (Flandreau et al., 2009a; 2009b). According to the available empirical evidence, the efficiency of private capital markets in Spain was far below that of the core European financial centres.

Outside the bill-of-exchange credit system that connected national and international merchant-bankers, notarized mortgage-backed loans provided domestic credit in the different kingdoms of Spain. Long-term loans were supported by the credit instrument *censos consignativos*. The debtor of the *censo* obliged himself to pay a rent from certain specified properties in return for a sum of money. Sometimes he promised to pay in perpetuity, sometimes for the life of the creditor, and, most commonly, until he redeemed the *censo* by repaying at any time in one lump sum, the capital value of the loan (*censo consignativo al quitar*) (Álvarez Vázquez, 1987: 221–223; Fiestas Loza, 1993: 582). The interest rates of

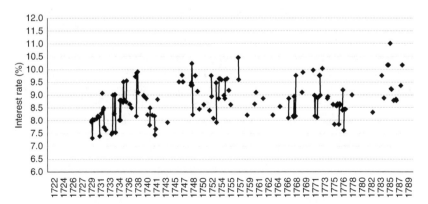

Figure 13.4 Commercial annual interest rates (%), Cádiz, 1729–1789.
Source: Nogues-Marco (2011: 65–92). Outliers have been removed.

censos consignativos decreased from 7.1% to 4% between 1570 and 1698 (Yun-Casalilla, 1987: 237; 352–356). In the early eighteenth century, the rate was limited by the usury laws to a maximum of 3% in Castile and 5% in Aragon (Milhaud, 2018: 87). However, this interest rate is not comparable with that of plain financial instruments because *censos consignativos* were financial derivatives; the opportunity for the debtor to redeem the *censo* at any time implies the existence of embedded options, which does not facilitate a simple yield calculation (see Nogues-Marco & Vam Malle-Sabouret, 2007).

Similarly, short-term credit known as obligation contracts – whose maturity was usually less than a year – were registered by notaries and usually collateralized by mortgages. Peña-Mir (2016) has documented obligation contracts at the end of the eighteenth century (1779–1792) as being oriented to fund agrarian activities in Málaga (Andalusia). Notarized registers do not document the payment of interests for these loans, although indirect evidence declares its existence. There were similar occurrences in France, where notaries hid the interest rates of obligations because usury laws had established a ban on interest for such financial instruments until the time of the French Revolution (Hoffman et al., 2000: 14–16).

In Portugal, a variety of institutions supplied credit to private debtors, but there is no evidence of primitive banks of deposit. Our survey on private credit thus relies on bilateral contracts, notarized or recorded in probate inventories, as well as on the credit activities of the *Misericórdia*. Given its charitable purpose, this lay brotherhood was often bequeathed substantial legacies. The frequent use of these funds to provide public and private credit makes it an illustrative case with which to examine the credit business.

Both probate inventories and notarial deeds show the common use of short-term obligations (IOUs) with different maturities (usually one year) albeit often including a prorogation clause. Explicit indication of the rate of interest was common and occurred alongside the request for assets or sources of income as collateral. The former seems to be a unique feature of the Portuguese notarized credit with this information being available in any deed. A recent study was able to extract a market interest rate from bilateral contracts, after expunging the idiosyncratic variables (Costa et al., 2018a). It shows a downward trend, with interest rates falling from 6.25% to 5% between 1715 and 1755, the year of the Lisbon earthquake (see Figure 13.5). The wording of thousands of obligations drawn up by notaries in Lisbon attests to the widespread use of Brazilian gold as cash that was channelled to credit activities. Indeed, injections of cash could have had an endowment effect (the prospect of a future increase in income) on raising interest rates, but they were also a source of liquidity supply in a credit market, which reduced interest rates. The liquidity effect, rather than the substantial improvements in enforcement mechanisms through recourse to law courts, explains the downward

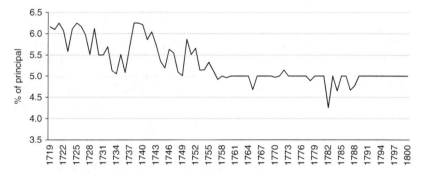

Figure 13.5 Annual market interest rates (%) – short-term obligations, Lisbon, 1719–1800.
Source: Costa et al. (2018a: 1161–1164).

trend in interest rates until 1757, as will be further illustrated by the *Misericórdia*'s problems in dealing with private credit through legal actions.

As far as the use of notarized credit is concerned, yet another feature differentiates the case study of Lisbon. While the participation of the nobility and professionals is a remarkable feature of notarized credit in Paris, as Hoffman et al. (2000) noted, in Lisbon it reports a significant participation by craftsmen and, although less so, by labourers. This suggests that the level of wealth needed for this trade was not critically high. Indeed, a great deal of retail distribution relied on selling on credit, which also explains the common use of informal notes of IOU listed in probate inventories.

The *Misericórdia*, on the other hand, displays distinct credit relationships with regard to the social rank of debtors as well as to the maturity of loans supplied. The Lisbon branch of the brotherhood is known to have met the demands of the aristocracy, thus corresponding with studies that have already noted the high level of indebtedness of that social group in the Iberian kingdoms (Yun-Casalilla, 2019). As in Spain, in the sixteenth and seventeenth centuries, aristocrats tended to find credit by issuing *censos consignativos* (Abadía Irache, 1998; Yun-Casalilla, 2002) with interest assigned to rents from real estate or seigneurial rights. This practice became less frequent in Portugal, during the century, thus resulting in that social group depending increasingly on credit from the *Misericórdia*. Some in-depth studies illuminate the problems caused by the biased credit relationships of the *Misericórdia* and have shown that judicial rulings determining the seizure of assets given by aristocrats as collateral were not effectively enforced, either because of the courts' lack of coercive means or because judges were reluctant to contend with a social group that enhanced the institution's prestige. The state intervened and interdicted the *Misericórdia* from lending to private borrowers in 1775, which in turn reinforced the institution's option of applying its liquidity in public credit or in short-term obligations to other social groups (Rodrigues, 2019b).

The working of the credit market in Portugal was affected by the 1755 earthquake, which created conditions for a new legal framework. The event was followed by the imposition of a 5% legal cap on interest rates, which put an end to a legal loophole. The legislation, however, explicitly excluded the bottomry loans used in the Cape of Good Hope route. The ruler's aim may have been to steer funds to Asian endeavours, rather than avoiding a steep rise of interest rates after a demand shock by virtue of the earthquake, which eventually also affected public credit (Costa et al., 2018a; 2018b).

The destruction of wealth caused by the earthquake had a variety of impacts on lenders and borrowers. For survivors, it offered the chance of returns, but also potentially involved high risk given the destruction of collateral, which possibly made 5% too low an interest rate and caused credit rationing. The state's intervention could have made supply more stringent and slowed down the pace of reconstruction. But it is also likely that the legal cap was close to the equilibrium interest rate; demand might have fallen due to the reduced wealth of borrowers. However, the high level of physical capital depletion was not matched by a loss in money wealth in the form of gold coins, mostly for two reasons. On the one hand, a great deal of the private remittances that had arrived in the most recent Brazilian fleets was still stored in the Mint House where 1% tax on remittances was collected. On the other hand, remittances did not stop in subsequent years. Hence, the liquidity effect attributed to gold influxes may have mitigated the impact of the legal cap after the earthquake. At the same time, in 1757 and 1763, the state sponsored the foundation of chartered companies to deal with the north and north-eastern regions of Brazil for 20 years. The stock market experienced outstanding periods of vitality in 1766–1767 and again in 1775 (Costa et al., 2019). In addition to the consequences of the earthquake, new investment options may have changed the landscape of the credit market in Portugal in the second half of the eighteenth century.

Despite the 5% legal cap, institutions increasingly sought to invest funds in short-term maturities. The church, hospitals and lay brotherhoods, such as *Misericórdias*, resorted to credit obligations more often than to *censos consignativos*, making the preference for the former the most significant change we observed in the long run in urban markets (Abreu, 1990: 57–58; Rocha, 1996: 190; Rodrigues, 2013; 2019a). This change in Portugal seems to have occurred earlier than in Aragon, where 73% of the income of the ecclesiastical institutions was still generated by *censos* in the mid-eighteenth century (Milhaud, 2018). In Portugal, as also found for other areas of the Iberian Peninsula (Yun-Casalilla, 1987: 357; Grafe, 2012: 223), the nominal interest rates of this credit instrument could have been below the legal ceilings, reaching 3%. Once the *censos* underwent a declining trend (Figure 13.6), 5% legal cap applied to short-term obligations seems to allow better remuneration.

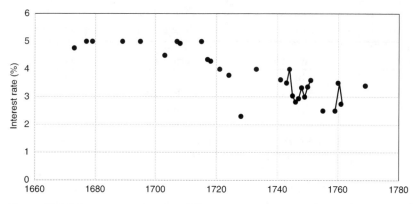

Figure 13.6 Interest rates at issuance (%): private perpetuities in Portugal.
Source: Rodrigues (2021).

A major institutional change in the working of credit markets was tried in the early 1800s when the state sought the foundation of a public bank as a joint-stock enterprise. It faced resistance from the greatest merchant-financiers of the kingdom who did not foresee any benefit in setting up a specialized banking institution (Cardoso, 1997). By that time, Portugal's financial system was still based on institutions that had already existed in the sixteenth century. If financial development can be assessed through interest rates' trends, such an institutional resilience did not have critical consequences, considering that interest rates of long-term maturities declined in Portugal as elsewhere, and the legal cap after the earthquake did not have long-term consequences in credit rationing. In any event, much research is needed for a full understanding of the financial hindrances the kingdom experienced when the royal court fled to Brazil in 1808.

13.5 Conclusions

This chapter has focused on early modern financial development in the Iberian Peninsula. The access to precious metals – gold and silver – was the major common denominator of the Iberian colonial experience. Remittances were not only a royal affair, but, primarily, a private business. For this reason, we have considered the relationship between liquidity and financial development by examining both public and private credit markets. Our approach has the advantage of considering a more complete scope of financial development contrary to traditional historiography that has generally considered *either* the public *or* the private credit market. At the same time, this approach has also highlighted the limits of our knowledge on the topic, and we hope this piece of research will encourage further study.

When analysing the development of public credit in the long run, the first common feature between Castile and Portugal is that both kingdoms used the same financial instruments. Public debt resorted to short-term credit in the form of contracts with syndicates of merchant-financiers (*asientos* for Castile and *assentos* for Portugal), and to long-term credit based largely on perpetuities (*juros al quitar* and *padrões de juro*, respectively). In the case of Castile, the debt service of *juros* was paid over a tax stream on ordinary taxes (excluding public remittances of precious metals), but *asientos* might be paid with public remittances of precious metals or converted to *juros*. It is difficult to disentangle the role precious metals played in the development of public credit from the Crown's bargaining power (*vis-à-vis* that of municipalities) to raise the tax ceiling that permitted the increased issuance of *juros*. In the case of Portugal, the debt service of the new *juros* issued in the eighteenth century was increasingly paid over a tax levied on gold remittances (1% tax), denoting the growing importance of the Brazilian colonial economy in collateralizing public debt. In any case, we know that the ratio of debt-to-tax revenues was much lower in Portugal than in the Habsburgs' Castile.

Another common feature of public credit development in Portugal and Castile is that both kingdoms experienced a long-term reduction of the interest rates on the nominal value of long-term bonds. Liquidity might have played a role. Other variables, such as the long-term reduction of transaction costs and investors' perception of default risk or financial repression, probably also contributed to market performance. More research is needed on the explanatory variables of the capital market development. The strategy we have followed to approach market development has been to consider the yields instead of the interest rates on the nominal value, as yields take into account market value.

Unfortunately, however, yields are elusive because public debt was traded in decentralized markets. In the case of Portugal, no information about yields is available so far. There is not enough data on market prices of *juros* in the Portuguese secondary market to have a consistent picture of the evolution of yields. The indications about transactions between private investors point to sales at par. In the case of Castile, anecdotal evidence shows a yield of 7.4–9% at the end of the sixteenth century and 8–9% at the end of the seventeenth century, which indicates a sustained investors' perception of country risk consistent with defaults, despite the reduction of interest rates on the nominal value. Similarly, yields on European sovereign debt traded in Amsterdam in 1771 and 1783 show that Spain had the highest yield; the country risk counteracted the potentially positive effects of liquidity in reducing the cost of public debt, although yields on Spanish debt decreased at the end of the eighteenth century as a result of an improvement in creditworthiness.

When analysing the development of private credit in the long run, there is a higher degree of complexity. Interest rates in the market of long-term maturities (*censos consignativos*) show a long-term downward trend and the legal ceilings seem to have adjusted to it. But usury laws established a maximum legal interest rate for credit that makes the measurement of private credit efficiency difficult. Simple devices camouflaged the effective interest rates in Spain, which means that the interest rates registered in official records are only a biased measure of the cost of capital.

The case of Portugal is different because usury laws did not affect the private credit market until 1757. Notarized credit explicitly indicated an interest rate, before and after the enactment of the regulation that established a 5% ceiling. Short-term obligations show a downward trend in the eighteenth century that is interpreted as the result of the increase in liquidity caused by the remittances of Brazilian gold. The earthquake, however, may have changed the credit market landscape in Portugal, and the 5% ceiling possibly caused credit rationing in the following decade. In the case of Spain, notarized credit did not document the payment of interests, although indirect evidence declares the existence of such. To measure the efficiency of the Spanish private credit market, we have focused on bills of exchange instead of notarized credit. Bills of exchange constitute the benchmark for the calculation of private interest rates because this instrument circumvented usury regulations with the interest rate hidden in the exchange rate at maturity. The hidden interest rate embedded in exchange rates for eighteenth-century Cádiz was above the interest rates of the main financial markets at that time, which indicates that the efficiency of the private capital market in Spain was far below that of the core European financial centres.

The divergent path of the evolution of private and public credit, on the one hand, and of the markets for long and short-term maturities, on the other hand, suggest that the capital market was still much segmented.

14

Science, Knowledge and Technology, 1500–1800

CARLOS ÁLVAREZ-NOGAL, ALEJANDRO GARCÍA-MONTÓN
AND PEDRO LAINS

14.1 Introduction

Science, knowledge and technological progress have had an increasing importance in economic activity since early times and the period from the early discoveries to the Industrial Revolution studied here was no exception. New instruments for the measurement of space and distance allowed the exploration of new trade routes across the globe, the invention of new machinery led to increases in productivity in many manufacturing sectors, such as metals, paper and textiles, as well as in means of transportation and infrastructure. Although economic historians interested in science and technology have long focused primarily on those economies that would first experience an Industrial Revolution, especially Britain, early modern developments in science or technology, as well as of their impact on economic performance, transformed other economies at the same time. Thus the central quest is to understand the reasons behind changes in the intensity with which inventions and other changes in production took place, and to understand how different parts of the world participated in that process.

One major issue in the field is to define the causal relationship between knowledge and economic performance. Was technological development a response to the needs of economic activity and thus mostly a consequence of economic growth? Alternatively, were the advances in knowledge the outcome of a favourable social, political and institutional environment and thus a primary cause of economic transformation? These are open-ended questions as it is hard to quantify the impact of science on the economy and determine the direction of causality. Yet, we can address them by studying the developments in science, knowledge and technology in relation to what we know about the economic performance of the Iberian economy. We may thus insert the experiences of the Iberian polities into the more general context of the connections between a broad span of 'scientific revolutions' and economic convergence and divergence at the world level (O'Brien, 2013). Our understanding is that the two processes are interconnected. Yet, we will argue that in the Iberian economies the causality link ran mostly from the needs to overcome bottlenecks in economic activity to changes in technology rather than the other way round and that technology was likely more important than science. Technological progress in Iberia supported Smithian growth but as in all other places except Britain it did not push beyond that before the later nineteenth century.

That is not to say that we dismiss the major role in scientific and technological change played by the institutional environment (Mokyr, 1990). But while the traditional historiography had supposed that Iberian institutions were a drag on progress in science and technology, we see little evidence for such factors, especially in the early part of the period under consideration. True, as the Industrial Revolution gained momentum in Britain and other parts of north-western Europe, Iberia was largely lagging behind in terms of technological development. Some authors (White, 1962; Landes, 1969; Pollard, 1981) saw late eighteenth-century Iberia as a land of unrealized economic growth potential, citing market and institutional failures as obstacles to growth. But their hypotheses about the supposedly low quality of Iberian technology were based on thin empirical foundations and reached without studying any specific economic sector or providing data and information about the performance of technology in the Iberian Peninsula. The notion that Iberia was somehow held back by religious fanaticism and obscurantism has not stood the test of actual empirical research on the development of science in the peninsula and the colonial world (Bleichmar et al., 2009). According to Cañizares-Esguerra (2018: 5), 'scholars are just now beginning to realize that the European Renaissance and Enlightenment were not European inventions but vast encyclopaedias of hybrid global knowledge processed and packaged in Europe', to which the Iberian kingdoms contributed in many different ways. That was particularly so, as we shall see below, in the sixteenth century.

One conclusion we can draw from the large amount of literature on the evolution of science and technology is precisely that knowledge has developed across political and cultural borders, within a framework where differences are more relevant in terms of intensity of developments than in terms of technological paradigms. Efforts for controlling markets and the spread of knowledge made by states or institutions such as guilds may have reduced the speed of international trade of ideas, but they also helped the development of technology and its diffusion within the affected jurisdictions. There is, for example, still an open debate about the effects of guilds on the economy. Some scholars claim that guilds were so widespread, and lived so long, that they must have generated economic benefits. Others are much less positive, because guilds acted as cartels and thus were in a position to extract benefits for their own members only, restricting human capital formation and limiting creativity and innovation (Epstein, 1998; Ogilvie, 2004). A second lesson from the literature is that science and technology did not evolve in a uniform way across regions and throughout the centuries, at least up to the end of the period studied here. Some advances in technology were not fully absorbed at the time of their appearance, only to re-emerge in other places and times under more favourable conditions.

That has raised another question, namely whether in Iberia the economic incentives to innovation were less intense or simply were not there, with the exception of areas around the more dynamic port cities such as Lisbon, Bilbao, Cádiz, Málaga and Barcelona. Throughout the sixteenth century, we observe developments in many sectors that bear witness to the dynamism of maritime activity, including navigation, shipbuilding and related industries. But we also witness progress in the interior in woollens, the introduction of new crops in agriculture, irrigation and also in the service sector, such as financial instruments. The pace of development faded during the seventeenth century, a period of deep and long economic decline in Castile, but it did not die out completely. What made the difference then? Was there a more favourable institutional environment in the sixteenth century than in the following centuries? Did the increase in scale provided by the overseas territorial expansion lead to technological advances?[57] Furthermore, was the eighteenth century a period of technological regression in Iberia or of expansion compared to previous centuries, or compared to the most progressive regions of the world? By addressing these questions, we can find additional clues regarding the reasons for technological progress in history.

This chapter looks at the evolution of science, knowledge and technology in the Iberian Peninsula from the beginning of the age of discoveries to the time of the Industrial Revolution. Through the ages, we have witnessed transformations in the use of land, the introduction of new crops and processes to reduce the impact of plant diseases, and the impact of changes in rainfall. In the production of energy and in manufacturing we have also observed crucial developments in the efficiency of different sources of power, such as animal, wind, water, and coal or charcoal, as well as in techniques for the production of consumption staples, from foodstuffs to textiles and building materials. We can also identify important technological developments in transport, the transmission of knowledge, financial services, road building, the production of printing materials and the minting of coins. We first analyse the improvements in the agrarian sector, not only because it remained the most important sector in terms of employment but also because a set of ecological constraints shaped progress in this sector. We then show some technological advances in the non-agrarian part of the economy. We describe especially the innovations in specific

---

[57] Van Zanden and van Leewen (2012: 138) find a similar decline in output expansion after the mid-seventeenth century, which they relate to a decline in the contribution of technological change that peaked in the Golden Age period (1550–1650), and the increasing strength of Iberia's competitors in the global markets.

areas of manufacturing, such as shipbuilding, textiles (woollens, silk and cotton) and mining. The final section discusses the role played by the institutional framework. As we will see, Iberian monarchies were actively seeking to help overcome some of the existing constraints by promoting technology and knowledge in different ways. While the impact of such interventions was ambivalent, they bear witness to a generally progressive attitude to technological change in contrast to an older literature that had interpreted government intervention as necessarily negative and backward looking.

14.2 Agriculture

Agriculture was by far the most important sector in early modern economies, including the Iberian ones, in terms of total population employed and the share of national output. It provided the food for the population and the raw materials for the manufacture of clothing and other consumer goods, as well as for producing tools and building materials. The pace of change in agriculture was thus crucial for the improvement of the material conditions of the population and the economy at large. The role of science, knowledge and technology is hard to gauge. But the little we know about the key features of agrarian development in this period suggests that change was limited. The advancement of the sector depended more on demographic dynamics, urbanization, changes in the degree of market integration, as well as access to long-distance trade. Such dependence was certainly not unidirectional, as changes in the rest of the economy could also be an outcome of improvements in the agrarian sector. This interpretation holds for most of the period covered in this chapter. But the picture changes slightly from the late seventeenth century onwards and particularly during the eighteenth century in some more fortunate parts of northern Europe. In Iberia, technological improvements made the difference in a limited number of regions only. Nonetheless, it is still important to investigate what the main transformations in knowledge and technology in agriculture were.

The base of the Iberian agrarian sector consisted overwhelmingly of the three traditional Mediterranean crops, namely wheat, wine and oil. Environmental frontiers and climate conditions were more important than political borders. The three products were the basis of a very successful economy with low prices and good quality. All of them had a significant impact on the population's diet. However, agricultural soils in the Iberian Peninsula were poor in comparison to Western Europe. The orography and harsh climate worked against agriculture in many regions. In Spain, 10% of the land is rock, 35% poor and unproductive, 45% moderately fertile and only about 10% is really rich and suitable for highly productive agriculture (Elliott, 1987: 7). The soil conditions in coastal Iberia were slightly better than in the interior, as was the case of Portugal, for which data suggest that by the late nineteenth century almost 35% of agricultural land was still unused (Lains, 2002b). The disparities of soil quality allowed for a certain degree of regional specialization and diversity of the structure of agrarian activity and thus opened up possibilities for internal trade. In some instances this connected to international trade flows. Such was the case with wine, wool, salt or minerals. International borders, including those between the two Iberian countries, remained largely open for a number of essential industrial inputs, such as wool and iron (imported from outside the Peninsula and from Spain into Portugal), lead and high-quality timber (Macedo, 1982: 125).

Most studies on agriculture have focused on the traditional cereal production of the Iberian Peninsula, where yields were very low. We have few quantitative studies on livestock, perhaps because of the scarcity of good sources. However, we have many historical references about its significant role in the local peasant economy. The importance of transhumance and the production of wool are well known (Fernández Albaladejo, 1994), but local livestock was also very important and a perfect complement to any agrarian expansion. All the disadvantages that arable agriculture had due to poor soil quality played in favour of livestock. Farmers had a wide variety of livestock (cows, oxen, horses, mules, pigs, goats, lambs and especially sheep) because the low population density allowed for large grazing areas. The animals not only helped to fertilize the soil, but also provided an extra source of power for many production and transportation activities. That would explain the high urban development of the northern *Meseta* plateau in a geographical area that lacks navigable rivers and canals, a common source of power in other areas of Europe. In addition to transportation, cattle, sheep and goats were a source of meat, milk and cheese, adding diversity to the population's diet.

Rural and urban activities often shared the same space thanks to an extensive network of transport services provided by *acemileros*, carters, *trajineros* and *arrieros*. Most transportation services used pack animals and were seasonal in nature, reflecting weather conditions and agrarian cycles, but some groups of carters demonstrated a high grade of specialization (Ringrose, 1969, 52). In the sixteenth century, many cities and towns in Castile were fed and provisioned thanks to the heavy traffic of these carriers (Bennassar, 1983), some of which specialized in the transport of heavy goods, such as wood, fish, wine, cereals, cloths and construction materials, and their presence was paramount in many regions (Rubio Pérez, 1995; Miguel López, 2000).

By 1500, parts of Iberia were finally recovering from the impact of the Black Death (1348–1350), which had left behind a vast, underpopulated and uncultivated territory (Álvarez-Nogal et al., 2020). The complete recovery, at least from the perspective of GDP per capita, arrived after 1600. Consequently, one major feature of the agrarian sector in the following decades and centuries was the recovery both of land for agricultural use and the population to work in this sector. This movement implied the use of a number of techniques, mostly of ancestral usage, which included improvements such as drying marshes, the building of irrigation canals or the recovery of the output of crops that involved more complex production methods, such as rice in the regions of Valencia (Franch Benavent, 2005) or later on in the surrounding region of the city of Coimbra. Putting new land to use implied an effort of organization and better knowledge of the terrain. The recovery of population growth was accompanied by increasing urbanization and the extension of the size of the market, as well as the structure of demand for agricultural products. All these changes created the incentives to rely more on innovation and new techniques. Simultaneously, the overseas expansion that commenced in the fifteenth century led to the expansion of traditional crops into new territories and to the introduction of a number of new crops in Iberia. Sugar, which was traditionally cultivated on the coast of the Muslim kingdom of Granada, was successfully expanded to Madeira and the Canary Islands (Díaz Hernández, 1982; Fábregas García, 2014; 2018). Maize was quickly introduced in the north-western part of the peninsula, having an important impact on the local agriculture (Anes, 1988). Elsewhere, the adaptation and expansion of the new crops were slower, and in many cases they only became relevant by the eighteenth century.

Yet, the relative importance of different sources for agrarian expansion varied throughout time and space. For the case of Spain, which has been studied in more detail, in the sixteenth century, the population increased both in the rural and urban areas and agriculture responded by increasing the degree of specialization and diversification of output. The growing demand for food in the urban centres pushed prices up thus increasing the incentive to exploit new lands, even some with lower levels of productivity. The fast growth of Madrid demanded large amounts of agrarian products, and it boosted the cereal economies of the centre of the Iberian Peninsula (Bernardos Sanz, 2003).

The once prosperous cities of Castile were in decline by the end of the sixteenth century and this had a considerable impact on the agrarian sector (Álvarez-Nogal et al., 2016). The decline in output was mostly a consequence of the fall in demand, and not a change in supply-side conditions. Many have blamed price controls (the so-called *tasa* on wheat prices) for the decline in agricultural output, mainly affecting cereals. However, all agricultural sectors contracted, not only grain production. At the same time the control of prices remained in place throughout the early modern period even during periods of output expansion.

Throughout the fifteenth century and the first half of the sixteenth century, the Iberian economy was increasingly opened up to the outside world, following the growth in demand for foodstuffs, and raw materials such as wool and minerals in north-western Europe. In the seventeenth century there were new opportunities in trade thanks to the specialization of different regions. The central *Meseta* plateau focused production on cereals and wool, while the Douro valley and Jerez de la Frontera, and their connected ports of Porto and Cádiz, specialized in wine as did Barcelona and its hinterland. However, exports were a small proportion of agricultural production. For Portugal, the share of total net food exports on total food consumption were quite low and declined from 1.4% to 0.4%, from 1700 to 1800; in the case of wine, the same share increased significantly in the same period from 1.0% to 3.8% (Costa & Reis, 2017; Lains, 2018: 185). The share of wine output in total agricultural output is estimated at 15% in 1515 and 19% in 1850.[58] Similar shares for sixteenth to eighteenth century Spain are not available, but they would certainly be lower at the aggregate level due to the larger size of the country. Yet the exports had a markedly positive impact on production methods in the wine sector, as it involved specialization in improving the output quality and the process of wine making, improvements in the production of casks, as well as improvements in transportation through the Douro River and overseas (Lains, 2018: 184). Salt was Portugal's main export, followed by wine and olive oil (Hanson, 1981: 199). As the war between Spain and Portugal (1640–1668) ended, by the end of the seventeenth century, Portuguese exports resumed revealing comparative advantages in olive oil, wine, wool and fruits like oranges, as well as sugar, tobacco and brazilwood re-exported from the colonies (Godinho, 1970: 519–520; Hanson, 1981: 129–130). Clearly, innovation in production, trade and services followed the increase in demand for higher quality products, and not the other way around.

For innovation to occur, adequate institutions are often as important as technical improvements, the advancement of knowledge, and scientific and technological breakthroughs. Their economic impact was important in different ways during the whole period we are covering here, but in the context of the early modern economy structural change derived largely from extensive growth and changes in the composition of demand – and less so from changes in technology – as fluctuations in population dynamics, urbanization and foreign trade opened up new commercial opportunities. Still, the Iberian agricultural sector suffered from a significant number of institutional and ecological constraints, such as a poorly integrated domestic market and low levels of output surplus and savings (not necessarily through high interest rates), resulting in low levels of available capital to invest in further improvements of land, tools and knowledge. Also, the importance of communal lands and the popular custom of the '*derrota de las mieses*' in Castile, that is, the collective use of straw that remained in the fields after harvesting (Vassberg, 1984), may have delayed innovation.

At the same time there were other institutions that helped output expansion, such as the *emphyteusis*. These types of rental contracts, dominant in Catalonia, Valencia and the Balearic Islands, guaranteed the tenant use of land throughout a lifetime of the planted grapevines in exchange for part of

---

[58] There are no estimates for the intermediate years (Reis, 2016: 174; Lains, 2018: 183).

the crop. A similar institution, the *colonia*, was developed on the island of Madeira (Câmara, 2006). A similar type of contract was also very successful for agrarian production around Barcelona. The presence of an important urban market around the city and its port encouraged the enclosure of farms and the lease of land with a specialization in vineyards. The *rabassa morta* sharecropping contract was a successful solution to reduce problems of moral hazard and opportunistic behaviour because of the extended duration of the contract (Carmona & Simpson, 1999). It was able to develop the trust and social capital needed to reduce conflicts between landowners and labourers, but it also provided incentives for peasants to respond to market opportunities. The agrarian expansion encouraged investment and technical innovation later on, even far beyond agriculture.

In the eighteenth century, the resurgence of population growth was intense in rural areas, implying a lower degree of agrarian diversification. Thus, while economic expansion during the sixteenth century was associated with trade and commercial services, and in the seventeenth century with specialization, the eighteenth century saw a return to extensive growth. The implications of those differences were paramount and reflected in the process of innovation and technological development (Álvarez-Nogal & Prados de la Escosura, 2013, 19–20). During the eighteenth century the number of people living and working in the countryside had increased without any substantial technological improvement, leaving no other alternative than to expand the land cultivated. Given the scarcity of quality soils in Spain, this second extensive growth process increased the pressure on resources and explains the lower productivity at the end of the eighteenth century. In some regions of the Peninsula, particularly in the north-west and the south-east, farmers introduced or reinvigorated crops with higher land productivity levels, particularly maize, potatoes and rice (Villares Paz, 1982; Anes, 1988; Neto, 2018), a process that had started in many areas at the beginning of the seventeenth century. Other products played an important role in local orchards (tomatoes, peppers or beans) and were cultivated for family self-consumption. One of the most important advantages of the introduction of these new products was that they meant an important alternative or complement to cereals. They helped to feed more people, but they did not contribute to any increase in the size of the agrarian market or to capital accumulation.

In the north, Galicia, Minho and Asturias experienced large population growth thanks to the introduction of these new crops, but they did not provide enough profits to improve their production methods and capital accumulation. However, in some places the introduction of maize led even in the eighteenth century to deep changes in some farming economies, and pushed for better irrigation and hydraulic systems, as well as the suppression of more traditional crops and a search for a more intensive agriculture (Maduro, 2018).

In areas like Murcia, with better access to land and markets, the new crops allowed the population to become more specialized in the production of vegetables. The plains of Tierras de Campos and the Alentejo specialized in cereals. Vineyards expanded in large areas of the *Meseta* plateau, as well as in Portugal, as did olive trees in Andalusia and Portugal. Valencia chose to specialize in fruit, vegetables and rice. In the Iberian Peninsula during the eighteenth century, areas with advanced agriculture coexisted with others that were much more backward. Portuguese agriculture went through a 'silent revolution' driven by the development of markets within an 'unchanged institutional and political context' (Serrão, 2009: 47-48).

In the sixteenth and early seventeenth century, before the agrarian revolution started in some areas of Holland and Britain, regional differences in agricultural factor productivity within Europe could be substantial, following the pattern of resource endowments, but they averaged out when we consider larger aggregates, such as nations. The differences in agrarian technology between the Iberian Peninsula and the rest of Western Europe were not significant, as methods of production were quite similar and there were no significant differences in the composition of output and demand. Agrarian technological frontiers within Europe were virtually absent and lower yields in the Iberian Peninsula were not a consequence of a technological gap, but rather due to fewer incentives to produce large quantities because of poorly developed and poorly integrated markets, the high transport costs of high-volume and low-value goods in many interior regions, or financial problems at a local level. In countries that lagged behind in the agrarian revolution, such as Spain and Portugal, innovation was held back by the lack of capital, adverse political conditions and poor access to the markets, factors that led farmers to focus on security and the minimizing risk rather than increasing long-term output and profits.

It is important to highlight the difficulties preventing the introduction of innovations in agriculture because a successful outcome depended on many factors. In fact, failures cost lives. Thus, where capital and access to markets were scarce, improvements in techniques had to be cautious and came as simple and small modifications, requiring little capital. For new techniques to be adopted it was necessary that they had a potential to provide undoubted benefits for the population that had to be fed and lodged. This aspect could explain the long persistence of the open field system and communal techniques, and the slow introduction of new products in many territories.

According to some estimates for 1500 and 1600 (Allen, 1988: 118), England and France had similar labour productivity rates in agriculture. Yet in the eighteenth century, productivity increased substantially in England, due to a number of factors, including enclosures, which implied large capital investments, an increase in the average size of farms and changes in property rights. To these factors, we also need to add the importance of innovations, successfully implemented because of adequate funding (King & Levine, 1993), and a political system that leveraged the power of innovators and protected them from those who benefitted from the status quo. Innovations were also dependent on an increase in access to the market, at the regional, national and international levels.

Enlightenment, physiocracy and the arrival of a new dynasty, the Bourbons, to the Spanish throne in the eighteenth century resulted in a renewed effort to promote knowledge and increase the production of agricultural and manufactured goods (López García & Santesmases Navarro de Palencia, 2006: 895). The Crown sponsored the use of new lands, the creation of new villages and the increase of public works. As we will see when looking at the manufacturing sector, we can observe the intervention by the government. However, the economic impact of all those changes was different depending on the regions.

Agriculture was also the main source of raw materials for manufacturing activity. One of the most dynamic and important sectors was food processing: the production of oil, biscuits for fleet crews, flour, wines and spirits, and fleece and the export of wool. All these activities require knowledge, skills, machines, tools and technology that go beyond simple agrarian tasks. In the north of Castile, the economy around shearing, packing and the transport of wool was one of the more dynamic areas (Phillips & Phillips, 1997; Ruiz Martín & García Sanz, 1998). This activity, again halfway between animal husbandry and manufacturing, made possible the use of marginal lands as pastures, providing a high-quality raw material to both local and foreign industry. The amount of wool exported tripled between 1512 and 1549 (Phillips & Phillips, 1997), but fell between the late sixteenth century and the mid-seventeenth and experienced a resurgence thereafter.

The production of biscuits, a dry and hard cake made with wheat bran, reached extraordinary volumes. It was the main food of thousands of sailors on board for months in the different monarchy's fleets that departed from Seville, Cádiz, Lisbon and Cartagena, but also in other ports of the peninsula (Domínguez Ortiz, 1984: 132-133: Serrano Mangas, 1990: 160-173). This activity required a large number of workers every year, but also capital and infrastructure such as ovens and warehouses. Linked to this were other large-scale food processing operations, such as the production of bacon, wine, oil, fish and cheese, all with the same destination: the provisioning of fleets and armies.

Agricultural physical capital consisted mostly of tools, harvesters, windmills, watermills and irrigation channels. The use of hydraulic power to drive flour and oil mills and wine presses was regular throughout Iberia, from the hills in the north to central Castile and the south. Evidence points to an increase in its importance across the period studied here, but tools regularly used by peasants at the beginning of 1800 were not very different from those used in 1500, except for a greater use of iron, and the use of fallow, which translated into a biennial or triennial rotation of cereal, fallow and grass. Productivity was low and stable over time, both per unit of seed and per cultivated area, so any increase in production required an expansion of the cultivated area and a larger population.

Andalucía and the Balearic Islands developed cooperative solutions to build the large infrastructures that were crucial in boosting productivity (Glick, 1970). In Murcia, for example, farmers had built irrigation systems with little intervention from the state since the Middle Ages, thus allowing the transformation of dry areas into irrigated cultures, turning it into one of the most highly productive territories in Mediterranean Iberia (Kirchner, 2009). Technology connected closely to the natural environment, not only in terms of the quantity of rainfall and the quality of soils, but also in terms of accessibility to urban markets and distant trade. These were features typical of the sector in the whole continent and Iberia was not different from the rest of Europe, which did in fact have a pattern of development that somehow differed from the rest of the world (Federico, 2005).

Irrigation and food processing represented an important technical and organizational challenge, only explained by an accumulation of experience and knowledge that the Iberian monarchies tried to protect. Producing olives and grapes is not the same as producing oil, salt and wine. It requires useful knowledge and tools that mercantilist governments tried to keep as an exclusive secret. Legislation prevented salt workers from leaving Portugal, particularly to the rest of the Peninsula, but also beyond (Hanson, 1981: 192), and was aimed at keeping the workers' unique production techniques within the country. In the opposite direction, foreign workers were excluded from engaging in salt production and processing to restrict the spread of knowledge to Portuguese subjects. Even though we know very little about the new technologies introduced in these sectors, they involved investments and technological changes in equipment to transform raw inputs into quality products. At the same time, the growth of these activities produced forward and backward linkages to other economic sectors – for example, wine provides a good incentive to produce barrels, bottles, carts and boxes to make possible its transport. Storage and food preservation also became another important sector.

14.3 The Non-Agrarian Sectors

Boundaries between sectors of economic activity are hard to define, particularly for early modern economies. Agricultural labour was most frequently seasonal, thus leaving room for other activities, mostly in manufacturing, but also in trade and commerce. Manufacturers used raw materials from agriculture and the transformation frequently occurred in the same place, such as the grinding of grain into flour or producing leather apparel from animal skins.

Regional specialization was a dominant feature of early societies, making it difficult to distinguish between rural and urban population, as many farmers lived in urban centres, and those who resided in the countryside devoted time to tasks in the service and manufacturing sectors. There were no clear boundaries between the rural and urban areas, and often we can see 'rural cities', where both manufacturing and agrarian products were made (Villalta i Escobar, 2003; Eiras Roel, 2004; Llopis Agelán & González Mariscal, 2006; Gómez Carrasco, 2007). The close interconnections between the agricultural and non-agricultural sectors imply that our study of the relevance of science, knowledge and technology has to be comprehensive and thus inferences from the study of the former are applicable to the later. This is advantageous, as the availability of information regarding the non-agricultural sector is much higher, not only because it was more concentrated locally and thus more visible, but also because manufacturing became increasingly important during the Industrial Revolution and thus its transformations have received more attention from historians. Therefore, the study of the non-agricultural sectors will provide valuable insights to our quest for the sources of technological change, whether stemming mostly from the demand side or the supply side.

Manufacturing catered mostly to the satisfaction of the basic needs of the population, as well as to military defence and luxury goods. The list of economic sectors remained relatively stable throughout the period covered here. Most of the secondary sector before the Industrial Revolution (90%) was linked to production of textiles (manufacturing of wool, flax-hemp, silk, cotton and esparto). There were also iron and steel, leather, pottery, glass, soap, paper and many other products. Many of these activities were carried out in cities, but rural areas were also very important in the Iberian Peninsula. From the geographical point of view, cotton was concentrated in Catalonia, flax in Galicia and wool in Castile (Segovia, Béjar, Alcoy, Antequera, Sierra de Cameros, Tierra de Campos, La Mancha). Silk was very popular in Valencia, Toledo, Granada and Barcelona. Iron and shipbuilding in the Basque Country and Cantabria, tanning in Catalonia and Galicia, soap-making in Andalucía and Mallorca, and pottery in Valencia and Andalucía (Casado Alonso, 2004: 310). The use of waterpower was widespread, though there is almost no systematic research available that would allow us to assess its contribution as a source of energy. While Iberia was desperately short of navigable rivers, the high elevations probably made for good conditions for the local use of waterpower.

A similar list of sectors can be described in Portugal: flour mills, bread, biscuits, wine and olive oil; pottery, bricks and glass; soap; woollens, hemps and silks; tannery and apparel; dyeing; paper; armament and gunpowder; ironworks; shipbuilding and related industries; coinage; later on sugar refining, tobacco, printing, cottons and bricks; as well as construction, transportation and mining (Madureira & Matos, 2005: 129). Small-scale units dominated most of the economic activity, with a few exceptions, such as shipbuilding or tobacco manufacturing. There are no estimates for the evolution of industrial output in the period, but the general perception is that manufacturing evolved positively during the sixteenth century, had a negative trend in the seventeenth century and recovered during the eighteenth century, with some timing differences between Spain and Portugal. Thus, manufacturing followed rather closely the rate of urbanization but the sector also developed in the countryside where there was more population (Pereira, 1979: 121–139; Sarasua García, 2019).

Scientific development in Iberia fell short of the high visibility of Copernicus, Galileo and Newton, but it was nevertheless a determinant and serves as a clear window to watch the Iberian society and economy responding to the challenges of a changing environment. In Portugal, cosmography and mathematics were taught at the University. Cartography was developed under the guilds system and maps were produced in many ateliers in Lisbon (Costa, 1988). The lower level of attention provided to what was happening in sixteenth-century Iberia relates to the 'age-old religious battles harking back to the Reformation', which provided the grounds to the vision of the Iberians as backwards and primitive (Cañizares-Esguerra, 2004: 89). Contrarily, at the time of the first voyages across the Atlantic and the Indian oceans, Iberian explorers created a 'culture of empirical, experimental, and utilitarian knowledge-gathering of massive proportions that did not get its cues from the classics or the learned but from merchants, enterprising settlers, and bureaucrats' (Cañizares-Esguerra, 2004: 89). Thus, Iberia positioned itself favourably in the European context in scientific knowledge around metallurgy, medicine, surgery, meteorology, cosmography, cartography, navigation, military technology and urban engineering (de Mesa, 2006).[59] These achievements were artisanal and low key in many instances but the outcome, that is, the ability to travel across the oceans in a precise manner, was 'remarkable' (Xavier & Županov, 2015: 288; Almeida, 2018; Leitão, 2018). Scientific contributions in Iberia will fall in the seventeenth century to re-emerge in the eighteenth century, although by that time they were behind what was happening elsewhere in northern Europe. In the eighteenth century, both the Spanish and Portuguese monarchies introduced reforms to foster the development and importation of new technology in order to reinvigorate the economy, in particular the sectors that were more relevant for the central administration and that could contribute more to the replace imports of manufactured goods and foodstuffs from foreign countries. According to Breen, in the early seventeenth century 'British imperial theorists could see themselves as

---

[59] The discussion regarding the religious, political or ideological grounds beyond the concept of Northern European scientific revolution goes beyond the scope of this chapter but see (Goodman, 1992: 171–175; Porter & Teich, 1992; Cañizares-Esguerra, 2004; 2017; O'Brien, 2013; Xavier & Županov, 2015: 288; Xavier, 2018: 329; Yun-Casalilla, 2018).

walking the same path to empire as the Portuguese'. Yet 'by the beginning of the eighteenth century British authors were elaborating racialized distinctions between northern and southern European constitutions and casting aspersions on the increasingly mixed demographics of the Portuguese tropical colonies' (Breen, 2018: 78). The flow of knowledge entering Portugal and Spain from north-western Europe, paradoxically or not, had roots in the contacts between British and other Europeans and the Iberian colonies.

The reasons for these changes are multiple and need further study, but the main hypothesis is a close connection to the economic fluctuations of the Iberian Peninsula. In addition, there is an exception to the seventeenth-century decline, which somehow confirms the rule: the technological developments in the Spanish American silver mines of Potosí, which are an example of how the 'circulation of knowledge provides a basis for the production of new knowledge' (Yun-Casalilla, 2018: 280). The new technology was indeed relevant as it involved the use of new products and processes, not too different from developments later on in the exploration of iron ores in northern Europe (Goodman, 1992: 171; Cañizares-Esguerra, 2004: 106; Yun-Casalilla, 2018: 278). Similarly, in seventeenth-century Castile we may also find technological improvements in 'roads, bridges, canals, aqueducts, watermills, looms, iron-works, public buildings, and water pumps' (Cañizares-Esguerra, 2004: 108–109). It is difficult to assess the true relevance and impact of such developments, but the main conclusion remains that what happened in the rest of Europe also happened in Iberia, albeit at different levels of intensity and timing. Concomitantly, what seems more important is not to assert whether the culture was different – whether the society was less keen on using new methods – but instead the most important factor to take into account is about the level, intensity and timing of the demand for innovations. This was something that changed over time, and it was very dependent on the economic performance.

The quest for the relevance of science and technology in manufacturing can thus follow the development of some of the most important sectors mentioned above and consider their relevance across time. We will start by looking at shipbuilding, which had been a major activity from the sixteenth century onward, followed by woollens and silk, which were predominant during most of the three centuries covered here, and end with the study of cottons. Cotton printing, in particular, is important because it was a fast-developing industrial sector by the end of the eighteenth century. We end with mining and other industrial sectors at the beginning of the first Industrial Revolution.

Shipbuilding was a crucial industry for the expansion of Iberian empires, but it also shows the high degree of dynamism achieved by the local peninsular economies in connection with technical and scientific knowledge. The construction of ships for overseas navigation was a technical challenge but it was also crucial for the development of the knowledge behind expeditions, which required developments in cosmography, cartography, astronomy or mathematics (Goodman, 1988; 1992).

From the Middle Ages, naval expertise and refined knowledge had circulated in Iberia among highly skilled shipwrights who used to belong to families with a long tradition in this technological sector. For example, the Basque littoral had the highest concentration of capable shipwrights, but Barcelona, Seville and Lisbon also saw important activity in this sector (Costa, 1997; Domingues, 2004; Valdez-Bubnov, 2011). It was a large-scale, capital-intensive industry with ramifications in other domestic sectors. Shipbuilding was a global industry, and knowledge and technology circulated across Atlantic Europe with the strong participation of other countries, such as the Netherlands, where it was one of the most dynamic sectors (Phillips, 1991: 94; Costa, 1997; Domingues, 2004; van Zanden & van Leeuwen, 2012: 128). The same can be said about the maritime dimension of the Spanish Empire in the Mediterranean, where Genoese knowledge and skills were behind the construction of galleys in Barcelona's shipyards (Gatti, 1990; Thompson, 2006; Aguilera López, 2018). Infrastructure was crucial for overseas explorations but there are grounds to defend that "science" was the handmaiden of the Iberian empires' (Cañizares-Esguerra, 2009: 1), particularly in the fields of cartography, cosmography, mathematics and natural history (Yun-Casalilla, 2018; 2019).

The Iberian crowns responded accordingly by providing a favourable institutional environment, in particular the *Casa da Índia* in Lisbon and the *Casa de la Contratación* in Seville in the sixteenth century (Goodman, 1992: 166; Costa, 1997; Xavier, 2018). The *Casa da Índia* was established in 1500 (abolished 1833), with the primary function of managing trade between Portugal and its empire and in the process producing 'written information and knowledge' (Xavier & Županov, 2015: 51) that 'contributed to the emergence of a science of administration' (Xavier, 2018: 28). Two other institutions regulated the commercial network of the empire.[60] The first, the Armazéns da Guiné e Índia, was the bureau where cartography and shipbuilding developed based on information from pilots and their practice at sea. It produced and controlled the nautical instruments and maps used in the navigation. At this bureau, theoretical solutions were provided by physicians and mathematicians – known as cosmographers – for problems reported by pilots, either derived from errors in maps or the inefficient sailing capabilities of the ships at sea (Costa, 1988). It was also at this bureau where pilots and cartographers were examined before being allowed to practice and enter the market. This was less visible but it still

---

[60] The *Casa da Índia*, established in 1501, followed the establishment of similar institutions, namely, the House of Ceuta (1434), Guinea (1443) and Mina (1482), and their main task was to manage the information coming from the different parts of the empire (Xavier & Županov, 2015: 51).

shows the important connection between science and the economy, before the better known 'scientific revolution' that would emerge in north-western Europe and that would be connected to the roots of the eighteenth-century Industrial Revolution (Mokyr, 1990). Costa and Leitão (2009) point further to the relevance of institutional developments that allowed for the development of scientific knowledge in Portugal. The second, the Ribeira das Naus, produced the ships and was one of the largest industrial units ever in Lisbon. The three sister institutions responded to the increasing complexity of the imperial administration. In the Spanish Empire, the *Casa de la Contratación* was founded in 1503. It managed all commercial and fiscal issues with the trade with the West Indies and Barbary, including among its services pilots and cosmographers similar to those provided in Portugal. Published manuals were used in other parts of Europe, including France, Holland, Italy and England (Goodman, 1992, 167). These imperial institutions were buoyant in the sixteenth century but they declined in the eighteenth century (Costa, 1997; Xavier, 2018).[61]

During the sixteenth century shipbuilding increased considerably in Iberia. According to one account in 1586, Iberia had 954 vessels (650 for Spain and 304 for Portugal) (Hanson, 1981: 130–131; Costa et al., 2016: 93). The tonnage of ships increased too. Until the mid-sixteenth century, the Spanish transatlantic fleet was mostly composed of ships ranging from 40 to 150 tons while from the mid-sixteenth century to late seventeenth century, the average ranged from 400 to 800 tons per ship (Alfonso Mola, 2002). The cost of building the vessels more than doubled in nominal terms in Lisbon between 1510–1520 and 1580–1604, which was the outcome of higher prices but also of the increase in the average size of the vessels. Incremental changes in technology and the organization of work accompanied the increase in the tonnage of ships built in Iberian shipyards. According to one estimation, by the mid-sixteenth century, Lisbon built an average of two ships of 400 tons per year. The turnover would amount to about 8.14 million *réis* per year, as each ship's costs per ton amounted to about 6,000 *réis* to build and 4,860 *réis* to equip, making the industry a highly concentrated one. Wood for the hulls, linen for the smaller sails, hemp for cords and pitch for caulking were provided by domestic producers from regions across the country, whereas wood for masts and linen for larger sails were imported from outside the Peninsula, namely from the Baltic region, and nails were imported from the region of Biscay (Costa, 1997: 298, 317–322; Costa et al., 2016: 74–75). According to Unger (2011), Portugal's sixteenth-century nautical cartography and shipbuilding technology developments had a decisive role in the development of similar activities in

---

[61] In a related history of science and knowledge in the empires, Xavier and Županov (2015: 339–340) refer to the decline of the once buoyant Catholic Orientalism in the same period, particularly in the second half of the eighteenth century.

the Dutch Republic, thus contributing to its rise in the global economy during the Golden Age.

The American expansion was also part of the history of Iberian technology for two reasons. First, because it shows the existence of a high level of technology, without which it would have been impossible to face such a large undertaking. The discovery and conquest of the new territory demanded nautical and cartographic knowledge, the ability to open new routes, build civil and military infrastructures, and new cities. Second, it was due to the significant technological transfer that took place in both directions.

Several historians agree with the idea that technological backwardness or the inability to compete with foreign technical developments, mostly Dutch, did not trigger the slowdown of the Basque shipbuilding sector (Phillips, 1991: 46-48; Grafe, 2011: 97-99). Deficient capitalization and the inflation of prices may have harmed the Spanish shipbuilding industry from the late sixteenth century onwards. The import of ships from abroad offset the scarcity of ships produced locally somewhat and in the second half of the seventeenth century, foreign ships represented circa 30% of all the merchant navy involved in the Spanish transatlantic official trade. This trend consolidated during the next century and from 1717 to 1778 foreign ships accounted for 60% of the number of vessels in use (Alfonso Mola, 2002: 374). Shipbuilding re-emerged following the War of the Spanish Succession as the new ruling Bourbons aimed to restore glory to the maritime industry with new docks built in Barcelona, as well as Cádiz, the later having received the *Casa de la Contratación* in 1717, and other developments that included the promotion of timber supply (López Arandia, 2018).

During the eighteenth century, the state became a central actor for shipbuilding as for many other manufacturing sectors, and fostered a policy in which the combination of local technology and international technological transfer played a major role. With the advent of the Bourbon dynasty to the Spanish throne, the royal fleet increased in order to reinvigorate Spanish naval power. Antonio Gaztañeta (1656-1728), who had already introduced and spread the use of the quadrant in the Spanish navy, designed a ship that did not require any ballast (Quintero González, 2009: 293). Spanish shipwrights frequently travelled to England and the Netherlands to acquire new expertise, while foreign shipwrights, mostly French and to a lesser extent English, were hired by the Crown. As a result, Spanish shipbuilding had a hybrid character, combining and improving aspects from local and international traditions alike. However, the effective adoption and adaptation of different models and techniques had more to do with rivalries between naval constructors and local carpenters, mercantile lobbies, admirals and political factions, than with technological choice. Nevertheless, if technology was a political decision, it is also clear that in Iberia the repertoire of knowledge and expertise was wide enough to offer different solutions to similar technical challenges (Valdez-Bubnov, 2011).

It is not surprising that the development of Iberian overseas trade led to the publication of the first treaties on shipbuilding. The first in the world was probably the one by Diego García de Palacio published in Mexico City in 1587 (Arróniz, 1980: 32–33). The progressive dissemination of technical and practical knowledge combined with the enactment by the Spanish Crown of ordinances on shipbuilding during the early seventeenth century, which standardized ships' dimensions and typologies, proportions and tonnage, probably had a positive impact on the costs of construction, reduced the risks of sailing and improved ships' quality. In setting these norms, the Crown gathered and contrasted knowledge from different nautical sectors, including shipwrights, practitioners, pilots, mathematicians and merchants' guilds (Valdez-Bubnov, 2009).

Moving on to textiles, within the overall stable regional distribution of manufacturing sectors there were some relevant changes starting in the seventeenth century. The production of woollens developed in the highlands of interior Portugal (Serra da Estrela), and linen and laces industries developed in the highly populated region of the north-west (Minho) (Pedreira, 1990: 526). These sectors were further helped by the protectionist measures that were first introduced in the later decades of the seventeenth century (there was also an integration of the markets across the border to Castile). Other regions such as the Alentejo in the south and Trás-os-Montes in the north-east, which were much less populated, also saw the development of industrial activity in the same period. The reasons for these changes were diverse. They include both the increase in population that allowed for larger markets, and the close availability of the most important resources, namely raw materials, water and wood (Pedreira, 1990: 528). Changes in the organization of production, distribution and commerce may have had some importance for the new industries, but there is not much to say about technological innovations. Moreover, the success of textile manufacturing into the nineteenth century was rather uneven. The Alentejo manufacturers virtually disappeared, as resources were diverted to agriculture, where the region had comparative advantages regarding the rest of the country. In the north, a few sectors remained and developed further by importing technology and adopting protectionist tariff policies. Overall, however, Portugal remained technologically underdeveloped throughout the period.

On the Spanish side the recovery of the Catalan wool industry in rural areas in the eighteenth century came from the introduction of new techniques aimed at manufacturing light wool fabrics mixed with other fibres, in the Dutch or French style. The silk industry also experienced a renewal at that time. Silk production had been a tradition in Spain from the Middle Ages. During the eighteenth century, international techniques were successfully adopted, local adaptations and improvements emerged, but rejection to innovation also took place. Several factors explain this mixed scenario. By the mid-eighteenth century, Valencia had 3,500 silk looms, falling to 2,600 by the 1780s. Contemporaries blamed international competition. Yet, there were multiple possible solutions to counteract the effects of international competition and the eventual decline in numbers of manufacturers. Guild members insisted on implementing severe quality controls to keep standards high, but this came at the cost of running a less flexible production system. For other artisans, the answer to relaunch local production was not necessarily a technological one. Instead, they proposed to adapt to consumers' preferences in a context in which the consumption of silks was spreading across more diverse social strata. Innovation in design and fostering the role of designers rather than investing in technological improvements was thought to be a more appropriate strategy to compete with foreign fabrics (Muñoz Navarro, 2014).

In the meantime, Barcelona's textile production was thriving thanks to the successful introduction of new technology. In 1750 the city hosted 111 silk looms, by 1780 the number had reached 3,000. Other towns like Manresa had up to 1,200 silk looms. From the late seventeenth century, new techniques like the multiple ribbon frame – invented in Gdansk one century before – were introduced in Catalonia. During the second half of the eighteenth century, knitted cotton stocks were also successfully introduced in northern Catalonia from France. Openness to novelties was important, but pre-existing mechanical knowledge among artisans was a greater determinant in explaining the success of the Catalan textile industry. Indeed, the failure of the Royal Factory of silk in Talavera, established in 1748, shows how importing new technology from abroad was not enough to guarantee a substantial technical improvement (Solà, 2010).

The introduction and development of technology in Iberia followed specific patterns in different regions. The case of cotton printing during the eighteenth century is illuminating in this regard. Lisbon was an entry port for Indian cottons from an early stage. During the seventeenth and eighteenth centuries, domestic production replaced Indian cottons in many parts of Europe and that eventually happened also in Lisbon, although with a considerable time lag. The introduction of cotton printing in Portugal dates from 1775 and developed from then onwards led by foreign entrepreneurs who founded industrial units that hired specialized labour from abroad, namely France, England and Switzerland. None of these manufacturers were mechanized and they followed artisanal methods. Yet, the size of the cotton printing units was comparatively large, second only to glass factories. Part of the output of printed cottons was exported, although mostly to neighbouring regions of Spain. The first steam engine and English printing machinery were introduced in Lisbon in 1847 and in 1881 one-third of the units still had no steam engines (Pedreira, 1991: 547–554).

The dependence on foreign capital, entrepreneurs and specialized labour in Lisbon contrasted markedly with what happened in Catalonia. Between 1736 and 1786, almost 166 workshops for cotton printing were established in

Barcelona. By the 1780s, the concentration of production in Barcelona was not only exceptional in the Iberian context but by European standards. The state fostered those developments through fiscal, commercial and legislative changes from which local entrepreneurs and investors benefited. The flow of French, German, Norwegian and Swiss experts towards Catalonia contributed to fill the initial lack of local expertise in the production process. However, printing techniques were quickly diffused among local workers, who acquired a leading role both as the labour force and in adapting and further developing foreign technology (Thomson, 2003: 17, 18, 40). Due to their expertise, Catalan workers were sought after in other areas of Spain which aimed at developing their own cotton printing workshops and factories, like in Cádiz Bay during the 1770s (Bernal Rodríguez, 2015: 56–57). Also, the first steam engine for cotton printing was introduced earlier in Barcelona (1833) than in Lisbon, although the commercial bonds between Portugal and England were traditionally stronger than in the Anglo-Spanish case. By 1833, 36 workshops and factories already had introduced steam engines. During the 1840s, animal force prevailed, but steam quickly replaced not only animal traction but also water as the main source of energy (Thomson, 2003: 33–36).

Grinding was part of many industrial processes, such as in the textile industry, where dyeing materials had to be previously ground. Mills were also used to operate bellows in forges and blacksmiths, and power saws, lathes and, in general, the machinery used in the production of all kinds of goods including paper mills, but also for making money, washing fabrics and tanning (the famous *batanes*). Hydraulic knowledge is evident in engineering texts, such as those written by Jerónimo Girava and Pedro Juan de Lastanosa in the sixteenth century (García Tapia, 1987; García Tapia & García Diego, 1987). In just the province of Valladolid, 424 mills were recorded in the middle of the eighteenth century (García Tapia, 1989a: 138), but we still lack a complete inventory of this kind of infrastructure.

Mining was another development area, with the adaptation of knowledge and techniques to the geological and mineral conditions of the 'New World'. If the Iberian Peninsula had not had those technologies, it would hardly have been able to transfer them. If the economic effects of all these new contributions to America were evident (Arroyo Abad & Van Zanden, 2016), the impact that technology had on the Iberian Peninsula, with a much more developed economy, needs to be stressed. There were also incentives to increase silver and gold production in American mines. The mercury amalgamation technique of silver refining was a major improvement applied by Bartolomé de Medina in 1554, being 'the result of a communal effort of pragmatic refiners', who drew upon central European, Spanish and African know-how and mining knowledge (Bargalló, 1955; Muro, 1964; Castillo Martos & Lang, 1995; Guerrero, 2017: 51–53, 103, 134–143). Mining was carried out by private entrepreneurs, but the Crown supported any effort to improve techniques and import technology and human capital from other European regions. Castile had inventors, such as Jerónimo de Ayán, who, among other ideas, proposed several diving machines and primitive steam engines. Probably there were spillover effects from military to civilian technology and to the rest of the economy, but so far they have not been studied. At the end of the sixteenth century, the Madrid Academy of Mathematics was founded, a technical school dedicated to mathematics, physics and engineering.

The macro-inventions of the first Industrial Revolution did not touch most of the Iberian Peninsula before the later nineteenth century. Industrial activity remained based on small-scale units using traditional machinery, such as the handloom, human labour and natural sources of energy. Given the characteristics of the Iberian economy, instead of macro-inventions many improvements derived from micro-inventions. Due to the high transport costs, industrial units were scattered across the territory according to the availability of natural resources, such as water, forests and pasturages, and the proximity of consumers. Transportation costs and the associated pattern of regional dispersion helped protect such industries from foreign competition until well into the end of the eighteenth century. Their technology was adopted to these conditions, more focused on reaching local needs and producing cheaply. Proto-industry played a very important role in those regions of the Peninsula with problems in finding large enough concentrations of capital, labour and resources. No industrial activity was detected in the late sixteenth century in the whole of the Algarve, the southernmost province of Portugal (Godinho, 1970, 183), and the same happened in the adjacent province, the Baixo Alentejo, in the second half of the eighteenth century (Marcadé, 1971: 157–158).

Moreover, even when technology was available, and demand existed, the lack of specialized workers could hamper industrial and manufacturing activities. For instance, after two unsuccessful attempts, a blast furnace was inaugurated in Sagardelos, in eastern Galicia, in 1792. This initiative was intended to satisfy the increasing demand for iron products and ammunition from the royal shipyards at Ferrol; a demand that had already boosted the development of the *Verlagssystem* in the region from the 1780s onwards. The design of Sagardelos' equipment was inspired by the installations of La Cavada and Liérganes, also in northern Spain (Carmona Badía, 1993). However, it took almost two years to find the appropriate experts to run the blast furnace adequately. Even technological transfer and the dissemination of practical knowledge within Iberia could result in slow and haphazard processes by the late eighteenth century.

14.4 The Institutional Framework and the Role of the State

In early modern Europe, the relevance of the state for the economy and the development of technology was mostly indirect, by means of the legal framework that it created, the ability to wage war or to keep peace and security, and as a consumer of goods and labour for the army and state services. Thus, the demand from the state for weapons, fortifications or for means of land and maritime transportation was relevant for the development of such sectors. Notably, in the sixteenth century, overseas expansion received attention from the kings of Spain and Portugal. For most of the seventeenth century, prolonged wars dominated the demands from the state, up to Westphalia (1648) and during the wars of independence that unfolded in Iberia (1640–1668). From the turn of the seventeenth and throughout most of the eighteenth century, it was the need to control silver and gold outflows and to promote agriculture and manufacturing that motivated state action in the realm of economic activity. Most European states, including the Iberian ones, were increasingly concerned with the supply of manufactured and agricultural goods and got more involved in the production of woollens, cottons, fine paper, weapons and ships.

There is no precise measure of the relevance of state activity for the performance of the economy and for the development of technology. But we can hypothesize that it was overall relatively small, even by the end of the period we are studying here. Thus, we cannot discuss to any great depth how state intervention affected growth at large. Moreover, we have to take into account that mercantilism was not necessarily the only option at hand, at least theoretically. In fact, in Portugal, for example, Colbertism or the 'French' model of intervention in manufacturing was supported by Ribeiro de Macedo, a seventeenth-century renowned mercantilist and ambassador to the French court, whereas a 'Dutch' model of commercial expansion was preferred by António Vieira, who spent most of his life in colonial Brazil (Hanson, 1981: 135–136). Mercantilism was the outcome of the political climate of international state competition, in both Portugal and Spain. Whatever the impact of the state on the economy and technological performance, the involvement of the state left an array of quantitative and qualitative information that provides a unique window on issues regarding the outcomes and constraints of technological development in both Portugal and Spain.

The institutional framework in which economic activity takes place is as important as the techniques and tools used because the incentives that drive people's work and technical progress depend on it. The institutional framework of the pre-industrial era was certainly not homogeneous, and there were many important differences, depending on the environment, war and peace, the political system and the overall performance of the economy. This dependence implied that innovation could appear in different places and points in time not necessarily connected, which implies that we may not find a sustained pattern of technological development through the period studied here.

From as early as the beginning of the sixteenth century, we can detect the impact of state action in the development of ocean-going ships and related nautical techniques, which were particularly relevant in Lisbon, Seville and

Cádiz. Lisbon vessels that reached India and Brazil implied the use and development of new technology and knowledge, taking advantage of the development of communication flows with Venice and other European port cities. Advanced military technology in shipbuilding, artillery, munitions, fortifications and siege machines were developed during Philip II's reign (Goodman, 1988). The Spanish monarchy used the best contemporary knowledge and technology available to get its main political goals. Spanish kings were aware of the importance of cosmography for their empire and there were relevant contributions to navigation techniques. The *Casa de la Contratación* produced remarkable geographic works and there was an impressive training program for qualified pilots to guide the empire's merchant and military fleets in the Universidad de Mareantes, later known as Colegio de San Telmo in Seville (García Garralón, 2007). The monarchy had an active interest in new techniques, importing foreign experts and founding training schools for engineers, gunners and mariners. The new Segovia mint employed specialized workers and machinery originated in Germany to produce high-quality coins. The Schools of Artillery and Military Engineering promoted knowledge of metallurgy, chemistry and architecture in the construction of new ports and fortifications (Capel Sáez, 1983).

The construction of infrastructures such as roads, bridges, reservoirs, lighthouses and ports, as well as the water supply of several towns, demonstrates the existence of sufficient technical expertise to build any type of machinery. The monarchy supported all these improvements. In sixteenth-century Iberia, most social overhead infrastructural work concerned the fortification of urban dwellings, ports and lighthouses, as well as canals for irrigation and transport. In 1561, Juan Bautista de Toledo began the construction of canals using the same type of locks used in the Lombardy canal. Canals were built in the area of Aranjuez, but also the Colmenar and Jarama ditch, and the irrigation network in Catalonia and Levante (García Tapia, 1989b). During the reign of Philip II, the navigation of the Pisuerga was explored (Helguera Quijada, 1983). In 1581 the Italian engineer Juan Bautista Antonelli, who navigated the Tajo to Toledo, made a proposal to make all the rivers in Spain navigable and to connect Porto with Burgos (Llaguno Amírola & Ceán Bermudez 1829: 67). These kind of improvements in infrastructure continued in the eighteenth century. The speed and prices of transportation were reduced over time (Grafe, 2012: 110–111).

Following the end of Portugal's Restoration War with Spain (1640–1668), the Portuguese Crown experienced a form of Colbertism, which implied state support for investment in manufacturing. Our knowledge does not allow any conclusions on the economic implications of such policies or even of their true motivations, but we can use the related information to conclude about the degree of technological advancement of manufacturing in the Peninsula. Such policies were to be closely tied to Count Ericeira (1632–1690), the

'Superintendent of the Workshops and Factories of the Realm', and the main declared goal was to foster the domestic manufacture of higher quality goods in order to replace imports. To achieve that, manufacturing in Portugal had to count on 'master craftsmen and workers from France, England and Venice – with their looms, frames, tools and drawings' (Godinho, 1970: 512) who ultimately trained the domestic labour force. In 1670, in Lisbon, a furnace to produce crystal and plate glass and glassware, using 'Venetian methods', was installed by two Portuguese merchants, supervised by Venetian masters. Godinho summarizes the steps of that installation as follows: 'the State provided a site, advanced money, exempted them from duties on the imported equipment and materials, and from other taxes, for ten years; the manufacturers, craftsman and other staff received various personal privileges; and the undertaking enjoyed a monopoly throughout the kingdom and the Atlantic islands.' In the following year, 'a master draper and eight female workers arrived from Rouen with looms for making serges, bolting-cloth and other light woollens at Estremoz, which had plentiful supplies of water and olive oil and easy access to supplies of Spanish wool founded by the State' (Godinho, 1970: 512–513).[62] This factory was handed over to private enterprise in 1672, concerning 'machinery for finishing raw silk, taffetas and linen imported from France or Venice, together with master dyers coming from the same places; woollens in Covilhã; "Castilian-style" bed coverlets. As well as the reopening of forges and foundries under the direction of a "French official", as imports from Biscay dwindle due to the war' (Godinho, 1970: 512–513). The foundation of these manufacturing units was accompanied by sumptuary laws concerning the sale of 'French hats, ribbons and luxury lace, Italian brocades, and the more expensive English and Dutch cloths' (Hanson, 1981: 131).

As far as trade flows can tell, Portugal had no competitive advantages in manufacturing and its exports were comprised mostly of colonial goods, such as sugar, tobacco and brazilwood, as well as re-exports of Spanish wool, whereas it imported 'silks, woollens, baizes, ribbons, spirits, and cod' (Godinho, 1970: 512). Colbertism meant the prohibition of such imports and led to public policies to protect the domestic production of many goods, catering mainly for the wealthier. The design of such policies helps us identify the differences between the levels of technological advancement in the various parts of Iberian Peninsula and between the Peninsula and the more advanced industrial regions of Europe. As Hanson (Hanson, 1981, 268) states: 'despite the importation of foreign expertise and equipment, the quality of Portuguese manufactured goods was generally inferior to that of nations with older, more firmly established industrial enterprises'. Whatever the relevance of various sectors, legislation provides a perspective on which sectors in Portugal and

---

[62] There are further examples of the need these new manufactured goods had for imported knowledge and machinery.

Spain did not have a comparative advantage and in which knowledge was imported from other parts of the Peninsula, England, France or Venice.

At the same time, the picture is not completely dark. There were other sectors where the intervention of the state led to the development of successful experiences. We have shown above the example of the development of wine in northern Portugal, but others have also been given, such as shipbuilding in Lisbon. The sumptuary laws forbidding the importation of higher grades of consumer goods and other import restrictions were lifted during the eighteenth century, and some of the protected manufacturers survived and progressed considerably. In Spain, the state founded factories that incorporated new machines, in order to foster manufacturing production and technical innovation. As described above, some of the new units were for military purpose, such as the Ferrol, Cádiz and Cartagena shipyards and arms factories, or intended to produce luxury goods, including porcelain, crystal, as well as textiles, such as those in Guadalajara, Brihuega and San Fernando (González Enciso, 1980; Barrio Moya, 2006). Cotton printing and shipbuilding in Barcelona benefitted from fiscal exemptions, tariffs and legal protection. The developments of the Basque iron industry during the early modern era also bear witness to that scenario. Among other products, since the Middle Ages, the Basque Country had provided high-quality anchors to the local and Iberian naval industry, as well as to the Flemish and English markets. However, this industry had been unable for some time to meet the demand caused by the development of larger battleships during the mid-seventeenth century, which required heavier anchors. Foreign anchors dominated until the 1730s, when Juan Fermín de Guilisasti improved and recycled traditional techniques regarding the use of sources of heat, allowing him to develop a new welding system. The diffusion of Guilisasti's methods allowed for the expansion of the local industry, which by the 1750s was again able to meet both Iberian and international demands, including the French and English markets. Guilisasti's method was cheap, but it was labour-intensive. A furnace with 7 to 10 specialized workers was able to produce in 5 to 24 days anchors weighing between 720 and 2610 kilograms. The demand posed by the royal navy and the Royal Company of Caracas, a Basque chartered company trading cocoa from Venezuela, stimulated technological development but it did not create *ex novo* (Carrión Arregui, 1995).

14.5 Conclusion

There was technological progress in the Iberian Peninsula in the early modern period. It is possible to find examples during this time that contributed to the development of many different economic sectors. Some technical solutions were invented in Spain and Portugal, but others came from other European countries, imported by private entrepreneurs or directly through royal initiative. Perhaps, the main difference with other parts of Europe was the gap that opened during the seventeenth century in the manufacturing sector. It was a time of crisis, in which economic openness and dynamic ideas were gradually replaced by protectionism and fragmented markets. Reversing this path was not an easy task.

A major problem of technological development in the Iberian Peninsula was the development of efficient knowledge, but this process stopped during the economic crisis of the seventeenth century. There is widespread consensus among economic historians about the importance of human capital in explaining technological progress (Kelly et al., 2014), but discussions around the Industrial Revolution have shown the need to define what we understand as such. Before the Industrial Revolution, human capital was mainly skills. Artisans did not have sophisticated mechanical and scientific knowledge, but they did have the expertise to produce and improve tools and machines – they learned by doing. Apprenticeships were much more important to transmit 'useful knowledge' from masters to young workers (Humphries, 2003). Unlike in France and other countries on the European continent, the apprenticeship system was not as widespread in Iberia. The institution was known, but manufacturing production by the early seventeenth century had entered into crisis in many Castilian cities (Moreno Claverías, 2015). Proto-industrial systems increased production, but they did so in low-quality goods that required fewer worker skills than the more complex goods manufactured in cities. In Iberia proto-industrial systems did not imply significant advances in productivity, nor did they aim to transmit knowledge; they simply met a growing demand for simple products at low prices.

A key aspect for technological progress to have an economic impact is the diffusion of innovations, especially micro-inventions. There was importation and technological transfer in Spain as indicated by the mobility of human capital, one of the traditional ways of transferring technology in the pre-industrial period, but it was not enough to transform important sectors of the economy. Tools were manufactured and repaired by those who used them, both in agriculture and in manufacturing, perhaps working secretly. People expected to profit by producing cheaper or with higher quality than their competitors and product differentiation was one driving force of production changes (MacLeod, 1992). With the exception of shipbuilding, specialized sectors dedicated to the production of capital goods were not developed in Spain until the nineteenth century, and even then, much of the machinery was imported (Deu Baigual & Llonch, 2008). The lack of specialization and the absence of an industrial sector dedicated to the construction of machines and tools can also explain, in part, the slowness of technological progress in manufacturing.

Resistance to change came not so much from organized groups who felt that their income was threatened, but instead was driven by a realistic and widespread fear of the risk arising from change (Mokyr, 1992). This resistance is usually greater in societies with inefficient markets. Lack of competition and difficulties in the flow of information favours conservative strategies. The government's weakness in carrying out fiscal reforms forced it to relinquish much of its functions to local groups, thus fragmenting the market and discouraging the productive expansion particularly required by industry. Innovation and technological improvements suffered from these conservative and protectionist strategies.

15

Living Standards, Inequality and Consumption, 1500–1800

ESTEBAN NICOLINI, FERNANDA OLIVAL AND FERNANDO RAMOS-PALENCIA[63]

15.1 Introduction

The objectives of this chapter are to provide an overview of living standards (measured mainly by prices and wages), levels of inequality and the evolution of consumption patterns in different regions of Iberia. Thus, it adopts a comparative approach to addressing the composition of demand and analyses how that demand was conditioned by these socioeconomic variables.

Some elements of the evolution of living standards in the Iberian Peninsula between 1500 and 1800 are relatively easy to describe: prices and nominal wages moved in long cycles with a peak at the beginning of the seventeenth century, and real wages were stagnant and lost ground compared with countries in Northern Europe. Other elements move along more blurred lines and require a more cautious approach: it seems that consumption patterns gained in sophistication (even for some families in the lower social strata) together with what looks like a reduction in leisure time; the trend in economic inequality (if there is any) is very difficult to identify within a combination of strong cyclical movements and a very large regional and even local variation.

The analysis of standards of living in the Iberian Peninsula in the early modern age should be understood on a stage defined by two main historical features. The first is the institutional complexity of the Habsburg period; until the arrival of the Bourbons in the eighteenth century, Spain did not exist as a political entity but rather it was under a composite and polycentric monarchy – which also included the kingdom of Portugal under the Crown of the Spanish Habsburgs between 1580 and 1640 – whose plurality was well known (see Chapter 12). This implied a very large regional and local variability in labour and land distribution traditions and regulations, high variations in the

---

[63] Esteban Nicolini (Universidad Carlos III de Madrid) and Fernando Ramos-Palencia (Universidad Pablo de Olavide, Seville) acknowledge support by grants from the Ministerio de Economía y Competitividad and FEDER (HAR2016-77794-R and PID2020-117468GB-I00). Fernanda Olival (Universidade de Évora; CIDEHUS) works in the context of UIDB/00057/2020, FCT – Portugal. We are grateful to Pedro Lains and Jaime Reis for helpful comments and suggestions.

relationship between the local powers and the Crown and, particularly, different fiscal and, sometimes, monetary institutions.

The second feature is that, after periods of certain economic growth, the seventeenth and eighteenth centuries marked the beginning of stagnation (for Spain first and then for Portugal) in terms of average 'national' GDP per capita (see Chapter 10). On the one hand, slow economic growth may have been contributing to modest and intermittent improvements in standards of living. On the other hand, the causality may also have run in the opposite direction: the low real wages and relatively high inequality in some regions limited aggregate demand and stymied earlier and more sustainable growth. It seems that the only modest expansion of market participation through a more sophisticated consumption pattern and an increased consumption of durable goods (and colonial products) were not enough to compensate for the other, more pessimistic, side of living standards.

15.2 Living Standards

In this section we offer a first look at living standards measured mainly by prices and wages. Regarding prices, their trends are similar in both countries of the Iberian Peninsula (see Figure 15.1(a) and (d)), although information for Spain during the early modern age is much more fragmented (Andrés-Ucendo & Lanza-García, 2014; González-Mariscal, 2015) than that for Portugal. There was a clear positive trend in price levels until the central decades of the seventeenth century, reaching a peak in the decades after 1600. From the mid-seventeenth century there had been a fall in prices that coincided with a crisis in colonial trade and, following the War of the Spanish Succession and especially after the 1750s, prices throughout the Iberian Peninsula began to rise again. The oscillations (bullish peaks) were greater in Portugal, as can be inferred from the evolution of prices in Lisbon and in Porto, and this may well be related to the degree of commercial opening, to difficulties in its colonial empire, and in some cases to political conflict.

As with prices, the wages of skilled and unskilled workers (in grams of silver) followed a strongly similar trend throughout the Iberian Peninsula with long-term cycles very similar to the ones observed for price levels. Figure 15.1(b) and (e) show unskilled nominal wages while Figure 15.1(c) and (f) show the evolution of skilled wages. Within this general pattern, there were some remarkable regional differences: between 1550 and 1800, wages of unskilled workers were higher in Andalusia and New Castile than in Catalonia and only wages of Old Castile were lower than their Catalan counterparts. Yet, wages in New Castile and Catalonia tended to converge from the mid-eighteenth century onward. Moreover, wages of skilled workers were higher in the territories of the former Crown of Castile (data for New Castile and Andalucía) than in the Crown of Aragon – specifically, for the

LIVING STANDARDS, INEQUALITY AND CONSUMPTION, 1500–1800   387

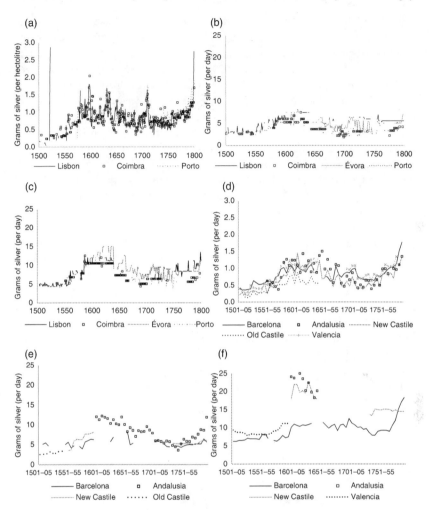

Figure 15.1 Prices and wages in Iberia, 1500–1800: (a) wheat prices in Portugal (in grams of silver per hectolitre); (b) unskilled wages in Portugal (day labourers: daily wages in grams of silver); (c) skilled wages in Portugal (mason master: daily wages in grams of silver); (d) wheat prices in Spain (in grams of silver per hectolitre); (e) unskilled wages in Spain (day labourers: daily wages in grams of silver); (f) skilled wages in Spain (mason: daily wages in grams of silver).
Sources: Spanish prices are authors' own calculations based on data from Feliu Monfort (1991); Portugal prices are from http://pwr-portugal.ics.ul.pt (accessed 20 March 2020).

periods 1600–1650 in Andalusia and 1735–1785 in New Castile (there are no data for the period between 1650 and 1735). Even within the Crown of Aragon, wages were higher in the kingdom of Valencia than in the Catalan principality between 1500 and 1600 (see Figure 15.1(f)). For Portugal, a distinction must be made between Lisbon and the rest of the country. From 1500 to 1800, a large part of Portuguese economic and political power was concentrated in Lisbon: the most populous city in the peninsula, the fifth largest city in Europe in 1750 and the ninth largest in 1800 (Bairoch et al., 1988: 278). This predominance must be taken into account when considering Portuguese economic history. The wages of skilled workers were always higher in Lisbon; for unskilled workers, they were higher in the interior of Portugal (Évora) between 1600 and 1750. Thereafter, unskilled wages, too, were higher in Lisbon (see Figure 15.1(b) and (c)).

Of great interest in all cases is the purchasing power of families. It is well known that, at the European level, the real wages of Dutch and English workers were appreciably higher than elsewhere in Europe from the end of the seventeenth century. In about 1800, the trailing countries – in order of decreasing real wages – were Spain, France, Austria, Portugal, Germany and Italy (Allen, 2003; Costa et al., 2015). The real wages of Spanish workers were always higher than those of their Portuguese counterparts and in the two countries they display a negative trend in the early modern period (see Figure 15.2). In Spain, they declined from the sixteenth to the eighteenth centuries, with long-term cycles that coincided between different regions: some decline until the second half of the seventeenth century, followed by a small rebound (or stagnation)

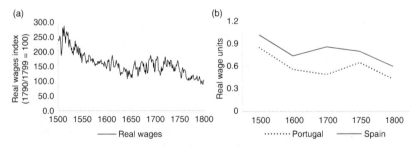

Figure 15.2 Real wages in Spain and Portugal, 1500–1800: (a) real wages in Spain (1790/1799 = 100); (b) real wages in Portugal and Spain (in units).
Sources: (a) Álvarez-Nogal and Prados de la Escosura (2013), online supporting information: Table S2. Real wage rates, 1277–1850 (1790/1799 = 100). (b) Costa et al. (2015), supplementary data online.
Note: Álvarez-Nogal and Prados de la Escosura (2013: 9) have noted that the use of unskilled wages does not alter their results significantly since most workers were unskilled.

until the first decades of the eighteenth century, and then further decline until the start of the nineteenth century (Álvarez-Nogal & Prados de la Escosura, 2013; López-Losa & Piquero-Zarauz, 2021).

These negative or stagnant trends in living standards took place in a context of large regional variation: Seville had substantially larger real incomes than Madrid and Valencia in the sixteenth century while Madrid had better incomes than the other two cities in the seventeenth century (López-Losa & Piquero-Zarauz, 2021). In fact, some good economic and welfare indicators for Madrid and the Seville–Cádiz–Jerez axis (both in the former Crown of Castile) featured two 'islands' amidst two types of rural misery (Vilar, 1999: 27–62). In this visualization, there is an imaginary line from Salamanca to Albacete: (i) above that line, farmers and day labourers lived in small and heavily indebted farms (in Galicia and León, scarcely 5% of the workforce were day labourers); (ii) below the line high seasonal unemployment combined with more than 70% of privately owned land worked by low-wage day labourers (Herr, 1989: 27–28).

In Catalonia, in light of the data provided by Feliu Monfort (1991) and according to Llopis (2004b: 18–20), the purchasing power (in wheat) of wages decreased between the periods 1501–1550 and 1751–1800 as follows: for master builders, by 21.9%; for builders, 20.8%; for day labourers, 44.4%; for master carpenters, 24.2%; and for senior carpenters, by 26.8%. From this information Llopis (2004b) concludes that real wages fell slightly less in Catalonia than in other Spanish regions, which is consistent with the information provided by López-Losa and Piquero-Zarauz (2021) suggesting a decline of 34% in Seville and of 31% in Madrid in that period.

Workers' earnings are particularly important in Catalonia given that it was the first Spanish region to industrialize and the only one that experienced meaningful pre-industrial growth (Marfany, 2012). The so-called high-wage hypothesis argues that mechanization served to replace expensive labour. However, in Catalonia it must be put into context. From the end of the seventeenth century, Catalonia enjoyed Smithian economic growth and a process of market development that intensified its agrarian and proto-industrial sectors, followed by rapid population growth during the next century. In this scenario, one of the keys was the structure of Catalan land and property rights (Torras, 1984), which enabled Catalan producers to take advantage of this opportunity. Using data from Barcelona city, Martínez-Galarraga and Prat (2016) show that Catalonia was not a high-wage economy like England in 1750, but they confirm the relevance of relative factor prices in the adoption of new technology in the cotton spinning sector.

For Portugal, real wages are estimated to have fallen by about 50% between 1500 and 1800: they decreased from 1500 to 1650, recovered from 1650 to 1750, and then fell sharply between 1750 and 1800 (Costa et al., 2015). These authors find no substantial differences between the evolution of wages of skilled and unskilled workers. At the same time as real incomes were low,

Portugal reaped significant colonial profits. Costa and colleagues consider that the Portuguese colonial empire helped the country's long-term economic growth; however, this was not enough to stop the decline of the Portuguese economy in relation to Europe's advanced countries.

In this context, the issue is whether low wages combined with high commodity price levels could be a consequence of an unequal society and what effect this might have on consumption patterns (or on aggregate demand). The answer is not easy. Between 1500 and 1550, the Crown of Castile and some areas of Portugal were – along with Flanders and the northern Italian cities – one of the richest areas in Europe (in terms of GDP per capita; see Chapter 10) and probably one with quite high standards of living in comparative terms. This period of economic expansion was notable for an increase in population, the impact of colonies, and for higher agricultural and manufacturing prices. However, from the second half of the sixteenth century productivity and real wages decreased. In the seventeenth century, the rupture of the commercial axis between Antwerp and Portugal–Castile, followed by the Eighty Years' War against the United Provinces of the Netherlands (1568–1648), meant that between 1640 and 1670 the Iberian Peninsula suffered its darkest period: (i) demographic decline in the cities and depopulation in rural areas, immigration of beggars to the cities and plague epidemics; (ii) poor harvests (aggravated by periods of droughts and torrential rains); (iii) landowners and farmers losing their properties; and (iv) pronounced unemployment among day labourers and artisans. Portugal started the process of economic recovery around 1670, followed by Spain in the first decades of the eighteenth century (see Chapters 10 and 11).

In the Portuguese case, growth was due to the new expectations generated in Brazil and also to agrarian expansion (Reis, 2017); in the Spanish case, it reflected the demographic and economic recovery of the coast, which moved the nexus of economic activity from Castile to the Mediterranean periphery and (though to a lesser extent) to the Basque–Cantabrian periphery (Grafe, 2012). A clear indicator of that shift was the country's changing demographics (Domínguez Ortiz, 2004: 219–220). At the beginning of the sixteenth century, almost 80% of Spaniards were Castilians. Two centuries later, the picture was radically different: Bilbao went from 5,000 to 10,000 inhabitants; Cartagena and El Ferrol grew significantly thanks to the activity of their shipyards; and Cádiz also grew at the expense of Seville, whose plague-stricken population declined from 150,000 inhabitants at the end of the sixteenth century to 85,000 a century later. Nevertheless, the most notable growth was that of Barcelona, whose increase from 37,000 inhabitants at the end of the Bourbon siege (1714) to 100,000 at the end of the eighteenth century was due to the expansion of its cotton industry. Meanwhile, Madrid (the capital of the monarchy from 1561) grew from 50,000 to 150,000 inhabitants between 1590 and 1630 thanks to the rural exodus from Castile, which also favoured Andalusian and Murcian lands.

Madrid's expansion then slowed considerably, and it became an essentially bureaucratic city of about 170,000 inhabitants. The royal factories created by the Bourbons outside Madrid (in Guadalajara, Ávila, Talavera and elsewhere) did nothing to change the dynamic created by the ruralization of Castile, which had the lowest urbanization rates in the entire Peninsula.

15.3 Inequality

The explanation of the variation in levels and the long-term changes in inequality in pre-industrial societies is usually linked to economic growth (van Zanden, 1995), demographic changes (Alfani, 2019), and social conflicts and unrest (Scheidel, 2017). Therefore, when trying to understand the evolution of economic inequality in Iberia, the following type of events should be considered: the appearance of the plague (there were severe epidemics in 1597–1602, 1647–1652 and 1676–1685; e.g. the plague claimed more than 60,000 victims in Seville during 1647–1652 and in 1676–1685 it claimed about 250,000 victims throughout the Spanish territory); natural catastrophes (earthquakes in Lisbon in 1531, 1755, 1761 and 1769); ethnic or religious tensions (Jews were expelled from Spain and Portugal in 1492 and 1496–1497, respectively, and Spanish Moors were expelled between 1609 and 1614); low-intensity conflicts (e.g. Revolt of the Comuneros in Castile, 1520–1522; Revolt of the Brotherhoods in Valencia and Mallorca, 1519–1523; Rebellion of the Alpujarras in Granada, 1568–1571); and wars in the Iberian territory (the Reapers' War in 1640–1652; the Spanish–Portuguese wars, 1640–1668; the War of the Spanish Succession, 1701–1714; the Fantastic War, 1762–1763; and the War of the Oranges, 1801).

Table 15.1 provides data on inequality from several places in Portugal between 1565 and 1776, and Table 15.2 does likewise for mid-eighteenth-century Spain. The Gini indices range between 0.2 and 0.8 depending on the year and the size of the locale. A comparison of eighteenth-century Portugal and Castile reveals that the former exhibited more inequality (a Gini index of between 0.45 and 0.74); in the latter, the highest Gini index was 0.68 in Granada City. Inequality was not uniform in either space or time, while the positive correlation between town size and inequality observed in Tables 15.1 and 15.2 (see also Nicolini & Ramos-Palencia, 2016; 2020; 2021) suggests that demographic or economic growth can have a nontrivial impact on inequality.

In Portugal there was a notable decrease in income inequality between the sixteenth and eighteenth centuries mainly due to significant changes in agricultural productivity (Reis, 2017). According to Palma and Reis (2019), the GDP per capita of Portugal doubled between 1550 and 1750 thanks to the primary sector's growth and, after 1700, it expanded also 'by burgeoning gains from colonial exploitation'. This growth reflected the introduction of corn (the

Table 15.1 *Inequality in Portugal, 1565–1770.*

Place	Date	Households	Gini index
Lisbon	1565	15,014	0.802
Porto	1565	3,500	—
Coimbra	1567	1,920	0.692
Loulé	1564	694	0.714
Loulé	1564	507	0.553
Coimbra	1599	1,334	0.696
Coimbra	1613	1,599	0.698
Avis	1690	311	0.656
Avis	1690	313	0.636
Vila do Conde	1698	714	0.583
Tavira	1699	446	0.576
Arraiolos	1700	552	0.650
Arraiolos	1700	374	0.650
Porto	1700	6,000	0.667
Lisbon	1700	45,000	—
Portalegre	1725	1,279	0.497
Portalegre	1725	682	0.472
Ponte de Sor*	1728	341	0.710
Galveias	1753	107	0.610
Guarda	1766	1,042	0.744
Viseu	1763	469	0.696
Caminha	1767	2,027	0.483
Caminha	1767	325	0.585
Vila do Conde	1763	706	0.559
Vila do Conde	1763	125	0.450
Porto	1776	9,000	0.700
Lisbon	1776	47,500	—

Source: all data are from Reis (2017); except *Ponte de Sor (Faísca, 2020).

'maize revolution') as well as the labour-intensive wine sector, which increased the supply of labour by 50% per capita. These developments could well explain a moderate decrease in income inequality in small cities and rural communities even as urban inequality barely changed in the long term. Thus, for example, in 1770: (i) inequality was higher in large towns than in 1565 and 1700; and (ii) inequality was lower in small towns and rural areas than in 1565 (Reis, 2017; Palma & Reis, 2019).

Table 15.2 *Income inequality in Spanish cities, towns and villages, c. 1750.*

Town/village	Province	Households	Population[*]	Annual income per capita	Gini index[**]
Granada city	Granada	11,907	47,628	1,296.1	0.686
Úbeda city	Jaén	2,563	10,252	896.4	0.661
Cúllar Baza	Granada	674	2,696	813.3	0.618
Guadalajara city	Guadalajara	1,301	5,204	988.1	0.613
Padul	Granada	258	1,032	1,245.4	0.608
Palencia city	Palencia	2,259	9,036	957.3	0.607
Paredes Nava	Palencia	722	2,888	1,107.7	0.600
Sigüenza city	Guadalajara	806	3,224	1,052.3	0.591
Carabaña	Madrid	182	728	934.4	0.563
Torredonjimeno	Jaén	841	3,364	633.0	0.551
Bustillo	Palencia	34	136	1,350.2	0.544
Azuqueca	Guadalajara	76	304	831.7	0.535
El Casar	Guadalajara	252	1,008	1,294.1	0.529
Motril city	Granada	2,174	8,696	483.3	0.510
Colmenar Viejo	Madrid	975	3,900	1,668.8	0.497
Marchamalo	Guadalajara	199	796	1,095.6	0.495
Santillana	Santander	170	680	489.8	0.466
Villabellaco	Palencia	32	128	900.8	0.444
Villabermudo	Palencia	77	308	943.6	0.409
Villarramiel	Palencia	377	1,508	1,057.2	0.407
Hontoria	Palencia	69	276	1,090.5	0.355
Resoba	Palencia	63	252	932.1	0.336
Cevico Navero	Palencia	132	528	1,071.5	0.304
Valberzoso	Palencia	30	120	957.2	0.289
Torre del Bierzo	León	32	128	650.9	0.179

[*] These figures are approximate, given that 'population' is obtained by multiplying the number of household heads by 4 and that members of the clergy are not included.
[**] This index is an approximation (via the Gini index) of the annual yields from the land properties held by household heads.
Source: authors' calculations based on *Ensenada Cadastre* (see Nicolini & Ramos-Palencia, 2020).

Between 1565 and 1700, the wages of skilled workers remained unchanged or decreased; the ratio of land leases to wages fell throughout the seventeenth century and did not begin to recover until the 1770s. In this analysis, the impact of the Lisbon earthquake in 1755 – which claimed some 50,000 victims altogether in Portugal, Spain and Morocco – should not be ignored. Pereira (2009) estimates that direct earthquake costs accounted for between 30% and 50% of Portuguese gross domestic product. In this context, during 1755–1777, certain property rights changed, the tax system was reformed, entire cities were restructured and even the nobility's power was addressed; however, these changes had a limited effect on wealth inequality. Enriched traders came to the fore as new wealth owners; but at the same time, there was no less distance between the richest and poorest citizens (Santos & Serrão, 2013).

Using the ratio of land rent to wages (i.e. the index of inequality proposed by Williamson, 2002), Álvarez-Nogal and Prados de la Escosura (2007a; 2013) show that economic inequality in Spain was cyclical during the early modern age: it periodically rose and fell in response to epidemics, disease and wars; and the fluctuations were apparently not driven by the Kuznets hypothesis. What does this mean? In 1955, Kuznets suggested that – mainly in rich countries – inequality first increases and then decreases during the course of a growth process (Kuznets, 1955). Since then, this hypothesis has been extensively used as a benchmark to analyse the relationship between growth (and/or development) and inequality. However, Milanovic (2016) suggests that 'the Kuznets curve gradually fell out of favour because its prediction of low inequality in very rich societies could not be squared with the sustained increase in income inequality that started in the late 1970s in practically all developed nations'. Álvarez-Nogal and Prados de la Escosura (2013: 20–21) document that inequality in Spain increased in the long term from (approximately) 1530 to 1650 and 1730 to 1800. Between 1650 and 1730, the levels of inequality fluctuated in concert with different events. For instance, following the destructive plague epidemic of the mid-seventeenth century, a new plague epidemic (1676–1685) and the adoption of deflationary monetary policies (1680–1686), inequality decreased during 1650–1670 and 1680–1700; however, it increased considerably during 1670–1680 and the War of the Spanish Succession (1700–1714). Other studies address the impact of Spanish inequality in more detail but restrict themselves to a specific area of the Iberian Peninsula. For example, Santiago-Caballero (2011) estimated income concentration during the last third of the eighteenth century in central Spain (Guadalajara) using grain tithes as a proxy. He argues that inequality decreased because the redistribution of communal lands after the Esquilache Riots in 1766 allowed many small peasants to produce above the subsistence level and hence to take advantage of trade and high grain prices. Using annual income data from the *Catastro de Ensenada* (c. 1750) in Castile (Palencia province), Nicolini and Ramos-Palencia (2016) show how different income sources and returns to productive factors affected inequality. For these authors, the leading cause of income inequality was land distribution and they estimate that land (resp. livestock) ownership was responsible for 52% (resp. 15%) of inequality (Nicolini &

Ramos-Palencia, 2016: 763-764). Oto-Peralías and Romero-Ávila (2017) explain how the medieval Christian conquest conditioned the ownership of land and thereby led to extremely persistent levels of inequality over time.

These results are in line with other European income patterns observed in pre-industrial societies, where the distribution of non-human wealth is usually the main determinant of economic inequality but, at least for the Spanish case, it seems differences in human capital levels and the dispersion of labour incomes can have a role in income inequality. Nicolini and Ramos-Palencia (2016) report that, despite the land factor's importance, labour income accounted for almost a fifth (18.5%) of inequality, and according to Álvarez and Ramos-Palencia (2018), human capital could have contributed to inequality of income (and hence of household income) prior to the nineteenth century's industrialization in north and central Spain (in the provinces of Palencia and Guadalajara). In theory, wage differentials associated with human capital should be greater in urban than in rural areas. Also, literacy made a difference in the tertiary sector – it was no accident that in the mid-eighteenth-century Madrid and Lisbon periodicals dedicated to advertising many candidates for the servant position highlighted their writing competence, while agricultural applicants stressed numerical skills. The implication is that reaching the highest level of professional qualification improved remuneration more in the primary and tertiary sectors than in the secondary sector; this outcome was consistent with Castilian manufacturers' low level of technological development. García-Montero (2016) uses anthropometric measures, as indicators of biological and nutritional welfare, to verify a significant correlation between height disparity and economic inequality in central Spain (Toledo Province) at the end of the eighteenth century; he reports differences of nearly five centimetres between the tallest individuals (large property owners and employees in services requiring extensive qualifications) and the shortest (servants).

In the Mediterranean periphery, Espín-Sánchez et al. (2019) state that – during the eighteenth century in the city of Murcia – levels of income inequality fell while the urbanization rate increased. These outcomes reflected an advanced 'de-skilling' process in the secondary sector. A similar trend is observed for the Barcelona area during the second half of the eighteenth century when, following economic growth, levels of inequality decreased. Brea-Martínez and Pujadas-Mora (2019) emphasize that, from 1810 to 1860, a process of *proletarianization*, which in Marxist terms means that the middle class becomes absorbed into the working class, was responsible for increased inequality between economic sectors and within the secondary sector of textiles. With regard to Catalonia, García-Montero (2015) likewise rules out a 'Kuznets curve' explanation of the wealth inequality in rural Catalonia between 1400 and 1800. According to this author, the growth of inequality ran parallel to GDP per capita growth starting in the mid-seventeenth century.

Yet, the trend of inequality in previous periods was not related to economic growth, and inequality fell during economic growth stages even during the second half of the sixteenth century.

In this context, women were one of the groups most affected by unfavourable economic conditions. Between 1500 and 1800, the alternatives for a woman coping with economic difficulties amounted to marriage, midwifery, becoming a baker or a seller of various products, dependent work (domestic service, wet-nursing and jobs related to the textile sector), joining a religious order, or prostitution. In general, women served a complementary function when both spouses were present and active but when the husband was absent they served a supplementary function to ensure continuity of the family economy (García, 2010; 2016).

Addressing the inheritance system, legislation was not the same throughout the Iberian Peninsula or even homogeneous within the same region: although Portugal and the former Crown of Castile advocated legal equality between men and women, the Catalan region, some parts of the Basque Country and Navarre opted for birthright (system of primogeniture). Consider Andalusia, which was governed by the Castilian inheritance system. In Córdoba, married women had no rights to any property acquired during marriage (Friedman, 1986). In Seville, a husband surviving his wife's death made use of the marital capital until his own death; however, if the husband died first then the jointly owned property was usually liquidated (Aguado de los Reyes, 1996). In that event, the wife retained half of the marital property as well as the dowry, the pledge, the marital bed and ordinary clothes; all remaining assets were distributed among the other heirs. Moreover, Castilian and Portuguese legislation established the *Mayorazgo* system whereby inherited goods were bequeathed according to birthright, defined in the charter of foundation (usually to the eldest male child).

When widowed, a woman became the family head even if she lived with a married adult male child. Often a woman continued her husband's business when he died, frequently relying on help from their children and other close relatives. In practice, widowhood was then considered to be a 'provisional period' between a new widow's marriage and her children's coming of age. Serious problems arose when the widow had no family support: in that case, the low remuneration that females received for their salaried work meant that widowed (and single) women were usually assumed to be poor.

According to the *Ensenada* population census (c. 1750), the percentage of poor widows (4.01%) and poverty-stricken women (1.14%) was almost twice the number of poor and poverty-stricken men (2.75% and 0.53%, respectively) in the former Crown of Castile (Vol. I, table 11, pp. 84–85).[64] López-Cordón Cortezo (1986: 64) underscores that female employment increased as social

---

[64] *Catastro de Ensenada. Vecindario de Ensenada* (1759). Vol. 1, Madrid, 1991.

status decreased and that female employment was (indirectly) correlated with employment in the active male population. During the eighteenth century, the Bourbon Enlightenment policy of Campomanes (1723-1802) and Jovellanos (1744-1811) promoted the presence of women in textile activities at the same time as the royal factories established a network of spinning schools that employed chiefly female and child labour. The French, English and Irish factory experiences led the Irish economist Ward – a board member and minister in the Royal Board of Commerce and Currency of Ferdinand VI – to initiate his 1762 economic project involving almost 1.5 million women working in yarn factories. In 1784, a Royal Certificate approved by Charles III allowed women to work in thread factories and to perform other activities. However, female workers were paid less than male workers.

Carbonell (2005: 253) cites the textile sector's continuous disputes – from the seventeenth century onward – between guild masters and apprentices; these disputes were occasioned by the hiring of female employees, which reduced the cost of labour. Portuguese wage differences between men and women were also large: in 1593 Coimbra, for example, the daily wages of women and boys in the olive harvest were fixed at 15 *réis* when they included meals and at 30 *réis* when they did not; yet on otherwise equal terms, men's wages were set at 25 *réis* (1.7 times as much) and 70 *réis* (2.3 times), respectively (Oliveira, 1972: 73). With regard to Lisbon's supply and commerce sectors in 1552, women had the humblest and least specialized occupations (Brandão, 1990). During the second half of the eighteenth century, lower rates were strongly associated with manufacturing and apprenticeship as well as with female and child labour (Pedreira, 1994: 404-405). Women were also the ones most likely to avail themselves of home assistance from holy 'houses of mercy' in Évora (1650-1750, 61.5%), Coimbra (1769-1785, 86%) and other places (see Lopes, 2000: 182; Sá, 2002: 316; Pardal, 2015: 184).

Another group that suffered many hardships was children (Bennassar, 1989). In Valladolid at the start of the seventeenth century, the proportion of abandoned children was slightly less than 10%; in 1641-1645 it was 15%, from 1665 to 1670 it was 17%, and during 1691-1695 it was 22%. In Seville from 1631 to 1640, the average number of abandoned children was 258; from 1650 to 1657, the number was less than 200; and from 1683 to 1690 it was more than 300, with a peak of 425 in 1684. In 1680, Madrid's *Inclusa* took in 926 newborns – a number that regularly exceeded 1,000 after that year. According to Domínguez Ortiz (2004: 246-247), of the 3,000-5,000 children abandoned annually throughout Spain, as many as four-fifths died before their first birthday. In Lisbon, the annual number of abandoned children tripled from an average of about 500 in 1689-1690 to 1,526 per year during 1790-1800; in Porto, that number grew by a factor of 6: the average increased from 141 to 853 between about 1700 and 1795 (Sá, 1995: 216; 2002: 333; Reis, 2016: 74).

Both the charity system organized during the *Ancien Régime* and a certain concept of charity and beneficence – the right of the poor to ask for alms freely and to receive assistance – contributed to avoiding rebellions, social demonstrations and other conflicts in the structurally unequal society of the Iberian Peninsula. Marcos Martín (2007: 43–44) refers to an 'unwritten social pact' whereby the rich had certain obligations to the poor and the poor had the right to receive alms and assistance. This system helped to create social and political equilibrium near the poorest sections of the population, despite their knowing that these institutions did not treat all the poor in the same way (Sá, 2002).

Recall from Chapters 12 and 13 that it is not clear whether the fiscal capacity of the different Iberian kingdoms, the volume of public debt and/or interest payment defaults (or the withholding of part of these) affected some of these processes of inequality and impoverishment. Portugal nearly went bankrupt between 1542 and 1555; Spain did go bankrupt in 1557, 1575, 1596, 1607, 1627 and 1647 (Reinhart & Rogoff, 2011: 114). Alfani and Di Tullio (2019) show that the growth of the fiscal-military state during the modern age led to increased economic inequality. In fact, all pre-industrial tax systems were regressive because they opted for an increase in fiscal pressure on less affluent social groups. In the opinion of these authors, most taxes were meant to finance armed conflicts to the detriment of social welfare. Reis (2017) points out that in the Portuguese case wars were few and relatively cheap; however, a variety of methods were used to achieve these ends. In theory, many services could be paid with honours, posts and pensions as well as with goods confiscated from families who fled to Castile between 1640 and 1668. In the short term, the Crown opted too many times for not paying wages while reducing provisions. It also made use of obligations and the Public Treasury's consequent indebtedness (Costa et al., 2016: 120). And starting in the mid-seventeenth century, Portugal's alliance with England allowed for some protection of its overseas sea lanes. The signing of several treaties with England, including that of Methuen in 1703, resulted in a 'double' political–commercial alliance that kept Portuguese foreign policy aligned with British interests (Costa et al., 2016). Meanwhile, Portugal tried to make its empire self-sufficient – even using tithes it received to generate the basis of a 'fiscal state' in its non-European territories (e.g. Brazil).

The Hispanic monarchy's story was more intricate. In theory, its need for financing required considerable fiscal pressure that must be analysed from a triple perspective that incorporates the territory, social groups and the city/town/village's jurisdictional category. It should be stressed that not all territories contributed identically to the Hispanic monarchy. The Crown of Castile, the territories attached to the Crown of Castile (the Lordship of Biscay and the so-called Exempt Provinces), Navarre, the Crown of Aragon (Aragon, Catalonia, Valencia and the Balearic Islands) and Portugal (between 1580 and 1640) each enjoyed their own institutions and tax regimes. Quevedo

(1580–1645), one of the most representative writers of the Spanish 'golden age', summed up the situation in 1638: 'In Navarre and Aragon, there is no-one who pays anything towards taxes; Catalonia and Portugal are the same; it is only Castile and León and the noble Andalusian kingdom that carry the burden' (Egido López, 1973). Thompson (1992) maintains that, following the Revolt of the Comuneros (1520–1522), a distinction must be made between Old Castile and León and the peripheral territories of the Crown of Castile: Galicia, New Castile, Extremadura and Andalusia. The latter were compensated for increased fiscal pressure by a hefty increase in public spending in the form of fleet supply, construction of fortifications, spending in Court (transfer from Toledo and Valladolid to Madrid) and payment of wages to the court bureaucracy (which offset all costs associated with the imperial policy of the Habsburgs). Upon the arrival in Spain of the Bourbons in the eighteenth century, the former territories of the Crown of Aragon continued to enjoy a different tax regime. After the end of the War of the Spanish Succession, a fixed amount (the *cadastre*) was finally applied to these areas. Since Valencia and especially Catalonia were the regions exhibiting the greatest economic and demographic growth, the effects of fiscal pressure continued to be more pronounced in the territories of the former Crown of Castile (Domínguez Ortiz, 2004: 215). In addition, between 1500 and 1700 the tax system used by the monarchy was based on indirect taxation imposed on consumption, commerce and production – taxes from which the aristocracy and clergy were exempt. The fiscal reform of the Marquess of Ensenada in the mid-eighteenth century sought to reverse this situation, but it was never implemented. Until about the mid-eighteenth century, 'privilege' in all of Iberia was equivalent to being exempt from tax burdens (Bluteau, 1720; *Diccionario de la lengua castellana, 1737*).

Finally, it is crucial to account for the jurisdictional category of 'royal, stately, and ecclesiastical'. The imperial policy of the Habsburgs devoured resources continuously, which affected all economic agents. Thus, for example, Charles I sold towns belonging to military orders; Philip II sold towns belonging to the bishoprics; Philip III did not sell anything because his *valido*, the Duke of Lerma, dedicated himself to real estate speculation with the temporary transfer of the court from Madrid to Valladolid; and Philip IV sold approximately 40,000 vassals who lived in 200 places. In reality, what was being sold was royal jurisdiction: the lord became a kind of perpetual ruler, albeit subject to the laws and royal authorities. The new owner or lord had the right to appoint municipal officers, had land-buying privileges and could manage his own and vacant property. At the end of Charles II's reign, when there was almost nothing left to sell, nearly 300 titles of marquis and count had been sold; the venality in this field continued into the eighteenth century, especially in the Indies (Domínguez Ortiz, 2004: 244–245; Andújar & Felices, 2007; Soria Mesa, 2007: 49–55; Felices, 2016). In short, the former Crown of Castile financed its public debt by turning up the fiscal pressure on peasants, artisans and merchants; when this was not enough, the monarchy – frequently conniving with individuals – resorted to the sale of municipal assets, tax collection rights (a.k.a. 'disposed' income), public positions (notaries and councillors), vassals and places. Although such events obviously created upward social mobility, they must also have had both direct and indirect effects on the increase in long-term inequality.

15.4 Consumption

The panorama described so far is a complex one: low and declining real wages combined with high levels of inequality, and Spain and Portugal were in an unstable equilibrium with wages barely above the subsistence level (see Allen et al., 2012; Palma & Reis, 2019). Yet, from the sixteenth century there had been in all social strata an upward trend throughout Europe in the possession of furniture, kitchen utensils and diverse clothes as well as in the consumption of 'exotic' foods.

The early modern diet benefited from the introduction of products from other continents and regions, although their effects were not the same in all social groups. In the sixteenth century, the most important of these products was maize (*Zea mays*) coming from America and spreading from the Mondego River to the north-west of France, in some areas of the Mediterranean coast (e.g. Valencia) and in the Atlantic archipelagos (Canary Islands and Madeira). In wheat-deficient areas, maize played a large role in reducing famine and thus in affecting demography from the eighteenth century onward. Maize was most often consumed as bread or in porridge with vegetables. Throughout the Iberian Peninsula, bread retained its leading position (since medieval times) in the diet. Bread and meat were the staples in all social strata, but with meat in the second position (as reported in 1552 – see Brandão (1990: 28)). However, bread became increasingly made of maize or from a mixture of several cereals; mixtures involving vegetables and fruits were also frequent. The Madrid 1818 edition of *General Agriculture* described maize bread as 'suitable for the livelihood of the working class of very hardworking and active life' (I, p. 210). Maize and its antecedents had traditionally been viewed as 'declassified' food. Thus in 1508, in the Portuguese area of Pombal, it was offered to the visiting Bishop of Coimbra to feed the dogs and for the woman who did the laundry (Gonçalves, 2006: 276). In some areas of Galicia, bread made only with maize was considered unsuitable for all but for the poorest inhabitants (Saavedra, 2018: 67–72). Across the Peninsula, white (wheat) bread was much more expensive and was consumed mostly by the elites.

In the Portuguese territory, a similar dynamic was evident with respect to rice – the most expensive of all cereals in the *Ancien Régime*. Portugal imported rice from several places on the Mediterranean coast of Castile and Aragon and from Italy; in the mid-eighteenth century rice came also from Carolina, on the other side of the Atlantic. In 1781, production in Portugal and overseas spaces exceeded consumption; hence rice imports were banned (by the *alvará* of 24 July) as a way to protect this crop. In the sixteenth to eighteenth centuries, male and female convents bought fair quantities of rice, and 'sweet rice' or 'milk rice' became a fashionable delight, on festive days, for those in the middle and higher social strata. In the Mediterranean regions mentioned, in the kingdom of Valencia, rice consumption was not rare enough to be socially differentiating.

Beginning in the early nineteenth century, potatoes became relevant to the diet of Iberia's general populace. At that time, it was considered to be 'without a doubt the most appreciable production that came to us from the New World', with positive impact on the Demography, being able to supply grains and feed the working people (Herrera, 1818, III, p. 248; Neto, 2018: 122). Yet, resistance to potato consumption was even greater and more prolonged than that recorded for maize – the elites resisted eating potatoes well into the early nineteenth century. However, consumption of this tuber was boosted by the increase in cereal prices in the late eighteenth century. Before then, potatoes were almost always cultivated to feed domestic animals (Pérez Samper, 2009: 58; Braga, 2012; Neto, 2018: 134).

Sugar was likewise not accessible to all social groups, despite its dissemination throughout the Iberian Peninsula and the rest of Europe from the fifteenth century onwards. Its high price meant that the poor consumed sugar only on special occasions or when sick or in hospitals, where it was distributed in the form of marmalade, confectionery, pink sugar or conserved fruits. In 1529–1530, a female weeding day worker in central Portugal (Tomar) would need at least 3.5 days of wages to buy an *arrátel* (0.4590 kg) of Madeira sugar (Arquivo Nacional Torre do Tombo, *Ordem de Cristo, Convento de Tomar*, L° 118, f. 11v, 16v). Two centuries later, in 1759, a male farm worker in Lisbon could buy the same quantity with only a single day's wages (see Figure 15.1). Even so, in 1593 the secretary of the apostolic Nuncio in Lisbon, Villalba y Estaña, recorded that the people of Lisbon used sugar at the same rate as the Lombards used cheese (Villalba y Estaña & Confalonieri, 2002: 183). The same consumption levels were evident in Castile's wealthiest cities. In Valladolid alone – not counting street sales and other services offering ready meals – there were more than a hundred shops where one could buy sweets when the Royal Court was there (c. 1601–1606). At that time, sugar and nougats (*'turrones'*) were abundant but all at high prices, affordable only to those of the courtier group (Veiga, 1911: 217–218).

Most other 'new food products' that appeared in the Iberian Peninsula following maritime expansion – including spices (pepper became more commonplace in Europe during the mid-seventeenth century, when its price declined – see Braudel (1992, I: 187–190)), cocoa, turkey, tomatoes and pineapple – did not change the eating habits of intermediate and privileged groups despite having the most impact there. Instead, they simply favoured diversification of the diet and slowly changing (from an exotic curiosity) palates and flavour impressions. Most of the aforementioned groups never visited colonial territories; yet their money, relationships and sociability, including offers and patronage (in Portugal, the Crown and the royal family offered regular amounts of sugar and spices to many monasteries), promoted the introduction of these new foods. In contrast, ordinary people depended heavily on producing for self-consumption; hence their purchases were generally limited to basic, low-priced products obtained at local markets.

Portuguese satirical verses from 1587 recall how money strongly affected living standards and social promotion: 'Money that gives comfort / chicken, partridge, deer / fat cow, & make honourable'.[65] Frequent access to these meats, especially beef, marked the dietary pattern of privileged groups across the Iberian Peninsula. But the general populace obtained its animal protein (when available) mostly from pork, bacon and eggs. River fish and sardines, mainly in the Iberian Atlantic areas, were also widely consumed even in conventual communities. As far as contemporary sources allow us to observe, Portuguese convents in the seventeenth and eighteenth centuries bought large quantities of cod fish in spite of its high price – and especially when other types of fresh fish were unavailable. Those residing in the Peninsula's interior consumed dried, salted and vinegar-marinated fish (Veiga, 1911: 338–339).

Tobacco was another product whose consumption started to expand in the seventeenth century and did not stop expanding until late in the eighteenth century. Diffusion was rapid; tobacco's first uses were medicinal, but it quickly became an addictive pleasure in the two Iberian Crowns. Until nearly the end of the 1770s, tobacco was consumed mostly in powder form not only in Spain but also in Portugal (although timelines for the latter are not known with certainty). In Spain, the regions of Galicia, Seville, Madrid and Valencia consumed the most tobacco during the eighteenth century (GRETA, 2002: 314, 331). Because tobacco was sold at the retail level, its use was widespread both geographically and socially including among women and the poor despite its high price. According to the (likely exaggerated) estimates published in an 'advice' (*arbítrio*) around 1698 tobacco was consumed in about 40% of Portuguese households (Hespanha, 2013: 125). The Englishman Thomas Cox's description of Lisbon in 1701 noted that 'all types of people, from the king to beggars, smell like powdered tobacco' and he considered it was a way to remove the disgusting stench from the streets (Cox & Macro, 2007: 166). There

---

[65] Quote is from Auto chamado do Desembargador in Primeira parte dos autos e comedias portuguesas feitas por Antonio Prestes, & por Luis de Camões, & por outros Autores Portugueses, cujos nomes vão nos principios de suas obras. Agora novamente juntas & emendadas nesta primeira impressão, ed. Afonso Lopes, s. l., & Andres Lobato, 1587.

is much evidence that, by the end of the seventeenth century, Lisbon had become the country's leading consumer of tobacco (Gonçalves, 2003: 139–141, 150).

The great contrast that existed in the diets of the Peninsula's various social groups was evident also in housing and comfort. The size of the houses, the existence of floors above ground and the number of windows were all clear indicators of a homeowner's social status and economic power – as were architectural quality as well as the existence of coats of arms or other marks of possession and ornaments on building facades.

For many, access to housing was possible only through contracts of '*emphyteusis*'[66]; leasing was less frequent. In several of the large urban agglomerations, expenditures were reduced by renting only parts of houses (e.g. rooms, attics). In Lisbon, the aristocracy itself provided rooms or areas in their palaces in the city centre for rent. These strategies were all means of adjusting the market to demographic pressures in the largest cities. In 1593, Villalba y Estaña observed that in the streets of Lisbon where the artisans lived there were 'four, five or six families per building, buildings that were narrow like sardines' (Villalba y Estaña & Confalonieri, 2002: 173). In Castile at the beginning of the seventeenth century, houses consisting only of a kitchen and one other room were exempt from compulsory accommodation (*aposentadoria*). For this reason, many houses in Madrid were also narrow (with little space on the facade facing the street but with great depth), built with a kitchen and an extremely long room that was later divided by wooden partitions or other ephemeral arrangements (Veiga, 1911: 331). Yet, in the south of Castile many houses were more spacious, and arranged around an interior courtyard.

At the beginning of the early modern age, interiors of the houses of commoners were not specialized and amounted more to a place of refuge than an area of sociability (if one excludes the working areas of artisanal groups). Some houses had just a single, multi-functional room. In Lisbon and other Portuguese towns, people would cook anywhere (even on the street) with clay pots and charcoal for combustion as documented in sixteenth-century paintings and in written sources. We conclude that many houses did not contain a space dedicated to cooking.

Throughout the Iberian Peninsula, most furniture (e.g. chests) served to hold items. For sleeping, families typically used mattresses stretched out directly or indirectly on the floor – that is, because not all houses had beds (viz., an elevated piece of furniture meant specifically for sleeping). During the day, mattresses could be stowed away to free up space. However, only the

---

[66] *Emphyteusis* was a contract that allowed the holder (*emphyteuta*) to enjoy a land or a house for a number of lives (usually three) or in perpetuity, paying an annual tax. The *emphyteuta* could not divide the property or alien it.

poorest slept on the floor. In 1611, Sebastian Covarrubias (1611: 178) recommended sleeping on a higher plane, to avoid moisture on the floor as a health measure.

Few houses had wells or holes that would guarantee a supply of water. Chimneys, another symbol of comfort, became more widely used in Italy during the fifteenth century; however, Thomas Cox reported in 1701 that some houses in Portugal lacked a chimney and had no interior light other than what came in through the door (Cox & Macro, 2007: 276). Also, in the rest of the Peninsula, the chimney was still a rare item at the end of the eighteenth century (Franco Rubio, 2009: 78). And according to Cox, most of the windows in 1701 Lisbon lacked glass panes (Cox & Macro, 2007: 53). Even in the urban centres, only a few monasteries and palaces had a sewage system.

A notorious extent of specialization was evident in the interiors of eighteenth-century houses, especially in the aristocratic palaces and in the homes of merchants and other wealthy individuals. The most striking changes were in fashioning of the 'cabinet'. The *Dictionary of Authorities*, published in 1734 by the Royal Spanish Academy, defined *cabinet* as a 'room, in the Palaces or houses of the lords, in the innermost part of them, destined for their withdrawal, or to deal with private businesses, and run on them'. In contrast, *saloons* were intended for mixed-gender socializing and exhibited sumptuous furniture and decoration (Franco Rubio, 2009: 93).

In the seventeenth and eighteenth centuries, social contrasts became even more pronounced in housing and between the most populated cities and the small rural villages despite an overall reduction in inequality in these latter areas. In particular, houses of the more affluent and of those positioned higher on the social scale were larger and more specialized, from stables, cellars and barns to dedicated areas for servants and cooking. In aristocratic palaces, such areas were almost always on the ground floor; the upper floor was the 'noble' floor, to which people climbed via an imposing staircase. On that floor there were saloons (specializing in games, music, etc.), antechambers, cabinets and dressing rooms or toilets, a dining room and sometimes a kitchen. Often a library was located in the private cabinet or office. From the seventeenth century onward, the fashion of attaching a private chapel to the house had spread among the noble groups. The most enriched middling social sectors tried to imitate the homes of the aristocracy.

A study of the post-mortem inventories of 70–80 traders in Lisbon between 1759 and 1827 revealed that their fortunes consisted of similar average values of objects in gold and silver and in other household items (accounting for, resp., 1.52% and 1.38% of all assets). Their investment was greatest in furniture (38.1%), clothing (27.4%) and crockery (9.3%) considering the household categories of objects (Pedreira, 1995: 307–310). However, the set of middle-rank groups in the same city were evidently less enamoured with furniture: after gold and silver, most of their investments were in clothing. Clothes were held in even higher esteem among those of the lowest socioeconomic stratum, accounting for more value than the household's accumulation of gold and silver (Gomes, 2017: 202). The same predominance of textiles can be seen in the matrimonial dowries of Valladolid in the eighteenth century (García, 2010: 123). Clothing is an essential component of the representation of the individual in the public sphere and the indicator of his social status, which is why it was so relevant in the society of the *Ancien Régime*. The most important domestic item in relation to the Portuguese aristocratic inventories was gold and silver, mainly silver, which was more differentiating (Monteiro, 2012: 37).

As we described in previous topics two material culture and consumption patterns prevailed in the pre-industrial world. One appears clearly in the European courts; the other pattern, which is more difficult to discern, is related to households in the upper to middle part of the income distribution. We can infer their nature and that of more modest houses by analysing post-mortem inventories, travel logs and the works of painters who portrayed the daily life of the middle and lower groups. The underlying question is obvious: Why did consumption of food and of durable (and semi-durable) goods increase if real wages decreased in the long term? We address this question as follows. First, wages were not the only component of family income; other components included the exploitation of agricultural properties and the use of livestock for family self-consumption. Second, family income grew because the number of hours worked increased. Thus in Catalonia (Barcelona and towns surrounding it) during the late eighteenth century the pattern of the distribution of meals, working hours and recreation changed: at first the working hours were from 5 a.m. to 7 p.m. (7-8 a.m. breakfast; 12-1 p.m. lunch; 3:30-4:30 p.m. snack; 8-9 p.m. dinner); but then it moved to a continuous day with occasional breaks for breakfast and lunch during a working timetable that ran from dawn until 8 p.m. (data from a survey conducted by Francisco de Zamora). Third, income increased because an increasing number of family members entered the labour market. Finally, one should not discount the general reduction in basic consumer prices due to continual increases in agricultural production.

The key to this entire process was the emergence of an 'industrious revolution' in many places in Europe in the eighteenth century, with epicentres in the Netherlands and in England, which affected the consumption of a wide variety of products. De Vries (2008) documents that north-west Europe and the British colonies in North America experienced an industrious revolution between 1650 and 1850 as more and more families increased their labour in the market, earning more money and thus increasing their demand for and consumption of goods. In summary, the greater variety of available assets increased the marginal utility of income; this, in turn, encouraged households to increase their income by working more, even though doing so reduced their leisure and free time. McCants (2007: 461) suggests that the European demand for luxury goods was driven not only by those of the richest social status but also by the less affluent (and, of course, far more numerous) social groups in urban and rural centres. The available data suggest that European demand for imports did not change solely because of increases in income or reductions in prices. There was a significant reorientation of people's tastes (and purchase preferences) toward imported products to the detriment of those selling items from local agriculture and industry. The most curious fact is that after the mid-eighteenth century this increase in luxury goods can be seen also in the most disadvantaged social groups. Thus the consumption of sugar, tobacco and porcelain, as well as of silk and cotton textiles, increased substantially in Western Europe from the end of the seventeenth century.

The appearance of the Iberian Peninsula's first advertising periodicals – in Madrid (1758), Lisbon (1763) and Barcelona (1772) – embody this dynamism of a socially extended demand for goods and services, whether local or from other countries and continents. What factors drove residents of the Iberian Peninsula to reduce their leisure and to work and consume more (see Chapter 14)? A 1788 chapbook described how, under the guise of birthdays or other reasons, the fashion of the assemblies had percolated down to the middle groups in Lisbon, with women visiting the saloon, playing the harpsichord and singing (Costa, 1788). In all of Goya's work painted before the Napoleonic Wars there is an unusual interest in and taste for leisure and sociability, as if the middle-ranking groups and the groups at the bottom of the social pyramid only discovered the value of leisure when they were losing it: men play with kites, smoke, drink, play music, play cards; women dance or ride on a swing; and children climb trees or play with animals. Likewise, the streets of Madrid were rife with gentlemen wearing three-cornered hats, artisans in wide hats, and poorer but well-dressed younger people wearing scarves and hairnets. The nobility imitated the fashions of the Court and tried to differentiate themselves from ordinary people by being seen in their saloons and carriages on avenues and streets (as depicted by Goya in the painting *San Isidro Meadow* [1788]). To account for this, García (2016) contends that the strength of Iberian societies should be placed in the middle of the sixteenth century and not in the second half of the eighteenth century. In his opinion, what happened in this last period was an expansion of consumption patterns driven by the dynamism of the Peninsula's coastal centres – the Seville–Cádiz and Lisbon–Porto axes with Madrid – and the networks that Catalan merchants wove were factors driving the expansion of consumption patterns during the eighteenth century. García (2016) underlines the importance of the commercial exchanges of Murcia merchants with the Mediterranean ports in Marseille, Genoa, Malta and the Ottoman Empire in order to understand the increase in consumption and refinement in certain patterns and manners. Aram and Yun-Casalilla (2014) emphasize the role played by the elites of the Atlantic world, showcasing the role of the privileged social strata of Creole origin in New Spain in the acquisition and consumption of manufactured goods from Asia (fans, spices, Japanese furniture, porcelain and Chinese silks, inter alia). Thus a simple circuit of consumption patterns was established that could respond effectively to Brazil in the Portuguese case as well as to New Spain – and its connections with the Viceroyalty of Peru and/or the Court of Madrid and Crown of Castile, especially after the opening of the Manila Galleon route in 1571.

Yet, the consumption of luxuries was not confined to the upper levels of society. López Barahona and Nieto Sánchez (2012) describe the paradoxical coexistence of rags and luxury goods among the poorest social groups in Madrid. The poor also consumed items and products that they did not, strictly speaking, need; even the lowest economic strata comprised hierarchies of the poor. Ramos-Palencia (2010: 88–96) suggests that the intermediate social strata of Palencia province (Castile and León) increased their amount of spending on durable and semi-durable items and also the quantity of those items purchased. Whereas families in 1752–1765 spent an average of 146 *reals* (in real terms), that average rose to 163 *reals* at the end of the eighteenth century (1785–1800). What is the contemporary economic magnitude of these amounts? Donézar (1996: 338–341) posits that, in the middle of the eighteenth century, the minimum/subsistence amount for a farmer and his family was 500 *reals* net, and Yun-Casalilla (1987: 463–464) estimates a subsistence income of 300 *reals* net for a family of 3.5 members per year. It follows that basic needs – in other words expenditures on personal clothing, bedding and household linen – absorbed almost three-quarters of a family's funds budgeted annually for the purchase of durable and semi-durable consumer goods.

15.5 Conclusion

After the bright political prospects of the sixteenth century the Iberian Peninsula suffered a long period of irregular but persistent decline in living standards. Even though there was significant variation across regions, real wages displayed a negative trend during the period with larger reductions before the central decades of the seventeenth century and after the second half of the eighteenth century. Large differences were noticeable also across income groups and social classes. Even though the general pattern of income inequality in Spain and Portugal was not radically different from the one observed in other areas of early modern Europe, it was very high in large cities like Lisbon and Granada. While income inequality decreased in Portugal between the sixteenth and eighteenth centuries, the picture in Spain is not so obvious, with many different regional patterns and no clear general trend. Across the Iberian Peninsula, the culturally disadvantaged groups of women, small children and poor people were the ones most affected by these living conditions.

Consumption patterns were similar in both countries and were strongly conditioned by the socioeconomic framework and living standards. However, the increased consumption was greater in Spain owing to that country's better conditions: the demographic growth of Cádiz and Barcelona in the eighteenth century amplified the demand for manufactured good and also the economic performance of the Mediterranean area more generally. The mid-eighteenth century is a turning point in the two countries, with the consolidation of traders as a social stratum and the changes in people's tastes. Expanding consumption relied on the reduction in prices of manufactured products, the greater openness to fashions and influences from abroad, and the emergence of critical thinking about the backwardness of Iberian countries. In Portugal and Castile, the experience of the colonial Empire also marked consumption patterns, especially the sumptuous consumption of the elites. Particularly in Portugal, hoarding (through the purchase of gold and silver products) continued throughout the *Ancien Régime* for different social groups, starting with the aristocracy. It simultaneously represented an investment in utility, status and hoarding that did not devalue over time. It was an asset that easily converted into liquidity or that could easily be used as a pledge.

Despite high levels of wealth in the upper classes that lived in large urban centres such as Madrid, Lisbon or Seville, it seems that Iberian consumption patterns did not experience a consumer revolution. In the Iberian Peninsula the consumption of the majority of families was concentrated on cheap durables and semi-durables goods; even though the demand for these products increased between the seventeenth and eighteenth centuries and there was some progressive refinement of consumption patterns, the impact of these processes was rather limited and the proto-industrial systems were mostly focused on low-price products (see Chapter 14). In short, the panorama during the early modern period in Iberian Society was as follows: high income and wealth inequality, low wages that stimulated people to work more hours and days, high prices for essential commodities and some expansion of demand but focused on low-quality manufactures.

16

Trade and the Colonial Economies, 1500–1828

CÁTIA ANTUNES, REGINA GRAFE AND XABIER LAMIKIZ

16.1 Introduction

Economic historians have placed commercialization at the centre of Europe's early modern capitalism, emphasizing the importance of domestic and international trade, shipbuilding and concomitant industries, the financial sector and urbanization. As the Iberian polities extended geographically to Africa, Asia and the Americas during the early modern period, trade, whether domestic, international or colonial, had a critical effect upon economic development. However, as we will see, the economic impact of colonial expansion was uneven across Iberia. There is now a consensus among economic historians that in Iberia commercial exchange associated with the overseas empires produced surprisingly few backward and forward linkages in the European national economies (O'Brien & Prados de la Escosura, 1999; Costa et al., 2015). The question this chapter seeks to address is thus to what extent and how Iberian trade, especially colonial trade, supported or hindered economic development in the early modern period.

The general trends and cycles of economic and commercial expansion are clear. As seen in Chapters 10 and 11, the Iberian Peninsula emerged from the economic and demographic setback brought about by the Black Death (1347–1351) into a period of territorial and maritime expansion. In 1415 the Portuguese conquered Ceuta in Morocco. By 1500 the Portuguese population had recovered to pre-plague levels despite recurrent famines (see Chapter 11). Population growth picked up across the peninsula over the sixteenth century accompanied by an increase in agricultural output, the development of a significant manufacturing sector, and the Christian conquest of the last southern Islamic polity, Granada, coinciding with the early conquests in the Americas. In the last quarter of the sixteenth century, however, gradual changes in geographies of international trade and subsequent processing in the supply chains led the Iberian kingdoms first to stagnation, and then to a period of decline that found its nadir in the 1630s.

The Portuguese economy subsequently followed a path of gradual expansion of population and per capita income from the 1630s to the 1755 Lisbon earthquake (with the exception of years of the War of Spanish Succession, 1701–1714). This was followed by a slow-down during the second half of the eighteenth century. Spain recovered more slowly from the crisis in the seventeenth century. Overall the population grew from the 1640s onwards, with the highest annual rates occurring in the eighteenth century. In the aftermath of the post-1590s crisis a significant shift saw the centres of economic gravity move permanently from the interior to the coastal regions in the two largest reigns, Castile and Aragon (see Chapter 11 and Álvarez-Nogal & Prados de la Escosura, 2007b). The end of the eighteenth and beginning of the nineteenth century witnessed a relative decline of the Iberian economies, culminating in the French invasion and the ensuing Peninsular War (1807–1814), a conflict that seemed to confirm Portugal's and Spain's place as economically backward nations of the European periphery.

Recent research stresses the significant divergence in impact of colonial and intercontinental trades between Spain and Portugal. Without the empire, Portugal's per capita income may have been at least one-fifth lower (Costa, et al., 2015). Nevertheless, the assistance provided by the empire to the domestic economy was not sufficient to offset Portugal's relative decline in relation to Europe's advanced nations. Salary levels began to fall behind from the seventeenth century onwards and, after a recovery in the eighteenth century, worsened significantly at the beginning of the nineteenth century. Spain's domestic economy owed far less to colonial trade at any point in the early modern period. In macroeconomic terms the colonial empire had little weight in the great cycles of the Spanish economy. And yet 'the Indies were a vital cog in an institutional and economic system that shaped interregional relationships in the period of formation of a [Spanish] national economy' (Yun-Casalilla, 1998: 148).

In order to assess the importance of European trade and the empire in the development of the Iberian economies, this chapter starts by exploring the early geographies and main trading routes of the Iberian commercial expansion in the Atlantic World, Asia and the Pacific, including the rise of the transatlantic slave trade (Section 16.2). Section 16.3 looks at the institutional set up and the protagonists of the expanding extra-European trades. Section 16.4 analyses the eighteenth century reforms to the colonial political economy. Finally, Section 16.5 deals with the goods traded to and from the colonies. We conclude by examining the mutual economic impacts between the Iberian metropoles and their colonies, and between Iberia and Europe.

16.2 Iberians from Europe to the Atlantic, Indian and Pacific Oceans: First Steps

Since antiquity, the location of the Iberian Peninsula in south-western Europe, between the Mediterranean and the Atlantic Ocean, and close to the African continent, allowed its kingdoms and regions to participate in important international trading routes in the north and south of Europe, and the eastern Mediterranean. Geography is critical to understanding Iberians' head start in setting up transoceanic exchanges from the late fifteenth century onward. Grain-deficient coastal areas of the peninsula, especially in Portugal, sought supplies from beyond the sea. At the same time, the late medieval economic recovery coincided with the beginning of Ottoman control of both the eastern Mediterranean and the major overland routes that connected Europe and Asia. Iberians were to capitalize on both developments, and the Atlantic World was the natural arena for their commercial expansion.

The agricultural sector stood at the core of late medieval and early modern Iberian societies, with a focus on the production of wine, fruits (fresh, salted, in jam or dried), olive oil and grain, accompanied by extractive activities like salt extraction, timber, collection of cork, or iron winning and metallurgy, and last but not least shepherding. These products, produced or extracted domestically, were exported to other European countries; by the sixteenth century in particular to the Low Countries (north and south), England, France and the Italian peninsula. Return cargoes consisted often of specialized textiles and foodstuffs, in many regions grain, and from the later sixteenth century onwards large quantities of dried fish.

For Castile, wool exports to the Low Countries, France and Italian territories were particularly important in terms of their backward linkages in the domestic economy. Castilian merchants, particularly from Burgos, but also from other regions such as the Basques provinces, established themselves in Bruges and other major European commercial hubs (Casado Alonso, 1996; Priotti, 2005). Until the third quarter of the sixteenth century, the trade was carried in Iberian ships, departing from the different kingdoms in the Peninsula. However, the participation of vessels from the Spanish regions in European trade declined dramatically with the war interruptions of the late sixteenth century and would only become important again in the eighteenth century. Economic warfare repeatedly led to redirections of trade flows, such as the relative rise of English markets for Spanish wool in the mid-seventeenth century (Grafe, 2005).

Portuguese merchants also had an important presence in the main northwestern European and Mediterranean ports. Yet, domestically produced exports took second place behind the redistribution of overseas products that arrived from the empire as soon as the 1450s. The demographic expansion post-Black Death, the need for redistributive rents and lands for a growing nobility, and the economic incentives associated with a Papal Bull of Crusade led to the Portuguese conquest of North African strongholds after 1415. Aiming at participating and reaping the outputs of the east–west Saharan caravan trade, the Portuguese looked for cheap and readily available sources of grain to feed a growing population, military and religious posts for the nobility, and the rights and rents of plundering and enslavement associated with the Bull (Mendes, 2016).

Portuguese North African conquests stood as an extension to the discovery and settlement in the Azores Archipelago and Madeira, from where further expansion southwards along the West African coast ensued and came to include the Atlantic Archipelago of Cabo Verde and São Tomé. The Castilian monarchy meanwhile brought the Canaries Archipelago under its control in the late fifteenth century. Famously, Castilian armies in 1492 conquered the Kingdom of Granada, while Columbus's expedition reached the Caribbean, ushering in the conquest and colonization of the Americas. In 1497, the Portuguese Vasco da Gama sailed around the tip of Africa and along the eastern coast of Africa to reach India, and, in 1500, a Portuguese fleet commanded by Pedro Álvares Cabral arrived in Brazil.

Simple conquest quickly gave way to colonial exploitation and redistribution with the initiation and rapid increase of sugar production in the island of Madeira after 1455. Sugar became a cornerstone of Iberian colonial trade in the sixteenth and seventeenth centuries. Portuguese investors expanded sugar cultivation and the plantation complex in São Tomé and, after the 1520s, in Brazil as seen in Table 16.1. Their Castilian peers introduced the same practices in the Canaries. Sugars from Madeira, the Canaries, São Tomé and Brazil competed in the same Iberian and international markets, but consumers in Northern Europe apparently favoured the sugar from São Tomé and were willing to pay a premium. In order to impose its production, Brazilian sugar often initially had to be sold as if it originated from São Tomé. But, notwithstanding the cunning of Brazilian producers, Brazilian sugar began to dominate European consumption by the end of the sixteenth century mostly because of continuous slave revolts in São Tomé. The threats revolts posed to production together with the notoriously high death rates on the island, where malaria

Table 16.1 *Sugar production in the Portuguese colonial empire, 1515–1617 (arrobas).*

	Madeira	São Tomé	Brazil
1515–1525	200,000	100,000	
1527–1529	123,170		
1535–1536	135,860		
1550	40,000	150,000	
1578		175,000	
1581–1584	38,000–40,000	200,000	350,000
1610			735,000
1617			1,000,000

Source: Costa et al. (2016: 78).

is endemic to this day, provided a competitive advantage to Brazilian sugar production in detriment to that of São Tomé or Madeira.

As island sugar lost out to Brazilian production, Madeira and the Canaries turned to wine cultivation to first complement then substitute sugar. Early imports from the Spanish colonial territories in the Caribbean and the mainland were more varied than those from the Portuguese islands. Plantation production would not become an important part of the Spanish American economy until the late eighteenth century. In contrast to the early Portuguese expansion, Castilian colonizers focused mostly on the control of labour resources in America and the expansion of the 'domestic' American market, rather than production for export to the peninsula. The early expansion of the Spanish American economy was therefore less export driven. Cochineal and indigo dyes, hides, pearls, cocoa, non-plantation produced sugar and various other products made up the list of Iberian imports until silver production from Potosi (today's Bolivia) and Zacatecas (Mexico) took off after the mid-sixteenth century. Silver quickly began to dominate imports to Castile, if not in terms of volume certainly in terms of value. After 1572 imports of Asian textiles and porcelain were trans-shipped via Manila and Acapulco to Seville, though a significant part of the cargoes in fact remained in the Americas and found their way to the major consumption centres of the viceroyalties of New Spain and Peru (Bonialian, 2020).

For Portugal, commodified sugar was joined early on by gold imports from Castelo da Mina (today's Ghana), which increased significantly between 1480 and the 1560s to *c.* 25 million *réis* per annum (Godinho, 1982–1984, I: 286). This abundant and continuous influx of gold stimulated conspicuous consumption on the part of the Crown, increased the income of the Exchequer through taxation and, above all, provided Portugal with enough specie to pay for foreign imports, particularly from Flanders, to supply Portuguese consumption of northern manufactured goods. Though gold imports from Castelo da Mina declined by the last quarter of the sixteenth century, a second cycle of Atlantic gold ensued after the discovery of gold mines in Brazil by the end of the seventeenth century. Following a similar trading circuit as sugar, and certainly before large-scale sugar production, brazilwood became a major colonial import in the Iberian Atlantic. The dyewood, in high demand in the textile producing areas of the Low Countries, England and Italy, became a significant source of wealth for the Portuguese Crown and a major colonial export onto the European domestic markets (Antunes et al., 2016: 26). It was the dyewood that stood as collateral for the conspicuous consumption of the Portuguese Crown at the Portuguese Factory of Antwerp and as guarantee for Portuguese public debt in the Antwerp market.

The Portuguese so-called Cape Route to Asia was originally organized as a yearly fleet, the *Carreira da Índia*. The fleet sailed from Lisbon to Goa with some European products, but mostly administrative, military and church personnel, as well as convicts and emigrants. On the return voyage, the *Carreira* transported luxury goods (pepper, nutmeg, cinnamon, textiles, precious stones, etc.) from Goa to Lisbon, which were also re-exported to European markets. Cotton textiles and silk grew in importance towards the end of the sixteenth century as other Europeans entered the Indian Ocean exchanges and competed in the pepper trade (Godinho, 1982–1984, III: 17, 21, 24, 49; Boyajian 1993: 203). Throughout the sixteenth and seventeenth century, Asian trade was of enormous importance for Portugal and for Portugal's economic relations with the rest of Europe. After 1572, the Manila galleon from Acapulco to Manila was the purest expression of a global pattern of trade, in which Europeans had few goods but silver to offer to Asian markets in exchange for mostly luxury manufactured goods, such as porcelain and silks, which were highly sought after in the Spanish American and European markets.

The degree of integration and overlap between Castilian and Portuguese Atlantic trading routes differed by region and product. On the whole, in Asia separate interests were jealously guarded, though economic actors often ignored them. Yet, from the start, one new trade depended on the closest cooperation between the Iberian reigns. First the Caribbean islands and then the densely populated areas of Meso- and South America experienced an unprecedented demographic collapse throughout the sixteenth and early seventeenth centuries (Livi Bacci, 2008). As the arrival of European epidemic diseases dramatically increased mortality, conquest-related social, cultural and economic dislocation and labour exactions decreased fertility. The land–labour ratio increased dramatically, resulting in an ever-growing demand for labour, which from the start was overwhelmingly met by the forced migration of enslaved Africans. In the Spanish territories, enslaved people were employed in urban households, small farms, cattle raising, non-plantation sugar production and as skilled labour in the crafts. Silver mining in Mexico and the viceroyalty of Peru relied mostly on paid free and coerced indigenous labour (*mita*) and interestingly only marginally on enslaved labour. In 1597 enslaved Africans might have accounted for 14% of the labour force in New Spain's mines and the share fell thereafter (Tutino, 2018). Only the small gold mining sector in today's Colombia drew heavily on enslaved labour among Hispanic American mining centres. By contrast, in Brazil plantation production and later mining dominated the demand for enslaved labour throughout. Portuguese sugar imports relied heavily on a circuit of trade in enslaved Africans that grew concomitantly to the increase and expansion of the sugar production in the Atlantic.

Portuguese access to the African coasts especially on the Gold Coast and in Angola, combined with Portuguese shipping and Spanish and Portuguese capital and a trans-Iberian legal and contractual structure drove the initial expansion of the transatlantic slave trade. The first cycle of cross-Iberian

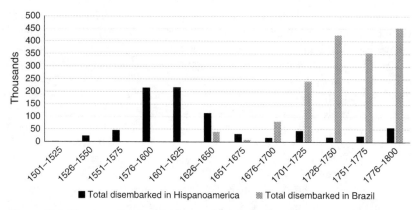

Figure 16.1 Number of enslaved Africans disembarked in Iberoamerica, 1500–1800. Source: Trans-Atlantic Slave Database (www.slavevoyages.org) (accessed March 2018).

collaboration in the slave trade collapsed after 1640 partially due to events in West Africa, partially due to the Portugal's War of Restoration (Rodrigues, M. G., 2019). By then more than half a million enslaved Africans had been taken to the Spanish territories. The total number of enslaved people arriving in Brazil thereafter, though expanding rapidly, would not exceed that in Spanish America until the early to mid-eighteenth century, when the trade in humans experienced another dramatic acceleration as seen in Figure 16.1.

The first transatlantic trade in enslaved Africans dated back to the fifteenth-century colonization of Madeira, Cabo Verde and São Tomé by the Portuguese. Patterns developed here were expanded and adapted to the trade with the Americas from the start. Thus, what we now refer to as the transatlantic slave trade was created in the fifteenth, sixteenth and early seventeenth centuries in the Iberian Atlantic (Borucki et al., 2020). It was the only trading circuit that in various forms persisted during the Iberian early modern colonial period, extending still into the nineteenth century with Portugal, Brazil and Angola as by far the largest traders, in demographic terms and voyages, of the transatlantic slave trade, according to the recent findings of the Trans-Atlantic Slave Database. Spanish American demand for enslaved Africans would rise again in the late eighteenth century and the early nineteenth, when also for the first time, Spanish, especially Andalusian and Catalan, investors would be important participants in the trade to Cuba and Puerto Rico.

16.3 Institutional Foundations and Actors

In the Iberian empires the control over maritime and colonial expansion was a royal prerogative and, as such, Iberian Monarchs claimed sovereignty over territories and maritime frontiers overseas (*mare clausum*).

However, the capital to be invested in the new colonial territories was entirely private in the Castilian case and overwhelmingly so in Portugal. Hence the distribution of rights over labour services to be performed by subject indigenous populations, the taxation of subsoil natural resources, trade and consumption, and the deployment of jurisdictions (religious, military, mercantile, civil and criminal) were almost always commodified as a way to provide income and redistributive capacity to the colonial polity as part of royal prerogative. The institutional implementation of such revenue-raising powers took a variety of forms, from proper economic monopolies, to licensing structures, different forms of public–private partnerships and, later on, joint-stock enterprises.

As conquered territory, the Spanish *Indias* became politically subject to the laws of the conqueror and were incorporated into the Castilian monarchy. While Spanish conquerors and settlers recreated familiar political organizations through the foundation of towns, the monarchy rolled out a structure of viceroyalties (initially Peru and New Spain), *audiencias* and regional treasuries in an attempt to curb the power of the *conquistadores*. The Portuguese expansion in the Atlantic World and Asia combined territorial control over Brazil and to a lesser extent Angola with a much more complex, dynamic pattern of trading routes across Asia. Brazil was first divided into donatary captaincies, which included religious, military and administrative jurisdictions, bestowed upon donatary captains as reward for their service to the Crown. Since the Portuguese presence on much of the west coast of Africa, in the brim of the Indian Ocean, the South China Sea, the Straits of Malacca, the Indonesian Archipelago, China and Japan rarely went beyond more or less urbanized strongholds on the coast and some land exploitation in the hinterlands, municipal and urban institutions stood at the forefront of colonization. In those areas where Portuguese control was more consolidated, the Crown named the highest officials, such as viceroys (Goa, the seat of the administration for the *Estado da Índia*), captain majors (Macao, Castelo da Mina, Cabo Verde and São Tomé) or governors (Brazil, Angola).

In their own minds, Iberians' claim of sovereignty over conquered territories was at least partially justified by a duty to convert indigenous populations transferred to them by the papacy. In that sense, monarchs had the right of *Padroado* or *patronato*, meaning the jurisdictional right to appoint clergymen in the empire and carve a societal space for religious courts, including the Inquisition. The latter, however, had no jurisdiction over the indigenous population in Spanish America, which was considered under the tutelage of the monarchy. As a consequence of that legal conception, which likened indigenous people to minors, the enslavement of indigenous populations was legally banned in the 1540s in Spanish America (though the practice never totally disappeared in the remoter parts of the empire). Recent research suggests that the legislation for Brazil by contrast was kept deliberately ambiguous. As Portuguese settlers and Jesuits vied for control of indigenous labour in the interior, the former captured and traded large numbers of indigenous people declared unwilling to bow to colonial rule until the mid-eighteenth century, while the latter restricted indigenous people's movement by binding them to the land (Perrone-Moisés, 1992; Zeron, 2011).

The political economy of the Portuguese empire was based on an institutional principle of exploitation that had royal exclusive rights at its core, which were often referred to as monopolies. Contrary to the modern economics usage of the word, royal monopolies provided Portuguese kings mostly with the exclusive right to extract, ship, trade or export a specific product. Legally akin to the right to subsoil mineral resources, which in continental Europe since the high Middle Ages was a royal right, this exclusive right was very often transferred to a selective choice of private entrepreneurs by means of a royal privilege, license or contract. The Crown outsourced the costs and risks of colonial exploitation, but also reserved it to its subjects. In this determination of subjecthood stood implicit the exclusivity of the empire for the Portuguese subjects (colonial exclusive), whether they resided in the Peninsula or abroad, and whether the latter were European or non-European by birth. This premise also implied that 'foreigners' were automatically excluded from colonial exploitation. However, royal exemptions and privileges allowed many Italians, Germans, Dutch and Englishmen to heavily and continuously participate in Portugal's colonial enterprises (Costa, 2002a).

From the perspective of the entrepreneurs, being associated with the state increased social capital and boded well for social upward mobility, while also offering significant profit opportunities. The Portuguese king was thus a manager of incomes accruing from the colonial riches rather than a direct operator. This management was effected through a hierarchy of institutions in Lisbon and the main administrative centres of the empire. The *Casa da Índia*, in Lisbon, functioned as customs, clearing and administrative house for the overseas possessions, while Praia (Cabo Verde), Luanda (Angola), Bahia (Brazil), Ormuz (Arabian Peninsula), Goa (India), Cochin (India) and Malacca functioned as customs houses and taxation offices. More often than not, the revenues controlled by these institutions were also farmed out to (local) private traders and entrepreneurs who became entangled with the Portuguese empire as subjects of the king, although not always part of the empire, particularly in Asia.

Even if the *Carreira da Índia* was created as a royal monopoly, very soon privileges were given to private merchants to transport their own goods in the bottoms of the fleet against the obligation to declare all imports to the *Casa da Índia* (Customs House for Overseas Trade) in Lisbon. The high returns in these exchanges and the intensification of the *Carreira* offered the king an opportunity to share risks and gains with a privileged minority of businessmen in Lisbon and, at the same time, enforced a monopoly for the Crown on specific products, especially pepper. The *Carreira* transitioned thus from a general royal monopoly to a public service bestowed upon private entrepreneurs who were expected to respect the royal monopoly over specific products. It was quite efficient in including all Portuguese (and some foreign) merchants trading to Asia. The supremacy of the fleet was only challenged in the beginning of the seventeenth century. The entry of the Dutch and the English East India companies to the Cape Route was, however, not the only reason why the *Carreira* declined. The *Carreira* was already sending fewer ships by the end of the sixteenth century. Simultaneously, Dutch and English competition resulted directly in heavy losses in the trade in spices, especially pepper, for the *Carreira*. But textiles and dyestuffs remained extremely profitable endeavours for private merchants transporting their imports in the *Carreira* bottoms.

Beyond the *Carreira* there was a Portuguese inter-Asian system of trade that was only slightly linked to it. The *Estado da Índia* claimed control and as such imposed taxes on specific Portuguese strongholds and maritime mobility throughout the Indian Ocean, But Goa was unable to control all Portuguese subjects in Asia and their endeavours. Many served Asian polities and later European competitors, some chose to be only slightly or remotely connected to the *Estado*, as was the case of Macau or Malacca, while others opted to form alliances with local interest groups, like those involved in the raiding and trading of Bengali slaves together with the Arakanese. Others still, invoked their loyalty to the king (instead of to the viceroy in Goa) as a pretext to have privileged access to the *Carreira*, as was the case of the naturals and residents of Cochin. In this interconnected world of mobility and exchanges, the Portuguese interests were as important and strategic as the interests of the different Portuguese or Luso-Asian communities dispersed throughout the Indian Ocean, the South China Sea or the Pacific. In this sense, most investments, gains and losses by subjects of the Portuguese king in Asia were raised, accumulated or paid in Asia.

The degree of enforced exclusivity of trade also differed across trades and over time in the Portuguese East and West Atlantic. The production and commercialization of sugar, for example, was unregulated for much of the early modern period. But with the Dutch occupation of the north-eastern captaincies of Brazil between 1630 and 1652, the conquest of Luanda between 1641 and 1649, and the definitive conquest of Castelo da Mina, King John IV opted to form the *Companhia Geral do Comércio do Brasil* (1649–1663). The company had the monopoly of brazilwood imports. Meanwhile, merchants trading to and from Brazil were forced into a convoy system, which continued to exist until 1769, long after the *Companhia* had ceased to exist, and after Dutch pressure in the South Atlantic had disappeared. The convoy was supervised by the Junta do Comércio, under the jurisdiction of the royal *Armazens and Terecenas* (Costa, 2002b).

Similarly, the trade in gold from Mina, and the extraction and trade of brazilwood were officially royal monopolies, and the latter became increasingly regulated during the late sixteenth and early seventeenth century. But these regulations were often trespassed by private traders as was the case of the gold from Mina, where estimates place about 20% of the total imports in the hands of private investors (Godinho, 1982–1984, I: 58). In the case of dyewood, although a royal monopoly, it was only seldomly exploited directly by the Crown as more often than not it was auctioned as contract to private businessmen or given as payment for a different colonial contract (e.g. for the provisioning of the Portuguese forts in North Africa).

Portuguese colonial trade was carried by three types of actors. The metropolitan European traders, concentrated in Lisbon, and with few chronological exceptions in Porto, Viana do Castelo and Vila do Conde for the Atlantic trades can be separated into contractors (*contratadores*), wholesalers (*mercadores de grosso trato*) and retailers (*mercadores*) (Costa, 2002a; Polónia, 2007). The contractors were responsible for the central tax farming (over colonial products) and the logistics of maintenance of colonial settlements and supplying fleets. The wholesalers were often wealthy merchants who were responsible for the import of colonial products, cash crops and agro-industrial products for the domestic markets and their re-export to the Northern European and Mediterranean markets. This group often overlapped with the contractors or worked in close partnerships with them. Finally, the retailers were responsible for the supply of the urban and rural markets in Portugal and across the border to Spain. At times, they also participated in specific inter-European trade, but did so when in partnership with wholesalers or under contract with the contractors. Contractors and wholesalers were particularly important in colonial transactions as they were not only a bolt in the exchanges of colonial and European products in the Lisbon and European markets, but they were also responsible for the financial remittances, for private traders and the Crown, from the colonies to Portugal, from there to the colonies and in-between the colonies.

Beyond an exclusive metropolitan elite, Portuguese colonial trade was mostly carried within local systems by merchants born or long-settled in the overseas sphere (Alencastro, 2007; Bohorquez, 2020: 32). The development of the South Atlantic complex took place through joint initiative of traders born and/or settled in Brazil, Angola and Cabo Verde, whereas a circuit for the exchange of products and people ensued. Although this system of exchanges and transfers often took place without the heavy intervention of metropolitan traders, financial support, remittances and large tax farming remained in the hands of metropolitan firms, while local tax farming, credit and the bridging of production outlets and consumption markets remained in the hands of local investors. In the case of traders born in the South Atlantic, they reflected the principles of the societies of *métissage* whence they came. Similar cases developed in the Indian Ocean, the South China Sea and the Malacca Straights.

The third group of traders operating within the Portuguese empire was that of the non-Europeans. Some of these traders were considered by the Portuguese authorities as subjects of the Portuguese king, although many were not. Africans (especially in the areas between the Senegal and the Gambia rivers), the Loango and Benguela Coast, the Island of Mozambique, Arab traders in Ormuz, Hindu merchants in Goa, Araknese slave raiders and traders in Bengal, the Chinese of Macau or the Catholic Japanese of Nagasaki functioned as parts of the Portuguese empire and multiple spheres of influence in terms of trade, credit and long-term commercial and productive exchanges (Winius, 2011).

The large array of participants in Portugal's colonial exchanges resulted in three phenomena. On the one hand, a sharing of economic interests between Portuguese authorities and non-Europeans who were crucial to the success of different settlements or spheres of influence of the empire, even when the systemic intervention of Portugal as a colonial power decreased. The Portuguese *Estado da Índia* after the 1620s is a case in point. At the same time, the partnerships between non-Europeans and members of local Portuguese societies (either born in Portugal or locally) designed spheres of economic interest that often diverged from those of the empire as such (Halikowski-Smith, 2010: 12; Machado, 2014; Radhika Seshan, 2016: 351). For this reason, the local economic logic of empire superseded the general goals of the Portuguese Crown, with colonial trade feeding colonial markets and traders without intervention from Lisbon. The case of the South Atlantic or the exchanges between Goa and Brazil illustrate this. Finally, the overall nexus of the empire was kept intact through a localized, systemic and centralized system of tax farming (over production, trade and access to natural resources) that framed the empire as such, but accommodated greatly the interests of the other layers of the system. In such a context, sovereignty was a theoretical perception emanating from Europe, as authority was continuously (re-)negotiated ad hoc.

Following Columbus's first return to Spain from the Indies in March 1493, the Castilian monarchy considered creating a state trade monopoly similar to the one established by the Portuguese king to trade with Africa and Asia. But the idea was discarded at the turn of the century. On the one hand, to exert total control over the exchanges with and exploitation of the vastness of the conquered lands in the Americas, as opposed to a number of ports without much hinterland, required a bureaucratic apparatus that far exceeded the monarchy's capability. On the other hand, as the richness of silver deposits in Mexico and Peru became evident, it seemed obvious that the sinews of transatlantic trade (its routes, frequency and tonnage) were to be specifically designed to connect the metropole with the two main bullion-producing American regions. From the start, the Spanish kings left the daunting task to organize these transatlantic trades in the hands of private individuals, though they always kept a close eye on their activities.

The system of regulation that would become known as the *Carrera de Indias* eventually combined three well-known commercial institutions of its time: a staple port system, convoys and control over the trade in the hands of a merchant guild. The monarchy decided that both communications and commercial exchanges with the New World would be conducted exclusively from Seville, an important commercial hub located 52 miles up the River Guadalquivir in western Andalusia. The *Casa de la Contratación* or House of Trade was established here in 1503 to control trade, navigation and migration (Fernández-López, 2018). It granted licences to passengers, merchants and vessels, kept records of all the cargoes shipped to the Indies, and collected taxes, among other things. It also had a court of law to deal with all cases emanating from transatlantic communications and exchanges. In 1524 the Castilian Monarch created the Council of the Indies, the supreme governing body of the Spanish empire for nearly three centuries. It formulated and implemented policies concerning every aspect of life in the New World, from government and defence to trade and the administration of justice (Schäfer, 2003). In the tradition of Castilian governance (see Chapter 12) most regulations emanated from adjudication *ex post* between different interests, since it also served as the highest court of justice in all matters related to the Indies.

Similar to the Portuguese policy of creating a colonial exclusive, non-Castilians were legally forbidden from travelling to and establishing themselves in the Indies, and transatlantic trade was to be carried out exclusively by Castilians. The policy was first adopted in 1501 and reaffirmed in 1518, 1522, 1530 and 1539 to ensure that the colonies would be free of 'heretics' such as Jews, Moors, Protestants and their descendants (Martínez, 1983: 37–39). Yet, the status of 'Castilian subject' did not exist. In the peninsular reigns of the Spanish monarchy it was up to urban corporations to bestow that right on newcomers (Herzog, 2003), making it legally impossible to establish a colonial exclusive (Grafe & Pedreira, 2019) no matter the political intentions. Willing migrants to the Spanish Americas generally found a more or less legal way to board a ship and not return. Foreigners turned to *testaferros*, Spaniards who acted as representatives for their business to ship their goods.

As transatlantic traffic grew, the *cargadores* or merchants trading with the Indies in 1525 demanded a merchant court and guild similar to the Burgos *Consulado* (f. 1494), which had been the first of its kind in Castile to follow the model of the Mediterranean *consolats de mar* of Valencia (founded 1283) and Barcelona (founded 1347). The *cargadores* argued that the House of Trade's court was unable to deal with sufficient celerity with the increasing number of commercial litigations. In 1543 the monarchy finally allowed them to create a court specialized in mercantile matters whose three judges (a *prior* and two *cónsules*) would be elected among merchants trading with the Indies (Fernandez Castro, 2014). The court/guild's official name was *Consulado de Cargadores a Indias*. Gradually, along with the House of Trade, it became the other central institution governing transatlantic exchanges. Its functions were mirrored in Mexico City and Lima, where *consulados* were created in 1592 and 1613 respectively, indicating *criollo* merchants' maturity and independence from their peninsular counterparts (Hausberger & Ibarra, 2003).

The function of the wholesale merchants established in the viceregal capitals of Mexico City and Lima was to intermediate the trade in bullion and a few other colonial products for manufactured goods, mostly textiles, from their Peninsular counterparts. While the emerging mining centres articulated large interregional trade networks within the Americas (Assadourian 1982), intercolonial maritime trade was often forbidden or greatly hampered for fear that bullion would escape the official transatlantic channels, which it often did. Innumerable royal decrees and regulations issued by the Spanish monarchy were precisely intended to bolster a trading system meant to assure that bullion exports should reach Spain rather than other American or European destinations. Yet, silver mining was a private activity, and most bullion shipped was private and hard to control.

By the 1560s the Spanish Atlantic trading system had been laid out in the form of two armed commercial fleets departing from Seville and, due to increasing problems of fluvial navigation, the nearby Andalusian ports of Sanlúcar de Barrameda and Cádiz: one fleet destined for Veracruz (the main seaport of New Spain) and the other for Tierra Firme (the northern coast of the South American mainland). The merchandise and Peninsular merchants travelling in the latter would meet the Peruvian merchants and their silver (who would have previously come in another fleet sailing northwards from Callao along the Pacific rim) in the Isthmus of Panama, where a fair would take place on its Atlantic side at Nombre de Dios or, after 1597, at Portobelo. On the homeward leg, both fleets were meant to rendezvous at Havana before crossing the Atlantic (Stein & Stein, 2000: 8–19).

The number of merchant vessels that would form a fleet was not predetermined. For each fleet a total tonnage was put forward by the *Consulado* for the House of Trade's consideration and approval (García-Baquero, 1992: 88–104). Once the fleet's tonnage was sanctioned, two thirds of it were allocated to the *cargadores* of Seville and the remaining third to those of Cádiz. Total tonnage was also divided by type of cargo: two-thirds were for manufactured goods and re-exports, and one-third for domestic agricultural products such as wine, olive oil and brandy. As a result, the size of the fleets could vary greatly. In the mid-sixteenth century they were made up of 15 to 20 ships. Towards the end of the sixteenth and beginning of the seventeenth centuries fleets were comprised of 30 to as many as 70 vessels. The increasing size of the vessels themselves and the decline of the transatlantic trade (at least when measured in total tonnage and frequency of exchanges) brought the number down to 10 to 20 ships after

1650. Both fleets were meant to depart annually, but their frequency became erratic in the second half of the seventeenth century, with gaps of several years.

Other means of transatlantic communication remained marginal at best until the 1740s. Seville merchants in the sixteenth century had already started to send *navíos de registro* (single register ships) to the regions outside the regular fleet system (to places such as Buenos Aires, Caracas, Campeche and Honduras), although the *Consulado* always opposed these ventures. A royal licence was required to fit them out. Up to 1650, these vessels amounted to barely 15% of all the ships and 8.4% of total tonnage crossing the Spanish Atlantic (Chaunu & Chaunu, 1955–1956, VI-1: 404–409). From 1650 to 1700, at a time when transatlantic traffic shrank considerably, *navíos de registros'* share decreased even more, comprising 6.8% of all the ships bound for the colonies (García-Fuentes, 1980: 172, 211–213).

Economically speaking, neither the *Consulados*, nor the staple, nor the convoy system constituted a monopoly. There were hundreds of merchants fiercely competing with each other at any given time. Many were members of the guild and membership probably created costs typically associated with guild membership. However, it is important to stress that, for most of the colonial period, participation in trade was de facto not restricted to guild membership (Heredia Herrera, 2004: 179–180). The *Consulado*'s members enjoyed exclusive rights over the exchanges with the Indies from 1730 to 1742 only (García-Baquero, 1992: 275). Before and after that brief hiatus, ship registers show that any Spaniard, born in Iberia or the Indies, man or woman, could ship goods to and from the colonies. Nevertheless, the most important merchants gathered around the Seville/Cádiz, Mexico City and Lima *Consulados*. They would remain the single most important representative body of commercial interests of elite merchants until the end of the eighteenth century (and in some cases beyond the end of empire).

Spanish trade with Asia relied almost exclusively on intermediation via the Spanish-held port of Manila (Bjork, 1998), notwithstanding a small number of direct shipping ventures from both Peru and Mexico to Asian markets in the early and mid-sixteenth century. Since 1572 a regular and regulated galleon sailed between Mexico and the Philippines. The presence of Spanish colonial institutions in Manila remained weak, and the colony depended almost entirely on both local and a large Chinese population, which articulated exchange with the Chinese markets. Recurrent outbreaks of violence, which often resulted in massacres of and among the Chinese population, were followed by the re-establishment of trading relations. The Manila Galleon was quantitatively important for the flows of bullion in the early modern global economy and for luxury consumption in Mexico and Peru, but the trade expanded only modestly over time. It did, however, represent in many ways the global dimension of Iberian trade in the sixteenth to eighteenth centuries.

The regulatory frameworks in the Iberian colonial trades were not monolithic superstructures as has sometimes been suggested. There were important legal differences between Castilian and Portuguese commercial institutions. While the latter relied more strongly on a legal notion of royal monopoly, the outsourcing of most activities to private investors created de facto different forms of licencing systems that resembled fiscal rights rather than direct production by the Crown. On the Spanish side the Castilian colonial exclusive was always legally weak. De facto the regulatory framework was guild-run and managed fiscal resources for the monarchy. A traditional staple in turn served fiscal enforcement and monitoring purposes. But there was also diversity within each system. The Manila Galleon created in the 1570s gave economic rights to the Euro-descendent residents of Manila. Trade to the Rio de la Plata either escaped regulation or was opened to other forms of access quite often (Moutoukias, 1988). The merchants of Lima and Mexico City were a match for those in Seville, though the role of large Asian merchant houses in the Portuguese *Estado* had no equivalent in the Atlantic trades. In general terms, the Iberian Crowns did not issue proper monopoly charters to private companies, as opposed to what became common practice in the American and Asian expansions of their British, Dutch, French and Scandinavian counterparts in the seventeenth century. However, there are a few noteworthy exceptions. Portugal issued several charters in the seventeenth and eighteenth centuries, although the majority were short-lived. Also in the eighteenth century, a small number of monopoly companies would be active in the Spanish territories. Most of these were part of reform attempts, to which we will return below.

16.4 Eighteenth-Century Reforms and Their Impact on Colonial Trade

During the War of Spanish Succession (1701–1714), Spain lost control over a significant portion of its colonial trade. Transatlantic communications came to a virtual halt, with the French taking advantage of the Spanish monarchy's weakness. During the peace negotiations, however, the British were awarded what they believed to be two important concessions that were passed to the South Sea Company: the *asiento de negros* or monopoly on importing enslaved Africans into the Spanish colonies (which had previously been in the hands of Portuguese, Italians, Dutch, Spanish and, since 1701, French contractors) and, included in the contract, the right to send to either Veracruz or Portobelo a 500-ton merchant ship carrying British goods every year. After the war, the new Spanish Bourbon monarchy made efforts to regain control from foreigners and revitalize transatlantic exchanges. Trade was, in fact, one of the first targets of the so-called Bourbon reforms, which gradually were to encompass virtually all spheres of imperial administration and economy throughout the eighteenth century. Reforms affecting colonial trade were both proactive and reactive, war being the main driver of the latter (Kuethe & Andrien, 2014).

In 1717 both the House of Trade and the *Consulado de Cargadores* were relocated to Cádiz, which had become the official port of departure of the Indies fleets in 1680. In 1720, the old fleet system was bolstered by the publication of the *Proyecto para Galeones y Flotas*, a piece of legislation which, with minor tweaks, was to regulate transatlantic shipping and taxation until 1778 (García-Baquero, 1976, I: 195–215). Although very little was changed regarding the organization of trade, there were clear signs of recovery after 1720. A novelty was introduced in 1728 with the creation of the first Spanish joint-stock privileged trading company, the Royal Guipuzcoan Company of Caracas. It obtained a proper trading monopoly for Venezuela in 1742 that would last until 1784, with a clear mandate to recover from Dutch interlopers the control of cacao exports (Gárate Ojanguren, 1990). The king's decision to approve an initiative led by a group of Basque businessmen pursued another goal: to reduce the smuggling of colonial commodities (mostly tobacco) entering Castile from the Basque provinces.

The Caracas Company encouraged the production of crops such as cacao, tobacco and cotton, and constructed both war and merchant ships. Its relative success prompted the creation of other privileged companies, such as the Royal Havana Company (1740–1790), and the Royal Barcelona Trading Company to the Indies (1755–1785). Rather than monopoly rights they were awarded substantial tax cuts. The privileged companies were never seen as an alternative to either the fleet or single ships systems. Instead, they were a means to exert more control over and develop the economies of peripheral American regions or trades. From 1730 to 1778, approximately 20% of all the transatlantic voyages were carried out by ships belonging to these companies (García-Baquero, 1976, I: 136–137).

In that sense the first real break in the organization of colonial trade came in the 1740s, when war compelled the Spanish monarchy to suspend temporarily the departure of the Indies fleets. It allowed *navíos de registro* to depart from Cádiz for any American destination, including the major ports of Veracruz and Callao (Lima's seaport, which was now directly reached, for the first time, by sailing around Cape Horn). Freed from the time-consuming, costly preparations that fitting out a whole fleet entailed, transatlantic exchanges became far more frequent and dynamic, providing colonial consumers with a more extensive assortment of European goods at lower prices. Though trade (and competition) grew significantly under the system of single ships, yielding increasing fiscal income to the Crown, the government succumbed to the pressure from the Cádiz merchant elite (whose interests were aligned with those of the foreign merchant communities) and agreed to resume partially the traditional system in 1754: fleets would be resumed for the exchanges with New Spain, whereas the single ships system was permanently adopted in the trade with

Peru as well as with other destinations such as Buenos Aires, the Caribbean and Central America (Lamikiz, 2010: 81–94). The *flota* was meant to depart for New Spain every two years. The first fleet set sail for Veracruz in 1757. But before the system was finally abolished in 1778, only five additional fleets would depart from Cádiz in 1760, 1765, 1768, 1772 and 1776. These final fleets have gathered great historiographical attention, but de facto roughly 80% of Spanish transatlantic trade's total tonnage was carried by *navíos de registro* between 1755 and 1778, while the fleets to New Spain accounted for just 13% of the tonnage (García-Baquero, 1976, I: 173).

Insofar as their headquarters and trading routes fell outside the orbit of Cádiz, the privileged companies gradually began to undermine the long-held idea that the whole colonial trade should be conducted from a single Iberian staple port. By the 1750s, a growing number of government officials thought that transatlantic trade should be deregulated and opened to more ports on both sides of the Atlantic. The first major step in that direction was taken in 1765, when nine peninsular ports were allowed to trade directly with the Spanish Caribbean islands. In 1768 the permission was extended to Louisiana, and in 1770 to Yucatán and Campeche. This gradual liberalization of colonial trade culminated in October 1778 with the promulgation of the so-called *comercio libre* or free trade regulations. Colonial trade was now opened to 13 peninsular and many more American ports, though it was not applied to Venezuela and New Spain until 1788 and 1789, respectively (Baskes, 2013: 69–86).

Foreign participation remained banned. But *comercio libre* greatly simplified both taxation and the administrative paperwork to get a licence to cross the Atlantic. Its goal was to 'restore agriculture, industry, and population' in the Spanish empire. Although it led to commercial expansion, a new body of scholarship has demonstrated that the real growth of trade was a small fraction of that which historians have traditionally indicated (Cuenca-Esteban, 2008). At any rate, *comercio libre* was short-lived. It was only fully implemented after the war with Britain ended in 1783 and, although the *Carrera de Indias* would continue to exist until its final abolition in 1828, the 1797 British blockade of Cádiz marked the beginning of the end for Spain's colonial trade system. During the French Revolutionary, Napoleonic and Spanish American Independence wars, the Spanish monarchy had no option but to allow neutral foreign ships to carry out Spain's colonial trade. It was a desperate attempt to get access to the much needed American bullion and keep commercial lifelines open (Marichal, 2007).

Reforms in Portuguese colonial trade also started in the earlier eighteenth century. The Brazil convoys were heavily in debt and in 1720 taken into the Crown's general stores. A new small tax on gold imports from Brazil was used to deal with its financial liabilities and to finance the protection of the convoys. As the century progressed, measures multiplied to push back against the operation of single ships sailing outside the fleets and the presence of foreign ships on the Brazil run, driven in large parts by the dependence on British goods and merchants. As in the case of Spain measures to try and keep the bullion trade in Portuguese hands were of limited success. Ships travelling to the East were permitted to stop over in Brazil, but relatively few did so. At the same time, the growing trade in enslaved Africans became a South Atlantic direct trade dominated by Brazilian and Angolan interests (Florentino, 1995, 103; Candido, 2013; Lopes, 2015: 56).

The second half of the eighteenth century witnessed a wave of administrative reforms associated with the intervention of the Marquis of Pombal, minister of King Joseph I. Pombal's interventions were diverse and their impact domestically and in the colonial sphere were broad and deep. Commercially, Pombal sought to push back against British influence in Portugal's colonial trade through stricter controls on the shipment of staple products from Brazil and the creation of chartered monopoly companies. The Portuguese East India Company, the Portuguese Company for the Commerce with Brazil, the Company for Trade in Chacheu and the Company for Pernambuco and Grão Pará are but a few examples of these chartered companies. Most of them were created to emulate foreign developments, to work as means of protection for a specific territory, or as means of capital lock-in for the capital market in Lisbon. Those for the north-eastern region of Brazil did in addition transform the agricultural sector and trade significantly.

Perhaps the two most important reforms in economic terms were the attempt to develop a national textile manufacturing sector for the purpose of import substitution and the confiscation of the properties owned by the Society of Jesus in Europe and the empire. Pombal's measures to develop Portuguese metropolitan industries, in particular the textile industry, met with mixed success. The idea behind the policies was the substitution of imports of textiles from Great Britain into the metropolitan and Brazilian markets by nationally produced textiles, while at the same time Brazil was legally restricted to producer of primary products and the production of manufactured goods on a larger scale was outlawed. The Portuguese textile industries responded quickly and successfully to the Pombaline incentives, but, in practice, metropolitan textiles did not substitute British textiles. Both British and Portuguese textiles were bought in Portugal and exported to Brazil. De facto they served different segments in the consumption markets. Furthermore, the expansion of economic outputs in the interior of Brazil beyond the mining outputs and the usual cash crops, enlarged the markets that were being serviced by these Pombaline textiles (Costa et al., 2011).

The decision to supress the Society of Jesus in Portugal and its colonies in 1759, and force the return of its properties to the Crown, is one of the most notable political and economic achievements of Pombal's administration. Its extinction met with echoes throughout Europe, and Spain followed suit in

1767. However, the benefits of the confiscation of the assets of the order were less straightforward. Even if the Portuguese Crown confiscated all landed properties of the Society of Jesus in Europe and overseas, these assets were often sold below market value or rented out to local businessmen or civil servants. The returns to the Crown were thus short term and of little impact in the state's or imperial finances (Serrão, 2014: 13). In Spanish America the expropriation of the Jesuits led equally to a mixture of a sell off of their large-scale investments in real estate, *haciendas*, and large numbers of enslaved Africans owned by the Society, on the one hand, and increasingly desperate attempts by the appointed administrators of the former Jesuit property, the so-called *temporalidades*, to collect on the myriad of loans that Jesuit institutions had lent to Spanish Americans from all walks of life, on the other. The process foreshadowed the financial havoc that the disentailment policies of the late eighteenth century would wreak on the credit sector in Spanish America (Grafe, 2020).

16.5 Commodities

Up to the eighteenth century, there were two main differences between the structures of colonial import and export trades in Portugal and Spain. First, Portugal imported both agricultural commodities (spices and sugar) and manufactured goods (silks and ceramics) from its empire, and colonial trade had a large impact on the Portuguese economy and treasury. In Spain, by contrast, a single colonial import, bullion, had dominated colonial trade since the 1550s. Mercantile profits were mostly the result of re-exports of European manufactured goods to the Americas and the impact of the trade was more circumscribed, both because the internal Spanish American markets were more important and because less of the colonial taxation found its way into the peninsular treasuries (see Chapter 12). Second, Portugal's trading system was multipolar and Asian (and African) trade was initially much more important than transatlantic exchanges. Spain's trade was almost exclusively concentrated on the Americas. The Manila trade was not only a very distant second, but de facto controlled from New Spain.

Portugal's multipolar colonial trading system initially integrated three circuits of overlapping commodities. The first linked the colonial world to the metropolis. Lisbon imported refined and unrefined cash crops and natural resources from the South Atlantic (sugar, tobacco, coffee and brazilwood) and re-exported most of these goods to the European markets, before or upon their processing. This import and re-distribution system was also applied for the spices and luxury products (dyestuffs and textiles) imported from Asia. The second circuit linked western Africa to Brazil and the rest of the American continent. Merchants born in Portugal, Brazil, the Atlantic Islands (mostly from Cabo Verde) and Angola were active in the export of enslaved

Africans from different points on the west coast of Africa, but with particular intensity from Loango and Angola, to Brazil and the Spanish West Indies. African authorities tended to impose the rules for bartering for enslaved Africans, which meant merchants needed to bring cotton textiles with specific patterns, cowry shells, tobacco, alcoholic beverages and, at times, gold as means of exchange. They were supplied in a third circuit met by Portuguese, Brazilian, Cabo Verdian and Angolan traders who imported, sometimes via Bahia and Rio de Janeiro, textiles from Goa, cowry shells from Angola to other points on the west coast of Africa, tobacco, gold and *cachaça* (a type of rum) from Brazil.

By the eighteenth century, however, the differences between Portugal and Spain became less obvious. The ongoing difficulties in Asia caused by European competition and the discovery of gold in Brazil led Portugal to refocus its attention to the Atlantic World and to the export of staple commodities to be re-exported to the rest of Europe. Recent research has stressed that Goa remained a vital part of the Portuguese commercial network, but in relative terms Brazil became the tail that wagged the imperial dog. This also meant that Portuguese colonial trade became less diversified and more dominated by the cycles in particular commodity trades, such as gold and sugar. At the same time, Spain, though always giving priority to bullion, tried to expand non-bullion staple imports from the colonies. It also established direct trade with the Philippines from 1765 onward.

In terms of the commodities traded by the eighteenth century, Brazilian trade was dominated by the staples of tobacco, sugar, gold and cotton, while rice, hides and other products were also increasingly important. In some of these commodities clear cycles appear, most notably with regard to gold. Others were subject to less obvious swings but also to sometimes significant changes in terms of the regions that produced them. Thus, Bahia remained the main source of Brazilian tobacco in the eighteenth century, which was a crucial product in the exchanges for enslaved Africans. Alden suggests that in the mid-eighteenth century exports of Bahian tobacco to the Mina Coast almost matched those sent to Portugal for consumption in the metropolis and re-export to the rest of Europe (Alden, 1987: 632–633). Sugar production had expanded over the seventeenth century from maybe 700,000 *arrobas* to a high of 1.3 million *arrobas* in 1710, and fell back a bit thereafter (Schwartz, 2004: 168). A significant part of that production was transhipped directly to the Netherlands between 1635 and 1650 (Edel, 1969). Sugar production expanded again in the eighteenth century to an estimated 1.6 or 1.7 million *arrobas* by 1807, especially in Rio de Janeiro and Bahia, while Pernambuco's production probably stagnated (Alden, 1987: 630–631). Coffee, too, took off in the 1770s.

The two commodities that have attracted most attention with regard to their impact on the Portuguese colonial economy as a whole in the eighteenth century were gold and cotton. Gold-mining was important in both Spanish

America and Portuguese Brazil as seen in Figure 16.2. Yet, the discovery of gold in Brazil had a dramatically larger impact on the economy of Brazil and that of peninsular Portugal (see Chapter 13) than the Spanish American production. In the 1690s, prospectors and explorers from São Paulo found placers on several rivers in Minas Gerais. In 1718, *Paulista* prospectors discovered gold in the Mato Grosso. In 1725, significant deposits were also found in Goiás though Minas Gerais remained the most productive of the three regions throughout the eighteenth century, with 72% of the total output. Brazilian gold mining from the start was part of the slavery complex. Gold production rose from 4,327 kilograms in the 1690s to an all-time high record of over 145,000 kilograms in the 1740s. Then it dropped gradually to 38,000 kilograms in the first decade of the nineteenth century. Gold deposits were superficial and widely scattered. As a result, colonial gold mining was small-scale, transient and permeated with fraud and smuggled goods. The circulation of unregistered, un-assayed gold was widespread in Brazil, with the most realistic estimates placing it at above 50% of total output (TePaske, 2010: 23).

Just as gold production declined a new sector expanded, especially in Maranhao and Pernambuco, driven in part by the policies of the new Companies created by Pombal's reforms (Figure 16.3). Cotton stood for a new exchange that would see Brazil integrated into the expanding European cotton industries, and not only the English one, from the late eighteenth century onwards. Portuguese intermediation in the sector was key, as were its links with the ever-expanding trade in enslaved people.

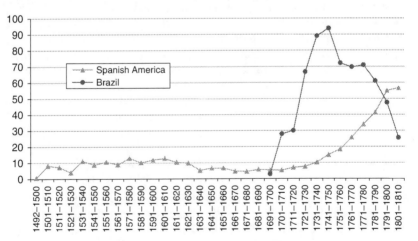

Figure 16.2 New World gold output, 1492–1810 (by decade, in millions of pesos of 272 *maravedís*).
Source: TePaske (2010: 54–55).

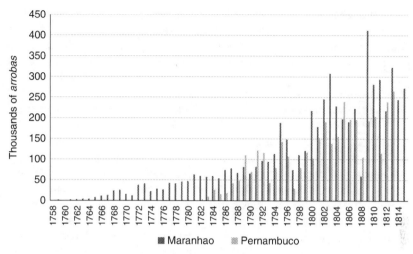

Figure 16.3 Cotton exports from Maranhao and Pernambuco, 1758–1815 (in *arrobas*). Sources: Melo and Martins (2022; 2023).

However, one ought to be careful not to see too simple a link between staple productions in Brazil and slavery: Melo & Martins (2022; 2023) show that slavery was crucial for the expansion of cotton in Maranhao, but not in Pernambuco.

The Spanish American imperial trade was, by comparison to Portugal, always mainly focused on the attempt to contain, control and tax transatlantic trade within the strict routes and parameters of the two commercial fleets of the *Carrera* system. As we have seen, the system was rarely completely closed to the prescribed routes and procedures. Nevertheless, the staple feature and the irregularity of the fleets had severe consequences for the colonial economy. By definition, vast regions were initially outside the main channels of exchange via new Spain and Portobelo/Lima. This encumbered regional specialization and made vital imports more expensive. Still, until 1630, the regularity of the fleets meant that secondary American areas not too distant from the transatlantic routes could still export part of their agricultural output to Spain. Thus, Central American indigo production and trade enjoyed significant prosperity from 1580 to 1620. Two or three vessels of the New Spain fleet would call at the main Central American ports and provided the means to export indigo and other commodities to Seville with acceptable regularity, notwithstanding Guatemalan complaints about insufficient tonnage. However, as the fleets became less frequent and carried smaller tonnages after 1630, indigo exports stagnated, even though indigo was a low bulk and high unit value commodity. In the second half of the century, the *cabildo* (municipal council) of Santiago de los Caballeros (present-day Antigua Guatemala) repeatedly complained that the by then irregular fleets included virtually no ships bound for the Gulf of Honduras (MacLeod, 2008: 199–200). However, it is difficult to generalize. Other regions, such as the Rio de la Plata, fared better and regions underserved by the fleet found ways around the problem, as we will see.

Silver dominated value but not volume. From 1560 to 1650, bullion and non-bullion commodities made up 82.2% and 17.8%, respectively, of the total value of Spain's colonial imports (Chaunu & Chaunu, 1955–1956, VI-1: 474). Unfortunately, there is no reliable data on cargo value for the second half of the seventeenth century, so we must turn to volume measures. These show that the total movement of gross register tonnage (i.e. ships' total internal volume) that criss-crossed the Spanish Atlantic shrank precipitously after the 1630s, as seen in Figure 16.4. The total tonnage of the 1700s amounted to less than a tenth of that of the 1610s (García-Baquero, 1992: 324–325) although the contraction of the outward tonnage was not as acute, as can be seen in Figure 16.4, probably due to the fact that between 1660 and 1708 registration of goods shipped to Spain was not compulsory. It stands to reason that this spectacular decrease reduced even more the share of non-bullion commodities, which occupied most of the shipping space even if we have little knowledge about how the qualities and prices of the shipped goods might have changed.

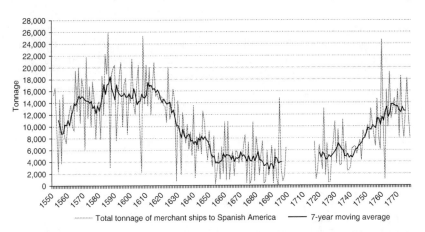

Figure 16.4 Total tonnage of merchant ships sailing from the western Andalusian ports (Seville, Sanlúcar and Cádiz) and the Canary Islands to Spanish America, 1550–1778 (tons of 1.376 m^3).
Sources: Chaunu and Chaunu (1955–1956, VI-2: 384–391), García-Baquero (1976, II: 126–128) and García-Fuentes (1980: 211–213, 224–225). The *tonelada de arqueo* used in the Spanish colonial trade (a ton that refers to a ship's cargo-capacity) had 1.376 m^3. For a discussion on tonnage measurements see García-Baquero (1976, I: 248–250).

The fall in trade was not caused by a fall in production of exportable agricultural commodities (bulky crops such as sugar, cacao, tobacco and dyewood trees, among others, but also less bulky ones such as indigo and cochineal) and cattle ranching (hides, tallow and dried meat) in the Spanish colonies. Instead, the Spanish American economy of the seventeenth century not only diverged from developments in Brazil, but also from English, Dutch and French Caribbean models. The latter began to develop plantation economies (alongside smuggling with the Spanish colonies), which by definition had a very high reliance on trade. Meanwhile, the Spanish colonial economy became even less trade dependent, with growing regional market integration within rather than between the two main viceroyalties (Assadourian, 1982). Paradoxically, the stronger development of Spanish American internal markets reinforced the role of bullion as the primary driver of Spanish commercial policies and thus the tensions between commercial regulations and the interests of regional elites in the Americas.

The prosperity of colonial elites was one of the driving forces of an increasing illegal integration between the Spanish colonies and the Dutch, English and Portuguese colonies in the Americas and towards the end of the eighteenth century between the Spanish islands and the USA. In the seventeenth century some regions began to specialize in exportable commodities that were then sold to foreign interlopers. Mexico continued to produce and export the most precious of all American dyes, cochineal, which had high unit value and therefore occupied little shipping space (in the 1630s cochineal was worth 30 times more than an equivalent weight of sugar) but it is unclear how much of it reached Seville. Cuba had perfect soil and climate for sugar and tobacco, but it soon became apparent that Cuba could not compete on price with the plantation sugar produced in English Jamaica, French Haiti and Portuguese Brazil, so it reduced sugarcane cultivation (which would regain importance only after the 1780s) and concentrated on tobacco throughout the seventeenth century. However, a large part of the tobacco was smuggled to non-Iberian European markets, since consumers considered it superior to that of Virginia. Likewise, cacao production (but also tobacco and hides) in Venezuela and parts of the viceroyalty of Peru expanded in the seventeenth and early eighteenth centuries. Dutch smugglers operating from Curaçao and Bonaire initially dominated the former, Spanish trading circuits the latter.

After the War of Spanish Succession, the Bourbon administration tried to curtail smuggling and promote colonial agriculture with the aim of increasing fiscal revenue. In the case of Cuba and Venezuela, the strategy adopted was to turn the production of tobacco and cacao into monopolies run by either the state or a privileged trading company such as that of Caracas. The increasing use of *navíos de registro* after the 1740s also had a positive effect on the overall volume and value of colonial non-bullion goods arriving in Spain. But, despite those efforts, overall agricultural and ranching exports likely remained lower

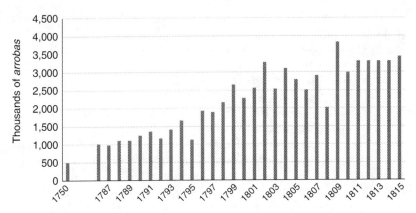

Figure 16.5 Sugar exports from Cuba, 1750–1815 (in *arrobas*).
Sources: Sims Taylor (1970), Klein (1975) and Bosma and Curry Machado (2012).

than they would have been had transatlantic trade been open to more American and Iberian regions or if Spain had copied Portugal's eighteenth-century policies of turning the colonies into producers of primary products dependent on European manufactured goods.

The so-called free trade regulations of the last third of the eighteenth century (particularly those of 1765 and 1778) finally removed the trade restrictions. The abolition or at least restriction of the triad of staple, convoy and guild power together with the deregulation of the trade in enslaved people (and the fall of French sugar production after the Haitian Revolution 1791) accelerated a shift to plantation production in Spanish America that had started around the 1760s. The main sites of this fast-expanding Spanish American plantation complex were Cuba and Puerto Rico. In Cuba, the economic model changed significantly after the shock of the short-lived English occupation of 1762. Between mid-century and 1800 the island began to develop a coffee producing sector for the first time. Tobacco production doubled between 1750 and 1800. Yet, the most dramatic transformation was the creation of a sugar plantation complex, which by the late eighteenth century exported almost 3 million *arrobas* of sugar annually, almost twice as much as the main sugar producing regions in Brazil (see Figure 16.5).

Although the peacetime existence of the new trade regime was relatively brief (1783–1796), it further contributed to expanding Spain's agricultural imports from the Americas. As Figure 16.6 shows, the gap between bullion and non-bullion commodities had begun to close from mid-century onward even though mining output grew very fast, too. From 1747–1750 to 1791–1795, the total value of Spain's colonial imports grew 83.8%, despite set-backs caused

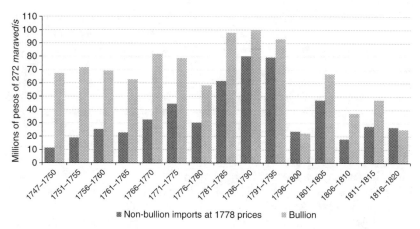

Figure 16.6 Spanish private imports from the Indies, 1747–1820 (by quinquennium in millions of pesos of 272 *maravedís*).
Source: Cuenca-Esteban (2008: 349).

by Spain's participation in both the Seven Years' War (1761–1763) and American Revolution (1779–1783). In 1747–1750, non-bullion commodities amounted to 14.4% of the value of Spain's colonial imports, a percentage slightly below the 17.8% estimated for the period from 1560 to 1650. By 1791–1795, the quinquennium that preceded the collapse of 1797, the value share of non-bullion commodities had steadily increased to 46%. After 1797 imports followed a downward trend (except for a 14-month respite during the Treaty of Amiens in 1802–1803), but the share of non-bullion commodities remained high as the Wars of Independence brought three centuries of colonial trade with the Spanish American mainland to a close.

The increasing importance of non-bullion imports in the second half of the eighteenth century translated into the expansion of shipping, particularly after the effective implementation of the free trade regulations in 1783, once the peace with Britain was signed. Even though Cádiz lost exclusive access to colonial trade, it still retained 84% of the total value of Spain's colonial imports between 1778 and 1796 (far behind Cádiz were La Coruña with 6.8%, Barcelona with 3.8% and Santander with 2.6%, which were the other important importers of colonial goods). Unfortunately, the existing literature provides no data on the evolution of tonnage during those years. There is, however, data on the total number of ships that participated in the transatlantic exchanges, showing that the previous record of 1608 (283 outward and return voyages) was now greatly surpassed (785 voyages in 1792). Between 1778 and 1796, a total of 4,102 ships sailed from Spanish American ports for Spain, of which 2,141 (or 53.4%) entered Cádiz, a percentage far lower than their share of the total value of imports (Fisher, 1985). The discrepancy in the percentages is presumably explained by both the presence of more substantial quantities of bullion in the ships bound for Cádiz and the larger average tonnage of those ships.

Figure 16.7 provides a long-term view of the total shipping movement (outward and inward) between the western Andalusian ports (the ones that held the exclusive right to trade with the colonies since the early sixteenth century) and Spanish America. Following the seventeenth-century collapse and similar to the evolution of tonnage, shipping began a steady recovery after 1715. However, it was the 1778 opening of trade to many more ports that catapulted its numbers to 7,821 ships in the years leading to the 1797 blockade. Figure 16.7 shows the 3,382 ships that departed from or arrived at Cádiz (Fisher, 1981; 1985). That shipping grew far more than the value of the cargoes can only be explained by the lowering of prices and transport costs (the consequence of more competition), a wider range of manufactured goods traded and the growing importation of non-bullion commodities (including those with low unit value).

With the benefit of hindsight, economic historians see clearly the importance of non-bullion goods for commercial development. However, there were good economic reasons why silver production and circulation remained at the forefront of commercial policy. In 1545, the richest silver deposit the world has ever known was discovered at the Cerro Rico de Potosí (present-day Bolivia), located at an altitude of over 4000 m. In New Spain, rich silver lodes were

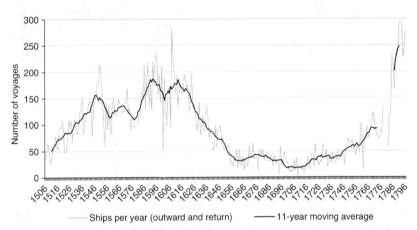

Figure 16.7 Total shipping movements between western Andalusian ports (Seville, Sanlúcar and Cádiz) and Spanish America, 1506–1796.
Source: Trans-Atlantic Slave Database (www.slavevoyages.org) (accessed March 2018).

discovered in the Zacatecas area (1546), Guanajuato (1550) and elsewhere. In the 1550s, miners in New Spain developed the amalgamation process, a cheap method of refining large amounts of pulverized low-grade silver ore by blending it with mercury or *azogue*. At the time there were only three known sizeable mercury deposits in the world. Castile had two of them, by far the largest ones, at Almadén (in Castile) and Huancavelica (in central Peru), in its realm (the third was in Idria, modern Slovenia). As a result, silver output took off in the second half of the sixteenth century. New veins and the abandonment of old ones, as well as the need for investment, would drive the familiar mining cycle of boom and bust originated precisely from the combined effect of the nature of the ore deposits and, at times, insufficient capital resources to counter their impact.

The two main silver producing regions, those of central and northern New Spain and Upper Peru were strikingly different and evolved rather dissimilarly. In New Spain, silver deposits were scattered over seven important *reales de minas* or mining districts. By contrast, in the viceroyalty of Peru production was highly concentrated at Potosí (and its district of Charcas). Excavation methods were also to some extent different. In New Spain the dimensions of shafts and adits were more substantial, the use of underground cartridge blasting more common, and the whims to keep the shafts drained had more capacity than in the latter – 'to construct a deep shaft cost as much as to build a factory or a church' – and the trend of increasing capital investments continued up to the end of the colonial period (Brading & Cross, 1972: 549). By contrast, in the Upper Peruvian mines, shafts were less profound, and the use of whims reduced. Since ore deposits were located in conical peaks, adits provided the best access for extraction. Most of these tunnels only allowed two miners to work with picks at any given time.

Differences between the two main silver producing regions also extended to refining. By the early seventeenth century the bulk of New World silver was yielded by amalgamation, and this continued to be so until the second half of the nineteenth century. However, smelting did not disappear and at times, when mercury was scarce (particularly in the seventeenth century), its share of total production could grow significantly. The type of silver extracted at Potosí, silver sulfide compounds, could be refined using either smelting and amalgamation. Aside from silver sulfide, New Spanish deposits also contained another type of silver, argentiferous galena, which could only be refined by smelting. As a result, the viceroyalty produced about a third of its silver by smelting. Mercury production and distribution was one of the very few proper state monopolies in Spain. Hence, the royal treasury could estimate, for taxation purposes, the silver that was produced using the method of amalgamation. But production by smelting was harder to control and estimate for the royal officials and, thus, it left more room for unregistered output. This appears to have been the case in the second half of the seventeenth century, particularly in New Spain. Half of the silver presented for taxation at the *Real Caja de Zacatecas* from 1670 to 1705 had been obtained by smelting (Bakewell, 1971: 248).

The temporary surge in smelting has profound ramifications for assessing real output and exports during the second half of the century, a period for which there are intensely contrasting historiographical interpretations. A shortage of mercury and the surge in smelting could explain, at least in part, the enormous amounts of unregistered silver reaching Spain at a time when the New World mines were officially producing less (Morineau, 1985; TePaske, 2010: 312). But then again, fraud in the Andean mines also appears to have been widespread in the same period, despite the fact that over there smelting was less important than in New Spain for the simple reason that the large quantities of fuel that smelting required were harder to come by in sites at extremely high altitudes.

For most of the colonial period, Upper Peruvian and New Spanish silver production also differed in fiscal pressure. As in continental Europe, subsoil resources were considered a royal domain. Exploitation was left to private initiative, for which the Crown levied a tax called *real quinto* (royal fifth or 20%). However, across different mining districts the actual tax applied differed between 5% and 10% de facto, as is clear from an evaluation of the tax receipts of different mining regions. Following the introduction of mercury amalgamation in 1573, Potosí's annual output went from 1 million to 7.6 million pesos in 1585. Between 1580 and 1650, its yearly output never fell below 4.2 million. But after the mid-seventeenth century production slipped steadily until it reached its nadir in the 1720s at about 1.1 million pesos a year (see Figure 16.8). There were several reasons for the decline: among them the exhaustion of silver ores and deepening of mines, and a contraction in the supply of mercury from Huancavelica.

Though initially smaller than the Peruvian production, Mexico overtook Peru in the late seventeenth century. Up to 1627, Mexico's mining industry grew at 2.5% a year. Over the eighteenth century, Spain used its mercury monopoly deliberately to support silver production (Dobado & Marrero, 2011). New silver deposits were discovered and exploited in the northern part of the viceroyalty, such as at Sombrerete, Bolaños and Santa Bárbara. By the end of the colonial period, from 1790 to 1810, it was refining 200 million pesos of silver per decade. Meanwhile, a tax reduction in 1736 brought about a revival of Potosí and other Upper Peruvian mines such as Pasco, Porco and Oruro, and was re-enforced here too by the significant lowering of the price of mercury. In the 1780s, total Peruvian production (including Upper and Lower Peru and Chile) reached the record output of the early seventeenth century (Garner, 1988: 903). Thus, the later eighteenth century was a phase of expansion in silver mining.

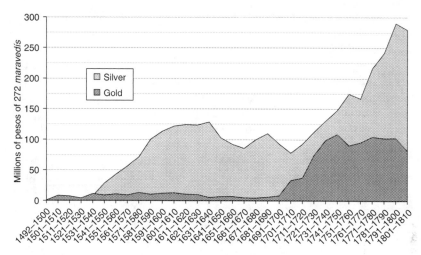

Figure 16.8 New World silver and gold output, 1492–1810 (by decade in millions of pesos of 272 *maravedís*)
Source: TePaske (2010: 20).

The same was true for gold, which had traditionally been marginal for Spanish America. By the end of the sixteenth century three main gold-mining regions had been identified in the northern Andes, in Nueva Granada (present-day Colombia): the drainage basin of the Cauca River, the upper Magdalena River, and the Pacific coast and lowlands. There were both vein and placer deposits in these regions, and also important differences in the timing of exploitation. The richest mines of Antioquía, in the Magdalena valley, saw their heyday in the late sixteenth and early seventeenth century, by which time most of them had been depleted. In the seventeenth century production dropped notably. In the eighteenth century, though, the Chocó and other mining districts of the Pacific coast increased total gold output considerably, to a large extent thanks to the importation of enslaved Africans.

Before 1810 total registered bullion output in the Indies adds up to 4.53 billion pesos or 113,000 tonnes of silver equivalent (i.e. silver plus gold expressed in silver value at a 1:16 ratio), 96,816 of which correspond to the Spanish colonies. These silver and gold estimates are conservative because they have no fraud percentage factored in. Illicit unregistered production was significant and it affected gold more than silver mining (TePaske, 2010: 52–53). Thus, other estimates, which include unregistered bullion, place total New World production before 1800 at between 130,000 and 150,000 tonnes of silver equivalent (Barrett, 1990: 237). These higher estimates suggest that the New World contributed more than 80% of the silver and 70% of the gold produced in the world between 1550 and 1800 (Cross, 1983: 397). More conservative estimates for the same period put those figures at 70% and 47%, respectively (TePaske, 2010: 67, 140).

The majority of the New World bullion was shipped to Iberia, but the relationship between stocks of bullion produced and flows of bullion to Europe, Africa and Asia changed over time. By the late eighteenth century the Spanish American economy was larger than the peninsular one, and more and more of the silver production remained within the Americas, as reflected by extremely high nominal prices and wages in many parts of the Americas (Grafe & Irigoin, 2012). Also, bullion remittances (see Chapter 13) were subject to fraud and the official records are often unreliable. Portuguese gold went mostly to England, its main trading partner. Around the second third of the eighteenth century gold accounted for between half and two-thirds of the value of Portuguese imports from Brazil even though production began to fall in the 1750s and about 80% of Brazil's gold production found its way to England (Fisher, 1971; Cross, 1983: 418).

However, the single largest difference between the flows of silver towards Spain and gold towards Portugal was likely their impact on the fiscal receipts from the colonial sphere on the peninsular polities. Around 40% of Portuguese revenue in the mid-eighteenth century derived from taxes on Brazilian trade, which included gold prominently; by the 1760s and 1770s the share was still above 20%. On the Spanish side, the same proportion of American revenue accounted for about 12–13% of royal receipts across the eighteenth century, of which silver taxes accounted only for a fraction (Irigoin & Grafe, 2008; Grafe & Pedreira, 2019)

16.6 Conclusion

It is impossible to understand the economic history of early modern Iberia without taking stock of its trade, and in particular its imperial expansion. Imperial trade contributed to a dramatic increase of openness of the peninsular economy, quite opposite to the image sometimes painted. The regulatory frameworks used for much of the period by Spain and Portugal differed significantly. Yet, neither constituted a monopoly in the modern economic sense or indeed in the sense of Dutch and English seventeenth-century trading companies. The legal basis for a colonial exclusive were stronger in the Portuguese case, but only in the later eighteenth century could reformers create the conditions for the metropolis to reap more of the benefits of such an exclusive. Generally, the benefits of empire for peninsular Portugal with its smaller European economy and larger empire were substantial, especially in fiscal terms. In Spain, the proportions were inverted, and the process of colonization of a large territorial mass with increasing internal markets meant the room for an 'imperial subsidy' was always modest. In addition, there was simply no legal basis for a colonial exclusive. The rents from the exploitation of indigenous and enslaved Afro-descendent labour in Spanish America went mostly to Spanish American elites, not to the metropolis until the late eighteenth century (Grafe & Irigoin, 2012).

Economic conditions account for some of the differences in the development of the two empires over the three centuries under consideration. It should be noted that even during the union of Crowns the regulatory frameworks for trade remained separate though in particular in the trade in enslaved Africans collaboration and inter-imperial trade drove the expansion to 1640. It is an interesting counterfactual to think how commodity flows might have developed had the Portuguese War of Restoration not raised the barriers between the hispanophone and lusophone regions of America. The orientation towards England in foreign policy in the case of Portugal shaped the eighteenth-century empire. In the case of Spain, the alliance with France made much less of a difference to American trade, though re-exports of French textiles to the Americas were one factor. One fact that is too rarely acknowledged is that the Iberians created the transatlantic slave trade long before the Dutch, English, French and other Europeans partook. It was the poisonous fruit of intra-Iberian cooperation first and foremost. But neither commodity cycles nor trade conditions would seem sufficient explanations for the very different role that enslaved people played in either empire until the late eighteenth century.

The Achilles heel of both empires was that exports to the Empire mostly consisted of re-exports of northern European manufactured goods. That limited the backward linkages of the trade, though there were impulses to shipbuilding and a large array of services from the start. Agriculture in the peninsula benefitted in the earlier periods. It is even harder to understand the forward linkages. Commodity re-exports were lucrative for Portuguese merchants, but to the extent that they depended on foreign finance the benefits were shared. Silver imports into Spain lubricated trade, but they also contributed to financial conditions that led to urban indebtedness and high local taxation (see Chapter 13 and Grafe, 2012). From the early seventeenth century onward, when primarily north-western European merchants took control of Iberia's international trade and the manufactured goods coming from their countries of origin flooded into Spain and Portugal, the bulk of the bullion arriving in Seville and Lisbon from the Iberian empires began to be increasingly reshipped to Antwerp, Amsterdam, London, Nantes and other ports. This feature of Iberia's international trade would continue unabated until the end of the colonial period.

A pattern of trade that had bullion at its core had massive ramifications for both European and global trade. A large part of the bullion was used to offset Western Europe's chronic trade deficits with three areas: the Baltic (whence basic commodities such as grain, timber, hemp, flax, wax, leather and potash were imported, a trade dominated by the Dutch and English), the Levant (which was primarily in the hands of French, Dutch and English merchants), and Asia or the Orient. The latter was the main destination of the American silver, and the two main players in that trade in the seventeenth and eighteenth centuries were the English and Dutch East Indies companies (Barrett, 1990: 250–253). The purpose of shipping silver to Asia was not only to offset Europe's trade deficit. Equally important was the price of silver itself.

The fact that more silver than gold was mined in the New World meant that the exchange or price ratio of silver to gold changed significantly. From the mid-sixteenth to the mid-seventeenth century the value of silver fell 60% relative to gold, setting the bimetallic ratio in the Spanish Empire at around 16:1, where it remained until the later nineteenth century. This meant that silver's purchasing power in the Spanish Empire decreased during the colonial period. But the silver to gold ratio differed substantially around the world, a fact that had implications in shaping not only commodity flows in the Atlantic World but also global trade. Differences in the bimetallic ratio gave rise to commercial exchanges between countries and continents. In the late seventeenth century, for instance, in north-western European ports the price of silver relative to gold was as much as 10% higher than in Spain. Similar differences generated trade between Spain and the rest of Europe, greatly contributing to draining silver away from Iberia. However, the most substantial exchange discrepancy was between the Spanish Empire and China. The relative price of silver to gold in China was about 8:1, that is, twice that of the Americas. This meant that Chinese goods such as silks and ceramics could be sold for silver in the New World or Europe at double the price paid for them in Asia, though transport costs reduced some of that difference. Such a price gap was a major force in generating trade between Europe and Asia via the Cape of Good Hope, and between Spanish America and Asia via the Pacific and the Philippines. As a result, a significant part of the New World silver ended up in China (Cross, 1983: 399–401).

17

The Economic History of Iberia in a Wider Context, 1500–1800

BARTOLOMÉ YUN-CASALILLA

17.1 Introduction

Placing the history of Spain and Portugal in a wider context implies revising much of the received wisdom about the history of both countries. It also implies explaining this history in a comparative perspective and without losing sight of the global contexts and, therefore, the empires they built.[67]

The fact that these countries were latecomers in the European Industrial Revolution triggered a series of negative views, some of which were already present in the writings of political thinkers (Castilian and Aragonese *arbitristas*, as well as Portuguese authors of *remedios*) of the sixteenth and seventeenth centuries, and would spread to enlightened politicians of the eighteenth, eager to justify their reform projects. Perhaps for these reasons, when Masson de Morvillers referred to Spain in his article in *l'Encyclopédie Méthodique*, he wrote: 'in two centuries, in four, or even in six, what has Spain done for Europe?' According to him it was a country in which it is necessary 'to ask priests for permission to read and think'. These visions, which by extension sometimes apply to Portugal, have been greatly nuanced and are changing thanks to research in recent decades.

17.2 The Iberian Peninsula, 1500: A Crossroads in a Wider Context

By 1500 Iberia was a crossroads and, therefore, a centre for the creation and transfer of knowledge and technology between some of the most advanced areas and cultures of the planet: the Islamic world, the Hebraic culture and the Italian Renaissance. This was reflected in the exceptional development of cartography, navigation sciences, mathematics, geometry, astronomy and even knowledge related to warfare, which experienced a particularly fast development in Portugal and in the other Iberian kingdoms (Parry, 1981). These advances – and many others of European origin for which Iberia served as a stage – were also transferred to America and Asia. Moreover, this

---

[67] For a more detailed analysis of Sections 17.2, 17.3 and 17.4 see Yun-Casalilla (2019).

crossroads condition that gave rise to important innovations was reflected in a fact of an ecological nature that is no less important, although it is sometimes forgotten. Today the concept of the Islamic green revolution – linked to the medieval technological revolution – is criticized (Horden & Purcell, 2000). But the truth is that agronomic knowledge and animal and plant species from Eurasia and Africa converged in the peninsula (Watson, 1981) and found here the bridge through which they were transferred to America, making the New World a crucial piece in the process of ecological globalization that would change American ecosystems just as American fauna and flora transformed Europe and Asia (Yun-Casalilla et al., 2021).

From medieval times, Iberia was also the meeting point between the Low Countries and Italy, the most urbanized regions of Europe, which gave it locational advantages for commercial development. Lisbon, Seville, Barcelona, Burgos, Valencia and other cities benefited from the last decades of the fifteenth century. Some of them were embedded in the hub of the Genoese commercial networks and connected with Asia, North Africa, the Atlantic islands (Canary Islands, Madeira and Azores) and also with Northern Europe (Fernández-Armesto, 1982; Thomaz, 1994). These networks were not only sources of benefits and financial possibilities – especially for the monarchs – but they also served to import the most advanced knowledge of Europe, both in commercial and navigational techniques and others. Barcelona and Valencia had been pioneers and rivalled Genoa in the genesis of institutions such as the *Taulas de Canvi*, a predecessor of today's public banks, and which would give rise to major innovations in the financial history of Europe.

One could imagine that the institutions that led the advance against Islam, oriented above all to war – razzias, or looting expeditions (Mackay, 1977) – were more efficient for the destruction of resources than for their maintenance and improvement. But this is a trait that can be extended to European feudal societies in general and that, in any case, should not hide the fact that Iberian local institutions, such as the *concejos* (councils) or the Portuguese *camaras*, developed very efficient agrarian organization formulas to improve production and productivity, as well as the silvopastoral balance and the use of the different regional ecosystems. The Muslim heritage in irrigated farming had been maintained in many areas of the south and east of the peninsula, thanks to institutions that regulated individual interests. The so-called *Real Concejo de la Mesta*, an association of transhumance sheep owners dominated by the nobility and the ecclesiastic institutions, has been considered a hindrance to growth (North & Thomas, 1973). But transhumance was also a way to take advantage of the complementarity of very diverse ecosystems. The abundance of land taken from the Islamic polities allowed the extensive agricultural system prevailing throughout Europe to be brought to its maximum potential. At the same time, the need for labour and vassals on the part of the great lords and the constant emigration of peasants towards the south forced forms of

ECONOMIC HISTORY OF IBERIA IN A WIDER CONTEXT, 1500–1800   445

exploitation and property rights that favoured both population increase and productive expansion. This was the case with some of the forms of emphyteusis common in Portugal, in some areas of the Douro Valley, or on the Mediterranean coasts from Catalonia to Valencia and the Kingdom of Granada.

Like France or England, the Crowns of Portugal, Castile and Aragon (the Principality of Catalonia and the kingdoms of Valencia and Aragon), and the Kingdom of Navarre constituted composite states that were beginning to develop forms of fiscal states within themselves. Despite the enormous differences, these polities articulated very large territories and created fiscal systems and political formations capable of guaranteeing social order and property rights at a level similar to that of any other country in Europe (and within the limitations of the time). The cities (which were also jurisdictional lordships) and the secular and ecclesiastical lordships maintained their own jurisdictions. By 1500, the Avis dynasty in Portugal and the Trastámara dynasty in Castile and Aragon had created systems of balance of power that guaranteed a remarkable political stability. In all these kingdoms the justice of the Crown was being reinforced and, although the king was not always an impartial third party (Owens, 2005), he was more than *primus inter pares*, and his judges could create some guarantees and security in the enforcement of contracts and compromises between parties. Although manorial jurisdictions had a high degree of independence, the possibility of appeal existed (for some more than for others) (Kagan, 1981; Hespanha, 1994) and the development of a system of notaries and legal compilations helped to lower transaction costs (Yun-Casalilla, 2019). In addition to the consulates of Burgos and Bilbao, institutions such as the *Casa da Índia* (1503) in Lisbon and, in imitation of it, the *Casa de la Contratación* in Seville (1504) were added, which served to regulate overseas trade, resolve conflicts between merchants and seek agreements that reduced risks and uncertainties in trade. A network of university institutions (Valencia, Alcalá, Salamanca, Valladolid, Coimbra, Évora, etc.), with a strong cross-border character, as evidenced by the frequent presence of Portuguese or Aragonese students in Castile and vice versa, was the basis of an educational revolution similar to others in Western Europe and would provide these states with a small but efficient bureaucracy by the standards of the time (Kagan, 1974).

17.3   The Iberian Empires in Early Globalization, 1492–1668

The economic history of Spain and Portugal would be marked by the imperial expansion of Portugal and Castile and, therefore, by the process of globalization that they speeded up, as well as by the composite character of the monarchies that were articulated in these territories. Traditional historiography emphasized the strongly centralized and absolutist character of these empires, which has also led some economists to emphasize a simplistic idea of parasitic absolutism (Acemoglu et al., 2005). These political systems, inefficient both economically and in their state capacity, were not suitable, it was also argued, to control and govern such distant and diverse societies scattered around the world. Today, historiography has swung in the opposite direction. Not only is the efficiency of this bureaucracy underlined, but emphasis is placed on the fact that the monarchic constitutional system itself imposed imperial models in which the Crown had to take into account the dissimilar norms and customs of the different territories and even the legal pluralism and the multiple colonial status of the societies and cultures under its dominions (Hespanha, 2001; Benton, 2002).

This vision seems to be corroborated by the doubts raised by some specialists about the real character of the military means used in colonial control (Thompson, 1999) and by the scarce capacity of territorial penetration of Europeans in other worlds until the eighteenth century (Ringrose, 2019). However, all of the above has also led to conceptual and terminological exaggerations that forget that all empires of the time were characterized by the multiplicity of centres of decision and power (Darwin, 2012; Burbank & Cooper, 2011), that the negotiated character is not a fact exclusive to the Iberian empires (Turner Bushell & Greene, 2002) and that, in any case, these negotiations were often very asymmetrical. But it is no less true that this vision of a more de-centralized empire opens interesting perspectives for economic historians.

Coercion and enforcement capacity, essential aspects in the functioning of any economy (North et al., 2009), could not fall only – and in fact did not fall – on the formal institutions created by the monarchy, even if these were more efficient than had once been assumed. Behind the formation and functioning of these empires was also the workings of self-regulated social networks (Antúnes & Polónia, 2016) or informal institutions (Yun-Casalilla, 2019), which through personal relationships, kinship and even prestige, created bonds of trust, they reduced risks and transaction costs, and acted as enforcement mechanisms in the fulfilment of agreements (Greif, 2006). They also articulated the different geopolitical and social spaces. All this is not at odds with the recognition of a high organizational capacity that is manifested, for example, in the management of the *Carrera de Indias*, or the *Carreira da Índia* in the Portuguese case, which testify to the ability of these states to use highly developed technologies and knowledge of geography and the physical environment to regulate trade and meet part of the protection costs involved in all empires. The aim was thus to provide traders and social agents with services indispensable for economic activity (Goodman, 1988; Cossart, 2021).

Within these similarities, the two empires were different. The Portuguese would develop first in Africa and Asia, where the conquerors used local knowledge to organize a system of theoretical monopoly by the monarch – the merchant king, as he has been called. At the same time the *Estado da Índia*, based in Goa, stood as a way of controling distant territories by giving them a high degree of autonomy from Lisbon (Miranda, 2010). The Portuguese also made use of informal mechanisms – often based on marital relations – that reveal a mixture of violence and negotiation with local societies and left in the hands of the conquerors a good deal of the possibilities of coercion on the ground. In Brazil, the plantation system that would characterize these empires during the early modern era, developed later and more slowly. The Spanish empire had one of its keys in the Indies trade and its administration from Seville (see Chapter 16). In this case, the king did not trade or claim a royal monopoly on imperial commerce. His benefits and those of a large part of colonial society came from the exploitation of the mines of Mexico and Peru. But a legally obligatory line of trade was created, between the Caribbean and Seville and later between Acapulco and Manila, also based on the organization of convoys protected by the royal fleets, with the Crown assuming the costs of protecting its cargoes and those of the merchants, who by law had to be Castilians. In turn, colonial control, projected over wide swathes of land, was based on the externalization of the costs of protection and administration, which were left in the hands of conquerors, religious orders and local elites in general, which was not an obstacle to the formation of a bureaucracy dependent on the viceroys, the representatives of the Crown.

Both empires were thus based on the sharing of the protection and administrative costs between private individuals and the Crown, in exchange for recognizing the colonial elite's *de jure* or de facto important powers. This formula would give rise to many frictions and problems of regulation, arbitration and monitoring, due to the blurred boundary between the rights and duties of the different agents and the confusion between public and private that was common in the societies of the time. The expansion of both imperial systems – and particularly in American lands – was largely due to one of the most important collateral effects of ecological globalization: the weakening of the original ecosystems and population (Crosby, 1972). Animals, plants and microbes mixed with the low efficiency of the Iberian institutions in preventing diseases and with the labour schemes implemented by miners and *econcomenderos* to unleash a true demographic and human disaster.

The weakness of the imperial administrations, already evident in the seventeenth century, has often been related only to their own functioning: the impossibility of maintaining the monopoly system of the king of Portugal, who had to sell trade licenses to attend to commerce and face the high management costs, on the one hand; and the inefficiency of the commercial control exercised from Seville with the infiltration of foreign merchants and merchandise there, in the case of Castile, on the other hand. Alternatively the difficulties of the empires have been blamed on the corruption and clientelist relations of the American officials and elites and on the attacks by European powers such as England and Holland.

All this is part of the truth; but it is only part of it. To a large extent, these problems were the consequence of the internal constitution of these empires and the way in which the public and private spheres were articulated within them. As for the weaknesses of the licensing system in Lisbon and the Sevillian trade, they are better understood in the broader context of globalization itself. Early globalization was not only the work of Iberian imperial formations, although they excelled in many ways. It was also due to a series of agents who, organized in social networks and often embedded in the imperial institutions themselves, created trade links that were difficult for the administrations of those empires to control. But in addition to this, the Iberian empires were not alone in this early globalization (Yun-Casalilla, 2019). Parallel to their expansion had developed the Ottoman Empire (both towards Europe and Asia), the Russian Empire (towards Siberia), the Safavid Empire (towards the Indian Ocean), the Mughal Empire (towards the Deccan) and China and Japan would clash in their respective expansionist policies in the China Sea and Korea. These are all actors to be added to the Dutch, English and French, usually recognized in this representation. As a consequence, the Iberian empires were beginning to be the scene of a trans-imperial tension that is typical of these political formations (Burbank & Cooper, 2011) and which would manifest itself not only in America but also in Asia.

The result of all this was also the formation of trans-imperial trade networks, often based on smuggling and multilateral trade, that made the Spanish and Portuguese attempts to control world trade impossible. A good example is the South Atlantic trade between Angola and America or the land and amphibious trade connecting Asia with Europe through Anatolia or the Black Sea. The result was also growing pressure on the income of the monarchs of Madrid – centre of both empires since the annexation of Portugal in 1580 by Philip II (Philip I of Portugal). An increasing proportion of global traffic and the potential taxes on it escaped the royal coffers. Such trade networks must include not only merchants, but also officials, pirates and privateers, and members of the colonial elites as well as the merchant communities of Seville and Lisbon, who often worked for their own benefit and to the detriment of the imperial systems. Globalization was thus having a corrosive effect and created increasing stress on the political formations that were so difficult to control and monitor (Yun-Casalilla, 2019).

In these circumstances, the empires would survive thanks to the fact that they were fiscally organized around Goa (Miranda, 2010) and the American system of *cajas reales*, respectively (Marichal, 1999), but also thanks to the alliance and permissiveness with respect to the local elites who enjoyed a relative degree of autonomy. Hence, a large part of the revenues remained increasingly in the colonies, where more effective defensive systems were organized. In addition, powers such as England and Holland were more likely to infiltrate the Iberian spaces through smuggling than to conquer large territories with the protection costs that this would have entailed (Yun-Casalilla, 2019).

17.4 Economic Trends and Political Economies in the Iberian Peninsula, 1500–c. 1668

17.4.1 Economic Trends from a Southern European Perspective

The evolution of the Iberian economies between c. 1500 and c. 1668 was not exceptional with respect to other areas of Europe, although the rhythms would be very different. The figures available on the evolution of GDP per capita in Spain and Portugal show different profiles (see Chapter 10). In Portugal, the growth of the 'sixteenth century' actually began towards the last decades of the century and continued with ups and downs throughout the seventeenth century. In Spain, growth began much earlier, slowing down from the end of the sixteenth century. It entered moments of recession in the seventeenth century in some regions, so that some estimates give a setback by 1700 (Carreras, 2009). Urbanization indexes corroborate this trend. They also show how the urban networks of medieval origin in the Iberian countries were reaching their peak of expansion to give way from the seventeenth century to the implementation of another pattern of development based on the dynamism of port cities, which, together with the rise of urban hubs in Northern Europe, would characterize Europe during the following centuries (de Vries, 1987: chapter 7).

But this evolution makes more sense, and is perhaps more explicable, if we also analyse it from a regional perspective and not only from national calculations. Solid and detailed research has shown that the latter could be underestimating the weight of agrarian transformations and, with it, the GDP per capita figures (Catalán, 2018). Unfortunately, we do not have many studies of this type, despite the fact that they are essential for countries like Spain, so internally diverse and without an integrated market, which makes it difficult to extrapolate local data, such as wages, prices and even urbanization, to the whole country. We are therefore guided by indirect indicators that measure, not growth in the current sense (income per capita), but the expansion of production and population of the different areas. The tentative result is that all the peninsular regions – each at its own pace and in different dimensions – experienced both demographic and productive increase during the sixteenth century. Perhaps even in Portugal it is possible to speak of extensive growth an increase in production no greater than that of the population – from earlier dates than those marked by the reconstructions of GDP per capita. It also seems evident that this expansion had a privileged setting in the Douro Valley (at least until the 1560s), New Castile, Andalusia and, with a different chronology, in Lisbon and the regions around it. During this period there are also many symptoms of a growing integration between the Castilian and Portuguese economies (Ribeiro, 2016). Though growth was extensive and one of its pillars was the enlargement of the cultivated area, it was also accompanied by the spread of improvements in agricultural organization, by an increase in peasant pluri-activity associated with the development of rural markets, by internal migrations, and by seasonal population movements that allowed increments in productivity per inhabitant (Yun-Casalilla, 2004: chapter 4; 2019: 118-138).

The regional data confirm the fact that during the seventeenth century there was a progressive shift towards a model of greater dynamism in the coastal areas. It is likely that there was a climatic crisis that affected the distinct regions differently. But the small gains or losses in each of them respond to additional factors, some of them associated with changes in the wider context. Regions such as Lower Andalusia or the coastal areas from Málaga to Catalonia had the advantage of their greater possibilities of supply by sea in a century of poor harvests. At the same time the cultivation of products for export such as raisins, brandies and others developed, all favoured by a cabotage trade network that would also benefit from the American traffic concentrated in Seville (García Espuche, 1998). Northern Portugal and the Spanish Cantabrian coast up to the Pyrenees were pioneers in the introduction of new species of American maize and potatoes. In the case of the aforementioned areas of Portugal, the development of vineyards dedicated to export would lead to technical innovations (or their diffusion), such as cultivation on terraces or specialization in higher-quality wines.

All these regions were favoured by the existence of Atlantic ecosystems with more abundant rainfall, by the existence of natural meadows of regulated use by the rural communities that allowed more efficient agro-livestock farming combinations, as well as by the seasonal emigration to the inland areas – including the migration of Portuguese workers to Castile – during the harvest months. The outcome was an increasing variety of available resources that allowed for more stable annual food cycles, thus raising the Malthusian ceilings. Although it is possible to speak of some areas in crisis and even of recession in the production of cereals, the seventeenth century was characterized above all by the beginning of a change in the weight of the different regional economies, and the slow displacement of economic dynamism to the coastal regions (Yun-Casalilla, 1999). All of this is not exclusive to Iberia. These phenomena would also be present in the economies of Southern Europe, such as Italy, where it is not possible to speak of a crisis in the northern and central regions of the country (Federico & Malanima, 2004). Spain and Portugal were not exceptions but variants, in intensity and in their cycles, with respect to other surrounding economies.

17.4.2 Empires, Institutions and State Building in the Peninsula

Given the scant commercial weight that even in 1600 the empires had in macroeconomic terms, their impact on the metropolitan economies was small. Neither the Spanish nor the Portuguese empires had created large markets for their domestic production (Costa et al., 2015; Yun-Casalilla, 2019). It was difficult and slow to create a powerful demand for European products among the native American and enslaved African populations, with consumption habits and forms of material culture so different from those of the Old World; especially when America witnessed a demographic and human catastrophe and emigration from the peninsula was insufficient to fill the void (Martínez Shaw, 1994). Situations such as that described by Pomeranz (2000) for eighteenth-century England, with high levels of emigration and demographic growth in the colonies that encouraged the demand for products from the metropolis and provided ghost acreage to supply the latter with goods necessary for industry, were unthinkable at the time. On the other hand, to the extent that Lisbon and Seville were transit ports for goods from other countries, colonial demand did not decisively affect Castilian or Portuguese production.

This does not mean that these were semi-peripheral economies, as has been said, since the reduced trade also made economic dependence impossible (Yun-Casalilla, 2019: 88–98). The stimuli of the colonial markets on the industrial sector in particular came more from the side of shipbuilding and military construction – whose technologies were ostensibly developed (Chapter 14; see also Cossart, 2021) – than from sectors such as textiles. This was despite the development of textile centres such as Porto, Seville or Segovia, associated with colonial demand. Nonetheless, the impact of the empires on the peninsular economies was undeniable. Regardless of the importance we want to give to the price revolution or the weight we want to give to the inflow of money, inflation created major social tensions. It contributed to increased income inequalities in the urban centres, decreased the income of the high nobility, and strengthened the merchant classes. These destabilizing effects on the social order were, however, cushioned by the empire's impact on institutions and state-building.

As early as the fifteenth century, colonial trade was an important source of income for the monarchs of Portugal and fed customs and trade tax revenues, particularly in Lisbon and its area of influence. One could even speak of a rentier state, insofar as the monarch did not live so much from the taxes of the kingdom, that is, from the formation of a tax state in the Schumpeterian sense, but above all from those coming from other political units, in this case the colonies (Yun-Casalilla, 2012). As far as Spain is concerned, at its best time, during the reign of Philip II, the silver from America did not exceed 25% of the crown of Castile's income, which has led to the belief that they were not relevant (Flynn, 1982). These amounts would, however, have their importance.

Associated with the agreement with the *Cortes* to guarantee stable and secure income for the consolidation of the debt, they made it possible to take loans from international bankers with the guarantee that those loans would be respected, while at the same time avoiding constitutional problems regarding the use by the Habsburgs of the kingdom's taxes, theoretically reserved to support the interests of the kingdom itself and not those of the king (Yun-Casalilla, 2019: 167–173). What was taking place in Castile was the beginning of an incomplete financial revolution endorsed by the *Cortes*, which made it possible to lower the cost of debt in a similar way to what had happened in cities such as Genoa in medieval times; with the advantage in Genoa's case that the Bank of San Giorgio would act as a public bank of the republic, which would be impossible in Castile, despite attempts to imitate the *Taulas* of Barcelona and Valencia, as well as the system of the Bank of Amsterdam.

The institutional impact of the empires is, therefore, undeniable. The empire made it easier for Portugal – which did not have the burden of defending dynastic interests in Europe, as was the case in Castile – to reach 1600 with a moderate fiscal contribution from the kingdom. In Spain, the fact that a large part of the military expenses for the defence of the European dynastic domains was paid with Castilian funds, allowed less pressure on the other kingdoms, whose elites established constitutional commitments based on the maintenance of pre-existing institutions. It was not that the military–fiscal state did not also exist in the territories of the Crown of Aragon, where fiscal pressure in the form of donations, taxes and services, as well as in military mobilizations on local scale, increased. But the empire, and the way in which the agreements with the *Cortes* of Castile facilitated the mechanisms of borrowing and debt consolidation, contributed to consecrate the preceding political-institutional systems of Aragon, Navarre, Catalonia and Valencia until the early eighteenth century.

Of course, these agreements on financial and fiscal matters between the Crown and the *Cortes* had effects. Their negotiations, despite the constant conflict involved, enabled the cities to maintain high degrees of autonomy in the collection of taxes. This strengthened their fiscal jurisdiction. Something similar occurred with the church, in exchange for whose resources – which also grew as its services were presented as a way of defending Christianity – not a few privileges were maintained and attacks on its properties and economic bases were reduced to a minimum. Moreover, both in Castile and Portugal, the empires and the possibilities of promotion created by the European dominions in the Castilian case allowed the nobility, always in financial dire straits, access to extraordinary resources. In all the Iberian kingdoms the abundance of currency made it possible to cheapen the debt of this social group and to create spaces of understanding with the king, who approved the mortgage loans (*censos*) on their entailed estates, as well as other grants, in exchange for military and diplomatic services (Abadía Irache, 1998; Monteiro, 1998; Yun-Casalilla, 2002; Vila-Santa, 2015). The concept of the 'crisis of aristocracy' has long been discussed for other European countries. In Iberia this discussion is out of place and acquires a particular meaning, since, despite their indebtedness, the stability of the fortunes of this social group would be the rule (Yun-Casalilla, 2002). At the same time and despite the ruptures in Portugal and Catalonia, the monarchy and the political order were reinforced, thus guaranteeing the social order, property rights and the institutional system. Nobel manorial estates, entitled properties, as well as the cities' jurisdictions, would continue to be an integral part of the architecture of the state and of the rules that regulated the allocation of productive factors. The system was all the more efficient as long as it favoured the rise of the secondary branches of the noble lineages and the ennoblement and social promotion of merchants, patricians of the cities and bankers, some of them of Genoese origin.

All this implied the maintenance of the coercive capacity of these social agents and a limit to the king's monopoly of power. The Habsburg military fiscal state thus maintained a decentralized character. A good part of the military mobilizations in the peninsular interior were satisfied – in troops or in money – by the seigniorial nobility and by the cities and towns, in the form of services and local militias. Although differences could be sought between Portugal, Castile and the territories of the Crown of Aragon, these were forms of absolutism that, as in other areas of Europe, combined a high degree of negotiation between political agents with the fragmentation of jurisdictional space (Beik, 1985). Except for the anti-fiscal rebellions, which did not affect the social order, none of these territories experienced internal convulsions such as the French *frondes* or the English revolutions that threatened to upset the balance of power within the kingdom. The equation empires = stability seems to have been fulfilled, for better and for worse.

Historians discuss some of the effects of all this on the fiscal and financial level. Recently, the sustainability of the debt at its moment of maximum stress has been defended and the success of Philip II in this regard has been emphasized (Drelichman & Voth, 2014). There is evidence for it, and certainly the increase of this monarch's revenues was much faster than that of his European counterparts (Comín & Yun-Casalilla, 2012: 237, 240, fig. 10.2). But the state structure I have just described, with its strong corporate component, implied the expansion of the debt of lordships, cities and towns to meet the king's requirements. The debt of these agents – part of the (corporate) state – whose management mechanisms were negotiated with the king, was in fact a consubstantial element of the political system and had a public character at the time. Although we do not have macroeconomic estimates, when this part of the 'public debt' is added to the available numbers, it is very likely that the figures would increase significantly, especially in Castile. At the same time, it is difficult, regardless of the figures, to attribute sustainability to a state that had to satisfy current debt and bankruptcies by alienating its own foundations and those of its coercive capacity. Manorial jurisdictions were sold to the nobility and to the towns, auctions of royal lands and of royal fiscal sources took place, etc. There is also speculation about a possible effect of absorption of capital that could have been invested in productive sectors. This hypothesis should be contrasted by putting the figures of the total debt –not only that of the king – not in relation to the GDP but also in relation to the industrial sector and the commercialized segment of the economy in which the currency circulated.

In the case of Castile, the effect of fiscal policy on the economy is also the subject of controversy. One could think that taxation was not at the root of the problems that the Castilian economy went through from the second half of the sixteenth century. This is correct if one considers that the taxes usually computed were a small proportion of GDP, and that expenditure – especially military and naval – that went to the regions of the northern coast of Castile, to Navarre and Catalonia and to Lisbon and Porto could have had positive effects on their economies. Perhaps the problem is not one of numbers, but of forms of taxation, since a good part of the taxes fell on consumption and mainly affected the artisans' workshops and their maintenance costs (Yun-Casalilla, 1990). The sale of jurisdictions as well as monetary devaluations – notwithstanding the criticism of 'tyranny' by writers such as Father Mariana – also delayed market integration and increased transaction costs (Mariana, 1987).

These state structures would face major problems in the seventeenth century. In Portugal, the needs of the monarchy served to justify the increase in fiscal demands and for Philip IV (Philip III in Portugal) to take decisive steps to strengthen the tax state. This was done at a time when the Crown's revenues from colonial trade were either declining or not growing at the pace of needs (Hespanha, 1993: 200–210). Such a trend would continue during the reigns of João (1640–1656) and Alfonso (1656–1683), due to the war and post-war needs at a time when the difficulties of Asian trade made it necessary (Hespanha, 1993: 207–210). Paradoxically, it was the Bragança, rebelling against the Habsburgs for this reason, who executed a clear fiscal state project in Portugal. In the case of Castile, it was also the decline in silver remittances which – not by itself, but because it no longer allowed the credit and debt consolidation circuit to be efficiently fed – led to policies that would break the constitutional consensus not only in this kingdom but, above all, in Catalonia (and, as mentioned above, in Portugal). Again, in one sense or another, the revenues derived from their imperial dominions had effects of a different nature on the political system and state-building in both countries.

The forms of political organization would have other consequences on the economy. The consolidation of *mayorazgos* and *morgadíos* as well as the amortized properties of the church – all of them inalienable – crystallized criteria for the management of large estates that did not always involve innovative investments or organizational and technological changes on their part. The political system and the possibilities opened up by war and diplomacy served to create mechanisms for the protection of the domestic economy, but also encouraged forms of rent seeking among the elites who benefited from royal patronage. Many members of these elites transferred part of their wealth to ecclesiastical institutions, which grew exponentially. The result was a high degree of rigidity in the land market. Although today the negative image of these forms of property ownership is revised, their opportunity costs compared to a more fluid system of property rights must have been high. Economic recovery would have to come from readjustments that did not involve structural reforms of the institutional framework.

17.5 Empires, Ecological Globalization, Global Tensions and Political Economies, 1668–1808

17.5.1 Empires and Global Tensions: Turning Their Backs on Each Other

If inter-imperial tension was already evident in the middle of the seventeenth century, from then until c. 1783, the Iberian worlds would be immersed in three processes that would only increase it: the advance of early globalization; the expansion of the Atlantic economy, which was part of it; and the growing warlike conflict that all this would bring with it.

World trade continued to grow during the eighteenth century at a rate of 1.26% per year, similar to that of the sixteenth century (1%) and much higher than the 0.6% of the seventeenth century (O'Rourke & Williamson, 2002a; 2002b). This figure may not impress today's economists, but it is significant for pre-industrial economies. Empires such as Mughal India, China and Russia became increasingly tied to the export of products such as tea, cotton fabrics, silk fabrics and raw silk, porcelain, furs and opium (Findlay & O'Rourke 2007: chapter 5). The development of the plantation economy in the Americas propelled the African slave trade and the expansion of frontier crops such as sugar, tobacco, cotton, cocoa and others that would form the basis of new ecosystems associated with world commerce and, above all, with Europe (Romano, 2004). This, while some original American products, such as potatoes – especially important for the Chinese economy (Pérez-García, 2017) – or corn and yucca, spread around the planet, facilitating population growth in spaces such as China. By the end of the century, not only these but also chili, peanuts, sugar cane or tobacco had become part of consumption patterns in some regions of Asia (Naquin & Rawski, 1987: 2).

All this was the consequence of a new leap in ecological globalization, which was going through the reconstruction of new ecosystems and new consumption patterns in America (Romano, 2004) and other areas of the planet, including China and Russia. Ecological change and that of consumption patterns and technology – especially to produce these new products – were thus closely linked (Yun-Casalilla, 2022). It is also a process that is not exclusively European, but had its manifestations in other areas of the globe, particularly in China (Clunas, 1999). In Europe, there has been talk of a consumer revolution and an expansion of luxury among the middle classes to refer to the increase in demand for products such as tea, coffee and chocolate, which also created backward linkages, and, accompanied by changes in sociability, affected many other segments of demand (Mackendrick et al., 1982; Roche, 1997; 1989; Berg & Eger, 2003). As a result, Europeans' desires for these goods skyrocketed and with them the interests of governments and merchants to preserve their trade and defend their interests in distant parts of the globe.

The available figures also show the growing importance of Atlantic traffic within this globalization process (de Vries, 2003), and the weight in this space of the aforementioned goods. For some authors, it is now clear that an authentic Atlantic system emerged in which, logically, the Iberian countries were heavily involved and which formed part of the triangular trade. The growing connections between Angola, Brazil, the Caribbean, Buenos Aires and Montevideo, with their derivations to Lima from Rio de la Plata, through Córdoba and Tucumán, and to Mexico became more intense and led to the exploitation of new lands and new products (Bonialian, 2016). Mexican mining gained new momentum and fed peaceful trade with Qing China (1644–1912), which had begun an irregular but perceptible policy of opening up to the exterior that would increase its exports notably (Rawski, 2004: 213). The development of gold mining in Brazil would also contribute to the impulse of international trade. The fur trade and the development of tobacco, sugar and cotton plantations boosted the French and British colonies in the Caribbean and North America. Since the second half of the seventeenth century, Colbert's mercantilist policy had put France in a privileged position in colonial development. Scholars have identified the existence of multiple poles of globalization and some have placed their respective epicentres in America or Asia (Frank, 1998; Hausberguer, 2018; Bonialian, 2020).

Although these products still accounted for a small proportion of the GDP of the countries involved (O'Brien, 1980) and were a small part of the total trade of countries such as India or China, their commerce affected the interests of powerful merchant groups, as well as states – especially European ones – whose fiscal systems were increasingly based on the taxes and monopolies associated with trade. The result was increased tensions between the various empires. Conflicts became evident in India, between Qing China and Russia and in the Indian Ocean. In the former, the internal crisis of the Mughal system was followed by the establishment of the British East India Company (1757), which implemented a mercantilist policy while creating a fiscal state aimed 'to fund the protracted military campaigns necessary to conquer India' (Richardson, 2012: 417). In China, the new Qing dynasty concentrated – at intervals – foreign trade in Canton, thus creating a highly regulated trade system, while at the same time radicalizing its conflicts with the Mughals of Central Asia and with Russia – which extended into Manchuria – over the fur trade (Findlay & O'Rourke, 2007: 296ff.). But, above all, and for what concerns us here, tensions became more intense on the American continent and in the Atlantic in general. In the Caribbean, where the interests of the Anglo-American colonists clashed with those of France, Holland, Spain and Portugal, the conflict manifested itself in the form of piracy, plunder, smuggling and confrontations between these countries. Attempts by the various powers to control colonial territories only accentuated this tension, as evidenced by the English Navigation Acts (1651) and the actions of British American settlers against London's policy (Lovejoy, 1987). The same could be said of the South Atlantic and the areas between the Río de la Plata, Brazil and the Gulf of Guinea and Portuguese Angola. The result was an unprecedented stress also in the Iberian colonies in Africa and America. This tension was especially virulent between Spain and England until the latter obtained the *Asiento* of the slave trade in the Peace of Utrecht (1713–1715). From then on, the latter country would hold the monopoly on the sale of enslaved Africans in Spanish America, while good relations with Portugal gave England privileged access to captives in Angola. The study of all these tensions, which would require a whole chapter on the political history of these regions, came to a head during the Seven Years' War (1756–1763), a truly global conflict, and during the American Revolutionary War (1775–1783).

If all of the above was already a problem for Spain and Portugal, things became even more complicated because of the multilateral character of world trade, which weakened the benefits of the routes linking Seville and Cádiz with the Caribbean and Mexico with Manila, as well as the one linking Lisbon with Brazil. As if that were not enough, this multilateralism was reflected in centrifugal forces within the imperial formations themselves. The predominant role of Lisbon and the income of the Braganzas associated with it, for example, was threatened by Brazil's direct trade with Angola, which was also activated by Brazilian mining, the development of the plantation economy and the consequent increasing demand for enslaved Africans. In the case of the Spanish Bourbons, Andalusian trade with the Caribbean suffered from the competition of Buenos Aires and Montevideo, associated also with African trade. The fiscal control of traffic between Acapulco and Manila was threatened by smuggling and the increase of fraudulently traded products from both Mexico and Lima. It should be borne in mind that this multilateral trade involved not only the other powers, but also a good part of the officials and the Creole and Spanish and Portuguese elites dominating the colonial system.

The conflicts in specific and dispersed points of these imperial formations made it necessary to prolong during the eighteenth century the policy of leaving in the colonies a good part of the tax revenues received in America, which, in the case of the Spanish empire, were used to attend to defensive and administrative needs (Marichal, 1999). In the Portuguese case this fact – although of a different nature – is reflected in the problems of the colonial administration to avoid the evasion of taxes generated by gold mining (Lochkart & Schwartz, 1988: chapter 10). The two empires were also crisscrossed in Europe by both legal and illegal trade networks dominated by merchants from other European countries (García-Baquero, 1992; Pedreira, 1998). Corrosive globalization thus continued to be the challenge for these empires, which were trying to grasp the water of an ocean that was slipping through their fingers and into those of their enemies.

Much of this tension materialized in a system of alliances that would confront Spain and Portugal for decades and that represented a decisive turning point in the economic and political history of Iberia. As we have seen, it all began in 1640 and was consolidated during the *Restauraçao*. The rapprochement between Portugal and England even before the Peace of Lisbon (1668) and the desire of the Braganza family to protect themselves from the Habsburgs, on the one hand, and the Treaty of Methuen (1703) and the Peace of Utrecht, which closed the War of the Spanish Succession, on the other, contributed to the creation of two great blocks that confronted each other during the eighteenth century. In Methuen, England sealed a pact with Portugal for the exchange of English textiles and naval protection for Portuguese wines, which also entailed substantial participation in Portugal's American trade and Brazilian gold. From 1715 onwards, and despite the subsequent confrontations between Spain and France, the fact that a Bourbon, Philip V (1683-1746), was recognized on the throne in Madrid, created the basis for the future Family Pacts by which Spain would align with France in many of the conflicts of the century.

With the reduced importance of the *Estado da Índia* in the Portuguese imperial system and the loss in Utrecht of some of the European old possessions of the Habsburgs, the domains of the Braganzas and the Spanish Bourbons were much more manageable and governable than those of their predecessors. Both Spain and Portugal were now political formations of territorial consistency and continuity, with their respective empires focused mainly on the Atlantic. And both would turn their backs on each other not only politically but also socially and economically. This would become evident during the first half of the century and above all, in the two great conflicts mentioned above.

17.5.2 Empires in Transition and Their Political Economies

In this context, the mercantilist policy of Bourbons and Braganza family must be understood as an attempt to centralize the control, and, therefore, the protection costs too, of their empires. To understand this situation, it is useful to describe the political economies of both empires and countries around 1700. In all the Iberian kingdoms, as in the rest of continental Europe, parliaments of medieval origin had entered into crisis during the seventeenth century. In both the Habsburg and Braganza domains, alternative representative infrastructures had been created – the *Junta dos Três Estados* in Portugal and the *Comisión de Millones* in Castile – which systematically collected taxes through schemes established during the sixteenth and seventeenth centuries. Monarchs could also resort to individualized – and sometimes very asymmetrical – negotiations with local entities or private agents for the concession of services (in Castile and Spanish America the famous *donativos* (Torres Sánchez, 2013; Del Valle, 2016). But all this also meant that the Iberian kingdoms were moving further and further away from a possible financial revolution in the style of England's, based on parliamentary control of spending to give security to the underwriters of public debt. In fact, it would be at the beginning of the eighteenth century – after the political changes of 1688 – when English debt securities would start to be cheaper than Castilian or Portuguese ones (Yun-Casalilla, 2019: 169–173).

At the same time, forms of the contractor state were being developed, based on large contracts (*asientos* in Spanish terminology) and advances of money to the Crown by financiers and leaseholders in exchange for privileges and exploitation of monopolies, very similar also to what was happening in other countries, such as France (Torres Sánchez, 2016). These state patterns would be perfected during the eighteenth century. In Spain the framework of the new territorial model created by the *Nueva Planta* Decrees (1706-1716) would impose Castilian and French forms of centralism (see Chapter 12).

In both countries, negotiation, sometimes implicit, with social actors was part of the political game and led to very refined forms of *do ut des*. In both countries, the ability of the urban oligarchies and the nobility and *fidalgos*, or the church, to make themselves heard before the king was maintained. This was due in part to their coexistence at Court and to the fact that the rules of the political legal game that benefited these elites were very clear and not always susceptible to change by the monarch. The development of centralized armies (Jiménez and Andújar, 2018), especially after the War of the Spanish Succession, in which Portugal was also involved alongside England, made increasingly unnecessary the military function of the manors, already overtaken by the advances of the military revolution, and the indebtedness of the entailed estates, as well as the local militias, which in some areas such as Catalonia would be banned.

Coercion increasingly resided in the king. This in turn was matched by improvements in the judicial system, which for many was the main arena for conflict resolution (Rodrigues, 2019b). However, this did not imply the disappearance of the power of local elites or the high nobility. On the contrary, although the privative jurisdiction of nobles and clergy was more subordinated to the king's justice, their survival (Camarinhas, 2012), combined with the extension of land under their possession (in the case of the church also of local credit), guaranteed the use of formal and informal mechanisms of power of great weight, especially in rural areas (Windler, 1997). And in both countries, more efficient tax systems were developed with a greater capacity to penetrate the social fabric (Paquette, 2013). Meanwhile, the shifting of tax pressure towards customs and monopolies associated with colonial and foreign trade (as in the case of the tobacco *estanco* in Spain), increased the credibility of the king as a debtor. It is not surprising then that, despite not having followed the path of the English financial revolution, interest rates on the public debt of both countries remained at low levels for much of the eighteenth century.

Globalization and the tensions associated with it were the reasons for the reforms in the financial as well as in the commercial system implemented by Charles II (1665–1700) in Spain, and in Portugal João IV (1640–1656) and Alfonso VI (1656–1683). But the pressure for change would grow even stronger throughout the eighteenth century. One of its clearest manifestations in Spain was the increase in spending on the navy and its reform, often based on the development of the contactor state (Torres Sánchez, 2013). Military spending increased dramatically in absolute numbers both on the peninsula and in the colonies (Pieper, 1992: 161ff.). The Spanish fleet had surpassed the English fleet in numbers by 1788 (Valdez-Bubnov, 2011). In the Portuguese case, these expenses were also high and increased with their participation in the War of the Spanish Succession. By 1766 they accounted for almost half of the state's total expenditure (Hespanha, 1993: 209–213).

By the end of the eighteenth century, both countries had taken important steps in the formation of empires in accordance with the assumptions of mercantilism and the struggle for the world market (to what extent they made their economies more competitive is another matter). In both, the system of self-regulated networks or informal institutions that served to maintain trust between traders and economic agents in general remained of great importance (Lamikiz, 2010; Antúnes & Polónia, 2016), and it may be thought that the efficiency of formal institutions had been improved and the infrastructural capacity of states had increased. Especially in the case of Spain, the occasional triumphs of the naval fleet – for example, in Menorca (1782) over the English – are an indication of this. In both empires, relations with local elites were intensifying and a more efficient administration was being put in place. Although different from those of other countries, trading companies were developing and strengthening intra-imperial relations (see

Chapter 16). While Andean and Mexican silver and Brazilian gold continued to be vital to imperial exploitation, the commercialization of goods from the plantation system had advanced from the situation in the sixteenth century. In other words, although to different degrees, these empires were facing and even overcoming one of their fundamental challenges: that of transforming themselves into the type of empire that could compete in the eighteenth century and would continue with the pertinent changes until the nineteenth century.

This is all the more evident if we take into account that recent historiography on empires such as the English one, perhaps the most economically efficient model of the time, also tends to qualify the features of its bureaucratic-administrative modernity and infrastructural capacity. In fact, the importance of self-regulated networks and informal institutions (Veevers, 2015), its unfinished and negotiated nature (Turner Bushell & Greene, 2002; Darwin, 2012), and even the possibilities for corruption that implied that difficult interweaving between private interests and personal networks and public management (Dirks, 2008) have also been emphasized in the British case. It is possible that the eighteenth-century British empire developed an unprecedented infrastructural capacity (Rosental & Wong, 2011; Vries, 2015). But it is no less true that the Iberian empires were witnessing a qualitative change, even if they did not reach the same levels. In any case, the crucial point would be to what extent there was a structural change that made Iberian economies competitive compared to their neighbouring countries.

17.6 Regional Models of Growth and Reformism in Comparative Perspective, 1668–1800

The economic expansion of the Iberian countries in the eighteenth century had fundamentally agrarian roots. But, like the previous fluctuations, it cannot be understood without considering the broader context and the regional models of economic growth that had emerged in the seventeenth century. General factors contributed to such an expansion. The fall in land rent, due to the demographic recession, especially in the interior of the peninsula, allowed the peasantry to have access to land under better conditions. The concentration of capital in the hands of the clergy and the increasing number of ecclesiastical institutions and foundations, such as pious endowments, confraternities, and *misericordias*, lowered the interest rates of *censos* and therefore improved the credit conditions for many peasants. As the eighteenth century progressed, population growth led to a rising peasant self-exploitation that in some areas manifested itself in various forms of pluri-activity – with an intensification of female labour (Sarasúa, 2019; 2021) – and in an industrious revolution of varying intensity according to the different regions (see among many others – Yun-Casalilla,

1987; Carmona, 1990; Pedreira, 2005; Torras, 2007). Though with a zenith by 1750 in the case of England, Portuguese foreign trade expanded during the eighteenth century (Costa, 2005) while the Spanish rose at a rate of 1.21% per year (Prados de la Escosura, 1985; 1988), thus paralleling the expansion of world trade.

Although we lack a more general assessment, recent research is also breaking with the idea of closed guilds unable to incorporate organizational or technological changes (Nieto, 2019; Fattacciu, 2020). The idea of the existence of low-dynamic consumption patterns, impervious to the effects of a consumer revolution, has also been revised, not only among the elites (Cruz, 1996), but even in rural areas that have long been considered as a hindrance to the formation of an internal market (García & Bartolomé, 1997; García & Yun-Casalilla, 1997; Torras & Yun-Casalilla, 1999; Llopis et al., 2003; Ramos-Palencia, 2010). Recent studies have drawn attention to the commercial networks – in which those created by the Catalans within the peninsula would stand out – which were articulating the internal market (Torras, 1991; Pérez Sarrión, 2016), and to the migrations of seasonal workers from the north who provided the necessary labour to the large farms of inland Spain and the Portuguese Tagus Valley or Alentejo during cereals and grapes harvest seasons. Likewise, this growth is usually dissociated from technological improvements, but the picture changes if, as we shall see below, we apply the broader concept of diffusion of useful knowledge.

But, as in the previous period, only a regional perspective also considering connections with the outside world can give us the keys to the process. Almost 30 years ago David Ringrose argued that a series of urban networks and economic regions had been defined in Spain – some on a small scale – whose dynamism obliges us to change the negative image of the country's economy in this century (Ringrose, 1998). The historiography on the agrarian sector has reinforced this opinion. It is not necessary to describe those regions in detail here (see Ringrose, 1998): a network on the Cantabrian coast that penetrated towards the Douro Valley; another one between Catalonia and Málaga very connected to the Mediterranean trade circuits and Cádiz; a third one around the Lower Guadalquivir Valley with Seville and Cádiz as its centre; and, finally, the one that articulated Madrid in the interior of the peninsula. The importance of economic relations with the exterior of these areas is evident. Some of them, the Cantabrian coast for example, continued with the diffusion of American crops introduced in the previous century (potatoes and maize above all). All of them articulated in some of their nodes axes of foreign or colonial trade that became denser with the timid liberalization of American commerce (1765–1778). Associated with this traffic, some were developing market-oriented crops, such as wine, raisins or brandy, or the production of linen (Galicia) or wool fabrics (Catalonia and Málaga). Although growing, foreign trade still did not represent a very high figure in relation to national income, a large part of exports concentrated their positive impact on coastal areas with benefits for them.

One can think of this scheme by adding Portugal to the equation. Indeed, the entire coastal area from the north of Portugal to Lisbon, with its surrounding region towards the Tagus valley and to the south of the capital, fulfilled the same conditions. As we have seen, it was a very active economic region thanks to the trade that was articulated around this city and around Porto, to the development of some industries such as linen (Pedreira, 2005) and the diffusion of American crops. After 1668 its positive evolution continued, at least until the 1750s. It is likely that this region was "crucial for" the increase in the GDP of the national aggregates. This expansion was helped by the expansion of trade with Brazil and the export of wines to England that accelerated technical improvements, such as reinforced terraced cultivation, well combined with emphyteusis (Serrão, 2017). Although it is quite possible that the effects of these circuits did not reach beyond the nearby areas of the Alentejo, some cities such as Évora, connected to trade with Castile and with wool textile production despite the tightening of customs policy, would be integrable in this economic region.

For many years, the permanence of archaic elements in the Iberian economies has been emphasized. Today historians do not pose the problem in terms of economic backwardness, but rather try to understand why growth was not faster. Probably, the figures available for the eighteenth century – at least for Spain (Catalán, 2018) – should be taken as minimums, especially when these are based on the analysis of urbanization processes, since some more dynamic peripheral areas grew over medium-sized but very active towns. In this context, there are also debates about the real scope of the Enlightenment's reforms (see Chapter 12). But it is also recognized that the economy of both countries reached productive ceilings that could only be overcome with the institutional transformations associated with the liberal revolution.

The truth is that some of the processes described above to explain the growth were late compared to other countries, at least for some regions. By the middle of the eighteenth century the entitled properties in the hands of the *mayorazgos*, the *morgadíos* and the church were very extensive. In Portugal, this property of 'dead hands', as Enlightenment thinkers called them, was in a notable proportion ceded in emphyteusis, which allowed peasants access to its cultivation and even the circulation of their possession rights (Monteiro, 2005). The model is similar to that of Galicia, but in this case, an overlapping cascade of levies for the use of the land by different holders ended up creating high pressure on the direct cultivators (Villares, 1982). In the Crown of Castile, the church owned more than 20% of the lands, not counting those ceded in emphyteusis (Grupo 75, 1977).

All this, together with other factors, had a negative effect on income distribution and on the demand for industrial products. Unfortunately, we do not have sufficiently representative analyses of income distribution (see Chapter 15). The most elaborate data are based on local studies in rural areas and do not consider income sources such as women's work, which could raise the revenues of some low-income families by 20–30%. In addition, income inequalities would be higher if the aristocracy and privileged classes, preferably urban and not well represented in these calculations, were taken into account. In any case, diachronic analyses suggest that disparities increased (Álvarez & Prados de la Escosura, 2013: 9). But even so, we could only get a clear idea with larger samples and more convincing international comparisons. Therefore, it is necessary to point out that, despite the growth, urbanization rates were by the eighteenth century among the lowest in Europe, and the urban map left very wide regional gaps, especially in the peninsular interior and on the border between Portugal and Castile (Figures 17.1 and 17.2).

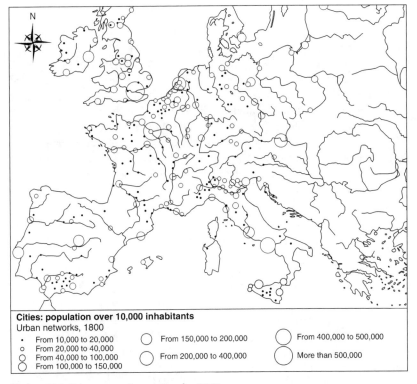

Figure 17.1 European urban networks, 1800.
Source: Redrawn based on a map published in Yun-Casalilla (2019).

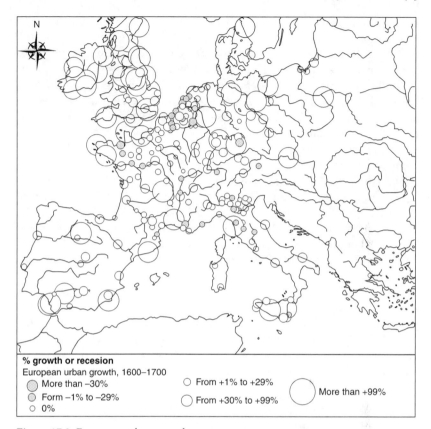

Figure 17.2 European urban growth.
Source: Redrawn based on a map published in Yun-Casalilla (2019).

Such gaps undoubtedly affected the formation of a more dynamic and more favourable internal market for peasant commercialization. Although Portuguese prices suggest a relative integration of the market, this fact is not so clear in Spain, at least until well into the century, which reflects the greater diversity of regional economies, the bigger extension of the country and the high interregional transport costs. In recent decades, attention has also been drawn to the fragmentation of the jurisdictional map and its effects on transaction costs and market integration (Yun-Casalilla, 2001; Grafe, 2012). And it should not be forgotten that the possibilities for the development of coastal areas to affect a wide hinterland were sometimes limited by geography and geopolitics. The Cantabrian Mountain range constrained the connections between the northern coasts, where trade and a bourgeoisie very active in relations with America developed, and the Castilian plateau. If we look at the most dynamic areas of Europe at the time, we will see that none – or few – had to face a problem of the same dimensions. At the same time, if some fluvial systems, such as the Tagus, made it possible to spread the positive effect of Lisbon upstream, the Spanish–Portuguese border created another obstacle to the exploitation of the Atlantic waterways from Castile: in addition to the streamflow difficulties that the navigation of the Douro, Tagus and Guadiana presented – which had not prevented small-scale navigation in the sixteenth century – there was also the fact that the political border impeded the outflow of Castile's production to the Atlantic. The construction of canals by the state aroused certain enthusiasm, but these never created a real web and did not cover the necessary distances until the end of the century or even the following one (Pérez Sarrión, 1975; Helguera et al., 1988).

It is in this context of difficulties that the reformist policy of the Marquis of Pombal (1699–1782) and of enlightened Spaniards such as Ensenada (1702–1781), Campomanes (1723–1802), Floridablanca (1829–1808) and others should be placed. Reformism manifested itself in Iberia in its maximum expression: in taxation, in trade, in the attempts to liberalize the grain market and to limit the negative effects of entitled property – at the end of the century the first disentailments would take place – and in the policy of industrial and technological promotion. Today it is even affirmed that this reformism was not a late phenomenon, but that it began already in the first decades of the century and that it had its precedent in initiatives taken in the previous century (Storrs, 2006; 2016). But there is still debate about its real effects and it is possible that these were very different depending on the cases, economic sectors and regions.

17.7 Global Conflicts and Crisis, 1778–1808: Portugal and Spain at the Door of Industrialization

As C. Bayly has said, by 1789 the world was witnessing a variety of industrious revolutions scattered in many areas, where family economies were increasingly dependent on the market and, consequently, on wider trade circuits (Bayly, 2004: 51–55). Perhaps the term industrious revolutions is excessive when applied to these vast territories, as it was not always accompanied by the development of solid urban networks. And perhaps one should speak of self-exploitation closer to the theories of Boserup and Chayanov in order to understand the differences that – among other factors – would explain the possibilities of each area in international competition. In any case, peasant pluriactivity increased and even – as would happen with the British in India – industrial competition between East and West would be resolved by mechanisms alien to the market and typical of coercion.

By the end of the eighteenth century, European empires had increased their territorial component, which heralded the imperialism of the nineteenth century, and the model of coastal occupation and commercial relations with local societies was coming to an end (Ringrose, 2018). The Iberian case is very clear. By 1778, the frontiers had been expanded and consolidated through Brazil, the Chaco (present-day Paraguay and northern Argentina) and Argentina, while present-day Florida, Louisiana and California had been occupied. Evidence of the importance of this territorial expansion is the way in which these latter domains formed part of the give and take of the peace treaties of the time. Portuguese expansion into the interior of Brazil had continued until at least 1750. Russia had added extensive domains in Manchuria to the routes that served for the provisioning of furs. China had extended into the continental interior and Tibet, reaching the greatest extent in its history. The British had used the platform provided by their control of Mughal India to spread throughout the Ganges Valley and along the east coast of the subcontinent. Only Africa seems to have resisted this process, and even the penetration by the Portuguese into Mozambique was still weak (Magalhães, 2005). All this only increased the tensions between these empires as it also gave an amphibious character to the conflicts, which expanded the military costs and strained the military-fiscal state in these countries.

This high degree of tension rose as a result of the French Revolution and the subsequent wars. The revolutionary cycle that was about to explode after 1778 was to a large extent a consequence of this conflict. As is well known, in the French case the trigger was the attempts to reform the fiscal financial system because of the stress caused by the Atlantic wars. Subsequent wars and the Napoleonic blockades – also very expressive of economic competition, especially in Europe – would further accentuate the pressure to which the economies of the different countries were exposed. The era of revolutions, which many regions of the planet would know, would have in this global context one of its most important reasons (Bayly, 2004: 88–100).

The Iberian empires would not be the exception, but, on the contrary, a privileged scenario of these processes. Today many historians tend to think that the changes that would take place in them had more to do with these convulsions in wider contexts than with endogenous transformations, and that their models of economic, social and political development had not exhausted their chances of survival in 1808 (Paquette, 2013). What is certain is that the imperial alliances were shaken. In the second half of the eighteenth century, peninsular Spain's demands regarding the income of the American treasury had become greater and the proportion of silver sent to the peninsula was progressively swinging in favour of the latter, thus breaking an essential piece of the pact between the metropolis and the colonial elites.

In the last decades of the century, the system of so-called *donativos* that maintained the alliance with the American elites was becoming strained (Marichal, 1999; 2007) and these, together with the demands due to the war, became a source of resistance and friction. On the peninsula itself, the dismantling of some of the institutions on which the state edifice was built began. The governments in Madrid were forced to adopt a policy with respect to the recently founded Banco de San Carlos that led to the depreciation of the securities it issued – the *vales reales* (Tedde, 1988). Also the first disentailment process materialized in the sale of properties that had belonged to confraternities and pious institutions. In any case, all these measures did not prevent the breakdown of the fiscal system (Fontana, 2002). The situation in Portugal was not very different. From the 1760s the decreasing amounts of gold arriving from Brazil led to some reforms but the financial crisis had also a strong impact in the public revenue and monetary circulation (Ferreira da Silva, 2005: 257–260). In 1796 reforms were carried out that attacked the immunity of the church and the clergy, *juros* were issued at higher than usual interest rates and could be used as fiduciary currency, and reforms were even planned that imitated the English financial revolution with the particularity that, instead of parliament, a syndicate of large creditors would control the public debt (Cardoso, 1989). The search for impossible models from the point of view of the structure of the state is but a symptom of how the political systems were in trouble.

Between 1500 and 1800 a gap had opened up in relation to the growth of other European countries, which we can understand as the 'Small Divergence'. But the Spanish and Portuguese economies had also evolved differently in the second half of the eighteenth century. In Portugal, expansion seems to have stopped around the 1760s and remained on a plateau with a downward slope until the fall of the last decade. Spain experienced a more continuous expansion that would last throughout the eighteenth century (see Chapter 10). Within the doubts that these variables might offer, what is certain is that the two countries were establishing some of the bases that explain their status as latecomers to the Industrial Revolution.

In both cases, the last years of the century had witnessed the development of the industrial sector. In both cases, too, colonial demand was a positive lever for some manufacturing (Pedreira, 1994). Moreover, the protectionist policy of the state in Portugal and the free trade decrees in Spain, although still leaving much to be desired, increased the opportunities for national industries (García-Baquero, 1992; Pedreira, 1998). Even the wars, followed by the re-establishment of traffic, created opportunities for some sectors, such as the Catalan cotton printing industries (Thomson, 1992). But both countries were very active in the re-export of manufactured commodities from other European regions, which competed with their own and limited the positive effect of the mentioned measures (Costa, 2005; Delgado Rivas, 2007).

Therefore, the key to understanding these moments of pre-industrialization and its characteristics and rhythms lies in the domestic markets of both countries. Domestic demand developed largely due to the impact of external forces related to the spread of new ways of life, the arrival of new products such as cocoa and others, which affected forms of sociability and had collateral effects on other sectors (Fattacciu, 2021), the expansion of cities, where a new middle class showed a greater propensity to consume these products, and the rise of new forms of commercialization (García & Yun-Casalilla 1997; Cruz 1996; 2011; Moreno, 2007; Muñoz, 2018). In both countries, the consumer revolution would be slower and later than in countries such as England or France, but it was a fact, particularly in some regions. There were also processes of specialization such as those occurring in the linen sector in Galicia or the Minho region as well as in the wool sector of Beira or in the creation of proto-industrial districts around Catalan settlements such as those of Igualada (Pedreira, 1994; Torras, 2007). In both, the development of what would be the revolutionary sector of industrialization, that is, the cotton printing industry would begin, was central and there would even be initiatives of import substitution of English textiles during the years of economic blockade and war.

It is also in this area of domestic demand that one must look for the constraints to the industrial development that was beginning. In fact, the reasons for the slow pace of industrialization – not its failure, as was believed some time ago (Nadal, 1975) – should be sought in the lower rates of urbanization in comparison with other European countries and in the limits to the expansion of the domestic market, largely derived from agricultural growth models and income distribution. Thus, the industrious revolutions taking place on the Iberian Peninsula would also lead to industrial revolutions in the nineteenth century, unlike in many other areas of the planet. But, at the same time, and in comparison with its European competitors, this process would take place in the form of latecomers, or slow cumulative processes.

17.8 Conclusion

Historians have tried to measure the impact of empires on Iberian economies and have even reached a positive conclusion in the case of Portugal (Costa et al., 2015). It is possible, however, to think that these empires contributed to consolidate political and institutional arrangements that limited structural changes and thus underpinned the survival of institutions that, although favouring economic growth, had limitations when it came to creating economies capable of competing with the surrounding countries. Unfortunately it is very difficult – not to say impossible – to imagine a counterfactual scenario in which the two countries would not have had empires. During the early modern era economic expansion is evident and the negative views and sense of pessimistic exceptionalism of people like Movillers that has permeated much of the twentieth-century historiography is not tenable. But Iberian countries had lost ground to the growth of countries like France, Germany or England. The processes of property accumulation typical of the *Ancien Régime* had reached their maximum expression in many areas and, with it, income differences that profoundly affected the demand and the market for industrial products. The cutting edge of scientific and technological development had shifted from Southern to Northern Europe. At the same time, most of the agricultural innovations that would increase the productivity of the land to the point of favouring intensive growth were based on forms of crop rotation that presupposed richness of water, only present in some areas of the peninsula (González de Molina, 2001). Gone were the days when abundance of land and rural communities' regulations had been the key to European growth. Iberia would thus remain in relative backwardness for several decades, although in both countries the definitive crisis of the institutions that had been underpinned by the empires would create the appropriate framework for the establishment of capitalist forms of intensive growth. Regarding the next historiographical steps, it is maybe good to remember that 'a procura das causas do atraso é un exercício essencial na análise de economías como era a portuguesa do século XIX, mas esa procura nao pode obscurecer a análise do crescimento'[68] (Lains, 2005). These words – I believe – are equally valid for the early modern age and for Spain.

---

[68] 'The search for the causes of backwardness is an essential exercise in the analysis of economies such as the Portuguese economy of the nineteenth century, but this search cannot obscure the analysis of growth.'

PART III

Industrialization and Catching Up, 1800–2000

Edited by Alfonso Herranz-Loncán and Vicente Pinilla

18

Economic Growth and the Spatial Distribution of Income, 1800–2000

ALFONSO HERRANZ-LONCÁN, M. TERESA SANCHIS-LLOPIS
AND DANIEL A. TIRADO-FABREGAT

18.1 Introduction

This chapter surveys the economic growth experience of Spain and Portugal since the early nineteenth century. It starts by providing a periodization of both countries' economic growth from a comparative perspective. The text shows that Iberian long-term economic growth had a significant break point c. 1950. After more than a century dominated (except for some short episodes) by sluggish growth and divergence from Western Europe, there was a substantial acceleration in GDP and per capita GDP growth rates of both Iberian economies. This allowed Spain and Portugal to converge with the core countries and recover and even surpass their initial relative starting point. Growth, however, slowed down after 1974 and, as a consequence, convergence became slower until it ended in the early twenty-first century. As a result, in the very long term, Iberia has been unable to close the initial gap with the Western European core.

Second, on the basis of recent historical estimates of regional GDP, we offer a description of the changes in the spatial distribution of income in the Iberian Peninsula over the long term. According to the available evidence, current Iberian regional inequality emerged after the first long wave of Iberian modern economic growth, which started in the central decades of the nineteenth century. While regions with abundant natural resources or high agricultural productivity were among the richest ones in the mid nineteenth century, over time only those areas that managed to industrialize were able to reach and remain at the top positions of the ranking. By 1950, the geographical patterns of regional inequality in Iberia were well established, and since then, they have just been consolidated.

Third, based on historical growth accounting evidence, we provide a detailed presentation on the sources of economic growth in order to decompose, as far as possible, the recent growth experience of Spain, Portugal and the whole of Iberia into accumulation of production factors and total factor productivity (TFP) growth. This allows observing to what extent the periods of modest economic growth and divergence can be explained by insufficient investment in human and physical resources or by low increases in productivity. In this respect, we show that, in the case of Spain, the early 1950s represent a divide between a hundred years of moderate growth dominated by factor accumulation, and half a century of fast growth led by TFP. By contrast, this intensive model of growth was not shared by Portugal, where GDP per capita increases so far have been mainly associated with factor accumulation, rather than with TFP increases.

18.2 The Iberian Growth Experience

The breakthrough to modern economic growth is characterized by a sustained increase in per capita income supported by the integration of markets and a strong incorporation of technological progress in production. This explains the impressive improvement in the standards of living in the most developed countries since the Industrial Revolution and through the last two centuries, which has been shared with some delay by Spain and Portugal. This section reviews the economic growth experience of Iberia since the early nineteenth century, with a focus on its long-term evolution, and in comparison to Western Europe.

The different stages of Iberian economic growth since 1800 can be identified based on the most recent per capita GDP estimates available for both countries. For Portugal, Pedro Lains (2006b) provided estimates since 1850, while the first half of the nineteenth century has been covered in recent research by Nuno Palma and Jaime Reis (2019). For Spain, Leandro Prados de la Escosura (2017) offers updated GDP estimates from 1850 onwards whereas figures for 1800–1850 have been estimated by the same author in a joint work with Carlos Álvarez-Nogal and Carlos Santiago-Caballero (Prados de la Escosura et al., 2022). Figure 18.1 presents the evolution of per capita GDP for both countries since 1800.

As may be observed in Figure 18.1, the stages of growth were rather different in Spain and Portugal from the early nineteenth century until 1950. In the case of Portugal, during most of the nineteenth century the economy stagnated. Such stagnation represented the continuation of a period of zero growth that started around 1750 and was followed by a fast decline in the last years of the eighteenth century. As described in Chapter 10, the decline of the Portuguese economy was largely associated with the exhaustion of the previously available engines of economic growth (such as the spread of new crops and the establishment of an overseas Empire) without their substitution by new sources. Stagnation would not end until 1880, when a process of moderate and rather unstable economic growth started, which coincided with slow institutional and infrastructure development, in a context of increasing international integration. However, growth did not last and the first two decades of the twentieth

Figure 18.1 Spanish and Portuguese GDP per capita, 1800–2018 (Geary–Khamis 'international' 1990 dollars).
Sources: for Spain until 1850, Prados de la Escosura et al. (2022) and from 1850 onwards, Prados de la Escosura (2017), available at: https://espacioinvestiga.org/bbdd-chne/. Figures for Portugal from 1800 to 1849 come from Palma and Reis (2019) and, for 1850–2010, from the Maddison Project database (2013 version), projected forward to 2018 based on the Maddison Project database (2018 version) and World Bank data (https://data.worldbank.org/).

century were, once more, characterized by negative growth rates. As a consequence, by 1920, Portuguese GDP per capita was only 33% higher than the average of 1800–1850.

By contrast, the Spanish economy undertook moderate growth since the beginning of the nineteenth century, which consolidated the previous growth trend of the eighteenth century (see Chapter 10), and a gradually increasing gap with Portugal opened up as a consequence, which contrasted with the Portuguese advantage in income per capita in earlier times. Although at relative low rates, Spanish GDP per capita kept on growing at least until 1883, with a clear acceleration from the 1840s, once the worst episodes of the conflict underlying liberal reforms were overcome. Economic growth, which was only temporarily interrupted by some deep but short-lived crises (such as those of 1856–1857 and, especially, 1868–1869), was fuelled by institutional change, infrastructure investment and increasing economic integration. In the early 1880s, however, the Spanish economy entered a new phase of stagnation associated with the late-nineteenth-century recession and the subsequent upsurge of protectionist policies in Europe and Spain. Growth only resumed, at moderate rates, at the end of the century.

During the interwar period, both countries experienced a rather intense and unprecedented growth episode in the 1920s, to suffer afterwards the (relatively mild) consequences of the Great Depression in the 1930s. Then, however, while Portugal gradually started a slow recovery, the Spanish economy collapsed due to the Civil War and the early Francoist policies and economic isolation.

As mentioned before, Portugal and Spain's long-term economic growth registered a significant break point *c.* 1950, involving a substantial increase in GDP per capita growth rates, which in 1950–1974 would be 11 (Portugal) and 7 (Spain) times as large as in the previous century and a half. This acceleration came to an end *c.* 1975, and growth rates would never go back to the previous levels. After that year both economies would alternate growth periods with crises, with the most serious of the latter being the Great Recession of the early twenty-first century, when economic growth became negative in both countries for several years, until recovery arrived in 2011 in Portugal and in 2013 in Spain.

The different stages of Portuguese and Spanish economic growth can also be identified in Figure 18.2, which depicts the evolution of the ratio between the GDP per capita of the Iberian economies and the average GDP per capita of a varying (according to the available evidence) sample of Western European countries. Starting from the 'little divergence' generated in the previous centuries (see Chapter 10), the picture shows that Iberia, despite the aforementioned episodes of moderate growth, did not stop losing ground with Western Europe until the late 1930s (in the case of Portugal) or the late 1940s (in the case of Spain). In Spain, divergence was only temporarily interrupted in the 1870s and the 1920s, but just to be resumed later on at a very intense pace.

Divergence was replaced from the late 1950s onwards by a period of fast convergence with the Western European economies. This was temporarily interrupted by the crisis of the 1970s, but was then resumed after the integration of the two states into the European Union in 1986. As a consequence, Portuguese and Spanish relative per capita incomes reached their absolute maximum in 2001 and 2003, respectively (66% of the Western European average in Portugal and 76% in Spain). However, the Great Recession, once more, affected more seriously the Iberian economies and, as a result, their relative levels of GDP per capita diverged again from Western Europe.

As a consequence of this long cycle of divergence and convergence, by 2018 Portuguese and Spanish GDP per capita amounted to 66% and 72% of the European average, respectively, percentages that were similar to or, in the case of Portugal, even lower than those of the 1830s. In other words, convergence during the second half of the twentieth century just allowed the loss that had been accumulated since the end of the Napoleonic Wars to be overcome. However, it has not been intense enough to close the initial gap between Iberia and Western Europe.

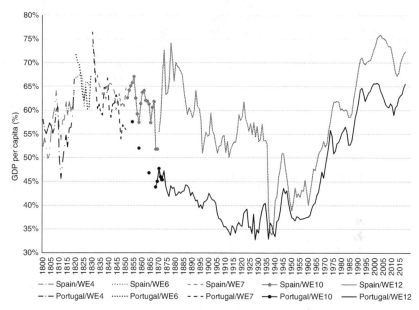

Figure 18.2 Portuguese and Spanish GDP per capita as a percentage of the average of Western European economies.
Sources: for Portugal and Spain, see Figure 18.1. For the Western European countries, the Maddison Project database (2013 version), projected forward to 2018 based on the Maddison Project database (2018 version) and World Bank data (https://data.worldbank.org/).
Notes: WE4 includes Italy, the Netherlands, Sweden and the UK; WE6 includes WE4 plus France and Denmark; WE7 includes WE6 plus Norway; WE10 includes WE7 plus Belgium, Germany and Switzerland; WE12 includes WE10 plus Finland and Austria. All figures for Western Europe are simple averages.

18.3 The Geography of Iberian Economic Growth

By comparing the evolution of the Spanish and Portuguese economies, the information presented in the previous section offers a first glimpse of the diversity of growth experiences within the Iberian space. This section enters into the detail of that diversity, presenting some evidence that allows the relative evolution of the different areas of the peninsula to be compared. The first salient feature is that the Spanish economy has always been much larger than the Portuguese one. Spain's participation in the Iberian GDP fluctuated between 76% and 86% from 1820 to 2018. In accordance with the different growth stages described in the previous section, Spain reached its highest participation in the Iberian economy between the mid nineteenth century and the late 1920s, when Portugal stagnated or grew at lower rates than Spain and the Spanish share fluctuated between 80% and 86% of Iberian GDP. Nevertheless, the Spanish economy sank in the late 1930s, and its relative weight declined to 76% in 1937–1938. It remained at that level until *c.* 1960, when it started a slow recovery, but without ever regaining its former participation.

Things become much more complex when the comparison is carried out in GDP per capita terms. During the first half of the nineteenth century, Portuguese and Spanish GDP per capita were very similar. On average, the Spanish GDP per capita was just 4% higher than the Portuguese one. Then, the combination of Spanish moderate growth and Portuguese stagnation opened up a huge distance between both economies, and by 1880 Spain's GDP per capita was 66% higher than Portugal's. Portugal closed part of that gap during the Spanish depression of the last two decades of the nineteenth century, and by 1900 the Spanish advantage had been reduced to 29% as a result. The Portuguese slowdown of the early twentieth century and the Spanish recovery, especially during the 1920s, opened up a new gap between both economies, which amounted again to 66% in 1928.

The situation, however, changed dramatically in the late 1930s. The Spanish economy collapsed during the Civil War of 1936–1939, at the end of which Spain's GDP per capita was only 3% higher than Portugal's. The distance between both countries increased again after the war, but has remained on average at 13% between 1940 and the present. As a consequence, the current distance in GDP per capita levels between both countries is significantly lower than in 1880 or 1928.

The existence of substantial differences and cycles of divergence and convergence in terms of GDP per capita between both countries constitutes preliminary evidence of the geographical dimension of the process of economic development, which not only increases income levels generally, but also provokes the emergence of significant differences between territories. This points to the importance of analysing whether economic growth has followed a differentiated regional pattern both in Iberia and in each of its individual economies.

From a theoretical perspective, regional income differences could be the consequence of two main mechanisms. First, throughout the process of economic growth and domestic market integration, some regions may specialize in high-productivity sectors. Second, some regions can have a better performance than the average in all industries. So, aggregate labour productivity can differ as a result of regional specialization but, beyond the effects of differences in economic structure, there might still be variations in regional aggregate productivity due to differences in regional productivity within each sector. In this regard, labour productivity can be higher in some regions due to differences in the relative endowment of cumulative factors like human and physical capital. Additionally, the agglomeration economies associated with certain production processes mean that labour productivity can be higher in regions with higher volumes of production of these types of goods. However, spatial differences in factor endowments or agglomeration economies only give way to increasing geographical inequality if the degree of market integration is high enough to allow regional specialization.

Thus, one of the main forces of regional economic differentiation is market integration. In the case of Portugal, domestic market integration advanced relatively slowly, compared with other Western European economies (see e.g. Justino, 1989). In fact, only the improvement of the transport networks during the last third of the nineteenth century and, especially, the expansion of the railway network, allowed the reduction of transport costs between the main urban areas (Porto and Lisbon) and the rural inner and southern regions. This was accompanied by the expansion of secondary transport networks within each region during the first decades of the twentieth century. However, the construction and the improvement of roads in Portugal was clearly delayed by European standards. Although the first highways were built just before the Second World War and the roads between major cities were finished during the 1950s and 1960s, the complete expansion of the modern road network would not happen until the 1980s.

As for the integration of the Portuguese economy into the international markets, after the liberal period extending from the mid nineteenth century to the 1880s, Portuguese trade policy was characterized by a high degree of protection of domestic industrial and agrarian production. This shift had its roots in the crisis of the late nineteenth century and was reinforced by the 1886 tariff. From then until the timid attempt at trade liberalization initiated at the end of the 1950s, the ruling feature of Portuguese trade policy was the high protection of domestic production. However, from the early 1960s, the country started a process of gradual economic liberalization. Thus, Portugal was a founding member of EFTA in 1960, signed a preferential treaty with the EEC in 1972 and finally joined the EEC in 1986.

In the Spanish case, domestic market integration received a strong push in the mid nineteenth century. Before the 1840s, the presence of barriers to interregional trade and capital and labour flows were ubiquitous: local tariffs and regulations on domestic commerce were widespread; weights and measures differed across regions; transport costs were very high due to low public investment in transport infrastructure and the particular geography of Spain, which lacked an extensive water transport system; economic information moved slowly across regions; the banking system was underdeveloped; and many regions had their own currencies (although all currencies were based on a bimetallic monetary system). Both market liberalization and transport improvements, particularly the construction of Spain's road and railway networks, induced the creation of a national market for the most important commodities from the 1840s, and domestic market integration progressed steadily until the Spanish Civil War. The war and the first years of Franco's regime put a brake on both Spanish economic growth and domestic integration. The regulation of markets for goods and factors of production and government control of prices and quantities in final and intermediate goods, energy, capital markets and wages reduced the mobility of factors and resources. From the end of the 1950s, new investments in infrastructure, such as roads, railways, communication networks and energy supply and distribution, led to further reductions in domestic transport costs. During the last 15 years of the twentieth century a new wave of investment in infrastructure helped to further reduce transport costs across Spanish regions through the implementation of huge investment programs in motorways, high-speed railways and telecommunications.

The work by Tirado-Fabregat and Badia-Miró (2014) allows a closer study of the evolution of regional inequality in Iberia from 1900 to 2000 and the analysis of its relationship with this long-term pattern of reduction of domestic transport costs. That research offers a description of regional economic inequality in Spain and Portugal in the long term, based on recent historical estimates of regional GDP at the level of the Portuguese historical districts and Spanish provinces. A summary of their results is provided in Figure 18.3, which shows the evolution of income inequality among the Iberian regions through the twentieth century.

Figure 18.3 indicates that, during the early twentieth century, Portuguese and Spanish economic growth was accompanied by increasing regional income inequality. By contrast, regional disparities started to decrease from the 1920s. According to this data, Iberian regional income inequality followed an inverted U-shaped pattern during the twentieth century, with a substantial growth in inequality before 1920, followed by a long phase of declining regional disparities that lasted until the end of the century.[69]

The Iberian experience also shows the existence of clear geographical patterns in the spatial distribution of regional GDP per capita levels. Figures 18.4–18.6 provide a first approach to those patterns. The grayscale used in the maps represents per capita income levels relative to the average of the whole region, with the darkest tones corresponding to those regions in the first quartile of the regional distribution, while the white regions are those in the bottom quartile of the distribution.[70]

Figure 18.4 indicates the absence of a well-defined geography of relative wealth and poverty in 1900. Poor and rich regions were spread everywhere,

---

[69] A detailed description of the long-term regional inequality patterns in Portugal can be found in Badia-Miró et al. (2012). For the Spanish case, see Díez-Minguela et al. (2018).
[70] Quartiles were obtained by considering the whole sample.

Figure 18.3 Regional inequality in Iberia, 1900–2000 (Williamson index).
Source: Tirado-Fabregat and Badia-Miró (2014).

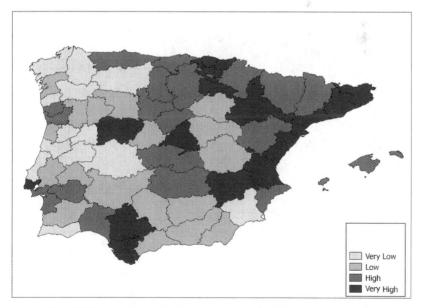

Figure 18.4 GDP per capita in the Iberian regions, 1900 (quartiles).
Source: redrawn based on a map originally published in Tirado-Fabregat and Badia-Miró (2014).

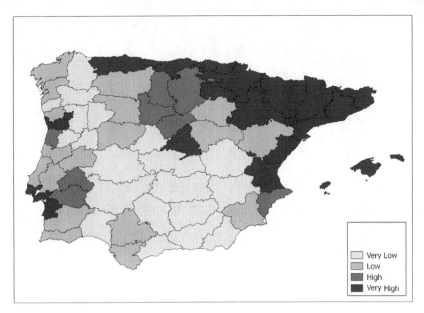

Figure 18.5 GDP per capita in the Iberian regions, 1960 (quartiles).
Source: redrawn based on a map originally published in Tirado-Fabregat and Badia-Miró (2014).

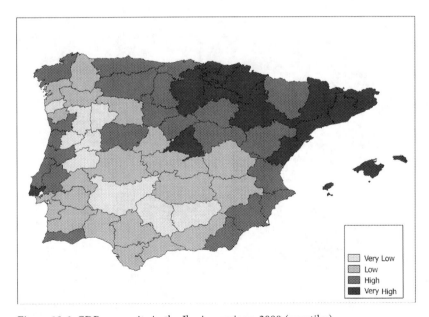

Figure 18.6 GDP per capita in the Iberian regions, 2000 (quartiles).
Note: Different grey intensities indicate the GDP per capita distribution of Spanish provinces and Portuguese districts by quartiles (darker grey represents higher GDP per capita).
Source: redrawn based on a map originally published in Tirado-Fabregat and Badia-Miró (2014).

being present both in coastal and interior areas and also scattered between the north and the south. Nevertheless, this picture gradually changed during the twentieth century, with a very distinct pattern of regional economic inequality arising in the middle of the century (Figure 18.5). By 1960 it was possible to observe the emergence of clusters of rich and poor regions. Moreover, regional income levels were not randomly distributed across the territory. Instead, rich and poor clusters had specific locations, which tended to consolidate over time. During the second half of the twentieth century, regions in the north-east quadrant of the peninsula and in the coastal regions exhibited higher per capita income levels than those located in inland areas, especially in the south of the peninsula and on both sides of the border between Spain and Portugal. The formation of this group has its roots in the first half of the twentieth century, and seems to have been consolidated over time, in parallel to the process of integration of Iberia into the European economy.

To sum up, during the twentieth century, and in parallel to domestic market integration, the initial increase in Iberian regional inequality was followed by a long (although never completed) process of regional convergence. At the same time, a distinct geographical pattern of regional inequality gradually emerged, with the poorest regions clustering in the south and on both sides of the border between Spain and Portugal, and the richest regions concentrating along the coasts, especially in the north-east corner of the peninsula. The available data show that this geographical structure was well established in the middle of the twentieth century, before opening up to the international economy. In this respect, the accession of both countries into the EEC in 1986 seems to have just consolidated this geographical distribution (Figure 18.6). Thus, the most recently available evidence clearly shows that each region's level of income has been closely associated with its location, and that the poorest districts and provinces have tended to concentrate in a large region crossing the border between both countries.

18.4 The Proximate Causes of Economic Growth: Growth Accounting in the Iberian Economies

The historical experience of the more advanced economies describes a pattern of economic growth based on intense capital deepening in the early stages of modern economic growth and on TFP growth thereafter (Collins & Bosworth, 1996). For instance, the US economy moved from an extensive growth process based on the exploitation of abundant natural resources and tangible capital in the nineteenth century, to a model of growth largely dependent upon investment in intangible capital in the twentieth century (Abramovitz & David, 2001). In this section, we aim at analysing to what extent the Iberian economies adapted to these different stages, using the available evidence for Spain and Portugal to provide comparable growth accounting exercises for both countries and for the whole of Iberia. Our estimates allow identifying the relative contribution of productive factors (capital, labour and human capital) and overall productivity to GDP increases across the different phases of modern economic growth.

Generally speaking, the long-term analysis of the Iberian case hardly adapts to the stylized facts observed by Collins and Bosworth (1996). The main reason is the opposite patterns observed in each country. While the long-term analysis for Spain would tend to follow the general model, Portugal's economic growth has been mainly based on factor accumulation, with just a very small contribution of productivity growth (see Table 18.1 below). On the other hand, given that Spain has represented more than three quarters of the Iberian GDP during the period, the Spanish experience clearly dominates the estimates for the whole of Iberia.

18.4.1 The Growth Accounting Approach

The growth accounting approach offers a structured framework for assessing the role of various factors in the economic growth process. It distributes output growth between the contributions of increases in the quantity of factor inputs and changes in the efficiency with which they are used. This methodology is based on the neoclassical model of Solow (1957), whose starting point is the standard Cobb–Douglas production function:

$$Y = F(K, L) = AK^{\alpha}L^{\beta}, \qquad (18.1)$$

where Y, K and L represent total output, capital and labour, respectively; A is the state of technology; and α and β represent the elasticity of output with respect to capital and labour. After differentiating and taking logarithms, Eq. (18.1) can be expressed as:

$$\frac{\Delta A}{A} = \frac{\Delta Y}{Y} - \alpha\left(\frac{\Delta K}{K}\right) - \beta\left(\frac{\Delta L}{L}\right). \qquad (18.2)$$

Under the assumption of perfect competition and constant returns to scale, α and β will sum to unity and could be proxied by the share of each factor returns in total income. This way, Eq. (18.2) allows calculating the contributions of capital and labour inputs to output growth and also obtaining, as a residual, the growth in total factor productivity ($\Delta A/A$, thereafter TFP), which represents a combination of changes in efficiency in the use of inputs, improvements in the quality of inputs and technological change. Although the assumptions underlying this exercise must be taken with caution, it provides a preliminary estimation of the contribution of factors and technology to output growth.[71]

The growth accounting analysis has been profusely applied to the growth experience of the two Iberian countries, not only from a long-term perspective, but also for short time spans.[72] The available long-term study for Portugal focuses on the years 1910–1990 and was carried out by Lains (2003a), while for Spain Prados de la Escosura and Rosés (2009, 2020) provided a long-term analysis for 1850–2000 and 1850–2019. In Portugal, the lack of data on capital investment before the Great War confined the starting year to 1910. As a consequence, in our analysis for Iberia we can only analyse the period after 1910. On the other hand, these two studies apply different versions of the growth accounting approach. Since the analysis for Spain is much more demanding empirically and requires data that are not available for Portugal, for the sake of comparability we have applied to both countries the standard growth accounting approach and periodization followed by Lains (2003a) for Portugal,[73] but using the data provided by Prados de la Escosura and Rosés (2010a) for hours worked and human capital, Prados de la Escosura (2020a) for capital stock and Prados de la Escosura (2017) for real GDP.[74] Moreover, in order to arrive to the present, the study has been complemented with data on

---

[71] The basic papers on growth accounting are Solow (1957), Kendrick (1961), Denison (1962) and Jorgenson and Griliches (1967), while a critical look is offered by Barro (1999). For a suggestive growth accounting exercise and discussion about the relative role of factor inputs accumulation and productivity growth in explaining the impressive performance of the East Asian countries see Collins and Bosworth (1996). Similarly, Abramovitz and David (2001) made use of this methodology to explain two centuries of US economic growth.

[72] For a long-term perspective, see Lains (2003a) for Portugal and Prados de la Escosura and Rosés (2009, 2020) for Spain. Additionally, other studies for both countries tackled this issue over shorter periods in the official National Accounts statistics era. See, for instance, for Spain, Myro (1983), Suárez (1992), Cebrián (2001) and, from a comparative perspective with other countries, Timmer et al. (2003), Mas and Quesada (2006) and van Ark et al. (2003, 2009). For Portugal, see Mateus (1995), Almeida and Félix (2006), Amador and Coimbra (2007), Amaral (2010a) and Gomes da Silva (2011), among others.

[73] While Lains (2003a) uses the classical Solow approach presented in Eq. (18.2), Prados de la Escosura and Rosés (2009) apply the extended version suggested by Jorgenson (1990). There are remarkable differences between both exercises in terms of the number of factors, the factor weights (α and β) and the input measurement (K, L).

[74] Lains (2003b) uses a standard measure of human capital, the average years of schooling of active population, whereas Prados de la Escosura and Rosés (2010a) compute a measure of 'labour quality' made up of different categories of workers weighted by their average nominal earnings. In order to use the same human capital variable for both countries, for Spain here we use a measure of human capital based on education data, which are provided by Prados de la Escosura and Rosés (2010a) following Mincer's (1958) parametric approach. Notwithstanding, Prados de la Escosura and Rosés (2010a) demonstrate that for Spain the 'labour quality' variable based on income gives similar results to 'human capital' based on education but obtained parametrically.

GDP, hours worked, and physical and human capital extracted from the Penn World Table 9.1 for 1990–2017.[75]

The results of our growth accounting exercise are summarized in Tables 18.1 and 18.2. We have applied the customary income shares of 1/3 for each factor (capital stock, labour and human capital) in the two countries to obtain the residual factor. The available evidence for Spain, however, reveals that income shares have not remained stable across time (Prados de la Escosura & Rosés, 2009, 2020). More concretely, Spanish capital share increased from the mid nineteenth century up to the First World War, and it was not until the interwar period that income distribution moved into a trend more favourable to labour. Such pattern of income distribution is similar to that observed in other advanced countries through the process of modern economic growth, although the turning point in favour of labour income started in Spain some decades later than, for instance, the UK or France, where it took place in the 1880s and 1890s, respectively. Thereafter, between 1920 and 1936 the Spanish labour share soared from 50% to 70%, which was consistent with the decrease in inequality that took place at the time (see Chapter 23). After the setback represented by the Civil War (1936–1939) and the autarkic years (1939–1955), labour revenues have increased their share of total income steadily since the mid 1950s. On average, taking the whole period together, the Spanish evidence gives some support to the conventional weights of 1/3 for capital and 2/3 for labour observed in other countries and used in the present study. Since the 1980s, the trend of income distribution has moved again to favour capital, as in other European countries (Piketty, 2014).

18.4.2 The Growth of Factors of Production

Before focusing on the contributions of production factors to GDP growth, Table 18.1 summarizes how each factor has evolved across time. During the period 1910–2017, Iberian capital stock grew at an annual rate of 3.78%, a weighted average of the Portuguese (3.97%) and Spanish (3.69%) rates. On average, as happened with GDP growth, capital accumulation rates were much higher during the second half of the twentieth century than during the first half. Before 1910, the absence of capital stock data for Portugal prevents analysing the growth of the whole Iberian capital stock. However, the available evidence for Spain provides a partial (and arguably upward biased, given the differences in growth rates) picture of Iberian capital accumulation.[76]

---

[75] The corresponding data for growth accounting provided by the Penn World Table 9.1 were constructed by Feenstra et al. (2015).
[76] Prados de la Escosura (2010b, 2020) provide detailed information on the construction of the long-term series of capital in Spain from 1850 to the present and its evolution.

Table 18.1 *Iberian growth accounting: annual average growth rates.*

	Portugal				
	Capital stock	Labour quantity	Human capital	TFP	GDP
1910–1934	1.25	1.00	2.08	0.73	2.17
1934–1947	3.89	1.31	1.14	−0.02	2.09
1947–1973	7.73	0.70	2.47	1.54	5.17
1973–1990	5.21	0.05	4.83	0.56	3.93
1990–2017	2.04	0.08	0.91	0.09	1.10
1910–2017	3.97	0.58	2.20	0.65	2.90

	Spain				
	Capital stock	Labour quantity	Human capital	TFP	GDP
1850–1884	2.21	0.50	0.20	0.77	1.74
1884–1910	1.93	0.20	0.10	0.12	0.86
1910–1934	2.34	0.93	1.23	0.71	2.21
1934–1947	0.77	0.40	0.80	−0.76	−0.10
1947–1973	5.45	0.60	1.21	3.39	5.81
1973–1990	5.05	−3.35	1.28	2.64	3.63
1990–2017	3.78	1.02	0.71	0.30	2.14
1910–2017	3.69	0.13	1.05	1.37	3.00

	Iberia				
	Capital stock	Labour quantity	Human capital	TFP	GDP
1910–1934	1.95	0.95	1.54	0.71	2.19
1934–1947	1.97	0.75	0.93	−0.47	0.74
1947–1973	6.22	0.63	1.63	2.77	5.60
1973–1990	5.11	−2.01	2.68	1.82	3.75
1990–2017	3.09	0.96	0.80	0.14	1.75
1910–2017	3.78	0.38	1.48	1.08	2.96

Sources and notes: for Portugal, data come from Lains (2003a): 376, table 4; for Spain, capital stock from Prados de la Escosura (2020a), labour quantity and human capital from Prados de la Escosura and Rosés (2010a), and real GDP from Prados de la Escosura (2017, updated in 2019). For comparative purposes, data for Spain follow the same periodization as Lains (2003a) uses for Portugal. Iberian average rates are computed by weighting each country by its share in total Iberian GDP, which has been calculated from the Maddison Project 2018 database. We use 1910 weights for 1910–1934; 1934 weights for 1934–1947; 1947 weights for 1947–1973; and 1973 weights for 1973–1990. For 1990–2017 data on hours worked, capital stock and human capital have been taken from the Penn World Table 9.1 (Feenstra et al., 2015).

Thus, from 1850 to the early 1880s, there was a first period of intense capital accumulation, when capital grew at a yearly 2.21%, driven by investment in railway construction and mining. This boom coincided with a period of liberal policies favourable to trade openness and foreign capital inflows. In fact, the attraction of foreign capital was crucial for funding railway construction. Additionally, the abundance of some natural resources, highly demanded by the new industrial technologies, attracted the interest of European investors and companies towards Spanish mining. But this phase of prosperity and economic integration was partly interrupted between 1884 and the First World War. Then capital stock growth slowed down to a yearly 1.93%, seriously affected by the late-nineteenth-century recession and the subsequent upsurge of protectionist policies in Europe and Spain.

Between 1910 and 1934, the average growth rate of Iberian capital was 1.95%. This figure masks notable differences in the pace of capital accumulation between Spain and Portugal. While in Spain capital grew at 2.34%, improving its late-nineteenth-century record, Portugal exhibited a very low rate of 1.25%. In Spain, the highest accumulation rates were reached in the 1920s. The Primo de Rivera dictatorship (1923–1929) was a period of intense economic growth and capital grew at a yearly rate of 3.5%. During those years, high public infrastructure investment encouraged private investment in transport equipment, while substantial inflows of external capital allowed the acquisition of foreign capital goods (Tena-Jungito, 1999). Foreign investment gave impetus to the development of the electricity network and to the renewal of equipment with advanced technologies (Betrán, 2005). This expansion, though, was interrupted by the Civil War and its aftermath in the 1940s, when investment languished and reached the lowest historical record of 1850–2000.

Portuguese investment in equipment and infrastructures grew much more slowly than in Spain from 1910 to 1934 (1.25%). In fact, the increasing gap in GDP per capita between the two countries may be largely explained by the low dynamism of capital accumulation in Portugal during the interwar period. The situation was partly overcome by Portugal in 1934–1947 thanks to a much higher capital growth rate (3.89%), reached while investment in Spain was collapsing as a consequence of the Civil War and the autarchic economic policies and, consequently, the capital stock grew at 0.77%.

During the second half of the twentieth century capital growth rates in Iberia were twice as high as in the first half. More specifically, since the mid-1950s Iberia tended to follow Western European trends. Thus, there was an expansionary investment period during the Golden Age, followed by a drop in capital growth rates since the oil shock and the subsequent crisis. Finally, there was a new expansionary period after the entry in the ECC in 1986, that lasted until the 2008 financial crisis. The Golden Age represents the fastest phase of capital accumulation in Iberia, with a maximum yearly growth rate of

6.22%. Both Spain and Portugal stood at the top positions in terms of capital accumulation among the industrial countries, with rates of 5.45% for Spain and 7.73% for Portugal, which were only lower than the Japanese and Greek ones.[77] Private companies' investment in more sophisticated capital goods required increases in complementary capital, such as infrastructure and labour skills, in order to make a more efficient use of the new equipment.

After 1973 capital growth declined, although it remained higher than before the Second World War. The Iberian economies were shaken not only by the oil crisis but also by the political and institutional instability derived from the change from dictatorship regimes to democracy. In 1986, when political stability had been restored in both countries, the entry in the European Economic Community offered additional incentives to invest in infrastructure and private productive capital, in order to confront the higher exposure to international competition. The integration in the EEC also attracted foreign private investors towards the Iberian markets of goods and factors. Additionally, the inflow of EEC structural funds invigorated public investment in transport infrastructure and equipment. The consolidation of the new democracies brought also the expansion of the Welfare State and, consequently, the expansion of public investment in buildings and equipment to provide public education and health services.

Moving to the evolution of labour, Table 18.1 shows that Iberian economic growth has not been associated with high job creation in the long term. The total hours worked has increased moderately, at rates far below those experienced by capital and output. Interestingly, low job creation went hand in hand with a contraction in the hours worked by employees, as a consequence of the gradual adoption of the 8-hour working day, especially during the second half of the twentieth century. Labour reallocation from agriculture towards industry and services, as well as the parallel urbanization process, are among the main factors explaining this reduction. On average, labour quantity grew at a yearly rate of 0.38% between 1910 and 2017. The most intense phase of employment creation was the interwar period, with an average annual rate of 0.95%. During the Golden Age, despite the high rates of output growth, the pace of job creation decreased considerably due to the generalization of labour-saving technologies. Hence, employment growth rates halved in comparison to previous expansionary periods. For instance, in Spain employment grew at a yearly 0.93% in the 1920s but just at 0.6% in 1947–1973. In Portugal, annual labour growth rates were 1.31% in 1934–1947 but declined to 0.70% in 1947–1973. The crisis of the 1970s provoked a dramatic process of employment destruction in Spain, with an average contraction of –3.35% per year in 1973–1990, and a negligible increase in Portugal of 0.05% per year in 1973–1990. Employment destruction in Iberia has been the natural adjustment

---

[77] See Bosworth et al. (1995), table 6.

mechanism in times of economic crisis. Again, during the last financial crisis the hours worked were reduced at an annual average rate of –0.33 % in 2008–2017 in Iberia, which corresponds to –0.41 % for Spain and –0.27 % for Portugal.

The contribution of workers to GDP growth depends not only on the quantity of hours worked but also on their skills. A broad definition of human capital refers to any kind of investment that improves human skills, including formal education provided by schools and informal education received at home or acquired by job experience. There are two main ways to account for human capital: the first is based on formal education measures or indirect education indicators, such as literacy or numeracy rates; and the second relies on labour incomes and skill premia. Measuring human capital as years of education tends to underestimate it during the first stages of development, when investment in education is still low and skills are mainly acquired at the workplace.

Human capital for Portugal is measured as the average years of schooling of active population taken from Lains (2003a). Figures for Spain are from Prados de la Escosura and Roses (2010a)'s parametric estimates of human capital based on education for 1850–1950, while data for 1950–2017 are the education attainment levels, obtained from Barro and Lee (2013, updated in 2018).[78] Whichever the approach followed, human capital in Iberia progressed more slowly prior to 1950 than thereafter. The prosperity of the interwar period was accompanied by a significant effort in human capital formation, similar to what happened during the Golden Age. But the interruption of the previous growth episode due to the Great Depression and the wars left also a footprint in terms of schooling years lost for the whole Iberian population.

Later on, investment in education has increased in line with per capita income. Hence, human capital has soared since the 1950s, and especially since the 1980s, when the new democratic regimes devoted more resources to public education, made high school education compulsory up to the age of 16 and made university access more affordable to people with lower incomes. Since then up to the present day, Iberian countries have closed part of the gap in years of schooling with the most advanced economies, according to Barro and Lee's (2013) database.

18.4.3 The Contribution of TFP and Production Factors to Output Growth

The contributions of production factors to output growth are displayed in Table 18.2. Over the entire period 1910–2017, Iberian GDP growth was the joint result of the almost equal contributions of capital stock growth (42.6%) and TFP growth (36.5%), complemented by the use of more qualified workers

---

[78] See www.barrolee.com for the update.

Table 18.2 *Contribution of factors and TFP to GDP growth (%).*

	Portugal				
	Capital stock	Labour quantity	Human capital	TFP	GDP
1910–1934	19.2	15.4	32.0	33.5	100
1934–1947	62.0	20.9	18.2	−1.1	100
1947–1973	49.8	4.50	15.9	29.7	100
1973–1990	44.3	0.4	41.1	14.2	100
1990–2017	61.6	2.39	27.5	8.4	100
1910–2017	45.7	6.7	25.3	22.3	100
	Spain				
	Capital stock	Labour quantity	Human capital	TFP	GDP
1850–1884	42.3	9.6	3.8	44.3	100
1884–1910	74.8	7.7	3.9	13.6	100
1910–1934	35.4	14.0	18.6	32.0	100
1934–1947	−251.4	−130.9	−261.9	744.2	100
1947–1973	31.3	3.4	6.9	58.4	100
1973–1990	46.3	−30.7	11.7	72.7	100
1990–2017	58.9	15.9	11.1	14.2	100
1910–2017	41.0	1.4	11.7	45.9	100
	Iberia				
	Capital stock	Labour quantity	Human capital	TFP	GDP
1910–1934	29.6	14.4	23.4	32.6	100
1934–1947	88.4	33.6	41.7	−63.7	100
1947–1973	37.0	3.8	9.7	49.5	100
1973–1990	45.4	−17.9	23.8	48.6	100
1990–2017	58.7	18.3	15.2	7.8	100
1910–2017	42.6	4.3	16.7	36.5	100

Source: authors' own calculations, based on data in Table 18.2.

(16.7%) and a rather low capacity to generate employment (4.3%). However, these average results mask important differences between both countries. While in Spain TFP growth had a much more relevant role (45.9%), in Portugal the dominant growth source was capital accumulation (45.7%), and the TFP contribution was much less important (22.3%).

In Spain, the early 1950s represent a divide between a century (1850–1950) of moderate growth dominated by factor accumulation and fast growth driven by TFP. Improvements in efficiency explain roughly one-fourth of growth in the first hundred years, and almost three-fourths since 1950. As Prados de la Escosura and Rosés (2009) outline, these results are in line with the pattern postulated by Collins and Bosworth (1996) and observed in other Western European economies and the US.[79] By contrast, unlike Spain and other developed countries, in Portugal TFP has not performed a dominant role since the Second World War. Instead, Portuguese growth has mostly been based on the accumulation of physical and human capital, with a minor role of TFP during the twentieth century.[80]

As was indicated before, the Spanish economic expansion of 1850–1883 was largely linked to railway construction and investment in other infrastructure and the mining sector. In this stage capital deepening made the highest contribution to overall growth and efficiency gains were trifling. However, as time went by the importance of the capital deepening effect decreased and improvements in efficiency became more relevant (Herranz-Loncán, 2006). As indicated before, it is not possible to carry out a growth accounting exercise for Portugal before the First World War because capital stock data are not available. However, data for output and labour force reveal a relatively poor performance before 1910 in terms of labour productivity, with a yearly growth rate of 0.50% for 1860–1910 (Lains, 2003b), which would indicate a comparatively small contribution of both capital accumulation and TFP increases, jointly explaining the sluggish growth of the period.[81]

The 1920s represented for Spain an expansionary phase, linked to the expansion of the electricity network and the development of the second industrial revolution technologies. During those years, output growth thrived, assisted by capital accumulation and the highest TFP growth observed so far. The complementarity between investment in new equipment, road transport, electricity infrastructures and human capital had a visible impact on overall efficiency. For the first time, TFP growth outperformed the contribution of capital. Data for Portugal in 1910–1934 describe also a balanced contribution of capital (19.2%), labour (15.4 %), human capital (32%) and TFP (33.5 %). In this period, Portugal registered the highest contribution of TFP to output growth of the whole twentieth century. However, the late 1930s put an end to that expansion in both Iberian economies, with negative contributions of TFP to output growth. The autarkic industrial policies promoted by Franco's and Salazar's authoritarian regimes, combined with protectionism and restrictions to the inflow of foreign capital

---

[79] See Maddison (1987) and Crafts (2004) for the UK; and Kendrick (1961) and Abramovitz and David (2001) for the US.

[80] Bosworth et al. (1995) report growth accounting analysis for 88 developing and industrial economies over the period 1960–1992 and show that increases in TFP were small in developing countries, where accumulation of physical and human capital had a more relevant role in explaining growth.

[81] Own calculation from Lains (2003b), table 9, page 139.

help to explain why economic growth was based during those years on extensive accumulation of capital but at the cost of losses in efficiency.

Fortunately, during the Golden Age Iberia recovered part of the ground lost with respect to Western Europe since the late 1930s, with TFP becoming the main growth force (49.5%). In Spain, TFP growth accounted for nearly two-thirds of overall output growth while in Portugal its contribution was just one-third. Capital deepening was the second source of growth for Iberia (37%) and the contribution of job creation was positive but comparatively weak (3.8%).[82] Underlying this process, there was intense structural change towards industries that could take advantage of the technological gap between the Iberian economies and the industrial leaders. In Spain, electric utilities, machinery and equipment industries, transport equipment, chemicals, rubber and plastic, and communications registered TFP growth that was more than twice the average.[83] They benefited not only from industry specific technological change but also from spillovers derived from the final phase of expansion of the electricity network across the country (Sanchis, 2016). Advances in electricity generation and distribution supplied the whole economy with a cheap essential input. Additionally, the implementation of such technologies put in motion subsequent changes in business management, manufacturing organization or inter-firm relations. All these changes improved efficiency in a way that cannot be classified as embodied technological change or human capital, and hence are accounted inside the residual, increasing the contribution of TFP to output growth. All this explains why TFP growth made its highest historical contribution to GDP growth in this period.

Meanwhile, the Portuguese experience, with a TFP contribution to output growth of only 29.7% for 1947–1973, has been compared with the East Asian and Latin American experiences.[84] In Portugal, extensive growth was therefore clearly different from the intensive growth model of Western European countries during the post-war period (Lains, 2003a) and, despite the development in Portugal of the same industries as in Spain, efficiency gains were disappointing (Amaral, 1998).

The 1973 oil shock provoked drastic drops in output and TFP growth in Iberia. In the period 1973–1990, the contraction of output growth rates had a deep impact on employment, whose contribution to overall growth was negative (−17.9%). Job destruction was especially dramatic in Spain (−30.7%).

---

[82] Several empirical studies report similar results; see, for instance, Myro (1983), Suárez (1992), Cebrián (2001) and Sanchis (2006).

[83] Sanchis (2006) provides a growth accounting study for 22 industries in 1958–1975 based on Jorgenson et al. (1987)'s approach.

[84] For instance, Hong Kong, China and Taiwan had a TFP contribution of 30% in 1966–1990 (Young, 1995) and in some Latin American economies, such as Argentina, Brazil, Chile and Mexico, the TFP contribution runs between 30% and 40%. Mateus (1995) compares Portugal with the Asian countries. Amaral (1998) obtains also contributions around 30% for TFP and 40% for capital in 1951–1973.

Firms confronted the economic crisis and the start of the new globalization era by devoting more resources to improve efficiency and incorporate new equipment, rather than to generate new employment. Meanwhile, the public sector invested in education and made more affordable the upgrading of human capital. Membership of the European Union opened a new period of vigorous output growth, although it was not translated into TFP improvement at the level of the Golden Age.

Some available growth accounting studies for Spain and Portugal for the period 1990–2015 conclude that Iberian countries registered notable inefficiencies, and even years with very low TFP growth during the boom of the 2000s. Only the ICT-intensive industries escaped from this disappointing situation and allowed a modest resurgence of labour productivity growth over the 2000–2004 period (Mas & Quesada, 2006; Cavalcanti, 2007). Actually, the use of ICT intermediate inputs and investment in ICT capital has had a modest but positive contribution to output and productivity growth in both Iberian countries since the mid-1990s (Hernando & Núñez, 2004; Silva, 2011). Nevertheless, this result is partly masked by a too low share of the ICT sector within total industry in Iberia, that halves the share of EU-10. As a consequence, the contribution of ICT industries to labour productivity, on one side, and that of ICT capital to aggregate labour productivity growth, on the other, are lower than in more advanced Western European countries (van Ark et al., 2003; 2009). This fact is even more distressing if one takes into account that it is the same reason that explains the enlargement of the productivity gap between Western Europe and the US over the last few decades. The Iberian countries, as other Western European economies, still lag behind the US in terms of ICT adoption and ICT equipment production.[85] The low penetration of ICT industries in the productive structure and the comparatively low rate of investment in ICT equipment are preventing this technology from displaying its full potential and making a more efficient contribution to output growth (Timmer et al., 2003).

18.5 Conclusion

The economic growth of Portugal and Spain during the last two centuries has many common features. In both cases, after a long century of stagnation or slow progress, economic growth substantially accelerated around 1950, which resulted in the main period of Iberian convergence with the Western European countries. Convergence, however, slowed down since 1975 and, as a consequence, both Iberian economies have been unable to completely close their distance from their richer neighbours. Economic growth was accompanied in both cases by the emergence of clusters of rich and poor territories. One of the main results of

---

[85] See Timmer et al. (2003), Van Ark et al. (2003) and Timmer and Van Ark (2005).

this process of geographical differentiation has been the gradual emergence of a poor Iberia, spreading over a continuous area around the border between Spain and Portugal.

Those common features, however, hide also some significant differences between both countries. The available growth accounting exercises clearly show that the proximate causes of the Portuguese and Spanish growth experience have been very different, especially during the second half of the twentieth century. Whereas in Spain, the TFP contribution to economic growth has been predominant since 1950, in Portugal growth has been mainly associated with factor accumulation, rather than TFP increases. The difference was greatest during the Golden Age, when the Portuguese economy was unable to keep pace with the Spanish in capturing efficiency gains from new technologies. After the crisis of 1970s, however, this difference has been mitigated and both economies have found similar difficulties in taking full advantage of technological change.

19

Population Growth, Composition and Educational Levels

AMÉLIA BRANCO AND FERNANDO COLLANTES

19.1 Introduction

The history of European populations was radically transformed during the nineteenth and twentieth centuries. All across Europe, population numbers grew at an unprecedented rate and the demographic structures of the past broke down. There was a transition from a demographic regime of high mortality and high fertility to one of low mortality and low fertility. There was large-scale occupational change, as agricultural populations shifted to industrial and service occupations. Occupational change, in turn, was connected to great changes in the territorial distribution of populations, among them urbanization. Finally, there was a huge increase in educational levels (Bairoch, 1997, vols. I and II).

The aim of this chapter is to provide a synthetic view of these demographic changes in modern Portugal and Spain (henceforth, 'Iberia'). The chapter is organized in four main sections. Following this introduction, Section 19.2 deals with population growth and its sources, with a particular focus on the demographic transition. Sections 19.3 and 19.4 succesively discuss the occupational and territorial distribution of the population. Section 19.5 considers education. Throughout the chapter, our focus will not be on making reciprocal comparisons between Portugal and Spain, or between different regions in Iberia, but rather on unifying the main features of the Iberian experience into a single, joint narrative.

We are grateful to our funding agencies (Ministerio de Ciencia e Innovación, project PID2022-138886NB-I00; Gobierno de Aragón, cofinanced by FEDER 2014-2020, 'Construyendo Europa desde Aragón', research group, S55_23R; and the Portuguese National Funding Agency for Science, Research and Technology, FCT, Project UID/SOC/ 04521/2013); to Cláudia M. Viana, Tiago Lima Quintanilha and Raquel Rocha for their help with data collection and references; to Albert Herreria for his revision of our English; and to Dulce Freire and Daniel Lanero. Participants at the Zaragoza meeting on Iberian economic history (May 2019) made helpful suggestions.

19.2 The Demographic Transition

Between 1800 and 2018, Iberia's population grew from 13 to 57 million inhabitants (Table 19.1). There were three distinct phases in this evolution. During the first phase, the nineteenth century, population grew at a modest rate. Population growth gained some momentum during much of the twentieth century, even if it never had an explosive magnitude. Finally, after having

Table 19.1 *Basic population figures for Portugal, Spain and 'Iberia' (Portugal + Spain).*

	1800[a]	1860[b]	1900	1930	1950	1980	2000	2018
Population numbers (million)								
Portugal	2.9	4.0	5.4	6.8	8.4	9.9	10.2	10.3
Spain	10.5	15.6	18.6	23.5	27.9	37.5	40.2	46.7
Iberia	13.4	19.6	24.0	30.3	36.3	47.4	50.4	56.9
Population growth[c]								
Portugal		0.5	0.8	0.8	1.1	0.5	0.2	0.0
Spain		0.7	0.4	0.8	0.9	1.0	0.3	0.8
Iberia		0.6	0.5	0.8	0.9	0.9	0.3	0.7
Age structure (%)								
Portugal								
Less than 15	33	34	34	32	29	26	16	14
15 to 64	61	61	60	62	64	63	67	64
More than 64	5	5	6	6	7	11	16	22
Spain								
Less than 15	35	35	33	32	26	26	15	15
15 to 64	59	62	61	62	67	63	68	66
More than 64	5	3	5	6	7	11	17	19
Iberia								
Less than 15	35[d]	35	34	32	27	26	15	15
15 to 64	60	62	61	62	66	63	68	66
More than 64	5[e]	3[e]	5	6	7	11	17	20

Notes: [a] 1801 for Portugal, 1797 for Spain; [b] 1864 for Portugal's age structure; [c] annual compound rate (%) – the figure for 1860 refers to the period 1800–1860, and so on; [d] less than 16 for Spain; [e] for Spain, we assume (in line with the data available for 1877) that two-thirds of the 60–69 age group corresponds to the 65–69 subgroup.
Sources: Baganha and Marques (2001: 33, 51–53, 55–56); Instituto Nacional de Estatística (2003; www.ine.pt); Nicolau (2005: 124–127, 144–147); Instituto Nacional de Estadística (www.ine.es).

reached a peak in the 1970s, population growth began to decelerate and, except for a booming period in the years prior to the 2008 recession, became slower than ever before in the modern era.

Natural change (the difference between births and deaths) was the main driver of population growth for almost all of the period (Figure 19.1 and Table 19.2). Slow growth during the nineteenth century was associated with low rates of natural growth, while the acceleration of population growth during much of the twentieth century was driven by an acceleration of natural growth. The deceleration of population growth from 1980 onwards was also closely related to a reduction of the rates of natural growth. Only in the 1990s and especially in the 2000s, with close-to-zero natural growth, did foreign migrations come to drive demographic change.

Therefore, Iberia's population growth was strongly linked to the unfolding of the demographic transition (Figure 19.2). For most of the nineteenth century, population growth was slow because the risk of mortality remained high in most of Iberia, especially in the inland regions of the Peninsula. True, there was some progress in the escape from premature death. For instance, episodes of catastrophic mortality, which were still common and severe in the

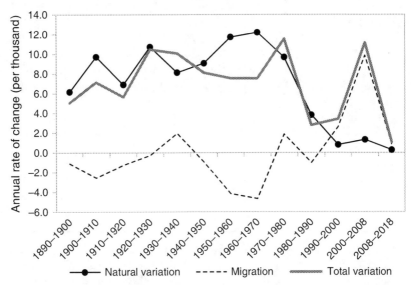

Figure 19.1 Iberian population change and its sources. Note: natural variation = births – deaths; migration = total variation – natural variation.
Sources: Baganha and Marques (2001: 51–53, 55–56, 59–62); Instituto Nacional de Estatística (2003; www.ine.pt); Veiga (2004); Nicolau (2005: 124–127, 144–147); Instituto Nacional de Estadística (www.ine.es).

Table 19.2 Sources of population change (average annual per thousand rates).

	Portugal		Spain		Iberia			
							Contribution to population change (%)	
	Natural variation	Migration	Natural variation	Migration	Natural variation	Migration	Natural variation	Migration
1890–1900	9.3	−2.2	5.2	−0,8	6.2	−1.1	122	−22
1900–1910	11.5	−2.9	9.2	−2.5	9.7	−2.6	136	−36
1910–1920	8.8	−6.7	6.4	0.3	6.9	−1.3	122	−22
1920–1930	12.5	−0.2	10.2	−0.3	10.7	−0.3	103	−3
1930–1940	11.4	0.9	7.2	2.2	8.1	1.9	81	19
1940–1950	10.4	−1.5	8.7	−0.8	9.1	−1.0	112	−12
1950–1960	12.6	−7.9	11.4	−3.1	11.7	−4.2	155	−55
1960–1970	12.3	−15.6	12.2	−1.7	12.2	−4.7	162	−62
1970–1980	8.5	5.5	10.0	0.9	9.7	1.9	84	16
1980–1990	3.6	−3.5	3.8	−0.4	3.8	−1.0	137	−37
1990–2000	0.9	2.7	0.8	2.6	0.8	2.6	23	77
2000–2008	0.3	4.0	1.6	11.3	1.3	9.8	12	88
2008–2018	−1.7	−2.1	0.7	1.4	0.3	0.8	25	75

Sources: Baganha and Marques (2001: 51–53, 55–56, 59–62); Instituto Nacional de Estatística (2003; www.ine.pt); Veiga (2004); Nicolau (2005: 124–127, 144–147); Instituto Nacional de Estadística (www.ine.es).

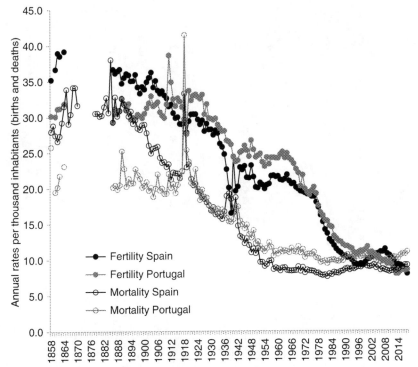

Figure 19.2 The demographic transition.
Sources: Baganha and Marques (2001: 33, 51–53, 55–56, 59–62); Instituto Nacional de Estatística (2003; www.ine.pt); Veiga (2004); Nicolau (2005: 124–127, 144–147); Instituto Nacional de Estadística (www.ine.es).

early years of the century (especially during the French invasion), came to be less dramatic as the century progressed. All in all, ordinary mortality remained high and both its structure, dominated by infant mortality, and its geography, with the interior regions performing worse than the coastal ones (and Spain performing worse than Portugal), were still very traditional (Pérez Moreda, 1999b; Barbosa & Godinho, 2001).

Why did mortality remain so high during the nineteenth century? An important factor was, of course, the state of medical science and technology at the time. For most of the century, the scientific understanding of some of the main diseases remained somewhat blurred, which was detrimental to the pace and direction of practical technological innovation in the area. Nor were there active pro-health policies. Partly due to budget constraints, partly due to a conscious non-interventionist policy stance, public spending in health (by central or local governments) remained low. In most cities, there was not much urban planning either, at least until around the 1870s and 1880s. Especially in working-class neighbourhoods, health and housing conditions deteriorated as population grew and effective systems of water supply, waste disposal and urban management were lacking (Cosme, 2006).

The economic evolution of Iberia was not propitious either. Economic growth lagged behind that of the rest of Western Europe and social inequality was on the rise (see Chapters 18 and 23). As a result, most households did not have the chance to substantially improve their diets, calorie intakes were close to subsistence for the lower classes and there were widespread deficiencies in proteins, vitamins and minerals. Moreover, the low productivity of Iberian agriculture (see Chapter 22) and the weakness of the rest of the food chain further constrained diet change. During much of the century, and particularly in its central decades, there were even nutritional crises during which the relative prices of basic foodstuffs (namely, cereal-based products) would rocket and major (even if local) episodes of social unrest would take place. It is unlikely that the shortcomings of Iberian diets had a direct impact on mortality, but they must have had an indirect impact through its effect on personal health and resistance to disease (Barbosa & Godinho, 2001; Cussó, 2005).

A new era took shape between around 1890 and 1980. Mortality began to fall substantially in Spain, which by the time of the First World War had bridged its gap with Portugal in this respect. From the 1920s onwards, the levels and trends of mortality became fairly similar in both countries. With some time lag, fertility also decreased. This gave way to a period of faster population growth, which was only occasionally interrupted by late episodes of catastrophic mortality such as the influenza of 1918–1919 and the Spanish Civil War of 1936–1939 (Ortega & Silvestre, 2006; Henrique & Rodrigues, 2008; Echeverri, 2018). Between around 1950 and 1975, in particular, Iberia experienced a baby boom similar to that in other parts of Western Europe, as mortality reached an all-time low while fertility was more resistant to change.

This new trend was made possible by the removal of the obstacles that for a long time had hampered the unfolding of the demographic transition. There was substantial progress in the scientific understanding of disease, and new vaccines, antibiotics and cures were made available. There was also a reorientation of public policies. From the late nineteenth century onwards, most local governments shifted towards a more active policy stance, including crucial areas for health such as water supply, waste disposal, urban planning and protection against epidemic contagion. Moreover, as the twentieth century progressed, both central governments constructed a network of modern hospitals oriented towards the provision of health care on a massive scale. This allowed for a rapid incorporation of new territories and social groups to the benefits of a modern public health system. There were also more efforts made to spread new ideas about personal hygiene, especially when it came to childrearing, by means of public information campaigns (Cosme, 2006; Pérez Moreda et al., 2015).

The economic situation was also more favourable. With some short-term exceptions, economic growth was faster and social inequality decreased (see Chapter 18 and 23). Therefore, household incomes increased substantially. Furthermore, there was substantial technological change in agriculture and a new food system emerged – one that was led by a relatively small number of food industries involved in mass production and capable of eliminating most inflationary pressures from food consumer markets. As a result, consumers' increasing purchasing power allowed them to transition to richer, more diversified diets. This reinforced the effect of technological change and pro-health public policies. Yet, it probably was a minor factor, as is suggested by the striking continuity in Spain's mortality decline during the 1940s, which was a period of falling household incomes and deteriorating diets (Pérez Moreda et al., 2015).

From the mid-1970s onwards there was a sudden decline in fertility that started a new demographic period. In the late twentieth century, natural growth became almost zero, which stood in sharp contrast to any other period in the modern history of the Iberian population. Of course, by 1975 fertility had already fallen well below its nineteenth-century levels. The Iberian demographic transition was not an explosive one and, with a moderate time lag in relation to the decline in mortality, couples had begun to adjust their fertility behaviour. Much of this adjustment had been based on rudimentary strategies of family planning that, as was the case with sexual abstinence and the interruption of intercourse, could be incorporated more or less harmoniously into the dominant Catholic value structure. The fertility decline was also underpinned by some secularization, especially in urban areas, as well as by shorter-term shifts towards lower nuptiality and a higher age at marriage (Leite, 2005; Henriques and Rodrigues, 2008).

What happened after 1975 was more radical, though. There was a steep decline in fertility as a result of both a decrease in the number of children per household and an increase in the mother's age at first birth (Mendes et al., 2016). This reflected forces that were also operating in other European countries. The male-breadwinner household model declined. On the basis of expanding educational levels and more widespread employment opportunities in the service sector, more and more women participated in the labour force in a stable way, which reduced their orientation towards reproduction and childrearing (Nunes, 1991; Gálvez, 2006). Moreover, childrearing itself increasingly became an activity that required a solid economic base. Whereas in the traditional society of the nineteenth century children had an economic function (as workers and as a future source of old-age economic support), in the late twentieth-century society children were mostly draining resources from the household during ever longer periods of formal schooling (and even during the early stage of their adult working life).

Still, the fall of fertility in Iberia went further than in other European countries and seems to require additional explanation. In the particular case of Spain, the trajectory of secularization may have played a part. In Spain and elsewhere in most of Europe, there was a history of secularization already going on prior to the 1970s or the 1980s. However, the death of Francisco Franco in 1975 led to the end of a dictatorship that for almost four decades had strongly advocated traditional Catholic values. The transition towards democracy accelerated a change in values that would have probably taken place anyway. Beyond values, the end of the dictatorship also implied a more ready access to modern contraceptives.

Furthermore, we should consider the fact that public policies in both Spain and Portugal were only weakly oriented towards the promotion of fertility. In the late twentieth century, both Iberian countries constructed welfare states that made a remarkable contribution to social cohesion and justice but were primarily oriented towards classical social protection (i.e. retirement pensions, transfers to the unemployed), health and education. In comparison to the rest of the European Union, public spending addressed to the promotion of fertility was low (Comín & Díaz, 2005). Nor were active policies set to make it easier for parents to find the right balance between working life and family life. A related problem was the segmented nature of the labour market and the way in which gender discrimination in the less attractive segments of that market discouraged fertility.

The steep decline in fertility accelerated the trend towards ageing, which in the previous decades had become noticeable (Table 19.1). Around 1980 Iberia had one of the youngest age structure in Europe. By 2000, and following particularly rapid changes at both the bottom and top of the age pyramid, the population older than 64 outnumbered (for the first time ever) the population younger than 15 (Moreira & Gomes, 2014). Barely one century earlier, before the full development of the demographic transition, the ratio between these two population groups had stood at 1 to 7. Ageing will be crucial for the demographic future of Iberia, but it is important to note that during the twentieth century the most prominent change was not extreme ageing, but rather the advent of 'mass maturity' (Pérez Díaz, 2003). By the start of the present century, the proportion of people aged between 15 and 64 was actually higher than ever before.

Foreign migration has become the main driver of population growth in Iberia during the last three decades. It is true that both Portugal and Spain had a previous history of emigration abroad. An early cycle of emigration had been directed towards Latin America in the late nineteenth and early twentieth centuries, while a more significant, second cycle had been oriented towards Latin America and especially Western Europe during the decades after the

Second World War. None of them, however, came even close to driving Iberia's population change. The remarkable inflow of returning migrants coming back to Iberia in the 1970s from both Western Europe and the Portuguese ex-colonies was also secondary compared with natural population growth (Sánchez Alonso, 1995; Baganha & Góis, 1999; de la Torre & Sanz, 2008; Marques & Góis, 2012).

The inflow of foreign migrants starting in the 1990s was another matter, though. Foreign migrants from Latin America, Eastern Europe and Africa became the new drivers of population growth in both countries (Peixoto, 2007; Reher & Requena, 2009). This was not simply because natural growth had become close to zero in both countries: the size of these new immigration flows was remarkable on its own terms. In the particular case of Spain, the country in which these flows were more massive, the magnitude of foreign immigration in the 2000s went well beyond the orders of magnitude of the country's past experience as a country of emigration. However, immigration has greatly receded after 2008 and both countries are facing again the prospect of little, if any, population growth. After 2008 Portugal has actually started to lose population as a result of both negative natural growth and net emigration.

19.3 Occupational Change

We can identify three distinct stages in the evolution of Iberia's occupational structure. The chronology is similar to the one we have found for the demographic transition. During the first stage, the nineteenth century, Iberia was a predominantly agrarian society (Table 19.3). Even though industrialization and modern economic growth had started, there was no substantial movement of population out of agriculture and into the other sectors. The available data, which must be handled with great caution due to the lack of homogeneity of occupational categories through time, would even suggest some increase in the proportion of agricultural employment. Regardless of this possible late growth, it is clear that by the early twentieth century the agrarian population was still dominant in Iberia. This was in contrast to the situation in the rest of Western Europe, where the movement of population out of agriculture had already started.

Why was Iberia different in this respect? Obviously, industrial growth was much weaker than in the rest of Western Europe. As in most other countries, in Iberia the industrial and service sectors had productivity levels that were higher than that of agriculture, so that they could offer the prospect of higher average earnings (Lains, 2009: 335; Prados de la Escosura, 2017: 341–345). This could potentially be the basis for a massive transfer of agricultural populations into industrial and service occupations. However, during the nineteenth century the weakness of Iberian industrialization prevented the demand for non-agricultural labour from expanding rapidly (Silvestre, 2005). We must also take

Table 19.3 *Occupation and activity.*

	1800[a]	1887[b]	1910	1930	1950	1981	2011
Occupation (%)							
Portugal							
Primary	55	62	58	51	49	19	3
Secondary	18	18	22	19	24	39	26
Tertiary	27	20	21	30	26	42	70
Spain							
Primary	61	69	68	47	50	16	4
Secondary	15	15	15	26	26	37	21
Tertiary	23	15	17	27	25	47	74
Iberia							
Primary	60	67	65	48	49	17	4
Secondary	16	16	17	24	25	38	22
Tertiary	24	17	18	28	25	46	73
Gross activity rate (%)[c]							
Portugal							
Total		50	43	37	38	39	50
Male		66	65	56	61	54	53
Female		35	22	19	17	26	47
Spain							
Total		40	38	37	39	34	50
Male		65	67	65	67	52	56
Female		16	10	9	12	17	45
Iberia							
Total		42	39	37	38	35	50
Male		65	67	63	66	52	55
Female		20	13	11	13	18	45

Notes: [a] 1797 for Spain. For Portugal we have assumed that activity rates were similar in urban and rural areas, that the total occupied population was a proportion of Iberia's similar to the one that we can actually observe in the earliest data available (1887), and that the breakdown of non-agricultural populations between secondary and tertiary occupations was similar to that of Spain in 1797; [b] 1890 for Portugal; [c] active population / total population.
Sources: Nunes (2001: 164); Llopis (2002a: 147); Nicolau (2005: 147–150); Palma and Reis (2019: 10); www.pordata.pt ('Emprego e mercado de trabalho'); Instituto Nacional de Estadística (www.ine.es); Instituto Nacional de Estatística (www.ine.pt).

into account that during the nineteenth century both countries became specialized in agriculture in the new international division of labour, while the technological conditions of farming remained traditional. Iberian agriculture was among the least productive in Western Europe and absorbed large amounts of labour. As a matter of fact, agriculture acted as some sort of 'employer of last resort' – a fraction of the agricultural labour force was made up of underemployed populations (Veiga, 2004; Leite, 2005; Silvestre, 2007).

The transformation of Iberia's occupational structure took place later, from around 1910 onwards. During this second stage, there was a massive transfer of agricultural populations to secondary and tertiary occupations. This change was already remarkable during the period 1910–1930 and, after coming to a halt during the 1930s and 1940s, it resumed with even greater force after 1950. By 1980, the agricultural population represented less than 20 per cent of the labour force.

The key to occupational change was that economic growth was on average much faster than in the nineteenth century. As a matter of fact, the chronology of occupational change mirrors that of economic growth, which slowed down in the years of the Great Depression, the Spanish Civil War and the Second World War, and later experienced a golden age. The periods of economic growth greatly expanded the demand for non-agricultural labour and, since labour productivity remained much higher in industry and services than in agriculture, large amounts of agricultural labour had the chance to increase their earnings by shifting to the other sectors. Complementarily, occupational change was favoured by intense technological change within agriculture. What in the nineteenth century had been an organic, labour-intensive activity became (especially after 1950) an increasingly mechanized activity in which innovations such as tractors substantially reduced agriculture's capacity for labour absorption (see Chapter 22).

The rapid decline of agricultural employment after 1950 allowed Iberia to complete in barely a few decades a structural transformation that had taken around a century in the rest of Western Europe. All in all, the path was slightly different. While in early developers occupational change had been driven by the growth of industrial employment, in Iberia it was mostly the service sector that took the lead. In both cases, it was of course a combination of industry and services that took people out of the land, but in Iberia this combination was more biased towards services. To some extent, this prefigures the later experience of the Global South, in which the dominance of service employment over industrial employment has been even stronger (Bairoch, 1997, vol. III). There has not been a systematic analysis of this feature, but we can refer to a weaker process of industrialization in Iberia and a higher relevance of some service activities (i.e. tourism) within Iberia's model of economic growth (see Chapter 22). As a hypothesis, we should also consider the fact that the delay in Iberia's occupational change implied that the latter eventually took place at a time when public policies (in Iberia and elsewhere) were favouring job creation in activities such as administration, education and health, to a much larger extent than in the nineteenth century.

Finally, during the last two decades of the twentieth century we can identify the start of a third stage. Agriculture continued to decline, but now it was joined by industry. Services became the only expanding sector and by 2000 they amounted to more than 60 per cent of employment. Similarly to other parts of Western Europe, a new era of deindustrialization and tertiarization started.

Unlike in the case of classical occupational change during most of the twentieth century, intersectoral productivity gaps played now a minor role. Average labour productivity was actually lower in services than in industry. There were, however, crucial differences in the evolution of the demand for labour (Gonçalves, 2005; Collantes, 2017). Industry was hit hard by the oil crisis of the 1970s and, more generally, had much trouble at facing the competition coming from low-cost producers in the developing world. This was particularly clear in some of the sectors that had driven occupational change in the past, such as textiles, iron and steel production, and shipbuilding. Services, on the contrary, went on expanding. The consolidation of consumer societies in Iberia favoured a persistent expansion of employment in all sorts of commerce-related pursuits, ranging from supermarkets to specialized retailers. In a business environment of increasing functional specialization, there was also much growth in the area of services to firms. In connection with the expansion of Iberian welfare states, public service employment also increased notably.

During this period there was also a remarkable increase in women's participation in the labour force (Table 19.3). Similarly to other European countries, this must be put in relation to cultural changes in gender roles, rising educational levels among the female population, the expansion of employment opportunities in the tertiary sector and the mechanization of domestic work, made possible by the diffusion of electric home appliances (Nunes, 1991; Gálvez, 2006). The current state of research, however, does not allow us to be precise about the longer-term evolution of the female activity rate. The studies available at a micro level suggest that in the nineteenth and early twentieth centuries women were more involved in labour markets than the official, macro-level statistics show (Sarasúa and Gálvez, 2003). Moreover, in Iberia as elsewhere, quantifying female labour participation in agriculture is difficult, particularly in those regions where family farms were dominant.

19.4 The Geography of Population

The spatial distribution of Iberia's population followed a chronology that is very similar to that of occupational change. During the nineteenth century, Iberia's population was mostly rural (Table 19.4). The urbanization rate was not particularly low for the region's level of economic development, but a number of cities, especially in the southern half of the peninsula, were actually 'agro-towns' with many farmers and agricultural workers. During the nineteenth century urbanization progressed slowly. There was of course net rural–urban migration, but the cities only absorbed a minor share of the countryside's natural population growth (Collantes & Pinilla, 2011; Rodrigues, 2010). Rural and urban populations grew then at fairly similar rates, at least until well into the nineteenth century. Nor were there great changes in the spatial distribution of population. There were a number of major, expanding cities, with the agglomerations around Madrid, Lisbon and Barcelona, in particular, growing from 100,000–200,000 to 400,000–600,000 inhabitants as the century passed (Reher, 1994: 26). There were also important regional differences, the coastal regions being more densely populated than the interior regions. This was a population geography that had started to take shape in the seventeenth century and remained relatively stable during the nineteenth century (Ayuda et al., 2010). Population growth seems to have been a bit faster in the southern regions than in the northern ones, at least in Portugal (Veiga, 2004).

Why was internal migration so limited? Iberia was a slow-growing economy, and this limited the capacity of cities and dynamic regions to attract population from the countryside and other, more backward regions. Only around Barcelona, Iberia's main industrial city at the time, had a migration basin emerged that was wide enough to spread beyond Catalonia and into other regions. Outside the remaining, smaller-scale migration basins, the cost of internal migration was a constraining factor, especially for the large number

Table 19.4 *Percentage share of population living in nuclei of 5,000 inhabitants or more.*

	1801	1860	1900	1930	1960	1981	2011
Portugal	16.1	13.4[a]	20.8	26.7	30.1	35.8	51.6
Spain	24.0[b]	22.5	29.3	37.0	50.6	68.4	74.9
Iberia	22.0	20.7	27.5	35.1	46.5	62.2	70.6

Notes: [a] 1864; [b] 1787.
Sources: Reher (1994: 25); Instituto Nacional de Estadística (www.ine.es); Instituto Nacional de Estatística (www.ine.pt).

of low-income households prevailing in much of Iberia. Distance implied a high transport cost and made it less likely that there would be relatives and acquaintances at the destination to facilitate the social and economic assimilation of migrants (Silvestre, 2005). By making potential migrants less responsive to economic opportunities emerging in other regions, widespread illiteracy may have also hampered internal migration (Núñez, 1992; Beltrán & de Miguel, 2017).

In the case of rural–urban migration, moreover, we must realize that, even though the city was undoubtedly ahead of the countryside in terms of access to infrastructures and services, its advantage was not as prominent as it would be at a later stage. Educational and health services were still very rudimentary and, therefore, their provision was not subject to large economies of scale. Rural areas often had an endowment of schools or health posts that was mediocre but not much worse than that of cities. As a matter of fact, during the nineteenth century many cities experienced a deterioration of public health conditions, as was discussed in a previous section. All this contributes to explaining why the sizeable productivity gap between agriculture and the rest of the economy was not enough to move Iberia's rural population to massive internal migrations (Collantes & Pinilla, 2011).

Major changes would take place, again, between 1900 and 1980. It was then when Iberian society ceased to be predominantly rural and became predominantly urban. Rural–urban migration became massive, particularly during the 1920s and the period 1950–1975. Rural–urban migration basins became much wider and spread over hundreds of kilometres. In Spain, migrants from southern regions such as Andalusia would eventually flow towards northern destinations such as (for instance) Catalonia. Migrants from Alentejo would also move long distances in order to reach Lisbon, Setúbal or Porto. There would also be much interregional migration originating from other southern and interior regions, such as both Castiles in Spain and Trás-os-Montes in Portugal, towards destinations such as Catalonia, Madrid, the Basque Country, the Valencia region, Lisbon, Setúbal, Porto or Faro. This was joined by persistent flows of rural–urban migration within each region (Reher, 1994; Moreira and Rodriguez, 2008).

Consequently, there was impressive growth in both the size and the number of cities. The agglomerations of Madrid and Barcelona reached around four million inhabitants, while Lisbon came close to two million and another agglomeration (Valencia) exceeded one million (Reher, 1994: 26; Rodrigues, 2010: 332–345). The other side of this was the depopulation of rural communities all across Iberia, a process that became extreme and painful in many regions (Collantes & Pinilla, 2011).

The widening of migration basins also led to a substantial deepening of regional disparities in population distribution. The geography of population remained similar to the previous period, but the concentration in coastal regions and around Madrid went much further than in the past, as coastal regions grew much faster than the interior ones. This was perceptible in the early part of the twentieth century, but became particularly drastic during the quarter century after 1950. The Gini coefficient of provincial disparities in population density, which had been in the 0.27–0.33 interval for both countries around 1860, jumped from 0.36–0.39 in 1950 to a remarkable 0.51–0.54 in 1981 (Ayuda et al., 2010: 32).

What had changed in comparison to the nineteenth century? To begin with, industrialization and economic growth gained momentum and expanded the demand for non-agricultural labour at a generally faster rate. Contrary to the British experience of precocious occupational change, in Iberia, as in most other parts of Europe, there was not much occupational change in the countryside until well into the twentieth century. Most non-agricultural growth was heavily concentrated on a small number of industrial districts located in urban areas, and the rural economy remained highly dependent on farming until well into the twentieth century. Therefore, occupational change was tightly linked to urbanization. On the other hand, rapid urbanization was also favoured by the relative deterioration of living standards in the countryside. During the twentieth century (and especially after 1950) a more pronounced 'rural penalty' in the access to infrastructures and services took shape. In an era of rising expectations, scale economies in the provision of new educational and health services (such as secondary education and specialized health provision) mattered and made it much more difficult for rural communities to stand comparison to the urban lifestyle (Collantes & Pinilla, 2011).

Simultaneously, migration basins became wider and more fluid. The cost of moving was no longer so crucial, as household income was now generally higher than in the nineteenth century. The transition towards literacy (more on this later in this chapter) made populations become more responsive to migration as a means to seize new economic opportunities. Furthermore, as internal migration gained some momentum, it started a feedback mechanism – migration chains made it easier for immigrants to face the challenge of finding their place far away from home. All this contributed, especially after 1950, to the movement from some of Iberia's backward regions (especially in the south) to the migration basins structured around the urban systems of distant, more dynamic regions (Collantes & Pinilla, 2011).

All in all, in the last two decades of the twentieth century there were signs of a change of phase. 'Classic' urbanization ceased to progress so rapidly, particularly in Spain, and the bigger cities actually started to lose population while other, medium-sized cities and newly created residential peripheries gained it. Rural depopulation ceased to be so intense, and some rural areas even managed to grow in population again. Iberia entered thus an era of counter-urbanization and diffused urbanization (Collantes & Pinilla, 2011). In the main cities, especially in Spain, as the relative price of housing tended to rise rapidly, many middle-class households moved towards smaller cities and residential peripheries. Many of these households, moreover, had housing preferences that were different from those of most urban dwellers in the twentieth century and wanted to leave the environmental and psychological costs of urban life behind. This change in residential patterns was also favoured by the rise of dual income households and the spread of female drivers.

The regional distribution of population remained very unequal. The coastal regions and Madrid had population densities well beyond those of the interior regions, which in some cases came close to becoming 'demographic deserts' (Rodrigues & Oliveira, 2008). Yet, regional population disparities ceased to grow as rapidly as it had been the case during most of the twentieth century. Interregional migrations, in particular, were not so prominent. A crucial difference in relation to the previous period is that now the demand for labour was expanding in a much slower and more selective way. Unemployment rates actually reached very high levels, especially in Spain. Moreover, labour markets tended to become dual. There was a segment of stable, quality jobs that were safely protected by employment legislation alongside another segment of opposite characteristics (Gálvez, 2006). The latter could hardly be taken by much of the population as a reasonable basis for long-distance, interregional migration. Furthermore, at a time when (as we have seen) foreign immigration became important, the geography of the latter was not very similar to the traditional geography of Iberian populations. Some of the backward regions with a traditionally negative internal migration balance, such as Andalusia, received a sizeable inflow of immigrants, ranging from middle-class European retirees to Maghrebi labourers in search of work in export-oriented, highly intensive agricultural enclaves.

19.5 Education

As our two indicators in Table 19.5 show, the educational level of Iberian populations increased greatly during the nineteenth and twentieth centuries. The first indicator is the literacy rate. The second is the number of schooling years, which allows us to track educational progress beyond the basics. In both cases there is steady and clear progress. Yet, similarly to other areas reviewed in this chapter (and in Iberia's socioeconomic history more generally), there is a contrast between the slow progress of the nineteenth century and the faster progress of the twentieth century.

During the nineteenth century, educational progress was slow basically as a consequence of weak public policies. In the absence of strong compensatory policies, educational outcomes depended on family and community dynamics. But, as Iberia's poor educational record during the pre-1800 period had already shown, these dynamics were not as conducive to literacy as in north-western Europe. During the nineteenth century, this negative inertia remained

Table 19.5 *Education.*

	1860	1900	1930	1950	1981	2010
Net literacy rate (%) [a]						
Total						
Portugal		27	40	58	79	95
Spain	26	43	71	88	94	98
Iberia		39	64	81	91	97
Male						
Portugal		36	50	67	85	96
Spain	40	55	80	93	96	99
Iberia		51	73	87	94	98
Female						
Portugal		18	31	51	75	93
Spain	12	32	63	83	91	97
Iberia		29	56	76	88	96
Average years of education						
Portugal	0.5[b]	1.4	2.0	2.5	5.7[c]	7.8
Spain	1.5[b]	3.1	3.8	4.9	7.3[c]	10.3
Iberia	1.3[b]	2.7	3.4	4.3	7.0[c]	9.8

Notes: [a] literate population / population of 10 or more years (15 or more years for 2010); [b] 1870; [c] 1980.
Sources: Candeias (2004: 519); Núñez (2005: 250), www.clio-infra.eu (*Human capital*, 'Average years of education'); UNESCO (www.uis.unesco.org).

influential especially in southern Spain and most of Portugal. Many families were not very interested in education and literacy. Economic growth was slow and only in the central part of the century a market society emerged that would reward the acquisition of basic skills for the purpose of conducting transactions and seizing economic opportunities. To this we must add a longer-term cultural inertia that devalued education and made it difficult for illiterate populations to perceive the potential benefits of education (Ramos, 1988; Núñez 1992; Reis, 1993a).

Overcoming these problems called for an active educational policy, but nineteenth-century governments in Portugal and Spain did not achieve consistent results in this area. In both countries, in the 1840s and 1850s laws were promulgated in order to make schooling compulsory, but there was a long distance between the legal and the real (Candeias, 2004; Núñez, 1992). For different reasons, ranging from financial difficulties to lack of political will, central governments did not enforce compulsory schooling effectively.

This made the transition to literacy highly dependent on the characteristics of different types of rural societies. In southern Iberia, the consolidation of latifundia-type rural societies and the consequent increase in social inequality may well have damaged the lower classes' incentives to invest in education. The concentration of local political power in a landowning elite oriented local government spending away from the pursuit of mass literacy. In many of these rural societies, additionally, the settlement structure was dominated by large municipalities, which implied that much of the rural population was physically remote from the rural towns in which the formal educational system was developing. In northern Iberia, in contrast, there were less unequal rural societies (with a greater role for family farms) and smaller municipalities, which contributed to a better provision of schools and teachers by local communities and parishes (Ramos, 1988; Pérez Moreda, 1997a; Beltrán & Martínez-Galarraga, 2018).

In the absence of stronger public policies, there was also a remarkable gender gap in the literacy transition. The cultural values prevailing in most households privileged the education of boys. In addition, the characteristics of the business environment and the labour market made many families perceive as economically rational the decision to allocate more resources to the education of boys than to the education of girls (Sarasúa, 2002).

Educational progress gained momentum in the twentieth century because it was then when more ambitious and effective educational policies were implemented. This happened earlier in Spain than in Portugal, where the gap between the legal and the real remained substantial until well into the century, as did the role of informal sources of access to literacy such as the family. In both countries, however, there eventually was a move towards the mass provision of education, which eradicated illiteracy almost completely and secured an increasing number of compulsory schooling years for both boys and girls. In Spain, in 1903 the State shifted to a more active policy, reducing the relevance that local characteristics had had until then on the trajectory of literacy. Some of the governments of the short-lived Spanish Second Republic regime (1931–1936) also envisioned education as a key policy area within a broader pro-equality, pro-democracy programme. Although the pro-democracy element was dropped by the Franco dictatorship, educational opportunities went on increasing in Spain, especially from the 1950s onwards. In Portugal, the Salazar dictatorship implemented a more effective educational policy than its predecessor Republican regime (Gomes & Machado, 2020; Palma & Reis, 2021). Later on, the transition to democratic governments in both countries brought about a restructuring of educational systems and a leap forward in budgetary terms.

Educational progress was also favoured by the economic context. It is true that the role of economic returns to education must not be overstressed. The turning point in both countries seems to have followed a chronology more closely related to the aforementioned educational policies than to the evolution of the skill premium. In Spain, the skill premium does not seem to have increased significantly during the early decades of the twentieth century; in key sectors such as the textile industry, it even seems to have been substantially lower than it was in the late nineteenth century (Betrán & Pons, 2004). In Portugal, the connection between the evolution of the skill premium and attitudes towards schooling may have been stronger (Amaral, 2002; Palma & Reis, 2021), but even so families seem to have increased their interest in literacy well before economic change provided abundant opportunities for skilled populations. All in all, an expanding economy in which progress opportunities were made available to a large majority of the population was a more propitious environment for education than that of the nineteenth century. Another of the changes reviewed previously in this chapter, the decline of fertility, made it easier for households to bear the opportunity cost involved in their children spending more time in the educational system. There were also major cultural changes, so that education came to be widely seen as a key element in personal development.

As the twentieth century progressed (and especially from the 1950s onwards), the educational attainment of Iberian populations expanded beyond literacy and basic capabilities (Núñez, 2005). There was a marked increase in the number of schooling years. More and more children (eventually all of them) finished successfully their time at primary school, while an increasing proportion of teenagers enrolled in non-compulsory secondary school. Secondary education actually became a building block in the making of a new, distinct middle-class identity in Iberia. In the final decades of the twentieth century, the middle class even became increasingly involved in university-level studies, which until then had shown an indisputably elitist profile. Similarly to the nineteenth century, Iberia was lagging behind the rest of Western Europe in educational terms, but from the standpoint of 2000 the degree up to which two societies that were mostly illiterate by 1900 had managed to progress in educational terms was remarkable.

19.6 Conclusion

The modern history of Iberian populations can be read in terms of the notion of 'structural periods'. Each structural period is a long-term period during which structures remain stable or structural change proceeds along a stable path. Transitions between structural periods result from the destabilization of previously stable structures or of the path that had until then characterized structural change. According to the evidence presented in this chapter, in the population history of Iberia we can find three of these periods, which are broadly coincidental with the structural periods of economic history (see Collantes, 2017, for Spain).

The first of them covers most of the nineteenth century and features relatively stable structures. Population grew at a moderate rate, in large measure because a high-mortality, high-fertility demographic regime prevailed in most regions. Most people lived in rural areas, were employed in agriculture and did not know how to read or write. Migration, both internal and external, had a limited relevance as a source of population change. None of this changed much through the nineteenth century. In demographic terms, there certainly was much more continuity in relation to the 1500–1800 period than, say, in economic or political terms. In the area of demography, there was not a historical break comparable to industrialization, the railways or the making of a liberal state.

We can identify a second structural period between around 1890 and 1980. Population grew faster as a result of the unfolding of the demographic transition. Most population came to be employed in occupations other than agriculture and, following massive internal migrations, came to be concentrated in cities and in a small number of regions (all of them coastal with the only exception of Madrid). Literacy became almost completely widespread. In other words, the demographic structures of the nineteenth century were blown away.

During the last two decades of the twentieth century, demographic change shifted to a different path. A low-mortality, low-fertility regime set in, and the population came to grow less than ever before in the modern era. The inflow of foreign immigrants actually became the main driver of population growth. Most of the population was employed in service activities and, contrary to what had been happening previously during the twentieth century, industrial employment declined. The degree of regional concentration of the population remained high, but did not grow fast anymore. Classic urbanization, based on a few large, compact cities, gave way to diffuse urbanization, with a large presence of middle-sized cities and newly created residential peripheries. Educational progress, finally, moved to the area of secondary and university-level studies.

Throughout all these three structural periods, Iberia lagged behind the rest of the developed countries (Table 19.6). The demographic transition, de-agrarianization and urbanization started later, and full literacy was achieved later as well. By the start of the twenty-first century, Iberia had converged in these traditional indicators, but was lagging behind in others that were defining the new path of demographic change; for instance, employment in those activities with a greater technological content was low, and educational attainment remained (in spite of remarkable progress) comparatively modest. Yet, a comparison with the Global South undoubtedly positions Iberia within the North. In contrast to the Global South, in Iberia by the mid twentieth century the demographic transition was close to coming to an end and was not

Table 19.6 Iberian demographic and economic change in a comparative perspective.

	Crude fertility rate (°/₀₀)[a]	Crude mortality rate (°/₀₀)[a]	Agricultural employment (%)[b]	Urban population (%)	Average years of education[c]	GDP per capita (1990 dollars)[c]
1900						
Global North	24.7	15.8	40	30	4.1	2,520
Iberia	32.4	22.1	65	28	2.7	1,677
Global South	38.6	32.2	78	9	0.6	643
1950						
Global North	17.9	11.9	23	46	6.8	4,987
Iberia	21.0	11.1	49	47[d]	4.3	2,165
Global South	45.0	23.1	76	16	1.7	911
2000						
Global North	11.4	10.3	5	68	11.5	16,744
Iberia	9.5	9.1	10	66	9.1	15,365
Global South	32.0	9.8	55	37	6.2	3,583

Notes: [a] Global North: Western Europe (1911/1913, 1949/1951 and 1995); Global South, 1900: Egypt (1917), India (1911) and Mexico (1910); Global South, 1950 and 2000: China not included (1951/1955 and 1990/1995); [b] Global North: Japan and planned economies not included (1913, 1950 and 1995); Global South: China not included (1900, 1950 and 1990); [c] Global North: Western Europe, Eastern Europe and Western offshoots; Global South: rest of the world; [d] 1960.

Sources: Bairoch (1997, vol. II: 157, 188, 196–197; vol. III: 724–725, 740, 759); Mitchell (2007a: 6, 10, 74, 77; 2007b: 5, 72); van Leeuwen and van Leeuwen-Li (2014: 95); Maddison Project Database version 2018 (www.rug.nl/ggdc). For Iberia, see the sources in Figure 19.2 and Tables 19.3, 19.4 and 19.5.

explosive, the twin processes of de-agrarianization and urbanization were at an advanced stage, and a massification of educational attainment was clearly under way. In spite of all the important progress made by the Global South during the second half of the twentieth century, by 2000 there were still remarkable differences between Iberia and the Global South. This is in line with the historical position of Iberian economies: backward in the context of the North, but clearly differentiated from Southern trends.

The main reason why we find these correspondences between different dimensions of demographic change, and between them and economic change, is that there were many interactions involved. These interactions favoured both the stability of the nineteenth century and the profound transformations of the twentieth century. In this respect, a crucial nexus between demographic and economic change was probably urbanization. Yet, this should not be taken to imply that demographic change was just a mere collateral effect of economic change, though. The history of Iberian populations rather suggests that demography is a semi-autonomous sphere, that is, one governed by a combination of mechanisms shared with the economic sphere and mechanisms that are autonomous from it. This chapter has presented some of these autonomous forces, such as scientific and technological advances in health and cultural changes in secularization, the value given to education and the spread of new ideas about the role of women in society and in the economy. We would like to conclude by reflecting on one of those autonomous elements: public policy.

The demographic transformations of the period 1890–1980, which put an end to premature mortality and mass illiteracy and created an urban society, were not just the outcome of Iberia's economic transformation. They resulted from consciously active public policies. The reduction of mortality was not just a consequence of technological innovations in health and the kind of diet change made possible by economic growth and the strengthening of the food chain. It also resulted from public policies implemented at different scales (from local to central) in order to improve the water supply and the waste disposal systems, secure consistent urban planning, construct a modern hospital network and spread new ideas about hygiene and diets among the population. The role of public policy is also clear in the area of education, where, in spite of economic growth, progress would not have been so remarkable under the weak, inconsistent policy stances of the nineteenth century. In general terms, the contrast between the nineteenth and the twentieth centuries is not just an economic contrast, but also a political one. With all its shortcomings and deficiencies, demography-related public policies were more active and effective in the twentieth than in the nineteenth century.

Maybe one of the challenges ahead for Iberia in the current structural period, which started around 1980, is not to repeat the mistakes made in the nineteenth century. Similarly to the nineteenth century, an important trend since the late twentieth century is the rise of a pro-market, anti-intervention policy stance. While this may be reasonable in some areas, it is dubious that we can face our new demographic challenges without active public policies. It is dubious that the fertility decline can be mitigated unless public social spending is reoriented towards pro-family policies. It is dubious that occupational change will be led by knowledge-intensive activities unless we implement policies that strengthen our regional systems of innovation. It is dubious that genuine educational progress can continue unless educational policies are reoriented from quantity and massification to quality. It is dubious, finally, that the serious imbalances currently affecting the spatial distribution of the population will correct themselves spontaneously. Our demographic challenges today are different from those of the past, but we should keep in mind that our successes of the past resulted not only from economic change, scientific progress or cultural change. They also resulted from public policies that consciously sacrificed some short-term allocational efficiency in favour of other, more relevant social objectives.

20

Economic Policies and Institutions

JOSÉ LUÍS CARDOSO AND FRANCISCO COMÍN

20.1 Introduction

The aim of this chapter is to present and discuss the role played by both private and public institutions in decision-making processes related to the implementation of economic policies encouraging economic growth.

As far as the process of institution making is concerned, this comparative approach to the two Iberian countries is quite appealing, given the simultaneous occurrence of historical events that had similar consequences. Notwithstanding the differences that naturally existed between Spain and Portugal, the close similarities detected help us to understand the specificity of the Iberian experience within the wider European context.

The analysis developed in this chapter starts from a basic assumption, not always made explicit, that should be kept in mind: economic growth is not possible without good institutions. It is certainly true that the causal connection between institutions and economic growth is not always easy to discern. However, the study of institutional changes and continuities in the Iberian Peninsula throughout the nineteenth and twentieth centuries offers multiple opportunities to better understand the articulation between the economic and business environment, the dynamics of the markets and the economic policies designed or implemented by the state, in fulfilment of its regulatory role. It is important to recognize that the intensity and the scope of this state intervention is subject to variation, which justifies different rates of industrialization and economic growth, both during the period under analysis and in the context of the comparative analysis between Portugal and Spain.

The political decision-making processes, in the sphere of the functions of the state, have significant repercussions on the definition of the legal framework of the economic and financial activities and play a decisive influence in the promotion of incentives and in the removal of obstacles or constraints to the adequate performance of the market and business sector. Therefore, special attention needs to be given to the way in which the state has defined its structure of expenditure and revenues in different stages and in each of the

Iberian countries, and has contributed, in a positive or negative way, to the process of economic growth.

It is undeniable that institutions – formal and informal, public and private, secular and religious, material and symbolic in their diversity of statutes and attributions – interfere in the organization of economic and business life. The theme has become commonly accepted by economic historians, given the relevance of the efficiency-enhancing effects of institutions to explain processes of economic growth and development. The seminal works of Ronald Coase, Douglass North, Elinor Ostrom and Oliver Williamson have largely contributed to the establishment of a conventional canon concerning the study of the relationship between institutions and economic performance through time and the distributional and welfare effects of institutional change.[86] The efforts to disseminate this approach have been rewarded by the public impact of works explaining the crucial importance of good institutions as a guarantee of economic growth at both the local and global levels.[87]

Throughout the nineteenth century, in a process that saw many advances and setbacks, liberal revolutions established the basic institutions of the modern capitalist economic system, based on private ownership and initiative respected by political power, free access to markets and efficient division of labour in industry. This happened in many European and international contexts, including of course Spain and Portugal. First, through the very configuration of the division of powers into a new constitutional order according to which the executive power of the government and the king was submitted to the scrutiny of the sovereignty of the nation represented by the legislative power and remained under the control of the judiciary power. Second, by defining the limits of the economic functions of the liberal state, which, as systematized by Adam Smith and later developed and refined by the economists of the classical and neoclassical schools, should essentially help to solve market failures, namely: (1) to secure property rights and laissez-faire on domestic and foreign trade; (2) to ensure the provision of pure public goods (external defence, internal security, system of justice); (3) to provide other assets with benefits to society as a whole (education, public health and social assistance); and (4) to promote the implementation of infrastructures with positive external economies (public works).

Although it was not easy to maintain a strict program of non-economic intervention by the state, the nineteenth-century liberal ideologues remained

---

[86] For an overview of the topic, as addressed by some of the most relevant contributors, see North (1990) and Williamson (2000). Although in this chapter we do not follow a strict new institutionalist approach, we acknowledge its relevance as an implicit framework for our straightforward narrative.

[87] Such relevance is illustrated by the success of the best-seller by Acemoglu and Robinson (2012), notwithstanding the lack of historical accuracy displayed in several chapters of the book.

faithful to the principle that the state should not play a role in the productive sphere and should limit its redistributive functions. The inevitable growth of the state's administrative machinery for the management of the provision of public goods should not contaminate economic sectors that required the participation of private agents and enterprises. This explains why, for the construction of public works and provision of services of public interest, the liberal state resorted to concessions to private companies.

When liberal institutions functioned properly, transaction costs were reduced, legal guarantee was secured to entrepreneurs and consumers, social cohesion was strengthened and efficient allocation of resources was favoured. However, the Iberian case clearly demonstrates that liberal institutions often did not function as expected, either because of the persistence and weight of the informal rules of *Ancien Régime* societies or because of the subversion of basic principles and rules by acting on their own interest or benefit.

The way in which in Spain and Portugal, in the mid-nineteenth century, former landowners and new possessors reconciled their strategies to mutually benefit from the sale of land and property that belonged to religious orders, is very elucidating on how the liberal state could become a clientelist state. In fact, the liberal political system was marked by practices of political *caciquismo* in which the social groups that acquired property and voting power elected those who could best defend their interests. In this context, liberal laws and institutions did not produce the expected effects, since clientelist practices, coupled with the complexity of laws, did not allow justice to be exercised impartially and led to frequent processes of illicit favouritism, fraud and corruption, in addition to inhibiting the state from fulfilling its essential attributes (Almeida, 1991; Comín, 2018).

The political crisis that hit Europe with the outbreak and aftermath of the First World War, the ensuing reconfiguration of national states, and the Great Depression of the early 1930s revealed the weaknesses and difficulties of a global development model based on the foundations of the liberal state. The dictatorial regimes of the inter-war period and the policies of reconstruction and economic recovery based on strong state intervention in the period after the Second World War were particularly successful, as well illustrated by the Iberian case. In the generality of the countries of the Western world, the crisis of the liberal state explains the emergence and development of the welfare state with reinforced functions in the creation and distribution of income. The direct intervention in the productive sphere through public companies and the increase of regulatory functions of the state were accompanied by a significant increase in public expenditures of social scope (education, health, housing, subsidies and social pensions). In order to promote the development of national production, protectionist measures and import substitution policies were adopted.

This return to the centrality of the role of the state in guaranteeing the defence of national interests implied a strengthening of the institutions of tax extraction and of the framing and regulation of the private sector of the economy. Therefore, it is not surprising that the market failures were replaced by the failures of the state. This explains the revolt against the state and its fiscal pressure in the early 1980s, which marked the return to a process of liberalization of markets and privatization of economic sectors under public tutelage. This new liberalizing process has come to be seen as an essential institutional condition to achieve increases in efficiency and competitiveness and consequent growth of integrated economies on a global scale. The evolution of the institutions of the European Community – which since 1986 has come to count on Spain and Portugal as new member states – provides a good example of the importance of greater integration resulting from greater economic openness guaranteed by the single market and the single currency.

Throughout this chapter, we try to keep in mind the simultaneously harmonious and conflictual relationship between the state and private economic agents, distinguishing three fundamental stages or periods: the first stage corresponds to the long nineteenth century (1807–1914), during which the basic institutions of the new regimes of constitutional monarchy were put in place and consolidated; the second stage, between 1914 and 1974, encompasses a period characterized by crisis and disbelief in liberal institutions and by the emergence and strengthening of dictatorial political regimes; finally, the third stage, covering the years 1974 (1976 in Spain) to 2000, corresponds to the period of construction of the institutions which allow for the consolidation of democracy and integration into the European Community.[88]

In the following sections of this chapter we try to address economic policies and institutions in both Iberian countries throughout the period from 1800 to 2000 by stressing their common and distinctive features. However, it is inevitable to present specific elements relative to each country in order to explain the interaction between political realities and the course of economic events.

20.2 Emergence and Consolidation of Capitalist Institutions

The first phase considered here covers the period between 1807 and 1914, that is, between the invasions and French occupation of the Iberian Peninsula and the eve of the First World War. We shall divide the presentation of the main institutional reforms and economic policies into two sub-periods: first, the years 1807–1850, which were decisive for overcoming the political, economic

---

[88] For a summary and general overview of the institutional setting in Portugal during the nineteenth and twentieth centuries, see Lains and Silva (2005a; 2005b), especially the chapters on public finance, economic policy and institutional and legal framework, and Lains (2002a). For Spain see Comín (1996).

and social institutions of the *Ancien Régime* and for the emergence and triumph of the liberal revolutions; and second, the years 1851 to 1914, during which the liberal institutions that supported and framed capitalist economic structures were consolidated, as is the case in most countries of the Western world.

20.2.1 The Wars of Independence and the Liberal Revolutions, 1807–1850

At the beginning of the century, Portugal and Spain were with their backs turned and playing in opposite political and diplomatic fields. Portuguese alignment with Britain and the Franco–Spanish alliance provoked the unhappy military outcome of the 'War of Oranges' (1801), which penalized Portugal and served to demonstrate the risks and threats inherent in the Napoleonic pretensions to European dominance. However, soon the two Iberian countries would simultaneously fall victim to this expansionist drift, suffering the vicissitudes of a prolonged war of resistance and independence from the invading and occupying French power.

This phase of strong political and military instability in Europe (which only calmed after the beginning of the Congress of Vienna in 1814) was also accompanied by turbulence in the colonial domains in Central and South America that had sustained the Spanish and Portuguese empires for about three centuries. The example of the American Revolution of 1776 encouraged a vast movement of independence that forced the European colonial metropolises to rethink the bases of support of their economies, already weakened by the Napoleonic Wars.

In this context, the movements of rejection of the regimes of political absolutism and of the economic structures grounded on a social and colonial order that was close to its ending, gained momentum. The triumph of the liberal revolutions of 1820 (in January in Spain, in August in Portugal) was inevitable and had been symbolically announced by the promulgation of the Constitution of Cádiz (1812) during the period of French occupation in Spain. This constitution had a clear liberal vein. The new ideas of sovereignty, citizenship and division of powers, and the strong attachment to freedom as a mobilizing force in the multiple spheres of human life, pointed the way to meaningful structural changes.

The Portuguese Constitution of 1822 was clearly inspired by the model of Cádiz, which contributed to reinforce the convergence of the political options assumed by both countries in their liberal triennials (1820–1823). The absolutist restoration occurred almost simultaneously in Portugal (May 1823) and Spain (October 1823), with the inevitable approval of the European powers united in the Holy Alliance. There followed years of intense turbulence and conflict between liberal supporters of the regime of constitutional monarchy and absolutists rooted in the principles of the old monarchical order.

The liberal triumph would occur in both countries after intense civil wars (1832–1834 in Portugal and 1833–1840 in Spain). Despite the momentary successes and setbacks naturally associated with a political environment marked by strong turmoil between liberals and absolutists, the institutions of the *Ancien Régime* were gradually dismantled, in two fundamental dimensions: at the political level, through forms of representation of sovereignty according to which the legislative and parliamentary power came to assume a clear preponderance; and at the economic and social level, through the construction of new forms of access to property and means of production with the rise of new social groups and economic interests that replaced the previous predominance of the traditional orders of the clergy and nobility.

It was at this stage that the liberal constitutions were launched, always having as a reference the pioneering and symbolic example of the Constitution of Cádiz of 1812. In Portugal, after the repeal of the Constitution of 1822 following the absolutist counterrevolution of 1823, the more moderate Constitutional Charter of 1826 was conceded. Except for the short period of validity of a new radical constitution adopted in 1838 (following a revolutionary coup in September 1836) and repealed in 1842, the Constitutional Charter of 1826, subject to an amendment in 1852, remained in force as a structuring document of the regime of constitutional monarchy until the republican revolution of 1910. The victory of the supporters of the Charter in 1842 began a troubled period that also witnessed several popular revolts (namely the revolts of *Maria da Fonte* and the *Patuleia* War between 1846 and 1847). This prolonged the climate of tension and civil war between supporters of and opponents to liberal constitutional principles, or between supporters of more radical solutions and defenders of more gradual reforms, in relation to the pace and intensity of the institutional changes to be promoted. The dilemmas associated with the construction of the liberal state in Portugal saw a period of relaxation and appeasement after 1851, following one of several political-military coups that proved decisive in establishing the political peace that Portuguese political history consecrated with the expression of Regeneration. The Constitutional Charter of 1826 remained as a document inspiring rotation among parties that respected the king's authority and were interested in creating consensus on the need to consolidate liberal institutions and strengthen their attributes as instruments of construction of a modern capitalist economy.

In Spain, after the absolutist restoration of 1823, there was a similar setback in the constitutional framework that culminated with the concession of the Charter of 1834, which provoked the animosity of the liberals. As in the case of Portugal, in 1836 the Constitution of Cádiz was re-established until a compromise solution was again found with the approval of the more moderate Constitution of 1845, which managed to accommodate the support of great landowners. In this succession of advances and retreats in relation to the constitutional model of Cádiz, it is important to recognize two fundamental changes, regarding the acceptance of the liberal doctrine: on the one hand, a vision of sovereignty that implied sharing power between the Crown and the nation, recognizing that Queen Isabel II had the capacity to establish the balance between political parties and maintain the stability of the social order; on the other hand, the substitution of the universal suffrage of the *Cortes* of Cádiz by a census voting system, significantly limiting the participation of the low-income population.

It should be noted that this victorious emergence of the liberal state was, above all, a movement of elites led by a political class with privileged access to power and with the inevitable marginalization of disadvantaged social groups. The very nature of census voting (reserved for the population with access to property and sources of income) generated a clientele system in which the elite who participated in the political decision-making processes and in the state regulatory power also formed an interest group that could benefit from those decisions, hence paving the way to *caciquismo*, to the manipulation of electoral processes, to the purchase of votes and the corruption of political agents. It is not surprising, therefore, that the absolutist opposition (*Miguelista* in Portugal, *Carlista* in Spain) had as its privileged source of recruitment the social groups from below, peasants and salaried workers who did not benefit from the outcome of a bourgeois revolution that substantially limited representation and access of such disadvantaged groups to the exercise of sovereign power. This characteristic feature of the Iberian liberal revolutions was kept throughout the second half of the nineteenth century, worsening the social tension arising from the growth of the workers' organization and protest.[89]

Despite the political instability and the setbacks inherent in the vicissitudes of the alternation of revolution and counterrevolution, which took place both in Spain and Portugal during the first half of the nineteenth century, the economic and political institutions that characterize the essence of the liberal state were nevertheless firmly launched.

Subject to the specificities and nuances of each country, it is possible to establish a set of common features, namely: an annual budget, which was publicly discussed and voted, and based on a minimum government revenue and expenditure to ensure state functions and on revenues borne by customs duties and direct proportional taxes on property and production; the reform of local institutions (municipalities and councils) with administrative powers delegated by the central state; a regular army with the capacity to intervene in the national territory and overseas; a financial system based on a national central bank and several deposit banks of a private nature; a monetary system based on a national currency; an educational system gradually extended to the whole country, especially at the level of basic instruction; national and local

---

[89] For a general appraisal of the course of the liberal revolution in Portugal, see Bonifácio (2010). For Spain, see Comín (2020).

institutions willing to build up and maintain transport and communication networks, as well as to create urban public services, generally through concessions to private companies; a system of legislation, defence and jurisdiction of private property (ending of the *Ancien Régime*'s property system based on the tied property of the church and religious orders, private landlords and municipalities); the gradual establishment of systems of economic freedom in trade and industry; the maintenance of integrated colonial territories (in the Portuguese case, especially in the African regions of Angola and Mozambique, in the Spanish case, especially in the islands of Cuba and Puerto Rico and in the Philippines and also in the protectorate of Morocco after 1912); and a system of freedom of the press and scrutiny of political debate in the public sphere (Cardoso & Lains, 2010b).

Regarding the reforms of the tax system, it is important to take into account the Spanish case and the vicissitudes of approval and successive amendments to the Law of 1845. Despite the rigour of the formal principles defining liberal taxation, the changes introduced were quite revealing of one of the facets crucial to the survival of the Iberian constitutional monarchies, that is, the need to harmonize multiple economic interests (agriculture, industry and commerce) that could be benefited or harmed by the introduction of new taxes (Llopis, 2002b).

In both countries, the structure of taxation and the management of state returns has kept a regular pattern throughout the long nineteenth century, as we shall further discuss in the next section. The weight of indirect taxation (consumption and tariffs) and the regular increase of revenues originated by the introduction of income tax and taxes on property and on production have similarly occurred in both Portugal and Spain. As far as the composition of public expenditure is concerned, there has also been a stable allocation throughout the period, up to 1910, with a regular increase of debt servicing, a sharp decrease of military expenses and a sustained growth of expenditure in the main economic sectors requiring state intervention, namely infrastructures and public works, as well as in education and social assistance.[90]

The evolution of public expenditure and public revenues as a percentage of GDP is depicted in Figures 20.1 and 20.2, which also serve to illustrate the analysis and discussion referring to the whole period under consideration.[91]

---

[90] Due to length restrictions, it is not our aim here to discuss with detail the composition of public expenditure and state returns. The subject has been analysed in the chapters on Spain and Portugal included in Cardoso and Lains (2010a). On Portugal, see also Esteves (2005) and Lopes (2005). For the Spanish case, see Comín (1996; 2010; 2014a). For the evolution of the structure of public social spending and the tax structure in Spain, see also Espuelas (2013) and Torregrosa-Hetland (2016b). This long-term evolution of the structure of public revenues and expenses in Portugal and Spain is also shared by Italy (see Comín, 2014b).

[91] Source of Figures 20.1–20.4: International Monetary Fund, Fiscal Affairs Department. Historical Public Debt Database. Version September 2012. Abbas, S. M. Ali, Nazim

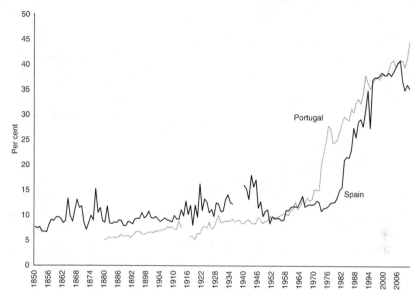

Figure 20.1 Government revenue/GDP (%).
Source: see footnote 91.

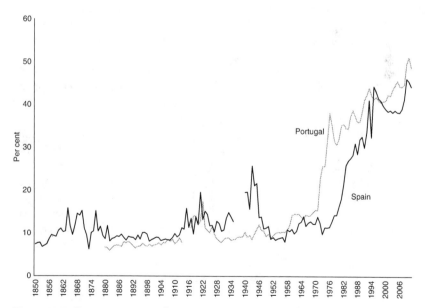

Figure 20.2 Government expenditures/GDP (%).
Source: see footnote 91.

20.2.2 Consolidation and Crisis of the Liberal State, 1851–1910

The consolidation of liberal state institutions favoured the process of industrialization and economic growth which, however, was largely based on private companies and institutions. The amount of public expenditure as a percentage of GDP remained practically stable between 1880 and 1900 (around 6.74% in Portugal and 8.68% in Spain) (Figure 20.2). The Iberian liberals were aware of the recommendations of the classical economists to maintain a minimal state. Nonetheless, the liberal state played a key role in the process of industrialization leading to economic growth in both Iberian countries. Among the set of reforms and economic policies that took place in this period, the following should be particularly taken into account: the definitive dissolution of the seigniorial and ecclesiastical institutions of the *Ancien Régime* (the end of the entail, *morgadio* system); the consolidation of legal regimes and legal codes regulating private ownership of land and the functioning of financial markets; the creation of public debt restructuring and consolidation procedures; the abolition of restrictive foreign trade policies with a mercantilist blueprint, and their substitution by customs tariffs fixed according to governmental guidelines and circumstances more or less favourable to protectionist measures; the creation of banking laws allowing the strengthening of private banks that played a pivotal role in funding public works, namely through investment in transport infrastructures (especially railways); and the strengthening of local education systems, which allowed a significant reduction in illiteracy rates (see Chapter 19).

The institutional changes that occurred in Portugal in the Regeneration period under the leadership of Fontes Pereira de Melo (both as Minister of Public Works in 1852–1856 and as Prime Minister on three separate occasions between 1871–1886) were fundamental to guaranteeing the international financing of the Portuguese public debt and the flow of foreign investments that allowed the state and public works which induced the gradual growth of important industrial sectors. Portugal's entry into the gold standard system in 1854 provided added credibility when negotiating external borrowing in the international stock markets of Paris and London. With regard to reforms of the framework of customs protection, its liberalizing scope was never fully achieved, as was well documented by the customs protection measures enacted in the 1850s (Reis, 1993b).

The time frame of 1851 is also relevant for Spain, as this year Bravo Murillo promoted fundamental administrative reforms, notably a new public accounting law and legislation on public debt consolidation. Aware of the power conceded to her by the Constitution of 1845, Isabel II behaved like a capricious queen who never properly understood the responsibilities

---

Belhocine, Asmaa El-Ganainy and Mark Horton (2010). A Historical Public Debt Database, IMF Working Paper WP/10/245, Washington, DC. Available at: www.imf.org/external/pubs/ft/wp/2010/data/wp10245.zip.

required by the exercise of power. In fact, her sympathies and political choices provoked the animosity of the Progressive Party, which resorted to two revolutionary coups (in 1854 and 1868) in order to impose its orientation on matters of economic policy (Pascual & Sudrià, 2002).

Between 1854 and 1856, the governments of the *Bienio Progresista* (Progressive Biennium) promoted a set of fiscal reforms that led to some fall in revenue collection, since no new taxes had been introduced to compensate for the abolished consumption tax. But the most important reforms of this progressive period were the policies designed for the industrial and banking sectors, which made possible a significant increase in investment, especially foreign investment. The main beneficiaries were not the traditional sectors of industry but rather the construction of railways and banking. In fact, capital invested in railway companies doubled between 1859 and 1866, while industrial investment fell by one-third. In turn, banking legislation allowed the creation of an issuing bank in each provincial capital, as well as credit companies especially aimed at investment in the railway sector.[92]

The remarkable railway investment in Spain was behind the construction of lines subsidized by the state, which granted large customs benefits for the import of all the materials and equipment necessary for the lines' construction and operation. This process resulted in an excess of infrastructure that could not be profitable due to the shortage of passengers and goods (Herranz-Loncán, 2007). The inevitable railway bubble led to the economic crisis of 1864–1868, which caused the bankruptcy of many of the banks created in the previous decade (Martín-Aceña & Nogués, 2013). The Spanish economic crisis created a situation of social unrest that was one of the main causes of the *coup d'état* and Revolution of 1868, which approved the new Constitution of 1869, of a progressive liberal character. Following this revolution, the spread of free-trade ideas intensified, helping to counteract measures of a prohibitionist nature which, however, were replaced by protectionist customs duties, in order to guarantee competitive conditions favourable to the nascent industry. At the turn of the following decades the debate (both in Spain and in Portugal) was intense on the aims and scope of free-trade policies that impeded the emergence and growth of national industrial sectors. The rhetoric of public debates (including parliamentary debates), on the faithfulness to liberal principles, could not be matched by concrete measures that almost always collided with the economic interests of social groups on which governments depended (Comín, 1996).

The Spanish Revolution of 1868 was also responsible for a monetary reform of great institutional impact, the creation of a new currency, the peseta, which lasted until its replacement by the euro. Another relevant institutional change

---

[92] On the influence of the institutions created by the liberal revolution on the industrial revolution in Spain during the nineteenth century, see Gutiérrez-Poch (2018).

was the granting of the banknote issuing monopoly to the Bank of Spain, as a counterpart of credit granted to the public treasury, which opened the door to the process of monetization of the public deficit.

The effort to centralize and regulate the state accounts, in the Portuguese case (in 1859 and 1863), as well as the founding of banking institutions specialized in the management of mortgage loans, were signs of economic reform with strong political implications. Equally important was the reforms of the taxation system of 1852 and 1860 with the introduction of two new types of direct taxes (tax on property and tax on production) that would be the main sources of state revenues until the late 1880s. However, the changes and reforms of the fiscal system were a focus of permanent tension and political instability (helping to explain many of the riots and *coups d'état*) in Portugal until the early 1870s.

In 1871 Portuguese politics entered a period of relative calm, witnessing a process of alternation in power of the main political parties. However, the beginning of the 1890s would unleash a new and sharp political crisis, driven by colonial disputes in Africa that were the reason for a British ultimatum and a consequent banking and financial crisis aggravated by the fall of Baring Brothers (the main Portuguese financier in London) and by the drop in emigrants' remittances from Brazil. Portugal was forced to abandon the gold standard and to suspend the service of its internal and external debt in 1892, entering bankruptcy and undermining its credibility before international partners and financiers. This situation forced Portugal to change its economic and financial policies, by reducing its dependence on foreign capital flows, intensifying customs protectionism and increasing fiscal discipline and the tax burden. The exit from the gold standard system created room for the Bank of Portugal to guarantee new forms of access to credit and devaluation policies that contributed to minimizing the negative effects of the 1891–1892 crisis and allowed the survival of protected industrial sectors. However, the political management of the crisis demonstrated the difficulties of survival of a liberal-minded state ruled by the institutions of a parliamentary monarchy.

In Spain, the coup of 1874 put an end to the *Sexenio Democratico* (Democratic Sexennium) and restored the Bourbon dynasty, initiating the Restoration period. This was a period of political stability, alternating between the conservative and liberal parties, which continued until the *coup d'état* of Primo de Rivera in 1923. With regard to economic policy measures, emphasis should be given to the implementation of customs protectionism, which was partly justified by the consequences of the colonial wars (1868–1878), especially the Cuban War of Independence (1895–1898). The financial effort required to maintain military expenditures led to the creation of public debt, whose management forced the new tax reform and the devaluation of the peseta. However, protectionism in foreign trade relations, associated with exchange rate devaluation, was not justified only by the colonial crisis. It was the typical response, involving both Spain and Portugal, by the less developed European countries that sought, through high

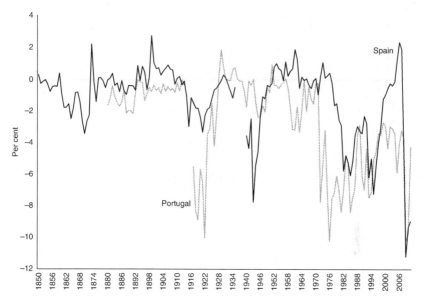

Figure 20.3 Budget balance/GDP (%).
Source: see footnote 91.

custom duties, to monitor the possibilities of industrial growth. It was for this reason, after all, that institutions and institutional reforms could be useful.

In 1880, the tax revenue/GDP ratio was rather low, as mandated by the liberal canon: 5.1% in Portugal and 8.6% in Spain (Figure 20.1). In the absence of wars and revolutions, the budget deficits of the liberal state (as a percentage of GDP) were small. In fact, on the eve of the First World War both countries managed to balance their public budgets (Figure 20.3). Until the First World War, the outstanding public debt/GDP ratio (Figure 20.4) was higher in Spain than in Portugal, due to the country's greater budget deficits and greater recourse to the central bank, and due to the fact that Spain was not included in the gold standard (Cardoso & Lains, 2010b; Comín, 2010).

20.3 Protectionism, Nationalism and State Intervention

The first three decades of the second phase considered here (1914 to 1974/1975) were characterized by a change in economic policy towards protectionism and nationalism, and a greater state economic interventionism. Like other countries in southern Europe, Portugal and Spain were affected by the first globalization and their reaction was to isolate themselves from abroad. The social changes experienced during the First World War and

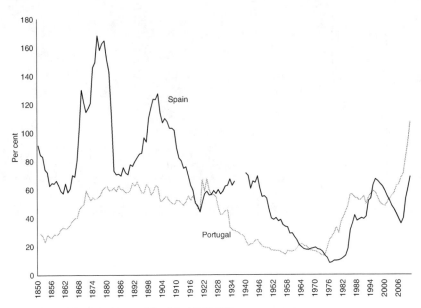

Figure 20.4 Outstanding public debt/GDP (%).
Source: see footnote 91.

the post-war period created a growing social and political instability that led to the dictatorships in Portugal (1926–1974) and Spain (1923–1930 and 1939–1975).

The dictatorships of Primo de Rivera and Salazar created significant institutional changes. Politically, they established two authoritarian, corporatist political regimes of a fascist-like nature. The economic institutions were aimed at increasing the intervention of the state in the economy through market regulation, public spending and the foundation of public companies.

Later, from the 1950s on, Spain and Portugal adopted indicative planning in imitation of the French model, which implied an indirect intervention through tax exemptions, subsidies and privileged credit at interest rates much lower than those of the market.[93]

20.3.1 Warfare, Autarchy, Corporatism and Dictatorship

The proclamation of the Republic in Portugal in 1910 did not allow the new regime, eager to affirm its difference to the constitutional monarchy that was

---

[93] For a general overview of the main features of institutional and economic change during the twentieth century in Portugal, see Cardoso (2015) and Pinto (2015), especially the chapters on political life and economic process. For Spain, see Betrán and Pons (2020).

then in crisis, sufficient time to demonstrate its institutional capacity before the financial disruption caused by the First World War overturned any prospects of significant changes in the conduct of economic policy. At a time when the country had not yet solved the negative effects of the financial crisis of 1891–1892, the significant increase in military expenditure associated with the traumatic involvement in the European conflict of 1914–1918, the worsening public deficit, the increase of public debt and the policy of monetary depreciation that generated strong inflationary tensions all combined to supplant the rhetoric of institutional change that the republican regime was supposed to bring.

It was in the name of the need for financial discipline that the Portuguese republican regime would eventually be deposed in May 1926. For the mentors of a new political order and authority, republican institutions had not only failed to solve the problems of deficit and debt but had further aggravated such problems with the wrong solutions of monetary issuing and exchange rate devaluation.

Spain did not participate in the First World War, but the Spanish economy was considerably affected by the war and suffered a deep industrial crisis in the post-war period. The Cambó tariff of 1921 was a protectionist measure intended to solve the crisis. In the post-war period, the Law of Productive Coordination, also a work of Cambó, was approved and state support to the railway companies was promoted. The social conflicts of the post-war period caused a military coup in 1923, which established the dictatorship of Primo de Rivera, who deepened the nationalist, protectionist and interventionist policies through the formation of corporatist institutions in imitation of Mussolini's Italy. Some public companies were also set up, in the banking sector and fiscal monopolies. The law of 1917 strengthened the National Production Protective Commission (set up in 1908), which was the predecessor of the National Economic Council, created in 1924 to command economic activity. Primo de Rivera deepened the strategy of support provided to national production, with the Royal Decree of 30 April 1924 aiming at a new institutional setting to foster the development of industrial firms. It also consolidated the regulation of the production and trade sectors: in 1926, the National Production Regulatory Committee was established, with the power to authorize the establishment of new industrial firms and the extension or transfer of existing ones; and numerous intervening agencies were established in which the interests of national production were represented.

Labour and social legislation advanced in Spain during the First World War due to pressure from the unions and strikes. A 10-hour business day was approved in 1918, followed by an 8-hour work day in industry in 1919. In the same year, a compulsory retirement age and adhesion to the League of Nations and the ILO were approved. An important step was the establishment of the Ministry of Labour in 1920. During the dictatorship of Primo de Rivera, in

1926 the National Corporate Organization was established, consisting of the local joint committees, in which businesspeople, workers and government were represented. Labour contracts were also regulated for the first time in 1926.

In interwar Spain some public companies were created. The Railway Statute of 1924 established a process of public funding for the acquisition of material for the companies, carried out by the Caja Ferroviaria (Railway State Fund) from 1926. The dictatorship of Primo de Rivera established, in 1924, a telephone monopoly, with its management granted to the Compañia Telefónica Nacional de España (Spanish National Telephone Company), a private company whose main shareholder was the ITT. In 1928 a petroleum monopoly was created in Spain, with its management leased to the Compañía Arrendataria del Monopolio de Petróleos SA (Leasing Company of the Monopoly of Petroleum), a company created by the main banks of the country (Comín, 2002).

The neutralization or minimization of the immediate effects of the Great Depression in Portugal is associated with the policy of financial stabilization developed under the iron command of António de Oliveira Salazar, who took over the direction of the Ministry of Finance in April 1928. In particular, the policies of budgetary balance and exchange rate and monetary stabilization, the fiscal reform of 1928–1929, and the restructuring of internal and external public debt were instrumental in putting an end to a long cycle of deficit budgets and in ensuring the control of the outflow of capital before the signs of the international crisis had been felt (Silva, 2015).

However, in addition to these preventive measures, there was also a decisive and reactive response in the area of economic policy, notably through decisions of the following types: the containment of private and public consumption, in the light of principles of budgetary equilibrium; a stimulus to exports through a competitive exchange rate policy; private investment (through lower interest rates, which also alleviated public debt burdens) and public investment (through increased public spending, especially in the road and port construction sectors); and the creation of special social assistance and welfare schemes designed to protect unemployed and disadvantaged social groups.

The managing of the conjuncture of the Great Depression allowed Salazar to take advantage of a unique opportunity to strengthen the economic instruments to consolidate the authoritarian regime of the corporatist New State (*Estado Novo*). The Portuguese Constitution of 1933 conferred special attention to the economic component and the specific attributes of the state in this matter, aimed at the coordination and direction of social activities as a whole and expressly claiming the objective of promoting social harmony through the submission of individual interests to the superior interests of the nation. The regulatory purpose was not limited to the generic principles of balancing the distribution of population by a diversity of professions and jobs; it even announced that it was the state's objective to defend the national economy in the face of the threat posed by competition among agricultural, industrial and commercial enterprises (Lopes, 2004a).

Also in 1933 a legislative package was enacted which included a strategic document called the National Labour Statute (inspired by Mussolini's fascist *Carta del Lavoro*), as well as a set of five diplomas that regulated the functioning of corporatist bodies with direct implications for the organization of the labour force and social security regimes. Among the measures enacted for the construction of the legal system of the corporatist regime, it is important to highlight the legislation on industrial conditioning (Brito, 1989).

Beginning in 1931, the industrial conditioning regime was to become one of the main instruments of the *Estado Novo*'s economic policy over the next two decades. In essence, conditioning consisted of creating an administrative barrier to the entry of new firms into the market or to an increase in installed production capacity. In spite of the exemptions applied to some sectors that were relieved from bureaucratic control, conditioning measures mainly covered industrial sectors with a strong component of imports of raw materials or intermediate products, or industrial sectors considered strategic for national economic development and, in particular, the country's export sector. In this sense, it functioned both as a measure of import substitution and protection of the domestic market. The conditioning regime was especially relevant until the end of the 1940s, leaving indelible marks in the formation of a business economic culture that has become accustomed to protected competition environments and to the special privileges granted by the state (Almodovar & Cardoso, 2005).

In 1935 a Law of Economic Reconstitution was enacted with the objective of defining an integrated program of public investments aimed at the consolidation and guarantee of better functioning of the internal market. This investment program focused on areas of activity essential to the performance of the various sectors of economic life, namely transport and communications infrastructures, electricity production, irrigation systems and public facilities.

The implementation of this program was surrounded by the doctrinal rhetoric of corporatism. Unconditional enemies of laissez-faire and of neo-classical economic principles based on the idea of free competition, corporatist ideologues advocated the notion of a self-directed economy which, however, had nothing to do with processes of spontaneous market equilibrium. In the corporatist ideal model, the direction of economic organization was not imposed from above but assumed by agents who were naturally involved in the decision-making procedures of corporatist bodies, with the state having a global surveillance function over the entire economic process. It was precisely the failure to realize this ideal model of corporatism until the end of the 1940s that conferred on the institutional structure of the *Estado Novo* the character of a blocking force against free initiative and individual economic freedom. The authoritarian regime imposed serious restrictions on the exercise of basic civil liberties (in addition to drastic limitations on political freedom of association and representation and on freedom of thought and expression) and reduced its scope to the defence and conservation of the interests of economic and traditional social groups that naturally felt comfortable within a regime that depended on them and supported their actions. The weak competitiveness of the Portuguese economy was compensated by protectionist policies, raising the state as a factor of conservation and reproduction of a weak economic structure and echoing adherence to Keynesian ideas (Almodovar & Cardoso, 2005). This institutional design served to protect and accommodate interests that were based on the benefits of a regime characterized by discipline, dictatorship and repression of individual liberties in both civic and political terms (Rosas & Garrido, 2012).

Spain did not participate in the Second World War, but suffered a bloody civil war (1936–1939) that was won by Franco, who created a personal dictatorship, reinforced by the fascist powers during the war, and an autarkic economy. In the post-war period, Franco's governments established fascist-like political and economic institutions, in imitation of Nazi Germany and Fascist Italy. Between 1936 and 1957, the institutions and economic policies were those of a war economy, with the autarky to fight against external markets and the command economy at the domestic level.

The autarchic policy took to the limits the protectionism and the interventionism rehearsed by the dictatorship of Primo de Rivera. It was basically a policy of import substitution, which contrasted with the policies implemented by the post-war European democracies. In addition to protectionism, Franco implemented an interventionist policy, creating regulatory bodies for production, prices and trade, as well as ration cards to deal with shortages. The economic policy of autarky was not carried out by professional economists but by the military, lawyers, engineers and neo-mercantilist economists, who lacked the most elementary training in economics.

Franco's governments controlled foreign trade through state trading, quantitative restrictions (quotas and licenses), bilateral agreements, capital controls, exchange controls and a monopoly on foreign exchange. Imports and exports were decided by the government, which granted import licenses and foreign currency to pay for imports. The Franco regime also rejected foreign investors and the main foreign companies were nationalized: Renfe, Rio Tinto, Telefónica, La Canadiense. The law of monetary crimes punished those who evaded currencies or traded on their own. Like other dictators, Franco kept the peseta highly appreciated (Barciela, 2002).

Franco's industrialization policy was very interventionist. To replace the market, different regulators and auditors were established, with the role of setting both the prices and quantities that the sectors and firms had to produce, and with the privilege of buying at monopoly prices to sell at official prices. The

Comisaría de Abastecimientos y Transporte (Comissariat for Supply and Transport) controlled the fixing of official prices and distributed the guides for the transportation of the products. The circulation of products without a guide was deemed a black market crime (i.e. smuggling), and punished with harsh penalties, whenever producers did not have the necessary political influences. The Servicio Nacional del Trigo, or SNT (National Wheat Service) controlled the wheat market by fixing the area of sowing allocated to farmers and the prices for which they had to sell their production, which the SNT stored in silos for future selling to the flour manufacturers.

The intervention in the labour market from 1939 onward prohibited free trade unions and created a single or vertical trade union with compulsory membership, controlled by the Falangists.[94] The labour market was totally commanded by the vertical union and strikes were banned, punishable even with the death penalty. The government set nominal wages at very low levels, which were eroded by rising inflation. As compensation, dismissal was practically prohibited.

Between 1950 and 1959 there was a 'mercantilist industrialization' that generated a slight economic growth, thanks to the enormous technological backwardness accumulated in the previous decade and the moderate reforms of the 1951 government. But the autarchic model continued, and immediately showed its limitations, since the pursuit of growth required an increase in the imports of raw materials, for whose payment the necessary foreign currency was not available. Therefore, the system collapsed due to two economic imbalances: domestic inflation and the external deficit, which depleted foreign currency reserves (Barciela, 2002).

20.3.2 Post-War Development and New Growth Pathways

The favourable conditions and obstacles to the growth of the Portuguese economy became evident during the Second World War and in the immediate post-war period. Portugal had no direct involvement in the conflict and did not suffer the adverse effects of destruction experienced by the major world powers. But the pace of industrialization was slow, in tune with the effects of inertia caused by the protectionist framework and the regime of industrial conditioning.

A new policy that would allow Portugal to converge with European economic growth, now that the war was over, was implemented by the Law of Industrial Development and Reorganization of 1945, considered as a new and more solid support for Portuguese industrial policy. The Development Plans

---

[94] Falange Española was a Spanish fascist political organization founded by José Antonio Primo de Rivera in 1933. In 1937, General Franco merged it with the monarchist ultracatholic Traditionalist Communion, becoming the sole party of the Franco regime.

conceived and implemented up to the end of the 1950s embody and express well the continuity and consistency of the guidelines drawn in the post-war context.

In the final year of the First Development Plan, in 1958, one of the most important instruments of public and private investment policy was created, which would play a major role in the process of Portuguese economic growth in the 1960s: the Bank of National Development. The total amount of investment involved in the initial program of the II Development Plan more than tripled in relation to the amount of the previous plan.

The II Development Plan added a broader view of the coordination and articulation of sectoral policies that also extended to the social dimension of economic development policies, especially with regard to employment and social protection issues. It introduced a less imperative and less authoritarian attitude towards the modalities of direct state intervention in the economy, benefiting from a climate of openness that participation in international organizations – from the negotiations under the Marshall Plan for Europe in 1948 to the accession to the European Free Trade Association (EFTA) in 1959 and to the International Monetary Fund (IMF) and the World Bank in 1961 – necessarily favoured.

Although Portugal initially dispensed with US aid for European reconstruction established through the Marshall Plan, it participated as a founding member of the European Economic Cooperation Organization (OECD) and the European Union of Payments, bodies with responsibility for administering this aid plan. The exchange and financial difficulties experienced at the end of 1948 obliged Portugal to take a new attitude of express acceptance of the aid and led to the abandonment of the principles of economic autarchy, which were no longer feasible. There is also no doubt that Portugal was a net beneficiary of the Marshall Plan and the financial programs that were able to correct the balance of payments imbalances and help it implement economic recovery and development projects.

The interaction of the Portuguese technical delegations that participated in the negotiations related to foreign aid and European integration were crucial for the modernization of the country's economic and financial administration, and for the learning of the instruments and languages of international cooperation (namely the language of Keynesian economic policies), especially with regard to the use and comparison of statistical and national accounting systems.

The integration option offered by EFTA turned out to be more advantageous and profitable for Portugal. The weight of the colonial markets, combined with the need not to disturb the stability of social and political balances between representatives of interests of the agricultural and industrial sectors, were factors that weighed in the choice of alignments in the European framework. The Portuguese convergence effort would require favourable conditions and incentives, which were guaranteed by EFTA on preferential terms. Europe was beginning to be understood as the main force to open up and modernize the framework of the national economy (Amaral, 2015a).

This was also the way that opened the doors to the golden period of Portuguese economic growth in the 1960s (an annual average rate of GDP growth of 6.4% in the period 1960–1973) and to other processes of opening up and liberalizing trade relations with its main European economic partners. However, the unprecedented increase in GDP was not reflected in the growth of social expenditure or in opening up labour relations and trade union organization (Lopes, 2004a).

Unlike Portugal, Spain was not allowed to participate in the Marshall Plan aid and was not a member of EFTA. Nevertheless, in September 1953, Spain and the United States signed the Defense and Mutual Aid Pacts: in exchange for US aid valued at US$1,523 million until 1963, Spain ceded land for the United States to establish military bases in Spain. The Stabilization Plan of 1959 put an end to the autarchic regime and opened the economy abroad (Prados de la Escosura et al., 2011; Martínez-Ruiz & Pons, 2020). In 1958 Spain had been integrated into the IMF and the World Bank; then Spain joined the OECD (1959), followed by the General Agreement on Tariffs and Trade (GATT) in 1963. These organizations promoted the Spanish external opening up by providing technical and economic assistance to overcome the opposition of the Falangists. They also provided financial coverage, with grants and loans in foreign currency to cover the balance of payments deficits.

Spain had been trying to integrate into Europe since 1962, but the initial applications were rejected due to the dictatorship nature of Franco's regime. The European Economic Community (EEC) only offered a Preferential Agreement that was signed in 1970. The 1960 tariff ended quantitative protection by moving to liberalized trade with tariff protection. The Spanish gradual external liberalization continued with the agreements of the GATT and the negotiations with the EEC.

In 1959, long-term capital inflows were allowed and the extraction abroad of foreign companies' profits obtained in Spain were authorized. Spain ended its monetary isolation by declaring the convertibility of the peseta in 1961 and its integration into the Bretton Woods system, setting a more realistic exchange rate, subject to the discipline of the IMF.

Between 1964 and 1974, three Development Plans were approved in Spain. The plans were mandatory for public agencies and indicative for the private sector, with increased regulation in financial markets, the labour market and industry.

The financial control had two basic regulations: the privileged funding of credit to companies and the official credit. In 1974, 43% of the funding of the credit system to the private sector was regulated. Labour market intervention hardly changed and employers and workers were offered a combination of low wages and job security. This forced production adjustments to be made through overtime, at the expense of employment levels and by reducing the savings from social security contributions. The industrial policy was based on the granting of credit, financial, fiscal and customs advantages, as well as on direct aid to firms that invested in privileged sectors selected by the government. The industrial policy was developed by the law of preferential interest industries of 1963, combined with Concerted Actions and the Development Poles framed by the Development Plans.

Public companies lost the role they had obtained during the autarchy period. The National Institute of Industry (INI) became a kind of 'hospital' for bankrupt companies in coal mining, the steel industry and shipbuilding. Public companies were inefficient and generated large losses that were financed through the state budget.

The state hardly increased public expenditure to meet the demands of development plans and society. The tax reforms of 1959 and 1964 continued with the tax principles established in 1845 but hardly increased the collection of revenues. From 1965 the state expenses in economic and social services grew slowly: education was assumed by the state as its responsibility, while health and pensions were funded by the Social Security system, which was created in 1967. The new social benefits were financed by contributions from companies and workers to the Social Security system (Serrano Sanz & Pardos Martínez, 2002).

20.4 Democracy Building and European Integration

This third stage corresponds to the period of transition from authoritarian regimes to mature democracies (1974–2000), breaking the isolation in which Portugal and Spain were living within democratic Europe. The exceptional character that the Iberian countries (together with Greece) represented in the early 1970s arrived at its desired and inevitable outcome.

The end of dictatorships allowed the political change towards democracy and the institutional transformations that allowed the standardization of policies and institutions with those of the EEC and, later, both countries' integration into the club of European democracies. Integration in the EEC and the euro allowed the establishment of democratic institutions, the development of the welfare state, the modernization of the financial monetary system and the opening up to the outside world.[95] Two subperiods will be considered: the first deals with the transition to democracy, while the second concerns the integration in the EEC.

---

[95] On the similarities and the interrelationship between the two Iberian transitions to democracy and to the institutions with similar patterns to the EEC, see Sabater Navarro (2019).

20.4.1 Transition to Democracy

After the Portuguese revolution of April 1974, two of the essential assumptions of the successful growth model of the previous decade were altered: first, the loss of the African colonial market, which until then had functioned as a structural element in the formation of a wider national and international market for economic agents that supported the political regime; and, second, the loss of an authoritarian political background that imposed limits on the freedom of action of economic, social, political and cultural agents and which prevented the modernization of the Portuguese economy and society. The shy attempts of Marcelo Caetano's government (1968–1973) to bring change into the regime could not succeed while the political system was kept in a non-democratic framework. Therefore, the main challenges that confronted Portugal in the period immediately following the April 1974 revolution involved the strengthening of institutions which would guarantee the full functioning of a political regime based on principles of freedom and democracy.

The political opening up inaugurated with the revolution of April 1974 introduced immediate changes in labour institutions, with a significant increase in wages, with benefits for workers including new hiring systems and freedom of trade union enrolment. In this initial period (1974–1975), marked by the strong political influence of the Communist Party and its charismatic leader Álvaro Cunhal, there was a profound (although ephemeral) institutional change, namely through the nationalization of the main sectors of economic activity controlled by private groups (industry, banking and insurance) and collective appropriation of a large number of agricultural estates in the southern region of the country.

After an initial phase of natural turbulence, Portugal took firm steps towards one of the main purposes inherent in the construction of the democratic regime: full integration into the European Community. The main signs that the decision-making process would have to be framed in the European economic and political space were promptly given by Mário Soares, leader of the Socialist Party and Minister of Foreign Affairs of the First Interim Government, who in early May 1974 went to Brussels for first contacts with the European Community. The slogan 'Europe with us', launched by Mário Soares in 1976, set the tone for a long-lasting commitment in which, more important than the financial support that could result from Portugal's integration, Europe was able to dispel the spectre of totalitarian experiences. The formal support of the European Community to the fragile Portuguese democracy was given in September 1976 with the signing of an economic and financial cooperation protocol (Amaral, 2010a).

In Spain, the transition to democracy occurred between 1975 and 1985, when the institutional reforms needed to prepare integration into the EEC took place. After the death of Franco in 1975, the regime change was agreed and peaceful. The political parties signed the Pacts of Moncloa in 1977, and in 1978 the Constitution was approved, which defined a 'social state of law' (Cuevas & Pons, 2020).

The Pacts of Moncloa (1977) modernized the institutions of the state and the instruments of economic policy. Monetary policy adopted a floating exchange rate and exchange control was liberalized in 1985. The full liberalization of capital movements was achieved in 1992. In 1977, the financial market was deregulated, with the liberalization of interest rates, the repeal of mandatory investment ratios and the equalization of financial operations of savings banks and commercial banks. In November 1977, the Deposit Guarantee Fund of Credit Institutions was established. From the Pacts of Moncloa an income policy was agreed to contain wages and create a Welfare State. Tax reform was carried out to homogenize the Spanish tax system with the European one, establishing progressive income tax, corporate tax and a wealth tax. This process was completed in 1986, when entry into the EEC forced the introduction of VAT (Rojo, 2002)

In the twilight of their dictatorships, both Spain and Portugal had budgetary figures more typical of a liberal state than of the welfare states that were dominant in democratic Europe. First, low tax pressure: in 1966, the fiscal revenue/GDP ratio was 12.4% in Portugal and 11.8% in Spain (Figure 20.1). On the other hand, in 1971, the public expenditure/GDP ratio remained low: 15.45% in Portugal and 13.96% in Spain (Figure 20.2). Likewise, in 1970, both countries had the state budget practically balanced, with the budget balance/GDP ratio being −0.24% in Portugal and 0.09% in Spain (Figure 20.3). The dictatorships reduced the public debt/GDP ratio to 13.5% in both countries in 1974 (Figure 20.4).

The effort of institutional convergence towards the EU, including the consolidation of the welfare state, increased the size of the government in both countries to very similar figures: in 1996 the public revenue/GDP ratio was 37.53% in Portugal and 37.72% in Spain, while the public expenditure/GDP ratio was 42.07% in Portugal and 43.23% in Spain. The institutional changes were accompanied in both countries by the doubling of the size of their respective public sectors. The construction of the welfare state created strong budget deficits: in 1996, the budget balance/GDP ratio reached −4.54% of GDP in Portugal and −5.51% in Spain. The budget deficits were financed on credit, which increased the outstanding public debt/GDP ratio to 58.29% in Portugal and 67.48% in Spain in 1996. Afterwards, the fiscal consolidation policy to enter the euro forced both countries to reduce their budget deficits and stabilize the size of their public debt, which increased again with the 2008 depression and the euro crisis.

20.4.2 The Challenges of European Integration

The long pre-accession period faced by Portugal was to some extent justified by the increased difficulties resulting from the enlargement of the European Community to include the Southern countries, each with its own agenda of problems to be solved. Thus, Portugal had to await the outcome of negotiations that proved to be particularly complex in the Spanish case. This experience of enlargement brought important lessons for the internal process of adaptation of the structures and institutions of the European Community, which aimed for a progressive and intensified economic and political integration that would culminate in the preparation of the single market and the European single currency. There is no doubt that Portugal's participation in this process had very positive outcomes.

Portugal's entry into the European Community brought immediate economic and financial benefits. From 1986 onwards there was a strong increase in exports (especially to Spain), a sharp recovery of the balance of payments and a fast influx of foreign investment. In addition, access to European structural funds allowed a set of public investments in areas decisive for the development of the Portuguese economy. All these factors combined led to the launching of a new convergence process to European growth rates (Comín, 1995).

The new rules and the European institutional framework led to constitutional revision and structural reform processes that contributed to Portugal's insertion into an increasingly globalized world. Thus, a new golden decade of growth of the Portuguese economy (between 1986 and 1995) took place. However, full integration into the euro zone would reveal the difficulties of a small and non-competitive open economy, which had to face the challenges of increasing external indebtedness, an accumulated deficit and a marked imbalance in public accounts (Amaral, 2010a).

In the period 1986–1992, Spain joined the EEC and the single market. A fundamental institutional change was the opening up to external competition (through the Treaty of Accession, 1985) and internal competition (through the Internal Market Agreement, 1986). By the terms of the Treaty of Accession to the Community, Spain had to remove commercial protection in seven years. In 1993, Spain liberalized trade in goods, with the exception of agrarian commodities (which were covered by the Common Agricultural Policy) and coal. The openness index increased from 29.2% to 62.2% between 1975 and 2000. The lack of protection allowed imports of goods and services from the EEC to flood the Spanish market. To increase industrial competitiveness, the government expanded the flexibility of the labour market, allowing temporary employment, and also addressed industrial reconversion, which included the privatization of INI public enterprises (iron and steel, automobiles, shipbuilding) with losses since 1985. The EEC forced the privatization and liberalization of network services, which involved the liquidation of public monopolies such as Renfe, Campsa, Tabacalera and Iberia. In the 1990s, liberalization and deregulation affected telecommunications, air, maritime and road transport, professional associations, and the electricity and gas sectors (Rojo, 2002).

Democracy involved the generalization of unemployment benefits and the universalization of pensions, health and education. In the period 1975–2000, the consolidation of the welfare state increased social expenditures from 17.5% to 22.4% of GDP, health expenses from 3.7% to 5.1%, and those of education from 3.9% to 4.3%.

The monetary integration of Spain and Portugal into the euro took place between 1992 and 2000. The peseta was incorporated into the exchange mechanism of the European Monetary System in 1989 and the same occurred with the escudo in 1990. The convergence to the euro began with the Treaty of Maastricht (February 1992) and in 1994 the second phase of the creation of the Monetary Union began. Compliance with the criteria of monetary convergence required great efforts by Portugal and Spain, both of which benefited from the Cohesion Fund (created by the European Union in 1992 as aid to countries with a low per capita income), and this was added to the already existing Structural Funds. In 1994, the Bank of Spain was granted autonomy for monetary policy.

Spain and Portugal were incorporated into the new single currency area on its creation on 1 January 1999, and the national central banks (Banco de Portugal and Banco de España) passed their accounts to euros, while the markets and financial institutions denominated their clients' balances in euros. In order to be able to produce euro coins and banknotes, their entry into circulation was postponed until 1 January 2002. At the beginning of 1999, the common monetary policy became operational and Spain and Portugal ceded their monetary sovereignty to the European Central Bank.

20.5 Conclusion

The evolution of public and private political and economic institutions in Portugal and Spain during the nineteenth and twentieth centuries has some similarities, notwithstanding the temporal mismatches and the natural differences resulting from the smaller size, in the Portuguese case, of the territory, population and economy. In a way, the Iberian Peninsula can be seen as a totality formed by two unequivocally distinct countries, with their own historical and cultural identities, but with characteristics of geographical proximity that make them capable of facing the same type of external shocks, both natural and climatic, or of military or political nature. Also in economic, commercial and financial terms, differences in resource and capacity allocations do not conceal a common position in the geography of global economic development. It was also the historical and geographical neighbourhood between Portugal and Spain that made it possible for both countries to experience a period of dynastic union (between 1580 and 1640) or to be simultaneous victims of Napoleonic expansionism between 1807 and 1814.

The experiences of the liberal triennium (1820–1823) and the resistance to the absolutist restoration (*Miguelista* and *Carlista*) were also similarly shaped in Portugal and Spain. In the middle of the twentieth century, Portugal and Spain joined in an Iberian Pact signed by the dictators Salazar and Franco in 1939 that sealed a political compromise between authoritarian political regimes. But it was the victory of the republican democratic regime in Portugal in 1974 and the democratic regime of the Spanish monarchy in 1976 that allowed a new and reinforced rapprochement between the two countries that on the same day (12 June 1985) signed the treaty of adhesion and on the same day (1 January 1986) joined the European Community as full members.

Throughout the historical narrative presented in this chapter, notwithstanding the main purpose of discussion of the common features of both Iberian countries, we have also separately dealt with the specificities of the course of political events and their connection with the creation of new institutions.

In conclusion, we can affirm that the institutions created and maintained in the Iberian countries during the nineteenth and twentieth centuries were and are the result of political processes marked by the sharing of common experiences of resistance to the invader, of construction of the liberal constitutionalism framework, of traumatic acceptance of authoritarian regimes and of enthusiasm for the opportunities created by European integration. These various moments have proved crucial to the design and implementation of policy decisions with implications for economic growth and convergence with developed Western economies.

21

Iberian Financial System, 1800–2000

PABLO MARTÍN-ACEÑA AND RITA MARTINS DE SOUSA

21.1 Introduction

This chapter covers the history of banking in the Iberian Peninsula from the early nineteenth century to the beginning of the twenty-first century. The narrative provides a complete, albeit brief, historical overview of how the financial structures of the two countries have evolved. It also offers a comparative perspective of the two financial systems, pointing out to their similarities and their differences.

The first part of the chapter describes the formation of the Portuguese and Spanish banking systems. Special attention is given to the main changes that took place from their early beginnings to the consolidation and modernization of the banking structure in both countries. By 1900 the number of institutions had increased substantially, and some of the banks were much bigger than when they started activity. The first half of the twentieth century was hazardous and complicated for the financial system, as elsewhere in Europe. After the Second World War the banking system, strictly regulated, increased its dimension, and played a major role in fostering the industrialization of the two countries. Liberalization began in the mid-1970s and by the end of the 1990s financial legislation had adapted to the Single European Act and to the common banking legislation enacted by the European Union.

The second part traces the history of the two Iberian central banks: the Bank of Portugal and the Bank of Spain. The Bank of Portugal was established in 1846, after the merger of the Banco de Lisboa with Companhia Confiança Nacional, a 'near bank' company,[96] while the Bank of Spain was founded in 1782 as Banco de San Carlos. By the end of the nineteenth century both were the only issue institutions in their respective countries and began to play the role of central banks. Both joined the euro system from the very beginning in 1999.

---

[96] A near bank is a financial company with some of the characteristics of a bank. In this case, Companhia Confiança Nacional was an investment company that specialized in financing public debt.

The last section compares the banking structure and development of the two Iberian nations, and brings out their similarities and differences. First, attention is focused on comparing the main features of the Portuguese and Spanish private commercial and investment institutions. The chapter finishes with a brief evaluation of the historical role played by the Bank of Portugal and the Bank of Spain.

21.2 The Origin and Development of Iberian Banking

21.2.1 The Creation of Modern Banking in Portugal

Despite some proposals to create a bank at the end of the eighteenth century (Cardoso, 1997), a modern banking system began only in the first half of the nineteenth century. The first Portuguese bank,[97] Banco de Lisboa, was created in 1821 with two targets. The first was to be a privileged bank of issue to help the state with its financial problems. The acquisition of public debt was one of its goals (though not its most important one), as was redeeming the paper money created in 1797 when a public loan was issued as small bonds and circulated as money. The introduction of paper money implied some disturbances in monetary circulation because it was not accepted by some economic units and circulated with discounts. The second purpose was to be a commercial bank and issue convertible banknotes.

In this period, branches of the Banco de Lisboa and the Banco Comercial do Porto (1835) were also established in Portugal's north (1825). The latter was also an issuing bank. However, their convertible notes were not accepted for payments made to the state. Some savings banks, banking houses and a number of individual bankers also emerged in this epoch of turmoil and public financial difficulty, including the creation of several financial companies during the 1840s to deal with public debt (Reis, 1996).

Until the financial crisis of 1891, the second half of the nineteenth century can be described as a period of political and monetary stability (with Portugal joining the gold standard) and some banking freedom. During this epoch, public investments grew, although the link between the banking system and the state financial debt was, to some extent, broken. Funded debt in foreign and domestic markets increased, and special bank loans diminished (Esteves, 2005).

Other features were the expansion and diversification of the banking system, mainly between 1850 and 1870. This enlargement involved creating new commercial banks, banks specializing in mortgage lending, banking houses and savings banks, as well as increasing the number of issuing banks. Despite this expansion and in contrast to other European countries, Portugal did not

---

[97] Earlier on, the Banco do Brasil was founded in Rio de Janeiro, in 1808.

have an investment bank, and 'the attempt to create specialized mortgage banks and banks that addressed agricultural and industrial credit was a poor substitute' (Valério et al., 2007, vol. I: 149).

By 1858, there were a total of six banks and issuing banks combined. By 1892, the number of banks had reached 44, and there were eight issuing banks. Issuing notes became competitive, and the number of banks increased broadly in the north, which was primarily related to emigrant remittances. This meant a higher concentration in the south and greater competition in the north. Nevertheless, if we compare the equity capital of commercial banks, we find that in Lisbon banks had a higher capital – in 1875, the average was 1,879 *contos* in Lisbon, 1,469 *contos* in Porto and 711 *contos*[98] in other regions. Despite this geographical spread, the number of banks per 10,000 inhabitants was 0.1 compared with 0.5 in France and 1.83 in England (Reis, 2003).

The Caixa Geral de Depósitos (CGD), a state savings bank founded in 1876, with several branches, and the Banco Nacional Ultramarino (BNU), a colonial bank founded in 1864, with branches in all Portuguese overseas possessions except Macao, were the banks with the highest number of branches. The presence of foreign banks was minimal, with only two institutions. Another feature of Portuguese banks was a low degree of specialization. The ratio between long- and short-term credit was below one for almost all banks (Reis, 2003).

Two crises interrupted the banking prosperity of this period. First, the crisis of 1876 can be explained by the amount of Spanish public debt that Portuguese banks had in their portfolios. The devaluation of three percentage points in the interest of these assets implied difficulties mainly to northern banks. Consequently, if we compare 1875 to 1878, the number of banks declined (54 to 51), and the total amount of deposits dropped (26,000 *contos* to 18,000 *contos*). The role assumed by the Bank of Portugal helped avoid a more severe crisis (see Section 21.3.1). After a period of stability during the 1880s, a new banking crisis occurred in 1891, caused by a combination of international and domestic factors. A decrease in emigrant remittances, the Baring Brothers Crisis (a crisis involving Portugal's state bankers in London) and political instability were responsible for the financial turmoil that obliged the government to declare the inconvertibility of banknotes (it was also the end of the gold standard in Portugal). In 1892, the government of Portugal announced partial bankruptcy.

Although the data do not allow us to draw conclusions about the financing of economic activity, the low effects of both crises on Portuguese economic performance can possibly be explained by the weak link between the financial system and productive activity (Valério et al., 2007). Between 1891 and the First World War, the CGD's role as a treasury lender increased, as did its

---

[98] The Portuguese monetary unit was the *real* (plural, *reis*). For large amounts, the *conto* was employed. One *conto* was equal to a million *reis*.

importance in the banking sector (Lains, 2002b). At the same time, legal regulations began for joint-stock companies (1894-1896), which did not include banking houses and private bankers. The requirement of a cover deposit ratio, the obligation to publish a monthly balance sheet and the attempt to limit the banks' exposure to long-term operations are the main rules to highlight. During this period, deposits and credit to the private sector increased, and the number of banks was nearly stable (41 in 1914).

After the First World War, high inflation (in 1924, prices were around 24 times higher than before the war) characterized the Portuguese macroeconomic environment, and a new wave of banking institutions was created and quickly fell. This period can be compared to the 1870s, with some speculation involved in the boom-and-bust movements of provincial banking institutions. Nevertheless, the CGD, BNU and Bank of Portugal remained among the Big Five in terms of deposits.

A new legal framework and some measures adopted for financial stabilization after 1922 (fiscal reform, no monetization of debt, intervention in foreign exchange markets) resulted in a decrease in turbulence in the banking industry. The legislation of 1925 was an important step in Portuguese banking activity and was applied to joint-stock banks and banking houses. Unlike the legislation of the 1890s, minimum capital and reserve amounts were required, and government control of banking activity increased because entry into the market, mergers and acquisitions, and opening branches were dependent on authorization by the Minister of Finance. During the second half of the 1920s, the creation of clearing houses in Lisbon and Porto, as well as the reorganization of the CGD as an investment bank, completed the changes of this period. The reform of the CGD in 1929 aimed at putting an end to public deficit financing, applying resources through the Caixa Nacional de Crédito for economic modernization. The establishment of this service annexe to the CGD can be justified by the difficulties firms faced in obtaining credit from commercial banks. This can be considered an original solution because it established a single development bank, not a bank by activity sector (Reis, 1995).

During the 1920s, credit rose fourfold, deposits rose fivefold and banks' assets rose almost sixfold. On the eve of the 1930 crisis, Portugal had 96 banks and a widespread banking system. The sum of credits and deposits represented almost 10% of GDP.

With the 1930s Depression, Portuguese banking activity concentrated in the south after the liquidation of two important banks in the north. The colonial bank, the BNU, received financial assistance from the government to avoid a financial crisis. At the beginning of the 1930s, the banking market was dominated by the CGD, with almost 54% of the total gross deposits, and its position increased during the decade. Credit for economic activity rose from 20,000 *contos* in 1929 to 1.5 million *contos* in 1939, with agriculture as the main activity financed by the CGD during this period. The growth rate of CGD assets was higher than GDP growth (9% vs 3.3%).

In the authoritarian political regime period, known as *Estado Novo*, a new legal framework began under Oliveira Salazar as Minister of Finance that included the banking sector in a framework known as 'corporatist'. A new legislation was published in 1935, aimed at promoting the removal of small banking institutions and foreign exchange offices to have a higher concentration in the banking sector. Market entry was also frozen. Additionally, this legislation aimed to centralize the regulation of credit under the Minister of Finance. A National Credit Council was created to deliver opinions about credit, creations, mergers, closures and alterations of credit institutions' capital.

During the 1930s and 1940s, the rise in the number of branches and the greater link between the banking system and economic agents can explain the increase in demand deposits as means of payment (Santos, 1994). If we consider the whole banking system, between 1930 and 1947, the deposits grew tenfold and the credit sixfold, with a higher percentage in commercial banks – almost 44% of the total deposits and 57% of the credit. A favourable Portuguese macroeconomic environment justified the increase in deposits, credits and assets in the global banking sector. In the report written by Henry Wallich (1951), President of the Special Mission of Economic Cooperation in Portugal, the substantial changes in the Portuguese banking system during the 1930s were highlighted. The main features were the composition of the money supply that had an increased proportion of commercial bank deposits, the large excess of reserves in commercial and savings banks, and the growth of a substantial Treasury cash balance. The system's weakness was long-term loans, except for the CGD, which granted loans in the medium and long term. This report also considered interest rates to be very low for a country with capital scarcity.

After the Second World War, until 1974, the Portuguese banking sector increased its importance in the financial system during a period of economic growth. The sector's legal framework changed in 1957, 1959, 1965 and 1969. The law of 1957 reorganized the Portuguese banking structure, dividing the institutions into state credit institutions (the CGD), issue banks (the BdP), commercial banks and special credit institutions (investment banks, savings banks and credit cooperatives). In this law, high initial capital requirements were established as a barrier to entrance, and rules about the composition of cash reserves and credit were established to increase regulation. Commercial banks' cash reserves needed to include cash in hand, and deposits at the issuing bank and other interbank deposits were forbidden. The Credit and Insurance Corporation was also created with this legislation. The 1957 law was regulated by the law of 1959, in which the key innovation was the standardization of bank accounting. In 1965, the provisions included the composition of compulsory reserves and, for the first time, established limits on interest rates for time deposits of between 1.25% and 3.5%. Finally, in 1969, a law authorized commercial banks to develop credit operations with a period between two and five years to finance agriculture and industry, and grant credits to the export sector. Therefore, this was a change in the principle of specialization for the Portuguese banking system. Despite the period's legal restrictions, recent research showed that Portuguese commercial banks competed with each other, particularly after the mid-1960s, through interest rates and deposits (Amaral, 2013; 2015a).

The second broad feature of these decades was the decrease in the number of commercial banks (14 in 1974), explained by mergers and the transformation of small banking houses into joint-stock banks. However, an opposite movement occurred if we consider the banking system's geographical expansion with the rise of the number of branches. During the 1950s, 121 branches were authorized. This increased to 364 by 1964, and by 1972, 778 branches had been authorized. The regions of Lisbon and Porto were privileged in this expansion because the competition between banks rose in the regions with higher industrial activity (Carvalho, 1973). This enlargement can also explain the growth in demand deposits and the decrease in the currency ratio. At the same time, term deposits increased in importance in the banking system, which was likely justified by the low level of development of the capital market.

Despite the competition increase, the CGD was still the largest institution, with a market share of 27% in 1950 and approximately 18% in 1973. The legal framework supported the market position of the CGD. The requirement for certain deposits to be done through this banking institution (i.e. the deposits of all state services) and the tax-free interest rates paid on deposits benefited the bank's ranking.

In this epoch, the first investment bank was created – the Banco de Fomento Nacional (BFN) - in 1958, with 60% of its initial capital subscribed by the state. This bank's main objective was to grant loans to activities defined by the government in its Development Plans. The indicative planning coordinated the policy of economic development, including the principal sectors to finance. The credit of commercial banks also increased but with short-term rollover credits. The evolution of credit for commercial banks ranged from 36.52% in 1947 to almost 50% of the total assets in 1959 and 1973. For the investment bank (BFN), credit rose from 66% to 72% of total assets with values that increased almost sixfold for the same period. However, if we consider credits with a term up to one year, the percentage was 9–12% of the credit total volume. As term deposits in 1965 represented 25% of the total deposits, the amount of credit was very low, and the system's liquidity was very high (Simões, 1967).

The data does not allow us to evaluate the credit structure, but considering commercial banks in 1970, credit to the productive sector amounted to almost

80%, and consumption credit to 14% of total credit. Industry represented only 27% of the productive sector, while construction and real estate transactions had higher relative importance (48%) (Gonçalves, 1971).

After 1960, it can also be observed that the major banks established close connections with the most important economic and industrial groups (CUF and Champalimaud were two of these groups). The financial system's diversification increased with new types of para banking institutions, namely, securities of property investment fund management companies and securities portfolio management companies. However, there were not enough of these to compete with the banking institutions.

Near the end of this period, the U-shaped pattern of money's income velocity reached a turning point (1969). The falling trend during the 1950s and 1960s can be explained by the take-off of modern economic growth and the change in economic agents' attitudes towards the financial system (Nunes et al., 2018).

The transition to a democratic political regime was the main feature of Portugal's political environment after 1974. In the first phase, the new regime imposed profound transformations on the banking system. A new regulation determined the nationalization of the issuing banks and all credit institutions and, in 1977, the financial sector was blocked to the private sector. In the nationalization period, the economic groups lost importance, and the nationalized banking sector was restructured with the acquisition of small banking organizations by the largest banks. Another consequence was the financing of public expenditure by the Bank of Portugal and banking institutions in general. The banking system was responsible for more than half of the total domestic credit to the state. This is why some authors suggest that the banking sector's nationalization did not have a structural impact on the economy (Valério et al., 2010). The CGD preserved the banking system's leadership with roughly a quarter of the total of the deposits and the loan market. After credit to the state, real estate credit was the most relevant loan form.

When Portugal adhered to the Single European Act, a slow deregulation process occurred. All restrictions concerning entry regulations, interest rates and branching restrictions were abolished at the end of 1992. In fact, the legislation published in 1985 changed the institutional background of the Portuguese banking system. This new regulation authorized the establishment of private banking entities, and the consequences were threefold. First, private banks were created, and some of the economic groups of the 1970s re-emerged (CUF, Champalimaud, Espírito Santo). Second, the state-owned banks were privatized, leaving only three state-owned banks – the Bank of Portugal, CGD and BNU (integrated in the CGD in 2001). Third, the internationalization of the banking system was reflected in the establishment of foreign banks in Portugal and in the expansion of Portuguese banks abroad (Cunha, 2002).

The share of deposits of state-owned banks dropped from 90% in 1989 to 45% in 1993, and the Portuguese market for deposits became increasingly competitive (Barros & Modesto, 1999; Pinho, 2000; 2002). The competition also increased with the rise in the number of banks (68 in 1998) and branches. New types of para banking organizations were authorized, such as risk capital companies and business development companies. In 1992, a new legislation was published for financial institutions and companies. The main rules that were established were the distinction between banks and special credit institutions. The concept of 'universal banking' was also adopted. Additionally, the Bank of Portugal had a new role in the supervision of financial companies and a Guarantee Fund for deposits made at credit institutions was established. In 1993, the CGD was transformed into a universal bank and a state-owned public limited company. Internationally, it was the largest Portuguese bank, with 31.6% of the deposits and 25.1% of the credit (Lains, 2011).

At the end of the twentieth century, the total number of banks was 68 with 5,192 branches (5.1 banks per 10,000 inhabitants). During this period, deposits and credit rose, achieving values 70 times higher when comparing 1973 with 1998. The turn of the century brought a new picture with mergers and acquisitions, which implied an increased concentration, with supervisory bodies playing an ever more important role.

21.2.2 Banking in Spain

The history of the modern Spanish banking system begins in 1856 with the passing of the Issuing Banks Law and the Credit Companies Law. The first enshrined the principle of plurality of issue and led to the establishment of 21 banks. The second facilitated the creation of institutions which could perform a wide range of activities, from bill discounting and trade credit, through to long-term lending and investments in company shares and bonds. In addition to the banks established as corporations, and the savings banks, there was also a class of merchant private bankers who had provided foreign exchange and ordinary credit operations since the eighteenth century. The presence of foreign banks was minimal, with just three foreign-owned institutions.

Although at the end of the nineteenth century the business of the banks, savings banks (examined later), credit unions and private bankers had clearly taken off, their level of development and modernization still lagged a long way behind that of Europe's leaders. With little regulation, as the legislation did not impose restrictions on the activities of credit institutions, they had nevertheless been unable to go beyond being relatively simple non-specialist deposit-takers. According to Raymond Goldsmith's 'Financial Intermediation Ratio', which is defined as the ratio between total assets issued by financial institutions and the market value of national wealth, the degree of development of the structure of the Spanish banking system in 1900 was well below the European average.

The most significant phenomenon in the banking sector during the early years of the twentieth century was the opening of numerous entities across the country. Between 1900 and 1914 around 50 banks were created, although many of them were the outcome of the transformation of old commercial houses and the conversion of some well-known banking firms into corporations. Most of the banks continued to be small, and their sphere of activity was circumscribed to the town or city in which they were based. The expansion of the banks during this first decade and a half of the twentieth century was not, however, free of difficulties and even of occasional setbacks. Together with the wave of newly founded banks, the period was also marked by some significant closures.

The First World War gave a fresh boost to the financial system. Spain's neutrality placed its economy in an advantageous position to meet demand from abroad arising as a result of the conflict: exports of goods and services boomed, leading to a balance of payments surplus and an influx of gold and foreign currency into credit institution's accounts; firms made extraordinary profits. The banking sector was not unaffected by these changes: between 1915 and 1920 the number of institutions grew to 120. The war also encouraged the largest banks to embark on a policy of expansion by opening branches at a wide range of locations across the country as a means of expanding their deposits base and their business.

The post-war period brought radical changes to the business world. The preceding upward trend gave way to a downward phase in the cycle, leading to widespread paralysis of industry and trade. In the financial sector, the post-war difficulties put a stop to the creation of new banks, and exposed the fragility of many institutions that had emerged during an unusually favourable period which proved unsustainable beyond the armistice of November 1918. A year after the hostilities had ended a number of institutions began to face liquidity and solvency difficulties, followed by a number of resounding crises. Fear of a general financial collapse, and the conviction that credit firms ought to be under some form of control led to the passing of the Banking Ordering Law of 1921, which remained in force, with amendments introduced in 1931, until the Spanish Civil War.

In the 1920s, the financial system expanded and underwent significant structural changes. Banks' assets grew rapidly and above the rate of growth of national income during those years. As a consequence, the intermediation coefficient rose to 75%, which was high, but still a long way short of 100, which is the minimum level at which a financial system can be classified as advanced.

The expansion of the 1920s ended in 1930. In the spring of 1931 the collapse of the central European banking system and the advent of the Second Spanish Republic provoked a massive withdrawal of deposits, which shrank by 20% in just two months. Some institutions failed, but the majority managed to obtain the funds they needed to meet their short-term commitments and obligations, and to re-establish their normal levels of liquidity. This was made possible by the attitude of the authorities at the Ministry of Finance and the credit policy adopted by the Bank of Spain, which enabled a rapid and 'orthodox' solution to the crisis. Another important factor explaining the absence of bankruptcies was that public debt securities could be automatically monetized to obtain cash reserves. The rest of the decade was characterized by economic stagnation and hence the volume of loans, credit and the portfolio of bills stagnated or contracted. The same was true of the portfolio of private securities and only the public debt investment portfolio, a safer and more stable investment, remained unchanged.

One significant new feature in this period was the emergence of official credit institutions, which aimed to meet the financing needs of special sectors. Up until their nationalization in 1962, all these banks had private capital, though they were regulated and controlled, directly or indirectly, by the state. The authorities kept the right to appoint the governor, who became their official representative. Apart from their public nature, another feature that characterized these official entities was their high degree of specialization. Their operations followed special, and complex, administrative procedures. A distinctive feature of the official banking system was the source of funds. Indeed, although these institutions were called banks, this was not, strictly speaking, true, as they did not take deposits from private individuals. Instead they used alternative mechanisms to obtain the resources they needed. In 1929 they were already on the list of the country's 12 largest credit institutions.

The military uprising in July 1936 divided the country into two opposing sides from which two antagonistic states emerged, splitting the financial system in two, and brought massive state intervention in the economy. The conflict's financial needs consumed the Bank of Spain's gold reserves, drove up public debt and swelled the supply of cash in circulation, leading to rampant inflation and a decline in the internal and external value of both currencies. The conflict dislocated Spanish commercial life. The country's being divided in two affected the majority of its banking institutions. Given that their head offices were mainly located in the republican sector, a plethora of branches scattered across the territory under Franco's control lost their links to their respective parent banks.

After the civil war, it was necessary to rebuild the fabric of the financial system. The first significant piece of legislation was the adoption of the so-called banking status quo introduced by the Ministerial Order of 19 October 1939, establishing a 'numerus clausus'. It not only prevented the creation of new credit institutions but also prohibited the opening of new agencies and branches without the relevant government permission. The postwar legislative framework was completed in 1946 with a new Banking Ordering Law, which was intended to regulate the ensemble of credit institutions, and commercial and official banks, although excluding the savings banks. One interesting feature of the act was how it divided the financial system into three types of institution: official banks, private-sector banks (national, regional, local and foreign) and savings banks. The extreme interventionism of these years did not prevent significant changes in the bank census, nor was it an obstacle to the strong growth of the financial system.

The passing and implementation in 1962 of the Basic Law on Credit and Banking Organization put an end to the long period of the status quo and opened the way for a phase of reforms and changes in the Spanish financial industry. With this new provision, the government was authorized to reorganize the whole system, including the Bank of Spain (which was nationalized), private-sector banks, savings banks, official credit institutions, collective investment entities, long-term sales finance institutions and the stock exchanges. The financial sector underwent significant changes in its structure, with the creation of new institutions and a series of mergers, takeovers and liquidations. The level of intermediation rose as a result of the gradual deregulation and expansion of banking business, the diversification of operations and the creation of an extensive network of branches. Despite the 1962 Law's reforming and renewing intent, the degree of state intervention was barely reduced and was only relaxed in later years, and then very gradually: asset and liability operations remained subject to controls and regulations, and interest rates were still set by the authorities. Privileged credit circuits remained, with obligatory coefficients for the banks and savings banks. The official banks also took on a more central role in the financing of public investments and activities the state considered strategic.

In 1969 timid steps began to be taken to deregulate interest rates. A basic rediscount rate was set by the Bank of Spain and the rates applicable to lending and borrowing by other credit institutions were linked to it by positive or negative marginal differences. In 1970 and 1971 reserve ratios for banks and savings banks were put in place, replacing the existing liquidity coefficient. A more important step towards the deregulation of the financial system came with the regulations approved in 1974, when a series of measures were enacted, introducing an increasing degree of deregulation.

The banking crisis that struck three years later brought the banking industry's expansion to a halt and overturned the map of the Spanish financial system. With the crisis, which endured until the mid-1980s, no new institutions were created, and numerous institutions disappeared, including almost all of those created during this first phase of financial deregulation. Of the 110 banks in operation in Spain in 1977, the crisis affected 56 banks and 23 banking firms, that is, 52% of Spanish banking institutions and more than 27% of savings banks, with an associated cost that reached 15% of GDP.

The causes of the banking crisis were a combination of exogenous and endogenous factors. Among the former, the economic difficulties of the mid-1970s, after the increase in oil prices, the collapse of the Bretton Woods agreements, and the rise in world interest rates can be mentioned. Financial costs increased, firms' profits fell, and companies of all sizes could not meet their obligations with their lenders. Non-performing assets in the balance sheets of the banks increased and solvency problems emerged. Rates of returns were reduced, and new capital stopped flowing. Banks' prices in the stock market began slide down from 1974 on and aggravated the financial position of many institutions. Bankruptcies were widespread and the risk of a meltdown of the system increased.

The end of the status quo and the uncontrolled liberalization of the financial markets was also a contributing factor. Deregulation was not accompanied by the introduction of surveillance mechanisms, supervision was faulty, and the Bank of Spain was not given sufficient instruments to monitor the banking system. In addition, the new banks erected after the partial liberalization were undercapitalized, many promoters were alien to the financial sphere and managers lacked experience in the field. Moreover, they assumed excessive risks in order to expand and capture a larger share of the market. Balance sheets became overloaded with dubious investments and instead of increasing the own resources of banks, managers preferred to resort to the capital market at a time when interest rates were escalating. Operational margins were reduced, and profits vanished.

The authorities faced the usual dilemma in these cases: either allow the market to perform its disciplinary role and let the 'rotten banks' fall or put in place mechanisms to rescue institutions in trouble in order to avoid a general collapse of the banking system. The latter was chosen, and the Bank of Spain began a series of interventions, taking charge of the insolvent banks, dismissing their management, examining their financial situation and, if feasible, restructuring their balance sheets. Later, once the banks´ portfolio had been cleaned up, they were sold in public auctions to other well capitalized and solvent institutions.

The direct cost of the financial rescue was huge. Eighty per cent of the funds consumed came out of the various government bodies involved in the lifeboat operations, and the rest from the vaults of the banks themselves. The fiscal deficit multiplied by a factor of 50, jumping from 0.5% of GDP in 1975 to 6.0% in 1985. The sovereign debt increased by 80% between 1977 and 1985. On the other hand, the crisis brought about significant changes in the sphere of banking regulation and supervision. The Bank of Spain's capacity in both areas was reinforced, two Deposit Guarantee Funds were established, new and modern rules in book-keeping were introduced, and banks were compelled to provide more and better financial information.

Once the crisis was over, during the so-called Great Moderation of the following years, Spanish banks enjoyed a period of expansion and prosperity. Three main features characterized the evolution of the system: a process of consolidation and concentration, with multiples mergers and takeovers; diversification and increasing efficiency; and a significant process of internationalization, particularly in the Latin American market.

The history of Spanish savings banks begins in 1835 when the first institution was founded. From that date onward the number of savings banks increased. Many of them were promoted by wealthy local patrons, the church and charitable organizations. By 1900 there were about 55 savings banks scattered throughout the country. Between 1900 and 1935 the number had increased to 171, due to new foundations sponsored by municipalities and provincial councils. Savings banks specialized in mortgage credit and in personal short-term loans of small amount. Management was usually prudent and conservative, and not subjected to the pressure of stakeholders demanding high returns for their share. The principle of territoriality was paramount, and hence their operation was generally restricted to a single province.

During Franco's long dictatorship savings banks were subject to strict government control, even more extreme than the surveillance exerted over commercial banks. However, despite all the restrictions on their operations, the savings banks sector expanded considerably, not in number (88 in 1975), but in their share of the national credit market, which reached 30%. However, they lost the autonomy they had enjoyed since their origin. The orientation of their investment was dictated by the government and directed towards the economic and industrial priorities of the dictatorship. Their portfolio was loaded with government bonds and public enterprise securities, and the rest of their investments consisted of long-term credit to the building sector at official interest rates. The absence of crises during this period was the result of the strict regulations imposed on the financial system.

In 1977, when the banking sector crisis began to unfold, the savings banks went through a period of notable institutional changes. The functioning of the old and traditional savings banks became similar to that of the commercial banks. Its financial activities were liberalized, and the range of their operations enlarged. They were also allowed to open branches all over the country, which put an end to the territoriality principle. A first reform in 1988 modified the government structure of the savings banks, which until then was formed, according to their particular statutes, by a small number of individuals and composed almost exclusively of the original members of the founding institutions and corporations. They were replaced by members representing the interests of various stakeholders groups: founding entities, depositors, employees, trade unions, and public authorities. In 1985 a new act altered the composition of the governing bodies by increasing the presence of the public authorities. The boards of directors fell into the hands of the local and regional (Autonomous Communities) corporations controlled by the political parties and the trade unions connected to them.

For some time, savings banks were very successful in capturing the excess resources of small and medium-size investors and in lending to also small and medium-size firms. They multiplied their presence by opening branches all over the country, as well as by expanding beyond their traditional business products to reach new customers. While the economic cycle lasted the savings banks sector showed its better face and all entities, whether big or small, seemed to have a bright future.

During the so-called Great Moderation and thanks to the early integration into the Eurogroup, the Spanish economy enjoyed a decade of steady growth. Fuelled by low interest rates and a constant flow of external capital, the financial sector expanded and a huge amount of resources were channelled to real estate development and construction. To finance the expansion of their balance sheets, instead of reinforcing their own resources or increasing the volume of deposits they resorted to the wholesale international financial market, primarily based on the emission of mortgage bonds.

Before long, an important segment of the sector accumulated imbalances of various kinds whose magnitude was evident when the economic environment changed. The most serious problems were its high exposure to the real estate development and construction sectors, dependence on wholesale external financial markets, excess capacity, and the fragmentation of the industry composed of a large number of small entities. And although Spain's banking institutions avoided the worst excesses of 'the originate to distribute model', the truth is that savings banks had made widespread use of securitization and covered bonds to refinance mortgage portfolios. When the real estate boom collapsed, it left in its wake a huge amount of unsold housing and unfinished development and a mountain of unrecovered loans.

A second explanation to understand the crisis of the savings banks has to do with their peculiar nature. Savings banks are (or rather were) not banks. Their mission, the outcome of a historical evolution of the institutions, was focused on providing financial services to avoid financial exclusion, conducting community welfare activities and pursuing the economic development of the region in which they operated. Their internal organization had become complex and rigid and far from the international practices of corporate governance. With the impetus of their founding fathers long gone, the process of appointment of senior executives degenerated into corruption, nepotism and inefficiency. On the other hand, legal restrictions to obtain core capital posed a serious obstacle to their urgent need of capitalization in order to increase their solvency ratios. As the crisis deepened, their profit margins declined and so did their accumulated reserves, their most important source of core capital, since savings banks, which are basically foundations, cannot issue shares. While the savings banks maintained a business model based on the geographical proximity to their customer, marketing of non-complex financial products and moderate growth strategies, it was sufficient to obtain equity by capitalizing self-generated profits. But when they deviated from this model, traditional funding sources were insufficient.

The difficulties began in March 2009 when the Bank of Spain rescued the first savings banks, and the crisis reached its climax in 2012. The consequences of the crisis have been devastating, if measured by the number of entities that have been rescued by the government, and in the number of units: from 45 independent savings banks of various sizes in 2010, the sector now has only 13 institutions.

The nature of the savings banks has been radically altered. A main reform took place in November 2010, introducing new organizational models and affecting the governance of the institutions. With the new corporate formulas, savings banks may choose to exercise their financial activity directly, indirectly through a bank, or become a foundation and transfer their financial business to a bank. The reform also changed the composition of the board of directors, reducing the weight of public authorities, whether national, autonomous or municipal, and the presence of representatives of political parties and trade unions.

Although these changes have yet to prove their virtues, it is apparent that the crisis has in fact dismantled the old savings banks system. Its present structure does hardly resemble the structure in place before the crisis. The main features of what five years ago defined a 'savings bank' are no longer there. It is true that both the surviving savings banks and those that have been consolidated into a major group retain their old and traditional denomination as '*cajas de ahorros*', but they are in fact '*bancos*'. As a matter of fact, the difference between banks and savings banks has been blurred. The crisis has meant the liquidation (by transformation) of a financial sector that had been in existence for more than 150 years.

21.3 Central Banking in Iberia

21.3.1 The Bank of Portugal

The Banco de Portugal/Bank of Portugal was created in 1846 after a crisis that resulted in the Banco de Lisboa's merger with Companhia Confiança Nacional. Ten years (1857) later, after conflicts with the government and with a new legal framework, the bank gained the trust of the markets and began a more equanimous relationship with the state (Reis, 1996). It always dominated the country's south; however, it wasn't until 1888 that the Bank of Portugal was given the monopoly of issue, although it wasn't until the crisis of 1891 that it became effective. This dominance over note issuance, which resulted from privileges granted by the government, can be explained by the bank's role as the lender of last resort during the crises of 1876 and 1891. Under the gold standard, the Bank of Portugal overcame the short-term difficulties of importing gold from London. These imports avoided a decrease in the reserves below 30% and discount rate changes (Reis, 1999). In 1891, the notes' convertibility was suspended (suspension of the gold standard), and in the next years, the bank's discount rate became the reference for interest rates.

After the crisis and until the end of the First World War, the banking sector became dominated by the Bank of Portugal. It continued to operate as a commercial bank, although with a strong link to the state's financing through monetizing the public deficit. The stabilization of the inflationary process in 1924 was also explained by the government's and the Bank of Portugal's intervention in foreign exchange markets. The government created a surcharge on exports, and the Bank of Portugal managed the fund established with this revenue. In the legislation of 1925, the role of the bank in the direct-discount market was reduced, which can be considered a step towards taking on the role of central bank.

Nevertheless, this role was legally assumed only in 1931 when Portugal adopted the gold-exchange standard and a new legislation reform was passed (Decree with the force of Law No. 19870, of 9 June). Under this reform, the Bank of Portugal was responsible for the currency's internal and external value (monetary stability) and became the Portuguese Central Bank (Valério, 2001a). At the same time, rules were defined to limit financing to the state.

We can discuss whether crowding out was effective in Portugal because the state absorbed many resources during the nineteenth century, the First World War and the 1920s. Between 1919 and 1931, medium- and long-term internal loans to the state, considering the Bank of Portugal and the CGD, totalled (in nominal values) 1,267,400 *contos* (Valério et al., 2007). In 1931, the Bank of Portugal's deposits represented 68% of the total deposits of the savings banks, or 41% if we include the commercial banks. However, we should remember that the Portuguese banking sector, unlike the financial systems of other European countries, had no universal banks, and that the period of inflation (1919–1924) could have affected economic agents' assessments.

After the Second World War and until 1974, the bank continued to perform the functions of a central bank, but only the 1962 legislation defined it as an issuing, central and reserve bank. As capital increased, a new Legal Reserve Fund was created, and the Special Reserve Fund was maintained. The limit of the current account opened in favour of the state increased, and the state's debt to the bank was extinguished by applying the nominal valuation of the assets.

During this period, the priorities of the bank were monetary stability and economic development (Amaral, 2018). For the first target, the stabilization of the exchange rate was the intermediate variable, and concerning the second, the Bank of Portugal kept its discount and rediscount rates as low as possible and in line with inflation. Regarding supervision, the Bank of Portugal did not have as important a role as the Minister of Finance.

The Bank of Portugal was a private bank until the entry into force of the Decree Law of 1975, when the capital was entirely subscribed by the state during the banking system nationalization period (see Section 21.2.1). This legislation gave the bank greater powers to supervise and control the banking sector. The Central Bank authorized the creation of new banks and new branches for existing banks, defined the limits to interest rates, defined credit ceilings, and oversaw the level and composition of the reserves to be held by monetary and financial institutions. The other important provision was to end the limits to monetary issue according to reserves. In this period of high regulation of the banking industry, the Bank of Portugal financed the government's credit demands. Therefore, it was assumed that increased public expenditure and money supply were two macroeconomic measures to surpass short-term problems. This is why this legislation reflects a Keynesian perspective of the functions of a central bank (Valério, 2001a; Nunes & Valério, 2005).

During this period, and before Portugal became a member of the European Communities (1986), the Portuguese economy had external payment problems that justified two International Monetary Fund interventions (in 1978 and 1983). At this time, and according to the negotiations of the Communities Directives, the financial system had two important innovations: the creation of an interbank money market and the creation of treasury bills for open market operations.

The legislation of 1990 and the period of deregulation determined the central bank's independence. They put an end to the public sector's financing, as the only way to finance public expenditures was through the acquisition of treasury bills. Any influence on the bank by the government was also forbidden. A supervisory role was defined that consisted of regulations, accounting, the collection of statistics and prudential supervision.

During the 1990s, the Bank of Portugal was also important in the market interventions concerning the exchange rate mechanism (ERM). In 1992, the liberalization of exchange operations was concluded, and the Portuguese currency was integrated into the ERM of the European Monetary System. Therefore, the Bank of Portugal's market interventions were crucial to maintaining the Portuguese currency throughout these fluctuations.

In 1998, the Bank of Portugal was included in the European System of Central Banks. In 1999, Portugal's integration in the Economic and Monetary Union implied an active role for the bank in updating information and exchanging the old currency with the new European currency. The Bank of Portugal also belongs to the Single Supervisory Mechanism, a first step and a key process of the Banking Union.

21.3.2 The Bank of Spain

The Banco de España/Bank of Spain is one of the oldest European central banks. It was originally founded in 1782 as Banco de San Carlos, renamed Banco de San Fernando in 1829, and finally became the Banco de España in 1856. It was formed as a private joint-stock company, which held the privilege of issuing banknotes. In 1874 a decree conferred on the institution the monopoly of issue for the whole country. A new revision of the charter in 1891 extended this privilege for another 30 years. The 1921 Banking Law (partially amended in 1931) included various provisions to transform the institution into a genuine central bank, with responsibilities in the field of monetary policy and as lender of last resort. In 1946, when the exclusive privilege of issuing notes expired, the Bank of Spain was de facto nationalized and its banknotes became legal tender. It was *de jure* nationalized in 1962. Finally, in 1994, under the terms of the Maastricht Treaty of 1992, the Law of Autonomy of the Bank of Spain established its independence from the government and conferred full responsibility for monetary policy on the institution. Also, in 1994, the Bank of Spain joined the European System of Central Banks.

During its first 150 years, from its foundation in 1782 to the outbreak of the civil war in 1936, the Bank of Spain, being a private company, enjoyed a significant degree of autonomy. Nevertheless, its role as an issuing credit institution was closely linked to the Treasury. Indeed, the Banco de San Carlos was founded to sustain the market value of the kingdom's public debt (*vales reales*) and to meet the financial needs of the Treasury, and its survival until 1962 depended on the government's will.

Until its nationalization, the Bank of Spain's paramount objective as a private joint-stock company was profit maximization. This involved managing the bank to distribute the highest possible annual dividend to the shareholders, to ensure the highest market prices for its stock and to guarantee the convertibility of its notes into cash at all times. The board of directors was far from concerned about the bank's duties as a 'central bank'; that is to say, being responsible for financial stability (lender of last resort), and monetary stability (exchange rate or price stability). The bank's owners and board members always considered that these were the government's duties, not theirs. There was for more than a century a long-running and sometimes bitter dispute between the institution's directors and shareholders and the government (in particular, the Treasury officials). The former defended the bank's autonomy as a private financial company, while the latter insisted on its duties as an institution with issuing privilege. The disputes reached their zenith at times of banking crises or exchange rate instability; on some occasions, they were resolved in favour of the government, but on many others, the bank had the upper hand.

The first charter was the only one that formally established a clear mandate for the Bank of Spain: to sustain the market value of the *vales reales* (the special debt issued by the Treasury to finance the continental wars at the end of the eighteenth century) by converting them into cash (metallic coins) at par value on request of the bearer. Neither of the ensuing charters set out well-defined objectives, such as the convertibility of notes and deposits into metal (gold or silver), Treasury financing or monetary or financial stability. If the Bank of

Spain fulfilled some of these functions before 1939, it did so because it suited its own interests as a private credit company or because it feared that the monopoly of issue would not be renewed. The bank thus assumed central bank policies from a sense of convenience or threat.

After 1939, this situation changed: the Bank of Spain was placed under state control, subject to the close supervision of the Ministry of Finance. Indeed, it became a mere appendix of the Treasury. Some independence was regained in the mid-1970s, after the death of Franco. The economic reforms undertaken during the political transition to democracy and the fact that Spain was moving closer to the European Economic Community allowed a new generation of bank officials to transform the institution from within and to assume central bank policy objectives. From 1977, it effectively assumed responsibility for monetary policy and financial stability. In 1988, it was assigned full supervisory functions over all types of credit institutions. In 1994, it finally gained the full autonomy it never had, and was given a unique and complex mandate: price stability.

Three main historical forces have driven the history of the Bank of Spain. First, wars, because they meant temporary increases in government expenditures that the bank, as the official or semi-official issue institution, was called to finance. A second force modelling the life of the bank has been its links with the Treasury, because central banks have almost invariably been established by an act of government and have been designated as banker to the government. Even in peace times, the bank has been called to cover the fiscal needs of the government. Treasury policy and objectives have as well shaped the historical trajectory of the bank. There has been always a permanent tension between its objectives as private maximizing commercial institution and its function as banker of the government. Third, because institutions and their functions do not develop in a vacuum, it has been profoundly influenced by the development of ideas, theories and perceptions about its proper role.

The monopoly of issue in 1874 did not mark the beginning of the Bank of Spain as a truly or genuine central bank. The main objective of the bank was profit maximization. Banknote convertibility into gold or silver was seen as essential to guarantee the financial respectability of the bank. Until its nationalization, monetary policy was not a major concern of the bank. The maintenance of the (domestic or international) value of the currency was considered a government responsibility. The fact that Spain was off the gold standard during its long period of domination was due, among other causes, to the non-collaborative stance of the bank. The gold standard required the central bank to use its financial resources (gold and foreign exchange) and monetary instruments (interest rate) to maintain the stability of the exchange rate. The bank never assumed such responsibility, neither before 1914 nor thereafter.

The stability of the financial system was not a responsibility that the Bank of Spain assumed while it was a private commercial company. Rivalry more than cooperation was a feature of the relationship of the bank with the commercial banking system. The assumption of the lender of last resort function was delayed at least until the beginning of the twentieth century, if not later. The first operations in this regard were undertaken under pressure from the government, and unwillingly. Only in 1931, when the combination of the European banking crisis and the political crisis (the demise of the monarchy and the proclamation of the Second Republic) threatened the financial fabric of the country, did the bank intervene as lender of last resort, jointly with the Treasury, to avoid a complete breakdown.

After its de facto nationalization in 1939 and for more than three decades, the Bank of Spain lost its autonomy and became an agent or branch of the Treasury. It changed its 'profit-maximizing' objective for whatever goal the government decided: cheap and abundant money to foster economic growth; low interest rates to reduce the public debt burden; aid to rescue individual banks. On a few occasions, such as the Stabilization Plan of 1959, monetary policy was used to combat inflation or any other economic imbalances.

Despite its long history as an issue institution, the Bank of Spain did not assume the roles of a real central bank until late in the twentieth century. From 1977 onward, it regained its lost institutional autonomy and took full responsibility (the duties) for monetary policy. In fact, the transformation of the Bank of Spain into a modern fully fledged central bank only occurred in 1999 when it became part of the Eurosystem.

21.4 A Comparison: Similarities and Differences

The comparative banking history of Portugal and Spain is an interesting case study. The beginning of commercial banking in the two countries harks back to the same epoch, the mid-nineteenth century. The first establishments in both countries were common deposit and issue banks, although the plurality of issue lasted more in Portugal than in Spain. The presence of foreign banks was limited in the two countries until very recently. By developed European standards, Iberian banking was backward. Credit institutions were smaller and the level of penetration into the real economy was below that of other Central and Western European countries. For Iberian financial institutions, the First World War and the decade of the 1920s were a period of considerable expansion. Thereafter and until the early 1970s, the banking sector, under strict regulations, grew slowly. It accelerated in the second part of the decade and in both cases the 1980s and 1990s were characterized by deregulation and privatization. Moreover, legislative changes were frequent and took place in relatively close dates.

There were some differences. Portugal did not have a 'public banking investment sector' (the CGD through the Caixa Nacional de Crédito can be considered a public investment bank after 1929), while in Spain a significant group of 'official banks' were created in the 1920s. Credit institutions were nationalized in Portugal between 1975 and 1977. In Spain nationalization came earlier in 1962 but only included the so-called 'official banks', and the Bank of Spain.

With regard to central banking, Spain possessed a 'national' bank from early on, in 1782, when the Banco de San Carlos (later baptized in 1856 as Banco de España/Bank of Spain) was established. The Bank of Portugal was born later, in 1821, with the Banco de Lisboa. The Bank of Spain was granted the monopoly of issue in 1874 and nationalized in 1962. The Bank of Portugal was entrusted with the monopoly of issue in 1891 and nationalized in 1975. Neither of them was 'stricto sensu' a modern central bank until recently, which implies performing the role of Treasury's bank, lender of last resort and conductor of monetary policy.

22

Economic Growth and Structural Change in the Iberian Economies, 1800–2000

LUCIANO AMARAL, CONCHA BETRÁN AND VICENTE PINILLA

22.1 Introduction

The Iberian countries followed the typical path of structural change of contemporary economies, with most resources (including labour) being transferred from agriculture to industry and services. These changes in the composition of employment and production are important parts of the development process. However, they took place in the Iberian countries at a later stage than in the core European economies. The latter started their industrialization processes in the late eighteenth century while peripheral countries did so in the mid-nineteenth century, especially in Southern Europe. This chapter examines the main stages of economic growth and structural change in the two Iberian economies and explains the main differences between them and the core European countries. Industrialization and the modern economic growth process began in the two countries in the middle of the nineteenth century (1850–1860); the interwar years were a period of significant transformations (especially 1913–1929) and industrialization concluded in the twentieth century during the golden age of capitalism (1960–1973). Both countries experienced post-1950 growth miracles as a consequence of being rapid industrializers, similar to other European latecomers (such as Greece, Ireland and Italy).

The Iberian countries had common characteristics which made it difficult for them to catch up with the European core, such as being on the periphery of Western Europe, with difficult access by land to the core European countries, not being very well endowed with land for cereal agriculture, and having a poor supply of fuel resources, although Spain was well endowed with metallic-mineral resources (but not Portugal). The educational level of the labour force was relatively low, and neither of the countries was very densely populated. These factors explain the late start and the slow pattern of development during the late eighteenth century and the nineteenth century. However,

---

This study has received financial support from the Ministry of Science, Innovation and Universities of Spain, projects PID2022-138886NB-I00, ECO2015-66782-P and PID2019-108645 GB-100, from the Government of Aragon (S55_23R) and from the Generalitat Valenciana (AICO/2018/130).

technological change, especially from the late nineteenth century onwards, was more adapted to the factor endowments and conditions of the Iberian countries, such as in the case of electricity (Betrán, 2005; Henriques & Sharp, 2020). Industries using these new technologies transferred their productivity gains by means of lower relative prices, which in turn produced a positive market pecuniary externality. This promoted demand spillovers that were sufficient to increase the market size of the whole industry and economy, and established a path for economic transformation and growth. In addition, foreign demand for agricultural products such as olive oil, wine, cork, fruits and vegetables, and those related to Iberian comparative advantages, improved agriculture productivity and trade specialization. However, the most significant changes in the demand side were biased in favour of industrial and services sectors due to the higher increase in these sectors' demand as a result of income rise (Engel's law), and their greater contribution to economic growth.

Besides presenting the stages of structural change between the three main sectors of the two economies, we will also measure the contribution of structural change to economic growth in the long term. Then, we will disaggregate further within the three sectors to determine the leading industries at each stage of economic transformation. Finally, we will study the contribution of these sectors to economic growth.

22.2 Stages of Economic Growth and the Contribution of Structural Change to Productivity and Economic Growth

Modernization and industrialization began in Spain in the mid-nineteenth century. In the 150 years from 1850 to 2000, the three periods of greater economic growth were 1850–1883, the 1920s and 1950–1974 (Prados de la Escosura, 2003) (see Table 22.1). Per capita growth surged in the interwar period and in 1950–1974 in Spain compared to the core European countries. Portugal also entered into the process of modern economic growth in the second half of the nineteenth century. The pace was, however, generally disappointing in comparison with the rest of Western Europe, and even with Spain (Table 22.2). This was, indeed, a very negative period: between the 1850s and the early twentieth century, the Portuguese economy diverged strongly in relation to the European first-comers. Only in the 1920s did it show any signs of change in behaviour, something that was only completely reversed between 1945 and 1973, when it caught up rapidly (Amaral, 2002; Lains, 2003a). The period between 1973 and 2000 was one of relative slowdown and milder convergence (Table 22.2).

In Spain, the stages of high economic growth were accompanied by a shift in resource allocation towards more productive industries, and for this reason structural change made an important contribution to labour productivity and economic growth. Using shift-share analysis, Prados de la Escosura (2007) calculated the part of the increase in aggregate productivity due to the increase

Table 22.1 *Economic growth, structural change and labour productivity (%), Spain.*

	GDP	GDP/L	Internal productivity	Structural change
1850–2000	2.5	1.7	1.6	0.1
1850–1883	1.8	1.3	1.1	0.2
1920–1929	3.8	2.4	2.1	0.4
1958–1974	6.9	6	5.4	0.6
1974–1986	2.5	4	3.9	0.1
1986–2000	3.5	1.4	1.7	−0.3

Note: Growth rates in percentages. L = number of workers.
Source: Prados de la Escosura (2007).

Table 22.2 *Economic growth, structural change and labour productivity (%), Portugal.*

	GDP	GDP/L	Internal productivity	Structural change	Interaction (internal – structural)
1862–1910	0.6	−0.2	0.2	−0.5	0.1
1910–1950	2.4	1.7	1.4	0.2	0.1
1950–1973	5.5	5.4	3.9	0.4	1.1
1973–1985	2.7	1.0	0.7	0.6	−0.3
1986–2002	3.7	2.2	2.0	0.5	−0.3
1862–2002	2.5	2.6	2.0	0.4	0.2

Note: Growth rates in percentages. L = number of workers.
Sources: GDP: 1862–1910: Maddison (2006); 1910–1950: Batista et al (1997); 1950–2002: Amaral (2009); Shift-share: 1862–1910: authors' calculations using data from Lains (1995), Nunes (2001) and Reis (2005); 1910–1950, 1950–1973 and 1973–1985: Aguiar and Martins (2005); 1986–2002: Amaral (2010b).

in output per worker in each industry (internal productivity) and the part due to the shift of labour from less productive to more productive industries (structural change).[99] As we can see in Table 22.1, the contribution of

---

[99] The intra-sectoral effect or internal productivity shows the growth of labour productivity that would have occurred if there had not been any structural change and it corresponds

structural change to productivity growth is around 6% for the whole period 1850–2000.[100] Contribution was higher in the years 1920–1929, amounting to 17%, which is related to an important structural change associated with inter-industry transformation. This structural change is due to the reduction of the share of agriculture in the total economy, and also to the increasing share of leading industries with higher productivity, due to their relationship with new industrial technologies (electricity, chemicals and equipment goods). In the golden age period, 1958–1974, corresponding to the highest growth of labour productivity, the contribution of structural change was 10%.

The contribution of structural change to the growth of the Portuguese economy for the whole period 1862–2002 was 15%, according to the shift-share analysis presented column 3 of in Table 22.2, more than double than in Spain but with differences in intensity throughout the period. The contribution coming from the transference of resources from sectors with relatively low productivity levels to sectors with relatively higher ones was negative between 1862 and 1910 (this could explain the exceptionally low growth rate of the Portuguese economy in this period) but reached 12% in the period 1910–1950. It was again of some significance during the 1950–1973 period, with a contribution of 7% (as industrialization accelerated), only slightly lower than in Spain. The contribution of structural change to productivity growth became systematically positive from 1973 onwards, as the economy continued to industrialize, first, and then deindustrialized. Despite this positive role played by structural change productivity improvements within sectors were much more significant.

Tables 22.3 and 22.4 provide each sector's share of GDP and total employment, respectively. Portugal and Spain were among the least industrialized countries of Europe in the second half of the nineteenth century and at the beginning of the twentieth century. Moreover, they were also among those where structural change was less important. The change in pattern occurred mainly in the twentieth century.

Agriculture's share of GDP in Spain reached its highest point at around 40% in the nineteenth century (1873–1883). In the period 1920–1929,

to the productivity gains due to the increase in productivity in each sector. The difference between total productivity and internal productivity is the contribution of structural change, which is due to the re-allocation of labour between sectors.

[100] However, this conventional shift-share analysis method used would be a lower bound, when labour shift between sectors occurs. Together with this traditional form of calculation, Prados de la Escosura (2007) also provides a different one which calculates internal productivity by means of the weight of the contribution of each sector at the initial level of employment. The result obtained is considered an upper bound, given that it is calculated in terms of total factor productivity instead of in terms of labour productivity. Using this metric, the results are more realistic and similar to those obtained in other countries, assigning greater importance to structural change, being near to a half (two-fifths) during the whole 150-year period, also a half for the period 1920–1929, and one third for the period 1958–1974. Unfortunately, no similar exercise exists for Portugal.

Table 22.3 *Share of each sector in GDP (%).*

	Spain					Portugal		
	Agric.	Ind.	Cons.	Serv.		Agric.	Ind.	Serv.
1850–1880	41.9	18.1	3.0	39.3	1850–1880	39.6	15.8	42.3
1920–1929	26.8	28.0	3.7	41.5	1920–1930	31.0	26.9	42.2
1958–1974	16.7	30.8	5.3	47.2	1960–1973	17.0	39.1	43.8
1974–1986	7.7	28.2	7.2	56.9	1974–1986	11.9	39.6	48.5
1986–2000	4.9	24.2	8.0	62.9	1986–2000	7.5	35.5	57.0

Sources: Spain: Prados de la Escosura (2003). Portugal: 1850–1930: Lains (2006b); 1960–1995: Pinheiro et al. (1997) spliced with AMECO for 1995–2000.

Table 22.4 *Share of each sector in employment (%).*

	Spain					Portugal		
	Agric.	Ind.	Cons.	Serv.		Agric.	Ind.	Serv.
1850-1883	63.6	13.2	3.7	19.5	1841–1878	66.5	16	17.4
1920-1929	50	20.3	4.6	25	1920–1930	60.9	21	18.2
1958-1974	32	23.1	8.1	36.8	1960–1973	33.7	32	34.3
1974-1986	18	24.7	8.5	48.8	1974–1986	20.2	36.1	43.6
1986-2000	9.3	20.8	9.5	60.4	1986–2000	13.2	34.5	52.3

Sources: Spain: Prados de la Escosura (2003). Portugal: 1850–1930: Lains (2006b); 1960–1995: Pinheiro et al. (1997) spliced with AMECO for 1995–2000.

manufacturing overtook agriculture, reaching 28%. The highest GDP share of manufacturing was reached in 1958–1974, with 30.8%. Services represented 56.9% in 1974–1986 and 62.9% in 1986–2000 while construction accounted for 8% in 1986–2000 (Prados de la Escosura, 2003).

Within total employment, agriculture's share was over 50% until 1920–1929, decreasing from around 64% in the middle of the nineteenth century. Manufacturing's share of employment reached its highest percentage in 1976 with around 26%, surpassing agriculture. This share is close to the percentage considered by Rodrik (2013) as the highest during the industrialization process (30%). Services accounted for 50% in 1982. In addition, at the end of the twentieth century agriculture accounted for 7% of employment, manufacturing for 20% and services for 63% (Prados de la Escosura, 2003). This is a particularity of Spain: the late exodus of the agricultural labour force to other sectors and the decline in industrial employment in the 1980s perhaps constituted one of the main origins of the high structural unemployment of the Spanish economy during the late twentieth century. As a consequence of the observed trends in production and employment, and given that agriculture had a lower labour productivity than manufacturing and services, structural change made a higher contribution to labour productivity and growth during the stages of higher growth.

With respect to Portugal, we should note that the services sector contributed most to GDP until 1929 (Table 22.3). In the second half of the nineteenth century, agriculture was the largest sector in Spain but not in Portugal. Agriculture then lost weight, when the industrialization process began and, consequently, industry increased its weight in the economy. The years of the highest contribution of industry to GDP were those between the 1960s and the 1980s. Then, de-industrialization began, although later than in Spain: the loss of weight of industry started in the 1970s in Spain, one decade before Portugal. Services increased in proportion, but, by the late twentieth century, the structure of the Portuguese economy had changed less than that of the Spanish one. The importance of agriculture is still one-third higher than in Spain, and that of services is still lower.

As for employment, a similar picture seems to apply. In the second half of the nineteenth century, the Spanish and Portuguese economies seemed to have a similar structure. However, from then on, the process of relocation of labour from agriculture to industry and, later, services, was quicker in Spain than in Portugal (Table 22.4). Rather interesting is the still quite high proportion of employment in agriculture in Portugal in the late twentieth century (13%).

22.3 Sectoral Developments and the Contribution of Different Sectors to Growth

One of the reasons why we need to study the sources of economic growth and the nature of structural change at the sectoral level is because the innovations leading to long-term economic growth are concentrated in a relatively small number of sectors. Manufacturing before 1976 and services after 1976 had the highest growth rates and made the largest contributions in the subsequent stages of economic growth and development. However, agriculture was the main sector during a great part of the period and its dynamics explains a significant part of the GDP trend.

22.3.1 Agriculture

The majority of the Iberian Peninsula has a Mediterranean climate. This represents a severe obstacle to the development of agriculture due to the irregularity and scarcity of rain, conditioning the crops that can be cultivated.

Vineyards and olive groves adapt excellently to these agro-ecological conditions while cereal crops, although well adapted, generate very low yields per hectare. However, the high amount of sunshine received due to the latitude of the peninsula means that with the addition of water to counteract the natural aridity, the conditions are ideal for growing horticultural products (Table 22.5). Only the west and northern coasts of the peninsula are more humid and are therefore better suited to other crops that require larger volumes of water. These conditions also limited the development of livestock farming due to the poor pastureland. Nomadic sheep farming was the adaptive response that sought to exploit the pastureland of the lower southern areas in the winter and of the northern mountains in the summer.

In the nineteenth century, agricultural production grew in the Iberian Peninsula, driven mostly by the increasing population and also by a growing insertion into the international markets of agricultural production that were taking shape in the first globalization. Before this expansion in production could take place, an important institutional change had to be implemented in both countries in order to enable the formation of a market economy. Furthermore, the restrictions imposed by the institutions of the *Ancien Régime* had to be eliminated. Both in Portugal and Spain, the liberal reforms were met with a high level of resistance from the absolutists, who delayed their definitive implementation (Amaral, 2012; Pinilla, 2023). The privatization of land belonging to the church and local governments and communal land and its sale by public auction in the successive disentailment processes was particularly relevant, although the property structure did not change substantially in either of the two countries.

The population of the Iberian Peninsula grew by approximately five million people during the second half of the nineteenth century and feeding it without resorting to imports required a tremendous increase in production. The most important structural change of Iberian agriculture in the second half of the nineteenth century was, undoubtably, the rapid conversion of unused land into cultivated land. The cultivated area grew in Portugal between 1867 and 1902 by approximately 1.2 million hectares and in Spain between 1800 and 1900 by almost six million hectares. This turned out to be a period of very strong growth in agricultural output, as shown by Lains (2003b). In Portugal, output increased during the second half of the nineteenth century at an average annual rate of 1.4% and in Spain it increased throughout the whole of the nineteenth century at an annual rate of 0.7%. In both countries, wheat, grapes and olives were the principal crops, together with Mediterranean horticultural products.

In the second half of the nineteenth century, there was a growing presence of Iberian agricultural exports in international markets, particularly from Spain. The star product was wine. The shaping of an international market for wine, arising from the growth in demand in industrialized countries in the American

Table 22.5 Structure of agricultural output (%).

	Spain								Portugal				
	1891–1895	1900–1910	1931	1950–1955	1971–1975	1981–1985	1991–1995	1861–1870	1900–1909	1935–1939	1954–1958	1970–1973
Cereals & pulses	45.2	44.25	34.2	24	20.5	16.1	13	34.7	32.1	32.6	29.8	19.5
Wine	12.2	8.85	6	14.5	5.3	4.3	5.8	22.0	24.2	14.0	13.9	12.7
Olive oil	5.5	5	5.7	10.1	3.4	6.3	6	5.9	8.4	8.2	7.2	4.6
Fruits and vegetables	7.6	9.1	13.9	11.4	23.4	22.3	29.9	7.9	6.7	6.7	13.9	16.5
Roots and Potatoes	6	7.05	11	17	5	5.5	3	4.5	4.7	9.4	8.8	9.0
Crops	79.7	79	76.2	80.5	65.6	63.5	64.6	75.0	76.0	71.0	73.6	62.3
Meat	9.8	9.65	11.4	5.8	17.7	22.9	22.7	15.4	16.8	19.4	25.5	22.2
Dairy	5.1	5.4	6.9	8.3	12.2	9.2	9.4	7.6	5.8	8.1	11.1	8.9
Wool	0.9	0.8	0.6	1.2	0.2	0.1	0	2.2	0.8	1.6	2.5	6.6
Animal products	20.3	21	23.8	19.4	34.4	36.5	35.4	25.0	24.0	29.0	26.4	37.7
Total agriculture	100	100	100	100	100	100	100	100	100	100	100	100

Sources: Clar and Pinilla (2009); Lains (2009).

continent and in France due to the phylloxera plague, gave rise to interesting opportunities for the traditional producers. Between 1850 and 1890, Portugal tripled the volume of wine exported and Spain multiplied its exports fifteen-fold. The exports of other agricultural products also expanded significantly, such as cork or olive oil in Portugal and olive oil or fresh fruits and vegetables in Spain (Gallego & Pinilla, 1996; Branco & Silva, 2017).

The large expansion of production was accompanied by a moderate increase in productivity. Even so, there was a notable intensification process which moved resources into higher productivity sectors (from unused land or pastures to crops). Total factor productivity (TFP) in the agricultural sector grew very slowly during the first half of the nineteenth century (the annual growth rate for Spain was 0.16% between 1800 and 1857), but faster in the second half (the annual growth rate for Portugal was 0.63% between 1865 and 1902, and 0.95% for Spain between 1857 and 1905) (Bringas, 2000; Lains, 2009). A severe obstacle limiting the growth of productivity was the inability of the agricultural sector to adapt to technological change ('the first green revolution'), given the environmental conditions prevailing in much of the Iberian Peninsula. Starting from relatively low levels of agricultural productivity, the gap between Iberian productivity and the already high levels found in other European countries could only widen.

The beginning of the agricultural depression at the end of the nineteenth century marked the start of a certain divergence between the Iberian agricultures. In Portugal, the early twentieth century was a period of slower growth, mostly marked by a traditionalist turn of agricultural policy, as protection and stimulus were given to wheat cultivation (Reis, 1979). Although during this period the use of fertilizers and machinery was gaining importance, Portugal did not incorporate these innovations to modernize its agriculture at a sufficiently fast pace. However, its orientation towards the foreign market weakened as a result of the difficulties in the wine market and the decline in British purchases of other products, which was not compensated by a reorientation towards products with a higher income elasticity (Lains, 1995). TFP in the sector grew at a much slower rate than during the second half of the nineteenth century (Lains, 2009).

In contrast, although it was facing serious difficulties as a result of the depression and its problems in foreign markets, Spanish agriculture experienced significant changes in the first third of the twentieth century. Agricultural productivity improved, initially in terms of the yield from the land itself and, after the First World War, in labour productivity. TFP also grew faster than in the previous century (Bringas, 2000). The consumption of fertilizers grew sharply, and their use quadrupled between 1907 and 1935 (Gallego, 2001). Agricultural mechanization finally took off, particularly when, after the First World War, real wages began to increase appreciably, which constituted an incentive to substitute capital investment for labour

(Clar & Pinilla, 2009). The strong wheat protectionism gave farmers a margin to allow them to modernize their production. Meanwhile, in foreign markets, the most important Spanish export products faced serious difficulties. Wine, which had represented the fundamental part of exports in the second half of the nineteenth century, had many difficulties in accessing its traditional markets either due to the protectionist policies of countries such as France, the United States or Argentina or because it had not become a mass consumption product in industrialized countries (Pinilla & Ayuda, 2002).

However, a subsequent reorientation in the development of Spanish agriculture consisted of increasing the production and exports of fresh fruit and vegetables. Nevertheless, the development of these crops required the extension of irrigated land to counteract the effects of aridity. This was remarkably successful, since increased production and exports were an unquestionable source of improvement and growth for Spanish agriculture (Pinilla & Ayuda, 2010).

The Spanish Civil War and the Second World War marked a further divergence in the trajectory of the two countries. While in Portugal structural changed continued, with cereals and wine declining and animal products, fruits and vegetables, especially the latter, increasing their weight in agricultural output, in Spain, the process of agricultural modernization was interrupted between 1936 and 1951, within a context of erroneous interventionist policies and foreign isolation due to the Franco dictatorship. This resulted in a severe fall in productivity and a notable inability to adequately feed the Spanish population, while agriculture exports decreased significantly.

After 1951, both countries began a period of strong economic and industrial growth, with a significant increase in income per capita and urbanization, which had an appreciable impact on consumption. Initially, the traditional agriculture of the Iberian Peninsula found it difficult to adapt to the new diet, giving rise to surpluses in some products (wheat) and deficits in others (meat).

The industrialization process generated push and pull effects that were strong enough to cause a mass rural exodus. The demand for labour in the more developed European countries also contributed to this exodus, particularly in Portugal. The increase in wages in rural areas promoted mechanization, although in Portugal the public policies sought to maintain the volume of the active population in agriculture higher than necessary (Amaral & Freire, 2017). This process was completed with the adoption of green revolution technologies, in particular the introduction of hybrid seeds, although more profoundly in Spain than in Portugal. The expansion of irrigation was also crucial, and irrigated land increased in Spain by over one million hectares between 1950 and 1978, although it hardly grew in Portugal.

The restructuring of Iberian farm production began around 1965 and was mainly concentrated in meat. Livestock farming became the paradigm for the transformation of agriculture. International connections favoured the introduction of technologically mature foreign species (particularly chickens and pigs, although also cattle). Intensive livestock farming was developed using industrial production systems and was increasingly vertically integrated, becoming one of the leading sectors in farm production in the second half of the 1960s.

In 1986, Portugal and Spain joined the EEC and, after a period of transition, they adopted the Common Agricultural Policy (CAP). However, the results of this integration were very different in each case. The type of policy implemented in Portugal was similar to that existing in the EEC: protection at the border, guaranteed prices and some (but little) structural reform. In this respect, there was, therefore, no major conceptual adaptation. Nevertheless, there were two main problems: the differences in guaranteed prices (lower in the CAP) and the structural development of agriculture (lower in Portugal). The Portuguese approach to negotiations was to make few demands on price levels but, at the same time, to ask for strong support for structural reform (Amaral & Freire, 2017).

The result of this transition process, together with various changes in the mechanisms of the CAP over the years, had a strong impact on Portuguese agriculture. The support mechanisms of the CAP had a natural impact on land use and product mix. The use made of land changed significantly. In 1970–1973, arable land occupied about 63% of used land and pasture 21%, but by 2000–2003 the proportions between the two were almost the same, with about 40% each – the area dedicated to permanent crops remained practically unaltered. Portuguese agriculture became much more extensive than it used to be, with a large percentage of the soil no longer dedicated to temporary or permanent crops. Under these circumstances, the product mix of Portuguese agriculture changed significantly. Cereals and wine followed by olive oil and fruits, which had been the traditional and most important Portuguese crops, lost weight. Milk and dairy products have become the clear front-runners, with a relevant increase in beef and other meats. The CAP changed the profile of Portuguese agriculture in a pronounced way, although it was not enough to make it converge, in terms of productivity, with the agricultural sectors of northern countries (Amaral & Freire, 2017).

The entrance of Spain into the EU represented a significant increase in the support given to Spanish farmers, which implied a significant stimulus for expanding production (Clar et al., 2018). Furthermore, gaining access to the European market initially represented excellent trade opportunities for those products, particularly Mediterranean horticultural ones, in which Spanish agriculture was competitive. Internal European agricultural trade increased substantially after the abolition of internal tariffs, and even more so with the creation of the single market and monetary union (Serrano & Pinilla, 2011). Spain, therefore, initially benefited from accessing a market with enormous potential under more favourable conditions. However, more interesting than these benefits, which we could classify as being static and derived exclusively from trade liberalization, is that the Spanish agri-food sector became highly dynamic after Spain's accession, with the introduction of technological improvements and its adaption to the new conditions of demand and consumer tastes. Spanish agri-food companies learnt how to raise and improve their productivity (Serrano et al., 2015). Consequently, agricultural production, integrated in the complex agri-food sector, has grown, and Spain has become one of the world's leading food exporters. Agricultural exports grew at a very fast rate after 1985, and their volume multiplied almost five-fold in only 20 years.

The results of the Iberian agricultures in the second half of the twentieth century are clearly divergent. Spanish agriculture shows quite outstanding results, with an average annual growth rate of 2.2% between 1950 and 2005, compared to a European average of 1.3%, the highest of the continent (Table 22.6). In contrast, the agricultural production of Portugal grew at a modest rate of 0.9%. The main difference in the pace of Spanish growth is due to the fact that although until 1985 its production increased at a high rate, similar to that of many other European countries, after this year it continued to grow vigorously. On the other hand, countries in Western Europe saw their production stagnate, while production in Eastern Europe fell as a result of the

Table 22.6 *Agricultural annual growth rates of outputs, inputs and TFP between 1950 and 2005.*

1950–2005	Output	Labour	Land	Capital	TFP
Portugal	0.9	−1.73	−1.09	2.24	1.34
Spain	2.34	−2.52	−0.2	3.64	2.37
Europe	1.26	−2.76	−0.31	2.18	1.8
1950–1985	Output	Labour	Land	Capital	TFP
Portugal	0.87	−1.2	−0.33	3.38	0.54
Spain	2.92	−2.2	0.09	5	2.36
Europe	2.07	−2.41	−0.2	3.92	1.98
1985–2005	Output	Labour	Land	Capital	TFP
Portugal	0.96	−2.64	−2.41	0.3	2.73
Spain	1.33	−3.08	−0.69	1.33	2.36
Europe	−0.15	−3.37	−0.5	−0.77	1.48

Source: Martín-Retortillo & Pinilla (2015).

collapse of the communist model and the transition to a market economy. Portuguese agriculture, however, maintained a very similar growth rate in both periods; much lower than the European average in the first period but clearly higher in the second (Martin-Retortillo & Pinilla, 2015).

22.3.2 Industry

The manufacturing sector followed the typical pattern of economies that started their industrialization process late, as there was a specific scarcity of raw materials, such as water and coal in both countries and iron in Portugal, a low educational level of the population, and protected domestic markets. The upswing of Spanish industrialization took off when the textile and, later the iron and steel industries developed due to the use of steam in the mechanization of their production processes. The origin of this industrial advance took place in the late eighteenth century in Catalonia. This region sold spirits and calico manufacturing (linen textile printing) to American colonial markets. Printing textiles was a growing industry, mostly concentrated in Barcelona, producing linen calicos for the colonies and cotton calicos for the domestic market. Thanks to the Atlantic trade, wine growing experienced a commercial and industrial expansion essential for the start of the Industrial Revolution. At the same time, the colonial trade of calicos allowed the import of cheaper raw cotton and the surge of cotton textile shops scattered across the countryside which were replacing wool manufacturers. Subsequently, cotton yarns were produced using the new spinning jenny and an improved adaptation of it, the so-called 'bergadana'.

After the Napoleonic Wars, the colonial markets were lost, and industry had to adapt. The loss of population due to the war, together with capital accumulation during the export boom and also the Royal decree forbidding cotton yarn imports from abroad in 1802, favoured the mechanization of cotton spinning by means of water-frames and mule-jennies, and later on with the first use of the Watt steam engine in 1833 in the Bonaplata factory. Mechanical spinning accounted for nearly 30% of total production in 1835 and reached almost 100% in 1861 (Sánchez, 2000). However, the mechanization of weaving was slow. Cotton textiles adopted the new technologies and gained importance and competitiveness in relation to old textile industries, such as linen and wool. Moreover, as a consequence of the use of steam power, the location of the factors changed from places near water resources to the coast. The advantages of being located close to the port of Barcelona included the import of raw cotton and coal and the agglomeration economies or Marshall externalities that are shared by industries located together: a skilled labour pool, specialized inputs and technological spillovers.

The iron and steel industry had different locations according to factor endowments. The first industry was established in Málaga in 1826 and produced 72% of Spanish cast iron. However, the change from charcoal to coal increased the competitiveness of the Asturias factories located near the coal mines and Britain during the 1864-1879 period. After 1879, the industry developed in Biscay (Basque Country) due to cheaper coal shipping from Great Britain, owing to the lower transport costs. These were a consequence of the abundance of high-quality iron in Biscay, which was massively exported, mainly to the British market, when Bessemer technology demanded non-phosphoric iron ore. In short, manufacturing was concentrated in the two provinces of Asturias and Biscay primarily due to the important role of access to natural resource endowments such as coal and other raw materials and mining inputs in production, but also due to external and internal economies of scale. In addition, the iron and steel industries were protected in 1869 and especially after 1891.

As mentioned, Spain was well endowed with metallic mineral resources and the mining sector experienced a boom thanks to the 1868 law for the exploitation of natural resources and the increase in foreign demand associated with European industrialization. The period from 1861 to 1913 coincided with the golden age of mining, which reached its highest level in 1900, representing 7.3% and 1.8% of industrial value added and GDP, respectively. From 1876 to 1900, Spain was at the forefront of the lead and copper industries (Harley & Taylor, 1987), producing more than 86% of iron ore and 90% of the sulphur sold abroad by European countries, and 40% of the world's mercury (Escudero, 1996). Lead, copper and mercury were mainly located in Andalusia and iron in the Basque Country, but during the interwar period the deposits were exhausted, which meant those regions became less important.

However, around 1910, the textile, food, beverage and tobacco industries were predominant. For Spain, manufacturing transformation at a lower level of disaggregation over the long term (1850-2000) can be followed with data drawn from corporate income taxes and estimations from national accounts.[101] Consumer goods industries constituted the most important manufacturing sector until 1913. Food, drinks and tobacco represented the highest share in manufacturing in 1856, with 56%, although with a decreasing share in favour of textiles and clothing, and leather and shoes, which had its maximum share of 30% in the 1920s. With respect to Portugal, the biggest difference was the larger concentration of the Portuguese textiles industry, rather than food and beverages, despite some change throughout the period. As a matter of fact, textiles had an overwhelming weight in the Portuguese industrial structure, although with a declining trend: from nearly 60% in 1845 to 45% in 1896 (Table 22.7), with a more or less equi-proportional distribution between cotton and wool. The most important changes in structure came

---

[101] See sources for the different years in Table 22.7.

Table 22.7 *Share of manufacturing valued added (%).*

Spain		1856	1900	1913	1929	1958	1980	2000
1	Food, beverages and tobacco	55.8	40.3	38.4	29.6	17.0	14.9	14.0
2	Textiles, clothing and footwear	27.4	29.6	28.9	21.4	21.2	12.0	7.2
3	Wood, cork and furniture	1.2	3.2	7.6	11.3	7.1	6.6	5.5
4	Paper printing and graphic arts	2.3	5.0	2.2	1.7	4.4	6.5	8.8
5	Chemical industry	3.5	5.6	2.5	4.3	10.2	10.6	14.5
6	Stone, clay, glass and cement	5.3	4.0	0.7	4.4	4.4	9.4	8.6
7	Basic metallurgic	–	–	6	6.6	6.2	15.1	14.4
8	Metal transformation	3.2*	8.1*	6.3	12.7	17.3	16.3	15.3
9	Transport equipment	–	–	5	6.6	7.6	7.7	10.6
10	Diverse industry	1.1	4.1	2.4	1.4	4.6	0.9	1.1
	Total manufacturing	100	100	100	100	100	100	100

Portugal		1845	1896	1910	1929	1960	1980	2000
1	Food, beverages and tobacco	10	24	21	25	17	16	20
2	Textiles, clothing and footwear	58	45	44	36	20	22	25
3	Wood, cork and furniture	1	10	18	10	11	10	5
4	Paper printing and graphic arts	10	3	3	4	5	7	8
5	Chemical industry	–	–	11	14	20	10	10
6	Stone, clay, glass and cement	–	–	1	2	7	9	10
7	Basic metallurgic	–	–	1	1	1	3	2
8	Metal transformation and transport equipment	7*	6*	2	5	12	20	17
9	Diverse industry	–	–	1	1	1	1	1

* Basic metals, metal transformation and transport equipment together.
Sources: Spain: Nadal et al. (2003) for 1856 and 1900 from corporate income taxes (Basque country and Navarre are not included); Prados de la Escosura (2003) and own calculation from Nadal et al. (2003) for 1913, 1929 and 1958; for 1980 and 2000 from *INE, Encuesta industrial*. Portugal: 1845 and 1896: Pedreira (2013), based on employment shares; 1910–2000: Aguiar & Martins (2005).

about thanks to the growth of the cork and tinned fish industries, the former increasing from almost 2% to 9.5% in 1896, and the latter from virtual non-existence to 10% in the same period (Table 22.7). As could be expected for these two new sectors, most of the industry depended on the internal market and most of it was technologically traditional. Domestic industry continued to represent the largest part of the sector, with just a few islands of more modern units.

The Portuguese industrial sector was practically unable to profit from the environment of the 'first age of globalization' of the second half of the nineteenth century (expression coined by O'Rourke & Williamson, 1999), which had a lot to do with the adoption of a deliberate protectionist policy (Lains, 2006b). According to Lains (1995), the specialization in textiles went against the country's comparative advantages, which existed in some agricultural goods but also in the new industrial sectors of tinned fish and cork products. This prevented Portugal from adopting the pattern followed in Spain but also in Italy or even France: specializing in food and beverages allowed these countries to compensate for the disadvantage of not being well endowed with the raw materials and fuel typical of industrialization in Northern Europe. However, according to Reis (1984), even that sort of specialization would not have been enough to put the Portuguese economy on a different path. The country simply did not possess the natural resources or a viable specialization pattern that could have broken the cycle of backwardness: no coal or iron existed in sufficient amounts and all potential specializations based on the economy's comparative advantages (wine, tin sardines or cork) were not viable due to various supply limits. As noted by Reis (1993a), one of the resource endowments seriously limiting not only the overall productivity of the economy but also the ability to move resources from less to more sophisticated industrial sectors was human capital. Portugal had one of the highest illiteracy rates in Europe in the second half of the nineteenth century. Not only was the initial level high but it decreased very slowly in comparison with other similar low-literacy countries such as Spain or Italy: 88% in 1864, compared to 76% in Spain and 73% in Italy, and 78% in 1900, compared to 60% in Spain and 56% in Italy (see Chapter 19).

During the interwar period, 1913–1929, there was a decline in traditional industries in favour of a more diversified industrial structure. For Spain, in the 1920s, the share of traditional lighter industries lost ground to chemicals, building materials and metal transformation. During the golden age and the growth miracle years of the Spanish economy, metallurgic and transformed metal, including transport equipment, represented the greatest share of total manufacturing, at around 40% (see Table 22.7). These changes came together with important transformations and innovations within a common protectionist and regulatory context. The important innovations at the end of the nineteenth century were electricity and other technological changes and goods associated with this general purpose technology (GPT). The industries related to these technological changes contributed to growth through transferring their productivity gains, by means of lower relative prices and the resulting positive market pecuniary externality, which promoted demand spillovers that were enough to increase the market size of the whole industry and economy

(Betrán, 1997). These industries included electricity, industries related to the first processing of metal and non-metal minerals (aluminium, lead, copper, cement), equipment goods (electric materials, engines, machinery and transport equipment) and chemicals (fertilizers, artificial silk). By contrast, some industries delayed the process due to their high relative prices, with the coal, iron and steel industries, wheat flour and sugar among the most important ones (Betrán, 1997). These industries were the most highly protected after 1891, with the trade tariffs of 1891, 1906 and also 1922.

As a consequence of different contributions of coal and electricity, relative prices for coal were higher than those for electricity. Therefore, coal was replaced rapidly by electricity, especially in those industries that made intensive use of electric processes within chemicals and equipment goods. Electrical energy played a crucial role, especially in countries that lacked coal, as electricity could be created from different primary energies, for example water or coal. In general, the relative prices between electricity and coal were greater in countries with very few coal reserves, such as Spain, leading to more opportunities to use the new energy, as was the case in Italy and Scandinavian countries. Spain, where electricity was cheap compared to coal, had the opportunity for greater economic growth during this period. Moreover, the degree of electrification advanced substantially from the end of the nineteenth century until the Second World War. The height of the process was in 1925, after the First World War, when real electricity prices fell considerably, generating important consequences for economic growth (Betrán, 2005). The height of manufacturing concentration took place in the interwar period due to the importance of factor endowments in industry location and the location of industries in a few regions. However, increasing returns were also fundamental in certain industries, such as in the case of cotton textiles, due to Marshall's externalities during this period (Betrán, 2011). In addition, there was a process of formation of large corporations, initiated at the end of the nineteenth century through mergers to invest in capital and technology, access a growing market and take advantage of economies of scale, in industries such as iron and steel (Altos Hornos de Vizcaya), paper (Papelera Española) and sugar beet (Sociedad Azucarera de España). Other large firms were created in the electricity sector (e.g. Chade and Barcelona Traction), communications (Telefonica), the chemical industry (Cross and Unión Española de Explosivos) and in the equipment goods sector (Sociedad Española de Construcción Naval). There was substantial participation by foreign enterprises in technology-intensive industries through the establishment of affiliated companies jointly owned with the national producers, for example AEG, Siemens, General Electric and Westinghouse, among others, due to the economic advantages to be gained by the national industrial producers (following the industrial protection laws of 1907, 1917 and 1924).

In the case of Portugal, the industrial structure changed considerably. During the First World War, the 1930s crisis and the Second World War there was a return to protectionism at a global level – although in Portugal it was not a return but an increase. Governments used protectionism to foster new sectors that they identified with industrial and technical progress. Besides protectionism, governments used a series of other stimuli, especially between the 1930s and 1970s, such as reserved markets and fiscal incentives. This is how textiles declined from 44% of industrial value added in 1910 to 36% in 1929 and 20% in 1960; the same happened with wood and cork products, from 18% in 1910 to 11% in 1929 and 10% in 1960. The biggest increases took place in the chemical industry, from 11% in 1910 to 14% in 1929 and 20% in 1960 (thus reaching the size of textiles and food and beverages), and the metalworking industries, rising from a residual level of 2% in 1910 to 5% in 1929 and 12% in 1960. The biggest boost for the chemical industry came from the development of the oil refining industry, especially after the opening of a large refining infrastructure in Lisbon in 1939. In metalworking, the impulse came from a series of projects on industrial machinery and light vehicles (Aguiar & Martins, 2005). Governments, especially from the 1930s to the 1970s, were very active in providing incentives for these sectors. Industry was concentrated in coastal cities, mainly Lisbon and Porto, with the exception of Covilhã, a traditional centre for woollens since the eighteenth century. The advantages of access to international markets and agglomeration economies were behind this industrial location pattern.

The industrialization process accelerated during the 1960s – the so-called economic miracle. For Spain, the leading industries were electricity, machinery and equipment, transport equipment and the chemical industry thanks to the diffusion of US technologies across Europe. Sanchis (2006) estimated the disaggregated growth accounting of the industrial sector, separating the part explained by the growth of TFP from the intermediate, capital and labour inputs. TFP represented around half the overall production growth. This result is similar to the findings for the whole Spanish economy and other countries (see Chapter 18). As previously explained, these leading industries with a higher contribution in terms of TFP generated demand spillovers in the industrial sector and the economy. At the same time, manufacturing spread to more regions as a consequence of industrialization and the inter-regional convergence of factor endowments, particularly skilled labour, as well as thanks to the growing importance of mobile factors in relation to immobile ones (coal, minerals and land) in production. For example, internal and external migrations were extraordinarily high during the 1960s. In addition, there was an increase in the significance of market access, as a location factor, due to the importance of economies of scale in 1960–1973. Later on, its importance decreased in line with the reduction in transport costs (Betrán, 2011). This process was enhanced by industrial promotion policies and public intervention, through the application of development plans and the creation of public companies in selected industries (e.g. Ensidesa in iron and steel). These public companies were also the origins of some large companies in the leading industries, such as Seat in automobiles, Repsol in oil refining (a merger of Campsa, Encaso and other firms), and others that are among the most internationalized firms today. In addition, multinational companies, especially in the automobile and petrochemical sectors, also entered the Spanish market.

For Portugal, this advance also occurred after 1960, when the economy opened up and became increasingly connected with the rest of Europe. Portugal participated in the process of European integration from the start, joining the European Free Trade Association (EFTA) in 1960 and the European Economic Community (EEC) in 1986. This time, contrary to what had happened in the nineteenth century, the country was a full participant in the second wave of globalization. The sectors where Portuguese industry had the highest success in international markets were the previously protected textiles and metalworking sectors (Amaral, 2002; Lains, 2003b; Aguiar & Martins, 2005). The industrial structure experienced many changes in this period: textiles kept their share at around 20% to 25%, from 1960 to the end of the century, as did food and beverages, from 17% to 20% (Table 22.7), but the chemical industry declined, halving its weight from 20% to 10% between 1960 and 1980 and staying at that level until 2000. The weight of the metal industries nearly doubled, from 12% in 1960 to 20% in 1980, but declined to 17% in 2000. Most of those changes took place between 1960 and 1980, in contrast with the much more stable final 20 years of the twentieth century. Economic activity was still concentrated in coastal regions around Lisbon and the north-east until the 1970s, but after that the concentration decreased (see Chapter 18; and Badía et al., 2012), although later than in other countries, including Spain, where this happened before the Second World War.

This seems to indicate that Portugal found its specialization pattern under the conditions of European openness during the 1980s. In these conditions, many of the policies that had previously been followed, with the purpose of protecting and fostering certain sectors, had to be interrupted. This explains how the chemical and basic metal industries lost weight within the Portuguese industrial structure, and indicates an apparent confinement of the Portuguese economy to a relatively low-tech path, raising questions over its ability to integrate into the wider European market. Again, human capital played an important role in this transformation, as illiteracy declined to 60% in 1930, 26% in 1970 and 13% in 1990 (see Chapter 19). Therefore, changes in this respect allowed for labour to move to more sophisticated industrial sectors, although human capital remained low by international standards until the end of the twentieth century. This may explain why sectors with lower technological content still predominate in Portugal's industrial structure.

For Spain, the main international integration process came later on when it became a member of the EEC in 1986, which accelerated the changes in the industrial structure. Table 22.7 shows that, from 1980 to 2000, food, drink and tobacco, metallurgy, metal transformation, transport equipment and chemicals became the most important sectors, whereas textiles and footwear lost weight. Food and drink and transport equipment were the leading exporters to the EU. The previous interventionist policies had to be eliminated and it was necessary to take measures to adapt the Spanish economy to its entry into an open European market with a customs union. Spanish comparative advantages were located in the leading industries of the years before the entry into the EEC (especially in automobile and food and beverage).

This seems to indicate that Spain and Portugal found their specialization pattern under the conditions of European openness. When comparing the two countries, although food and beverages were important for both, there still seemed to be an excessive importance of textiles in the case of Portugal. The same goes for food and beverages, although to a lesser degree. The increasing importance of metal industries in Spain is significant, in contrast to its stability in Portugal. The chemical industry also increased in Spain and stabilized in Portugal, while basic metals had a relevance in Spain that Portugal never matched. The scarcity of factors used intensively in the metal and chemical industries – natural resources and human capital – and the different size of the markets of the two countries could explain the different patterns.

22.3.3 Services

Although it has been a long-neglected element in the explanation of modern economic growth, the services sector has acquired increasing relevance in some recent literature. Broadberry (2006) and Broadberry and Ghosal (2005) have noted how the productivity differential between the UK, the USA and Germany during the twentieth century was more due to the evolution of the services sector than to manufacturing and agriculture. The relevance of the sector is linked to the so-called process of 'industrialisation' of services', which involves 'the transition from a world of customised, low-volume, high-margin business organised on the basis of networks to a world of standardised, high-volume, low-margin business with hierarchical management' (Broadberry, 2006: 5). The process of industrialization of services started in the second half of the nineteenth century in the early developing countries and continued with increased intensity throughout the twentieth century, spreading progressively to latecomers.

Spain and Portugal were not left entirely outside of this process, but they followed it with a considerable delay on account of their limitations at both the supply and demand levels. On the supply side, the process of industrialization of services is highly intensive in physical capital, human capital and technology. On the demand side, it requires a relatively high degree of urbanization and complex patterns of consumption. The beginnings of the industrialization of services can be found in railways in the US, very closely followed by the wholesale and retail trade, both being at the origin of the modern, large business firm (Chandler, 1977). They also correspond to the beginnings of modern finance, with the expansion of commercial and savings banks, as well as insurance companies. All of these subsectors required strong physical capital expansion (rails, locomotives, carriages, buildings ...) and a high human capital stock (to deal with the new technologies and increasingly more complex management and accounting systems). They also required a high level of technological intensity, especially to process information: the

Table 22.8 *Share of service sector value added (%).*

Spain	1913	1929	1958	1980	2003
Transport and communications	18.2	23.3	16	11.9	13.7
Wholesale and retail trade	31.7	29.6	27.9	22.3	16.9
Banking and insurance	2.3	4.6	8.6	9.9	7.5
Real estate	7.7	6.9	7.6	12.2	11.1
Public administration	13.8	12.1	12.6	7.8	9.4
Education	2.6	2.4	2.9	6.2	7.1
Health	0.5	0.8	2.4	6.9	8.3
Hotels and restaurants	10.6	7	5.6	11.4	10.1
Housekeeping	3	3	4.2	5.9	6.3
Other services (liberal professions)	9.5	10.2	12.2	5.5	9.5
	100	100	100	100	100
Portugal	1910	1929	1958	1980	1995
Transport and communications	7.5	9.1	9.6	10.9	10.8
Wholesale and retail trade	29.2	26.0	34.6	33.6	22.7
Banking and insurance	1.4	1.7	5.4	9.4	9.3
Real estate	20.2	14.4	21.8	9.6	12.3
Public administration*	12.0	20.7	13.5	22.5	24.8
Hotels and restaurants	–	–	1.8	4.1	6.7
Other services	30.6	28.6	13.3	9.9	13.4
	100	100	100	100	100

* Includes education and health.
Sources: Spain: Prados de la Escosura (2003) for 1913, 1929, 1958 and Gordo et al. (2006) for 1980 and 2003. Portugal: Batista et al. (1997) for 1910, 1929 and 1958 and Pinheiro et al. (1997) for 1980 and 1995.

telegraph, the telephone, typewriters, calculating machines and other similar instruments were crucial for them.

Spain and Portugal could only follow this process in a moderate way in the late nineteenth century and early twentieth century. Table 22.8 shows how, in that period, wholesale and retail trade had the highest weight in both countries, at around one-third of the sector's value added. Although this was one of the subsectors where many innovations appeared in the USA or the UK, the Iberian countries did not adopt them with high intensity. Despite some examples of modern retail methods in the largest cities, on the whole the sector remained essentially traditional, based on small shops selling basic consumption goods (Martins, 1997; Cuñado, 2018). The same is true for transport and communications. Railways, the telegraph and the telephone expanded in the Iberian Peninsula in the second half of the nineteenth century, but to a lesser extent than in core countries (Mata, 1988; Alegria, 1990; Calvo, 2001; Herranz-Loncán, 2006). This subsector was the second most important service branch in Spain in the early twentieth century, although not in Portugal. Railways were initially based on steam power, but when electricity became widespread, not only did the railways electrify in order to profit from the new technology, but also new means of urban transport appeared, such as tramways, subways and the metro. Despite its relatively low importance in comparison with other countries (Caruana-Galizia & Martí-Henneberg, 2013), the contribution of railways to economic growth was substantial in the case of Spain: the social saving for the economy, as a percentage of GDP, calculated by Herranz-Loncán (2006) was 3.9–6.4% in 1878, increasing, as a consequence of technological progress, to 18.9% in 1912. No similar calculations exist for Portugal, but most probably the contribution of railways to economic growth was much less pronounced. On the one hand, its weight was substantially lower, and on the other hand, the few existing indications point to significant inefficiency in the installation of the railway network: under the influence of highly corrupt practices, the chosen routes do not seem to have favoured the best integration of the national market (Vieira, 1983). Modern banking institutions and methods were introduced in both countries in this period, following the path of core countries, but, as in the case of many other services, they remained less developed, in this instance reflecting their much lower financial intermediation (see Chapter 21; Malo de Molina and Martín-Aceña, 2012; Valério et al., 2006). The relatively low endogenous capacity of both Iberian countries to contribute to the industrialization of services is revealed by the fact that most modern activities depended on foreign direct investment, as demonstrated by the cases of railways, public transport, the telegraph and the telephone (Puig & Álvaro, 2016; Silva, 2016).

The third most important subsector in Spain, and fourth in Portugal, in the late nineteenth century and early twentieth century was that of public administration, representing a similar weight in value added in both countries. Spain and Portugal experienced similar processes of institutional development, as both installed a modern state in the period, with its associated bureaucratic and administrative structure. This process was common to the rest of Europe, as the liberal revolutions of the period not only meant the liberation of markets from old restrictions but also the creation of public authorities in the sense we understand them today (Cardoso & Lains, 2010a).

The process of industrialization of services was somehow interrupted, even in core countries, between 1914 and the 1940s, as a consequence of the world wars and the 1930s crisis, but resumed after the 1950s, this time affecting especially Europe, which adopted many management methods that had been in use for some time in the USA – a phenomenon sometimes defined as the 'Americanization' of European economies (Zeitin & Herrigel, 2004). The Iberian countries followed this process quite closely, as many of the supply and demand aspects that had hampered the industrialization of services in the nineteenth century and early twentieth century were now being overcome, continuing their rapid catching up with the core countries. Physical and human capital intensity grew at fast rates in the period, as did technological progress. At the same time, urbanization and more sophisticated consumption habits also developed. Many of the new management methods were introduced by large business groups, which had a visible expansion from the 1950s until the 1970s in both countries (Silva et al., 2016; Cuervo-Cazurra, 2018). A subsector where this was especially visible was in the retail trade, with the appearance of the first supermarkets and department stores (Cuñado, 2018). Loss of weight in the sector's value added (Table 22.8) did not mean a lack of substantial modernization. The same is true for transport and communications, a subsector that acquired similar relevance in both countries from the 1980s onwards. Another subsector that saw considerable expansion was banking and finance. This again depended a lot on the catching up processes of both economies, which led to substantially increased financial intermediation. As a consequence, the banking system grew and modernized from the 1950s onwards (Malo de Molina and Martín-Aceña, 2012; Valério et al. 2010). In the last couple of decades of the twentieth century, Spain was even able to develop some important multinational banks, with influence in Europe and outside of Europe (Santander and BBVA are cases in point). All of these activities were very much affected by the ICT revolution that started in the 1980s. According to some estimates, ICT technologies in Spain, as applied to communications, retail and banking represented a share of valued added of 2.8% in 1980, increasing to 5% in 2003 (see Gordo et al., 2006).

A subsector that became crucial for both economies, especially after the 1960s was that of tourism. This is reflected in Table 22.8 in the growth of the hotels and restaurants sector. The reason for this was the transformation of Spain and Portugal into popular beach destinations for many northern Europeans (mostly from the UK but also France, the Netherlands, Germany or Scandinavia). Foreign exchange originating in tourism reached a first peak of 5% of GDP in Portugal in 1966 and remained at about that level until the end of the century (Amaral, 2019). The weight was higher in Spain, reaching close to 8% of GDP in 1965 and increasing afterwards to 11% in the late twentieth century (Vallejo, 2002).

Public administration, including public provided social systems (such as health and education), grew slowly until the 1970s in both countries, mostly on account of the little attention devoted to social programmes by their respective authoritarian regimes (lasting between 1939 and 1975 in Spain, and between 1933 and 1974 in Portugal) (Espuelas, 2012). This changed considerably from the 1970s onwards, when both countries acquired democratic regimes that relied heavily on this sort of policy. Between the 1970s and the end of the century, the Iberian countries installed their own versions of the Welfare State, with a corresponding increase in social expenditure (Tanzi & Schuknecht, 2000). It is not possible to disaggregate the figures for Portugal in Table 22.8, but the figures for Spain reveal a process that was similar on the other side of the border: by the end of the twentieth century, public administration, together with education and health services, was the largest services subsector in both countries.

Finally, a note should be made about the importance of real estate in Spain and Portugal, which can be observed in Table 22.8. The figures reflect the fast pace of construction in both countries from the 1960s onwards (see also Tables 22.3 and 22.4 for Spain), sometimes leading to episodes of excessive growth culminating in speculative spells, particularly in Spain (Lourenço & Rodrigues, 2014).

22.4 Conclusion

Both Iberian countries were latecomers to industrialization and also to agricultural success. With a late start in the mid-nineteenth century in relation to the core European countries, due to both poor factor endowments and institutions, they advanced in terms of structural change during the interwar period and experienced post-1950 growth miracles. Major changes took place when technological change and foreign markets were adapted to their factor endowments.

The main differences between both countries were the slow path of Portugal in relation to Spain, and the less intense Portuguese structural change, with agriculture having a lower and services a higher share of GDP and employment during the nineteenth century, with the opposite being the case in the twentieth century. Within the industrial sector, light industries and industries that were less intensive in skilled labour and capital had a higher importance in Portugal than in Spain. Moreover late-twentieth-century de-industrialization also took place a decade later in Portugal than in Spain. Agriculture displayed a different trend, shifting from a specialization in olive oil, wine and cork towards a higher importance of cattle and dairy products in Portugal and towards an integrated agri-food sector with a higher growth in Spain. The successful exporters in both countries were heavy industry, especially automobile, and food and beverages, as well as clothing and footwear in Portugal, while banking and finance and tourism were the predominant services.

The main challenges for both countries, although more pressing in Portugal, are increasing human capital, research and development investments, and changes in regulations and institutions to upgrade to higher value-added in all sectors, but particularly in services where the role of the new IT-based communications technologies and human capital are decisive.

23

Living Standards in Iberia, 1800–2010

ALFONSO DÍEZ-MINGUELA, JORDI GUILERA AND JULIO MARTINEZ-GALARRAGA

23.1 Introduction

In the nineteenth century, modern economic growth was well under way in Western Europe. New ideas and knowledge rooted in the Enlightenment and the ensuing scientific revolution gave rise to technological change and industrialization. Together with productivity growth and structural change, progress was made in other areas too. Medical advances and sanitation, for instance, brought about a steady decline in mortality while the population grew. This time, however, population growth did not lead to falling living standards. Although debate on the social question marked the final decades of the nineteenth century, living standards on the whole ultimately improved.

In this chapter our aim is to analyse the evolution of living standards in Iberia over the last two centuries. However, measuring well-being is far from trivial, and so we present a number of indicators capturing different dimensions. Our selected indicators include average income, consumption patterns, height, life expectancy at birth, and the Human Development Index (HDI).[102] We also examine income distribution by looking at alternative inequality indicators: the Gini coefficient, the extraction ratio and top income shares. In so doing we should make it clear that, as is often the case in historical studies, data availability is an issue. Information on such indicators usually begins in the mid-nineteenth century, often constraining the time span of the analysis, and geographical coverage also differs in some cases between Portugal and Spain.[103] Bearing this in mind, we assess the long-term evolution of living standards in Iberia and, when possible, look at its Western European counterparts for the purposes of comparison. As we will see, economic progress and well-being improved significantly in Iberia over the last two centuries, although this occurred some years later than elsewhere in Western Europe.

---

[102] Other measures such as mortality rates, infant mortality rates and educational variables, which may complement this analysis, can be found in Chapter 19.
[103] We believe, however, that this asymmetry in the availability of information over time and across Iberian countries does not compromise the analysis conducted in this chapter.

23.2 From Wealth to Health

23.2.1 A First Approach to Material Living Standards: Income

Since well-being is a multidimensional concept, one of the usual starting points is to explore how per capita income evolved over time. Of the various aggregate measures of income, we focus on gross domestic product (GDP). GDP per inhabitant essentially captures the average distribution of output – or aggregate production – and income in a particular country. One advantage of this indicator is its availability for long historical periods, thus allowing us to present its long-term evolution.[104] Figure 23.1 shows the evolution of Iberian per capita income on a yearly basis since 1850 using GDP and population data from the Maddison Project Database (2013). To shed additional light on the subject, Figure 23.1 also shows a smoothed average of the maximum and minimum values reported for Western Europe, excluding Spain and Portugal.[105]

Although average income in Iberia has risen by a factor of 16 over the last 150 years, this growth was not a steady process. From 1850 it took approximately 70 years for per capita income to double. After the Great War (1914–1918) political instability and internal conflict had a negative effect on economic progress. While in Spain the dictatorship of Primo de Rivera (1923–1930) was followed by the Second Republic (1931–1939) and a Civil War (1936–1939), in Portugal a military coup ended the First Republic in 1926 and gave rise to the *Estado Novo*. Per capita income then rapidly increased in the context of the Golden Age, especially in the 1960s. However, this came to a halt in the mid-1970s and early 1980s, but then resumed afterwards. Despite these ups and downs, material living standards improved substantially from the mid-nineteenth century. Nevertheless, it can also be seen in Figure 23.1 that Iberia drifted away from its Western European counterparts.

Using per capita income can give us a first glimpse of living standards, but it may leave out other important dimensions (Stiglitz et al., 2009).[106] Well-being is not just about average income or material living standards, but is also related to

---

[104] A detailed analysis of the evolution of per capita income and growth in Iberia can be found in Chapter 18.

[105] Spain saw a moderate improvement in per capita income throughout the eighteenth century, and this intensified in the first half of the nineteenth. However, this was not enough to halt the secular relative decline of the economy, and by the mid-nineteenth century Spain had fallen behind its main European counterparts. The story of Portugal was even more disappointing. Although a relatively prosperous economy in the early modern period, from the 1750s onwards it underwent intense economic decline. By 1850 per capita income there was below that of other countries on the European periphery, including Spain (Álvarez-Nogal & Prados de la Escosura, 2013; Palma & Reis, 2019; see also Chapter 10).

[106] For a review of the pros and cons of GDP per capita as a measure of well-being, see, for example, Deaton (2013: 167–180).

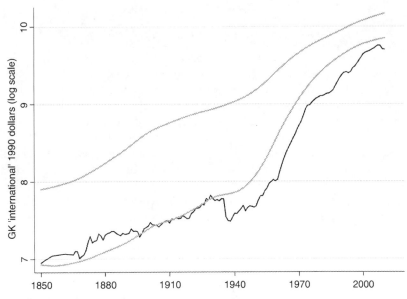

Figure 23.1 Real per capita income in Iberia (Spain and Portugal), 1850–2010 (Geary-Khamis 'international' 1990 dollars).
Note: The solid grey lines show a smoothed average of maximum and minimum real per capita income (in logarithmic scale) in Western Europe (Austria, Belgium, Denmark, Finland, France, Germany, Italy, the Netherlands, Norway, Sweden, Switzerland and the UK), while the solid black line shows real per capita income (in logarithmic scale) in Iberia.
Source: Maddison Project Database (2013).

health, education, political freedom and personal relationships, to mention but a few aspects (Sen, 1993). In the following sections we explore some of these dimensions.

23.2.2 The Household Budget: Changes in Consumption Patterns

One of the effects of economic progress, previously tracked through average income, is the increase in the amount of household disposable income that can be used for consumption. The relevance of consumption to well-being is that, unlike income, it is a key variable linked to living standards and poverty measurement in low-income countries. It is also therefore worth looking at the evolution of the relationship between expenditure and income. Using several sources including Ballesteros (1997), the Spanish Instituto Nacional de Estadística (INE) and Eurostat, Figure 23.2 shows the shares of household expenditure for Spain and Iberia in four major categories (food, clothing, housing and other expenses).

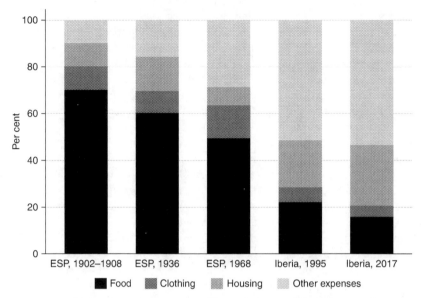

Figure 23.2 Share of consumption expenditure in Spain and Iberia by category.
Note: Food also includes non-alcoholic and alcoholic beverages. Housing refers only to renting in 1902–1908, 1936 and 1968, while in 1995 and 2017 it includes housing, water, electricity, gas and other fuels, furnishings and household equipment. Up to 1968 the data refer only to Spain, while for 1995 and 2017 Portugal is also considered. Information for Iberia for those years was obtained as a population-weighted average of the Eurostat data for Spain and Portugal.
Sources: 1902–1908 from Ballesteros (1997: Table 2); 1936 and 1968 from INE (https://www.ine.es/); and 1995 and 2017 from Eurostat (https://ec.europa.eu/eurostat/web/main/data/database).

Because of data limitations, our analysis focuses on Spain from the early twentieth century, with Portugal being included only after 1995 to enable Iberia as a whole to be considered.[107] The decrease in the share of basic items such as food and to a lesser extent clothing is clear to see.

This information allows us to monitor for Engel's law, which states that as income rises the proportion of it that households spend on food (i.e. the share devoted to food consumption) decreases (Stigler, 1954; Houthakker, 1957;

---

[107] Data limitations have not allowed us to delve further into the Portuguese economy (e.g. see da Costa Júnior, 1917a; 1917b). Nevertheless, it is worth noting that in 1995 the differences in consumption expenditure between the two Iberian countries were negligible. For instance, following Eurostat, the share of household expenditure on food and beverages in 1995 was 21.9% in Spain and 22.0% in Portugal.

Chai & Moneta, 2010). Although it is widely accepted that Spanish households on average allocated around 60-80% of their income to food at the start of the twentieth century, the gradual rise in income between the mid-nineteenth century and the Civil War (1936-1939) seems not to have brought about much change in consumption patterns (Reher & Ballesteros, 1993; Ballesteros, 1997). This, however, stands in contrast to what happened from the 1950s. As income grew, the composition of expenditure changed radically. In the late 1960s food already accounted for less than 50% of the household budget and continued to decrease steadily. By the early 1990s food represented only a quarter of expenditure. Nevertheless, there is still some catching up to do. According to information from Eurostat,[108] Iberian households currently spend on average around 15-16% on food, while countries with higher per capita incomes such as Sweden and the UK spend around 14-15% and 10-11%, respectively.

While the food's share of the consumption basket was falling over time, significant improvements in nutrition were nevertheless taking place. The nineteenth-century diet was essentially based on products of vegetable origin and the intake of animal proteins was still meagre. In the case of Iberia, the intake of sufficient calories was a persistent problem, as shown by the recurrent mortality crises of the nineteenth century. Even in the mid-twentieth century a large fraction of the Iberian population continued at subsistence levels.

Several studies have recently examined the nutrition transition. Although environmental conditions differ markedly within Iberia and therefore significant differences between regional diets can also be found (Nicolau & Pujol-Andreu, 2006), substantial progress has been made in all regions. In short, nutrition has slowly changed since the early twentieth century with the introduction of a more diversified diet including more vegetal foodstuffs (legumes, olive oil, green vegetables, fruits and wine) and a larger intake of fish and eggs (Cussó & Garrabou, 2007; Pujol-Andreu & Cussó, 2014). Meat and milk consumption, however, remained relatively limited, although the latter eventually gained in importance over time.[109]

From the 1960s consumption of food of animal origin became predominant in the diet and Iberia witnessed the culmination of the so-called nutrition transition in a period when the average income, as we have seen, was also rising noticeably. It is usually assumed that there is a positive relationship between increased income and the nutrition transition. Consumption of animal foodstuffs shows a high demand elasticity, and thus the improvement in income prompts consumption of these products, whose share in food consumption increases. All in all, the increase in average income and the changes in consumption patterns and diet had a significant impact on biological well-being too. The

---

[108] Eurostat, https://ec.europa.eu/eurostat/web/main/data/database.
[109] In the case of Spain, the two decades between 1930 and 1950 also represented a major setback in food consumption and calorie intake.

improvement was felt in many ways, one of which, as we will see next, affected the physiognomy of Iberians.

23.2.3 Stature or Height: Still a Long Way to Grow?

Anthropometric studies have made an important contribution to the historical analysis of living standards. There is a well-established literature that uses adult height as a proxy for biological living standards (e.g. Fogel, 1986; Komlos & Baten, 2004; Steckel, 2009; Komlos & Kelly, 2016). Apart from the genetic potential, height is affected by net nutrition from conception and early childhood to maturity. The concept of net nutrition is related to diet, the amount and quality of nutrients, and also to the intensity of physical effort and disease, which may generate a significant drain of calories. Height therefore reflects both the economic and disease environment of a society. If, for example, economic progress brings greater food intake and reduces childhood disease through better hygiene or sanitation (from medical advances to health systems), then adult heights would be expected to reflect this. As summarized by Deaton (2007: 13232):

> Because of the link to gross nutrition, and because, particularly in poor countries, gross nutrition is tied to income, the link from income per head to gross nutrition and population height has often been used by historians as an indicator of the material standard of living, although the link is importantly contingent on the disease environment, most famously during the early industrial revolution in Britain.

Data on adult height is often collected from military sources. Conscription, for instance, provides information on the height of young adult males around 20 years old. Table 23.1 shows the evolution of the average height of male adults by birth decade in Western Europe and Iberia from 1860 to 1980. Generally speaking, this evolution follows a similar pattern to that marked out by income. While Western Europeans generally grew steadily taller from the mid-nineteenth century, the stature of people in Iberia increased very slowly over the first hundred years and it has been estimated that those born in the 1940s were on average only 3.3 cm taller than those born in the 1860s. Indeed, the height gap between Western Europeans and Iberians reached its maximum (more than 9 cm) in the 1940s, as Table 23.1 illustrates.

Since then, however, heights have soared in Iberia. The average height increased by 8.7 cm in four decades – a remarkable improvement – and the average height of 20-year-old males in 2000 reached 175 cm. Nevertheless, Iberians are still shorter than most of their counterparts. Those born in the 1980s, for instance, are 7–9 cm shorter than the tallest Western Europeans in Denmark and the Netherlands. In short, there seems to be a clear relationship between economic progress and increases in height in Western Europe,

Table 23.1 *Average male adult height by birth decade in Western Europe and Iberia, 1860–1980.*

Decade of birth	Western Europe max.	Western Europe min.	Iberia average	Gap (WE – Iberia) max.	Gap (WE – Iberia) min.	Portugal	Spain
1860s	169.7	163.1	163.0	6.6	0.1	164.1	162.7
1880s	171.2	163.9	164.0	7.3	−0.1	164.2	163.9
1900s	172.8	165.6	164.4	7.2	1.2	163.8	164.6
1920s	176.3	167.3	165.4	8.9	1.9	164.9	165.6
1940s	178.5	169.3	166.3	9.2	3.0	166.4	166.3
1960s	182.2	173.0	173.2	9.2	−0.2	169.2	174.2
1980s	183.2	174.5	175.0	8.7	−0.5	172.1	175.6

Note: Iberia is the population-weighted average of Portugal and Spain. Western Europe comprises Austria, Belgium, Denmark, Finland, France, Germany, Italy, the Netherlands, Norway, Sweden, Switzerland and the UK.
Source: Authors' own elaboration based on Clioinfra (https://clio-infra.eu/). Population data is from the Maddison Project Database (2013).

whereby becoming wealthier also means becoming taller. However, increasing stature in Iberia is confined to the second half of the twentieth century and, although some convergence has occurred, there continues to be a considerable height gap.

Interestingly, there are marked differences within Iberia itself. In the case of Portugal the performance is particularly disappointing (Padez, 2007; Stolz et al., 2013), but this was not always the case. In 1860 the Portuguese were relatively well positioned in terms of height – they were taller than the Spanish and not so far from the average stature of Western Europe. However, during the second half of the nineteenth century the mean height in Portugal stagnated and by the 1900s the situation had reversed – in the early decades of the twentieth century the heights for Spain were above those for Portugal. The Spanish Civil War represented a setback that also affected stature, with both countries levelling off. From then on, the average height increased more rapidly in Spain, thus widening the gap between the two countries – of those born in the 1980s, for example, the Portuguese are 3.5 cm shorter. Overall there appears to be a stronger correlation between income and height in Spain (Quiroga, 2002; María-Dolores and Martínez-Carrión, 2011). In the case of Portugal, the performance in terms of average income has been more positive than in terms of height, given the particularly disappointing evolution of the latter since the mid-nineteenth century (Stolz et al., 2013).

Anthropometric studies have examined various other dimensions associated with living standards, such as the rural–urban gap, territorial differences, inequality between social groups and the gender gap. While there is a consensus that economic growth in the long term has a positive impact on living standards, it is arguable whether such an improvement was beneficial in the early stages of modern economic growth. The debate about living standards during the British industrial revolution is probably the most famous example (Floud & Steckel, 1997; Komlos, 1998; Pamuk & Van Zanden, 2010). Providing food for a growing population was not always feasible, working conditions in the factories were harsh, and living conditions for the working classes generally deteriorated in the new crowded industrial cities. As a result of inadequate public sanitation, disease spread, and mortality rates increased in urban settings.

In the case of Spain and Portugal, the literature has pointed out the serious difficulties involved in improving biological living standards in the second half of the nineteenth century (Reis, 2002; Pérez Moreda et al., 2015). The early stages of industrialization saw a worsening of nutritional status in places such as Alcoi and Igualada during their industrial take-off in the nineteenth century. In Alcoi, for example, average heights remained stagnant between the 1830s and 1900s (García-Gómez & Escudero, 2018), while in Igualada they actually fell between the 1830s and 1870s (Ramon-Muñoz & Ramon-Muñoz, 2016). In general, industrial cities also presented lower life expectancy and higher infant mortality.

Nevertheless, the evidence available shows that there was a persistent rural height penalty that marked the late nineteenth century. Living conditions in the countryside were just as difficult if not even harder than in industrial cities. Poverty and malnutrition were widespread and in some rural areas in the south-east this was aggravated by disease, particularly malaria.[110] The rural penalty only began to decrease in the early decades of the twentieth century, although it reappeared temporarily in Spain during the years of autarky after the Civil War. The rural–urban gap finally disappeared from Spain in the 1950s (Martínez-Carrión, 2016). However, a rural–urban gap also existed in southern Portugal, and the rural penalty there did not decrease between 1930 and 1980 but expanded instead (Sobral, 1990).

The countryside in Iberia is a very diverse space with marked differences in environmental conditions and agricultural systems. From the early stages of economic development there were differences in diet across regions, affected by, for example, the availability of nutrients such as cereals and the intake of proteins of animal origin. In addition, industrialization and structural change occurred unevenly. As a result lower statures were recorded in predominantly

---

[110] Though the rural penalty has often been attributed to living conditions, selective migration may also have played an important role.

agricultural and poor regions, while industrialized regions performed better. In the long term, therefore, industrialization seems to have had a positive effect on living standards insofar as the more industrialized areas recorded higher average statures.

The eastern part of Iberia and western Andalusia, for example, had higher average statures in the mid-nineteenth century. Furthermore, territorial differences continued to grow until the First World War, reaching a maximum of around 7 cm, as the north-east of the peninsula (the triangle above the Ebro Valley) and Madrid secured their positions as the main economic centres (Díez-Minguela et al., 2018). This regional gap was also present in the case of Portugal. In the early twentieth century the difference in mean heights between districts was around 4.5 cm, ranging from the 160.5 cm of Guarda in the north to the 165.0 cm of Faro in the south. By the 1960s, however, the district of Lisbon was already recording the highest stature of 171.6 cm (Padez, 2007). In addition, between 1930 and 1980, in the southern districts 'gains in stature were greater in the littoral than in the hinterland regions, where agriculture still employs a large percentage of the population' (Sobral, 1990: 491). As the twentieth century advanced, heights gradually converged and today the regional gap between the extremes is less than 2 cm (Padez, 2007; Martínez-Carrión, 2016).

Apart from these territorial disparities, interpersonal inequality in height was also important given the sizable differences between social groups, these being particularly marked in the nineteenth century. Agricultural labourers, low-skilled industrial workers and miners were systematically shorter than white-collar and semi-skilled workers. For instance, in the region of Valencia the difference between skilled and manual workers remained at around 4 cm from the 1860s to the 1910s (Ayuda & Puche-Gil, 2014). Significant differences also appear for groups with different levels of education. Illiterates were at a definite disadvantage while university students, who traditionally formed part of a social elite, were taller than average and much taller than the most disadvantaged groups in society (in some cases the gap could reach 7–8 cm) (Martínez-Carrión, 2016).

Gender differences were also noteworthy. Based on data collected from an alternative source – the Spanish National Health Survey – the stature of the generations born between the 1910s and the 1970s, including females, has been estimated for Spain (Cámara, 2015). The results show that at the beginning of the twentieth century females were on average 10 cm shorter than males, and these differences increased to more than 12 cm in the late 1970s. Thus the gender gap grew wider over the course of the century, particularly after the 1950s, and this was despite the remarkable growth experienced by females over that period, totalling almost 8 cm (from 156 cm to nearly 164 cm).

23.2.4 The Remarkable Increase in Life Expectancy

A longer life is a good indicator of living standards, which means that life expectancy is another way of measuring well-being. According to the latest data published by the Organisation for Economic Co-operation and Development (OECD), Spain and Portugal are among the countries with the longest life expectancy at birth, 83.4 and 81.5 years respectively. While Spain is in the world's top 10, life expectancy at birth in Portugal is still greater than in Germany or Denmark. Disaggregating by gender sheds further light, since Spain and Portugal would both be in the top 10 for female life expectancy, which stands at 86.1 and 84.6 years respectively.

However, in the mid-nineteenth century things were rather different. Studies have pointed out that in Spain at that time life expectancy at birth was around 30 years (Dopico & Reher, 1998; Pérez Moreda et al., 2015) and a similar value has been estimated for Lisbon (Leite, 2005). In the space of about a century and a half, therefore, life expectancy has almost tripled, increasing by more than 50 years. To put it in another way, over the last century alone, that is, within the space of around three or four generations, life expectancy has doubled, rising from 40 to 80 years. This is undeniably an astonishing improvement. And indeed, longevity is one of the most valuable outcomes of economic progress.

To trace the dynamics of this improvement, Figure 23.3 shows the long-term evolution of life expectancy in Spain (mid-nineteenth century to 1940) and Iberia (1940–2011). Using information from Clioinfra, Figure 23.3 also shows the maximum and minimum values reported in Western Europe. In this case it should be pointed out that data availability is an issue. While annual data for Spain since 1861 comes from Felice and Pujol (2016), for Portugal the yearly estimates only begin in 1940 (Clioinfra).[111]

If we first focus on the period running from the mid-nineteenth century to the 1930s, life expectancy at birth increased from 30 to 50 years. Thus the rather modest growth in income and height came with an extraordinary improvement in longevity, resulting mainly from falling infant and maternal mortality rates (Pérez Moreda et al., 2015). By 1950 life expectancy had already reached 60 years (doubling the levels of 1860) and has continued to rise ever since. Indeed, despite the income and height patterns described above, Iberians today enjoy a longer life expectancy than most of their Western European counterparts. In other words, even if Iberians continue to languish at the bottom of the table of Western European countries in terms of per capita income or height, they nevertheless enjoy longer lives.

---

[111] For the period 1920–1940 for Portugal there is decadal information by sex in Veiga (2005), see Table 23.2, while data for the nineteenth century are scarcer (Leite, 2005).

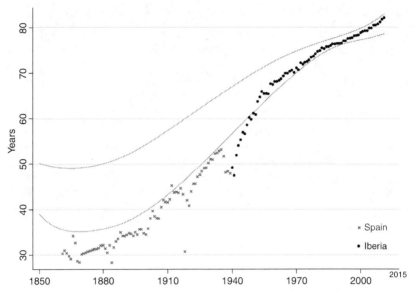

Figure 23.3 Life expectancy at birth (years) in Spain/Iberia and Western Europe, 1850–2011.
Note: The grey lines are a smoothed average of maximum and minimum life expectancy at birth reported in Western Europe (Austria, Belgium, Denmark, Finland, France, Germany, Italy, the Netherlands, Norway, Sweden, Switzerland and the UK), while the crosses and dots represent life expectancy in Spain and Iberia.
Source: authors' own elaboration based on Felice and Pujol (2016) and Clioinfra (https://clio-infra.eu/).

If we look at the two Iberian countries separately, we find that between 1940 and 2010 life expectancy in Spain was on average around 3.5 years higher than in Portugal, although today the gap is less than 2 years. In addition, as previously mentioned there are large differences in life expectancy between males and females. If the information is broken down by sex, the relative position of Iberian females improves, making it clear that there is a considerable gender gap in life expectancy. Table 23.2, however, presents a number of different stories. For example, the gender gap seems to show a tendency to increase over time. In Portugal the gap widened from 4.2 years in 1920 to 7.1 in 2000. In Spain the evolution is even more pronounced. While the gap was almost negligible (less than 1 year) in the 1860s, it widened to more than 6 years in the 1940s and was above 7 years in 2000. However, it would appear that in recent decades the gender gap has begun to decrease in both countries, although only slowly. Nevertheless, females in Iberia today live around 6 years longer than

Table 23.2 *Life expectancy at birth by sex.*

	Portugal			Spain		
	Male	Female	Gap	Male	Female	Gap
1860s				29.1	29.9	0.8
1900				33.9	35.7	1.8
1910				40.9	42.6	1.7
1920	35.8	40.0	4.2	40.3	42.1	1.8
1930	44.8	49.2	4.4	48.4	51.6	3.2
1940	48.6	52.8	4.2	47.1	53.2	6.1
1950	55.5	60.5	5.0	59.8	64.3	4.5
1960	60.7	66.8	6.1	67.4	72.2	4.8
1970	64.2	70.8	6.6	69.6	75.1	5.5
1980	69.1	76.7	7.6	72.5	78.6	6.1
1990	70.4	77.4	7.0	73.4	80.5	7.1
2000	73.3	80.4	7.1	75.8	82.9	7.1
2010	76.8	83.2	6.4	79.2	85.5	6.3
2017	78.4	84.6	6.2	80.6	86.1	5.5

Sources: For Portugal 1920–1990, Veiga (2005); for Spain 1863/1870–1990, Nicolau (2005); for 2000–2017, OECD (www.oecd.org).

males, thereby showing remarkable longevity, high enough to occupy the world's top positions.

23.2.5 A Multidimensional Approach: The Human Development Index

To obtain a synthetic view of living standards, various novel approaches have recently been introduced. One of these, and possibly the most popular, is the Human Development Index. Launched by the United Nations (UN) in 1990 for the Human Development Report,[112] this composite index considers three basic dimensions of human development: (i) longevity, as measured by life expectancy at birth; (ii) education, as captured by the average and expected years of schooling;[113] and (iii) income, as measured by gross national income (GNI). The upper limit of the HDI is 1. In the Human Development Report for

---
[112] Human Development Report, https://hdr.undp.org/.
[113] Iberian countries have historically lagged behind their Western European counterparts in education levels in terms of both literacy rates and average years of schooling, although substantial progress has been made over the twentieth century. On this issue, see Chapter 19.

2019 both Portugal and Spain were considered 'very high development countries' (above 0.8) – Spain ranked 25th, just above Czechia and France, while Portugal was 40th, immediately above Qatar and Chile.[114]

The long-term evolution of living standards in Spain/Iberia in relation to Western Europe as measured by the HDI is presented in Figure 23.4. Several features stand out. First, the gap between Spain and Western Europe in the second half of the nineteenth century was significant. The HDI for Spain was only around 60–70% that of Western Europe. Its absolute values, which over that period ranged from 0.227 to 0.349, were even lower than those for

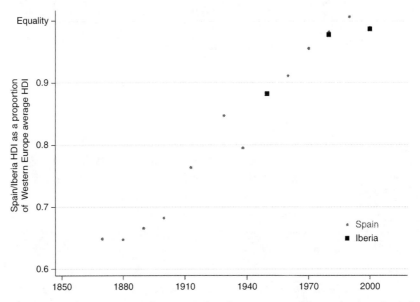

Figure 23.4 The Human Development Index: the narrowing of the gap between Spain/Iberia and Western Europe.

Note: Portugal 1980 refers to 1975. The grey dots and black squares represent the position of Spain/Iberia proportionally in relation to equality with Western Europe (Austria, Belgium, Denmark, Finland, France, Germany, Greece (since 1913), Italy, the Netherlands, Norway, Sweden, Switzerland and the UK).

Sources: For Portugal 1950–2000, Crafts (2002); for Spain 1870–2000, Carreras et al. (2005); for Western Europe, Carreras et al. (2005).

---

[114] A change in the calculation methodology in 2010 means that we are unable to compare HDI levels with past values. The pros and cons of the HDI as a welfare index and the main changes made to the methodology used to compute it are summarized in Prados de la Escosura (2010a).

most countries in the world in 2000. To put that in perspective, Niger's HDI in 2000, which earned it bottom position that year, was 0.321. Second, Spain has made significant progress over the last 150 years, steadily closing the gap with Western Europe. Its HDI for 1870 had doubled by the interwar years and grew by a factor of 4 over the whole period analysed. Third, by 1950 the HDIs for Portugal and Spain were very similar: 0.603 and 0.605 respectively. Such values place Iberia at around 88% of the values achieved in Western Europe at the time, that is, slightly higher than those recorded for India in 2000. Fourth, the evolution of Portugal in the second half of the twentieth century also shows a remarkable improvement (from 0.6 of the Western European rate in 1950 to 0.9 in 2000), although it lags slightly behind the Spanish trajectory. Finally, both Spain and Portugal entered the twenty-first century having almost achieved convergence with the main Western European countries and secured a place among the 'very high development countries'.

This long-term evolution indicates a rapid improvement in Iberian living standards over the last two centuries, particularly during the second half of the twentieth century. It is worth noting that the area's convergence with its main Western European counterparts in terms of human development occurred before convergence in income. In this regard its advances in health played a very significant role. However, this general improvement was not evenly distributed. Progress may also be accompanied by inequality. In the following section the focus will be on the distribution of income, and to this end we will describe the evolution of personal income inequality in Iberia.

23.3 Income Inequality

According to David Ricardo, understanding the distribution of income was 'the principal problem in Political Economy'.[115] The study of income distribution was nevertheless somewhat sidelined, and it was not until the late twentieth century that it reappeared as an important issue. Inequality today is at the forefront of academic research, political agendas and social debates. There are various possible explanations for this renewed interest, including the recent upsurge in inequality in the wealthiest countries after the Great Recession that started in 2008 and the sluggish growth that followed.

In this regard, the way income is distributed is particularly important as it has a direct effect on household expenditure and thus consumption. Studying inequality is therefore of great relevance since it affects the satisfaction of wants. In short, a more egalitarian distribution of income might provide more opportunities for consumption and also well-being. Other reasons for concern about income distribution in addition to economic matters are related to ethics, because high levels of inequality could be considered morally wrong.

---

[115] See Ricardo (1821, preface to the 3rd edition).

Also, taking inequality as a wider concept and not just restricting it to economics and income, it could be argued that high levels of inequality may affect (by reducing them) an individual's chances of self-realization (Sen, 1992).

Certainly inequality can be considered the result of a series of imbalances that ultimately depend on the characteristics of an economic and political system designed by humans. Levy and Temin (2007), for instance, argue that the increase in income inequality in the USA since 1980 is largely related to the institutional context, which is shaped politically. Inequality may thus be a cause and at the same time a consequence of the concentration of political power in the hands of a small elite. Acemoglu and Robinson (2012) argue that extractive institutions may have an impact on economic progress in the long term. However, given that economic and political systems (and institutions in general) are shaped by human beings, especially in democratic societies, it should be possible to correct such imbalances with the use of redistributive policies (Stiglitz, 2012; Piketty, 2014).

23.3.1 A Standard Approach to Inequality: The Gini Coefficient and the Kuznets Curve

Bearing all this in mind, concerns over the dynamics of income distribution are also present in Iberia, and there are good reasons for it. Both Portugal and Spain are currently among the most unequal countries in Western Europe. The analysis of income distribution typically relies on information provided by household budget surveys. In particular, the most recent studies have looked into the evolution of disposable income, that is, considering household incomes once taxes and government transfers have been paid and received respectively. The data contained in household budget surveys usually serve as the basis for the computation of Gini coefficients.[116] According to Eurostat's latest estimates, Portugal and Spain have Gini coefficients of 0.33 and 0.34 respectively. In Western Europe, only the UK, Italy and Greece have Gini coefficients similar to those of the Iberian countries. Other large countries such as Germany (0.29) and France (0.29) are more egalitarian, while the least unequal countries are Belgium (0.26), Norway (0.26) and Finland (0.25).

But was it always like this? In Section 23.2 we showed that living standards in a wide variety of dimensions in Iberia have improved since the mid-nineteenth century and we have seen how this compares with other Western European countries. So, have these achievements been equally distributed across the Iberian population? What were the levels of inequality in the past? How has

---

[116] It is also normal to find several entropy indices such as the Theil index (Theil, 1967; Milanovic, 2011) in the literature. Yet measurement is still an issue. The quality of the various sources used to construct inequality measures is hotly debated (e.g. Deininger & Squire, 1998; Gallup, 2012).

it evolved over the long term? Did it change substantially over the course of economic development? If so, when? Which historical periods saw more marked reductions in inequality? When did it increase? Recent research into economic history has given us a better understanding of all these questions.[117]

The relationship between inequality and economic development over time has usually been analysed following the Kuznets (1955) hypothesis, that is, that inequality increases during the first stages of modern economic growth but then declines afterwards as the economy develops further (the well-known inverted-U curve). Long-term country studies in most cases provide empirical support for the so-called Kuznets curve.[118] In Britain, inequality seems to have increased in the first half of the nineteenth century during the early stages of industrialization and started to fall from then on (Lindert & Williamson, 1985; Williamson, 1985; Lindert, 2000a; Allen, 2009). A similar trend is found for the USA, with a substantial rise in inequality between 1800 and 1860 (Lindert & Williamson, 2016). In other Western countries such as France, Germany and Sweden, inequality also followed an inverted-U pattern (Morrison, 2000), although in the case of Italy no evidence is found of an increase in inequality in the early stages of development (Rossi et al., 2001; Amendola, 2017). Nevertheless, despite the fact that the Kuznets curve often shows up in long-term country studies, a new wave of increasing inequality has been detected for recent decades (Bértola, 2005; Lindert, 2000b; Milanovic, 2016).

In the case of Iberia, for a long time we were unable to empirically test these issues due to a lack of information. Recent work has begun to fill this gap, especially with the construction of a long-term series of inequality. Since the mid-1990s there has been information about levels of inequality, and Gini coefficients are available on a yearly basis from official sources (Eurostat; OECD). In addition, in both countries the first official Household Budget Surveys were published in 1973, 1980 and 1990, which means that the series after the 1980s in Portugal and the 1970s in Spain come from official sources (see World Income Inequality Database – WIID).[119] For the period before this we now have the information provided by Guilera (2013) and Prados de la Escosura (2008) for Portugal and Spain respectively.[120] These studies, covering

---

[117] Until very recently we knew little about the long-term evolution of inequality in Europe, and the case of Iberia was no exception. However, this situation has changed substantially, although there is still a long way to go.

[118] The empirical results are nonetheless mixed, at least in cross-country studies focusing on the second half of the twentieth century (Deininger & Squire, 1998; Li et al., 1998; Barro, 2000; 2008; Gallup, 2012).

[119] Eurostat, https://ec.europa.eu/eurostat/web/main/data/database; OECD, www.oecd.org; WIID, https://widworld/.

[120] Álvarez-Nogal and Prados de la Escosura (2013) estimate inequality for Spain from 1280 to 1850. These authors present alternative measures including the ratios between land rents and wage rates and between nominal output per worker and nominal wages (the Williamson index).

a period of time before household budget surveys existed, were carried out using the statistical information available, essentially population censuses, wages and fiscal data.

On the basis of the information contained in these works, Figure 23.5 shows the evolution of the Gini index for Spain starting in 1850 and for Portugal from 1921 onwards. For Spain it is noteworthy that inequality in the early twenty-first century seems to be rather similar to that in the early stages of modern economic growth. However, if we focus instead on how it evolved, Figure 23.5 shows that inequality increased between the mid-nineteenth century and the Great War (1914–1918) and then decreased afterwards. This downward trend was interrupted during the autarkic decades (1940s–1950s) that followed the Civil War (1936–1939), although the decrease in inequality continued during the Golden Age of economic growth and reached a minimum in 1990. It then began to increase again, especially from the turn of the century. Considering all

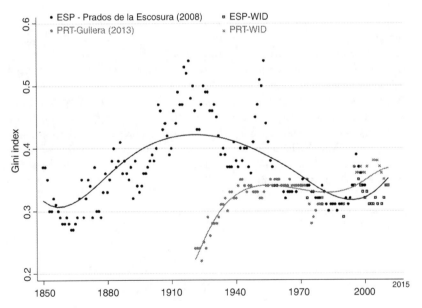

Figure 23.5 Gini indices for Portugal and Spain.
Sources: For Portugal 1921–1979: Guilera (2013); for Spain 1850–1972: Prados de la Escosura (2008); for Portugal 1980–2010 and Spain 1973–2010: WIID (https://wid.world).

the above, it can be argued that, in line with Kuznets' hypothesis, the long-term evolution of inequality in Spain describes an inverted-U curve over time.

It is nonetheless worth mentioning that the decline between the 1970s and 1990s in Spain is obtained on the basis of information supplied by the Household Budget Surveys (*Encuestas Continuas de Presupuestos Familiares*) for 1973, 1980 and 1990 (see e.g. Goerlich & Mas, 2001; Ayala et al., 2006). However, there are some methodological issues that need to be considered. For instance, following the recommendations of the Canberra Group and the Luxembourg Income Study (LIS), Gini coefficients are calculated on the basis of income, which in the case of these Spanish household surveys suffers from a well-known problem of under-reporting. Torregrosa-Hetland (2016b) corrects this potential underestimation of income and concludes that the decline in inequality between 1973 and 1990, that is, during the Spanish transition to democracy, was much weaker, in line with the evolution of the Gini series by Prados de la Escosura (2008).

Certainly the emergence of a Kuznets curve appears more clearly when changes in the level of inequality are compared to changes in per capita income, as shown by Prados de la Escosura (2008: 300). In addition, this author concludes that 'absolute poverty experienced a long-run decline. Growth prevailed over falling inequality as the main cause of poverty reduction, but a more egalitarian income distribution played a non-negligible part in crucial phases of absolute poverty decline' (Prados de la Escosura 2008: 312). In this respect the case of Spain is in line with the mainstream literature. There seems to be a consensus among economists that economic growth is beneficial for reducing poverty. Dollar and Kraay (2002) and Dollar et al. (2013) argue that growth in average incomes as a whole and growth in average incomes in the bottom quintile of the income distribution are highly correlated, thus concluding that economic growth is pro-poor and therefore central to improving the living standards of the lower segments of the population. Another strand of the literature, however, recognizes the importance of both growth and distribution in determining poverty levels (Ravallion, 1997; Bourguignon, 2004; Ferreira & Ravallion, 2008).

The case of Portugal is quite different. While the evidence in this case is limited to the twentieth century, it appears that in the 1920s Portugal was already a relatively egalitarian country. This view is strengthened when a comparison is made with Spain. However, inequality increased greatly from the mid-1920s to the 1940s and remained high until the mid-1970s, then fell dramatically during the transition to democracy and increased again during the democratic period. A couple of conclusions can be highlighted. First, no evidence of an evolution following an inverted-U curve is observed in this period. If anything, there is a sustained upward trend in levels of inequality. And second, it appears that levels of inequality in Portugal today are higher than they were in the early decades of the twentieth century.

From the evidence contained in Figure 23.5 it can be concluded that, although inequality levels are nowadays somewhat similar in Spain and Portugal, the paths followed by both countries over time before reaching these levels have been rather different. Leaving aside short-term fluctuations, it could be said that there has been a reversal of fortunes, given that inequality increased significantly in Portugal, erasing the memory of an egalitarian country in the 1920s, whereas Spain today has historically low levels of inequality. Finally, the effect of the Great Recession also seems to have been different in the two countries – while a reduction in inequality is observed for Portugal after 2008, an increasing trend is observed in the case of Spain.

The forces behind inequality are varied and may also change over time. Economic growth, globalization and skill-biased technological change or policies, among other things, have been at the centre of the issue (Atkinson, 2000; Easterly, 2004). Some of these can be synthetically summarized. To begin with, the rapid economic growth of the 1920s and during the Golden Age of capitalism in Spain was related to a decline in inequality, in a process of rapid structural change that fits the Kuznets hypothesis. In Portugal, rapid economic growth and structural change took place from the 1950s onwards, but if anything this was only able to halt the ongoing upward trend in inequality.

Globalization, by increasing demand for abundant factors (i.e. labour in the case of Iberia), should theoretically have led in turn to less inequality. This was the case during the periods of trade openness of 1850–1860 and 1880–1890 in Spain and from the 1960s in Iberia as a whole, where inequality fell (or stopped growing) partly as a result of Stolper–Samuelson forces.[121] The protectionist period, on the other hand, which began in the 1890s and was at its strongest in the early decades of the major Iberian dictatorships, brought significant increases in inequality. However, growing inequality also marked the liberal years that stretched from 1860 to 1880 in Spain, and the impact of the current wave of globalization also seems to be radically different, since cheaper labour has shifted production away from Western Europe – including Iberia – towards emerging economies, which in turn has brought rising inequality.

Political factors also seem to have had a definite but varied impact. During the first decades of the Salazar and Franco dictatorships, for example, inequality soared, but during the Iberian transitions to democracy in the mid-1970s, it fell. Then again, inequality decreased during the Primo de Rivera dictatorship in the 1920s and increased in Portugal during the democratic era. The increase in inequality in recent decades in Iberia may be related to global events that

---

[121] The Stolper–Samuelson theorem (Stolper & Samuelson, 1941) postulates that changes in the prices of goods have an effect on the prices of factors of production. In this framework, tariffs may affect the final prices of goods by favouring scarce production factors (e.g. capital and land) while being detrimental to abundant production factors (e.g. labour). This has an impact on the functional distribution of income.

also affect other OECD countries. Such events would include the policy changes introduced after the oil crisis of the 1970s, the neoliberal revolution led by Reagan and Thatcher in the USA and the UK in the early 1980s that gradually spread to other countries, the fall of the Berlin Wall in 1989 and the failure of communism, all of which are cited in the literature to explain the increase in inequality.

23.3.2 The Extraction Ratio: How Much Surplus Can the Elite Extract as the Economy Develops?

Income distribution, being such a broad concept, can be approached from different angles. While the Gini coefficient, as presented in the previous paragraphs, is commonly used to analyse inequality, alternative approaches and indicators have been suggested to capture different dimensions of it. Of these, the extraction ratio (ER) has occupied a prominent place in the inequality literature in recent years. Introduced by Milanovic et al. (2007; 2011), this index measures the capacity of the elites to extract the economic surplus of an economy. The ER is obtained as the ratio of actual inequality to maximum feasible inequality.[122] This maximum feasible inequality is in turn calculated assuming that 99% of the population in a society receives a subsistence income and the remaining 1% captures all the surplus. Maximum inequality therefore tends to rise as GDP per capita rises, and as a result the ER also tends to fall in the long term because the denominator increases.

As a measure of inequality, the extraction ratio has some appealing advantages. First, it relies on the fact that, as an economy develops, the maximum feasible inequality increases. When levels of income per capita are low, the surplus that can be captured by the elites – along with levels of inequality – will also be relatively small. Economic growth will then expand the surplus that the wealthier classes may potentially extract, while keeping the bottom part of the population at subsistence level. The ER thus measures how much of the surplus was actually extracted, an outcome that will provide a better idea of the levels of inequality in a dynamic context characterized by changing income and that will depend on the relative economic and political power enjoyed by the elites and the rest of population. The extraction ratio is therefore particularly suitable for conducting a long-term analysis of a country over the course of its transition from a Malthusian pre-industrial stagnant economy to a Solow-type society enjoying modern economic growth and democracy. If the actual level of inequality is close to the maximum feasible inequality at that

---

[122] Milanovic et al. (2007; 2011) infer inequality through the use of the ER employing social tables for different pre-industrial societies such as the Roman Empire, Byzantium, England in 1688, Mughal India in 1750 and China in 1880, to mention just a few examples.

time, the extraction ratio will be close to one (or 100%, given that it can be expressed in percentage points). Alternatively, the lower the actual inequality levels relative to the maximum potential inequality, the lower the ER will be, approaching zero if no economic surplus is extracted by the elites.

Figure 23.6 shows the evolution of the extraction ratio in Iberia. It can be seen that it fluctuated greatly in Spain following the pattern of the Gini index. However, from the 1950s it declined more sharply than the Gini index and in the twenty-first century reached historical minimums. Its evolution during Spain's transition to democracy thus shows a decline. This view is in line with the investigation by Torregrosa-Hetland (2016b), in which the income data from the household budget surveys are corrected, although her revised figures show higher ER levels between 1973–1990 (falling from 45.2% to 41.5%) than the Prados de la Escosura's figures we have used. The case of Portugal is more puzzling. The trend is similar to the evolution of the Gini index but, in contrast to the Spanish case, the ER does not decline in the long term. Indeed, in 2006 it reached almost historical maximums. In other words the capacity of the Portuguese elites to extract the surplus was higher at the start of the twenty-first century than it was 90 years before, and not far from the maximum reached in the

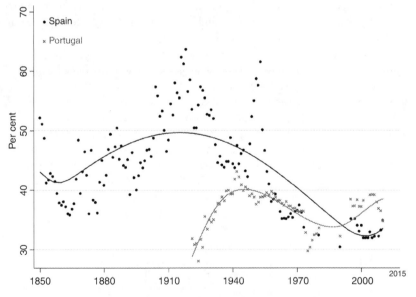

Figure 23.6 Extraction ratio in Spain and Portugal.
Sources: For Portugal, Guilera (2013). For Spain, authors' own elaboration from Prados de la Escosura (2008), WIID (https://wid.world) and Maddison Project Database (2013).

1940s. Nevertheless, in recent years and in line with the evolution of the Gini index, the extraction ratio has declined significantly in Portugal since the Great Recession of 2008, while the opposite is true for Spain.[123]

23.3.3 The Upper Tail of the Distribution: How Rich are the Rich?

Recent research on income distribution has also focused on the evolution of top income shares (Piketty & Saez, 2006; Atkinson et al., 2011; Alvaredo et al., 2013).[124] In this approach the main indicator is the share of national income in the hands of the top fractiles (10%, 5%, . . ., 0.01%) of the population. However, this does have certain limitations. For example, the top fractiles are computed using tax data and it has been acknowledged that tax evasion is an issue, especially for those on the upper side of the income distribution. Also, top income shares are only a partial measure of inequality because they do not include all the population and thus remain silent about changes in the lower or middle part of the distribution. However, it has been argued that the usual inequality measure, the Gini coefficient, is sensitive to the evolution of top income shares and that these are therefore a good proxy for inequality (Atkinson et al., 2011; Leigh, 2007). From a historical perspective, top income shares also have a definite advantage insofar as they allow the evolution of inequality to be tracked in the past, although this information is usually restricted to the post-First World War period, when income tax was introduced in most countries. Nevertheless, there are data available for some countries that go back to the nineteenth century.

Atkinson, Piketty and co-authors provide information based on tax data for more than 20 countries over the twentieth century. These studies show that the income accruing to the top one per cent in most countries declined during the first half of the century. Although there was no clear trend in the decades immediately after the Second World War, the evolution of inequality during the post-1970 period saw marked differences between regions – while English-speaking countries experienced an upsurge in top income shares, the evolution in continental Europe and Japan has been almost flat or characterized by just

---

[123] However, the use of the subsistence minimum ($300–400) in developed economies may not be representative (i.e. the ER and Gini index are highly correlated). Therefore, Milanovic (2013) proposed the inclusion of a social minimum that changes with increases in the average income of a society. Following this approach, Remohí Rius (2016) shows that the decline in the ER during the Spanish transition would be more intense (although it presented large regional variations). His work also shows that the ER using the social minimum would have undergone a steeper increase in Spain after the Great Recession.

[124] Interestingly, these works are based on the pioneering study by Kuznets (1953), who was the first to combine data on income tax records and national accounts to estimate top income shares.

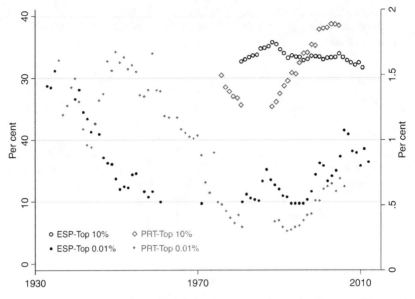

Figure 23.7 Top income shares (10% left axis; 0.01% right axis) in Spain and Portugal. Sources: For Portugal, Guilera (2010); for Spain, Alvaredo and Saez (2009).

a modest increase. As a result, income concentration in these latter countries has become much lower than in the former and is below pre-First World War levels.

As can be seen in Figure 23.7, the top 0.01% income share in Portugal fell between 1936 and the 1980s. Rapid structural change since the 1950s could be behind this decline, which would fit with the classic Kuznets hypothesis that, apart from the inverted-U curve, the top 20% income share will decline during the industrialization process as a whole. In the case of Spain and using individual tax statistics, Alvaredo and Saez (2009) have presented top income shares between 1933 and 2005. According to their results, after peaking in the 1930s, income concentration declined strongly up to 1960 and this was then followed by two decades of stability.[125]

---

[125] Artola Blanco et al. (2018) have recently reconstructed national wealth for Spain from 1900 to 2014. Overall, it is argued that the national wealth to income ratio follows a J-shaped trend. It is also documented that agricultural land and housing in Spain played a much more important role in the national and personal sector balance sheets than in other countries. This is particularly relevant in a country such as Spain with large differences in land access across the territory.

The evolution of top income shares has been different in Portugal and Spain during recent decades. In Spain the modest increase experienced since the beginning of the 1980s is in line with the continental European pattern. However, top income shares took off in Portugal, thus following the pattern of the English-speaking countries explained earlier. This is particularly visible in the top 10% income share, which increases from 25% in 1989 to 38% in 2006.

Finally, an alternative way of looking at the top income shares is to find out who has benefited from economic growth.[126] On this subject the case of Portugal since 1989 is particularly interesting. The Portuguese series shows that the richest 10% captured 66% of all economic growth between 1989 and 2006. To put it another way, their real per capita incomes increased at an annual rate of 3.3%, whereas the real per capita incomes of the remaining 90% of citizens decreased at a yearly rate of 0.6%. This strong regressive redistribution process is obviously related to the increase in the Gini coefficient and the extraction ratio.

23.4 Conclusion

One of the main challenges currently facing societies is to improve the well-being of their citizens. However, there is a lack of general consensus about which policies should be carried out to achieve this. In addition, the concept of well-being is complex and therefore measuring it becomes an issue. The OECD has recently suggested that: 'although there is no single definition of well-being, most experts and ordinary people around the world would agree that it requires meeting various human needs, some of which are essential (e.g. being in good health), as well as the ability to pursue one's goals, to thrive and feel satisfied with their life' (OECD, 2011: 18). It also underlined the difficulty of the task: 'Everyone aspires to a good life. But what does a "good" (or better) life mean?' (OECD, 2011: 14). From a historical perspective, this endeavour becomes even more challenging.

The indicators presented in this chapter clearly show that economic and social progress has occurred in Iberia over the last two centuries, regardless of the dimension or indicator chosen. This progress by any measure has been remarkable, which is probably the most important outcome of the transition from a preindustrial society to a modern economy. Iberians are now healthier and wealthier than previous generations, but they are still relatively poorer and, despite the improvements recorded, shorter than their Western European

---

[126] Such an exercise has been carried out for the USA between 1976 and 2007. The top 1% of income earners captured 58% of total economic growth. Their real per capita incomes increased at an annual rate of 4.4%, whereas the annual growth of incomes for the remaining 99% was just 0.6% (see Atkinson et al., 2011).

neighbours. In addition, according to the economic inequality measures presented, Iberia is one of the most unequal places in Western Europe, at least as far as personal income is concerned. Furthermore, the Great Recession that began in 2008 has uncovered great economic weakness. Destruction of employment, wage cuts and uncertainty have marked the last decade. Given the circumstances, a good number of young skilled adults have looked for a better life abroad.

The story is rather different, however, when we consider longevity or life expectancy or global measures of well-being such as the HDI. Not only are both Portugal and Spain among the most advanced economies, but their inhabitants also enjoy a longer lifespan than those of most other countries in Western Europe (and indeed the world). This could be driven by culture (diet, lifestyle) and also by a fine universal public health system. Interestingly, the development of the so-called welfare state in Iberia occurred later than in the rest of the continent. Similarly, the political and individual liberties of its citizens were severely restricted due to long fascist dictatorships until the last quarter of the twentieth century, which also affected human development. In fact it has been argued that the young Iberian democracies only reached modernity with their entry into the European Economic Community (EEC) in 1986.

Along with political freedom there are two other elements that merit careful analysis and consideration. First, gender and the changing role played by women in the economy and society as a whole, which is crucial for a better understanding of the improvements in well-being since the mid-nineteenth century. And second, the environment and the effect on it of economic growth also require further thought. In a context marked by environmental sustainability, ecological aspects are crucial for the future. Beyond Iberia, the progress and well-being of humankind is closely and inevitably linked to our ability to care for and conserve the planet we inhabit.

24

Iberian Globalization and Catching Up in the Poor South European Periphery, 1830–2010

ANTONIO TENA-JUNGUITO, GIOVANNI FEDERICO AND ESTER G. SILVA

24.1 Introduction

In this chapter, we address the effects of commodity, labour and capital market integration on the growth patterns observed in the Iberian Peninsula during the nineteenth and twentieth centuries. On the one hand, we explore the conventional wisdom that posits a definite link between greater economic integration and growth, despite the challenge of quantitative testing. On the other hand, we also ascertain whether other long-term forces, such as structural changes in products and markets, comparative advantage specialization and the distribution of gains from trade and financial integration, have positively or negatively impacted growth.

To this purpose, we rely on a comparative data set on the leading international trends of trade of commodities, capital and labour flows in the two countries, taking into account a broader comparative European and global context. Changes in the product composition of trade and trading partners explain the different aggregate trade dynamics of the Iberian countries driven by the variations in comparative advantage over the last 180 years. Along with this exercise, we discuss the main institutional changes driven by international conflicts, trade agreements, protectionist measures and monetary regimes that have influenced the international movement of commodities, labour and capital, to explore the role of globalization in explaining economic backwardness and the catching up of the Southern European periphery.

The story told in this chapter is that of two major waves of liberalization and globalization, occurring in the second halves of the nineteenth and twentieth centuries. The Iberian economies participated in both waves, but in a way that was different from the core European economies. During the first globalization boom, despite the smaller domestic market, Portugal was more protectionist than Spain, which probably discouraged export competitiveness in international markets and promoted a bigger dynamism in pushing more labour and pulling more capital lending from abroad. During the second globalization, Portugal was slightly more trade-friendly and better integrated in the international labour flows than its Iberian neighbour, as expected for an economy with a small domestic market and a robust global migration network. Finally, after a fast industrialization and welfare convergence process to the more prosperous Europe, both Iberian countries have recently enjoyed, within the scope of European institutions, more balanced growth and active participation in the international economy, at least until the financial crisis of 2008.

The chapter is structured as follows. Section 24.2 gives an account of the Iberian path in openness against the background of the international economy. Section 24.3 provides an analysis of the displayed trade patterns, based on structural transformation trends in the two countries, changes in revealed comparative advantage and institutional changes that prompted alterations in significant trade markets. Sections 24.4 and 24.5 examine the changes in factor market integration in a comparative perspective, to find some clarification for the analysis of the international financial capacity of the Iberian economy. A final section discusses the main findings, providing a tentative interpretation of the links between integration policies and the processes of catching up in the Iberian Peninsula.

24.2 Iberian Trade Globalization in the Context of the International Economy

An essential expansion of the world economy followed the decline of the Spanish and Portuguese mercantilist empires, accompanying the spread of industrialization around the world during the nineteenth century. World exports quickly started to grow after the end of the French Wars. The early rise in trade reflects to some extent the return to normal trading conditions after peace but is more commonly related to the transport technological improvements and the industrialization spread across Europe and other parts of the world (O'Rourke & Williamson, 1999; Findlay & O'Rourke, 2007). The outbreak of the First World War caused disruption to trade at the global level, while the international monetary system that had evolved during the previous half-century under the gold standard broke down. Exports returned to the pre-war level in 1924, increasing steadily until 1929, reaching in this year a figure about one-third higher than in 1913. The emergence of the Great Depression and the enforcement of autarkic policies in Europe, the Americas and other parts of the world led, however, to a new downturn in globalization. At the trough of the Great Depression in 1933, world trade was 30% lower than in 1929 and 5% lower than in 1913. Nevertheless, in the subsequent four years, about two-thirds of the ground lost were recovered, so that by 1937 it was only below the 1929 level by a tenth.[127]

---

[127] For chronological and comparative purposes, in this section we use the recent world trade estimations from Federico and Tena-Junguito (2018): World Trade Historical Database (http://www.uc3m.es/tradehist_db).

After the Second World War world trade recovered quite fast, and by 1950 it was already 10% higher than in 1929. It grew at breakneck speed during the Golden Age, under the new institutional regime established at the Bretton Woods conference, with an increasing number of countries and regions entering the global markets. Thus, by the early 1970s, the recovery was (almost) complete, and trade was again following its pre-1913 growth path. Growth slowed down markedly in the 1970s, when a worldwide crisis put an end to the overall post-Second World War economic expansion, but accelerated again after 1980. World trade growth has exceeded the pre-1913 growth path since the mid-1990s, and its trend growth rate was significantly higher in 1950–2007 (5.10) than in 1817–1913 (3.62), the period of the first globalization boom (Federico & Tena-Junguito, 2017).

The movement towards greater trade integration did not occur, however, at the same time around the world. Figure 24.1 shows the exceptionality of the Iberian Peninsula relative to Western Europe in this regard.[128] In the early

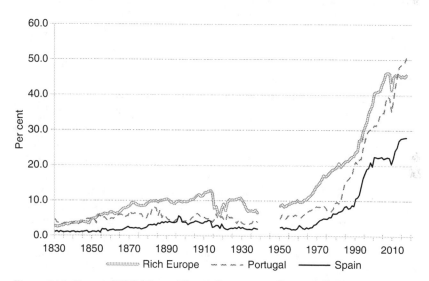

Figure 24.1 Exports/GDP (Geary–Khamis 'international' 1990 dollars).
Note: Rich Europe includes Belgium, Denmark, France, Germany/Zollverein, Netherlands, Switzerland and the UK.
Sources: Exports and GDP constant Geary–Khamis 'international' 1990 dollars. 1815–1938: Federico and Tena-Junguito (2017; 2019); 1950–2017: World Bank (2019).

---

[128] We use constant prices since Portuguese GDP nominal historical series from Valério (2001b) are not consistent with the available export current prices series before the First World War.

nineteenth century, when the first global trade boom erupted, Spain was at a short distance from the Rich Europe countries' export share in GDP (gross domestic product). In contrast, Portugal presented a similar figure, given its relatively small economic size. However, from 1830 onwards a growing gap emerged, reflecting the rising relevance of exports in fuelling the expansion of the manufacturing sector in rich countries accompanying the first period of industrialization before 1870. This expansion sharply contrasted with Portuguese (especially), but also with Spanish exports, which increased at a slower rate, about 1.0% and 3.7% per year, respectively, between 1830 and 1870, figures considerably below the European average (4.7%). The following years, between 1870 and 1913, were more equitable at least concerning Spain, which experienced an exceptional export performance: real exports grew faster than in the preceding period and even at higher rates than the European ones. The liberalization of the extractive sector and the favourable occasion enjoyed by common wine exports during 1879–1891, when phylloxera affected the French wine production, seem to have played an essential role in this exporting apogee (Simpson, 1996). The protectionist backlash to the grain invasion in prosperous continental Europe in the late nineteenth century negatively affected Iberian agrarian exporters in the initial years, but commodity price increases from 1895 reduced ad valorem tariff barriers before the First World War (Tena-Junguito, 2007).

During the interwar period, the two Iberian economies followed a trend of relative stagnation in globalization: exports were less dynamic than in the rest of Europe during the 1920s but experienced a lower decline afterwards. In Europe, and around the world, the 1920s and 1930s witnessed a rise and then a reduction in global integration, following the economic instability and the enforcement of autarkic policies of the Great Depression.

After 1950, growth in international trade expanded rapidly. Although Rich Europe countries did not recover the 1913 level of openness until the early 1970s, by 1950 world trade was already 10% higher than in 1929 and grew at breakneck speed during the Golden Age. Arguably, part of this growth was a recovery of the pre-1913 growth trend from the war-time shocks and the Great Depression.

During this second globalization boom, the two Iberian countries showed a distinct pattern. Although they were both under dictatorship regimes not politically aligned with the new democratic Europe – the Francoist dictatorship and the *Estado Novo* – Portugal made more efforts towards European integration during the 1950s and early 1960s, thus exhibiting more export dynamism.

The Spanish Civil War winners had close political and ideological connections with the Second World War losers. After the end of the Second World War they were not welcomed into the new Bretton Woods international economic institutions at least until the second half of the 1950s

(Guirao, 1998).[129] From the 1959 Stabilization Plan and until 1973, quantitative restrictions on foreign trade were gradually replaced with tariffs, and economic integration was more friendly than previously (Serrano Sanz & Pardos Martínez, 2002).

The Portuguese dictatorship gradually changed its economic approach in favour of the country's industrialization, and a more liberal approach to foreign economic relations was established by the end of the 1940s. In the late 1950s, the country embraced an export-oriented strategy of growth, subscribing to the European Free Trade Association (EFTA) convention (1960) and becoming a member of the General Agreement on Tariffs and Trade (GATT), the International Monetary Fund (IMF) and the World Bank afterwards (Lopes, 2004b).

Trade globalization in Portugal was thus more vigorous than in Spain in the early 1960s and subsequent years, a period marked by the internationalization of the economy and by an impressive rate of economic growth. However, it stagnated during the political transition to democracy in the early 1970s. The more appeased political change in Spain allowed for some continuity in the country's pattern of openness.

Portugal's recovery was very fast from the end of the 1970s to the late 1980s, showing a more dynamic early reaction to the European integration in the second half of the 1980s. Spain responded later, presenting an excellent performance in the 1990s. After the turn of the twenty-first century and until the emergence of the 2008 financial crisis there was again an asymmetric response by the two countries, with Spain showing rapid GDP growth (although one that was not led by exports), and Portugal presenting a more open, but unbalanced growth performance, marked by real divergence vis-à-vis the wealthier Eurozone countries, significant current account imbalances and a sharp increase in foreign indebtedness (Lopes, 2004a).

Figure 24.2 offers a complementary picture, describing Iberian per capita export trends relative to the rich European norm in constant prices between 1830 and 2017. Once again, Portugal's level of per capita exports stands visibly close to the European core at the beginning of the period, but afterwards experiences a marked decline. During the long nineteenth century, which encompasses the period from the 1830s to the First World War, Portugal shows persistent divergence with Europe, presenting less than a third of its initial relative export per capita level on the eve of the First World War. As happened with other peripheral countries, Portugal did not possess the early

---

[129] It is true that the new Cold War context fostered US aid to Spain with the Pact of Madrid (September 1953) in return to the right to establish four military bases. Thereafter the most extreme interventionist measures on commodity markets were relaxed and corrected and, in July 1959, following the convertibility of major European currencies in December 1958, the peseta became integrated into the Bretton Woods system (Prados de la Escosura et al., 2010b).

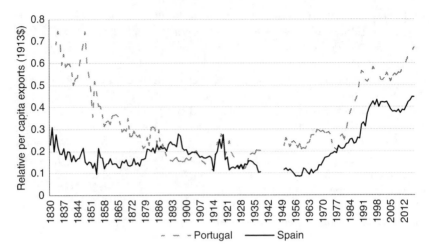

Figure 24.2 Per capita exports relative to Rich Europe (1913$; Rich Europe = 1).
Note: Rich Europe includes Belgium, Denmark, France, Germany/Zollverein, Netherlands, Switzerland and the UK.
Sources: 1830–1938: Federico and Tena-Junguito (2016; 2019); 1950–2017: World Bank (2019).

advantages in factor endowments that prompted a successful specialization, and thus exports increased slowly over time (Reis, 1984; Lains, 2006b).

As previously seen, the years spanning the First World War show some convergence to the rich European countries, followed by a negative trend in the 1920s and a positive one in the 1930s, the latter mostly due to the more significant fall in global integration experienced in European countries. After the Second World War, in the 1950s, there was a period of very moderate divergence followed by moderate convergence during the 1960s until the early 1970s, when Portugal made the political transition to democracy. From 1977 to 1992, Portugal's export dynamism was also exceptional, closing the gap with the European norm. Finally, during the expansive international trade decade of the 1990s and until the financial crisis of 2008, Portugal reinforced its integration within Europe, showing a very similar path to the European norm along with a severe drop in population growth (Sternberg, 2015).

Spain's initial export per capita levels in 1830 were around half the Portuguese levels, reflecting the larger size of its domestic economy. From the early 1830s to the mid-1850s Spain experienced an accelerated divergence relative to Europe. From this latter period until the second half of the 1870s, Spanish exports per capita followed the same trend as Rich Europe, even if remaining about one-fifth of the European norm. In the second half of the 1870s, Spain surpassed the Portuguese levels of exports per capita, increasing its dynamism over the European norm and the divergence with Portuguese levels. This period of trade expansion came to an end in 1897 and was followed by a long divergence trend with the European norm that only finished in the early 1960s, except for a short interruption during the First World War.

Contrary to Portugal, the 1950s were a period of trade globalization divergence for Spain, but from the early 1960s onwards Spanish per capita exports showed a long-term trend of export dynamism, converging from one-fifth to almost one-third of the European norm in the second half of the 1990s. This period of strong convergence allowed the relative levels of exports per capita observed during the early decades of the nineteenth century to be overcome for the first time. In contrast, the inception of the European Union's economic and monetary union (EMU) after the turn of the twenty-first century retarded the previously positive path of openness convergence with Rich Europe, which was only resumed after 2014.

The analysis of broad movements of trade globalization produced so far has taken the degree of openness as a proxy for market integration. However, the use of this indicator has some caveats, since the pace of economic development affects the structure of output across sectors, and the degree of international tradability varies across them. Public service administration and other non-tradable service had exceptional growth during the golden epoch of 1950–1973, and afterwards, that mainly affect the openness figures, introducing a bias in intertemporal and geographical comparisons in that period.

To achieve greater homogeneity and better understand changes in export openness, a recalculation of this indicator is thus carried out, measuring it on tradable sectors only, by removing the service sector from total GDP. That by definition is bound to be higher than the conventional openness ratio, as can be seen in Figure 24.3: the indicator of openness based on tradable goods is about 70% higher than the conventional one in 1870, double in 1913 and 1938, 160% higher in 1972 and almost four times higher in 2007 (74.1 vs 19.5%). Broad trends remain similar, however.[130] The major difference regards the widening of Spain's gap relative to Rich Europe in the post-war period, which reflects the processes of structural change within countries and, more precisely, the increase in the share of non-tradable services driven by the expansion of education, health and leisure services that accompanied the development of modern economies.

Before 1950, the tradable index broadly confirms the profile showed earlier for Spain. Convergence with Rich Europe between 1850 and 1895 was even more intense than that displayed by the conventional openness index. It was then followed by a long divergence trend of more than half a century until the

---

[130] Figure 24.3 does not provide data for Portugal before 1950 (see note 2). For this reason, during the nineteenth century and the interwar period, the analysis is based only on Spanish data.

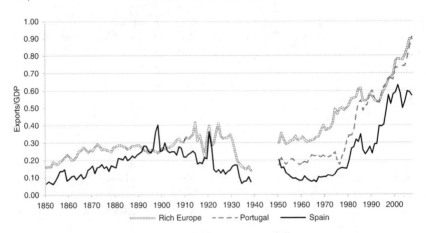

Figure 24.3 Exports/GDP ratio of tradables in current dollars, 1850–2007.
Note: Rich Europe includes Denmark, France, Germany/Zollverein, Netherlands and the UK.
Sources: 1830–1938: Federico and Tena Junguito (2017; 2019); 1950–2017: World Bank (2019).

early 1960s. During this period, Spain not only increased its distance relative to the European core but also reduced to one-third its level of integration in tradables (from 28% in the 1890s to 8% in 1960–1965). In the decade that followed, Spain reversed this trend, pursuing a path of integration that was slower than in Rich Europe but faster than in Portugal. Integration continued with no visible interruption during the political transition at the end of the 1970s until the shock of European Common Market integration in 1985. Since then, Spanish tradable openness has followed a rapid trend of convergence that was only interrupted by the inception of the EMU in 1999.

Portuguese tradable integration, on the other hand, was higher than that of Spain in the 1950s and early 1960s, but not remarkable at all by European standards. Contrary to the isolationist policies of Spain, by the end of the 1940s Portugal was following a more liberal path concerning foreign economic relations, with the country being accepted into the Marshall Plan in 1947 and becoming a charter member of the Organisation for European Economic Co-operation (OEEC) and North Atlantic Treaty Organization (NATO) in 1948 and 1949, respectively. However, it was only by the late 1950s that an export-oriented strategy of growth was embraced, when Portugal subscribed to the EFTA convention (1960), leading to a gradual increase in the internationalization of the economy (Lopes, 2004a; 2004b).

The transition to democracy in both countries in the 1970s had a positive affect on tradable openness, although with different timings and degrees of intensity. Portuguese tradable integration was faster and more vigorous in the years following the country's accession to the European Economic Community (EEC), partly due to the more rapid increase in the Portuguese services sector. As the tradable GDP depends on the size of the service sector, a faster service sector growth implies a lower tradable GDP and a more significant openness. That was the case with the Portuguese service sector after the revolution, which grew faster than the Spanish one.[131]

Spanish tradable sector convergence with both Rich Europe and Portugal, on the other hand, occurred only in the 1990s but stopped afterwards with the introduction of the single European currency. Portugal, in contrast, has followed its tradable convergence process in a rather smoother manner, which has been fostered by a renewed growth of the services sector from the turn of the century until the outbreak of the financial crisis.

24.3 Iberian Structural Change, Trade Policy and Markets

24.3.1 Changes in the Composition of Trade and Comparative Advantage

During the period under study, the two Iberian economies underwent broad processes of structural change, starting essentially as agrarian societies and gradually becoming industrialized ones (see Chapter 22). Changes in the structure of domestic production went hand in hand with changes in the composition of trade with other countries, as can be seen by the evolution of import and export shares displayed in Tables 24.1 and 24.2. These tables offer an homogenization of export and import product groups of commodities using the WTO classification for both countries in some benchmark years. We distinguish between primary products (differentiated by subcategories), semi-manufactured goods, industrial manufactured goods (separating between equipment goods and consumer manufactured goods) and other goods.

Industrial exports were almost non-existent in the nineteenth century, even though domestic production of textiles survived under the protection of trade barriers (Tena-Junguito, 2006b). In 1877, both countries exported mainly primary products (mostly food). From the last quarter of the nineteenth century, the share of primary products in total exports declined steadily in both countries, first at a rather moderate rate, and later at a breakneck pace. The moment at which deceleration became faster was different, however: it started earlier in Portugal, with the share of food products declining by more

---

[131] The rate of growth of the Spanish and Portuguese service sectors between 1970 and 1990 were 0.4% and 1.2%, respectively. Computation of the ratio service sector/GDP was based on data from UNCTAD-STAT Database (GDP by type of expenditure and value added by type of economic activity, annual).

Table 24.1 Composition of exports: main WTO categories (Portugal and Spain, 1877–2014).

	1877	1897	1913	1926	1951	1959	1967	1973	1984	1995	2001	2012–2014
Portugal												
1 Primary products	85.4	69.5									13.5	25.2
Food	68.3	53.7	65.0	64.0	22.5	28.1	23.1	17.0	24.3	14.8	7.1	13.9
Raw materials	8.9	12.9							11.0	7.1		
Fuels	8.2	2.9	0.3	6.1	0.2	4.0	1.4	1.2	5.0	3.0	3.7	13.8
2 Semi-manufactured goods	1.6	2.9	30.4	26.9	66.7	53.3	53.7	47.5		5.7	6.7	13.0
3 Industrial manufactured goods	2.6	6.3	4.4	3.1	10.0	13.9	21.2	33.6		50.0	53.6	61.8
Equipment goods	0.0	0.0	0.6	0.7	3.2	5.1	6.9	15.1		26.9	34.8	
Consumer manufactured goods	2.6	6.3	3.8	2.4	6.8	8.8	14.2	18.5	27.9	23.0	18.8	52.8
Other goods	10.4	21.2	0.0	0.0	0.7	0.6	0.6	0.8	0.0	0.0	0.0	
Spain												
1 Primary products	88.6	73.1	79.5	77.5	81.6	79.4	62.3	35.9	31.2	21.2	19.8	23.7
Food	56.1	43.5	47.1	57.2	50.1	61.5	48.3	27.9	15.8	15.6	14.6	12.2
Raw materials	4.4	4.5	5.7	5.8	4.8	3.2	1.5	1.5	1.8	1.4	1.0	1.0
Fuels	0.0	0.1	0.8	0.7	13.4	8.1	6.3	4.5	9.4	1.7	3.3	2.7
2 Semi-manufactured goods	6.7	11.3	9.1	13.6	5.1	10.8	12.5	18.3	26.7	21.5	22.1	16.8
3 Industrial manufactured goods	4.7	15.2	10.3	7.3	13.2	9.8	25.2	45.8	42.0	57.3	56.8	59.8
Equipment goods	0.0	0.2	0.6	0.3	2.1	3.3	11.5	28.5	28.5	45.7	46.1	55.5
Consumer manufactured goods	4.6	15.1	9.7	7.0	11.2	6.5	13.7	17.3	13.5	11.6	10.7	4.0
Other goods	0.0	0.4	1.0	1.5	0.0	0.0	0.0	0.0	0.0	0.0	1.3	0.0

Sources: Spain: 1877–2001 from Tena-Junguito (2007); 2012–2014 from WTO Statistical data sets. Portugal: (a) 1842–1913 from Lains (2007b); (b) 1914–1948 from Batista et al. (1997); (c) 1948–1995 from Bank of Portugal (2000); (d) 1980–2014 from WTO Statistical data set.

Table 24.2 Composition of imports: main WTO categories (Portugal and Spain, 1877–2014).

	1877	1897	1913	1926	1951	1959	1967	1973	1984	1995	2001	2012–2014
Portugal												
1 Primary products	50.7	60.2	51.0		5.4	6.4	6.1	2.7	23.3	26.5	36.3	33.1
Food	34.7	38.2	29.8	15.9					13.5	12.1	16.6	14.4
Raw materials	9.2	14.5	11.7	7.8	11.8	8.0	6.8	28.7	8.4	9.8	9.2	12.8
Fuels	6.9	7.5	9.5								6.9	16.4
2 Semi-manufactured goods	9.1	10.4	12.9	57.6	57.0	52.3	48.1	43.4	14.2	13.0	11.9	17.4
3 Industrial manufactured goods	20.2	11.5	11.4	18.7	24.7	33.2	39.1	24.3	42.1	43.4		68.0
Equipment goods	2.2	3.0	5.4	7.4	22.2	28.9	33.4	21.9	33.7	36.4	62.7	44.5
Consumer manufactured goods	18.0	8.5	6.0	11.3	2.5	4.3	5.7	2.4	8.4	7.0	18.0	20.6
Other goods	20.0	17.8	24.7		1.0	0.0	0.0	0.9				
Spain												
1 Primary products	51.4	59.1	54.8	48.7	70.9	50.6	46.4	63.7	29.8	24.4	18.7	30.7
Food	27.9	28.5	27.6	20.5	18.5	21.7	16.6	12.2	13.9	9.9	7.2	8.8
Raw materials	18.9	19.2	15.8	17.5	18.2	8.5	8.7	4.9	2.9	1.6		1.1
Fuels	3.4	8.9	8.1	7.4	30.6	13.7	13.3	40.5	8.8	11.2	3.4	6.5
2 Semi-manufactured goods	22.3	20.0	18.5	26.3	11.6	19.3	18.1	13.3	22.7	20.8	22.3	17.5
3 Industrial manufactured goods	26.0	19.2	26.6	23.7	17.5	30.1	35.5	23.0	47.5	53.9	68.0	51.8
Equipment goods	5.4	9.4	19.5	16.3	17.0	26.2	31.3	20.2	37.8	44.2	65.4	47.1
Consumer manufactured goods	20.6	9.8	7.1	7.4	0.5	3.9	4.2	2.9	9.7	9.7	3.5	4.7
Other goods	0.4	1.7	0.1	0.0	0.0	0.0	0.0	0.0	0.0	1.0	0.0	0.0

Sources: Spain: 1877–2001 from Tena-Junguito (2007); 2012–2014 from WTO Statistical data sets. Portugal: (a) 1842–1913 from Lains (2007b); (b) 1914–1948 from Batista et al. (1997); (c) 1948–1995 from Bank of Portugal (2000); (d) 1980–2014 from WTO Statistical data set.

than half between 1926 and 1959, whereas in Spain food remained the primary source of exports until at least the 1960s. Between 1926 and 1951, Portugal increased the share of semi-manufactured goods exports (66% in 1951) markedly, experiencing a more gradual increase in industrial manufactured goods. A significant boost occurred in these products in the late 1960s, following the process of internationalization of the economy initiated the decade before. From this period onwards, industrial manufactured goods exports increased sustainedly, representing more than half of Portuguese exports at the turn of the twentieth century. In Spain, the period with the most substantial boost of manufactured goods exports was also the 1960s, but equipment goods played a more prominent role. Inter-industrial and intra-industrial demand changes in the international economy affected this process, as shown by the changes in the import composition of both countries towards the main sources of industrial demand. The analysis of imports evidences also the meagre figure of consumer manufactured goods imports in the 1950s (0.5% and 2.5% of total imports in Spain and Portugal, respectively), which is representative of the two countries' attempt to promote self-sufficiency in the first years of the dictatorship period (cf. Section 24.3.2).

Both patterns reflect the computation of revealed comparative advantage (RCA) indices based on the Lafay index (Lafay, 1992):

$$\text{LF}_i = 100 \left[\left(\frac{x-m}{x+m} \right) - \left(\frac{X-M}{X+M} \right) \left(\frac{x+m}{X+M} \right) \right], \quad (24.1)$$

where x and m are the exports and imports of commodity i, and X and M are the total exports and imports, respectively, of the country under analysis. The index computes the difference between the normalized net balance of commodity i and the total normalized net balance weighted with the share of the product on total trade. If positive, it indicates specialization in commodity i; if negative, it reflects the lack of competitiveness in that specific commodity. The higher the index, the better the trading behaviour of the sector.[132]

Figure 24.4 displays the results for Portugal during the whole period under analysis, whereas Table 24.3 provides the RCA indices for Spain in selected years.

RCA indices reflect the process of structural transformation of the Portuguese economy, showing the gradual deterioration of comparative advantage in food products and, inversely, the increase in competitiveness in

---

[132] The Spanish computations of RCA use a slightly different indicator of comparative advantage following Tena-Junguito (2007). The formula has a very similar interpretation to that of the Lafay index, however, since the formulation is equivalent: RCA = [((x − m)/(x + m)) − ((X − M)/(X + M))].

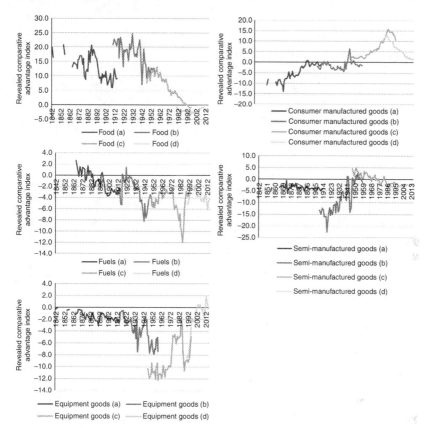

Figure 24.4 Revealed comparative advantage indices (Portugal, 1842–2014).
Sources: Based on export and import annual data from the same references as (a), (b), (c), (d) in Tables 24.1 and 24.2.

consumer manufactured goods and, more recently, in equipment goods. An increase in the relative competitiveness of semi-manufactured goods is also found after the 1920s and until the 1950s, which was followed by a declining trend until the 1980s, and a situation of relative stagnation afterwards.

A similar path is evidenced for Spain from the late nineteenth century onwards. Like Portugal, the Spanish historical comparative advantage in primary products, most notably in food, was gradually lost. On the other hand, Spain shows a positive comparative advantage on some textile consumer manufactured goods at the turn of the nineteenth century that persisted until the second half of the twentieth century. However, it was not until the 1970s that semi-manufactured goods and industrial products acquired relative competitiveness.

Table 24.3 Revealed comparative advantage indices (Spain, 1877–2014).

	1877	1889	1897	1913	1926	1951	1967	1973	1984	1989	1995	2001	2012–2014
1 Primary products	**37**	**50**	**37**	**46**	**48**	**7**	**9**	**−11**	**−33**	**−1**	**−16**	**−10**	**−4**
Food	49	88	78	90	109	44	37	25	13	25	6	19	3
Raw materials	−66	−66	−72	−52	−52	−60	−45	−55	−43	−21	−35	−21	−2
Ore and other minerals	91	88	81	94	68	51	−18	−53	−61	−25	−50	−27	−12
Fuels	−103	−101	−107	−75	−65	−40	−27	−40	−58	−26	−62	−49	−9
Ferrous metals	83	72	59	69	66	88	12	−35	53	18	−2		
2 Semi-manufactured goods	**−59**	**−41**	**−32**	**−39**	**−33**	**−39**	**−16**	**0**	**34**	**16**	**−3**	**3**	**−1.5**
Iron and steel	−101	−79	−82	−88	−77	−57	−48	20	68	33	12	2	3
Chemicals	−32	−49	−45	−46	−11	−65	−16	−36	−2	−1	−20	−6	−2
Other semi-manufactured goods	−47	−24	−12	−17	−35	47	21	45	58	31	14	20	−2
3 Industrial manufactured goods	**−69**	**−42**	**−4**	**−24**	**−36**	**−14**	**−7**	**12**	**30**	**−5**	**9**	**3**	**1**
Equipment goods	−104	−97	−108	−89	−81	−83	−28	−4	17	−10	9	2	1
3.1.1 industrial machinery	−105	−105	−110	−90	−81	−73	−45	−32	−12	−38	−11	−13	1
3.1.2. Office and telecom equipment				−90	−84	−92	−39	−48	−90	−73	−89	−31	−17
3.1.3 Road vehicles	−106	−104	−109	−80	−82	−105	−4	33	53	28	32	17	5
3.1.4 Other equipment goods	−106	−105	−110	−89	−79	−80	−22	5	6	−14	−6	−4	−3
3.1.5 Other durable consumer goods	−97	4	−91	−79	−82	−107	−18	18	3	−19	−21	14	3
Consumer manufactured goods	**−65**	**−35**	**21**	**16**	**−10**	**86**	**60**	**68**	**69**	**21**	**9**	**5**	**−3**
3.2.1 Textiles	−85	−50	8	4	−4	86	18	25	58	13	8	9	0
3.2.2 Clothes	−84	−76	2	−77	−84	90	58	84	62	−10	−29	7	−4
3.2.3 Other consumer manufactured goods	19	15	45	43	−22	63	86	83	75	33	23	1	

Sources: See Tables 24.1 and 24.2, for Spain.

24.3.2 Trade Policy

After the Napoleonic Wars, most European countries had either high levels of protection or prohibitions on most manufactured goods. In Britain, the Corn Laws of 1815 prohibited the import of wheat, creating a conflict of interest between agriculture and industry that culminated with the repeal of the Corn Laws in 1846, marking the decades that followed in both Britain and the continent.[133]

In the case of Spain, prohibitive tariffs were maintained throughout most of the first half of the nineteenth century on entire manufacturing groups (as leather and pieces of cotton), inducing smuggling and other illegal activities. The 1849 tariffs and other liberalizing measures implemented in the mid-1850s, related to the allowance of duty-free imports for the construction of railways, promoted an early decline in average nominal protection (Tena-Junguito, 2006b). This liberalization process stagnated in the 1860s since the influence of the British–French Cobden–Chevalier tariff agreement in the European periphery was much smaller than in the rest of Europe. Even if average tariffs in the European periphery show some liberalization before and after 1860, and despite the extension of commercial treaties signed under the most favoured nation clause, duties on ordinary manufactured goods remained much higher than those of the European core. In Spain, the return to protectionism was led by the protection of industrial interests, although tariffs also affected profoundly the imports of agricultural products. The Canovas 1891 tariff law increased tariffs on manufactured goods and agrarian products, but later increases in international prices reduced its ad valorem impact until the new 1922 Cambo tariff raised volume duties (Tena-Junguito, 2006a).

The return towards autarkic policies after the Great Depression in combination with the Civil War destruction and the isolationist policies applied in the 1940s almost entirely inhibited trade integration (Figure 24.5). Monetary and quantitative controls lasted until the 1950s, and exchange controls and import licenses were used until 1959. Spain was the only Western European country (along with Finland) that did not take part in the Marshall Plan and, by extension, in the OEEC and other organizations created in the wake of the US post-war reconstruction policy in Europe (Powell, 2015). In 1957, when the Treaty of Rome was signed, Spain sold almost one-third of its exports to and bought one-quarter of its imports from the six founding member countries of the EEC. Europe was increasing its trade liberalization when Spain was still implementing hard import substitution policies. The move to a more open conventional trade policy started in the 1960s, when protection was smoothly and gradually moderated until the political democratic transition in the late

---

[133] See Tena-Junguito et al. (2012).

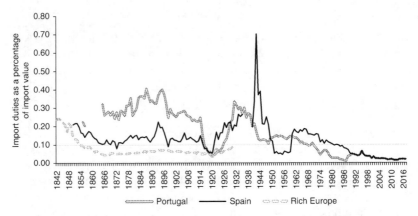

Figure 24.5 Tariff average in Spain and Portugal, 1842–1980 (import duties as a percentage of import value).
Sources: Portugal: Valério (2001a: Table 10.1) for 1842–1990; Spain: 1850–1980, Tena-Junguito (2007: 626, Chart 8.8); 1980–1990, Busain and Gordo (1994: 25, Chart I2.1); 1990–2017: tariff rate applied is a weighted mean, all import products (%) from WDI, World Bank (2019). Rich Europe (simple tariff average of Denmark, France, Germany and the UK), 1842–1930, from Tena-Junguito (2006a).

1970s. Negotiations to join the EEC gave another impulse to additional trade liberalization. EEC membership implied full liberalization of trade within the Community and a significant decrease of protection towards the rest of the world. Since then, competitiveness in international markets has become a key policy guideline.

Portugal raised trade barriers in 1837 and, with the new treaty signed with Britain, in 1842. The 1852 tariff reduced specific duties, and most quantitative restrictions and import licensing schemes were dropped until the mid-1860s. Notwithstanding, volume duties remained rather high, not only for protectionist reasons but also as a source of state revenue (Reis, 1993b). Tariffs remained very high during the nineteenth century, even though the dominant political ideology could be described as liberal and favourable to free trade. Portuguese average tariffs remained high during the second half of the century, and reacted in the 1870s to the reduction of oceanic transport cost and cheap grain arrival to Europe, increasing specific duties in the 1880s and early 1890s. Only later, the 1895 international price increase reduced the tariff average ad valorem impact until the First World War. The war period and subsequent years witnessed a decrease in the ratio of import duties to imports (due to price increases and stable volume duties). Still, ad valorem tariffs increased again in the late 1920s and the early 1930s, after the Great Depression. The post-Second World War years saw significant changes in Portuguese foreign trade, with the country presenting a more

European profile of trade liberalization (cf. Section 24.2). Unlike Spain, during this period Portugal not only reduced the average degree of tariff protection but also dropped most quantitative restrictions and import licensing schemes from the early 1950s. At the same time, Portugal managed to establish a system of imperial preference with its African colonies, despite the instability and war conflict experienced until decolonization in 1974–1975. Portugal became an EEC member in 1986, and foreign trade liberalization prompted a gradual change in the traditional pattern of specialization. The more recent decades have witnessed a progressive shift to export-led growth based on medium- and high-technology goods, in competition with the most developed EEC partners and other developed economies (Fontoura-Valério, 2000).

24.3.3 Commercial Markets

Changes in the composition of trade were also accompanied by changes in the sources and destinations of commodities. The geographical distribution of external trade was strongly influenced by significant institutional changes that took place in the most important trade partners of both countries, in particular those relating to the independence of former colonies in the 1820s.

The colonial system furnished relevant tariff revenues to the Iberian metropolises, along with commercial re-exports and transport and financial monopolies better sited in other countries after independence. Between 1784/1796 and 1815/1820 total Spanish exports fell around 25% (Prados de la Escosura, 1988: 72), but colonial trade suffered a deeper decline of about 40% (in real prices), which implied a sizeable change in the Spanish secular geographical trade equilibrium between the Americas and Europe that persisted until the independence of Cuba and Puerto Rico in 1898.

During the Napoleonic Wars, Portugal reinforced its previous intense commercial and political relationship with Great Britain, which would endure for the whole of the nineteenth century. The Portuguese–British treaty of 1810 established free trade relations between both countries and gave the British power of intervention in Portuguese government decisions at least until 1820. The drop in Portuguese exports following Brazil's independence in 1822 was less steep, being compensated with a move towards the UK market, which in the mid-nineteenth century absorbed more than half of Portuguese exports (Figure 24.6).[134] France, on the other hand, played only a marginal role, accounting for less than 5% of Portuguese trade through most of the nineteenth century.[135]

---

[134] Portugal exports to Brazil dropped by 22.4% between 1796–1806 and 1808–1813 according to Pedreira (1993: 234–235).
[135] France was only a relevant market for Portugal in the 1880s, around 20%, because of a sharp increase in the French demand for wine imports due to the attack on its vineyards by the phylloxera (Costa et al., 2016: 291–344).

Geographical proximity did not foster the bilateral commercial integration between Spain and Portugal. Between 1842 and 1900 trade figures were rather low, about 3.6% and 8.6% of Spanish and Portuguese total exports, respectively. Other than Europe, Latin American markets accounted for a significant amount (one-fifth) of total Iberian exports, with Brazil receiving about 20% of total Portuguese exports and Cuba standing as the leading market for Spain (Figures 24.6 and 24.7).[136] African colonies became only essential export destinations for Portugal after the new discriminatory protective tariff law of 1892.[137] The new tariff regime fostered a significant increase in Portugal's exports to Africa, as well as African exports to third countries, shipped through Portugal as re-exports. In the early twentieth century, African markets already accounted for 15% of total Portuguese exports, ranking second to Brazil in Portuguese non-European export destinations. The relevance of African markets increased

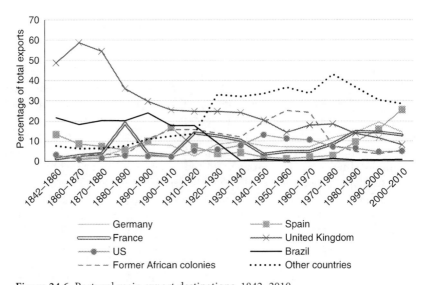

Figure 24.6 Portugal main export destinations, 1842–2010.
Sources: 1842–1910: Lains (2007b); 1910–2010: INE- Estatísticas do Comércio Externo (www.ine.es).

---

[136] Cuba represented 15% of total Spanish exports before political independence and 10% afterwards.
[137] Under the new regime, exports from Portugal to African colonies paid between 10% and 20% of the rights established on the general tariff, while foreign products re-exported to the colonies through Lisbon paid 80% and direct exports from other countries to the colonies paid the total general tariff (Lains, 1998).

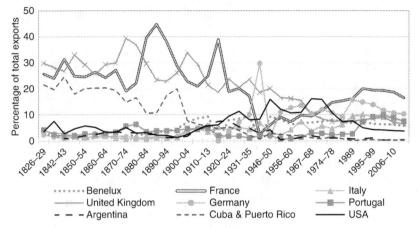

Figure 24.7 Spain main export destinations, 1826–2010.
Sources: Benchmarks are yearly averages. 1826–1829 to 1995–1999 from Tena-Junguito (2007: Chart 8.7); 2006–2010 and 2011–2013 yearly averages from INE (several years), Anuario Estadistico (www.mapa.gob.es/es/estadistica/temas/publicaciones/anuario-de-estadistica/).

steadily after the Great Depression, reaching about a quarter of total exports between 1950 and 1970, until the Portuguese African colonial independence in 1974.[138]

Nevertheless, throughout the nineteenth century, European markets remained the major destination for Iberian exports, representing 60–80% of total exports, led by France and the UK. From the turn of the century, the USA and the rest of the world increased their presence in both Iberian economies' markets at the expense of Europe and Latin America. Later on, the collapse of the fixed exchange rate system offered a new rival to Japan and the Middle Eastern and North African petroleum and gas producers. A renewed strength of the European market arrived with the formal entrance of Iberia in the European Common Market in the second half of the 1980s, which increased both European and Iberian bilateral trade integration.[139] During the twenty-first century, both economies lost markets in the USA and Europe in favour of other emerging markets in China, South-East Asia and Africa.

---

[138] See p. 239 and Tables 1 and 2 in Lains (1998). Portuguese exports to African colonies share increased after the Second World War reaching around a quarter of total Portuguese exports in the 1950s and 1960s and 17.8% during the early 1970s.

[139] The Spanish share in Portuguese exports was 2.9% in 1974–1985; 13.8% in 1987–1997; 23.8% in 1998–2008; and 24.8% in 2009–2015. *Exportações (Série desde 1974 - €) de bens por Local de destino.* INE, Estatísticas do Comércio Internacional de bens.

24.4 Capital and Labour Markets' Integration

The significant technological advances in steamships, railroads, telegraph networks and telephone connections that took place through the nineteenth century favoured not only the trade of commodities across countries but also other components of globalization, notably the international mobility of capital and labour. Benefiting from the stability and credibility conveyed by the gold standard monetary system, global capital mobility increased considerably in the post-1870 era up to 1914 (Obstfeld & Taylor, 2003), in conjunction with the age of 'mass migration' (Williamson, 1995). This globalization trend was nevertheless interrupted by the disruptions caused by the First World War and the Great Depression during the interwar years. Return to autarky became the rule, with monetary policy being used as an instrument to finance domestic goals, in particular war expenditures. After the Second World War, the Golden Age of growth in Europe was accompanied by a gradual recovery of globalization, first through tariff liberalization under the GATT, and later by a surge of migration starting in the 1960s and an increase of capital movements, following the abandonment of capital controls after the breakdown of the Bretton Woods system in the 1970s.

How do Iberian countries compare with this general pattern? A simple analysis of capital and labour market integration in Portugal and Spain can be performed based on the quantification of capital and labour flows. Concerning capital movements, the current account balance provides the difference between national saving and domestic investment: if positive, it measures the portion of a country's savings invested abroad; if negative, it measures the share of domestic investment financed by foreigners' savings. Since country aggregation between positive and negative flows does not allow changes in the level of factor integration over time to be shown, we use the average absolute values of a country's current account balance to GDP ratio, following Obstfeld (1998). The objective is to get a useful comparative index of the level of integration (whether positive or negative) of the capital movement in relative terms to European and world patterns. Concerning labour, we will use net migration flows over time in absolute terms.

24.4.1 Financial Integration

In the late nineteenth century, Spain presented a modest degree of international financial integration when compared both to Rich Europe and to the world (Figure 24.8). According to the literature, Spain and Portugal's poor financial integration in the late nineteenth century was because both countries remained out of the gold standard international club. The Portuguese currency

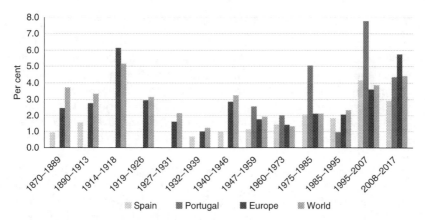

Figure 24.8 Net capital flows (absolute value of the current account as a percentage of GDP, Spain, Portugal, Italy, Europe and world, 1870–2017).
Sources: Current account balance (absolute values)/GDP. Europe: Denmark, France, Germany, Italy, Norway, UK (Obstfeld, 1998): 1870 to 1990–1995; Spain: Prados de la Escosura (2017); Portugal: Valério (2003: table 10.4); 2005–2010 and 2010–2015 all from WDI (Word Bank, 2019); world: Europe plus Argentine, Australia, Canada, Japan, USA; Obstfeld (1998) for 1870 to 1990–1995; 2005–2010 and 2010–2015 from WDI (Word Bank, 2019).

(*escudo*) was pegged to gold from 1854 to 1891. In contrast, Spain was the only Western country that never joined the gold standard, maintaining only a stable relationship with the dollar from 1960 to 1970.

In the twentieth century, the *escudo* was pegged to sterling from 1931 to 1949, and to the dollar from 1949 until 1973 (Bordo & Santos, 1995). Capital flows were regulated during the Bretton Woods Agreement period, which lasted from the mid-1940s to the early 1970s. During this period, Spain showed a lower trade and political integration than Portugal, especially in the 1950s, which explains its relative financial isolation.

Portugal remained more financially integrated than Spain through the late 1970s and early 1980s, and even after the integration of both countries in the EMU in 1999 (Figure 24.8). Portugal's remarkable financial integration, partially explained by its small domestic market and chronic trade deficit, is notable both by European and world standards.

A gradual increase in capital flows occurred in Spain from the 1960s onwards, compensating for its initial current account deficits and showing a trend similar to Rich Europe (which contrasts with the poorly financially integrated Italy).

24.4.2 Migrations

Labour flows are estimated based on the net migration rate, defined as the absolute value of the number of immigrants minus the number of emigrants over a period, per 1,000 population. In Figure 24.9 we compare this rate in the Iberian countries and the world, which represents the arithmetic average of 10 countries, including the leading settler economies of America (the USA, Argentina and Canada) and Oceania (Australia) and five rich European countries (Denmark, France, Germany, Netherlands and the UK), taken as an absolute value.

At the global level, mass migration started only in the second half of the nineteenth century, with strong intercontinental outflows from Europe towards the New World, made possible by ongoing developments in sea travel technology (Hatton & Williamson, 2008). Net migration increased decisively from the 1870s onwards, peaking just before the First World War, with a rate of 10 per 1,000, slumping to 0.5 at the end of the 1930s, and increasing

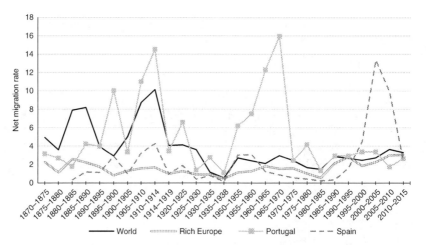

Figure 24.9 Net migration rate per 1,000 population (absolute figures).
Notes: Net migration rates per 1,000 population (absolute figures). Net migration rates are the number of immigrants minus the number of emigrants over a period, divided by the person-years lived by the population of the receiving country over that period in absolute figures).
Sources: Rich Europe: Denmark, France, Germany, Netherlands, UK, 1870–1960 from Mitchell (2013); Spain from Nicolau (2005); Portugal from Mitchell (2007c); 1960–2015 from WDI (World Bank, 2019). The world is composed of Rich Europe plus Argentina, USA, Canada and Australia.

moderately in the 1950s and 1960s to around 3.0, before finally settling on a rate of 3.7 at the end of the first decade of the twenty-first century.[140]

In Iberia, emigration showed a considerable upsurge in the late nineteenth century, following the first tide of emigration to the Americas originating from north-west Europe (Hatton & Williamson, 2008). Portugal, in particular, displayed an exceptional movement of people across its borders during the years of the Atlantic mass emigration before the First World War, with a top rate of 14.5 per 1,000 in 1910–1914, directed mainly to Brazil. During the golden years of European growth, there was again a massive outflow of people in Portugal, with a top rate of 15.9 in the late 1960s. Spain showed a similar emigration cycle, but with much more moderate peaks of 4.3 and 3.1 in 1910–1914 and 1955–1960, respectively.

From 1950 to 1973, both countries went through deep structural transformation (cf. Chapter 22), moving from an agrarian economy to a modernized industrial one. Spain's active agrarian population plummeted from around 40% to less than one-quarter, and more than one million people moved abroad. In Portugal, the movement of people from the countryside to towns was as important as in Spain, but in relative terms, people emigrating abroad doubled the Spanish figures in the 1950s and reached levels of more than thirteenfold the Spanish net migration in the 1960s. This was partially due to attempts by part of the youth to avoid the African colonial wars in a period in which the European growth boom pulled for new employment opportunities. Although Portugal had long been a source of labour outflow, emigration accelerated significantly in the mid-1960s, and by 1973 about 14% of the Portuguese labour force was employed in the European Community.[141]

Both countries reduced their net migration rates in the 1970s and 1980s, and from the 1990s onwards a renewed economic dynamism took the form of net immigration. In both countries, the available evidence reveals vigorous net migration rates, but in the case of Spain, these rates were exceptional in the first decade of the twenty-first century, with a top rate of 13.4% in its early years. Spain went from having a total foreign population of 2% in 2000 to approximately 12% in 2011. The magnitude of this phenomenon can be seen from a EU-15 perspective. According to Eurostat data, 1 in 5 migrants that moved to

---

[140] The movement of people in the world was much less dynamic after the Second World War than it was at the end of the nineteenth century. Quantity-based measurements of labour mobility show a lower degree of integration in the twenty-first century than in the years before 1914 (Lains & Silva, 2015). However, there has been a moderate upward trend in the European rich countries, which arrived at a 3.1 rate in the second decade of the twenty-first century, whereas showing a peak of 2.3 in the early 1870s and a minimum of 0.5 in the late 1930s.

[141] Between 1964 and 1974, the average annual number of departures was about 118,000, with a considerable share of the departures taking place clandestinely (Baganha, 2003).

the EU-15 between 2002 and 2013 went to Spain.[142] In this period the Spanish economy was booming and demanding young, 'low-skilled' workers willing to take relatively low salaries. Immigration raised employment figures and promoted economic growth. A consequence of the financial crisis was that immigration rates rapidly became moderate and migration outflows in the next decade overcame inflows, not only in Spain but also in Portugal.[143]

24.5 Balance of Payments and Financial Capacity

A relevant part of the nineteenth century historical capital imports in the Iberian periphery is related to the contracting of foreign loans to finance government deficits or to invest in social overhead capital. In Portugal, capital imports appeared at an earlier stage, following the financial distress associated with the civil war of 1832–1834 that obliged the country to contract a foreign loan (Costa et al., 2016).

The Portuguese government raised the first loan of a new era in 1856, to be invested in the first railway line. By 1890, with a total debt of 1,129 million French francs, Portugal had more difficulties in borrowing abroad, and thus in 1910 the effective interest rate paid by the Portuguese governments on foreign loans was among the highest from 1890 (see Lains 2002a: 37). British investment dominated the Portuguese urban transport and railway-building investment sector during the third quarter of the nineteenth century, and also later, when foreign companies diversified into other sectors such as telegraphs, gas, water supply and telephones in the last quarter of the nineteenth century (see Mata, 2008).

The balance of payments data available for Portugal reveal a structural problem of the Portuguese economy: its chronic lack of competitiveness (see Figure 24.10). Trade deficits are an almost permanent feature, although between the 1930s and the early 1970s Portugal was either able to find external loans to cover existing current account deficits or to achieve current account surpluses through tourist revenues and remittances from emigrants, especially between 1964 and 1973. During the 1960s and until 1973 remittances constituted the main factor that supported the surplus, covering about 30% of the imports of goods and services in 1973. The Portuguese balance of payments benefited also from the privileged market relations with former colonies, particularly Angola and Mozambique. The structural difficulties in external accounts became a serious problem, with pervasive effects throughout the entire economy after 1974, when the combination of the external energy crisis

---

[142] Based on Spanish National Institute of Statistics (www.ines.es) and Eurostat Migration data (https://ec.europa.eu/eurostat/statistics-explained/index.php?title=Migration_and_migrant_population_statistics).

[143] See Jaumotte and Saxena (2016).

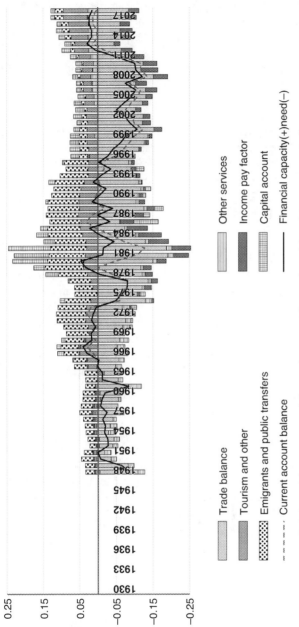

Figure 24.10 Portugal's balance of payments and financial capacity/financial need (% of GDP; 1948–2018).

Note: Data on the Portuguese balance of payments are only available from 1948 onwards.

Sources: Balance of payments: 1948–1996, Valério (2001a: table 6.6C); 1997–2018, Bank of Portugal (www.bportugal.pt/en/page/estatisticas). GDP and its variations, according to the Bank of Portugal.

with the domestic economic turbulence following the 1974 revolution produced a current account deficit of 6% of GDP (Lopes, 2004b). Along with a decline in emigrants' remittances, there was a drastic decrease in the coverage of imports by exports, which materialized as a widening of the deficit on the external current account to the equivalent of 8–9% of GDP in 1976 and 1977. Such a serious deterioration in the country's external accounts led to the signing of a stabilization program with the IMF and to the implementation of several austerity measures in order to improve the trade balance. The recovery of the Portuguese balance of payments was at the time extremely rapid: the external deficit on the current account was totally eliminated by 1979. However, new problems would arise in the same year, following a second oil shock, which lead again to a sharp deterioration in terms of trade (the current account showed a deficit of about 13% of GDP), leading to a new stabilization adjustment mechanism under the leadership of the IMF in 1983. After 1985 and until the early 1990s there was a comfortable equilibrium, this time benefiting from a positive external shock – the reduction in world petroleum prices – which determined an improvement in terms of trade, although it did not materialize as an accumulation of reserves similar to what happened in the 1960s. From the 1980s onwards the relative importance of remittances started to decline. However, this reduction was compensated by an increase in European Funds transfers. Capital flows, including short-, medium- and long-term loans, along with foreign direct investment, remained positive most of the time. After 1995 the situation worsened again: between 1995 and 1998 – just prior to joining the EMU – Portugal experienced a large deficit (7.6% of GDP) that was only progressively moderated from 1999 onwards. By 2007, prior to the emergence of the crisis, Portugal showed large external deficits on its current account, which reflected its economic vulnerability.

In the case of nineteenth-century Spain (Figure 24.11(a)), foreign capital inflows were also related to the need to finance government budget deficits and the construction of urban and railway infrastructures, but they also reflected the attraction of foreign capital towards the modern banking business and the exploitation of mineral resources. The net capital inflow was strongly positive between 1850 and 1870 and moderately positive until 1890, while between 1891 and 1913 foreign investment growth slowed down at a time of positive current account balances (Prados de la Escosura, 2010b).

Emigration remittances tended to exhibit a countercyclical role in the Iberian economies. A decline in domestic economic activity was sometimes accompanied by an increase in emigrants' flows and subsequent remittances. This was the case for Spain during the upswing of 1877, when a drop of 19% occurred in remittances, and inversely, during the crises of 1899 and 1913,

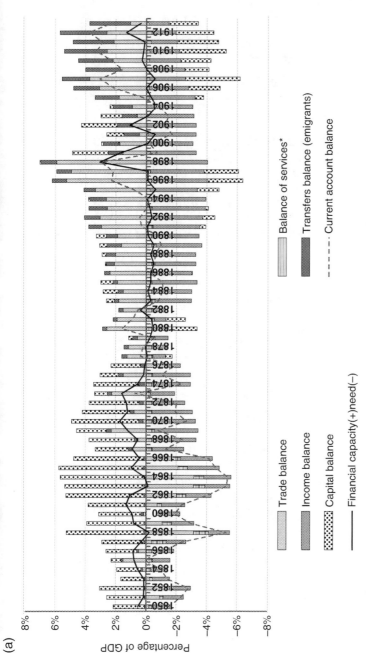

Figure 24.11 Spain's balance of payments and financial capacity/financial need (% of GDP; 1850–2018): (a) 1850–1913; (b) 1931–2018. Sources: Current account (trade, service, income, transfers and capital balance, 1850–1913, indirect 'residual' estimates', Prados de la Escosura (2020b); 1931–1995, Tena-Junguito (2007); 1996–2018, Bank of Spain (2020). GDP at market prices: Prados de la Escosura (2018).

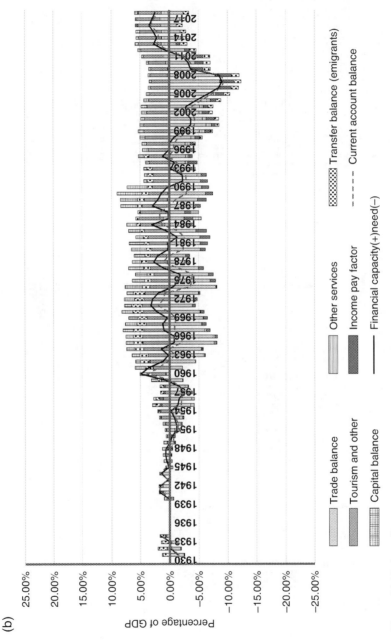

Figure 24.11 (cont.)

when an increase in remittances of 42% and 18%, respectively, took place.[144]

The trade deficit persisted in Spain during the interwar period, resulting in a negative current account balance (see Figure 24.11(b)). Capital inflows were reduced to less than half of the pre-war years' levels, showing a pattern similar to overall international trends. This trend persisted during the autarkic policy stance imposed by the Franco regime at the end of the Spanish Civil War, in 1939, and during the 1940s and 1950s. During General Franco's dictatorship, market-oriented reforms were very limited, and authorities adopted a system of multiple exchange rates in 1948, which lasted until the peseta devaluation of July 1959 that followed more open trade policies.[145] Between 1954 and 1958, the number of foreigners entering Spain increased by a factor of 2.5, but according to official records tourism revenue fell from $100 to less than $25 per tourist, because illegal networks for securing foreign currency extended their areas of influence to Algeria and Southern France (Martínez-Ruiz, 2003). Spain's commitment to openness continued during the remaining years of the high-growth period of the 1960s and early 1970s, bringing about a huge increase in trade deficits. Spaniards moved from the countryside to the cities, and more than one million went abroad, contributing with foreign capital and tourism inflows to finance the huge growth of imports. The massive increase in tourism to Spain since the early 1950s was made possible thanks to the improved European road network and the growing availability of private cars for the rising European upper-middle classes (Cirer-Costa, 2019). From 1960 to 1973, export coverage rate never rose above 50%, and tourism and emigrant remittances financed 79% and 32%, respectively, of the Spanish massive trade deficit (cf. Figure 24.11).

Trade deficits boomed with the international crisis in the 1970s because of the drop in international demand for Spanish products and the strong rise in the prices of gasoline and other price-inelastic import products. The export coverage rate grew to 70% during the first half of the 1980s. Emigrants' remittances showed an increasing trend until 1977, after which they began to decline. Remittances peaked in 1973 with a rate of 2% of GDP and reached their lowest point in 1994 with 0.28%, becoming negative thereafter. Following the European Common Market entrance, a renewed economic growth sustained by capital inflows helped to finance the new large trade and service deficits. Capital inflows compensated for the decline in remittances, but tourism remained the major source of foreign revenue between 1984 and 1994, covering on average about 80% of the trade deficit (cf. Figure 24.11). Finally, once Spain joined the EMU in 1999, borrowing in the international markets became easier. Accordingly, until the beginning of the financial crisis in 2007, the Spanish economy ran the highest current account deficits in its

---

[144] See Esteves and Khoudour-Castéras (2011: 453).
[145] See Tena-Junguito (2007: 586–587).

history (9.1 % of GDP). However, in a monetary union, such disequilibria should be corrected by wage and price deflation and not by nominal exchange rate depreciation, as happened during the years that followed the financial crisis and until the current account balance became positive in 2012 (Bajo-Rubio & Esteve, 2021).

24.6 Catching Up and Integration Policies: A Balance

After the devastating 'Peninsular War' that followed Napoleon's invasion, Portugal and Spain probably had similar levels of income per capita, representing around 60% of the level in Rich European countries around 1830, and most likely a percentage similar to the one Iberia had relative to Great Britain more than two centuries earlier.[146] The widening of the gap with the more developed European countries occurred in parallel with the acceleration of globalization during the 'long nineteenth century', ending with the First World War, when the GDP per capita ratio decreased to 50% and 30% in Spain and Portugal, respectively (see also Chapter 18). In the nineteenth century, the old Iberian monarchies continued, with difficulty, the process of trade liberalization started by the UK, as happened with most of the European latecomers.

Conventional wisdom would state a positive causal link between higher commercial openness, global financial and labour opportunities and economic growth, but this virtuous mechanism is complex and depends on the point of departure of a vast array of factors, including the level of development, market size, sectoral structure, endowment of human capital and the quality of domestic institutions. In this sense, the backlash to international competition in the nineteenth century was partially endogenous to the initial level of economic development of the Iberian Economies. Liberalization of trade barriers in the 1840s was shared in Europe by rich and poor countries, but not in the same dimension. For instance, Portugal, in an apparent contradiction with its smaller domestic market, maintained a very high tariff average of around 30% in the 1860s, in contrast with average levels of 12% and 5% in Spain and rich European countries, respectively. The Iberian economies did not participate wholly in the gold standard club, and in both cases the repercussions of the 'grain invasion' of the late nineteenth century were severe. Portugal reacted very early in the 1870s, increasing ad valorem tariffs to 40% at the end of the 1880s, and Spain reacted later reaching a maximum level of 20% of tariff average, during the early 1890s. Spain surpassed Portuguese tariff levels in the 1920s, and the Spanish response to the Great Depression was also more vigorous.

Portugal's high tariffs and low dynamism of international trade integration during the nineteenth century contrast with an extraordinary movement of

---

[146] See Álvarez-Nogal and Prados de la Escosura (2013) and Palma and Reis (2019).

labour out of its borders, with exceptional migration rates. This combination of forces confirms to some extent the well-known Mundell (1957) proposition that trade acts as a substitute for the movement of factors. Less free trade would reduce the equalization of relative incomes coming from land and labour in Portugal and abroad, stimulating migration from low-wage to high-wage regions. Spain was a relatively severe protectionist country in the late nineteenth century, interwar years and post-war years by European standards, as shown by its reduction in relative trade openness (Figures 24.1 and 24.2). Nevertheless, capital and labour flows were less vigorous, albeit not modest.

The disintegration of the international economy during the interwar years slowed down growth in the rich European countries and, as a consequence, their divergence process with the Iberian economies. Portugal and, especially, Spain did not participate initially in the European Bretton Woods Golden Age of growth, partially because of their international political isolation. The well-known convergence in Iberian economies is clearly a phenomenon of the second half of the twentieth century, when the bottleneck created by the initial commercial isolation forced more open policies towards international economic integration. The rapid structural industrialization of the Iberian economies in the second half of the twenty century was fostered by the rapid shift in the composition of exports towards industrial manufactured goods from around 10% in the late 1950s to more than 60% in the twenty-first century. European integration and the new inter- and intra-industrial international trade demand encouraged this process, which continued to mature during the late 1980s to the turn of the century. This process of convergence was apparently rudely interrupted in 2008 with the financial crisis. Following this course of events, both countries clearly overcame the initial 1830 historical ratio of 60% in the 1990s, but the improvement of such a modest target has been partially put into question after the crisis (Prados de la Escosura 2017; Peiró-Palomino et al., 2019).

25

The Iberian Economy in Comparative Perspective, 1800–2000

STEPHEN BROADBERRY AND RUI PEDRO ESTEVES

25.1 Perspectives on Iberian Economic Performance

In 1800, Spain and Portugal were fading imperial powers on the periphery of Europe, with per capita incomes less than half the level of Great Britain. During the nineteenth century, the Iberian economies failed to catch up with Britain, which was going through the first Industrial Revolution, which opened up opportunities for other economies to industrialize and make the transition to modern economic growth. As the United States overtook the United Kingdom to emerge as the leading economic power at the turn of the century, Spain and Portugal fell further behind, falling to a nadir of around 20% of US GDP per capita by 1950. Both Iberian economies then entered a dramatic new phase of growth which propelled them to around 50% of the US level and 70% of the UK level by 1980, after which the catching up process stalled. The chapters in Part III provide a number of different perspectives on this roller coaster performance.

The simplest perspective is to examine the path of Spanish and Portuguese GDP per capita as a measure of the rise in living standards on the Iberian Peninsula, without reference to the level in the rest of the world. This is the perspective adopted in Figure 25.1, which plots the level of GDP per capita in Spain and Portugal in 1990 international dollars, using the same sources as Herranz-Loncán, Sanchis-Llopis and Tirado-Fabregat (Chapter 18). The two economies began the nineteenth century with almost identical levels of GDP per capita but then followed very different trajectories to arrive once more at about equal levels of GDP per capita in the late 1940s. Spain grew at more than 1% per annum from around 1850 until the mid-1930s, then experienced a sharp decline during the Civil War and had still not recovered the 1929 peak level of GDP per capita by 1947. Portugal, by contrast, stagnated through most of the nineteenth century, then grew slowly from 1880 to 1920 before entering a phase of more than 1% growth between 1920 and 1947. Both economies then experienced a phase of very rapid growth of nearly 5% per annum between 1947 and 1973, followed by a reduction to around 2.5% between 1973 and 1990, and a further reduction to around 1% after 1990.

IBERIAN ECONOMY IN COMPARATIVE PERSPECTIVE, 1800–2000   649

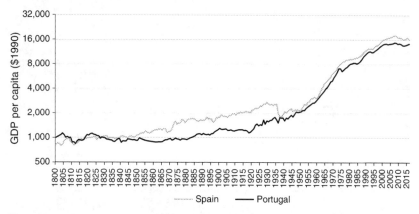

Figure 25.1 GDP per capita in Spain and Portugal, 1800–2016.
Sources: Maddison Project Database (2013; 2018); Palma and Reis (2019); Prados de la Escosura et al. (2020).

A second perspective comes from considering Iberian performance in relation to the leading economies of the world, which represent the technological frontier. The further behind the technological frontier that an economy falls, the easier it is to grow rapidly. This can be interpreted in at least two ways. First, rapid growth may be the result of importing superior technology from abroad, so long as the society has the appropriate social capabilities (Abramovitz, 1986). Alternatively, low levels of output per worker due to low levels of capital per worker will lead to a high marginal product of capital, thus inducing the capital investment that will close the productivity gap. During the nineteenth century, the UK is normally seen as the technological leader, with the USA forging ahead around the turn of the century and remaining the world leader throughout the twentieth century and into the twenty-first. Hence Figure 25.2 displays Spanish and Portuguese GDP per capita as a percentage of the UK and US levels. Spain remained at around 50% of the UK level from 1800 to the mid-1930s, then crashed to around 30% during the Civil War and remained at this level until 1950 (Figure 25.2(a)). Portugal declined gradually relative to the UK during the nineteenth century and remained at around 30% of the UK level during the first half of the twentieth. Both Spain and Portugal then caught up rapidly from 1950, but the catching up process stalled from around 1980 at 70% of the UK level. Turning to the comparison with the USA in Figure 25.2(b), Iberian relative performance follows a U-shaped pattern, with a low point of 20% of the US level around 1950, and the catching up process stalling at 50% of the US level around 1980. The reason for the J-shaped pattern in Figure 25.2(a) and the U-shaped pattern in Figure 25.2(b) is that the USA was catching up with the

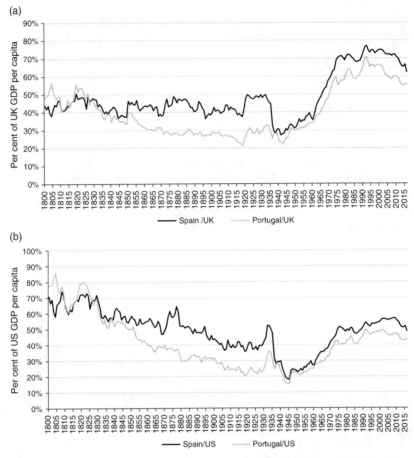

Figure 25.2 Spanish and Portuguese GDP per capita as a percentage of the UK and US economies: (a) comparison with the UK; (b) comparison with the US.
Sources: Maddison Project Database (2013; 2018); Palma and Reis (2019); Prados de la Escosura et al. (2020).

UK during the nineteenth century. This reminds us that the overall assessment of relative economic performance depends on careful choice of the reference country. Using the Iberia/US yardstick tends to give an unduly pessimistic picture of Iberian performance, indicating relative decline during the period to 1950, and the persistence of a very large gap after 1980. On the other hand, using the Iberia/UK yardstick reduces Iberian relative decline during the nineteenth century, and narrows the gap in the late twentieth century. Perhaps a fairer assessment is obtained by comparison with the UK during

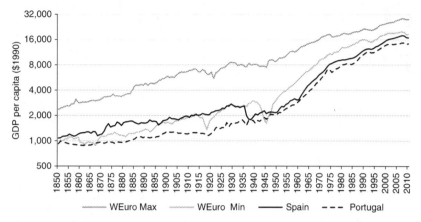

Figure 25.3 Spanish and Portuguese GDP per capita compared with the maximum and minimum in the rest of Western Europe.
Source: Maddison Project Database (2013; 2018).

the period of UK economic leadership in the nineteenth century, and with the USA during the period of US economic leadership from the twentieth century.

A third perspective is offered by comparison with a wider sample of West European economies in Figure 25.3, suggested by Díez-Minguela, Guilera and Martinez-Galarraga (Chapter 23). The grey lines in this graph track the maximum and minimum levels of GDP per capita in 12 West European economies in each year, covering the whole of Western Europe excluding Spain and Portugal. This tends to put a less optimistic interpretation on Iberian performance over time, which more or less tracks the worst-performing West European economy over time between 1850 and 1950, but then lags behind during the post-1950 period. Against this yardstick, the apparently good performance of catching up with the leaders between 1950 and 1980 is turned into a disappointing performance compared with other West European economies that were equally poor in 1950.

Comparing Spain and Portugal with a sample of today's poorer countries offers a fourth and more optimistic perspective on Iberian economic performance, since much of the world still lives in poverty. India and China are not among the very poorest of the world's economies, particularly since their rapid growth from the 1980s. Figure 25.4 thus makes clear that things could have been a lot worse in Spain and Portugal during the nineteenth and twentieth centuries. India and China showed no sign of catching up with Spain and Portugal before the 1980s despite being substantially poorer, and despite their subsequent improved performance they remain a long way behind.

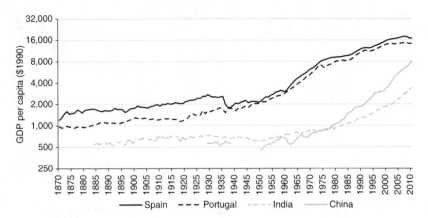

Figure 25.4 Spanish and Portuguese GDP per capita compared with India and China. Source: Maddison Project Database (2013; 2018).

25.2 Accounting for Growth: Proximate Sources

Maddison (1988) made a useful distinction between proximate and ultimate sources of economic growth. The proximate sources such as capital, human capital and technology are useful in exploring the mechanics of growth or describing the changes that characterize a growing economy. But they do not shed much light on why those changes occurred in one economy but not in another at a particular point in time. To the extent that the accumulation of physical or human capital can be identified as crucial sources of growth in the leading economy, we would still want to know why the lagging economy did not increase its investment. That requires us to delve into the deeper underlying sources of growth such as institutions and geography.

To assess the contribution of the proximate sources, growth accounting begins with a production function to assess whether economic growth came from the use of more factor inputs or from the more effective use of existing inputs. Aggregate output (Y) is produced using inputs of capital (K), labour (L) and human capital (H), and A is a measure of efficiency, or total factor productivity (TFP):

$$Y = AF(K, L, H). \qquad (25.1)$$

The growth rate of output ($\Delta Y/Y$) can be related to the growth rates of the inputs of capital ($\Delta K/K$), labour ($\Delta L/L$) and human capital ($\Delta H/H$), and the growth rate of TFP ($\Delta A/A$):

$$\Delta Y/Y = \alpha \Delta K/K + \beta \Delta L/L + \gamma \Delta H/H + \Delta A/A. \qquad (25.2)$$

The weights α, β and γ reflect the relative importance of inputs in the production process, measured by their shares in the costs of production.

The growth accounting equation can also be written in intensive rather than extensive form, to show how the growth of labour productivity (output per worker or per hour worked) can be explained by the growth of physical or human capital per unit of labour (capital deepening) or total factor productivity growth:

$$\Delta y/y = \alpha \Delta k/k + \gamma \Delta h/h + \Delta A/A, \qquad (25.3)$$

where y is output per unit of labour, k is capital per unit of labour and h is human capital per unit of labour. This is useful because it focuses attention on the factors underpinning the rise in living standards rather than just the size of the economy.

Herranz-Loncán, Sanchis-Llopis and Tirado-Fabregat (Chapter 18) report results for Spain and Portugal using the extensive growth accounting equation. Output is measured by the GDP data used in Figure 25.1. Capital stock data are available for Spain covering the period from 1850, but for Portugal they are available only from 1910 (Lains, 2003a; Prados de la Escosura & Rosés, 2009). The labour input is measured not just by the number of workers, but also takes into account the number of hours worked per person per year, while human capital is measured by the years of education of the labour force. The growth of the labour input was driven by the growth of population, which was in turn affected by the demographic transition, analysed by Branco and Collantes (Chapter 19). The demographic transition can also be seen as affecting the growth of human capital as society moved from an equilibrium of fairly stable population with high birth rates and death rates to a new equilibrium of fairly stable population with low birth rates and death rates. This both extended the length of time spent in the labour force by women and made it more affordable for families to invest in the education of their children, which became ever more important as technology played an increasingly important role in the economy. This is broadly consistent with the model of development proposed in unified growth theory (Galor & Weil, 2000; Galor, 2005).

The extensive growth accounts in Table 25.1 yield a number of interesting results. First, concentrating on the final three columns, it is clear that GDP growth was driven largely by weighted factor input growth in Portugal throughout the period 1910–2017, and also in Spain during most of the longer period 1850–2017. However, there was an exception to this dominance of factor input growth in Spain between 1947 and 1990, when TFP growth was briefly more important than weighted factor input growth. Second, focusing on the first four columns of Table 25.1, physical capital was the key driver of weighted factor input growth in both Spain and Portugal. Capital accumulation was particularly strong during the railway construction and mining boom

Table 25.1 *Accounting for the growth of output: average annual growth rates (%).*

(a) Spain

	Physical capital	Labour quantity	Human capital	Weighted factor inputs	TFP	GDP
1850–1884	2.21	0.50	0.20	0.97	0.77	1.74
1884–1910	1.93	0.20	0.10	0.74	0.12	0.86
1910–1934	2.34	0.93	1.23	1.50	0.71	2.21
1934–1947	0.77	0.40	0.80	0.66	−0.76	−0.10
1947–1973	5.45	0.60	1.21	2.42	3.39	5.81
1973–1990	5.05	−3.35	1.28	0.99	2.64	3.63
1990–2017	3.78	1.02	0.71	1.84	0.30	2.14
1910–2017	3.69	0.13	1.05	1.62	1.37	3.00

(b) Portugal

	Physical capital	Labour quantity	Human capital	Weighted factor inputs	TFP	GDP
1910–1934	1.25	1.00	2.08	1.44	0.73	2.17
1934–1947	3.89	1.31	1.14	2.11	−0.02	2.09
1947–1973	7.73	0.70	2.47	3.63	1.54	5.17
1973–1990	5.21	0.05	4.83	3.36	0.57	3.93
1990–2017	2.04	0.08	0.91	1.01	0.09	1.10
1910–2017	3.97	0.58	2.20	2.25	0.65	2.90

Note: Weights are one-third for each of physical capital, labour and human capital.
Sources: Lains (2003a); Prados de la Escosura and Rosés (2009); Herranz-Loncán, Sanchis-Llopis and Tirado-Fabregat (Chapter 18).

between 1850 and 1884, and again during the intense period of catching up by both Portugal and Spain between 1947 and 1973. Third, the labour quantity played a relatively modest role in the growth of weighted factor input as hours per worker declined to offset the effects of population growth before the completion of the demographic transition. Fourth, although literacy and average years of education increased during the nineteenth century and the first half of the twentieth, human capital made a relatively limited contribution to the growth of weighted factor input before the rapid expansion of secondary and tertiary education during the post-war catching up phase (see Chapter 19).

The intensive growth accounts in Table 25.2 provide some additional insights into the growth process, by highlighting the sources of labour productivity growth, which underpins the rising standard of living. In Spain, there is a clear divide between the modest labour productivity growth before 1947 and the subsequent period of faster growth. During the pre-1947 period, labour productivity growth was driven largely by physical capital deepening, as the physical capital stock grew faster than the quantity of labour, while TFP growth was relatively modest. After 1947, although capital deepening continued, labour

Table 25.2 *Accounting for the growth of labour productivity: average annual growth rates (%).*

(a) Spain

	Physical capital intensity	Human capital intensity	Weighted capital intensity	TFP	Labour productivity
1850–1884	1.71	−0.30	0.47	0.77	1.24
1884–1910	1.73	−0.10	0.54	0.12	0.66
1910–1934	1.41	0.30	0.57	0.71	1.28
1934–1947	0.37	0.40	0.26	−0.76	−0.50
1947–1973	4.85	0.61	1.82	3.39	5.21
1973–1990	8.40	4.63	4.34	2.64	6.98
1990–2017	2.76	−0.31	0.82	0.30	1.12
1910–2017	3.56	0.92	1.49	1.38	2.87

(b) Portugal

	Physical capital intensity	Human capital intensity	Weighted capital intensity	TFP	Labour productivity
1910–1934	0.25	1.08	0.44	0.73	1.17
1934–1947	2.58	−0.17	0.80	−0.02	0.78
1947–1973	7.03	1.77	2.93	1.54	4.47
1973–1990	5.16	4.78	3.31	0.57	3.88
1990–2017	1.96	0.83	0.93	0.09	1.02
1910–2017	3.39	1.62	1.67	0.65	2.32

Note: Weights are one-third for each of physical capital, labour and human capital.
Sources: Lains (2003a); Prados de la Escosura and Rosés (2009); Herranz-Loncán, Sanchis-Llopis and Tirado-Fabregat (Chapter 18).

productivity growth was driven more by an increase in TFP growth. In Portugal, by contrast, there was a greater role for capital deepening throughout the period 1910–2017, with TFP growth playing a minor role, apart from during the period 1910–1934.

25.3 Structure: Agriculture, Industry and Services

We have so far focused on macroeconomic aggregates, but an important proximate source of growth is structural change, which is discussed in Chapter 22. The broad trends of structural change in Iberia between 1800 and 2011 can be tracked in parts (a) and (b) of Table 25.3, which set out the shares of employment in Spanish and Portuguese agriculture, industry and services. Parts (c) to (g) of Table 25.3 provide data on other economies for comparison. Between 1800 and 1910, agriculture was the dominant activity in Spain and Portugal, absorbing around 60 to 70% of employment. This is in striking contrast to the UK, the nineteenth-century economic leader, where agriculture accounted for just 12% of employment in 1911. The share of agriculture was also substantially lower in the USA and Germany on the eve of the First World War. A high share of the labour force in agriculture thus seems to indicate a relatively low level of GDP per capita. This is confirmed by the data for Italy and India in parts (f) and (g) of Table 25.3. Spain and Portugal on the eve of the First World War were in a similar situation to Italy on the periphery of Europe, but not as poor as India, where around three-quarters of the labour force remained in agriculture. To the extent that Spain and Portugal were participating in the international economy at this time, trading with the advanced nations, their position reflected the international division of labour, with the Iberian nations specializing in agricultural products.

Since agriculture was a relatively low-value-added activity, it accounted for a substantially smaller share of GDP at this time, around 40% in both countries (see Chapter 22). Catching up would clearly require a substantial shift of labour from agriculture into more productive activities in industry and services, and this began between 1910 and 1930, but was followed by a pause between 1930 and 1950, when agriculture still accounted for around half of all employment in both Spain and Portugal. The shift away from agriculture resumed at a more rapid pace after 1950, with labour moving into both industry and services in roughly equal proportions until 1981, before a process of deindustrialization set in. This structural shift away from agriculture occurred much later than in the UK, the USA and Germany, but at about the same pace as in Italy, and faster than in India, where agriculture continued to account for more than 60% of employment at the end of the twentieth century.

After 1981, as the decline in agricultural employment continued, it was joined by a decline of industrial employment, and services became the

Table 25.3 *Sectoral shares of employment (headcount), 1870–2007 (%)*

(a) Spain	Agriculture	Industry	Services	(b) Portugal	Agriculture	Industry	Services
c. 1800	61	15	23	c. 1800	55	18	27
c. 1890	69	15	15	1890	62	18	20
1910	68	15	17	1910	58	22	21
1930	47	26	27	1930	51	19	30
1950	50	26	25	1950	49	24	26
1981	16	37	47	1981	19	39	42
2011	4	21	74	2011	3	26	70

(c) USA	Agriculture	Industry	Services	(d) UK	Agriculture	Industry	Services
1870	50.0	24.8	25.2	1871	22.2	42.4	35.4
1910	32.0	31.8	36.2	1911	11.8	44.1	44.1
1930	20.9	30.2	48.9	1930	7.6	43.7	48.7
1950	11.0	32.9	56.1	1950	5.1	46.5	48.4
1973	3.7	28.9	67.4	1973	2.9	41.8	55.3
1990	2.5	21.8	75.7	1990	2.0	28.5	69.5
2005	1.5	16.7	81.8	2005	1.4	18.4	80.2

(e) Germany	Agriculture	Ind	Services	(f) Italy	Agriculture	Industry	Services
1871	49.5	29.1	21.4	1871	68.1	15.8	16.2
1913	34.5	37.9	27.6	1911	59.1	23.5	17.4
1930	30.5	37.4	32.1	1931	53.8	25.4	20.8
1950	24.3	42.1	33.6	1951	44.3	31.0	24.8
1973	7.2	47.3	45.5	1973	17.7	38.4	43.9
1990	3.4	39.7	56.9	1993	6.6	31.3	62.2
2005	2.1	25.5	72.4	2007	3.9	27.9	68.2

(g) India	Agriculture	Industry	Services
1875	73.4	14.5	12.1
1910/1911	75.5	10.3	14.2
1929/1930	76.1	9.1	14.8
1950/1951	73.6	10.2	16.2
1970/1971	73.8	11.1	15.1
1999/2000	64.2	13.9	21.9

Sources: Spain, Portugal: Branco and Collantes (Chapter 19); USA, UK, Germany: Broadberry (1998); Italy: Broadberry et al. (2013); India: Broadberry et al. (2015b).

Table 25.4 *Structural change and labour productivity growth (% per annum).*
(a) Spain

	Labour productivity growth	Internal productivity growth (shift–share)	Structural change (lower bound)	Internal productivity growth (revised)	Structural change (upper bound)
1850–1883	1.3	1.1	0.2	1.1	0.2
1883–1920	0.7	0.6	0.1	0.4	0.3
1920–1929	2.4	2.1	0.4	1.1	1.3
1929–1952	−0.5	−0.5	0.0	−0.5	0.0
1952–1958	3.0	2.3	0.7	1.3	1.7
1958–1974	6.0	5.4	0.6	3.8	2.2
1974–1986	4.0	3.9	0.1	3.0	0.9
1986–2000	1.4	1.7	−0.3	0.9	0.5
1850–2000	1.7	1.6	0.1	1.1	0.7

(b) Portugal

	Labour productivity growth	Internal productivity growth (shift–share)	Structural change (lower bound)
1862–1910	−0.2	0.2	−0.4
1910–1950	1.7	1.4	0.3
1950–1973	5.4	3.9	1.5
1973–1985	1.0	0.7	0.3
1966–2002	2.2	2.0	0.2
1910–1995	2.8	2.4	0.4

Sources: Spain: Prados de la Escosura (2007). Portugal: Amaral, Beltrán and Pinilla (Chapter 22).

dominant sector. By 2011, services accounted for 70 to 75% of all employment. This shift to services was accompanied by growing female participation, rising from as low as 13% in Iberia as a whole in 1950 to 45% by 2011 (see Chapter 19).

The effects of structural change on labour productivity performance have traditionally been analysed using shift–share analysis. However, this normally yields the surprising result that the dramatic structural shift away from low-productivity agriculture had very little effect on labour productivity growth. In the case of Spain, this conventional approach can be seen in the first three columns of Table 25.4(a), yielding a lower bound measure of the contribution of structural change to labour productivity growth. However, this is also accompanied by an alternative approach in the last two columns of Table 25.4(a), yielding an upper bound measure. For Portugal, there are only results for the traditional shift–share calculation in Table 25.4(b), but it is likely that structural change was just as important for labour productivity performance in Portugal as it was in Spain.

The standard shift–share approach begins from the observation that the level of aggregate labour productivity in year t (A_t) can be obtained not only by dividing aggregate output (Q_t) by labour for the economy as a whole (L_t), but also by summing labour productivity in each sector (A_{it}) weighted by that sector's share of total employment (S_{it}):

$$A_t = Q_t/L_t = \sum A_{it} S_{it}. \tag{25.4}$$

Taking time derivatives, denoted by hats above variables, we have

$$\hat{A}_t = \sum \hat{A}_{it} S_{it} + \sum A_{it} \hat{S}_{it}, \tag{25.5}$$

where aggregate labour productivity growth is made up of two parts, with the first term representing internal labour productivity growth and the second term representing structural change.

In standard shift–share analysis, internal productivity growth is obtained as the weighted sum of the growth of output per worker in each sector:

$$\sum \hat{a}_{it}(A_{it}/A_t)S_{it}, \tag{25.6}$$

where $\hat{a}_{it}$ is the log growth rate of labour productivity in each sector, A_{it}/A_t is the relative labour productivity in each sector and S_{it} is the share of each sector in total employment. The contribution of structural change is then obtained as the difference between aggregate productivity growth and internal productivity growth. However, this procedure assumes that productivity growth rates in each sector would be unaffected by the absence of structural change. Thus, for example, during the period between the 1950s and the 1970s, agriculture experienced extremely rapid labour productivity growth in both Spain and Portugal. But it is hard to believe that agricultural labour productivity would have continued to grow so rapidly if half of the labour force had remained in agriculture instead of shrinking to less than one-fifth, since all the economies that remained committed to agriculture on this scale remained poor. The contribution of structural change in the standard shift–share analysis must therefore be regarded as a lower bound measure.

The revised contribution of internal productivity growth in Table 25.4(a) follows the approach of Broadberry (1998: 387–388). This is obtained as

$$\sum \hat{\alpha}_{it}(A_{it}/A_t)S_{it}, \qquad (25.7)$$

where
$$\hat{\alpha}_{it} = \hat{a}_{it} - (\hat{L}_t - \hat{L}_{it}) \text{ if } \hat{S}_{it} < 0, \qquad (25.8a)$$

$$\hat{\alpha}_{it} = \hat{a}_{it} \text{ if } \hat{S}_{it} \geq 0. \qquad (25.8b)$$

In a declining sector such as agriculture, the actual labour productivity growth rate is reduced by the difference between the growth rate of aggregate employment ($\hat{L}_t$) and the growth rate of employment in the particular sector $\hat{L}_{it}$, as in Eq. (25.8a). In expanding sectors, the actual labour productivity growth rate is used, as in Eq. (25.8b). The use of the revised internal productivity growth in Table 25.4(a) results in a substantially larger contribution from structural change in the upper bound measure for Spain. As Prados de la Escosura (2007) notes, structural change can account for over 40% of the aggregate productivity growth over the whole period 1850–2000 using the upper bound measure, compared with less than 6% using the lower bound measure. The reason for the difference is that in the upper bound measure, the surplus labour that was redeployed from agriculture to industry, and thus raised industrial output without reducing industrial productivity growth, is put back into agriculture without producing any more agricultural output, thus slowing down productivity growth in agriculture.

One way of understanding the existence of this surplus labour in declining sectors is to think in terms of the role of demand constraints in structural transformation (Broadberry, 1998: 389). The demand for output of sector i (Q_i) can be split into the following components:

$$Q_i = D_i + X_i - M_i, \qquad (25.9)$$

where D_i is domestic demand, X_i is export demand and M_i is total imports of products classified in sector i. Slow growth of domestic demand may act as a constraint on the expansion of employment in sector i if output in that sector is geared largely to the home market and if there is technical progress in that sector. The structural transformation during the nineteenth and twentieth centuries involved a reduction in the importance of agriculture. Domestic demand played an important role here, with the low income elasticity of demand for food acting as a constraint on the further expansion of agriculture. This is consistent with Engel's Law, which states that the proportion of income spent on food declines as income rises. However, this shift occurred rather later in Iberia than in the core European economies, as Spain and Portugal specialized in exporting agricultural products as part of the international division of labour before 1950. After 1981, a higher income elasticity of demand for services than for industrial goods combined with rapid technological progress in industry to produce a declining share of employment in industry as well as agriculture (Table 25.3).

Iberian agriculture was able to take its place in the international division of labour during the nineteenth century and the first half of the twentieth, as it shifted increasingly from peasant agriculture to a market orientation (see Chapter 22). As farmers became increasingly responsive to market incentives, the resulting growth in exports offset the limited growth of domestic demand due to modest growth of GDP per capita and a low income elasticity of the demand for food. Agriculture received an additional boost from reforms to privatize land belonging to the church and local governments as well as communal land via a succession of disentailment processes. These trends combined with limited technological progress to delay the reduction in the share of agricultural employment. The key export product at this time in both Iberian economies was wine, supplemented by exports of olive oil, fresh fruit and vegetables in the case of Spain, and by cork and olive oil in the case of Portugal.

From the 1950s, productivity within Iberian agriculture received a boost from a number of sources, including the adoption of Green Revolution technologies (such as the introduction of hybrid seeds), the expansion of irrigation and the growth of intensive livestock farming. These developments were consolidated after Spain and Portugal joined the European Economic Community (EEC) in 1986, with the subsidies of the Common Agricultural Policy (CAP) providing a significant stimulus to agricultural production, and trade liberalization yielding access to a market with enormous potential. However, the benefits have been spread unevenly across the Iberian Peninsula, with the Spanish agri-food sector becoming highly competitive so that Spain has become one of the world's leading food exporters, while agricultural output and productivity have grown below the European average in Portugal (see Chapter 22).

Before the dramatic improvement of Iberian agricultural productivity performance in the mid-twentieth century, economic historians often explained the poor economic performance of Spain and Portugal in the nineteenth century and the first half of the twentieth by their natural endowments such as a shortage of land suitable for cereal production. The subsequent experience of these same economies, however, suggests that the problem may have been more one of second-nature geography, encompassing human-made factors such as market access. As the Iberian Peninsula became more integrated into the European continent, culminating in EEC entry in 1986, productivity performance improved dramatically and much of the productivity lag with the rest of Western Europe was eliminated.

Similar issues are apparent in the performance of Iberian industry. During the nineteenth century, Spanish and Portuguese industry specialized in textiles and food, drink and tobacco, lacking sufficient quantities of key natural resources such as coal and iron to be competitive in heavy industries such as metals, engineering and chemicals. As a result, heavy industry accounted for less than 10% of industrial value added during the nineteenth century, with production limited to coastal locations, where coal could be obtained from the UK at relatively low prices. The resource constraint was to some extent relaxed by the introduction of electricity as a source of power, but the growth of heavy industry remained muted in Spain and Portugal during the first half of the twentieth century, as low levels of education restricted the availability of human capital. Although Iberian protectionism provided a captive domestic market, the protectionist climate in the rest of the world also limited the growth of export demand. Nevertheless, Iberian industry began to take on a more modern shape with the formation of large corporations, sometimes in joint ventures with multinational producers. These modern business enterprises began the process of Chandler's (1977) three-pronged investment in large-scale capital-intensive production facilities, product-specific marketing, and distribution and professional management.

Iberian industrial performance improved dramatically during the second wave of globalization from the 1950s. Important developments here included the reforms associated with Spain's 1959 Stabilization and Liberalization Plan and Portugal's decision to join the European Free Trade Area (EFTA) in 1960, culminating in both countries joining the EEC in 1986. US technology diffused across Europe, facilitating a process of catching up in which both Spain and Portugal participated (Figure 25.2(b)). In Spain, this led to rapid TFP growth, explaining about half of industrial output growth during the period 1958–1975 (Sanchis, 2006: 413). Revealed comparative advantage changed substantially in both Spain and Portugal away from light industries such as textiles and food, drink and tobacco towards heavy industries such as electrical and mechanical engineering, transport equipment and chemicals.

Services have received much less attention in economic history than agriculture and industry but have often played a crucial part in the modernization process. As noted earlier, services have always accounted for a substantial proportion of output and employment, and their share increased dramatically in the period after 1950 in both Spain and Portugal, reaching half of all employment in the 1980s and around three-quarters by the 2010s. The main reason for the rising share of services in economic activity is that the income elasticity of demand for services is greater than the income elasticity of demand for agricultural and industrial goods. In an extension of Engel's Law, as people get richer, they spend a growing share of their income on services. For a long time, economists focused on the rising share of expenditure on industrial rather than agricultural goods, but the share of services has increased still more. Put simply, everyone wants to own a washing machine, but rich people also want someone to do their washing for them.

The origins of modern business enterprise in the USA are to be located not in industry but rather in services (Chandler, 1977). The 'industrialization' of services involved a reorganization of business from a low-volume, high-margin basis to a high-volume, low-margin basis, in a process running in parallel with the move to mass production in industry (Broadberry, 2006). The process began on the railways and soon spread to other parts of transportation and communications, and to wholesale and retail distribution and financial services such as banking and insurance. These developments required not just reorganization, but heavy investment in physical capital (transport and communications infrastructure and equipment, retail outlets, warehouses and office buildings) and in technology to process information more efficiently (the telegraph, the telephone, typewriters and calculating machines). They also required investment in human capital to operate the new technologies and more complex management and accounting systems.

Railways expanded on the Iberian Peninsula in the second half of the nineteenth century. The impact of railways on the integration of the Portuguese economy was probably quite limited, given the possibilities of coastal transport by water, but social savings calculations for Spain suggest a substantial gain, rising from 3.9% to 6.4% of GDP in 1878 to 18.9% by 1912 (Herranz-Loncán, 2006: 854). Although there were isolated examples of modern retail methods in the largest cities, distribution remained dominated by small-scale shops selling basic consumption goods in the period before 1914. In financial services, modern banking institutions and methods were introduced, but again the extent of financial intermediation remained less than in much of Western Europe during this period.

As in other Western economies, the industrialization of services was interrupted in Spain and Portugal between 1914 and the 1940s, as a consequence of the deglobalization arising from the world wars and the Great Depression, but with the additional dislocation of the Civil War in Spain. However, the process resumed at an accelerated pace from the 1950s against a backdrop of greater investment in human capital and the importation of technology from abroad (see Figure 25.5). The revolution in information and communications technology (ICT) significantly affected the main service sectors, particularly from the 1980s. In distribution, supermarkets and department stores began to appear from the 1950s, while in financial services the banking system grew and modernized, producing strong banks such as Santander and BBVA that developed a multinational presence in the last decades of the twentieth century. From the 1960s, the relatively new sector of mass tourism developed

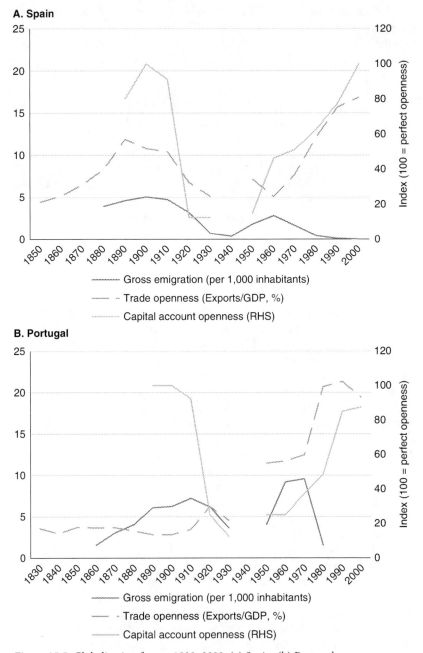

Figure 25.5 Globalization forces, 1830–2000: (a) Spain; (b) Portugal.
Sources: Emigration rates from Carreras and Tafunell (2005) and Valério (2001b); trade openness from Federico and Tena Junguito (2018); and capital account openness from Quinn (2003).

strongly as Spain and Portugal became popular beach destinations for many northern Europeans. Public services also grew strongly as a result of the expansion of health and education, particularly after the end of the Franco and Salazar regimes in the 1970s.

25.4 Institutions: Fundamental Sources of Growth

Political scientists and economic historians have long identified institutions as one of the ultimate sources of long-term growth. A clear understanding of what we mean by institutions is key here. Douglass North coined a pithy definition: 'Institutions are the rules of the game in a society, or, more formally, are the humanly devised constraints that shape human interaction' (North, 1990: 3). The emphasis in North's concept lies in the rules of interaction in society, which may be devised to favour the interests of groups (religious, political, ethnic, economic) that control political power.

Avner Greif (2006) introduced a useful distinction between rules/norms, beliefs about their enforcement and the human organizations that are allowed by those rules (e.g. corporations, political parties) or that enforce them, such as the courts. Clearly, only norms that are perceived as legitimate (or fairly enforced) are followed by the population, otherwise formal institutions may coexist with fragile states and fragmented authority. Modernity has long been associated with the concentration of political power in a unitary entity, the state, which enjoys a 'monopoly of violence' as Max Weber defined it. This transformation occurred in both Iberian nations prior to the period covered in Part III, although one of its corollaries – administrative and fiscal centralization – was only accomplished in the 1840s (Dincecco, 2009). Political and administrative centralization are first-best solutions for economic efficiency, as they allow for the integration of internal markets and uniformity in standards regulating economic exchange. However, the other side of the coin is that a unitary and centralized state can use its 'monopoly of violence' to extract rents from the population and distribute them to the elites that control it.

North et al. (2009) reframe the fundamental problem of development as the transition from limited access to open access orders. In the former, political stability is guaranteed through the sharing of economic rents among the political elites that could upset that stability. Barriers to entry are required to co-opt these elites but disenfranchise (politically and economically) the majority of the population. The authors find this as a 'natural state' of human societies, which is consistent with long periods of economic growth, as shown by the many cases of growth-friendly autocratic regimes in history. At some point, most advanced nations, starting with the UK and the USA, traversed to an open access order, where stability and growth are achieved through political and economic competition and equal access to the creation of organizations (political parties, corporations, associations, etc.). This concept is broader than the research on democratization as it specifically connects political competition in stable democracies with economic competition in open markets where rents are limited by pro-competition regulation. Unlike political scientists, who code scales of democracy and autocracy, these authors have not provided a cross-country list of transition dates to open access orders, but their framework is very useful to understand the institutional history of the Iberian nations since the nineteenth century.

In this framework, similar formal institutions (markets, elections, incorporation laws) may end up having very different outcomes depending on whether they operate in a context of a limited or open access order. As described by Cardoso and Comín (Chapter 20), the two Iberian nations have mostly followed a common institutional path since the nineteenth century, which we can summarize in four periods separated by three main political transitions: the 1910 Republican revolution in Portugal, the 1923 Spanish Dictatorship and the transition to democracy since 1975.

Politically, the Napoleonic Wars and the loss of their American empires spurred the adoption of liberal institutions in the 1820s, consolidated, after two decades of on-and-off civil war and repeated coups, in relatively conservative parliamentary monarchies. Key in this settlement was a limited franchise, but this is an imperfect representation of the real degree of participation in the political process. Franchise rules in the Iberian nations were deceptively similar to their peers in Western Europe or North America (see Table 25.5). But elections were regularly rigged by local political agents (*caciques*) or outright vote buying. An index of election fairness, computed by a consortium of political scientists, is a more accurate measure of electoral competition (Table 25.5). Dissatisfaction with this political stalemate was behind several progressive coups and revolutions, the most important being those that were the origin of the three Republican regimes in Portugal (1910–1926) and Spain (1873–1874 and 1931–1936).

These radical attempts at institutional reform gave way to a conservative reaction, initially driven by the traditional landowning elites in alliance with the army, but that later co-opted other economic elites. Compared with the human scars of the Spanish Civil War, the Portuguese coup of 1926 was relatively painless, but the long-lasting consequences for the two nations were similar. The regimes of Salazar in Portugal and Franco in Spain (with a precursor in Primo de Rivera), while preserving the trappings of the electoral system or republican institutions, effectively reasserted the forces of a new limited access order that protected the interests of political and economic incumbents. Their longevity confirms the strength of the underlying political alliances. In exchange for support for the new regimes, economic elites received protection against foreign and domestic competition (industrial conditioning), suppression of labour activism, and privileged access to credit in the context of a top-down industrial policy aiming at import substitution and economic autarky (see Chapter 20). This autarkic phase was more successful in

Table 25.5 *Political and economic institutions, 1800-2019.*

		1800– 1909	1910– 1922	1923– 1974	1975– 2019
Franchise	Spain	16.7	50.0	91.3	100.0
	Portugal	17.6	28.5	48.1	100.0
	Western Europe/North America*	15.7	56.3	87.0	100.0
Electoral fairness	Spain	0.1	0.1	0.1	0.9
	Portugal	0.2	0.3	0.1	0.9
	Western Europe/North America*	0.3	0.6	0.7	0.9
Coups	Spain	10	0	2	0
	Portugal	8	3	2	0
Economic liberty	Spain	7.3†	7.3	5.6	8.1‡
	Portugal	6.8†	6	6.4	7.8‡

Notes: Franchise = percentage of adult population eligible to vote. Electoral fairness is an index ranging from 0 to 1 (fair elections). * Also includes Australia, New Zealand, and Cyprus, but excludes the German Democratic Republic. † 1850–1909; ‡ 1975–2007. The Historical Index of Economic Liberty varies from 0 to 10 (maximum economic liberty).
Sources: Varieties of Democracy (V-Dem) dataset available at www.v-dem.net and Prados de la Escosura (2016b).

promoting political stability than economic growth, however, and was replaced from the late 1950s by a progressive reopening to the international economy, which, together with large-scale public investment in infrastructure, ushered in one of the fastest convergence periods of the two economies (Figure 25.5).

This spread of relative economic prosperity (added to the burden of a long-drawn-out colonial war in the case of Portugal) weakened the political coalitions supporting the regimes and led, in the mid-1970s, to a bloodless democratic transition. The period since has been dominated by the process of European integration, which allowed a second burst of economic growth and convergence until the introduction of the Euro. The 'European lottery' was equally important as a means of consolidating the two Iberian democracies, which finally committed to free elections, the rule of law and a market economy in expectation of joining the EEC in 1986. The last rows in Table 25.5 report the averages of an index of economic liberty compiled by Prados de la Escosura (2016b) for 21 OECD economies since 1850. The progress on this measure has been remarkable since the 1970s as the two Iberian nations transitioned to open access orders. Nevertheless, their rank in the same group of nations has barely changed over the long period. In the last year with data, 2007, Portugal and Spain still ranked 20th and 18th, respectively, among the 21 nations. Similarly, in the latest vintage (2019) of the corruption perception index, compiled by the NGO Transparency International, the two Iberian countries still rank midway among European nations, though better than other comparable democracies such as Italy and Greece. Even after more than four decades of democracy, the two countries continue to face challenges in living up to the expectations of an open access order.

25.5 First and Second Nature Geography

The role of geography in economic performance can be analysed using the distinction between first and second nature geography. First nature geography covers natural endowments such as mineral deposits, soil quality or climate, while second nature geography covers human-made factors such as access to markets and agglomeration economies. First nature geography has traditionally featured heavily in explanations of the lagging performance of Spain and Portugal behind the richer core European economies during the nineteenth century and the first half of the twentieth. The Iberian Peninsula has a Mediterranean climate, with scarce and irregular rainfall, leading to arid soil that tends to generate low yields with cereal crops, but is better suited to vineyards and olive groves. The dry conditions also limited the availability of pastureland, leading to the development of transhumance or nomadic sheep farming to exploit the lowland pastures of the south during winter and the mountainous northern regions during the summer. While it is possible to see these conditions as limiting the response of Iberian farmers to the innovations of the agricultural revolution that occurred in north-west Europe during the eighteenth and nineteenth centuries, geared to heavy clay soils and mixed arable and livestock farming, it is also clearly the case that Iberian agriculture managed to overcome these constraints during the second half of the twentieth century.

A similar argument has already been noted concerning the performance of Iberian industry, where it is possible to see natural resource constraints such as lack of coal and iron as a major constraint holding back the process of industrialization following the innovations of the British Industrial Revolution. But again, this argument becomes less persuasive when it is placed against the dramatic period of industrial catching up by Spain and Portugal during the second half of the twentieth century.

Part of the reason for the slow adaptation of Iberian agriculture and industry to the innovations of north-west European agriculture and industry may be found in institutional factors, as noted in the previous section. However, there may also be a role for second nature geography, with catching up delayed until the increased integration of the Iberian Peninsula with the rest of the European continent from the 1950s. Spain and Portugal saw some domestic and international market integration during the nineteenth century, with the spread of railways and the growth of exports. However, the Iberian Peninsula remained peripheral to the European core, with Spanish and Portuguese exports growing more slowly than in the European core (Belgium, Denmark, France, Germany, the Netherlands, Switzerland and the UK) during the nineteenth century and at about the same reduced rate during the interwar period.

Recently, a new literature has arisen, emphasizing the importance of second nature geography (Krugman & Venables, 1995). The basic idea here is that when trade costs are high, industrial production has to occur close to the market, so that industry is spread fairly evenly around the world. As trade costs fall, however, it becomes possible to supply consumption of industrial goods through trade rather than local production, and in a world of agglomeration economies this naturally tends to happen. Thus, as transport costs fall from a high level to an intermediate level, this results in the industrialization of core countries with high productivity and wages, and deindustrialization in peripheral countries with low productivity and wages. However, as trade costs fall further still, the penalty for being in a location remote from the large markets and suppliers in the core regions is reduced, and eventually it becomes possible for industry to spread out from the established centres to some more peripheral regions to take advantage of the lower wages. Agglomeration economies in these formerly peripheral locations then tend to raise productivity and wages, producing a process of convergence of per capita income levels.

Falling trade costs during the nineteenth century may thus have reinforced Spain and Portugal's resource disadvantages, leading to a specialization in primary rather than secondary products, which preserved the relative backwardness of the Iberian economies within the European economy. Similarly, the further reduction in transport costs from the 1950s may be seen as allowing the Iberian Peninsula to become more integrated within the European economy as an exporter of industrial goods. This interpretation seems to be consistent with the international trade data analysed by Tena-Junguito, Federico and Silva (Chapter 24). The revealed comparative advantage of Spain and Portugal in the late nineteenth century was decisively in primary products, especially food, with a switch to industrial manufactured goods occurring only later. Portugal's index of revealed comparative advantage became positive in consumer manufactured goods and semi-manufactured goods from the 1940s and in equipment goods from the 1990s. In Spain, a similar shift in revealed comparative advantage occurred, but a higher level of disaggregation allows Federico, Tena and Silva to identify an earlier positive revealed comparative advantage index in textiles around the turn of the nineteenth century, which persisted in the second half of the twentieth century.

Spain's revealed comparative advantage index became positive in semi-manufactured goods from the 1970s and in equipment goods from the 1990s.

This second nature geography interpretation of Iberian economic performance is consistent with the changing regional distribution of GDP per capita in Figure 25.6, taken from Herranz-Loncán, Sanchis-Llopis and Tirado-Fabregat (Chapter 18). This is based on a series of maps presented by Tirado-Fabregat and Badia-Miró (2014) showing the shifting distribution at 20-year intervals between 1900 and 2000. In a grey scale representing the quartiles of the GDP per capita distribution, the darkest regions have the highest per capita incomes, while the lightest regions have the lowest per capita incomes. The 1900 snapshot in Figure 25.6(a) shows how the richest regions were fairly evenly spread geographically. There were poor and rich regions in all parts of both Spain and Portugal, with many regions at intermediate levels of per capita income. By 2000, however, the snapshot in Figure 25.6(b) paints a very different picture, with the richest regions highly concentrated in the north-east quadrant of the Iberian Peninsula. Other rich regions were concentrated in the coastal areas, leaving the poorest regions concentrated in the interior areas of the south and west. The very poorest regions were concentrated on both sides of the border between Spain and Portugal. This group had its roots in the first half of the twentieth century but was consolidated during the second half of the century as Iberia became more integrated into the European economy.

The Krugman and Venables (1995) model helps to explain this shifting pattern of regional income distribution. The Iberian economies specialized according to their comparative advantage in primary products and food and drink during the nineteenth century globalization as falling transport costs favoured the concentration of industrial production in the core economies of north-west Europe. As transport costs fell further during the second wave of globalization from the 1950s, however, Spain and Portugal were able to develop a full range of industrial capabilities, shifting comparative advantage away from primary products to a wider range of consumer manufactured goods, semi-manufactured goods and equipment goods. However, we have also noted that services have come to play an increasingly important role in recent decades, and the growth of tourism can surely be seen as helping to explain the relatively high-income levels in the Balearic Islands and along the south-east coast of Spain.

One other aspect of second nature geography that deserves attention is the effects of Latin American independence on nineteenth-century Spain and Portugal. The colonial system provided tariff revenue, commercial re-exports and monopolies in transportation and finance which were lost after independence. The independence of the Spanish colonies during and after the Napoleonic Wars had a sizeable impact on market access, with Prados de la Escosura (1988: 72) showing that while total Spanish exports fell by around 25% between 1784/1796 and 1815/1820, colonial trade fell by as much as 40%.

IBERIAN ECONOMY IN COMPARATIVE PERSPECTIVE, 1800–2000

(a)
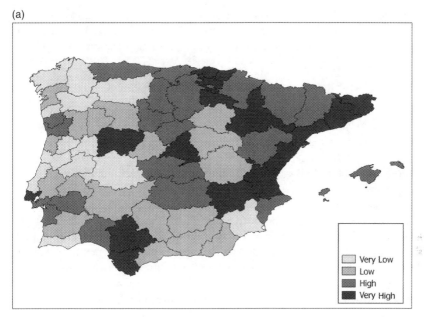

(b)
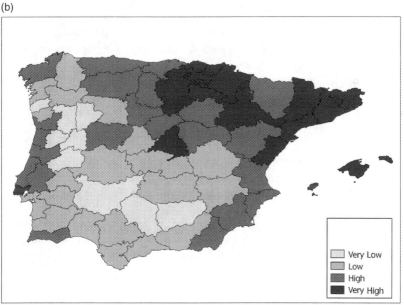

Figure 25.6 GDP per capita in Iberian regions, relative to the average: (a) 1900; (b) 2000.
Note: Different grey intensities indicate the GDP per capita distribution of Spanish provinces and Portuguese districts by quartiles (darker grey represents higher GDP per capita).
Source: Herranz-Loncán, Sanchis-Llopis and Tirado-Fabregat (Chapter 18), based on maps published in Tirado Fabregat and Badia-Miró (2014).

The decline of Portuguese exports to Brazil after independence was less steep, and the market access effects were offset by Portugal's relationship with the UK, which absorbed more than half of all Portuguese exports by the mid-nineteenth century.

25.6 Consequences of Growth

After surveying the trends in aggregate GDP over time and in comparative terms, it is important to understand how economic growth translated into the well-being of the Iberian populations. Using the proverbial metaphor, the glass here is half-full or half-empty, depending on which indicators we use.

Today's Iberians are certainly wealthier and healthier than their forebears. The data collected by Díez-Minguela, Guilera and Martínez-Galarraga (Chapter 23) consistently point to increasing living standards since the nineteenth century. Iberian households spent a progressively smaller share of their incomes on basic needs (especially food), and each new generation (barring war periods) added to the life expectancy of the population. Indeed, the Portuguese and Spanish are now among the populations with the highest life expectancy. Rising income levels are certainly behind this progress, but so are universal health care systems operating in both nations since the 1970s.

Puzzlingly, no such progress is evident in the median heights of the population, which are often taken as a portmanteau indicator of biological standards of living. Despite the radical changes in standards of living and economic structure that traversed the Iberian nations since the nineteenth century, median heights increased at a disappointing rate in the two nations, so much so that the gap with the rest of Western Europe has remained the same or even increased since the mid-nineteenth century. The literature has proposed several explanations for this outcome ranging from a relatively late industrialization to inequality, though biology may also be a factor.

More worrying are the trends in inequality, especially since the 1980s, when inequality has trended upward in most developed nations. Díez-Minguela, Guilera and Martínez-Galarraga (Chapter 23) find that the long-term behaviour of income inequality in Spain broadly confirms Kuznets's inverted U curve, whereby inequality increased in the early stages of modern economic growth and later fell as the fruits of growth were more evenly distributed, particularly through structural transformation that released large swathes of the labour force from low-productivity agricultural employment. The authors are intrigued about Portugal, however, as the country appears to follow a trend of rising inequality since the 1920s until today, only interrupted by the fast economic growth of the 1960s and 1970s. However, it is unclear whether we can draw any conclusion about Portugal, since the disaggregated data on Portuguese incomes necessary to calculate the Gini index only start in the 1920s, precisely. In any case, it is hard to imagine a pre-1920 egalitarian economy in Portugal, considering what is known in terms of land tenure and real wages for the period. The authors duly relate the observed changes in the Gini index and other inequality measures over time to the main hypotheses in the literature, namely, globalization, policy and skill-biased technical change. In the Iberian case, globalization helped to reduce inequality in income through two mechanisms that bid up unskilled wages: the Stolper–Samuelson effect of international trade and the high flows of emigration in the late nineteenth century and the 1960s and 1970s (see Figure 25.5). Economic policy left its marks as well, either through the protectionism that increased income inequality after 1890, and especially during the autarkic phase of the Iberian dictatorships, or through the creation of a welfare state and redistributive taxation after the transition to democracy.

The skill bias in the technologies of the 'third industrial revolution' is probably the most convincing explanation for the return of higher inequality in the Western world since the 1970s and also in the Iberian economies (Acemoglu, 2002). Much attention has been pored over this issue, especially as the new wave of technical change (AI and robotization) threatens to replace all manner of workers, not just unskilled ones. While these changes threaten long-held perceptions about inter-personal equity and the distribution of the fruits of economic growth, another issue, perhaps more pressing, strains the bonds of inter-generational equity. Now that anthropogenic climate change is universally recognized, economies and societies will have to adapt to avoid bequeathing a possibly catastrophic environmental dividend to future generations. Uncertainty about future scenarios is still rife, though, and more reflection on this is better left to a future edition of this book.

25.7 Macroeconomic Fluctuations and Policy

Built on the long-term growth trends of Figure 25.1 there were cyclical fluctuations that interrupted growth trajectories, sometimes for long periods. As small and mostly open economies, the Iberian nations were not immune to the overarching fluctuations in the world economy, bookended by major systemic crises or policy regimes. For this reason, it makes sense to organize the history of Iberian business cycles in five main sub-periods. Table 25.6 summarizes some stylized facts about macro policy and business cycles in the two nations in 1870–2007.

To begin with, the currencies of the two nations largely followed international monetary arrangements, with steady pegs to the US dollar in the Bretton Woods period, followed by using the Deutschmark as nominal anchor. Prior to joining the Euro, both nations found it easier to import price stability by holding a peg against more credible monetary authorities. Both countries were forced off a stable peg by the collapse of the gold exchange standard in the interwar period, but Portugal was also an early member of the gold standard

Table 25.6 *Macroeconomic policy and imbalances.*
(a) Spain

Period	1870–1913	1914–1945	1946–1973	1974–1985	1986–2007
Pegs§	0/44	6/32	24/28	12/12	22/22
Inflation	0.3%	3.3%	6.0%	14.8%	3.8%
Average credit growth	7.7%	6.8%	10.0%	0.2%	7.8%
Inv rate	6.4%	10.7%	19.1%	22.2%	24.7%
CA	0.3%	0.5%	−0.5%	−1.6%	−3.3%
Budget balance	−0.7%	−1.5%	−0.3%	−2.7%	−2.3%
Correlations					
CA and inv rate	0.29	0.10	0.03	−0.77***	−0.94**
CA and budget bal	0.33**	0.44	−0.08	−0.58**	−0.86***

(b) Portugal

Period	1870–1913	1914–1945	1946–1973	1974–1985	1986–2007
Pegs§	21/44	6/32	27/28	5/12	22/22
Inflation	0.6%	9.0%	2.1%	20.8%	4.8%
Average credit growth	1.5%	6.4%	9.1%	0.5%	9.1%
Inv rate		6.2%	25.0%	30.6%	25.6%
CA	−2.1%	−6.7%	−1.6%	−5.3%	−4.8%
Budget balance	−0.7%	−1.8%	−0.9%	−6.7%	−5.0%
Correlations					
CA and inv rate		0.06	.53*	−0.45	0.31
CA and budget bal		0.57**	0.53**	−0.26	−0.41

Notes: § Number of years in a peg out of total years. *** (**) significant at 1% (5%). Average credit growth in real terms per annum. CA = current account (as percentage of GDP). Inv rate = investment rate (as percentage of GDP).
Sources: Batista et al. (1997) and Jordà et al. (2017).

(joined in 1854), until it left during a systemic financial crisis in 1890–1892. Remarkably, Spain was one of the few nations that never joined the classical gold standard. Martin-Aceña and Sousa (Chapter 21) explain this with the resistance of the Bank of Spain, a private company, to take on the responsibilities of a central bank, particularly, the money-losing burden of defending the gold parity of the currency by keeping a large gold reserve. Similar conflicts played out between the government and the Bank of Portugal, but the latter was able to extract sufficient compensation from the government for acting as a central banker, be it by defending the peg or providing liquidity to the banking sector during crises (Reis, 2007; Esteves et al. 2009). Both institutions were de facto nationalized in the 1930s and slowly adopted the trappings of modern central banks until their incorporation in the Eurosystem in 1999.

This monetary stance translated into different growth rates of credit since, unfettered by a peg, the Spanish banking sector extended credit to the real economy before 1914 at a much faster rate than its Portuguese equivalent. Credit also grew especially fast during the Bretton Woods period as part of the developmental agenda of the dictatorial governments on both sides of the border. After a pause caused by the financial and macro imbalances of the 1970s, credit growth recovered, especially following entry into the European communities. Gross investment rates (as a percentage of GDP) also trended upward from relatively low levels pre-war to over a fifth of GDP, pulled by the forces of growth, convergence and specialization, once both economies started reopening to international trade in the 1960s. In the last two periods, investment decoupled from domestic credit growth, implying a greater access to foreign investment, which is confirmed by the scale of current account deficits.

Across all periods, the possibilities of growth in both economies were either limited by their domestic savings (and the ability of the financial sector to mobilize them) or by their ability to fund a current account deficit. Figure 25.7 compares the growth in bank credit in Spain and Portugal to the contemporary trend in the 17 advanced economies surveyed by Jordà et al. (2017). From modest beginnings, the Iberian banking sector quickly converged or even superseded the average share of credit in GDP after the Second World War. This growth was almost exclusively concentrated in credit to businesses and was reversed in Spain after the 1977 systemic crisis, when non-performing loans to companies brought down more than half of Spanish banks (see Chapter 21). In Portugal, the retrenchment came six years later, mandated by an IMF adjustment programme in exchange for averting a financial crisis.

Figure 25.7 shows how other systemic crises were preceded by excessive credit growth, the more salient being the Global Financial Crisis that hit Iberian banks from 2008. By then the banking sector had outgrown the average size of banks in the 17 advanced economies, only to be forced to reverse back to this benchmark through a new wave of bank failures or forced mergers and the write-down of non-performing assets. The novelty in this crisis was the importance of credit to families, mostly driven by mortgages that inflated a large housing bubble in the two nations.

Even though it is fair to say that both Portugal and Spain have had bank-based financial systems, we should not ignore the development of their capital markets. Though growing much slower than its peers in Europe, market capitalization reached close to a third of GDP in both Portugal and Spain by

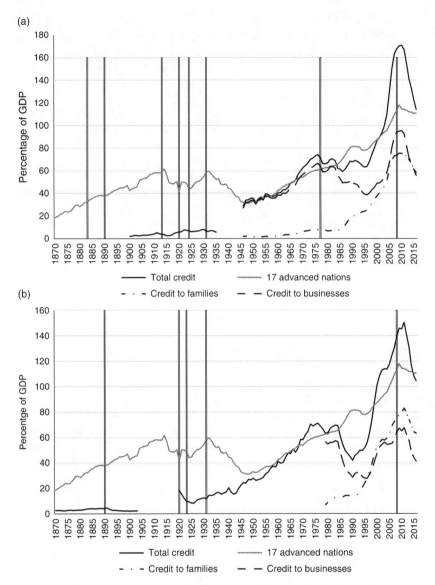

Figure 25.7 Growth of the credit system, 1870–2016: (a) Spain; (b) Portugal.
Sources: Credit to non-financial sector and its components from Jordà et al. (2017).
Vertical lines mark systemic financial crises as defined by Jordà et al. (2017).

the early 1970s (Kuvshinov & Zimmermann, 2020). Even though the markets were almost wiped out by the Portuguese nationalizations and the 1977 financial crisis in Spain, they recovered with financial openness in the 1990s, reaching another maximum in the 2000s (two thirds of GDP). The Great Financial Crisis of 2008–2009 then took the wind out of the sails of the Iberian stock markets, once more.

Throughout the period, fiscal policy was only moderately counter-cyclical given that the two nations were late adopters of Keynesianism, as described by Cardoso and Comín (Chapter 20). Only after the transition to democracy in the 1970s did governments commit to the entitlements and relief programmes of the social welfare state. On top of this, limited domestic savings soon led governments to borrow abroad, often in foreign currencies, which added an external constraint to their ability to spend. This problem of 'twin deficits' was responsible for the 1890 crisis that forced Portugal off the gold standard and into its last external default. The positive correlations between current account deficits and budget balances until the 1970s confirm this external constraint (Table 25.6). The correlation turned negative in the last two sub-periods as firms and families started borrowing abroad, while governments had to keep their deficits under the Maastricht limits. This also explains the negative correlation between domestic investment rates and current account deficits, at least in Spain. In Portugal, the lack of correlation is due to the greater weight of consumption credit granted to families by domestic banks that funded themselves abroad, especially in the Eurozone.

25.8 Conclusions

In the early 1960s, the Spanish tourist board came up with the slogan 'Spain is different'. Not quite European and somewhat exotic, the slogan was supposed not only to attract tourists from Europe and the USA but also help with rebranding the country away from its recent past of civil war and association with the Axis powers. In 1965, the Portuguese dictator reacted to international criticism of the ongoing colonial war in Africa by stating that Portugal stood 'proudly alone'. As in the case of the UK, imperial links and perhaps cultural differences appeared to offer an alternative to deeper integration with the European economy. At different points, the two nations embarked on autarkic development plans or tried growing by building an overseas economic area. And yet, two centuries worth of evidence show that trying to fight economic geography was not in the Iberian nations' favour. The two relatively small economies were only able to make significant strides in terms of convergence of standards of living and lowering inequality when they opened up to international trade, capital and migration. The 1960s and the pre-Euro integration in the European communities, in particular, stand to date as the fastest growth periods in the history of both nations.

To be sure, both nations faced other obstacles to growth – in terms of endowments, the modest size of their internal markets and savings, and the inefficient distribution of property they had inherited from the *Ancien Régime*. Notwithstanding, none of these were set in stone but were endogenous to the growth process itself. This led the authors of Part III to look for deeper explanations for the economic retardation and late industrialization of the Peninsula. Institutions and the political equilibria that underpin them loom large here. Political history is the dimension where the peninsula is indeed 'different' from its European neighbours. After a century of fragile liberal monarchies and radical republican regimes, the two Iberian nations stood out for their long-lasting authoritarian regimes. While taking a cue from other contemporary authoritarian regimes (Italian Fascism, above all), the two dictatorships were not cut short by the Second World War, as elsewhere in Europe. The inward-looking economic policies promoted by the dictators since the 1930s favoured domestic incumbents in farming and industry but harmed the long-term growth potential of the two countries. Only the gradual reopening of the economies from the 1960s unleashed, as mentioned, this potential.

And yet, the fruits of growth through openness are not equally distributed today as they were not in the 1920s or 1930s. Despite a successful integration in the European Communities, the two nations have entered the new millennium with a weaker growth outlook (in the case of Portugal), or an unbalanced growth built on real estate speculation (Spain). The Global Financial Crisis then exposed the economic and financial imbalances built by the two economies since the 1990s. The introduction of the Euro is clearly connected to these developments and led to a renewed debate about the need for a 'fiscal union' to complement the monetary union. This has long been resisted by some member countries as a 'transfer union'. However, the need for a European-wide fiscal instrument that transcended individual countries' fiscal spaces was finally made obvious by the Covid-19 pandemic, which, though exogenous, was especially punishing for countries such as Spain and Italy. It is clear that the future of economic growth and political stability in Iberia and elsewhere in Europe will depend on the successful use of the EU's new-fangled fiscal power.

REFERENCES

Abadal, R. (1926). *Catalunya carolíngia. Els diplomes carolingis a Catalunya*, vol. 1. Geneve, Barcelona: Institució Patxot de Catalunya.
Abadal, R. (1952). *Catalunya carolíngia. Els diplomes carolingis a Catalunya*, vol. 2. Geneve, Barcelona: Institució Patxot de Catalunya.
Abadía Irache, A. (1998). *La enajenación de rentas señoriales en el reino de Aragón*. Zaragoza: Institución Fernando el Católico.
Abadía Irache, A. (2017). El régimen señorial en Aragón en la Edad Moderna. In J. Arrieta, X. Gil & J. Morales, eds., *La diadema de Rey. Vizcaya, Navarra, Aragón y Cerdeña en la Monarquía de España (siglos XVI–XVIII)*. Bilbao: Universidad del País Vasco, pp. 449–566.
Abd Allāh. (1980). *El siglo XI en primera persona, Las memorias de 'Abd Allāh, último rey zirí de Granada, destronado por los almorávides (1090)*. E. García Gómez & É. Lévi-Provençal, Spanish trans. Madrid: Alianza Tres.
Abramovitz, M. (1986). Catching-up, forging ahead and falling behind. *Journal of Economic History*, 46, 385–406.
Abramovitz, M. & David, P. (2001). Two centuries of American Macroeconomic growth from exploitation of resource abundance to knowledge-driven development. *SIEPR Discussion Paper*, 01–05.
Abreu, L. (1990). *A Santa Casa da Misericórdia de Setúbal de 1500 a 1755: aspectos de sociabilidade e poder*. Setúbal (ed. Santa Casa da Misericórdia de Setúbal).
Abreu, L. (2016). *The Political and Social Dynamics of Poverty, Poor Relief and Health Care in Early-Modern Portugal*. London: Routledge.
Abulafia, D. (2002). *A Mediterranean Emporium: The Catalan Kingdom of Majorca*. Cambridge: Cambridge University Press.
Abulafia, D. (2008). Sugar in Spain. *European Review*, 16(2), 191–210.
Abulafia, D. & Garí, B. (1996). *En las costas del Mediterráneo occidental: las ciudades de la Península Ibérica y del reino de Mallorca y el comercio mediterráneo en la Edad Media*. Barcelona: Ediciones Omega.
Acemoglu, D. (2002). Technical change, inequality, and the labor market. *Journal of Economic Literature*, 40(1), 7–72.
Acemoglu, D., Johnson, S. & Robinson, J. (2005). The rise of Europe: Atlantic trade, institutional change and economic growth. *American Economic Review*, 95(3), 546–579.
Acemoglu, D. & Robinson, J. (2012). *Why Nations Fail: The Origins of Power, Prosperity, and Poverty*. New York: Crown.

Aguado de los Reyes, J. (1996). La mujer y la riqueza en la Sevilla del barroco. In D. Ramos Palomo & M. T. Vera Balanza, eds., *El trabajo de las mujeres, pasado y presente: Actas del Congreso Internacional del Seminario de Estudios Interdisciplinarios de la Mujer*, vol. 1. Málaga: Diputación de Málaga-Universidad de Málaga, pp. 91–104.

Aguiar, A. & Martins, M. M. F. (2005). A indústria. In P. Lains & Á. Ferreira da Silva, eds., *História Económica de Portugal: 1700–2000*, vol. III. Lisbon: Imprensa de Ciências Sociais, pp. 259–282.

Aguilera López, J. (2018). La maestranza de las Atarazanas Reales de Barcelona durante el siglo XVI. *Pedralbes: Revista d'història moderna*, 38, 51–85.

Albareda Salvadó, J. (2012). El debate sobre la modernidad del reformismo borbónico, *Revista HMiC: Història Moderna i Contemporània*, 10, 6–19.

Alden, D. (1987). Late colonial Brazil, 1750–1808. In L. Bethell, ed., *Colonial Brazil*. Cambridge: Cambridge University Press, pp. 284–343.

Alegria, M. F. (1990). *A Organização dos Transportes em Portugal. As Vias e o Tráfego*, Lisbon: Centro de Estudos Geográficos.

Alencastro, L. F. de (2007). The economic network of Portugal's Atlantic world. In F. Bethencourt & D. R. Curto, eds., *Portuguese Oceanic Expansion, 1400–1800*. Cambridge: Cambridge University Press, pp. 109–137.

Alfani, G. (2019). Wealth and income inequality in the long run of history. In C. Diebolt & M. Haupert, eds., *Handbook of Cliometrics*. Berlin: Springer-Verlag, pp. 1173–1201.

Alfani, G. & di Tullio, M. (2019). *The Lion's Share: Inequality and the Rise of the Fiscal State in Preindustrial Europe*. Cambridge: Cambridge University Press.

Alfonso Antón, I. (1982). Sobre la organización del terrazgo en Tierra de Campos durante la Edad Media. *Agricultura y sociedad*, 23, 217–232.

Alfonso Mola, M. (2002). The Spanish colonial fleet (1492–1828). In H. Pietschmann, ed., *Atlantic History: History of the Atlantic System 1580–1830*. Göttingen: Vandenhoeck & Ruprecht, pp. 365–374.

Allen, R. C. (1988). The growth of labor productivity in early modern English agriculture. *Explorations in Economic History*, 25(2), 117–146.

Allen, R. C. (2003). Progress and poverty in early modern Europe. *The Economic History Review*, 56(3), 403–443.

Allen, R. C. (2005). Real wages in Europe and Asia: a first look at the long-term patterns. In R. C. Allen, T. Bengtsson & M. Dribe, eds., *Living Standards in the Past. New Perspectives on Well-Being in Asia and Europe*. Oxford: Oxford University Press.

Allen, R. C. (2009). Engels' pause: technical change, capital accumulation, and inequality in the British Industrial Revolution. *Explorations in Economic History*, 46(4), 418–435.

Allen, R. C. (2017). Absolute poverty: when necessity displaces desire. *American Economic Review*, 107(12), 3690–3721.

Allen, R. C., Murphy, T. E. & Schneider, E.B. (2012). The colonial origins of the divergence in the Americas: a labor market approach. *The Journal of Economic History*, 72(4), 863–894.

Almeida, O. T. (2018). *O Século dos Prodígios. A Ciência no Portugal da Expansão*. Lisbon: Quetzal.

Almeida, P. Tavares (1991). *Eleições e Caciquismo no Portugal Oitocentista (1868–1890)*. Lisbon: Difel.

Almeida, V. & Félix, R. (2006). Computing potential output and output gap for the Portuguese economy. *Economic Bulletin and Financial Stability Report and Banco de Portugal Economic Studies*, 73–88.

Almodovar, A. & Cardoso, J. L. (2005). Corporatism and the economic role of Government. *History of Political Economy*, 37(Suppl. 1), 333–354.

Alvaredo, F., Atkinson, A., Piketty, T. & Saez, E. (2013). The top 1 percent in international and historical perspective. *Journal of Economic Perspectives*, 27(3), 3–20.

Alvaredo, F. & Saez, E. (2009). Income and wealth concentration in Spain in a historical and fiscal perspective. *Journal of the European Economic Association*, 7(5), 1140–1167.

Álvarez, A., Ariza, M. & Mendoza, J. (2001). *Un padrón de Sevilla del siglo XIV. Estudio filológico y edición*. Seville: Ayuntamiento de Sevilla.

Álvarez, B. & Ramos-Palencia, F. (2018). Human capital and earnings in eighteenth-century Castile. *Explorations in Economic History*, 67(1), 105–133.

Álvarez Borge, I. (2003). *La Plena Edad Media*. Madrid: Síntesis.

Álvarez Borge, I. (2016). Patrimonio, rentas y poder de la nobleza bajomedieval peninsular. In *Discurso, memoria y representación: la nobleza peninsular en la Baja Edad Media*. XLII Semana de Estudios Medievales de Estella. Pamplona: Gobierno de Navarra, pp. 83–140.

Álvarez de Cienfuegos Campos, I. (1958). Sobre la economía en el reino naṣrī granadino. *Miscelánea de Estudios Árabes y Hebraicos*, VIII(1), 85–97.

Álvarez-Nogal, C. (2005). Incentivos económicos y derechos de propiedad en la Castilla del siglo XVI. *Cuadernos económicos de ICE*, 70, 77–96.

Álvarez-Nogal, C. (2009). *Oferta y demanda de deuda pública en Castilla. Juros de Alcabalas (1540–1740)*. Madrid: Banco de España.

Álvarez-Nogal, C. (2017). Los bancos públicos de Castilla y el decreto de 1575. *Cuadernos de Historia Moderna*, 42(2), 527–551.

Álvarez-Nogal, C. & Chamley, C. (2014). Debt policy under constraints: Philip II, the Cortes and Genoese bankers. *Economic History Review*, 67(1), 192–213.

Álvarez-Nogal, C. & Chamley, C. (2016). Philip II against the Cortes and the Credit Freeze of 1575–1577. *Revista de Historia Economica – Journal of Iberian and Latin American Economic History*, 34(3), 351–382.

Álvarez-Nogal, C. & Chamley, C. (2018). Refinancing short-term debt with a fixed monthly interest rate into funded juros under Philip II: an asiento with the Maluenda brothers. *Economic History Review*, 71(4), 1100–1117.

Álvarez-Nogal, C. & Prados de la Escosura, L. (2007a). The decline of Spain (1500–1850): conjectural estimates. *European Review of Economic History*, 11, 319–366.

Álvarez-Nogal, C. & Prados de la Escosura, L. (2007b). Searching for the roots of retardation: Spain in European perspective, 1500–1850. *Carlos III Working Paper in Economic History*, 07–06.

Álvarez-Nogal, C. & Prados de la Escosura, L. (2013). The rise and fall of Spain (1270–1850). *The Economic History Review*, 66(1), 1–37.

Álvarez-Nogal, C., Prados de la Escosura, L. & Santiago-Caballero, C. (2016). Spanish Agriculture in the Little Divergence. *European Review of Economic History*, 20(4), 452–477.

Álvarez-Nogal, C., Prados de la Escosura, L. & Santiago-Caballero, C. (2020). Economic effects of the Black Death: Spain in European perspective. *Investigaciones de Historia Económica*, 16(4), 35–48.

Álvarez-Ossorio Alvariño, A. (2016). Del reino al palacio real: la negociación del embajador de la ciudad de Nápoles en la Corte de Carlos II. *Revista de Historia Moderna*, 42, 9–34.

Álvarez Vázquez, J. A. (1987). *Rentas, Precios y Crédito en Zamora en el Antiguo Régimen*. Zamora: Colegio Universitario de Zamora.

Amador, J. & Coimbra, C. (2007). Characteristics of the Portuguese economic growth: What has been missing? *Estudos e Documentos de Trabalho Working Papers*, 8.

Amaral, L. (1998). Convergência e crescimento económico em Portugal no pós-guerra. *Análise Social*, 33(148), 741–776.

Amaral, L. (2002). How a country catches up: explaining economic growth in Portugal in the post-war period (1950s to 1973). PhD thesis, European University Institute.

Amaral, L. (2009). New Series of Portuguese population and employment, 1950–2007: implications for GDP per capita and labor productivity, *Análise Social*, XLIV (193), 767–791.

Amaral, L. (2010a). *A Economia Portuguesa. As Últimas Décadas*. Lisbon: Fundação Francisco Manuel dos Santos.

Amaral, L. (2010b). The state and the economy: economic growth and structural change in Taiwan and Portugal, *Économies et Sociétés*, 6(44), 1095–1126.

Amaral, L. (2012). Institutions, property and economic growth: back to the passage from ancien régime to liberalism in Portugal. *Análise Social*, LXVII(4), 28–55.

Amaral, L. (2013). Imperfect but true competition: innovation and profitability in Portuguese banking during the golden age (1950–1973). *Financial History Review*, 20(3), 305–333.

Amaral, L. (2015a). O processo económico. In A. C. Pinto, ed., *História Contemporânea de Portugal, vol. V. Em Busca da Democracia, 1960-2000*. Lisbon: Objectiva, pp. 81–110.

Amaral, L. (2015b). Measuring competition in Portuguese commercial banking during the Golden Age (1960–1973). *Business History*, 57(8), 1192–1218.

Amaral, L. (2018). A monetary plethora and what to do with it: the Bank of Portugal during the Second World War and the Post War period (1931–1960). *Economic History Review*, 71(3), 795–822.

Amaral, L. (2019). *The Modern Portuguese Economy in the Twentieth and Twenty-First Centuries*. Cham, Switzerland: Palgrave Macmillan.

Amaral, L. & Freire, D. (2017). Agricultural policy, growth and demise, 1930-2000. In D. Freire & P. Lains, eds., *An Agrarian History of Portugal, 1000-2000: Economic Development on the European Frontier*. Leiden: Brill, pp. 245-276.

Amasuno Sárraga, M.V. (1996). *La Peste en la Corona de Castilla durante la segunda mitad del siglo XIV*. Salamanca: Junta de Castilla y León.

Amendola, N. (2017). Inequality. In G. Vecchi, ed., *Measuring Wellbeing: A History of Italian Living Standards*. Oxford: Oxford University Press.

Amorim, M. Norberta (2004). Comportamentos demográficos de Antigo Regime na Península Ibérica. *Ler História*, 47, 147-170.

Amorim, M. Norberta, Silva, C. Guardado da & Silva, P. Correia da (2016). Microanálise de longa duração em demografia urbana: Santa Maria de Torres Vedras entre os séculos XVII e XX. *Revista de Guimarães*, 120-121, 129-156.

Andrade, A. A. & Miranda, F. (2017). Lisbon. Trade, urban power and the king's visible hand. In W. Blockmans, M. Krom & J. Wubs-Mrosewicz, eds., *The Routledge Handbook of Maritime Trade Around Europe 1300-1600*. London and New York: Routledge, pp. 333-351.

Andrés Ucendo, J. I. (1999). *La fiscalidad en Castilla en el siglo XVII: los servicios de millones, 1601-1700*. Bilbao: Universidad del País Vasco-EHU.

Andrés Ucendo, J. I. & Lanza García, R. (2009). Estructura y evolución de los ingresos de la Real Hacienda de Castilla en el siglo XVII. *Studia Historica. Historia moderna*, 30, 147-190.

Andrés Ucendo, J. I. & Lanza García, R. (2014). Prices and real wages in seventeenth century Madrid. *Economic History Review*, 67(3), 607-626.

Andújar, F. & Felices, M. del M. (2007). Nobleza y venalidad: el mercado eclesiástico de venta de titulos nobiliarios durante el siglo XVIII. *Chronica Nova*, 33, 131-153.

Anes Alvarez, G. (1970). *Las crisis agrarias en la España moderna*. Madrid: Taurus.

Anes Alvarez, G. (1974). Antecedentes próximos del motín contra Esquilache. *Moneda y Crédito*, 128, 219-224.

Anes Alvarez, G. (1988). *Economía y sociedad en la Asturias del antiguo régimen*. Barcelona: Ariel.

Ansón Calvo, M. del C. (1977). *Demografía y sociedad urbana en la Zaragoza del siglo XVII*. Zaragoza: Caja de Ahorros de Zaragoza, Aragón y Rioja.

Antúnes, C. & Polónia, A. (2016). *Beyond Empires: Global, Self-Organizing, Cross-Imperial Networks, 1500-1800*. Leiden and Boston, MA: Brill.

Antunes, C., Salvado, J. P. & Post, R. (2016). Het omzeilen van monopoliehandel: smokkel en belastingontduiking bij de handel in brazielhout, 1500-1674. *Tijdschrift voor Sociale en Economische Geschiedenis*, 13(1), 23-52.

Aram, B. & Yun-Casalilla, B., eds. (2014). *Global Goods and the Spanish Empire, 1492-1824. Circulation, Resistance and Diversity*. London: Palgrave.

Ardit Lucas, M. (1991). Un ensayo de proyección inversa de la población valenciana (1610-1899). *Boletín de la Asociación de Demografía Histórica*, IX(3), 27-47.

Ardit Lucas, M. (1997). Una societat agrária. In B. de Riquer, ed., *Crisi institucional i canvi social. Segles XVI i XVII. Història, política, societat i cultura dels Països Catalans*. Barcelona: Enciclopèdia Catalana, pp. 90-103.

Argilés, C. (2010). *Una ciutat catalana en època de crisi: Lleida, 1358-1500: El treball, els salaris, la producció agrícola i els preus a través dels llibres d'obra de la Seu Vella*. Lleida: Institut d'Estudis Ilerdencs – Diputació de Lleida.

Arié, R. (1965). Quelques remarques sur le costume des Musulmans d'Espagne au temps des Nasrides. *Arabica*, 12(3), 244-261.

Arié, R. (1977). La vie économique dans l'Espagne musulmane. *Handbuch der Orientalistic*, 239-254.

Arié, R. (1992). *El reino nasrí de Granada*. Madrid: Mapfre.

Armenteros Martínez, I. (2012). *Cataluña en la era de las navegaciones: La participación catalana en la primera economía atlántica (c. 1470-1540)*. Lleida: Milenio.

Arróniz, O. (1980). *El despertar científico en América: la vida de Diego García de Palacio: documentos inéditos del Archivo de Sevilla*. México D.F.: Universidad Autónoma Metropolitana.

Arroyo Abad, L. & Palma, N. (2021). The fruits of El Dorado: the global impact of American precious metals. In R. Dobado-González & A. García-Hiernaux, eds., *The Fruits of the Early Globalization: An Iberian Perspective*. Cham, Switzerland: Palgrave Macmillan, pp. 95-131.

Arroyo Abad, L. & van Zanden, J. L. (2016). Growth under extractive institutions? Latin American per capita GDP in colonial times. *The Journal of Economic History*, 76(4), 1182-1215.

Artola, M. (1982). *La Hacienda del Antiguo Régimen*. Madrid: Alianza Editorial.

Artola Blanco, M., Bauluz, L. E. & Martínez-Toledano, C. (2018). Wealth in Spain, 1900-2014: a country of two lands. *WID.world Working Paper Series*, 2018/05, 1-102.

Asenjo González, M. (1986). *Segovia. La ciudad y su tierra a fines del Medievo*. Segovia: Diputación Provincial.

Asenjo González, M. (1991). Transformación de la manufactura de paños en Castilla. Las Ordenanzas Generales de 1500. *Historia. Instituciones. Documentos*, 18, 1-38.

Asenjo González, M. (2008). Urban systems as an oligarchy structuring process in fifteenth-century Castilian society. In M. Asenjo González, ed., *Oligarchy and Patronage in Late Medieval Spanish Urban Society*. Turnhout: Brepols, pp. 29-50.

Assadourian, C. S. (1982). *El sistema de la economía colonial: El mercado interior, regiones y espacio económico*. Lima: Instituto de Estudios Peruanos.

Atkinson, A. (2000). The changing distribution of income: evidence and explanations. *German Economic Review*, 1, 3-18.

Atkinson, A., Piketty, T. & Saez, E. (2011). Top incomes in the long run of history. *Journal of Economic Literature*, 49(1), 3–71.

Aurell i Cardona, J. (1996). *Els mercaders catalans al quatre-cents: mutació de valors i procés d'aristocratització a Barcelona (1370–1470)*. Lleida: Pagès editors.

Aventín i Puig, M. (1996). *La societat rural a Catalunya en temps feudals*. Barcelona: Columna.

Ayala, L., Jurado, A. & Pedraja, F. (2006). Desigualdad y bienestar en la distribución intraterritorial de la renta. *Investigaciones Regionales*, 8, 5–30.

Ayala Martínez, C. de (2003). *Órdenes militares hispánicas en la Edad Media (siglos XI–XV)*. Madrid: La Torre Literaria.

Ayala Martínez, C. de, Cantera, E., Caunedo, B. & Laliena, C. (2004). *Economía y sociedad en la España medieval*. Madrid: Istmo.

Ayuda, M. I., Collantes, F. & Pinilla, V. (2010). From locational fundamentals to increasing returns: the spatial concentration of population in Spain, 1787–2000. *Journal of Geographical Systems*, 12(1), 25–50.

Ayuda, M.I. & Puche-Gil, J. (2014). Determinants of height and biological inequality in Mediterranean Spain, 1859–1967. *Economics and Human Biology*, 15, 101–119.

Azevedo, J. L. (1973). *Épocas de Portugal económico*, 3rd edn. Lisbon: Clássica Editora.

Aznar Vallejo, E. (1983). *La integración de las islas Canarias en la Corona de Castilla (1478–1526). Aspectos administrativos, sociales y económicos*. La Laguna: Universidad de La Laguna.

Badia-Miró, M., Guilera, J. & Lains, P. (2012). Regional incomes in Portugal: industrialisation, integration and inequality, 1890–1980. *Revista de Historia Económica – Journal of Iberian and Latin American Economic History*, 30(2), 225–244.

Baganha, M. I. (2003). From closed to open doors: Portuguese emigration under the Corporative Regime. *Journal of Portuguese History*, 1(1), 1–16.

Baganha, M. I. & Góis, P. (1999). Migrações internacionais de e para Portugal: o que sabemos e para onde vamos?. *Revista Crítica de Ciências Sociais*, 52–53, 229–280.

Baganha, M. I. & Marques, J. C. (2001). População. In N. Valèrio, ed., *Estatísticas históricas portuguesas*. Lisbon: Instituto Nacional de Estatística.

Bairoch, P. (1997). *Victoires et déboirs: histoire économique et sociale du monde du XVIe siècle à nos jours*. Paris: Gallimard.

Bairoch, P., Batou, J. & Chèvre, P. (1988). *La Population des Villes Européennes de 800 à 1850*. Geneva: Librairie Droz.

Bajo-Rubio, O. & Esteve, V. (2021). The current account of the Spanish economy, 1850–2016: was it optimal? *Revista de Historia Económica – Journal of Iberian and Latin American Economic History*, 39(2), 329–354.

Bakewell, P. (1971). *Silver Mining and Society in Colonial Mexico, Zacatecas 1546–1700*. Albuquerque, NM. Revised and reprinted by Cambridge University Press (2002).

Ballesteros, E. (1997). Una estimación del coste de la vida en España, 1861-1936. *Revista de Historia Económica - Journal of Iberian and Latin American Economic History*, 15 (2), 363-395.

Banegas López, R. A. (2016). *Sangre, dinero y poder. El negocio de la carne en la Barcelona bajomedieval*. Lleida: Milenio.

Bank of Portugal (2000). Séries longas para a economia portuguesa – pós II Guerra Mundial. www.bportugal.pt/publicacao/series-longas-para-economia-portuguesa-pos-ii-guerra-mundi

Bank of Spain (2020). Balanza de Pagos y Posición de Inversión Internacional. Boletín Estadístico. www.bde.es/webbde/es/estadis/infoest/bolest17.html

Barata, F. T. (1998). *Navegação, Comércio e Relações Políticas: Os Portugueses no Mediterrâneo Ocidental (1385-1466)*. Lisbon: Fundação Calouste Gulbenkian – Junta de Investigação Científica e Tecnológica.

Barbosa, M. H. Vieira & Godinho, A. de Deus (2001). *Crises de mortalidade em Portugal desde meados do século XVI até ao início do século XX*. Guimarães: Universidade do Minho, Núcleo de Estudos de População e Sociedade (NEPS).

Barbosa, P. Gomes (1991). *Documentos, lugares e homens: estudos de história medieval*. Lisbon: Edições Cosmos.

Barciela López, C. (2002). Guerra civil y primer franquismo (1936-1959). In F. Comín, M. Hernández & E. Llopis, eds., *Historia económica de España, siglos X-XX*. Barcelona: Crítica, pp. 331-367.

Bargalló, M. (1955). *La minería y la metalurgia en la América española durante la época colonial*. México D.F.: Fondo de Cultura Económica.

Barrett, W. B. (1990). World bullion flows. In J. Tracy, ed., *The Rise of Merchant Empires: Long-Distance Trade in the Early Modern World, 1350-1750*. Cambridge: Cambridge University Press, pp. 224-254.

Barriendos, M. (1994). Climatología histórica de Catalunya. Aproximación a sus características generales (ss. XV-XIX). PhD thesis, Departamento de Geografía Física y Análisis Geográfico Regional de la Universidad de Barcelona.

Barrio Gozalo, M. (2002). *La sociedad en la España Moderna*. Madrid: Editorial Actas.

Barrio Moya, J. L. (2006). Carlos IV y la Real Fábrica de Paños de San Fernando de Henares. *Anales Complutenses*, 18, 77-94.

Barro, R. J. (1999). Notes of growth accounting. *Journal of Economic Growth*, 4, 119-137.

Barro, R. J. (2000). Inequality and growth in a panel of countries. *Journal of Economic Growth*, 5(1), 5-32.

Barro, R. J. (2008). Inequality and growth revisited. *Asian Development Bank Working Paper Series on Regional Economic Integration*, 11, 1-14.

Barro, R. J. & Lee, J.-W. (2013). A new data set of educational attainment in the world, 1950-2010. *Journal of Development Economics*, 104, 184-198.

Barros, F. & Modesto, L. (1999). Portuguese banking sector: a mixed oligopoly? *International Journal of Industrial Organization*, 17, 869-886.

Barros, M. F. de (2007). *Tempos e Espaços de mouros. A minoria muçulmana no reino de Portugal (séculos XII a XV)*. Lisbon: Fundação Calouste Gulbenkian-Fundação para a Ciência e Tecnologia.
Barros, M. F. de & Viana, M. (2012). *Posturas municipais Portuguesas (séculos XIV–XVII)*. Ponta Delgada: CEGF e CIDEHUS.
Basas, M. (1964). *Banqueros burgaleses en el siglo XVI*. Burgos: Diputación Provincial.
Baskes, J. (2013). *Staying Afloat: Risk and Uncertainty in Spanish Atlantic World Trade, 1760–1820*. Stanford, CT: Stanford University Press.
Batista, D., Martins, C., Pinheiro, M. & Reis, J. (1997). *New Estimates for Portugal's GDP, 1910–1958*. Lisbon: Banco de Portugal.
Bayly, C. A. (2004). *The Birth of the Modern World, 1780–1914*. Oxford: Blackwell.
Beik, W. (1985). *Absolutism and Society in Seventeenth-Century France: State Power and Provincial Aristocracy in Languedoc*. Cambridge: Cambridge University Press.
Beltrán, F. J. & de Miguel, S. (2017). Migrants' self-selection in the early stages of modern economic growth, Spain (1880–1930). *Economic History Review*, 70(1), 101–121.
Beltrán, F. J. & Martínez-Galarraga, J. (2018). Inequality and education in pre-industrial economies: evidence from Spain. *Explorations in Economic History*, 69, 81–101.
Benaboud, M. (1994). La economía y la moneda. I. La economía. In R. Menéndez Pidal ed., *Historia de España, vol. VIII-I*. M. J. Viguera Molins & J.-M. Jover Zamora, eds., *Los reinos de taifas. Al-Andalus en el siglo XI*. Madrid: Espasa Calpe. pp. 229–272.
Benito i Monclús, P. (2003). *Senyoria de la terra i tinença pagesa al comtat de Barcelona (segles XI–XIII)*. Barcelona: Institució Milà i Fontanals – CSIC.
Benito i Monclús, P. (2008). Casa rural y niveles de vida en el entorno de Barcelona a fines de la Edad Media. In *Col·loqui internacional 'Pautes de consum i nivells de vida al món rural medieval'*. Valencia: Universitat de València. Unpublished paper.
Bennassar, B. (1969). *Recherches sur les grandes épidémies dans le Nord de l'Espagne à la fin du XVIe siècle*. Paris: SEVPEN.
Bennassar, B. (1983). *Valladolid en el siglo de oro: una ciudad de Castilla y su entorno agrario en el siglo XVI*. Valladolid: Fundación Municipal de Cultura.
Bennassar, B. (1989). *Historia de los Españoles, Siglos VI–XX*, vol. I. Barcelona: Crítica.
Bensch, S. P. (1995). *Barcelona and its Rulers, 1096–1291*. New York: Cambridge University Press.
Benton, L. (2002). *Law and Colonial Cultures: Legal Regimes in World History, 1400–1900*. Cambridge and New York: Cambridge University Press.
Berg, M. & Eger, E., eds. (2003). *Luxury in the Eighteenth Century: Debates, Desires and Delectable Goods*. Basingstoke and New York: Palgrave Macmillan.
Bernal Rodríguez, A. M. (1999). Las finanzas imperiales: expansión del oro y la plata por Europa. In C. Lopezosa Aparicio, ed., *El oro y la plata de las Indias en la época de los Austrias*. Madrid: Fundación ICO, pp. 551–576.

Bernal Rodríguez, A. M. (2015). De lanas andaluzas y algodones americanos. Prolegómenos al proceso industrializador en Andalucía. *Revista de Historia Industrial*, 58, 43–60.

Bernardos Sanz, J. U. (2003). *Trigo castellano y abasto madrileño: los arrieros y comerciantes segovianos en la Edad Moderna*. Valladolid: Junta de Castilla y León.

Berry, B. J. L. (1961). City size distribution and economic development. *Economic Development and Cultural Change*, 9(4), 573–588.

Bértola, L. (2005). A 50 años de la curva de Kuznets: crecimiento económico y distribución del ingreso en Uruguay y otras economías de nuevo asentamiento desde 1870. *Investigaciones de Historia Económica*, 1(3), 135–176.

Bethencourt, F. & D. R. Curto, eds. (2007) *Portuguese Oceanic Expansion, 1400–1800*. Cambridge: Cambridge University Press.

Betrán, C. (1997). Tamaño de mercado y crecimiento industrial en España durante el primer tercio del siglo XX. *Revista de Historia Industrial*, 11, 119–148.

Betrán, C. (2005). Natural resources, electrification and economic growth. From the end of the XIXth century until WWII. *Revista de Historia Económica – Journal of Iberian and Latin American Economic History*, 23, 47–81.

Betrán, C. (2011). Regional specialisation and economic growth: Spain in the US mirror, 1856–2002. *Cliometrica*, 5(3), 259–290.

Betrán, C. & Pons, M. A. (2004). Skilled and unskilled wage differentials and economic integration. *European Review of Economic History*, 8(1), 29–60.

Betrán, C. & Pons, M. A., eds. (2020). *Historical Turning Points in Spanish Economic Growth and Development, 1808–2008*. Cham, Switzerland: Palgrave Macmillan.

Betrán, J. L. (1996). *La peste en la Barcelona de los Austrias*. Lleida: Milenio.

Bilbao Bilbao, L. M. & Fernández de Pinedo, E. (2018). La producción agrícola en el País Vasco peninsular, 1537–1850: tendencia general y contrastes comarcales: una aproximación. *Vasconia: Cuadernos de historia-geografía* (2), 83–198.

Biraben, J.-N. (1975). *Les hommes et la peste en France et dans les pays Européens et Méditerranéens*, 2 vols. Paris: Mouton.

Bishko, Ch. J. (1996). Sesenta años después: la Mesta de Julius Klein a la luz de la investigación subsiguiente. In P. García Martín & J. M. Sánchez Benito, eds., *Contribución a la historia de la trashumancia en España*. Madrid: Ministerio de Agricultura, pp. 19–82.

Bisson, T. N. (1991). *The Medieval Crown of Aragon. A Short History*. Oxford: Clarendon Paperbacks.

Bjork, K. (1998). The link that kept the Philippines Spanish: Mexican merchant interests and the Manila trade, 1571–1815. *Journal of World History*, 9(1), 25–50.

Blanco Rodríguez, J. A. & Bragado Toranzo, J. M. (2003). *El sector vitivinícola en Castilla y León. Historia y claves de una recuperación*. Zamora: Centro de la UNED.

Bleichmar, D., de Vos, P., Huffine, K. & Sheehan, K. J., eds. (2009). *Science in the Spanish and Portuguese Empires, 1500–1800*. Stanford, CT: Stanford University Press.

Bluteau, R. (1720). *Vocabulario portuguez e latino, aulico, anatomico, architectonico, bellico, botanico ... autorizado com exemplos dos melhores escritores Portuguezes, e latinos ...*, vol. VI. Lisbon: na Officina de Pascoal da Sylva.

Bohorquez, J. (2020). Linking the Atlantic and Indian Oceans: Asian textiles, Spanish silver, global capital, and the financing of the Portuguese-Brazilian slave trade (c. 1760–1808). *Journal of Global History*, 15 (1), 19–38.

Bonachía Hernando, J. A. (1994). La ciudad de Burgos en la época del Consulado. In F. Ballesteros Caballero et al., eds., *Actas del V Centenario del Consulado de Burgos (1494–1994)*, vol. 1. Burgos: Diputación Provincial, pp. 69–146.

Bonet Donato, M. & Pavón Benito, J. (2013). Los Hospitalarios en la Corona de Aragón y Navarra. Patrimonio y Sistema Comendaticio (Siglos XII y XIII). *Aragón en la Edad Media*, 24, 5–54.

Bonialian, M. A. (2016). La 'ropa de la China' desde Filipinas hasta Buenos Aires. Circulación, consumo y lucha corporativa, 1580–1620. *Revista de Indias*, 76 (268), 641–672.

Bonialian, M. A. (2020). *La América española: entre el Pacífico y el Atlántico: globalización mercantil y economía política, 1580–1840*. México: Colegio de México, Centro de Estudios Históricos.

Bonifácio, M. de F. (2010). *A Monarquia Constitucional, 1807–1910*. Lisbon: Texto.

Bonnassie, P. (1975). *La organización del trabajo en Barcelona a finales del siglo XV*. Barcelona: CSIC.

Bonney, R., ed. (1995). *Economic Systems and State Finance*. Oxford: Clarendon Press.

Bordo, M. D. & Santos, F. Teixeira dos (1995). Portugal and the Bretton Woods International Monetary System. In J. Reis, ed., *International Monetary Systems in Historical Perspective*. London: Palgrave Macmillan, pp. 181–208.

Borrero Fernández, M. (1983). *El mundo rural sevillano en el siglo XV: Aljarafe y Ribera*. Seville: Diputación Provincial.

Borrero Fernández, M. (1998). La mujer en la gestión de las explotaciones agrícolas. Diferentes grados de actuación en el ámbito rural de la Baja Edad Media sevillana. In C. Segura Graiño and Á. Muñoz Fernández, eds., *El trabajo de las mujeres en la Edad Media hispana*. Madrid: Asociación Al-Mudayna, pp. 69–82.

Borucki, A., Eltis, D. & Wheat, D. (2020). *From the Galleons to the Highlands: Slave Trade Routes in the Spanish Americas*. Albuquerque, NM: University of New Mexico Press.

Bosma, U. & Curry-Machado, J. (2012). Two islands, one commodity: Cuba, Java, and the global sugar trade (1790–1930). *NWIG: New West Indian Guide/Nieuwe West-Indische Gids*, 86(3/4), 237–262.

Bosworth, B., Collins, S. & Chen, Y. C. (1995). Accounting for differences in economic growth. Paper presented at Conference on 'Structural adjustment policies in the 1990s: Experience and Prospects'. Institute of Developing Economies, Tokyo, Japan, 5–6 October.

Bourguignon, F. (2004). The poverty-growth-inequality triangle. Paper presented at the Indian Council for Research on International Economic Relations, 1–30.

Boyajian, J. (1993). *Portuguese Trade in Asia under the Habsburgs, 1580–1640*. Baltimore, OH: The John Hopkins University Press.

Brading, D. & Cross, H. (1972). Colonial silver mining: Mexico and Peru. *Hispanic American Historical Review*, 52(4), 545–579.

Braga, I. D. (2012). Produits Américains dans l'alimentation Portugaise. In J.-P. Poulain, ed., *Dictionnaire des Cultures Alimentaires*. Paris: PUF.

Bramon, D. (2000). *De quan érem o no musulmans. Textos del 713 al 1010*. Vic: Eumo.

Branco, A. & Silva, E. Gomes da (2017). Growth, structural change and innovation, 1820–1930. In D. Freire & P. Lains, eds., *An Agrarian History of Portugal, 1000–2000*. Leiden: Brill, pp. 219–244.

Branco, M. J. (2006). *D. Sancho I*. Lisbon: Círculo de Leitores.

Brandão (de Buarcos), J. (1990). *Grandeza e abastança de Lisboa em 1552*. Lisbon: Livros Horizonte.

Braudel, F. (1992). *Civilization and Capitalism. 15th–18th century*, vols. I–III. Berkeley, CA: University of California Press.

Braunstein, Ph. (2007). Production et travail dans les villes à la fin du moyen âge. *História. Revista da Faculdade de Letras*, 8, 11–23.

Brea-Martínez, G. & Pujadas-Mora, J.M. (2019). Estimating long-term socioeconomic inequality in southern Europe: the Barcelona area, 1481–1880. *European Review of Economic History*, 23(4), 397–420.

Breen, B. (2018). Empires on drugs: pharmaceutical go-betweens and the Anglo-Portuguese alliance. In J. Cañizares-Esguerra, ed., *Entangled Empires: The Anglo-Iberian Atlantic, 1500–1830*. Philadelphia, PA: University of Pennsylvania Press, pp. 63–81.

Bringas Gutiérrez, M. Á. (2000). *La productividad de los factores en la agricultura española (1752–1935)*. Madrid: Banco de España.

Bringas Gutiérrez, M. Á. (2012). La productividad de la tierra en la Corona de Castilla a mediados del siglo XVIII. In M. J. Pérez Álvarez & A. Martín García, eds., *Campo y campesinos en la España Moderna: culturas políticas en el mundo hispano*, vol. 2. Madrid: Fundación Española de Historia Moderna, pp. 945–956.

Brito, J. M. Brandão de (1989). *A industrialização Portuguesa no pós-Guerra (1948–1965). O Condicionamento Industrial*. Lisbon: Publicações Dom Quixote.

Broadberry, S. (1998). How did the United States and Germany overtake Britain? A sectoral analysis of comparative productivity levels, 1870–1990. *Journal of Economic History*, 58, 375–407.

Broadberry, S. (2006). *Market Services and the Productivity Race, 1850–2000: British Performance in International Perspective*. Cambridge: Cambridge University Press.

Broadberry, S., Campbell, B. M. S., Klein, A., Overton, M. & van Leeuwen, B. (2015a). *British Economic Growth 1270–1870*. Cambridge and New York: Cambridge University Press.

Broadberry, S., Custodis, J. & Gupta, B. (2015b). India and the great divergence: an Anglo-Indian comparison of GDP per capita, 1600–1871. *Explorations in Economic History* 55, 58–75.

Broadberry, S. & Ghosal, S. (2005). Technology, organisation and productivity performance in services: lessons from Britain and the United States since 1870. *Structural Change and Economic Dynamics*, 16, 437–466.

Broadberry, S., Giordano, C. & Zollino, F. (2013). Productivity. In G. Toniolo, ed., *The Oxford Handbook of the Italian Economy Since Unification*. Oxford: Oxford University Press, 187–226.

Broadberry, S., Guan, H. & Li, D. D. (2018). China, Europe, and the great divergence: a study in historical national accounting, 980–1850. *Journal of Economic History*, 78(4), 955–1000.

Burbank, J. & Cooper, F. (2011). *Empires in World History: Power and the Politics of Difference*. Princeton, NJ: Princeton University Press.

Busain, A. and Gordo, E. (1994). Funciones de importación y exportación de la economía española. *Investigaciones Económicas*, 18(1), 165–192.

Bustelo, F. (1972). Algunas reflexiones sobre la población española de principios del siglo XVIII. *Anales de Economía*, 15, 89–106.

Bustelo, F. (1973–1974). El vecindario General de España de 1712–1717 o Censo de Campoflorido. *Revista Internacional de Sociología*, XXXII, 83–103; XXXIII, 7–35.

Bustelo, F. (1975). La població del País Valencià al segle XVIII. *Recerques. Història, economía i cultura*, 5, 73–96.

Cabrera Muñoz, E. (1999). Nobleza y señoríos en Andalucía durante la Baja Edad Media. In *La nobleza peninsular en la Edad Media*. Ávila: Fundación Sánchez-Albornoz, pp. 89–120.

Calvo, A. (2001). Los inicios de las telecomunicaciones en España: el telégrafo. *Revista de Historia Económica – Journal of Iberian and Latin America Economic History*, 3, 613–635.

Cámara, A. (2015). A biosocial approach to living conditions: inter-generational changes of stature dimorphism in 20th-century Spain. *Annals of Human Biology*, 42(2), 168–178.

Câmara, B. (2006). The Portuguese civil code and the colonia tenancy contract in Madeira (1867–1967). *Continuity and Change*, 21(2), 213–233.

Camarinhas, N. (2012). *Les magistrats et l'administration de la justice. Le Portugal et son empire colonial (XVIIe–XVIIIe siècle)*. Paris: L'Harmattan.

Campbell, B. M. S. (2005). The agrarian problem in the early fourteenth century. *Past & Present*, 188(1), 3–70.

Camps i Surroca, M. & Camps i Clement, M. (1985). *La pesta de meitats del segle XVII a Catalunya*. Lleida: Dilagro.

Cañavate Toribio, J. (2006). *Granada, de la madina nazarí a la ciudad cristiana*. Granada: Universidad de Granada.
Candeias, A. (2004). Literacy, schooling and modernity in twentieth-century Portugal: what population censuses can tell us. *Paedagogica Historica*, 40(4), 509-530.
Candido, M. (2013). *An African Slaving Port and the Atlantic World: Benguela and its Hinterland*. Cambridge: Cambridge University Press.
Cañizares-Esguerra, J. (2004). Iberian science in the Renaissance: ignored how much longer? *Perspectives on Science*, 12(1), 86-124.
Cañizares-Esguerra, J. (2009). Introduction. In D. Bleichmar, P. de Vos, K. Huffine, & K. J. Sheehan, eds., *Science in the Spanish and Portuguese Empires, 1500-1800*. Stanford, CT: Stanford University Press, pp. 1-5.
Cañizares-Esguerra, J. (2017). On ignored global 'scientific revolutions'. *Journal of Early Modern History*, 21(5), 420-432.
Cañizares-Esguerra, J. (2018). Introduction. In J. Cañizares-Esguerra, ed., *Entangled Empires: The Anglo-Iberian Atlantic, 1500-1830*. Philadelphia, PA: University of Pennsylvania Press, pp. 1-15.
Cantera Montenegro, E. (1986). *Los judíos en la Edad Media hispana*. Madrid: AZ.
Canto García, A. (2012). Al-Andalus: dinero, monedas y medios de intercambio. In P. Sénac, ed., *Villa 4. Histoire et archéologie de l'occident musulman (VIIe-XVe siècle): Al-Andalus, Maghreb, Sicile*. Toulouse: CNRS-Université de Toulouse-Le Mirail, pp. 67-80.
Capel Sáez, H. (1983). *Los ingenieros militares en España, siglo XVIII: repertorio biográfico e inventario de su labor científica y espacial*. Barcelona: Edicions Universitat Barcelona.
Carande, R. (1987). *Carlos V y sus banqueros. La Hacienda Real de Castilla*, 3rd edn, 3 vols. Barcelona: Editorial Crítica y Junta de Castilla y León.
Carbajo Isla, M. F. (1987). *La población de la villa de Madrid. Desde finales del siglo XVI hasta mediados del siglo XIX*. Madrid: Siglo XXI.
Carbonell, M. (2005). Trabajo femenino y economías familiares. In I. Morant, ed., *Historia de las Mujeres en España y América Latina*, vol. II. Madrid: Cátedra, pp. 237-262.
Cardim, P. (1998). *Cortes e Cultura Política no Portugal do Antigo Regime*. Lisbon: Cosmos.
Cardim, P., Feros, A. & Sabatini, G. (2019). The political constitution of the Iberian Monarchies. In F. Bouza, P. Cardim & A. Feros Carrasco, eds. *The Iberian World (1450-1820)*. London: Routledge, pp. 34-61.
Cardim, P. & Hespanha, A. M. (2018). A estrutura territorial das monarquias ibéricas. In A. B. Xavier, F. Palomo & R. Stumpf, eds. *Monarquias Ibéricas em Perspectiva Comparada (Sécs. XVI-XVIII)*. Lisbon: Imprensa Ciências Sociais, pp. 51-95.
Cardon, D. (1999). *La draperie au Moyen Âge. Essor d'une grande industrie européenne*. Paris: CNRS.

Cardoso A. C. & Sequeira J. (2020). Michele da Colle's account books (1462–63): the first example of double entry in Portugal? *De Computis – Revista Española de Historia de la Contabilidad*, 17(1), 158–190.

Cardoso, H. F. & Garcia, S. (2009). The not-so-Dark Ages: ecology for human growth in medieval and early twentieth century Portugal as inferred from skeletal growth profiles. *American Journal of Physical Anthropology*, 138(2), 136–147.

Cardoso, J. L. (1989). *O pensamiento economico em Portugal nos finais do século XVIII, 1780–1808*. Lisboa: Editorial Estampa.

Cardoso, J. L. (1997). *Novos elementos para a história bancária de Portugal – Projectos de banco 1801–1803*. Lisbon: Banco de Portugal.

Cardoso, J. L., ed. (2001). *Dicionário Histórico de Economistas Portugueses*. Lisbon: Temas & Debates.

Cardoso, J. L., ed. (2015). *Olhando para Dentro 1930–1960 (História Contemporânea de Portugal 1808–2010*, Vol. 4). Lisbon: Penguin Random House/ Fundación Mapfre, pp. 109–143.

Cardoso, J. L. & Lains, P., eds. (2010a). *Paying for the Liberal State: The Rise of Public Finance in Nineteenth-Century Europe*. Cambridge: Cambridge University Press.

Cardoso, J. L. & Lains, P. (2010b). Public finance in Portugal, 1796–1910. In J. L. Cardoso & P. Lains, eds., *Paying for the Liberal State: The Rise of Public Finance in Nineteenth-Century Europe*. Cambridge: Cambridge University Press, pp. 251–278.

Carlomagno, A. (2010). Il banco Salviati di Pisa: commercio e finanza di una compagnia fiorentina tra il 1438 e il 1489, 2 vols. PhD thesis, Università degli Studi di Pisa.

Carmona Badía, X. (1990). *El atraso industrial de Galicia. Auge y liquidación de las manufacturas textiles (1750–1900)*. Barcelona: Ariel.

Carmona Badía, X. (1993). Sargadelos en la historia de la siderurgia española. *Revista de Historia Industrial*, 3, 11–40.

Carmona, J. & Simpson, J. (1999). The 'Rabassa Morta' in Catalan viticulture: the rise and decline of a long-term sharecropping contract, 1670s–1920s. *The Journal of Economic History*, 59(2), 290–315.

Carrasco Pérez, J. (1973). *La población de Navarra en el siglo xiv*. Pamplona: Universidad de Navarra.

Carrasco Pérez, J. (2000). Moneda metálica y moneda crediticia en el Reino de Navarra (siglos XII–XV). In *Moneda y monedas en la Europa medieval (siglos XII–XV): XXVI Semana de Estudios Medievales*. Pamplona: Gobierno de Navarra, pp. 399–456.

Carrasco Pérez, J. (2001). Acuñaciones y circulación monetaria en el reino de Navarra: estancamiento y crisis. In *La moneda en Navarra*. Pamplona: Gobierno de Navarra-Caja Navarra.

Carrasco Pérez, J. (2003). Sociedades mercantiles en los espacios urbanos del camino de Santiago (1252–1425): de San Juan de Pie de Puerto a Burgos. In

Las sociedades urbanas en la España Medieval. Pamplona: Gobierno de Navarra, pp. 243–276.

Carrasco Pérez, J. (2006). El mundo urbano en la Navarra del siglo xiii. In M. González Jiménez, ed., *El mundo urbano en la Castilla del siglo xiii.* Seville: Ayuntamiento de Ciudad Real, Fundación El Monte, pp. 219–242.

Carrasco Pérez, J. (2009). Crisis, ordenanzas monetarias y 'Tabla de cambios' en el reino de Navarra (1329–1360). *Príncipe de Viana*, 70(246), 107–120.

Carrasco Pérez, J. (2019). *Dinero y deuda: Crédito judío en las villas navarras del Camino de Santiago (1266–1413).* Zaragoza: Liber Ediciones.

Carreras, A. (2009). Problemi di stima del PIL nell'Europa Moderna: il caso Spagnolo. *Studi Storici: rivista trimestrale dell'Istituto Gramsci*, 50(3), 653–694.

Carreras, A., Prados de la Escosura, L. & Rosés, J. R. (2005). Renta y riqueza. In A. Carreras & X. Tafunell, eds., *Estadísticas históricas de España: siglos XIX–XX.* Bilbao: Fundación BBVA, pp. 1297–1376.

Carreras, A. & Tafunell, X., eds. (2005). *Estadísticas Históricas de España. Siglos XIX–XX*, 3 vols. Bilbao: Fundación BBVA.

Carrère, C. (1967). *Barcelone, centre économique à l'époque des difficultés, 1380–1462*, 2 vols. Paris-La Haye: Mouton.

Carrión Arregui, I. M. (1995). Tecnología tradicional y desarrollo de una industria pesada: la fabricación de anclas en Guipúzcoa (siglos XVI–XVIII). *Revista de Historia Industrial*, 7, 199–216.

Caruana-Galizia, P. & Martí-Henneberg, J. (2013). European regional railways and real income, 1870–1910: a preliminary report. *Scandinavian Economic History Review*, 61(2), 167–196.

Carvajal, A. (2017). *Bajo la máscara del regnum: la monarquía asturleonesa en León (854–1037).* Madrid: CSIC.

Carvajal de la Vega, D. (2015). En los precedentes de la banca castellana moderna: cambiadores al norte del Tajo a inicios del siglo XVI. In E. García Fernández & J. A. Bonachía Hernando, eds., *Hacienda, mercado y poder al norte de la Corona de Castilla en el tránsito del medievo a la modernidad.* Valladolid: Castilla Ediciones, pp. 17–38.

Carvajal de la Vega, D. (2017). Crédito privado en Castilla a fines del siglo XV. Una introducción a su estudio. *Anuario de estudios medievales*, 47(1), 3–36.

Carvajal de la Vega, D. (2018). The economic and social bases of urban credit. Valladolid in the later Middle Ages. *Histoire Urbaine*, 51, 131–150.

Carvalho, G. Ribeiro (1973). A Cobertura Bancária da Metrópole. *Revista Bancária*, 34, 5–28.

Casado Alonso, H. (1987). *Señores, mercaderes y campesinos: la comarca de Burgos a fines de la Edad Media.* Valladolid: Junta de Castilla y León.

Casado Alonso, H. (1990). El comercio del pastel: datos para una geografía de la industria pañera española en el siglo XVI. *Revista de Historia Económica*, 8(3), 523–548.

Casado Alonso, H. (1991). Evolución de la producción agraria, precios y coyuntura económica en los obispados de Burgos y Palencia a lo largo del siglo XV. *Studia Historica. Historia Medieval*, 9, 67–110.

Casado Alonso, H. (1996). La nation et le quartier des Castillans de Bruges (XVe et XVIe siècles). *Genootschap voor geschiedenis handelingen*, 133(1–3), 61–77.

Casado Alonso, H. (2001). Medina del Campo fairs and the integration of Castile into 15th to 16th century European economy. In *Fiere e mercati nella integrazione delle economie europee, secc. XIII–XVIII. Atti della 'Trentaduesima settimana di studi,' 8–12 maggio 2000*. Florence: Le Monnier, pp. 495–517.

Casado Alonso, H. (2003). *El triunfo de Mercurio. La presencia castellana en Europa. Siglos XV y XVI*. Burgos: Cajacírculo.

Casado Alonso, H. (2004). Guilds, technical progress and economic development in preindustrial Spain. In P. Massa & A. Moioli, eds., *Dalla corporazione al mutuo soccorso: organizzazione e tutela del lavoro tra XVI e XX secolo*. Milano: Franco Angeli, pp. 309–327.

Casado Alonso, H. (2008). Cultura material y consumo textil en Castilla a fines de la Edad Media e inicios de la Edad Moderna. In *Pautes de consum i nivells de vida al món rural medieval, Col·loqui internacional* (València, 18–20 September 2008), unpublished proceedings.

Casado Alonso, H. (2012). Comercio y hombres de negocios castellanos y navarros en los inicios de la 'Primera Edad Global'. In *En los umbrales de España. La incorporación del Reino de Navarra a la monarquía hispana. XXXVIII Semana de Estudios Medievales de Estella*. Pamplona: Gobierno de Navarra, pp. 333–370.

Casado Alonso, H. (2014). Il mondo spagnolo della mercatura e le Americhe nei secoli XV e XVI. In G. Pinto, L. Rombai & C. Tripodi, eds., *Vespucci, Firenze e le Americhe*. Florence: Leo S. Olschki, pp. 87–104.

Casado Soto, J. L. (2002). Construcción naval y navegación. In L. García Ballester, ed., *Historia de la Ciencia y de la Técnica en la Corona de Castilla*, vol. 2. Valladolid: Junta de Castilla y León, pp. 433–501.

Casey, J. (1983). *El reino de Valencia en el siglo XVII*. Madrid: Siglo XXI.

Castán Esteban, J. L. (1994). Trashumancia aragonesa en el reino de Valencia (s. XVI y XVII). *Estudis. Revista de Historia Moderna*, 20, 303–310.

Castán Lanaspa, G. (2000). *Política económica y poder político. Moneda y fisco en el reinado de Alfonso X el Sabio*. Valladolid: Junta de Castilla y León.

Castán Lanaspa, G. (2020). *La construcción de la idea de la Peste Negra (1348–1350) como catástrofe demográfica en la historiografía española*. Salamanca: Universidad de Salamanca.

Castells Calzada, N. (1987). La peste de mediados del siglo XVII en Cataluña. In *Actas del I Congrés Hispano-Luso-Italià de Demografia Històrica*. Barcelona: ADEH, pp. 104–112.

Castillo Martos, M. & Lang, M. F. (1995). *Metales preciosos: unión de dos mundos: tecnología, comercio y política de la minería y metalurgia iberoamericana*. Seville and Bogotá: Muñoz Moya y Montraveta Editores.

Catalán, E. (2018). El crecimiento del producto agrario por habitante de La Rioja en la Edad Moderna. *Investigaciones de Historia Económica – Economic History Research*, 14, 82–93.

Cavalcanti, T. V. (2007). Business cycle and level accounting: the case of Portugal. *Portuguese Economic Journal*, 6, 47–64.

Cebrián Villar, M. (2001). Las fuentes del crecimiento económico español, 1964–1973. *Revista de Historia Económica – Journal of Iberian and Latin American Economic History*, 19(Extra 1), 277–299.

Cermeño, A. & Santiago-Caballero, C. (2020). All roads lead to market integration: lessons from a spatial analysis of the wheat market in 18th century Spain. *Instituto Figuerola Working Papers in Economic History*.

Chai, A. & Moneta, A. (2010). Engel curves. *Journal of Economic Perspectives*, 24 (1), 225–240.

Chalmeta, P. (1973). *El 'señor del zoco' en España: edades media y moderna, contribución al estudio de la historia del mercado*. Madrid: Instituto Hispano-Árabe de Cultura.

Chalmeta, P. (1992). An approximate picture of the economy of al-Andalus. In S. K. Jayyusi, ed., *The legacy of Muslim Spain*. Leiden: Brill, pp. 741–758.

Chandler, A. D., Jr. (1977). *The Visible Hand: The Managerial Revolution in American Business*. Cambridge, MA: Harvard University Press.

Chaney, E. & Hornbeck, R. (2016). Economic dynamics in the Malthusian Era: evidence from the 1609 Spanish expulsion of the Moriscos. *The Economic Journal*, 126(594), 1404–1440.

Charotti, C., Palma, N. & Santos, J. Pereira dos (2022). American treasure and the decline of Spain. CEPR Discussion Paper No. 17020.

Chaunu, H., Chaunu, P. & Arbellot, G. (1955–1956). *Séville et l'Atlantique, 1504–1650*. Paris: A. Colin.

Childs, W. R. (1978). *Anglo-Castilian Trade in the Later Middle Ages*. Manchester: Manchester University Press.

Childs, W. R. (2013). *Trade and Shipping in the Medieval West: Portugal, Castile, and England*. Porto: Fédération Internationale des Instituts d'Études Médiévales.

Cipolla, C. M. (1974). *Storia economica dell'Europa pre-industriale*. Bologna: Il Mulino.

Cirer Costa, J. C. (2019). The crumbling of Francoist Spain's isolationism thanks to foreign currency brought by European tourists in the early years of the Golden Age. *MPRA Paper*, 95578, 1–31.

Clar, E., Martín-Retortillo, M. & Pinilla, V. (2018). The Spanish path of agrarian change, 1950–2005: from authoritarian to export-oriented productivism. *Journal of Agrarian Change*, 18(2), 324–347.

Clar, E. & Pinilla, V. (2009). The contribution of agriculture to Spanish economic development. In P. Lains & V. Pinilla, eds., *Agriculture and Economic Development in Europe since 1870*. London: Routledge, pp. 311–332.

Clemente Ramos, J. (1989). *Estructuras señoriales castellanoleonesas: el realengo (siglos XI–XIII)*. Cáceres: Universidad de Extremadura.

Clemente Ramos, J. (2003). *La economía campesina en la corona de Castilla (1000–1300)*. Barcelona: Crítica.

Clemente Ramos, J. (2004). Propiedad, producción y paisaje agrarios en Pozuelo, a finales de la Edad Media. *Anuario de Estudios Medievales*, 34(1), 249–278.

Clemente Ramos, J. (2005). La organización del terrazgo agropecuario en Extremadura (siglos XV–XVI). *En la España medieval*, 28, 49–80.

Clemente Ramos, J. (2011). Niveles de vida y pautas de consumo en el campesinado (Corona de Castilla, 1200-c. 1550). In E. López Ojeda, ed., *Comer, beber, vivir. Consumo y niveles de vida en la Edad Media hispánica*. Logroño: Instituto de Estudios Riojanos, pp. 215–244.

Clunas, C. (1999). Modernity global and local: consumption and the rise of the West. *The American Historical Review*, 104(5), 1497–1511.

Coelho, M. H. da Cruz (1989). *O Baixo Mondego dos Finais da Idade Média*, 2 vols. Lisbon: Imprensa Nacional Casa da Moeda.

Coelho, M. H. da Cruz (1990). *Homens, Espaços e Poderes (Séculos XI–XVI). I – Notas do Viver Social*, 2 vols. Lisbon: Livros Horizonte.

Coelho, M. H. da Cruz (1995). A pesca fluvial na economia e sociedade medieval portuguesa. *Cuadernos Históricos*, 6, 81–102.

Coelho, M. H. da Cruz (1996a). Os Homens ao longo do tempo e do espaço. In M. H. Coelho & A. L. Homem, ed., *Portugal em definição de fronteiras. Do condado portucalense à crise do século XIV*. Lisbon: Presença, pp. 166–184.

Coelho, M. H. da Cruz (1996b). Concelhos. In M. H. Coelho & A. Carvalho Homem, eds., *Portugal em definição de fronteiras. Do condado portucalense à crise do século XIV*. Lisbon: Presença, pp. 554–584.

Coelho, M. H. & Magalhães, J. R. (2008). *O poder concelhio: das origens às Cortes Constituintes. Notas de História Social*, 2nd edn, Coimbra: Centro de Estudos e Formação Autárquica.

Collantes, F. (2017). *La economía española en 3D: oferta, demanda y largo plazo*. Madrid: Pirámide.

Collantes, F. & Pinilla, V. (2011). *Peaceful Surrender: The Depopulation of Rural Spain in the Twentieth Century*. Newcastle-upon-Tyne: Cambridge Scholars Publishing.

Collantes de Terán Sánchez, A. (1977). *Sevilla en la Baja Edad Media: la ciudad y sus hombres*. Seville: Ayuntamiento de Sevilla.

Collantes de Terán Sánchez, A. (1979). Los señoríos andaluces. Análisis de su evolución territorial en la Edad Media. *Historia. Instituciones. Documentos*, 6, 89–112.

Collantes de Terán Sánchez, A. (1984). Oligarquía urbana, explotación agraria y mercado en la Andalucía bajomedieval. In *Congreso de historia rural: siglos XV–XIX*. Madrid: Casa de Velázquez, 53–62.

Collantes de Terán Sánchez, A. (1991). Los mercados de abasto en Sevilla: permanencias y transformaciones (siglos XV y XVI). *Historia. Instituciones. Documentos*, 18, 57–70.

Collantes de Terán Sánchez, A. (2007). El modelo meridional: Sevilla. In *Mercado inmobiliario y paisajes urbanos en el Occidente europeo (siglos XI-XV)*. Pamplona: Gobierno de Navarra, pp. 591-630.
Collins, S. M. & Bosworth, B. P. (1996). Economic Growth in East Asia: Accumulation versus Assimilation. *Brooking Papers in Economic Activity*, 2, 135-196.
Comas, M., Muntaner, C. & Vinyoles, T.M. (2008). Elles no només filaven: producció i comerç en mans de dones a la Catalunya baixmedieval. *Recerques*, 56, 19-45.
Comín, F. (1995). La difícil convergencia de la economía española: un problema histórico. *Papeles de Economía Española*, 63, 78-92.
Comín, F. (1996). *España (1808-1995)*. Vol. II of *Historia de la Hacienda pública*. Barcelona: Crítica.
Comín, F. (2002). El período de entreguerras (1919-1935). In F. Comín, M. Hernández & E. Llopis, eds., *Historia económica de España, siglos X-XX*. Barcelona: Crítica, pp. 285-329.
Comín, F. (2010). Public finance and the rise of the liberal state in Spain, 1808-1914. In J. L. Cardoso & P. Lains, eds., *Paying for the Liberal State: The Rise of Public Finance in Nineteenth-Century Europe*. Cambridge: Cambridge University Press, pp. 214-250.
Comín, F. (2014a). La Hacienda Pública durante el franquismo: el retroceso en la modernización del Estado (1936-1975). In C. Barciela, J. Melgarejo & A. di Vittorio, eds., *La evolución de la Hacienda Pública en Italia y España (siglos XVIII-XXI)*. Alicante: Publicacions de la Universitat d'Alacant, pp. 335-361.
Comín, F. (2014b). La evolución de la Hacienda pública en Italia y España: dos historias casi paralelas. In C. Barciela, J. Melgarejo & A. di Vittorio, eds., *La evolución de la Hacienda Pública en Italia y España (siglos XVIII-XXI)*. Alicante: Publicacions de la Universitat d'Alacant, 11-74.
Comín, F. (2016). *Las crisis de la deuda soberana en España (1500-2015)*. Madrid: Catarata.
Comín, F. (2018). Presupuesto y corrupción en la España contemporánea (1808-2017): lecciones de la historia. In B. de Riquer i Permanyer et al., eds., *La corrupción política en la España contemporânea*. Madrid: Marcial Pons, pp. 81-109.
Comín, F. (2020). 1808: the Napoleonic Wars and the loss of the American colonies. In C. Betrán & M. A. Pons, eds., *Historical Turning Points in Spanish Economic Growth and Development, 1808-2008*. Cham, Switzerland: Palgrave Macmillan, pp. 15-51.
Comín, F. & Díaz, D. (2005). Sector público administrativo y estado del bienestar. In A. Carreras & X. Tafunell, eds., *Estadísticas históricas de España, siglos XIX-XX*. Bilbao: Fundación BBVA.
Comín, F. & Yun-Casalilla, B. (2012). Spain: from composite monarchy to nation-state, 1492-1914. An exceptional case?. In B. Yun-Casalilla & P. O'Brien, eds.,

The Rise of Fiscal States: A Global History, 1500–1914. Cambridge: Cambridge University Press, pp. 233–266.

Conklin, J. (1998). The theory of sovereign debt and Spain under Philip II. *Journal of Political Economy*, 106(3), 483–513.

Constable, O. R. (1994). *Trade and Traders in Muslim Spain: The Commercial Realignment of the Iberian Peninsula, 900–1500*. New York: Cambridge University Press.

Contreras y López de Ayala, J. (1921). *Historia de las corporaciones de menestrales en Segovia*. Segovia: Mauro Lozano Impresor.

Córdoba de la Llave, R. (1995). Transportes y albergues en el reino de Córdoba a fines de la Edad Media. *Historia. Instituciones. Documentos*, 22, 87–118.

Córdoba de la Llave, R. (2002). Las técnicas preindustriales. In L. García Ballester, ed., *Historia de la Ciencia y de la Técnica en la Corona de Castilla*, vol. 2. Valladolid: Junta de Castilla y León, pp. 221–432.

Córdoba de la Llave, R. (2006). Los instrumentos de la relación comercial: medios, técnicas y útiles de transporte en la España bajomedieval. In J. I. de la Iglesia, ed., *El comercio en la Edad Media. XVI Semana de Estudios Medievales, Nájera y Tricio 2005*. Logroño: Instituto de Estudios Riojanos, pp. 189–251.

Córdoba de la Llave, R. (2007). Industrial techniques in al-Andalus: a long-lasting legacy. In S. Cavacciochi, ed., *Relazione economiche tra Europa e mondo islamico (secc. XIII–XVIII). Atti della 'Trentottesima Settimana di Studi', 1–5 maggio 2006*, vol. II. Florence: Le Monnier, pp. 739–768.

Córdoba de la Llave, R. (2009). *Ciencia y técnica monetarias en la España bajomedieval*. Madrid: Fundación Juanelo Turriano.

Córdoba de la Llave, R. (2017a). Industria y artesanía rural en la Corona de Castilla a fines de la Edad Media. In G. Navarro & C. Villanueva, eds., *Industrias y mercados rurales en los reinos hispánicos (siglos XIII–XV)*. Murcia: Sociedad Española de Estudios Medievales, pp. 37–62.

Córdoba de la Llave, R. (2017b). *Los oficios medievales*. Madrid: Síntesis.

Cosme, J. (2006). As preocupações higio-sanitárias em Portugal (2.ª metade do século XIX e princípio do XX). *História: Revista da Faculdade de Letras da Universidade do Porto*, 7, 181–195.

Cossart, B. (2021). *Les Artilleurs et la Monarchie hispanique (1560–1610). Guerre, savoirs techniques, État*, Paris: Classiques Garnier.

Costa, J. D. Rodrigues da (1788). *Petas da vida ou a terceira parte dos ópios*. Lisbon: Na off. de Simão Thaddeo Ferreira.

Costa, J. P. O. (2013). *Mare Nostrum. Em Busca de Honra e Riqueza nos Séculos XV e XVI*. Lisbon: Círculo de Leitores.

Costa, L. Freire (1988). Acerca da Produção Cartográfica no Século XVI. *Revista de História Económica e Social*, 23, 1–26.

Costa, L. Freire. (1997). *Naus e Galeões na Ribeira de Lisboa. A Construção Naval para a Rota do Cabo no Século XVI*. Cascais: Patrimonia Histórica.

Costa, L. Freire (2002a). *Império e grupos mercantis. Entre o Oriente e o Atlântico (século XVII)*. Lisbon: Livros Horizonte.

Costa, L. Freire (2002b). *O transporte no Atlântico e a Companhia Geral do Comércio do Brasil*. Lisbon: National Commission for the Commemoration of the Discoveries.

Costa, L. Freire (2005). Relaçoes económicas com o exterior. In P. Lains & Á. Da Silva, eds., *História Económica de Portugal 1700-2000*, vol. I, *O Século XVIII*. Lisboa: Imprenta de Ciências Sociais, pp. 263-291.

Costa, L. Freire (2013). A Restauração de Portugal: serviço da dívida, crises financeiras e recursos do império. In A. Galán Sanchez & J. M. Carretero Zamora, eds., *El alimento del Estado y la salud de la res publica: orígenes, estructura y desarrollo del gasto público en Europa*. Madrid: Ministerio de Hacienda y Administraciones Públicas – Instituto de Estudios Fiscales, pp. 169-188.

Costa, L. Freire, Henriques, A. & Palma, N. (2022). Anatomy of a Premodern State. University of Manchester, Economics Discussion Paper 2208.

Costa, L. Freire, Lains, P. & Miranda, S. M. (2014). *História Económica de Portugal: 1143-2010*, 3rd ed. Lisbon: A Esfera dos Livros.

Costa, L. Freire, Lains, P. & Miranda, S. M. (2016). *An Economic History of Portugal, 1143-2010*. Cambridge: Cambridge University Press.

Costa, L. Freire & Miranda, S. Munch (2023). Reputational recovery under political instability: public debt in Portugal, 1641-83. *Economic History Review* 76(3), 871-891.

Costa, L. Freire, Neves, P. & Albuquerque, T. P. (2019). A alteração da estrutura acionista das companhias coloniais pombalinas: impactos do mercado secundário de títulos em Portugal no século XVIII. *GHES Working Paper*, 60, 1-32.

Costa, L. Freire, Palma, N. & Reis, J. (2015). The great escape? The contribution of the empire to Portugal's economic growth, 1500-1800. *European Review of Economic History*, 19(1), 1-22.

Costa, L. Freire & Reis, J. (2017). The chronic food deficit of early modern Portugal: curse or myth? *Analise Social*, 52(223), 416-429.

Costa, L. Freire, Rocha, M. M. & Brito, P. B. (2018a). The alchemy of gold: interest rates, money stock, and credit in eighteenth-century Lisbon. *The Economic History Review*, 71(4), 1147-1172.

Costa, L. Freire, Rocha, M. M. & Brito, P. B. (2018b). Os impactos do terramoto de 1755 no mercado de crédito de Lisboa. *Ler História*, 72, 77-102.

Costa, L. Freire, Rocha, M. M. & Sousa, R. M. de (2013). *O ouro do Brasil*. Lisbon: Imprensa Nacional-Casa da Moeda.

Costa, L. Freire & Salvado, J. P. (2018). Consumo, inovação organizacional e fiscalidade do tabaco em Portugal (1701-1803). In S. de Luxán Meléndez & J. Figueirôa-Rego, eds., *El tabaco y la esclavitud en la rearticulación imperial ibérica (s. XV-XX)*. Évora: Publicações do Cidehus.

Costa, M. J. de Almeida (1961). *Raízes do censo consignativo: para a história do crédito medieval português*. Coimbra: Atlântida.

Costa, P. & Leitão, H. (2009). Portuguese imperial science, 1450-1800: a historiographical review. In D. Bleichmar, P. de Vos, K. Huffine & K. J. Sheehan, eds., *Science in the Spanish and Portuguese Empires, 1500-1800*. Stanford, CT: Stanford University Press, pp. 35-53.

Covarrubias, S. (1611). *Tesoro de la lengua castellana, o española*. Madrid: Luis Sánchez.

Cox, T. & Macro, C. (2007). *Relação do Reino de Portugal: 1701*. Lisbon: Biblioteca Nacional.

Crafts, N. F. R. (2002). The Human Development Index, 1870-1999: some revised estimates. *European Review of Economic History*, 6, 395-405.

Crafts, N. F. R. (2004). Productivity growth in the Industrial Revolution: a New Growth Accounting Perspective. *Journal of Economic History*, 64 (2), 521-535.

Crespo Álvarez, M. (2002). Judíos, préstamos y usuras en la Castilla medieval. De Alfonso X a Enrique III. *Edad Media: revista de historia*, 5, 179-215.

Crosby, A. (1972). *The Columbian Exchange: Biological and Cultural Consequences of 1492*. Westport, CT: Greenwood Press.

Cross, H. E. (1983). South American bullion production and export, 1550-1750. In J. F. Richards, ed., *Precious Metals in the Later Medieval and Early Modern Worlds*. Durham, NA: Carolina Academic Press, pp. 397-423.

Crusafont i Sabater, M. (2015). *Història de la moneda de la Corona catalano-aragonesa medieval (excepte els comtats catalans) (1067/1162-1516)*. Barcelona: Societat Catalana d'Estudis Numismàtics, Institut d'Estudis Catalans.

Cruselles Gómez, E. (2019). *Fortuna y expolio de una banca medieval: la familia Roís de Valencia (1417-1487)*. Valencia: Publicacions de la Universitat de València.

Cruz, J. (1996). *Gentlemen, Bourgeois, and Revolutionaries: Political Change and Cultural Persistence among the Spanish Dominant Groups, 1750-1850*. Cambridge and New York: Cambridge University Press.

Cruz, J. (2011). *The Rise of Middle-Class Culture in Nineteenth-Century Spain*. Baton Rouge, LA: Louisiana State University Press.

Cuadrada, C. (1990-1991). Sobre les relacions camp-ciutat a la Baixa Edat Mitjana. Barcelona i les comarques de l'entorn. *Acta historica et archaeologica mediaevalia*, 11-12, 161-185.

Cuenca-Esteban, J. (2008). Statistics of Spain's colonial trade, 1747-1820: new estimates and comparisons with Great Britain. *Revista de Historia Económica*, 26(3), pp. 323-354.

Cuervo-Cazurra, A. (2018). Business groups in Spain: regulation and ideology drivers for transformation. *Northeastern University D'Amore-McKim School of Business Research Paper Series*, 317778.

Cuevas, J. & Pons, M. A. (2020). 1977: Hopes fulfilled: building democracy in turbulent economic times. In C. Betrán & M. A. Pons, eds., *Historical Turning Points in Spanish Economic Growth and Development, 1808-2008*. Cham, Switzerland: Palgrave Macmillan, pp. 159-193.

Cuñado, J. H. (2018). Factores de modernización de la comercialización en España. Tendencias y retos futuros. *ESIC Market Economics and Business Journal*, 49(1), 193-209.

Cunha, A. da Silva (2002). *Internacionalização da Banca Portuguesa: opções estratégicas*. Lisbon: Universidade Autónoma de Lisboa.

Cunha, P. (2019). As feiras no Portugal Medieval (1121-1521): Evolução, Organização e Articulação. Master thesis, Faculty of Arts of the University of Porto.

Cussó Segura, X. (2005). El estado nutritivo de la población española, 1900-1970: análisis de las necesidades y disponibilidades de nutrientes. *Historia Agraria: Revista de agricultura e historia rural*, 36, 329-358.

Cussó Segura, X. & Garrabou, R. (2007). La transición nutricional en la España contemporánea: las variaciones en el consumo de pan, patatas y legumbres (1850-2000). *Investigaciones de Historia Económica*, 7, 69-100.

d'Arienzo, L. (2010). *La presenza italiana in Spagna al tempo di Colombo*. Rome: Istituto Poligrafico dello Stato.

Darwin, J. (2012). *Unfinished Empire: The Global Expansion of Britain*. London: Allen Lande.

de Francisco Olmos, J. M. (1999). La moneda castellana de los Reyes Católicos: Un documento económico y político. *Revista general de información y documentación*, 9(1), 85-115.

de la Torre, J. & Sanz, G., eds. (2008). *Migraciones y coyuntura económica del franquismo a la democracia*. Zaragoza: Prensas Universitarias de Zaragoza.

de la Torre Gonzalo, S. (2018). *Grandes mercaderes de la Corona de Aragón en la Baja Edad Media: Zaragoza y sus mayores fortunas mercantiles 1380-1430*. Madrid: CSIC.

de Mesa Gallego, E. (2006). Innovaciones militares en la Monarquía Hispánica durante el siglo XVI: origen y desarrollo. In E. García Hernán & D. Maffi, eds., *Guerra y sociedad en la Monarquía Hispánica: Política, estrategia y cultura en la Europa moderna (1500-1700)*, vol. 1. Madrid: Laberinto - MAPFRE - CSIC, pp. 537-552.

de Roover, R. A. (1948). *Money, Credit and Banking in Medieval Bruges*. Cambridge, MA: The Mediaeval Academy of America.

de Roover, R. (1968). *The Bruges Money Market Around 1400*. Bruselas: Paleis der Academiën.

de Vries, J. (1987). *La Urbanización de Europa 1500-1800*. Barcelona: Editorial Crítica.

de Vries, J. (1995). Problems in the measurement, description and analysis of historical urbanization. In A. van der Woude, A. Hayami & J. de Vries, eds., *Urbanization in History: A Process of Dynamic Interactions*. Oxford: Clarendon Press, pp. 43-60.

de Vries, J. (2003). Connecting Europe and Asia: a quantitative analysis of the Cape-route trade, 1497-1795. In D. O'Flynn, A. Giráldez & R. Von Glahn, eds., *Global Connections and Monetary History, 1470-1800*. Aldershot: Ashgate.

de Vries, J. (2008). *The Industrious Revolution: Consumer Behavior and the Household Economy, 1650 to the Present*. Cambridge: Cambridge University Press.

Deaton, A. (2007). Height, health, and development. *Proceedings of the National Academy of Sciences*, 104(33), 13232–13237.

Deaton, A. (2013). *The Great Escape: Health, Wealth, and the Origins of Inequality*. Princeton, NJ: Princeton University Press.

Deaton, A. & Heston, A. (2010). Understanding PPPs and PPP-based national accounts. *American Economic Journal: Macroeconomics*, 2, 1–35.

Dedieu, J. P. (2000). La Nueva Planta en su contexto. Las reformas del aparato del Estado en el reinado de Felipe V. *Manuscrits*, 18, 113–139.

Dedieu, J. P. (2011). El aparato de gobierno de la Monarquía española en el siglo XVIII. In G. Pérez Sarrión, ed., *Más estado y más mercado. Absolutismo y economía en la España del siglo XVIII*. Madrid: Sílex, pp. 53–73.

Deininger, K. & Squire, L. (1998). New ways of looking at old issues: inequality and growth. *Journal of Development Economics*, 57(2), 259–287.

del Val Valdivieso, M. I. & Jiménez Alcázar, J. F., eds. (2013). *Las mujeres en la Edad Media*. Murcia: Sociedad Española de Estudios Medievales.

del Valle Pavón, G. (2016). *Donativos, préstamos y privilegios. Los mercaderes y mineros en la Ciudad de México durante la Guerra Anglo-Española de 1779–1783*. Ciudad de México: Instituto Mora.

Delgado Rivas, J. M. (2007). *Dinámicas imperiales (1650–1796). España, América y Europa en el cambio institucional del sistema colonial español*. Barcelona: Ediçions Bellaterra.

Denison, E. F. (1962). *The Sources of Economic Growth in the United States and the Alternatives Before Us*. Washington, DC: Committee for Economic Development.

Denzel, M. A. (1995). *Europäische Wechselkurse von 1383 bis 1620. Währungen der Welt*, vol. IX. Stuttgart: Verlag.

Deu Baigual, E. & Llonch, M. (2008). La maquinaria textil en Cataluña: de la total dependencia exterior a la reducción de importaciones, 1870–1959. *Revista de Historia Industrial*, 38, 17–49.

Dias, J. Alves (1985). Um documento financeiro do século XVII. *Nova História*, 3–4, 107–148.

Dias, J. Alves (1998). A População. In J. Serrão & A. H. Oliveira Marques, eds., *Nova História de Portugal*, vol. V. Lisbon: Editorial Presença, pp. 11–52.

Díaz de Durana, J. R. & García Fernández, E. (1991). *Demografía y sociedad: la población de Logroño a mediados del siglo XV*. Logroño: Instituto de Estudios Riojanos.

Díaz Hernández, R. F. (1982). *El azúcar en Canarias: (s. XVI–XVII)*. Las Palmas de Gran Canaria: Mancomunidad de Cabildos.

Diccionario de la lengua castellana en que se explica el verdadero sentido de las voces, su naturaleza y calidad, con las phrases o modos de hablar, los proverbios o refranes, y otras cosas convenientes al uso de la lengua, vol. V. Madrid:

Imprenta de la Real Academia Española por los Herederos de Francisco del Hierro (1737).
Díez de Salazar, L. M. (1985). La industria del hierro en Guipúzcoa (siglos XIII–XIV). Aportación al estudio de la industria urbana. *En la España Medieval*, 6, 251–276.
Díez-Minguela, A., Martinez-Galarraga, J. & Tirado-Fabregat, D. A. (2018). *Regional inequality in Spain 1860–2015*. Cham, Switzerland: Palgrave Macmillan.
Dincecco, M. (2009). Fiscal centralization, limited government, and public revenues in Europe, 1650–1913. *Journal of Economic History*, 69, 48–103.
Dirks, Nicholas B. (2008). *The Scandal of Empire India and the Creation of Imperial Britain*. Cambridge, MA: Harvard University Press.
Dobado, R. & Marrero, G. (2011). The role of the Spanish imperial state in the mining-led growth of Bourbon Mexico's economy. *Economic History Review*, 64(3), 855–884.
Dollar, D., Kleineberg, T. & Kraay, A. (2013). Growth is still good for the poor. *The World Bank Policy Research Working Paper*, 6568, 1–33.
Dollar, D. & Kraay, A. (2002). Growth is good for the poor. *Journal of Economic Growth*, 7, 195–225.
Doménech-Belda, C. (2016). Fatimíes y taifas: la moneda de oro fatimí en al-Andalus. *Al-qantara: Revista de estudios árabes*, 37(2), 199–232.
Domingues, F. C. (2004). *Os Navios do Mar Oceano: Teoria e Empiria na Arquitectura Naval Portuguesa dos Séculos XVI e XVII*. Lisbon: Centro de História da Universidade de Lisboa.
Dominguez Ortiz, A. (1960). *Política y Hacienda de Felipe IV*. Madrid: Editorial de Derecho Financiero.
Domínguez Ortiz, A. (1963). *La Sociedad Española en el siglo XVII*. Madrid: Consejo Superior de Investigaciones Científicas.
Domínguez Ortiz, A. (1973). *El Antiguo Régimen: los Reyes Católicos y los Austrias*. Madrid: Alianza Editorial-Alfaguara.
Domínguez Ortiz, A. (1984). *Historia de Sevilla: la Sevilla del siglo XVII*. Seville: Universidad de Sevilla.
Domínguez Ortiz, A. (2004). *España: Tres milenios de historia*. Madrid: Marcial Pons.
Domínguez Ortiz, A. & Vincent, B. (1978). *Historia de los moriscos. Vida y tragedia de una minoría*. Madrid: Revista de Occidente.
Donézar, J. M. (1996). *Riqueza y propiedad en la Castilla del Antiguo Régimen. La provincia de Toledo del siglo XVIII*. Madrid: Ministerio de Agricultura, Pesca y Alimentación.
Dopico, F. & Reher, D. S. (1998). *El declive de la mortalidad en España, 1860–1930*. Huesca: Asociación de Demografía Histórica.
Dopico, F. & Rowland, R. (1990). Demografía del Censo de Floridablanca. Una aproximación. *Revista de Historia Económica*, VIII(3), 591–618.
Drelichman, M. & Voth, H.-J. (2010). The sustainable debts of Philip II: a reconstruction of Castile's fiscal position, 1566–1596. *Journal of Economic History*, 70(4), 813–842.

Drelichman, M. & Voth, H.-J. (2011). Serial defaults, serial profits: returns to sovereign lending in Habsburg Spain, 1566–1600. *Explorations in Economic History*, 48(1), 1–19.

Drelichman, M. & Voth, H.-J. (2014). *Lending to the Borrower from Hell: Debt, Taxes, and Default in the Age of Philip II*. Princeton, NJ and Oxford: Princeton University Press.

Duarte, L. M. (1998). Contrabandistas de gado e 'Passadores de cousas defesas' para Castela e 'Terra de Mouros'. *História: revista da Faculdade de Letras da Universidade do Porto*, 15(1), 451–473.

Duarte, L. M. (2001). O comércio proibido. In *Estudos en Homenagem a Joao Francisco Marques*, vol. 1. Porto: University of Porto, pp. 407–424.

Duarte, L. M. (2003). Quando as casas se queriam pequenas (espaço e medidas na Idade Média). In J. Vitor Oliveira, ed., *Arquitectando espaços: da natureza à Megapólis*. Porto-Coimbra: Universidade do Porto-Universidade de Coimbra, pp. 183–192.

Dubet, A. (2003). *Hacienda, arbitrismo y negociación política: los proyectos de erarios públicos y montes de piedad en los siglos XVI y XVII*. Valladolid: Universidad de Valladolid.

Dubet, A. (2008). *Un estadista francés en la España de los Borbones- Juan Orry y las primeras reformas de Felipe V (1701-1706)*. Madrid: Biblioteca Nueva.

Durand, R. (1982). *Les campagnes portugaises entre Douro et Tage aux XIIe et XIIIe siècles*. Paris: Fondation Calouste Gulbenkian.

Easterly, W. R. (2004). Globalization, inequality, and development: the big picture. *Monetary and Economic Studies*, 22(S1), 57–87.

Echeverri, B. (2018). En el centenario de la gripe española: un estado de la cuestión. *Revista de Demografía Histórica*, 36(1), 17–42.

Edel, M. (1969) The Brazilian sugar cycle of the seventeenth century and the rise of West Indian competition. *Caribbean Studies*, 9(1), 24–44.

Edvinsson, R. (2013). Swedish GDP 1620–1800: stagnation or growth?. *Cliometrica*, 7, 37–60.

Edwards, J. (1987). 'Development' and 'underdevelopment' in the Western Mediterranean: the case of Córdoba and its region in the late fifteenth and early sixteenth centuries. *Mediterranean Historical Review*, 2(1), 3–45.

Egido López, T. (1973). *Sátiras políticas de la España Moderna*. Madrid: Alianza Editorial.

Egido López, T. (1980). El motín madrileño de 1699. *Investigaciones Históricas. Época Moderna y Contemporánea*, 2, 253–294.

Egido López, T. (2011). La Iglesia y los problemas religiosos. In A. Floristán Samanes, ed., *Historia de España en Edad Moderna*. Barcelona: Ariel, pp. 335–358.

Eiras Roel, A. (2004). Demografía rural en la España moderna: evolución, variantes y problemas. In F. J. Aranda Pérez, eds., *El mundo rural en la España moderna: actas de la VIIa Reunión Científica de la Fundación Española de Historia Moderna*. Cuenca: Universidad de Castilla La Mancha, pp. 19–78.

Elía Munárriz, A. (1995). El crédito cristiano en el mercado de Pamplona (1330–1369). *Huarte de San Juan. Geografía e Historia*, 2, 9–58.

Elliott, J. H. (1963). *The Revolt of the Catalans*. Cambridge: Cambridge University Press.

Elliott, J. H. (1987). *La España Imperial, 1469–1716*. Barcelona: Vicens Vives.

Elliott, J. H. (1990). *El conde-duque de Olivares*. Barcelona: Editorial Crítica.

Elliott, J. H. (1992). A Europe of composite monarchies, *Past & Present*, 137, 48–71.

Elliott, J. H. (2007). *Empires of the Atlantic World: Britain and Spain in America 1492–1830*. New Haven, CT: Yale University Press.

Elliott, J. H. (2018). *Scots and Catalans: Union and Disunion*. New Haven, CT: Yale University Press.

Epalza, M. de (1989). Nota sobre la etimología árabe-islámica de riesgo. *Sharq Al-Andalus. Estudios Árabes*, 6, 185–192.

Epalza, M. de (1991a). Origines du concept de risque: De l'Islam à l'Occident. In L. Faugères & C. Villain-Gandossi, eds., *Le risque et la crise*. Malta: Foundation for International Studies, pp. 63–70.

Epstein, S. R. (1998). Craft guilds, apprenticeship, and technological change in preindustrial Europe. *The Journal of Economic History*, 58(3), 684–713.

Epstein, S. R. (2000). *Freedom and Growth: The Rise of States and Markets in Europe, 1300–1750*. London: Routledge.

Escobedo Romero, R. (2008). El monopolio fiscal del tabaco en la España del siglo XVIII. *Tiempos Modernos: Revista Electrónica de Historia Moderna*, 6 (17).

Escudero A. (1996). Pesimistas y optimistas ante el 'boom' minero. *Revista de Historia Industrial*, 10, 69–92.

Espín-Sánchez, J. A., Gil-Guirado, S., Giraldo-Paez, W. D. & Vickers, C. (2019). Labor income inequality in pre-industrial Mediterranean Spain: The City of Murcia in the 18th century. *Explorations in Economic History*, 73, 101274.

Espuelas, S. (2012). Are dictatorships less redistributive? A comparative analysis of social spending in Europe (1950–1980). *European Review of Economic History*, 16(2), 211–232.

Espuelas, S. (2013). *La evolución del gasto social público en España, 1850–2005*. Madrid: Banco de España.

Estepa Díez, C. (2003). *Las behetrías castellanas*. Valladolid: Junta de Castilla y León.

Esteves, R. P. (2005). Finanças públicas. In P. Lains and Á. Ferreira da Silva, eds., *História Económica de Portugal: 1700–2000*, vol. II. Lisbon: Imprensa de Ciências Sociais, pp. 305–335.

Esteves, R. P. & Khoudour-Castéras, D. (2011). Remittances, capital flows and financial development during the mass migration period, 1870–1913. *European Review of Economic History*, 15, 443–474.

Esteves, R. P. & Nogues-Marco, P. (2021). Monetary systems and the global balance-of-payments adjustment in the pre-gold standard period, 1700–1870. In S. Broadberry & K. Fukao, eds., *The Cambridge Economic History of the Modern World*, vol. 1. Cambridge: Cambridge University Press, pp. 438–467.

Esteves, R. P., Reis, J. & Ferramosca, F. (2009). Market integration in the golden periphery: the Lisbon/London exchange, 1854–1891. *Explorations in Economic History*, 46(3), 324–345.

Fabregas García, A. (2007). Actividad comercial de los reyes nazaríes y su implicación con los representantes del gran comercio occidental a finales de la Edad Media. *Studia Historica. Historia medieval*, 25, 171–190.

Fábregas García, A. (2013). Other markets: complementary commercial zones in the Naṣrid world of the western Mediterranean (seventh/thirteenth to ninth/ fifteenth centuries). *Al-Masaq: Islam and the Medieval Mediterranean*, 25(1), 135–153.

Fábregas García, A. (2014). Azúcar e italianos en el reino nazarí de Granada. Del éxito comercial a la intervención económica. *Cuadernos del CEMYR*, 22, 133–153.

Fábregas García, A. (2017). Las industrias y los mercados rurales en el reino de Granada. In G. Navarro Espinach & C. Villanueva Morte, eds., *Industrias y mercados rurales en los reinos hispánicos (siglos XIII–XV)*. Murcia: Sociedad Española de Estudios Medievales, pp. 63–92.

Fábregas García, A. (2018). Commercial crop or plantation system? Sugar cane production from the Mediterranean to the Atlantic. In T. F. Glick, A. Malpica, F. Retamero & J. Torró, eds., *From Al-Andalus to the Americas (13th–17th Centuries): Destruction and Construction of Societies*. Boston, MA and Leiden: Brill, pp. 301–331.

Faísca, C. M. (2020). Desigualdades de rendimento na zona norte do Alentejo: Arraiolos, Avis, Portalegre e Ponte de Sor (1690–1728). In M. F. L. de Barros & A. P. Gato, eds., *Desigualdades*. Évora: Publicações do Cidehus.

Falcão, L. F. (1859). *Livro em que se contém toda a fazenda e real património dos reinos de Portugal, Índia e Ilhas adjacentes*. Lisbon: Imprensa Nacional.

Falcón Pérez, I. (2011). *Zaragoza en el siglo XV: morfología urbana, huertas y término municipal*. Zaragoza: Institución Fernando el Católico.

Farelo M. (2018). Um coletor apostólico 'in remotis finibus mundi'. Bertrand du Mazel em Portugal (1368–1371). In F. J. Hernández, R. Sánchez Ameijeiras & E. Falque Rey, eds., *Medieval Studies in Honour of Peter Linehan*. Florence: Sismel, pp. 523–556.

Fattacciu, I. (2020). *Empire, Political Economy, and the Diffusion of Chocolate in the Atlantic World*. New York, NY: Routledge.

Federico, G. (2005). *Feeding the World: An Economic History of Agriculture, 1800–2000*. Princeton, NJ: Princeton University Press.

Federico, G. & Malanima, P. (2004). Progress, decline, growth: product and productivity in Italian agriculture, 1000–2000. *Economic History Review*, LVII (3), 437–464.

Federico, G. & Tena-Junguito, A. (2016). World trade. 1800–1938: a new data-set. *EHES Working paper in Economic History*, 93, 1–297.

Federico. G & Tena-Junguito, A. (2017). A tale of two globalizations: gains from trade and openness 1800–2010. *Review of World Economics*, 153(3), 601–626.

Federico, G. & Tena-Junguito, A. (2018). Federico-Tena World Trade Historical Database: Openness. e-cienciaDatos. www.uc3m.es/ss/Satellite/UC3MInstitucional/es/TextoMixta/1371246237481/Federico-Tena_World_Trade_Historical_Databa-se

Federico. G & Tena-Junguito, A. (2019). World trade, 1800–1938: a new synthesis. *Revista de Historia Económica – Journal of Iberian and Latin American Economic History*, 37(1), 9–41.

Feenstra, R. C., Inklaar, R. & Timmer, M.P. (2015). The next generation of the Penn World Table. *American Economic Review*, 105(10), 3150–3182.

Felice, E. & Pujol Andreu, J. (2016). GDP and life expectancy in Italy and Spain over the long-run: a time-series approach. *Demographic Research*, 35(1), 813–866.

Felices, M. del M. (2016). Hacia la nobleza titulada: los 'méritos' para titular en el siglo XVII. In P. Ponce & F. Andújar, eds., *Mérito, venalidad y corrupción en España y América: siglos XVII y XVIII*. Valencia: Albatros, pp. 19–40.

Feliu Montfort, G. (1991). *Precios y salarios en la Cataluña Moderna*. Madrid: Banco de España – Servicio de Estudios.

Feliu Monfort, G. (1992). Activitats econòmiques. In J. Sobrequés i Callicó, ed., *Història de Barcelona, vol. II. La formació de la Barcelona medieval*. Barcelona: Ajuntament de Barcelona, pp. 137–272.

Feliu Monfort, G. (1998). La funció de la ciutat i el mercat. L'impuls urbà i mercantil. In J. M. Salrach i Marés, ed., *Història, política, societat i cultura dels Països Catalans*, vol. 2. Barcelona: Enciclopèdia Catalana, pp. 138–153 and 252–269.

Feliu Monfort, G. (2010). Evolución y asentamiento de la población. In J. Á. Sesma Muñoz, ed., *La Corona de Aragón en el centro de su Historia. 1208-1458. Aspectos económicos y sociales*. Zaragoza: Grupo CEMA, pp. 31–60.

Feliu Monfort, G. (2014). Moneda y coyuntura monetaria en la Corona de Aragón en torno a 1300. In M. Bourin, F. Menant & Ll. To Figueras, eds., *Dynamiques du monde rural dans la conjoncture de 1300: échanges, prélèvements et consommation en Méditerranée occidentale*, Rome: École française de Rome, pp. 397–426.

Feliu Monfort, G. (2016a). *Els primers llibres de la Taula de Canvi de Barcelona*, 2 vols. Barcelona: Fundació Noguera.

Feliu Monfort, G. (2016b). Finances, currency and taxation in the 14th and 15th centuries. *Catalan Historical Review*, 9, 25–44.

Fernández Albaladejo, P. (1992). *Fragmentos de Monarquía*. Madrid: Alianza Editorial.

Fernández Albaladejo, P. (1994). Historia de La Mesta. El gremio y la Corona. Mesta y Monarquía. In P. García Martín *Por los caminos de la trashumancia*. Valladolid: Junta de Castilla y León, pp. 177–194.

Fernández Castro, A. B. (2014). *Juzgar las Indias: La práctica de la jurisdicción de los oidores de la audiencia de la Casa de la Contratación de Sevilla (1583–98)*. PhD tesis, European University Institute.

Fernández López, F. (2018). *La Casa de la Contratación: una oficina de expedición documental para el gobierno de las Indias, 1503-1717*. Seville: Universidad de Sevilla.

Fernández-Armesto, F. (1982). *The Canary Islands after the Conquest: The Making of a Colonial Society in the Early Sixteenth Century*. Oxford: Oxford University Press.

Ferreira, A. M. Pereira (1983). *A importação e o comércio têxtil em Portugal no século XV (1385 a 1481)*. Lisbon: Imprensa Nacional-Casa da Moeda.

Ferreira, F. H. G. & Ravallion, M. (2008). Global poverty and inequality: a review of the evidence. *The World Bank Policy Research Working Paper*, 4623, 1–42.

Ferreira, S. Carlos. (2014). Preços, salários e níveis de vida em Portugal na Baixa Idade Média. PhD thesis, Universidade do Porto.

Ferreira da Silva, Á. (2005). Finanças públicas. In P. Lains, P. and Á. Ferreira da Silva, eds., *História Económica de Portugal: 1700-2000*, vol II. Lisbon: Imprensa de Ciências Sociais, pp. 237–262.

Ferrer Alòs, Ll. (2011). Acceso y distribución de los medios de producción. Herencia y reproducción social. In F. Chacón & J. Bestard, *Familias. Historia de la sociedad española (del final de la Edad Media a nuestros días)*. Madrid: Ed. Cátedra, pp. 255–324.

Ferrer Mallol, M. T. (2002). Las comunidades mudéjares de la Corona de Aragón en el siglo xv: la población. In *De mudéjares a moriscos: una conversión forzada*. Teruel: Instituto de Estudios Turolenses, pp. 27–153.

Ferrer Mallol, M. T. (2012). El comerç català a la baixa edat mitjana. *Catalan Historical Review*, 5, 159–193.

Fiestas Loza, A. (1993). El censo consignativo, según la fórmula castellana del Antiguo Régimen. *Anuario de historia del derecho español*, 63-64, 549–614.

Findlay, R. & O'Rourke, K. H. (2007). *Power and Plenty: Trade, War, and the World Economy in the Second Millennium*. Princeton, NJ: Princeton University Press.

Fisher, H. E. S. (1971). *The Portugal Trade: A Study of Anglo-Portuguese Commerce, 1700-1770*. London: Methuen.

Fisher, J. (1981). Imperial 'free trade' and the Hispanic economy, 1778-1796. *Journal of Latin American Studies*, 13(1), 21–56.

Fisher, J. (1985). The imperial response to 'free trade': Spanish imports from Spanish America, 1778-1796. *Journal of Latin American Studies*, 17(1), 35–78.

Flandreau, M., Galimard, C., Jobst, C. & Nogues-Marco, P. (2009a). The bell Jar: commercial interest rates between two revolutions, 1688–1789. In J. Atack & L. Neal, eds., *The Origins and Development of Financial Markets and Institutions. From the Seventeenth Century to the Present*, Cambridge: Cambridge University Press, pp. 161–208.

Flandreau, M., Galimard, C., Jobst, C. & Nogues-Marco, P. (2009b). Monetary geography before the industrial revolution. *Cambridge Journal of Regions, Economy and Society*, 2(2), 149–171.

Florentino, M. (1995). *Em costas negras: uma história do tráfico de escravos entre a África e o Rio de Janeiro (séculos XVIII e XIX)*. São Paulo: Companhia das Letras.

Floud, R. & Steckel, R. (1997). *Health and Welfare During Industrialization*. Chicago, IL: University of Chicago Press.

Flynn, D. O. (1982). Fiscal crisis and the decline of Spain (Castile). *The Journal of Economic History*, 42(1), 139–147.

Flynn, D. O., Giráldez, A. & von Glahn, Richard, eds. (2003). *Global Connections and Monetary History, 1470–1800*. Aldershot and Burlington: Ashgate.

Fogel, R. W. (1986). Physical growth as a measure of the economic well-being of populations: the eighteenth and nineteenth centuries. In F. Falkner & J. M. Tanner, eds., *Human Growth: A Comprehensive Treatise*, vol. 3. New York: Plenum, 263–281.

Fonseca, H. & Reis, J. (2011). The limits of agricultural growth in a fragile ecosystem: total factor productivity in Alentejo, 1750–1850. In M. Olsson & P. Svensson, eds., *Growth and Stagnation in European Historical Agriculture*. Turnhout: Brepols, 37–66.

Fonseca, J. (1997). *Escravos em Évora no século XVI*. Évora: Câmara Municipal de Évora.

Fonseca, J. (2010). *Escravos e Senhores na Lisboa Quinhentista*. Lisbon: Colibri.

Font Rius, J. M. (1969). *Textos*. Vol. I of *Cartas de población y franquicia de Cataluña*. Madrid-Barcelona: CSIC.

Fontana, J. (2002). *La quiebra de la Monarquía absoluta, (1814–1820)*, 2nd edn. Barcelona: Crítica.

Fontes, J. & Roriz, A. (2007). *Património arquitectónico e arqueológico de Vieira do Minho*. Vieira do Minho: Câmara Municipal.

Fortea Pérez, J. I. (1981). *Córdoba en el siglo XVI. Las bases demográficas y económicas de una expansión urbana*. Córdoba: Monte de Piedad y Caja de Ahorros de Córdoba.

Fortea Pérez, J. I. (1995). Las ciudades de la Corona de Castilla en el Antiguo Régimen una revisión historiográfica. *Revista de Demografía Histórica – Journal of Iberoamerican Population Studies*, 13(3), 19–60.

Fortea Pérez, J. I. (2008). *Las cortes de Castilla y León bajo los Austrias. Una interpretación*. Valladolid: Junta de Castilla y León.

Fortún Pérez de Ciriza, L. J. & Jusué Simonena, C. (1993). *Antigüedad y Alta Edad Media*. Vol. I of *Historia de Navarra*. Pamplona: Gobierno de Navarra.

Franch Benavent, R. (2005). La intervención de la Junta de Comercio de Valencia en la política arrocera de la monarquía en la segunda mitad del siglo XVIII: los informes emitidos sobre la naturaleza de las tierras de la ribera del Xúquer. *Revista de historia moderna: Anales de la Universidad de Alicante*, 23, 391–414.

Franch Benavent, R. & Navarro Espinach, G., eds. (2017). *Las rutas de la seda en la historia de España y Portugal*. Valencia: Publicacions de la Universitat de València.

Franco Rubio, G. A. (2009). La vivienda en el Antiguo Régimen: de espacio habitable a espacio social. *Chronica nova: Revista de historia moderna de la Universidad de Granada*, 35, 63–103.

Franco Sánchez, F. (1999). Consideración jurídica y religiosa de los territorios de la Meseta y el Norte peninsular por el poder musulmán de al-Andalus. *Al-Andalus -Magreb. Estudios árabes e islámicos*, 7, 101-133.
Franco Sánchez, F. (2010). La concepción de la soberanía en el Islam del Occidente Musulmán. In *Homenaje al profesor Eloy Benito Ruano*, vol. I. Madrid – Murcia: Editum Universidad de Murcia – Sociedad de Estudios Medievales, 285-290.
Frank, A. G. (1998). *ReOrient: Global Economy in the Asian Age*. Berkeley, CA: University of California Press.
Freire, D. & Lains, P., eds. (2017). *An Agrarian History of Portugal, 1000-2000: Economic Development on the European Frontier*. Leiden: Brill.
Friedman, E. G. (1986). El estatus jurídico de la mujer castellana durante el Antiguo Régimen. In J. García-Nieto, ed., *Ordenamiento jurídico y realidad social de las mujeres: siglos XVI a XX: actas de las IV Jornadas de Investigación Interdisciplinaria*. Madrid: Universidad Autónoma de Madrid, pp. 41-54.
Fuentes Quintana, E., ed. (2005). *Economía y economistas españoles. De los orígenes al mercantilismo*, vol. 2. Madrid: Galaxia Gutenberg/Círculo de Lectores.
Furió Diego, A. (1995). *Història del País Valencià*. Valencia: Edicions Alfons El Magnànim.
Furió Diego, A. (1998). Endettement paysan et crédit dans la Péninsule Ibérique au Bas Moyen Âge. In M. Berthe, ed., *Endettement paysan et crédit rural dans l'Europe médiévale et moderne*. Toulouse: Presses universitaires du Mirail, pp. 139-167.
Furió Diego, A. (2010a). Producción agraria, comercialización y mercados rurales en la Corona de Aragón. In J. Á. Sesma Muñoz, ed., *La Corona de Aragón en el centro de su historia, 1208-1458. Aspectos económicos y sociales*. Zaragoza: Grupo de Investigación CEMA, pp. 363-425.
Furió Diego, A. (2010b). La crisis de la Baja Edad Media: una revisión. In *Las crisis a lo largo de la historia*. Valladolid: Universidad de Valladolid, pp. 13-46.
Furió Diego, A. (2015a). València, 'mare e cap de tot lo regne'. *Afers. Fulls de recerca i pensament*, 30, 149-179.
Furió Diego, A. (2015b). I paesaggi dell'acqua nella Spagna mediterranea: le huertas e l'agricultura irrigua. In *I paesaggi agrari d'Europa (secoli XIII-XV)*. Rome: Viella, pp. 323-384.
Furió Diego, A. (2017). La crescita economica medievale: progressi qualitativi e quantitativi nella produzione agricola. In *La crescita economica dell'Occidente medievale. Un tema storico non ancora esaurito*. Rome: Viella, pp. 107-136.
Furió Diego, A. (2019). Le consommateur paysan, agent des mutations économiques? Le cas de la Péninsule Ibérique au bas Moyen Âge. In G. Ferrand & J. Petrowiste, ed., *Le nécessaire et le superflu. Le paysan consommateur. Actes des XXXVIes Journées internationales d'histoire de l'abbaye de Flaran, 17 et 18 octobre 2014*. Toulouse: Presses Universitaires du Midi, pp. 147-188.

Furió Diego, A. (2021). Teoría y práctica de la agricultura en la Baja Edad Media. Leyendo a los autores agronómicos latinos y árabes en la Corona de Aragón. In I. Ait & A. Esposito, eds., *Agricoltura, lavoro, società. Studi sul medioevo per Alfio Cortonesi*. Bologna: Clueb, pp. 251–288.

Fynn-Paul, J. (2015a). *The Rise and Decline of an Iberian Bourgeoisie: Manresa in the Later Middle Ages, 1250–1500*. Cambridge: Cambridge University Press.

Fynn-Paul, J. (2015b). Occupation, family, and inheritance in fourteenth-century Barcelona: a socio-economic profile of one of Europe's earliest investing publics. *European History Quarterly*, 45(3), 417–445.

Fynn-Paul, J. (2017). *Family, Work, and Household in Late Medieval Iberia: A Social History of Manresa at the Time of the Black Death*. London: Routledge.

Galán Sánchez, Á. (1991). *Los mudéjares del Reino de Granada*. Granada: Universidad de Granada.

Gallego, D. (2001). Historia de un desarrollo pausado: integración mercantil y transformaciones productivas de la agricultura española (1800–1936). In J. Pujol et al., *El pozo de todos los males. Sobre el atraso de la agricultura española contemporánea*, Barcelona: Editorial Crítica, pp. 147–214.

Gallego, D. & Pinilla, V. (1996). Del librecambio matizado al proteccionismo selectivo: el comercio exterior de productos agrarios y alimentos en España entre 1849 y 1935. *Revista de Historia Económica*, XIV(2), 371–420.

Gallup, J. L. (2012). Is there a Kuznets curve? *Portland State University Journal*, 575–603.

Galor, O. (2005). From stagnation to growth: unified growth theory. In P. Aghion & S. N. Durlauf, eds., *Handbook of Economic Growth*, vol. 1A. Amsterdam: Elsevier, pp. 171–285.

Galor, O. & Weil, D. N. (2000). Population, technology and growth: from the Malthusian regime to the demographic transition. *American Economic Review*, 90, 806–828.

Gálvez, L. (2006). Los mercados de trabajo en la España del siglo XX. In J. M. Matés & A. González Enciso, eds., *Historia económica de España*. Madrid: Ariel.

Gárate Ojanguren, M. (1990). *La Real Compañía Guipuzcoana de Caracas*. San Sebastián: Sociedad Guipuzcoana de Ediciones y Publicaciones.

García, M. (2010). La dote femenina: posibilidades de incremento del consumo al comienzo del ciclo familiar: cultura material castellana comparada (1650–1850). In I. dos Guimarães Sá & M. García Fernández, eds., *Portas adentro: comer, vestir, habitar (ss. XVI–XIX)*. Valladolid: Universidad de Valladolid-Imprensa da Universidade de Coimbra, pp. 117–148.

García, M. (2016). La cultura material cotidiana: la complejidad de la vida privada en Castilla y Portugal durante el Antiguo Régimen. *Revista Portuguesa de Historia*, XLVII, 109–127.

García, M. & Bartolomé, Y.-C. (1997). Pautas de consumo, estilos de vida y cambio político en las ciudades castellanas a fines del Antiguo Régimen (Sobre algunas teorías del crecimiento económico desde la perspectiva de la demanda). In J. I. Fortea Pérez, ed., *Imágenes de la diversidad. El mundo urbano en la Corona de Castilla (ss. XVI–XVIII)*. Santander: Universidad de Cantabria.

García-Baquero González, A. (1976). *Cádiz y el Atlántico (1717-1778): el comercio colonial español bajo el monopolio gaditano*, 2 vols. Seville: Escuela de Estudios Hispano-Americanos de Sevilla.
García-Baquero González, A. (1992). *La Carrera de Indias. Suma de negociación y océano de negocios*. Seville: Algaida.
García-Baquero González, A. (1996). Las remesas de metales preciosos americanos en el siglo XVIII: una aritmética controvertida. *Hispania*, 56(1), 203–266.
García de Cortázar, J. Á., ed. (1985). *Organización social del espacio en la España medieval. La Corona de Castilla en los siglos VIII al XV*. Barcelona: Ariel.
García de Cortázar, J. Á (1988). *La sociedad rural en la España medieval*. Madrid: Siglo XXI de España.
García de Cortázar, J. Á. (1994). La ruptura del ritmo de la comunidad: el viaje. In R. Menéndez Pidal, ed., *Historia de España* vol. 16, J. M. Jover Zamora, ed., *La Época del Gótico en la Cultura Española (c. 1220-c. 1480)*. Madrid: Espasa-Calpe, pp. 245–262.
García Díaz, J. (2011). El fenómeno del mercado en la obra legislativa de Alfonso X el Sabio. *Historia. Instituciones. Documentos*, 38, 111–140.
García Espuche, A. (1998). *Un siglo decisivo. Barcelona y Cataluña, 1550-1640*. Madrid: Alianza.
García Fitz, F. (2002). *La experiencia castellano-leonesa frente al Islam. Siglos XI-XIII*. Seville: Universidad de Sevilla.
García-Fuentes, L. (1980). *El comercio español con América, 1650-1700*. Seville: Diputación de Sevilla.
García Garralón, M. (2007). *La Universidad de Mareantes de Sevilla (1569-1793)*. Seville: Diputación de Sevilla.
García-Gómez, J. J. & Escudero, A. (2018). The standard of living of the workers in a Spanish industrial town: wages, nutrition, life expectancy and heigh in Alcoy (1870-1930). *Social Indicators Research*, 140(1), 347–367.
García Herrero, M. del C. (2009). La contribución de las mujeres a la economía de las familias dedicadas a actividades no agrarias en la Baja Edad Media española. In S. Cavaciocchi, ed., *La famiglia nell'economia europea, secc. XIII-XVIII. Atti della 'Quarantesima settimana di studi,' 6-10 aprile 2008*. Florence: Firenze University Press, pp. 569–598.
García Marsilla, J. V. (1993). *La jerarquía de la mesa: los sistemas alimentarios en la Valencia bajomedieval*. Valencia: Diputació de València.
García, Máximo. & Bartolomé Yun-Casalilla, (1997) "Pautas de consumo, estilos de vida y cambio político en las ciudades castellanas a fines del Antiguo Régimen. (Sobre algunas teorías del crecimiento económico desde la perspectiva de la demanda)". In J. I. Fortea Pérez, (ed.) *Imágenes de la diversidad. El mundo urbano en la Corona de Castilla (ss. XVI-XVIII)*, Santander: Universidad de Cantabria.
García Marsilla, J. V. (2002). *Vivir a crédito en la Valencia medieval. De los orígenes del sistema censal al endeudamiento del municipio*. Valencia: Publicacions de la Universitat de València.
García Marsilla, J. V. (2012). Vestit i aparença en els regnes hispanics del segle XIII. In R. Narbona Vizcaíno, ed., *Jaume I i el seu temps 800 anys després*. Valencia: Universitat de València, pp. 621–646.

García-Montero, H. (2015). Long-term trends in wealth inequality in Catalonia, 1400–1800: initial results. *Dondena Working Paper*, 79.
García-Montero, H. (2016). The nutritional status of manufacturing workers and craftsmen in central Spain in the eighteenth century. *Revista de Historia Industrial*, 64(2), 51–75.
Garcia-Oliver, F. (1991). *Terra de feudals: el País Valencià en la tardor de l'Edat Mitjana*. Valencia: Edicions Alfons el Magnànim – Institució Valenciana d'Estudis i Investigació.
Garcia-Oliver, F. (2004). Els cultius. In J. M. Salrach Marés, ed., *Història agrària dels Països Catalans*, vol. 2. Barcelona: Enciclopèdia Catalana, pp. 301–334.
García Sánchez, E. (1986). La alimentación en la Andalucía islámica. Estudio histórico y bromatológico. II: Carne, pescado, huevos, leche y productos lácteos. *Andalucía Islámica. Textos y Estudios*, 4–5, 237–278.
García Sánchez, E. (1996). La alimentación popular urbana en al-Andalus. *Arqueologia medieval*, 4, 219–236.
García Sanjuan, A. (1997). La organización de los oficios en Al-Andalus a través de los manuales de 'hisba'. *Historia. Instituciones. Documentos*, 24, 201–234.
Garcia Sanz, A. (1982). La producción de cereales y leguminosas en Castilla la Vieja. Los diezmos del Obispado de Segovia de 1570 a 1800. In J. Goy & E. Le Roy Ladurie, eds., *Prestations Paysannes, Dîmes, Rente Foncière et Mouvements de la Production Agricole à l'époque Préindustrielle*. Paris: Éditions de l'École des Hautes Études en Sciences Sociales.
Garcia Sanz, A. (1985). Auge y decadencia en España en los siglos XVI y XVII: economía y sociedad en Castilla. *Revista de Historia Economica-Journal of Iberian and Latin American Economic History*, 3(1), 11–27.
García Tapia, N. (1987). Pedro Juan de Lastanosa y 'Pseudo-Juanelo Turriano'. *Llull: Revista de la Sociedad Española de Historia de las Ciencias y de las Técnicas*, 10(18), 51–74.
García Tapia, N. (1989a). *Ingeniería y arquitectura en el renacimiento español*. Valladolid: Universidad de Valladolid.
García Tapia, N. (1989b). *Técnica y poder en Castilla durante los siglos XVI y XVII*. Valladolid: Junta de Castilla y León.
García Tapia, N. & García Diego, J. A. (1987). *Vida y técnica en el renacimiento: manuscrito que escribió, en el siglo XVI, Francisco Lobato vecino de Medina del Campo*. Valladolid: Universidad de Valladolid.
Garner, R. L. (1988). Long term silver mining trends in Spanish America: a comparative analysis of Peru and Mexico. *The American Historical Review*, 93(4), 898–935.
Garzón Pareja, M. (1972). *La industria sedera en España: El arte de la seda de Granada*. Granada: Archivo de la Real Chancillería.
Gatti, L. (1990). *L'arsenale e le galee: pratiche di costruzione e linguaggio tecnico a Genova tra medioevo ed età moderna*. Genova: Centro di studio sulla storia della tecnica del Consiglio nazionale delle ricerche.

Gerrard, C. M., Gutiérrez, A. & Vincent, A. G. (1995). *Spanish Medieval Ceramics in Spain and the British Isles*. Oxford: British Archaeological Reports Oxford Ltd.

Gil Pujol, X. (2012). Integrar un mundo. Dinámicas de agregación y de cohesión en la Monarquía de España. In Ó. Mazín & J. J. Ruiz Ibáñez, eds., *Las Indias Occidentales. Procesos de incorporación a las Monarquías Ibéricas, (siglos XVI a XVIII)*. México: El Colegio de México-Red Columnaria, pp. 69–108.

Gilliodts-van Severen, L. (1904–1905). *Cartulaire de l'Ancienne Estaple de Bruges. Recueil de documents concernant le commerce intérieur et maritime, les relations internationales et l'histoire économique de cette ville*, 2 vols. Bruges: Imprimerie de Louis de Plancke.

Gimpel, J. (1982). *La revolución industrial en la Edad Media*. Madrid: Taurus.

Glick, T. F. (1970). *Irrigation and Society in Medieval Valencia*. Cambridge, MA: Belknap Press of Harvard University Press.

Godinho, V. Magalhães (1970). Portugal and her empire, 1680–1720. In J. S. Bromley, ed., *The New Cambridge Modern History*. Cambridge: Cambridge University Press, pp. 509–539.

Godinho, V. Magalhães (1977). *A Estrutura da Antiga Sociedade Portuguesa*. Lisbon: Arcádia.

Godinho, V. Magalhães (1982–1984). *Os descobrimentos e a economia mundial*, 2nd edn, 4 vols. Lisbon: Presença.

Godinho, V. Magalhães (2008). *A Expansão Quatrocentista Portuguesa*. Lisbon: Dom Quixote.

Goerlich, F. J. & Mas, M. (2001). Inequality in Spain, 1973-91: contribution to a regional dabase. *Review of Income and Wealth*, 47(3), 361–378.

Goitein, S. D. (1967). *A Mediterranean Society: The Jewish Communities of the Arab World as Portrayed in the Documents of the Cairo Geniza. Vol. 1: Economic Foundations*. Berkeley, CA: University of California Press.

Gomes, A. M. D. (2017). Casas de cidade: processo de privatização e consumo de luxo nas camadas intermédias urbanas (Lisboa na segunda metade do século XVIII e inícios do século XIX). PhD thesis, Universidade do Minho.

Gomes, J. C. (1883). *Collecção de leis da dívida pública portuguesa*. Lisbon: Imprensa Nacional.

Gomes, P. & Machado, M. P. (2020). Literacy and primary school expansión in Portugal: 1940–62. *Revista de Historia Económica – Journal of Iberian and Latin American Economic History*, 38(1), 111–145.

Gomes, S. A. (2009). *Vinhos e História na Alta Estremadura entre os séculos XII e XVI*. Leiria: Folheto.

Gomes, S. A. (2017). As feiras e as indústrias rurais no Reino de Portugal. In G. Navarro Espinach & C. Villanueva Morte, eds., *Industrias y mercados rurales en los reinos hispánicos (siglos XIII–XV)*. Murcia: Sociedad Española de Estudios Medievales, pp. 17–35.

Gómez-Blanco, V. M. (2021). When safety becomes risky. Essays on venality, safe assets, and the bubble for offices in early modern Spain. PhD thesis, Universidad Carlos III de Madrid.

Gómez Carrasco, C. J. (2007). *Entre el mundo rural y el mundo urbano: familia, parentesco y organización social en la villa de Albacete (1750-1808)*. Albacete: Instituto de Estudios Albacetenses.

Gonçalves, C. M. (2005). Evoluções recentes do desemprego em Portugal. *Sociologia: Revista da Faculdade de Letras da Universidade do Porto*, 25, 125-163.

Gonçalves, D. Oehen (1971). A Selectividade do Crédito. *Revista Bancária*, 34, 5-28.

Gonçalves, I. (1989). *O património do mosteiro de Alcobaça nos séculos XIV e XV*. Lisbon: Universidade Nova de Lisboa – Faculdade de Ciências Sociais e Humanas.

Gonçalves, I., ed. (2006). *Tombos da Ordem de Cristo: comendas do Vale do Mondego (1508)*. Lisbon: Centro de Estudos Históricos da Universidade Nova de Lisboa.

Gonçalves, P. (2003). Usos e consumos de tabaco em Portugal nos séculos XVI e XVII. Master thesis, Universidade Nova de Lisboa.

González Arce, J. D. (2009). *Gremios y cofradías en los reinos medievales de León y Castilla siglos XII-XV*. Palencia: Región Editorial.

González Arévalo, R. (2020). *Ad terram regis Castelle*: comercio, navegación y privilegios italianos en Andalucía en tiempos de Alfonso X el Sabio. *Alcanate: Revista de Estudios Alfonsíes*, 12, 125-162.

González de Molina, M. (2001). Condicionamientos ambientales del crecimiento agrario español (siglos XIX y XX). In J. Pujol Andreu, ed., *El pozo de todos los males. Sobre el atraso de la agricultura española contemporánea*. Barcelona: Crítica, pp. 43-94.

González Enciso, A. (1980). *Estado e industria en el siglo XVIII: la fábrica de Guadalajara*. Madrid: Fundación Universitaria Española.

González Enciso, A. (2003). La Hacienda castellana y la economía en el siglo XVIII. *Estudis: Revista de historia moderna*, 29, 21-41.

Gonzalez Enciso, A., de Vicente Algueró, F.-J., Floristan Imízcoz, A. & Torres Sánchez, R. (1992). *Historia Económica de la España Moderna*. Madrid: Actas.

González Jiménez, M. (1995). Del Duero al Guadalquivir: repoblación, despoblación y crisis en la Castilla del siglo XIII. In *Despoblación y colonización del valle del Duero. Siglos VIII-XX*. Ávila: Fundación Sánchez-Albornoz, pp. 209-224.

González Mariscal, M. (2015). Inflación y niveles de vida en Sevilla durante la revolución de los precios. *Revista de Historia Economica – Journal of Iberian and Latin American Economic History*, 33(3), 353-386.

Gonzalvo Bou, G. (1994). *Les constitucions de Pau i Treva de Catalunya (segles XI-XIII)*. Barcelona: Departament de Justícia de la Generalitat de Catalunya.

Goodman, D. (1988). *Power and Penury: Government, Technology, and Science in Philip II's Spain*. Cambridge and New York: Cambridge University Press.

Goodman, D. (1992). The scientific revolution in Spain and Portugal. In R. Porter & M. Teich, eds., *The Scientific Revolution in National Context*. Cambridge: Cambridge University Press, pp. 158–177.
Gordo, E., Jareño, J. & Urtasun, A. (2006). Radiografía del sector servicios en España. Madrid: Banco de España.
Gouveia, M. (2012). *Ilduara Mendes e a vila de Nogueiró. Gestão feminina de uma exploração agrária (século XI)*. Lisbon: s.n.
Grafe, R. (2005). *Entre el mundo ibérico y el Atlántico. Comercio y especialización regional, 1550–1650*. Bilbao: Bizkaiko Foru Aldundia.
Grafe, R. (2011). The strange tale of the decline of Spanish shipping. In R. W. Unger, ed., *Shipping and Economic Growth 1350–1850*. Leiden: Brill, pp. 81–115.
Grafe, R. (2012). *Distant Tyranny: Markets, Power, and Backwardness in Spain, 1650–1800*. Princeton, NJ: Princeton University Press.
Grafe, R. (2020). An empire of debt? The Spanish empire and its colonial realm. In N. Barreyre & N. Delalande, eds., *A World of Public Debts: A Political History*. Cham, Switzerland: Palgrave Macmillan, pp. 5–35.
Grafe, R. & Irigoin, A. (2012). A stakeholder empire: the political economy of Spanish Imperial rule in America. *Economic History Review*, 65(2), 609–651.
Grafe, R. & Pedreira, J. M. (2019). New imperial economies. In F. J. Bouza Alvarez, P. Cardim & A. Feros, eds., *The Iberian World*. Abingdon and New York: Routledge, pp. 582–614.
Greif, A. (2006). *Institutions and the Path to the Modern Economy: Lessons from Medieval Trade*. Cambridge: Cambridge University Press.
GRETA (Grupo de Estudios del Tabaco). (2002). El consumo de tabaco en España en el siglo XVIII. *Cuadernos de Investigación Histórica*, 19, 313–345.
Grupo '75. (1977). *La economía del Antiguo Regimen: La 'renta nacional' de la Corona de Castilla*. Madrid: Universidad Autónoma de Madrid.
Guerrero, S. (2017). *Silver by Fire, Silver by Mercury: A Chemical History of Silver Refining in New Spain and Mexico, 16th to 19th Centuries*. Leiden and Boston, MA: Brill.
Guichard, P. (2001). *Al-Andalus frente a la conquista cristiana. Los musulmanes de Valencia (Siglos XI–XIII)*. Valencia: Universitat de València.
Guichard, P. & Lagardère, V. (1990). La vie sociale et économique de l'Espagne musulmane aux XI–XII siècles à travers les *fatwā-s* du *Mi'yār* d'al-Wanšarišī. *Mélanges de la Casa de Velázquez*, XXVI(1), 197–236.
Guidi-Bruscoli, F. (2014). *Bartolomeo Marchionni «Homem de grossa Fazenda» (ca. 1450–1530). Un mercante fiorentino a Lisbona e l'impero portoghese*. Florence: Leo S. Olschki Editrice.
Guilera, J. (2010). The evolution of top income and wealth shares in Portugal since 1936. *Revista de Historia Económica – Journal of Iberian and Latin American Economic History*, 28(1), 139–171.
Guilera, J. (2013). Income inequality in historical perspective. Portugal (1890–2006). PhD thesis, Universitat de Barcelona.

Guinot Rodríguez, E. (2014). La construcción de una nueva sociedad feudal: la repoblación del Reino de Valencia en el siglo XIII. In C. Estepa Díez & M. A. Carmona Ruiz, ed., *La Península Ibérica en tiempos de las Navas de Tolosa*. Murcia: SEEM, pp. 367–391.

Guirao, F. (1998). *Spain and the Reconstruction of Western Europe, 1945–57: Challenge and Response*. London and Nueva York: Macmillan-St. Martin's Press.

Gutierrez Nieto, J. I. (1986). El pensamiento económico, político y social de los arbitristas. In R. Menéndez Pidal, ed., *Historia de España*. Vol. 28, t. 1. *El siglo del Quijote (1580–1680): Religión, filosofía, ciencia*. Madrid: Espasa-Calpe, pp. 235–354.

Gutiérrez-Poch, M. (2018). Oh, industria madre fecundísima. La 'doble revolución': Revolución Liberal, cambio político y Revolución Industrial en España (1808–1874). *Áreas*, 37, 44–58.

Hajnal, J. (1965). European marriage patterns in perspective. In D. V. Glass & D. E. C. Eversley, eds., *Population in History. Essays in Historical Demography*, vol. I. New Brunswick: Aldine Transaction, pp. 101–143.

Halikowski-Smith, S. (2010). No obvious home: the flight of the Portuguese 'tribe' from Makassar to Ayutthaya and Cambodia during the 1660s. *International Journal of Asian Studies*, 7(1), 1–28.

Hamilton, E. J. (1934). *American Treasure and the Price Revolution in Spain, 1501–1650*. New York: Octagon Books.

Hamilton, E. J. (1936). *Money, Prices and Wages in Valencia, Aragon and Navarre (1351–1500)*. Cambridge, MA: Harvard University Press.

Hanson, C. A. (1981). *Economy and Society in Baroque Portugal, 1668–1703*. Minneapolis, MN: University of Minnesota Press.

Haring, C. H. (1939). *Comercio y navegación entre España y las Indias en la época de los Habsburgos*. Mexico D.F.: Fondo de Cultura Económica.

Harley, Ch. & Taylor, P. (1987). Mineral wealth and economic development: foreign direct investment in Spain, 1851–1913. *The Economic History Review*, 40(2), 185–207.

Hatton, T. J. & Williamson, J. G. (2008). *Global Migration and the World Economy: Two Centuries of Policy and Performance*. London and Cambridge, MA: The MIT Press.

Hausberguer, B. (2018). *Historia mínima de la globalización temprana*. México: El Colegio de México.

Hausberger, B. & Ibarra, A., eds. (2003). *Comercio y poder en América colonial. Los consulados de comerciantes, siglos XVII–XVIII*. Madrid: Iberoamericana.

Helguera Quijada, J. (1983). El Canal de Castilla como factor de desarrollo económico regional, en el siglo XVIII. In *El pasado histórico de Castilla y León. Actas del I Congreso de Historia de Castilla y León celebrado en Valladolid, del 1 al 4 de diciembre de 1982*, vol. 2. Valladolid: Junta de Castilla y León, pp. 493–515.

Helguera Quijada, J., García Tapia, N. & Molinero Hernando, F. (1988). *El Canal de Castilla*. Valladolid: Junta de Castilla y León.

Henriques, A. Castro (2003). O Rei e a Terra de Barroso. Poder Régio, Montanha e Periferia. Master thesis. Lisbon: Universidade Nova de Lisboa.
Henriques, A. Castro (2008). State finance, war and redistribution in Portugal, 1249-1527. PhD thesis, University of York.
Henriques, A. Castro (2014). The rise of a tax state: Portugal, 1371-1401. *e-journal of Portuguese History*, 12, 49-66.
Henriques, A. Castro (2015). Plenty of land, land of plenty: the agrarian output of Portugal, 1311-20. *European Review of Economic History*, 19(2), 149-170.
Henriques, A. Castro (2017). The Reconquista and its legacy, 1000-1348. In D. Freire & P. Lains, eds., *An Agrarian History of Portugal, 1000-2000. Economic Development on the European Frontier*. Leiden: Brill, pp. 13-44.
Henriques, A. Castro (2019). Taming Leviathan: constitution, representation and taxation in fifteenth-century Portugal. *População e Sociedade*, 31, 69-82.
Henriques, A. Castro (2020). Capital in a frontier economy: Portugal, 1230-1500. *Revista de Historia Economica - Journal of Iberian and Latin American Economic History*, 38, 11-44.
Henriques, A. Castro & Palma, N. (2023). Comparative European institutions and the Little Divergence, 1385-1800. *Journal of Economic Growth*, 28, 259-294.
Henriques, A. Castro, Palma, N. & Reis, J. (2021). A bumpy ride: economic growth in Portugal from the reconquest to the present. Unpublished manuscript.
Henriques, A. Castro & Reis, J. (2015). 'From horn to corn': the two regimes of Portuguese agriculture, 1250-1850. Semantic Scholar. Available at: https://lisbon2016rh.files.wordpress.com/2015/12/0005-onw3.pdf [accessed 5 May 2023].
Henriques, F. & Rodrigues, T. Ferreira (2008). O século XX: a transição. In T. Ferreira Rodrigues, ed., *A População Portuguesa. Das longas permanências à conquista da modernidade*. Porto: Afrontamento.
Henriques, S. T. & Sharp, P. (2020). Without coal in the age of steam and dams in the age of electricity: an explanation for the failure of Portugal to industrialize before the Second World War. *European Review of Economic History*, 25(1), 85-105.
Heredia Herrera, A. (2004). Casa de la Contratación y Consulado de Cargadores a Indias: afinidad y confrontación. In A. Acosta Rodríguez, A. L. González Rodríguez & E. Vila Vilar, eds., *La Casa de la Contratación y la navegación entre España y las Indias*. Seville: Universidad de Sevilla - CSIC - Fundación El Monte, pp. 161-181.
Herlihy, D. & C. Klapisch-Zuber (1985). *Tuscans and their Families: A Study of the Florentine Catasto of 1427*. New Haven, CT: Yale University Press.
Hernández, B. (1997). Hombres de negocios y finanzas públicas en la Cataluña de Felipe II. *Revista de Historia Económica*, 15(1), 51-86.
Hernández, B. (2003). *Fiscalismo y finanzas en la Cataluña moderna. La fiscalidad catalana en época de Felipe II*. Barcelona: Taller de Estudios Hispánicos e Hispanoamericanos.
Hernández García, R. (2013a). Women's labor participation rates in the kingdom of Castilla in the 18th century. *Feminist Economics*, 19(4), 181-199.

Hernández García, R. (2013b). La mano de obra infantil en la Castilla rural del siglo XVIII. In J. M. Borrás Llop, ed., *El trabajo infantil en España (1700-1950)*. Barcelona: Universitat de Barcelona, pp. 91-115.

Hernández López, A. (2011). Una aproximación a las prácticas usurarias en las ciudades andalusíes. In V. Martínez Enamorado, ed., *I Congreso Internacional. Escenarios Urbanos de al-Andalus y el Occidente Musulmán (Vélez-Málaga, 16-18 de junio de 2010)*. Vélez-Málaga: Ayuntamiento de Vélez-Málaga, pp. 369-383.

Hernández López, A. (2016). *El valor del tiempo. Doctrina jurídica y práctica de la usura (ribā) en el Occidente islámico medieval*. Helsinki: Academia Scientiarum Fennica.

Hernando, I. & Núñez, S. (2004). The contribution of ICT to economic activity: A growth accounting exercise with Spanish firm-level data. *Investigaciones Económicas*, 28(2), 315-346.

Herr, R. (1989). *Rural Change and Royal Finances in Spain at the End of the Old Regime*. Berkeley, CA: University of California Press.

Herranz-Loncán, A. (2006). Railroad impact on backward economies: Spain, 1850-1913. *Journal of Economic History*, 66(4), 853-881.

Herranz-Loncán, A. (2007). Infrastructure investment and Spanish economic growth, 1850-1935. *Explorations in Economic History*, 44, 452-468.

Herrera, Gabriel Alonso de (1818). *Agricultura General*, 4 vols. Imprenta Real.

Herrero Sánchez, M., ed. (2017). *Repúblicas y republicanismo en la Europa moderna (siglos XVI-XVIII)*. Madrid: Fondo de Cultura Económica.

Herzog, T. (2003). *Defining Nations: Immigrants and Citizens in Early Modern Spain and Spanish America*. New Haven, CT: Yale University Press.

Hespanha, A. M. (1993). Os poderes do centro: a fazenda. In J. Mattoso & A. M. Hespanha, eds., *História de Portugal, vol. IV. O Antigo Regime (1620-1807)*. Lisbon: Estampa, pp. 202-239.

Hespanha, A. M. (1994). *As vésperas do Leviathan. Instituições e poder político. Portugal (Século XVII)*. Coimbra: Almedina.

Hespanha, A. M. (2001). A constituçao do Império português de alguns enviesamentos correntes. In J. Fragoso, M. F. Bicalho & M. F. Gouvêa, eds., *O antigo regime nos trópicos. A dinâmica imperial portuguesa (séculos XVI-XVIII)*. Rio de Janeiro: Civilização Brasileira, pp. 163-188.

Hespanha, A. M. (2013). As finanças portuguesas nos séculos XVII e XVIII. *Cadernos do Programa de Pós-Graduações em Direito/ UFRGS*, VIII(2), 79-132.

Hilaire-Pérez, L. & Verna, C. (2006). Dissemination of technical knowledge in the middle ages and the early modern era: new approaches and methodological issues. *Technology and Culture*, 47, 537-563.

Hillgarth, J. N. (1976). *1250-1410, Precarious Balance. The Spanish Kingdoms, 1250-1516*, vol. 1. New York: Oxford University Press.

Hoffman, P. T., Postel-Vinay, G. & Rosenthal, J. L. (2000). *Priceless Markets: The Political Economy of Credit in Paris, 1660–1870*. Chicago, IL: The University of Chicago Press.

Hoffmann, R. C. & Johnson, H. B. (1971). Un village portugais en mutation: Povoa del Rey à la fin du XIVe siècle. *Annales. Économies. Sociétés. Civilisations*, 26(5), 917–940.

Hoffmann. W. (1965). *Das Wachstum der Deutschen Wirtschaft Seit der Mitte des 19. Jahrhunderts*. Berlin: Springer.

Hohenberg, P. M. & Lees, L. H. (1985). *The Making of Urban Europe, 1000–1950*. Cambridge, MA: Harvard University Press.

Horden, P. & Purcell, N. (2000). *The Corrupting Sea: A Study of Mediterranean History*. Oxford and Malden: Blackwell.

Hough, J. & Grier, R. (2015). *The Long Process of Development: Building Markets and States in Pre-Industrial England, Spain and their Colonies*. Cambridge and New York: Cambridge University Press.

Houthakker, H. S. (1957). An international comparison of household expenditure patterns, commemorating the century of Engel's Law. *Econometrica*, 25(4), 532–551.

Hugon, A. (2014). *La insurrección de Nápoles, 1647–1648: la construcción del acontecimiento*. Zaragoza: Prensas de la Universidad de Zaragoza.

Humphries, J. (2003). English apprenticeship: a neglected factor in the first industrial revolution. In P. A. David & M. Thomas, eds., *The Economic Future in Historical Perspective*. London: British Academy, pp. 73–102.

Humphries, J. & Sarasúa, C. (2012). Off the record: reconstructing women's labor force participation in the European past. *Feminist Economics*, 18(4), 39–67.

Ibn Hawqal (1964). *Configuration de la Terre (Kitāb Ṣūrat al-Arḍ)*, J. H. Kramers & G. Wiet., French transl. Beyrouth-Paris: Éditions G.P. Maisonneuve & Larose.

Ibn Ḥayyān (2001). *Crónica de los emires Alhakam I y 'Abdarrahman II entre los años 796 y 847 [Almuqtabis II-1]*, M. 'Ali Makki & F. Corriente, eds. Zaragoza: Instituto de Estudios Islámicos y del Oriente Próximo.

Ibn Ṣāḥib aṣ-Ṣalā (1969). *Al-Mann bi-l-imāma*, A. Huici, Spanish transl. Zaragoza Anubar.

Igual-Luis, D. (2000). Los agentes de la banca internacional: cambistas y mercaderes en Valencia. *Revista d'Història Medieval*, 11, 105–138.

Igual-Luis, D. (2001). La difusión de productos en el Mediterráneo y en Europa occidental en el tránsito de la Edad Media a la Moderna. In S. Cavaciocchi, ed., *Fiere e mercati nella integrazione delle economie europee. Secc. XIII–XVIII. Atti della 'trentaduesima settimana di studi,' 8–12 maggio 2000*. Florence: Le Monnier, pp. 453–494.

Igual-Luis, D. (2005). La emigración genovesa hacia el Mediterráneo bajomedieval. Algunas reflexiones a partir del caso español. In L. Gallinari, ed., *Genova, una 'porta' del Mediterraneo*, vol. 1. Genoa: Brigati, pp. 295–328.

Igual-Luis, D. (2014). Los grupos mercantiles y la expansión política de la Corona de Aragón: nuevas perspectivas. In L. Tanzini & S. Tognetti, eds.,

Il governo dell'economia. Italia e Penisola Iberica nel basso Medioevo. Rome: Viella, pp. 9-32.

Igual-Luis, D. (2017a). Los mercados rurales en la Corona de Castilla. In G. Navarro Espinach & C. Villanueva Morte, eds., *Industrias y mercados rurales en los reinos hispánicos (siglos XIII-XV)*. Murcia: Sociedad Española de Estudios Medievales, pp. 125-144.

Igual-Luis, D. (2017b). Valencia: opportunities of a secondary node. In W. Blockmans, M. Krom & J. Wubs-Mrosewicz, eds., *The Routledge Handbook of Maritime Trade Around Europe 1300-1600*. London and New York: Routledge, pp. 210-228.

Igual-Luis, D. (2018). The Christian kingdoms of the Iberian Peninsula (1100-1500): concepts, facts and problems concerning social mobility. In S. Carocci & I. Lazarinni, eds., *Social Mobility in Medieval Italy (1100-1500)*. Roma: Viella, pp. 101-126.

Igual-Luis, D. (forthcoming). La Corona de Aragón. In M. Asenjo González, ed., *La ciudad viva. El mundo urbano en el Medievo hispanocristiano (siglos XI-XV)*. Madrid: Universidad Complutense.

Igual-Luis, D. & Navarro Espinach, G., eds. (2018). *El País Valenciano en la Baja Edad Media. Estudios dedicados al profesor Paulino Iradiel*. Valencia: Publicacions de la Universitat de València.

Instituto Nacional de Estatística (2003). *Portugal Social, 1991-2001*. Lisbon: Instituto Nacional de Estatística.

Instituto Nacional de Estatística (INE). Área, Produção e Produtividade das Principais Culturas. www.ine.pt/xportal/xmain

Iradiel Murugarren, P. (1974). *Evolución de la industria textil castellana en los siglos XIII-XVI. Factores de desarrollo, organización y costes de la producción manufacturera de Cuenca*. Salamanca: Universidad de Salamanca.

Iradiel Murugarren, P. (2003). Metrópolis y hombres de negocios (siglos XIV y XV). In *Las sociedades urbanas en la España medieval*. Pamplona: Gobierno de Navarra, pp. 277-310.

Iradiel Murugarren, P. (2017). *El Mediterráneo medieval y Valencia. Economía, sociedad, historia*. Valencia: Publicacions de la Universitat de València.

Iradiel Murugarren, P., Moreta, S. & Sarasa, E. (1989). *Historia Medieval de la España cristiana*. Madrid: Cátedra.

Irigoin, A. & Grafe, R. (2008). Bargaining for absolutism: a Spanish path to empire and nation building. *Hispanic American Historical Review*, 88(2), 173-210.

Isla Frez, A. (1992). *La sociedad gallega en la Alta Edad Media*. Madrid: CSIC.

Izquierdo Benito, R. (1983). *Precios y salarios en Toledo durante el siglo XV (1400-1475)*. Toledo: Caja de Ahorros Provincial.

Jaumotte, F., Koloskova, K. & Saxena, S. C. (2016). *Impact of Migration on Income Levels in Advanced Economies*. Washington, DC: International Monetary Fund.

Jiménez Estrella, A. & Andújar, A. (2018). Ejército y reformas militares en la Monarquía Hispánica a ambos lados del Atlántico. Un análisis en perspectiva comparada (siglos XVI-XVIII). In A. Barreto, F. Palomo & R. Stumpf, eds.,

REFERENCES

Monarquias ibéricas em perspectiva comparada (Sécs. XVI-XVIII). Dinâmicas imperiais e circulação de modelos administrativos. Lisbon: Imprensa de Ciências Sociais-Universidade de Lisboa, pp. 387-430.

Jong, H. & Palma, N. (2018). Historical national accounting. In M. Blum & C. Colvin, eds., *An Economist's Guide to Economic History*. Cham, Switzerland: Palgrave Macmillan, pp. 395-403.

Jordà, O., Schularick, M. & Taylor, A. (2017). Macrofinancial history and the new business cycle facts. In M. Eichenbaum & J. Parker, eds., *NBER Macroeconomics Annual 2016*. Chicago, IL: University of Chicago Press.

Jorgenson, D. W. (1990). Productivity and economic growth. In E. R. Berndt & J. E. Tripplett, eds., *Fifty Years of Economic Measurement: The Jubilee of the Conference on Research and Income and Wealth*. Chicago, IL: Chicago University Press, 19-118.

Jorgenson, D. W., Gollop, F. M. & Fraumeni, B. (1987). *Productivity and U.S. Economic Growth*. Cambridge, MA: Harvard University Press.

Jorgenson, D. W. & Griliches, Z. (1967). The Explanation of Productivity Change. *Review of Economic Studies*, 34, 249-280.

Jover Avellà, G. (1997). *Societat rural i desenvolupament econòmic a Mallorca. Feudalisme, latifundi i pagesia, 1500-1800*. Barcelona: Universitat de Barcelona.

Júnior, J. T. A. da Costa (1917a). Inquérito às condições da vida económica do operariado português. *Boletim da Previdência Social*, 3, 103-109.

Júnior, J. T. A. da Costa (1917b). O custo de vida em Portugal. *Boletim da Previdência Social*, 3, 195-199.

Junyent, E. (1992). *Diplomatari i escrits literaris de l'abat i bisbe Oliba*. Barcelona: Institut d'Estudis Catalans.

Justino, D. (1989). *A formação do espaço económico nacional: Portugal (1810-1913)*. Lisbon: Vega.

Kagan, R. (1974). *Students and Society in Early Modern Spain*. Baltimore, OH: Johns Hopkins University Press.

Kagan, R. (1981). *Lawsuits and Litigants in Castile, 1500-1700*. Chapel Hill, NC: University of North Carolina Press.

Kamen, H. (1981). *La España de Carlos II*. Barcelona: Crítica.

Kassis, Hanna E. (1997). La economía. II: La moneda, pesos y medidas. In R. Menéndez Pidal, ed., *Historia de España*, Vol. VIII-II, M. J. Viguera Molins, ed. *El retroceso territorial de al-Andalus. Almorávides y almohades. Siglos XI al XIII*. Madrid: Espasa Calpe, pp. 301-337.

Kasl, R. (2012). The making of Hispano-Flemish style: art, commerce, and politics in fifteenth-century Castile. PhD thesis, New York University.

Kedar, B. Z. (1976). *Merchants in Crisis: Genoese and Venetian Men of Affairs and the Fourteenth Century Depression*. New Haven, CT and London: Yale University Press.

Kedrosky, D. & Palma, N. (2021). The Cross of Gold: Brazilian Treasure and the Decline of Portugal. CAGE working paper no. 574.

Kelly, M., Mokyr, J. & Ó Gráda, C. (2014). Precocious Albion: a new interpretation of the British industrial revolution. *Annual Review of Economics*, 6(1), 363–389.
Kelly, P. (1835). *The Universal Cambist*, 2nd edn. London: Printed for the author.
Kendrick, J. W. (1961). *Productivity Trends in the United States*. Princeton, NJ: Princeton University Press.
King, R. G. & Levine, R. (1993). Finance and growth: Schumpeter might be right. *The Quarterly Journal of Economics*, 108(3), 717–737.
Kirchner, H. (2009). Original design, tribal management and modifications in medieval hydraulic systems in the Balearic Islands (Spain). *World Archaeology*, 41(1), 151–168.
Klein, H. S. (1975). The Cuban slave trade in a period of transition, 1790–1843. *Revue française d'histoire d'outremer*, 62.
Komlos, J. (1998). Shrinking in a growing economy? The mystery of physical stature during the Industrial Revolution. *The Journal of Economic History*, 58(3), 779–802.
Komlos, J. & Baten, J. (2004). Looking backward and looking forward: anthropometric research and the development of social science history. *Social Science History*, 28, 191–210.
Komlos, J. & Kelly I. R., eds. (2016). *The Oxford Handbook of Economics and Human Biology*. Oxford: Oxford University Press.
Krantz, O. (2017). Swedish GDP 1300–1560: a tentative estimate. *Lund Papers in Economic History*, 152, 1–28.
Krugman, P. & Venables, A. J. (1995). Globalization and the inequality of nations. *The Quarterly Journal of Economics*, 110(4), 857–880.
Kuethe, A. J. & Andrien, K. J. (2014). *The Spanish Atlantic World in the 18th Century: War and the Bourbon Reforms, 1713–1796*. Cambridge: Cambridge University Press.
Kuvishnov, D. & Zimmermann, K. (2020). The Big Bang: stock market capitalization in the long run. *CEPR Discussion Paper*, 14468.
Kuznets, S. (1953). *Shares of Upper Income Groups in Income and Savings*. New York: National Bureau of Economic Research.
Kuznets, S. (1955). Economic growth and income inequality. *American Economic Review*, 45(1), 1–28.
Kuznets, S. (1966). *Modern Economic Growth: Rate, Structure, and Spread*. New Haven, CT: Yale University Press.
Lacarra de Miguel, J. M. (1981). Dos tratados de paz y alianza entre Sancho el de Peñalén y Moctadir de Zaragoza (1069 y 1073). In *Colonización, parias, repoblación y otros estudios*. Zaragoza: Anúbar, pp. 79–94.
Ladero Quesada, M. Á. (1969). *Granada. Historia de un país islámico (1232–1571)*. Madrid: Gredos.
Ladero Quesada, M. Á. (1978). *España en 1492*. Madrid: Hernando.
Ladero Quesada, M. Á. (1988a). La política monetaria en la Corona de Castilla (1369–1497). *En la España Medieval*, 11, 79–123.

Ladero Quesada, M. Á. (1988b). El crecimiento económico en la Corona de Castilla en el siglo XV: algunos ejemplos andaluces. In *Los mudéjares de Castilla y otros estudios de historia medieval andaluza*. Granada: Universidad de Granada, pp. 257–288.

Ladero Quesada, M. Á. (1990–1991). Crédito y comercio de dinero en la Castilla medieval. *Acta historica et archaeologica mediaevalia*, 11–12, 145–159.

Ladero Quesada, M. Á. (1992). El crecimiento económico de la Corona de Castilla en el siglo XV: ejemplos andaluces. *Medievalia*, 10, 217–235.

Ladero Quesada, M. Á. (1994). *Las ferias de Castilla. Siglos XII a XV*. Madrid: Comité Español de Ciencias Históricas.

Ladero Quesada, M. Á. (1997). Las reformas fiscales y monetarias de Alfonso X como base del 'Estado Moderno'. In M. Rodríguez Llopis, ed., *Alfonso X: aportaciones de un rey castellano a la construcción de Europa*. Murcia: Editora Regional de Murcia, pp. 31–54.

Ladero Quesada, M. Á. (2010). Los mudéjares de Castilla cuarenta años después. *En la España Medieval*, 33, 383–424.

Ladero Quesada, M. Á. (2011). *Fiscalidad y poder real en Castilla (1252–1369)*. Madrid: Real Academia de la Historia.

Ladero Quesada, M. Á. (2017). *Población. Economía*. Vol. 1 of *España a finales de la Edad Media*. Madrid: Dykinson.

Ladero Quesada, M. Á. & González Jiménez, M. (1978). *Diezmo eclesiástico y producción de cereales en el reino de Sevilla (1408–1503)*. Seville: Universidad de Sevilla.

Lafay, G. (1992). The measurement of revealed comparative advantage. In M. G. Dagenais & P. A. Muet, eds, *International Trade Modelling*. London: Chapman & Hall.

Lafuente Gómez, M. (2018). El consumo doméstico de armas en Aragón en la Baja Edad Media. In M. Lafuente Gómez & J. Petrowiste, eds., *Faire son marché au Moyen Âge. Méditerranée occidentale, XIIIe–XVIe siècle*. Madrid: Casa de Velázquez, pp. 47–68.

Lagardère, V. (1993). *Campagnes et Paysans d'al-Andalus (VIIIe–XVe s.)*. Paris: Éditions Maisonneuve & Larose.

Lahon, D. (2001). Esclavage et Confréries Noires au Portugal durant l'Ancien Régime (1441–1830). PhD thesis, École des Hautes Études en Sciences Sociales.

Lains, P. (1995). *A Economia Portuguesa no Século XIX. Crescimento Económico e Comércio Externo, 1851–1913*. Lisbon: Imprensa Nacional-Casa da Moeda.

Lains, P. (1998). An account of the Portuguese African empire, 1885–1975. *Revista de Historia Económica – Journal of Iberian and Latin American Economic History*, 16(1), 235–263.

Lains, P. (1999). *L'Économie Portugaise au XIX siècle*. Paris: L'Harmattan.

Lains, P. (2002a). *Os Progressos Do Atraso. Uma Nova História Económica de Portugal: 1842–1992*. Lisbon: Imprensa de Ciências Sociais.

Lains, P. (2002b). *História da Caixa Geral de Depósitos, 1876–1910. Política e finanças no liberalismo português*. Lisbon: Imprensa de Ciências Sociais.

Lains, P. (2003a). Catching-up to the European core: Portuguese economic growth (1910-1990). *Explorations in Economic History*, 40, 369-386.

Lains, P. (2003b). New wine in old bottles: output and productivity trends in Portuguese agriculture, 1850-1950. *European Review of Economic History*, 7 (1), 43-72.

Lains, P. (2005). A Indústria. In P. Lains and Á. Ferreira da Silva, eds., *História Económica de Portugal: 1700-2000*, vol II. Lisbon: Imprensa de Ciências Sociais.

Lains, P. (2006a). *Los Progresos del Atraso. Una Nueva Historia Económica de Portugal, 1842-1992*. Zaragoza: Prensas Universitarias de Zaragoza.

Lains, P. (2006b). Growth in a protected environment: Portugal. 1850-1950. *Research in economic history*, 24, 121-163.

Lains, P. (2007a). *O Economista Suave. Ensaios*. Lisbon: Edições Cosmos.

Lains, P. (2007b). New series of Portuguese foreign trade 1850-1914. *Universidad Carlos III Working Papers in Economic History*, 17-04, 1-33.

Lains, P. (2008). *História da Caixa Geral de Depósitos, 1910-1974. Política, finanças e economia na República e no Estado Novo*. Lisbon: Imprensa de Ciências Sociais.

Lains, P. (2009). Agriculture and economic development in Portugal, 1870-1973. In P. Lains & V. Pinilla, eds., *Agriculture and Economic Development in Europe Since 1870*. London: Routledge, pp. 333-352.

Lains, P. (2011). *História da Caixa Geral de Depósitos, 1974-2010.Política Nacional e Banca Pública na Integração Europeia*. Lisbon: Imprensa de Ciências Sociais.

Lains, P. (2014). *O Economista Suave Outra Vez: Ensaios sobre Portugal e a Grande Recessão, 2008-2013*. Coimbra: Actual Editora.

Lains, P. (2018). Portugal. In V. Pinilla & K. Anderson, eds., *Wine Globalization: A New Comparative History*. Cambridge: Cambridge University Press, pp. 178-207.

Lains, P. & Pinilla, V. (2009). *Agriculture and Economic Development in Europe Since 1870*. London: Routledge.

Lains, P. & Silva, Á. Ferreira da, eds. (2005a). *História Económica de Portugal: 1700-2000*, vol. II. Lisbon: Imprensa de Ciências Sociais.

Lains, P. & Silva, Á. Ferreira da, eds. (2005b). *História Económica de Portugal: 1700-2000*, vol. III. Lisbon: Imprensa de Ciências Sociais.

Lains, P. & Silva, Á. Ferreira da, eds. (2005c). *História Económica de Portugal: 1700-2000*, vol. I. Lisbon: Imprensa de Ciências Sociais.

Lains, P. & Silva, Ester G. (2016). Globalization, growth and inequality. In C. Antunes & K. Fatah-Black, eds., *Explorations in History and Globalization*. London: Routledge, pp. 231-249.

Laliena Corbera, C. (2010a). Dinámicas de crisis: la sociedad rural aragonesa al filo de 1300. In J. Á. Sesma Muñoz, ed., *La Corona de Aragón en el centro de su Historia. 1208-1458. Aspectos económicos y sociales*. Zaragoza: Grupo CEMA, pp. 61-88.

Laliena Corbera, C. (2010b). La metamorfosis del Estado feudal. Las estructuras institucionales de la Corona de Aragón en el periodo de expansión (1208-1283). In J. Á. Sesma Muñoz, ed., *La Corona de Aragón en el centro de su historia. 1208-1458. La monarquía aragonesa y los reinos de la Corona*. Zaragoza: Grupo CEMA, pp. 65–96.

Laliena Corbera, C. (2014). Cambio social y reorganización institucional en la Corona de Aragón. In C. Estepa Díez & M. A. Carmona Ruiz, eds., *La Peninsula Ibérica en tiempos de las Navas de Tolosa*. Murcia: SEEM, pp. 337–366.

Laliena Corbera, C. (2016). Una edad de oro? Transformaciones económicas en la Corona de Aragón en el siglo XV. In P. Iradiel Murugarren, G. Navarro Espinach, D. Igual-Luis & C. Villanueva Morte, eds., *Identidades urbanas Corona de Aragón-Italia: redes económicas, estructuras institucionales, funciones políticas (siglos XIV–XV)*. Zaragoza: Prensas universitarias de Zaragoza.

Laliena Corbera, C. & Iranzo Muñío, M. T. (1998). Poder, honor y linaje en las estrategias de la nobleza urbana aragonesa (siglos XIV y XV). *Revista d'Història Medieval*, 9, 41–80.

Lamikiz, X. (2010). *Trade and Trust in the Eighteenth-Century Atlantic World: Spanish Merchants and their Overseas Networks*. Woodbridge: Royal Historical Society.

Landes, D. S. (1969). *The Unbound Prometheus: Technological Change and Industrial Development in Western Europe from 1750 to the Present*. Cambridge: Cambridge University Press.

Leigh, A. (2007). How closely do top income shares track other measures of inequality? *Economic Journal*, 117(524), 619–633.

Leitão, H. (2018). Instruments and artisanal practices in long distance oceanic voyages. *Centaurus*, 60(3), 189–202.

Leite, J. da Costa (2005). Populaçao e crescimento económico. In P. Lains & Á. Ferreira da Silva, eds., *História Económica de Portugal: 1700–2000*, vol. II. Lisbon: Imprensa de Ciências Sociais.

Leite, M. T. (2014). O espaço da Mouraria na cidade de Évora, séculos XIV e XV. Master thesis, Universidade de Évora.

Levy, F. & Temin, P. (2007). Inequality and institutions in 20th century America. *NBER Working Paper Series*, 13106, 1–53.

Li, H., Squire, L. & Zou, H. (1998). Explaining international and intertemporal variation in income inequality. *Economic Journal*, 108(446), 26–43.

Lindert, P. H. (2000a). When did inequality rise in Britain and America?. *Journal of Income Distribution*, 9, 11–25.

Lindert, P. H. (2000b). Three centuries of inequality in Britain and America. In A. Atkinson & F. Bourguignon, eds., *Handbook of Income Distribution*, vol. 1. Amsterdam: Elsevier, pp. 167–216.

Lindert, P. H. & Williamson, J. G. (1985). Growth, equality and history. *Explorations in Economic History*, 22(4), 341–377.

Lindert, P. H. & Williamson, J. G. (2016). *Unequal Gains: American Growth and Inequality Since 1700*. Princeton, NJ: Princeton University Press.

Livi-Bacci, M. (1968). Fertility and nuptiality changes in Spain from the late 18th to the early 20th century. *Population Studies*, XXII(1), 83–102 and XXII(2), 211–234.

Livi-Bacci, M. (2008). *Conquest: The Destruction of the American Indios*. Cambridge and Malden: Polity.

Llaguno Amírola, E. & Ceán Bermúdez, J. A. (1829). *Noticias de los arquitectos y la arquitectura de España desde su Restauración*, 3 vols. Madrid: Imprenta Real.

Llopis Agelán, E. (2001). El legado económico del Antiguo Régimen desde la óptica regional. In L. G. Germán Zubero *et alii*, eds., *Historia Económica Regional de España, siglos XIX y XX*. Barcelona: Crítica, pp. 507–524.

Llopis Agelán, E. (2002a). Expansión, reformismo y obstáculos al crecimiento (1715–1789). In E. Llopis, ed., *Historia económica de España: siglos X–XX*. Barcelona: Crítica.

Llopis Agelán, E. (2002b). La crisis del Antiguo Régimen y la Revolución liberal (1790–1840). In F. Comín, M. Hernández & E. Llopis, eds., *Historia económica de España, siglos X–XX*. Barcelona: Crítica, pp. 165–202.

Llopis Agelán, E. (2004a). El crecimiento de la población española, 1700–1849: Índices regionales y nacional de bautismos. *Áreas. Revista Internacional de Ciencias Sociales*, 24, 10–24.

Llopis Agelán, E. (2004b). España, la 'Revolución de los Modernistas' y el legado del Antiguo Régimen. In E. Llopis, ed., *El legado económico del Antiguo Régimen en España*. Barcelona: Crítica.

Llopis Agelán, E. & González Mariscal, M. (2006). La tasa de urbanización de España a finales del siglo XVIII: el problema de las agrociudades. *Documentos de trabajo de la Asociación Española de Historia Económica*, 0602, 1–25.

Lopes, G. A. (2015). Brazil's colonial economy and the Atlantic slave trade: supply and demand. In D. Richardson & F. Ribeiro da Silva, eds., *Networks and Trans-Cultural Exchanges. Slave Trading in the South Atlantic, 1590–1867*. Leiden and Boston, MA: Brill, pp. 31–70.

Lopes, J. da Silva (2004a). *A Economia Portuguesa no Século XX*. Lisbon: Imprensa de Ciências Sociais.

Lopes, J. da Silva (2004b). *A Economia Portuguesa desde 1960*. Lisbon: Gradiva.

Lopes, J. da Silva (2005). Finanças públicas. In P. Lains & Á. Ferreira da Silva, eds., *História Económica de Portugal: 1700–2000*, vol. III. Lisbon: Imprensa de Ciências Sociais, pp. 265–304.

Lopes, M. A. (2000). *Pobreza, assistência e controlo social em Coimbra (1750–1850)*, vol. II. Viseu: Palimage Editores.

López Arandia, M. A. (2018). Timber supplying in the South Spanish dockyards during the 18th century. In A. Polónia & F. Cotente Domingues, eds., *Shipbuilding: Knowledge and Heritage*. Porto: CITCEM, pp. 135–157.

López Barahona, V. & Nieto Sánchez, J. (2012). Dressing the poor: the provision of clothing among the lower classes in eighteenth-century Madrid. *Textile History*, 43(1), 24–43.

López Beltrán, M. T. (2010). El trabajo de las mujeres en el mundo urbano medieval. *Mélanges de la Casa de Velázquez*, 40(2), 39–57.

López-Cordón Cortezo, M. V. (1986). La situación de la mujer a finales del Antiguo Régimen (1760–1860). In M. Á. Durán Heras & R. M. Capel Martínez, eds.,

Mujer y Sociedad en España, 1700–1975. Madrid: Ministerio de Cultura-Instituto de la Mujer, pp. 47–107.

López-Cordón Cortezo, M. V. & Monteiro, N. Gonçalo (2019). Enlightened politics in Portugal and Spain. In F. Bouza, P. Cardim & A. Feros, eds., *The Iberian World (1450–1820)*. London: Routledge, pp. 475–499.

López García, S. M. & Santesmases Navarro de Palencia, M. J. (2006). La ciencia en España. In A. González Enciso & J. M. Matés Barco, eds., *Historia económica de España*. Barcelona: Ariel, pp. 891–918.

López-Losa, E. & Piquero-Zarauz, S. (2021). Spanish subsistence wages and the Little Divergence in Europe, 1500–1800. *European Review of Economic History*, 25(1), 59–84.

López Piñero, J. M. et al. (1981–1986). *Los impresos científicos españoles de los siglos XV y XVI*, 4 vols. Valencia: Universidad de Valencia.

Lorenzana de la Puente, F. (2014). *La representación política en el Antiguo Régimen. Las Cortes de Castilla, 1655–1834*. Madrid: Congreso de los Diputados.

Lorenzo Sanz, E. (1979). *Comercio de España con América en la época de Felipe II*. Valladolid: Instituto Cultural Simancas.

Lourenço, R. F. & Rodrigues, P. M. M. (2014). The dynamics and contrasts of house prices in Portugal and Spain. *Economic Bulletin and Financial Stability Report Articles and Banco de Portugal Economic Studies*, 39–52.

Lovejoy, D. (1987). *The Glorious Revolution in America*, 2nd edn. Hanover, NH: Wesleyan University Press.

Macedo, J. Borges de (1982). *Problemas de História da Indústria Portuguesa no Século XVIII*, 2nd edn. Lisbon: Querco.

Machado, P. (2014). *Ocean of Trade: South Asian Merchants, Africa and the Indian Ocean, c. 1750–1850*. Cambridge: Cambridge University Press.

Macías Hernández, A. M. (2011). Población, producción y precios del trigo, 1498–1560. *Anuario de Estudios Atlánticos*, 57, 327–384.

MacKay, A. (1977). *Spain in the Middle Ages: From Frontier to Empire, 1000–1500*. London: Macmillan.

MacKay, A. (1981). *Money, Prices and Politics in Fifteenth-Century Castile*. London: Royal Historical Society.

MacLeod, Ch. (1992). Strategies for innovation: the diffusion of new technology in nineteenth-century British industry. *The Economic History Review*, 45(2), 285–307.

MacLeod, M. J. (2008). *Spanish Central America: A Socioeconomic History, 1520–1720*. Austin, TX: University of Texas Press.

Maddison, A. (1987). Growth and slowdown in advanced capitalist economies: tenchiques of quantitative assessment. *Journal of Economic Literature*, 25(2), 649–668.

Maddison, A. (1988). Ultimate and proximate growth causality: a critique of Mancur Olson on the rise and decline of nations. *Scandinavian Economic History Review*, 36, 25–29.

Maddison, A. (2006). *The World Economy*, 2 vols. Paris: Organisation for Economic Cooperation and Development (OECD).

Maddison Project Database 2013. (2013). www.rug.nl/ggdc/historicaldevelop ment/maddison/releases/maddison-project-database-2013
Maddison Project Database 2018. (2018). www.rug.nl/ggdc/historicaldevelop ment/maddison/releases/maddison-project-database-2018
Madureira, N. L. (1997). *Mercado e Privilégios: A indústria portuguesa entre 1750 e 1830*. Lisbon: Editorial Estampa.
Madureira, N. L. & Matos, A. Cardoso de (2005). A tecnologia. In P. Lains and Á. Ferreira da Silva, eds., *História Económica de Portugal: 1700–2000*, Vol. I. Lisbon: Imprensa de Ciências Sociais, pp. 123–144.
Maduro, A. Valério (2018). La difusión del maíz y las transformaciones en el sistema agropecuario del dominio cisterciense de Alcobaça, siglos XVIII y XIX. *Obradoiro de historia moderna*, 27, 81–111.
Magalhães, J. Romero (1987). Alguns aspectos da produção agrícola no Algarve: fins do século XVIII – princípios do século XIX. *Revista Portuguesa de História*, XXII. Coimbra: Faculdade de Letras da Universidade de Coimbra.
Magalhães, J. Romero (1993). *O Algarve económico: 1600–1773*. Lisbon: Estampa.
Magalhães, J. Romero (1994). As estruturas sociais de enquadramento da economia portuguesa de Antigo Regime: os concelhos. *Notas económicas: Revista da Faculdade de Economia da Universidade de Coimbra*, 4, 30–47.
Magalhães, J. Romero (2009). O açúcar nas ilhas portuguesas do Atlântico, séculos XV e XVI. *Varia Historia*, 25(41), 151–175.
Magalhães, J. Romero (2010). Do tempo e dos trabalhos: a agricultura portuguesa no século XVII. *Revista Portuguesa de História*, 41, 59–72.
Makkari [Al-Maqqarī] (1840–1843). *The History of the Mohammedan Dynasties in Spain*. Pascual de Gayangos, partial translation into English. London: Oriental Translation Fund of Great Britain and Ireland.
Malanima, P. (1988). *I piedi di legno. Una macchina alle origini dell'industria medioevale*. Milano: Franco Angeli.
Malanima, P. (2005). Urbanisation and the Italian economy during the last Millennium. *European Review of Economic History*, IX(1), 97–122.
Malanima, P. (2011). The long decline of a leading economy: GDP in central and northern Italy, 1300–1913. *European Review of Economic History*, 15, 169–219.
Mallorquí Garcia, E. (2011). *Parròquia i societat rural al Bisbat de Girona, segles XIII i XIV*. Barcelona: Fundació Noguera.
Malo de Molina, J. L. & Martín-Aceña, P., eds. (2012). *The Spanish Financial System. Growth and Development Since 1900*. Basingstoke: Palgrave Macmillan, pp. 145–181.
Malpica Cuello, A., ed. (1996). *Agua, trabajo y azúcar. Actas del VI Seminario Internacional sobre la caña de azúcar. Motril, 19–23 September 1994*. Granada: Diputación Provincial de Granada.
Malpica Cuello, A. (2010). Urban life in al-Andalus and its role in social organization and the structure of settlement. *Imago Temporis. Medium Aevum*, IV, 25–49.

Maltas Montoro, J. (2019). Caresties, fams i crisis de mortalitat a Catalunya: 1283–1351. Anàlisi d'indicadors i reconstrucció dels cicles econòmics i demogràfics. PhD thesis, Universitat de Lleida.
Mansuy-Diniz Silva, A., ed. (1993). *D. Rodrigo de Souza Coutinho. Textos políticos, económicos e financeiros: 1783–1811*, vol. I. Lisbon: Banco de Portugal.
Manzano Moreno, E. (2015). *Épocas medievales*. Vol. 2 of *Historia de España*. Madrid: Crítica-Marcial Pons.
Marcadé, J. (1971). *Une comarque portugaise – Ourique-entre 1750 et 1800*. Lisbon: Fundação Calouste Gulbenkian-Centro Cultural Português.
Marcos, R. F. (1997). *As companhias pombalinas: Contributo para a história das sociedades por acções em Portugal*. Coimbra: Almedina.
Marcos Martín, A. (2000). *España en los siglos XVI, XVII y XVIII: economía y sociedad*. Barcelona: Crítica.
Marcos Martín, A. (2006). Deuda pública, fiscalidad y arbitrios en la Corona de Castilla durante los siglos XVI y XVII. In C. Sanz Ayán & B. J. García, eds., *Banca, Crédito y Capital. La Monarquía Hispánica y los antiguos Países Bajos (1505–1700)*. Madrid: Fundación Carlos de Amberes, pp. 345–375.
Marcos Martín, A. (2007). Movilidad social ascendente y movilidad social descendente en la Castilla Moderna. In I. Gómez González & M. L. López-Guadalupe Muñoz, eds., *La movilidad social en la España del Antiguo Régimen*. Granada: Comares.
Marfany, J. (2012). *Land, proto-industry and population in Catalonia, c. 1680–1829. An Alternative Transition to Capitalism?* Abingdon: Routledge.
María-Dolores, R. & Martínez-Carrión, J.M. (2011). The relationship between height and economic development in Spain, 1850–1958. *Economics and Human Biology*, 9(1), 30–44.
Mariana, Juan de (1987). *Tratado y discurso sobre la moneda de vellón*. Madrid: Instituto de Estudios Fiscales (edited by Lucas Beltran, first edition in Latin 1609).
Marichal, C. (1999). *La bancarrota del virreinato, Nueva España y las finanzas del imperio español, 1780–1810*. México: El Colegio de México and Fondo de Cultura Económica.
Marichal, C. (2007). *Bankruptcy of Empire: Mexican Silver and the Wars Between Spain, Britain, and France, 1760–1810*. Cambridge: Cambridge University Press.
Marques, A. H. de Oliveira (1965). A Pragmática de 1340. In *Ensaios de História Medieval Portuguesa*. Lisbon: Editorial Vega, pp. 125–160.
Marques, A. H. de Oliveira (1978). *Introdução à História da Agricultura em Portugal: A Questão Cerealífera Durante a Idade Média*, 3rd edn. Lisbon: Edições Cosmos.
Marques, A. H. de Oliveira (1987). *Portugal na Crise dos séculos XIV e XV*. Vol. IV of *Nova História de Portugal*. Lisbon: Ed. Presença.
Marques, J. (1988). *A Arquidiocese de Braga no século XV*. Lisbon: Imprensa Nacional-Casa da Moeda.

Marques, J. (1999). A vila rústica de Deão em 1284. In M. Barroca, ed., *In Memoriam Carlos Alberto Ferreira de Almeida*, vol. 2. Porto: Faculdade de Letras do Porto, pp. 15-26.

Marques, J. d. S., ed. (1944). *Descobrimentos Portugueses. Documentos para a sua História*, vol. 1. Lisbon: Instituto Nacional de Investigação Científica.

Marques, J. C. & Góis, P. (2012). A evolução do sistema migratório lusófono. Uma análise a partir da imigração e emigração portuguesa. *Revista Internacional em Língua Portuguesa*, 24, 213-231.

Marques, M. Gomes (1996). *História da moeda medieval portuguesa*. Sintra: Instituto Universitário de Sintra.

Martín-Aceña, P. (2012). Central banking in the Iberian Peninsula: a comparison. In J. A. Consiglio et al., eds., *Banking and Finance in the Mediterranean: A Historical Perspective*. Surrey: Ashgate.

Martín-Aceña, P. & Nogues-Marco, P. (2013). Crisis bancarias en la historia. Del Antiguo Régimen a los orígenes del capitalismo moderno. In F. Comín & M. Hernández, eds., *Las crisis económicas en España, 1300-2012. Lecciones de la Historia*. Madrid: Alianza Editorial, pp. 141-167.

Martín Cea, J. C. (1996). El trabajo en el mundo rural bajomedieval castellano. In Á. Vaca Lorenzo, ed., *El trabajo en la historia*. Salamanca: Universidad de Salamanca, pp. 91-128.

Martín Rodríguez, J. L. (1993). *La España medieval*. Madrid: Historia 16.

Martín Rodríguez, M. (1984). *Pensamiento económico español sobre la población. De Soto a Matanegui*. Madrid: Pirámide.

Martínez, J. L. (1983). *Pasajeros a Indias: Viajes transatlánticos en el siglo XVI*. Madrid: Alianza.

Martínez-Carrión, J. M. (2016). Living standards, nutrition and inequality in the Spanish industrialisation: an anthropometric view. *Revista de Historia Industrial*, 64, 11-50.

Martínez-Galarraga, J. & Prat, M. (2016). Wages, prices, and technology in early Catalan industrialization. *Economic History Review*, 69(2), 548-574.

Martínez García, S. (2006). Obras en el palacio de la Aljafería a finales del siglo XIV. Un apunte documental. *Aragón en la Edad Media*, XIX, 381-390.

Martinez-Ruiz, E. (2003). *El Sector Exterior durante la Autarquía: Una Reconstrucción de las Balanzas de Pagos de España (1940-1958)*. Madrid: Banco de España.

Martínez-Ruiz, E. & Pons, M. A. (2020). 1959: the stabilization plan and the end of autarky. In C. Betrán & M. A. Pons, eds., *Historical Turning Points in Spanish Economic Growth and Development, 1808-2008*. Cham, Switzerland: Palgrave Macmillan, pp. 123-157.

Martínez Shaw, C. (1994). *La emigración española a América (1492-1824)*. Colombres: Archivo de Indianos.

Martínez Sopena, P. (1995). Repoblaciones interiores. Villas nuevas de los siglos XII y XIII. In *Despoblación y colonización del valle del Duero. Siglos VIII-XX*. Ávila: Fundación Sánchez-Albornoz, pp. 161-188.

Martínez Sopena, P. (2004). Los francos en la España de los siglos XI al XIII. In Á. Vaca, ed., *Minorías y migraciones en la Historia*. Salamanca: Universidad de Salamanca, pp. 25-66.

Martín-Retortillo, M. & Pinilla, V. (2015). Patterns and causes of growth of European agricultural production, 1950-2005. *Agricultural History Review*, 63, 132-159.

Martins, C. A (1997). Trabalho e condições de vida em Portugal (1850-1913). *Análise Social*, XXXII(142), 483-535.

Mas, M. & Quesada, J. (2006). The role of ICT in the Spanish productivity slowdown. *FBBVA Documentos de Trabajo*, 5, 1-24.

Mata, M. E. (1988). As três fases do fontismo. Projectos e realizações. In *Estudos em Homenagem a Vitorino Magalhães Godinho*: Lisbon: Livraria Sá da Costa Editora, pp. 412-439.

Mata, M. E. (2008). A forgotten country in globalisation? The role of foreign capital in nineteenth-century Portugal. In M. Müller & T. Myllyntaus, eds., *Pathbreakers: Small European Countries Responding to Globalisation and Deglobalisation*. Bern: Peter Lang Publishing Group, pp. 177-184.

Mateus, A. M. (1995). O sucesso dos Tigres Asiáticos, que lições para Portugal?. *FEUNL Working Paper*, 254, 1-60.

Mattoso, J. (1985). *Ricos homens, infanções e cavaleiros. A nobreza medieval portuguesa nos séculos XI e XII*. Lisbon: Guimarães Editores.

Mattoso J. (1993). *A Monarquia Feudal (1096-1480)*. Vol. 2 of *História de Portugal*. Lisbon: Ed. Círculo de Leitores.

Mauro, P., Sussman, N. & Yafeh, Y. (2006). *Emerging Markets and Financial Globalization: Sovereign Bond Spreads in 1870-1913 and Today*. Oxford: Oxford University Press.

McCants, A. E. C. (2007). Exotic goods, popular consumption, and the standard of living: thinking about globalization in the early modern world. *Journal of World History*, 18(4), 433-462.

Medeiros, Carlos A. (1993). Environnement, agriculture et élevage au Portugal a l'époque des découvertes maritimes. In R. Durand, ed., *L'homme, l'animal domestique et l'environnement: du Moyen Âge au XVIIIe siècle*. Nantes: Ouest Editions, pp. 307-313.

Medrano Adán, J. (2006). *Puertomingalvo en el siglo XV: iniciativas campesinas y sistema social en la montaña turolense*. Teruel: Instituto de Estudios Turolenses.

Medrano Fernández, V. (2010). *Un mercado entre fronteras: las relaciones comerciales entre Castilla y Portugal al final de la Edad Media*. Valladolid: Universidad de Valladolid.

Melo, A. Sousa (2009). *Trabalho e Produção em Portugal na Idade Média: O Porto, c.1320 - c.1415/Travail et Production au Portugal au Moyen Âge: Porto, c.1320-*

c.1415, 2 vols. Braga-Paris: Universidade do Minho-École des Hautes Études en Sciences Sociales.

Melo, A. Sousa (2018). Entre trabalho ordenado e trabalho livre: regulamentação e organização dos mesteres em Portugal nos séculos XIV e XV. In J. Á. Solorzano Telechea & A. Sousa Melo, eds., *Trabajar en la Ciudad Medieval Europea. XIII Encuentros Internacionales del Medievo*. Logroño: Instituto de Estudios Riojanos, pp. 23–37.

Melo, A. Sousa & Ribeiro, M. do C. Franco (2012). Os materiais empregues nas construções urbanas medievais. Contributo preliminar para o estudo da região do Entre Douro e Minho. In A. Sousa Melo & M. do C. Franco Ribeiro, eds., *História da Construção – Os Materiais*. Braga-Paris: Ed. CITCEM-LAMOP, pp. 127–164.

Melo, A. Sousa & Ribeiro, M. do C. Franco (2015). Late-medieval construction site management: the Monastery of Jerónimos in Lisbon. *Construction History*, 30 (1), 23–37.

Melo, F. Souza & Martins Cambraia, D. de. (2022) Cotton exports from Brazil, 1758–1815 dataset. EUI Research Data, Department of History and Civilisation. https://hdl.handle.net/1814/74724.

Melo, F. Souza & Martins Cambraia, D. de. (2023). Reassessing the productivity of enslavement on large-scale plantations and small farms in Brazilian cotton production (C.1750–C.1810). *Historical Research*, 96, 193–221.

Mendes, A. de Almeida (2016). Le Portugal et l'Atlantique. Expansion, esclavage et race en perspective (XIVe–XVIe siècles). *Rives Méditerranéennes*, 53, 137–157.

Mendes, M. F., Infante, P., Afonso, A. et al. (2016). *Determinantes da fecundidade em Portugal*. Lisbon: Fundação Francisco Manuel dos Santos.

Mendo Carmona, C. (1990). La industria del cuero en la Villa y tierra de Madrid a finales de la Edad Media. *Espacio, Tiempo y Forma. Serie III: Historia Medieval*, 3, 181–211.

Menéndez Pidal, R., Lapesa, R., García, C. & Seco, M. (2003). *Léxico Hispánico Primitivo (siglos VIII al XII)*. Madrid: Fundación Ramón Menéndez Pidal – Real Academia Española.

Merino Navarro, J. P. (1987). *Las Cuentas de la Administración Central Española: 1750-1820*. Madrid: Servicio de Publicaciones del Ministerio de Economía y Hacienda.

Miguel López, I. (2000). *El mundo del comercio en Castilla y León al final del antiguo régimen*. Valladolid: Sever-Cuesta.

Milanovic, B. (2011). A short history of global inequality: the past two centuries. *Explorations in Economic History*, 48(4), 494–506.

Milanovic, B. (2013). The inequality possibility frontier: extensions and new applications. *Policy Research Working Paper, World Bank Development Research Group*, 6449, 1–31.

Milanovic, B. (2016), *Global Inequality: A New Approach for the Age of Globalization*. Cambridge, MA: Harvard University Press.

Milanovic, B., Lindert, P. H. & Williamson, J. (2007). Measuring ancient inequality. *National Bureau of Economic Research Working Paper Series*, 135050, 1–86.

Milanovic, B., Lindert, P. H. & Williamson, J. (2011). Pre-industrial inequality. *Economic Journal*, 121(551), 255–272.
Milhaud, C. (2018). Interregional flows of capital and information in Spain: a case study of the Theresian Carmelite order. *Revista de Historia Económica – Journal of Iberian and Latin American Economic History*, 37(1), 81–110.
Mincer, J. (1958). Investment in human capital and personal income distribution. *Journal of Political Economy*, 66(4), 281–302.
Mira Jódar, A. J. (1997). Administrar los drets al senyor rey pertanyents. La gestión de la fiscalidad real en el País Valenciano en la Baja Edad Media. In M. Sánchez Martínez & A. Furió, eds., *Corona, municipis i fiscalitat a la Baixa Edat Mitjana*. Lleida: Institut d'Estudis Ilerdencs, pp. 527–553.
Miranda, F. & Casado Alonso, H. (2018). Comércio entre o porto de Bristol e Portugal no final da Idade Média, 1461–1504. *Anais de História de Além-Mar*, 19, 11–36.
Miranda, F. & Faria, D. (2016). Lisboa e o comércio marítimo com a Europa nos séculos XIV e XV. In J. L. Inglês Fontes et al., eds., *Lisboa medieval. Gentes, Espaços e Poderes*. Lisbon: Instituto de Estudos Medievais, pp. 241–266.
Miranda, S. M. (2010). Organización financiera y práctica política en el estado de la India durante la Unión Ibérica. In G. Sabatini, ed. *Comprendere le monarchie iberiche. Risorse materiali e rappresentazioni del potere*. Roma: Viella, pp. 261–229.
Miranda, S. M. (2016). Coping with Europe and the empire, 1500–1620. In D. Freire & P. Lains, eds., *An Agrarian History of Portugal, 1000–2000: Economic Development on the European Frontier*. Leiden: Brill.
Miranda García, F. & Guerrero Navarrete, Y. (2008). *Medieval. Territorios, sociedades y culturas*. Vol. III of *Historia de España*. Madrid: Sílex.
Mitchell, B. R. (2007a). *International Historical Statistics: The Americas 1750–2005*. Basingstoke: Palgrave Macmillan.
Mitchell, B. R. (2007b). *International Historical Statistics: Africa, Asia and Oceania 1750–2005*. Basingstoke: Palgrave Macmillan.
Mitchell, B. R. (2007c). *International Historical Statistics: Europe 1750–2005*. Basingstoke: Palgrave Macmillan.
Mitchell, B. R. (2013). *International Historical Statistics; Africa, Asia and Oceania 1750–2005*, 6th ed. New York: Palgrave Macmillan.
Mokyr, J. (1990). *The Lever of Riches: Technological Creativity and Economic Progress*. New York and Oxford: Oxford University Press.
Mokyr, J. (1992). Technological inertia in economic history. *The Journal of Economic History*, 52(2), 325–338.
Molas i Ribalta, P. (1978). La Junta General de Comercio y Moneda: la institución y los hombres. *Hispania: Revista Española de Historia*, 8–9, 1–38.
Molas i Ribalta, P. (1996). Las Juntas de Comercio en la Europa Moderna. *Anuario de Historia del Derecho Español*, 66, 497–518.
Molina López, E. (1997). La economía. I. Economía, propiedad, impuestos y sectores productivos. In R. Menéndez Pidal, ed., *El Historia de España*, vol.

VIII-II, M. J. Viguera Molins, ed., *El retroceso territorial de al-Andalus. Almorávides y almohades. Siglos XI al XIII*. Madrid: Espasa Calpe, pp. 211–300.
Monsalvo Antón, J. M. (1985). *Teoría y evolución de un conflicto social. El antisemitismo en la Corona de Castilla en la Baja Edad Media*. Madrid: Siglo XXI.
Monsalvo Antón, J. M. (1997). Las dos escalas de la señorialización nobiliaria al sur del Duero. Concejos de villa y tierra frente a la señorialización 'menor'. (Estudio a partir de casos del sector occidental: señoríos abulenses y salmantinos). *Revista d'història medieval*, 8, 275–338.
Monsalvo Antón, J. M. (2010). *Atlas histórico de la España medieval*. Madrid: Síntesis.
Monsalvo Antón, J. M., ed. (2014). *Historia de la España medieval*. Salamanca: Universidad de Salamanca.
Monteano Sorbet, P. J. (1996). Navarra de 1366 a 1428: población y poblamiento. *Príncipe de Viana*, 208, 307–344.
Monteano Sorbet, P. J. (2000). La población de Navarra en los siglos xiv, xv y xvi. *Revista de Demografía Histórica*, 18(1), 29–70.
Monteano Sorbet, P. J. (2001). La Peste Negra en Navarra. La catástrofe demográfica de 1347–1349. *Príncipe de Viana*, 222, 87–120.
Monteiro, N. G. (1996). Os poderes locais no Antigo Regime. In C. de Oliveira, ed. *História dos Municípios e do Poder Local*. Lisbon: Círculo de Leitores, pp. 17–175.
Monteiro, N. G. (1998). *O crepúsculo dos grandes: a casa e o património da aristocracia em Portugal, 1750–1832*. Lisbon: Imprensa Nacional-Casa da Moeda.
Monteiro, N. G. (2001). Identificação da política setecentista. Notas sobre Portugal no início do período joanino. *Análise Social*, 157, 961–987.
Monteiro, N. G. (2003). *Elites e Poder: entre o Antigo Regime e o Liberalismo*. Lisbon: Imprensa de Ciências Sociais.
Monteiro, N. G. (2005). A ocupaçao da terra. In P. Lains & A. Ferreira da Silva, eds., *História Económica de Portugal, 1700–2000*, vol. I, o século XVIII. Lisboa: Impresa de Ciências Sociais, pp. 68–91.
Monteiro, N. G. (2010). A ocupação da terra. In P. Lains & Á. Ferreira da Silva, eds., *História Económica de Portugal: 1700–2000*, vol. I. Lisbon: Imprensa Ciência Sociais, pp. 67–91.
Monteiro, N. G. (2012). Os 'consumos culturais' da aristocracia na dinastia de Bragança: algumas notas. In M. A. P. de Matos, ed., *Um gosto português. O uso do azulejo no século XVII*. Lisbon: Babel-Museu Nacional do Azulejo, pp. 31–39.
Moreira M. J. Guardado (2008). O século XVIII. In T. Rodrigues, ed., *História da População Portuguesa*. Porto: CEPESE; Edições Afrontamento, pp. 247–287.
Moreira M. J. Guardado & Gomes, C. S. (2014). Evolução da população portuguesa. In M. L. Bandeira, ed., *Dinâmicas demográficas e envelhecimento da população portuguesa: 1950–2011, evolução e perspectivas*. Lisbon: Fundação Francisco Manuel dos Santos.

Moreira M. J. Guardado & Rodrigues, T. F. (2008). As regionalidades demográficas do Portugal contemporáneo. *CEPESE Working Papers*, 1-38.
Moreira, M. J. Guardado & Veiga, T. Rodrigues (2005). A evolução da população. In P. Lains & Á. Ferreira da Silva, eds., *História Económica de Portugal: 1700-2000*, vol. I. Lisbon: Imprensa de Ciências Sociais, pp. 35-65.
Moreno Claverías, B. (2007). *Consum i condiçions de vida a la Catalunya Moderna. El Penedès, 1670-1790*. Vilafranca del Penedès: Edicions Andana.
Moreno Claverías, B. (2015). El aprendiz de gremio en la Barcelona del siglo XVIII. *Áreas. Revista Internacional de Ciencias Sociales*, 34, 63-75.
Morineau, M. (1985). *Incroyables gazettes et fabuleux métaux: Les retours des trésors américains d'aprés les gazettes hollandaises (XVIe-XVIIIe siécles)*. London and Paris: Cambridge University Press and Editions de la Maison des Sciences de l'Homme.
Morrison, C. (2000). Historical perspectives on income distribution. In A. Atkinson & F. Bourguignon, eds., *Handbook of Income Distribution*, vol. 1. Amsterdam: Elsevier, pp. 217-260.
Moutoukias, Z. (1988). *Contrabando y control colonial en el siglo XVII. Buenos Aires, el Atlántico y el espacio peruano*. Buenos Aires: Bibliotecas Universitarias-Centro Editor de América Latina.
Mueller, R. C. (1977). *The Procuratori di San Marco and the Venetian Credit Market*, New York: Arno Press.
Mugueta Moreno, Í. (2008). *El dinero de los Evreux: Hacienda y fiscalidad en el Reino de Navarra (1328-1349)*. Pamplona: Gobierno de Navarra.
Mugueta Moreno, Í. (2017). Mercados locales e industrias rurales en Navarra (1280-1430). In G. Navarro Espinach & C. Villanueva Morte, eds., *Industrias y mercados rurales en los reinos hispánicos (siglos XIII-XV)*. Murcia: Sociedad Española de Estudios Medievales, pp. 145-174.
Mundell, R. (1957). International trade and factor mobility. *American Economic Review*, 47(3), 321-335.
Munro, J. H. (2003). Industrial energy from water-mills in the European economy, 5th to 18th centuries: the limitations of power. In S. Cavacciochi, ed., *Economia e Energia, secc. XIII-XVIII. Atti della 'Trentaquattresima Settimana di Studi,'* 15-19 aprile 2002. Florence: Le Monnier, pp. 223-269.
Munro, J. H. (2013). Rents and the European 'financial revolution'. In G. Caprio, ed., *Handbook of Key Global Financial Markets, Institutions, and Infrastructure*, vol. 1. Oxford: Elsevier, pp. 235-249.
Muñoz, M. R., Navarro, G., Igual, D. & Villanueva, C., eds. (2019). *Els llibres de la col·lecta del Dret Portugués de València (1464-1512)*. Valencia: Publicacions de la Universitat de València.
Muñoz Navarro, D. (2014). El artesanado sedero valenciano a finales del Antiguo Régimen. Crisis sedera, proletarización social y declive progresivo del Colegio del Arte Mayor de la Seda (1759-1836). In R. Franch Benavent, F. Andrés Robres & R. Benítez Sánchez-Blanco, eds., *Cambios y resistencias sociales en la*

Edad Moderna: un análisis comparativo entre el centro y la periferia mediterránea de la Monarquía Hispánica. Madrid: Sílex Ediciones, pp. 85–96.

Muñoz Navarro, D. (2018). *Los escaparates de la moda. Sistemas de comercialización, espacios de consumo y oferta textil en la Valencia preindustrial (1675–1805)*. Madrid: Sílex.

Muro, L. (1964). Bartolomé de Medina, introductor del beneficio de patio en Nueva España. *Historia Mexicana*, 13(4), 517–531.

Myro, R. (1983). La evolución de la productividad global de la economía española en el período 1965–1981. *Información Comercial Española*, 549, 115–127.

Nadal, J. (1975). *El fracaso de la Revolución Industrial en España, 1814–1913*. Esplugues de Llobregat: Editorial Ariel.

Nadal, J. (1984). *La población española (Siglos XVI a XX)*. Barcelona: Ariel.

Nadal, J. (1992a). La última epidemia de peste en Cataluña, 1650-1654. In J. Nadal, *Bautismos, desposorios y entierros. Estudios de historia demográfica*. Barcelona: Ariel, pp. 55–76.

Nadal, J. (1992b). La población catalana a lo largo del último milenio. In J. Nadal, *Bautismos, desposorios y entierros. Estudios de historia demográfica*. Barcelona: Ariel, pp. 95–121.

Nadal, J., Benaul, J. P. & Sudrià, C. (2003). *Atlas de la industrialización de España, 1750-2000*. Madrid: Crítica-BBVA

Nadal, J. & Giralt, E. (1960). *La population catalane de 1553 à 1717. L'immigration française et les autres facteurs de son développement*. Paris: SEVPEN.

Naquin, S. & Rawski, E. S. (1987). *Chinese Society in the Eighteenth Century*. New Haven, CT: Yale University Press.

Navarro Espinach, G. (1999). *Los orígenes de la sedería valenciana (siglos XV–XVI)*. Valencia: Ajuntament de València.

Navarro Espinach, G. (2004). Las etapas de la vida en las familias artesanas de Aragón y Valencia durante el siglo XV. *Aragón en la Edad Media*, XVIII, 203–244.

Navarro Espinach, G. (2012). Estudios sobre industria y artesanado en la España medieval. *Actas y Comunicaciones del Instituto de Historia Antigua y Medieval de la Universidad de Buenos Aires*, 8(1), 1–9.

Navarro Espinach, G. & Villanueva Morte, C., eds. (2017). *Industrias y mercados rurales en los reinos hispánicos (siglos XIII–XV)*. Murcia: Sociedad Española de Estudios Medievales.

Navarro Palazón, J. & Jiménez Castillo, P. (2001). El urbanismo islámico y su transformación después de la conquista cristiana: el caso de Murcia. In J. Passini, ed., *La ciudad medieval: de la casa al tejido urbano*. Toledo: Universidad de Castilla la Mancha, pp. 71–131.

Negro Cortés, A. E. (2020). Las parias pagadas a Castilla por la taifa aftasí de Badajoz. *Revista de Estudios Extremeños*, 76(Extra 1), 41–64.

Neto, M. Sobral (2018). La difusión del cultivo de la patata en Portugal, siglos XV–XIX. *Obradoiro de Historia Moderna*, 27, 113–138.

Nicolau, R. (2005). Población, salud y actividad. In A. Carreras i Odriozola & X. Tafunell Sambola, eds., *Estadísticas históricas de España: siglo XIX–XX*, 2nd edn, 3 vols. Bilbao: Fundación BBVA.

Nicolau, R. & Pujol-Andreu, J. (2006). Variaciones regionales de los precios de consumo y de las dietas en España, en los inicios de la transición demográfica. *Revista de Historia Económica – Journal of Iberian and Latin American Economic History*, 24(3), 521–553.

Nicolini, E. & Ramos-Palencia, F. (2016). Decomposing income inequality in a backward pre-industrial economy: Old Castile (Spain) in the middle of the eighteenth century. *The Economic History Review*, 69(3), 747–772.

Nicolini, E. & Ramos-Palencia, F. (2020). Inequality in early modern Spain: new evidence from the Ensenada Cadastre in Castile, c. 1750. In G. Nigro, ed., *Disuguaglianza economica nelle società preindustriali: cause ed effetti/ Economic Inequality in Pre-industrial Societies: Causes and Effects*. Florence: Firenze University Press, pp. 259–277.

Nicolini, E. & Ramos-Palencia, F. (2021). Comparing income and wealth inequality in pre-industrial economies: lessons from 18th-century Spain. *European Review of Economic History*, 25(4), 680–702.

Nieto, J. (2006). *Artesanos y mercaderes. Una historia social y económica de Madrid (1450–1850)*. Madrid: Editorial Fundamentos.

Nogues-Marco, P. (2010). Bullionism, specie-point mechanism and bullion flows in the early 18th century Europe. PhD thesis, Institut d'études politiques de Paris.

Nogues-Marco, P. (2011). *Tipos de cambio y tipos de interés en Cádiz en el siglo XVIII (1729–1788)*. Banco de España – Estudios de Historia Económica, 58.

Nogues-Marco, P. (2018). Money markets and exchange rates in preindustrial Europe. In S. Battilossi, Y. Cassis & K. Yago, eds., *Handbook of the History of Money and Currency*. Singapore: Springer, pp. 245–268.

Nogues-Marco, P. & vam Malle-Sabouret, C. (2007). East India bonds, 1718–1763: early exotic derivatives and London market efficiency. *European Review of Economic History*, 11 (3), 367–394.

North, D. C. (1990). *Institutions, Institutional Change and Economic Performance*. Cambridge: Cambridge University Press.

North, D. C. & Thomas, R. P. (1973).*The Rise of the Western World: A New Economic History*. Cambridge: Cambridge University Press.

North, D. C., Wallis, J. J. & Weingast, B. R. (2009). *Violence and Social Orders: A Conceptual Framework for Interpreting Recorded Human History*. Cambridge: Cambridge University Press.

North, D. C. & Weingast, B. R. (1989). Constitutions and commitment: the evolution of institutions governing public choice in seventeenth-century England. *Journal of Economic History*, 49(4), 803–832.

Nuez, F., ed. (2002). *La herencia árabe en la agricultura y el bienestar de Occidente*. Valencia: Editorial Universidad Politécnica de Valencia.

Nunes, A. Bela (1991). A evolução da estrutura, por sexos, da população activa em Portugal—um indicador do crescimento económico (1890-1981). *Análise Social*, 26(112/113), 707-722.

Nunes, A. Bela (2001). Actividade económica da população. In N. Valério, ed., *Estatísticas históricas portuguesas*. Lisbon: Instituto Nacional de Estatística.

Nunes, A. Bela, St. Aubyn, M., Valério, N. & Sousa, R. Martins de (2018). Determinants of the income velocity of money in Portugal: 1891-1998. *Portuguese Economic Journal*, 17(2), 99-115.

Nunes, A. Bela & Valério, N. (2005). Moeda e Crédito. In P. Lains & Á. Ferreira da Silva, eds., *História Económica de Portugal: 1700-2000*, vol. II. Lisbon: Imprensa de Ciências Sociais.

Núñez, C. E. (1992). *La fuente de la riqueza: educación y desarrollo económico en la España contemporánea*. Madrid: Alianza.

Núñez, C. E. (2005). Educación. In A. Carreras & X. Tafunell, eds., *Estadísticas históricas de España: siglos XIX-XX*. Bilbao: Fundación BBVA.

O'Brien, P. (1980). European economic development: the contribution of the periphery. *Economic History Review*, 35, 1-18.

O'Brien, P. (2013). Historical foundations for a global perspective on the emergence of a Western European regime for the discovery, development, and diffusion of useful and reliable knowledge. *Journal of Global History*, 8(1), 1-24.

O'Brien, P. K. & Prados de la Escosura, L. (1999). Balance sheets for the acquisition, retention and loss of European empires overseas. *Itinerario*, XXIII(3/4), 25-52.

Obstfeld, M. (1998). The global capital market: benefactor or menace. *Journal of Economic Perspectives*, 12(4), 9-30.

Obstfeld, M. & Taylor, A. (2003). Globalization and capital markets. In M. D. Bordo, A. M. Taylor & J. G. Williamson, eds., *Globalization in Historical Perspective*. Chicago, IL: University of Chicago Press, pp. 121-188.

OECD. (2011). *How's Life? Measuring Well-being*. Paris: OECD Publishing.

Ogilvie, S. (2004). Guilds, efficiency, and social capital: evidence from German proto-industry. *The Economic History Review*, 57(2), 286-333.

Oliva Herrer, H. R. (2000). Sobre los niveles de vida en Tierra de Campos a fines del medievo. *Edad Media. Revista de Historia*, 3, 175-226.

Oliva Herrer, H. R. (2001). La industria textil en Tierra de Campos a fines del medievo. *Studia Historica. Historia Medieval*, 18-19, 259-285.

Oliva Herrer, H. R. (2002). *La Tierra de Campos a fines de la Edad Media: economía, sociedad y acción política campesina*. Valladolid: Universidad de Valladolid.

Oliva Herrer, H. R. (2003). The peasant domus and the material culture in northern Spain in the later Middle Ages. In A. M. Cordelia Beattie, ed., *The Medieval Household in Christian Europe, c.850-1550. Managing Power, Wealth and the Body*. Turnhout: Brepols, pp. 469-86.

Oliva Herrer, H. R. (2007). El mundo rural en la Corona de Castilla en la Baja Edad Media: dinámicas socioeconómicas y nuevas perspectivas de análisis. *Edad Media. Revista de Historia*, 8, 295–328.

Oliva Herrer, H. R. (2013). De nuevo sobre la crisis del XIV: carestías e interpretaciones de la crisis en la Corona de Castilla. In P. Benito Monclùs, ed., *Crisis alimentarias en la Edad Media. Modelos, explicaciones y representaciones*. Lleida: Milenio, pp. 87–114.

Oliva Herrer, H. R. & Benito i Monclús, P., eds. (2007). *Crisis de subsistencia y crisis agrarias en la Edad Media*. Seville: Universidad de Sevilla.

Oliveira, A. de (1972). *A vida económica e social de Coimbra de 1537 a 1640*, vol. II. Coimbra: Inst. Est. Históricos.

Oliveira, A. de (1991). *Poder e Oposição Política em Portugal no Período Filipino (1580–1640)*. Lisbon: Difel.

Oliveira, A. de (2002). *Movimentos sociais e poder em Portugal no século XVII*. Coimbra: Instituto de História Económica e Social – Faculdade de Letras da Universidade de Coimbra.

Oliveira, L. F. (2009). *A Coroa, os mestres e os comendadores: as ordens militares de Avis e de Santiago, 1330–1449*. Faro: Universidade do Algarve.

O'Rourke, K. H. & Williamson, J. G. (1999). *Globalization and History: The Atlantic Economy in the Nineteenth Century*. Cambridge, MA: The MIT Press.

O'Rourke, K. H. & Williamson, J. G. (2002a). After Columbus: explaining Europe's overseas trade boom, 1500–1800. *Journal of Economic History*, 62(2), 417–456.

O'Rourke, K. H. & Williamson, J. G. (2002b). When did globalisation begin? *European Review of Economic History*, 6(1), 23–50.

Ortega, J. A. & Silvestre, J. (2006). Las consecuencias demográficas. In P. Martín-Aceña & E. Martínez, eds., *La economía de la Guerra Civil*. Madrid: Marcial Pons.

Ortí Gost, P. (1999). Una primera aproximació als fogatges catalans de la dècada de 1360. *Anuario de Estudios Medievales*, 29, 747–773.

Ortí Gost, P. & Verdés Pijuan, P. (2016). The crisis of public finances in the cities of late medieval Catalonia (1350–1500). In *XLVII Settimana di Studi. Le crisi finanziari: gestione, implicazioni sociali e conseguenze nell'età preindustriale (Prato, 10–13 maggio 2015)*. Florence: Firenze University Press, pp. 119–221.

Oto-Peralías, D. & Romero-Ávila, D. (2017). Historical frontiers and the rise of inequality: the case of the frontier of Granada. *Journal of the European Economic Association*, 15(1), 54–98.

Owens, J. B. (2005). *By My Absolute Royal Authority: Justice and the Castilian Commonwealth at the Beginning of the First Global Age*. Rochester, NY: University of Rochester Press.

Padez, C. (2007). Secular trend in Portugal. *Journal of Human Ecology*, 22, 15–22.

Palma, N. (2020a). American precious metals and their consequences for early modern Europe. In S. Battilossi, Y. Cassis & K. Yago, eds., *Handbook of the History of Money and Currency*. Singapore: Springer, pp. 363–382.

Palma, N. (2020b). Historical account books as a source for quantitative history. In G. Christ & P. Roessner, eds., *History and Economic Life: A Student's Guide to*

Approaching Economic and Social History Sources. London and New York: Routledge, pp. 184-197.

Palma, N. & Reis, J. (2019). From convergence to divergence: Portuguese economic growth, 1527-1850. *Journal of Economic History*, 79(2), 477-506.

Palma, N. & Reis, J. (2021). Can autocracy promote literacy? Evidence from a cultural alignment success story. *Journal of Economic Behaviour and Organization*, 186, 412-436.

Palma, N., Reis, J. & Zhang, M. (2020). Reconstruction of regional and national population using intermittent census-type data: the case of Portugal, 1527-1864. *Historical Methods: A Journal of Quantitative and Interdisciplinary History*, 53(1), 11-27.

Palop Ramos, J. M. (1982). El producto diezmal valenciano durante los siglos XVII y XVIII. Aproximación a su estudio. In J. Goy & E. Le Roy Ladurie, eds., *Prestations Paysannes, Dîmes, Rente Foncière et Mouvements de la Production Agricole à l'époque Préindustrielle*. Paris: Éditions de l'École des Hautes Études en Sciences Sociales, pp. 407-416.

Pamuk, S. & van Zanden, J.L. (2010). Standards of living. In S. Broadberry & K. H. O'Rourke, eds., *The Cambridge Economic History of Modern Europe*, vol. 1. Cambridge: Cambridge University Press, pp. 217-234.

Paquette, G. (2013). *Imperial Portugal in the Age of Atlantic Revolutions: The Luso-Brazilian World, c. 1770-1850*. Cambridge: Cambridge University Press.

Pardal, R. (2015). *Práticas de caridade e assistência em Évora (1650-1750)*. Lisbon: Publicações do Cidehus-Edições Colibri.

Parry, J. H. (1981). *The Discovery of the Sea*. Berkeley, CA: University of California Press.

Pascual, P. & Sudrià, C. (2002). El difícil arranque de la industrialización, 1840-1880. In F. Comín, M. Hernández & E. Llopis, eds., *Historia económica de España, siglos X-XX*. Barcelona: Crítica, pp. 203-241.

Passini, J. (2015). Visión diacrónica del espacio de la casa medieval en la ciudad de Toledo: aporte de las fuentes escritas del siglo XV. In M. E. Díez Jorge & J. Navarro Palazón, ed., *La casa medieval en la Península Ibérica*. Madrid: Casa Velázquez, pp. 597-611.

Pavón, J. & García de la Borbolla, M. (2000). Hospitalarios y Templarios en Navarra. Formación patrimonial (1134-1194). In *Las Ordenes Militares en la Península Ibérica. Edad Media*. Cuenca: Ediciones de la Universidad de Castilla-La Mancha, pp. 571-587.

Pedreira, J. M. V. (1987). Indústria e atraso económico em Portugal (1800-25). Uma perspectiva estrutural. *Análise Social*, 23, 563-596.

Pedreira, J. M. V. (1990). Social structure and the persistence of rural domestic industry in XIXth century Portugal. *Journal of European Economic History*, 19 (3), 521-547.

Pedreira, J. M. V. (1991). Indústria e negócio: a estamparia da Região de Lisboa, 1780-1880. *Análise Social*, 26(112/113), 537-559.

Pedreira. J. M. V. (1993). La economía portuguesa y el fin del imperio luso-brasileño (1800–1860). In L. Prados de la Escosura & S. Amaral, eds., *La independencia americana: consecuencias económicas*. Madrid: Alianza Editorial.

Pedreira, J. M. V. (1994). *Estrutura industrial e mercado colonial: Portugal e Brasil (1780–1830)*. Lisbon: Difel.

Pedreira, J. M. V. (1995). Os homens de negócio da praça de Lisboa de Pombal ao vintismo (1755–1822): diferenciação, reprodução e identificação de um grupo social. PhD thesis, Universidade Nova de Lisboa.

Pedreira, J. M. V. (1998). To have or to have not: the economic consequences of empire: Portugal (1415–1822). *Revista de Historia Económica*, 16(1), 93–122.

Pedreira, J. (2005). A industria. In P. Lains & A. Ferreira da Silva, eds., *História Económica de Portugal, 1700–2000*, vol. I, o século XVIII. Lisboa: Impresa de Ciências Sociais, pp. 177–208.

Pedreira, J. M. V. (2007). Costs and financial trends in Portuguese empire, 1415–1822. In F. Bethencourt & D. Ramada Curto, eds., *Portuguese Oceanic Expansion, 1400-1800*. Cambridge: Cambridge University Press, pp. 49–87.

Pedreira, J. M. V. (2013). O processo económico. In A. Costa Pinto, N. Gonçalo Monteiro & P. Tavares de Almeida, eds., *História Contemporânea de Portugal, Vol. II, A Construção Nacional, 1834–1890*. Carnaxide: Fundación MAPFRE/ Editora Objectiva, pp. 111–157.

Peiró-Palomino, J., Perugini, F. & Picazo-Tadeo, A. (2019). Well-being and the great recession in Spain. *Applied Economics Letters*, 26(15), 1279–1284.

Peixoto, J. (2007). Dinâmicas e regimes migratórios: o caso das migrações internacionais em Portugal. *Análise Social*, 42(183), 445–469.

Peña-Mir, J. L. (2016). Financiación y especialización productiva: el mercado de crédito malagueño a finales del siglo XVIII. *Investigaciones en Historia Económica – Economic History Research*, 12, 133–143.

Pereira, Á. S. (2009). The opportunity of a disaster: the economic impact of the 1755 Lisbon earthquake. *Journal of Economic History*, 69(2), 466–499.

Pereira, J. M. Esteves (1979). *Subsídios para a história da indústria portuguesa*. Lisbon: Guimarães Editores.

Peres, D. (1971). *História do Banco de Portugal, 1821–1846*. Lisbon: Banco de Portugal.

Pérez Díaz, J. (2003). *La madurez de masas*. Madrid: Instituto de Migraciones y Servicios Sociales.

Pérez-Garcia, J. M. & Ardit Lucas, M. (1988). Bases del crecimiento de la población valenciana en la Edad Moderna. In C. Pérez Aparicio, ed., *Estudis sobre la població del País Valencià*, vol. I. Valencia: Edicions Alfons el Magnànim-Institut d'Estudis Juan Gil-Albert, pp. 199–228.

Pérez-García, M. (2017). Challenging national narratives: on the origins of sweet potato in China as global commodity during the early modern period. In M. Pérez García & L. de Sousa, eds., *Global History and New Polycentric*

Approaches: Europe, Asia and the Americas in a World Network System. Singapore: Palgrave Macmillan.

Pérez Moreda, V. (1980). *Las crisis de mortalidad en la España interior (siglos XVI–XIX)*. Madrid: Siglo XXI.

Pérez Moreda, V. (1986). Matrimonio y familia. Algunas consideraciones sobre el modelo matrimonial español en la Edad Moderna. *Boletín de la Asociación de Demografía Histórica*, IV(1), 3–51.

Pérez Moreda, V. (1987). La peste de 1647–1657 en el Mediterráneo occidental. *Boletín de la Asociación de Demografía Histórica*, V(2), 14–25.

Pérez Moreda, V. (1988a). La población española. In M. Artola, ed., *Economía y Sociedad*. Vol. I of *Enciclopedia de Historia de España*. Madrid: Alianza Editorial, pp. 345–431.

Pérez Moreda, V. (1988b). La población de la España interior en el siglo XVIII: evolución, características y contrastes regionales. In C. Pérez Aparicio, ed., *Estudis sobre la població del País Valencià*, vol. I. Valencia: Edicions Alfons el Magnànim-Institut d'Estudis Juan Gil-Albert, pp. 587–598.

Pérez Moreda, V. (1995). Cuestiones demográficas en la transición de la Edad Media a los tiempos modernos en España. In *El Tratado de Tordesillas y su época. Congreso Internacional de Historia*, vol. I. Madrid: Sociedad V Centenario del Tratado de Tordesillas, pp. 227–243.

Pérez Moreda, V. (1997a). El proceso de alfabetización y la formación de capital humano en España. *Papeles de Economía Española*, 73, 243–253.

Pérez Moreda, V. (1997b). La péninsule ibérique: I. La population espagnole à l'époque moderne. In J.-P. Bardet & J. Dupâquier, eds., *Histoire des populations de l'Europe*. vol. I. Paris: Fayard, pp. 463–479.

Pérez Moreda, V. (1999a). La evolución demográfica española en el siglo XVII. In *La popolazione italiana del Seicento*. Bologna: CLUEB, pp. 141–1169.

Pérez Moreda, V. (1999b). Población y economía en la España de los siglos XIX y XX. In G. Anes, ed., *Historia económica de España: siglos XIX y XX*. Barcelona: Gutenberg.

Pérez Moreda, V. (2002). La población española en tiempos de Isabel I de Castilla. In J. Valdeón, ed., *Sociedad y Economía en tiempos de Isabel la Católica*. Valladolid: Ámbito, pp. 13–38.

Pérez Moreda, V. (2017). Spain. In G. Alfani & C. Ó Gráda, eds., *Famine in European History*. Cambridge: Cambridge University Press, pp. 48–72.

Pérez Moreda, V. & Reher Sullivan, D. S. (1997). La población urbana española entre los siglos XVI y XVIII. Una perspectiva demográfica. In J. I. Fortea Pérez, ed., *Imágenes de la diversidad. El mundo urbano en la corona de Castilla (siglos XVI–XVIII)*. Santander: Universidad de Cantabria, pp. 129–163.

Pérez Moreda, V. & Reher Sullivan, D. S. (2003). Hacia una definición de la demografía urbana: España en 1787. *Revista de Demografía Histórica*, XXI(1), 113–140.

Pérez Moreda, V., Reher, D. S. & Sanz Gimeno, A. (2015). *La conquista de la salud: mortalidad y modernización en la España contemporánea*. Madrid: Marcial Pons.

REFERENCES

Pérez Samper, M. Á. (2009). La alimentación cotidiana en la Cataluña del siglo XVIII. *Cuadernos de Historia Moderna. Anejos*, 8, 33–65.

Pérez Sarrión, G. (1975). *El Canal Imperial de Aragón y la navegación hasta 1812*. Zaragoza: Institución Fernando el Católico.

Pérez Sarrión, G. (2016). *The Emergence of a National Market in Spain, 1650–1800: Trade Networks, Foreign Powers and the State*. London and New York: Bloomsbury Academic.

Peribáñez Otero, J. (2014). *La villa de Aranda de Duero y su comarca en los inicios de la modernidad*. Burgos: Ayuntamiento de Aranda de Duero.

Perrone-Moisés, B. (1992). Índios livres e índios escravos: os princípios da legislação indigenista no período colonial. In M. Carneiro da Cunha, ed., *História dos Índios no Brasil*. São Paulo: Companhia das Letras, pp. 115–132.

Persson, K. G. (1991). Labour productivity in medieval agriculture: Tuscany and the 'Low Countries'. In B. M. S. Campbell & M. Overton, eds., *Land, Labour and Livestock*. Manchester: Manchester University Press, pp. 124–143.

Petrowiste, J. & Lafuente Gómez, M., eds. (2018). *Faire son marché au Moyen Âge: Méditerranée occidentale, XIIIe–XVIe siècle*. Madrid: Casa de Velazquez.

Pfister, U. (2011). Economic growth in Germany, 1500–1850. Paper presented at the 'Quantifying Long Run Economic Development' conference, University of Warwick in Venice, May 2011.

Phillips, C. R. (1990). The growth and composition of trade in the Iberian empires, 1450–1750. In J. D. Tracy, ed., *The Rise of Merchant Empires: Long-Distance Trade in the Early Modern World 1350–1750*. Cambridge: Cambridge University Press, pp. 34–101.

Phillips, C. R. (1991). *Seis galeones para el rey de España: La defensa imperial a principios del siglo XVII*. Madrid: Alianza Editorial.

Phillips, C. R. & Phillips, W. D. (1997). *Spain's Golden Fleece: Wool Production and the Wool Trade from the Middle Ages to the Nineteenth Century*. Baltimore, OH: Johns Hopkins University Press.

Phillips, W. D. Jr. (1986). Local integration and long-distance ties: the Castilian community in sixteenth-century Bruges. *The sixteenth century journal*, 17(1), 33–49.

Phillips, W. D. Jr. (1992). Africa and the Atlantic Islands meet the Garden of Eden: Christopher Columbus's view of America. *Journal of World History*, 3(2), 149–164.

Pieper, R. (1992). *La Real Hacienda bajo Fernando VI y Carlos III (1753–1788)*. Madrid: Instituto de Estudios Fiscales.

Piketty, T. (2014). *Capital in the 21st century*. Cambridge, MA: Harvard University Press.

Piketty, T. & Saez, E. (2006). The evolution of top incomes: a historical and international perspective. *American Economic Review*, 96(2), 200–205.

Pinheiro, M. et al. (1997). *Séries Longas para a Economia Portuguesa, Pós-II Guerra Mundial*, vol. I. Lisbon: Banco de Portugal.

Pinho, P. Soares de (2000). The impact of deregulation on price and non-price competition in the Portuguese deposits market. *Journal of Banking & Finance*, 24, 1515-1533.

Pinho, P. Soares de (2002). Portugal. In E. P. M. Gardener, P. Molyneux & B. Moore, eds., *Banking in the New Europe: The Impact of the Single European Market Programme and EMU on the European Banking Sector*. London: Palgrave Macmillan, pp. 230-252.

Pinilla, V. (2023). Agricultural crisis in Spain (19th and 20th centuries). In G. Beaur and F. Chiapparino, eds., *Agriculture and the Great Depression*, London: Routledge, pp. 39-56.

Pinilla, V. & Ayuda, M. I. (2002). The political economy of the wine trade: Spanish exports and the international market, 1890-1935. *European Review of Economic History*, 6(1), 51-86.

Pinilla, V. & Ayuda, M. I (2007). The international wine market, 1850-1938: an opportunity for export growth in Southern Europe? In G. Campbell & N. Gibert, eds., *Wine History, Development and Globalization. Multidisciplinary Perspectives on the Wine Industry*. New York: Palgrave Macmillan, pp. 179-199.

Pinilla, V. & Ayuda, M .I. (2010). Taking advantage of globalization? Spain and the building of the international market in Mediterranean horticultural products, 1850-1935. *European Review of Economic History*, 14(2), 239-274.

Pinto, A. Costa, ed. (2015). A busca da democracia, 1960-2000. Vol. V of *História Contemporânea de Portugal*. Lisbon: Penguin Random House/Fundación Mapfre.

Pinto, M. L. Rocha, Rodrigues, J. Damião & Madeira, A. Boavida (2001). A base demográfica. In J. Serrão & A. H. Oliveira Marques, eds., *Nova História de Portugal*, vol. VII. Lisbon: Presença, pp. 385-403.

Pinto, M. L. Rocha & Rodrigues, T. Ferreira (2013). O povoamento das ilhas da Madeira e do Porto Santo nos séculos XV e XVI. In C. Santos & P. T. de Matos, ed., *A Demografia das Sociedades Insulares Portuguesas. Séculos XV a XXI*. Braga: CITCEM, pp. 15-53.

Pleijt, A. M. de & van Zanden, J. L. (2016). Accounting for the 'Little Divergence': what drove economic growth in pre-industrial Europe, 1300-1800? *European Review of Economic History*, XX(4), 387-409.

Pollard, S. (1981). *Peaceful Conquest: The Industrialization of Europe 1760-1970*. Oxford and New York: Oxford University Press.

Polónia, A. (2007). *A expansão ultramarina numa perspective local: o porto de Vila do Conde no século XVI*, 2 vols. Lisbon: Imprensa Nacional Casa da Moeda.

Pomeranz, K. (2000). *The Great Divergence: China, Europe, and the Making of the Modern World Economy*. Princeton, NJ: Princeton University Press.

Pontes, R. M. (2006). Povoamento e desenvolvimento económico do senhorio de Coina (estuário do Tejo) nos séculos XIII e XIV: a construção de uma paisagem rural. In I. Gonçalves, ed., *Paisagens Rurais e Urbanas. Fontes, Metodologias, Problemáticas*, vol. 2. Lisbon: CEH-UNL, pp. 213-239.

Porter, R. & Teich, M. (1992). Introduction. In R. Porter & M. Teich, eds., *The Scientific Revolution in National Context*. Cambridge: Cambridge University Press, pp. 1-10.

Postan, M. (1973). *Medieval Trade and Finance*. Cambridge: Cambridge University Press.

Powell, C. (2015). La larga marcha hacia Europa: España y la Comunidad Europea, 1957-1986. Real Instituto Elcano. www.realinstitutoelcano.org/documento-de-trabajo/la-larga-marcha-hacia-europa-espana-y-la-comunidad-europea-1957-1986/

Prados de la Escosura, L. (1988). *De imperio a nación. Crecimiento y atraso económico en España (1780-1860)*. Madrid: Alianza Editorial.

Prados de la Escosura, L. (2000). International comparisons of real product, 1820-1990: an alternative data set. *Explorations in Economic History*, 37(1), 1-41.

Prados de la Escosura, L. (2003). *El progreso económico de España (1850-2000)*. Bilbao: Fundación BBVA.

Prados de la Escosura, L. (2007). Growth and structural change in Spain, 1850-2000: a European perspective. *Revista de Historia Económica - Journal of Iberian and Latin American Economic History*, 25, 147-181.

Prados de la Escosura, L. (2008). Inequality, poverty, and the Kuznets curve in Spain, 1850-2000. *European Review of Economic History*, 12(3), 287-324.

Prados de la Escosura, L. (2010a). Improving human development: a long-run view. *Journal of Economic Surveys*, 24(5), 841-894.

Prados de la Escosura, L. (2010b). Spain's international position, 1850-1913. *Revista de Historia Económica - Journal of Iberian and Latin American Economic History*, 28(1), 173-215.

Prados de la Escosura, L. (2016a). Mismeasuring long-run growth: the bias from splicing national accounts – the case of Spain. *Cliometrica*, 10(3), 251-275.

Prados de la Escosura, L. (2016b). Economic freedom in the long run: evidence from OECD countries (1850-2007). *Economic History Review*, 69(2), 435-468.

Prados de la Escosura, L. (2017). *Spanish Economic Growth, 1850-2015*. Cham, Switzerland: Palgrave Macmillan.

Prados de la Escosura, L. (2020a). Capital in Spain, 1850-2019. *Working Papers in Economic History of the Universidad Carlos III de Madrid*, 20-09, 1-61.

Prados de la Escosura, L. (2020b). Spain's balance of payments, 1850-1913: direct and indirect estimates. Unpublished paper.

Prados de la Escosura, L., Álvarez-Nogal, C. & Santiago-Caballero, C. (2020). Growth recurring in preindustrial Spain: half a millennium perspective. *CEPR Discussion Paper*, 14479.

Prados de la Escosura, L., Álvarez-Nogal, C. & Santiago-Caballero, C. (2022). Growth Recurring in Preindustrial Spain? *Cliometrica*, 16, 215-241.

Prados de la Escosura, L. & Rosés, J. R. (2009). The sources of long run growth in Spain, 1850-2000. *Journal of Economic History*, 69(4), 1063-1091.

Prados de la Escosura, L. & Rosés, J. R. (2010a). Human capital and economic growth in Spain, 1850–2000. *Explorations in Economic History*, 47(4), 520–532.

Prados de la Escosura, L. & Rosés, J. R. (2010b). Capital accumulation in the long run: the case of Spain, 1850–2000. *Research in Economic History*, 27, 141–200.

Prados de la Escosura, L. & Rosés, J. R. (2020). Accounting for growth: Spain, 1850–2019. *Journal of Economic Surveys*, 35(3), 804–832.

Prados De La Escosura, L., Rosés, J. R. & Sanz-Villarroya, I. (2011). Economic reforms and growth in Franco's Spain. *Revista de Historia Económica – Journal of Iberian and Latin American Economic History*, 30(1), 45–89.

Priotti, J.-P. (2005). *Bilbao y sus mercaderes en el siglo XVI. Génesis de un crecimiento*. Bilbao: Bizkaiko Foru Aldundia.

Puig, N. & Álvaro-Moya, A. (2016). The long-term impact of foreign multinational enterprises in Spain: new insights into an old topic. *Journal of Evolutionary Studies in Business*, 2(1), 14–39.

Pujol, M. (2015). La construcció naval a la Catalunya baixmedieval. PhD thesis, Universitat Autònoma de Barcelona.

Pujol-Andreu, J. & Cussó X. (2014). La transición nutricional en Europa Occidental, 1865–2000: una nueva aproximación. *Historia Social*, 80, 133–155.

Quinn, D. (2003). Capital account liberalization and financial globalization, 1890–1999: a synoptic view. *International Journal of Finance and Economics*, 8, 189–204.

Quintero González, J. (2009). La construcción naval española en el siglo XVIII. En busca del equilibrio en los sistemas constructivos. In C. Martínez Shaw & M. Alfonso Mola, eds., *España en el comercio marítimo internacional (siglos XVII–XIX): quince estudios*. Madrid: UNED, pp. 289–318.

Quiroga, G. (2002). Medidas antropométricas y condiciones de vida en la España del siglo XX. PhD thesis, Universidad de Alcalá de Henares.

Radhika Seshan, R. (2016). Transnational and informal networks in the seventeenth century Coromandel coast. In A. Polónia & C. Antunes, eds., *Seaports in the First Global Age: Portuguese Agents, Networks and Interactions (1500–1800)*. Porto: Porto University Press, pp. 347–356.

Ramírez Vaquero, E. (2006). Finanzas municipales y fiscalidad de Estado. Tudela en la transición al siglo XVI. In D. Menjot & M. Sánchez Martínez, eds., *Fiscalidad de Estado y fiscalidad municipal en los reinos hispánicos medievales*. Madrid: Casa de Velázquez, pp. 413–432.

Ramon-Muñoz, R. & Ramon-Muñoz, J.M. (2016). The biological standard of living in nineteenth-century industrial Catalonia: a case study. *Revista de Historia Industrial*, 75, 77–118.

Ramos, R. (1988). Culturas da alfabetização e culturas do analfabetismo em Portugal: uma introdução à história da alfabetização no Portugal contemporáneo. *Análise Social*, 24 (103–104), 1067–1145.

Ramos-Palencia, F. (2010). *Pautas de consumo y mercado en Castilla, 1750–1850. Economía familiar en Palencia al final del Antiguo Régimen*. Madrid: Sílex.

Rau, V. & De Macedo, J. (1962). *O açúcar da Madeira nos fins do século XV. Problemas de produção e comércio.* Funchal: Junta Geral do Distrito Autónomo do Funchal.

Ravallion, M. (1997). Can high inequality development countries escape absolute poverty?. *Economic Letters,* 56(1), 51–57.

Rawski, E. S. (2004). The Qing Formation and the early-modern period. In L. A. Struve, ed., *The Qing Formation in World-Historical Time.* Cambridge, MA, and London: Harvard University Asian Studies, pp. 205–241.

Reglero de la Fuente, C. M. (1994). *Espacio y poder en la Castilla medieval. Los montes de Torozos (siglos X-XIV).* Valladolid: Diputación Provincial.

Reglero de la Fuente, C. M. (2001). Señores y vasallos en una aldea castellana medieval: Fuenteungrillo (siglos XIII–XIV). *Edad Media. Revista de Historia,* 4, 113–139.

Reher, D. S. (1990).*Town and Country in Pre-Industrial Spain: Cuenca, 1540–1870.* Cambridge: Cambridge University Press.

Reher, D. S. (1994). Ciudades, procesos de urbanización y sistemas urbanos en la Península Ibérica, 1550–1991. In M. Guardia, F. J. Monclús & J. L. Oyón, eds., *Atlas histórico de las ciudades europeas,* vol. 1. Barcelona: Salvat Editores – Centre de Cultura Contemporània de Barcelona, pp. 1–29.

Reher, D. S. & Ballesteros, E. (1993). Precios y salarios en Castilla la Nueva: la construcción de un índice de salarios reales, 1501–1991. *Revista de Historia Económica – Journal of Iberian and Latin American Economic History,* 11(1), 101–151.

Reher, D. S. & Requena, M., eds. (2009). *Las múltiples caras de la inmigración en España.* Madrid: Alianza.

Reinhart, C. M. & Rogoff, K. S. (2011). *This Time is Different: Eight Centuries of Financial Folly.* Princeton, NJ: Princeton University Press.

Reis, A. M. (2007). *História dos Municípios (1050–1383).* Lisbon: Livros Horizonte.

Reis, J. (1979). A 'Lei da Fome': as origens do proteccionismo cerealífero (1889–1914). *Análise Social,* XV(60), 745–793.

Reis, J. (1984). O atraso económico português em perspectiva histórica (1860–1913). *Análise Social,* XX(80), 7–28.

Reis, J. (1993a). O analfabetismo em Portugal no século XIX: uma interpretação. In *O atraso económico português.* Lisbon: Imprensa Nacional Casa da Moeda.

Reis, J. (1993b). *O atraso económico português em perspectiva histórica: estudos sobre a economia portuguesa na segunda metade do século XIX, 1850–1930.* Lisbon: Imprensa Nacional Casa da Moeda.

Reis, J. (1995). Portuguese banking in the inter-war period. In C. H. Feinstein, ed., *Banking, Currency, and Finance in Europe between the Wars.* Oxford: Clarendon Press, 472–501.

Reis, J. (1996). *História do Banco de Portugal,* vol. 1. Lisbon: Banco de Portugal.

Reis, J. (1999). The Bank of Portugal's first century: from 1846 to the Second World War. In C.-L. Holtfrerich, J. Reis & G. Toniolo, eds., *The Emergence of Modern Central Banking from 1918 to the Present.* Aldershot: Ashgate.

Reis, J. (2002). Crescimento económico e estatura humana. Há um paradoxo antropométrico em Portugal no século XIX?. *Memórias da Academia das Ciências de Lisboa, Classe de Letras*, XXXV, 153–169.

Reis, J. (2003). Bank structures, Gerschenkron and Portugal (pre-1914). In D. J. Forsyth & D. Verdier, eds., *The Origins of National Financial Systems. Alexander Gerschenkron Reconsidered*. London: Routledge, pp. 182–204.

Reis, J. (2005). O trabalho. In P. Lains & A. Ferreira da Silva, eds., *História Económica de Portugal: 1700–2000*, vol. II. Lisbon: Imprensa de Ciências Sociais, pp. 119–151.

Reis, J. (2007). An 'art', not a 'science'? Central bank management in Portugal under the gold standard, 1863–1887. *Economic History Review*, 60(4), 712–741.

Reis, J. (2016). Gross agricultural output: a quantitative, unified perspective, 1500–1850. In D. Freire & P. Lains, eds., *An Agrarian History of Portugal, 1000–2000: Economic Development on the European Frontier*. Leiden and Boston, MA: Brill, pp. 172–216.

Reis, J. (2017). Deviant behaviour? Inequality in Portugal 1565–1770. *Cliometrica*, 11(3), 297–319.

Remohí Rius, C. (2016). De la Dictadura a la crisis. La evolución de la desigualdad en España y sus regiones a través de la Ratio de Extracción (1973–2013). Unpublished work. Universitat de València.

Ribeiro, A. S. (2016). *Early Modern Trading Networks in Europe: Cooperation and the Case of Simon Ruiz*. Abingdon and New York: Routledge.

Ribeiro, O. (1986). *Portugal, o Mediterrâneo e o Atlântico. Esboço de relações geográficas*, 4th edn, Lisbon: Ed. João Sá da Costa.

Ricardo, D. (1821). *On the Principles of Political Economy and Taxation*, 3rd edn, Kitchener: Batoche Books.

Ridolfi, L. (2016). The French economy in the longue durée. A study on real wages, working days and economic performance from Louis IX to the Revolution (1250–1789). PhD thesis, IMT School for Advanced Studies Lucca.

Riera Melis, A. (1992). La aparición de las corporaciones de oficios en Cataluña (1200–1350). In *Cofradías, gremios y solidaridades en la Europa medieval*. Pamplona: Gobierno de Navarra, pp. 285–318.

Riera Melis, A. (1993). Estructura social y sistemas alimentarios en la Cataluña bajomedieval. *Acta historica et archaeologica mediaevalia*, 14–15, 193–217.

Riera Melis, A. (1995). Jerarquía social y desigualdad alimentaria en el Mediterráneo Nor-occidental en la baja Edad Media. La cocina y la mesa de los estamentos privilegiados. *Acta historica et archaeologica mediaevalia*, 16–17, 181–205.

Riera Melis, A. (1998). Panem nostrum quotidianum da nobis hodie: los sistemas alimenticios de los estamentos populares en el Mediterráneo Noroccidental en la Baja Edad Media. In J. I. de la Iglesia Duarte, ed., *La vida cotidiana en la Edad Media – VIII. Semana de Estudios Medievales, Nájera, del 4 al 8 de agosto de 1997*. Logroño: Instituto de Estudios Riojanos, pp. 25–46.

Riera Melis, A. (2000). Monedas y mercados en la Edad Media: el Mediterráneo Noroccidental (c. 1190–1350). In *Moneda y monedas en la Europa medieval*

REFERENCES

(siglos XII–XV): *XXVI Semana de Estudios Medievales*. Pamplona: Gobierno de Navarra, pp. 193–256.

Riera Melis, A. (2005). Els orígens de la manufactura textil a la Corona catalanoaragonesa (c. 1150–1298). In R. Narbona Vizcaíno, ed., *La Mediterrània de la Corona d'Aragó, segles XIII–XVI. VII Centenari de la Sentència Arbitral de Torrellas, 1304-2004: XVIII Congrés d'Història de la Corona d'Aragó*, vol. 1. Valencia: Universitat de València, pp. 821–902.

Riera Melis, A. (2017). The beginnings of urban manufacturing and long distance trade. Crises and changes in the late middle ages. In F. Sabaté Curull, ed., *The Crown of Aragon: A Singular Mediterranean Empire*. Leiden and Boston, MA: Brill, pp. 201–236 and 237–278.

Riesco Chueca, P. (2015). Antecedentes y primeros pasos del cultivo en hojas en Zamora y provincias vecinas. *Stvdia Zamorensia*, 14, 109–132.

Ringrose, D. R. (1969). The government and the carters in Spain, 1476–1700. *The Economic History Review*, 22(1), 45–57.

Ringrose, D. R. (1983). *Madrid and the Spanish Economy*. Berkeley, CA: University of California Press.

Ringrose, D. R. (1998). *Spain, Europe, and the 'Spanish Miracle', 1700–1900*. Cambridge: Cambridge University Press.

Ringrose, D. R. (2018). *Europeans Abroad, 1450–1750 (Exploring World History)*. Lanham, MD: Rowman & Littlefield.

Ringrose, D. R. (2019). *Europeans Abroad, 1450–1750*. Lanham, MD: Rowman & Littlefield.

Rocha, M. M. (1996). Crédito privado num contexto urbano: Lisboa, 1770–1830. Ph.D. thesis, European University Institute, Florence.

Roche, D. (1989). *La culture des apparences: une histoire du vêtement (XVIIe–XVIIIe siècle)*. Paris: Fayard.

Roche, D. (1997). *Histoire des choses banales: naissance de la consommation dans les sociétés traditionnelles (XVIIe–XIXe siècle)*. Paris: Fayard.

Rodrigo, F. S., Pozo-Vázquez, D., Esteban-Parra, M. J. & Castro-Díez, Y. (2001). A reconstruction of the winter North Atlantic Oscillation index back to AD 1501 using documentary data in southern Spain. *Journal of Geophysical Research: Atmospheres*, 106(D14), 14805–14818.

Rodrigo, F. S., Esteban-Parra, M. J., Pozo-Vázquez, D. & Castro-Diez, Y. (1999). A 500-year precipitation record in southern Spain. *International Journal of Climatology*, 19, 1233–1253.

Rodrigo Estevan, M. L. (2009). Fresco, frescal, salado, seco, remojado: abasto y mercado de pescado en Aragón (siglos XII–XV). In B. Arizaga Bolumburu & J. Á. Solórzano Telechea, eds., *Alimentar la ciudad en la Edad Media: Nájera, Encuentros Internacionales del Medievo 2008, del 22 al 25 de junio de 2008*. Logroño: Instituto de Estudios Riojanos, pp. 547–577.

Rodrigues, L. (2013). Os hospitais portugueses no Renascimento (1480–1580): o caso de Nossa Senhora do Pópulo das Caldas da Rainha. PhD thesis, Univsersidade do Minho, Braga.

Rodrigues, L. (2019a). Os padrões de juro da Misericórdia, 1767–1797. *Ler História*, 74, 137–160.

Rodrigues, L. (2019b). Debt litigation and the performance of law courts in eighteenth-century Portugal. *Journal of Interdisciplinary History*, 50(2), 237–264.

Rodrigues, L. (2021). Between private and public credit: institutional investors in Portugal, 1580–1800. *GHES Working Paper*.

Rodrigues, M. G. (2019). Between West Africa and America: the Angolan slave trade in the Portuguese and Spanish Atlantic Empires (1560–1641). PhD thesis, European University Institute.

Rodrigues, T. Ferreira (2008). As vicissitudes do povoamento nos séculos XVI e XVII. In T. F. Rodrigues, ed., *História da População Portuguesa. Das longas permanências à conquista da modernidade*. Porto: Afrontamento, pp. 159–246.

Rodrigues, T. Ferreira (2010). *Dinâmicas migratórias e riscos de segurança em Portugal*. Lisbon: Instituto da Defesa Nacional.

Rodrigues, T. Ferreira & Oliveira, P. Violante (2008). Migrações e mobilidade. In T. F. Rodrigues, ed., *História da população portuguesa. Das longas permanências à conquista da modernidade*. Porto: Afrontamento pp. 490–507.

Rodríguez, L. (1973). The Spanish riots of 1766. *Past & Present*, 52, 76–136.

Rodríguez Gómez, M. D. (2016). Emires, linajes y colaboradores: el traspaso de la tierra en la Vega de Granada (Alitaje, s. XV). In A. Echevarría Arsuaga & A. Fábregas García, eds., *De la alquería a la aljama*. Madrid: UNED, pp. 37–70.

Rodrik, D. (2013). Structural change, fundamentals, and growth: an overview. Unpublished manuscript.

Rojo, L. Á. (2002). La economía española en la democracia (1976–2000). In F. Comín, M. Hernández & E. Llopis, eds., *Historia económica de España, siglos X–XX*. Barcelona: Crítica, pp. 397–435.

Roldán, A. (2018). Spain and the classical gold standard: short-and long-term analyses. *U.B. Economics Working Papers*, E18/385.

Roma Valdés, A. (2000). *Moneda y sistemas monetarios en Castilla y en León durante la Edad Media (1087–1366)*. Barcelona: Asociación Numismática Española.

Romano, R. (2004). *Mecanismo y elementos del sistema económico colonial americano. Siglos XVI–XVIII*. México: Colegio de México.

Rosas, F. & Garrido, Á., eds. (2012). *Corporativismo, Fascismos, Estado Novo*. Coimbra: Livraria Almedina.

Rosés, J. R. (2003). Why isn't the whole of Spain industrialized? New economic geography and early industrialization, 1797–1910. *The Journal of Economic History*, 63(4), 995–1022.

Rossi, N., Toniolo, G. & Vecchi, G. (2001). Is the Kuznets curve still alive? Evidence from Italian household budgets, 1881–1961. *The Journal of Economic History*, 61(4), 904–925.

Rowland, R. (1989). Sistemas matrimoniais na Península ibérica: uma perspectiva regional. *Estudos Econômicos*, 19(3), 497–553.

Rowland, R. (1997). *População, Família, Sociedade. Portugal, séculos XIX–XX*. Lisbon: Etnográfica Press.

Rucquoi, A. (1997). *Valladolid en la Edad Media*. Valladolid: Junta de Castilla y León.
Ruiz, T. F. (1994). *Crisis and Continuity: Land and Town in Late Medieval Castile*. Philadelphia, PA: University of Pennsylvania Press.
Ruiz, T. F. (2014). The Mediterranean and the Atlantic. In P. Horden & S. Kinoshita, eds., *A Companion to Mediterranean History*. Oxford: Wiley-Blackwell, pp. 411–424.
Ruiz, T. F. (2015). Castilian merchants in England, 1248–1350. In W. C. Jordan, B. McNab & T. F. Ruiz, eds., *Order and Innovation in the Middle Ages*. Princeton, NJ: Princeton University Press, pp. 173–186.
Ruiz Martín, F. (1967). La población española al comienzo de los tiempos modernos. *Cuadernos de Historia, anexos de Hispania*, I, 189–207.
Ruiz Martín, F. (1968). Las finanzas españolas durante el reinado de Felipe II. *Cuadernos de Historia. Anexos de la Revista Hispania*, 2, 109–174.
Ruíz Martín, F. (1970). La banca en España hasta 1782. In *El Banco de España. Una historia económica*. Madrid: Banco de España, pp. 1–196.
Ruíz Martín, F. (1990). *Las finanzas de la Monarquía Hispánica en tiempos de Felipe IV (1621–1665)*. Madrid: Real Academia de la Historia.
Ruiz Martín, F. & García Sanz, Á., eds. (1998). *Mesta, trashumancia y lana en la España moderna*. Barcelona: Crítica.
Ryder, A. (2007). *The Wreck of Catalonia: Civil War in the Fifteenth Century*. Oxford: Oxford University Press.
Sá, I. dos Guimarães (1995). *A circulação de crianças na Europa do Sul: o exemplo da Casa da Roda do Porto no século XVIII*. Lisbon: Gulbenkian.
Sá, I. dos Guimarães (1997). *Quando o rico se faz pobre: misericórdias, caridade e poder no império português*. Lisbon: Comissão Nacional para as Comemorações dos Portugueses.
Sá, I. dos Guimarães (2002). Estatuto social e discriminação: formas de selecção de agentes e receptores de caridade nas misericórdias portuguesas ao longo do Antigo Regime. In *Actas do Colóquio Internacional Saúde e discriminação social*. Braga: Universidade do Minho, pp. 303–334.
Sá, I. dos Guimarães (2005). O trabalho. In P. Lains & Á. Ferreira da Silva, eds., *História Económica de Portugal: 1700–2000*, vol. I. Lisbon: Imprensa de Ciências Sociais, pp. 93–121.
Saavedra, P. (2018). El maíz en el sistema agrario y en la alimentación en Galicia, siglos XVII–XIX. *Obradoiro de Historia Moderna*, 27, 49–80.
Sabaté Curull, F. (2015). El Compromiso de Caspe: ruptura dinástica o modelo de estado. In F. Sabaté i Curull, ed., *Ruptura i legitimació dinástica a l'Edat Mitjana*. Lleida: Pagés editors, pp. 279–290.
Sabaté Curull, F., ed. (2017). *The Crown of Aragon. A Singular Mediterranean Empire*, Leiden and Boston, MA: Brill.
Sabater Navarro, G. (2019). *Las Transiciones Ibéricas. Influjos y convergencias en la democratización peninsular*. Madrid: UAM.

Sáinz Guerra, J. Á. (1994). La falsificación de moneda en el derecho castellano de la Baja Edad Media. In M. D. Gutiérrez Calvo & R. Pérez Bustamante, eds., *Estudios de historia del derecho europeo*, vol. 3. Madrid: Universidad Complutense de Madrid, pp. 215–226.

Sales Favà, Ll. (2014). Suing in a local jurisdictional court in late medieval Catalonia. The case of Caldes de Malavella (1328–1369). *Continuity and Change*, 29(1), 49–81.

Salgado, A. A. (2009). Portugal e o Atlântico Organização militar e acções navais durante o período Filipino (1580–1640). PhD thesis, Universidade de Lisboa.

Salicrú i Lluch, R. (2007). *El sultanato nazarí de Granada, Génova y la Corona de Aragón en el siglo XV*. Granada: Universidad de Granada.

Salvado, J. P. (2014). O Estanco do Tabaco em Portugal: contrato-geral e consorcios mercantilistas (1702–1755). In Santiago de Luxán, ed. *Política y Hacienda del Tabaco en los Imperios Ibéricos (siglos XVII–XIX)*. Madrid: Centro de Estudios Políticos y Institucionales, pp. 133–153.

Salvado, J. P. (2019). Repartição Fiscal no Império Luso-atlântico, 1720–1760. Paper presented at the XXXIX meeting of APHES, Faro.

Sánchez, A. (2000). Crisis económica y respuesta empresarial. Los inicios del sistema fabril en la industria algodonera catalana, 1797–1839. *Revista de Historia Económica – Journal of Iberian and Latin American Economic History*, 18(3), 485–523.

Sánchez-Albornoz, C. (1980). *Una ciudad de la España cristiana hace mil años: estampas de la vida en León*. Madrid: Rialp.

Sánchez Alonso, B. (1995). *Las causas de la emigración española, 1880–1930*. Madrid: Alianza.

Sánchez Martínez, M., Furió, A. & Sesma Muñoz, Á. (2008). Old and new forms of taxation in the crown of Aragon (13th–14th centuries). In *La fiscalità nell'economia europea (sec. XIII–XVIII), 39 Settimana di Studi dell'Istituto Internazionale di Storia Economica 'Francesco Datini' di Prato*. Florence: Firenze University Press, pp. 99–130.

Sánchez Martínez, M. & Menjot, D., eds. (2006). *Fiscalidad de Estado y fiscalidad municipal en los reinos hispánicos medievales*. Madrid: Casa de Velázquez.

Sánchez Sarto, M. (1934). Les Banques Públiques en Espagne jusqu'à 1815. In J. G. Van Dillen, ed., *History of the principal public banks*. The Hague: Martinus Nijhoff, pp. 1–14.

Sanchis Llopis, M. T. (2006). The Spanish economic miracle: a disaggregated approach to productivity growth, 1958–1975. *Revista de Historia Económica – Journal of Iberian and Latin American Economic History*, 24(2), 383–419.

Santiago-Caballero, C. (2011). Income inequality in central Spain, 1690–1800. *Explorations in Economic History*, 48(1), 83–96.

Santiago-Caballero, C. (2014). Tithe series and grain production in central Spain (1700–1800). *Rural History*, 25(1), 15–37.

Santos, F. Teixeira dos (1994). Stock monetário e desempenho macroeconómico durante o Estado Novo. *Análise Social*, 19(128), 981–1003.

Santos, M. E. M. & Lobato, M., eds. (2006). *O domínio da distância: comunicação e cartografia*. Lisbon: Instituto de Investigação Científica Tropical.

Santos, M. J. Azevedo (2006). O azeite e a vida do homem medieval. In *Estudos em Homenagem ao Prof. Doutor José Amadeu Coelho Dias*, vol. II. Porto: Faculdade de Letras, pp. 139–157.

Santos, R. (2003). *Sociogénese do Latifundismo Moderno: Mercados, Crises e Mudança Social na Região de Évora, Séculos XVII a XIX*. Lisbon: Banco de Portugal.

Santos, R. & Serrão, J. V. (2013). Land policies and land markets. Portugal, late eighteenth and early nineteenth century. In G. Béaur, P. R. Schofield, J. M. Chevet & M.T. Pérez-Picazo, eds., *Property Rights, Land Markets and Economic Growth in the European Countryside (13th–20th Centuries)*. Turnhout: Brepols Publishers, pp. 317–342.

Sanz Gimeno, A. & Ramiro Fariñas, D. (2002). Infancia, mortalidad y nieles de vida en la España interior. Siglos XIX y XX. In J. M. Martínez Carrión, ed., *El nivel de vida en la España rural, siglos XVIII–XX*. Alicante: Servicio de Publicaciones de la Universidad de Alicante, pp. 359–403.

Sarasúa García, C. (1997). The role of the State in shaping women's and men's entrance into the labour market. Spain, 18th and 19th centuries. *Continuity and Change*, 12(3), 347–371.

Sarasúa García, C. (2002). El acceso de los niños y niñas a los recursos educativos en la España rural del siglo XIX. In J. M. Martínez Carrión, ed., *El nivel de vida en la España rural, siglos XVIII–XX*. Alicante: Servicio de Publicaciones de la Universidad de Alicante pp. 549–612.

Sarasúa García, C. (2013). Activos desde cuándo? La edad de acceso al mercado de trabajo en la España del siglo XVIII. In J. M. Borrás Llop, ed., *El trabajo infantil en España (1700–1950)*. Barcelona: Universitat de Barcelona, pp. 63–89.

Sarasúa García, C. (2019). Women's work and structural change: occupational structure in eighteenth-century Spain. *The Economic History Review*, 72(2), 481–509.

Sarasúa García, C., ed. (2021). *Salarios que la ciudad paga al campo. Las nodrizas de las inclusas en los siglos XVIII y XIX*. Alicante: Publicacions de la Universitat d' Alacant.

Sarasúa García, C. & Gálvez, L. (2003). *Privilegios o eficiencia? Mujeres y hombres en los mercados de trabajo*. Alicante: Servicio de Publicaciones de la Universidad de Alicante.

Saunders, A. C. de C. M. (1982). *A Social History of Black Slaves and Freedmen in Portugal 1441–1555*. Cambridge: Cambridge University Press.

Schäfer, E. (2003). *El Consejo Real y Supremo de las Indias. Su historia, organización y labor administrativa hasta la terminación de la Casa de Austria*. Valladolid: Junta de Castilla y León-Marcial Pons.

Scheidel, W. (2017). *The Great Leveler: Violence and the History of Inequality from the Stone Age to the Twenty-First Century*. Princeton, NJ: Princeton University Press.

Schön, L. & Krantz, O. (2012). The Swedish economy in the early modern period: constructing historical national accounts. *European Review of Economic History*, 16(4), 529-549.

Schwartz, S. B. (2004) *Tropical Babylons: Sugar and the Making of the Atlantic World, 1450-1680*. Chapel Hill, NC: University of North Carolina Press.

Sen, A. (1992). *Inequality Reexamined*. Oxford: Clarendon Press.

Sen, A. (1993). *The Quality of Life*. Oxford: Clarendon Press.

Sequeira, J. (2014). *O pano da terra. Produção têxtil em Portugal nos finais da Idade Média*. Porto: Universidade do Porto Edições.

Sequeira, J. (2017). A indústria da seda em Portugal entre os séculos XIII e XVI. In R. Franch Benavent & G. Navarro Espinach, eds., *Las rutas de la seda en la historia de España y Portugal*. Valencia: Universitat de València, pp. 343-373.

Sequeira, J. & Melo, A. Sousa (2012). A mulher na produção têxtil portuguesa tardo-medieval. *Medievalista*, 11, 1-26.

Sequeira, J. & Miranda, F. (2019). 'A port of two seas': Lisbon and European maritime networks in the fifteenth century. In G. Nigro, ed., *Reti marittime come fattori dell'integrazione europea*. Florence: Firenze University Press, pp. 339-354.

Serrano, R., García-Casarejos, N., Gil-Pareja, S., Llorca-Vivero, R. & Pinilla, V. (2015). The internationalisation of the Spanish food industry: the home market effect and European market integration. *Spanish Journal of Agricultural Research*, 13(3), 1-13.

Serrano, R. & Pinilla, V. (2011). Agricultural and food trade in European Union countries, 1963-2000: a gravity equation approach. *Economies et Sociétés. Série 'Histoire Economique Quantitative'*, AF, 43(1), 191-219.

Serrano Mangas, F. (1990). *Armadas y flotas de la plata, 1620-1648*. Madrid: Banco de España.

Serrano Sanz, J. M. & Pardos Martínez, E. (2002). Los años de crecimiento del Franquismo (1959-1975). In F. Comín, M. Hernández & E. Llopis, eds., *Historia Económica de España, Siglos X-XX*. Barcelona: Crítica, pp. 369-397.

Serrão, J. V. (1970). Conspecto histórico da emigração portuguesa. *Análise Social*, XVIII (32), 597-617.

Serrão, J. V. (1993). O quadro humano. In J. Mattoso, ed., *História de Portugal*, vol. 4. Lisbon: Editorial Estampa, pp. 49-69.

Serrão, J. V. (1994). Demografia portuguesa na época dos descobrimentos e da expansão. In L. Albuquerque, ed., *Dicionário de História dos Descobrimentos Portugueses*. Lisbon: Círculo de Leitores, pp. 342-352.

Serrão, J. V. (1996). População e rede urbana nos séculos XVI-XVIII. In C. Oliveira, ed., *História dos Municípios e do Poder Local*. Lisbon: Círculo de Leitores, pp. 63-77.

Serrão, J. V. (2009). Land management responses to market changes: Portugal, seventeenth-nineteenth centuries. In V. Pinilla, ed., *Markets and Agricultural Change in Europe from the Thirteenth to the Twentieth Century*. Turnhout: Brepols, pp. 47-73.

Serrão, J. V. (2014). Introduction. In J. V. Serrão, B. Direito, E. Rodrigues & S. Münch Miranda, eds., *Property Rights, Land and Territory in the European Overseas Empires.* Lisbon: CEHC-IUL, pp. 7-20.
Serrão, J. V. (2017). Extensive growth and market expansion, 1703-1820. In D. Freire & P. Lains, eds., *An Agrarian History of Portugal, 1000-2000. Economic Development on the European Frontier.* Leiden and Boston, MA: Brill, pp. 132-171.
Sesma Muñoz, J. Á. (2003). La población urbana en la Corona de Aragón (siglos XIV-XV). In *Las sociedades urbanas en la España medieval.* Pamplona: Gobierno de Navarra, pp. 151-193.
Sesma Muñoz, J. Á. (2004a). Sobre los fogajes generales del reino de Aragón (siglos XIV-XV) y su capacidad de reflejar valores demográficos. In J. Á. Sesma Muñoz & C. Laliena Corbera, eds., *La población de Aragón en la Edad Media (siglos XIII-XV). Estudios de demografía histórica.* Zaragoza: Grupo CEMA, pp. 23-54.
Sesma Muñoz, J. Á. (2004b). Las ciudades de Aragón y Cataluña interior: población y flujos económicos (1150-1350). In J. Á. Sesma Muñoz & C. Laliena Corbera, eds., *La población de Aragón en la Edad Media (siglos XIII-XV). Estudios de demografía histórica.* Zaragoza: Grupo CEMA, pp. 55-90.
Sesma Muñoz, J. Á. (2006). El mundo urbano en la Corona de Aragón (siglo XIII). In M. González Jiménez, ed., *El mundo urbano en la Castilla del siglo XIII*, vol. 1. Seville: Ayuntamiento de Ciudad Real, Fundación El Monte, pp. 203-218.
Sesma Muñoz, J. Á. (2013). *Revolución comercial y cambio social. Aragón y el mundo mediterráneo (siglos XIV-XV).* Zaragoza: Universidad de Zaragoza.
Sesma Muñoz, J. Á. (2014). Parlamentarismo y sucesión al trono en la Corona de Aragón. El compromiso de Caspe. *Hidalguía: la revista de genealogía, nobleza y armas*, 362, 55-84.
Silva, A. C. Nogueira da (1998). O modelo espacial do Estado Moderno. *Reorganização territorial em Portugal nos finais do Antigo Regime.* Lisbon: Editorial Estampa.
Silva, Á. Ferreira da (1997). A evolução da rede urbana portuguesa (1801-1940). *Análise Social*, XXXII(143-144), 779-814.
Silva, Á. Ferreira da (2010). As finanças públicas. In P. Lains & Á. Ferreira da Silva. *História Económica de Portugal: 1700-2000*, vol. I. Lisbon: Imprensa de Ciências Sociais, pp. 237-261.
Silva, Á. Ferreira da (2015). O processo económico. In N. Severiano Teixeira, ed., *História Contemporânea de Portugal*, vol. III. Lisbon: Penguin Random House/ Fundación Mapfre, pp. 117-157.
Silva, Á. Ferreira da (2016). Multinationals and foreign direct investment: the Portuguese experience (1900-2010). *Journal of Evolutionary Studies in Business*, II(1), 40-68.
Silva, Á. Ferreira da, Amaral, L. & Neves, P. (2016). Business groups in Portugal in the Estado Novo period (1930-1974). *Family, Power and Structural Change. Business History*, 58(1), 49-68.

Silva, E. Gomes da (2011). Portugal and Spain: catching up and falling behind: a comparative analysis of productivity trends and their causes, 1980-2007. *Faculdade de Economia do Porto Working Papers*, 409.

Silva, F. Ribeiro da & Carvalhal, H. (2017). Trends, methods and sources for the study of labour, labour relations and occupational structures in early modern Portugal. Paper presented at the 37th Meeting of the Portuguese Association of Economic and Social History (APHES): The Atlantic in Economic and Social History, 17-18 November 2017. Funchal, Madeira, Portugal.

Silva, M. Santos (1996). *Óbidos e a sua Região na Baixa Idade Média*. Lisbon: University of Lisbon.

Silveira, L. E. (1987). Aspectos da evolução das finanças públicas portuguesas nas primeiras décadas do século XIX (1800-27). *Análise Social*, XXIII(97), 505-529.

Silvestre, J. (2005). Internal migrations in Spain, 1877-1930. *European Review of Economic History*, 9(2), 233-265.

Silvestre, J. (2007). Temporary internal migrations in Spain, 1860-1930. *Social Science History*, 31(4), 539-574.

Simões, I. (1967). Política Monetária e Conjuntura. *Revista Bancária*, 10.

Simpson, J. (1996). *Spanish Agriculture: The Long Siesta, 1765-1965*. Cambridge: Cambridge University Press.

Sims Taylor, K. (1970). The economics of sugar and slavery in northeastern Brazil. *Agricultural History*, 44(3).

Smith, C. A. (1995). Types of city-size distributions: A comparative analysis. In A. van der Woude, A. Hayami & J. de Vries, eds., *Urbanization in History: A Process of Dynamic Interactions*. Oxford: Clarendon Press, pp. 20-42.

Smits, J. P. H., Horlings, E. & van Zanden, J. L. (2000). *Dutch GNP and its components, 1800-1913*. Groningen: Groningen Growth and Development Centre.

Sobral, F. (1990). Secular changes in stature in Southern Portugal between 1930 and 1980 according to conscript data. *Human Biology*, 62(4), 491-504.

Solà, Á. (2010). Silk technology in Spain, 1683-1800: technological transfer and improvements. *History of Technology*, 30, 111-120.

Solórzano Telechea, J. Á. (2013). 'Commo uno más del pueblo': acción colectiva y ambiciones políticas del Común en las villas portuarias de Cantabria en la Baja Edad Media. *Edad Media. Revista de Historia*, 14, 239-257.

Solórzano Telechea, J. Á. (2018). Integración económica, competencia y jerarquización de los puertos atlánticos del norte de España (siglos XIII-XV). *Anuario de Estudios Medievales*, 48(1), 213-242.

Solow, R. J. (1957). Technical change and the aggregate production function. *Review of Economics and Statistics*, 39, 312-320.

Soria Mesa, E. (2007). *La nobleza en la España moderna: cambio y continuidad*. Madrid: Marcial Pons.

Sousa, A. de (1990). *As Cortes Medievais portuguesas* (1385-1490), 2 vols. Porto: INIC.

REFERENCES

Sousa, A. de (1993). 1325-1480. In J. Mattoso, ed., *História de Portugal*, vol. II. *A Monarquia Feudal (1096-1480)*. Lisbon: Ed. Círculo de Leitores, pp. 312-389.

Sousa, F. de (1979). A população portuguesa nos inícios do século XIX. PhD thesis, University of Porto.

Sousa, I. Coelho de (2007). Tensões e interações entre judeus e cristãos em Portugal no final do século XV. M.S. thesis, Universidade Federal de Goiás.

Spufford, P. (1988). *Money and Its Use in Medieval Europe*. Cambridge: Cambridge University Press.

Spufford, P., Wilkinson, W. & Tolley, S. (1986). *Handbook of Medieval Exchange*. London: Royal Historical Society.

Stasavage, D. (2011). *States of Credit: Size, Power, and the Development of European Polities*. Princeton, NJ: Princeton University Press.

Steckel, R. H. (2009). Heights and human welfare: recent developments and new directions. *Explorations in Economic History*, 46(1), 1-23.

Stein, S. J. & Stein, B. H. (2000). *Silver, Trade, and War: Spain and America in the Making of Early Modern Europe*. Baltimore, OH and London: Johns Hopkins University Press.

Sternberg, E. (2015). Defining capitalism. *Economic Affairs*, 35: 380-396. https://doi.org/10.1111/ecaf.12141

Stigler, G. J. (1954). The early history of empirical studies of consumer behavior. *Journal of Political Economy*, 62(2), 95-113.

Stiglitz, J. (2012). *The Price of Inequality*. New York: W.W. Norton and Company.

Stiglitz, J. E., Sen, A. & Fitoussi, J.P. (2009). *Report by the Commission on the Measurement of Economic Performance and Social Progress*. París: INSEE.

Stolper, W. & Samuelson, P. A. (1941). Protection and real wages. *Review of Economic Studies*, 9, 58-73.

Stolz, Y., Baten, J. & Reis, J. (2013). Portuguese living standards, 1720-1980, in European comparison: heights, income, and human capital. *The Economic History Review*, 66(2), 545-578.

Storrs, C. (2006). *The Resilience of the Spanish Monarchy 1665-1700*. Oxford: Oxford University Press.

Storrs, C. (2016). *The Spanish Resurgence, 1713-1748*. New Haven, CT: Yale University Press.

Suárez, F. J. (1992). Economías de escala, poder de mercado y externalidades: medición de las fuentes del crecimiento español. *Investigaciones Económicas*, 26 (3), 411-441.

Subtil, J. (1993). Governo e administração. In José Mattoso & A. M. Hespanha, eds., *História de Portugal. O Antigo Regime*, vol. IV. Lisbon: Editorial Estampa, pp. 157-193.

Subtil, J. (2007). Evidence for *Pombalism*: reality or pervasive clichés? *e-Journal of Portuguese History*, 5(2), 1-5.

Subtil, J. (2010). Instituições e quadro legal. In P. Lains and Á. Ferreira da Silva, eds. *História Económica de Portugal: 1700-2000*, vol. I. Lisbon: Imprensa de Ciências Sociais, pp. 369-388.

Tanzi, V. & Schuknecht, L. (2000). *Public Spending in the Twentieth Century: A Global Perspective.* Cambridge: Cambridge University Press.

Tavares, M. J. F. (1982-1984). *Os judeus em Portugal no século XV*, 2 vols. Lisbon: Universidade Nova de Lisboa and Instituto Nacional de Investigação Científica.

Tedde de Lorca, P. (1988). *El Banco de San Carlos, 1782-1829.* Madrid: Banco de España-Alianza.

Tena-Junguito, A. (1999). Un nuevo perfil del proteccionismo español durante la Restauración, 1875-1930. *Revista de Historia Económica*, 17(3), 579-621.

Tena-Junguito, A. (2006a). Assessing the protectionist intensity of tariffs in nineteenth-century European trade policy. In J.-P. Dormois & P. Lains, eds., *Classical Trade Protectionism 1815-1914.* London and New York: Routledge, pp. 99-120.

Tena-Junguito, A. (2006b). Spanish protectionism during the Restauración 1875-1930. In J.-P. Dormois & P. Lains, eds., *Classical Trade Protectionism 1815-1914: Fortress Europe.* London and New York: Routledge, pp. 265-297.

Tena-Junguito, A. (2007). New series of the Spanish foreign sector. 1850-2000. *Universidad Carlos III Working papers in Economic History*, 07-14.

Tena-Junguito, A., Lampe, M. & Tamega, F. (2012). How much trade liberalization was there in the World before and after Cobden-Chevalier. *Journal of Economic History*, 72(3), 708-740.

TePaske, J. J. (2010). *A New World of Gold and Silver.* Ed. by Kendall Brown. Leiden and Boston, MA: Brill.

Theil, H. (1967). *Economics and Information Theory.* Amsterdam: North-Holland.

Thomaz, L. Fernandes (1994). *De Ceuta a Timor.* Lisbon: DIFEL.

Thomaz, L. Fernandes (1988). As finanças do estado pombalino 1762-1776. In J. R. D. Magalhães, D. Justino, N. Valério & M. E. Mata, eds., *Estudos e ensaios em homenagem a Vitorino Magalhães Godinho.* Lisbon: Sá da Costa, pp. 355-388.

Thompson, I. A. A. (1992). Taxation, military spending and the domestic economy in Castile in the later sixteenth century. In I. A. A. Thompson, ed., *War and Society in Habsburg Spain. Selected Essays.* Aldershot: Variorum, pp. 1-21.

Thompson, I. A. A. (2006). Las galeras en la política militar española en el Mediterráneo durante el siglo XVI. *Manuscrits: Revista d'història moderna*, 24, 95-124.

Thomson, J. K. J. (1992). *A Distinctive industrialization: Cotton in Barcelona, 1728-1832.* Cambridge: Cambridge University Press.

Thomson, J. K. J. (2003). Transferencia tecnológica en la industria algodonera catalana: de las indianas a la selfactina. *Revista de Historia Industrial*, 24, 13-50.

Thompson, W. (1999). The military superiority thesis and the ascendancy of western Eurasia in the world system. *Journal of World History*, 10(1), 143-178.

Timmer, M. P. & Van Ark, B. (2005). Does information and communication technology drive EU-US productivity growth differentials?. *Oxford Economic Papers*, 57, 693-716.

REFERENCES

Timmer, M. P., Ypma, G. & Van Ark, B. (2003). IT in the European Union: Driving productivity divergence? *Groningen Growth and Development Centre. Research Memorandum* GD-67, 1–67.

Tinoco Rubiales, S. (1979). Mercaderes, banqueros y bancos públicos. Aproximación a la problemática del trato y la banca en la Sevilla del siglo XVI. Tesis de Licenciatura, Universitat de Barcelona.

Tinoco Rubiales, S. (1988). Crédito y banca en la Sevilla del siglo XVI. PhD thesis, Universitat de Barcelona.

Tirado-Fabregat, D. A. & Badia-Miró, M. (2014). New evidence on regional inequality in Iberia (1900–2000): a geographical approach. *Historical Methods: A Journal of Quantitative and Interdisciplinary History*, 47(4), 180–189.

To Figueras, Ll. (1997). *Família i hereu a la Catalunya nord-oriental (segles X–XII)*. Barcelona: Publicacions de l'Abadia de Montserrat.

To Figueras, Ll. (2016). Wedding trousseaus and cloth consumption in Catalonia around 1300. *The Economic History Review*, 69(2), 522–547.

Toboso Sánchez, P. (1987). *La deuda pública castellana durante el Antiguo Régimen (juros) y su liquidación en el siglo XIX*. Madrid: Instituto de Estudios Fiscales.

Tomás Faci, G. (2015). Geografía de la población infanzona en Aragón (ss. XIII–XV). *Aragón en la Edad Media*, 26, 321–349.

Tomás Faci, G. (2016). *Montañas, comunidades y cambio social en el Pirineo medieval. Ribagorza en los siglos x–xiv*. Toulouse-Zaragoza: Méridiennes.

Tomás Valiente, F. (1982). El gobierno de la Monarquía y la administración de los reinos en la España del siglo XVII. In *La España de Felipe IV: el gobierno de la monarquía, la crisis de 1640 y el fracaso de la hegemonía europea*. Madrid: Espasa Calpe, pp. 1–214.

Tomz, M. (2007). *Reputation and International Cooperation: Sovereign Debt Across Three Centuries*. Princeton, NJ: Princeton University Press.

Torras, J. (1984). Especialización agrícola e industria rural en Cataluña en el siglo XVIII. *Revista de Historia Económica*, 2, 113–127.

Torras, J. (1991). The old and the new, marketing networks and textile growth in eighteenth-century Spain. In M. Berg, ed., *Markets and Manufacture in Early Industrial Europe*. London: Routledge.

Torras, J. (2007). *Fabricants sense fàbrica: els Torelló, d'Igualada (1691–1794)*. Vic, Eumo Editorial (Spanish translation: *Fabricantes sin fábrica: en el camino de la industrialización: los Torelló, 1691–1794*, Barcelona, Crítica, 2018).

Torras, J. & Yun-Casalilla, B. eds. (1999). *Consumo, condiciones de vida y comercialización. Cataluña y Castilla, siglos XVII–XIX*. Valladolid: Consejería de Cultura de la Junta de Castilla y León.

Torregrosa-Hetland, S. (2016a). Tax system and redistribution: the Spanish fiscal transition (1960–1990). PhD thesis, Universitat de Barcelona.

Torregrosa-Hetland, S. (2016b). Sticky income inequality in the Spanish transition (1973–1990). *Revista de Historia Económica – Journal of Iberian and Latin American Economic History*, 34(1), 39–80.

Torres Balbás, L. (1971). *Ciudades Hispano-musulmanas*. Madrid: Instituto Hispano-Árabe de Cultura.

Torres Delgado, C. (2000). El territorio y la economía. In R. Menéndez Pidal, ed., *Historia de España*. Vol. VIII-III, M. J. Viguera Molins, ed., *El reino nazarí de Granada (1232-1492). Política, instituciones. Espacio y economía*. Madrid: Espasa Calpe, pp. 479-561.

Torres Sánchez, R. (2013). *El precio de la guerra. El estado fiscal-militar de Carlos III (1779-1783)*. Madrid: Marcial Pons.

Torres Sánchez, R. (2015). *Constructing a Fiscal-Military State in Eighteenth-Century Spain*. Basingstoke: Palgrave.

Torres Sánchez, R. (2016). *Military Entrepreneurs and the Spanish Contractor State in the Eighteenth Century*. Oxford: Oxford University Press.

Torró Abad, J. (2009). Formas de poblamiento y urbanismo. Cómo se organizaron los lugares de habitación de los musulmanes del reino de Valencia (siglos XIII-XIV). In R. Benítez Sánchez-Blanco, J. V. García Marsilla & N. Piqueras Sánchez, eds., *Entre terra i fe. Els musulmans al regne cristià de València, 1238-1609*. Valencia: Publicacions de la Universitat de València, pp. 201-218.

Torró Abad, J. (2014). Emisión de moneda y recaudación de impuestos hacia 1300. Observaciones desde el reino de Valencia y la Corona de Aragón. In M. Bourin, F. Menant & Ll. To Figueras, eds., *Dynamiques du monde rural dans la conjoncture de 1300: échanges, prélèvements et consommation en Méditerranée occidentale*. Rome: École Française de Rome, pp. 535-560.

Tortella Casares, G. & Comín, F. (2001). Fiscal and monetary institutions in Spain (1600-1900). In M. D. Bordo & R. Cortés-Conde, eds., *Transferring Wealth and Power from the Old to the New World: Monetary and Fiscal Institutions in the 17th Through the 19th Centuries*. Cambridge: Cambridge University Press, pp. 140-186.

Tracy, J. D. (1985). *A Financial Revolution in the Habsburg Netherlands*. Berkeley, CA: University of California Press.

Trillo San José, M. del C. (2000). Las actividades económicas y las estructuras sociales. In R. G. Peinado Santaella, ed., *Historia del reino de Granada*, vol. I. *De los orígenes a la época mudéjar (hasta 1502)*. Granada: Universidad de Granada-Fundación El Legado Andalusí.

Trillo San José, M. del C. (2000-2001). El mundo rural nazarí: una evolución a partir de al-Andalus. *Studia Historica. Historia Medieval*, 18-19, 121-161.

Trindade, L. (2002). *A casa corrente em Coimbra, dos finais da Idade Média aos inícios da Época Moderna*. Coimbra: Câmara Municipal.

Turner Bushell, A. & Greene, J. (2002). Introduction. In Ch. Daniels & M. V. Kennedy, eds., *Negotiated Empires: Centres and Peripheries in the Americas, 1500-1820*. New York and London: Routledge, pp. 1-14.

Tutino, J. (2018). *The Mexican Heartland: How Communities Shaped Capitalism, a Nation, and World History, 1500-2000*. Princeton, NJ: Princeton University Press.

Udovitch, A. L. (1979). Bankers without banks: commerce, banking, and society in the Islamic world of the middle ages. In *The Dawn of Modern Banking*. New Haven, CT: Yale University Press, pp. 255-273.

UNCTAD-STAT Database. http://unctadstat.unctad.org/

Unger, R. W. (2011). Dutch nautical sciences in the golden age: the Portuguese influence. *e-Journal of Portuguese History*, 9(2), 68-83.

United Nations. (n.d.). *The Yearbook of the United Nations*. https://unyearbook.un.org/

Usher, A. P. (1934). The origins of banking: the primitive bank of deposit, 1200-1600. *Economic History Review*, 4(4), 399-428.

Usher, A. P. (1943). *The Early History of Deposit Banking in Mediterranean Europe*, vol. I. Cambridge, MA: Harvard University Press.

Vaca Lorenzo, A. (2014). Cambios económicos y conflictos sociales de la Baja Edad Media. In J. M. Monsalvo Antón, ed., *Historia de la España medieval*. Salamanca: Universidad de Salamanca, pp. 393-438.

Valdeón Baruque, J. & Esteban Recio, A. (1985). Esbozo de una geografía social. Palencia a fines de la Edad Media. *Studia Historica. Historia Medieval*, 3, 117-142.

Valdez-Bubnov, I. (2009). War, trade and technology: the politics of Spanish shipbuilding legislation, 1607-1728. *International Journal of Maritime History*, 21(2), 75-102.

Valdez-Bubnov, I. (2011). *Poder naval y modernización del Estado: política de construcción naval española (siglos XVI-XVIII)*. México: Universidad Nacional Autónoma de México.

Valério, N. (2001a). The role of the Bank of Portugal as a central bank (1931-1999). *The Journal of European Economic History*, special issue, pp. 215-240.

Valério, N., ed. (2001b). *Estatísticas Históricas Portuguesas*. Lisbon: INE.

Valério, N., Nunes, A. Bela, Bastien, C., Sousa, R. Martins de (2007). *History of the Portuguese Banking System. From the First Portuguese Bank to the Bank of Portugal's Role as Central Bank (1822-1931)*, vol. I. Lisbon: Banco de Portugal.

Valério, N., Nunes, A. Bela, Bastien, C. & Sousa, R. Martins de (2010). *History of the Portuguese Banking System. From the Bank of Portugal's Role as a Central Bank to the European Monetary Union (1931-1998)*, vol. II. Lisbon: Banco de Portugal.

Valério, N., Nunes, A. B., Bastien, C., Sousa, R. Martins & Costa, S. D. (2006). *Da Formação do Primeiro Banco Português à Assunção pelo Banco de Portugal das Funções de Banco Central, 1822-1931*. Vol. I of *História do Sistema Bancário Português*. Lisbon: Banco de Portugal.

Valero Lobo, Á. (1984). Edad media de acceso al matrimonio en España. Siglos XVI-XIX. *Boletín de la Asociación de Demografía Histórica*, II(2), 39-48.

Vallejo Pousada, R. (2002). Economía e historia del turismo español en el siglo XX. *Historia Contemporánea*, 25, 203-232.

Van Ark, B., Hao, J., Corrado, C. & Hulten, C. (2009). Measuring intangible capital and its contribution to economic growth in Europe. *EIB Papers*, 14(1), 63-94.

Van Ark, B., Inklaar, R. & McGukin, R. H. (2003). Changing gear, productivity, ICT and services: Europe and the United States. In E. F. Christensen & P. Maskell, eds., *The Industrial Dynamics of the New Digital Economy*. Cheltenham: Edward Elgar Publishers.

van Leeuwen, B. & van Leeuwen-Li, J. (2014). Education since 1820. In J. L. van Zanden, J. Baten, M. Mira d'Ercole, A. Rijpma, C. Smith & M. Timmer, eds., *How was Life? Global Well-being Since 1820*. Paris: OECD.

van Zanden, J. L. (1995). Tracing the beginning of the Kuznets curve: Western Europe during the early modern period. *The Economic History Review*, 48(4), 643–664.

van Zanden, J. L. (2009). *The Long Road to the Industrial Revolution: The European Economy in a Global Perspective, 1000–1800*. Leiden: Brill.

van Zanden, J. L. & van Leeuwen, B. (2012). Persistent but not consistent: the growth of national income in Holland 1347–1807. *Explorations in Economic History*, 49(2), 119–130.

Vaquerizo Gil, D. (2017). La alimentación en al-Andalus a partir del registro arqueofaunístico. Estado de la cuestión. *Lucentum*, 36, 341–358.

Varieties of Democracy (V-Dem) Dataset. www.v-dem.net

Vassberg, D. E. (1984). *Land and Society in Golden Age Castile*. Cambridge: Cambridge University Press.

Veevers, D. (2015). 'Inhabitants of the universe': global families, kinship networks, and the formation of the early modern colonial state in Asia. *Journal of Global History*, 10, 99–121.

Veiga, T. Pinheiro da (1911). *Fastigímia*. Porto: Bibliotheca Publica Municipal do Porto.

Veiga, T. Rodrigues da (2004). *A população portuguesa no século XIX*. Porto: Afrontamento.

Veiga, T. Rodrigues da (2005). A transição demográfica. In P. Lains & A. Ferreira da Silva, eds., *História Económica de Portugal, 1700–2000, vol. III*. Lisbon: Imprensa de Ciências Sociais, pp. 37–65.

Verdés Pijuan, P. (2015). El mercado de la deuda pública en la Cataluña de los siglos XIV–XV. In *Estados y mercados financieros en el Occidente cristiano (siglos XIII–XVI)*. XLI Semana de Estudios Medievales, Estella, 15–18 July 2014. Pamplona: Gobierno de Navarra, pp. 243–272.

Verna, C. (2011). Innovations et métallurgies en Méditerranée occidentale (XIIIe–XVe siécles. *Anuario de Estudios Medievales*, 41, 623–644.

Viana, M. (1998). *Os vinhedos medievais de Santarém*. Cascais: Patrimonia.

Viana, M. (2007). *Espaço e povoamento numa vila portuguesa (Santarém, 1147–1350)*. Lisbon: Centro de História da Universidade de Lisboa.

Viciano, P. (2012). *Els peus que calciguen la terra. Els llauradors del País Valencià a la fi de l'edat mitjana*. Valencia: Publicacions de la Universitat de València.

Vieira, A. (n.d.). *O Açúcar na Madeira: Produção e comércio nos séculos XV a XVII*. Funchal: Centro de Estudos de História do Atlântico.

Vieira, A. L. (1983). The role of Britain and France in the finance of the Portuguese railways 1845–1890: a comparative study in speculation, corruption and inefficiency. PhD thesis, Leicester University.

Vilar, H. Vasconcelos (2012). Da vilania à nobreza: trajetórias de ascensão e de consolidação no Sul de Portugal (séculos XIII–XIV). In H. Vasconcelos Vilar & M. F. Lopes de Barros, eds., *Categorias Sociais e Mobilidade Urbana na Baixa Idade Média. Entre o Islão e a Cristandade*. Lisbon: CIDEHUS/Ed. Colibri, pp. 145–161.

Vilar, H. Vasconcelos (2019). Em torno de Évora como espaço de fronteira (1190–1217). In I. C. Fernandes & M. J. Branco, eds., *Da Conquista de Lisboa à conquista de Alcácer – 1147–1217. Definição e dinâmicas de um território de fronteira*. Lisbon: Edições Colibri, pp. 317–335.

Vilar, P. (1972). El Motín de Esquilache y las crisis del Antiguo Régimen. *Revista de Occidente*, 107, 199–249.

Vilar, P. (1999). *Hidalgos, Amotinados y Guerrilleros*. Barcelona: Crítica.

Vila-Santa, N. (2015). *Entre o Reino e o Imperio: a carreira político-militar de D. Luís de Ataide (1516–1581)*. Lisbon: ICS.

Villalba y Estaña, B. & Confalonieri, G. (2002). *Por terras de Portugal no século XVI*. Lisbon: CNPCDP.

Villalta i Escobar, M. J. (2003). 'Ciudades rurales' en la España Moderna: el protagonismo de las continuidades. *Revista de Demografía Histórica-Journal of Iberoamerican Population Studies*, 21(1), 15–43.

Villares Paz, R. (1982). *La propiedad de la tierra en Galicia: 1500–1936*. Madrid: Siglo XXI.

Vincent, B. (1976). La peste atlántica de 1596–1602. *Asclepio*, XXVIII, 5–25.

Vogt, J. (1979). *Portuguese Rule of the Gold Coast, 1469–1682*. Athens: University of Georgia Press.

Wallerstein, I. (2011). *The Modern World-System I*. Berkeley, CA: University of California Press.

Wallich, H. C. (1951). *O Sistema Financeiro Português, Administração de segurança Mútua, Missão Especial de Cooperação Económica em Portugal*. Lisbon: Banco de Portugal.

Watson, A. M. (1981). A medieval green revolution: new crops and farming techniques in the early Islamic world. In A. Udovitch, ed., *The Islamic Middle East, 700–1900: Studies in Economic and Social History*. Princeton, NJ: The Darwin Press.

White, L. (1962). *Medieval Technology and Social Change*. London: Oxford University Press.

Wickham, C. (2005). *Framing the Early Middle Ages: Europe and the Mediterranean, 400–800*. Oxford: Oxford University Press.

Wickham, C. (2016). *Medieval Europe*. New Haven, CT: Yale University Press.

Williamson, J. G. (1985). *Did British Capitalism Breed Inequality?* Boston, MA: Allen & Unwin.

Williamson, J. G. (1995). The evolution of global labor markets since 1830: background evidence and hypotheses. *Explorations in Economic History*, 32 (2), 141-196.

Williamson, J. G. (2002). Land, labor, and globalization in the Third World, 1870-1940. *Journal of Economic History*, 62(1), 55-85.

Williamson, O. (2000). The new institutional economics: taking stock, looking ahead. *Journal of Economic Literature*, 38(3), 595-613.

Windler, Ch. (1997). *Élites locales, señores, reformistas: redes clientelares y monarquía hacia finales del antiguo régimen*. Córdoba: Universidad de Córdoba.

Winius, G. D. (2011). 'The shadow empire' of Goa in the Bay of Bengal. *Itinerario*, 7(2), 83-101.

World Bank (2019). World Development Indicators. https://databank.worldbank.org/source/world-development-indicators

Wrigley, E. A. (1987). Urban growth and agricultural change: England and the Continent in the early modern period. In E. A. Wrigley eds., *People, Cities and Wealth: The Transformation of Traditional Society*. Oxford: Basil Blackwell, pp. 157-193.

Wrigley, E. A. (1990). Brake or accelerator? Urban growth and population growth before the industrial revolution. In A. van der Woude, A. Hayami & J. de Vries, eds., *Urbanization in History: A Process of Dynamic Interactions*. Oxford: Clarendon Press, pp. 101-112.

Xavier, Â. Barreto (2018). The Casa Da Índia and the emergence of a science of administration in the Portuguese empire. *Journal of Early Modern History*, 22 (5), 327-347.

Xavier, Â. Barreto & Olival, F. (2018). O Padroado da Coroa de Portugal: fundamentos e práticas. In A. B. Xavier, F. Palomo & R. Strumpf, eds., *Monarquias ibéricas em perspectiva comparada (sécs. XVI-XVIII): dinâmicas imperiais e circulação de modelos administrativos*. Lisbon: Imprensa de Ciências Sociais, pp. 123-60.

Xavier, Â. Barreto & Županov, I. G. (2015). *Catholic Orientalism: Portuguese Empire, Indian Knowledge (16th-18th Centuries)*. Oxford and New York: Oxford University Press.

Young, A. (1995). The tyranny of numbers: confronting the statistical realities of the East Asian growth experience. *Quarterly Journal of Economics*, 110(3), 641-680.

Yun-Casalilla, B. (1987). *Sobre la transición al capitalismo en Castilla. Economía y sociedad en Tierra de Campos 1500-1814*. Salamanca: Junta de Castilla y León.

Yun-Casalilla, B. (1990). Estado y estructuras sociales en Castilla. Reflexiones para el estudio de la «crisis del siglo XVII» en el Valle del Duero (1550-1630). *Revista de Historia Economica -Journal of Iberian and Latin American Economic History*, 8(3), 549-574.

Yun-Casalilla, B. (1998). The American empire and the Spanish economy: an institutional and regional perspective. *Revista de Historia Económica/ Journal of Iberian and Latin American Economic History*, 16, 123–156.

Yun-Casalilla, B. (1999). Del centro a la periferia: la economía española bajo Carlos II. *Studia Historica. Historia Moderna*, 20, 45–76.

Yun-Casalilla, B. (2001). Manufacturas, mercado interior y redes urbanas: recesión, reajustes y rigideces. In J. Alcalá-Zamora & E. Belenguer Cebrià, eds., *Calderón de la Barca y la España del Barroco*, vol. I. Madrid: Centro de Estudios Políticos y Constitucionales, pp. 111–128.

Yun-Casalilla, B. (2002). *La gestión del poder. Corona y economías aristocráticas en Castilla (siglos XVI–XVIII)*. Madrid: Akal.

Yun-Casalilla, B. (2004). *Marte contra Minerva. El precio del imperio español, c.1450–1600*. Barcelona: Editorial Crítica.

Yun-Casalilla, B. (2012). The rise of the fiscal state in Eurasia from a global comparative and transnational perspective. In B. Yun-Casalilla & P. O'Brien, eds., *The Rise of Fiscal States: A Global History, 1500–1914*. Cambridge: Cambridge University Press, pp. 1–38.

Yun-Casalilla, B. (2018). Social networks and the circulation of technology and knowledge in the global Spanish empire. In M. Pérez García & L. De Sousa, eds., *Global History and New Polycentric Approaches: Europe, Asia and the Americas in a World Network System*. Singapore: Springer, pp. 275–291.

Yun-Casalilla, B. (2019). *Iberian World Empires and the Globalization of Europe 1415–1668*. Singapore: Palgrave Macmillan.

Yun-Casalilla, B. (2022). From goods to commodities in Spanish America: structural changes and ecological globalization from the perspective of the European history of consumption. In B. Yun-Casalilla, I. Berti & O. Svriz-Wucherer, eds., *American Globalization, 1492–1850: Trans-Cultural Consumption in Spanish Latin America*. London: Routledge.

Yun-Casalilla, B. & O'Brien, P. K. (2012). *The Rise of Fiscal States: A Global History, 1500–1914*. New York: Cambridge University Press.

Yun-Casalilla, B. & Ramos, F. (2012). El Sur frente al Norte. Instituciones, economías políticas y lugares comunes. In F. Ramos & B. Yun, eds., *Economía Política. Desde Estambul a Potosí: Ciudades estado, imperios y mercados en el Mediterráneo y el Atlántico ibérico, c. 1200–1800*. Valencia: Universitat de València, pp. 11–38.

Zeitin, J. & Herrigel, G. (2004). *Americanization and Its Limits: Reworking US Technology and Management in Postwar Europe and Japan*. Oxford: Oxford University Press.

Zeron, C. A. d. M. R. (2011). *Linha de fé: A Companhia de Jesus e a escravidão no processo de formação da sociedade colonial (Brasil, séculos XVI e XVII)*. São Paulo: Editora USP.

Zulaica Palacios, F. (1994). *Fluctuaciones económicas en un período de crisis. Precios y salarios en Aragón en la Baja Edad Media (1300–1430)*. Zaragoza: Institución Fernando el Católico.

INDEX

Index entries are grouped under topics, so for example all entries for cities are grouped under 'cities', with each new topic formatted in bold for ease of navigation.

absolutism, 17, 20, 310, 446, 453, 523–525, 545, 573
accounting, 20, 60, 124–126, 136, 163, 169, 174, 214, 226, 237, 296, 325, 331, 334, 350, 528, 538, 550, 562, 587, 663
administration, 8, 15, 31, 41, 104–106, 113, 118–121, 125, 150, 156, 182, 210, 224, 237, 271, 310, 313–315, 325, 328–332, 334, 370, 372–373, 399, 413, 416–417, 420–421, 424, 427–428, 433, 445–448, 458, 460–461, 507, 521, 525, 528, 538, 588–590, 623, 665, *See* state
meritocracy, 328, 332, 334
official and civil servant, 84, 93, 104, 106–107, 119, 127, 149, 187, 224, 255, 314–316, 330, 332, 353, 381, 416, 426, 428, 437, 445, 448, 457, 563–564
secretary, 318, 329–332, 401
treasury, 30, 105, 111, 119, 124, 126, 313–314, 320, 322–325, 327, 330, 332, 334, 398, 413, 416, 428, 437, 530, 548, 550, 562–566
agriculture, 3, 8–9, 11, 13–14, 21, 26, 33, 35–37, 41, 49, 51, 56–59, 65, 69–70, 72–74, 76, 83–85, 89, 91, 93–94, 98–99, 103, 110, 116–117, 126, 129, 149, 160–162, 165, 174–175, 180–182, 184–186, 193, 202, 204–206, 216, 221, 223–227, 241, 255–263, 267–271, 288, 293, 302, 304, 306–308, 324, 326, 352, 360–369, 375, 379, 383, 390–391, 395, 400–401, 406, 411, 422, 426–427, 433, 441, 461, 469, 473, 489, 501–502, 504, 506–507, 509–510, 515, 526, 538, 549, 551, 567–568, 570–573, 575–579, 586, 590, 600, 631, 656, 658–662, 668, 678
agricultural or green revolution, 49, 74, 366, 444, 575–576, 661, 668
agronomy, 61, 74, 160, 444
Common Agricultural Policy, 543, 577, 661
corn revolution, 296, 392
extensive agriculture, 36, 47, 51, 56–57, 109, 161, 261, 444, 450, 577
huerta and orchard, 54, 56–58, 61–62, 64, 160–161, 179, 183, 189, 191, 365
intensive agriculture, 33, 57, 110, 161, 269, 365, 470, 511
irrigation, 33, 35, 48–49, 51, 53, 56–57, 59–61, 73, 98, 109, 144, 160–162, 186–187, 191, 222–223, 261, 269, 360, 363, 365, 367–368, 380, 444, 535, 576, 661
olive and olive grove, 54, 57, 61, 98, 366, 573, 668, *See also* oil in food and beverages

INDEX

sugar cane and sugar cultivation, 54, 73, 109, 160–161, 165, 214, 231, 412, 433–434, 455–456, *See also* sugar in food and beverages

vinegrape and vineyard, 35, 41, 46, 51–53, 57, 61–62, 73, 161, 163, 183, 185–186, 189, 241, 261, 269–270, 364–366, 450, 462, 573, 620, 633, 668, *See also* wine in food and beverages

agrotown, 58, 302, 369, 508

al-Andalus, 5–9, 25–34, 41, 44, 47–49, 71, 73, 80, 82, 91, 93, 98–99, 103, 105, 108, 110, 117, 124, 131, 133, 137, 143–145, 152, 161–162, 165–166, 172–173, 175–176, 191–192, 199–201, 203, 206–207, 219, 235

Almohads, 5, 8, 26, 29–32, 49, 92, 98, 105, 107–109, 132–134

Almoravids, 5, 8, 26, 28–29, 31, 33–34, 42–43, 49, 98, 105, 107–110, 132–134, 139

Nasrid kingdom of Granada, 5, 7, 48, 80, 86, 98–99, 103, 109–110, 114, 133, 144–146, 156, 160, 165, 173, 176, 186–187, 190–191, 193, 196, 204–205, 207, 212, 223, 243, 363, 409, 412

taifa kingdoms, 5, 7–8, 25, 28, 30–31, 33, 42, 49, 91, 103, 105, 108–111, 132–134, 137, 140, 145, 156, 201, 223, 235

Umayyad Caliphate and Emirate, 25, 27–29, 31, 33, 49, 80, 98, 103, 105–106, 110, 132–134, 156, 165, 175, 222–225, 235, 246

animal husbandry and livestock, 36–37, 41, 49, 51–53, 59, 62–63, 70, 74, 85–86, 91–92, 111, 117, 129, 144, 160–162, 169, 179, 183, 185–186, 189, 193, 204, 258, 260–261, 268–269, 362, 367, 394, 405, 411, 414, 433, 450, 573, 576, 661, 668

sheep farming, 36, 50, 53, 62–63, 74, 117, 161–162, 241, 260, 362, 367, 444, 573, 668

draft animals, 11, 35, 64, 151

anthropometry, 395, 592, 597–601, 672

apprenticeship, 65, 95, 166, 184, 383, 397

arbitrismo, 328, 334, 443

archaeology, 32, 76, 161, 232, 234

art, 160, 192, 232, 240, 242

autarky and self-sufficiency, 109, 168, 316, 476, 486, 488, 492, 536–540, 599, 608, 618, 620, 624, 628, 631, 636, 645, 666, 673, 677

authoritarism, 534, *See* dictatorship

autocracy, 666, *See* dictatorship

banditry, 241

banking and finance, 3, 8, 15, 19, 21, 43, 75, 97, 105, 121–125, 130–131, 143–145, 147–148, 152–157, 174, 183, 214, 216, 226, 228–230, 236–237, 241–242, 255, 314, 335, 340, 343, 346, 349–352, 355–356, 360, 366, 409, 426, 428, 441, 452, 459, 467, 479, 519, 522, 525, 528–530, 533–534, 538, 541, 546–557, 561–562, 565, 587–589, 591, 617–618, 636–637, 642, 645–646, 663, 670, 675, 677

Banco de Lisboa, 546–547, 560, 566

Banco de San Carlos, 350, 468, 546, 562–563, 566

Bank of Portugal, 530, 544, 546–547, 549, 552–553, 560–562, 566, 674

Bank of Spain, 530, 544, 546–547, 555–557, 560, 562–566, 674

banking and financial crisis, 565, 618, 621–622, 625, 640, 645–647, 674–675, 677–678

bankruptcy, 150, 237, 343–345, 350, 356, 398, 454, 529–530, 540, 548, 555, 557, 677

central bank, 21, 525, 531, 544, 546, 554, 561–566, 674–675

commercial and deposit bank, 349–350, 352, 525, 542, 547–551, 555, 558, 561, 565, 587

credit union, 548–550, 553

banking and finance (cont.)
  deposit, 146, 148, 155
  giro, 350
  International Monetary Fund (IMF),
    528, 538–539, 562, 621, 642, 675
  liquidity, 14–15, 155, 335, 340, 344,
    347, 352–356, 408, 551,
    554–557, 559, 675
  merchant-banker (private banker),
    129, 145–157, 228, 255, 350,
    356, 452, 453, 547–553
  moneychanger, 143, 145, 151–154,
    157, 183, 208
  public bank and *Taula de Canvi*, 152,
    154–155, 157, 350, 355, 444,
    452, 565
  reserve fund, 537, 550–551, 555–556,
    559, 561–562, 642, 674
  savings, 148, 152, 349, 364, 540, 588,
    636, 663, 675, 677–678
  savings bank, 542, 547–548, 550, 553,
    556, 558–561, 565, 587
  security, 346, 459, 468, 552, 555, 558
  speculation, 123, 226, 231, 399, 549,
    590, 678
  World Bank, 538–539, 621
battle, 114, 370
  battle of Alfarrobeira, 120
  battle of Ksar el Kebir, 10
  battle of Las Navas de Tolosa, 114,
    117
  battle of Muret, 224
  battle of Simancas, 40
bill of exchange, 148, 215, 226, 345,
    350–351, 357
bookkeeping, 124, 126, 215, 225, 237,
    242, 557
bullion, *See* precious metals

capital, 22, 65–66, 69, 96, 150, 152,
    157–159, 167, 176, 208, 223,
    226, 228, 230, 236–237, 239,
    242–244, 247, 256, 263, 269,
    345, 351, 354, 364, 366–367,
    372, 374, 376, 378, 396, 414,
    416, 427, 437, 454, 461, 479,
    483–486, 488–489, 492–494,
    529–530, 534, 536, 542,
    548–551, 553, 555, 557, 559,
    561, 575, 583–584, 587, 590,
    617, 636–637, 640, 642, 645,
    647, 649, 652–653, 662, 677
  capital accumulation, 365, 486,
    488–489, 491–493, 579,
    653
  capital deepening, 653, 655–656
  cost of capital, *See also* interest rate,
    16, 335, 344, 350, 357
capitalism, 159, 242, 351, 409, 523–524,
    567, 610
Carolingians, 9, 25, 38, 40, 48, 112, 132,
    134, 136–137, 156, 224
cartography, 169–170, 174, 215, 370,
    372–374, 443
charity and beneficence, 176, 183, 187,
    352, 397–398
  alms, 155, 398
  charitable institution, 155, 264, 354,
    401, 468, 558
chemical industry, 570, 583–586, 662
  oil refining, 584–585
Church (catholic), 44, 111, 125, 129,
    135, 153, 167, 181, 223, 227, 230,
    240, 242, 299, 316–317,
    327–328, 333, 348, 354, 413,
    444, 452, 455, 459–461, 463,
    468, 526, 558, 573, 661
  clergy, 35, 38, 42, 77, 84, 94, 98, 116,
    123, 127, 138, 148, 188, 316, 318,
    324, 327, 399, 416, 460–461,
    468, 524
  convents and monasteries, 35–36,
    40–41, 43, 50, 52, 116–117, 166,
    264, 327, 401–402, 404
  Inquisition, 313, 416
  Jesuits, 417, 427–428
  Papacy, 112, 125, 129, 153, 212, 416
  Papal bull, 112, 125, 129, 411
  religious order, 396, 447, 521, 526
cities, 20, 25–26, 32–35, 37–38, 40–45,
    51, 54, 57–59, 61, 64–70, 72–74,
    76, 80, 82–100, 103, 110–112,
    118–120, 122–125, 133, 135,
    148–151, 153–156, 160,
    163–165, 168–170, 175–176,
    178, 183–184, 187–192,
    194–195, 208, 216, 222–223,
    226–227, 229, 231–236, 238,

INDEX

240–242, 245, 255, 259,
262–264, 282, 287, 300, 303,
308, 316, 318–319, 333, 360,
362–363, 365, 369, 374, 380,
383, 389–392, 394, 398, 401,
403–404, 407, 444–445, 449,
452–453, 463, 468, 479, 501,
508–511, 515, 554, 584, 588,
599, 645, 663
Badajoz, 32
Barcelona, 1, 35, 37–38, 42–45, 59,
64–65, 71, 73–74, 88–89, 95–96,
111–112, 118–119, 128,
134–137, 142, 149–150, 153,
155, 157, 168, 170, 179, 181, 184,
188, 194, 208, 212, 216–217,
219, 231, 243–244, 303, 345,
349, 360, 364–365, 369, 372,
374, 376–377, 382, 389–390,
395, 405–406, 408, 421, 425,
435, 444, 452, 508–509, 579, 583
Bilbao, 88, 128, 240, 360, 390, 445
Coimbra, 28, 44, 50, 90, 161, 192,
264, 363, 397, 400, 445
Évora, 3, 27, 91–92, 112, 192, 264,
288, 388, 397, 445, 463
Faro, 69, 91, 201–202, 509, 600
La Coruña, 115, 124, 435
Las Palmas, 129
Lisbon, xvi, 1–3, 33, 50–51, 59, 64,
68–69, 72–73, 83, 85, 90–91,
112, 118–119, 153–154, 161,
164, 166, 168, 170–171, 201,
203–205, 208–210, 216,
218–219, 264, 287–288, 292,
303, 305, 336, 346, 348–349,
352–353, 360, 367, 370,
372–373, 376–377, 379–382,
386, 388, 391, 394–395, 397,
401–404, 406–409, 413–414,
417, 419–420, 427–428, 441,
444–445, 447–448, 450–451,
454, 457–458, 463, 466, 479,
508–509, 548–549, 551,
584–585, 600–601, 634
Logroño, 62, 93, 128
Madrid, 1–2, 4, 72, 256–257, 263,
281, 288, 294, 302, 349, 363, 378,
385, 389–391, 395, 397,

399–400, 402–403, 406–408,
448, 458, 462, 467, 508–511,
515, 600, 621
Mallorca, 89, 149, 155, 236, 243,
391
Mérida, 32–33, 232, 234
municipal council, 50, 151, 313, 315,
400, 431
Murcia, 33, 56, 62, 66, 73, 114, 160,
171, 281, 395, 406
Oviedo, 42–43, 52, 87
Palma de Mallorca, 59, 65, 88, 92, 95,
118, 128, 170, 202, 212, 245, 303
Pamplona, 35, 38, 40, 43–45, 77,
88–89, 96–97, 113, 146, 151,
153, 155, 313
Porto, 90–91, 168, 170–171, 218, 264,
305, 336, 363, 380, 386, 397, 406,
419, 451, 454, 463, 479, 509,
547–549, 551, 584
Santander, 240, 435
Santiago de Compostela, 44–45, 135,
202
Seville, 30, 32–34, 54, 59, 66, 71–73,
92–93, 108, 114, 118, 124–125,
145, 148, 151, 154, 164,
170–171, 173, 189, 192, 202,
208, 210, 212, 216, 224–225,
228, 230, 233, 236, 239, 263, 281,
302, 336, 349, 367, 372,
379–380, 389–391, 396–397,
402, 406, 408, 413, 421–424,
431, 433, 441, 444–445,
447–448, 450–451, 457, 462
Tenerife, 61, 129
Toledo, 32, 43, 66, 72, 124, 151, 154,
166, 171, 178, 192, 208, 281, 349,
369, 380, 399
Valencia, 33–34, 56, 65, 73, 89, 92,
95–96, 114, 128, 149, 153, 155,
157, 160–161, 165, 167–168,
170–171, 194, 202, 204,
208–210, 212, 216–219, 231,
243–245, 263, 303, 349, 369,
389, 391, 402, 421, 444–445,
452, 509
Valladolid, 73, 88, 118, 151, 154, 208,
257, 349, 397, 399, 401, 403, 405,
445

772 INDEX

cities (cont.)
  Zaragoza, 1, 30, 32–33, 38, 59, 65,
    88–89, 92, 95–96, 111–112, 118,
    128, 161, 164, 208, 216, 232, 245,
    303, 349
clientelism, 447, 521
climate, 4, 57, 165, 199, 246, 253, 256,
    260, 361, 433, 450, 668, 673
  Atlantic climate, 56–57, 162
  climate change, 57, 255
  Mediterranean climate, 56–57, 572,
    668
Colbertism, 379–381
colonies, 12–13, 16–17, 19, 98, 129, 219,
    232, 271, 278, 282–283, 287,
    291, 312, 317, 335–336, 339,
    348, 350, 355–356, 359, 364,
    371, 381, 390–391, 402, 405,
    410, 415–417, 419–421, 423,
    429, 434, 436, 440–441, 446,
    448, 451, 454, 456–458, 460,
    523, 526, 530, 538, 541, 633,
    639–640, 677
  colonisation, 11, 14, 16–17, 41,
    50–51, 53, 80, 86, 127, 161–162,
    170, 172, 183, 229, 232, 236,
    242–243, 253, 261, 292, 294,
    308, 311, 333, 335, 339, 374, 379,
    409, 411–416, 419, 440, 445,
    448, 457, 466–467, *See also*
    conquest
  decolonisation, 633
  empire, 11, 14, 16–17, 20, 28–29, 31,
    43, 103, 157, 229–230, 233–234,
    236–237, 242, 244, 252–253,
    263–264, 269–271, 296,
    311–313, 325, 336, 348–349,
    371–373, 380, 386, 390, 398,
    406, 408–412, 415–417,
    420–421, 423–424, 426–428,
    440–443, 446–448, 451–453,
    455–456, 458–461, 466–467,
    469–470, 474, 523, 611, 618,
    648, 666
  independence, 272, 435, 633–635,
    670, 672
  loss of colony, 267, 270
  Portuguese colony, 229–230, 287,
    311–312, 371, 379–380, 390,
    398, 407, 416–417, 420, 427,
    430, 433, 504, 633–635
  Spanish colony, 11, 169, 229,
    311–313, 315, 320, 324–325,
    336, 373, 399, 407, 410, 413, 416,
    420–421, 423–424, 428–431,
    433–436, 439, 442, 447, 458, 670
commerce, *See* trade
  commercialisation, 48, 53, 58, 61–62,
    70, 90, 179, 186, 194, 197, 409,
    418, 461, 465, 469
commodity, 11, 14, 69, 72, 201, 234,
    238–239, 241–242, 253, 264,
    322, 325, 336, 339–340, 390,
    408, 410–411, 414, 422, 425,
    428–429, 431–436, 441–442,
    468, 480, 543, 617, 620, 625, 628,
    633, 636
company, 75, 96, 108, 129, 144–145,
    153–154, 207–210, 215–216,
    218–219, 245, 382, 418–420,
    424–427, 430, 433, 440, 460,
    488–489, 493–494, 507, 521,
    526, 528–529, 532–536,
    539–540, 547, 552–554, 557,
    559, 563–564, 578, 583, 585,
    587, 640, 674–675, 677
  chartered company, 354, 382, 424,
    427
  Companhia das Naus, 212
  Dutch East India company, 243, 418,
    442
  Dutch West India company, 12
  English East India company, 243,
    418, 442
  joint venture, 662
  joint-stock company, 349, 355, 416,
    425, 549, 562–563
  limited liability partnerships, 237
  multinational, 585, 589, 662–663
comparative advantage, 375, 382,
    617–618, 628–629, 662,
    669–670
conquest, 30, 42–43, 88, 117, 129, 150,
    157, 216, 229, 244, 312, 314, 409,
    411–412, 414, 416, 418
  Christian conquest, 7, 10, 31–34, 40,
    42, 48–51, 53, 59, 61–62, 80,
    82–84, 86, 91–92, 99, 102–103,

112, 114, 116–119, 122–123, 125, 127, 139, 156, 160–162, 166, 175, 180–181, 186–187, 192–193, 202, 219, 224–225, 236, 244, 312, 336, 395, 409
Muslim conquest, 4–5, 8, 25–26, 28–29, 31, 34, 45, 103, 105, 108, 222–223, 234–235
consumption, 9, 11, 16, 29, 32, 34, 38, 54, 56, 60, 62, 74, 100, 125, 149, 151–152, 175–180, 183, 187–191, 194–197, 203, 214, 220, 230, 239, 255, 319–320, 328, 360, 364, 376, 385–386, 390, 399–402, 405–408, 412–413, 416, 419, 423, 427, 429, 451, 454–456, 462, 468, 526, 529, 534, 552, 575–576, 578, 587–589, 592, 594–596, 605, 663, 669, 677
consumer, 30, 64, 158, 179, 201, 204, 209, 376, 378–379, 403, 412, 425, 433, 502, 507, 521
consumer price index (CPI), 264
mass consumption, 189, 576
self-consumption, 64, 66, 68, 74, 261, 365, 402, 405
corporation, 88, 155, 533, 535, 665
coup d'état, 524, 529–530, 533, 555, 593, 666
credit, 6, 8, 21, 38, 44, 53, 90, 96, 130–131, 142–157, 184–185, 194, 207, 215, 226, 237, 241, 335, 343, 345–346, 349–357, 398, 419–420, 428, 454, 460–461, 529–530, 532, 539–540, 542, 549–556, 558–559, 562–566, 640, 666, 675
asiento, 332, 343–345, 356, 459
censo consignativo, 351–354, 357
consumer credit, 97, 143, 149, 353, 677
credit ceiling, 347, 350, 354, 357, 562
creditor, 146–148, 185, 333, 346, 349, 351, 468
interest rate, 16, 38, 131, 143–145, 147–149, 151–152, 155, 237–238, 335, 344–357, 364, 398, 460–461, 468, 532, 534,

542, 550–552, 556–559, 561–562, 564–565, 640
juro, 148, 151, 343–349, 356, 468
long-term credit, 15–16, 150–152, 155–156, 344, 346–347, 548, 550, 553, 558, 642
mortgage, 14, 146, 226, 351–352, 452, 530, 547–548, 558–559
mutuum, 146, 148–149
perpetuity and annuity, 147–152, 226, 245, 346–347, 349
private credit, 15, 340, 348, 355–357
public credit, 15, 335, 340, 352, 354–357
short-term credit, 15, 146, 148–152, 156, 343, 347, 352, 356, 548, 551, 558, 642
usury, 94, 107, 130, 143–145, 147–148, 152, 156, 345, 350, 352, 357
crops, 11, 36, 41, 53–54, 56–57, 60–62, 98, 128, 145, 160–161, 165, 185, 243, 260–261, 361, 363, 365, 401, 425, 433, 455, 463, 474, 572–573, 575–577, 668
crop rotation, 50, 59–60, 161, 368, 470
industrial or cash crop, 54, 160–162, 174, 222, 226, 230, 233, 243, 419, 427–428, 462
introduction of new crops, 11, 15, 48–49, 53, 73, 109, 160, 222, 260–261, 269, 291, 360, 363, 365–366, 450, 462

debt, 107, 136, 145–151, 182, 333, 343–344, 346–348, 350–353, 356, 426, 452, 454, 459–460, 526, 530, 533, 547, 549, 640
debt restructuring, 528
indebtedness, 67, 183, 353, 398, 441, 452–453, 459, 543, 621
public or sovereign debt, 111, 121, 123, 125, 138, 141, 143, 150–152, 155–156, 182, 236–238, 335, 342–344, 346, 348, 350, 356, 398, 400, 413, 453–454, 459–460, 468, 528, 530–531, 533–534, 542–543, 547–549, 552, 555, 557, 561, 563, 565, 640, 642

demand, 16, 36, 53–54, 58, 61–67, 70, 73–75, 96–98, 115, 132, 138, 143–144, 150–152, 158, 167, 175, 183–184, 189, 194–195, 197, 208, 214, 218, 225, 227, 234–235, 237–239, 241, 246, 256, 259, 344, 353–354, 363–364, 366, 369, 371, 378–379, 382–383, 385–386, 390, 405–406, 408, 413–415, 451, 456–457, 464, 468–469, 504, 506–507, 510–511, 551, 554, 568, 573, 576, 578, 580, 582, 584, 587, 589, 596, 610, 628, 633, 645, 647, 660–662
  money, 133–134, 137–138, 141–142, 156
democracy, 21, 489–490, 513, 522, 536, 541–542, 544–545, 590, 609–611, 616, 666–668, See also politics
  limited suffrage, 525
  transition to democracy, 18, 489, 503, 513, 540–541, 552, 564, 609–610, 612–613, 621–622, 624, 631, 666–667, 673, 677
  universal suffrage, 525
demography, 80, See also population
  demographic transition, 20, 281, 293, 496, 498, 501–502, 504, 515, 653–654
desiccation, 51, 56–57
dictatorship, 18, 20–22, 489, 521–522, 532, 536, 538, 540–542, 545, 590, 610, 616, 620, 628, 673, 675, 678
  Franco's dictatorship, 480, 492, 503, 513, 536, 539, 545, 558, 576, 610, 620, 645, 665–666
  Primo de Rivera's dictatorship, 18, 488, 530, 532–534, 536, 593, 610, 666
  Salazar's dictatorship or *Estado Novo*, 492, 513, 532, 534–535, 545, 550, 593, 610, 620–621, 665–666, 677
diet, 58, 176, 187–191, 197, 361–362, 400–403, 501–502, 517, 576, 596–597, 599, 616, See also food
diplomacy, 210–211, 215, 231, 240, 455

Economic and Monetary Union, 544, 562, 577, 623–624, 637, 642, 645, 678
economies of scale, 105, 219, 509, 580, 583–584
education, 485, 489–490, 494, 496, 502–503, 507, 509–515, 517–518, 520–521, 525–526, 528, 540, 544, 567, 579, 590, 592, 594, 600, 603, 623, 653–654, 662, 665, See also public education in welfare
  literacy, 222, 490, 509–515, 517, 528, 582, 585, 600, 654
  numeracy, 222, 267, 395, 490
  school, 268, 378, 380, 397, 490, 509, 513
  teacher, 98, 106, 227, 513
  university, 370, 380, 490, 514–515, 600
employment, 306, 360, 397, 489, 491, 493–494, 502, 504, 506–507, 511, 515, 538, 540, 543, 567, 570–572, 590, 616, 639–640, 656, 658–662, 672
  unemployment, 389–390, 489, 503, 511, 534, 544
energy, 9, 68, 159, 163–164, 360, 369, 377–378, 480, 640
  1973 Oil Crisis, 476, 488–489, 493, 495, 507, 611, 645
  coal, 164, 360, 540, 543, 579–580, 582–584, 662, 668
  electricity, 492–493, 535, 544, 568, 570, 582–584, 588, 662
  electrification, 488, 492–493, 583
  fuel and gasoline, 567
  gas, 635, 640
  hydraulic energy, 159, 163–166, 174, 360, 369, 377, 579, 583
  oil or petroleum, 534, 556, 635, 642
  steam energy, 579, 588
  water energy, 36
  wind energy, 164, 166, 360
engineering, 169, 370, 377–378, 380, 662

INDEX

Enlightenment, 4, 13, 329–330, 333–334, 359, 367, 397, 443, 463, 466, 592

European Economic Community (EEC), 479, 483, 488–489, 522, 539–543, 564, 577, 585–586, 631–633, 639, 661

European integration, 3, 18, 21–22, 476, 522, 543, 545, 559, 562, 577, 585–586, 616, 621, 625, 633, 661–662, 667, 678

European Union (EU), 3–4, 494, 503, 544, 546, 586

exploration, 127, 129, 169, 219, 229–230, 243

factor accumulation, 474, 484, 492, 495

factor endowment, 21, 479, 568, 579, 583–584, 590, 622

fair, 69–71, 74–75, 90, 116–117, 127, 133, 151, 203, 211–212, 215–216, 256, 315, 422
  fair of Champagne, 200, 228, 238, 243
  fair of Medina del Campo, 71–72, 75, 151, 203, 215

farmer, *See* peasant

fashion, 166, 196–197, 241, 401, 404, 406, 408

fertiliser, 35, 160, 362, 575, 583

feudalism, 25, 38, 41, 46, 50–51, 77, 86–88, 91, 112, 118, 146, 159–160, 168, 180–182, 185, 224
  feudal society, 26, 34, 92, 112, 444
  serfdom, 26, 231

fiscality, 12–15, 28, 30–31, 70–71, 77, 81, 94–95, 120, 122, 124, 133, 135, 151, 153, 176, 182–183, 198, 211, 216, 222, 225, 227, 236–237, 253, 310, 316, 329, 332–334, 373, 386, 398, 424, 440, 445, 452, 454, 456–457, 467–468, 529–530, 584, 608, 665, 678

fishing, 57, 91, 186, 189

food and beverages, 9, 37, 49, 51, 58, 70, 93, 107, 144, 161, 175, 179, 184, 187–190, 204–205, 214, 223, 269, 291–292, 360–364, 367–368, 370, 400–402, 405, 411, 422, 429, 450, 501–502, 578, 580, 582, 585, 594–597, 599, 625, 628–629, 660–662, 670, 672

bread, 37, 60, 176, 187–191, 197, 369, 400

cocoa and chocolate, 11, 382, 401, 413, 425, 433, 455–456, 468

coffee, 428–429, 434, 456

fasting and Lent, 187–189

fish, 70, 168, 183, 185, 188–189, 191, 204–205, 218, 233, 240, 245, 362, 367, 381, 402, 411, 581–582, 596

industry, 580, 584, 586, 591, 661–662, 669

meat, 37, 64, 178, 183, 187–191, 197, 245, 255, 319, 362, 367, 400, 402, 433, 576–577, 596

oil, 13, 55, 62, 72–73, 161, 165, 182, 191, 201–202, 204–205, 218, 233, 240, 255, 258, 268, 319, 361, 364, 367–369, 381, 411, 422, 568, 573, 575, 577, 591, 596, 661, *See also* olive and olive grove in agriculture

potato, 11, 365, 401, 450, 455, 462

spice, 53, 71, 73, 127, 161, 183, 191, 201, 206, 214, 216, 218, 220, 223, 229–230, 243, 245, 325, 401–402, 407, 414, 418, 428

sugar, 11, 53, 58, 69, 72–73, 165–166, 204–205, 217–218, 231, 239, 243, 245, 260, 363–364, 369, 381, 401–402, 406, 412–414, 418, 428–429, 433–434, 455, 583, *See also* sugar cane and sugar cultivation in agriculture

tea, 455–456

wine, 13, 37–38, 54, 72–73, 168, 174, 187–189, 191, 201–202, 205, 214, 218, 231, 233, 240, 255, 258, 260–261, 268, 319, 361–362, 364, 367–369, 382, 392, 411, 413, 422, 450, 458, 462–463, 568, 573, 575–577, 579, 582, 591, 596, 620, 633, 661

forest and woodland, 37, 49, 57–58, 62, 159, 161, 164, 179, 186, 189, 240, 378
   deforestation, 51, 56–58
fraud, 315, 339–340, 430, 433, 438–440, 457, 521, 666
   contraband, 430
   corruption, 332, 447, 461, 521, 525, 559, 588
   corruption perception index, 668
   electoral fraud, 17
   smuggling, 63, 204, 339–340, 433, 457, 537
furniture, 176, 184, 192–193, 214, 239, 400, 403–404, 407

gender, 176, 185, 307, 404, 503, 507, 599–602, 616
   gender gap, 513
globalisation, 2, 4, 22, 200, 220, 230, 242, 444–445, 447–448, 455–456, 458, 460, 494, 531, 573, 582, 585, 610, 617–621, 623, 636, 646, 662–663, 670, 673
   internationalisation, 2, 22, 552, 621, 624, 628
governance, 12, 104, 114, 121–122, 312–316, 318–320, 328, 332–333, 421, 559–560
grain, 35–38, 41, 46, 49, 51–52, 54, 59–62, 70–71, 73, 98, 125, 161–163, 181, 183, 186, 188–191, 201, 206, 210, 240, 258, 268, 283, 287, 296, 362–363, 365–366, 368, 394, 400–401, 411, 450, 462, 466, 501, 567, 573, 576–577, 599, 620, 632, 646, 661, 668
   barley, 35, 60–61, 190
   maize, 11, 261, 267–270, 291, 363, 365, 392, 400–401, 450, 455, 462
   millet, 35, 60, 190, 268
   rice, 53–54, 58, 73, 161, 201, 205, 260–261, 363, 365–366, 400–401, 429
   rye, 35, 60, 190, 268
   supply, 51, 59, 70, 85, 188
   wheat, 35, 54, 60–61, 73, 151, 188–190, 204–205, 260, 268, 361, 363, 367, 389, 400, 537, 573, 575–576, 583, 631
Great Depression, 476, 490, 506, 521, 534, 549, 618, 620, 631–632, 636, 646, 663
gross domestic product (GDP), 18, 21–22, 222, 233, 251, 253, 256, 264, 268, 275, 362, 386, 390–391, 394–395, 449, 454, 456, 463, 473–478, 480, 484–488, 490–491, 493, 526, 528, 531, 539, 542, 544, 549–550, 556–557, 570, 572, 580, 588, 590, 593, 611, 619–621, 623, 625, 636, 642, 645–646, 648–649, 651, 653, 656, 661, 663, 670, 672, 675
growth accounting, 473, 484–486, 492–495, 584, 652–653
guild and confraternity, 63, 67, 115, 145, 151, 183–185, 210, 213, 227, 231, 313, 333, 348, 352–354, 359, 370, 376, 397, 421, 423–424, 434, 461–462, 468
   ligallo, 63
   merchant guild, 375, 421
   Mesta, 52, 62–63, 74, 115, 162, 240–241, 260, 262, 444
   Misericórdia, 155, 333, 348–349, 352–354, 461
   ṭarīqāt, 106

health, 93, 317, 395, 404, 489, 500–502, 507, 509–510, 517, 521, 540, 544, 590, 594, 597, 605, 615, 623, 665, *See also* health care in welfare
   disease, 360, 394, 414, 447, 500–501, 597, 599
   epidemic, 52, 57, 100, 107, 126, 161, 177–178, 180, 245, 269, 279, 281, 283, 287–293, 296–297, 302, 390–391, 394, 409, 501
   Black Death, 51–53, 56, 78–82, 85, 89, 98, 100, 161, 175, 178–180, 196, 225, 227, 231, 239, 241, 243–244, 254, 277, 283, 287, 362, 409, 411

INDEX

cholera, 297
diphtheria, 289, 291
flu, 281, 287, 291, 501
malaria, 289, 293, 412
smallpox, 287, 291, 293
syphilis, 287
typhus, 281, 289, 291–292, 297
yellow fever, 297
malnutrition, 501, 599
medicine, 62, 93, 172, 190, 370, 402, 500–501, 592, 597
household budget, 596, 606–607, 609, 612
household economy, 176, 178, 183–184, 198, 464, 466, 502
housing and construction, 30, 614
human capital, 20–21, 159, 222, 224, 228, 230, 242, 247, 264, 331, 359, 378, 383, 395, 474, 479, 484–486, 490, 492–494, 582, 585–587, 589, 591, 646, 652–654, 662–663
hunting, 35, 57, 179, 186
hygiene, 188, 315, 502, 517, 592, 597, 599

import-substitution, 13, 370, 381, 427, 469, 521, 529, 535–536, 631, 666
income, 4, 14–16, 18, 20, 27, 31, 42, 46, 52, 71, 96, 98, 103, 105–106, 110–111, 113–118, 123–127, 149, 155, 178–184, 186–187, 198, 251, 253, 256–257, 266, 268–271, 273–278, 319–320, 322–324, 326–328, 330, 332, 346, 352, 354, 383, 389, 391–392, 394–395, 400, 405–410, 413, 416–417, 425, 448–449, 451–452, 457, 463–464, 467, 469, 474–476, 478, 480, 483–486, 490, 502, 509–511, 521, 525–526, 542, 544, 552, 554, 568, 575–576, 580, 592–598, 601, 603, 605–606, 609, 611–616, 646–648, 660–663, 669–670, 672–673
distribution, 9, 176, 180, 185–187, 277, 394, 405, 464, 469, 473, 486, 592, 605–606, 609–611, 613, 670

Industrial Revolution, 158, 164, 275, 277, 358–360, 369, 371, 373, 378, 383, 443, 468–469, 474, 492, 529, 579, 597, 599, 648, 668, 673
industrialisation, 13, 17, 19–21, 389, 395, 468–469, 473, 504, 506, 510, 515, 519, 528, 536–537, 546, 567–568, 570–572, 576, 579–580, 582, 584, 586–590, 592, 599–600, 607, 614, 618, 620–621, 625, 647–648, 663, 668–669, 672, 678, *See also* Industrial Revolution
deindustrialisation, 21, 268, 507, 656, 669
industry, 21, 115
cottage industry, 110
proto-industry, 307, 378, 383, 389, 408, 469
rural industry, 58, 65–67, 176, 227, 241
inequality, 4, 16, 19, 21, 31, 35, 110, 182, 186–187, 255–256, 324, 385–386, 390–392, 394–396, 398, 400, 404, 407–408, 451, 464, 473, 479–480, 483, 486, 501–502, 513, 592, 599–600, 605–613, 616, 672–673, 677
extraction ratio, 592, 611–613, 615
Gini coefficient, 510, 592, 606–607, 609, 611, 613, 615, 672–673
Kuznets Curve, 266, 394–395, 607, 609–610, 613–614, 672, 747
Theil index, 606
information and communication, 38, 159, 169, 210, 215, 218–219, 221, 238, 246, 336, 345, 352, 369, 372, 380, 384, 421, 423–424, 480, 493, 502, 526, 535, 544, 557, 562, 588–589, 591, 663
telegraph, 588, 636, 640, 663
telephone, 534, 583, 588, 636, 640, 663
infrastructure, 18, 41, 106, 163, 169, 176, 183, 210, 222, 233, 247, 305, 331, 358, 367–368, 371–372, 374, 377, 380, 459–461, 474–475, 479–480, 488–489, 492, 509–510, 520, 526, 528–529, 535, 584, 642, 663, 667

infrastructure (cont.)
  ports, 70, 72, 89, 108, 115, 124, 128, 149, 169–170, 183, 185, 189, 201, 203–204, 216–218, 227–228, 231, 240–241, 243, 267, 272, 287, 325, 363, 367, 380, 406, 411, 420–423, 436, 441–442, 451, 534, 579
  railways, 241, 479–480, 488, 492, 515, 528–529, 533–534, 587–588, 631, 636, 640, 642, 653, 663, 669
  roads, 39, 72, 106, 169, 171, 183, 222, 360, 371, 380, 479–480, 492, 534, 544, 645
  waste disposal, 501, 517
  water supply, 380, 501, 517
inheritance, 59, 105–106, 181–182, 184–186, 228, 239, 256, 326, 396
innovation, 11, 14–16, 53, 59, 65, 95, 125, 138, 158–160, 164–166, 170–171, 173–174, 176, 226–227, 359–360, 363–367, 371, 375–376, 378–379, 382–384, 444, 450, 470, 500, 506, 517–518, 550, 562, 572, 575, 582, 588, 668
Inquisition, 317
insurance, 107–108, 212, 215, 242, 350, 541, 550, 587, 663
investment, 11–12, 21, 28, 30, 33–34, 38, 45, 48–49, 52, 59, 61, 65, 67, 70, 135, 148–149, 152, 167, 175–176, 184–185, 187, 207–208, 226, 231, 238, 245, 256, 270, 336, 339, 345–346, 349–350, 354, 356, 364–366, 368, 376–377, 380, 404, 408, 416, 418–419, 424, 428, 437, 454–455, 474–475, 479–480, 485, 488–490, 492, 494, 528–529, 534–536, 538, 540, 542–543, 547–549, 552–553, 555–559, 565, 575, 583, 588, 591, 636, 640, 642, 649, 652, 662–663, 667, 675, 677

Jews, 44, 64, 83, 90–94, 96, 98, 100, 123, 126–127, 138, 143–144, 147–148, 150–152, 154, 156, 172, 187, 207–208, 219, 288, 391, 421
jurisdiction, 11–13, 15, 41, 69–70, 77, 87, 114, 116–117, 120, 128, 134, 181–182, 310–317, 327, 331–334, 348, 359, 416, 418, 465

Keynesianism, 536, 538, 562, 677
knowledge, 1, 3–4, 16, 18, 76, 95–96, 100, 110, 143, 160, 166, 170, 173, 176, 215, 235, 308, 328, 355, 358–361, 363–364, 367–378, 380, 382–383, 443–444, 446, 462, 518, 592

labour, 11, 22, 52, 65, 67–68, 85, 158–161, 167, 177–178, 184, 208, 231, 233, 254, 268, 308, 366, 377–379, 381–382, 385, 389, 392, 395, 397, 405, 408, 413–414, 417, 444, 447, 462, 478–479, 484–486, 489–490, 492, 494, 502, 504, 506–507, 510–511, 533–535, 539, 541, 567–572, 575–576, 584–585, 610, 617–618, 636, 638–639, 646–647, 652–656, 658–660, 666, 672, *See also* employment, labour market in market, wage, work
  child labour, 93, 306–307, 397
  day labourer, 65, 389–390, 401
  division of labour, 506, 520, 656, 661
  enslaved labour, 11, 414, 441, *See also* slavery
  labour service, 11, 181, 185, 414, 416
  seasonal labour, 184–185, 389, 462
  skill premium, 386, 388, 490, 514
  skilled labour, 21, 92, 159, 166–167, 201, 376, 378, 382, 386, 388–389, 393, 414, 490, 579, 584, 590, 616, 640
  trade union, 533, 537, 539, 541, 558, 560
  strike, 533, 537

unskilled labour, 167, 184, 383, 386, 388–389, 397, 600, 673
women's labour, 93, 95, 176, 184–185, 195, 198, 306–307, 381, 396–397, 401, 461, 464, 502, 507, 511, 653, 658
land, 15, 26, 30, 35–36, 38, 40–41, 48–53, 57–62, 73, 84, 88–89, 105, 109, 112–114, 116–117, 148–149, 160–161, 170, 179–182, 184–187, 202, 221, 223, 225–226, 228–229, 241, 246, 256, 260–261, 268–269, 323, 327–328, 359–367, 389–390, 393–395, 399, 411, 416–417, 428, 444, 447–448, 454, 456, 460–461, 463, 470, 506, 521, 539, 567, 573, 575–577, 584, 607, 614, 647, 661
demesne, 52, 181
land distribution, 14, 30, 53, 59, 86, 255, 385, 394
land ownership, 59–60, 318, 326–327, 389, 394–395, 513, 528, 666, 673
landowner, 36, 61, 129, 140, 146, 181, 190, 228, 241–242, 315, 317, 326, 365, 390, 521, 524, 526
ownership, 15, 26, 36, 53, 86–87, 114, 182–183, *See* property
sharecropping, 187, 261, 365
law, 31–32, 75, 94, 104–105, 115–116, 122–123, 128, 130, 134–135, 142–144, 146–148, 186, 188, 195, 212, 215, 244, 256, 267, 312–313, 315, 326–327, 330, 332, 345, 350, 352, 357, 399, 416, 447, 512, 521, 526, 528, 533, 535–537, 540, 542, 550–551, 553–556, 561, 563, 580, 583, 631, 634, 665–667
arbitration, 237–238, 447
charter, 61, 84, 111, 114, 118–119, 146, 170, 315, 320, 396, 424, 524, 563, 624
constitution, 134, 136, 139, 310–311, 313, 323, 328, 330, 334, 371, 446, 448, 452, 454, 520, 523–524, 543, 545

Constitution of 1822, 523–524
Constitution of 1826, 524
Constitution of 1834, 524
Constitution of 1838, 524
Constitution of 1845, 524, 528
Constitution of 1869, 529
Constitution of 1933, 534
Constitution of 1978, 542
Constitution of Cádiz, 523–524
courts, 147–149, 313–314, 318, 328, 352–353, 416, 421, 459, 665
mercantile courts, 115, 212, 218, 421
custom, 75, 244, 312, 334, 364, 446
decree of *Nueva Planta*, 12, 318, 330, 459
fuero, 45, 146, 312, 330
jurisdiction, 75, 398–399, 416, 445, 452–454, 526
justice, 122, 181, 313–314, 333–334, 421, 445, 460, 503, 520–521
law enforcement, 105, 267–268, 352–353, 445–446, 618, 620, 665
legislation, 36, 38, 146, 152–153, 228, 328, 332, 336, 354, 368, 381, 396, 416, 425, 511, 526, 528–529, 533, 535, 546, 549–550, 552–553, 555, 561–562, 565
litigation, 147, 421
privilege, 94, 146, 154, 312–313, 316, 329–330, 332, 334, 381, 399, 417, 452, 459, 464, 535–536, 560, 562–563
sumptuary law, 115, 188, 195, 197, 381–382
League of Nations, 533
leather and hides, 38, 64, 68, 72–73, 93, 95–97, 167–168, 173, 201, 204–206, 218, 226, 241, 245, 271, 294, 368–369, 413, 429, 433, 441, 580, 631
cordovan, 64, 173, 201
tanning, 68, 163, 166–167, 173, 206, 245, 369, 377
levy, 176, *See* taxation
liberalisation, 479, 522, 528, 542, 544, 546, 557–558, 562, 565, 573, 589, 617, 620–621, 631, 662

liberalism, 17, 19-20, 324-325, 329, 334, 426, 488, 518, 520-526, 529, 531, 535, 545, 610, 624, 632, 666, 678
neoliberalism, 611
luxury, 27-32, 38, 44, 65-66, 99-100, 183, 187, 191, 195-196, 201, 205, 214, 222, 239, 243, 271, 328, 369, 381-382, 405-407, 414, 423, 428, 456

machinery and mechanical devices, 164-165, 224, 358, 367, 376, 378, 380-383, 493, 575, 583-584
clock, 168
mechanisation, 389, 506, 575-576, 579
spinning jenny, 579
steam engine, 376-378, 579
Malthus, Thomas Robert, 84, 223, 254, 260, 264, 266, 276, 299, 450, 611
markets, 7, 15, 21, 27, 29, 31-35, 37, 42, 44-46, 53-54, 64, 66-70, 72-74, 89-90, 92, 98-99, 109, 116-118, 127-131, 133, 135, 138-139, 141-142, 146-148, 151, 154, 157-158, 161-162, 167, 170, 173-176, 179, 182, 184-185, 188-190, 197, 199-200, 203-206, 210-212, 215-218, 220, 229, 231, 235, 237, 239-240, 243, 245-246, 252, 254, 261, 263, 267, 270-272, 305, 315, 330, 334, 340, 343-347, 349, 352, 354, 356, 359, 363, 365-368, 372, 375, 382-384, 386, 389, 402-403, 405, 411-414, 419, 423, 427-428, 433, 440, 450-451, 460, 462, 465-466, 468-469, 479, 489, 503, 512, 517, 519-520, 522, 532, 535-538, 541, 543-544, 547, 549-551, 553, 557-558, 560-563, 568, 573, 575-577, 579-586, 588-590, 617-619, 632-635, 637, 640, 645-646, 660-662, 665-666, 668-670, 672, 675, 677-678
capital market or financial market, 150, 152, 244, 335, 350-351, 356-357, 427, 480, 528, 539, 542, 549, 551, 557, 559, 561, 617, 636, 675, *See also* capital
colonial market, 420, 451, 541, 579
commodity market, 238, 419, 427, 469, 480, 502, 617, 621
credit market, 15, 97, 100, 130, 147-148, 150, 182, 237, 270, 335, 340, 349, 352, 354-355, 357, 552, 558
European single market, 522, 543, 577, 586, 624, 635, 645
labour market, 95, 177, 245, 264, 405, 503, 507, 511, 513, 537, 539, 543, 617, 636
land market, 14, 35, 37, 59, 176, 226, 455
market economy, 34, 150, 255, 573, 579, 667
market integration, 4, 11, 13, 264, 305, 361, 364, 366, 375, 433, 449, 454, 465, 474, 478-480, 483, 617-618, 623
second hand market, 194, 346
slave market, 28, 231, *See also* slavery
souk, 32-33, 105-107, 203
stock market, 346, 354, 528, 557, 677
marketing, 88, 190, 559, 662
marriage, 15, 111, 194, 240, 278, 290-291, 297-300, 309, 396, 447, 502
dowry and trousseau, 106, 126-127, 176, 184, 194, 396, 405
Marshall Plan, 538-539, 624, 631
material culture, 29-30, 176, 187, 240, 405, 451
mercantilism, 328-329, 368, 379, 456-457, 459-460, 528, 536-537, 618
merchants, 38, 44, 53, 58, 63, 65-67, 72, 75, 87-88, 92, 96-99, 115, 119, 128-129, 140, 142-144, 148-149, 151, 153-154, 157, 162, 167-168, 170, 172, 183, 187-188, 199-200, 202, 204-209, 211-220, 226-231, 236-245, 255, 262, 327, 336,

INDEX

339, 347, 351, 370, 374, 380–381, 394, 400, 404, 406, 408, 411, 415, 417–425, 427–429, 441–442, 445–448, 451, 453, 456, 458, 460, 553
metallurgy, 36, 64, 68–69, 93, 96–99, 151, 163–164, 206, 226, 232–233, 241, 270, 336, 358, 369–371, 377–378, 380–382, 411, 507, 540, 543, 579–580, 582–586
Altos Hornos de Vizcaya, 583
migration, 11, 20, 22, 44–45, 50, 64, 82, 85, 109–110, 119, 159–160, 208–209, 223, 260–261, 269, 278, 281–283, 287–289, 291–292, 294, 296, 309, 390, 421, 444, 450–451, 462, 479, 498, 503–504, 508–511, 515, 548, 584, 599, 618, 636, 638–640, 642, 645, 647, 673, 677
forced migration, 11, 41, 414
rural-to-urban migration, 65, 185, 508–509, 576
military orders, 50, 83–84, 86, 113, 116–118, 129, 320, 326, 399
mill, 35–36, 41, 53, 55, 58–59, 69, 163–164, 166, 367, 369, 377
fulling mill, 163–164, 166
hydraulic mill, 59, 109, 166, 367, 371
windmill, 59, 164, 166, 367
mining, 11–12, 97, 99, 109, 126, 163, 222, 232, 292, 320, 335–336, 340, 343, 361, 369, 371, 377, 413–414, 422, 427, 429–430, 434, 437–439, 442, 447, 456–458, 488, 492, 580, 642, 653
amalgamation, 377, 437–438
Potosí, 371, 436–438
minting, 7, 9, 26–29, 31–32, 38, 43–44, 108–109, 111, 113, 124, 126–127, 130–131, 133–142, 156, 340, 360, 380
mint house, 90, 336, 340, 354
mobility, 52, 480, 636
geographical mobility, 8, 383, 418, 639, *See also* migration
social mobility, 113, 119, 183, 327, 400, 417, 453

monarchy, 8, 10, 12, 14, 17–18, 25, 35, 38, 42, 77, 97, 102–103, 113, 115–116, 119, 122, 124–126, 128–129, 131, 134–135, 138–139, 142, 150–155, 180, 182, 222, 224–225, 227–228, 237, 244, 253, 281, 310–318, 320, 322–334, 343, 361, 367–368, 370, 374–375, 379–380, 385, 390, 398–400, 416–418, 420–422, 424–426, 446, 453–454, 459, 565, 646, 678
Astur-Leonese dynasty, 27
Bourbon dynasty, 12–13, 17–18, 329–330, 342, 367, 374, 380, 385, 391, 397, 399, 424, 457–459, 525, 528, 530
Capetian dynasty, 126
Carolingian dynasty, 37
Castilian House of Ivrea, 43–44, 62, 71, 109, 112, 114–115, 119, 121, 124–125, 135, 138, 142, 162, 182, 195, 228
Catholic Monarchs, 67, 103, 125, 128–129, 134–135, 137–138, 152–153, 164, 211, 237, 244, 279, 412
composite monarchy, 11, 15, 312, 328–330, 445
constitutional monarchy, 522–524, 526, 530, 532, 545, 666
dynastic union, xv, 10–11, 112, 173, 225, 230, 253, 273, 329, 346, 441, 545
Habsburg dynasty, 10, 12, 237, 244, 281, 288, 312, 316, 322–324, 343–344, 346, 380, 385, 399, 448, 451–454, 458–460
House of Aviz, 10, 140, 153, 169, 229, 445
House of Barcelona, 150, 195, 228
House of Braganza, 17–18, 273, 314, 329, 331, 346, 418, 427, 454, 457–460
House of Évreux, 126–127
House of Jiménez, 113–114
House of Trastámara, 125, 127, 135, 137–138, 142, 154, 229, 244, 445
Jimena dynasty, 42–43, 111, 140

INDEX

monarchy (cont.)
  Navarrese House of Blois, 125–126
  Portuguese House of Burgundy, 29,
    44, 100, 112–114, 120, 123, 135,
    139, 148, 153, 201
money, 6–9, 11, 19, 26, 28–29, 34–35,
  38, 42–44, 56, 67, 74–76, 92,
  106–108, 111, 115, 128,
  130–143, 145, 148, 153,
  156–157, 177–178, 184, 207,
  225, 255, 259, 269, 312, 319, 331,
  335, 340, 349–352, 354, 377,
  381, 386, 394, 402, 405, 451, 453,
  459, 468, 525, 529, 534,
  536–537, 539–540, 542, 544,
  547, 550–552, 554–555,
  561–566, 617–618, 621, 631,
  636, 645, 673–675, 677
  banknote and paper money, 108, 530,
    544, 547–548, 560–561, 563–564
  bimetallism, 29, 132, 138–139, 226,
    442, 479
  Bretton Woods, 539, 556, 619–621,
    636–637, 647, 673, 675
  coinage, 27–29, 34, 38, 42–44, 71, 104,
    108, 110–111, 113, 124–127,
    130–133, 135–142, 145, 152, 156,
    166, 226, 235, 255, 336, 340, 354,
    360, 369, 380, 454, 563, 665
  dinar and *dirham*, 26–27, 29–31,
    108, 111, 133, 135, 145
  dollar, 253, 273–275, 539, 637, 648,
    673
  escudo, 141, 544, 636–637
  euro, 522, 529, 540, 542–544, 546,
    562, 565, 625, 667, 673, 675, 678
  florin and *ducat*, 133–134,
    137–138, 140–142
  morabatí and *maravedí*, 28–29, 44,
    109, 113, 136, 138–140, 142
  peseta, 529–530, 536, 539, 544, 645
  real, 138, 140–141, 324, 348–349,
    373, 397, 407, 548
  vellón, 255, 324
  debasement, 71, 115, 122, 124, 130,
    132–142, 156, 178, 255, 324,
    346, 454
  devaluation, 530, 533, 645

exchange rate, 139–140, 145, 273,
  350–351, 357, 530, 533–534,
  539, 542, 549, 561–564, 635,
  645–646
  falsification, 141–142
  monetisation, 102, 133, 139, 178, 530,
    549
  monetised economy, 29, 34, 152, 226,
    270
  money of account, 38, 132–133,
    135–136, 138–141, 226
  monometallism, 136, 140
  ratio of silver to gold, 27, 439, 442
  shortage, 26, 139, 141–142, 156
monopoly, 53, 126, 209, 212, 236, 238,
  310, 320, 324–325, 332, 339,
  348–349, 381, 416–420,
  423–425, 427, 433, 437–438,
  440, 446–447, 453, 456–457,
  459, 530, 533–534, 536, 560,
  563–564, 566, 633, 665, 670
Morisco
  expulsion, 261, 263, 288–290, 294, 391
Mozarabic, 98
Mudejar, 50, 83–84, 93–94, 96, 98, 193

natural resource, 4, 56, 65, 158–159, 168,
  186, 375, 378, 416, 420, 428, 473,
  483, 488, 580, 582, 586, 662, 668
  mining or mineral resource, 99, 232,
    336, 417, 438, 567, 580, 642
  resource endowment, 253, 261, 264,
    366, 580, 582, 661, 668
navigation, 11, 33, 132, 174, 202, 220,
  242–243, 370, 380, 443
nobility, 35, 38, 40, 71, 77, 87, 94, 98,
  100, 111–113, 116, 121, 123,
  125–127, 129, 135, 138, 142,
  148, 150–151, 153, 156,
  175–176, 180–182, 184–185,
  188–189, 195, 197, 208, 210,
  224, 227–228, 230, 239, 242,
  316–318, 326–328, 332–333,
  353, 394, 399, 404, 406, 411, 444,
  451–454, 459–460, 524
  Count-Duke of Olivares, 329, 334
  Marquess of Ensenada, 293, 330, 332,
    394, 396, 399, 466

Marquess of Pombal, 13, 329, 331–332, 400, 427, 430, 466
North, Douglass C., 277, 310, 444, 446, 520, 665
nuptiality, 290, See also marriage

occupational structure, 8, 93–94, 271, 278–279, 301, 305, 307–308, 496, 504, 506
Organisation for Economic Cooperation and Development (OECD), 539, 601, 607, 611, 615, 631, 667
output, 181, 254, 257–259, See also production

paper, 108, 163, 166, 169, 223, 245, 358, 369, 377, 379, 583, 707
parliament, 18, 227, 236, 312–313, 316, 319, 322–323, 325, 330, 333, 459, 468, 524, 529
  Cortes, 77, 115, 120–127, 134–136, 140, 142, 146, 154, 156, 195, 270, 312, 316, 318–319, 322–324, 343–344, 452
Partidas of Alfonso X, *Las*, 135, 142, 146
path-dependency, 225, 233
patronage, 35, 78, 320, 402, 455
pawning, 146, 150, See also credit
peasant, 26, 35–36, 39–40, 50, 52–53, 56–60, 62, 66–67, 70, 85, 113, 116, 127, 151, 175, 179–181, 185–191, 193–197, 207–208, 215, 255–256, 260, 317, 362, 365–369, 389–390, 394, 400, 407, 444, 450, 461, 463, 465–466, 508, 525, 537, 576–577, 661, 668
pilgrimage, 37, 45, 87, 183
  Camino de Santiago, 43–46, 87, 89, 94, 96, 153–154, 183, 202, 209, 219, 223–224
  ḥaǧǧ, 103
pillage and plunder, 111–113, 132, 139, 411, 457
piracy, 236, 262, 448, 457
plantation economy, 11, 165, 231, 412–414, 433–434, 447, 455–457, 461

politics
  minister and ministry, 528, 533–534, 541, 549–550, 555, 561, 564
  political participation, 310, 319
  political party, 530, 542, 558, 560, 665
polycentrism, 11–12, 385
polysynodial system, 314, 318, 328, 331
population, 6, 8, 11, 16, 19–21, 26, 32–33, 38–41, 43, 48–50, 54, 56, 65, 70, 76–86, 88–95, 98–100, 104, 109, 114, 124, 126–127, 138, 151, 175–176, 178, 184, 186–187, 189–194, 196–198, 203, 217, 223–224, 235, 241, 244, 246, 253, 258, 262–263, 266, 268–269, 278–279, 281, 283–284, 288–294, 296–297, 299–303, 305–309, 316, 327, 361–366, 368–370, 375, 388–390, 396, 398, 400, 409–411, 414–416, 423, 426, 445, 447, 449–451, 461, 490, 496–498, 501–504, 506–511, 513–515, 517–518, 525, 534, 544, 567, 573, 576, 579, 592–593, 596–597, 599–600, 606, 608–609, 611, 613, 622, 638–639, 653–654, 665, 672
  active population, 58, 73, 94–95, 260, 397, 485, 490, 576
  baptism, 287, 290–291, 293–294
  Becerro de las Behetrías, 77, 86
  birth, 283, 288, 290–294, 297, 300, 597, 653
  celibacy, 283, 290, 298–299
  census of Floridablanca, 293, 305
  census of Godoy, 293, 299, 306
  density, 36, 41, 50, 76, 78, 82–83, 86, 88, 90, 158, 162, 180, 197, 215, 235, 284, 297, 305, 309, 362
  depopulation, 52, 82, 84–85, 186, 288, 509–510
  distribution, 80–82, 99
  fertility, 20, 232, 246, 278, 283, 289–290, 297–300, 414, 496, 501–503, 514–515, 518
  hearth census or *fogaje*, 77–78, 81, 84, 100

population (cont.)
life expectancy, 21, 293, 297, 592, 599, 601–603, 616, 672
mortality, 20, 51, 178, 185, 278, 281, 284, 287, 289, 291–293, 296–298, 308, 412, 414, 496, 498, 500–502, 515, 517, 592, 596, 599, 601, 653
Numeramento, 78–79, 284, 303
overpopulation, 106, 110
repopulation, 40–41, 47, 49–50, 64, 69, 82, 84, 87, 261
pottery, 30, 35, 39, 64, 69–70, 93–94, 99, 159, 166, 187, 193, 201, 226, 232, 234, 241, 369, 428, 442
porcelain, 382, 406–407, 413–414
poverty, 34, 241, 389, 396, 398, 480, 599, 609, 651
pauperization, 180
poor, 245, 267, 394, 396, 398, 401–402, 407, 480, 483, 609, 651, 659
precious metals and bullion, 71, 99, 108, 110, 130, 132, 141, 220, 335–336, 339–340, 349, 356
gold, 11, 27–29, 34, 42–44, 67, 108, 113, 125, 127, 129, 132–142, 153, 166, 196, 203, 222, 226, 230, 232–233, 235, 237, 269–270, 320, 335–336, 339–340, 348, 354–356, 377, 379, 404–405, 408, 413–414, 419, 429, 439–440, 442, 458, 554–555, 561, 563–564, 637, 674
gold standard, 528, 530–531, 547–548, 560–561, 564, 618, 636–637, 646, 673–674, 677
scarcity or shortage, 9, 38, 138, 140–142, 156, 336, 442
silver, 11, 26–30, 56, 97, 108, 125, 132–133, 136–142, 153, 166, 179, 193, 195, 203, 222, 226, 232, 237, 255, 320, 335–336, 339–340, 343, 347, 355, 377, 379, 386, 404–405, 408, 414, 422, 432, 436–442, 454, 563–564
American silver, 12, 242, 260, 320, 326, 335–336, 343, 371, 413–414, 420, 422, 436–440, 442, 461, 467

prices, 9, 36, 66, 72, 74, 115, 139, 175, 177–179, 189–191, 194–197, 224, 237–238, 264, 273, 275, 315, 322, 325, 349, 356, 361, 363, 373, 380, 383, 385–386, 389–390, 394, 401–402, 405–406, 408, 425, 432, 436, 438, 440, 442, 449, 465, 480, 501, 510, 536–537, 556–557, 563–564, 568, 577, 582–583, 610, 619–621, 631–633, 642, 645, 662, 673
deflation, 394, 646
grain price, 51, 177–179, 198, 401, *See also* grain
inflation, 51, 71, 115, 138, 374, 451, 502, 533, 537, 549, 555, 561, 565
printing, 166, 172, 360, 369
production, *See also* output
agricultural production, 8, 14–15, 33, 36–37, 40, 49, 52–58, 108, 144, 176, 186, 215, 252, 254, 257–261, 268–269, 317, 327, 361–365, 367, 405, 409, 431, 479, 573, 576, 578, 660–661
high value-added production, 239
mass production, 67, 233–234, 502, 663
production costs, 60, 159, 167, 653
productivity, 8, 11, 14–16, 18, 48, 52, 55, 159, 164–165, 171, 176, 185, 253, 279, 301, 304, 308, 332, 358, 363, 365–366, 368, 383, 390–391, 444, 450, 470, 473–474, 478–479, 483–485, 492, 494, 501, 504, 506–507, 509, 568–570, 572, 575–578, 582, 586, 592, 649, 652–653, 655, 658–661, 669, 672
total factor productivity (TFP), 20, 473–474, 484, 487, 490–495, 570, 575, 584, 652–653, 655–656, 662
profit, 38, 40, 42–43, 65, 127, 134, 159, 168, 184, 189, 336, 339, 343, 365–366, 390, 417, 428, 539, 554, 557, 559–560, 563–565, 582, 588
profitability, 142

proletarianisation, 395
property, 26, 35, 106, 122, 125, 151, 179, 181, 183–184, 186–187, 319, 324, 326–328, 339–340, 390, 396, 399, 403, 427–428, 452, 463, 466, 469, 521, 524–526, 530, 552, 573
  allodial property, 35, 41
  communal property, 35, 57–58, 62, 186, 315–316, 323, 364, 541, 573
  demesne, 150, 327
  disentailment, 328, 346, 428, 466, 468, 573, 661
  distribution, 106, 678
  emphyteusis, 14, 185, 256, 326–327, 364, 403, 445, 463
  entailment, 452–453, 455, 459, 463
  latifundium or large estate, 36, 146, 187, 255, 326, 455, 513, 541
  lease, 187, 256, 327, 349, 364–365, 393, 403
  mayorazgo or *morgadío*, 14, 182, 396, 454, 463, 528
  minifundium, 36
  rent, 29, 45–46, 53, 116, 136, 140, 150, 181, 184–185, 190, 264, 276, 351, 353, 394, 403, 411, 461, 607, 665–666
  waqf property, 106, 110
property rights, 13, 36, 41, 123, 152, 215, 226, 325, 327–328, 333, 349, 366, 389, 394, 396, 445, 453, 455, 463, 520
protectionism, 19, 63, 65, 71, 115, 128, 331, 375, 381, 383–384, 468, 476, 479, 488, 492, 521, 528–531, 533, 535–537, 543, 575–577, 579, 582–585, 610, 617, 620, 625, 631–634, 647, 662, 666, 669, 673
purchasing power, 67, 178, 189, 217, 222, 275, 388–389, 442, 502
putting-out system, 67, See also *Verlagssystem*

raid, 39, 111
ransom, 42, 139, 231

ratio
  land–labour ratio, 51, 84, 186, 269, 414
  rent–wage ratio, 393–394
real estate and construction, 44, 69, 118, 146, 171, 183–184, 240, 271, 349, 353, 362, 369, 380, 399, 428, 466, 479–480, 488, 492, 521, 529, 534, 552, 559, 582, 590, 631, 642, 653, 678
  housing, 77, 84, 113, 120, 125, 175, 187, 191–194, 212, 222, 234, 239–240, 242, 403–405, 501, 510–511, 521, 559, 594
  palace, 33, 168, 192, 403–404
religion, 31, 359, 404
  Catholicism, 267, 502–503
  Christianity, 4, 62, 224, 452
  freedom, 30
  Gregorian reform, 45
  Islam, 31, 62, 98, 104–105, 107, 224
  Protestantism, 267, 421
  Reformation, 370
  religious order, 116, 187
Renaissance, 49, 166, 235, 359, 443, 692
republic and republicanism, 374, 452, 666, 678
  Portuguese First Republic, 18, 513, 532–533, 593, 666
  Portuguese Third Republic, 545
  Spanish Second Republic, 18, 513, 554, 565, 593
revolt and uprising, 289, 323, 333, 394, 412, 453, 522, 524, 530
  rebellion of the Alpujarras, 391
  revolt of the *Germanies*, 391
  revolt of the *Comuneros*, 255, 391, 399
revolution, 38, 49–50, 74, 232, 235, 238, 241, 243, 276, 296, 366, 392, 434, 444–445, 467, 524–525, 531, 589, 611, 663, 666, See also Industrial Revolution
  American revolution, 435, 523
  Carnation revolution, 541, 625, 642
  commercial revolution, 236
  consumer revolution, 408, 456, 462, 469
  English revolution, 453
  financial revolution, 226, 237, 244, 452, 459–460, 468

revolution (cont.)
  French revolution, 16, 352, 426, 467
  Industrious Revolution, 11, 16, 158,
    164, 239, 275, 277, 358–360,
    369, 371, 373, 378, 383, 405, 443,
    461, 466, 468–469, 474, 492,
    529, 579, 597, 599, 648, 668, 673
  liberal revolution, 463, 475, 520, 523,
    525, 529, 589
  price revolution, 451
  Scientific revolution, 358, 373, 592
risk, 65, 70, 107–108, 148, 153, 226, 238,
  306, 349–350, 354, 356, 366,
  375, 384, 417, 445–446, 498,
  523, 553, 557

salt, 70, 97, 109, 168, 204–205, 218, 240,
  245, 320, 325, 362, 364, 368, 411
Schumpeter, Joseph, 451
science and mathematics, 105, 166, 168,
  171–172, 215, 358–361, 364,
  369–373, 375, 378, 380, 383, 443,
  446, 469, 500–501, 518, 592
  chemistry, 166, 380, 493, 582–583
secularisation, 502–503, 517
service industry, 21, 65, 69, 92–93, 95,
  169, 184, 268, 271, 360, 364,
  395–396, 401, 441, 489, 502,
  504, 506–507, 515, 567–568,
  571–572, 586–591, 623, 625,
  656, 661–663, 670
shipbuilding, 58, 69–70, 91, 170, 172,
  174, 215, 228, 231, 240, 244, 271,
  360–361, 369–375, 379–380,
  382–383, 409, 441, 451, 507,
  540, 543
  shipyard, 168, 170, 215, 372–374,
    378, 382, 390
  shipwright, 372, 374–375
slavery, 11, 16, 28–29, 35, 44, 65, 107,
  111, 127, 145, 201, 206, 220, 231,
  233, 243, 245, 287, 325, 412,
  414–415, 418, 420, 430–431,
  434, 441, 455
  asiento de negros, 424, 457
  enslaved African, 11, 231, 288,
    414–415, 424, 427–429, 439,
    441, 457
  enslavement, 231, 411, 414, 416

Smith, Adam, 359, 389
social emulation, 175, 184, 197
social hierarchy or stratification, 25,
  36, 40, 42, 60, 112, 118, 175, 181,
  188, 407
sovereignty, 104, 330, 415–416, 420,
  520, 523–525, 544
specialisation, 13, 15–16, 53, 95–97, 130,
  161, 173, 183, 199, 207, 222, 226,
  267–268, 362–366, 369, 383, 404,
  431, 433, 450, 469, 478–479,
  506–507, 548, 551, 555, 568, 582,
  585–586, 591, 617, 622, 628, 633,
  656, 660, 669, 675
standards of living, 6, 9, 16, 18, 21,
  175–179, 192, 196–198, 243,
  247, 275, 299, 361, 385–386,
  389–390, 402, 407, 474, 501,
  510, 592–594, 597, 599–601,
  603–606, 609, 648, 653, 655,
  672, 677, *See also* living
  conditions
  Human Development Index (HDI),
    21, 592, 603–605, 616
state, 4, 7, 26, 29–31, 33–35, 77, 95,
  103–109, 114, 130–131, 135, 139,
  150, 152, 176, 186–187, 211, 222,
  225–226, 229–231, 235–238,
  242–243, 246–247, 292, 310, 313,
  318, 324, 328–329, 331–332,
  339–340, 343, 346, 348–349,
  353–355, 359, 368, 374, 377–379,
  381–382, 398, 417, 420, 428, 433,
  437, 445–446, 451–454, 456–457,
  459–460, 466–468, 513, 519–522,
  525–526, 528, 530–536, 538, 540,
  542, 547–548, 550–553, 555–556,
  560–561, 564, 589, 632, 665
  city-state, 223
  Estado da Índia, 416, 418, 420, 424,
    447, 458
  liberal state, 3, 21, 328, 515, 520–521,
    524–525, 528, 530–531, 542
  nation-state, 4, 17, 236
  state building, 3, 17, 20, 29, 32, 48,
    451, 454
  state manufacture, 32, 110, 376,
    380–382, 391, 397
  subsidy, 529, 532

tributary state, 29–30
welfare state, 489, 503, 507, 521, 540, 542, 544, 590, 616, 673, 677, *See also* welfare
subsistence crisis and famine, 47, 51–52, 57, 80, 82, 85, 100, 106, 161, 176, 178, 180, 183, 189–190, 198, 283–284, 287, 289, 291–293, 296–297, 390, 400, 409

tax, 7, 27, 30, 37, 53, 77, 104–105, 107, 109–110, 113, 116, 122–125, 127, 134–135, 182, 184, 186, 204, 216, 316, 319–320, 322–325, 327, 330, 332–333, 336, 339–340, 348–349, 354, 356, 398–399, 418, 426, 431, 438, 440, 448, 451–452, 454, 456, 459, 525–526, 529, 542, 577, 580, 583, 606, 613–614
  alcabala, 67, 120, 124–125, 127, 255, 316, 322, 327, 343
  customs duties, 72, 123–124, 320, 324–325, 330, 348–349, 417, 451, 460, 463, 525, 528–531, 540, 586, 632
  direct tax, 120, 124–125, 182–183, 324, 330, 343, 530
  extraordinary tax, 122, 124–127
  indirect tax, 15, 124–125, 183, 320, 322, 324, 348, 399, 526
  poll tax, 105
  sisas, 78, 123, 316, 322, 327
  tithes, 53–55, 116–117, 123–125, 181, 257–258, 276, 316–317, 324, 327, 339, 394, 398
  toll, 37, 113, 117, 123, 126
tax burden, 11–12, 14, 30–31, 37, 41, 119, 123, 127, 183, 186, 227, 238, 252, 255, 259, 261, 263, 323–324, 330, 398–400, 438, 452, 454, 460, 463, 522, 530, 542
tax ceiling, 344, 356
tax collection, 8, 30, 103, 108–109, 113, 119–120, 122–125, 127, 311, 314–315, 319, 322–324, 330–334, 340, 400, 419–421, 452, 529, 540
tax evasion, 458, 613

tax exemption, 77, 90, 117, 126, 210, 227, 316, 334, 381–382, 399, 532, 551
tax privilege, 330
tax reform, 30, 113, 325, 399, 530, 534, 540, 542
tax revenue, 8, 30–31, 105, 108, 123–126, 181, 216, 225, 315, 320, 322–325, 327, 329–331, 348, 356, 416–417, 433, 440, 448, 451, 453–454, 458, 468, 525, 530–531, 542, 632–633, 670
taxation, 8, 14–15, 27, 29, 31–32, 40, 49, 69, 76–78, 93, 95, 114–115, 119–120, 124, 136, 151, 176, 180–183, 186, 236, 238, 261, 263, 311–312, 314–315, 319, 323–324, 326–327, 330, 339, 348, 394, 398–399, 413, 416–417, 425–426, 428, 437–438, 441, 452, 454, 460, 463, 466, 526, 542, 613, 673
taxpayer, 76–77, 122, 227
technology and techniques, 6, 9, 15–16, 18, 20–21, 33, 48, 53, 56, 59, 61, 67–68, 73, 95–96, 154, 158–160, 162, 164–167, 170–174, 191, 194, 214, 220, 222, 228, 241–242, 269, 331, 358–384, 389, 395, 443–444, 446, 450–451, 455–456, 462–463, 466, 469, 474, 484–485, 488–489, 492–495, 500, 502, 506, 515, 517, 537–539, 568, 570, 575–580, 582–584, 586–592, 610, 618, 633, 636, 638, 649, 652–653, 660–663, 673, *See also* knowledge, innovation
  dissemination and transfer, 9, 16, 26, 34, 59, 64, 73, 159, 163–164, 166, 172–173, 214–215, 219, 374–375, 378, 383
textile industry, 44, 53, 62, 64–67, 70, 74, 92–93, 95, 97, 99, 110, 128, 151, 159, 162–165, 167–168, 176, 178, 184, 197, 200, 206, 226, 240, 263–264, 358, 361, 369, 375–377, 382, 395–397, 413, 427, 451, 507, 514, 579–580, 582, 584–586, 625, 629, 662, 669

textile industry (cont.)
cloth, 64–68, 74, 252, 369, 371, 375, 379, 381, 462–463, 579, 584
cotton, 38, 68, 196, 206, 369, 371, 376–377, 382, 389–390, 430–431, 468–469, 579–580, 583
dyeing, 66, 72, 166, 195, 206, 218, 369, 381
flax and hemp, 369
knitting, 376
linen and hemp, 166, 204, 271, 369, 373, 375, 381, 463, 469, 579
loom, 110, 165, 371, 376, 378, 381
printing, 376–377, 382, 468–469, 579
shearing, 65–66, 367
silk, 33, 38, 44, 53–54, 64, 68, 73–74, 96, 99, 110, 160–161, 164–165, 195–196, 204, 206, 223, 245, 260–261, 263, 369, 371, 375–376, 583
spinning, 164–165, 185, 389, 397, 579
weaving, 65–66, 97, 165, 579
wool, 68, 70–72, 89, 95, 168, 195, 201, 205–206, 225, 228, 240–241, 252, 256, 260–262, 271, 363–364, 367, 369, 375, 469, 580

textile raw materials, 204
cotton, 98, 109, 160–161, 425, 429–430, 455–456, 579
dye, 11, 54, 58, 62, 72, 161–162, 194–195, 201, 205–206, 214, 218, 241, 348, 377, 413, 418–419, 428, 431, 433
mordent, 162–163
flax and hemp, 35, 53–54, 62, 98, 109, 162, 185, 441
silk, 54, 72–74, 109, 201, 206, 381, 455
wool, 13, 53, 62–63, 73–74, 128, 162, 182, 190, 195, 218, 362, 381, 411
merino wool, 73, 214, 241

textiles, 243
cloths, 38, 97, 192, 194–197, 201, 204–206, 216, 240–241, 245, 360, 362, 376, 405, 411, 413–414, 418, 422, 427–429
cottons, 194, 361, 376, 379, 406, 414, 429, 455, 579, 631

linens, 68, 195, 462, 579
silks, 30, 44, 194, 201, 361, 376, 381, 406–407, 414, 428, 442, 455
clothing, 9, 144, 175, 187, 192–196, 241, 361, 376, 396, 400, 404–405, 407, 580, 591, 594–595
tobacco, 11, 325, 348–349, 364, 369–370, 381, 402–403, 406, 425, 428–429, 433–434, 455–456, 460, 580, 586, 662
tourism, 506, 589–591, 640, 645, 663, 670, 677
trade, 6, 9–10, 13–14, 16, 19, 22, 27, 31–34, 37, 41–42, 44–45, 47–49, 53, 64, 69–72, 75, 87, 89, 91–94, 96–97, 99, 102–103, 107–108, 110, 117–118, 123, 125, 127–129, 132–133, 135, 140, 142, 144–146, 148–149, 151, 154–156, 162, 168–172, 174–175, 183–184, 186, 193–194, 197, 199–222, 224, 226, 228–230, 232–246, 256, 259, 261–262, 264, 267, 269–271, 303, 320, 323, 325–326, 330–331, 335–336, 339–340, 348, 359, 361–365, 368, 372–373, 375, 379, 381–382, 394, 397, 399, 409–411, 413–429, 431, 433–434, 436, 440–442, 445–448, 451, 454, 456–457, 460, 462–463, 465–466, 479, 520, 526, 528, 530, 533, 536, 539, 553–555, 568, 577, 583, 587–589, 617–623, 625, 628, 631–637, 642, 645–647, 669, 673, 675, 677
Atlantic trade, 71–72, 174, 183, 200, 202, 204–205, 216–218, 221, 229, 242, 246, 414, 419–420, 422, 424, 448, 579
Atlantic trade system, 231, 374, 420–426, 428, 431, 434–435, 456
balance of trade or trade deficit, 115, 220, 441–442, 637, 640, 642, 645
Baltic trade, 240
Carreira da Índia or *Carrera de Indias*, 11, 339, 413–414, 417–418, 421, 426, 431, 446
Casa da Índia, 372, 445

Casa de Contratación, 336, 339,
    372–374, 380, 421–422, 425, 445
colonial trade, 12, 14, 16, 219–220,
    270, 336, 339, 349–350, 372,
    386, 409–410, 412–413,
    419–420, 422, 424–429, 431,
    435, 440–441, 447–448, 451,
    454, 458, 460, 462, 579, 633, 670
Consulados, 115, 128, 210, 212, 215,
    217, 219, 238, 242, 421–423, 425
  Consolat del Mar, 212–213, 238,
    244, 421
  Consulado de Bilbao, 128
  Consulado de Burgos, 128, 218,
    421, 445
  *Universidad de Mercaderes de
    Bilbao*, 128, 218
domestic trade, 69, 118, 479, 520
English Navigation Acts, 457
European Free Trade Association
    (EFTA), 479, 538–539, 585, 621,
    624, 662
free trade or trade liberalisation, 71,
    272, 324–325, 336, 426,
    434–435, 462, 468, 479, 488,
    526, 529, 539, 543, 578, 610,
    631–633, 636, 646–647, 661
global or world trade, 72, 200, 223,
    247, 414, 441–442, 448, 455,
    457, 462, 618–620
license, 421, 447, 536, 631–633
Manila Galleon route, 11, 407,
    413–414, 423–424, 428, 447, 457
Mediterranean trade, 33, 45–46,
    71–72, 88, 108, 144, 170, 172,
    174, 183, 200–201, 204–206,
    214, 216–219, 221, 225, 228,
    234, 236, 243, 462
prohibition, 63, 66, 115, 145, 204,
    339, 529, 631
route, 9, 38, 117, 127, 171–172,
    199–207, 211–212, 217–218,
    223, 229, 236, 247, 410–411,
    414, 416, 420, 431
Saharan trade, 108, 229, 336,
    411
slave trade, 16, 415, 418, 430, 434,
    441, 457, *See also* slavery

trade network, 11, 26, 34, 99, 128,
    154–155, 197, 218, 222, 227,
    229–230, 234–236, 238, 245,
    247, 259, 261–263, 372, 422,
    429, 444, 448, 450, 458, 462
trading cost, 69, 669
trading house, station and post, 127,
    203–204, 212, 232, 424
Trans-Atlantic slave trade, 410,
    414–415, 427, 429, 455, *See also*
    slavery
trader, *See* merchant
transaction cost, 210, 215, 238, 270,
    356, 445–446, 454, 465, 521
transhumance, 36, 62–63, 67, 74, 162,
    171, 241, 362, 444, 668
transport, 9, 64, 69, 93, 161–162,
    168–169, 189, 204, 210, 215,
    222, 226, 241–242, 256, 271,
    358, 360, 362, 364, 367–369,
    380, 414, 417–418, 479,
    488–489, 492–493, 526, 528,
    535, 537, 584, 586, 588–589,
    618, 633, 640, 663, 670
  air transport, 544
  car, 585–586, 591, 645
  coastal transport, 663
  cartage, 169, 215, 241, 362, 437
  fluvial transport, 88, 171, 202, 362,
    364, 369, 380, 422, 466
  land transport, 169, 171, 202, 205,
    215, 219, 222, 362, 379, 544
  maritime transport, 170–171, 174,
    201–202, 204–206, 212, 215,
    231, 236, 240, 246, 320, 340, 343,
    348, 364, 372, 374–375, 379,
    413, 417, 421–423, 425, 427,
    429, 432, 435–436, 440–442,
    544, 580, 634, 638
  muleteer, 69, 169, 215
  rafting, 171
  ship, 11, 108, 157, 168, 170–171, 215,
    372–375, 379, 411, 418,
    421–427, 432, 435–436, 636
    navíos de registro, 423, 425–426, 433
  subway, 588
  train, 587
  tramway, 588

transport (cont.)
  transport cost, 163, 366, 378, 436, 442, 465, 479–480, 509, 580, 584, 632, 669–670
  transport equipment, 582–583, 662
treatise, 107, 160, 169, 172, 190, 207, 375
  hisba, 31–32, 107, 143, 145, 190
treaty, 230, 467, 479, 545, 631–633
  Peace of Utrecht, 457–458
  Treaty of Accession, 543
  Treaty of Alcaçovas, 129
  Treaty of Alcañices, 114
  Treaty of Amiens, 435
  Treaty of Cazola, 112
  Treaty of Maastricht, 544, 563, 677
  Treaty of Methuen, 12, 270, 272, 398, 458
  Treaty of Rome, 631
  Treaty of Tordesillas, 230
tribute, 111, 116, 132–133
  parias, 7, 28, 31, 34, 42–43, 108, 110–111, 117, 133, 137, 139

urbanisation, 20, 26, 48, 96, 175, 197, 222, 224, 233, 235, 253, 261–263, 278–279, 300–305, 308–309, 361, 363–364, 370, 391, 395, 409, 449, 463–464, 469, 489, 496, 508, 510, 515, 517, 576, 587, 589
  ruralisation, 35, 263, 309, 391

Verlagssystem, 92, 195, 197, 378,
  See also putting-out system
Visigoths, 9, 25–26, 34–35, 38, 42, 134, 156, 221–222, 224, 235

wage, 9, 16, 115, 133, 175, 177–180, 196–198, 237, 264, 270, 276, 283, 385–386, 388–390, 393–395, 397–401, 405, 407–408, 410, 440, 449, 480, 537, 539, 541–542, 575–576, 607–608, 616, 640, 646–647, 669, 673
  gender wage gap, 185, 397
war, 10, 12, 14, 17, 29, 34, 47, 52, 57, 73, 80, 82, 92, 100, 108, 111–114, 119–120, 125, 135, 162, 176, 180, 182, 209, 211, 225, 228, 236–237, 244, 287, 290, 293, 296–297, 313–314, 324, 342–343, 369, 378–381, 391, 394, 398, 411, 424–426, 435, 444, 454–455, 467–469, 490, 523–524, 530–531, 533, 536–537, 554, 563–564, 589, 633, 636, 639, 654, 666–667, 677
  American Revolutionary War, 457
  Castilian Civil War, 52, 138
  Catalan Civil War, 128–129, 137, 142, 231, 244
  Cold War, 621
  Crimean War, 236
  Crusade, 116, 125, 236, 411
  Eighty Years' War, 12, 390
  Fantastic War, 391
  Fernandine Wars, 139, 182
  First World War, 485–486, 488, 492, 501, 521–522, 531, 533, 548–549, 554, 561, 565, 575, 583–584, 593, 600, 608, 613–614, 618–623, 632, 636, 638–639, 646, 656, 663
  Hundred Years' War, 211
  independence war, 426
  liberal wars, 640
  Napoleonic invasion or Napoleonic Wars, 12, 17, 253, 257, 270, 348, 406, 410, 426, 467, 476, 500, 522–523, 545, 579, 618, 631, 633, 646, 666, 670
  Portuguese Miguelista war, 17
  Portuguese War of Restoration, 12, 14, 291, 314, 324, 346, 364, 379, 391, 415, 441, 454
  Reapers' War, 391
  revolutionary wars, 320
  Second World War, 479, 489, 504, 506, 521, 536–537, 546, 550, 561, 576, 583–585, 613, 619–620, 622, 632, 635–636, 639, 663, 675, 678
  Seven Years' War, 324, 435, 457
  Spanish Carlista war, 17
  Spanish Civil War, 18, 296, 476, 478, 480, 486, 488, 501, 506, 536,

554–555, 563, 576, 593, 596,
    598–599, 608, 620, 631, 645,
    648–649, 663, 666, 677
spoils, 28, 31, 73, 105, 113, 117, 180,
    230
war between Castile and Navarre, 141
War of the Oranges, 391, 523
War of the Spanish Succession, 12,
    14, 330, 347, 374, 386, 390–391,
    394, 399, 410, 424, 433, 458–460
War of the Two Peters, 52, 177, 228,
    245
wealth, 7, 41–45, 53, 65, 70, 73, 107, 111,
    113, 116, 118–119, 131, 161,
    181–184, 188, 216, 222–224, 226,
    229, 232–234, 244–246, 259, 316,
    319, 330, 336, 353–354, 394–395,
    408, 413, 455, 480, 542, 553, 598,
    614
petrification of wealth, 111
weights and measures, 70, 74–75, 107,
    166, 267, 479
standardization, 115, 169, 267
welfare, 110, 348, 389, 395, 398, 503,
    520, 535, 559, 618
health care, 501, 510, 520, 540, 600,
    616, *See also* health
pension, 521, 534, 540, 544
retirement, 503, 533

social assistance and social security,
    106, 184, 212, 520, 526, 540
work, 16, 30, 36, 64–68, 73, 83, 93–95,
    97, 99, 106, 110, 151, 159–160,
    166, 176, 185–186, 208, 268,
    271, 307–308, 315, 327, 362,
    365, 367, 373, 379–380, 383,
    396–397, 405–406, 408, 427,
    437, 448, 464, 503, 507, 511,
    520–521, 526, 528, 599, *See also*
    labour
workday, 178, 198, 405, 408, 485–486,
    489–490, 533, 653–654
worker, 66, 92, 95–96, 126, 159, 163,
    165–167, 177–180, 184–185,
    189, 195, 201, 260, 271, 353,
    365, 367–368, 377–378,
    381–383, 386, 388–390, 397,
    401, 450, 462, 485, 490, 502,
    508, 511, 525, 534, 539–541,
    569, 600, 607, 640, 649,
    653–654, 659, 673

yield, 159, 222, 343, 352,
    658
agricultural yield, 48, 61, 73,
    161, 362, 366, 573, 575,
    668
bond yield, 344–347, 349, 356

Printed in the United States
by Baker & Taylor Publisher Services